SECOND EDITION

The Making of the West

PEOPLES AND CULTURES

SECOND EDITION

The Making of the West

PEOPLES AND CULTURES

Lynn Hunt
University of California,
Los Angeles

Thomas R. Martin
College of the Holy Cross

Barbara H. Rosenwein
Loyola University Chicago

R. Po-chia Hsia
Pennsylvania State University

Bonnie G. Smith
Rutgers University

BEDFORD/ST. MARTIN'S
Boston ◆ New York

FOR BEDFORD/ST. MARTIN'S

Executive Editor for History: Mary Dougherty
Director of Development for History: Jane Knetzger
Developmental Editor: Sara Wise
Senior Production Editor: Anne Noonan
Senior Production Supervisor: Dennis Conroy
Senior Marketing Manager: Jenna Bookin Barry
Editorial Assistant: Rachel L. Safer
Production Assistant: Kristen Merrill
Copyeditor: Janet Renard
Text Design: Wanda Kossak
Page Layout: DeNee Reiton Skipper
Photo Researchers: Elsa Peterson and Judy Brody
Cover Design: Billy Boardman
Cartography: Mapping Specialists Limited
Composition: TechBooks
Printing and Binding: R.R. Donnelley & Sons Company

President: Joan E. Feinberg
Editorial Director: Denise B. Wydra
Director of Marketing: Karen Melton Soeltz
Director of Editing, Design, and Production: Marcia Cohen
Managing Editor: Elizabeth M. Schaaf

Library of Congress Control Number: 2004102164

9 8 7 6 5 4
f   e   d   c   b   a

For information, write: Bedford/St. Martin's, 75 Arlington Street, Boston, MA 02116
(617-399-4000)

ISBN: 0–312–40959–1 (hardcover edition)   EAN: 978–0–312–40959–3
ISBN: 0–312–41740–3 (paperback Vol. I)   EAN: 978–0–312–41740–6
ISBN: 0–312–41761–6 (paperback Vol. II)   EAN: 978–0–312–41761–1
ISBN: 0–312–41767–5 (paperback Vol. A)   EAN: 978–0–312–41767–3
ISBN: 0–312–41768–3 (paperback Vol. B)   EAN: 978–0–312–41768–0
ISBN: 0–312–41769–1 (paperback Vol. C)   EAN: 978–0–312–41769–7

Cover Art: *Musical Company* (known as *The Young Suitor*) by Jan Havicksz Steen (1625/26 –1679). Harold Samuel Collection, Corporation of London, UK/Bridgeman Art Library.

Preface

THE IDEA OF "THE WEST" is now urgently under discussion. The end of the cold war after 1989 presented new challenges for historical interpretation, but these had hardly been digested when the shock of September 11, 2001, reverberated throughout the world. These momentous events present extraordinary challenges for authors of Western civilization textbooks. We welcome the challenges, for they have deepened our commitment to our project's basic goal and approach. From the very beginning, we have insisted on an expanded vision of the West that includes the United States, fully incorporates eastern Europe, and emphasizes Europe's relationship with the rest of the world, whether through trade, colonization, migration, cultural exchange, or religious and ethnic conflict.

Every generation of students needs new textbooks that synthesize recent findings. Textbooks conceived during the era of the cold war are, of course, oriented toward explaining the clash between a West unquestionably identified as western Europe and the United States and its eastern-bloc opponents, eastern Europe and the Soviet Union. Since much of eastern Europe has now joined the European Union, the notion of Europe—and the West—has to change. Conflict now takes place on a global stage, and globalization of the economy and culture has become a subject of passionate debate. Nowhere is that debate more crucial than over relations between the West and Islam precipitated by the September 11, 2001, attacks by Islamic radicals. How to respond to such global threats sharply divides the West. The United States and Great Britain's decision to invade Iraq despite strong opposition from allies in western Europe tests long-standing alliances and suggests significant international realignments. New histories must reflect these dramatic changes, and we feel confident that ours meets the challenge. In every chapter, we develop these new perspectives and show how they offer a more coherent and convincing view of the important issues in the making of the West.

Central Themes and Approach

Our title, *The Making of the West: Peoples and Cultures*, makes two enduring points about our themes and approach: (1) that the history of the West is the story of a process that is still ongoing, not a finished result with only one fixed meaning; and (2) that "the West" includes many different peoples and cultures, that is, that there is no one Western people or culture that has existed from the beginning until now. To understand the historical development of the West and its position in the world today, it is essential to place the West's emergence in a larger, global context that reveals the cross-cultural interactions fundamental to the shaping of the Western identity. Our task as authors, moreover, is to integrate the best of social and cultural history with the enduring developments of political, military, and diplomatic history, offering a clear, compelling narrative that sets all the key events and stages of the West's evolution in a broad, meaningful context.

We know from our own teaching that introductory students need a solid chronological framework, one with enough familiar benchmarks to make the material readily assimilable, but also one with enough flexibility to incorporate the new varieties of historical research. That is one reason why we present our account in a straightforward, chronological manner. Each chapter treats all the main events, people, and themes of a period in which the West significantly changed; thus students are not required to learn about political events in one chapter, then backtrack to concurrent social and cultural developments in the next. The chronological organization also accords with our belief that it is important, above all else, for students to see the interconnections among varieties of historical experience—between politics and cultures, between public events and private experiences, between wars and diplomacy and everyday life. Our chronological synthesis allows students to appreciate these relationships while it, we hope, captures the spirit of each age and sparks students' historical imaginations. For teachers, our chronological approach ensures a balanced account, allows the flexibility to stress themes of one's own choosing, and perhaps best of all, provides a text that reveals history not as a settled matter but as a process that is constantly alive, subject to pressures, and able to surprise us. In writing *The Making of the West: Peoples and Cultures*, it has been our aim to communicate the vitality and excitement as well as the fundamental importance of history. If we have succeeded in conveying some of the vibrancy of the past and the thrill of historical investigation, we will be encouraged to start rethinking and revising—as historians always must—once again.

Pedagogy and Features

More and more is required of students these days, and not just in Western civilization courses. We know from our own teaching that students need all the help they can get in assimilating information, acquiring skills, learning about historical debate, and sampling the newest approaches to historical thinking. With these goals in mind, we retained the class-tested learning and teaching aids that contributed to the first edition, but we have also added more such features.

Each chapter begins with a ***vivid anecdote*** that draws readers into the atmosphere and issues of the period and raises the chapter's main themes, supplemented by a full-page illustration that echoes the anecdote and similarly reveals the temper of the times. We have added **new chapter outlines** and **timelines** to introduce students to each chapter. As they read, students now encounter **review questions** strategically placed at the end of each major section to check their comprehension of main ideas, plus bolded **key terms** in the text with corresponding **glossary** definitions at the end of the book and a running **pronunciation guide**. Each chapter closes with a strong **chapter conclusion** that reviews main topics and ties together the chapter's thematic strands. An all-new **chapter review** section provides a clear study plan with a table of important events, list of key terms, review questions, and "Making Connections" questions, which encourage students to analyze chapter material or make comparisons within or beyond the chapter.

But like a clear narrative synthesis, strong pedagogical support is not enough on its own to encourage active learning. To reflect the richness of the themes in the text and to enliven the past with many more original sources, in the second edition we have added **sixty new single-source documents** (two per chapter). Nothing can give a more direct experience of the past than original voices, and we have each endeavored, sometimes through our own retranslation, to let those voices speak, whether it is Seneca describing everyday life in the Roman Empire, Frederick Barbarossa replying to the Romans when they offer him the emperor's crown, or an ordinary person's account of one of Stalin's pogroms. At the same time, we have retained our unique, proven features that extend the narrative by revealing the process of interpretation, providing a solid introduction to the principles of historical argument, and capturing the excitement of historical investigation:

- ***Contrasting Views*** provide three or four often conflicting eyewitness accounts of a central event, person, or development, such as Martin Luther, the English Civil War, and late-nineteenth-century migration.
- ***New Sources, New Perspectives*** show students how historians continue to develop

new kinds of evidence about the past, from tree rings to Holocaust museums.

- **Terms of History** explain the meanings of some of the most important and contested terms in the history of the West and show how those meanings have developed—and changed—over time. For example, the discussion of *progress* shows how the term took root in the eighteenth century and has been contested in the twentieth.

- **Did You Know?** is a short, illustrated feature that emphasizes the interactions between the West and the broader world, offering unexpected and sometimes startling examples of cultural interchange, from the invention of "smoking" (derived from the New World) to the creation of polo (adapted from South Asia).

- **Taking Measure** highlights a chart, table, graph, or map of historical statistics that illuminates an important political, social, or cultural development.

The map program of the first edition was widely praised as the most comprehensive in any survey text. In each chapter we offer a set of three types of maps, each with a distinct role in conveying information to students. Four to five **full-size maps** show major developments, two to four **"spot" maps**—small maps that emphasize a detailed area from the discussion—aid students' understanding of specific but crucial issues, and **"Mapping the West"** summary maps at the end of each chapter provide a snapshot of the West at the close of a transformative period and help students visualize the West's changing contours over time. For this edition, we have carefully considered each map, improved the colors for better contrast, and clarified and updated borders and labels where needed.

It has been our intention to integrate art as fully as possible into the narrative and to show its value for teaching and learning. **Over 400 illustrations**, carefully chosen to reflect this edition's broad topical coverage and geographic inclusion, reinforce the text and show the varieties of visual sources from which historians build their narratives and interpretations. All artifacts, illustrations, paintings, and photographs are contemporaneous with the chapter; there are no anachronistic illustrations—no fifteenth-century peasants

tilling fields in a chapter on the tenth century! We know that today's students are very attuned to visual sources of information, yet they do not always receive systematic instruction in how to "read" or think critically about such visual sources. Our substantive captions for the maps and art help them learn how to make the most of these informative materials, and now in the second edition, we have frequently included specific questions or suggestions for comparisons that might be developed. Specially designed visual exercises in the *Online Study Guide* supplement this approach in an especially thought-provoking fashion. A new page design for the second edition supports our goal of intertwining the art and the narrative and lends more interest and dynamism to the page.

Textual Changes

A textbook, unlike most scholarly books, offers historians the rare chance to revise the original work, to keep it fresh, and to make it better. It has been a privilege to bring our own scholarship and teaching to bear on this rewriting. In this second edition, we have kept our emphasis on a strong central story line that incorporates the best of new research, but we have worked to make the narrative even more focused and accessible by reviewing every line of text and recrafting the headings to provide better signposts for readers.

Our book now begins with a new prologue that examines the lives of early human beings in the Paleolithic and Neolithic eras. Here we discuss the archeological evidence that points to the technology, trade, religious practices, and social traditions of people who left no written history. The prologue is designed for maximum flexibility. It contains full chapter pedagogy to support instructors who choose to assign this period. Alternatively, it can be used as introductory or extra reading for those instructors who begin their courses with Mesopotamia.

To illustrate our conception of the history of the West as an ongoing process, the first chapter opens with a new section on the origins and contested meaning of *Western civilization.* In this conversation, we emphasize our theme of cultural borrowing between the peoples of Europe and their neighbors that has characterized Western civilization from the beginning. We continue to incorporate the experiences of borderland regions and the importance of global interactions into the historical narrative and in many of our new art selections.

Of course, the recent past is the most pressing arena in which to examine the West as an evolving construct. The impact of recent events is reflected most dramatically in the last two chapters, which have been completely rewritten and now divide at 1989, the year that marks the beginning of a new era after the cold war.

Throughout each chapter, we've added new material and drawn on new scholarship on topics such as the demise of the Akkadian Empire and the succeeding Ur III dynasty (Chapter 1); Zoroastrianism and the influence of Persian religion on later faiths (Chapter 2); criticisms of radical democracy (Chapter 3); diversity among the non-Roman peoples who flooded into the Roman Empire (Chapter 7); the origins of Islam (Chapter 8); Byzantine court culture and the *dynatoi* (Chapter 9); the prominence of the flagellant movement (Chapter 13); Spanish exploration of the Pacific Coast of North America (Chapter 16); the promotion of women's emigration to the new colonies (Chapter 17); sugar grinding in the colonies (Chapter 18); the role of peasants in the French Revolution (Chapter 20); nineteenth-century French efforts to transform Saigon (Chapter 23); Japan's imperialist activity in the 1920s (Chapter 26); discontent in the colonies during the depression (Chapter 27); postwar recovery in Scandinavia and the contributions of immigrants to postwar European economies (Chapter 28); the rise in the study of social sciences (Chapter 29); and the impact of global outsourcing (Chapter 30).

Supplements

As with the first edition, a well-integrated ancillary program supports *The Making of the West: Peoples and Cultures.* Each print and electronic resource has been carefully revised to provide a host of practical teaching and learning aids.

For Students

***Sources of* The Making of the West, Second Edition**—Volumes I (to 1740) and II (since 1500)—by Katharine J. Lualdi, University of Southern Maine. For each chapter in *The Making of the West*, this companion sourcebook features four or five important political, social, and cultural documents that reinforce or extend discussions in the textbook, encouraging students to make connections between narrative history and primary sources. Short chapter summaries and document headnotes contextualize the wide array of sources and perspectives represented, while discussion and comparative questions guide students' reading and promote historical thinking skills. The second edition provides instructors with even more flexibility, as the nearly one-third new selections feature visual sources for the first time. This edition also features more attention to geographic areas beyond Europe and includes an improved balance between traditional documents and selections that provide a fresh perspective.

***Study Guide to Accompany* The Making of the West, Second Edition**—Volumes I (to 1740) and II (since 1500)—by Victoria Thompson, Arizona State University, and Eric Johnson, University of California, Los Angeles. For each chapter in the textbook, the *Study Guide* offers overview questions; a chapter summary; an expanded timeline with questions; a glossary of key terms with a related exercise; multiple-choice and short-answer questions; plus map, illustration, and source exercises that help students synthesize information and practice analytical skills. Answers for all exercises are provided.

Online Study Guide at **bedfordstmartins .com/hunt** The popular *Online Study Guide* for *The Making of the West* is a free and uniquely personalized learning tool to help students master themes and information in the textbook and improve their historical skills. Instructors can monitor student progress through the online *Quiz Gradebook* or receive e-mail updates.

The Bedford Series in History and Culture—Advisory Editors Natalie Zemon Davis, Princeton University; Ernest R. May, Harvard University; David W. Blight, Yale University; and Lynn Hunt, University of California, Los Angeles. European titles in this highly praised series combine first-rate scholarship, historical narrative, and important primary documents for undergraduate courses. Each book is brief, inexpensive, and focused on a specific topic or period. Packaged discounts are available. European titles include *Spartacus and the Slave Wars, Utopia, Candide, The French Revolution and Human Rights, The Enlightenment,* and *The Communist Manifesto.*

DocLinks at bedfordstmartins.com/ doclinks This Web site provides over 400 annotated Web links with single-click access to primary documents online, including speeches, legislation, treaties, social commentary, essays, travelers' accounts, personal narratives and testimony, newspaper articles, visual artifacts, songs, and poems. Searchable by topic, date, or specific chapter of *The Making of the West.*

HistoryLinks at bedfordstmartins.com/ historylinks HistoryLinks directs instructors and students to over 500 carefully selected and annotated history-related Web sites, including those containing image galleries, maps, and audio and video clips for supplementing lectures or making assignments. Searchable by date, subject, medium, keyword, or specific chapter in *The Making of the West.*

A Student's Online Guide to History Reference Sources at bedfordstmartins .com/benjamin This collection of links provides access to history-related electronic reference sources such as databases, indexes, and journals, plus contact information for state, provincial, local, and professional history organizations. Based on the appendix to Jules Benjamin's *A Student's Guide to History,* Ninth Edition.

For Instructors

***Instructor's Resource Manual to Accompany* The Making of the West, Second Edition**—Volumes I (to 1740) and II (since 1500)—by Dakota Hamilton, Humboldt State University. This helpful manual offers both first-time and experienced teachers a wealth of tools for structuring and customizing Western civilization history courses of different sizes. For each chapter in the textbook, the *Instructor's Resource Manual* includes an outline of chapter themes; a chapter summary; lecture and discussion topics; film and literature suggestions; writing and class-presentation assignments; research topic suggestions; and in-class exercises for working with maps, illustrations, and sources.

Transparencies A set of over 200 full-color acetate transparencies for *The Making of the West* includes all full-sized maps and many images from the text.

Computerized Test Bank—by Joseph Coohill, Pennsylvania State University at New Kensington, and Frances Mitilineos, Loyola University Chicago; available on CD-ROM. This fully updated test bank offers over 80 exercises per chapter, including multiple-choice, identification, timelines, map labeling and analysis, source analysis, and full-length essay questions. Instructors can customize quizzes, edit both questions and answers, as well as export them to a variety of formats, including WebCT and Blackboard. The disc includes answer keys and essay outlines.

Instructor's Resource CD-ROM This disc provides instructors with ready-made and easily customized PowerPoint multimedia presentations built around chapter outlines, maps, figures, and selected images from the textbook. The disc also contains images in JPEG format, an electronic version of the *Instructor's Resource Manual,* outline maps in PDF format for quizzing or handouts, and quick-start guides to the *Online Study Guide.*

Book Companion Site at bedfordstmartins .com/hunt The companion Web site for

The Making of the West gathers all the electronic resources for the text, including the *Online Study Guide* and related *Quiz Gradebook*, at a single Web address. It provides convenient links to such helpful lecture and research materials as PowerPoint chapter outlines from the textbook, DocLinks, HistoryLinks, and Map Central.

Map Central at bedfordstmartins.com/mapcentral Map Central is a searchable database of more than 750 maps from Bedford/St. Martin's history texts for classroom presentations and more than 50 basic political and physical outline maps for quizzes or handouts.

Using the Bedford Series in History and Culture with The Making of the West, Second Edition This short guide gives practical suggestions for using the volumes in The Bedford Series in History and Culture in conjunction with *The Making of the West*. This reference supplies connections between the text and the supplements and ideas for starting discussions focused on a single primary-source volume. Available in print as well as online at **bedfordstmartins.com/usingseries**.

Blackboard and WebCT content is available for *The Making of the West*.

Videos and Multimedia A wide assortment of videos and multimedia CD-ROMs on various topics in European history is available to qualified adopters.

Acknowledgments

In the vital process of revision, the authors have benefited from repeated critical readings by many talented scholars and teachers. Our sincere thanks go to the following instructors, whose comments often challenged us to rethink or justify our interpretations and who always provided a check on accuracy down to the smallest detail.

Stephen J. Andrews, *Albuquerque Technical Vocational Institute*

Laetitia Argenteri, *San Diego Mesa College*

Sharon Arnoult, *Midwestern State University*

Wayne C. Bartee, *Southwest Missouri State University*

S. Jonathan Bass, *Samford University*

Joel D. Benson, *Northwest Missouri State University*

Marjorie Berman, *Red Rocks Community College*

Lyn A. Blanchfield, *Le Moyne College*

Stephen Blumm, *Montgomery County Community College*

Ronald G. Brown, *College of Southern Maryland*

J. Laurel Carrington, *St. Olaf College*

Joseph Coohill, *Pennsylvania State University, New Kensington*

Cassandra B. Cookson, *Brazosport College*

Paul Cullity, *Keene State College*

Marianne Eve Fisher, *South Dakota State University*

Malia Formes, *Western Kentucky University*

James Genova, *Indiana State University*

Karen Graubert, *Cornell University*

William G. Gray, *Texas Tech University*

Ginger Guardiola, *Colorado State University*

David Halahmy, *Cypress College*

Paul Halsall, *University of North Florida*

Dakota Hamilton, *Humboldt State University*

Carmen Harris, *University of South Carolina, Spartanburg*

L. Edward Hicks, *Faulkner University*

Christine Holden, *University of Southern Maine*

David Hood, *California State University, Long Beach*

Chris Howell, *Red Rocks Community College*

David Hudson, *California State University, Fresno*

Paul J. Hughes, *Sussex County Community College*

Marsh W. Jones, *Parkland College*

Erin Jordan, *University of Northern Colorado*

Gerald Kadish, *State University of New York, Binghamton*

Ruth Mazo Karras, *University of Minnesota*

Frances A. Kelleher, *Grand Valley State University*

Jason Knirck, *Humboldt State University*

Anne Kelly Knowles, *Middlebury College*

John Krapp, *Hofstra University*

David Kutcha, *University of New England*

Ann Kuzdale, *Chicago State University*

Michelle Laughran, *Saint Joseph's College of Maine*

Alison Williams Lewin, *St. Joseph's University*

Janice Liedl, *Laurentian University*

Paul Douglas Lockhart, *Wright State University*

David W. Madsen, *Seattle University*

Steven G. Marks, *Clemson University*

Andrew McMichael, *Western Kentucky University*

Gary M. Miller, *Southern Oregon University*

Eva Mo, *Modesto Junior College*

David B. Mock, *Tallahassee Community College*

Scott Morschauser, *Rowan University*

Johanna Moyer, *State University of New York, Oswego*

Peter Parides, *New York City College of Technology*

Paulette L. Pepin, *University of New Haven*

Norman Raiford, *Greenville Technical College*

Salvador Rivera, *State University of New York, Cobleskill*

Kenneth W. Rock, *Colorado State University*

Anna Marie Roos, *University of Minnesota, Duluth*

Patricia C. Ross, *Columbus State Community College*

Jon Rudd, *Prince George's Community College*

Brian Rutishauser, *Fresno City College*

Daniella Sarnoff, *Xavier University*

Lynn Schibeci, *University of New Mexico*

Kim Schutte, *Missouri Western State College*

David Shafer, *California State University, Long Beach*

Jessica A. Sheetz-Nguyen, *Oklahoma City Community College*

William A. Sherrard, *Creighton University*

Charlie R. Steen, *University of New Mexico*

Nicholas Steneck, *Ohio State University*

Robert E. Stiefel, *University of New Hampshire*

Ann Sullivan, *Tompkins Cortland Community College*

Paul Teverow, *Missouri Southern State College*

Michael E. Thede, *Florida Gulf Coast University*

Frances Titchener, *Utah State University*

Tracey Trenam, *Aims Community College*

David G. Troyansky, *Texas Tech University*

Timothy Vogt, *University of San Francisco*

James J. Ward, *Cedar Crest College*

Theodore Weeks, *Southern Illinois University*

Michael Weiss, *Linn-Benton Community College*

Stephen J. White Sr., *College of Charleston*

Anne Will, *Skagit Valley College*

Andrea Winkler, *Whitman College*

Robinson Yost, *Kirkwood Community College*

Each of us has also benefited from the close readings and valuable criticisms of our coauthors, though we all assume responsibility for our own chapters. Thomas Martin has written Chapters 1–7; Barbara Rosenwein, Chapters 8–12; Ronnie Hsia, Chapters 13–15; Lynn Hunt, Chapters 16–22; and Bonnie Smith, Chapters 23–30.

Many colleagues, friends, and family members have helped us develop this work as well. They know how grateful we are. We also wish to acknowledge and thank the publishing team at Bedford/St. Martin's who did so much to bring this revised edition to completion: Joan Feinberg, Denise Wydra, Elizabeth Welch, Mary Dougherty, Jane Knetzger, Sara Wise, Anne Noonan, Kristen Merrill, Jenna Bookin Barry, Rachel Safer, Bryce Sady, Jan Fitter, Dale Anderson, Gretchen Boger, Elsa Peterson, and Judy Brody.

Our students' questions and concerns have shaped much of this work, and we welcome all our readers' suggestions, queries, and criticisms. Please contact us at our respective institutions or via **history@bedfordstmartins.com**.

L.H.   T.R.M.   B.H.R.   R.P.H.   B.G.S.

Brief Contents

Contents

Unity and Diversity in Three Societies, 750–1050

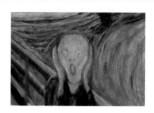

Remaking Europe in the Shadow of Cold War, c. 1945–1965 *1097*

Postindustrial Society and the End of the Cold War Order, 1965–1989 *1139*

The New Globalism: Opportunities and Dilemmas, 1989 to the Present 1185

Maps and Figures

Maps

Figures

Special Features

Individual Documents

Contrasting Views

New Sources, New Perspectives

Terms of History

Did You Know?

Taking Measure

To the Student

This guide to your textbook introduces the unique features that will help you understand the fascinating story of Western civilization.

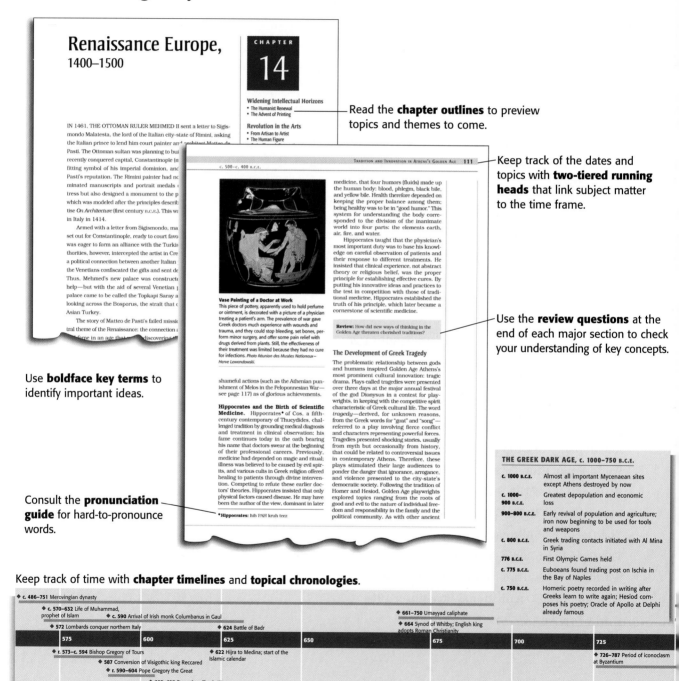

Read the **chapter outlines** to preview topics and themes to come.

Keep track of the dates and topics with **two-tiered running heads** that link subject matter to the time frame.

Use the **review questions** at the end of each major section to check your understanding of key concepts.

Use **boldface key terms** to identify important ideas.

Consult the **pronunciation guide** for hard-to-pronounce words.

Keep track of time with **chapter timelines** and **topical chronologies**.

Special features show you how historians think and work.

The document program reveals the range of sources that historians use to learn about the past and to draw conclusions.

Numerous **individual documents** offer direct experiences of the past including personal letters, poems, songs, political statements, and speeches.

Contrasting Views provide three or four often-conflicting eyewitness accounts of a central event, person, or development.

New Sources, New Perspectives show how new evidence leads historians to fresh insights—and sometimes new interpretations.

A Merchant's Advice to His Sons

Giovanni Rucellai, one of the most successful merchants of fifteenth-century Florence, kept an extensive diary that reveals life among the city's urban elite. In this selection, Rucellai warns his sons against pursuing political power for self-serving reasons. Rucellai's comments on political of-

in order to convert the treasure of the state into your own, for such an action is not good and I shall not approve it. He who aspires to a political position with this goal in mind has always been destroyed by the state itself regardless of the power of ingenuity which he might command. Everyone who

CONTRASTING VIEWS

Christians in the Empire: Conspirators or Faithful Subjects?

Ancient Romans worried that new religions might disrupt the long-standing "peace with the gods" that guaranteed their national safety and prosperity. Groups whose religious creed seemed likely to offend the traditional deities could therefore be accused of treason, but Christians insisted that they were loyal subjects who prayed for the safety of the em

Looking up to heaven, the Christians—with hands outspread, because innocent, with head bare because we do not blush, yes! and without a prompter because we pray from the heart—are ever praying for all the emperors. We pray for a fortunate life for them, a secure rule, a safe house, brave armies, a faithful senate, a virtuous people.

NEW SOURCES, NEW PERSPECTIVES

The Cairo Geniza

What do historians know about the daily life of ordinary people in the Middle Ages? Generally speaking, very little. We have writings from the intellectual elite and administrative documents from monasteries, churches, and courts. But these rarely mention ordinary folk, and if they do, it is always from the standpoint of those who are not ordinary themselves. Glimpsing the concerns, occupations, and family relations of medieval people as they went about their daily lives is very difficult (a dicipline called paleography). They also needed to organize the material. Dispersed among various libraries, the documents were a

Many of these documents were purchased by American and English collectors and ended up in libraries in New York, Philadelphia, and Cambridge, England, where they remain. As is often the case in historical research, the questions that scholars ask are just as important as the sources themselves. At first, historians did not ask what the documents could tell them about everyday life. They wanted to know how to transcribe and read them; they wanted to study the evolution of their writing style (a dicipline called paleography). They also needed to organize the material. Dispersed among various libraries, the documents were a

called Fustat), in Egypt.
Cairo is exceptional because of a cache of un-

Other engaging features investigate historical terms, evidence of cultural exchange, and qualitative data.

Terms of History identify a term central to history writing yet hotly debated.

Did You Know? features offer unexpected examples of cultural interchange between the West and the wider world.

Taking Measure data reveal how individual facts add up to broad trends and introduce important quantitative analysis skills.

TERMS OF HISTORY

Progress

Believing as they did in the possibilities of improvement, many Enlightenment writers preached a new doctrine about the meaning of human history. They challenged the traditional Christian belief that the original sin of Adam and Eve condemned human beings to un-

you was a bottomless pit." In the movement toward postmodernism, which began in the 1970s, critics argued that we should no longer be satisfied with the modern: the modern brought us calamity and disaster, not reason and freedom. They wanted to go beyond the modern, hence the term postmodern. The most influential was the Frenchman Michel ... 970s and 1980s that

DID YOU KNOW?

Tobacco and the Invention of "Smoking"

In the early seventeenth century, a "new astonishing fashion," wrote a German ambassador, came to the Dutch Republic from the New World. The term *smoking* gradually evolved in the seventeenth century out of "a fog-drinking bout," "drinking smoke," or "drinking tobacco." One Jesuit preacher called it "dry drunkenness." The analogy to inebriation is not entirely far-fetched, for nicotine (named after the French ambassador to Portugal,

panded their exports of tobacco sixfold between 1663 and 1699. Until 1700, Amsterdam dominated the curing process; half the tobacco factories in Amsterdam were owned by Jewish merchants of Spanish or Portuguese descent.
Smoking spread geographically from western to eastern Europe, socially from the upper classes downward, and from men to women. At first the Spanish preferred cigars, the British pipes, and

TAKING MEASURE

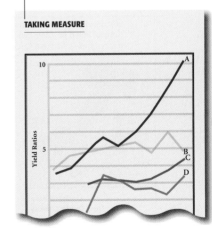

Read the **art and map captions** to help you analyze images and place events.

MAP 17.2 State Building in Central and Eastern Europe, 1648–1699
The Austrian Habsburgs had long contested the Ottoman Turks for dominance of eastern Europe, and by 1699 they had pushed the Turks out of Hungary. In central Europe, the Austrian Habsburgs confronted the growing power of Brandenburg-Prussia, which had emerged from relative obscurity after the Thirty Years' War to begin an aggressive program of expanding its military and its territorial base. As emperor of the Holy Roman Empire, the Austrian Habsburg ruler governed a huge expanse of territory, but the emperor's control was in fact only partial because of guarantees of local autonomy.

Full-size maps show major historical developments and carry informative captions.

Mapping the West summary maps provide a snapshot of the West at the close of each chapter.

The Exotic as Consumer Item
This painting by the Venetian artist Rosalba Carriera (1675–1757) is titled *Africa*. The young black girl wearing a turban represents the African continent. Carriera was known for her use of pastels. In 1720, she journeyed to Paris where she became an associate of Antoine Watteau and helped inaugurate the rococo style in painting. Why did the artist choose to paint an African girl for this picture? **For more help analyzing this image,** see the visual activity for this chapter in the Online Study Guide at **bedfordstmartins.com/hunt.** *Staatliche Kunstsammlungen Dresden, Gemaldegalerie Alte Meister.*

Web references direct you to visual activities at the Online Study Guide.

"Spot" maps offer geographic details right where you need them.

officers, in fact the dukes of Benevento and Spoleto ruled on their own behalf. Although many Lombards were Catholics, others, including important kings and dukes, were Arian. The "official" religion of **Lombard Italy** varied with the ruler in power. Rather than signal a major political event, the conversion of the Lombards to Catholic Christianity occurred gradually, ending only around the mid-seventh century. Partly as a result of this slow development, the Lombard kings, unlike the Visigoths, Franks, or even the

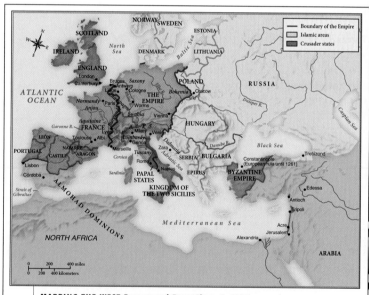

Lombard Italy, Early Eighth Century

MAPPING THE WEST Europe and Byzantium, c. 1215
The major transformation in the map of the West between 1150 and 1215 was the conquest of Constantinople and the setting up of European rule there until 1261. The Byzantine Empire was now a mere shell. A new state, Epirus, emerged in the power vacuum to dominate Thrace. Bulgaria once again gained its independence. If Venice had hoped to control the Adriatic by conquering Constantinople, it must have been disappointed, for Hungary became its rival over the ports of the Dalmatian coast.

Organize your study plans with review sections at the end of each chapter.

Chapter conclusions tie together the chapter's thematic strands, review main topics, and point you onward.

Annotated lists of suggested references provide print and web resources for papers, research projects, or further study.

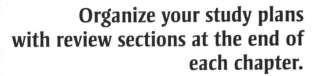

Important Events lists help you review key happenings at a glance.

Key terms highlight important concepts with page references that point to the text discussion. Each term is defined in the **glossary** at the end of the book.

Review Questions offer section-by-section comprehension prompts.

Making Connections analytical questions help you link ideas within or across chapters.

For Further Exploration points you to free online activities that help you master the chapter material and to additional chapter-related primary sources.

See the preface for a full list of student resources, including the Online Study Guide, that accompany *The Making of the West: Peoples and Cultures*, Second Edition.

How to Read Primary Sources

In each chapter of this textbook you will find many primary sources to broaden your understanding of the development of the West. Primary sources refer to firsthand, contemporary accounts or direct evidence about a particular topic. For example, speeches, letters, diaries, song lyrics, and newspaper articles are all primary sources that historians use to construct accounts of the past. Nonwritten materials such as maps, paintings, artifacts, and even architecture and music can also be primary sources. Both types of historical documents in this textbook—written and visual—provide a glimpse into the lives of the men and women who influenced or were influenced by the course of Western history.

To guide your interpretation of any source, you should begin by asking several basic questions, listed below, as starting points for observing, analyzing, and interpreting the past. Your answers should prompt further questions of your own.

1. **Who is the author?** Who wrote or created the material? What was his or her authority? (Personal? institutional?) Did the author have specialized knowledge or experience? If you are reading a written document, how would you describe the author's tone of voice? (Formal, personal, angry?)

2. **Who is the audience?** Who were the intended readers, listeners, or viewers? How does the intended audience affect the ways that the author presents ideas?

3. **What are the main ideas?** What are the main points that the author is trying to convey? Can you detect any underlying assumptions of values or attitudes? How does the form or medium affect the meaning of this document?

4. **In what context was the document created?** From when and where does the document originate? What was the interval between the initial problem or event and this document, which responded to it? Through what form or medium was the document communicated? (For example, a newspaper, a government record, an illustration.) What contemporary events or conditions might have affected the creation of the document?

5. **What's missing?** What's missing or cannot be learned from this source, and what might this omission reveal? Are there other sources that might fill in the gaps?

Now consider these questions as you read the following document, "Columbus Describes His First Voyage, 1493." Compare your answers to the sample observations provided.

Columbus Describes His First Voyage, 1493

In this famous letter to Raphael Sanchez, treasurer to his patrons, Ferdinand and Isabella, Columbus recounts his initial journey to the Bahamas, Cuba, and Hispaniola (today Haiti and the Dominican Republic), and tells of his achievements. This passage reflects the first contact between Native Americans and Europeans; already the themes of trade, subjugation, gold, and conversion all emerge in Columbus's own words.

Indians would give whatever the seller required; …Thus they bartered, like idiots, cotton and gold for fragments of bows, glasses, bottles, and jars; which I forbad as being unjust, and myself gave them many beautiful and acceptable articles which I had brought with me, taking nothing from them in return; I did this in order that I might the more easily conciliate them, that they might be led to become Christians, and be inclined to entertain a regard for the King and Queen, our Princes and all Spaniards, and that I might induce them to take an interest in seeking out, and collecting, and delivering to us such things as they possessed in abundance, but which we greatly needed. They practise no kind of idolatry, but have a firm belief that all strength and power, and indeed all good things, are in heaven, and that I had descended from thence with these ships and sailors, and under this impression was I received after they had thrown aside their fears. Nor are they slow or stupid, but of very clear understanding; and those men who have crossed to the neighbouring islands give an admirable description of everything they observed; but they never saw any people clothed, nor any ships like ours. On my arrival at that sea, I had taken some Indians by force from the first island that I came to, in order that they might learn our language, and communicate to us what they know respecting the country; which plan succeeded excellently, and was a great advantage to us, for in a short time, either by gestures and signs, or by words, we were enabled to understand each other. These men are still travelling with me, and although they have been with us now a long time, they continue to entertain the idea that I have descended from heaven.

Source: Christopher Columbus, *Four Voyages to the New World.* Translated by R. H. Major (New York: Corinth Books, 1961), 8–9.

1. **Who is the author?** The title and headnote that precede each document contain information about the authorship and date of its creation. In this case, the Italian explorer Christopher Columbus is the author. His letter describes events in which he was both an eyewitness and a participant.

2. **Who is the audience?** Columbus sent the letter to Raphael Sanchez, treasurer to Ferdinand and Isabella—someone who Columbus knew would be keenly interested in the fate of his patrons' investment. Because the letter was also a public document written to a crown official, Columbus would have expected a wider audience beyond Sanchez. How might his letter have differed had it been written to a friend?

3. **What are the main ideas?** In this segment, Columbus describes his encounter with the native people. He speaks of his desire to establish good relations by treating them fairly, and he offers his impressions of their intelligence and naiveté—characteristics he implies will prove useful to Europeans. He also expresses an interest in converting them to Christianity and making them loyal subjects of the crown.

4. **In what context was the document was created?** Columbus wrote the letter in 1493, within six months of his first voyage. He would have been eager to announce the success of his endeavor.

5. **What's missing?** Columbus's letter provides just one view of the encounter. We do not have a corresponding account from the Native Americans' perspective nor from anyone else travelling with Columbus. With no corroboration evidence, how reliable is this description?

Note: You can use these same questions to analyze visual images. Start by determining who created the image—whether it's a painting, photograph, sculpture, map, or artifact—and when it was made. Then consider the audience for whom the artist might have intended the work and how viewers might have reacted. Consult the text for information about the time period, and look for visual cues such as color, artistic style, and use of space to determine the central idea of the work. As you read, consult the captions in this book to help you evaluate the images and to ask more questions of your own.

Authors' Note

The B.C.E./C.E. Dating System

"When were you born?" "What year is it?" We customarily answer questions like these with a number, such as "1987" or "2004." Our replies are usually automatic, taking for granted the numerous assumptions Westerners make about how dates indicate chronology. But to what do numbers such as 1987 and 2004 actually refer? In this book the numbers used to specify dates follow a recent revision of the system most common in the Western secular world. This system reckons the dates of solar years by counting backward and forward from the traditional date of the birth of Jesus Christ, over two thousand years ago.

Using this method, numbers followed by the abbreviation B.C.E., standing for "before the common era" (or, as some would say, "before the Christian era"), indicate the number of years counting backward from the assumed date of the birth of Jesus Christ. B.C.E. therefore indicates the same chronology marked by the traditional abbreviation B.C. ("before Christ"). The larger the number following B.C.E. (or B.C.), the earlier in history is the year to which it refers. The date 431 B.C.E., for example, refers to a year 431 years before the birth of Jesus and therefore comes earlier in time than the dates 430 B.C.E., 429 B.C.E., and so on. The same calculation applies to numbering other time intervals calculated on the decimal system: those of ten years (a decade), of one hundred years (a century), and of one thousand years (a millennium). For example, the decade of the 440s B.C.E. (449 B.C.E. to 440 B.C.E.) is earlier than the decade of the 430s B.C.E. (439 B.C.E. to 430 B.C.E.). "Fifth century B.C.E." refers to the fifth period of 100 years reckoning backward from the birth of Jesus and covers the

years 500 B.C.E. to 401 B.C.E. It is earlier in history than the fourth century B.C.E. (400 B.C.E. to 301 B.C.E.), which followed the fifth century B.C.E. Because this system has no year "zero," the first century B.C.E. covers the years 100 B.C.E. to 1 B.C.E. Dating millennia works similarly: the second millennium B.C.E. refers to the years 2000 B.C.E. to 1001 B.C.E., the third millennium to the years 3000 B.C.E. to 2001 B.C.E., and so on.

To indicate years counted forward from the traditional date of Jesus' birth, numbers are followed by the abbreviation C.E., standing for "of the common era" (or "of the Christian era"). C.E. therefore indicates the same chronology marked by the traditional abbreviation A.D., which stands for the Latin phrase *anno Domini* ("in the year of the Lord"). A.D. properly comes before the date being marked. The date A.D. 1492, for example, translates as "in the year of the Lord 1492," meaning 1492 years after the birth of Jesus. Under the B.C.E./C.E. system, this date would be written as 1492 C.E. For dating centuries, the term "first century C.E." refers to the period from 1 C.E. to 100 C.E. (which is the same period as A.D. 1 to A.D. 100). For dates C.E., the smaller the number, the earlier the date in history. The fourth century C.E. (301 C.E. to 400 C.E.) comes before the fifth century C.E. (401 C.E. to 500 C.E.). The year 312 C.E. is a date in the early fourth century C.E., while 395 C.E. is a date late in the same century. When numbers are given without either B.C.E. or C.E., they are presumed to be dates C.E. For example, the term *eighteenth century* with no abbreviation accompanying it refers to the years 1701 C.E. to 1800 C.E.

No standard system of numbering years, such as B.C.E./C.E., existed in antiquity. Different people in different places identified years with varying names and numbers. Consequently, it was difficult to match up the years in any particular local system with those in a different system. Each city of ancient Greece, for example, had its own method for keeping track of the years. The ancient Greek historian Thucydides, therefore, faced a problem in presenting a chronology for the famous Peloponnesian War between Athens and Sparta, which began (by our reckoning) in 431 B.C.E. To try to explain to as many of his readers as possible the date the war had begun, he described its first year by three different local systems: "the year when Chrysis was in the forty-eighth year of her priesthood at Argos, and Aenesias was overseer at Sparta, and Pythodorus was magistrate at Athens."

A Catholic monk named Dionysius, who lived in Rome in the sixth century C.E., invented the system of reckoning dates forward from the birth of Jesus. Calling himself *Exiguus* (Latin for "the little" or "the small") as a mark of humility, he placed Jesus' birth 754 years after the foundation of ancient Rome. Others then and now believe his date for Jesus' birth was in fact several years too late. Many scholars today calculate that Jesus was born in what would be 4 B.C.E. according to Dionysius's system, although a date a year or so earlier also seems possible.

Counting backward from the supposed date of Jesus' birth to indicate dates earlier than that event represented a natural complement to reckoning forward for dates after it. The English historian and theologian Bede in the early eighth century was the first to use both forward and backward reckoning from the birth of Jesus in a historical work, and this system gradually gained wider acceptance because it provided a basis for standardizing the many local calendars used in the Western Christian world. Nevertheless, B.C. and A.D. were not used regularly until the end of the eighteenth century. B.C.E. and C.E. became common in the late twentieth century.

The system of numbering years from the birth of Jesus is far from the only one in use today. The Jewish calendar of years, for example, counts forward from the date given to the creation of the world, which would be calculated as 3761 B.C.E. under the B.C.E./C.E. system. Under this system, years are designated A.M., an abbreviation of the Latin *anno mundi,* "in the year of the world." The Islamic calendar counts forward from the date of the prophet Muhammad's flight from Mecca, called the *Hijra,* in what is the year 622 C.E. The abbreviation A.H. (standing for the Latin phrase *anno Hegirae,* "in the year of the Hijra") indicates dates calculated by this system. Anthropology commonly reckons distant dates as "before the present" (abbreviated B.P.).

History is often defined as the study of change over time; hence the importance of dates for the historian. But just as historians argue over which dates are most significant, they disagree over which dating system to follow. Their debate reveals perhaps the most enduring fact about history—its vitality.

About the Authors

LYNN HUNT, Eugen Weber Professor of Modern European History at the University of California, Los Angeles, received her B.A. from Carleton College and her M.A. and Ph.D. from Stanford University. She is the author of *Revolution and Urban Politics in Provincial France* (1978); *Politics, Culture, and Class in the French Revolution* (1984); and *The Family Romance of the French Revolution* (1992). She is also the coauthor of *Telling the Truth about History* (1994); coauthor of *Liberty, Equality, Fraternity: Exploring the French Revolution* (2001, with CD-ROM); editor of *The New Cultural History* (1989); editor and translator of *The French Revolution and Human Rights* (1996); and coeditor of *Histories: French Constructions of the Past* (1995), *Beyond the Cultural Turn* (1999), and *Human Rights and Revolutions* (2000). She has been awarded fellowships by the Guggenheim Foundation and the National Endowment for the Humanities and is a fellow of the American Academy of Arts and Sciences. She served as president of the American Historical Association in 2002.

THOMAS R. MARTIN, Jeremiah O'Connor Professor in Classics at the College of the Holy Cross, earned his B.A. at Princeton University and his M.A. and Ph.D. at Harvard University. He is the author of *Sovereignty and Coinage in Classical Greece* (1985) and *Ancient Greece* (1996, 2000) and one of the originators of *Perseus 1.0: Interactive Sources and Studies on Ancient Greece* (1992, 1996, and www.perseus.tufts.edu), which, among other awards, was named the EDUCOM Best Software in Social Sciences (History) in 1992. He also wrote the lead article on ancient Greece for the revised edition of the *Encarta* electronic encyclopedia. He serves on the editorial board of STOA (www.stoa.org) and as co-director of its DEMOS project (online resources on ancient Athenian democracy). A recipient of fellowships from the National Endowment for the Humanities and the American Council of Learned Societies, he is currently conducting research on the comparative historiography of ancient Greece and ancient China.

BARBARA H. ROSENWEIN, professor of history at Loyola University Chicago, earned her B.A., M.A., and Ph.D. at the University of Chicago. She is the author of *Rhinoceros Bound: Cluny in the Tenth Century* (1982); *To Be the Neighbor of Saint Peter: The Social Meaning of Cluny's Property, 909–1049* (1989); *Negotiating Space: Power, Restraint, and Privileges of Immunity in Early Medieval Europe* (1999); and *A Short History of the Middle Ages* (2001). She is the editor of *Anger's Past: The Social Uses of an Emotion in the Middle Ages* (1998) and coeditor of *Debating the Middle Ages: Issues and Readings* (1998) and *Monks and Nuns,*

Saints and Outcasts: Religion in Medieval Society (2000). A recipient of Guggenheim and National Endowment for the Humanities fellowships, she is currently working on a history of emotions in the early Middle Ages.

R. PO-CHIA HSIA, Edwin Erle Sparks Professor of History at Pennsylvania State University, received his B.A. from Swarthmore College and his M.A. and Ph.D. from Yale University. He is the author of *Society and Religion in Münster, 1535–1618* (1984); *The Myth of Ritual Murder: Jews and Magic in Reformation Germany* (1988); *Social Discipline in the Reformation: Central Europe 1550–1750* (1989); *Trent 1475: Stories of a Ritual Murder Trial* (1992); and *The World of the Catholic Renewal* (1997). He has edited *The German People and the Reformation* (1998); *In and Out of the Ghetto: Jewish-Gentile Relations in Late Medieval and Early Modern Germany* (1995); *Calvinism and Religious Toleration in the Dutch Golden Age* (2002); and *A Companion to the Reformation World* (Blackwell Companion Series, 2004). An academician at the Academia Sinica, Taiwan, he has also been awarded fellowships by the Woodrow Wilson International Society of Scholars, the National Endowment for the Humanities, the Guggenheim Foundation, the Davis Center of Princeton University, the Mellon Foundation, the American Council of Learned Societies, and the American Academy in Berlin. Currently he is working on the cultural contacts between Europe and Asia between the sixteenth and eighteenth centuries.

BONNIE G. SMITH, Board of Governors Professor of History at Rutgers University, earned her B.A. at Smith College and her Ph.D. at the University of Rochester. She is the author of *Ladies of the Leisure Class* (1981); *Confessions of a Concierge: Madame Lucie's History of Twentieth-Century France* (1985); *Changing Lives: Women in European History Since 1700* (1989); *The Gender of History: Men, Women, and Historical Practice* (1998); and *Imperialism* (2000). She is also the coauthor and translator of *What Is Property?* (1994); editor of *Global Feminisms since 1945* (2000); and coeditor of *Objects of Modernity: Selected Writings of Lucy Maynard Salmon, Gendering Disability* (2004) and the forthcoming *Oxford Encyclopedia of Women in World History*. She has received fellowships from the Guggenheim Foundation, the National Endowment for the Humanities, the National Humanities Center, the Davis Center of Princeton University, and the American Council of Learned Societies. Currently she is studying the globalization of European culture since the seventeenth century.

The Making of the West

PEOPLES AND CULTURES

Prologue:
Before Civilization,
to c. 4000 B.C.E.

IN 1997, A TEAM OF ARCHAEOLOGISTS IN ETHIOPIA spied pieces of fossilized bone embedded in hard sand. They scraped away the dirt to reveal the fragments, which fit together to form an adult skull, missing its lower jaw. Deep cut marks scarred the surface of the skull. The archaeologists soon found pieces of other skulls, including a much smaller one. Radioisotope analysis of the bones produced a startling analysis: dated to about 160,000 years ago, they were the oldest remains ever found of the species **Homo sapiens** ("wise human being")—people whose brains and appearances were similar (though not identical) to ours today. Before this, no one had ever discovered fossils near as old as these that could be securely identified as *Homo sapiens*. The discovery excited scientists because it seemed to confirm what previously had been only a theory: that *Homo sapiens* first appeared in Africa around 160,000 to 200,000 years ago and spread from there all over the world.

New discoveries keep making new history, which means that answers to important questions, such as those concerning human origins, can change. Also, past discoveries can be reinterpreted through new research, which means that historians regularly open new debates over the meaning of what has already been found. As part of doing history, therefore, experts argue and often disagree over the significance of evidence. Some scientists, for example, contest the "out of Africa" theory of human origins, arguing for a multiregional model according to which human beings arose in different parts of the world. They hope that future discoveries of fossilized human bones in widely different places will prove them correct. Research concerning the periods, locations, and ways in which human beings came into existence and populated the world thus fuels one of the hottest topics in contemporary archaeology and anthropology.

The Paleolithic Age,
c. 200,000–c. 10,000 B.C.E.
- The Life of Hunter-Gatherers
- Trade, Technology, Religion, and Hierarchy

The Neolithic Age,
c. 10,000–c. 4000 B.C.E.
- The Neolithic Revolution
- Neolithic Origins of Modern Life
- Daily Life in the Neolithic Village of Çatalhöyük
- Social Change in the Neolithic Age

Stone Age Handaxe
Archaeologists found this stone cutting tool, called a handaxe, at the site in Ethiopia where they also discovered the bones of the oldest known ancestors of the species Homo sapiens—people closely resembling modern human beings. These early people probably used a hammer made from bone or wood to chip off flakes from the stone to create knifelike edges for cutting. This sharp tool would have been especially useful for butchering animals, such as the hippopotamuses that these hunter-gatherers killed for meat. Shown here at its full size (seven and a half inches top to bottom), the tool would have fit into the palm; perhaps users wrapped it in a piece of hide to protect their hands from cuts. *Paleoanthropology Laboratory, National Museum of Ethiopia, Addis Ababa. Photo © 2001 David L. Brill/Atlanta.*

A crucial point on which researchers agree is that the deepest roots of human history tunnel far into the past. The scientific dating of fossilized bones supports genetic studies on human mitochondrial DNA to suggest that human beings developed slowly over millions of years before the emergence of *Homo sapiens*. Researchers disagree on precisely how long it took for the descendents of *Homo sapiens* to become the most recent type of human being—people exactly like us. They call this modern type *Homo sapiens sapiens* ("wise, wise human being"). Originating in sub-Saharan Africa more than fifty thousand years ago, bands of these modern-type human beings had moved out of Africa by some forty-five thousand years ago to settle across the Near East,[1] Europe, and Asia, becoming the ancestors of everyone alive today.

---

[1]The term *Near East*, like *Middle East*, has undergone several changes in meaning over time. Both terms reflect the geographical point of view of Europeans. Today, the term *Middle East*, more commonly employed in politics and journalism than in history, usually refers to the area encompassing the Arabic-speaking countries of the eastern Mediterranean region, Israel, Iran, Turkey, Cyprus, and much of North Africa. Ancient historians, by contrast, generally use the term *ancient Near East* to designate Anatolia (often called Asia Minor, today occupied by the Asian portion of Turkey), Cyprus, the lands around the eastern end of the Mediterranean, the Arabian peninsula, Mesopotamia (the lands north of the Persian Gulf, today Iraq and Iran), and Egypt. In this book we will observe the common usage of the term *Near East* to mean the lands of southwestern Asia and Egypt.

❖ The Paleolithic Age, c. 200,000–c. 10,000 B.C.E.

Archaeology is our only source of information about the extended period of human history before 10,000 B.C.E.; there are no documents to inform us about the lives of early human beings because people did not invent writing until about 4000–3000 B.C.E. For this reason, historians sometimes label the time before the invention of writing as "prehistory," because "history" traditionally implies having written sources about the past. It is also possible to label this period "precivilization" because these early people did not live in cities, the main characteristic that historians use to distinguish the word *civilization*. (The first cities emerged about the same time as writing, as we will see in Chapter 1.) Both *prehistory* and *precivilization* are contested terms because they can be taken to mean that people without writing or cities were "primitive," when in fact they developed complex ways of life.

The period in which these early peoples lived is called the Stone Age because they made their most durable tools from stone. The Stone Age saw the most significant change in all of ancient human history: people learned how to produce their own food by farming instead of only hunting for it in the wild. This discovery changed almost everything about how people have lived since. To mark this momentous turning point, archaeologists divide the Stone Age into two periods, one before people farmed for a living—the **Paleolithic** ("Old Stone") period and one after, the **Neolithic** ("New Stone") period.

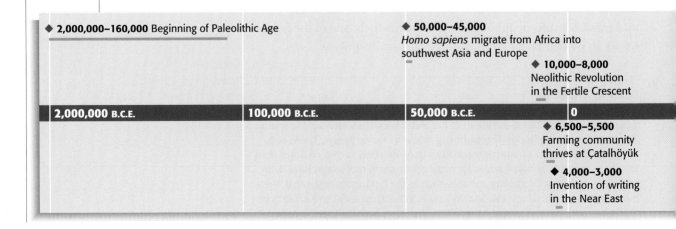

◆ **2,000,000–160,000** Beginning of Paleolithic Age

◆ **50,000–45,000**
Homo sapiens migrate from Africa into southwest Asia and Europe

◆ **10,000–8,000**
Neolithic Revolution in the Fertile Crescent

| 2,000,000 B.C.E. | 100,000 B.C.E. | 50,000 B.C.E. | 0 |

◆ **6,500–5,500**
Farming community thrives at Çatalhöyük

◆ **4,000–3,000**
Invention of writing in the Near East

The Life of Hunter-Gatherers

Paleolithic peoples lived a radically different life from the settled existence most of us now take for granted: they roamed all their lives, never settling permanently in one place, always moving around because they had to hunt and gather their food in the wild. Although they knew a great deal about how to survive in the natural environment, they had not yet learned to produce their own food by growing crops and raising animals. Instead, they hunted wild game for meat, fished in lakes and rivers, collected shellfish along the shore, and gathered wild grains, fruits, and nuts. Historians refer to human beings who obtained their food in these ways as **hunter-gatherers**.

Archaeology reveals that the movement of the later *Homo sapiens sapiens* out of Africa around 50,000–45,000 B.C.E. was a crucial period in human history because it coincided with what some scientists call an explosion of inventiveness. People began devising new forms of tools, weapons, and jewelry and more elaborate burial customs. Climate change probably impelled people to leave Africa. Long periods without rain would have driven game animals into southwest Asia and then Europe to find water, and at least some of the mobile human populations who hunted them in African lands would have followed this moving food into new continents. There is no evidence explaining why some hunter-gatherers left Africa in the Paleolithic period while others stayed behind.

When *Homo sapiens sapiens* first appeared in Europe and Asia, they encountered earlier types of human beings that had migrated out of Africa long before, such as the heavy-browed, squat-bodied Neanderthal type (named after the Neander Valley in Germany, where their fossil remains were first found; their body type is often used to represent "cave men" in popular art). Eventually *Homo sapiens sapiens* completely replaced all earlier types of people around the globe, traversing then-existent land bridges to reach the Americas and Australia.

Archaeological exploration of early humans' campsites tells us about their lives on the move. In addition, anthropologists speculate about the lives of ancient hunter-gatherers on the basis of comparative study of the scattered groups of people who lived on as hunter-gatherers into modern times, such as the !Kung♦ San of Africa's Kalahari Desert in southern Africa, the Aborigines in Australia, and the Coahuiltecans♦ in the American Southwest. These two categories of evidence suggest that Paleolithic hunter-gatherers banded together in groups numbering around twenty or thirty people to hunt and forage for food that they shared with each other. Their average life expectancy was about twenty-five to thirty years. Since they had not learned to domesticate animals or to make wheels for carts, they walked everywhere. Because women of childbearing age had to carry and nurse their babies, they would have found it difficult to roam far from camp. They and the smaller children therefore gathered edible plants, fruits, and nuts close to camp and caught small animals such as frogs and rabbits. The plant food that they gathered provided the majority of the group's diet. Men did most of the hunting of large animals, which frequently took them a great distance away from camp to kill prey at close range with rocks and spears; butchered hippopotamus bones found near the skulls in Ethiopia show that early humans hunted these large and dangerous animals. Women probably participated in some hunts, especially when the group used large nets to ensnare game.

Although early people tended to divide their main labor—finding food—by gender, they recognized that both women and men did essential work in feeding their band. In fact, hunter-gatherers probably lived originally in societies that we would characterize as egalitarian, meaning that all adults enjoyed a general equality in making decisions for the group. Nevertheless, differences in social status probably existed. Older people of both genders gained prestige because of their wisdom, gained from long experience of life in an era when most people died of illness or accidents before they were thirty years old. Women past childbearing age earned respect by helping out wherever needed around camp, while strong and clever men may have also enjoyed higher status from their prominent role in hunting dangerous game.

♦**!Kung:** (clicking sound) kung
♦**Coahuiltecans:** koh uh WEEL tehk uhns

Paleolithic hunter-gatherers did not roam randomly in their search for food. Each group tended to stay within its own territory. If they behaved anything like the hunter-gatherers of modern times, they ranged over an area that averaged roughly sixty miles across in any one direction. Their constant walking, bending, and lifting kept them in robust condition, but they counted on their knowledge as well as their strength. Most important, they planned ahead for cooperative hunts at favorite spots, such as river crossings or lakes with shallow banks, where experience taught they were likely to find herds of large game animals fording the stream and drinking water.

They also used their knowledge to establish makeshift camps year after year in the locations that experience showed to be particularly good spots for gathering wild plants to eat. They took shelter from the weather in caves or rough dwellings made from branches and animal skins. On occasion, they built more elaborate shelters, such as the dome-like hut found in Ukraine that was constructed from the bones of mammoths. Nevertheless, their temporary dwellings could never become permanent homes; they had to roam to survive.

Trade, Technology, Religion, and Hierarchy

Over time, Paleolithic people developed skill at shaping tools such as hammers and blades from stone, wood, and bone. When they encountered other bands, they could exchange these worked goods or valued natural objects such as flint or seashells. The objects exchanged in this way could travel great distances from their point of origin: for example, ocean shells worn as jewelry made their way inland through repeated swaps from one group to another. This process of exchange, for which there is archaeological evidence from the late Paleolithic period, foreshadowed the development of long-distance trade that would forge connections among distant parts of the world in later times.

Technological innovation helped Paleolithic people increase their chances for survival. Learning how to chip sharp edges and points in stone created better cutting tools and weapons for hunting, digging out roots, and making clothes from animal skins. The discovery of how to kindle fire proved invaluable, especially because Paleolithic people had to endure the cold of extended ice ages, when the northern European glaciers moved much farther south than usual. The coldest part of the most recent Ice Age started about twenty thousand years ago and created a harsh climate in much of Europe for nearly ten thousand years. Their control of fire also helped hunter-gatherers to flourish by making it possible for them to cook. Cooking was a crucial innovation because it turned indigestible wild plants, such as grains, into edible and nutritious food.

Archaeological discoveries hint that Paleolithic hunter-gatherers had religious beliefs that began very long ago. Researchers interpret the missing jaws and the marks on the skulls found in Ethiopia and elsewhere as evidence that these early people cut away the flesh from dead persons' heads as part of a careful burial ritual (and not for cannibalism, as some have said). Even the small Ethiopian skull, that of a child six or seven years old, received this treatment. Another indication of belief is the care with which later Paleolithic bands buried their dead, decorating the corpses with red paint, flowers, and seashells. This elaborate procedure points to a concern with the mystery of death and perhaps some notions about an afterlife.

Important evidence for early religious beliefs also comes from the discovery of striking female figurines in excavations of late Paleolithic sites all over Europe. These statuettes of women with extra-large breasts,

A Paleolithic Shelter

This is a reconstruction of a hut that Paleolithic people built around fifteen thousand years ago from the bones of giant mammoths in what is now Ukraine. Animal hides would have been used to cover the poles. It was small group to survive structure, like a tent on big enough for a to huddle inside cold weather.
Novosti   *(London).*

abdomens, buttocks, and thighs were called Venus figurines by modern archaeologists after the Roman goddess of sexual love (see the Venus of Willendorf, shown here). These sculptures' exaggerated features suggest that the people who made them had a special set of beliefs and rituals about fertility and birth. Comparative evidence from early Japan suggests that women played a role in these religious activities.

The colorful late Paleolithic cave paintings found in Spain and France hint at hunter-gatherers' religious ideas and display their artistic ability. Using strong, dark lines and earthy colors, Paleolithic artists painted on the walls of caves that were set aside as special places, not used as day-to-day shelters. The paintings, which depict primarily large animals, suggest that these powerful beasts and the dangerous hunts for them played a significant role in the life and religion of Paleolithic hunter-gatherers. Still, there remains a great deal we cannot yet understand about their beliefs, such as the meaning of the dots, rectangles, and hands that they often drew beside their paintings of animals.

Burials reveal more than religious beliefs: they show that by late Paleolithic times hunter-gatherers recognized differences in status and marked them with physical objects.

Prehistoric Venus Figurine
This limestone statuette, eleven centimeters high, was found at Willendorf in Austria. Carved in the later Paleolithic period and originally colored red, it probably was meant to have symbolic power expressing the importance of women's fertility. The striking depiction of the woman's breasts and pubic area have led scholars to call such statuettes Venus figurines after the Roman goddess of love and sex; archaeologists have uncovered many of them all across Europe. Since no contemporary texts exist to explain the significance of the figurine's hairstyle, obesity, and pronounced sexual characteristics, we can only speculate about the complex meanings that prehistoric peoples extracted from it. How would you explain the figurine's appearance? *SuperStock.*

People who were buried with weapons, tools, animal figurines, ivory beads, and bracelets must have had special social standing for their band to bury these valuable items along with the body. These object-rich burials suggest that some late Paleolithic groups organized themselves into **hierarchies**,

Bison Painting in the Cave at Lascaux
Stone Age people painted these bison on the rock walls of a large cave at Lascaux in central France about 15,000 B.C.E., to judge from radiocarbon dating of charcoal found on the floor. Using black, red, yellow, and white pigments, the artists made the deep cave into an art gallery by filling it with pictures of large animals such as these European buffaloes, horses, deer, bears, and wooly rhinoceroses. Some scholars have suggested that the scenes were meant to symbolize the importance of hunting to the people who painted them, but this guess seems wrong because the bones from butchered animals found in the cave are 90 percent reindeer, while no reindeer pictures exist in the cave. **For more help analyzing this image**, see the visual activity for this chapter in the Online Study Guide at **bedfordstmartins.com/hunt**. *Bridgeman Art Library.*

the technique of smelting metal from ore. This tricky process—the basis of true metallurgy and the foundation of much modern technology—required temperatures of seven hundred degrees centigrade, and it took centuries for metalworkers to perfect. Other workers at Çatalhöyük specialized in weaving textiles, and the scraps of cloth discovered there are the oldest examples of this craft ever found. Like other early technological innovations, metallurgy and the production of cloth apparently also developed independently in other places.

In addition to craft specialization, trade also figured prominently in the economy of this early farming community. Trade allowed the people of Çatalhöyük to acquire goods from far away, such as shells from the Mediterranean Sea to wear as ornaments and a special flint from far to the east to shape into ceremonial daggers. The villagers acquired these prized materials by offering obsidian in exchange, a local volcanic glass whose glossy luster and capacity to hold a sharp edge made it valuable. The trading contacts the Neolithic villagers made with other settlements increased the level of economic interconnection among far-flung communities that had begun in the Paleolithic period.

The nearby volcano that provided obsidian for the villagers to trade proved in the end to be as dangerous as it had been profitable. Çatalhöyük never recovered from a volcanic eruption that overwhelmed it about a thousand years after its foundation. A remarkable wall painting suggests that the people of Çatalhöyük regarded the volcano as an angry god whom they needed to propitiate, and shrines uncovered by archaeologists show how much their religious beliefs meant to the villagers. They outfitted these special rooms with representations of bulls' heads and female breasts, perhaps as symbols of male and female elements in their religion. Like the hunter-gatherers before them, they sculpted figurines depicting amply endowed women, who perhaps represented goddesses of birth. This evidence for their fascination with the secret of life and fertility, so essential to maintain their population, finds its mirror image in the evidence for their deep interest in the mystery of death: skulls displayed in the shrines and wall paintings of vultures devouring headless corpses.

We cannot tell whether the village had priests or priestesses with special authority for religious matters, just as we cannot tell what sort of political organization the villagers had for making decisions. We can feel confident, however, that the people of Çatalhöyük had a social and political hierarchy. The need to plan and regulate irrigation, trade, and the exchange of food and goods between farmers and crafts producers created a need for leaders with more authority than was required to maintain peace and order in hunter-gatherer bands. Furthermore, households that were successful in farming, herding, crafts production, and trade generated surpluses in wealth that distinguished them from others whose efforts proved less fortunate. In short, the villagers did not live in an undifferentiated, egalitarian, or leaderless society.

Social Change in the Neolithic Age

The equality between men and women that existed in hunter-gatherer society had also disappeared by the late Neolithic period. The reasons for this shift remain uncertain, but they perhaps involved gradual changes in agriculture and herding over many centuries. Plows pulled by animals began to be used after about 4000 B.C.E. to cultivate land that was more difficult to sow than the areas cultivated in the earliest period of agriculture. Men apparently operated this new technology of plowing, probably because it required more physical strength than digging with sticks and hoes. They also predominated in the tending of the larger herds that had become more common in settled communities; people were now keeping cattle as sources of milk and raising sheep for wool. The herding of a community's large groups of animals tended to take place at a distance from the home settlement because the animals continually needed new grazing land. As with hunting in hunter-gatherer populations, men, free from having to nurse children, took on this task that required ranging a long way from home.

Women, on the other hand, probably became more tied to the central settlement because they had to bear and raise more children to support agriculture as it became more intensive and therefore required more and more labor than had foraging for food or the earliest forms of farming. The responsibility for new labor-intensive tasks related to processing the secondary products of larger herds also fell to women. For example, they now turned milk into cheese and yogurt and made cloth by spinning and weaving wool. The predominance of men in agriculture in the late Neolithic period combined with women's lessened mobility and decreased time away from housebound tasks apparently led to women's loss of equality with men. The changes in people's lives that occurred during the Neolithic Revolution prepared the way for the first civilizations.

All these transformations of human life eventually combined to create cities and **political states**, people living in a definite territory and organized under a system of government with powerful leaders, officials, and judges. These marks of civilization first appeared in the Near East, but they subsequently emerged at various other distant places around the world, including India, China, and the Americas—whether through independent development or some process of mutual influence we cannot yet say. Either way, the innovations in human life created by the Neolithic Revolution spurred the development of civilization as we know it today.

> **Review:** In what major ways did the Neolithic Revolution change people's lives?

Conclusion

Permanent homes, relatively reliable food supplies from agriculture and animal husbandry, specialized occupations, and hierarchical societies in which men have held the most power have characterized Western history from the Neolithic period forward. For this reason, the broad outlines of the life of Neolithic villagers might seem unremarkable to us today. But the Neolithic way of life in built environments surrounded by cultivated fields and herds would have seemed astounding, we can guess, to Paleolithic hunter-gatherers, such as the roaming African hippopotamus hunters who now rank as the earliest known *Homo sapiens*. The Neolithic Revolution was the most pivotal change in the early history of human beings; it literally overturned the ways in which people related to and affected the natural environment and the ways in which they related to and affected one another. Now that farmers and herders could produce a surplus of food to support other people, specialists in art, architecture, crafts, religion, and politics could multiply as never before. Hand in hand with these developments came an increasing social differentiation and a new division of labor by gender that saw men begin to take over agriculture and women to take up new tasks at home. These developments reflected the apportionment of power in the society.

Suggested References

Çatal Höyük archaeological site: http://catal
.arch.cam.ac.uk/index.html.

Clark, J. Desmond, et al. "Stratigraphic, Chronological and Behavioural Contexts of Pleistocene *Homo Sapiens* from Middle Awash, Ethiopia," *Nature* 423 (June 12, 2003): 747–52.

Diamond, Jared. *Guns, Germs, and Steel: The Fates of Human Societies.* 1999.

Fagan, Brian M. *People of the Earth: An Introduction to World Prehistory.* 10th ed. 2000.

Klein, Richard G. *The Dawn of Human Culture.* 2002.

Lewis-Williams, David. *The Mind in the Cave: Consciousness and the Origins of Art.* 2002.

Rudgley, Richard. *The Lost Civilizations of the Stone Age.* 1999.

Wenke, Robert J. *Patterns in Prehistory: Humankind's First Three Million Years.* 4th ed. 1999.

White, Tim D., et al. "Pleistocene *Homo Sapiens* from Middle Awash, Ethiopia," *Nature* 423 (June 12, 2003): 742–47.

CHAPTER REVIEW

IMPORTANT EVENTS

c. 200,000–160,000 B.C.E.	Beginning of the Paleolithic ("Old Stone") Age
c. 50,000–45,000 B.C.E.	*Homo sapiens* migrate from Africa into southwest Asia and Europe
c. 10,000–8000 B.C.E.	The Neolithic ("New Stone") Revolution in the Fertile Crescent
c. 8000 B.C.E.	Walled settlement at Jericho (in modern Israel)
c. 6500–5500 B.C.E.	Farming community thrives at Çatal-höyük (in modern Turkey)
c. 4000–3000 B.C.E.	Invention of writing in the Near East

KEY TERMS

demography (P–11)

hierarchies (P–7)

Homo sapiens (P–3)

hunter-gatherers (P–5)

Neolithic (P–4)

Neolithic Revolution (P–8)

Paleolithic (P–4)

political states (P–15)

REVIEW QUESTIONS

1. How would you describe the daily activities of Paleolithic hunter-gatherers, male and female?

2. In what major ways did the Neolithic Revolution change people's lives?

MAKING CONNECTIONS

1. Explain whether you think human life was more stressful in the Paleolithic period or the Neolithic period.

2. What do you think were the most important differences and similarities between Stone Age life and modern life? Why?

FOR FURTHER EXPLORATION

To assess your mastery of the material in this prologue, see the Online Study Guide at **bedfordstmartins.com/hunt**.

CHAPTER 1

Foundations of Western Civilization, c. 4000–c. 1000 B.C.E.

ANCIENT EGYPTIANS BELIEVED that the gods judged them after death, to decide their fate in the afterlife, and that the stakes were high. In *Instructions for Merikare*, for example, written sometime around 2100–2000 B.C.E., Merikare's father, the king, warns his son to rule with justice because even a king would face a day of judgment when divine inquisitors would determine whether his choices had been good or evil: "Make secure your place in the cemetery by being upright, by doing justice, upon which people's hearts rely.... When a man is left over after mourning, his deeds are piled up next to him as treasure." Being judged pure of heart led to an eternal reward; if the dead king reached the judges "without doing evil," he would be transformed so that he would "abide [in the afterlife] like a god, roaming [free] like the lords of time."

Being judged impure, however, meant disaster for all eternity. The illustrated manual containing instructions for mummies on how to travel safely in the underworld, commonly called the *Book of the Dead*, explained that on the day of judgment the jackal-headed god Anubis would weigh the dead person's heart in a scale against the goddess Maat✦ and her feather of Truth, with the ibis-headed god Thoth carefully writing down the result (see the illustration at left). Pictures in the *Book of the Dead* also show the "Swallower of the

---

✦**Maat:** MAH aht

Weighing of the Heart on Judgment Day
This painting on papyrus (paper made from a river reed) from about 1275 B.C.E. illustrates a main concern of ancient Egyptian religious belief: the day of judgment when the gods decided a person's fate after death. Here, a man named Any is having his heart (in the left balance) weighed against the feather of Truth of the goddess Maat. The feather stands for "What Is Right." The jackal-headed god Anubis works the scales, while the bird-headed god Thoth records the result. The standing male figure on the left symbolizes Any's destiny, and the seated figures above are the jury of gods. The painting formed part of Any's copy of the *Book of the Dead*, a collection of instructions and magic spells to help the dead person in the afterlife, on the assumption that the verdict would be positive and bestow a blessed eternal life. *British Museum, London, UK/Bridgeman Art Library.*

Damned"—a hybrid monster featuring a crocodile's head, a lion's body, and a hippopotamus's hind end—who crouched behind Thoth ready to devour the heart of anyone who failed the test of purity. These stories, like the many others with a similar message preserved in Egyptian mythology, taught that living a just life was the highest human goal because it was the key to a blessed existence after death.

The Egyptians' neighbors in the ancient Western world—the Mesopotamians, those inhabiting the eastern Mediterranean coast (called the Levant,[1] today Syria, Lebanon, Palestine, and Israel), the Cretans, and the Greeks—did not all share this optimism about the chances for a delightful afterlife. Some, like the Greeks, believed that most people could expect only a gloomy, shadow-like existence following their deaths. All these peoples, however, agreed that justice was the ideal by which they should organize their societies and guide their personal lives. At the same time, they disagreed over whether the gods paid close attention to how human beings treated one another.

These are the peoples whose beliefs, customs, and accomplishments historians call the foundations of Western civilization. It is essential to acknowledge from the start that these early peoples living around the Mediterranean Sea and in the Near East had diverse ideas on issues as fundamental as the

---

[1] The term *Levant*, French for "rising (sun)"—that is, the East—reflects the European perspective on the region's location. It is the term commonly used in professional writing to refer to these lands.

nature of justice. This sort of cultural diversity has always characterized what historians call Western civilization. It is also true that trade and travel kept these peoples in frequent contact with other populations elsewhere on the globe, exchanging goods, technologies, and ideas. This tendency toward interconnectivity raises the question of what historians mean by the concept *Western civilization*, a term that is sometimes taken to imply separateness or even isolation from the rest of the world.

❖ The Controversial Concept of Western Civilization

Technically, a study of the history of Western civilization focuses on the peoples living on and near the continent of Europe from ancient to modern times, beginning with the history of Sumer in Mesopotamia and of Egypt in Africa. In practice, the historical idea of Western civilization mixes together three ambiguous topics: the contested historical concept of civilization, the geographic notion of the West, and—most controversial of all—the value of Western culture (that is, the West's particular ways of life and ideas).

Debating the Meaning of Western Civilization

Historians traditionally define the term **civilization** as a way of life that includes political states based on cities with dense populations, large buildings constructed for communal activities, diverse economies,

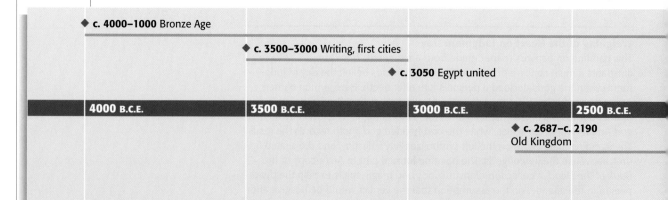

◆ **c. 4000–1000** Bronze Age

◆ **c. 3500–3000** Writing, first cities

◆ **c. 3050** Egypt united

4000 B.C.E.	**3500 B.C.E.**	**3000 B.C.E.**	**2500 B.C.E.**

◆ **c. 2687–c. 2190** Old Kingdom

a sense of local identity, and some knowledge of writing. The implications of this definition are controversial (see "Terms of History," page 6). Although we often use *civilization* and related terms such as *civilized behavior* as if everyone agreed that civilization was not a problematic idea, some social critics of modern life ask whether civilization in fact represents a better and more just way of life than does human history "before civilization." They argue that people were healthier, more equal in power, and more peaceful before civilization. Such comparisons are hard to evaluate meaningfully because there is so little evidence about life before civilization (see the Prologue, pages P-3–P-16). If there were indeed fewer conflicts then, it might be simply because so many fewer people existed and they were spread so much farther apart.

The geographic notion of the West comes to us from the Greeks. Building on ideas they probably derived from their Near Eastern neighbors, they gave us the term *Europe* to indicate the West (where the sun sets) as distinct from the East (where the sun rises). The Greeks, like modern historians, were not sure exactly where to draw the boundaries of the West because the geographical content of the term was, and is, too open-ended to allow precise definition. The boundaries shift depending on what era is being described, and the *West* in *Western civilization* sometimes refers to peoples and places beyond Europe and sometimes not. For example, the region that is today Turkey was certainly part of Western civilization at the time of the Roman empire; yet in the opening years of the twenty-first century, Europeans and Turks alike are debating what changes in Turkish life and politics it would take—and what the financial and cultural costs would be—for Turkey to be judged Western enough to join the European Union.

The idea that one culture might be superior in value to another is the most contested issue surrounding the concept of Western (or indeed any) civilization. This idea is old. The Greeks inherited from their neighbors in the Near East the idea that regional differences meant that one people's way of life was better than another's. Merikare's father, for instance, sternly warned him to beware of the "miserable Asiatic [Near Easterner], wretched because of where he's from, a place with no water, no wood.... He doesn't live in one place, hunger propels his legs.... He doesn't announce the day of battle, like a thief darting around a crowd."

Modern commentators continue to argue over the relative merits of different cultures as part of the murky debate over the meaning of *Western* (or, for that matter, *Eastern*) *civilization*. One thing, however, is clear about the story of Western civilization: cultural borrowing between the peoples of Europe and their neighbors near and far has characterized Western civilization from the beginning, whether that borrowing involved ideas, technologies, or goods. In fact, the story of Western civilization concerns cultural and political interaction both among the West's diverse peoples and between them and the peoples of the rest of the globe. Therefore, we should not understand the word *Western* to mean "fenced off in the West from the rest of the world."

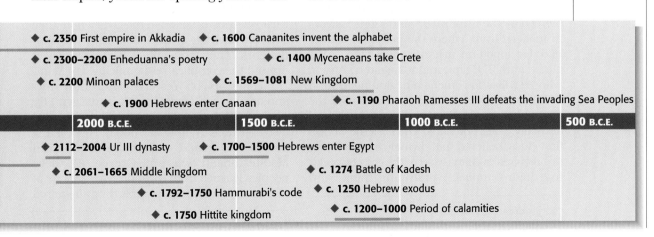

♦ **c. 2350** First empire in Akkadia   ♦ **c. 1600** Canaanites invent the alphabet

♦ **c. 2300–2200** Enheduanna's poetry   ♦ **c. 1400** Mycenaeans take Crete

♦ **c. 2200** Minoan palaces   ♦ **c. 1569–1081** New Kingdom

♦ **c. 1900** Hebrews enter Canaan   ♦ **c. 1190** Pharaoh Ramesses III defeats the invading Sea Peoples

| **2000** B.C.E. | **1500** B.C.E. | **1000** B.C.E. | **500** B.C.E. |

♦ **2112–2004** Ur III dynasty   ♦ **c. 1700–1500** Hebrews enter Egypt

♦ **c. 2061–1665** Middle Kingdom   ♦ **c. 1274** Battle of Kadesh

♦ **c. 1792–1750** Hammurabi's code   ♦ **c. 1250** Hebrew exodus

♦ **c. 1750** Hittite kingdom   ♦ **c. 1200–1000** Period of calamities

TERMS OF HISTORY

Civilization

Our term *civilization* comes from the Latin word *civilis*. For ancient Romans, civilis meant "suitable for a private citizen" and "behaving like an ordinary, unpretentious person." To be "un-civilis" was to behave in a showy and arrogant way that suggested you thought yourself superior to others.

Ironically, then, the modern term *civilization* expresses the judgment that becoming civilized meant achieving a superior way of life. Consider, for example, these definitions from a widely used reference work, *The Random House Webster's College Dictionary*.[1]

civilization: 1. an advanced state of human society, in which a high level of culture, science, and government has been reached. 2. those people or

nations that have reached such a state. 3. any type of culture, society, etc. of a specific place, time, or group: *Greek civilization*. 4. the act or process of civilizing or being civilized. 5. cultural and intellectual refinement. 6. cities or populated areas in general, as opposed to unpopulated or wilderness areas. 7. modern comforts and conveniences, as made possible by science and technology.

civilize: to bring out of a savage, uneducated, or rude state; make civil; enlighten; refine: *Rome civilized the barbarians*.

civilized: 1. having an advanced or humane culture, society, etc. 2. polite, well-bred; refined.

The common thread among these definitions is the idea that *civilization* implies an "advanced" or "refined" way of life compared to a "savage" or "rude" way. Ancient peoples often drew this sort of comparison between themselves and others whom

---

[1] *The Random House Webster's College Dictionary*, 2nd ed. (New York, 1997), 240.

Locating Western Civilization's Foundations

If we accept the traditional definition of *civilization*, Western civilization's deepest foundations lie in two places: (1) Mesopotamia (the region pierced by the Euphrates◆ and Tigris◆ Rivers in modern Iraq), where the people of Sumer had developed an urban society by c. 3000 B.C.E., and (2) Egypt, in northeastern Africa, whose civilization emerged beginning around 3050 B.C.E., when a strong ruler unified the country along the Nile River under a central authority. The Sumerians, who built the world's first cities, believed that divinely imposed justice required humans to serve the gods by building them temples, worshiping them, and

bringing them gifts, even though the deities seemed unpredictable and arbitrary. The Egyptians employed their extraordinary architectural skills and their country's natural wealth in agriculture and minerals to build magnificent temples and pyramids that expressed their religious devotion to the gods whom they believed lovingly provided them with life's delights. Their concept of justice revolved around the complicated significance of Maat.

The story of Western civilization next spreads beyond Mesopotamia and Egypt. By around 2000–1900 B.C.E., civilizations had also appeared in Anatolia◆ (today Turkey), the Levant, the island of Crete in the eastern Mediterranean Sea, and Greece. All these peoples learned from the older civilizations of Mesopotamia and Egypt, and they all shared

---

◆**Euphrates:** yu FRAY teez
◆**Tigris:** TY gruhs

◆**Anatolia:** a nuh TOH lee uh

they saw as crude; the urban dwellers of the Near East, Greece, and Rome, for example, applied this judgment to those who did not build cities. Much later, this notion of superiority became especially prominent in European thought after voyagers to the New World and colonial settlers reported on what they saw as the savage or barbarous life of the peoples they called Indians. Because Europeans of the times saw Indian life as lacking discipline, government, and, above all, Christianity, it seemed to them to be primitive and raw and therefore an inversion of their idea of civilized life.

Thus, the term *civilization* entered the English language in a "sense opposed to *barbarity*," as James Boswell in 1772 advised Samuel Johnson to define it in the latter's famous and influential *Dictionary of the English Language*. It became common to compare "the lower races of man" with "civilized peoples."[2] The word's built-in sense of comparative superiority became so accepted that it could even be used to express this notion in nonhuman contexts, such as in the following startling comparison: "some communities of ants are more advanced in civilization than others."[3]

Historians in recent times have been reluctant to confront explicitly the difficult issues that the term raises. For example, they shy away from the troubling question of how, or indeed whether, to evaluate the relative merits of one civilization versus another. Tellingly, there is no mention of the topic in the standard guide to scholarly work issued by the major professional organization for historians.[4]

Ultimately, the failure to consider what the term should mean can lead to its being used without much definitional content at all, as in the Random House dictionary's third definition under *civilization*. Does the term have any deep meaning if it can be used to mean "any type of culture, society, etc. of a specific place, time, or group"? This empty definition reveals that studying civilization still presents daunting challenges to students of history today. It should be their task to make *civilization* a term with intellectual content and a reality with meaning for improving human life, as those who first used the word thought that it was.

---

[2] Sir John Lubbock, *The Origin of Civilisation and The Primitive Condition of Man. Mental and Social Condition of Savages*, 5th ed. (New York, 1889), 1–2.

[3] Sir John Lubbock, *On the Origin and Metamorphoses of Insects*, 2nd ed. (London, 1874), 13.
[4] *The American Historical Association's Guide to Historical Literature*, 3rd ed. (New York, 1995).

the sense that nothing in life was more important than religion. Comparably complex societies also emerged in India, China, and the Americas in different eras starting around 2500 B.C.E.; however, these societies pursued independent paths of development before coming in contact with people from Europe and the Mediterranean in much later times.

Early civilizations developed and changed both intentionally and unintentionally. The invention of increasingly sophisticated metallurgical technology, for example, led to the creation of ever better tools and weapons, but it also turned out to be one factor promoting differences in social status; that is, people constructed status for themselves in part by acquiring metal objects. In every known civilization people insisted on establishing hierarchies, or status differences, among themselves. Some contemporary scientists claim that this development was inevitable because human beings are by nature "status-protecting organisms." In any case, early civilizations evolved to a large extent through cultural interaction provoked by international trade and war. Contact with unfamiliar ways and technologies spurred people to learn from one another and to adapt for themselves the traditions, beliefs, and inventions of others.

Understanding the history of Western civilization therefore requires us to trace the mingling and conflicts of diverse peoples and regions. We will begin with the early civilizations of Mesopotamia, Egypt, the Levant, Crete, and Greece. We will be reminded of the potential fragility of what we traditionally call civilization when we see that a mysterious era of widespread violence lasting from about 1200 to 1000 B.C.E. nearly put an early end to civilization in the West.

❖ Mesopotamia, Home of the First Civilization, c. 4000–c. 1000 B.C.E.

The Neolithic Revolution (see the Prologue, pages P-3–P-16) opened the way to civilization, as historians define it, by creating the first permanent settlements that, over millennia, grew into cities and by providing enough surplus agricultural resources to allow many people to work full-time at crafts, not just farming. Metal became an ever more important component of wealth and power from around 4000 to 1000 B.C.E. Historians label this period the Bronze Age because bronze, an alloy of copper and tin, was the most important metal for weapons and tools. The ownership of objects produced by the new technology of metallurgy increased the division in society between men and women and rich and poor. Long-distance commerce developed to satisfy people's desire for goods and materials not available in their homelands, while rulers created systems of law to convince their subjects that their power had divine backing and to show the gods that they were promoting justice in their increasingly complex societies.

Early farming villages gradually grew larger until, by around 3000 B.C.E., the people of Sumer, the name for southern Mesopotamia, built settlements big enough to be called the first cities. Each of these large urban communities controlled its surrounding territory and remained politically independent. The cities' residents grew bounteous crops by irrigating marginal land, built great temples to honor their gods, lived in a hierarchical society with slaves at the bottom and kings at the top, and invented writing to keep track of economic transactions and record their stories and beliefs. The rulers of these cities constantly battled one another for glory, territory, trade, and, especially, access to metal ores.

Cities and Society, c. 4000–c. 2350 B.C.E.

The first cities and thus the first civilization emerged in Sumer because its inhabitants figured out how to raise crops on the fertile but dry land between and around the Tigris and Euphrates Rivers (Map 1.1). Agriculture had begun in the well-watered hills of the Fertile Crescent, but these slopes offered too little habitable land to support the growth of cities. The plains along the rivers were huge, but they presented serious challenges to farmers: little rain fell, temperatures soared to 120 degrees Fahrenheit, and devastating floods occurred unpredictably. First Sume-

The "Standard of Ur" of Sumer
This wooden box, about twenty inches long and eight inches high, was found in a large grave in the Royal Cemetery at Ur dating to about 2600–2400 B.C.E. Its pictures, inlaid in white shell, red limestone, and blue lapis lazuli on all sides of the box, have made this mysterious object famous because they provide some of our earliest visual evidence for Sumerian life. This side shows animals being led to a banquet scene, where a musician playing a lyre entertains men in their characteristic woolen fleeces or fringed skirts. The large figure at the left is probably the king, here celebrating his role as the gods' representative to his subjects. The other side shows a Sumerian army. **For more help analyzing this image**, see the visual activity for this chapter in the Online Study Guide at **bedfordstmartins.com/hunt**.
British Museum.

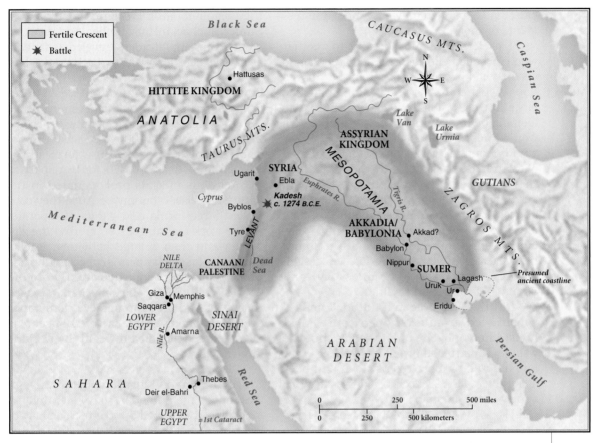

MAP 1.1 The Ancient Near East, c. 4000–3000 B.C.E.
The diverse region we call the ancient Near East encompassed many different landscapes, climates, peoples, and languages. Kings ruled its independent city-states, the centers of the world's first civilizations, beginning around 4000–3000 B.C.E. Trade by land and sea for natural resources, especially metals, and wars of conquest kept the peoples of the region in constant contact and conflict with one another.

rians and then other Mesopotamians turned this marginal environment into lush farmland by using the Tigris and Euphrates to irrigate the plains. Intricate canal systems that required constant maintenance turned the desert green and helped limit flooding. The surpluses of food produced by Mesopotamian farmers allowed the population to swell, the number of crafts producers to increase rapidly, and cities to emerge. The necessity of organizing labor to maintain the canals promoted the growth of monarchy to exercise centralized authority in Mesopotamian cities. Each city controlled agricultural land outside its fortification walls and built large temples inside them. Historians call this arrangement—an urban center

exercising political and economic control over the countryside around it—a **city-state**.

The Cities of Sumer. The origins of the Sumerians are obscure; unlike many other Mesopotamian peoples, they spoke a language whose background remains unknown, except that it was not one of the Semitic languages (which include Akkadian, Hebrew, and Arabic). By around 3000 B.C.E. the Sumerians lived in twelve independent city-states—including Uruk, Eridu,♦ and Ur—which remained fiercely separate communities warring over land and natural resources. By around 2500 B.C.E., each of the Sumerian

♦**Eridu:** EHR ih doo

cities had expanded to twenty thousand residents or more.

Travelers from one city-state to another would first come to the irrigated green fields on the outskirts of the city, then the villages housing agricultural workers, and finally the city's fortress walls and the high buildings looming behind. Outside the gates, travelers would find a bustling center of trade, either a harbor on the river or a marketplace on the overland routes leading to the city. Once they were inside the walls, their eyes would be drawn to the royal family's palace and, above all, to the immense temples. To be close to the gods, Sumerians built great **ziggurats**✦ (see The Ziggurat of Ur in Sumer below), temple towers with a stair-step design, which soared up to ten stories high and dominated the urban skyline.

City dwellers lived in mud-brick houses constructed around an open court. Most houses had only one or two rooms, but the wealthy constructed two-story dwellings that had a dozen or more rooms. Rich and poor alike suffered the ill effects of a domestic water supply often contaminated by sewage because no system of waste disposal existed. Pigs and dogs scavenged in the streets and areas where garbage was unceremoniously dumped.

Agriculture and trade made Sumerians prosperous. They constantly bartered grain, vegetable oil, woolens, and leather with one another and with foreign regions, from which

they acquired natural resources not found in Sumer, such as metals, timber, and precious stones. Sumerian traders traveled as far east as India, sailing for weeks to reach that distant land, where the Indus civilization's large cities emerged about five hundred years after Sumer's. Technological innovation strengthened the early Mesopotamian economy, especially beginning around 3000 B.C.E., when Sumerians invented the wheel in a form sturdy enough to be used on carts for transport.

Religious officials predominated in the early Sumerian economy because they controlled large farms and gangs of laborers, whose work for the gods supported the ziggurats and their related activities. Priests and priestesses supervised considerable property and economic activity. By around 2600 B.C.E., however, the kings had leveraged their war leadership to achieve dominance over the economy; some private households also amassed significant wealth by working large fields.

Kings in Sumer.   Kings and their royal families topped the Sumerian social hierarchy. A king formed a council of older men as his advisers and acknowledged the gods as his ruler and the guarantors of his power. This claim to divinely justified power gave priests and priestesses political influence. Patriarchy—domination by men in political, social, and economic life—was already the rule in these first cities. Although a Sumerian queen was respected because she was the

---

✦**ziggurats:** ZIH guh rats

The Ziggurat of Ur in Sumer

King Ur-Nammu and his son Shulgi built this massive temple as an architectural marvel for their city of Ur (in what is today southern Iraq) in the early twenty-first century B.C.E. Its three massive terraces, one above another and connected by stairways, were constructed with a mud-brick core covered by a skin of baked brick, glued together with tar. Compare the angular outline of its structure with that of the minaret of the Great Mosque at Samarra. The ziggurat's walls were more than seven feet thick to sustain its enormous weight. Its original height is uncertain, but the first terrace alone soared some forty-five feet above the ground. The enormous bulk of the Great Pyramid in Egypt, however, dwarfed it (see page 22). *Hirmer Fotoarchiv.*

wife of the king and the mother of the royal children, the king held the supreme power. Still, women had more legal rights under Sumerian law than they would in later Mesopotamian societies; only Egypt would give women a greater legal standing than Sumer.

The king's supreme responsibility was to ensure justice, which meant pleasing the gods, developing law, keeping order among the people, and defending his city-state from attacks by rival rulers eager to seize its riches and irrigated land. In return, the king extracted surpluses from the working population as taxes to support his family, court, palace, army, and officials. If the surpluses came in regularly, the king mostly left the people alone to live their daily lives.

As befitted his status atop the hierarchy, a Sumerian king and his family lived in an elaborate palace that rivaled the scale of the great temples. The palace served as the city-state's administrative center and the storehouse for the ruler's enormous wealth. Members of the royal family dedicated a significant portion of the community's economic surplus to displaying their superior status. Archaeological excavation of the immense royal cemetery in Ur, for example, has revealed the dazzling extent of the rulers' riches—spectacular possessions crafted in gold, silver, and precious stones. These graves also yielded grislier evidence of the exalted status of the king and queen: the bodies of the servants sacrificed to serve their royal masters after death. The spectacle of wealth and power that characterized Sumerian kingship reveals how great the gap was between the upper and lower ranks of Sumerian society.

Slaves in Sumer. Sumerian society confined slaves to its lowest level. No single description of slavery covers all its diverse forms or its social and legal consequences. Both the gods (through their temple officials) and private individuals could own slaves. People lost their freedom by being captured in war, by being born to slaves, by voluntarily selling themselves or their children to escape starvation, or by being sold by their creditors to satisfy debts. Foreigners enslaved as captives in war or by raiding parties were considered inferior to citizens who fell

into slavery to pay off debts. Children whose parents dedicated them as servants to the gods, although counted as slaves, could rise to prominent positions in the temple administrations.

In general, slaves existed in a state of near-total dependency on other people. Legally, they were excluded from normal social relations, usually worked without compensation, and lacked almost all rights. Although slaves sometimes formed relationships with free persons and frequently married each other and had families, their masters could sell their family members at will. Their masters could buy, sell, beat, or even kill them because slaves counted as property, not humans. Sumerians, like later Mesopotamians, apparently accepted slavery as a fact of nature, and there is no evidence of any sentiment for abolishing it.

Slaves worked in domestic service, craft production, and farming, but historians dispute their economic significance compared with that of free workers. Most state labor seems to have been performed by free persons who paid their taxes through labor rather than with money (which consisted of measured amounts of food or precious metal; coins were not invented until around 700 B.C.E. in Anatolia). Under certain conditions slaves could gain their freedom: masters' wills could liberate them, or they could purchase their freedom from the earnings they could sometimes accumulate.

The Invention of Writing. Beginning around 3500 B.C.E. the Sumerians invented writing to do accounting because their economic transactions had increased in complexity as their populations swelled. Before writing, people drew small pictures on clay tablets to represent objects. At first, these pictographs symbolized concrete objects only, such as a cow. Over several centuries of development, nonpictorial symbols and marks were added to the pictographs to stand for the sounds of spoken language. The final version of Sumerian writing was not an alphabet, in which a symbol represents the sound of a single letter, but a mixed system of phonetic symbols and pictographs that represented the sounds of entire syllables or entire words.

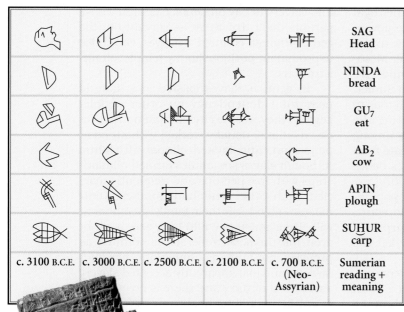

					SAG Head
					NINDA bread
					GU$_7$ eat
					AB$_2$ cow
					APIN plough
					SUHUR carp
c. 3100 B.C.E.	c. 3000 B.C.E.	c. 2500 B.C.E.	c. 2100 B.C.E.	c. 700 B.C.E. (Neo- Assyrian)	Sumerian reading + meaning

FIGURE 1.1 Cuneiform Writing
The earliest known form of writing developed in different locations in Mesopotamia in the 3000s B.C.E. when people began linking meaning and sound to signs such as these. The scribes who mastered the system used sticks or reeds to press dense rows of small wedge-shaped marks into damp clay tablets or chisels to engrave them on stone. Cuneiform was used for at least fifteen Near Eastern languages and continued to be written for three thousand years. Written about 1900 B.C.E., this cuneiform text records a merchant's complaint that a shipment of copper contained less metal than he had expected. His letter, impressed on a clay tablet several inches long, was enclosed in an outer clay shell, which was then marked with the sender's private seal. This envelope (photo above) protected the inner text from tampering or breakage. *British Museum.*

Archaeologists call the Sumerians' fully developed script **cuneiform**♦ (from *cuneus*, Latin for "wedge") because they used wedge-shaped marks impressed into clay tablets to record spoken language (Figure 1.1). Other Mesopotamian peoples subsequently adopted cuneiform to write their own languages. For

a long time, only a few professionally trained men and women, known as scribes, mastered the new technology of writing. Schools sprang up to teach aspiring scribes, who could then find jobs as accountants. Kings, priests, and wealthy landowners employed scribes to keep records that let them control their workers carefully by keeping precise track of who had paid their taxes, who still owed, and how much.

Writing soon proved useful for purposes other than accounting. The scribal schools extended their curriculum to cover nature lore, mathematics, and foreign languages. Writing also created a new way to hand down stories and beliefs previously preserved only in memory and speech. This written literature provided a powerful new tool for passing on a culture's traditions to later generations. Enheduanna,♦ an Akkadian woman of the twenty-third century B.C.E., composed the world's oldest written poetry whose author is known. She was a priestess, prophetess, and princess, the daughter of King Sargon♦ of the city of Akkad.♦ Her poetry, written in Sumerian, praised the awesome power of the life-giving goddess of love, Inanna: "the great gods scattered from you like fluttering bats, unable to face your intimidating gaze . . . knowing and wise queen of all the lands, who makes all creatures and people multiply." Later princesses, who wrote love songs, lullabies, dirges, and prayers, continued the Mesopotamian tradition of royal women as authors and composers.

Mesopotamian Mythology and Religion.
Writing was a crucial technology for passing down Mesopotamian myths about the gods and their actions toward human beings. Mesopotamian religion was a form of **polytheism** (the worship of multiple gods). Various gods were thought to have power in different areas affecting human existence, such as war,

♦**cuneiform:** kyoo NEE uh fawrm

♦**Enheduanna:** en hed oo AH na
♦**Sargon:** SAHR gahn
♦**Akkad:** AH kahd

fertility, and the weather. The more critical a divinity's sphere of influence over people's well-being, the more important the god. Each city-state honored a particular major deity as its special protector.

Realizing that human beings could not control nature, Mesopotamians viewed the gods as absolute masters to whom they owed total devotion. They believed that their deities looked like human beings and had human emotions, especially anger and an arbitrary will. Myths emphasized the gods' awesome but unpredictable power and the limits of human control over what the gods might do to them. If human beings offended them, Mesopotamian divinities such as Enlil, god of the sky, and Ishtar (also called Inanna♦), goddess of love and war, would punish worshipers by causing disasters, like floods and famine.

The *Epic of Gilgamesh*, a long poem usually read today as a combination of its many versions, relates the adventures of the hero Gilgamesh, who sought to cheat death and achieve immortality. As king of the city of Uruk,♦ he forced the city's young men to construct a temple and fortification wall and all the young women to sleep with him. When the distressed inhabitants implored Anu, lord of the gods, to grant them a rival to Gilgamesh, Anu called on Aruru, the mother of the gods, to create a man of nature, Enkidu,♦ "hairy all over...dressed as cattle are." A week of sex with a prostitute tamed this brute, preparing him for civilization: "Enkidu was weaker; he ran slower than before. But he had gained judgment, was wiser." After wrestling to a draw, Enkidu and Gilgamesh became friends and set out to conquer Humbaba (or Huwawa), the ugly, giant monster of the Pine Forest. Gilgamesh later insulted the goddess Ishtar, however, who sent the Bull of Heaven to challenge him and Enkidu. The two comrades prevailed, but when Enkidu made matters worse by hurling the dead bull's haunch at Ishtar, the gods condemned him to death. In despair over human failure and frailty, Gilgamesh tried to find the secret of immortality, only to have his quest foiled by a thieving snake. He subsequently realized that

immortality for human beings comes only from the fame generated by their achievements, above all building a great city such as Uruk, which encompassed "three square miles and its open ground." Only memory and gods live forever, he found.

A late version of the *Epic of Gilgamesh* includes a description of a huge flood that covered the earth, recalling the devastating inundations that often struck Mesopotamia. When the gods sent the flood, they warned one man, Utnapishtim, of the impending disaster, telling him to build a boat. He loaded his vessel with his relatives, artisans, possessions, domesticated and wild animals, and "everything there was." After a week of torrential rains, he and his passengers disembarked to repopulate and rebuild the earth. This story foreshadows the biblical account of the flood and the story of Noah's ark. The themes of Mesopotamian mythology, which lived on in poetry and song, also powerfully influenced the mythology of distant peoples, most notably the Greeks.

Since religion meant so much to Mesopotamians, the priest or priestess of a city's chief deity enjoyed extremely high status. The most important duty of Mesopotamian priests was to discover the will of the gods by divination. To perform this function, they studied natural signs by tracking the patterns of the stars, interpreting dreams, and cutting open animals to examine their organs for deformities signaling trouble ahead. These inspections helped the people decide when and how to please their fickle gods, whether by placing wondrous gifts in their sanctuaries or by celebrating festivals in their honor. During the New Year holiday, for example, the reenactment of the mythical marriage of the goddess Inanna and the god Dumuzi was believed to ensure successful reproduction by the city's residents, animals, and plants for the coming year.

Metals, the Akkadian Empire, and the Ur III Dynasty, c. 2350–c. 2000 b.c.e.

The drive to acquire metals from distant sources was one important factor impelling the kings of the Akkadians,♦ a Mesopotamian

♦**Inanna:** in AH na
♦**Uruk:** OO ruk
♦**Enkidu:** EHN kee doo

♦**Akkadians:** uh KAY dee uhns

not the first time in history that private entrepreneurs conducted business in a way that we might label early capitalism—maximizing profits as a reward for the risk of business—but it provides the best-known example from this period.

Hammurabi of Babylon and Written Law. The expansion of private commerce and property ownership in Mesopotamia created a pressing need to guarantee fairness and reliability in contracts and other business agreements. The king had the sacred duty to make divine justice known to his subjects by rendering judgments in all sorts of cases, from commercial disputes to crime. Once written down, the record of the king's decisions amounted to what historians today call a law code, even though the Mesopotamians did not use that term. King Hammurabi◆ (r. c. 1792–c. 1750 B.C.E.) of Babylon, a great city on the Euphrates River in what is today Iraq, built an empire rivaling that of Sargon. The fifth king of the Babylonian Amorite dynasty, he instituted the most famous law code of the era by building on earlier Mesopotamian legal traditions, such as those of the Akkadian monarchs and the Ur III dynasty. Hammurabi's code stands as a prime example of the sophistication that Mesopotamian legal traditions achieved (see "Hammurabi's Laws for Physicians," page 17).

In his code Hammurabi proclaimed that his goals as ruler were to support "the principles of truth and equity" and to protect the less powerful members of society from exploitation. The code legally divided society into three categories: free persons, commoners, and slaves. We do not know what made the first two categories different, but they reflect a social hierarchy in which some people were assigned a higher value than others. An attacker who caused a pregnant woman of the free class to miscarry, for example, paid twice the fine levied for the same offense against a commoner. In the case of physical injury between social equals, the code specified "an eye for an eye" (an expression still used today). But a member of the free class who killed a commoner was not executed, only fined.

◆**Hammurabi:** ha muh RAH bee

Most of the laws concerned the king's interests as a property owner who leased many tracts of land to tenants in return for rent or services. The laws imposed severe penalties for offenses against property, including mutilation or a gruesome death for crimes as varied as theft, wrongful sales, and careless construction. Women had only limited legal rights in this patriarchal society, but they could make business contracts and appear in court. A wife could divorce her husband for cruelty; a husband could divorce his wife for any reason. The inequality of the divorce laws was tempered in practice, however, because a woman could recover the property she had brought to her marriage, a considerable disincentive for a man to end his union.

Hammurabi's laws publicized a royal ideal of justice guaranteed by a righteous king; they did not necessarily reflect everyday reality. Indeed, Babylonian documents show that legal penalties were often less severe than the code specified. The people themselves assembled in courts to determine most cases by their own judgments. Why, then, did Hammurabi have his laws written down? He announces his reasons at the beginning and end of his code: to show Shamash, the Babylonian sun god and god of justice, that he had fulfilled the social responsibility imposed on him as a divinely installed monarch—to ensure justice and the moral and material welfare of his people: "So that the powerful may not oppress the powerless, to provide justice for the orphan and the widow...let the victim of injustice see the law which applies to him, let his heart be put at ease." The king's moral responsibility for his society's welfare corresponded to the strictly hierarchical and religious vision of society accepted by all Mesopotamian peoples.

City Life and Learning. The situations covered by Hammurabi's laws illuminate many aspects of the lives of city dwellers in Mesopotamia's Bronze Age kingdoms. For example, crimes of burglary and assault apparently plagued urban residents. The bride's father and the groom arranged a marriage, sealing the agreement with a legal contract. The detailed laws on surgery make clear that doctors practiced in the cities.

Hammurabi's Laws for Physicians

In Hammurabi's collection of 282 laws, the following statutes set the fees for successful operations and the punishment for physicians' errors. The prescription of mutilation of a surgeon as the punishment for mutilation of a patient from the highest social class (law number 218) squares with the legal principle of equivalent punishment ("an eye for an eye") that pervades Hammurabi's collection.

215. If a physician performed a major operation on a freeman with a bronze scalpel and has saved the freeman's life, or he opened up the eye-socket of a freeman with a bronze scalpel and has saved the freeman's eye, he shall receive ten shekels[1] of silver.

216. If it was a commoner, he shall receive five shekels of silver.

217. If it was a freeman's slave, the owner of the slave shall give two shekels of silver to the physician.

218. If a physician performed a major operation on a freeman with a bronze scalpel and has caused the freeman's death, or he opened up the eye-socket of a freeman and has destroyed the freeman's eye, they shall cut off his hand.

219. If a physician performed a major operation on a commoner's slave with a bronze scalpel and has caused his death, he shall make good slave for slave.

220. If he opened up [the slave's] eye-socket with a bronze scalpel and has destroyed his eye, he shall pay half his value in silver.

---

[1] A shekel is a measurement of weight (about 3/10 oz.), not a coin. A hired laborer earned about a shekel per week. The average price of a slave was about twenty shekels.

Source: Adapted from James B. Pritchard, *Ancient Near Eastern Texts Relating to the Old Testament*, 3rd ed. with supplement (Princeton, NJ: Princeton University Press, 1969), 175.

Because people believed that angry gods or evil spirits caused serious diseases, Mesopotamian medicine included magic as well as treatment with potions and diet. A doctor might prescribe an incantation as part of his therapy. Magicians or exorcists offered medical treatment that depended primarily on spells and on interpreting signs, such as the patient's dreams or hallucinations.

Archaeological evidence supplements the information on urban life found in Hammurabi's code. City dwellers evidently enjoyed alcoholic drinks in a friendly setting because cities had many taverns and wine shops, often run by women proprietors. Contaminated drinking water caused many illnesses because sewage disposal was rudimentary. Relief from the odors and crowding of the streets could be found in the city's open spaces. The oldest known map in the world, an inscribed clay tablet showing the outlines of the Babylonian city of Nippur about 1500 B.C.E., indicates a substantial area set aside as a city park.

Creating maps required sophisticated techniques of measurement and knowledge of spatial relationships. Mesopotamian achievements in mathematics and astronomy had a profound effect that endures to this day. Mathematicians used algebra to solve complex problems, and they could derive the roots of numbers. They invented place-value notation, which makes a numeral's position in a number indicate ones, tens, hundreds, and so on. We have also inherited from Mesopotamia the system of reckoning based on sixty, still used in the division of hours and minutes and degrees of a circle. Mesopotamian expertise in recording the paths of the stars and planets probably arose from the desire to make predictions about the future, in accordance with the astrological belief that the movement of celestial bodies directly affects human life. Astrology never lost its popularity in Mesopotamia, and the charts and tables compiled by Mesopotamian stargazers laid the foundation for later advances in astronomical knowledge.

> **Review:** How did life change for people in Mesopotamia when they began to live in cities?

❖ The Egyptians, Canaanites, and Hebrews, c. 3050–c. 1000 B.C.E.

Africa was home to the second great civilization to shape the West—that of the Egyptians. Egypt was located close enough to Mesopotamia to learn from its peoples but geographically protected enough to develop its own distinct culture. Egyptians created a wealthy, profoundly religious, and strongly traditional civilization ruled by kings. Unlike Mesopotamia, Egypt became a united state whose prosperity and stability depended on the king's success in maintaining strong central authority. The Egyptians' deep concern for the immortality of their souls and the afterlife motivated the construction of some of the most imposing tombs in history, the pyramids, while their architecture and art inspired later Mediterranean peoples, especially the Greeks.

The early civilizations of the Levant never rivaled Egypt's splendor, but they transmitted lasting legacies to Western civilization, especially the Canaanites' alphabet and the monotheism of the Hebrews (or Israelites). The Hebrews' religion, known as Judaism, took a long time to develop and reflected influences from their polytheistic neighbors in Canaan (ancient Palestine), but it initiated the most important religious movements in Western history.

From Egyptian Unification to the Old Kingdom, c. 3050–c. 2190 B.C.E.

Geography treated the Egyptians kindly: the Nile River irrigated their farms, the deserts beyond their rich fields yielded metal ores

and protected them from invasion, their Mediterranean ports supported seaborne commerce, and their southern neighbors in Africa offered trade and cultural interaction. The first large-scale Egyptian state began to emerge about 3050 B.C.E., when King Narmer (also called Menes)[2] united the previously separate territories of Upper (southern) Egypt and Lower (northern) Egypt. (*Upper* and *Lower* derive from the direction of the Nile River, which begins south of Egypt and flows northward to the Mediterranean.) The Egyptian ruler therefore referred to himself as "King of the Two Lands." By around 2687 B.C.E., the monarchs had forged a strong, centralized state, called the Old Kingdom by historians, which lasted until around 2190 B.C.E. (Map 1.2). The Old Kingdom's rulers established Egypt as an international power and a cultural beacon for the ancient world.

Narmer's unification created a state from a territory resembling a long green ribbon, zigzagging seven hundred miles southward from the Mediterranean Sea along the Nile. Lush agricultural fields extending several miles away from the river's banks formed this fertile strip. Under normal weather conditions, the Nile created Egypt's fertility by overflowing its channel for at least several weeks each year, when melting snow from the mountains of central Africa swelled its volume of water. This annual flood enriched the soil with nutrients from the river's silt and prevented the accumulation of harmful deposits of mineral salts. Unlike the random and catastrophic floods of the Mesopotamian

---

[2]Representing ancient Egyptian names and dates presents serious problems. Since the Egyptians did not include vowel sounds in their writing, we are not sure how to spell their names. The spelling of names here is taken from *The Oxford Encyclopedia of Ancient Egypt,* edited by Donald B. Redford (2001), with alternate names given in cases where they might be more familiar. Dates are approximate and controversial; the scattered evidence for Egyptian chronology embroils scholars in "a world of uncertainty and acrimonious debate" (Redford, *The Oxford Encyclopedia*, vol. 1, p. xi; for an explanation of the problems, see the article on "Chronology and Periodization," vol. 1, pp. 264–68). The dates appearing in this book are compiled with as much consistency as possible from articles in *The Oxford Encyclopedia* and in the "Egyptian King List" given at the back of each of its volumes.

rivers, the flooding of the Nile was predictable and beneficial. Trouble came only if dry weather in the mountains kept the flood from occurring and therefore reduced the year's crops to dust.

Deserts east and west of the river protected Egypt from attack by land, except through the Nile's delta at its mouth and its valley on the southern frontier with Nubia. The surpluses that a multitude of hardworking farmers produced in the lush Nile valley made Egypt prosperous. Date palms, vegetables, grass for pasturing animals, and grain grew in abundance. From their ample supplies of grain the Egyptians made bread and beer, a staple beverage.

Egypt comprised a diversity of people, whose skin color ranged from light to very dark. A significant proportion of Egyptians would be regarded as black by modern American racial classification, a distinction ancient people did not observe. The heated modern controversy over whether Egyptians were people of color is therefore anachronistic; if asked, ancient Egyptians would presumably have answered that they identified themselves by geography, language, religion, and traditions. Like many ancient groups, the Egyptians called themselves simply "The People." Later peoples, especially the Greeks, admired Egyptian civilization for its great antiquity and piety. There is merit to the modern accusation that some nineteenth-century historians minimized the Egyptian contribution to Western civilization, but it is important to remember that ancient peoples did not.

Early Egyptians learned from both the Mesopotamians and their southern African neighbors the Nubians.♦ Egyptians may have originally learned the technology of writing from the Sumerians, but they developed their own scripts rather than using cuneiform. To write formal and official texts they used an ornate pictographic script known as **hieroglyphs**♦ (Figure 1.2, page 20). They also developed other scripts for everyday purposes.

Some historians believe that Nubian society deeply influenced early Egypt. At places

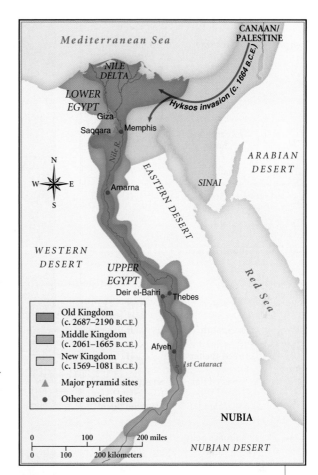

MAP 1.2 Ancient Egypt
Arid deserts closely embraced the Nile River, which provided Egyptians with water to irrigate their fields and a highway for traveling north to the Mediterranean Sea and south to Nubia. The only easy land route into and out of Egypt lay through the northern Sinai peninsula into the coastal area of the eastern Mediterranean; Egyptian kings therefore always fought to control this region to secure the safety of their land.

such as Afyeh, near the Nile's First Cataract, a Nubian social elite lived in dwellings much grander than the small huts housing most of the population. Egyptians interacted with Nubians while trading for raw materials such as gold, ivory, and animal skins, and some scholars argue that a hierarchical political and social organization in Nubia influenced the development of Egypt's politically centralized Old Kingdom. Eventually, however, Egypt's power overshadowed that of its southern neighbor.

♦**Nubians:** NOO bee uhns
♦**hieroglyph:** HY ruh glihf

Hieroglyph	Meaning	Sound value
	vulture	glottal stop
	flowering reed	consonantal I
	forearm and hand	ayin
	quail chick	W
	foot	B
	stool	P
	horned viper	F
	owl	M
	water	N
	mouth	R
	reed shelter	H
	twisted flax	slightly guttural
	placenta (?)	H as in "loch"
	animal's belly	slightly softer than h
	door bolt	S
	folded cloth	S
	pool	SH
	hill	Q
	basket with handle	K
	jar stand	G
	loaf	T

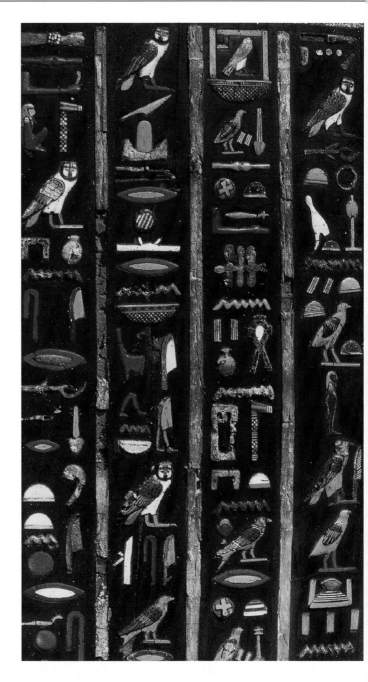

FIGURE 1.2 Egyptian Hieroglyphs
Ancient Egyptians used pictures such as these to develop their own system of writing about 3000 B.C.E. Egyptian hieroglyphs employ around seven hundred pictures in three categories: ideograms (signs indicating things or ideas), phonograms (signs indicating sounds), and determinatives (signs clarifying the meaning of the other signs). Because Egyptians employed this formal script mainly for religious inscriptions on buildings and sacred objects, Greeks referred to it as *ta hieroglyphica* ("the sacred carved letters"), from which comes the modern word *hieroglyphic,* used for this system of writing. Eventually, Egyptians also developed the handwritten cursive script called demotic (Greek for "of the people"), a much simpler and quicker form of writing. The hieroglyphic writing system continued until about 400 C.E., when it was replaced by the Coptic alphabet. The Egyptian language continued to be widely spoken until Arabic displaced it in medieval times. (It is preserved today in the liturgy of the Coptic Church.) Compare hieroglyphic writing with cuneiform (see page 12). *Victor Boswell, Jr. © National Geographic Society Image Collection. Giraudon/Art Resource, NY.*

Religion and the Old Kingdom's Central Authority.

The waxing and waning of strong central authority determined the course of Egyptian political history. When the kings were strong, as during the Old Kingdom, the country was stable and rich, with flourishing international trade, especially along the eastern Mediterranean coast. However, political instability resulted when the governors of different regions refused to support the king.

The king's power and success depended on his properly fulfilling his religious obligations. Like the Mesopotamians, Egyptians both royal and ordinary centered their lives on religion. They worshiped a great variety of gods, who were often shown in paintings and sculpture as creatures with both human and animal features, such as the head of a jackal or a bird atop a human body. This style of depicting deities did not mean that people worshiped animals but rather that they believed the gods each had a particular animal through which they revealed themselves to mortals. A picture or a statue of a divinity included the animal so that the depiction would have meaning to the human observer. Egyptian religion told complicated stories about the daily lives of the gods to explain their powers and their significance for human beings. At the most basic level, deities were associated with powerful natural objects, emotions, qualities, and technologies—examples are Re, the sun god; Isis, the goddess of love and fertility; and Thoth, the god of wisdom and the inventor of writing.

Egyptians regarded their king as a divinity in human form, identified with the hawk-headed god Horus.♦ In the Egyptian view, the king's rule was divine because it represented on earth the supernatural, eternal force that created harmony and stability in human life. The goddess **Maat** (literally, "What Is Right"), who stood for cosmic order, embodied this force; for Egyptians, order brought justice. As a divine being, the king had the heavy responsibility of ruling according to Maat's principles, which meant promoting law and keeping the forces of nature in balance for the benefit of his people.

This included regulating his daily activities very strictly: he had to have a specific time to take a bath, go for a walk, or make love to his wife. Most crucially, he had to ensure fertility and prosperity. These depended on a proper flooding of the Nile, which he guaranteed by performing his duties justly and in accordance with traditional order. A failure to make the flood happen could gravely weaken the king's authority.

Pyramids and the Afterlife.

Successful Old Kingdom rulers used expensive building programs to demonstrate their piety and exhibit their status atop the social hierarchy. Unlike their Mesopotamian counterparts ruling independent states in a divided land, Egyptian kings built only a few large cities in their united country. The first capital of the united country, Memphis (south of modern Cairo), grew into a metropolis packed with mammoth structures. In the desert outside Memphis, the Old Kingdom rulers erected the most stunning manifestations of their status and their religion— their huge tombs.

These tombs—the pyramids (see The Pyramids at Giza)—formed the centerpieces of elaborate groups of buildings for royal funerals and religious ceremonies. Although the pyramids were not the first monuments in the world built from enormous worked stones (that honor goes to temples on the Mediterranean island of Malta), they rank as the grandest. Old Kingdom rulers spent vast resources on these huge complexes to proclaim their divine status and protect their mummified bodies for existence in the afterlife. Imhotep, chief architect of King Djoser (r. 2687–2668 B.C.E.), became famous for overseeing the construction of the first large stone pyramid, the Step Pyramid at Saqqara.♦ King Khufu♦ (r. 2609–2584 B.C.E.; also known as Cheops♦) commissioned the hugest of them all—the Great Pyramid at Giza. At about 480 feet high, it stands taller than a forty-story skyscraper. Covering more than thirteen acres and 760 feet long on each side, it required more than two million

♦**Horus:** HAWR uhs

♦**Saqqara:** suh KAHR uh
♦**Khufu:** KOO foo
♦**Cheops:** CHEE ahps

blocks of limestone, some of which weighed fifteen tons apiece. Its fine exterior blocks were quarried along the Nile and then floated to the site on barges. Free workers (not slaves) dragged them up ramps into position using rollers and sleds.

The kings' lavish preparations for death reflect the strong Egyptian belief in an afterlife. More than any other ancient people, the Egyptians devoted material resources to preparing for eternity. A hieroglyphic text addressed to the god Atum◆ expresses the hope that the ruler will have a secure afterlife: "O Atum, put your arms around King Neferkare Pepy II [r. c. 2300–2206 B.C.E.], around this construction work, around this pyramid. . . . May you guard lest anything happen to him evilly throughout the course of eternity." The royal family equipped their tombs with elaborate delights for their existence in the world of the dead. Gilded furniture, sparkling jewelry, exquisite objects of all kinds—the dead kings had all this and more placed beside their coffins, in which rested

---

◆**Atum:** AH tuhm

their mummies. Archaeologists have even uncovered two full-sized cedar ships buried next to the Great Pyramid, meant to carry King Khufu on his journey into eternity.

Hierarchy and Order in Egyptian Society. Old Kingdom rulers organized Egyptian society into a tightly structured hierarchy to preserve their authority and therefore support what they regarded as the proper order. The king and queen, whose roles included producing children to continue the ruling dynasty, topped the social order. Brothers and sisters in the royal family could marry each other, perhaps because such matches were believed necessary to preserve the purity of the royal line or to imitate the marriages of the gods. The priests, royal administrators, provincial governors, and commanders of the army came next in the hierarchy, but they ranked far below the king and queen. The common people, who mostly worked in agriculture, constituted the massive base of this figurative pyramid of free people in Egypt. Although not slaves, workers had heavy obligations to the state. For example, in a system

The Pyramids at Giza in Egypt
The kings of the Egyptian Old Kingdom constructed massive stone pyramids for their tombs, the centerpieces of large complexes of temples and courtyards stretching down to the banks of the Nile or along a canal leading to the river. The inner burial chambers lay at the end of long, narrow tunnels snaking through the pyramids' interiors. The biggest pyramid shown here is the so-called Great Pyramid of King Khufu (aka Cheops), erected at Giza (in the desert outside what is today Cairo) in the twenty-sixthcentury B.C.E. and soaring almost 480 feet high, several times taller than the famous Parthenon temple in fifth-century B.C.E. Athens (see page 93). © John Lawrence/Super Stock.

called corvée labor, the kings could and did command commoners to work on the pyramids during slack times for agriculture. The state fed, housed, and clothed them while they performed this seasonal work, but their labor was a way of paying taxes. Rates of taxation reached 20 percent on the produce of free farmers. Slaves captured in foreign wars served the royal family and the priests in the Old Kingdom, but privately owned slaves working in free persons' homes or on their farms did not become prevalent until after the Old Kingdom.

Women generally enjoyed the same legal rights as free men in ancient Egypt. They could own land and slaves, inherit property, pursue lawsuits, transact business, and initiate divorces. Old Kingdom portrait statues show the equal status of wife and husband: each figure is the same size and sits on the same kind of chair. Men dominated public life, while women devoted themselves mainly to private life, managing their households and property. When their husbands went to war or were killed in battle, however, women often took on men's work. Some women could therefore serve as priestesses, farm managers, or healers.

The formalism of Egypt's art illustrates how much the civilization valued order and predictability. Almost all Egyptian sculpture and painting comes from tombs or temples, testimony to its people's consuming interest in maintaining proper relations with the gods. Old Kingdom artists excelled in stonework, from carved ornamental jars to massive portrait statues of the kings. These statues represent the subject either standing stiffly with the left leg advanced or sitting on a chair or throne, stable and poised. The concern for decorum also appears in the Old Kingdom literature the Egyptians called instructions, known today as **wisdom literature**. These texts conveyed instructions for appropriate behavior for high officials. In the *Instruction of Ptahhotep,*◆ for example, the royal minister Ptahhotep instructs his son, who will succeed him in office, not to be arrogant or overconfident just because he is well educated and to seek advice from ignorant people as well as the wise.

◆**Ptahhotep:** tah HOH tehp

The Middle and New Kingdoms in Egypt, c. 2061–c. 1081 B.C.E.

The Old Kingdom's ordered stability began to disintegrate in the late third millennium B.C.E. The causes remain mysterious. One suggestion is that climate changes caused the annual Nile flood to shrink and the ensuing agricultural failure discredited the regime—it had betrayed Maat. Economic hard times probably fueled rivalry for royal rule between ambitious families, and civil war between a northern and a southern dynasty then ripped apart the Kingdom of the Two Lands. This destruction of the Old Kingdom's unity allowed regional governors to increase their power. Some governors, who had supported the kings while times were good, seized independence for their regions. It was the troubles of this period that made Merikare's father's advice so pressing: famine and civil unrest during the so-called First Intermediate Period (c. 2190–c. 2061 B.C.E.) thwarted all attempts to reestablish political unity.

The Middle Kingdom. The monarchs of what historians label the Middle Kingdom (c. 2061–c. 1665 B.C.E.) gradually restored the strong central authority their Old Kingdom predecessors had lost. They pushed the boundaries of Egypt farther south, while to the north they expanded diplomatic and trade contacts in Canaan and Syria and with the island of Crete.

Middle Kingdom literature reveals that the reclaimed national unity contributed to a deeply felt pride in the homeland. The Egyptian narrator of the famous tale *The Story of Sinuhe*, for example, reports that he lived luxuriously during a forced stay in Syria but still longed to return: "Whichever deity you are who ordered my exile, have mercy and bring me home! Please allow me to see the land where my heart dwells! Nothing is more important than that my body be buried in the country where I was born!" For this lost soul, love for Egypt outranks even personal riches.

From the Hyksos Invasion to the New Kingdom. The Middle Kingdom lost its unity during the Second Intermediate Period (c. 1664–c. 1570 B.C.E.), when the kings proved too weak to repel foreign invaders who violently disrupted the Egyptians' ordered world. A Semitic people from the eastern Mediterranean coast expanded into Lower Egypt around 1664 B.C.E. The Egyptians called these foreigners Hyksos♦ (literally, "rulers of the foreign countries"). Recent archaeological discoveries have emphasized the role of Hyksos settlers in transplanting elements of foreign culture to Egypt: their capital, Avaris, boasted wall paintings done in the Minoan style current on the island of Crete. Some historians think the Hyksos also introduced such innovations as bronze-making technology, horses and war chariots, more powerful bows, new musical instruments, humpbacked cattle, and olive trees; they certainly promoted frequent contact with other Near Eastern states. As with the empire of the Akkadians, violent invasion indirectly promoted cultural interchange.

Eventually, the leaders of Thebes in southern Egypt reunited the kingdom by overcoming the Hyksos in a long struggle; their dynasties are called the New Kingdom (c. 1569–c. 1081 B.C.E.). The kings of this period, known as *pharaohs* (meaning "the great house" and referring to the royal palace and estate) rebuilt central authority by restricting the power of regional governors and promoted a renewed sense of national identity. To prevent invasions, the pharaohs created a standing army and a military elite to lead it. Recognizing from the Hyksos invasion that knowledge of the rest of the world was necessary for safety, they engaged in regular diplomacy with neighboring monarchs to increase their cosmopolitan contacts. In fact, the pharaohs regularly exchanged letters on matters of state with their "brother kings," as they called them, in Mesopotamia, Anatolia, and the eastern Mediterranean region.

Warrior Pharaohs. The New Kingdom pharaohs sent their reorganized military into foreign wars to promote Egypt's interests. They earned the epithet *warrior pharaohs* by waging many campaigns abroad and modifying their royal religious stature by presenting themselves as the incarnations of warrior gods. They invaded Nubia and the Sudan to the south to win access to gold and

other precious materials, and they fought in the lands of the Levant to control the land route to Egypt.

Massive riches supported the power of the warrior pharaohs. Egyptian traders exchanged local fine goods, such as ivory, for foreign luxury goods, such as wine and olive oil transported in painted pottery from Greece. Egyptian royalty displayed its wealth most conspicuously in the enormous sums spent to build stone temples. Queen Hatshepsut♦ (opposite) (r. 1502–1482 B.C.E.), for example, built her massive mortuary temple at Deir el Bahri near Thebes, including a temple dedicated to the god Amun (or Amen), to buttress her claim to divine birth and the right to rule. After her husband (who was also her half brother) died, Hatshepsut proclaimed herself "female king" as co-ruler with her young stepson. In this way, she shrewdly sidestepped Egyptian political ideology, which made no provision for a queen to reign in her own right. She therefore often had herself represented in official art as a man, sporting a king's beard and male clothing.

Religious Tradition and Upheaval. The many gods of Egyptian polytheism oversaw all aspects of life and death, with particular emphasis on the afterlife. Glorious temples honored the traditional gods, and their cults (that is, worship traditions and rituals) enriched the religious life of the entire population. The principal festivals of the gods, for example, involved lavish public celebrations. A calendar based on the moon governed the dates of religious ceremonies. (The Egyptians also developed a calendar for administrative and fiscal purposes that had 365 days, divided into 12 months of 30 days each, with the extra 5 days added before the start of the next year. Our modern calendar derives from it.)

The early New Kingdom pharaohs from Thebes promoted their state god Amun-Re♦ until he overshadowed the other gods. This Theban cult incorporated and subordinated the other gods without denying either their existence or the continued importance of their priests. The pharaoh Akhenaten♦

♦**Hyksos:** HIHK sahs

♦**Hatshepsut:** hat SHEHP soot
♦**Amun-Re:** AH muhn RAH
♦**Akhenaten:** AH kehn AH tehn

(r. 1372–1355 B.C.E.) went a step further, however; because he believed so fervently that traditional belief was misguided, he forcibly reformed official religion by making Aten, who represented the shining disk of the sun, the only true god. Some scholars identify Akhenaten's religion as the first **monotheism** (belief in only one god, as in Judaism, Christianity, and Islam). Akhenaten made the king and the queen the only people with direct access to the cult of Aten, using his new religion as a tool to reassert power over the nobles. Ordinary people had no part in the cult.

To showcase the royal family and the concentration of power that he sought, Akhenaten built a new capital for his god at Tell el-Amarna (see Map 1.2). He tried to force his revised religion on the priests of the old cults, but they resisted stubbornly. Historians have blamed Akhenaten's religious zeal for leading him to neglect the practical affairs of ruling the kingdom, weakening its defense, but recent research on international correspondence found at Tell el-Amarna has shown that the pharaoh used diplomacy to try to pit foreign enemies against each other to prevent them from becoming strong enough to threaten Egypt. His policy failed, however, when the Hittites defeated the Mitanni, Egypt's allies in eastern Syria. His religious reform also died with him. During the reign of Akhenaten's successor, Tutankhamun◆ (r. 1355–1346 B.C.E.)—famous today through the discovery in 1922 of his rich, unlooted tomb—the cult of Amun-Re reclaimed its leading role. The crisis created by Akhenaten's attempted reform emphasizes the overwhelming importance of religious conservatism in Egyptian life and the control of religion by the ruling power.

Life and Belief in the New Kingdom.

Despite the period's many upheavals, the rhythm of ordinary Egyptians' daily lives still revolved around their labor and the annual flood of the Nile. During the months when the river stayed between its banks, they worked their fields, rising early in the morning to avoid the searing heat. Their obligation to labor on royal building projects came due when the flooding halted agricultural work

Queen Hatshepsut of Egypt as Pharaoh
This famous New Kingdom monarch of the fifteenth century B.C.E. had to adopt the male trappings of Egyptian kingship to claim legitimacy because her land's tradition had no place for women as sole rulers. Here she is depicted wearing the distinctive garb of a pharaoh. She had this statue placed in a temple she built outside Thebes in Upper Egypt. *Metropolitan Museum of Art, Rogers Fund and contribution from Edward Harkness, 1929.*

◆**Tutankhamun:** too tang KAH muhn

become because it did not deny the existence of other gods. Because in the ensuing centuries some Hebrews worshiped other gods as well, such as Baal of Canaan, it seems that the covenant with Yahweh and fully formed Hebrew monotheism did not emerge until well after 1000 B.C.E.

The Hebrews who fled from Egypt with Moses made their way back to Canaan, but they were still exposed to attacks by the Egyptian army. The first documentation of their return to Canaan comes from an inscribed monument erected by the pharaoh Merneptah in the late thirteenth century B.C.E. to commemorate his victory in a military expedition there. The Hebrew tribes joined their relatives who had remained in Canaan and somehow carved out separate territories for themselves there. The twelve tribes remained politically distinct under the direction of separate leaders, called judges, until the eleventh century, when their first monarchy emerged. Their monotheism gradually developed over the succeeding centuries.

> **Review:** How did religion guide the lives of people in the early civilizations of Egypt and the Levant?

❖ The Hittites, Minoans, and Mycenaeans, c. 2200–c. 1000 B.C.E.

The first civilizations in the central Mediterranean region emerged in Anatolia, dominated by the warlike Hittite kingdom (see Map 1.1); on the large island of Crete, home to the famously artistic Minoan civilization; and on the Greek mainland, where Mycenaean civilization grew rich from raiding and trade (Map 1.3).

These peoples enjoyed advanced technologies, elaborate architecture, striking art, a marked taste for luxury, and extensive trade contacts with Egypt and the Near East. They also inhabited a dangerous world in which regional disruptions from around 1200 to 1000 B.C.E. ultimately overwhelmed their prosperous cultures. Nevertheless, their accomplishments paved the way for the later civilization of Greece, which would dramatically influence the course of Western history.

The earliest central Mediterranean civilizations arose on islands located on antiq-

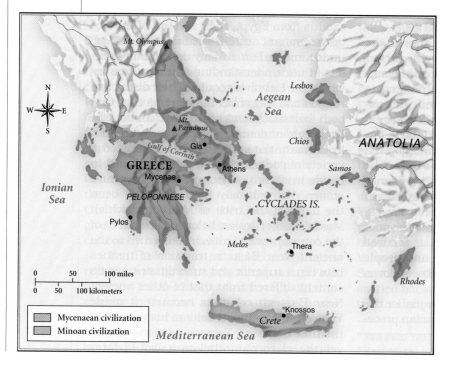

MAP 1.3 Greece and the Aegean Sea, c. 1500 B.C.E.
A closely packed jumble of mountains, islands, and seas defined the geography of Greece. The distances between settlements were mostly short, but rough terrain and seasonally stormy sailing made travel a chore. The distance from the mainland to the largest island in this region, Crete, where Minoan civilization arose, was sufficiently long to keep Cretans isolated from the turmoil of most of later Greek history.

Hittite Royal Couple Worshiping the Weather God

This relief sculpture from Alaca Höyük in north central Anatolia shows a Hittite king and queen worshiping the weather god, as he was called, who is represented here by his sacred animal, the bull, standing on an altar. In Hittite mythology, the weather god was thought to ride over the mountains in a chariot pulled by bulls. He was a divine hero who overcame evil by slaying a great dragon. At first the monster defeated him, but the goddess Inaras tricked the dragon into getting drunk so that the weather god could kill him. What characteristics of bulls and dragons made them relevant for expressing religious ideas? *Hirmer Fotoarchiv.*

uity's interstate highway, the sea. People, trade goods, and ideas from other places could reach islands easily. As early as 6000 B.C.E., people from Anatolia began migrating westward and southward to inhabit islands in the Mediterranean Sea. By around 2200 B.C.E., the rich civilization of the Minoans had emerged on the island of Crete. The Anatolian peoples who stayed on the mainland also developed civilizations, of which the most aggressive and ambitious was the kingdom of the Hittites, who came into conflict with New Kingdom Egypt.

The Hittite Kingdom, c. 1750–c. 1200 B.C.E.

By around 1750 B.C.E. the Hittites had made themselves the most powerful people of central Anatolia. They had migrated from the Caucasus area, between the Black and Caspian Seas, and overcome indigenous peoples to set up their kingdom. It flourished because they inhabited a fertile upland plateau in the peninsula's center, excelled in war and diplomacy, and controlled trade in their region and southward. The Hittites' military campaigns knifing into the Levant threatened Egypt's possessions in Syria.

Since the Hittites spoke an Indo-European language, they belonged to the linguistic family that eventually populated most of Europe. The original Indo-European speakers, who were pastoralists and raiders, had migrated as separate groups into Anatolia and Europe, including Greece, from somewhere in western Asia. Recent archaeological discoveries there of graves of women buried with weapons suggest that women in these groups originally occupied positions of leadership in war and peace alongside men; the prominence of Hittite queens in documents, royal letters, and foreign treaties perhaps sprang from that tradition.

As in other early civilizations, rule in the Hittite kingdom depended on religion. Hittite religion combined worship of the gods of Indo-European religion with worship of deities inherited from the original Anatolian population. The king served as high priest of the storm god, and Hittite belief therefore demanded that he maintain a strict purity in his life as a demonstration of his justice and guardianship of social order. His drinking water, for example, always had to be strained. So strong was this insistence on purity that the king's water carrier was executed if so much as one hair was found in the water. Like Egyptian kings, Hittite rulers felt responsible for maintaining the gods' goodwill toward their subjects. King Mursili♦ II (r. 1321–1295 B.C.E.), for example, issued a set of prayers begging the gods to end a plague: "What is this, o gods, that you have done? Our land is dying. . . . We have lost our wits, and we can do nothing right. O gods, whatever sin you behold, either let a prophet come forth to identify it . . . or let us see it in a dream!"

The kings conducted many religious ceremonies in their capital, Hattusas, which grew into one of the most impressive cities of its era. Ringed by massive defensive walls and towers of stone, it centered on huge palaces aligned along straight, gravel-paved streets. Sculptures of animals, warriors, and, especially, the royal rulers decorated public spaces. The Hittite kings maintained their rule by forging personal alliances—cemented by marriages and oaths of loyalty—with the noble families of the kingdom.

These rulers aggressively employed their troops to expand their power. In the periods during which ties between the kings and the nobles remained strong and the kingdom therefore preserved its unity, they launched extremely ambitious military campaigns. In 1595 B.C.E., for example, the royal army raided as far as Babylon, destroying that kingdom. Scholars no longer accept the once popular idea that the Hittites owed their success in war to a special knowledge of making weapons from iron, although their craftsmen did smelt iron, from which they made ceremonial implements. (Weapons made from iron did not become common in the Mediterranean world until well after 1200 B.C.E.—at the end of the Hittite kingdom.) Their army excelled in the use of chariots, and perhaps this skill gave them an edge.

The economic strength of the Hittite kingdom flowed from control over long-distance trade routes for essential raw materials, especially metals. The Hittites worked mightily to dominate the lucrative trade moving between the coast and inland northern Syria. The Egyptian New Kingdom pharaohs fiercely resisted Hittite expansion and power in this region. The Anatolian kingdom proved too strong, however, and in the bloody battle of Kadesh,♦ around 1274 B.C.E., the Hittites checked the Egyptians in Syria, leading to a stalemate. Fear of Assyria eventually led the Hittite king Hattusili♦ III to negotiate with his Egyptian rival Ramesses II, and the two warweary kingdoms became allies sixteen years after the battle of Kadesh by agreeing to a treaty that is a landmark in the history of international diplomacy. Remarkably, both Egyptian and Hittite copies of the treaty survive. In it, the two monarchs pledged to be "at peace and brothers forever." The alliance lasted, and thirteen years later the Hittite king gave his daughter to his Egyptian "brother" as his wife.

Minoan Crete, c. 2200–c. 1400 B.C.E.

Study of early Greek civilization traditionally begins with the people today known as Minoans, who inhabited the island of Crete by the late third millennium. The word *Minoan* was applied after a famous archaeologist, Arthur Evans (1851–1941), searched the island for traces of King Minos, renowned in Greek myth as a fierce ruler who built the first great navy. Scholars today are not sure whether to count the Minoans as Greek ancestors because they are uncertain whether the Minoan language, whose decipherment remains controversial, was related to Greek.

Cretans wrote in a script today called Linear A. Recent research suggests that, despite the long-held assumption to the contrary, Minoan may have been a member of the Indo-European family of languages, the ancestor of many languages, including Greek, Latin, and, much later, English. If this idea is confirmed by future research, then Minoan history will confidently rank as the earliest Greek history. Unfortunately, no Minoan literature survives, nor do any documents revealing Cretan ideas about the nature of justice.

Crete's large, fertile plains, adequate rainfall, and sheltered ports for fishing and

♦**Mursili:** mur SIHL ih

♦**Kadesh:** KAH dehsh
♦**Hattusili:** hat uh SIHL ih

Wall Painting from Akroteri on Thera
Minoan artists painted with vivid colors on plaster to enliven the walls of buildings. They depicted a wide variety of subjects, from lively animals and flowering plants to young boxers and women of the court in splendid dress. Unfortunately, time and earthquakes have severely damaged most Minoan wall paintings, and the versions we see today are largely reconstructions painted around surviving fragments of the originals. The fragmentary paintings from Akroteri on the island of Thera, south of Crete, were preserved by deep layers of ash spewed out by a massive volcanic eruption. *Julia M. Fair.*

seaborne trade offered a fine home for settlers. By around 2200 B.C.E., the Minoans had exploited these natural resources to create what scholars call a **palace society**, in recognition of its sprawling, many-chambered buildings that apparently housed both the rulers and their political, economic, and religious administration. The Cretan rulers combined the functions of chief and priest, dominating both politics and religion but without the unchallenged power of kings. The palaces seem to have been largely independent, with no one imposing unity on the island. Minoan rulers, their families, and their servants lived in the palaces. The general population clustered around the palaces in houses adjacent to one another; some of these settlements reached the size of cities, with thousands of inhabitants. Knossos♦ is the most famous such palace complex, which Evans thought had been Minos's headquar-

ters. Other, smaller settlements dotted outlying areas of the island.

The emergence in Minoan farming of what is called **Mediterranean polyculture**—the cultivation of olives, grapes, and grains in a single, interrelated agricultural system—profoundly affected Minoan society. The idea was to make the best use of a farmer's labor by growing crops together that required intense work at different seasons. This system, which still dominates Mediterranean agriculture, had two major consequences. First, the combination of crops provided a very healthy diet (the "Mediterranean diet," as it is called in today's medical community), which in turn stimulated population growth. Second, agriculture became both more diversified and more specialized, increasing production of the valuable products olive oil and wine.

The production of agricultural surpluses on Minoan Crete led to growth in specialized crafts, just as it had in Mesopotamia and

♦**Knossos:** NAH suhs

Egypt. Because old methods were inadequate for storing and transporting surplus food, Cretan artisans began to invent and manufacture huge storage jars (the size of a modern refrigerator) that could accommodate these products, in the process creating another specialized industry. Crafts workers, producing their sophisticated wares using time-consuming techniques, no longer had time to grow their own food or make the goods, such as clothes and lamps, they needed for everyday life. Instead, they had to exchange the products they made for food and other goods. In this way, Cretan society experienced increasing economic interdependence.

The vast storage areas in Cretan palaces suggest that Minoan rulers, like some Mesopotamian kings before them, controlled this interdependence through a redistributive economic system. The Knossos palace, for example, held hundreds of gigantic jars capable of storing 240,000 gallons of olive oil and wine. Bowls, cups, and dippers crammed storerooms nearby. Palace officials would have decided how much each farmer or crafts producer had to contribute to the palace storehouse and how much of those contributions would then be redistributed to each person in the community for basic subsistence or as an extra reward. In this way, people gave the products of their labor to the local authority, which redistributed them as it saw fit. There would have been almost no free markets.

The Minoan economy apparently worked peacefully until at least 1400 B.C.E. Although contemporary settlements elsewhere around the Aegean Sea and in Anatolia had elaborate defensive walls, Crete had none. The palaces, towns, and even isolated country houses apparently saw no need to fortify themselves. The remains of the newer palaces—such as the one at Knossos, with its hundreds of rooms in five stories, indoor plumbing, and colorful scenes painted on the walls—have led some historians to the controversial conclusion that Minoans spurned war. Others object to the romanticizing of Minoans as peaceful because they dominated neighboring Aegean islands. Recent discoveries of tombs have revealed weapons caches, and a find of bones cut by knives has raised the possibility of human sacrifice. The promi-

nence of women in palace frescoes and the numerous figurines of buxom goddesses found on Cretan sites have also prompted speculation that Minoan society was female-dominated, but no texts have come to light to verify this. Minoan art certainly depicts women prominently and nobly, but the same is true of contemporary civilizations that men controlled. More archaeological research is needed to resolve the controversies about the nature of Minoan civilization.

Mycenaean Greece, c. 1800–c. 1000 B.C.E.

The Greeks were Indo-European speakers whose ancestors had moved into the region by 8000 B.C.E.; the first mainland civilization definitely identified as Greek because of its language arose about the same time as the Hittite kingdom, in the early second millennium B.C.E. These early Greeks are called Mycenaeans, a name derived from the hilltop site of Mycenae,♦ famous for its rich graves, multiroomed palace, and massive fortification walls. Located in the Peloponnese♦ (the large peninsula forming southern Greece; see Map 1.3), Mycenae dominated its local area, but neither it nor any other settlement ever ruled all of Bronze Age Greece. Instead, the independent communities of what we call Mycenaean civilization vied with one another in a fierce competition for natural resources and territory.

Since the hilly terrain of Greece had little fertile land but many useful ports, settlements tended to spring up near the coast. Greeks from the earliest times depended on the sea: for food, for trade with one another and foreign lands, and for naval raids on rich targets. Palace records inscribed on clay tablets reveal that the Mycenaeans had a redistributive economy. Scribes wrote on the tablets to make detailed lists of goods received and goods paid out, tirelessly recording stored material, livestock, land holdings, and personnel. They recorded everything from chariots to perfumes, even broken equipment taken out of service. The records of goods distributed from the storerooms

♦**Mycenae:** my SEE nee
♦**Peloponnese:** PEH luh puh nee

covered ritual offerings to the gods, rations to personnel, and raw materials for crafts production, such as metal issued to bronze smiths. As on Minoan Crete, however, no written documents have survived to tell us about Mycenaean literature or ideas of justice.

The first excavator of Mycenae, a nineteenth-century German millionaire named Heinrich Schliemann, made the site famous by discovering treasure-filled graves there. The burial objects revealed a warrior culture organized in independent settlements and ruled by aggressive kings. Constructed as stone-lined shafts, the graves contained entombed dead, who had taken hordes of valuables with them: golden jewelry, including heavy necklaces festooned with pendants, gold and silver vessels, bronze weapons decorated with scenes of wild animals inlaid in precious metals, and delicately painted pottery.

In his excitement at finding treasure, Schliemann proudly informed the international press that he had found the grave of Agamemnon, the legendary king who commanded the Greek army against Troy, a city in northwestern Anatolia, in the Trojan War. Homer, Greece's first and most famous poet, immortalized this war in his epic poem *The Iliad*. Archaeologists now know the shaft graves date to around 1700–1600 B.C.E., long before the Trojan War could have taken place. Schliemann, who paid for his own excavation at Troy to prove to skeptics that the city had really existed, infuriated scholars with his self-promotion. But his passion to confirm that Greek myth preserved a kernel of historical truth spurred him on to the work at Mycenae, which provided the most spectacular evidence for mainland Greece's earliest civilization.

The Lion Gate to the Citadel at Mycenae
The hilltop fortress and palace at Mycenae was the capital of Bronze Age Greece's most famous kingdom. Above its main gate stood a sculpture of lions flanking a column, a design imitating the royal art of the Near East that shows that the Mycenaean kings admired the power and traditions of that region. What do you think the column between the lions signifies? In the circle of graves beyond the gate, Heinrich Schliemann found a treasure that he thought had belonged to King Agamemnon, the leader of the Greeks in the Trojan War. *Dimitrios Harissiades/© Photographic Archive, Benaki Museum Athens.*

Mycenaean Interaction with Minoan Crete. Mycenaean rulers enriched themselves by dominating local farmers, conducting raids near and far, and participating in seaborne trade. Underwater archaeology has disclosed that international commerce in this period promoted vigorous cultural interaction. Divers have discovered, for example, that a late-fourteenth-century B.C.E. shipwreck off Uluburun♦ in Turkey carried such a mixed cargo and varied personal

---

♦**Uluburun:** ou lou boor UHN

possessions—from Canaan, Cyprus, Greece, Egypt, Babylon, and elsewhere in the Near East—that attaching a single nationality to this tramp freighter makes no sense.

A special kind of burial chambers, called *tholos* tombs—spectacular underground domed chambers built in beehive shapes with closely fitted stones—shows that some Mycenaeans had become very rich by about 1500 B.C.E. The architectural details of the tholos tombs and the style of the burial goods placed in them testify to the far-flung raiding and trading that Mycenaean rulers conducted throughout the eastern Mediterranean. Above all, however, they show a close connection with the civilization of Minoan Crete because they display many motifs clearly inspired by Cretan designs.

Yet the Mycenaean and Minoan civilizations remained distinctly different in important ways. The Mycenaeans spoke Greek and made burnt offerings to the gods; the Minoans did neither. The Minoans scattered sanctuaries across the landscape in caves, on mountaintops, and in country villas; the mainlanders did none of this. When the Mycenaeans started building palaces in the fourteenth century B.C.E., unlike the Minoans they designed them around *megarons*—rooms with prominent ceremonial hearths and thrones for the rulers. Some Mycenaean palaces had more than one megaron, which could soar two stories high with columns to support a roof above the second-floor balconies.

This evidence demonstrates that the Mycenaeans were originally a separate people from the Minoans. A startling find of documents in the palace at Knossos shows, however, that Mycenaeans eventually achieved dominance over Crete, possibly in a war over commerce in the Mediterranean. The documents were tablets written in a script called **Linear B**, which was a pictographic script based on Minoan Linear A. A brilliant twentieth-century architect named Michael Ventris proved that Linear B was used to write not Minoan, but a different language: Greek. Because the Linear B tablets date from before the final destruction of Knossos in about 1370 B.C.E., they indicate that the palace administration had been keeping its records in a foreign language for some time

and, therefore, that Mycenaeans were controlling Crete well before the end of Minoan civilization.

In the end, then, the Mycenaeans conquered the Minoan culture whose art they had so highly admired, and by the middle of the fourteenth century B.C.E., they had displaced the Cretans as the Aegean region's preeminent civilization. The Greeks later recalled this reversal of power in the myth about Theseus♦ and the Minotaur:♦ The Cretan king Minos had forced Athenian youths, sent to him as a form of tribute, into his labyrinth, where the half-man, half-bull Minotaur devoured them. Theseus of Athens, however, slew the beast in its lair and backtracked to freedom through the labyrinth's dark corridors, guided by the thread that the king's daughter Ariadne, who had fallen in love with the dashing hero, had told him to leave to mark his way in the maze.

War in Mycenaean Society. By the time Mycenaeans took over Crete, war at home and abroad was the principal concern of well-off Mycenaean men, a tradition that they passed on to later Greek civilization. Contents of Bronze Age tombs in Greece reveal that no wealthy man went to his grave without his war equipment. The expense of these grave goods shows that armor and weapons were so central to a Mycenaean male's identity that he could not do without them, even in death. Warriors rode into battle in expensive hardware—lightweight, two-wheeled chariots pulled by horses. These revolutionary vehicles, perhaps introduced by Indo-Europeans migrating from Central Asia, first appeared in various Mediterranean and Near Eastern societies not long after 2000 B.C.E.; the first picture of such a chariot in the Aegean region occurs on a Mycenaean grave marker from about 1500 B.C.E. Wealthy people evidently desired this new form of transportation not only for war but also as proof of their social status.

The Mycenaeans seem to have spent more on war than on religion. In any case, they did not construct any giant religious buildings like Mesopotamia's ziggurats or

♦**Theseus:** THEE see uhs
♦**Minotaur:** MIH nuh tawr

Egypt's pyramids. Their most important deities were male gods concerned with war. The names of gods found in the Linear B tablets reveal that Mycenaeans passed down many divinities to the Greeks of later times.

The Period of Calamities, c. 1200–c. 1000 B.C.E.

A state of political equilibrium, in which kings corresponded with one another and traders traveled all over the area, characterized the Mediterranean and Near Eastern world around 1300 B.C.E. Within a century, however, calamity had struck not only small, loosely organized groups such as the Hebrews but also almost every major political state in the region, including Egypt, some kingdoms of Mesopotamia, and the Hittite and Mycenaean kingdoms. Explaining all the catastrophes that occurred around 1200–1000 B.C.E. remains one of the most fascinating puzzles in ancient Western history.

The best clue to what happened comes from Egyptian and Hittite records. They document many foreign invasions in this period, especially from the sea. According to an inscription, the pharaoh Ramesses III around 1190 B.C.E. defeated a fearsome coalition of seaborne invaders from the north, who had fought their way to the edge of Egypt. These **Sea Peoples**, as historians call them, comprised many different groups. Some had been mercenary soldiers in the armies of rulers whom they deserted; some were raiders by profession. Many may have been Greeks. The famous story of the Trojan War probably recalls this period of calamities because it portrays a seaborne Greek army attacking Troy and the surrounding region in Anatolia.

Apparently no single, unified group of Sea Peoples launched a tidal wave of violence. Rather, many different bands devastated the region. A chain reaction of attacks and flights in a recurring and expanding cycle put even more bands on the move. The turmoil reached far inland. The Kassite kingdom in Babylonia collapsed, and the Assyrians were confined to their homeland. Invasions by the Semitic peoples known as Aramaeans and Chaldeans devastated western Asia and Syria.

The reasons for these widespread calamities remain mysterious, but their dire consequences for the eastern Mediterranean region are clear. The once mighty Hittite kingdom fell about 1200 B.C.E., when raiders cut off its trade routes for raw materials. Invaders razed its capital city, Hattusas, which never revived. Egypt's New Kingdom repelled the Sea Peoples with a tremendous military effort, but these raiders reduced the Egyptian long-distance trade network to a shambles. Power struggles between the pharaohs and the priests only made the situation worse. By the end of the New Kingdom, around 1081 B.C.E., Egypt had shrunk to its original territorial core along the Nile's banks. The calamities ruined Egypt's credit. For example, when the eleventh-century B.C.E. Theban temple official Wenamun traveled to Byblos in Phoenicia to buy cedar for a ceremonial boat, the city's ruler demanded cash in advance. Although the Egyptian monarchy struggled on, ongoing power struggles between pharaohs and priests, made worse by frequent attacks from abroad, prevented the reestablishment of centralized authority. No Egyptian dynasty ever again became an aggressive international power.

The calamities of this time also afflicted the copper-rich island of Cyprus in the eastern Mediterranean and the flourishing cities of the eastern Mediterranean coast. Raiders from the north, called Philistines, settled in Canaan and attacked the Canaanites and the Hebrews repeatedly in the eleventh century B.C.E. The Hebrew tribes appointed rulers called judges in an attempt to unify their loose confederation during this period of near anarchy. One of these judges, Deborah, led an Israelite coalition force to victory over a Canaanite army, but the Hebrews remained weak militarily.

In Greece, the troubles were homegrown. The Mycenaeans reached the zenith of their power around 1400–1250 B.C.E. The enormous domed tomb at Mycenae, called the Treasury of Atreus, testifies to the riches of this period. The tomb's elaborately decorated facade and soaring roof reveal the self-confidence of the Mycenaean warrior princes. The last phase of the extensive palace at Pylos♦ on

♦**Pylos:** PY lahs

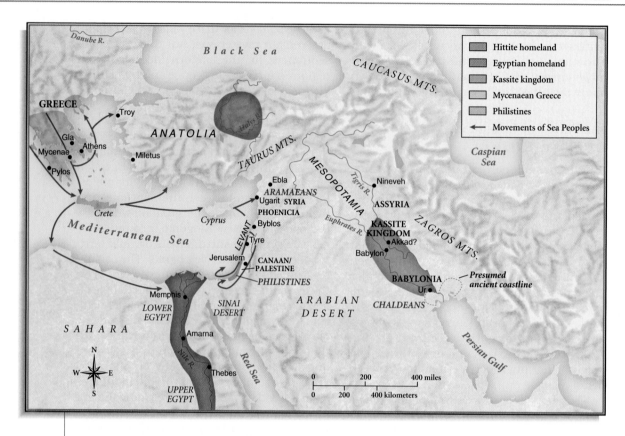

MAPPING THE WEST The Period of Calamities, c. 1200–1000 B.C.E.
Bands of wandering warriors and raiders set the eastern Mediterranean aflame at the end of the Bronze Age. This violence displaced many people and ended the power of the kingdoms of the Egyptians, the Hittites, and the Mycenaeans. Even some of the Near Eastern states well inland from the eastern Mediterranean coast felt the effects of this period of unrest, whose causes remain mysterious.

the west coast of the Peloponnese also dates from this time. It boasted glorious wall paintings, storerooms bursting with food, and a royal bathroom with a built-in tub and intricate plumbing. But these prosperous Mycenaeans did not escape the widespread calamities that began around 1200 B.C.E. Linear B tablets record the disposition of troops to the coast to guard the palace at Pylos at this time. The palace inhabitants of eastern Greece now constructed such massive defensive walls that the later Greeks thought giants had built them. These fortifications would have protected coastal palaces against seafaring attackers, who could have been either outsiders or Greeks. The wall around the inland palace at Gla in central Greece, however, which foreign raiders could not easily reach, confirms that, above all,

the Mycenaeans had to defend themselves against other Mycenaeans.

In Greece itself, then, the Sea Peoples apparently did relatively little damage. Rather, internal turmoil and major earthquakes destroyed Mycenaean civilization. Archaeology offers no evidence for the ancient tradition that Dorian Greeks invading from the north caused the destruction. Near-constant civil war by jealous local rulers overburdened the elaborate administrative balancing act necessary for the palaces' redistributive economies and hindered recovery from earthquake damage. The violence killed many Mycenaeans and put many others on the road to starvation through the disappearance of the palace-based redistributive economy. The calamity uprooted many of the remaining Greeks from their homes and forced them to wander abroad in search of new places to settle. Like people from the earliest times, these devastated ancestors of Western civilization had to move to build a better life.

> **Review:** How did war determine the fates of the early civilizations of Crete, Anatolia, and Greece?

Conclusion

Western civilization emerged in Mesopotamia and Egypt; these cultures in turn influenced the later civilization of Greece. Cities first arose in Mesopotamia by around 3000 B.C.E. Hierarchy characterized society to some degree from the very beginning, but it grew more pronounced once civilization emerged.

Trade and war were constants, both aiming in different ways at profit and glory. Indirectly, they often generated energetic cultural interaction by putting civilizations into close contact to learn from one another. Technological innovation was also a prominent characteristic of this long period. The invention of metallurgy, monumental architecture, mathematics, and alphabetic writing greatly affected the future. Religion was at the center of people's lives, with the gods seen as demanding just and righteous conduct from everyone. The emergence of monotheism set the stage for the leading faiths of later Western history.

The Mediterranean Sea was a two-edged sword for the early civilizations that grew up around and near it: as a highway for transporting goods and ideas, it was a boon; as an artery for conveying attackers, it was a bane. Ironically, the raids of the Sea Peoples that smashed the prosperity of the eastern Mediterranean region around 1200–1000 B.C.E. also set in motion the forces that led to the next step in our story, the resurgence of Greece. Strife among Mycenaean rulers turned the regional unrest of those centuries into a local catastrophe; fighting each other for dominance, they so weakened their monarchies that they could not recover after natural disasters. To an outside observer, Greek society by around 1000 B.C.E. might have seemed destined for irreversible economic and social decline, even oblivion. Chapter 2 shows how wrong this prediction would have been. After a dark period of economic and population decline called the Dark Age, Greeks invented a new form of social and political organization and breathed renewed life into their culture, inspired by their neighbors in the Near East and Egypt.

Suggested References

Mesopotamia, Home of the First Civilization, c. 4000–c. 1000 B.C.E.

Archaeological exploration in Mesopotamia (present-day Iraq) has been almost completely halted for more than a decade. Scholars have therefore been limited to studying already excavated material and texts. Modern translations have made Mesopotamian myths more accessible to today's readers.

Alcock, Susan, et al., eds. *Empires.* 2001.

Ancient Near East: http://www.etana.org/abzu.

Aruz, Joan, ed. *Art of the First Cities: The Third Millennium B.C. from the Mediterranean to the Indus.* 2003.

Bertman, Stephen. *Handbook to Life in Ancient Mesopotamia.* 2003.

Bienkowski, Piotr, and Alan Millard, eds. *Dictionary of the Ancient Near East.* 2000.

Bottéro, Jean. *Everyday Life in Mesopotamia.* Trans. Antonia Nevill. 2001.

Collins, Billie Jean. *A History of the Animal World in the Ancient Near East.* 2002.

Crawford, Harriet. *Sumer and the Sumerians.* 1991.

*Dalley, Stephanie, trans. *Myths from Mesopotamia: Creation, The Flood, Gilgamesh, and Others.* 1991.

Matthews, Roger. *Archaeology of Mesopotamia: Theories and Approaches.* 2003.

*Richardson, M. E. J. *Hammurabi's Laws: Text, Translation and Glossary.* 2000.

Stiebing, William H., Jr. *Ancient Near Eastern History and Culture.* 2003.

Sumerian literature. http://www-etcsl.orient .ox.ac.uk.

---

*Primary sources.

The Egyptians, Canaanites, and Hebrews, c. 3050–c. 1000 B.C.E.

Research and writing on ancient Egypt continue at a furious pace, while scholars studying the eastern Mediterranean region increasingly emphasize the interaction of its various cultures in trade and in war.

Assmann, Jan. *The Search for God in Ancient Egypt.* Trans. David Lorton. 2001.

Baines, John. *Religion and Society in Ancient Egypt.* 2003.

Dever, William. *Who Were the Early Israelites and Where Did They Come From?* 2003.

Hawass, Zahi. *Silent Images: Women in Pharaonic Egypt.* 2000.

Healy, John F. *The Early Alphabet.* 1990.

*Lichtheim, Miriam. *Ancient Egyptian Literature.* 3 vols. 1973.

Meskell, Lynn. *Private Life in New Kingdom Egypt.* 2002.

Morkot, Robert G. *The Black Pharaohs: Egypt's Nubian Rulers.* 2000.

Partridge, Robert B. *Fighting Pharaohs: Weapons and Warfare in Ancient Egypt.* 2002.

Redford, Donald B., ed. *The Oxford Encyclopedia of Ancient Egypt.* 2000.

*Simpson, William Kelly, ed. *The Literature of Ancient Egypt. An Anthology of Stories, Instructions, and Poetry.* 3rd ed. 2003.

Thebes in ancient Egypt: http://www.thebanmappingproject.com.

Tubb, Jonathan N. *Canaanites.* 1998.

Tyldesley, Joyce. *Hatshepsut: The Female Pharaoh.* 1996.

Virtual Museum of Nautical Archaeology (including the Uluburun shipwreck): http://ina.tamu.edu/vm.htm.

The Hittites, Minoans, and Mycenaeans, c. 2200–c. 1000 B.C.E.

Archaeology provides the securest evidence for the emergence of Greek and Anatolian civilizations. It has not yet, however, revealed what initiated the period of calamities around 1200–1000 B.C.E.

Bryce, Trevor. *Life and Society in the Hittite World.* 2002.

Crete and the Aegean Islands: http://harpy.uccs.edu/greek/crete.html.

Dickinson, Oliver. *The Aegean Bronze Age.* 1994.

Drews, Robert. *The End of the Bronze Age: Changes in Warfare and the Catastrophe ca. 1200 B.C.* 1993.

Farnoux, Alexandre. *Knossos: Searching for the Legendary Palace of King Minos.* Trans. David J. Baker. 1996.

Minoan civilization: http://www.culture.gr/2/21/211/21123m/e211wm01.html.

Mycenaean civilization: http://harpy.uccs.edu/greek/mycenae.html.

Sanders, N. K. *The Sea Peoples: Warriors of the Ancient Mediterranean, 1250–1150 B.C.* Rev. ed. 1985.

*Singer, Itamar. *Hittite Prayers: Writings from the Ancient World.* 2002.

CHAPTER REVIEW

IMPORTANT EVENTS

c. 4000–1000 b.c.e.	Bronze Age in southwestern Asia, Egypt, and Europe
c. 3500–3000 b.c.e.	Mesopotamians invent writing and establish first cities
c. 3050 b.c.e.	Narmer (Menes) unites Upper and Lower Egypt into one kingdom
c. 2687–c. 2190 b.c.e.	Old Kingdom in Egypt
c. 2350 b.c.e.	Sargon establishes the world's first empire in Akkadia
c. 2300–2200 b.c.e.	Enheduanna, princess of Akkad, composes poetry
c. 2200 b.c.e.	Minoans build their first palaces on Crete
2112–2004 b.c.e.	Ur III dynasty rules in Sumer
c. 2061–1665 b.c.e.	Middle Kingdom in Egypt
c. 1900 b.c.e.	Hebrews migrate from Ur in Mesopotamia to Canaan
c. 1792–1750 b.c.e.	Hammurabi rules the kingdom of Babylon and issues his law code
c. 1750 b.c.e.	Hittites establish their kingdom in Anatolia
c. 1700–1500 b.c.e.	Hebrews migrate from Canaan into Egypt
c. 1569–c. 1081 b.c.e.	New Kingdom in Egypt
c. 1600 b.c.e.	Canaanites invent the alphabet
c. 1400 b.c.e.	The Mycenaeans build their first palaces in Greece and take over Minoan Crete
c. 1274 b.c.e.	The Hittites war with Pharaoh Ramesses II at Kadesh in Syria
c. 1250 b.c.e.	Hebrews leave Egypt on their Exodus back to Canaan
c. 1200–1000 b.c.e.	Period of Calamities ends many kingdoms
c. 1190 b.c.e.	Pharaoh Ramesses III defeats an invasion of Egypt by Sea Peoples

KEY TERMS

city-state (9)

civilization (4)

cuneiform (12)

empire (14)

hieroglyphs (19)

Linear B (36)

Maat (21)

Mediterranean polyculture (33)

monotheism (25)

palace society (33)

polytheism (12)

redistributive economy (15)

Sea Peoples (37)

wisdom literature (23)

ziggurat (10)

REVIEW QUESTIONS

1. How did life change for people in Mesopotamia when they began to live in cities?

2. How did religion guide the lives of people in the early civilizations of Egypt and the Levant?

3. How did war determine the fates of the early civilizations of Crete, Anatolia, and Greece?

MAKING CONNECTIONS

1. Compare and contrast the environmental factors affecting the emergence of the world's first civilizations in Mesopotamia and Egypt.

2. What were the similarities and the differences in the notion of justice in the earliest civilizations?

FOR FURTHER EXPLORATION

To assess your mastery of the material in this chapter, see the Online Study Guide at **bedfordstmartins.com/hunt**.

To read additional primary-source material from this period, see Chapter 1 in *Sources of The Making of the West*, Second Edition.

CHAPTER 2

New Paths for Western Civilization, c. 1000–500 B.C.E.

HOMER, THE MOST FAMOUS GREEK POET, told violent stories from the period of calamities (c. 1200–c. 1000 B.C.E) in his epic poem *The Iliad*, composed in the eighth century B.C.E. His bloody tale of the Trojan War was rich with legends born from mingled Greek and Near Eastern traditions, such as the story of the Greek hero Bellerophon.◆ Driven from his home by a false charge of sexual assault, Bellerophon had to serve as "enforcer" for a king in Lycia (a region south of Troy), combating the king's most dangerous enemies. He had to fight—and kill—fierce tribesmen, Amazons, and even the king's own warriors, but his most famous contest pitted him against a monster. As Homer tells it, Bellerophon was ordered "to defeat the Chimera,◆ an inhuman freak created by the gods, horrible with its lion's head, goat's body, and dragon's tail, breathing fire all the time." Bellerophon triumphed by swooping down on the beast in an aerial attack, riding on the winged horse Pegasus. So amazing were Bellerophon's heroics that the king gave him his daughter in marriage and half his kingdom.

Both the multiform Chimera in Homer and the horse-headed, hawk-bodied, lion-footed beast painted on the vase from Corinth shown in the chapter opening illustration were creatures from Near Eastern myth taken over by Greeks. They provide evidence for the intercultural contact that characterized the far-flung world of ancient Western civilization. People were eager to trade and to discover new technology in other places. Inevitably, contact exposed people

---

◆**Bellerophon:** buh LEHR uh fahn
◆**Chimera:** ky MIHR uh

Black-Figure Vase from Corinth
This vase was made in Corinth about 600 B.C.E. and then shipped to the island of Rhodes, where it was found. The drawing is in the so-called black-figure style, in which artists carved details into the dark-baked clay. In the late sixth century B.C.E., this style gave way to red-figure, in which artists painted details in black on a reddish background instead of engraving them; the result was finer detail (compare this vase painting with that on page 55). The animals and mythical creatures on this vase follow Near Eastern models, which inspired Archaic Age Greek artists to put people and animals into their designs again after their absence during the Dark Age. Why do you think the artist depicted the animal at the lower right with two bodies but only one head? *British Museum.*

not only to others' products but also to their ideas. New paths for civilization emerged as people traded, traveled, innovated, and adapted for their own purposes things that they had learned or acquired from foreigners.

Even the turmoil and economic distress that ended the Bronze Age around 1000 B.C.E. did not suppress people's craving for trade and cross-cultural interaction. This drive only increased as conditions slowly improved in the following centuries. The Near East recovered more quickly than Greece, retaining monarchy as its traditional form of social and political organization. Following the model of the earlier Assyrian and Babylonian empires, Near Eastern kings in this period extracted surpluses from subject populations to support their palaces and their armies. They also continually sought new conquests to win glory, exploit the labor of conquered peoples, seize raw materials, and conduct long-distance trade.

In Greece, by contrast, politics and society in the period after 1000 B.C.E. emerged in radically different forms. The wars and subsequent economic collapse of 1200–1000 B.C.E. had destroyed the political and social organization of Minoan and Mycenaean Greece. Powerful rulers controlling the population no longer existed. During Greece's slow recovery from poverty and depopulation from about 1000 to 750 B.C.E., its Dark Age, Greeks maintained trade and cross-cultural contact with the older civilizations of the Near East. Their mythology, as in Homer, and their art, as on the Corinthian vase, reveal that they imported ideas as well as goods during this difficult era.

By the eighth century B.C.E., Greeks had begun to create the polis as a new form of political and social organization in the city-state. It was novel because it made citizenship the basis for society and politics, with legal—but not political—rights for women and with slavery for some. With the exception of occasional tyrannies, Greek city-states depended on the agreement among male citizens to share power in governing and in contributing surpluses to the state for common purposes. The extent of the power sharing varied, with small groups of upper-class men dominating in some places. In other places, however, the polis shared power among all free men, even the poor, creating the world's first democracy (literally, " rule by the people"). The invention of the democratic polis stands as a landmark in the history of Western civilization.

One experience that Greeks and Near Eastern peoples shared during this period of recovery was frequent warfare. In Greece, the gradual process of creating independent city-states created violent clashes over the mainland's limited supply of fertile land, while in the Near East the desire for empire and the control of trade made war as common as sunshine in that arid region. With the clash of arms constantly ringing in their ears, thinkers in the Near East and Greece developed new patterns in religion and philosophy that make up the foremost legacies of this period to later Western civilization: the Persians' Zoroastrian beliefs about life as a struggle between good and evil, the monotheism of the Hebrews, and the Greeks' development of philosophic rationalism to compete with mythological explanations of nature.

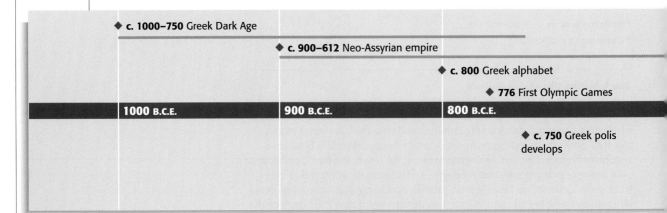

◆ **c. 1000–750** Greek Dark Age

◆ **c. 900–612** Neo-Assyrian empire

◆ **c. 800** Greek alphabet

◆ **776** First Olympic Games

| **1000 B.C.E.** | **900 B.C.E.** | **800 B.C.E.** |

◆ **c. 750** Greek polis develops

❖ From Dark Age to Empire in the Near East, c. 1000–500 B.C.E.

The widespread violence in 1200–1000 B.C.E. had weakened or obliterated many communities and populations in the eastern Mediterranean. We know little about the period of recovery that followed because few sources exist to supplement archaeological evidence. Both because economic conditions were so gloomy for so many people and because our view of what happened is so obscured, historians refer to the era in which conditions were hardest for a particular region as its **Dark Age**. Recent archaeological excavation suggests that the Dark Age in the Near East lasted less than a century, a much shorter period than Greece experienced.

By 900 B.C.E., a powerful and centralized Assyrian kingdom had once again emerged in Mesopotamia. From this base, the Assyrians ruthlessly carved out a new empire even larger than before. The riches and power of this Neo-Assyrian empire inspired first the Babylonians and then the Persians to build their own empires when Assyrian power collapsed. The traditional strife for empire remained constant in the Near East. The relatively powerless Hebrews, however, established a new path for civilization during this period by changing their religion. They developed monotheism and produced the Hebrew Bible, known to Christians as the Old Testament.

The New Empire of Assyria, c. 900–612 B.C.E.

When the Hittite kingdom fell around 1000 B.C.E., the Neo-Assyrian empire gained power by seizing supplies of metal and controlling trade routes in the eastern Mediterranean (Map 2.1). By 900 B.C.E., its armies were

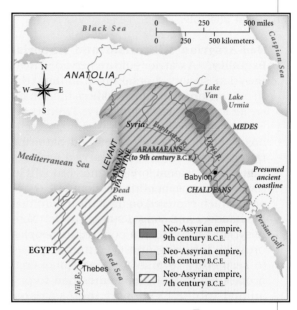

MAP 2.1 Expansion of the Neo-Assyrian Empire, c. 900–650 B.C.E.
Like their Akkadian, Assyrian, and Babylonian predecessors, the Neo-Assyrian kings dominated a vast region of the Near East to secure a supply of metals, access to trade routes on land and sea, and imperial glory. In so doing, they built the largest empire the world had yet seen. Also like their predecessors, they treated disobedient subjects harshly and intolerantly to try to prevent their diverse territories from rebelling.

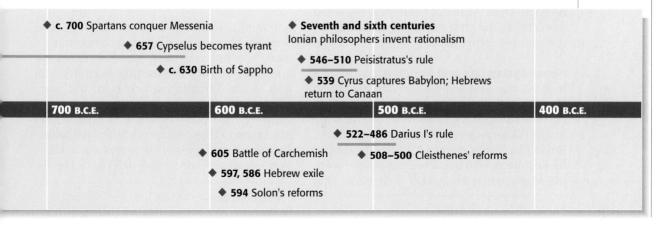

◆ **c. 700** Spartans conquer Messenia

◆ **657** Cypselus becomes tyrant

◆ **c. 630** Birth of Sappho

◆ **Seventh and sixth centuries**
Ionian philosophers invent rationalism

◆ **546–510** Peisistratus's rule

◆ **539** Cyrus captures Babylon; Hebrews return to Canaan

700 B.C.E.	**600 B.C.E.**	**500 B.C.E.**	**400 B.C.E.**

◆ **522–486** Darius I's rule

◆ **605** Battle of Carchemish

◆ **508–500** Cleisthenes' reforms

◆ **597, 586** Hebrew exile

◆ **594** Solon's reforms

striking westward against the Aramaean states in Syria until they punched through to the coast. In the eighth century B.C.E., the Neo-Assyrian kings extended their control into southern Mesopotamia by conquering Babylon, and they added Egypt to their empire in the seventh century. The weakness that had plagued Egypt since the New Kingdom's collapse in 1081 B.C.E. made this conquest possible.

Neo-Assyrian Militarism and Imperial Brutality. A warrior culture pervaded Neo-Assyrian society. Forsaking tradition, the Neo-Assyrians made foot soldiers their main strike force in place of cavalry. Trained infantrymen excelled in using military technology such as siege towers and battering rams, while swift chariots carried archers. Campaigns against foreign lands brought in revenues supplementing the domestic economy, which centered on agriculture, animal husbandry, and long-distance trade. Neo-Assyrian kings treated conquered peoples brutally, torturing and executing captives to keep order by instilling fear. Conquered peoples left in their homelands had to pay annual tribute to support the Assyrians' prosperity; these tributes included raw materials and luxury goods such as incense, wine, dyed linens, glasswork, and ivory. Worse was the fate of the large number of defeated people whom the kings routinely deported to Assyria for work on huge building projects—temples and palaces—in main cities. One unexpected consequence of this harsh policy was that the kings undermined their native language: so many Aramaeans, for example, were deported from Canaan to Assyria that Aramaic◆ largely replaced Assyrian as the land's everyday language by the eighth century B.C.E.

Neo-Assyrian Life and Religion. When not making war, Neo-Assyrian men spent much time hunting wild animals; the more dangerous the quarry, the better. The king hunted lions as proof of his vigor and power. Royal lion hunts provided a favorite subject for sculptors, who mastered the artistic technique of carving long relief sculptures that

◆**Aramaic:** ar uh MAY ihk

Neo-Assyrian Guardian Creature
This human-headed bull and lion creature (called a lamassu) stood guard over a gate at the palace of the Neo-Assyrian King Ashurnasirpal (r. 883–859 B.C.E.) in his capital city Kalhu (today Nimrud). Carved from alabaster, the guardian stood ten feet tall, with a cap to signify its divine power. The sculptor gave it five legs so it would look natural when viewed either from the side or the front. Ashurnasirpal reported in an inscription that he hosted 69,574 people at a party celebrating his new capital: "I feasted, wined, bathed, and honored them for ten days before sending them home in peace and joy." *Gift of John D. Rockefeller Jr., 1932 (32.143.1-.2). Photograph (c) 1981 The Metropolitan Museum of Art.*

narrated a connected story. Although the Neo-Assyrian imperial administration meticulously preserved many documents in its archives, literacy apparently mattered far less to the kingdom's men than did war, hunting, and practical technology. King Sennacherib◆ (r. 704–681 B.C.E.), for example, boasted that he invented new irrigation equipment and a novel method of metal casting. Ashurbanipal◆ (r. 680–626 B.C.E.) is the

◆**Sennacherib:** suh NA kuh ruhb
◆**Ashurbanipal:** ah shur BAH nuh pahl

only Assyrian ruler to proclaim his scholarly accomplishments: "I have read complicated texts, whose versions in Sumerian are obscure and in Akkadian hard to understand. I do research on the cuneiform texts on stone from before the Flood." Women of the social elite probably had a chance to become literate, but they were excluded from the male dominions of hunting and war.

Public religion, which included deities adopted from Babylonian religion, reflected the prominence of war in Assyrian culture: even the cult of Ishtar (the Babylonian name for Inanna), the goddess of love and fertility, glorified warfare. The Neo-Assyrians' passion for monumental architecture led them to build huge temples for the gods. The temples' staffs of priests and slaves grew so numerous that the revenues from temple lands could no longer support them, so the kings had to supply extra funds from the spoils of conquest.

The Neo-Assyrian kings' harshness made even their own people, especially the social elite, dislike their rule. Rebellions were common throughout the history of the kingdom; a seventh-century B.C.E. revolt fatally weakened it. The Medes,♦ an Iranian people, and the Chaldeans,♦ a Semitic people who had driven the Assyrians from Babylonia, combined forces to invade the tottering kingdom. When they destroyed its capital at Nineveh in 612 B.C.E., they forever blotted out the Neo-Assyrian kings' dreams of empire.

The Neo-Babylonian Empire, c. 605–562 B.C.E.

Since the Chaldeans had captained the allies who overthrew the Neo-Assyrian empire, they seized the lion's share of territory. Sprung from seminomadic herders along the Persian Gulf, they established the Neo-Babylonian empire, the most powerful in Babylonian history. King Nebuchadnezzar♦ II (r. 605–562 B.C.E.) made the Neo-Babylonians the Near East's leading power by driving the Egyptian army from Syria at the battle of Carchemish in 605 B.C.E.

Nebuchadnezzar spent lavishly to turn Babylon into an architectural showplace, rebuilding the great temple of its chief god, Marduk, creating the famous Hanging Gardens—so named because lush plants drooped over its terraced sides—and constructing an elaborate city gate dedicated to the goddess Ishtar. Blue-glazed bricks and lions molded in yellow, red, and white decorated the gate's walls, which soared thirty-six feet high.

The Chaldeans adopted traditional Babylonian culture and preserved much Mesopotamian literature, such as the *Epic of Gilgamesh*. They also created many new works of prose and poetry, which the educated minority would often read aloud publicly for the enjoyment of the illiterate. Particularly popular were fables, proverbs, essays, and prophecies teaching morality and proper behavior. This so-called wisdom literature, a Near Eastern tradition going back at least to the Egyptian Old Kingdom, would greatly influence the later religious writings of the Hebrews.

The Chaldeans also passed on their knowledge to others outside their region. Their advances in astronomy became so influential that the Greeks used the word *Chaldean* to mean "astronomer." As in the past, the Chaldeans' primary motivation for observing the stars was the belief that the gods communicated their will to humans through natural phenomena, such as celestial movements and eclipses, abnormal births, the way smoke curled upward from a fire, and the trails of ants. The interpretation of these phenomena as messages from the gods exemplified the mixture of science and religion characteristic of ancient Near Eastern thought and proved influential on the Greeks.

The Persian Empire, c. 557–500 B.C.E.

Cyrus (r. c. 557–530 B.C.E.) founded the Near East's next great kingdom in Persia (today Iran) through his skills as a general and a diplomat who respected others' religious beliefs. He continued the region's tradition of kings warring to gain territorial empires when he conquered Babylon in 539 B.C.E.; a rebellion there had weakened the Chaldean dynasty

---

♦**Medes:** meeds
♦**Chaldeans:** kal DEE uhns
♦**Nebuchadnezzar:** neh byuh kuhd NEH zur

when King Nabonidus (r. c. 555–539 B.C.E.) provoked a revolt among the priests of Marduk by promoting the cult of Sin, the moon god of the Mesopotamian city of Harran. Cyrus capitalized on this religious strife by presenting himself as the restorer of traditional Babylonian religion, thereby winning local support. An ancient inscription has him proclaim: "Marduk, the great lord, caused Babylon's generous residents to adore me."

His successors expanded Persian rule on the same principles of military strength and cultural tolerance. At its greatest extent, the empire extended from Anatolia (today Turkey), the eastern Mediterranean coast, and Egypt on the west to Pakistan on the east (Map 2.2). The kings' faith that they had a divine right to rule everyone in the world could provoke great conflicts, above all the war between Persians and Greeks that would break out around 500 B.C.E.

Persian Royal Magnificence and Decentralized Rule. The Persian monarchy's revenues produced wealth beyond imagination, and everything about the king emphasized his grandeur. His purple robes outshone everyone else's; only he could step on the red carpets spread for him to walk on; his servants held their hands before their mouths in his presence so that he would not have to breathe the same air as they; he appeared larger than any other person in the sculpture adorning his immense palace at Persepolis. To display his concern for his loyal subjects, as well as the gargantuan scale of his resources, the king provided meals for fifteen thousand nobles, courtiers, and followers every day—although he himself ate hidden from his guests' view. Those who committed serious offenses against his laws or his dignity the king punished brutally, mutilating their bodies and executing their families. Contemporary Greeks, in awe of the Persian

The Great King of Persia
Like their Assyrian predecessors, the Persian kings decorated their palaces with large relief sculptures emphasizing royal dignity and success. This one from Persepolis shows officials and petitioners giving the king proper respect when entering his presence. To symbolize their elevated status, the king and his son, who stands behind the throne, are depicted as larger than everyone else. Do you think the way the sculptors portrayed the figures from the side is more or less artistic than the way the Egyptian painters did it in the picture of the day of judgment on page 2? Why?
For more help analyzing this image, see the visual activity for this chapter in the Online Study Guide at **bedfordstmartins.com/hunt**. *Courtesy of the Oriental Institute of the University of Chicago.*

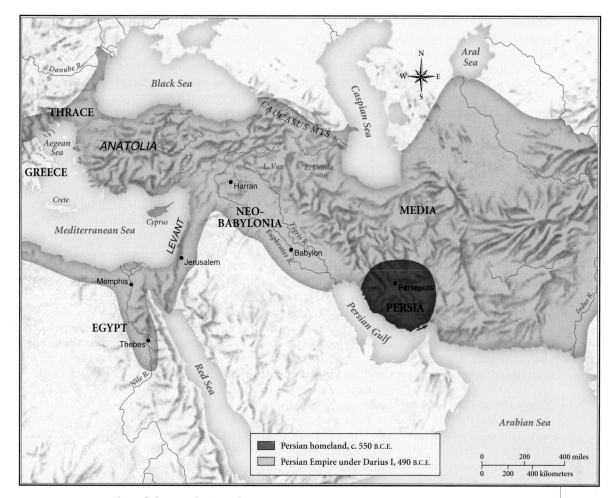

MAP 2.2 Expansion of the Persian Empire, c. 550–490 B.C.E.
Cyrus (r. c. 557–530 B.C.E.) initiated the Persian empire, which his successors expanded to be even larger than the Neo-Assyrian empire that it replaced. The Persian kings pressed hard outward from their inland center to gain coastal possessions for access to seaborne trade and naval bases. By the later years of Darius's reign (r. 522–486 B.C.E.), the Persian empire had expanded eastward as far as the western edge of India, while to the west it reached Thrace, the eastern edge of Europe. Unlike their imperial predecessors, the Persian kings won their subjects' loyalty with tolerance and religious freedom, although they treated rebels very harshly.

monarch's power and his lavish lifestyle, called him the Great King.

So long as his subjects—numbering in the millions and of many different ethnicities—remained peaceful, the king left them alone to live and worship as they pleased. The empire's smoothly functioning administrative structure sprang from Assyrian precedents: **satraps**♦ (regional governors) ruled enormous territories with little interference from

the kings. In this decentralized system, the governors' duties included keeping order, enrolling troops when needed, and sending revenues to the royal treasury.

Darius I (r. 522–486 B.C.E.) vastly extended Cyrus's conquests by pushing Persian power eastward to the Indus valley and westward to Thrace. Organizing this vast territory into provinces, he assigned each region taxes payable in the medium best suited to its local economy—precious metals, grain, horses, slaves. He also required each

♦**satraps:** SAY trap

region to send soldiers to the royal army. A network of roads and a courier system for royal mail provided communication among the far-flung provincial centers. The Greek historian Herodotus◆ reported that neither snow, rain, heat, nor darkness slowed the couriers from completing their routes as swiftly as possible, a feat transformed centuries later into the U.S. Postal Service motto.

Zoroastrian Religion. Ruling as absolute autocrats, the Persian kings believed themselves superior to everyone. They claimed not to be gods but rather to be the agents of Ahura Mazda◆ (literally, "Wise Lord"), the supreme god of Persia. As Darius said in his autobiography, carved into a mountainside in three languages, "Ahura Mazda gave me kingship.... By the will of Ahura Mazda the provinces respected my laws."

Persian religion made Ahura Mazda the center of its devotion and took its doctrines from the teachings of the legendary prophet Zarathustra, who may have lived as long ago as 1200–1000 B.C.E. (The religion is called Zoroastrianism◆ today from Zoroaster, the Greek name for this holy man.) Zarathustra proclaimed Ahura Mazda to be "the father of Truth" and "creator of Good Thought," who demanded purity from his worshipers and promised help to those who lived with truthfulness and justice. The most important doctrine of Zoroastrianism was its monotheism, which explained the origin of evil through **moral dualism**: perceiving the world as the arena of an ongoing battle between the opposing divine forces of good and evil. Ahura Mazda as the embodiment of good and light constantly struggled against the evil darkness represented by the Satan-like figure Ahriman. Human beings had to choose between the way of the truth and the way of the lie, between purity and impurity. Only those judged righteous after death made it across "the bridge of separation" to heaven and avoided falling from its narrow span into hell. The Persian religious emphasis on ethical behavior had a lasting influence on others, especially the Hebrews.

◆**Herodotus:** heh RAH duh tuhs
◆**Ahura Mazda:** ah hur uh MAZ duh
◆**Zoroastrianism:** zor oh AHS tree uhn iz uhm

The Consolidation of Hebrew Monotheism, c. 1000–539 B.C.E.

The Hebrews achieved their first national organization with the creation of a monarchy in the late eleventh century B.C.E. Saul became their first king by fighting to limit Philistine power in Palestine (the southern Levant), and his successors David (r. 1010–970 B.C.E.) and Solomon (r. c. 961–922 B.C.E.) brought the nation to the height of its prosperity. The kingdom's wealth, based on international commerce conducted through its cities, was displayed above all in the great temple richly decorated with gold leaf that Solomon built in Jerusalem to be the house of the Hebrews' god, Yahweh. This temple was the Hebrews' premier religious monument.

After Solomon's death, the monarchy split into two kingdoms: Israel in the north and Judah in the south. The more powerful Mesopotamians later subjugated these kingdoms. Tiglath-pileser III of Assyria forced much of Palestine to become a tribute-paying, subject territory, destroying Israel in 722 B.C.E. and deporting its population to Assyria. In 597 B.C.E., the neo-Babylonian king Nebuchadnezzar II conquered Judah and captured its capital, Jerusalem. In 586 B.C.E. he destroyed its temple to Yahweh and banished the Hebrew leaders and much of the population to Babylon. The Hebrews always remembered the sorrow of this exile.

When the Persian king Cyrus overthrew the Babylonians in 539 B.C.E., he permitted the Hebrews to return to their part of Canaan, which was called Yehud from the name of the southern Hebrew kingdom Judah. From this geographical term came the word *Jew*, a designation for the Hebrews after their Babylonian exile. Cyrus allowed them to rebuild their main temple in Jerusalem and to practice their religion. After returning from exile, the Jews were forever a people subject to the political domination of various Near Eastern powers, save for a period of independence during the second and first centuries B.C.E.

Jewish prophets, both men and women, preached that their defeats were divine punishment for neglecting the Sinai covenant and mistreating their poor. Some prophets also predicted the coming end of the present world following a great crisis, a judgment by Yahweh, and salvation leading to a new and better world. This **apocalypticism** ("uncovering" of the future), reminiscent of Babylonian prophetic wisdom literature, would greatly influence Christianity later. Yahweh would save the Hebrew nation, the prophets thundered, only if Jews strictly observed divine law.

Jewish leaders therefore developed complex religious laws to maintain ritual and ethical purity in all aspects of life. Marrying non-Jews was forbidden, as was working on the Sabbath (the week's holy day). Fathers had legal power over the household, subject to intervention by the male elders of the community; women gained honor as mothers. Only men could initiate divorce proceedings. Ethics applied not only to obvious crimes but also to financial dealings; cheating in business transactions was condemned. Jews had to pay taxes and offerings to support and honor the sanctuary of Yahweh, and to forgive debts every seventh year.

The Jews' hardships had taught them that their religious traditions and laws gave them the strength to survive even when separated from their homeland. Gradually, they came to believe that Yahweh was the only god and that to abide by divine will they had to behave ethically toward everyone, rich and poor alike. They thus created the first complete monotheism, with laws based on ethics. Jews retained their identity by following this religion, regardless of their personal fate or their geographical location. A remarkable outcome of these religious developments was that Jews who did not return to their homeland, instead choosing to remain in Babylon or Persia or Egypt, could maintain their Jewish identity while living among foreigners. In this way, the **Diaspora** ("dispersion of population") came to characterize the history of the Jewish people.

Hebrew monotheism made the preservation and understanding of a sacred text, the Bible, the center of religious life. The chief priests compiled an authoritative scripture by forming the **Torah** (also referred to as the Pentateuch, or first five books of the Hebrew Bible), to which were eventually added the books of the prophets, such as Isaiah, and other writings, including Psalms

Goddess Figurines from Judah
Many small statues of this type, called Astarte figurines after a popular Canaanite goddess, have been found in private houses in Judah dating from about 800 to 600 B.C.E. Hebrews evidently kept them as magical tokens to promote fertility and prosperity. The prophets fiercely condemned the worship of such figures as part of the development of Hebrew monotheism and the abandoning of polytheism. Compare the shape of these figurines to the body shape of the Venus figurine on page P-5. What do you think these shapes represented? © *Israel Museum, Jerusalem. Artifact Collection of the Israel Antiquities Authority.*

and wisdom literature. Making scripture the focus of religion proved the most crucial development for the history not only of Judaism but also of Christianity and Islam, because these later religions made their own sacred texts, the Christian Bible and the Qur'an, respectively, the centers of their belief and practice.

Although the ancient Hebrews never formed a militarily powerful nation, their religious ideas created a new path for Western civilization. Through the continuing vitality of Judaism and its impact on the doctrines of Christianity and Islam, the early Jews passed on ideas—the belief in monotheism and the notion of a covenant bestowing a divinely ordained destiny on a people if they obey divine will—whose effects have endured to this day. These religious concepts constitute one of the most significant legacies to Western civilization from the Near East in the period 1000–500 B.C.E.

Review: In what ways did religion affect the history of the Near East from c. 1000 B.C.E. to c. 500 B.C.E.?

Cyrene Records Its Foundation as a Greek Colony

The Greeks living in Cyrene in North Africa (in modern Libya) set up this inscription recording the foundation of their polis by colonists dispatched about 630 B.C.E. from Thera (a polis on an island north of Crete). The text we have, which is damaged and therefore uncertain in places (marked by brackets), comes from the fourth century B.C.E., but it was based on earlier documents. Cyrene was one of the few colonies originally established by a polis instead of entrepreneurs.

The Oath of the Colonists

The assembly of Thera decided:

Since the god Apollo of Delphi spontaneously instructed Battus and the Therans to settle Cyrene, the Therans decided to send Battus to North Africa as leader and king and for the Therans to sail as his companions. They are to sail on equal and fair terms according to their households and one adult son [from each household] is to be selected, and grown young men [are to be selected], and of the other Therans only those who are free can sail. And if the colonists establish a colony, a man from the

households who subsequently sails to North Africa shall share in citizenship and public office and shall be given a portion from land that has no owner. But if they do not establish a colony and the Therans are unable to provide aid, but the colonists suffer hardship for five years, they are allowed to leave the land without fear and return to Thera and their property and to be citizens. If any man is not willing to sail when the polis sends him, he will be subject to the death penalty and his property shall be confiscated. Any man who harbors or hides such a man, whether a father his son, or a brother his brother, will be subject to the same penalty as the man who is not willing to sail. Those who stayed at home and those who sailed to found the colony swore oaths on these terms, and they invoked curses against those who break the oaths and fail to keep them, whether they were those who settled in North Africa or those who remained at home.

Source: R. Meiggs and D. Lewis, eds., *A Selection of Greek Historical Inscriptions to the End of the Fifth Century B.C.* (1969), no. 5. Translation by Thomas R. Martin.

stiffly and stared straight ahead, imitating Egyptian statuary. When the improving economy of the later Archaic Age allowed Greeks again to afford monumental architecture in stone, their rectangular temples on platforms with columns reflected Egyptian architectural designs.

Historians have traditionally called the settlement process of this era Greek colonization, but recent research questions this term's accuracy because the word *colonization* implies the process by which modern European governments officially installed colonies abroad. The evidence for these Greek settlements suggests rather that private entrepreneurship initiated most of them; official state involvement was minimal, at least in the beginning. Most commonly, a Greek city-state in the homeland would establish ties with a settlement originally set up by its citizens privately and then claim it as its colony

only after the community had grown into an economic success. Few instances are clearly recorded in which a Greek mother city officially sent out a group to establish a formally organized colony abroad.

Citizenship and Freedom in the Greek City-State

The creation of the polis filled the political vacuum left by Mycenaean civilization's fall. The Greek city-state was unique because it was based on the concept of citizenship for all its free inhabitants. Moreover, except in tyrannies, at least some degree of shared governance was common; this power sharing reached its purest form in democratic Greek city-states. Some historians argue that knowledge of the older cities of the island of Cyprus and of Phoenicia influenced the Greeks in creating their new political systems; since monarchs dominating subjects ruled those eastern states, however, this theory cannot explain the origin of citizenship in all Greek city-states and the sharing of power in many, especially democracies. The most famous ancient analyst of Greek politics and society, the philosopher Aristotle (384–322 B.C.E.), insisted that the forces of nature had created the city-state: "Humans are beings who by nature live in a city-state." Anyone who existed outside such a community, Aristotle remarked, must be either a simple fool or superhuman.

Religion in the Greek City-State. Greek city-states were officially religious communities: as well as worshiping many deities, each city-state honored a particular god or goddess, such as Athena at Athens, as its special protector. Different communities could choose the same deity: Sparta, Athens's chief rival in later times, also chose Athena as its defender. Greeks envisioned the twelve most important gods banqueting atop Mount Olympus, the highest peak in mainland Greece. Zeus headed this pantheon; the others were Hera, his wife; Aphrodite,◆ goddess of love; Apollo, sun god; Ares, war god; Artemis, moon goddess; Athena, goddess of wisdom and war; Demeter, earth goddess; Dionysus, god of pleasure, wine, and disorder; Hephaestus, fire god; Hermes, messenger god; and Poseidon, sea god. Like Homer's proud warriors, the Olympian gods resented any slights to their honor. "I am well aware that the gods are competitively envious and disruptive towards humans," remarked the sixth-century Athenian statesman Solon. The Greeks believed that their gods occasionally experienced temporary pain or sadness in their dealings with one another but were immune to permanent suffering because they were immortal.

Greek religion's core belief was that humans, both as individuals and as communities, must honor the gods to thank them for blessings received and to receive more blessings in return. Furthermore, the Greeks believed that the gods sent both good and bad into the world. The relationship between gods and humans generated sorrow as well as joy, punishment in the here and now, and an uncertain hope for favored treatment in this life and in the underworld after death. Greeks did not expect to reach paradise at some future time when evil forces would finally be vanquished forever.

The idea of reciprocity between gods and humans underlay the Greek understanding of the nature of the gods. Deities did not love humans. Rather, they supported people who paid them honor and did not offend them. Gods offended by humans could punish them by sending calamities such as famine, earthquake, epidemic disease, or defeat in war.

City-states honored gods by sacrificing animals such as cattle, sheep, goats, and pigs, decorating their sanctuaries with works of art, and celebrating festivals with songs, dances, prayers, and processions. A seventh-century B.C.E. bronze statuette, which a man named

A Greek Woman at an Altar

This red-figure vase painting (contrast the black-figure vase on page 55) from the center of a large drinking cup shows a woman in rich clothing pouring a libation to the gods onto a flaming altar. In her other arm, she carries a religious object that we cannot securely identify. This scene illustrates the most important and frequent role of women in Greek public life: participating in religious ceremonies, both at home and in community festivals. Greek women (and men) commonly wore sandals; why do you think they are usually depicted without shoes in vase paintings? *The Toledo Museum of Art, Toledo, Ohio; Purchased with funds from the Libbey Endowment, Gift of Edward Drummond Libbey.*

◆**Aphrodite:** a fruh DY tee

Mantiklos◆ gave to a sanctuary of Apollo to honor the god, makes clear why individuals gave such gifts. On its legs Mantiklos inscribed his understanding of the transaction: "Mantiklos gave this from his share to the Far Darter of the Silver Bow [Apollo]; now you, Apollo, do something for me in return."

People's greatest religious difficulty lay in anticipating what might offend a deity. Mythology hinted at the gods' expectations of proper human behavior. For example, the Greeks told stories of the gods demanding hospitality for strangers, proper burial for family members, and punishment for human arrogance and murderous violence. Oracles, dreams, divination, and the prophecies of seers were all regarded as clues to what humans might have done to anger the gods. Offenses could be acts such as performing a sacrifice improperly, violating the sanctity of a temple area, or breaking an oath or sworn agreement. People believed that the deities were attentive to some wrong doings, such as violating oaths, but generally uninterested in common crimes, which humans had to police themselves. Homicide was such a serious offense, however, that the gods were thought to punish it by casting a miasma (ritual contamination) on the murderer and on all those around him or her. Unless the members of the affected group purified themselves by punishing the murderer, they could all expect to suffer divine punishment, such as bad harvests or disease.

The community and individuals alike paid homage and respect to the deities through cults, the prescribed sets of publicly funded religious activities for each deity overseen by priests and priestesses. To carry out their duties, people prayed, sang hymns of praise, offered sacrifices, and presented gifts at the deity's sanctuary. In these holy places a person could honor and thank the deities for blessings and beg them for relief when misfortune struck the community or the petitioner. Individuals could also offer sacrifices at home with the household gathered around; sometimes the family's slaves were allowed to participate.

Priests and priestesses chosen from the citizen body conducted the sacrifices of public

◆**Mantiklos:** MAN tee klahs

cults; they did not use their positions to influence political or social matters. Their special knowledge consisted in knowing how to perform traditional religious rites. They were not guardians of correct religious thinking because Greek polytheism had no scripture or uniform set of beliefs and practices. It required its adherents only to support the community's local rituals and to avoid religious pollution.

Citizenship for Rich and Poor. Greeks devised the concept of citizenship to organize their city-states; it meant free people agreeing to form a political community that was supposed to be a partnership of privileges and duties in common affairs under the rule of law. Citizenship was a distinctive political concept because, even in Greek city-states organized as tyrannies or oligarchies, it bestowed a basic level of political and legal equality. Most important, it carried the expectation (although not always the fulfillment) of equal treatment under the law for male citizens regardless of their social status or wealth. Women had the protection of the law, but they were barred from participation in politics on the grounds that female judgment was inferior to male. Regulations governing sexual behavior and control of property were stricter for women than for men.

The most dramatic version of political equality was having all free, adult male citizens in an oligarchic or democratic Greek city-state share in governance by attending and voting in a political assembly, where the laws and policies of the community were ratified. The degree of power sharing was closer to equality in some places than in others. In city-states where the social elite had a stranglehold on politics, small groups or even a single family could dominate the process of legislating. Other city-states introduced the revolutionary innovation of direct democracy, which gave all free men the right to propose laws and policies in the assembly and to serve on juries. Even in democratic city-states, however, citizens did not enjoy perfect political equality. The right to hold office, for example, could be restricted to citizens possessing a certain amount of property. Equality prevailed most strongly in the justice system, in which all male citizens were treated the same, regardless of wealth or status.

Because monarchy and legal inequality had characterized the history of the ancient Near East and Greece in earlier times, it is remarkable that a notion of equality became a principle for the reorganization of Greek society and politics in the Archaic Age. The polis—with its emphasis on equal protection of the laws for rich and poor alike—remained the preeminent form of political and social organization in Greece until the beginning of Roman control six centuries later.

The Greek city-states' free poor enjoyed the privileges and duties of citizenship alongside the rich throughout this long period. How the poor gained that status remains an important mystery. The greatest population increase in the late Dark Age and the Archaic Age came in the ranks of the poorer section of the population. These families raised more children to help farm more land, which had been vacant after the depopulation brought on by the worst of the Dark Age. (See "Taking Measure," below.) There was no precedent for extending the principle of even

TAKING MEASURE

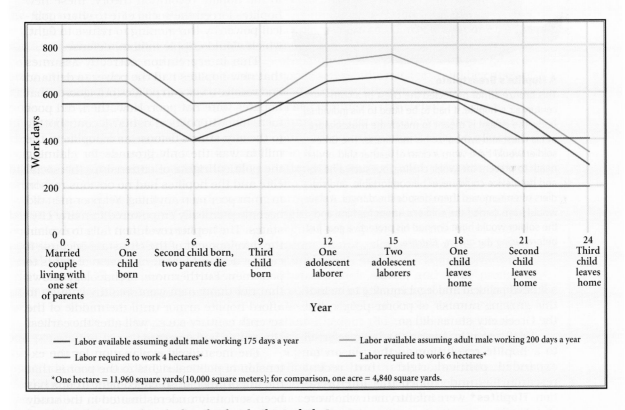

—— Labor available assuming adult male working 175 days a year	—— Labor available assuming adult male working 200 days a year
—— Labor required to work 4 hectares*	—— Labor required to work 6 hectares*

*One hectare = 11,960 square yards (10,000 square meters); for comparison, one acre = 4,840 square yards.

Greek Family Size and Agricultural Labor in the Archaic Age

Modern demographers have calculated the changing relationship in the Archaic Age between a farm family's productive capacity to work the land and the number of people in the family over time. The graph shows how valuable healthy teenage children were to the family's well-being. When the family had two adolescent laborers available, it could farm over 50 percent more land, increasing its productivity significantly and thus making life more prosperous. *Adapted from Thomas W. Gallant, Risk and Survival in Ancient Greece: Reconstructing the Rural Domestic Economy (1991), Fig. 4.10. Reprinted with the permission of Stanford University Press.*

laws and administering justice. Democracy has remained so important in Western civilization that understanding why and how Athenian democracy worked remains a vital historical quest.

Athens's early development of a populous middle class was a crucial factor in opening this new path for Western civilization. The Athenian population apparently expanded at a phenomenal rate when economic conditions improved rapidly from about 800 to 700 b.c.e. The ready availability of good farmland in Athenian territory and opportunities for seaborne trade along the long coastline allowed many families to achieve modest prosperity. These hardworking entrepreneurs evidently felt that their self-won economic success entitled them to a say in government. The cohesiveness forged by the Athenian masses was evident as early as 632 b.c.e., when the people rallied "from the fields in a body," according to Herodotus, to foil the attempt by an elite Athenian named Cylon to install a tyranny.

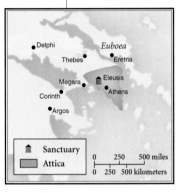

Athens and Central Greece, c. 750–500 b.c.e.

By the seventh century b.c.e., all freeborn adult male citizens of Athens had the right to vote on public matters in the assembly. They also elected magistrates called archons, who headed the government and the judicial system by rendering verdicts in disputes and criminal accusations. Members of the elite dominated these offices at the time because they carried no pay, meaning poor men could not afford to serve.

An extended economic crisis beginning in the late seventh century b.c.e. almost suffocated Athens's infant democracy. The first attempt to solve the problem was the emergency appointment around 621 b.c.e. of a man named Draco (literally, "the Serpent") to revise the laws. Like the Mesopotamian kings before them, Athens's leaders believed that reforming and clarifying the laws would bring social harmony through justice. Unfortunately, Draco's changes proved too harsh to work because they made death the penalty

for even minor crimes; later Greeks said he had written his laws in blood, not ink. By 600 b.c.e., the situation had become critical, with poorer farmers forced to borrow constantly from richer neighbors and deeply mortgage their land. Finally, the crisis became so bad that impoverished citizens were sold into slavery to pay off debts. Civil war seemed next.

Solon's Democratic Reforms. Desperate, the Athenians appointed another emergency official in 594 b.c.e., a war hero named Solon. To head off violence, Solon gave both rich and poor something of what they wanted, a compromise called the "shaking off of obligations" that canceled private debts, which helped the poor but displeased the rich; Solon's decision not to redistribute land had the opposite effect. He also banned selling citizens into slavery to settle debts and liberated citizens who had become slaves in this way. His elimination of debt slavery was a significant recognition of what today would be called citizen rights, and Solon celebrated his success in poetry: "To Athens, their home established by the gods, I brought back many who had been sold into slavery, some justly, some not."

Solon balanced political power between rich and poor by reforming Athens's traditional ranking of citizens into four groups. Most important, he made the top-ranking division depend solely on wealth, not birth. This change eliminated formal aristocracy at Athens. The groupings did not affect a man's treatment at law, only his eligibility for government office. The higher a man's ranking, the higher the post to which he could be elected; men at the poorest level, called laborers, were not eligible for any office. Solon did, however, confirm the laborers' right to participate in the legislative assembly. His revised classification scheme was another step toward democracy because it allowed for upward social mobility: if a man increased his wealth, he could move up the scale of eligibility for office.

To make the assembly more efficient, Solon created a council of four hundred men to prepare the assembly's agenda. He prevented the social elite from capturing too many places by having council members chosen annually by lottery. Over time, the council became the institution that kept Athenian direct democracy functioning efficiently; it organized the assembly's deliberations while preserving its freedom of action.

Even more than his changes to the government, Solon's two changes in the judicial system promoted democratic principles of equality. First, he mandated that any male citizen could bring charges on behalf of any crime victim. Second, he gave people the right to appeal a magistrate's judgment to the assembly. With these two measures, Solon empowered ordinary citizens in the administration of justice. Characteristically, he balanced these democratic reforms by granting broader powers to the "Council which meets on the Hill of the god of war Ares," a judicial body we call the Areopagus◆ Council. This select body, limited to ex-archons, wielded great power because its members judged the most important cases concerning public justice—accusations against archons themselves.

Solon's reforms broke the traditional pattern of government limited to the elite; they extended power broadly through the citizen body and created a system of law applying more equally than before to all the community's free men. An anecdote reported by the later biographer Plutarch offers a glimpse of how remarkable Solon's innovations seemed at the time: when a visiting foreign king, Anacharsis from Scythia,◆ discovered what Solon was doing, he burst into laughter, scoffing at Athenian democracy. Observing the procedure in the Athenian assembly, the king expressed his amazement that elite politicians could only recommend policy in their speeches, while the male citizens as a whole voted on what to do. "I find it astonishing," he remarked, "that here wise men speak on public affairs, while fools decide them." The king then added, "Do you actually believe your fellow citizens' injustice and greed can be kept in check this way? Written laws are more like spiders' webs than anything else: they tie up the weak and the small fry who get stuck in them, but the rich and the powerful tear them to shreds." Solon replied that communal values assure

the rule of law: "People abide by their agreements when neither side has anything to gain by breaking them. I am writing laws for the Athenians in such a way that they will clearly see it is to everyone's advantage to obey the laws rather than to break them."

Some elite Athenians vehemently disagreed with Solon because they wanted oligarchy. Their jealousy of one another kept them from uniting, and the unrest they caused opened the door to tyranny at Athens. Peisistratus,◆ helped by his upper-class friends and the poor whose interests he championed, made himself tyrant in 546 b.c.e. Like the Corinthian tyrants, he promoted the economic, cultural, and architectural development of Athens and curried the masses' favor. He helped poorer men, for example, by hiring them to build roads, a huge temple to Zeus, and fountains to increase the supply of drinking water. He boosted Athens's economy and its image by minting new coins stamped with Athena's owl and organizing a great annual festival honoring the god Dionysus that attracted people from near and far to see its musical and dramatic performances.

Peisistratus's family could not maintain public goodwill after his death. When Hippias, his eldest son, ruled harshly, a rival family, the Alcmaeonids,◆ denounced him as unjust toward the people. They convinced the Spartans, the self-proclaimed champions of Greek freedom, to "liberate" Athens from tyranny by expelling Hippias and his family in 510 b.c.e.

Cleisthenes, "Father of Athenian Democracy." Expelling the tyrants opened the way to the most important step in developing Athenian democracy, the reforms of Cleisthenes.◆ Himself a member of the social elite, in 508 b.c.e. he promised greater democracy to the masses to win political support for his election to office. Ordinary people favored his plan so strongly that they spontaneously rallied to repel a Spartan army that Cleisthenes' bitterest rival had convinced Sparta's leaders to send to block the reforms.

◆**Areopagus:** a ree AH puh guhs
◆**Scythia:** SIH thee uh

◆**Peisistratus:** pie SIS truh tuhs
◆**Alcmaeonids:** alk MEE uhn ihds
◆**Cleisthenes:** KLYS thuh neez

Vase Painting of a Music Lesson
This sixth-century B.C.E. red-figure vase shows a young man (seated on the left, without a beard) holding a lyre and watching an older, bearded man play the same instrument, while an adolescent boy and an older man listen. They all wear wreaths to show they are in a festive mood. The youth is evidently a pupil learning to play. Instruction in performing music and singing lyric poetry was considered an essential part of an upper-class Greek male's education. The teacher's lyre has a sounding board made from a turtle shell, as was customary for this instrument. *Staatliche Antikensammlungen und Glypothek.*

By about 500 B.C.E. Cleisthenes had ensured direct participation in government by as many adult male citizens as possible. First he assembled constituent units for the city-state's new political organization by grouping country villages and urban neighborhoods into units called demes◆ ("peoples"). The demes chose council members annually by lottery in proportion to the size of their populations. To allow for greater participation, Solon's Council of Four Hundred was expanded to five hundred members. Finally, Cleisthenes required candidates for public office to be spread widely throughout the demes.

Cleisthenes helped his reforms succeed by basing them in preexisting social conditions favorable to democracy. Using demes, most of which were country villages, suggests that democratic notions stemmed from traditions of village life. There, each man was entitled to his say in running local affairs and had to persuade, not force, others to

agree. Cleisthenes' reforms caused Athenians to remember him as the father of their democracy, but it took another fifty years of political struggle before Athenian democracy reached its full development.

New Ways of Thought and Expression, c. 630–500 B.C.E.

The idea that persuasion, rather than force or status, should drive political decisions in democracy matched the spirit of intellectual change rippling through Greece in the late Archaic Age. In city-states all over the Greek world, new ways of thought inspired artists, poets, and philosophers. The Greeks' ongoing contacts with the Near East supplied traditions to learn from and, in some cases, to alter dramatically.

Archaic Age Art and Literature. Early in the Archaic period Greek artists took inspiration from the Near East. By the sixth century B.C.E., they had introduced innovations of their own. In ceramics, painters experimented with different clays and colors to depict vivid scenes from mythology and daily life. They became expert at rendering fully three-dimensional figures in an increasingly realistic style. Sculptors gave their statues balanced poses and calm, smiling faces.

Greek poets built on the Near Eastern tradition of poetry expressing personal emotions by creating a new form, called **lyric poetry**. This poetry sprang from popular song and was always performed to the accompaniment of the lyre (a kind of harp that gives its name to the poetry). Greek lyric poems were short, rhythmic, and diverse in subject. Lyric poets wrote songs both for choruses and for individual performers. Choral poems honored deities on public occasions, celebrated famous events in a city-state's history, praised victors in athletic contests, and enlivened weddings.

Solo lyric poems generated controversy because they valued individual expression and opinion over conventional views. Solon wrote poems justifying his reforms. Other poets criticized traditional values, such as strength in war. Sappho,◆ a lyric poet from

◆**demes:** deems

◆**Sappho:** SA foh

Lesbos born about 630 B.C.E. and famous for her poems on love, wrote, "Some would say the most beautiful thing on our dark earth is an army of cavalry, others of infantry, others of ships, but I say it's whatever a person loves." In this poem Sappho was expressing her longing for a woman she loved, who was now far away. Archilochus of Paros,♦ who probably lived in the early seventh century B.C.E., became famous for poems mocking militarism, lamenting friends lost at sea, and regretting love affairs gone wrong. He became infamous for his lines about throwing away his shield in battle so that he could run away to save his life: "Oh, the hell with it; I can get another one just as good." When he taunted a family in verse after the father had ended Archilochus's affair with one of his daughters, the power of his ridicule reportedly caused the father and his two daughters to commit suicide.

Greek Philosophy and Science. The discipline of philosophy (literally, "love of wisdom") began in the seventh and sixth centuries B.C.E. when Greek thinkers whom we call pre-Socratic ("before Socrates") philosophers created prose writing to express their innovative ideas. These thinkers developed radically new explanations of the human world and its relation to the gods. Most pre-Socratic philosophers lived in Ionia, on Anatolia's western coast. This location gave them contact with Near Eastern knowledge in astronomy, mathematics, and myth. Because there were no formal schools in the Archaic Age, philosophers communicated their ideas by teaching privately and giving public lectures. Some also composed poetry to explain their theories. People who studied with these philosophers or heard their presentations helped spread the new ideas.

Working from Babylonian discoveries about the regular movements of the stars and planets, Ionian philosophers such as Thales♦ (c. 625–545 B.C.E.) and Anaximander♦ (c. 610–540 B.C.E.), both of Miletus, reached the revolutionary conclusion that unchanging laws of nature governed the universe rather than gods' whims. Pythagoras,♦ who emigrated from the island of Samos to the Greek city-state Croton in southern Italy about 530 B.C.E., taught that numerical relationships explained the world and initiated the Greek study of mathematics and the numerical aspects of musical harmony.

Ionian philosophers insisted that natural phenomena were neither random nor arbitrary. They applied the word *cosmos*—meaning "an orderly arrangement that is beautiful"—to the universe. The cosmos encompassed not only the motions of heavenly bodies but also the weather, the growth of plants and animals, and human health. Because the universe was ordered, it was knowable; because it was knowable, thought and research could explain it. Philosophers therefore looked for the first or universal cause of all things, a problem that scientists still pursue. These first philosophers firmly believed they needed to give reasons for their conclusions and to persuade others by arguments based on evidence; that is, they believed in logic. This new way of thought, called **rationalism**, became the foundation for the study of science and philosophy. This rule-based view of the causes of events and physical phenomena contrasted sharply with the traditional mythological view. Naturally, many people had difficulty accepting such a startling change in their understanding of the world, and the older tradition explaining events as the work of deities lived on alongside the new approach. Magic remained an important preoccupation in the lives of most people.

The first Greek philosophers deeply influenced later times by separating scientific thinking from myth and religion. Their idea that people must give reasons to justify their beliefs, rather than just make assertions that others must believe without evidence, was their

Ionia and the Aegean, c. 750–500 B.C.E.

♦**Archilochus of Paros:** ahr KIHL uh kuhs (of) PAR ahs
♦**Thales:** THAY leez
♦**Anaximander:** an nak suh MAN dur

♦**Pythagoras:** pie THAG uhr ahs

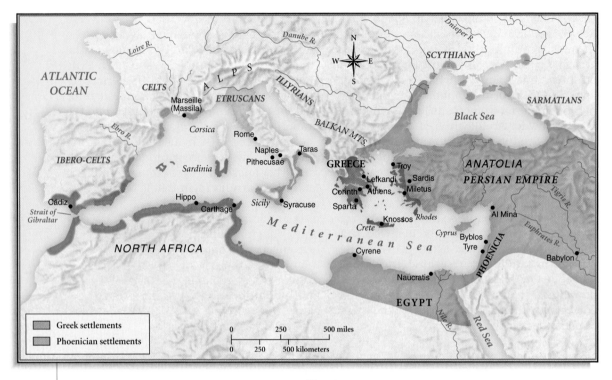

MAPPING THE WEST Mediterranean Civilizations, c. 500 B.C.E.
At the end of the sixth century B.C.E., the Persian empire was far and away the most power-ful civilization touching the Mediterranean. Its riches and its unity gave it resources that no Phoenician or Greek city could match. The Phoenicians dominated economically in the west-ern Mediterranean, while the Greek city-states in Sicily and southern Italy rivaled the power of those in the heartland. In Italy, the Etruscans were the most powerful civilization; the Romans were still a small community struggling to replace monarchy with a republic.

most important achievement. This insistence on rationality, coupled with the belief that the world could be understood as something other than the plaything of divine caprice, gave people hope that they could improve their lives through their own efforts. As Xenophanes of Colophon♦ (c. 580–480 B.C.E.) concluded, "The gods have not revealed all things from the beginning to mortals, but, by seeking, hu-man beings find out, in time, what is better." This saying expressed the value Archaic Age philosophers gave to intellectual freedom, corresponding to the value that citizens gave to political freedom in the city-state.

Review: What were the main differences between the various forms of government in the Greek city-states?

♦**Xenophanes of Colophon:** zih NAH fuh neez (of) KAH luh fuhn

Conclusion

Over different spans of time and with differ-ent results, both the Near East and Greece recovered from their Dark Ages, which the calamities of the period 1200–1000 B.C.E. had caused. After its Dark Age the Near East quickly revived its traditional pattern of social and political organization: empire with a strong central authority. The Neo-Assyrians, the Neo-Babylonians, and the Persians succeeded one another as imperial powers. The moral dualism of Persian religion, Zoroastrianism, influenced later religions. The Jews developed their monotheism based on scripture.

Greece's recovery from its Dark Age pro-duced the polis, a city-state based on citi-zenship as a new form of political and social organization. The rapidly growing popula-tion of the Archaic Age developed the sense of communal interests, personal freedom, and divine justice that underlay the city-state. Greek city-states were ruled by tyranny, oligarchy, and—for the first time in history—democracy. Athens developed the most thoroughgoing democracy, but it took more than a century to do so.

Just as revolutionary as the invention of democracy were the new ways of thought that Greek philosophers developed. Arguing that laws of nature controlled the universe and that humans could discover these laws through reason and research, they established rationalism as the conceptual basis for science and philosophy.

The political and intellectual innovations of the Greek Archaic Age, which so profoundly affected later Western civilization, were almost lost to history. The grave threat to the Greek world and its new values came from Persia's awesome empire by about 500 B.C.E.

Suggested References

From Dark Age to Empire in the Near East, c. 1000–500 B.C.E.

Recent surveys of ancient Near Eastern history take an integrative approach to the subject, treating its various empires comparatively. The significance of Persian religion for later faiths has also been an active field of study.

Briant, Pierre. *From Cyrus to Alexander: A History of the Persian Empire.* 2002.

Brown, John Pairman. *Ancient Israel and Ancient Greece: Religion, Politics, and Culture.* 2003.

Brosius, Maria. *Women in Ancient Persia, 559–331 B.C.* 1996.

Cohn, Norman. *Cosmos, Chaos, and the World to Come: The Ancient Roots of Apocalyptic Faith.* 1993.

Kugel, James. *The God of Old: Inside the Lost World of the Bible.* 2003.

*Lieber, David L., ed. *Etz Hayim: Torah and Commentary.* 2001.

*Malandra, William W. *An Introduction to Ancient Iranian Religion: Readings from the Avesta and the Achaemenid Inscriptions.* 1983.

Nigosian, S. A. *The Zoroastrian Faith: Tradition and Modern Research.* 1993.

*Primary source.

Persepolis and Ancient Iran: http://www.oi.uchicago.edu/OI/MUS/PA/IRAN/PAAI/PAAI_Persepolis.html.

Silberman, Neil, and Israel Finkelstein. *The Bible Unearthed: Archaeology's New Vision of Ancient Israel and the Origin of Its Sacred Texts.* 2002.

Snell, Daniel C. *Life in the Ancient Near East, 3100–332 B.C.E.* 1997.

Stiebing, William H., Jr. *Ancient Near Eastern History and Culture.* 2003.

Remaking Greek Civilization, c. 1000–750 B.C.E.

Scholarship on the Dark Age, such as by Sarah Morris, emphasizes that it was not as dark as sometimes asserted in the past because Greece was never completely cut off from contact with the Near East. Scholars agree that the Archaic Age was a period of tremendous activity and change, but they dispute the trustworthiness of the (later) ancient sources that inform us about it. The date of the first Olympic Games, for example, is much debated (see the article by Hugh Lee in the collection edited by Rashcke).

Hanson, Victor Davis. *The Other Greeks: The Family Farm and the Agrarian Roots of Western Civilization.* 1995.

*Hesiod. *Theogony; Works and Days.* Trans. M. L. West. 1999.

Kriwaczek, Paul. *In Search of Zarathustra: The First Prophet and the Ideas That Changed the World.* 2003.

Miller, Stephen G. *Ancient Greek Athletics.* 2004.

Morris, Sarah P. *Daidalos and the Origins of Greek Art.* 1992.

Olympia: http://harpy.uccs.edu/greek/olympia.html.

Osborne, Robin. *Greece in the Making, 1200–479 B.C.* 1996.

Raschke, Wendy J., ed. *The Archaeology of the Olympics: The Olympics and Other Festivals in Antiquity.* 1988.

Snodgrass, Anthony. *The Greek Dark Age.* 1971.

Social justice in Homer's *Odyssey:* http://www.fas.harvard.edu/%7Echs/HCJ/index.html.

The Creation of the Greek Polis, c. 750–500 B.C.E.

The Greek city-state did not spring up in a cultural vacuum, but the scarcity of sources for this period makes it difficult to evaluate the importance of various influences on it. Recent research persuasively argues for a greater role for individual entrepreneurs in what is usually regarded as state-initiated colonization (see the article by Robin Osborne in the collection edited by Fisher and van Wees).

Burkert, Walter. *The Orientalizing Revolution: The Near Eastern Influence on Greek Culture in the Early Archaic Age.* Trans. Margaret E. Pinder and Walter Burkert. 1992.

Fisher, Nick, and Hans van Wees, eds. *Archaic Greece: New Approaches and Evidence.* 1998.

Garlan, Yvon. *Slavery in Ancient Greece.* Rev. ed. Trans. Janet Lloyd. 1988.

Garland, Robert. *Religion and the Greeks.* 1994.

Starr, Chester. *Individual and Community: The Rise of the Polis, 800–500 B.C.* 1986.

Wees, Hans van, ed. *War and Violence in Ancient Greece.* 2000.

New Directions for the Polis, c. 750–500 B.C.E.

Contemporary scholarship stresses the diversity of city-state governance and customs, but, as always in ancient history, the scarcity of hard evidence hinders our gaining a clear picture.

Anhalt, Emily Katz. *Solon the Singer: Politics and Poetics.* 1993.

Archaic Greek sculpture: **http://harpy.uccs .edu/greek/archaicsculpt.html**.

*Barnes, Jonathan. *Early Greek Philosophy.* 1987.

*Campbell, David A. *Greek Lyric.* Five volumes. 1982–1993.

Cartledge, Paul. *Spartan Reflections.* 2001.

Emlyn-Jones, C. J. *The Ionians and Hellenism: A Study of the Cultural Achievements of Early Greek Inhabitants of Asia Minor.* 1980.

Gottlieb, Anthony. *The Dream of Reason: A History of Philosophy from the Greeks to the Renaissance.* 2000.

Halperin, David M. *One Hundred Years of Homosexuality and Other Essays on Greek Love.* 1990.

Hurwitt, Jeffrey M. *The Art and Culture of Early Greece, 1100–480 B.C.* 1985.

Kennell, Nigel M. *The Gymnasium of Virtue: Education and Culture in Ancient Sparta.* 1995.

McGlew, James F. *Tyranny and Political Culture in Ancient Greece.* 1993.

*Robinson, Eric W. *Ancient Greek Democracy: Readings and Sources.* 2003.

CHAPTER REVIEW

IMPORTANT EVENTS

c. 1000–750 B.C.E.	Greece experiences its Dark Age
c. 900 B.C.E.	Neo-Assyrian empire emerges
c. 800 B.C.E.	Greeks learn to write with an alphabet
776 B.C.E.	Olympic Games founded in Greece
c. 750 B.C.E.	Greeks begin to create the polis
c. 700 B.C.E.	Spartans conquer Messenia and enslave its inhabitants
700–500 B.C.E.	Ionian philosophers invent rationalism
657 B.C.E.	Cypselus becomes tyrant in Corinth
c. 630 B.C.E.	The lyric poet Sappho is born
612 B.C.E.	Medes and Chaldean destroy Neo-Assyrian empire
605 B.C.E.	Neo-Babylonian King Nebuchadnezzar II defeats the Egyptians at the battle of Carchemish in Syria
597 and 586 B.C.E.	Nebuchadnezzar II deports Hebrews to exile in Babylon
594 B.C.E.	Solon's reforms promote early democracy in Athens
546–510 B.C.E.	Peisistratus's family rules Athens as tyrants
539 B.C.E.	Persian King Cyrus captures Babylon and permits the Hebrews to return to Canaan
522–486 B.C.E.	Rule of Persian king Darius I
508–500 B.C.E.	Cleisthenes' reforms secure democracy at Athens

KEY TERMS

apocalypticism (51)

aretê (53)

Dark Age (45)

Diaspora (51)

hoplite (66)

lyric poetry (76)

moral dualism (50)

polis (57)

rationalism (77)

satrap (49)

Torah (51)

REVIEW QUESTIONS

1. In what ways did religion affect the history of the Near East from c. 1000 B.C.E. to c. 500 B.C.E.?

2. What factors proved most important in the Greek recovery from the economic troubles of the Dark Age?

3. What degrees of freedom existed for the different categories of people in the Greek city-state?

4. What were the main differences between the various forms of government in the Greek city-states?

MAKING CONNECTIONS

1. What made the Greek city-state a new form of political and social organization?

2. How were the ideas of the Ionian philosophers different from mythic traditions?

FOR FURTHER EXPLORATION

To assess your mastery of the material in this chapter, see the Online Study Guide at **bedfordstmartins.com/hunt**.

To read additional primary-source material from this period, see Chapter 2 in *Sources of The Making of the West*, Second Edition.

of Athens's population, but they lacked political rights. Women who were citizens enjoyed legal privileges and social status denied slaves and foreigners, and they earned respect through their roles in the family and in religion. Upper-class women managed their households, visited female friends, and participated in religious cults at home and in public. Poor women worked as small-scale merchants, crafts producers, and agricultural laborers. Slaves' and metics' work also contributed much to Athens's prosperity, but they always remained outsiders in the city-state.

Property, Inheritance, and Marriage. Bearing children in marriage earned women status because it was literally the source of family—the heart of Greek society. To defend this fundamental social institution, men were expected to respect and support their wives. Childbirth was dangerous under the medical conditions of the time. In *Medea*, a play of 431 B.C.E. by Euripides, the heroine shouts in anger at her husband, who has selfishly betrayed her: "People say that we women lead a safe life at home, while men have to go to war. What fools they are! I would much rather fight in battle three times than give birth to a child even once."

Athenian wives were expected to be partners with their husbands in owning and managing the household's property to help the family thrive. (See "Contrasting Views," page 100.) Rich women acquired property, including land—the most valued possession in Greek society because it could be farmed or rented out for income—through inheritance and dowry (the family property a daughter received at marriage). The husband was legally required to preserve the dowry and use it to support his wife and their children. A man often had to put up valuable land of his own as collateral to guarantee the safety of his wife's dowry.

Like fathers, mothers were expected to hand down property to their children to keep it in the family line. This expectation shows up most clearly in Athenian law about heiresses (daughters whose fathers died without any sons, which happened in about one in every five families): the heiress's father's closest male relative—her official guardian

after her father's death—was required to marry her. The goal was to produce a son to inherit the father's property himself. This rule applied regardless of whether the heiress was already married (unless she had sons) or whether the male relative already had a wife; the heiress and the male relative were both supposed to divorce their present spouses and marry each other. In real life, however, people often used legal technicalities to get around this requirement so that they could remain with their loves.

Requiring property to be passed down in this way met two traditional goals of male-dominated Greek society: continuing the father's blood line and preventing property from piling up in the hands of unmarried women (and therefore out of the control of men). At Sparta, the renowned scholar Aristotle (384–322 B.C.E.) reported, the inheritance laws were different (and in his opinion deficient); he claimed that women came to own 40 percent of Spartan territory.

Women's Daily Lives. Tradition restricted women's freedom of movement in public; men claimed this restriction protected women by limiting opportunities for seducers and rapists. Men wanted to ensure that their children were truly theirs, that family property went only to genuine heirs, and that the city had only legitimate citizens. Well-off women in the city were expected to avoid contact with men outside their family and to spend most of their time at home or with women friends in their houses. Recent research has exploded the idea that Greek homes had a set "women's quarter" to which women were confined; rather, women were granted privacy in certain rooms. If the house included an interior courtyard, women could walk there in the open air and talk with other members of the household, male and female. In the safety of her home a well-to-do woman would spin wool for clothing, converse with visiting friends, direct her children, supervise the slaves, and present her opinions on various matters, including politics, to the men of the house as they came and went. Poor women had little time for such activities because they—like their husbands, sons, and brothers—had to leave their homes, usually crowded rental apartments, to set up small stalls to sell bread, vegetables, simple clothing, or trinkets they had made.

An elite woman careful of her reputation left home only for appropriate reasons, such as religious festivals, funerals, childbirths at the houses of relatives and friends, and trips to workshops to buy shoes or other domestic articles. Often her husband escorted her, but sometimes she took only a slave, setting her own itinerary.

Women who bore legitimate children merited increased respect and freedom, as an Athenian man explained in his speech (written by Lysias) defending himself for having killed his wife's adulterer:

> After my marriage, I initially refrained from bothering my wife very much, but neither did I allow her too much independence. I kept an eye on her. . . . But after she had a baby, I started to trust her more and put her in charge of all my things, believing we now had the closest of relationships.

Bearing male children brought special honor to a woman because sons meant security. They could appear in court to support their parents in lawsuits and protect them in the streets of Athens, which for most of its history had no regular police force. By law, sons were required to support elderly parents. So intense was the pressure to produce sons that stories circulated of women who smuggled in male babies born to slaves and passed them off as their own. Substitution was possible, if unlikely, because husbands customarily stayed away at childbirth.

Most upper-class women probably viewed their limited contact with men outside the household as a badge of superior social status. For example, a pale complexion, from staying inside so much, was much admired as a sign of an enviable life of leisure and wealth. Unaware of the health risk, many women used powdered white lead as makeup to give themselves a fashionable pallor.

Extraordinary Women. A few women in Athens escaped traditional restrictions by working as what Greeks called a **hetaira**♦ (literally, "companion"). Companions, usually foreigners, were physically attractive, witty in speech, and skilled in music and poetry. Men hired them to entertain at **symposia** (drinking parties to which wives were not invited) with their playful conversation. Their much-admired skill at clever taunts and verbal snubs allowed companions a freedom of speech denied to "proper" women; they

---

♦**hetaira:** heh TYE rah

Vase Painting of a Woman Buying Shoes

Greek vases were frequently decorated with scenes from daily life instead of mythological stories. Here, a woman is being fitted for a pair of custom-made shoes by a craftsman and his apprentice. Her husband has accompanied her, as was often the case for shopping; and, to judge from his gesture, he is participating in the discussion of the purchase. This vase was painted in so-called black-figure technique, in which the figures are dark and have their details incised on a background of red clay. Over time, this technique was replaced by the red-figure style, as seen in the vase on page 111. **For more help analyzing this image**, see the visual activity for this chapter in the Online Study Guide at **bedfordstmartins.com/hunt**. *Museum of Fine Arts, Boston. Henry Lillie Pierce Fund. Photograph © 2004 Museum of Fine Arts, Boston (01. 80 35).*

CONTRASTING VIEWS

The Nature of Women and Marriage

Greeks believed that women had different natures from men and that both genders were capable of excellence, but in their own ways (Documents 1 and 2). Marriage was supposed to bring these natures together in a partnership of complementary strengths and obligations to each other (Document 3). Marriage contracts (Document 4), similar to modern prenuptial agreements, became common to define the partnership's terms.

1. THE POLITICAL LEADER PERICLES ADDRESSING THE ATHENIANS AT THE FUNERAL OF SOLDIERS KILLED IN THE FIRST YEAR OF THE PELOPONNESIAN WAR (WINTER OF 431–430 B.C.E.)

According to Thucydides, the famously stern Pericles concluded his Funeral Oration, a solemn public occasion commemorating the valor and virtues expected of citizens, with these terse remarks to the women in the audience. His comments reveal two ancient Greek assumptions: that women had a different nature from men and that women best served social harmony by not becoming subjects of gossip. He kept these comments to a bare minimum in his long speech.

If it is also appropriate now for me to say something about what constitutes excellence for women, I will signal all my thinking with this short piece of advice to those of you present who are now widows of the war dead: your reputation will be great if you don't fall short of your innate nature and men talk about you the least whether in praise of your excellence or blaming your faults.

Source: Thucydides, *History of the Peloponnesian War*, Book 2.45. Translation by Thomas R. Martin.

2. MELANIPPE, THE HEROINE OF *MELANIPPE THE CAPTIVE*, A LATE-FIFTH-CENTURY B.C.E. TRAGEDY BY EURIPIDES, EXPLAINING WHY MEN'S CRITICISM OF WOMEN IS BASELESS

The Athenian playwright Euripides often portrayed female characters as denouncing men for misunderstanding and criticizing women. In mythology, Melanippe is a mother who overcomes hardship and treachery to save her family and fight for justice. Preserved only on damaged papyrus scraps, Melanippe's speech unfortunately breaks off before finishing.

Men's blame and criticism of women are empty, like the twanging sound a bow string makes without an arrow. Women are superior to men, and I'll demonstrate it. They make contracts with no need of witnesses [to swear they are honest]. They manage their households and keep safe the valuable possessions, shipped from abroad, that they have inside their homes; without a woman, no household is elegant or happy. And then in the matter of people's relationship with the gods—this I judge to be most important of all—there we have the greatest role. For women prophesy the will of Apollo in his oracles, and at the hallowed oracle of Dodona by the sacred oak tree a woman reveals the will of Zeus to all Greeks who seek it. And then there are the sacred rites of initiation performed for the Fates and the Goddesses Without Names: these can't be done with holiness by men, but women make them flourish in every way. In this way women's role in religion is right and proper.

Therefore, should anyone put down women? Won't those men stop their empty fault-finding, the ones who strongly believe that all women should be blamed if a single one is found to be bad? I will make a distinction with the following argument: nothing is worse than a bad woman, but nothing is more surpassingly superior than a worthy one.

Source: Euripides, *Melanippe the Captive*, fragment 660 Mette. Translation by Thomas R. Martin.

3. THE PHILOSOPHER SOCRATES DISCUSSING GENDER ROLES IN MARRIAGE WITH A NEW HUSBAND TOWARD THE END OF THE FIFTH CENTURY B.C.E.

Socrates, who was dedicated to discovering the nature of human virtue, often discussed family life because it revealed the qualities of women as well as men. When his upper-class friend Ischomachus♦ married a young wife, as was common, the philosopher quizzed him about their marriage; the new husband, according to Xenophon, explained that it was a partnership based on the complementary natures of male and female.

ISCHOMACHUS: I said to her:…I for my sake and your parents for your sake [arranged our marriage] by considering who would be the best partner for forming a household and having children. I chose you, and your parents chose me as the best they could find. If god should give us children, we will then plan how to raise them in the best possible way. For our partnership provides us this good: the best mutual support and the best maintenance in our old age. We have this sharing now in our household, because I've contributed all that I own to the common resources of the household, and so have you. We're not going to count up who brought more property, because the one who turns out to be the better partner in a marriage has made the greater contribution.

ISCHOMACHUS'S WIFE (no name is given): But how will I be able to partner you? What ability do I have? Everything rests on you. My mother told me my job was to behave with thoughtful moderation.

ISCHOMACHUS: Well, my father told me the same thing. Thoughtful moderation for a man as for a woman means behaving in such a way that their possessions will be in the best possible condition and will increase as much as possible by good and just means.…So, you must do what the gods made you naturally capable of and what our law requires.…With great forethought the gods have yoked together male and female so that they can form the most beneficial partnership. This yoking together keeps living creatures from disappearing by producing children, and it provides offspring to look after parents in their old age, at least for people. [He then explains that human survival requires outdoor work—to raise crops and livestock—and indoor work—to preserve food, raise infants, and manufacture clothing.]…And since the work both outside and inside required effort and care, god, it seems to me, from the start fashioned women's nature for indoor work and men's for outdoor. Therefore he made men's bodies and spirits more able to endure cold and heat and travel and marches, giving them the outside jobs, while assigning indoor tasks to women, it seems, because their bodies are less hardy.…

But since both men and women have to manage things, [god] gave them equal shares in memory and attentiveness; you can't tell which gender has more of these qualities. And god gave both an equal ability to practice self-control, with the power to benefit the most from this quality going to whoever is better at it—whether man or woman. Precisely because they have different natures, they have greater need of each other and their yoking together is the most beneficial, with the one being capable where the other one is lacking. And as god has made them partners for their children, the law makes them partners for the household.

Source: Xenophon, *Oeconomicus* 7.10–30. Translation by Thomas R. Martin.

♦**Ischomachus:** iss KAH muh kuhs

(Continued)

(Continued)

4. A GREEK MARRIAGE CONTRACT FROM ELEPHANTINE IN EGYPT STATING THE LEGAL OBLIGATIONS OF HUSBAND AND WIFE (311–310 B.C.E.)

Greeks living abroad customarily drew up written contracts to define the duties of each partner in a marriage because they wanted their traditional expectations to remain legally binding regardless of the local laws. The earliest surviving such contract comes from the site of a Greek military garrison far up the Nile.

Marriage contract of Heraclides and Demetria.

Heraclides [of Temnos] takes as his lawful wife Demetria of Cos from her father Leptines of Cos and her mother Philotis. He is a free person; she is a free person. She brings a dowry of clothing and jewelry worth 1,000 drachmas. Heraclides must provide Demetria with everything appropriate for a freeborn wife. We will live together in whatever location Leptines and Heraclides together decide is best.

If Demetria is apprehended doing anything bad that shames her husband, she will forfeit all her dowry; Heraclides will have to prove any allegations against her in the presence of three men, whom they both must approve. It will be illegal for Heraclides to bring home another wife to Demetria's harm or to father children by another woman or to do anything bad to Demetria for any reason. If he is apprehended doing any of these things and Demetria proves it in the presence of three men whom they both approve, Heraclides must return her dowry in full and pay her 1,000 drachmas additional. Demetria and those who help her in getting this payment will have legal standing to act against Heraclides and all his property on land and sea.... Each shall have the right to keep a personal copy of this contract. [A list of witnesses follows.]

Source: *Elephantine Papyri*, ed. O. Rubensohn (Berlin, 1907), no. 1. Translation by Thomas R. Martin.

QUESTIONS TO CONSIDER

1. What evidence and arguments for differing natures for men and women do these documents offer?
2. Do you think Athenian women would have found these arguments convincing? Why or why not?

---

nevertheless lacked the social respectability and status that wives and mothers possessed.

Sometimes companions also sold sex for a high price, and they got to control their own sexuality by choosing their clients. Athenian men (but not women) could buy sex as they pleased without legal hindrance. "Certainly you don't think men father children out of sexual desire?" wrote the upper-class author Xenophon.◆ "The streets and the brothels are swarming with ways to take care of that." Men (but, again, not women) could also have sex freely with female or male slaves, who could not refuse their masters.

Less successful companions lived precarious lives of exploitation and even violence at the hands of their male customers, but the most skilled of them attracted admirers from the highest levels of society and earned enough to live in luxury on their own. The most famous companion in Athens was Aspasia from Miletus, who became Pericles's lover and bore him a son. She dazzled men with her brilliant talk and wide knowledge; Pericles fell so deeply in love with her that he wanted to make her an "honest woman" by marrying her, despite his own law of 451 B.C.E. restricting citizenship, which meant their children could not be citizens without a special law passed by the assembly.

Great riches could also free women from tradition, allowing them to speak to men openly and bluntly. The most outspoken Athenian woman of wealth was Elpinike, Cimon's sister. When controversy erupted over a speech by Pericles supporting Athens's attack on a rebellious Delian League ally, she publicly rebuked him by sarcastically remarking in front of a band of women who were praising him, "This really is wonderful, Pericles.... You have caused the loss of

◆**Xenophon:** ZEH nuh fuhn

many good citizens, not in battle against Phoenicians or Persians…but in suppressing an allied city of fellow Greeks."

Other sources, especially comic drama and fourth-century B.C.E. oratory, imply that not-so-rich women, too, had strong opinions about politics and foreign policy. They customarily expressed their views to their husbands and male relatives at home in private.

Slaves and Metics.   Traditional social and legal restrictions in Golden Age Athens made outsiders of slaves and metics, despite all the work they did in and for the city-state. Individuals and the city-state alike owned slaves, who could be purchased from traders or bred in the household. Unwanted newborns abandoned by their parents (the practice called infant exposure) were often picked up by others and raised as slaves. Athens's commercial growth in this period increased the demand for slaves, who in Pericles' time made up around 100,000 of the city-state's total of perhaps 250,000 inhabitants (an estimate compiled from ancient reports of the army's numbers and probable household sizes). Slaves worked in homes, on farms,

and in crafts shops; rowed alongside their owners in the navy; and, if they were really unlucky, toiled in Athens's dangerous silver mines. Unlike those at Sparta, Athens's slaves almost never rebelled, probably because they originated from too many different places to be able to unite. Many mining slaves did run away to the Spartan base established in Athenian territory during the Peloponnesian War; the Spartans resold them.

Golden Age Athens's wealth and cultural vitality attracted many metics, who flocked to the city from all around the Mediterranean, hoping to make money as importers, crafts producers, entertainers, and laborers. By the start of the Peloponnesian War in 431 B.C.E., metics constituted perhaps 50,000 to 75,000 of the approximately 150,000 free men, women, and children in the city-state. Metics paid for the privilege of living and working in Athens through a special foreigners' tax and military service. Athenians valued metics' contributions to the city's prosperity, but their insistence on exclusive citizenship meant they were unwilling to share its legal and financial benefits with immigrants.

Vase Painting of a Symposium
Upper-class Greek men often spent their evenings at symposia, drinking parties that always included much conversation and usually featured music and entertainers; wives were not included. The discussions could range widely, from literature to politics to philosophy. The man on the right is about to fling the dregs of his wine, playing a messy game called *kottabos*. The nudity of the female musician indicates she is a hired prostitute. *Reproduction by permission of the Syndics of the Fitzwilliam Museum, Cambridge. Master and Fellows of Corpus Christi College, Cambridge, The Parker Library.*

The Masculine Ideal
This sculpture of a male warrior/athlete was cast in bronze in the fifth century B.C.E.; bronze was preferred over marble for top-rank statues, but not many have survived because they were usually melted down in much later times to reuse their metal (e.g., to make guns). The relaxed pose displays the asymmetry—the head looking to one side, the arms in different positions, the torso tilted—that made Greek statues from the Classical Age appear less stiff than Archaic Age ones or their Egyptian predecessors (compare the illustration on pages 25 and 61). The body displays the ideal build that Greek men worked to achieve through daily workouts. For male statues, nudity indicated a heroic ideal. What do you think a female statue indicated depending on whether it was clothed (as on page 95) or nude (as on page 151)? *Erich Lessing/Art Resource, NY.*

Intellectual Innovation

New ways of thinking challenged accepted ideas about how people should live, creating social tension in the Golden Age. Innovative concepts in education, philosophy, historical writing, and medicine thrilled some fifth-century Greeks, but they deeply upset others, who feared that these startling changes from the old ways would undermine the traditions that held society together, especially religion, thereby provoking punishment from the angry gods. These controversial innovations had major consequences for Western civilization.

Education and philosophy provided the hottest battles between tradition and innovation. Earlier, education had stressed the preservation of old ways; parents controlled what children learned at home and from hired tutors (there were no public schools). Controversy erupted when Sophists appeared in the mid-fifth century B.C.E. and offered, for pay, classes to teenaged and young-adult males that taught nontraditional philosophic and religious doctrines and novel techniques for public speaking. Some philosophers' ideas about the nature of the cosmos challenged traditional religious views. The philosopher Socrates expounded ethical views on personal morality and responsibility and thus provoked an equally fierce controversy even though he did not work as a Sophist. In historical writing and medicine, innovators created models of interpretation and scientific method that also stimulated argument over how to understand human experience and the body.

Disagreement over whether these changes in intellectual life were dangerous for Athenian society contributed to the political tension that had arisen at Athens by the 430s B.C.E. concerning Athens's harsh treatment of its own allies and its economic sanctions against those allied with Sparta. This interaction occurred because the political, intellectual, and religious dimensions of life in ancient Athens were closely intertwined. Athenians would make connections between philosophic ideas about the nature of justice and decisions concerning what the city-state should do in domestic and foreign policy, while also being concerned about the attitude

Athenian Regulations for a Rebellious Ally

The city-state of Chalcis on the island of Euboea re-
belled from the Athenian-dominated Delian League
in 446 B.C.E. After defeating the rebels, the Athe-
nians forced the Chalcidians to swear compliance
with new regulations, which were inscribed on
stone in both cities. The text reveals that the terms
were not the same for the two sides.

The Athenian Council and the jurors shall swear
an oath in this form: "I will not expel Chalcidians
from Chalcis nor will I reduce the city to ruins nor
deprive any individual of his citizen rights nor
punish him with exile nor imprison him nor kill
him nor take property from anyone who has not
had a trial without approval from the People [i.e.,
the assembly] of the Athenians, nor will I have a
vote taken against the community or any single
individual without their being called to trial, and
when an embassy arrives, I will introduce them to
the Council and People within ten days when I am
in charge of the procedure, so far as I am able.
These things I will guarantee the Chalcidians if
they obey the People of the Athenians."

The Chalcidians shall swear an oath in this
form: "I will not rebel from the People of the Athenians either by cunning or by any way at all either
by word or by deed, and I will not obey anyone
who rebels, and if anyone does rebel, I will denounce him to the Athenians, and I will pay the
tribute to the Athenians which I persuade the
Athenians [to levy on me], and as an ally I will be
the best and most just that I am able, and I will
give support to and defend the People of the Athenians, if anyone wrongs the People of the Athenians,
and I will obey the People of the Athenians."

Source: *Inscriptiones Graecae*, 3rd ed. (1981), no. 40.
Translation by Thomas R. Martin.

---

of the gods toward the community. (See
"Athenian Regulations for a Rebellious Ally,"
above.)

Education. The only formal education
available came from private teachers, to
whom well-to-do families sent their sons to
learn to read, write, play a musical instrument or sing, and practice athletic skills
suitable for war. Physical training was considered a vital part of men's education because it both made their bodies beautiful
and prepared them for service in the militia
(to which they could be summoned from age
eighteen to sixty). Therefore, men exercised
nude every day in public open-air facilities
paid for by wealthy families. Men frequently
discussed politics and exchanged news at
these gymnasia.♦ The daughters of wealthy
families usually received instruction at home
from educated slaves, who were expensive

because they were rare. The young girls
learned reading, writing, and arithmetic so
that they would be ready to help their future
husbands by managing the household.

Poor girls and boys received no formal
education; they learned a trade and perhaps
a little reading, writing, and calculating by
assisting their parents in their daily work or
by serving as apprentices to skilled crafts
workers. Scholars disagree about how many
people could read well, but most likely they
were a minority. Weak reading skills were less
of a problem then than they are today because Greeks could always find someone to
read aloud any written text; in fact, oral
communication was at the center of Greek
life, whether in speeches about politics or in
songs, plays, and stories from literature and
history.

Traditionally, young men from prosperous families learned how to participate in
Athenian democracy by observing their fathers, uncles, and other older men as they

---

♦**gymnasia:** jihm NAY zee uh

debated in the Council of Five Hundred and the assembly, served in public office, and spoke in court. Often an older man would choose an adolescent boy as his special favorite to educate. The teenager would learn about public life by spending time with the older man. During the day the boy would listen to his mentor talking politics in the agora, help him perform his duties in public office, and work out with him in a gymnasium. They would spend their evenings at a symposium, whose agenda could range from serious political and philosophical discussion to riotous partying.

This older mentor–younger favorite relationship could lead to sexual relations between the youth and the older male, who would usually be married. Sex between mentors and favorites was considered acceptable in elite circles in many city-states, including Athens and Thebes; other places banned this behavior because they believed, as the Athenian author Xenophon suggests, that it sprang from a man's shameful inability to control his lustful desires. Sex between free adult men outside this sort of relationship was evidently regarded as disgraceful throughout the Greek world (too little evidence survives to reveal general Greek attitudes toward sex between women). These complicated attitudes about male homoerotic relations reflected the complexity of Greek ideas of masculinity—about what made a man a man and what unmade him. In any case, a mentor was expected never to exploit his younger companion just for pleasure, nor to neglect his political education.

Sophists and Philosophers as a Threat to Tradition. By the time of radical democracy in Athens, young men eager to develop the essential political skill of public speaking could pay a new kind of teacher to train them. **Sophists**, or "men of wisdom," sparked controversy because they strongly challenged traditional beliefs by teaching new skills of persuasion in speaking and new ways of thinking about philosophy and religion. The term sophist later acquired a negative connotation (preserved in the English word sophistry) because the Sophists were so clever in debate that they could make deceptive arguments using complex reasoning.

Starting about 450 B.C.E. Athens's booming economy and lively intellectual activity attracted Sophists from around the Greek world. They were individual entrepreneurs vying with one another to attract pupils who could pay the hefty prices they charged for their innovative courses. As in every part of Greek intellectual life, the competition for prominence was intense. Sophists competed by offering specialized training in rhetoric—the skill of speaking persuasively. Every ambitious young man craved rhetorical training because it promised power in Athens's assembly, council, and courts. The Sophists alarmed many tradition-minded Athenians, who feared their teachings would undermine established social and political traditions. Speakers trained by silver-tongued Sophists, they believed, might be able to mislead the assembly by persuading it to take bad decisions promoting their private interests.

Young men were not the only Athenians frequenting the Sophists; prominent leaders, Pericles among them, joined the Sophists for discussions of their new philosophical ideas. The most notorious sophist was Protagoras, a contemporary of Pericles from Abdera, in northern Greece. Protagoras moved to Athens around 450 B.C.E., when he was around forty, and spent most of his career there. His views on the nature of truth and morality outraged many Athenians: he denied that there could be an absolute standard of truth, asserting that every issue had two irreconcilable sides. For example, if one person feeling a breeze thinks it warm whereas another person thinks it cool, neither judgment can be absolutely correct because the wind simply is warm to one and cool to the other. Protagoras summed up this **subjectivism**—the belief that there is no absolute reality behind and independent of appearances—in the much-quoted opening of his work *Truth*: "The human being is the measure of all things, of the things that are that they are, and of the things that are not that they are not." The term *human being* (*anthropos* in Greek, hence our word *anthropology*) in this passage refers to the individual, male or female, whom Protagoras makes the sole judge of his or her own impressions.

The subjectivism of Protagoras and other Sophists contained two main ideas: (1) human

Sophists Arguing Both Sides of a Case

The Sophist Protagoras taught his students to argue both sides of any case, but he insisted he did not teach this skill for immoral purposes. Some teachers following in his footsteps were less ethical. This excerpt comes from an anonymous handbook of the late fifth century B.C.E. entitled Double Arguments, *which provided examples of how Sophists could make arguments in the fashion of Protagoras.*

Greek philosophers put forward double arguments concerning the good and the bad. Some say that the good is one thing and the bad another, but others say that they are the same, and that a thing might be good for some persons but bad for others, or at one time good and at another time bad for the same person. I myself agree with those who hold the latter opinion, which I shall examine using as an example human life and its concern for food, drink, and sexual pleasures: these things are bad for a man if he is sick but good if he is healthy and needs them. And, further, overindulgence in these things is bad for the one who overindulges but good for those who make a profit by selling these things. And again, sickness is bad for the sick but good for the doctors. And death is bad for those who die but good for the undertakers and makers of grave monuments....Shipwrecks are bad for the ship owners but good for the ship builders. When tools are blunted and worn away it is bad for others but good for the blacksmith. And if a pot gets smashed, this is bad for everyone else but good for the potter. When shoes wear out and fall apart it is bad for others but good for the shoemaker.... In the *stadium* race for runners, victory is good for the winner but bad for the losers.

Source: *Dissoi Logoi* 1.1–6. Translation adapted from Rosamund Kent Sprague, ed., *The Older Sophists* (Columbia: University of South Carolina Press, 1972), 279–80.

institutions and values are only matters of convention, custom, or law (*nomos*) and not creations of nature (*physis*), and (2) since truth is subjective, speakers should be able to argue either side of a question with equal persuasiveness. The first view implied that traditional human institutions were arbitrary and transient rather than natural and permanent, whereas the second made questions of right and wrong seem irrelevant. (See "Sophists Arguing Both Sides of a Case," above.)

The Sophists' critics therefore charged them with teaching moral relativism and threatening the shared public values of the democratic city-state. Aristophanes,◆ author of comic plays, satirized Sophists for harming Athens by instructing students in persuasive techniques "to make the weaker argument the stronger." Protagoras, for one, energetically responded that his doctrines were not hostile to democracy, arguing that every person had a natural capability for excellence and that human society depended on the rule of law based on a sense of justice. Members of a community, he explained, must be persuaded to obey the laws, not because they were based on absolute truth, which did not exist, but because it was advantageous for everyone to be law-abiding. A thief, for example, who might claim that stealing was a part of nature, would have to be persuaded that a man-made law forbidding theft was to his advantage because it protected his own property and the community in which he, like all humans, had to live in order to survive.

Even more disturbing than the Sophists' ideas about truth were their ideas about religion. Protagoras angered people with his agnosticism (the belief that supernatural phenomena are unknowable): "Whether the gods exist I cannot discover, nor what their

---

◆**Aristophanes:** a ruh STAH fuh neez

Socrates' ideas proved as disturbing as the Sophists' very different doctrines because they rejected the Athenians' usual, traditional way of life. His ridicule of commonly accepted ideas about the importance of wealth and public success infuriated many people. Unhappiest of all were the fathers whose sons, after listening to Socrates' questions reduce someone to utter bewilderment, came home to try the same technique on their parents by arguing that the accomplishments their family held dear were old-fashioned and worthless. Men who experienced this reversal of the traditional educational hierarchy—the father was supposed to educate the son—felt that Socrates was undermining the stability of society by making young men question Athenian traditions. Socrates evidently did not teach women, but Plato portrays him as ready to learn from exceptional women, such as Pericles' hyperintelligent companion Aspasia.

The worry that Socrates' ideas presented a danger to conventional society inspired Aristophanes to write his comedy *The Clouds* (423 B.C.E.). This play portrays Socrates as a cynical Sophist who, for a fee, offers instruction in the Protagorean technique of making the weaker argument the stronger. When the curriculum of Socrates' school ("The Thinkery") transforms a youth into a public speaker who argues that a son has the right to beat his parents, his father burns the place down. None of these plot details seems to have been real; what was genuine was the fear that Socrates' radical views on individual morality endangered the city-state's traditional practices. This anxiety only grew worse as the Peloponnesian War dragged on with ever more casualties and many citizens began to feel that their best hope for victory lay in strengthening tradition, not weakening it.

Historical Writing.   Just as the Sophists and Socrates antagonized many people with their new ideas, the inventors of historical writing drew attention because they took a critical attitude in their descriptions of the past. Herodotus of Halicarnassus♦ (c. 485–425 B.C.E.) and Thucydides of Athens (c. 455–399 B.C.E.) became Greece's most

♦**Halicarnassus:** ha luh kahr NA suhs

famous historians and established Western civilization's tradition of history writing. The fifth-century B.C.E.'s unprecedented events—a coalition Greek victory over the world's greatest power and then the longest war ever between Greeks—apparently inspired them to create history as a subject based on strenuous research. They explained that they wrote histories because they wanted people to remember the past and to understand why wars had taken place. In the 420s B.C.E., Herodotus finished a long, groundbreaking work called *Histories* (meaning "inquiries" in Greek) to explain the Persian Wars as a clash between the cultures of the East and West; by Roman times he had been dubbed the "Father of History." A typically competitive Greek intellectual, Herodotus made the justifiable claim that he surpassed all previous recording of the past by taking an in-depth and investigative approach to evidence, being interested in the culture of non-Greeks as well as Greeks, and expressing explicit and implicit judgments about people's actions. Because Herodotus recognized the necessity (and the delight) of studying other cultures for doing his historical research, he pushed his inquiries deep into the past, looking for long-standing cultural differences that helped explain the Persian-Greek conflict. Unlike poets and playwrights, he did not make the gods the driving force in history, instead putting the focus on human psychology and interaction.

Thucydides redirected historical inquiry—and overtly competed with Herodotus—by writing contemporary history and inventing the kind of analysis of power that today informs political science. His *History of the Peloponnesian War*, published after the end of the war, made power politics, not divine intervention, history's primary force. Deeply affected by the war's brutality, he used his experiences as a politician and failed military commander (he was exiled for losing a key outpost) to make his narrative vivid and frank in describing human moral failings. His insistence that historians should spare no effort in seeking out the most reliable sources and evaluating their testimony with objectivity set a high standard for later writers. Like Herodotus, he challenged tradition by revealing that Greek history was just as full of

Vase Painting of a Doctor at Work
This piece of pottery, apparently used to hold perfume or ointment, is decorated with a picture of a physician treating a patient's arm. The prevalence of war gave Greek doctors much experience with wounds and trauma, and they could stop bleeding, set bones, perform minor surgery, and offer some pain relief with drugs derived from plants. Still, the effectiveness of their treatment was limited because they had no cure for infections. *Photo Réunion des Musées Nationaux–Herve Lewandowski.*

shameful actions (such as the Athenian punishment of Melos in the Peloponnesian War—see page 117) as of glorious achievements.

Hippocrates and the Birth of Scientific Medicine. Hippocrates♦ of Cos, a fifth-century contemporary of Thucydides, challenged tradition by grounding medical diagnosis and treatment in clinical observation; his fame continues today in the oath bearing his name that doctors swear at the beginning of their professional careers. Previously, medicine had depended on magic and ritual; illness was believed to be caused by evil spirits, and various cults in Greek religion offered healing to patients through divine intervention. Competing to refute these earlier doctors' theories, Hippocrates insisted that only physical factors caused disease. He may have been the author of the view, dominant in later

♦**Hippocrates:** hih PAH kruh teez

medicine, that four humors (fluids) made up the human body: blood, phlegm, black bile, and yellow bile. Health therefore depended on keeping the proper balance among them; being healthy was to be in "good humor." This system for understanding the body corresponded to the division of the inanimate world into four parts: the elements earth, air, fire, and water.

Hippocrates taught that the physician's most important duty was to base his knowledge on careful observation of patients and their response to different treatments. He insisted that clinical experience, not abstract theory or religious belief, was the proper principle for establishing effective cures. By putting his innovative ideas and practices to the test in competition with those of traditional medicine, Hippocrates established the truth of his principle, which later became a cornerstone of scientific medicine.

Review: How did new ways of thinking in the Golden Age threaten cherished traditions?

The Development of Greek Tragedy

The problematic relationship between gods and humans inspired Golden Age Athens's most prominent cultural innovation: tragic drama. Plays called tragedies were presented over three days at the major annual festival of the god Dionysus in a contest for playwrights, in keeping with the competitive spirit characteristic of Greek cultural life. The word *tragedy*—derived, for unknown reasons, from the Greek words for "goat" and "song"—referred to a play involving fierce conflict and characters representing powerful forces. Tragedies presented shocking stories, usually from myth but occasionally from history, that could be related to controversial issues in contemporary Athens. Therefore, these plays stimulated their large audiences to ponder the danger that ignorance, arrogance, and violence presented to the city-state's democratic society. Following the tradition of Homer and Hesiod, Golden Age playwrights explored topics ranging from the roots of good and evil to the nature of individual freedom and responsibility in the family and the political community. As with other ancient

Theater of Dionysus at Athens
Tragedies, satyr plays, and comedies were produced at Athens during the daytime in this outdoor theater honoring the god Dionysus. The seating and stone stage building foundations that are visible today come from later eras; the seating, the stage, and the scenery were temporary, wooden installations during the Classical Age. The theater seated about fourteen thousand or more people, and subsidies kept ticket prices reasonable. Since Athens's drama festivals featured multiple plays each day, spectators spent long hours in the theater to see them all. *John Elk III/Bruce Coleman, Inc., New York.*

texts, most tragedies have not survived: only thirty-three still exist from the hundreds that were produced at Athens.

The competition took place every year, with a magistrate choosing three authors from a pool of applicants. Each of these finalists presented four plays during the festival: three tragedies in a row (a trilogy), followed by a semicomic play featuring satyrs (mythical half-man, half-animal beings) to end the day on a lighter note. Tragedies were written in verses of solemn language; they were often based on stories about the violent possibilities when gods and humans interacted. The plots often ended with a resolution to the trouble—but only after prolonged suffering.

Athenian tragedies in performance bore little resemblance to modern plays. They took place during the daytime in an outdoor theater sacred to Dionysus, built into the southern slope of Athens's acropolis. This theater held about fourteen thousand spectators overlooking an open, circular area in front of a slightly raised stage. A tragedy had eighteen cast members, all of whom were men: three actors to play the speaking roles (both male and female characters) and fifteen chorus members. Although the chorus leader sometimes engaged in dialogue with the actors, the chorus primarily performed songs and dances in the circular area in front of the stage, called the orchestra.

A successful tragedy offered a vivid spectacle. The chorus wore elaborate costumes and performed intricate dance routines. The actors, who wore masks, used broad gestures and booming voices to reach the upper tier of seats. A powerful voice was crucial to a tragic actor because words represented the heart of the plays, in which dialogue and long speeches predominated over physical action. Special effects were part of the spectacle. For example, a crane allowed actors playing the roles of gods to fly suddenly onto the stage. The actors playing lead roles, called the protagonists (literally, "first competitors"), competed against one another for the designation of best actor. So important was a first-rate protagonist to a play's success that actors were assigned by lottery to the competing playwrights to give all three an equal chance to have a winning cast. Great protagonists became enormously popular, although they were not usually members of the social elite.

Playwrights were from the elite because only men of some wealth could afford the amount of time and learning this work demanded: as author, director, producer, musical composer, choreographer, and sometimes even actor. As citizens, playwrights also fulfilled the normal military and political obligations of Athenian men. The best-known Athenian tragedians—Aeschylus♦ (525–456 B.C.E.), Sophocles♦ (c. 496–406 B.C.E.), and Euripides (c. 485–406 B.C.E.)—all served in the army, and Sophocles was elected to Athens's highest public office. Authors of plays competed from a love of honor, not money: the prizes, determined by a board of judges, awarded high prestige but little cash. The competition was regarded as so important that any judge who took a bribe to award a prize was put to death.

Athenian tragedy was a public art form subsidized by tax revenues and mandatory contributions by the rich. Tragedy's plots explored the difficulties of telling right from wrong when humans came into conflict with one another in the city-state and the gods became involved. Even though most tragedies were based on stories that referred to a legendary time before city-states existed, such as the period of the Trojan War, the moral issues the plays illuminated always pertained to the society and obligations of citizens in a city-state. To take only a few examples: Aeschylus in his trilogy *Oresteia*♦ (458 B.C.E.) uses the story of how the gods stopped the

murderous violence in the family of Orestes, son of Agamemnon, the Greek leader against Troy, to explain the divine origins of democratic Athens's court system. The plays suggest that human beings learn only by suffering but that the gods provide justice in the long run. Sophocles' *Antigone* (441 B.C.E.) presents the story of the cursed family of Oedipus of Thebes as a drama of harsh conflict between a courageous woman, Antigone, and the city-state's stern male leader, her uncle Creon. After her brother dies in a failed rebellion, Antigone insists on her family's

Theaters of Classical Greece

moral obligation to bury its dead in obedience to divine command, while Creon takes harsh action to preserve order and protect community values by prohibiting the burial of his nephew the traitor. In a horrifying story of raging anger and suicide that features one of the most famous heroines of Western literature, Sophocles exposes the right and wrong on each side of the conflict. His play offers no easy resolution of the competing interests of divinely sanctioned moral tradition and the state's political rules. Euripides' *Medea* (431 B.C.E.) reveals that the stability and prosperity of the city-state depend on men treating their wives and families with honor and trust: when Medea's husband, Jason, betrays her to marry a younger woman in a deal to gain political leadership, she takes revenge on him by using her magical powers to destroy the new bride and, in utter desperation, murders her own children to express her hatred of Jason.

Ancient sources tell us that the audiences reacted strongly to the messages of the tragedies presented in the drama competition of the Dionysian festival. For one thing, they could see that the central characters of the plays were figures who fell into disaster even though they held positions of power and prestige. The characters' reversals of fortune came about not because they were absolute villains but because, as humans, they were susceptible to a lethal mixture of error, ignorance,

---

♦**Aeschylus:** EHS kuh luhs
♦**Sophocles:** SAH fuh kleez
♦***Oresteia:*** awr ehs TYE uh

and **hubris**◆ (violent arrogance). The Athenian Empire was at its height when audiences at Athens attended the tragedies of these three great playwrights. Thoughtful spectators could reflect on the possibility that Athens's current power and prestige, managed as they were by humans, might fall prey to the same kind of mistakes and conflicts that brought down the heroes and heroines of tragedy. Thus, tragedies not only entertained through their spectacle but also educated through their stories and words. In particular, they reminded male citizens, who governed the city-state in its assembly, council, and courts, that success created complex moral problems that self-righteous arrogance never solved.

The Development of Greek Comedy

Golden Age Athens developed comedy as its second distinctive form of public theater. Like tragedies, comedies were written in verse, performed in a competition in the city's large outdoor theater during festivals honoring the god Dionysus, and subsidized with public funds and contributions from the rich. Unlike tragedies, comedies made direct comments about public policy and criticized current politicians and intellectuals. They did this with plots and casts presenting outrageous fantasies of contemporary life. For example, comic choruses, which had twenty-four dancing singers, could be colorfully dressed as talking birds or dancing clouds, or an actor could fly up on a giant dung beetle to visit the gods.

Comic playwrights competed for the honor of winning the award for the festival's best comedy by creating beautiful poetry, raising laughs with constant jokes and puns, and skewering pretentious citizens and political leaders. Much of the humor concerned sex and bodily functions, delivered in a stream of imaginative profanity. Well-known men of the day were targets for insults as

◆**hubris:** HYOO brihs

Statuettes of Comic Actors
Although these little statues portray comic actors dressed in the kinds of masks and costumes that came into vogue later than the style of comedy that Aristophanes and his contemporaries wrote in the fifth century B.C.E. (for which no such pieces exist), they give a vivid sense of the exaggerated buffoonery that characterized the acting in Greek comedy. In Aristophanes' day, the grotesque unreality of comic costumes would have been even more striking because the male actors wore large leather phalluses (penises) attached below their waists that could be props for all sorts of ribald jokes. The use of masks in certain kinds of theater performances continued into Roman times. *Staatliche Museen zu Berlin-Bildarchiv Preussischer Kulturbesitz/Art Resource, NY.*

cowards or effeminate weaklings. Women characters portrayed as figures of fun and ridicule seem to have been fictional, to protect the dignity of actual female citizens.

Athenian comedies often made fun of political leaders. As the leading politician of radical democracy, Pericles came in for fierce criticism in comedy. Comic playwrights mocked his policies, his love life, even the shape of his skull ("Old Turnip Head" was a favorite insult). So fiercely did Aristophanes (c. 455–385 B.C.E.), Athens's most famous comic playwright, ridicule Cleon, the city's most prominent leader early in the Peloponnesian War, in his comedy *Babylonians* in 426 B.C.E. that Cleon sued him. A citizen jury upheld free speech by returning the verdict in Aristophanes' favor. The author responded by pitilessly parodying Cleon as a scheming foreign slave in *The Knights* of 424 B.C.E., calling him a "mud-churning fraud who threw the whole city into chaos."

Several of Aristophanes's comedies have powerful women as their main characters, who compel the men of Athens to change their policy to preserve family life and the city-state. These plays even criticize the assembly's policy during wartime. Most famous is *Lysistrata* (411 B.C.E.), named after the female lead character of the play. In this fantasy, the women of Athens and Sparta unite to force their husbands to end the Peloponnesian War. To make the men agree to a peace treaty, they first seize the acropolis, where Athens's financial reserves are kept, to prevent the men from squandering them further on the war. They then use sarcasm and pitchers of cold water to beat back an attack on their position by the old men who have remained in Athens while the younger men are out on campaign. Although the women eagerly look forward to sex with their husbands, they steel themselves to refuse to sleep with those who were returning from battle. The effects of their strike on the men, portrayed in a series of sexually explicit comic episodes, finally compel the warriors to make peace.

Lysistrata presents women acting bravely and aggressively against men who seem bent on destroying their traditional family life— they are staying away from home for long stretches while on military campaign and are ruining the city-state by prolonging a pointless war. Lysistrata insists that women have the intelligence and judgment to make political decisions: "I am a woman, and, yes, I have brains. And I'm not badly off for judgment. Nor has my education been bad, coming as it has from my listening often to the conversations of my father and the elders among the men." Her old-fashioned training and good sense allow her to see what needs to be done to protect the community. Like the heroines of tragedy, Lysistrata is a conservative, even a reactionary; she wants to put things back the way they were before the war ruined family life. To do that, however, she has to act like an impatient revolutionary. That irony sums up the challenge that fifth-century Athens faced in trying to resolve the tension between the dynamic innovation of its Golden Age and the importance of tradition in Greek life.

The remarkable freedom of speech of Athenian comedy allowed frank, even brutal, commentary on current issues and personalities. It cannot be an accident that this energetic, critical drama emerged in Athens at the same time as radical democracy, in the mid-fifth century B.C.E. The feeling that all citizens should have a stake in determining their government's policies evidently fueled a passion for using biting humor to keep the community's leaders from becoming arrogant and aloof.

❖ The End of the Golden Age, 431–403 B.C.E.

A war between Athens and Sparta that lasted a generation (431–404 B.C.E.) ended the Golden Age; it is called the Peloponnesian War today because it pitted Sparta's Peloponnese-based alliance against Athens and its allies. The war started, according to Thucydides, because the growth of Athenian power alarmed the Spartans, who feared that their interests and allies would fall to the Athenians' restless drive. Pericles, the most powerful politician in Athens at the time, persuaded its assembly to take a hard line when the Spartans demanded that Athens ease restrictions on city-states allied with Sparta. Corinth and Megara, crucial Spartan allies, complained bitterly to Sparta about Athens; finally, Corinth told Sparta to attack Athens, or else Corinth and its navy would change sides to the Athenian alliance. Sparta's leaders therefore gave Athens an ultimatum—stop mistreating our allies—that Pericles convinced the Athenian assembly to reject on the grounds that Sparta had refused to settle the dispute through the third-party arbitration process called for by the 446–445 B.C.E. treaty. Pericles's critics claimed he was insisting on war against Sparta to revive his fading popularity; his supporters replied that he was defending Athenian honor and protecting foreign trade, a linchpin of the economy. By 431 B.C.E. these disputes had shattered the thirty-year peace between Athens and Sparta that Pericles had made in 446–445 B.C.E.

The Peloponnesian War, 431–404 B.C.E.

Lasting longer than any previous war in Greek history, the Peloponnesian War (Map 3.3) took place above all because Spartan

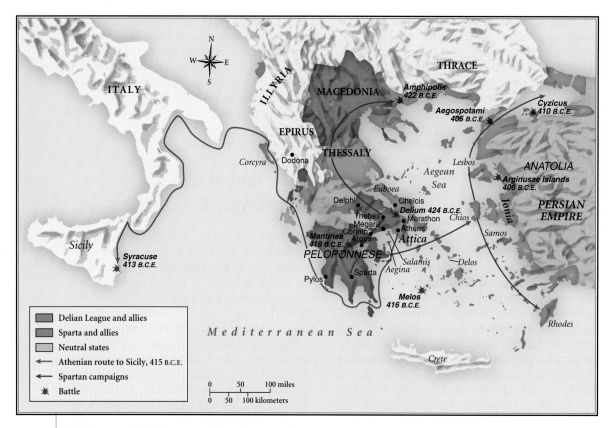

MAP 3.3 The Peloponnesian War, 431–404 B.C.E.

For the first ten years, the Peloponnesian War's battles took place largely in mainland Greece. Sparta, whose armies usually avoided distant campaigns, shocked Athens when its general Brasidas led successful attacks against Athenian forces in northeast Greece. Athens stunned the entire Greek world in the war's next phase by launching a huge naval expedition against Spartan allies in far-off Sicily. The last ten years of the war saw the action move to the east, on and along the western coast of Anatolia and its islands, on the boundary of the Persian Empire, which helped the Spartans build a navy there to defeat the famous Athenian fleet.

leaders believed they had to fight now to keep the Athenians from using their superior long-distance offensive weaponry—the Delian League's naval forces—to destroy Sparta's control of the Peloponnesian League. (See "Taking Measure," opposite.) The war opened with a Spartan first strike, but it dragged on so long because the Athenian assembly failed to negotiate and maintain peace with Sparta when it had the chance and because the Spartans were willing to deal with Persia to gain money to build a fleet to win the war.

Dramatic evidence for how angry the feelings were that fueled the war comes from Thucydides's version of Pericles's stern oration to the Athenian assembly about not yielding to Spartan pressure:

> If we do go to war, harbor no thought that you went to war over a trivial affair. For you this trifling matter is the assurance and the proof of your determination. If you yield to their demands, they will immediately confront you with some larger demand, since they will think that you only gave way on the first point out of fear. But if you stand firm, you will show them that they have to deal with you as equals.... When our equals, without agreeing to arbitration of the matter under dispute, make claims on us as neighbors and state those claims as commands, it would be no better than slavery to give in to them, no matter how large or how small the claim may be.

When Sparta began hostilities by invading Athenian territory, Pericles advised a two-pronged strategy to win what he saw would be a long war: (1) use the navy to raid the lands of Sparta and its allies, and (2) avoid large infantry battles with the superior land forces of the Spartans, even when the enemy hoplites plundered the Athenian countryside outside the city. The citizens could retreat to safety behind Athens's impregnable fortification walls, massive barriers of stone that encircled the city and the harbor, with the Long Walls protecting the land corridor between the urban center and the port. He insisted that Athenians should sacrifice their country property, which was vast and valuable, to save their population. In the end, he predicted, the superior resources of Athens would enable it to win a war of attrition, especially because without a base in Athenian territory the Spartans could not support long invasions.

Backed by Pericles' unyielding leadership, this strategy might have made Athens the winner in the long run, but chance intervened to deprive Athens of his guidance: an epidemic disease that struck Athens in 430 B.C.E. killed Pericles the next year. This plague ravaged Athens's population for four years, killing thousands as it spread like wildfire among the people packed in behind the walls to avoid Spartan attacks. Despite their losses and the fears of many that the gods had sent the epidemic to punish them, the Athenians fought on; over time, however, they abandoned the disciplined strategy that Pericles' prudent plan had required. The generals elected after his death pursued a much more aggressive strategy, but they failed to protect Athens's possessions in northern Greece, crippling the supply of timber and precious metals from this crucial region.

The most innovative and confident new general, Alcibiades,◆ persuaded the assembly to reject a peace that had been made in 421 B.C.E. and to attack Spartan allies in 418 B.C.E. In 416–415 B.C.E. the Athenians and their allies overpowered the tiny and strategically meaningless Aegean island of Melos because it refused to abandon its allegiance to Sparta. Thucydides dramatically represents Athe-

nian messengers telling the Melians they had to be conquered to show that Athens permitted no defiance to its dominance. Following their victory the Athenians executed the Melian men, sold the women and children into slavery, and colonized the island.

TAKING MEASURE

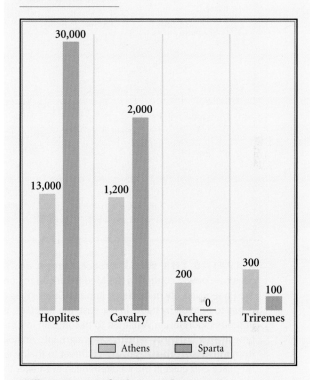

Military Forces of Athens and Sparta at the Beginning of the Peloponnesian War (431 B.C.E.)
These figures give estimates of the relative strengths of the military forces of the Athenian side and the Spartan side when the Peloponnesian War broke out in 431 B.C.E. The numbers come from ancient historical sources, above all the Athenian general and historian Thucydides, who fought in the war. The bar graphs starkly reveal the different characteristics of the competing forces: Athens relied on its navy of triremes and its archers (the fifth-century equivalent of artillery and snipers), while Sparta was preeminent in the forces needed for pitched land battles, hoplites (heavily armed infantry) and cavalry (shock troops used to disrupt opposing phalanxes). These differences dictated the differing strategies and tactics of the two sides, Athens trying guerrilla-fashion by launching surprise raids from the sea and Sparta trying to force decisive confrontations on the battlefield. *From Pamela Bradley,* Ancient Greece: Using Evidence *(Melbourne: Edward Arnold, 1990), 229.*

◆**Alcibiades:** al suh BY uh deez

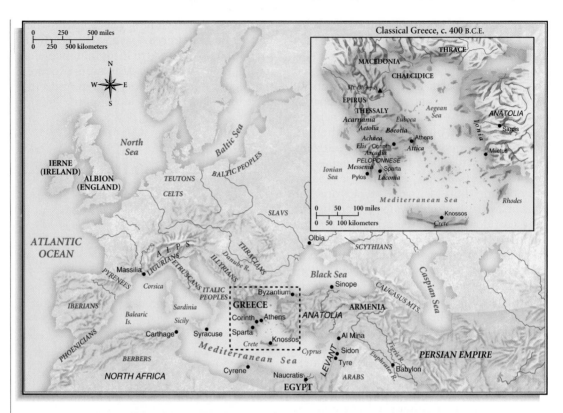

MAPPING THE WEST Greece, Europe, and the Mediterranean, c. 400 B.C.E.
No single power controlled the Mediterranean region at the end of the fifth century B.C.E. In the west, the Phoenician city of Carthage and the Greek cities of Sicily and southern Italy were rivals for the riches to be won by trade. In the east, the Spartans, emboldened by their recent victory over Athens in the Peloponnesian War, tried to become an international power outside the mainland for the first time in their history by sending campaigns into Anatolia. This aggressive action aroused stiff opposition from the Persians because it was a threat to their westernmost imperial provinces. There was to be no peace and quiet in the Mediterranean even after the twenty-seven years of the Peloponnesian War.

The turning point in the war came soon thereafter when in 415 B.C.E. Alcibiades persuaded the Athenian assembly to launch the greatest and most expensive campaign in Greek history. The expedition of 415 B.C.E. was directed against Sparta's allies in Sicily, far to the west; Alcibiades had dazzled his fellow citizens with the dream of conquering that rich island and especially its greatest city, Syracuse. Alcibiades' political rivals had him deposed from his command, however, and lesser generals blundered into catastrophic defeat in Sicily in 413 B.C.E. (see Map 3.3). The victorious Syracusans destroyed the allied invasion fleet and packed the survivors like human sardines into quarries under the blazing sun, with no toilets and only half a pint of drinking water and a handful of grain a day.

On the advice of Alcibiades, who had deserted to their side in anger at having lost his command, the Spartans seized a permanent base of operations in the Athenian countryside for year-round raids, now that Athens was too weak to drive them out. Athenian agriculture was then devastated by constant Spartan attacks, and twenty thousand slave workers crippled production in Athens's silver mines by deserting to the enemy. The democratic assembly became so upset over these losses that in 411 B.C.E. it voted itself out of existence in favor of an emergency government run by the wealthier citizens. When an oligarchic group illegally took charge, however, the citizens restored the traditional radical democracy and kept fighting. The end came when Persia gave the Spartans money to build a navy; the Persian king thought it was in his interest to see Athens defeated. Aggressive Spartan action at sea forced Athens to surrender in 404 B.C.E. After twenty-seven years of near-continuous war, the Athenians were at their enemy's mercy.

> **Review:** How did unexpected events contribute to the outcome of the Peloponnesian War?

Athens Humbled: Tyranny and Civil War, 404–403 B.C.E.

Following Athens's surrender, the Spartans installed a regime of antidemocratic Athenians who were willing to collaborate with the victors; they were members of the social elite, and some had been well-known pupils of Sophists. They became known as the Thirty Tyrants. Brutally suppressing democratic opposition, these oligarchs embarked on an eight-month period of terror and plundering in 404–403 B.C.E. The speechwriter Lysias, for example, reported that Spartan henchmen seized his brother for execution as a way of stealing the family's valuables, even ripping the gold earrings from the ears of his brother's wife. Outraged at the violence and greed of the Thirty Tyrants, citizens who wanted to restore democracy banded together outside the city to fight to regain control of Athens. Fortunately for them, the Spartans were paralyzed by a feud between their two most important leaders and did not send help to their Athenian collaborators. The democratic rebels defeated the forces of the Thirty Tyrants in a series of bloody street battles in Athens.

Democracy was therefore restored, but the city-state seethed with anger and unrest in the aftermath of the defeat by Sparta and the horrors the Thirty Tyrants perpetrated on their fellow citizens. To settle the internal strife that threatened to tear Athens apart, the newly restored democratic assembly voted the first known amnesty in Western history, a truce agreement forbidding any official charges or recriminations stemming from the crimes of 404–403 B.C.E. Agreeing not to pursue grievances in court was the price of peace. As would soon become clear, however, some Athenians harbored grudges that no amnesty could dispel. In addition, Athens's financial and military strength had been shattered. The end of the Golden Age left Athenians worriedly wondering how to remake their lives and restore the luster that their city-state's innovative accomplishments had produced.

Conclusion

When some Greek city-states temporarily united to resist the Persian Empire at the beginning of the fifth century B.C.E., they surprised themselves in the Persian Wars by defeating the invasion that had threatened their political independence. When the Persians retreated, so, too, did Greek unity. Athens's part in the victory made it a rival of Sparta for international power; the Athenian Golden Age that followed the war was based on empire and trade, and the city's riches funded the widening of democracy and cultural accomplishments that have remained influential ever since.

As the money poured in, the city-state built glorious temples, instituted pay for service in many government offices to strengthen democracy, and assembled the Mediterranean's most powerful navy. The poor men who rowed the ships demanded greater democracy; such demands led to legal reforms that guaranteed fair treatment for all. Pericles became the most famous politician of the Golden Age by leading the drive for radical democracy.

Religious practice and women's lives reflected the strong effect of tradition on everyday life, but intellectual life saw dramatic innovation that created tension in the society. Art and architecture broke out of old forms, promoting an impression of balanced motion rather than stability. Tragedy and comedy developed at Athens as public art forms commenting on contemporary social and political issues. The Sophists' relativistic views disturbed tradition-minded people, as did Socrates' definition of virtue, emphasizing his questioning of ordinary people's love of wealth and success.

Wars framed the Golden Age. The Persian Wars sent the Athenians soaring to imperial power and prosperity, but their high-handed treatment of allies and enemies combined with Spartan fears about Athenian power to bring on the disastrous Peloponnesian War.

Its nearly three decades of battle brought the stars of the Greek Golden Age crashing to earth: by 400 B.C.E. the Athenians found themselves in the same situation as in 500 B.C.E., fearful of Spartan power and worried whether the world's first democracy could survive. As it turned out, the next great threat to Greek stability and independence would once again come from a neighboring monarchy, this time not from Persia to the east but from Macedonia to the north.

Suggested References

Wars between Persia and Greece, 499–479 B.C.E.

Like many groups in history, the ancient Greeks defined their own identity by contrasting themselves with others, especially non-Greek-speaking peoples ("barbarians"). The Persian Wars strengthened their sense of difference from other peoples ruled by kings.

Georges, Pericles. *Barbarian Asia and the Greek Experience: From the Archaic Period to the Age of Xenophon.* 1994.

Hall, Jonathan M. *Ethnic Identity in Greek Antiquity.* 1997.

Hanson, Victor Davis. *The Wars of the Ancient Greeks.* 1999.

*Herodotus. *The Histories.* Translated Aubrey de Sélincourt. Revised by John Marincola. New edition, 1996.

Persian art: **http://www.oi.uchicago.edu/ OI/MUS/GALLERY/PERSIAN/ New_Persian_Gallery.html**.

Wees, Hans van, ed. *War and Violence in Ancient Greece.* 2000.

Athenian Confidence in the Golden Age, 478–431 B.C.E.

Athenian government remains significant for modern scholars in debates over direct versus representative democracy and the nature of citizenship. Online resources are also now available and important for studying the full context of Golden Age Athenian history.

Athenian democracy: **http://www.stoa.org/ projects/demos/home**.

Camp, John M. *The Archaeology of Athens.* 2001.

Cohen, Edward E. *The Athenian Nation.* 2000.

Ober, Josiah, and Charles W. Hedrick, eds. *Demokratia: A Conversation on Democracies, Ancient and Modern.* 1996.

Parthenon: **http://www.perseus.tufts.edu/ cgi-bin/vor?x=16&y=13&lookup=parthenon**.

Tradition and Innovation in Athens's Golden Age

Lively debates continue about how to measure and evaluate the difference between ancient Greek and modern Western customs. Davidson, for example, has rebutted the recent idea that Greeks considered sex a game of aggressive domination.

Blundell, Sue. *Women in Ancient Greece.* 1995.

Brunschwig, Jacques and Geoffrey E. R. Lloyd, eds. *Greek Thought: A Guide to Classical Knowledge.* 2000.

Davidson, James. *Courtesans and Fishcakes: The Consuming Passions of Classical Athens.* 1998.

Fisher, N. R. E. *Slavery in Classical Greece.* 1995.

Greek gods: **http://www.getty.edu/art/ collections/subjects/s23-1.html**.

Parker, Robert. *Athenian Religion: A History.* 1996.

Patterson, Cynthia B. *The Family in Greek History.* 1998.

Plutarch on Sparta. Trans. Richard J. A. Talbert. 1988.

The End of the Golden Age, 431–403 B.C.E.

Controversy still exists over whether to explain the Athenian defeat in the Peloponnesian War as caused by political disunity and failure of leadership at Athens, or by Persia's financial support of Sparta; Strassler's edition of Thucydides is the best resource for assessing the evidence of the most important ancient source.

Kagan, Donald. *The Peloponnesian War.* 2003.

Lazenby, J. F. *The Spartan Army.* 1985.

Munn, Mark. *The School of History. Athens in the Age of Socrates.* 2000.

The Peloponnesian War and Athenian Life: **http:// www.perseus.tufts.edu/cgi-bin/ ptext?doc=Perseus%3Atext%3A1999 .04.0009%3Ahead%3D%23212**.

*Strassler, Robert B., ed. *The Landmark Thucydides: A Comprehensive Guide to the Peloponnesian War.* 1996.

*Pseudo-Xenophon, *Constitution of the Athenians.* Trans. G. W. Bowersock, in *Xenophon VII. Scripta Minora.* 1971.

*Primary source.

CHAPTER REVIEW

IMPORTANT EVENTS

c. 500–323 B.C.E.	Classical Age of Greek History
499–479 B.C.E.	Wars between Persia and Greece
490 B.C.E.	Battle of Marathon
480–479 B.C.E.	Xerxes' invasion of Greece
480 B.C.E.	Battle of Salamis
479 B.C.E.	Battles of Plataea and Mycale
461 B.C.E.	Ephialtes reforms the Athenian court system
Early 450s B.C.E.	Pericles introduces pay for office holders in Athenian democracy
454 B.C.E.	Catastrophic defeat of Athenian fleet by Persians in Egypt kills tens of thousands of oarsmen
451 B.C.E.	Pericles sponsors law to restrict Athenian citizenship to children whose parents are both citizens
c. 450 B.C.E.	Protagoras and other Sophists begin to move to Athens to teach
446–445 B.C.E. (winter)	Peace treaty between Athens and Sparta; intended to last thirty years
431 B.C.E.	Euripides presents the tragedy *Medea*
431–404 B.C.E.	Peloponnesian War
420s B.C.E.	Herodotus finishes *Histories*, the first great Greek work of history writing
415–413 B.C.E.	Enormous Athenian military expedition against Sicily
411 B.C.E.	Aristophanes presents the comedy *Lysistrata*
404–403 B.C.E.	Rule of the Thirty Tyrants at Athens
403 B.C.E.	Restoration of democracy

KEY TERMS

agora (93)

Delian League (88)

frieze (95)

hetaira (99)

hubris (114)

metic (97)

mystery cult (97)

ostracism (91)

radical democracy (90)

Socratic method (109)

Sophists (106)

subjectivism (106)

symposium (plural "symposia") (99)

trireme (89)

REVIEW QUESTIONS

1. What differences in Greek and Persian political and military organization determined the course of the Persian Wars?

2. What factors prompted political change in fifth-century B.C.E. Athens?

3. How did new ways of thinking in the Golden Age threaten cherished traditions?

4. How did unexpected events contribute to the outcome of the Peloponnesian War?

MAKING CONNECTIONS

1. What were the most significant differences between Greece in the Archaic Age and in the Golden Age?

2. What did Greeks of the Golden Age believe it was worth spending public funds to pay for and why?

FOR FURTHER EXPLORATION

To assess your mastery of the material in this chapter, see the Online Study Guide at **bedfordstmartins.com/hunt**.

To read additional primary-source material from this period, see Chapter 3 in *Sources of The Making of the West*, Second Edition.

The Long Walls of Athens

In the fifth century B.C.E., at the height of its naval power, Athens had made itself impregnable to attack by extending its fortification walls in a corridor called the Long Walls that stretched from the ring around the city center to the harbor of Piraeus several miles to the west. This section, which stood near the water where the walls protected the port entrance, shows the close-fitting blocks forming the exterior of the walls. The victorious Spartans forced the Athenians to demolish the Long Walls after the Peloponnesian War ended in 404 B.C.E. When the Athenians regained their freedom in the following year, they set out to repair the walls. When they finished in 393 B.C.E., their city had regained its ability to defend itself against invasion, and the Athenians soon embarked on rebuilding their naval empire. *Craig and Marie Mauzy, mauzy@otenet.gr.*

and smocks, "the work considered the best and most fitting for women." He suggested they begin to sell the clothes outside the home. This plan succeeded financially, but the women complained that Aristarchus was the household's only member who ate without out working. Socrates advised his friend to reply that the women should think of him as sheep did a guard dog— he earned his share of the food by keeping the wolves away.

Athens's postwar economy recovered strength because private business owners and households engaged in trade and produced manufactured goods in their homes and small shops, such as metal foundries and pottery workshops. Greek businesses, usually run by families, never grew large; the largest known was a shield-making company employing 120 slaves. The return of prosperity, coupled with the greater flexibility in work roles for men and women that the war had produced, led to some change in occupations formerly

Athens's Long Walls as Rebuilt after the Peloponnesian War

defined by gender. For example, men began working alongside women in cloth production in this period, when the first commercial weaving shops outside the home sprang up. Later in the fourth century B.C.E., some women made careers in the arts, especially painting and music, which men had traditionally dominated.

The rebuilding by 393 B.C.E. of Athens's Long Walls, which connected the city to the port and had been destroyed at war's end, boosted the economy. These fortifications protected the ships importing grain to feed the population and made conducting business safe for international traders. A brisk commerce therefore resumed in grain, wine, pottery, and some silver from Athens's mines. The refortified harbor also allowed Athens to begin to rebuild its navy, which increased employment opportunities for poor men.

Daily life remained tough for working people even in an improving economy. Most workers earned only enough to feed and clothe their families. They usually ate two meals a day, a light one at midmorning and a heavier evening meal. Bread baked from barley provided their main food; only rich people could afford wheat bread. A family bought bread from small bakery stands, often run by women, or made it at home, with the wife directing the slaves in grinding the grain, shaping the dough, and baking it in a pottery oven heated by charcoal. People topped their bread with greens, beans, onions, garlic, olives, fruit, and cheese. Most people had meat only after animal sacrifices paid for by the state; the few households wealthy enough to afford meat at home boiled or grilled it over a fire. Everyone of all ages drank wine, diluted with water, with every meal. Women and slaves fetched drinking water in jugs from public fountains.

The Execution of Socrates, 399 B.C.E.

Even though most Athenians' daily lives returned to old patterns after the war, people remembered the horror of the reign of the Thirty Tyrants. Their bitter feelings created tensions that economic improvement did not relieve. The Athenian philosopher Socrates became the most famous victim of this bitterness. Since an amnesty prohibited prosecutions for crimes committed under the Thirty Tyrants, angry citizens had to find other charges against those they hated. Several prominent democratic Athenians felt this way about Socrates: they blamed him because his follower Critias had been one of the Thirty's most violent members.

Socrates's opponents charged him with impiety, a crime under Athenian law. His accusers said Socrates's philosophy angered the gods and therefore threatened divine punishment for the city. They argued their case in 399 B.C.E. before a jury of 501 male citizens, who had been chosen by lottery from that year's pool of eligible men. Their case presented religious and moral arguments: Socrates, they claimed, rejected the city-state's gods, introduced new divinities, and lured young men away from Athenian moral traditions. When Socrates spoke in his own defense, he refused to beg for sympathy, as was usual; instead, he repeated his dedication to goading his fellow citizens into examining their moral preconceptions. He vowed to remain their stinging gadfly no matter what.

When the jurors narrowly voted to convict, standard Athenian legal procedure required them to decide between alternative penalties proposed by the prosecutors and the defendant. The prosecutors proposed death. Everyone expected Socrates to offer exile as an alternative and the jury to accept it. The philosopher, however, said that he deserved a reward rather than a punishment, until his friends made him propose a fine as his penalty. The jury chose death. Socrates accepted his sentence calmly because, as he put it, "no evil can befall a good man either in life or in death." He was executed with a poisonous drink concocted from powdered hemlock. Executing Socrates did not resolve Athens's postwar tension. Ancient sources report that many Athenians soon came to regret his punishment as a tragic mistake and a severe blow to their reputation.

The Philosophy of Plato and Aristotle

Socrates' death made his most famous follower, Plato (c. 429–348 B.C.E.), hate democracy. From a well-to-do family, Plato started out trying to right what he saw as democracy's wrongs by promoting the rule of philosopher-tyrants as the best form of government. He served as political adviser to Dionysius, ruler of Syracuse in Sicily, but when he failed to turn him into an ideal ruler, Plato gave up hope that everyday politics could stop violence and greed. Instead, he devoted himself to talking and writing about philosophy as the guide to life and established a philosophical school, the Academy, in Athens around 386 B.C.E. It was not a school in the modern sense but rather an informal association of people who studied philosophy, mathematics, and theoretical astronomy under the leader's guidance. The Academy attracted intellectuals to Athens for the next nine hundred years, and Plato's ideas about the nature of reality, ethics, and politics have remained central to philosophy and political science to this day.

Plato's legacy also includes inspiring his most famous pupil, Aristotle (384–322 B.C.E.). The son of a wealthy doctor in northern Greece, Aristotle came to study in Plato's Academy at the age of seventeen. From 342 to 335 B.C.E. he earned a living by tutoring the young Alexander the Great in Macedonia. Returning to Athens, Aristotle founded his

Mosaic Depicting Plato's Academy

This Roman-era mosaic depicts philosophers—identified by their beards—at Plato's school (called the Academy after the name of a local mythological hero) in Athens holding discussions among themselves. The Academy, founded about 386 B.C.E., became one of Greece's most famous and long-lasting institutions, attracting scholars and students for more than nine hundred years until it closed under the Byzantine emperor Justinian in 529 C.E. The columns and the tree in the mosaic express the harmonious blend of the natural and built environment of the Academy, which was meant to promote productive and pleasant discussions. What message do the philosophers' bare chests convey? Compare the style of dress of the Spartan men on a hunt on page 71 and the Athenian men at a music lesson on page 76. *Erich Lessing/Art Resource, NY.*

own school, the Lyceum,◆ and taught his own life-guiding philosophy, based on logic, scientific knowledge, and practical experience. His vast writings made him one of the world's most influential thinkers.

Plato's Ethical Thought. Plato's intellectual interests covered astronomy, mathematics, political philosophy, ethics, and **metaphysics** (ideas about the ultimate nature of reality beyond the reach of the human senses). His innovative views on the nature of

reality underlay his ethics. He presented his ideas in dialogues, which usually featured Socrates conversing with a variety of people. Plato wrote to provoke readers into thoughtful reflection, not to prescribe a set of beliefs; nowhere did he offer a single set of doctrines. Nevertheless, he always maintained one essential idea based on his view of reality: ultimate moral qualities are universal, unchanging, and absolute, not relative.

Plato's dialogues teach that ethical qualities such as justice, goodness, beauty, or equality exist on their own outside our world and are not defined by our experience of them in our daily lives. Any earthly examples of them can always display the opposite quality. For example, returning what you have borrowed might seem like justice. But what if you borrow a friend's weapon and then discover your friend wants the weapon back to commit murder? Returning the borrowed item would then support injustice. For Plato, every virtue and every quality is relative in the context of the world that we humans experience with our senses.

Plato used the term *Forms* (or *Ideas*) to describe the abstract and ultimate realities of ethical qualities. Goodness, Justice, Beauty, Equality and exist as Forms. Forms are invisible, invariable, and eternal entities located in a higher realm beyond the daily world. According to Plato, the Forms are the only genuine reality; the qualities and other things that we perceive with our senses on earth are only dim and imperfect copies of these metaphysical realities. Our experiences, he said, are like us watching shadows of ultimate realities cast on the wall of a cave. The difficult notion of Forms, which made metaphysics an important issue for philosophers, exemplifies the complexity of Plato's philosophy.

Plato's ideas about the soul also had a profound influence on later thought. He believed that humans possess immortal souls distinct from their bodies; this idea established the concept of **dualism**, a separation between spiritual and physical being. Plato furthermore explained that the human soul possesses preexisting knowledge put there by a deity. Plato called this god the Demiurge◆ (literally, "craftsman") because the deity uses

◆**Lyceum:** lye SEE uhm

◆**Demiurge:** DEH mee urj

the Forms as his guide in crafting living beings out of raw matter. The world has order because a knowing, rational god created it. Furthermore, living beings have goals, such as animals adapting to their environments to survive. The Demiurge wanted to reproduce the Forms' perfect order in the material world, but the world turned out imperfect because matter is imperfect.

Plato believed our life's goal is to seek perfect order and purity in our own souls by using rational thought to control our irrational and therefore harmful desires. The desire to drink excessive alcohol, for example, is irrational and harmful because the one who binges fails to consider the hangover that follows. People who yield to irrational desires fail to consider the future of their body and soul. Finally, our present, impure existence is only a temporary stage in our cosmic existence because while the body does not last, the soul is immortal.

Plato's *Republic*.   Plato presented his most famous ideas on politics in his dialogue *The Republic*. This work, whose Greek title actually means "System of Government," primarily concerns the nature of justice and the reasons people should be just instead of unjust. For Plato, democracy cannot create justice because people on their own cannot rise above narrow self-interest to knowledge of any universal truth. Justice can come only under the rule of an enlightened oligarchy or monarchy. Therefore, a just society requires a strict hierarchy.

Plato's *Republic* envisions an ideal society stratified into three classes of people distinguished by their ability to grasp the truth of Forms. The highest class constitutes the rulers, or "guardians," who must be educated in mathematics, astronomy, and metaphysics. Next come the "auxiliaries," who defend the community. "Producers" make up the bottom class; they grow food and make objects for the whole population. Each class contributes to society by fulfilling its proper function in the hierarchy.

Women as well as men can be guardians because they possess the same virtues and abilities as men, except for a disparity in physical strength between the average woman and the average man. To minimize

distraction, guardians are to have neither private property nor nuclear families. Male and female guardians are to live in houses shared in common, to eat in the same mess halls, and to exercise in the same gymnasiums. They are to have sexual relations with various partners so that the best women can mate with the best men to produce the best children. The children are to be raised together in a common environment by special caretakers. The guardians who achieve the highest level of knowledge in Plato's ideal society qualify to rule as philosopher-kings.

Plato did not think that human beings could actually create this ideal society, but he did believe that imagining it was an important way to help people learn to live justly. That is, he passionately believed that philosophy mattered to human life.

Aristotle, Scientist and Philosopher.
Aristotle's reputation rests on his scientific investigation of the natural world and development of rigorous systems of logical argument. He regarded science and philosophy not as abstract subjects isolated from the concerns of ordinary existence but as the disciplined search for knowledge in every aspect of life. That search brought the good life and genuine happiness. Like Plato, Aristotle criticized democracy because it allowed uneducated instead of "better" people to control politics. He nevertheless chose Athens as the site of his school,

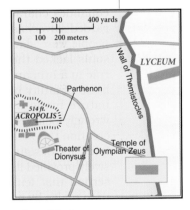

Aristotle's Lyceum, established 335 B.C.E.

the Lyceum (founded 335 B.C.E.), because the city's cosmopolitan atmosphere attracted the wealthy young men he needed as pupils. Later called the Peripatetic School after the covered walkway (*peripatos*) where his students conversed as they strolled, Aristotle's school became world famous. He lectured with dazzling intelligence on biology, medicine, anatomy, psychology, meteorology, physics, chemistry, mathematics, music, metaphysics, rhetoric, literary criticism, political science, and ethics. He also invented a system

alarmed his principal adviser by giving away virtually all his land and property to strengthen the army, thereby creating new landowners who would furnish troops. "What," the adviser asked, "do you have left for yourself?" "My hopes," Alexander replied. Alexander's hopes centered on making himself a warrior as splendid as the incomparable Achilles of Homer's *Iliad*; he always kept a copy of the *Iliad* under his pillow—along with a dagger.

Alexander displayed his heroic ambitions as his army advanced relentlessly through Persian territory. In Anatolia, he visited Gordion, where an oracle had promised the lordship of Asia to whoever could untie a massive knot of rope tying the yoke of an ancient chariot. The young king, so the story goes, cut the Gordian knot with his sword. When Alexander later captured King Darius's wives and daughters, he treated the women with respect. His honorable behavior toward the Persian royal women enhanced his reputation among the Persians.

Alexander complemented his personal qualities with an engineer's eye for better military technology. When Tyre, a heavily fortified city on an island off the eastern Mediterranean, refused to surrender to him in 332 B.C.E., he built a massive stone pier out into the sea as a platform for artillery towers, armored battering rams, and catapults flinging boulders to breach Tyre's walls. The successful use of this siege technology against Tyre showed that walls alone could no longer protect city-states. The knowledge that a technologically equipped army could break through their defenses made enemies much readier to negotiate a deal.

After Alexander conquered Egypt and the Persian heartland, he revealed his strategy for ruling this vast empire: establishing cities of Greeks and Macedonians in conquered territory while keeping an area's traditional administrative system. In Egypt, he established his first new city, naming it Alexandria after himself. In Persia, he proclaimed himself the king of Asia and left the existing governing units intact, retaining various Persian administrators. For the Persian Empire's local populations, therefore, the Macedonian Alexander's becoming the Per-

sian king changed their lives not a bit. They continued to send the same taxes to a remote master, whom they rarely if ever saw.

Marching to India and Back. So fierce was Alexander's heroic love of conquest and adventure that he led his army past the Persian heartland farther east into territory hardly known to the Greeks (Map 4.2). He apparently aimed to outdo the heroes of legend by marching to the end of the world. Paring his army to reduce the need for supplies, he led it northeast into the trackless steppes of Bactria and Sogdiana (modern Afghanistan and Uzbekistan). On the Jaxartes♦ River (Syr Darya), he founded a city called Alexandria the Furthest to show that he had penetrated deeper into this region than even Cyrus, the founder of the Persian Empire. When it proved impossible to subdue the highly mobile locals, however, Alexander settled for an alliance sealed by his marriage to the Bactrian princess Roxane.

Alexander then headed east into India. Seventy days of marching through monsoon rains extinguished his soldiers' fire for conquest. In the spring of 326 B.C.E., they mutinied on the banks of the Hyphasis♦ River in western India and forced Alexander to turn back. The return journey through southeastern Iran's scorching deserts cost many casualties from hunger and thirst; the survivors finally reached safety back in the Persian heartland in 324 B.C.E. Alexander immediately began planning an invasion of the Arabian peninsula and, after that, of all North Africa west of Egypt.

Alexander ruled more harshly after his return and began treating the Greeks as subjects instead of allies. Despite his earlier promise to respect the city-states' internal freedom, he ordered them to restore citizenship to the many exiles created by war, whose status as wandering, stateless persons was causing unrest. Even more striking was Alexander's announcement that he wished to receive the honors due a god. Initially dumbfounded by this request, most Greek city-states soon complied by sending honorary religious delegations to him. The Spartan

♦**Jaxartes:** jak SAHR teez
♦**Hyphasis:** Hy FAH sihs

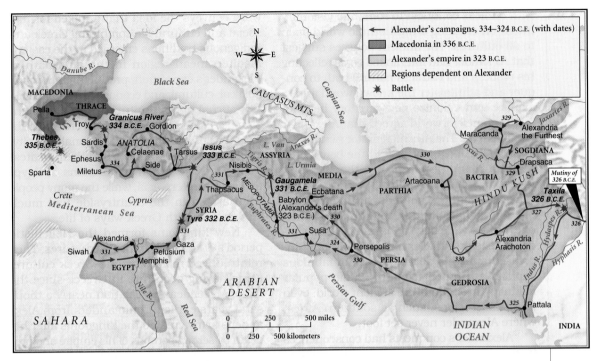

MAP 4.2 Conquests of Alexander the Great, 336–323 B.C.E.
The scale of Alexander's military campaigns in Asia made him a legend; from the time he led his army out of Macedonia and Greece in 334 B.C.E. until his death in Babylon in 323 B.C.E., he was continually on the move. His careful intelligence gathering combined with his charismatic and fearless generalship generated an unbroken string of victories, while his skillful choice of regional administrators, founding of garrison cities, and preservation of local governing structures kept his conquests stable after he moved on.

Damis pithily expressed the only prudent position on Alexander's deification: "If Alexander wishes to be a god, then we'll agree that he be called a god."

Personal rather than political motives best explain Alexander's announcement. He had come to believe he was actually the son of Zeus; after all, Greek mythology reported that Zeus had mated with many human females who produced children. Most of Zeus's legendary offspring were mortal, but Alexander's superhuman conquests proved that he had surpassed them. Since Alexander's accomplishments demonstrated that he had achieved godlike power, he therefore must be a god himself. Alexander's divinity was, in ancient terms, a natural consequence of his power.

Alexander's premature death from a fever and heavy drinking on June 10, 323 B.C.E., aborted his plan to conquer Arabia and North Africa. His death followed months of depression provoked by the death of his best friend, Hephaistion.♦ Close since their boyhood, Alexander and Hephaistion were probably lovers. Like Pericles, Alexander had made no plans about what should happen if he died unexpectedly. Roxane gave birth to their first child a few months after Alexander's death. The story goes that, when at Alexander's deathbed his commanders asked him to whom he bequeathed his kingdom, he replied, "To the most powerful."

Alexander's Impact. Modern scholars disagree on almost everything about Alexander, from whether his claim to divinity was meant to justify his increasingly authoritarian attitude toward the Greek city-states, to what his expedition was meant to achieve. They also offer different assessments of his character, ranging from bloodthirsty monster obsessed

♦**Hephaistion:** hih FEHST ee uhn

Mosaic Floor from Ai Khanoum◆
Archaeologists discovered this mosaic floor at the site of a city founded by Greeks and Macedonians in Afghanistan about 300 B.C.E.; since the city's original name is lost, it is referred to by its modern one, Ai Khanoum. Decorating floors with designs constructed from pebbles or colored pieces of stone was a favorite technique for giving visual interest to a room, while also providing a very durable surface. Like the other cities that Alexander the Great and the successor kings founded in the Near East and Asia, this one functioned as a defense point and an administrative center. To make their immigrant population feel more at home, its architects designed its buildings to replicate the Greek way of life. *Paul Bernard/Hellenisme et Civilizations Orientales.*

The price of these amenities was dependence on the king. Although Hellenistic cities often retained the polis's political institutions, such as councils and assemblies for citizen men, the requirement that they follow royal policy limited their freedom; they certainly made no independent decisions on international affairs. In addition, the cities also often taxed their citizens to send money demanded by the king.

Monarchy's reemergence in the Greek world therefore severely circumscribed the self-sufficiency and independence of the tradi-

tional city-states. At the same time, monarchy created a new relationship between rulers and the social elites, because the crucial element in the Hellenistic kingdom's political and social structure was the system of mutual rewards by which the kings and their leading urban subjects became partners in government and public finance. Wealthy people in the cities had the crucial responsibility of collecting taxes from the surrounding countryside as well as from their city and sending the money on to the royal treasury; the royal military and the administration were too small to perform these duties themselves. The kings therefore treated the cities con-

◆**Ai Khanoum:** aye kah NOOM

siderately because they needed the goodwill of the wealthiest and most influential city dwellers—the Greek and Macedonian urban elites—to ensure a steady flow of tax revenues. The kings honored and flattered the members of the cities' social elites to secure their help. When writing to a city's council, the king would express himself in the form of a polite request, but the recipients knew he expected his wishes to be fulfilled as commands.

This system continued the Greek tradition of requiring the wealthy elite to contribute to the common good, through the social interaction of the kings and the urban upper classes. Cooperative cities received gifts from the king to pay for expensive public works like theaters and temples or for reconstruction after natural disasters such as earthquakes. Wealthy men and women in the urban elites in turn helped keep the general population peaceful by subsidizing teachers and doctors, building public works, and providing donations and loans that secured a reliable supply of grain to feed the city's residents.

This organizational system also required the kings to establish relationships with well-to-do non-Greeks living in the old cities of Anatolia and the Near East, such as Sardis, Tyre, and Babylon. The kings had to develop cordial relations with the leading citizens of such indigenous cities because they could not keep their vast kingdoms peaceful and profitable without the help of local elites. In addition, non-Greeks and non-Macedonians from eastern regions began moving westward to the new Hellenistic Greek cities in increasing numbers. Jews in particular moved from their ancestral homeland to Anatolia, Greece, and Egypt. The Jewish community eventually became an influential minority in Egyptian Alexandria, the most important Hellenistic city. In Egypt the king also had to negotiate with the priests who controlled the temples of the traditional Egyptian gods because the temples owned large tracts of rich land worked by tenant farmers.

The Layers of Hellenistic Society

Hellenistic monarchy reinforced social hierarchy. The royal family and the king's friends topped the ranks. The Greek and Macedonian elites of the major cities ranked next. Just under them came indigenous urban elites, leaders of large minority urban populations, and local lords in rural regions. Merchants, artisans, and laborers made up the free population's bottom layer. Slaves remained where they had always been, without social status at all.

The kingdoms' growth increased the demand for slave labor throughout the eastern Mediterranean; the centrally located island of Delos established a market where up to ten thousand slaves a day were bought and sold. The fortunate ones were purchased as servants for the royal court and lived physically comfortable lives, so long as they pleased their owners; the luckless ones toiled, and often died, in the mines. Enslaved children could be taken far from home to work: for example, a sales contract from 259 B.C.E. shows that Zeno, to whom the camel trader wrote, bought a girl about seven years old named Sphragis ("Gemstone") to make her labor in an Egyptian textile factory. Originally from Sidon in the Levant, she had previously worked as the slave of a Greek mercenary soldier employed by a Jewish cavalry commander in the Transjordan region.

The Poor. Most people continued to live where the majority always had—in country villages. Poor people performed almost all the labor required to support the Hellenistic kingdoms' economies. Agriculture remained the economic base, and working conditions for farmers and laborers changed little over time. Many worked on the royal family's huge agricultural estates, but free peasants still worked their own small plots in addition to laboring for wealthy landowners. Rural people rose with the sun and began working before the heat became unbearable, raising the same kinds of crops and animals as their ancestors had with the same simple hand tools. Perhaps as many as 80 percent of all adult men and women, free as well as slave, had to work the land to produce enough food to sustain the population. In the cities, poor women and men could work as small merchants, peddlers, and artisans, producing and selling goods such as tools, pottery, clothing, and furniture. Men could sign on as deckhands on the merchant ships that sailed the Mediterranean Sea and Indian Ocean.

Poverty often meant hunger, even in fertile lands such as Egypt. Papyrus documents reveal that villagers at Kerkeosiris in the late second century B.C.E. had enough food for about 2,200 calories each per day in grain, supplemented by some lentils, onions, and other vegetables. They thus risked starvation: physically active adults require about 2,500 to 3,600 or more calories depending on size, gender, and the intensity of their activity. By comparison, slaves in the American South in 1860 received an average of 4,185 calories daily on a diet of mostly corn and pork (showing they could be worked harder than Hellenistic laborers); the general U.S. population in 1879 consumed about 3,741 calories per day (showing they were much richer than Hellenistic villagers).

A large portion of the rural population in the Seleucid and Ptolemaic kingdoms existed in a state of dependency between free and slave. The peoples, as they were called, were compulsory tenants who farmed the estates belonging to the king. Although they could not be sold like slaves, they were not allowed to move away or abandon their tenancies. They owed a certain quota of produce per area of land to the king, similar to rent to a landlord. The rent was so heavy that these tenant farmers had little chance to escape poverty.

Women's Lives. Hellenistic women's social and political status depended on their rank in the kingdom's hierarchy. Hellenistic queens, like their Macedonian predecessors, commanded enormous riches and honors. They usually exercised power only to the extent that they could influence their husbands' decisions, but they ruled on their own when no male heir existed. Because the Ptolemaic royal family observed the Egyptian royal tradition of brother-sister marriage, daughters as well as sons could rule. For example,

Emotion in Hellenistic Sculpture

Hellenistic sculptors introduced a new style into Greek art by depicting people not at the height of their glory or beauty but in realistic emotional terms. This statue of an elderly woman, for example, shows her with pain etched on her face, her clothing disheveled, and her body stooped from age and the burden of carrying her load of chickens and vegetables in a basket. The statue probably is intended to portray a poor woman desperately trying to survive by hawking food in the street. The artist apparently wanted to show the stress and strain caused by poverty. This new sort of art strove to produce an emotional response in its viewers. The statue's date is uncertain; this version may be a later copy of a Hellenistic original. *Rogers Fund, 1909 (09.39). Photograph © 1997 The Metropolitan Museum of Art.*

Arsinoe♦ II (c. 316–270 B.C.E.), the daughter of Ptolemy I, first married the Macedonian successor king Lysimachus, who gave her four towns as her personal domain. After Lysimachus's death she married her brother Ptolemy II of Egypt and exerted at least as much influence on policy as he did. The virtues publicly praised in a queen reflected traditional Greek values for women. When the city of Hierapolis♦ around 165 B.C.E. passed a decree honoring Queen Apollonis of Pergamum, it praised her piety toward the gods, reverence toward her parents, distinguished conduct toward her husband, and harmonious relations with her "beautiful children born in wedlock."

Some queens paid special attention to the condition of women. About 195 B.C.E., for example, the Seleucid queen Laodice♦ gave a ten-year endowment to the city of Iasus in

♦**Arsinoe:** ahr SIHN oh ee
♦**Hierapolis:** hy uh RA puh luhs
♦**Laodice:** lay AHD uh see

southwestern Anatolia to provide dowries for needy girls. That Laodice funded dowries shows that she recognized the importance to women of controlling property, the surest guarantee of respect in their households.

Most women still remained under the control of men. "Who can judge better than a father what is to his daughter's interest?" remained the dominant creed of fathers with daughters; once a woman married, the words *husband* and *wife's* replaced *father* and *daughter's* in the creed. Most of the time, elite women continued to be separated from men outside of their families, while poor women still worked in public. Greeks continued to abandon infants they could not or would not raise—girls more often than boys—but other populations, such as the Egyptians and the Jews, did not practice abandonment, or exposure, as it is often called. Exposure differed from infanticide because the parents expected someone else to find the child and rear it, albeit usually as a slave. The third-century B.C.E. comic poet Posidippos overstated the case by saying, "A son, one always raises even if one is poor; a daughter, one exposes, even if one is rich." Daughters of wealthy parents were not usually abandoned, but it has been estimated that up to 10 percent of other infant girls were.

In some ways, however, women achieved greater control over their lives in the Hellenistic period than in earlier periods. The rare woman of exceptional wealth could enter public life by making donations or loans to her city and in return be rewarded with an official post in her community's government. In Egypt, women acquired greater say in married life because the customary marriage contracts (see page 102) gradually evolved from an agreement between the bride's parents and the groom to one in which the bride made her own arrangements with the groom.

The Wealthy. Rich people showed increasing concern for the welfare of the less fortunate during the Hellenistic period. They were following the lead of the royal families, who emphasized philanthropy to build a reputation for generosity that would buttress their legitimacy. On the island of Samos, wealthy citizens funded a foundation to distribute free grain to all the citizens to

Egyptian-Style Statue of Queen Arsinoe II
Arsinoe II (c. 316–270 B.C.E.), daughter of Alexander's general Ptolemy, was one of the most remarkable women of the Hellenistic period. After surviving twenty-five years of political turmoil, dynastic intrigue, and family murders, she married her brother Ptolemy II to unify the monarchy. Hailed as Philadelphoi ("Brother-Loving"), the couple set a precedent for brother-sister marriages in the Macedonian dynasty, the Ptolemies, that ruled Egypt until the death of Cleopatra VII in 30 B.C.E. Arsinoe was the first Ptolemaic ruler whose image was placed in Egyptian temples as a "temple-sharing goddess." This eight-foot-tall, red granite statue portrays her in the traditional sculptural style of the pharaohs. Compare the statue of the Egyptian queen Hatshepsut on page 25. Why would a Hellenistic queen wish to be depicted in traditional Egyptian royal dress?
Vatican Museums.

eliminate food shortages. Wealthy citizens also funded state-sponsored schools for children in various Hellenistic cities. In some places, girls as well as boys could attend school. Many cities also began sponsoring doctors to improve medical care: patients still had to pay, but at least they could count on finding a doctor.

The donors funding these services were repaid by the respect and honor they earned from their fellow citizens. Philanthropy even touched international relations. When an earthquake devastated Rhodes, many cities joined kings and queens in sending donations to help the Rhodians recover. In return, Rhodes's citizens showered honors on their benefactors by appointing them to prestigious municipal offices and erecting inscriptions expressing the city's gratitude. In this system, the masses' welfare depended more and more on the voluntary generosity of the rich; without democracy, the poor had no political power to demand support.

The End of the Hellenistic Kingdoms

All the Hellenistic kingdoms eventually fell to the Romans. The trouble began when Philip V (238–179 B.C.E.), descendant of Antigonus and king of Macedonia, made a treaty in 215 B.C.E. to aid Hannibal of Carthage in a war against Rome (the Second Punic War). After the Romans won in 201 B.C.E., they sent an army to punish Philip. Rome repeatedly intervened in the squabbles of the Greek city-states to try to maintain peace on its eastern frontier, causing wars that established Roman dominance over Macedonia and Greece by the middle of the second century B.C.E. The city-state of Rhodes and the Attalid kings in Pergamum then convinced the Romans that preserving Rome's safety required Roman intervention farther east in the Mediterranean, to counterbalance Seleucid and Ptolemaic power.

The Seleucid kingdom finally fell to the Romans in 64 B.C.E. The Ptolemaic kingdom in Egypt survived a bit longer. By the 50s B.C.E., its royal family had split into warring factions; the resulting disunity and weakness forced the rivals for the throne to seek Roman support. The end came when the famous queen Cleopatra, a descendant of Ptolemy and the last Macedonian to rule Egypt, chose the losing side in the civil war between Mark Antony and the future emperor Augustus in the late first century B.C.E. An invading Roman army ended her reign and the long succession of Ptolemaic rulers in 30 B.C.E. Rome thus became the heir to all the Hellenistic kingdoms (see Map 4.3).

> **Review:** What were the biggest challenges facing the Hellenistic kings?

✦ Hellenistic Culture, 323–30 B.C.E.

Hellenistic culture reflected three principal characteristics: the overwhelming impact of royal wealth, increased emphasis on private life and emotion, and the increased interaction of diverse peoples. The fabulously rich kings drove developments in literature, art, science, and philosophy by deciding which scholars and artists to put on the royal payroll. Their obligation to the kings meant that authors and artists did not have freedom to criticize public policy; they therefore concentrated on everyday life and individual emotion.

Cultural interaction between Greek and Near Eastern traditions occurred most prominently in language and religion. These developments deeply influenced the Romans as they took over the Hellenistic world; the Roman poet Horace (65–8 B.C.E.) described the effect of Hellenistic culture on his own by saying that "captive Greece captured its fierce victor."

The Arts under Royal Patronage

Hellenistic kings became the patrons of scholarship and the arts on a vast scale, competing with one another to lure the best scholars and artists to their capitals with lavish salaries. They spent money supporting intellectual activity because they wanted to boost their reputations by having these famous people produce books, poems, sculptures, and other prestigious creations at their courts.

The Ptolemies assembled the Hellenistic world's most intellectually distinguished court by turning Alexandria into the Mediterranean's leading arts and sciences center. There the kings established the world's first scholarly research institute and a massive library to support its work. The librarians were instructed to collect all the books (that is, manuscripts) in the world. The library grew to hold half a million scrolls, an enormous number for the time. Linked to it was the building in which scholars hired to do research dined together and produced encyclopedias of knowledge such as *The Wonders of the World* and *On the Rivers of Europe* by Callimachus,✦ a learned prose writer as well as a poet. We still use the name of the research institute's building, the Museum (meaning "place of the Muses," the Greek goddesses of learning and the arts), to designate institutions preserving knowledge. The Alexandrian scholars produced prodigiously. Their champion was Didymus✦

✦**Callimachus:** kuh LIH muh kuhs
✦**Didymus:** DIH duh muhs

(c. 80–10 B.C.E.), nicknamed "Brass Guts" for writing nearly four thousand books. Sadly, not a single one has survived.

Literature at Court. The writers and artists whom Hellenistic kings paid necessarily had to please their patrons with their works. The poet Theocritus (c. 300–260 B.C.E.) spelled out the deal underlying royal patronage in a poem expressly praising his patron, King Ptolemy II: "The spokesmen of the Muses [that is, poets] celebrate Ptolemy in return for his benefactions." Poets such as Theocritus succeeded by avoiding overtly political subjects and stressing the division in society between the intellectual elite—to which the kings belonged—and the uneducated masses. They filled their new poetry with erudite references to make it difficult to understand and therefore exclusive. Only people with a deep literary education could appreciate the mythological allusions that studded these authors' elaborate poems.

Theocritus was the first Greek poet to express the divide between town and countryside, a poetic stance corresponding to a growing Hellenistic reality. His *Idylls* emphasized the discontinuity between urban life and the country bumpkins' bucolic existence, reflecting the Ptolemaic social division between the food consumers in the town and the food producers in the countryside. Theocritus presented a city dweller's idealized dream that country life was peaceful and stress-free, a fiction that deeply influenced later literature.

No Hellenistic women poets seem to have enjoyed royal patronage, but they practiced their art nevertheless. They excelled in writing **epigrams**, a style of short poem originally used for funeral epitaphs. Elegantly worded poems by women from diverse regions of the Hellenistic world—Anyte of Tegea♦ in the Peloponnese, Nossis of Locri♦ in southern Italy, Moero of Byzantium♦—still survive. They often wrote about women, from courtesans to respectable matrons, and their personal feelings. Love was their favorite subject.

♦**Anyte of Tegea:** ahn EE tay (of) TEH jee uh
♦**Nossis of Locri:** NAH sis (of) LOH kry
♦**Moero of Byzantium:** MAH ee ro (of) buh ZAN tee uhm

Nossis's poem on the power of Eros, for example, proclaimed, "Nothing is sweeter than Eros. All other delights are second to it—from my mouth I spit out even honey. And this Nossis says: whoever Aphrodite has not kissed knows not what sort of flowers are her roses." No other Hellenistic literature better conveys the depth of human emotion than the epigrams of women poets.

The Hellenistic theater, too, largely shifted its focus to stories about individual emotion; no longer did dramatists openly criticize political leaders, as they had in the Classical period. Comic dramatists now presented plays with timeless plots concerning the trials and tribulations of fictional lovers. These comedies of manners, as they are called, proved enormously popular because, like modern situation comedies, they offered a humorous view of situations from daily life. Recent papyrus finds have allowed us to recover comedies of Menander (c. 342–289 B.C.E.), the most famous Hellenistic playwright, and to appreciate his skill in depicting human personality. He presented his first comedy at Athens in 324 or 323 B.C.E. (See "New Sources, New Perspectives," page 148.) Hellenistic tragedy could take a multicultural approach: Ezechiel, a Jew living in Alexandria, wrote *Exodus*, a tragedy in Greek about Moses leading the Hebrews out of captivity in Egypt.

Emotion in Sculpture and Painting. Like their literary contemporaries, Hellenistic sculptors and painters featured personal feelings prominently in their works. Classical artists had consistently imbued their subjects' faces with an idealized serenity. Hellenistic sculptures, usually surviving only in later copies, depicted individual emotions. In portrait sculpture, Lysippus's famous bust of Alexander the Great captured the young commander's passionate dreaminess. A sculpture from Pergamum (page 150) by an unknown artist commemorated the third-century B.C.E. Attalid victory over the plundering Gauls (one of the Celtic peoples from what is now France) by showing a defeated Celtic warrior stabbing himself after having killed his wife to prevent her enslavement by the victors. A large-scale painting of Alexander battling with the Persian king Darius (see

NEW SOURCES, NEW PERSPECTIVES

Papyrus Discoveries and Menander's Comedies

Fourth-century B.C.E. Greek playwrights invented the kind of comedy that is today's most popular entertainment—the sitcom. In the Peloponnesian War's aftermath, they wrote comic plays that concentrated on the conflicts between human personality types as their characters suffered through everyday trials and tribulations. The rocky course of love and marriage drove most plots. Forsaking the bawdy political satire of earlier Greek comedy, comedians now created stereotypical characters such as addled lovers, cantankerous fathers, rascally servants, and boastful soldiers. Confusions of identity leading to hilarious misunderstandings were a frequent plot device, while jokes about marriage were another staple. The following is a typical exchange:

> FIRST MAN: "He's married, you know."
> SECOND MAN: "What's that you say? Actually married? How can that be? I just left him alive and walking around!"

The comedies' titles hinted at their tone: *The Country Boob, Pot-Belly, The Stolen Girl, The Bad-Tempered Man.*

By the end of the fourth century, these comedies had become wildly popular. Greek comic plays about daily life and social mix-ups inspired many imitations, especially Roman comedies, which eventually inspired William Shakespeare (1564–1616) in England and Molière (1622–1673) in France; their comedies, in turn, led to today's sitcoms.

The most famous author of this kind of comedy was Menander (343–291 B.C.E.) of Athens. Ancient critics ranked him as "second only to Homer" for his poetry's quality, and they praised his plots as "a mirror of life." Despite antiquity's unanimous "two thumbs up," none of Menander's comedies survived into modern times. Works of Greek and Roman literature had to be copied over and over by hand for centuries if they were to survive, until finally the invention of the printing press in the fifteenth century made mass production of books possible. For unknown reasons, people at some point stopped recopying comedies, including Menander's. Thus, although we knew Menander

Pompeian Wall Painting Depicting Menander
Four centuries after Menander's death, a wealthy Roman commissioned this painting of the playwright for a wall in his house at Pompeii, near Naples. Evidently the owner meant to proclaim his love for Greek drama because the room's other walls—now very damaged—were probably decorated with images of the tragedian Euripides and possibly the Muses of Tragedy and Comedy. This figure was identified by faded lettering on the scroll: "Menander: he was the first to write New Comedy." The ivy wreath on his head symbolizes the poet's victory in the contests of comedies presented at the festivals of the god Dionysus, the patron of drama. *Scala/Art Resource, NY.*

had been a star, we could not read the plays that made him so famous—until quite recently.

The situation changed dramatically when scholars in the late eighteenth century C.E. began finding ancient paper—papyrus—buried in Egypt's dry sands. In antiquity, Egyptians processed the reeds of the papyrus plant to make a thick, brownish paper for writing down everything from literature to letters to tax receipts. When papyrus texts were damaged or no longer needed, they were thrown out with the garbage or used to wrap mummies to help preserve the dried-out corpses for the afterlife. The super-arid climate of the Egyptian desert kept this waste paper from rotting away. The French emperor Napoleon's occupation of Egypt in 1798–1801 inspired a European mania for collecting papyrus. By excavating ancient Egyptian trash dumps and unwrapping mummies, scholars have discovered thousands and thousands of texts of all kinds. Papyrus experts estimate that the original production of papyrus texts was so enormous that it was more than 150,000 times greater than what has survived.

Incredibly, these discoveries have returned Menander to us from more than two thousand years ago: over the last several decades, painstaking study of often severely damaged papyrus sheets has uncovered texts of his comedies. When the so-called Bodmer Papyrus proved to contain a nearly complete copy of *The Bad-Tempered Man*, we could once again enjoy a Menander comedy for the first time since antiquity. Further detective work has yielded more, and today we can also read most of *The Girl from Samos* and parts of other plays. In this way, Menander's memorable and influential characters, stories, and jokes have been restored from the dead.

Rediscovering ancient comedy (or any other kind of writing) on papyrus is challenging. The handwriting is often crabbed and difficult to decipher, there are no gaps between words, punctuation is minimal at best, changes in speakers are indicated just by colons or dashes rather than by names, and there are no stage directions. The papyrus can be burned or torn into pieces or chewed by mice and insects. One part of a play can turn up in the wrapping of one mummy and another part in a different one. Incompletely preserved scenes and lines can be hard to understand.

The hard work required to make sense of papyrus texts pays off wonderfully, however, with

Books on Papyrus
Menander's works were written on sheets of papyrus like these that were glued together to make scrolls, the form of books used until the later Roman period. Holes and tears caused by age and use can destroy letters and words, making reconstruction of the original text a difficult task. The writing can also be hard to decipher; compared to most papyrus books from antiquity, this example is well preserved and has a very clear script. (Its words and drawings come from the works of the fourth-century B.C.E. astronomer and mathematician Eudoxus of Cnidos.) *Réunion des Musées Nationaux/ Art Resource, NY/Photo: Herve Lewandowski.*

discoveries like those that recovered Menander's comedies. In this case, the collaboration of archaeologists, historians, and literary scholars has brought back to life the distant beginnings of what remains our most enduring and crowd-pleasing form of comedy.

QUESTIONS TO CONSIDER

1. What makes situation comedy so appealing?
2. Why would Greeks living in the fourth century B.C.E. prefer situation comedy to political satire or darker forms of humor?

FURTHER READING

Roger Bagnall, *Reading Papyri, Writing Ancient History.* 1995.
Menander: Plays and Fragments. Translated with an introduction by Norma Miller. 1987.
Richard Parkinson and Stephen Quirke, *Papyrus.* 1995.

Gemstone Showing Diogenes in His Jar

This engraved gem from the Roman period shows the famous philosopher Diogenes (c. 412–c. 324 B.C.E.) living in a large storage jar and having a discussion with a man who holds a scroll. Diogenes was born at Sinope on the Black Sea but was exiled in a dispute over monetary fraud; he spent most of his life at Athens and Corinth, becoming famous as the founder of Cynic ("doglike") philosophy. He espoused an ascetic life of poverty ruled by nature, not law or tradition. In his defiance of social convention he was said to live like a dog, hence the name given to his philosophical views and the dog usually shown beside him in art, as in this engraving. What kind of person do you think would have wanted this gemstone as a piece of jewelry?
Thorvaldsen Museum, Copenhagen.

people's lives but that individuals should still make the pursuit of virtue their goal. Stoic virtue meant putting oneself in harmony with the divine, rational force of universal Nature by cultivating good sense, justice, courage, and temperance. These doctrines applied to women as well as men. In fact, some Stoics advocated equal citizenship for women and abolition of the conventions of marriage and families as the Greeks knew them. Zeno even proposed unisex clothing as a way to obliterate unnecessary distinctions between women and men.

The Stoic belief in fate created the question of whether humans truly have free will. Relying on subtle reasoning, Stoic philosophers concluded that purposeful human actions do have significance even if fate rules. Nature, itself good, does not prevent vice from occurring, because virtue would otherwise have no meaning. What matters in life is the striving for good, not the result. A person should therefore take action against evil by, for example, participating in politics. To be a Stoic also meant to shun desire and anger while enduring pain and sorrow calmly, an attitude that yields the modern meaning of the word *stoic*. Through endurance and self-control, adherents of Stoic philosophy at-

tained tranquillity. They did not fear death because they believed that people live the same life over and over again. This repetition occurred because the world is periodically destroyed by fire and then re-formed.

Competing Philosophies. Other Hellenistic philosophies competed with Epicureanism and Stoicism for people's minds and hearts. Some of these philosophies built on the work of earlier giants such as Plato and Pythagoras. Others struck out in idiosyncratic directions. Skeptics, for example, aimed at the same state of personal calm as did Epicureans, but from a completely different premise. Following the doctrines of Pyrrho (c. 360–270 B.C.E.) from Elis, in the Peloponnese, Skeptics believed that secure knowledge about anything was impossible because the human senses yield contradictory information about the world. All we can do, they insisted, is depend on appearances while suspending judgment about their reality. Pyrrho's thought had been influenced by the Indian ascetic wise men (the magi) he met while on Alexander the Great's expedition.

The philosophers called Cynics ostentatiously rejected every convention of ordinary life, especially wealth and material comfort.

They believed that humans should aim for complete self-sufficiency. Whatever was natural was good and could be done without shame before anyone; therefore, even public defecation and fornication were acceptable. Women and men alike were free to follow their sexual inclinations. Above all, Cynics disdained life's comforts. The most famous early Cynic, Diogenes (d. 323 B.C.E.) from Sinope, on the Black Sea, wore borrowed clothing and slept in a storage jar. Almost as notorious was Hipparchia,♦ a Cynic of the late fourth century B.C.E. She once bested an obnoxious philosophical opponent named Theodorus the Atheist with the following remarks: "That which would not be considered wrong if done by Theodorus would also not be considered wrong if done by Hipparchia. Now if Theodorus strikes himself, he does no wrong. Therefore, if Hipparchia strikes Theodorus, she does no wrong." The name *Cynic*, which meant "like a dog," reflected the common evaluation of this ascetic and unconventional way of life.

In the Hellenistic period, Greek philosophy reached a wider audience than ever before. Although the working poor had neither the leisure nor the resources to attend philosophers' lectures, the well-off members of society studied philosophy in growing numbers. Theophrastus lectured to crowds of two thousand in Athens. Most philosophy students continued to be men, but women could now join some groups. Kings competed to attract famous philosophers to their courts, and Greek settlers took their interest in philosophy with them to even the most remote Hellenistic cities. Archaeologists excavating a city located thousands of miles from Greece on the Oxus River in Afghanistan uncovered a Greek philosophical text as well as inscriptions of moral advice imputed to Apollo's oracle at Delphi.

Scientific Innovation

Scientific investigation was separated from philosophy in the Hellenistic period. Science so benefited from its widening divorce from philosophy that historians have called this era ancient science's golden age. Various factors contributed to a flourishing of scientific innovation: Alexander's expedition had encouraged curiosity and increased knowledge about the world's extent and diversity, royal patronage supported scientists financially, and the concentration of scientists in Alexandria promoted a fertile exchange of ideas.

Advances in Geometry and Mathematics. The greatest advances in scientific knowledge came in geometry and mathematics. Euclid, who taught at Alexandria around 300 B.C.E., made revolutionary discoveries in analyzing two- and three-dimensional space. The utility of Euclidean geometry still endures. Archimedes of Syracuse (287–212 B.C.E.) was a mathematical genius who calculated the approximate value of pi and devised a way to manipulate very large numbers. He also invented hydrostatics (the science of the equilibrium of fluid systems) and mechanical devices such as a screw for lifting water to a higher elevation. Archimedes's shout of delight when he solved a problem while soaking in his bathtub has been immortalized in the modern expression "Eureka!" (*heurēka* in Greek), meaning "I have found it!"

Advances in Hellenistic mathematics energized other fields that required complex computation. Aristarchus of Samos early in the third century B.C.E. became the first to

Bronze Astronomical Calculator
These fragments of a Hellenistic bronze astronomical calculator were discovered underwater in an ancient shipwreck off Anticythera, below the Peloponnese in southern Greece. The device was being transported to Italy in the early first century B.C.E. as part of a shipment of metalwork and other valuable objects. The product of sophisticated applied engineering and astronomical knowledge, it used a complex set of intermeshed gears, turned by hand, to control rotating dials that indicated the position of celestial phenomena. *National Archaeological Museum, Athens. Archaeological Receipts Fund.*

propose the correct model of the solar system: the earth revolves around the sun, which is far larger and more distant than it appears. Later astronomers rejected Aristarchus's heliocentric model in favor of the traditional geocentric one (with the earth at the center) because calculations based on the orbit he calculated for the earth failed to correspond to the observed positions of celestial objects. Aristarchus had assumed a circular orbit instead of an elliptical one, an assumption not corrected until much later. Eratosthenes of Cyrene (c. 275–194 B.C.E.) pioneered mathematical geography. He calculated the circumference of the earth with astonishing accuracy by simultaneously measuring the length of the shadows of widely separated but identically tall structures. Together, these researchers gave Western scientific thought an important start toward its fundamental procedure of reconciling theory with observed data through measurement and experimentation.

Scientific Discoveries. Hellenistic science flourished despite the enormous difficulties imposed by technical limitations. Rigorous scientific experimentation was not possible because no technology existed for the precise measurement of very short intervals of time. Measuring tiny quantities of matter was also next to impossible. The science of the age was as quantitative as it could be given these limitations. Ctesibius♦ of Alexandria (b. c. 310 B.C.E.), a contemporary of Aristarchus, invented pneumatics by creating machines operated by air pressure. He also built a working water pump, an organ powered by water, and the first accurate water clock. A later Alexandrian, Hero, continued the Hellenistic tradition of mechanical ingenuity by building a rotating sphere powered by steam. As in most of Hellenistic science, these inventions did not lead to viable applications in daily life. The scientists and their royal patrons were more interested in new theoretical discoveries than in practical results, and the metallurgical technology to produce the pipes, fittings, and screws needed to build powerful machines did not yet exist.

Hellenistic science did produce noteworthy new military technology. The kings hired engineers to design powerful catapults and wheeled siege towers many stories high; these weapons could batter down the defenses of walled cities. The most famous large-scale application of technology for non-military purposes was the construction of the Pharos, a lighthouse three hundred feet tall, for the harbor at Alexandria. Using polished metal mirrors to reflect the light from a large bonfire, the Pharos shone many miles out over the sea. Awestruck sailors called it one of the wonders of the world.

The Origins of Anatomy. Medicine also benefited from the Hellenistic quest for new knowledge. Increased contact between Greeks and people of the Near East made Mesopotamian and Egyptian medical knowledge better known in the West and promoted research on human health and illness. Around 325 B.C.E., Praxagoras♦ of Cos discovered the value of measuring the pulse in diagnosing illness. A bit later, Herophilus of Chalcedon♦ (b. c. 300 B.C.E.), working in Alexandria, became the first Western scientist to study anatomy by dissecting human cadavers and, it was rumored, condemned criminals while they were still alive; he had access to these subjects because the king authorized his research. Some of the anatomical terms Herophilus invented are still used. Other Hellenistic advances in anatomy included the discovery of the nerves and nervous system.

Like scientists of the time, Hellenistic medical researchers were limited by the lack of technology to detect and measure phenomena not visible to the naked eye. Unable to see what really occurred under the skin in living patients, doctors thought that many illnesses in women were caused by displacements of the womb, which they wrongly believed could move around in the body. These mistaken ideas could not be corrected because the technology to evaluate them was absent.

♦**Ctesibius:** teh SIHB ee uhs

♦**Praxagoras:** prak SAG uh ruhs
♦**Herophilus of Chalcedon:** huh RAHF uh luhs (of) KAL suh dahn

Cultural and Religious Transformations

Wealthy non-Greeks increasingly adopted Greek habits as they adapted to the Hellenistic world's social hierarchy. Diotimus of Sidon, for example, took a Greek name and pursued the premier Greek sport, chariot racing. He traveled to Nemea in the Peloponnese to enter his chariot in the race at the prestigious festival of Zeus. He announced his victory in an inscription written in Greek, which had become the Hellenistic world's common language for international commerce and cultural exchange. The explosion in the use of the Greek language in the form called **Koine**♦ (literally, "shared" or "common") reflected the emergence of an international culture based on Greek models; this was the reason that the Egyptian camel trader stranded in Syria had to communicate in Greek with a high-level official in Egypt. The most striking evidence of this cultural development comes from Afghanistan. There, King Ashoka (r. c. 268–232 B.C.E.), who ruled most of the Indian subcontinent, used Greek as one of the languages in his public inscriptions. These texts announced his plan to teach his subjects Buddhist traditions of self-control, such as abstinence from eating meat. Local languages did not disappear in the Hellenistic kingdoms, however. In one region of Anatolia, for example, people spoke twenty-two different languages. This sort of diversity remained the norm in the world that the Hellenistic kings ruled.

Changes in Greek and Egyptian Religion. The diversity of religious practice matched the variety in so many other areas of Hellenistic life. The traditional cults of Greek religion remained popular, but new cults, above all those that deified ruling kings, reflected changing political and social conditions. Preexisting cults that previously had only local significance, such as that of the Greek healing deity Asclepius♦ or the mystery cult of the Egyptian goddess Isis, gained adherents all over the Hellenis-

tic world. In many cases, Greek cults and local cults from the eastern Mediterranean influenced each other. Their beliefs meshed well because these cults shared many assumptions about how to remedy the troubles of human life. In other instances, local cults and Greek cults existed side by side and even overlapped. The inhabitants of villages in the Fayum♦ district of Egypt, for example, continued worshiping their traditional crocodile god and mummifying their dead according to the old ways but also paid homage to Greek deities. Since they were polytheists (believers in multiple gods), people could worship in both old and new cults.

New cults incorporated a prominent theme of Hellenistic thought: concern for the relationship between the individual and what seemed the controlling, arbitrary power of the divinities such as Tychê (literally "Chance"). The chaotic course of Greek history after the Peloponnesian War made human existence appear more unpredictable than ever. Since advances in astronomy revealed the mathematical precision of the celestial sphere of the universe, religion now had to address the seeming disconnection between that heavenly uniformity and the shapeless chaos of life on earth. One increasingly popular approach to bridging that gap was to rely on astrology for advice deduced from the movement of the stars and planets, thought of as divinities. Another very common choice was to worship Tychê as a god in the hope of securing good luck in life.

The most revolutionary approach in seeking protection from the capricious tricks of chance or luck was to pray for salvation from deified kings, who enjoyed divine status in what are now called **ruler cults**. Various populations established these cults in recognition of great benefactions. The Athenians, for example, deified the Macedonian Antigonus and his son Demetrius as savior gods in 307 B.C.E., when they liberated the city and bestowed magnificent gifts on it. Like most ruler cults, this one expressed both spontaneous gratitude and a desire to flatter the rulers in the hope of obtaining

♦**Koine:** koy NAY
♦**Asclepius:** as KLEE pee uhs

♦**Fayum:** fa yoom

Hellenistic Judaism. Cultural interaction between Greeks and Jews produced important changes in Judaism during the Hellenistic period. King Ptolemy II made the Hebrew Bible accessible to a wide audience by having his Alexandrian scholars produce a Greek translation—the Septuagint—in the early third century B.C.E. Many Jews, especially those in the large Jewish communities that had grown up in Hellenistic cities outside their homeland, began to speak Greek and adopt Greek culture. These Hellenized Jews did, however, retain traditional Judaism's rituals and rules, and they did not worship Greek gods. In other words, they did not simply become Greek but instead mixed Jewish and Greek customs.

Internal dissension among Jews erupted in second-century B.C.E. Palestine over how much Greek tradition was acceptable for traditional Jews. The Seleucid king Antiochus IV (r. 175–163 B.C.E.) intervened in the conflict to support an extreme Hellenizing faction of Jerusalem Jews, who had taken over the high priesthood that ruled the Jewish community with royal approval. In 167 B.C.E., Antiochus converted the great Jewish temple in Jerusalem into a Greek temple and outlawed the practice of Jewish religious rites, such as observing the Sabbath and circumcision. This provoked a revolt led by Judah the Maccabee, which won Jewish independence from Seleucid control after twenty-five years of war. The most famous episode in this revolt was the retaking of the Jerusalem temple and its rededication to the worship of the Jewish god, Yahweh, commemorated by the Hanukkah holiday. That Greek culture attracted some Jews in the first place provides a striking example of the transformations that affected many—though far from all—people of the Hellenistic world. By the time of the Roman Empire, one of those transformations would be Christianity, whose theology had roots in the cultural interaction of Hellenistic Jews and Greeks and their ideas on apocalypticism and divine human beings.

Review: How did the political changes of the Hellenistic period affect art and science?

Conclusion

The Peloponnesian War's violence and the decades of war that followed in the early fourth century B.C.E. led ordinary people as well as philosophers like Plato and Aristotle to question the basis of morality. The disunity of Greek international politics allowed Macedonia's aggressive leaders Philip II (r. 359–336 B.C.E.) and Alexander the Great (r. 336–323 B.C.E.) to make themselves the masters of the squabbling city-states. Inspired by Greek heroic ideals, Alexander the Great conquered the Persian Empire and set in motion the Hellenistic period's momentous political, social, and cultural changes.

When Alexander's generals transformed themselves into Hellenistic kings, they not only made use of the conquered lands' existing administrative structures but also added an administrative layer staffed by Greeks and Macedonians. Local elites as well as Greeks and Macedonians cooperated with the Hellenistic monarchs in governing and financing their society, which was divided along hierarchical ethnic lines. To enhance their own magnificence, the kings and queens of the Hellenistic world supported writers, artists, scholars, philosophers, and scientists, thereby energizing Hellenistic intellectual life. The traditional city-states continued to exist in Hellenistic Greece, but their freedom extended only to local governance; the Hellenistic kings determined international affairs.

Cultural diversity in the Hellenistic world encompassed much that was new, because interaction between different peoples became more common than ever before. Artists and writers expressed emotion in their works in novel ways, philosophers discussed ways to achieve true happiness, and scientists explored the mysteries of nature and the human body more deeply than ever before. Political and cultural change increased people's uncertainty and therefore their anxiety about the role of chance in life. In response, people looked for new religious experiences to satisfy their yearning for protection from perils. In the midst of so much novelty, however, the ancient world's fundamental elements remained unchanged—the labor, the poverty, and the necessarily limited horizons of the mass of ordinary people working in its fields, vineyards, and pastures.

What changed most of all was the Romans' culture once they took over the Hellenistic kingdoms' territory and came into close contact with their diverse peoples' traditions. Rome's rise to power took centuries, however, because Rome originated as a tiny, insignificant place that no one except Romans ever expected to amount to anything on the world stage.

Suggested References

Classical Greece's Decline, c. 400–350 B.C.E.

The works of Plato and Aristotle, unlike those of many ancient authors, have survived in quantity so that we can study their thought in detail. Xenophon's *Hellenica* and *Anabasis* offer action-packed accounts of the wars of the early fourth century B.C.E.

*Aristotle. *Complete Works*. Ed. Jonathan Barnes. 1985.

Barnes, Jonathan. *Aristotle*. 1982.

Garnsey, Peter. *Ideas of Slavery from Aristotle to Augustine*. 1996.

Greek archaeology: http://archnet.uconn.edu/regions/europe.php3.

*Plato. *The Collected Dialogues* (including *Apology*, *Crito*, and *Republic*). Eds. Edith Hamilton and Huntington Cairns. 1963.

Strauss, Barry S. *Athens after the Peloponnesian War: Class, Faction, and Policy, 403–386 B.C.* 1986.

Tritle, Lawrence A., ed. *The Greek World in the Fourth Century: From the Fall of the Athenian Empire to the Successors of Alexander*. 1997.

*Xenophon. *A History of My Times (Hellenica)*. Trans. Rex Warner. 1979.

———. *The Persian Expedition (Anabasis)*. Trans. Rex Warner. 1972.

The Rise of Macedonia, 359–323 B.C.E.

Modern scholars energetically debate Alexander's character; Bosworth, for example, brands him a natural-born killer, while O'Brien sees him as overcome by alcoholism.

*Arrian. *The Campaigns of Alexander (Anabasis)*. Trans. Aubrey de Sélincourt. 1971.

Borza, Eugene N. *In the Shadow of Olympus: The Emergence of Macedon*. 1990.

Bosworth, A. B. *Alexander and the East: The Tragedy of Triumph*. 1996.

———. *Conquest and Empire: The Reign of Alexander the Great*. 1988.

Carney, Elizabeth Donnelly. *Women and Monarchy in Macedonia*. 2000.

Macedonian royal tombs at Vergina: http://alexander.macedonia.culture.gr/2/21/211/21117a/e211qa07.html.

O'Brien, John Maxwell. *Alexander the Great, the Invisible Enemy: A Biography*. 1992.

*Plutarch. *The Age of Alexander*. Trans. Ian Scott-Kilvert. 1973.

Stoneman, Richard. *Alexander the Great*. 1997.

The Hellenistic Kingdoms, 323–30 B.C.E.

Recent research stresses the innovative responses of the successor kings to the challenges of ruling multicultural empires. Underwater archaeology has begun to reveal ancient Alexandria in Egypt, whose harbor district has sunk below the level of today's Mediterranean Sea.

*Austin, M. M. *The Hellenistic World from Alexander to the Roman Conquest: A Selection of Ancient Sources in Translation*. 1981.

*Burstein, Stanley M. *The Hellenistic Age from the Battle of Ipsos to the Death of Kleopatra VII*. 1985.

Ellis, Walter M. *Ptolemy of Egypt*. 1994.

Empereur, Jean-Yves. *Alexandria: Jewel of Egypt*. 2002.

Lewis, Naphtali. *Greeks in Ptolemaic Egypt*. 1986.

Ptolemaic Egypt: http://www.houseofptolemy.org.

Sherwin-White, Susan, and Amélie Kuhrt. *From Samarkhand to Sardis: A New Approach to the Seleucid Empire*. 1993.

Shipley, Graham. *The Greek World After Alexander 323–30 B.C.* 2000.

Hellenistic Culture, 323–30 B.C.E.

Old scholarship viewed Hellenistic culture as "impure" and less valuable than Classical Age culture because it mixed traditions. Scholars today identify the imaginative ways in which Hellenistic thinkers and artists combined the

---

*Primary source.

old and the new, the familiar and the foreign. Studying Hellenistic philosophers for the intrinsic interest of their ideas has become an important activity in the history of philosophy and ethics.

Ancient Alexandria in Egypt: http://ce.eng.usf.edu/pharos/alexandria.

*Bartlett, John R. *Jews in the Hellenistic World: Josephus, Aristeas, The Sibylline Oracles, Eupolemus.* 1985.

Chamoux, François. *Hellenistic Civilization.* Trans. Michel Roussel. 2003.

Inwood, Brad, ed. *The Cambridge Companion to the Stoics.* 2003.

Long, A. A. *Hellenistic Philosophy: Stoics, Epicureans, Sceptics.* 2nd ed. 1986.

*Menander. *The Plays and Fragments.* Trans. Maurice Balme. 2002.

Mikalson, Jon D. *Religion in Hellenistic Athens.* 1998.

Pollitt, J. J. *Art in the Hellenistic Age.* 1986.

Pomeroy, Sarah B. *Women in Hellenistic Egypt: From Alexander to Cleopatra.* Rev. ed. 1990.

Schäfer, Peter. *Judeophobia: Attitudes toward the Jews in the Ancient World.* 1997.

Sharples, R. W. *Stoics, Epicureans, and Sceptics: An Introduction to Hellenistic Philosophy.* 1996.

Snyder, Jane M. *The Woman and the Lyre: Women Writers in Classical Greece and Rome.* 1989.

Walker, Susan, and Peter Higgs, eds. *Cleopatra of Egypt: From History to Myth.* 2001.

CHAPTER REVIEW

IMPORTANT EVENTS

399 B.C.E.	Trial and execution of Socrates at Athens
C. 393 B.C.E.	Athens's Long Walls rebuilt
386 B.C.E.	Sparta makes a peace with Persia ceding control over the Anatolian Greek city-states; Plato founds the Academy in Athens
371 B.C.E.	Thebes defeats Sparta at the battle of Leuctra in Boeotia
362 B.C.E.	Power vacuum in Greece after the battle of Mantinea in the Peloponnese
338 B.C.E.	Philip II defeats a Greek alliance at the battle of Chaeronea to become the leading power in Greece
335 B.C.E.	Aristotle founds the Lyceum in Athens
334–323 B.C.E.	Alexander the Great leads an army of Greeks and Macedonians in a conquest of the Persian Empire
324 or 323 B.C.E.	The dramatist Menander presents his first comedy at Athens
C. 307 B.C.E.	Epicurus founds his philosophical group "the Garden" in Athens
306–304 B.C.E.	The successors of Alexander declare themselves to be kings
C. 300–260 B.C.E.	Theocritus writes poetry at the Ptolemaic court
C. 300 B.C.E.	Euclid teaches geometry at Alexandria in Egypt
C. 195 B.C.E.	Seleucid queen Laodice endows dowries for girls in Iasus
167 B.C.E.	Maccabee revolt after Antiochus IV converts the Jewish temple in Jerusalem to a Greek sanctuary
30 B.C.E.	Death of Cleopatra VII, queen of Egypt, and takeover of the Ptolemaic empire by Rome

KEY TERMS

dualism (128)

Epicureanism (151)

epigrams (147)

Hellenistic (124)

Koine (155)

materialism (150)

mean (130)

metaphysics (128)

ruler cults (155)

Stoicism (151)

successor kings (139)

REVIEW QUESTIONS

1. What were the major differences between Plato's philosophical ideas and Aristotle's?
2. How did innovation and tradition combine to sustain Macedonia's power during the reigns of Philip II and Alexander the Great?
3. What were the biggest challenges facing the Hellenistic kings?
4. How did the political changes of the Hellenistic period affect art and science?

MAKING CONNECTIONS

1. For people of all social classes, how did life in the Hellenistic kingdoms compare to that in the Greek city-state of the Classical Age?
2. What are the advantages and disadvantages of governmental support of the arts and sciences? Compare such support in the Hellenistic kingdoms to that in the United States today (e.g., through the National Endowment for the Humanities, National Endowment for the Arts, and the National Science Foundation).

FOR FURTHER EXPLORATION

To assess your mastery of the material in this chapter, see the Online Study Guide at **bedfordstmartins.com/hunt**.

To read additional primary-source material from this period, see Chapter 4 in *Sources of The Making of the West*, Second Edition.

The Rise of Rome,
c. 753–44 B.C.E.

THE ROMANS TREASURED LEGENDS describing their state's transformation from a tiny village to a world power. They especially loved stories about their legendary first king, Romulus, famous as a hot-tempered and shrewd leader. According to the legend later called the "Rape of the Sabine♦ Women," Romulus's Rome needed more women to bear children to increase its population and build a strong army. The king therefore begged Rome's neighbors for permission for Romans to marry their women. Everyone turned him down, scorning Rome's poverty and weakness. Enraged, Romulus hatched a plan to use force where diplomacy had failed. Inviting the neighboring Sabines to a religious festival, he had his men kidnap the unmarried women. The Roman kidnappers promptly married the Sabine women, promising to cherish them as beloved wives and new citizens. When the Sabine men attacked Rome to rescue their kin, the women rushed into the midst of the bloody battle, begging their brothers, fathers, and new husbands either to stop slaughtering one another or to kill them to end the war. The men immediately made peace and agreed to merge their populations under Roman rule.

This legend emphasizes that Rome, unlike the city-states of Greece, expanded by absorbing outsiders into its citizen body, sometimes violently, sometimes peacefully. Rome's growth became the ancient world's most dramatic expansion of population and territory, as a people originally housed in a few huts gradually created a state that swallowed up most of Europe, North Africa, Egypt, and the eastern Mediterranean lands. The social, cultural, political, legal, and economic traditions that Roman society and government developed

---

♦**Sabine:** SAY byn

The Wolf Suckling Romulus and Remus
This silver coin, dating from 269–268 B.C.E., belongs to the earliest issues of Roman coinage. A head of the Greek hero Hercules is on the other (front) side, while this side, the reverse, depicts the myth that a she-wolf suckled the twin brothers Romulus and Remus, the offspring of the war god Mars and the future founders of Rome. Romans treasured this story because it implied that Mars loved their city so dearly that he dispatched a wild animal to nurture its founders after a cruel tyrant had forced their mother to abandon the infants. The myth also taught Romans that their state had been born in violence: Romulus killed Remus in an argument over who would lead their new settlement. The word below the picture means "of the Romans." © 2003 The American Numismatic Society. All rights reserved.

163

in ruling this vast area created closer interconnections between its diverse peoples than ever before or since. Unlike the Greeks and Macedonians, the Romans maintained the unity of their state for centuries. Its political longevity meant that Rome deeply affected the course of later Western civilization.

Roman culture sprang from the traditions of ancient Italy's many peoples, but Greek literature, art, and philosophy influenced Rome's culture most of all. Some historians charge that Romans mindlessly took over the older civilization's traditions and changed them only in superficial ways, such as giving Latin names to Greek gods. It is more accurate, however, to think of the cross-cultural contact that so deeply influenced Rome as a kind of competition in innovation between equals rather than as imagining Greek culture to have been "superior" and improving "inferior" Roman culture. Like other ancient peoples, Romans often copied their neighbors, but they adapted whatever they learned to their own purposes and determined their own cultural identity.

The kidnapping legend belongs to Rome's earliest history, when kings ruled (c. 753–509 B.C.E.). Rome's most important history comes afterward, divided into two major periods of about five hundred years each—the republic and the empire. These terms refer only to the system of government in place at the time: under the republic (founded 509 B.C.E.), an oligarchy of the social elite governed; under the empire, monarchs once again ruled. Rome's greatest expansion came during the republic. The confidence that fueled this tremendous growth stemmed from Romans' belief in a divine destiny: the gods willed that the Romans should rule the world by military might and law and improve it through social and moral values. Their unshakable faith that heaven backed them is illustrated by the legend of the Sabine women, in which the earliest Romans used a religious festival as a ruse to commit kidnapping. Their firm belief that values should drive politics showed in their determination to persuade the Sabine women that loyalty and love would wipe out the crime that had forcibly turned them from captives into wives and Romans.

In addition to a determination to establish families, Roman values under the republic emphasized selfless service to the community, individual honor and public status, the importance of the law, and shared decision making. Unfortunately, these values conflicted with one another in the long run. During most of the republic, the conflicts never became fierce enough to threaten Rome's stability. By the first century B.C.E., however, power-hungry leaders such as Sulla and Julius Caesar had plunged Rome into civil war and destroyed the republic by putting their personal ambition before the good of the state.

❖ Roman Social and Religious Traditions

Roman social and religious traditions shaped the history of the Roman republic. Its citizens believed that eternal moral values connected them to one another and required them

◆ **753** Rome's founding as a monarchy		◆ **509** Roman republic established	
		◆ **509–287** Struggle of the orders	
			◆ **451–449** Twelve Tables created
700 B.C.E.	**600 B.C.E.**	**500 B.C.E.**	**400 B.C.E.**
			◆ **396** Defeat of Veii
			◆ **387** Gauls sack Rome

to honor the gods in return for divine support. Hierarchy affected every aspect of their lives: people in all social levels were obligated to patrons or clients; in families, fathers dominated; in religion, the gods' superiority demanded that people pray to them to protect the state and their families.

Roman Moral Values

Roman values involved complex ideas and often overlapped. Most important, they determined relationships with other people and with the gods. Romans guided their lives by the **mos maiorum** (literally, "the way of the elders"), or values handed down from their ancestors. The Romans treasured the antiquity of these values because, for them, *old* equaled "tested by time" whereas *new* implied "dangerous." Roman morality emphasized virtue, faithfulness, and respect; moral conduct earned public respect.

Virtus (literally, "virtue") was a primarily masculine quality comprising courage, strength, and loyalty. It also included wisdom and moral purity, qualities that members of the social elite were expected to display in their public and private lives. In this broader sense, virtus applied to women as well as men. In the second century B.C.E., the Roman poet Lucilius defined it in this way:

> Virtue is to know the human relevance of each thing,
> To know what is humanly right and useful and honorable,
> And what things are good and what are bad, useless, shameful, and dishonorable. . . .
> Virtue is to pay what in reality is owed to honorable status

> To be an enemy and a foe to bad people and bad values
> But a defender of good people and good values. . . .
> And, in addition, virtue is putting the country's interests first,
> Then our parents', with our own interests third and last.

Faithfulness (*fides*, from which our word *fidelity* derives) meant keeping one's obligations no matter the cost, whether the obligation was formal or informal. To fail to meet an obligation was to offend the community and the gods. Faithful women remained virgins before marriage and monogamous afterward. Men demonstrated faithfulness by never breaking their word, paying their debts, and treating everyone with justice—which did not mean treating everyone the same, but rather treating each person appropriately according to whether he or she was an equal, a superior, or an inferior.

Religious activity was a crucial part of faithfulness. Showing devotion to the gods and to one's family was its supreme form. Women and men alike respected the superior authority of the gods and of the elders and ancestors of their families. Performing religious rituals properly and regularly was crucial: Romans believed that they had to worship the gods faithfully and respectfully to maintain the divine favor that protected their community.

Roman values demanded that each person maintain self-control and limit displays of emotion. So strict was this value that not even wives and husbands could kiss in public without seeming emotionally out of control.

◆ 168–149 Cato, *The Origins*

◆ 149–146 Third Punic War

◆ 133 Tiberius Gracchus elected tribune, assassinated

◆ 44 Caesar appointed dictator, assassinated

◆ 49–45 Civil War; Caesar wins

◆ 264–241 First Punic War

300 B.C.E.   **200 B.C.E.**   **100 B.C.E.**

◆ c. 220 Rome controls Italy south of the Po River

◆ 218–201 Second Punic War

◆ 146 Carthage and Corinth destroyed

◆ 91–87 Social War

◆ 60 First Triumvirate

◆ 45–44 Cicero writes on *humanitas*

It also meant that a person should never give up no matter how hard the situation. Persevering and doing one's duty were thus basic Roman values.

The reward for living these values was respect from other people. Women earned respect by bearing legitimate children and educating them morally; their reward was a good reputation among their families and friends. Respected men relied on their reputations to help them win election to government posts. A man of the highest reputation commanded so much respect that others would obey him regardless of whether he held an office with formal power over them. A man with this much prestige was said to enjoy "authority."

The concept of authority based on respect reflected the Roman belief that some people were inherently superior to others; that is, they believed that society should be hierarchical. They therefore divided people up according to status, determined both by the history of their family and their wealth. Romans believed that aristocrats, or people born into the best families, automatically deserved high respect. In compensation, however, aristocrats were supposed to live strictly by the highest values and serve the community.

A Patrician Holding Death Masks of His Ancestors

This marble statue shows an elderly patrician man holding two death masks of his ancestors. It illustrates the Romans' commitment to the *mos maiorum*, the way of the ancestors. The second-century B.C.E. Greek historian Polybius, who learned about Roman customs while living in Rome for seventeen years, explains the use of the masks: "The masks are portraits, carefully made to resemble the dead person in shape and form. Romans display them at public sacrifices, and when a prominent family member dies, they carry them in the funeral procession, having them worn by those who most resemble the dead ancestor in stature and build." This particular version may have been sculpted in the first century C.E., but if so, it was a copy of an earlier statue dating to the republic. Compare its realistic style with that of the relief of an ex-slave family on page 167. *Scala/Art Resource, NY.*

In Roman legends about the early days, a person could be poor and still remain a proud aristocrat. Over time, however, money became overwhelmingly important to the Roman elite, for spending on showy luxuries, large-scale entertaining, and lavish gifts to the community. In this way, wealth became necessary to maintain high social status. By the later centuries of the Roman republic, ambitious men often trampled on other values to acquire riches and the status they now conveyed.

The Patron-Client System

The **patron-client system** provided the legal and moral basis for the status differences so key to Roman society. It was an interlocking network of personal relationships that obligated people to one another. A patron was a man of superior status who could provide benefits, as they were called, to lower-status people who paid him special attention. These were his clients, who in return owed him duties. In this hierarchical system, a patron was often himself the client of a more distinguished man. The Romans called the patron-client relationship a friendship; a patron would greet a social inferior as "my friend," not as "my client." A client, however, would honor his superior by addressing him as "my patron."

Benefits and duties centered on financial and political help to the other party. A patron would help a client get started in a political career by supporting his candidacy and would provide gifts or loans in hard times. A patron's most important obligation was to support a client and his family if they got into legal trouble, such as lawsuits involving property.

Sculpted Tomb of a Family of Ex-Slaves
The inscription on this tomb monument, which may date to the first century B.C.E., reveals that the husband and wife depicted on it started life as slaves but gained their freedom and thus became Roman citizens. Their son, shown in the background holding a pet pigeon, was a free person. One of the remarkable features of Roman civilization, and a source of its demographic strength, was the wholesale incorporation of ex-slaves into the citizen body. This family had done well enough financially to afford a sculpted tomb, and the tablets the man is holding and the carefully groomed hairstyle of the woman are meant to show that their family was literate and stylish. Compare the man's realistically lined face with the woman's softer, more idealized one. *German Archeological Institute/ Madeline Grimoldi.*

Clients had to aid their patrons' campaigns for public office by swinging votes their way. They also had to lend money when patrons serving as officials incurred large expenses to provide public works and fund their daughters' lavish dowries. Furthermore, a patron expected his clients to gather at his house early in the morning to accompany him to the forum, the city's public center, because it was a mark of great status to have numerous clients thronging around him. A Roman leader needed a large, fine house to hold this throng and to entertain his social equals; a crowded house signified social success.

Patrons' and clients' mutual obligations were supposed to endure over generations. Ex-slaves, who automatically became the clients for life of the masters who freed them, often passed this relationship on to their children. Romans with contacts abroad could acquire clients among foreigners; particularly distinguished Romans sometimes had entire foreign communities obligated to them. With its emphasis on duty and permanence, the patron-client system enshrined the Roman view that social stability and well-being were achieved by faithfully maintaining the established ties.

The Roman Family

The family was Roman society's bedrock because it taught values and determined the ownership of property. Men and women shared the duty of teaching their children values, though by law the father possessed the ***patria potestas***✦ (literally, "father's power") over his children, no matter how old, and his slaves. This power made him the sole owner of all his dependents' property. As long as he was alive, no son or daughter could officially own anything, accumulate money, or possess any independent legal standing. Unofficially, however, adult children did acquire personal property and money, and favored slaves could build up savings. Fathers also held legal power of life and death over these members of their households, but they rarely exercised this power on anyone except newborns. Abandoning unwanted babies (a practice called exposure)—so that they would die, be adopted, or be raised by strangers as slaves—was accepted to control the size of families and dispose of physically imperfect infants. Baby girls probably suffered this fate more often

---

✦***patria potestas:*** PAH tree uh   poh TEHS tahs

than boys because a family enhanced its power by investing its resources in its sons.

Since their values had a strong communal aspect, Romans regularly conferred with others to seek consensus on important family issues. Each Roman man had a council, a circle of friends and relatives whom he consulted before making significant decisions. A man contemplating the drastic decision to execute an adult member of his household, for example, would not have made the decision on his own. A father's council would certainly have advised him to think again if he proposed killing his adult son, except for an extremely compelling reason. In a rare instance of the violent exercise of a father's power, one outraged Roman had his son put to death in 63 B.C.E. because the youth had committed treason by joining a conspiracy to overthrow the government.

The patria potestas did not allow a husband to control his wife because "free" marriages—in which the wife formally remained under her father's power as long as the father lived—eventually became the most common. But in the ancient world, few fathers lived long enough to oversee the lives of their married daughters or sons; four out of five parents died before their children reached thirty. A woman without a living father was relatively independent. Legally she needed a male guardian to conduct her business, but guardianship was largely an empty formality by the first century B.C.E. Upper-class women could even on occasion demonstrate to express their opinions. In 195 B.C.E., for example, a group of women blocked Rome's streets for days, until the men rescinded a wartime law meant to reduce tensions between rich and poor by limiting the amount of gold jewelry and fine clothing women could wear and where they could ride in carriages. A later legal expert commented on women's freedom of action: "The common belief, that because of their instability of judgment women are often deceived and that it is only fair to have them controlled by the authority of guardians, seems more false than true. For women of full age manage their affairs themselves."

A Roman woman had to grow up fast to assume her duties as teacher of values to her children and manager of her household's resources. Tullia (c. 79–45 B.C.E.), daughter of the renowned politician and orator Marcus Tullius Cicero♦ (106–43 B.C.E.), was engaged at twelve, married at sixteen, and widowed by twenty-two. Like every other married woman of wealth in Rome, she oversaw the household slaves, monitored the nurturing of the young children by wet nurses, kept account books to track the property she personally owned, and accompanied her husband to dinner parties—something a Greek wife never did.

A mother's responsibility for shaping her children's values constituted the foundation of female virtue in Roman eyes. Women like Cornelia, a famous aristocrat of the second century B.C.E., won enormous respect for their accomplishments in raising outstanding citizens. When her distinguished husband died, Cornelia refused an offer of marriage from the Ptolemaic king of Egypt so that she could continue to oversee the family estate and educate her surviving daughter and two sons. (Her other nine children had died.) The boys, Tiberius♦ and Gaius Sempronius Gracchus,♦ grew up to be among the most influential and controversial political leaders in the late republic. The number of children she bore exemplified the fertility and stamina required of a Roman wife to ensure the survival of her husband's family line. Cornelia also became renowned for entertaining important people and for her stylish letters, which were still being read by the educated public a century later.

Roman women had no official political role, but wealthy women like Cornelia could wield indirect political influence by expressing their opinions privately to their husbands, male children, and other relatives. Marcus Porcius Cato♦ (234–149 B.C.E.), a famous politician and author, described the behind-the-scenes reality of women's influence: "All mankind rule their wives, we [Roman men] rule all mankind, and our wives rule us."

Women helped themselves and their families by accumulating property through in-

---

♦**Cicero** SIH suh roh
♦**Tiberius:** ty BEER ee uhs
♦**Gaius Sempronius Gracchus:** GAY uhs sehm PROH nee uhs GRAK uhs
♦**Porcius Cato:** PAWR key uhs KAY toh

Sculpture of a Woman Running a Store
This relief sculpture portrays a woman selling food from behind the counter of a small shop while customers make purchases or converse with each other. Since Roman women could own property, it is possible that the woman is the store owner. The man immediately to the left, behind the counter, could be her husband or a servant. The market areas in Roman towns were packed with small, family-run stores like this that sold everything imaginable, much like malls of today. Poor people did not own stores; they hawked cheap goods in the street. *Art Resource, NY.*

heritance and entrepreneurship; recent archaeological discoveries reveal that by the end of the republic some women owned large businesses. Most poor women, like poor men, had to toil for a living; often they held small-scale sales jobs, hawking vegetables, amulets, or ribbons from a stand (see illustration on this page). Women and men together performed the predominant form of Roman manufacturing: production in the home. The men worked the raw materials, cutting, fitting, and polishing wood, leather, and metal, while the women sold the finished goods. The poorest women often could earn money through prostitution, which was legal but considered disgraceful. Because both women and men could control property, prenuptial agreements determining the property rights of husband and wife were common. Divorce was legally simple, with fathers usually keeping the children.

Education for Public Life

Roman education aimed to make men and women exponents of traditional values and, for different purposes, effective speakers. As in Greece, most children received their education in the family; only the rich could afford to pay teachers. Wealthy parents bought literate slaves to educate their children; by the late republic, they often chose Greek slaves so that their children could learn to speak Greek and read that culture's literary classics, which most Romans regarded as the world's best. Wealthy parents might also send their children, from about seven years old, to classes offered by independent schoolmasters in their lodgings. Lessons usually consisted of rote memorization, and teachers frequently used corporal punishment to keep pupils attentive. In upper-class families, both daughters and sons learned to read. The girls were also taught literature and perhaps some music; they especially learned how to make educated conversation at dinner parties. The principal aim of women's education was to prepare them to instill traditional social and moral values in their children.

Sons received physical training and learned to fight with weapons—courage being a fundamental value—but the principal aim of a boy's education was to learn rhetoric—the skill of persuasive public speaking. Rhetorical training dominated an upper-class Roman boy's curriculum because it was crucial to a successful public career. A boy would hear rhetoric in action by accompanying his male relatives to public meetings, assemblies, and court sessions. By listening to the speeches, he would learn to imitate winning techniques. Cicero, Rome's most famous orator, agreed that young men must learn to "excel in public speaking. It is the tool for controlling men at Rome, winning them over to your side, and keeping them from harming you. You fully realize your own power when you are a man who can cause your rivals the greatest fears of meeting you in a trial." Wealthy parents paid advanced teachers to instruct their sons in the knowledge an effective speaker required, the same sort of education that the Sophists had offered in Greece. Roman rhetoric owed much to Greek techniques, and many Roman orators studied with Greek teachers. This was only one of the crucial ways in which Greek culture influenced Rome.

Public and Private Religion

Romans also followed Greek models in religion, worshiping many divinities identified with those of Greece. Romans viewed their chief deity, Jupiter, who corresponded to the Greek god Zeus, as a powerful, stern father. Juno (Greek Hera), queen of the gods, and Minerva (Greek Athena), goddess of wisdom, joined Jupiter to form the state religion's central triad. These three deities shared Rome's most revered temple on the Capitoline, the city's acropolis.

Guarding Rome's physical safety and prosperity was the gods' major function. Above all, they were supposed to help Rome defeat enemies in war, but divine support for agriculture was also indispensable. Many official prayers requested the gods' aid in ensuring good crops, warding off disease, and promoting healthy reproduction for animals and people. In times of crisis, Romans even sought foreign gods to protect them, such as when the government imported the cult of the healing god Asclepius from Greece in 293 B.C.E., hoping he would save Rome from a plague. Similarly, the Senate in 204 B.C.E. voted to bring to Rome the pointed black stone representing Cybele♦ ("the Great Mother"), whose chief sanctuary was in Phrygia♦ in Asia Minor (the Roman term for Anatolia). Her cult was believed to promote fertility.

The republic supported many other cults with special guardian features. The shrine of Vesta (Greek Hestia), the goddess of the hearth and therefore a protector of the family, housed Rome's official eternal flame, which guaranteed the state's permanent existence. The Vestal Virgins, six unmarried women sworn to chastity at ages six to ten for terms of thirty years, tended Vesta's shrine. Their chastity symbolized protection of the Roman family structure and thus the preservation of the republic itself. As members of Rome's only female priesthood, the Vestal Virgins earned high status and freedom from their fathers' control by performing their most important duty: keeping the flame from going out. As the Greek historian Dionysius of Halicarnassus♦ reported in the first century B.C.E., "The Romans dread the extinction of the fire above all misfortunes, looking upon it as an omen which portends the destruction of the city." On the rare occasions when the flame went out, the Romans assumed that one of the Vestal Virgins had broken her vow of chastity and buried her alive as the penalty.

Religion occupied a prominent place in Roman family life. Each household maintained a sacred space for small shrines housing statuettes of its Penates♦ (spirits of the household stores) and Lares♦ (spirits of the ancestors), who were believed to keep the family well and its moral traditions alive (see Household Shrine from Pompeii). Upperclass families kept death masks of distinguished ancestors hanging in the main room and wore them at funerals to commemorate the family's heritage and the current generation's responsibility to live up to the ancestors' values. This strong sense of family

---

♦**Cybele:** SIH buh lee
♦**Phrygia:** FRIH jee uh
♦**Dionysius of Halicarnassus:** dy uh NIH see uhs of ha luh kahr NA suhs
♦**Penates:** peh NAY teez
♦**Lares:** LAHR eez

tradition and instruction from parents (especially mothers) underlay Roman morality. The shame of losing public esteem, not the fear of divine punishment, was the strongest deterrent to immoral behavior.

Because Romans believed that divine spirits participated in crucial events such as birth, marriage, and death, they performed many rituals seeking protection from dangers. Rituals also accompanied everyday activities, such as breast-feeding babies or fertilizing crops. Many public religious gatherings promoted the community's health and stability. For example, during the February 15 Lupercalia festival (whose name recalled the wolf, *luper* in Latin, who legend said had reared Romulus and his twin, Remus), naked young men streaked around the Palatine hill, lashing any woman they met with strips of goatskin. Women who had not yet borne children would run out to be struck, believing this would help them to become fertile. The December 17 Saturnalia festival, honoring the Italian deity of liberation, Saturnus, temporarily inverted the social order to release tensions caused by the inequalities between masters and slaves. As the playwright and scholar Accius♦ (c. 170–80 B.C.E.) described the occasion, "People joyfully hold feasts all through the country and the towns, each owner acting as a waiter to his slaves." This social inversion reinforced the slaves' ties to their owners by symbolizing a benefit from the latter, which the former had to repay with faithful service.

Like the Greek gods, Rome's deities had few direct connections with human morality because Roman tradition did not regard the gods as the originators of society's moral code. Cicero's description of Jupiter's official titles explained public religion's closer ties to national security and prosperity than to individual morality: "We call Jupiter the Best *(Optimus)* and Greatest *(Maximus)* not because he makes us just or sober or wise but, rather, healthy, unharmed, rich, and prosperous." In keeping with this belief, Roman officials preceded important actions with the ritual called taking the auspices—seeking Jupiter's approval for their plans by observing natural signs such as the direction of the

Household Shrine from Pompeii
This colorfully painted shrine stood inside the entrance to a house at Pompeii known as the House of the Vettii, from the name of its owners. Successful businessmen, the Vettii spared no expense in decorating their home: with 188 frescoes (paintings done by applying pigments to damp plaster) adorning its walls, the interior blazed in a riot of color. This type of shrine, found in every Roman house, is called a *lararium* after the *lares* (deities protecting the household), who are shown here flanking a central figure. He portrays the spirit *(genius)* of the father of the family. What do you think it signifies that the lares seem to be dancing? The snake below, which is about to drink from a bowl probably holding milk set out for it, also symbolizes a protective force, the good daimon. The whole scene sums up the role Romans expected their gods to play: staving off harm and bad luck. *Scala/Art Resource, NY.*

flights of birds, their eating habits, or the appearance of thunder and lightning. Action proceeded only if the signs were favorable.

Romans linked values and religion by regarding central values as divine forces. *Pietas* (literally, "piety") for example, which meant devotion and duty to family, friends, the state, and the gods, had a temple at Rome. It housed a statue personifying pietas as a female divinity in human form. This personification of abstract moral qualities provided a focus for cult rituals. The religious aura attached to the cults of moral qualities emphasized that they were ideals to which every Roman should aspire.

♦**Accius:** AK key uhs

The duty of Roman religious officials, or priests, was to ensure the gods' goodwill toward the state; this the Romans called *pax deorum* (literally, "peace of or with the gods"). Men from the top of the social hierarchy served as priests by conducting frequent sacrifices, festivals, and other rituals conforming strictly to ancestral tradition. These priests were not professionals devoting their lives solely to religious activity; rather, they were citizens performing public service in keeping with Roman values. The most important official, the *pontifex maximus*♦ (literally, "highest priest"), served as the head of state religion and the ultimate authority on religious matters affecting government. The political powers of this priesthood motivated Rome's most prominent men to seek it.

Disrespect for religious tradition brought punishment. Naval commanders, for example, took the auspices by feeding sacred chickens on their ships: if the birds ate energetically before a battle, Jupiter favored the Romans and an attack could begin. In 249 B.C.E., the commander Publius Claudius Pulcher♦ grew frustrated when his chickens, probably seasick, refused to eat. Determined to attack, he finally hurled the birds overboard in a rage, sputtering, "Well then, let them drink!" When he promptly suffered a huge defeat, he was fined very heavily.

> **Review:** What was the most important common theme in Roman traditional values?

❖ From Monarchy to Republic, c. 753–287 B.C.E.

Rome's communal values provided the unity and stability necessary for its astounding growth from a tiny settlement into the Mediterranean's greatest power. This growth took place over centuries, as the Romans developed the republic's government and expanded their territory and population. Politically, Rome in the eighth through the sixth century B.C.E. adopted the ancient world's most common kind of political system: rule by kings. Disturbed by the later kings' violence, members of the social elite overthrew the monarchy to create a new political system—the republic—which lasted from the fifth through the first century B.C.E. The republic (from the Latin **res publica**, "the people's matter" or "the public business") distributed power more widely by electing officials in open meetings of male citizens. Rome gained land and population by winning aggressive wars and by absorbing other peoples. Its economic and cultural growth depended on contact with many other peoples around the Mediterranean.

Roman Society During the Monarchy, c. 753–509 B.C.E.

Legend taught that Rome's original government had seven kings, ruling in succession from 753 (the most commonly given date for the city's founding) to 509 B.C.E. The kings created Rome's most famous and enduring government body: the Senate, a group of distinguished men chosen as the king's personal council. The Senate helped the king rule in accordance with the Roman principle that important decisions should be thoroughly discussed with one's wisest friends. It played the same role—advising government leaders—for a thousand years, as Rome changed from a monarchy to a republic and back to a monarchy (the empire).

The kings laid the foundation for Rome's expansion by fighting enemies and taking in outsiders whom they conquered, as reflected in the story of Romulus's absorbing the Sabine women and their relatives into the Roman state. This inclusionary policy of making others into citizens, which contrasted sharply with the exclusionary laws of the contemporary Greek city-states, promoted ethnic diversity in early Rome and proved crucial for Rome's tremendous growth in power. Another important part of Roman policy—also different from Greek practice—was to grant citizenship to freed slaves. These freedmen and freedwomen, as they were called, still owed special obligations to their former owners, and they could not hold elective office or serve in the army. In all other

---

♦*pontifex maximus*: PAHN tih fehks MAK sih muhs
♦**Publius Claudius Pulcher:** PUHB lee uhs KLAW dee uhs PUHL kur

ways, however, ex-slaves enjoyed full civil rights, such as legal marriage. Their children possessed citizenship without any limitations. By the late republic, many Roman citizens were descendants of freed slaves.

Expansion and Cross-Cultural Contact. Over the 250 years of the monarchy, Rome's inclusionary policy produced tremendous expansion. By around 550 B.C.E., the Romans controlled three hundred square miles of the area around Rome, called Latium;◆ the tiny original settlement had grown to between thirty and forty thousand people. This growth under the kings foreshadowed Rome's future as a powerful imperialist state.

Rome's geography and contact with other cultures, especially Greek, helped propel its expansion and rise to power. Rome lay at the natural center of both Italy and the Mediterranean world. The historian Livy◆ (59 B.C.E.– 17 C.E.), who became famous for depicting Rome's early history as heroic, summed up the city's geographical advantages: "With reason did gods and men choose this site: all its advantages make it of all places in the world the best for a city destined to grow great." These advantages were fertile farmland, control of a river crossing on the major north–south route along the peninsula, and a nearby harbor on the Mediterranean Sea. Most important, Rome was ideally situated for contact with the outside world: the peninsula it was on stuck so far out into the Mediterranean that east–west traffic naturally encountered it (Map 5.1). The Romans' geographic term for the peninsula, Italia, came from an indigenous word meaning "calf land" and originally designated only the southern portion. Gradually Italia, or Italy, came to mean the entire peninsula south of the Alps.

The early Romans' contact with their diverse neighbors profoundly influenced their cultural development. Their closest neighbors, the people of Latium, were poor villagers like the Romans and spoke the same Indo-European language, an early form of Latin. To the south, however, lived Greeks, and contact with them had the greatest effect

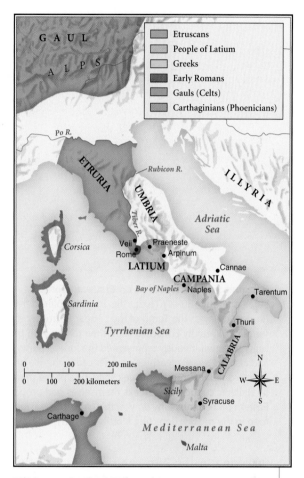

MAP 5.1 Ancient Italy, c. 500 B.C.E.
When the Romans ousted the monarchy to found a republic in 509 B.C.E., they inhabited a relatively small territory in central Italy between the western coast and the mountain range that bisects the peninsula from north to south. Many different peoples lived in Italy at this time, with the most prosperous occupying fertile agricultural land and sheltered harbors on the peninsula's west side. The early republic's most urbanized neighbors were the Etruscans to the north and the Greeks in the city-states to the south, including on the island of Sicily. Immediately adjacent to Rome were the people of Latium, called Latins.

on Roman cultural development. Greeks had established colonies on the Campanian◆ plain as early as the 700s B.C.E. These settlements, such as Naples, grew prosperous and populous thanks to their location in a fertile area and their participation in international trade. Greek culture reached its most famous

◆**Latium:** LAY shee uhm
◆**Livy:** LIH vee

◆**Campanian:** kam PAY ny uhn

Banquet Scene Painted in an Etruscan Tomb
Painted about 480–470 B.C.E., this brightly colored fresco decorated a wall in an Etruscan tomb (known today as the Tomb of the Leopards, from the animals painted just above this scene) at Tarquinia. Wealthy Etruscans filled their tombs with pictures such as these, which, some scholars suggest, simultaneously represented the funeral feasts held to celebrate the life of the dead person and also the social pleasures experienced in this life and expected in the next. Here the banqueters recline on their elbows in Greek style, one of the many ways in which Etruscans were influenced by Hellenic culture. The Greeks themselves had probably adopted their dining customs from Near Eastern precedents. Why do you think the mens' robes are more colorful than those worn by the men in the mosaic depicting Plato's Academy on page 128? *Scala/Art Resource, NY.*

flowering in the fifth century B.C.E., at the time when the Roman republic was just taking shape after the end of the monarchy and centuries before Rome had its own literature, theater, or monumental architecture. Romans developed a love-hate relationship with Greece, admiring its literature and art but despising its lack of military unity. They adopted many elements from Greek culture—from ethical values to deities for their national cults, from the model for their poetry and prose to architectural design and style.

The Etruscans. Cross-cultural influence also flowed to Rome from the Etruscans,◆ a people just to the north. Etruscan culture itself remains poorly known because the language has not yet been fully deciphered. The Etruscans became a prosperous people living in independent towns nestled on central Italian hilltops. Magnificently colored wall paint-

ings, which survive in some of their tombs, portray funeral banquets and games testifying to the splendor of their society (see the illustration on this page). While producing their own fine artwork, jewelry, and sculpture, the Etruscans nevertheless had a passion for importing luxurious objects from Greece and other Mediterranean lands. Most of the intact Greek vases known today, for example, were found in Etruscan tombs.

The Etruscans' international trade encouraged cultural interaction: gold tablets inscribed in Etruscan and Phoenician and discovered in 1964 at the port of Pyrgi◆ (thirty miles northwest of Rome) reveal that in about 500 B.C.E. the Etruscans dedicated a temple to the Phoenician goddess Astarte, whom they had learned about from trade with Carthage. That rich city, founded in western North Africa (modern Tunisia) by Phoenicians about 800 B.C.E., dominated seaborne commerce in the western Mediterranean.

◆**Etruscans:** ih TRUHS kuhns

◆**Pyrgi:** PEER ghee

The relationship between Etruscan and Roman culture remains a controversial topic. Until recently, scholars thought that the Etruscans had a huge influence on early Rome, assuming that the Etruscans conquered Rome and dominated it politically in the sixth century B.C.E. They also thought that the Etruscans were more culturally refined than the early Romans, mainly because archaeologists found so much Greek art at Etruscan sites. In short, they believed the Etruscans completely reshaped Roman culture during a period of supposed domination. New scholarship, however, stresses the Romans' independence in developing their own cultural traditions: they borrowed from the Etruscans, as from the Greeks, whatever appealed to them and revised these borrowings to fit their own circumstances.

Scholars agree that the Romans adopted ceremonial features of Etruscan culture, such as magistrates' elaborate garments, musical instruments, and procedures for religious rituals. The Romans also learned from the Etruscans to divine the will of the gods by looking for clues in the shapes of the vital organs of slaughtered animals. And they may have gotten their tradition of wives joining husbands at dinner parties from the Etruscans.

Other features of Roman culture formerly seen as deriving from Etruscan influence were probably part of the ancient Mediterranean's shared cultural environment. Rome's first political system, monarchy, was widespread in that world. The organization of the Roman army, a citizen militia of heavily armed infantry troops (hoplites) fighting in formation, reflected not just Etruscan precedent but that of many other peoples in the region. The alphabet, which the Romans certainly first learned from the Etruscans and used to write their own language, was actually Greek; the Greeks had gotten it through their contact with the earlier alphabets of eastern Mediterranean peoples. Trade with other areas of the Mediterranean and civil engineering leading to urbanization are other features of Etruscan life that Romans are said to have assimilated, but it is too simplistic to assume that cultural developments of this breadth resulted from one superior culture instructing another, less developed one. Rather, at this time in Mediterranean history, similar cultural developments were under way in many places. The Romans, like so many others, found their own way in navigating through this common cultural sea.

The Early Roman Republic, 509–287 B.C.E.

The Roman social elite's hatred of monarchy motivated the creation of the republic as a new political system. Aristocrats believed that a sole ruler and his family would inevitably become tyrannical and misuse their rule. This belief was enshrined in the most famous legend about the birth of the republic, Livy's story of the rape of Lucretia. Like most of Livy's stories about Roman history, it stressed moral virtue's role in the republic's founding. (See "Livy on Liberty in the Founding of the Roman Republic," page 176.) The end of the monarchy came when King Tarquin♦ the Proud's swaggering son raped Lucretia, a chaste wife in the social elite, to flaunt his superior power. Despite pleas from her husband and father not to blame herself, Lucretia committed suicide after denouncing her attacker and calling Roman women to remain faithful.

Declaring themselves Rome's liberators from tyranny, her relatives and their friends, led by Lucius Junius Brutus,♦ drove out Tarquin in 509 B.C.E. to end royal abuse of power. They then created the republic to ensure the sharing of power. Thereafter, the Romans prided themselves on having created a freer political system than that of many of their neighbors. The legend of the warrior Horatius at the bridge, for example, advertised the republic's dedication to national freedom. As Livy told the story, Horatius single-handedly blocked the Etruscan army's access to Rome over a bridge crossing the Tiber♦ River when they tried to reimpose a king on the city (Map 5.2). While hacking at his opponents, Horatius berated them as slaves who had lost their freedom because they

---

♦**King Tarquin:** [King] TAHR kwihn
♦**Lucius Junius Brutus:** LOO shuhs JOO nyuhs BROOT uhs
♦**Tiber:** TY bur

Livy on Liberty in the Founding of the Roman Republic

The Roman historian Livy, writing in the late first century B.C.E. at the time of Augustus (the first Roman emperor), describes the foundation of the Roman republic in 509 B.C.E. as successful because it did not occur before Rome's early kings had prepared the masses for liberty. Livy dates the first Roman king to 753 B.C.E., which implies that this preparation to live in liberty took two hundred years or more.

From this point I will be writing the history of the Roman people as a liberated people—their deeds in peace and war, their officials elected annually, and their rule of laws with greater power than human beings possessed. The excess pride of Rome's last king [Tarquin the Proud] made their liberty all the more full of joy. The earlier kings had ruled in such a way that they are deservedly counted certainly as founders of parts of the city, which they built as new residences for the population which they added. There is no doubt that the same Brutus who deserves so much glory for having driven out King Tarquin the Proud would have done the worst thing for the Roman people if he had torn away rule from one of the earlier kings through a desire for premature liberty. What would have happened, if that mass of shepherds and immigrants, all renegades from their own peoples and having gained liberty, or at least impunity, under the protection of an inviolable sanctuary, had been released from their fear of royal rule and began to be stirred up by stormy tribunes and instigate political fights with the senators in a city not their own, before their obligations to wives and children and love of the soil itself—which comes about only over a long time—had united their hearts? Their community, not yet grown to adulthood, would have been broken apart by disagreements, the very community that the peaceful moderation of the early kings' rule had fostered and nurtured to the point that with its mature strength it could bear the good fruit of liberty.

Moreover, one may count the origin of liberty as created more by fixing the consuls' term of office at a single year rather than by any lessening of royal authority. The first consuls possessed all the rights and all the insignia [of the kings]. . . . Brutus [one of the first consuls] guarded liberty just as fiercely as he had won it. First of all, while the people were eager for their new liberty, he impelled them to swear an oath that they would never allow anyone to rule Rome as a king, so that later they could not be won over by the pleas or gifts of a [would-be] king. Next, to make the Senate stronger from the number of its members—Tarquin had shrunk it by murdering "Fathers" [senators under the kings]—he filled out its ranks to three hundred by appointing leading men from the equestrian class. It is said that from that time on there was the tradition of convoking the Senate by summoning the "Fathers" and the "Enrolled," the latter being those senators who had been appointed. This proved marvelously positive for the concord of the citizen community and for linking the hearts of the masses to the "Fathers."

Source: Livy, *From the Foundation of the City*, Book 2.1. Translation by Thomas R. Martin.

were ruled by haughty kings. This legend made clear that the compelling reason to found the republic was to prevent monarchy's abuses.

The Struggle of the Orders. The Romans struggled for nearly 250 years to shape a stable government for the republic after its foundation in 509 B.C.E. Roman social hierarchy split the population into two **orders**— the patricians◆ (a small group of the most aristocratic families) and the plebeians◆ (the rest of the citizens). Bitter turmoil over political and legal power pitted the orders against one another in the republic's early centuries; historians call this turmoil the

◆**patricians:** puh TRIH shuhns
◆**plebeians:** plih BEE uhns

struggle of the orders. Finally, in 287 B.C.E., the plebeians forced the patricians to grant them the right to make laws in their own assembly.

Social and economic disputes fueled the struggle. Patricians constituted a tiny percentage of the population—numbering only about 130 families in all—but their inherited status entitled them to control essential religious activities. Soon after the republic's founding they used their religious importance to monopolize political office. In this early period, many patricians were much wealthier than most citizens. Some plebeians, however, were also rich, and they resented the patricians' dominance. They especially hated the patricians' ban on intermarriage with plebeians because it seemed a humiliating assertion of superiority. Patricians enflamed tensions by wearing special red shoes to set themselves apart; later they changed to black shoes adorned with a small metal crescent.

The struggle began when rich plebeians clamored for the right to marry patricians as social equals, while poor plebeians demanded an equitable distribution of farmland and relief from crushing debts. To pressure the patricians, the plebeians periodically left the city for a temporary settlement and then refused military service. This tactic of secession worked because Rome's army depended on plebeian manpower; the patricians were too few to defend Rome by themselves. The patricians therefore agreed to written laws guaranteeing greater equality and social mobility. The earliest Roman law code, the **Twelve Tables** (so named from the bronze tablets on which the laws were engraved for all to see), was enacted between 451 and 449 B.C.E. in response to a secession brought on by a patrician's violence against a plebeian woman. The Tables encapsulated early Rome's prevailing legal customs in simply worded provisions such as "If plaintiff calls defendant to court, he shall go," or "If a wind causes a neighbor's tree to be bent and lean over your farm, action may be taken to have that tree removed." These laws prevented the patrician public officials who judged most legal cases from, as Livy puts it, "arbitrarily giving the force of law to their own preferences." The laws contained in the Twelve Tables became so important a symbol of the commitment to justice for all citizens that

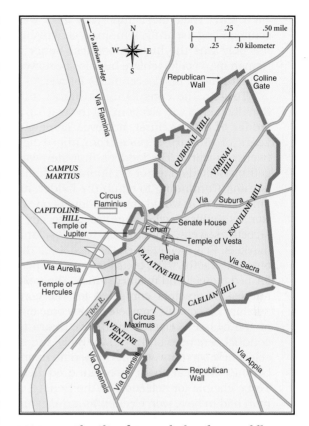

MAP 5.2 The City of Rome during the Republic
Roman tradition said that King Servius Tullius built Rome's first defensive wall in the sixth century B.C.E., but archaeology shows that the first wall completely encircling the city's center and seven hills on the east bank of the Tiber River belongs to the fourth century B.C.E. and covered a circuit of about seven miles. By the second century B.C.E. the wall had been extended to soar fifty-two feet high and had been fitted with catapults to protect the large gates. Like the open agora surrounded by buildings at the heart of a Greek city, the forum remained Rome's political and social heart.

children were required to memorize them. The Roman belief in clear, fair laws as the best protection against social unrest helped keep the republic united until Tiberius and Gaius Gracchus provoked murderous turmoil in the late second century B.C.E.

The Consuls, the Ladder of Offices, and the Senate. Elected officials ran Roman republican government. All posts operated as panels, numbering from two to more than a dozen members, in accordance with the Roman value that rule should be shared. The highest officials were called consuls; two were elected each year. Their most important duty was commanding the army. Winning a consulship not only was the highest political honor a Roman man could achieve but also bestowed high status on his descendants forever.

To gain the consulship, a man traditionally had to win elections all the way up a **ladder of offices**. First, however, came ten years of military service from about age twenty to thirty. The ladder's first step was getting elected quaestor,♦ a financial administrator. Continuing to climb the ladder, an ambitious man would gain election as one of Rome's aediles,♦ who supervised the city's streets, sewers, aqueducts, temples, and markets. Few men reached the next level, the office of praetor.♦ The board of praetors performed judicial and military duties. The most successful praetors competed for the consulship. Ex-consuls competed to become one of the censors, elected every five years to conduct censuses of the citizen body and to select new senators so that the Senate membership stayed at about three hundred men. To be eligible for selection to the Senate, a man had to have won election as a quaestor.

The patricians tried to monopolize the highest offices, but the plebeians resisted fiercely. After violent struggle from about 500 to 450 B.C.E., the plebeians forced the patricians to create a special panel of ten annually elected plebeian officials, called tribunes, whose only responsibility was to stop actions that would harm plebeians and their property. The tribunate did not count as a regular ladder office, and tribunes derived their power from the plebeians' sworn oath to protect them against all attacks. This inviolability, called *sacrosanctity*,♦ gave tribunes veto (a Latin word meaning "forbid") power to block officials' actions, prevent laws from being passed, suspend elections, and—most controversially—contradict the Senate's advice. The tribunes' extraordinary power to veto government action often made them the catalysts for bitter political disputes. By 367 B.C.E., the plebeians had smashed their way into the competition for high public office

♦**quaestor:** KWEH stur
♦**aediles:** EE dials
♦**praetor:** PREE tur
♦**sacrosanctity:** sa kroh SANK tuh tee

by forcing passage of a law requiring that at least one consul every year be a plebeian.

Roman values were supposed to motivate men to compete for high public office to win respect and glory, not money. Only well-off men could run for election because officials earned no salaries. In fact, they were expected to spend their own money lavishly to win popular support by paying for expensive public shows featuring gladiators (trained fighters) and wild beasts, such as lions imported from Africa. Financing such exhibitions could put a candidate deeply in debt. Once elected, a magistrate had to spend his money to subsidize public works, such as roads, aqueducts, and temples.

Early republican officials' only rewards were the esteem they won by service to the res publica. As the Romans gradually conquered more and more overseas territory, however, their desire for money to finance electoral campaigns overcame their emphasis on faithfulness and honesty. By the second century B.C.E., military officers enriched themselves not only legally by seizing booty from foreign enemies but also illegally by extorting bribes as administrators of newly conquered territories. Over time, acquiring money became more important than winning respect by upright public service.

The Senate under the republic retained the role it had enjoyed under the monarchy: shaping government policy by giving advice to its highest officials. Strictly speaking, the Senate did not make law. The senators' high social standing gave their opinions the moral force of law, however. If a consul rejected or ignored the Senate's advice, a political crisis ensued. The Senate thus guided the republic in every area: decisions on war, domestic and foreign policy, state finance, official religion, and all types of legislation. In keeping with the Roman tradition that status should be visible, the senators wore special black high-top shoes and robes embroidered with a broad purple stripe.

The Assemblies.   Male citizens meeting in a complicated system of differing assemblies officially determined legislation, government policy, election outcomes, and judgment in certain trials. Assemblies met outdoors and were only for voting, not discussion; a public gathering with speeches by leading men about the issues preceded every assembly. Everyone, including women and noncitizens, could listen to these speeches. The crowd expressed its agreement or disagreement with the speeches by applauding or hissing. Speakers therefore heard public opinion while forming the proposals that they put before the assemblies, which gave a small measure of democracy to the republic's oligarchic government. This was the extent of what some historians call the republic's mixed constitution. A significant restriction on democracy in the assemblies, however, was that voting took place by group, not individuals. Each assembly was divided into different groups, whose size was determined by status and wealth; a small group had the same vote as a large group.

The struggle of the orders led to a complex organization of the assemblies. Legend dated the earliest major one, the Centuriate Assembly, to the sixth century B.C.E., under the reign of Servius Tullius, Rome's fifth king. Its division into voting groups matched the army's organization and stuck the huge group of people too poor to afford military weapons, the **proletarians**,♦ into one group exercising only 1 vote out of the total of 193 votes. The groups of patricians and richer citizens therefore dominated this assembly. Conducting the elections for consuls and praetors became its main function.

To counterbalance the Centuriate Assembly, the plebeians in the fifth century B.C.E. created the Plebeian Assembly, which excluded patricians, divided plebeians into thirty-five groups according to where they lived, and elected tribunes. As plebeians gradually prevailed in the struggle of the orders, their assembly became more important; in 287 B.C.E., its resolutions, called *plebiscites*, became legally binding on all Romans. Soon after the Plebeian Assembly emerged, the Tribal Assembly was created to mix patricians with plebeians in voting groups according to where they lived. This assembly, in which plebeians greatly outnumbered patricians, eventually became the republic's most important institution for making policy, passing laws, and, until separate courts were created, conducting judicial trials.

♦**proletarians:** proh luh TEHR ee uhns

The Judicial System. The republic's judicial system developed slowly and with overlapping institutions. The praetors originally decided many legal cases, after listening to advice from their personal council; especially serious trials could be transferred to the assemblies. A separate jury system arose only in the second century B.C.E., and senators repeatedly clashed with other upper-class Romans over whether these juries should be manned only by Senate members.

As in Greece, Rome had no state-sponsored prosecutors or defenders. Accusers and accused had to speak for themselves in court or have friends speak for them. People of lower social status suffered a distinct disadvantage if they lacked a distinguished patron to plead their case. Priests dominated in legal knowledge procedures until the third century B.C.E. At that time, senators with legal expertise began to play a central role. Called jurists (from the Latin *juris*, "of the law"), they operated as private citizens, not as officials, in offering legal advice. Jurists' importance in the republican judicial system reflected the Roman tradition of consulting one's council in making decisions. Romans had a simple criminal law, but they formulated sophisticated civil law to regulate disputes over property and personal interests. Developed over centuries and gradually incorporating laws from other peoples, Roman civil law became the basis for many Western legal codes still in use today.

The republic's jumbled network of political and judicial institutions evolved in response to conflicts over power. Many different political bodies enacted laws, and legal cases could be decided in various ways. Rome had no highest judicial authority, such as the U.S. Supreme Court, to settle disputes about conflicting laws or controversial cases. The republic's stability therefore depended on a reverence for the mos maiorum. This tradition ensured that the most socially prominent and richest Romans dominated government and society—because they defined the way of the elders.

Review: Disputes over what issues fueled the struggle of the orders?

❖ Roman Imperialism and Its Consequences, Fifth to First Centuries B.C.E.

Expansion through war made conquest and military service central to Romans' lives. During the fifth, fourth, and third centuries B.C.E., the Romans fought war after war in Italy until they became the most powerful state on the peninsula. In the third and second centuries B.C.E., they also warred far from home in all directions, above all against Carthage to the south. Their success in these campaigns made Rome the premier power in the Mediterranean by the first century B.C.E.

Fear and the desire for wealth propelled Roman imperialism under the republic. The senators' worries about national security made them recommend preemptive attacks against foreign peoples they thought might attack Rome, while everyone longed to capture riches through conquest. Poorer soldiers hoped to pull their families out of poverty; the elite, who commanded the armies, expected to promote their chances for office by acquiring glory and greater wealth.

Nearly constant warfare in Italy and abroad transformed Roman life. Culturally, the contact with others that conquest brought stimulated the first Roman history and poetry; astonishingly, Rome had no literature until around 240 B.C.E. War's harsh reality also deeply influenced Roman art, especially portraiture. On the social side, endless military service away from home created stresses on small farmers and undermined the stability of Roman society; so, too, did the importation of huge numbers of war captives to work as slaves on rich people's estates. Rome's great victories in the third and second centuries B.C.E. thus turned out to be a two-edged sword: they brought expansion and wealth, but their unexpected social and political consequences disrupted traditional values and the community's stability.

Expansion in Italy, c. 500–c. 220 B.C.E.

The Romans believed they were successful militarily because they respected the gods' will. Cicero claimed, "We have overcome all the nations of the world, because we have realized that the world is directed and governed by the gods." Believing that the gods supported defensive wars as just, the Romans always insisted they fought only in self-defense, even when they attacked first.

After defeating their Latin neighbors in the 490s B.C.E., the Romans spent the next hundred years warring with the Etruscan town of Veii,♦ a few miles north of the Tiber River. Their 396 B.C.E. victory doubled Roman territory. By the fourth century B.C.E., the Roman infantry legion of five thousand men had surpassed the Greek and Macedonian phalanx as an effective fighting force. A devastating sack of Rome in 387 B.C.E. by marauding Gauls (Celts) from beyond the Alps proved only a temporary military setback, though it made Romans forever fearful of foreign invasion. By around 220 B.C.E., Rome controlled all of Italy south of the Po River.

The Romans combined brutality with diplomacy to control conquered people and territory. Sometimes they enslaved the defeated or forced them to surrender large parcels of land. Other times they struck generous peace terms with former enemies. Some defeated Italians immediately became Roman citizens, others gained limited citizenship without the right to vote, and still other communities received treaties of alliance. No conquered Italian peoples had to pay taxes to Rome. All, however, had to render military aid in future wars, for which they received a share of the booty, chiefly slaves and land, from victorious campaigns against a new crop of enemies. In this way, the Romans co-opted their former opponents by making them partners in the spoils of conquest, an arrangement that in turn enhanced Rome's wealth and authority.

Rome and Central Italy, Fifth Century B.C.E.

♦**Veii:** VAY

Aqueduct at Nîmes♦ in France
Like the Greeks, the Romans met the challenge of supplying drinkable water to towns by constructing aqueducts; they excelled at building complex delivery systems of tunnels, channels, bridges, and fountains to transport it from far away. Compare the Greek city fountain shown in the vase painting on page 125. One of the best-preserved sections of a major aqueduct is the so-called Pont-du-Gard near Nîmes♦ (ancient Nemausus) in France, erected in the late first century B.C.E. to serve the flourishing town there. Built of stones fitted together without clamps or mortar, the span soars 160 feet high and 875 feet long, carrying water along its topmost level from thirty-five miles away in a channel constructed to fall only one foot in height for every three thousand feet in length so that the flow would remain steady but gentle. What sort of social and political organization would be necessary to construct such a system? **For more help analyzing this image**, see the visual activity for this chapter in the Online Study Guide at **bedfordstmartins.com/hunt**.
Hubertus Kanus/Photo Researchers, Inc.

To buttress homeland security, the Romans planted colonies of citizens and constructed roads up and down the peninsula to allow troops to march faster. By connecting Italy's diverse peoples, these roads hastened the creation of a more unified culture dominated by Rome. Latin became the common language, although local tongues lived on, especially Greek in the south. The wealth captured in the first two centuries of expansion attracted hordes of people to the capital because it financed new aqueducts to provide fresh, running water—a treasure in the ancient world—and a massive building program that employed the poor. By 300 B.C.E., about 150,000 people lived within Rome's walls. Outside the city, around 750,000 free Roman citizens inhabited various parts of Italy on land taken from local peoples. Much conquered territory was declared public land, open to any Roman for grazing cattle.

Rich patricians and plebeians cooperated to exploit the expanding Roman territories; the old distinction between the orders had become largely a technicality. This merged elite derived its wealth mainly from agricultural land and plunder acquired during military service. Since Rome levied no regular income or inheritance taxes, families could pass down this wealth from generation to generation. Those who at some point had

Roman Roads, c. 110 B.C.E.

♦**Nîmes:** neem

a consul in the family enjoyed the highest status. They called themselves the nobles to set themselves apart from the rest of the elite.

Wars with Carthage and in the East, 264–121 B.C.E.

Since most of Rome's leaders, remembering the Gauls' attack, feared foreign invasions and also saw imperialism as the route to riches, it is hardly surprising that the republic fought its three most famous wars against the wealthy city of Carthage in North Africa. Governed, like Rome, as a republic, by the third century B.C.E. Carthage controlled an empire encompassing the northwest African coast, part of Libya, Sardinia, Corsica, Malta, and the southern portion of Spain. Geography decreed that an expansionist Rome would sooner or later infringe on Carthage's interests, which depended on the sea. The Carthaginians♦ possessed a large fleet but had to hire mercenaries to field a strong infantry. To Romans, Carthage seemed both a dangerous rival and a fine prize because it had grown so prosperous from agriculture and international trade. Roman hostility was also fueled by horror at the Carthaginian tradition of incinerating infants in the belief it would placate their gods in times of trouble.

First Wars Abroad.   A coincidence finally ignited conflict with Carthage, drawing Roman troops outside Italy for the first time; the three wars that ensued are called the Punic Wars, from the Roman term for Phoenicians, *Punici*. The First Punic War (264–241 B.C.E.) exploded when a desperate band of mercenaries in Messana at Sicily's northeastern tip appealed both to Rome and Carthage to aid them against their enemies. Both states sent troops. The Carthaginians wanted to protect their revenue from Sicilian trade; the Romans wanted to keep Carthaginian troops from moving close to their territory and to acquire war spoils. The Roman and Carthaginian forces clashed, starting a war that lasted a generation. Its bloody battles revealed why the Romans won wars: the Italian population provided deep manpower re-

serves, and the Roman government was prepared to sacrifice as many troops, spend as much money, and fight as long as it took to prevail. Previously unskilled at naval warfare, the Romans expended vast sums to build warships to combat Carthage's experienced navy; they lost more than five hundred ships and 250,000 men while learning how to win at sea. (See "Taking Measure," opposite.)

The Romans' victory in the First Punic War made them masters of Sicily, where they set up their first province (a foreign territory ruled and taxed by Roman officials). This innovation proved so profitable that they soon seized the islands of Sardinia and Corsica from the Carthaginians to create another province. These first successful foreign conquests whetted their appetite for more (Map 5.3). Fearing a renewal of Carthage's power, they cemented alliances with local peoples in Spain, where the Carthaginians were expanding from their southern trading posts.

A Roman ultimatum forbidding further expansion convinced the Carthaginians that another war was inevitable, so they decided to strike back. In the Second Punic War (218–201 B.C.E.), the daring Carthaginian general Hannibal (247–182 B.C.E.) astonished the Romans by marching troops and war elephants from Carthaginian territory in Spain over the snowy Alps into Italy. Slaughtering more than thirty thousand at Cannae in 216 B.C.E. in the bloodiest Roman loss ever, Hannibal tried to convince Rome's Italian allies to desert. But disastrously for him, most Italians remained loyal to Rome. His alliance in 215 B.C.E. with King Philip V of Macedonia (238–179 B.C.E.) forced the Romans to fight on a second front in Greece, but they refused to crack despite Hannibal's ravaging Italy from 218 to 203 B.C.E. The Romans finally won by turning the tables: invading the Carthaginians' homeland, the Roman general Scipio crushed them at the battle of Zama♦ in 202 B.C.E. and was dubbed "Africanus" to commemorate the victory. The Senate imposed a punishing settlement on the enemy in 201 B.C.E., forcing Carthage to scuttle its navy, pay huge war indemnities scheduled to last fifty years, and hand over its lucrative

---

♦**Carthaginians:** kahr thuh JIH nyuhns

♦**Zama:** ZAH muh

TAKING MEASURE

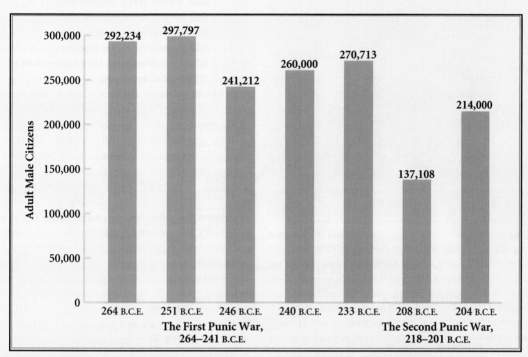

Census Records of Adult Male Roman Citizens during the First and Second Punic Wars
Livy (59 B.C.E.–17 C.E.) and Jerome (c. 347–420 C.E.) provide these numbers from Rome's censuses, which counted only adult male citizens (the men eligible for Rome's regular army), conducted during and between the first two wars against Carthage. The drop in the total for 246 B.C.E., compared with the total for 264 B.C.E., reflects losses in the First Punic War. The low total for 208 B.C.E. reflects both losses in battle and defections of citizenship-holding communities such as Capua in 216 B.C.E. Since the census did not include the Italian allies fighting on Rome's side, the census numbers understate the wars' total casualties; scholars estimate that they took the lives of nearly a third of Italy's adult male population, which would have meant perhaps a quarter of a million soldiers killed. *Tenney Frank,* An Economic Survey of Ancient Rome, *Vol. I (New York: Farrar, Straus, and Giroux, 1959), 56.*

holdings in Spain, which Rome made into provinces prosperous from their mines.

Dominance in the Mediterranean. The Third Punic War (149–146 B.C.E.) began when the Carthaginians, who had revived financially, retaliated against the aggression of their neighbor, the Numidian king Masinissa, who was a Roman ally. After winning the war, the Romans heeded the crusty senator Cato's repeated opinion, "Carthage must be destroyed!" They razed the city and converted its territory into a province. This dis-

aster did not obliterate Punic culture, however, and under the Roman empire this part of North Africa flourished economically and intellectually, displaying a synthesis of Roman and Punic traditions.

The Punic War victories extended Roman power beyond Spain and North Africa to Macedonia, Greece, and western Asia Minor. King Philip's alliance with Hannibal had brought Roman troops east of Italy for the first time. After thrashing Philip for revenge and to prevent any threat of his invading Italy, the Roman commander Flamininus

COMPARISON OF ANCIENT GREEK AND ROMAN DEVELOPMENTS, C. 750 B.C.E. – 146 B.C.E.

	GREECE	ROME
C. 750 B.C.E.	Polis begins to develop	
C. 750-700 B.C.E.	First Greek poetry (Homer and Hesiod)	
753 B.C.E.		Traditional date for the founding of Rome
509 B.C.E.		Overthrow of monarchy and establishment of the republic
508-c. 500 B.C.E.	Cleisthenes's reforms to strengthen Athenian democracy	
C. 500-c. 450 B.C.E.		Struggle to establish office of tribune to protect the people
461 B.C.E.	Ephialtes's reforms to democratize Athens's courts	
451-449 B.C.E.		Rome's first law code established (Twelve Tables)
420s B.C.E.	The first Greek history (Herodotus)	
C. 200 B.C.E.		First Roman history in Greek (Fabius Pictor)
C. 240-c. 210 B.C.E.		First poetry in Latin (Livius Andronicus's translation of Homer's Odyssey)
168-149 B.C.E.		First Roman history in Latin (Cato)
146 B.C.E.	Greece forced to become a Roman province	

Hellenistic Greek authors inspired Catullus◆ (c. 84–54 B.C.E.) to write witty poems that savaged prominent politicians for their sexual behavior and lamented his own disastrous love life. His most famous series of love poems detailed his passion for a married woman named Lesbia, whom he begged to think only of immediate pleasures:

◆**Catullus:** kuh TUH luhs

> Let us live, my Lesbia, and love;
>   the gossip of stern old men is not worth a cent.
> Suns can set and rise again;
>   we, when once our brief light has set,
>   must sleep one never-ending night.
> Give me a thousand kisses, then a hundred,
>   then a thousand more.

The great orator Cicero wrote speeches, letters, and treatises on political science, philosophy, ethics, and theology building on Greek philosophy. He adapted Hellenic ideas to Roman life and infused his writings with an appreciation of each human personality's uniqueness. His doctrine of **humanitas** (literally, "humanness, the quality of humanity") combined various strands of Greek philosophy, especially Stoicism, to express an ideal for human life based on generous and honest treatment of others and a commitment to morality based on natural law (the inherent rights of all people, independent of the differing laws and customs of different societies). The spirit of humanitas that he passed on to later ages was one of the ancient world's most attractive ideals.

Realistic Portraiture. Greece also influenced Rome's art and architecture, from the style of sculpture and painting to the design of public buildings. Romans adapted Greek models to their own purposes, as portrait sculpture reveals. Hellenistic sculptors had pioneered a realistic style showing the ravages of age and infirmity on the human body. They portrayed only stereotypes, however, such as the "old man" or the "drunken woman," not specific people. Individual portrait sculpture presented actual individuals in the best possible light, much like a retouched photograph today.

Roman artists in the later republic applied Greek realism to male portraiture, as contemporary Etruscan sculptors also did. They sculpted men without hiding their unflattering features: long noses, receding chins, deep wrinkles, bald heads, careworn looks. Portraits of women, by contrast, were more idealized, probably representing the traditional vision of the bliss of family life (see the image of the sculpted family tomb on page 167). Portraits of children were uncommon during the republic, perhaps because offspring were not seen as contributing to public life until they were grown. Because the men depicted in the portraits (or their families) paid for the busts, they must have wanted their faces sculpted realistically—showing the toll of age and effort—to emphasize how hard they had worked to serve the res publica.

Stresses on Republican Society, Third and Second Centuries B.C.E.

The republic faced grave social and economic difficulties when the successful wars of the third and second centuries B.C.E. produced disastrous side effects on small farmers. The long deployments abroad disrupted Rome's agricultural system, the economy's foundation. Before this time, Roman warfare had followed a pattern of short campaigns timed not to interfere with the fluctuating labor needs of farming. Now, however, a farmer absent on protracted military service had two unhappy choices: rely on a hired hand or slave to manage his crops and animals, or have his wife work in the fields in addition to her usual domestic tasks.

The story of the consul Regulus,♦ who led a Roman army to victory in Africa in 256 B.C.E., revealed the severe problems a man's prolonged absence could cause. When the man who managed Regulus's 4⅓-acre farm died while the consul was away fighting Carthage, a hired hand stole all the farm's tools and livestock. Regulus implored the Senate to send a general to replace him so that he could return home to save his wife and children from starving. The senators sent help to preserve Regulus's family and property because they wanted to keep him in the field, but ordinary soldiers' families could expect no such rescue. The republic's unceasing wars caused many of them to face disaster.

The Poor.   These troubles hit poor farmers particularly hard. When their families fell into debt, they were forced to sell their only source of income—their farmland. Not all regions of Italy suffered as severely as others, and some impoverished farmers managed to stay in the countryside by working as day laborers for others. Many ruined families, however, migrated to Rome, where the men looked for work as menial laborers and the

women did piecework making cloth—or became prostitutes.

This influx of desperate people swelled the poverty-level population at Rome, and the landless poor became an explosive element in Roman politics. They backed any politician who promised to address their need for food, and the government had to feed them to avert riots. Like Athens in the fifth century B.C.E., Rome by the late second century B.C.E. needed to import grain to feed its swollen urban population. The poor's demand for low-priced (and eventually free) food distributed at state expense became one of the most contentious issues in late republican politics.

The Rich.   Rome's elite reaped rich political and material rewards from imperialism. The increased need for commanders to lead military campaigns abroad created opportunities for successful generals to enrich themselves and their families. By using their gains to finance public works and services, the elite enhanced their reputations by benefiting the general population. Building new temples, for example, was thought to increase everyone's security because the Romans believed it pleased their gods to have many shrines. In 146 B.C.E., the victorious general Caecilius Metellus paid for Rome's first marble temple, finally bringing this Greek style to the capital city.

The economic distress plaguing farmers in Italy suited rich landowners because they could buy bankrupt small farms to create large estates. They further increased their holdings by illegally occupying public land carved out of the territory seized from defeated enemies. The rich worked their huge farms, called **latifundia,**♦ with slaves as well as free laborers. They had a ready supply of slaves in the huge number of captives taken in the same wars that displaced Italy's small farmers; as it turned out, the victories won by free but poor Roman soldiers created a slave workforce with which the poor could not compete. The growing size of the slave crews working on latifundia was a mixed blessing for their wealthy owners because the presence of so many slave workers in one place led to periodic revolts that required military intervention.

♦**Regulus:** REH gyuh luhs

♦**latifundia:** la tuh FUHN dee uh

Mosaic of the Riches of the Sea
Created in Pompeii about 100 B.C.E., this colorful mosaic was typical of the kind of exuberant decoration that Romans liked in their houses. It depicts the wide range of seafood popular at banquets in seaside towns like Pompeii. The details of the creatures shown, from fish to cephalopods to a spiny lobster, are accurate enough for scientists to identify their species. Super-wealthy Romans spent huge sums to build artificial salt-water ponds to raise favorite varieties of fish and eels to impress their guests at dinner parties. *Alinari/Art Resource, NY.*

The elite profited from Rome's expansion because they filled the governing offices in the new provinces and could get much richer than they already were if they ruled corruptly. Since provincial officials ruled by martial law, no one in the provinces could curb a greedy governor's appetite for graft, extortion, and plunder. Some governors ruled honestly, but others used their unsupervised power to squeeze all they could from the provincials. Often such offenders faced no punishment because their colleagues in the Senate excused one another's crimes.

The new opportunities for rich living strained the traditional values of moderation and frugality. Previously, a man like

Manius Curius◆ (d. 270 B.C.E.) became legendary for his life's simplicity: despite glorious military victories, he boiled turnips for his meals in a humble hut. Now, in the second century B.C.E., the elite acquired showy luxuries, such as large country villas for entertaining friends and clients. Money had become more valuable to them than the ancestral values of the res publica.

> **Review:** What were the unintended consequences of Rome's victories over foreign peoples?

❖ Upheaval in the Late Republic, c. 133–44 B.C.E.

In the late republic some ambitious members of the Roman elite set the republic on the road to war with itself by placing their own interests ahead of traditional communal values. When Tiberius and Gaius Gracchus used their powers as tribunes to agitate for reforms to help small farmers, the backbone of the army, the brothers' opponents in the Senate resorted to murder to curb them. When a would-be member of the elite, Gaius Marius,◆ opened military service to the poor to boost his personal status, his creation of "client armies" undermined faithfulness to the general good of the community. When the people's unwillingness to share citizenship with Italian allies sparked a war in Roman territory and then the clashing ambitions of the "great men" Sulla, Pompey, and Julius Caesar burst into civil war, the republic fractured, never to recover.

The Gracchi and Factional Politics, 133–121 B.C.E.

The upper-class brothers Tiberius and Gaius Sempronius Gracchus based their political careers on pushing the rich to make concessions to strengthen the state. They came from the acme of Roman society: their grandfather was the Scipio who had defeated Hannibal, and their mother was the Cornelia whom

---

◆**Manius Curius:** MAH nee uhs KOOR ee uhs
◆**Gaius Marius:** GAY uhs MAR ee uhs

the Ptolemaic king of Egypt had courted after their father died. Their policies supporting the poor angered many of their fellow elite. Tiberius, the older of the Gracchi (the plural of Gracchus), eloquently dramatized the tragic circumstances that motivated them politically, according to the biographer Plutarch (c. 50–120 C.E.):

> The wild beasts that roam over Italy have their dens. . . . But the men who fight and die for Italy enjoy nothing but the air and light; without house or home they wander about with their wives and children. . . . They fight and die to protect the wealth and luxury of others; they are styled masters of the world, and have not a clod of earth they call their own.

When Tiberius won election as a tribune in 133 B.C.E., his opponents blocked his attempts at reform. He therefore took the radical step of disregarding the Senate's advice by having the plebeian assembly pass reform laws to redistribute public land to landless Romans. He further broke with tradition by circumventing the senators to finance his agrarian reform: before they could decide whether to accept the king of Pergamum's bequest of his kingdom, Tiberius had the people pass a law to use the gift to equip new farms on the redistributed land.

Tiberius then announced he would run for reelection as tribune for the following year, violating the traditional prohibition against consecutive terms. His senatorial opponents boiled over: Tiberius's cousin Scipio Nasica, an ex-consul, led a band of senators and their clients in a sudden attack on him, shouting, "Save the republic." Pulling up their togas over their left arms so they would not trip in a fight, these illustrious Romans clubbed the tribune to death, along with many of his followers. Their assault made murder a political tactic.

Gaius, whom the people elected tribune for 123 B.C.E. and, contrary to tradition, again for the next year, followed his brother's lead by pushing measures that outraged the reactionary members of the elite: more agrarian reform, subsidized prices for grain, public works projects throughout Italy to provide employment for the poor, and colonies abroad with farms for the landless. His most revolutionary measures proposed Roman citizenship for

many Italians and new courts to try senators accused of corruption as provincial governors. The new juries would be manned not by senators but by **equites**✦ (literally, "equestrians" or "knights"). These were landowners who, in the earliest republic, had been what the word suggests—men rich enough to provide horses for cavalry service—but were now wealthy businessmen, whose careers in commerce instead of government set them at odds with senators. Because they did not serve in the Senate, the equites could convict criminal senators free of peer pressure. Gaius's proposal marked the equites' emergence as a political force in Roman politics, to the senators' dismay.

When in 121 B.C.E. the senators blocked Gaius's plans, he assembled an armed group to threaten them. They responded by telling the consuls "to take all measures necessary to defend the republic," meaning the use of force. To escape arrest and certain execution, Gaius had one of his slaves cut his throat; the senators then killed hundreds of his supporters and their servants.

The violence provoked by the Gracchi introduced factions (strongly aggressive interest groups) into Roman politics. From that point on, members of the elite identified themselves either as supporters of the people, the **populares** faction, or supporters of "the best," the **optimates** faction. Some chose a faction from genuine allegiance to its policies; others based their choice on political expediency, supporting whichever side better promoted their own political advancement. The elite's splintering into bitterly hostile factions remained a source of violent conflict until the end of the republic.

Gaius Marius and the Origin of Client Armies, 107–100 B.C.E.

The republic needed imaginative commanders to combat slave revolts and foreign invasions in the late second and early first centuries B.C.E. A new kind of leader arose to meet this need: the upper-class man without a consul among his ancestors, who relied on sheer ability to force his way to fame, fortune, and—his ultimate goal—the consulship. Called new men, these leaders challenged the nobles' political dominance.

✦**equites:** EHK wih tehs

Polybius on Roman Military Discipline in the Republic

In Histories, *Polybius, a Greek military officer of the second century* B.C.E. *who spent years on campaign with Roman armies, describes the ideal centurion— an experienced soldier appointed to discipline the troops—and the importance of harsh punishments and the fear of disgrace for maintaining discipline.*

The Romans want centurions not so much to be bold and eager to take risks but rather to be capable of leadership and steady and solid in character. Nor do they want them to initiate attacks and precipitate battle. They want men who will hold their position and stay in place even when they are losing the battle and will die to hold their ground. . . . Soldiers [convicted of neglecting sentry duty] who manage to live [after being beaten or stoned as punishment] don't thereby secure their safety. How could they? For they are not permitted to return to their homeland, and none of their relatives would dare to accept such a man into their households. For this reason men who have once fallen into this misfortune are completely ruined. . . . Even when clearly at risk of being wiped out by enormously superior enemy forces, troops in tactical reserve units are not willing to desert their places in the battle line, for fear of the punishment that would be inflicted by their own side. Some men who have lost a shield or sword or another part of their arms in battle heedlessly throw themselves against the enemy, hoping either to recover what they lost, or to escape the inevitable disgrace and the insults of their relatives by suffering [injury or death].

Source: Polybius, *Histories*, Book 6.24, 37. Translation by Thomas R. Martin.

Gaius Marius (c. 157–86 B.C.E.) set the pattern for this new kind of leader. He came from the equites class in Arpinum in central Italy. Ordinarily, a man of Marius's status had no chance to crack the ranks of Rome's ruling oligarchy of noble families. Fortunately for Marius, however, Rome at the end of the second century B.C.E. had a pressing need for men who could lead an army to victory. Capitalizing on his military record as a junior officer and on popular dissatisfaction with the nobles' war leadership, Marius won election as one of the consuls for 107 B.C.E. In Roman terms this election made him a new man— that is, the first man in his family's history to become consul. Marius's continuing success as a commander in great crises, first in North Africa and next against German tribes who attacked southern France and then Italy, led the people to elect him consul six times, an unprecedented honor.

Marius's victories led the Senate to vote him a triumph, Rome's ultimate military honor. On the day of his triumph, the successful general rode in a chariot through the streets of Rome. His face was painted red for reasons Romans could no longer remember. Huge crowds cheered him, while his army pricked him with off-color jokes, to ward off the evil eye at this moment of supreme glory. For a similar reason, a slave rode with him to keep whispering in his ear, "Look behind you, and remember that you are a mortal." For a former small-town member of the equites class like Marius to be granted a triumph was a supreme social coup.

Despite his triumph, the optimates faction never accepted Marius because they viewed him as an upstart and a threat to their preeminence. His support came from the common people, whom he had won over with his reform of entrance requirements for the army. Previously, only men with property could enroll as soldiers. Marius opened the ranks even to proletarians, men who owned little or nothing. For them, serving in the army under a successful general meant an opportunity to better their lot by acquiring booty and a grant of land to retire on. (See "Polybius on Roman Military Discipline in the Republic," above.)

Marius's reform changed Roman history by creating armies more loyal to their commander than to the republic. Proletarian troops felt immense goodwill toward a commander who led them to victory and then divided the spoils with them generously. The crowds of poor Roman soldiers thus began to behave like an army of clients following their commander as patron. In keeping with the patron-client system, they supported his personal ambitions. Marius was the first to promote his own career in this way. He lost his political importance after 100 B.C.E. when he was no longer consul and foolishly tried to win favor with the optimates. When commanders after Marius used client armies to advance their political careers more ruthlessly than he had, they accelerated the republic's disintegration.

Sulla and Civil War, 91–78 B.C.E.

An unscrupulous noble named Lucius Cornelius Sulla♦ (c. 138–78 B.C.E.) took advantage of uprisings in Italy and Asia Minor in the early first century B.C.E. to use his client army to seize Rome's highest offices and compel the Senate to support his policies. (See Bust of the General Lucius Cornelius Sulla.) His career revealed the dirty secret of politics in the late republic: traditional values no longer restrained commanders who prized their own advancement and the enrichment of their troops above peace and the good of the community.

The Social War. The uprisings in Italy occurred because Rome's Italian allies mostly lacked Roman citizenship and therefore had no vote in decisions concerning their own interests. They became increasingly unhappy as wealth from conquests piled up in the late republic; their upper classes wanted a greater share of the luxurious prosperity that war had brought the citizen elite. Romans rejected the allies' demand for citizenship, from fear that sharing that status would lessen their economic and political power.

The Italians' discontent finally erupted in 91–87 B.C.E. in the Social War (so named because the Latin word for "ally" is *socius*). Forming a confederacy to fight Rome, the allies demonstrated their commitment by the number of their casualties—300,000 dead. Although Rome's army eventually prevailed, the rebels won the political war: the Romans granted citizenship and the vote to all freeborn peoples in Italy south of the Po River. The Social War's bloodshed therefore reestablished Rome's tradition of strengthening the state by granting citizenship to outsiders. The war's other significant outcome was that Sulla's successful generalship against the allies won him election as consul for 88 B.C.E.

Plunder Abroad and Violence at Home. Sulla gained supreme power by taking advantage of events in Asia Minor in 88 B.C.E., when Mithradates♦ VI (120–63 B.C.E.), king of Pontus on the Black Sea's southern coast, instigated a murderous rebellion against Roman control. The peoples of Asia Minor hated Rome's rapacious tax collectors, who tried to make provincials pay much more than was required. After denouncing the Romans as "the common enemies of all mankind,"

♦**Mithradates:** mihth ruh DAY teez

Bust of the General Lucius Cornelius Sulla
Sulla (c. 138–78 B.C.E.) was the Roman commander who lit the match to the dynamite that was the political situation in the late republic. When he marched on Rome in 88 B.C.E., employing violence against his own countrymen to make the Senate give him the command in Asia Minor, he smashed beyond repair the Roman tradition that leading citizens should put the interests of the commonwealth ahead of their private goals. This bust, now in the Venice Archaeological Museum, is usually identified as Sulla—its harsh gaze at least corresponds to what the ancient sources report of his personality.
Scala/Art Resource, NY.

♦**Lucius Cornelius Sulla:**
LOO shuhs kawr NEEL
eeuhs SULL uh

Mithradates persuaded the locals to kill all the Italians there—tens of thousands of them—in a single day.

As retaliation for this treachery, the Senate advised a military expedition; victory would mean unimaginable booty because Asia Minor held many wealthy cities. Born to a patrician family that had lost much of its status and all of its money, Sulla craved the command against Mithradates. When the Senate gave it to him, his jealous rival Marius, now an old man, immediately connived to have it transferred to himself by plebiscite. Outraged, Sulla marched his client army against Rome itself. All his officers except one deserted him in horror at this unthinkable outrage, but his common soldiers followed him to a man. Neither they nor their commander shrank from starting a civil war. After capturing Rome, Sulla killed or exiled his opponents and let his men rampage through the city. He then led them off to fight Mithradates, ignoring a summons to stand trial and sacking Athens on the way to Asia Minor.

**The Kingdom of Mithradates VI,
c. 88 B.C.E.**

Sulla's ruthless violence only bred more. In Sulla's absence, Marius embarked on his own reign of terror in Rome to try to regain his former preeminence. In 83 B.C.E., Sulla returned after defeating Mithradates, having allowed his soldiers to strip Asia Minor bare. Civil war recommenced for two years until Sulla crushed his Roman enemies and their Italian allies. The climactic battle of the war took place in late 82 B.C.E. before the gates of Rome. An Italian general whipped his troops into a frenzy against Sulla's army by shouting, "The last day is at hand for the Romans! These wolves that have made such ravages upon our liberty will never vanish until we have cut down the forest that harbors them."

This passionate cry for freedom failed to carry the day. Sulla won and proceeded to exterminate everyone who had opposed him. To speed the process, he devised a horrific procedure called **proscription**—posting a list of those supposedly guilty of treasonable crimes so that anyone could hunt them down and execute them. (See "Contrasting Views," page 194.) Because proscribed men's property was confiscated, the victors fraudulently added to the list anyone's name whose wealth they coveted. The terrorized Senate appointed Sulla dictator—an emergency office supposed to be held only temporarily—without any limitation of term. He used the office to reorganize the government in the interest of the optimates—his social class—by making senators the only ones allowed to judge cases against their colleagues and forbidding tribunes to sponsor legislation or hold any other office after their term.

The Effects of Sulla's Career. Convinced by a prophecy that he would die soon, Sulla surprised everyone by retiring to private life in 79 B.C.E. and indeed dying in 78 B.C.E. His murderous career had uncovered the strengths and weaknesses of the republic's values. First, success in war had long ago changed its meaning from defense of the community to acquiring profits for common soldiers and commanders alike. Second, the patron-client system and its promise of material rewards led poor soldiers to feel stronger ties of obligation to their generals than to the republic.

Finally, the traditional desire to achieve status worked both for and against political stability. When that value motivated men to seek office to promote the community's welfare—the traditional ideal of a public career—it exerted a powerful force for social unity and prosperity. But pushed to its extreme, as in the case of Sulla, the drive for prestige and wealth could overshadow all considerations of public service. Sulla in 88 B.C.E. could not bear to lose the personal glory that a victory over Mithradates would bring, preferring to initiate a civil war rather than to see his status diminished.

The republic was doomed once its leaders and its followers forsook the mos maiorum, which had emphasized respect for the peace, prosperity, and traditions of the republic above personal gain. Sulla's career reveals that the republic's traditional values were not enough by themselves to restrain violently ambitious leaders who lusted after a dictator's power.

The Republic's Downfall, 83–44 B.C.E.

Powerful generals after Sulla took him as their model: while professing allegiance to the state, they ruthlessly pursued their own advancement. Their reasoning—that a Roman noble could never have too much glory or too much wealth—was a corruption of the republic's ancient values. Two Roman nobles' competition for power and money flared into a brutal civil war that ruined the republic and opened the way for the return of monarchy after an absence of nearly five hundred years. Those nobles were Pompey and Caesar.

Pompey's Irregular Career.   The career of Gnaeus Pompey♦ (106–48 B.C.E.) reveals how the traditional restraints on an individual's power ceased operating in the first century B.C.E. At twenty-three years old, Pompey gathered a private army from his father's clients to win victories for Sulla in the civil war in 83 B.C.E. So frightening was Pompey's power that Sulla could not refuse his astonishing demand for a triumph. Awarding the supreme honor to such a young man, who had held not a single public office, shattered the republic's ancient traditions. But as Pompey told Sulla, "People worship the rising, not the setting, sun."

In 71 B.C.E. Pompey won the final victories over a massive slave rebellion led by a fugitive gladiator named Spartacus, stealing the glory from the real victor, Marcus Licinius Crassus♦ (c. 115–53 B.C.E.). (For two years, Spartacus had terrorized southern Italy and defeated consuls with his army of 100,000 escaped slaves.) Pompey demanded and won election to the consulship in 70 B.C.E., years before he had reached the legal age of forty-two or even won any other office. Three years later, he received a command with unlimited powers to exterminate the pirates then infesting the Mediterranean, a task he accomplished in a matter of months. This success made him wildly popular with the urban poor, who depended on a steady flow of imported grain; with the wealthy commercial and shipping interests, which depended on safe sea lanes; and with coastal communities that had suffered from the pirates' raids. In 66 B.C.E., he defeated Mithradates, who was still stirring up trouble in Asia Minor. By annexing Syria as a province in 64 B.C.E., Pompey ended the Seleucid kingdom and extended Rome's power to the Mediterranean's eastern coast. In 63 B.C.E., Pompey captured the Jewish capital, Jerusalem. Jews had lived in Rome since the second century B.C.E., but most Romans knew little about Judaism; Pompey inspected the Jerusalem temple to satisfy his curiosity and confiscate its treasures.

Pompey's victories were so spectacular that people compared him to Alexander the Great and nicknamed him Magnus ("the Great"). He boasted that he had increased Rome's provincial revenues by 70 percent and distributed spoils equal to twelve and a half years' pay to each of his soldiers. His actions show the degree to which Roman foreign policy had become the personal business of "great men." On his eastern campaigns he ignored the tradition of commanders consulting the Senate about conquering and administering foreign territories, behaving like an independent king rather than a Roman official. He summed up his attitude when replying to some foreigners who criticized his actions as unjust: "Stop quoting the laws to us," he told them. "We carry swords."

Pompey's enemies at Rome sought popular support by proclaiming their concern for the common people's plight. By the 60s B.C.E., Rome's urban population had soared to more than half a million. Hundreds of thousands of the poor lived crowded together in slum apartment buildings and lived off subsidized food distributions. Jobs were scarce. Danger haunted the streets because the city had no police force. Even property owners were in trouble: Sulla's confiscations had caused land values to plummet and produced a credit crunch by flooding the real estate market with properties for sale. Overextended investors were trying to borrow their way back to liquidity, with no success.

The First Triumvirate.   Pompey's return to Rome in 62 B.C.E. lit the fuse to this political time bomb. The Senate, eager to curb his independence, blocked Pompey's eastern arrangements and his reward of land to his

---

♦**Gnaeus Pompey:** GNEE uhs PAHM pee
♦**Licinius Crassus:** lih SIHN ee uhs KRAS uhs

The Proscription Edict of 43 B.C.E.

Lucius Cornelius Sulla (c. 138–78 B.C.E.) initiated the brutal punishment known as proscription (from the Latin for "publishing a notice"). To take revenge on his enemies and raise money after capturing Rome in 82 B.C.E., he posted lists of Romans who were declared outlaws and whose property could therefore be confiscated. Those named in these notices could be killed by anyone with impunity; rewards were offered for their deaths, and their descendants were barred from public office. Sulla's associates added the names of innocent people to settle grudges or seize valuable properties. The victors in the civil wars of the later first century B.C.E. continued this practice (Document 1), making it difficult to achieve a secure peace because proscription caused such bitterness among its victims' families (Documents 2 and 3).

1. THE WINNERS IN THE CIVIL WAR JUSTIFY THEIR PROSCRIPTION EDICT OF 43 B.C.E.

Following the assassination of Julius Caesar in 44 B.C.E., Octavian (the future Augustus), Mark Antony, and Lepidus formed a triumvirate (coalition of three men) to rule Rome; their most infamous action was a proscription. Here, the second-century C.E. historian Appian reports the triumvirate's public justification for proscribing fellow citizens.

The proscription edict was in the following words: "Marcus Lepidus, Marcus Antonius, and Octavius Caesar [Octavian], chosen by the people to set in order and regulate the Republic, declare as follows:

"Had not perfidious traitors begged for mercy and when they had obtained it become the enemies of their benefactors and conspired against them, neither would Julius Caesar have been slain by those whom he saved by his clemency after capturing them in war, whom he admitted to his friendship, and upon whom he heaped offices, honors, and gifts, nor should we have been compelled to use this widespread severity against those who have in-sulted us and declared us public enemies. Now, seeing that the malice of those who have conspired against us and by whose hands Julius Caesar perished cannot be mollified by kindness, we prefer to anticipate our enemies rather than suffer at their hands. Let no one who sees what both Caesar and we ourselves have suffered consider our action unjust, cruel, or immoderate. . . .

"Some of them we have punished already; and by the aid of divine providence you shall presently see the rest punished. . . . One task still remains, and that is to march against Caesar's assassins beyond the sea. On the eve of undertaking this foreign war for you, we do not consider it safe, either for you or for us, to leave other enemies behind to take advantage of our absence and watch for opportunities during the war; nor again do we think that in such great urgency we should delay on their account, but that we ought rather to sweep them out of our pathway once and for all, seeing that they began the war against us when they voted us and the armies under us public enemies.

"What vast numbers of citizens have they, on their part, doomed to destruction with us, disregarding the vengeance of the gods and the reprobation of mankind! We shall not deal harshly with any multitude of men, nor shall we count as enemies all who have opposed or plotted against us, or those distinguished for their riches merely, their abundance or their high position, or as many as another man [i.e., Sulla] slew who held the supreme power before us when he too was regulating the commonwealth in civil convulsions, and whom you named the Fortunate on account of his success; and yet necessarily three persons will have more enemies than one. We shall take vengeance only on the worst and most guilty. This we shall do for your interest no less than for our own, for while we keep up our conflicts you will all be involved necessarily in great dangers, and it is necessary for us also to do something to quiet the army, which has been insulted, irritated, and decreed a public enemy by our common foes.

Although we might arrest on the spot whomsoever we had determined on, we prefer to proscribe rather than seize them unaware—and this too on your account, so that it may not be in the power of enraged soldiers to exceed their orders against persons not responsible, but that they may be restricted to a certain number designated by name and spare the others according to order.

"So be it then! Let no one harbor anyone of those whose names are appended to this edict, or conceal them, or send them away anywhere, or be corrupted by their money. Whoever shall be detected in saving, aiding, or conniving with them we will put on the list of the proscribed without allowing any excuse or pardon. Let those who kill the proscribed bring us their heads and receive the following rewards: to a free man 25,000 Attic drachmas per head, to a slave his freedom and 10,000 Attic drachmas and his master's right of citizenship. Informers shall receive the same rewards. In order that they may remain unknown the names of those who receive the rewards shall not be inscribed in our records."

Source: Appian, *Civil Wars*, Book 4.2.8–11, Loeb Classical Library (Cambridge: Harvard University Press, 1913).

2. THE FUTURE AUGUSTUS BETRAYS CICERO

The most famous victim of the proscription of 43 b.c.e. was the orator and politician Cicero, who had helped Octavian (the future Augustus) to power. Cicero had desperately underestimated Octavian's determination and ruthlessness when he planned to use the young man to promote the Senate's interest against Antony and then discard him. When Antony and Octavian unexpectedly united in the triumvirate, Cicero lost his gamble, with fatal consequences, as the Greek biographer Plutarch relates in this work from about 100 c.e.

Here, indeed, more than at any other time, Cicero was led on and cheated, an old man by a young man. He assisted Caesar [i.e., Octavian, Julius Caesar's adopted son] in his canvass and induced the Senate to favour him. For this he was blamed by his friends at a time, and shortly afterwards he perceived that he had ruined himself and betrayed the liberty of the people. For after the young man had waxed strong and obtained the consulship, he dropped Cicero, and after making friends with Antony and Lepidus and uniting his forces with theirs, he divided the sovereignty with them, like any other piece of property. And a list was made out by them of men who must be put to death, more than two hundred in number. The proscription of Cicero, however, caused most strife in their debates, Antony consenting to no terms unless Cicero should be the first man to be put to death, Lepidus siding with Antony, and Caesar holding out against them both. They held secret meetings by themselves near the city of Bononia for three days, coming together in a place at some distance from the camps and surrounded by a river. It is said that for the first two days Caesar kept up his struggle to save Cicero, but yielded on the third and gave him up. The terms of their mutual concessions were as follows. Caesar was to abandon Cicero, Lepidus his brother Paulus, and Antony Lucius Caesar, who was his uncle on the mother's side. So far did anger and fury lead them to renounce their human sentiments, or rather, they showed that no wild beast is more savage than man when his passion is supplemented by power.

Source: Plutarch, *Life of Cicero*, 46, Loeb Classical Library (Cambridge: Harvard University Press, 1919).

3. A GRIEVING HUSBAND DESCRIBES HIS DEAD WIFE'S VALOR

This eulogy emotionally describes the loss a husband felt at the death of his wife, who had saved his life during the proscription, first by helping him escape and then by confronting Lepidus when he tried to void her husband's pardon. Their story shows the victim's side of this notorious episode.

Rare indeed are marriages of such long duration, which are ended by death, not divorce. We had the good fortune to spend forty-one years together with no unhappiness. I wish that our long marriage had come finally to an end by *my* death,

(Continued)

Ides of March Coin
Celebrating Caesar's Murder

Roman coins were the most widely distributed form of art and communication in the Roman world. Usually the messages they carried expressed the mint officials' pride in their own ancestry, but during the crisis of the late republic, they became topical and contemporary. Caesar's assassins, led by Marcus Junius Brutus (85–42 B.C.E.), issued this coin celebrating the murder and their claim to be liberators. The daggers refer to their method, while the conical cap stands for liberation—it was the kind of headgear worn by slaves who had won their freedom. The inscription gives the date of the assassination, the Ides of March (March 15), according to the Roman calendar. What political message was intended by puting picture of murder weapons on coins? *British Museum.*

to rule a shattered republic. He apparently believed that only a sole ruler could end the chaotic violence of factional politics, but the republic's oldest tradition prohibited monarchy. The second-century B.C.E. senator Cato, notorious for his advice about destroying Carthage, had best expressed the Roman elite's view: "A king," he quipped, "is an animal that feeds on human flesh."

Caesar decided to rule as a king without the title. First, he made himself dictator in 48 B.C.E., using the traditional Roman title for a temporary emergency ruler. In 44 B.C.E., he said he would continue as dictator without a term limit. "I am not a king," he insisted. The distinction, however, was meaningless. As dictator, he controlled the government. Elections for offices continued, for example, but Caesar manipulated the results by recommending candidates to the assemblies, which his supporters dominated.

Caesar's policies as dictator were wide-ranging: a moderate cancellation of debts; a cap on the number of people eligible for subsidized grain; a large program of public works, including public libraries; colonies for his veterans in Italy and abroad; rebuilding Corinth and Carthage as commercial centers; and citizenship for more non-Romans, such as the Cisalpine Gauls (those on the Italian side of the Alps). He also admitted non-Italians to the Senate when he expanded its membership from six hundred (the number after Sulla) to nine hundred.

Unlike Sulla, Caesar did not proscribe his enemies. Instead, he exercised clemency; its beneficiaries were obligated to be his grateful clients. His not taking revenge earned him unprecedented honors, such as a special golden seat in the Senate house and the renaming of the seventh month of the year after him (our July). He also regularized the Roman calendar by having each year include 365 days, a calculation based on an ancient Egyptian calendar that roughly forms the basis for our modern one.

Caesar's dictatorship suited the people but outraged the optimates faction. They resented being dominated by one of their own, a "traitor" who had deserted to the people's faction. A conspiracy arose among a band of senators, led by Caesar's former close friend Marcus Junius Brutus and inspired by the memory of Brutus's ancestor Lucius Junius Brutus, who headed the overthrow of Rome's first monarchy five hundred years before. The conspirators cut Caesar to pieces with daggers in a shower of blood in the Senate house on March 15 (the Ides of March in the Roman calendar), 44 B.C.E. When his friend Brutus stabbed him, Caesar gasped his last words—in Greek: "You, too, child?" He collapsed dead at the foot of a statue of Pompey.

The "liberators," as they styled themselves, had no new plans for governing Rome. They apparently believed that the traditional republic would revive automatically after Caesar's murder; in their profound naïveté, they ignored the grisly political violence of the previous forty years and the deadly imbalance reigning in Roman values, with ambitious individuals valuing their private interests over the community's. The liberators were stunned when the people rioted at Caesar's funeral to vent their anger against the upper class that had robbed them of their generous patron. Instead of then forming a united front, the elite resumed their vendettas with one another to secure personal political power. By 44 B.C.E., the republic had suffered damage beyond repair.

Review: Who were the most important leaders in the republic's downfall and what were their policies?

CHAPTER REVIEW

IMPORTANT EVENTS

753 B.C.E.	Traditional date of Rome's founding as a monarchy
509 B.C.E.	Roman republic established
509–287 B.C.E.	Struggle of the orders
451–449 B.C.E.	Creation of the Twelve Tables, Rome's first written law code
396 B.C.E.	Defeat of the Etruscan city of Veii; first great expansion of Roman territory
387 B.C.E.	Gauls sack Rome
264–241 B.C.E.	First Punic War between Rome and Carthage
c. 220 B.C.E.	Rome controls Italy south of the Po River
218–201 B.C.E.	Second Punic War between Rome and Carthage
168–149 B.C.E.	Cato writes *The Origins*, the first history of Rome in Latin
149–146 B.C.E.	Third Punic War between Rome and Carthage
146 B.C.E.	Carthage and Corinth destroyed
133 B.C.E.	Tiberius Gracchus elected tribune; assassinated in same year
91–87 B.C.E.	Social War between Rome and its Italian allies
60 B.C.E.	First Triumvirate of Caesar, Pompey, and Crassus
49–45 B.C.E.	Civil war, with Caesar the victor
45–44 B.C.E.	Cicero writes his philosophical works on *humanitas*
44 B.C.E.	Caesar appointed dictator for life; assassinated in same year

KEY TERMS

equities (189)

First Triumvirate (196)

humanitas (186)

ladder of offices (178)

latifundia (187)

mos maiorum (165)

optimates (189)

orders (176)

patria potestas (167)

patron-client system (166)

plebiscites (179)

populares (189)

proletarians (179)

proscription (192)

res publica (172)

Twelve Tables (177)

REVIEW QUESTIONS

1. What was the most important common theme in Roman traditional values?

2. Disputes over what issues fueled the struggle of the orders?

3. What were the unintended consequences of Rome's victories over foreign peoples?

4. Who were the most important leaders in the republic's downfall and what were their policies?

MAKING CONNECTIONS

1. How do the political and social values of the Roman republic compare to those of the Classical Greek city-state?

2. What were the positive and the negative consequences of war for the Roman republic?

FOR FURTHER EXPLORATION

To assess your mastery of the material in this chapter, see the Online Study Guide at bedfordstmartins.com/hunt.

To read additional primary-source material from this period, see Chapter 5 in *Sources of The Making of the West*, Second Edition.

The Roman Empire,
c. 44 B.C.E.–284 C.E.

IN 203 C.E., VIBIA PERPETUA,♦ wealthy and twenty-two years old, nursed her infant in a Carthage jail while awaiting execution; she had received the death sentence for refusing to sacrifice to the gods for the Roman emperors' health and safety. One morning the jailer dragged her off to the city's main square, where a crowd had gathered. Perpetua described in a journal what happened when the local governor tried to persuade her to save her life:

> My father came carrying my son, crying "Perform the sacrifice; take pity on your baby!" Then the governor said, "Think of your old father; show pity for your little child! Offer the sacrifice for the imperial family's welfare." "I refuse," I answered. "Are you a Christian?" asked the governor. "Yes." When my father would not stop trying to change my mind, the governor ordered him flung to the earth and whipped with a rod. I felt sorry for my father; it seemed they were beating me. I pitied his pathetic old age.

The brutality of Perpetua's punishment failed to break her: gored by a wild cow and stabbed by a gladiator, she died professing her faith.

Perpetua went to her death as a martyr because she believed that her faith in Christ required her not only to disregard the traditional Roman value of faithfulness to her family obligations but even to refuse the state's demand for a demonstration of loyalty to the "way of the elders" in public religion. Her decision to put her personal religious commitment ahead of her civic duty was a different version of the republic's commanders' fighting civil wars because they valued their individual success above service to the common good.

♦**Vibia Perpetua:** VIB ee uh   per PET you ah

Executing a Criminal in the Amphitheater

This mosaic shows a condemned man being mauled by a leopard in the arena of an amphitheater. Romans believed that especially despicable criminals deserved disgraceful deaths before crowds of spectators. "Being condemned to the beasts," as the execution was called, was the most spectacularly gruesome of punishments. Martyrs charged with treason, such as Perpetua, were often executed in this way. Here the prisoner is tied to a stake on a small chariot so the handlers can propel him into the face of the leopard to provoke an angry leap; wild animals did not always attack without such provocation. This scene formed part of a larger mosaic showing gladiators and other performers in a huge show held in the arena. Dated to about 200 C.E., the mosaic covered a villa floor near the coast of North Africa in what is today Libya; it therefore belonged to the same time and general region of the Roman empire as did Perpetua. The villa's owner perhaps ordered these subjects for the mosaic to commemorate his sponsorship of the expensive public spectacle that included this grisly execution. *Roger Wood / Corbis.*

In the aftermath of Julius Caesar's assassination in 44 B.C.E., Augustus (63 B.C.E.–14 C.E.) eventually restored peace by developing a special kind of monarchy to reorient Romans' communal loyalty toward the ruling family. Ever after, however, Rome's rulers feared disloyalty above all because it threatened to reignite the fires of civil war that had consumed the republic. The refusal of Christians such as Perpetua to perform traditional sacrifice was considered treason—the ultimate disloyalty—because Romans believed the gods would punish the entire community for harboring such impious people.

The Roman Empire, the usual modern name applied to the period from Augustus onward, opened with a bloodbath: seventeen years of civil war followed Caesar's funeral. Finally, in 27 B.C.E., Augustus created his disguised monarchy—the *principate*—to end the violence. He ingeniously masked his creation as a restoration of the republic. He retained the republic's institutions for sharing power—the Senate, the consuls, the courts—while in truth making himself sole ruler. He enshrouded his monarchy in deft language: instead of calling himself *rex* ("king"), he used *princeps*◆ ("first man"), a traditional honorary title designating the leading senator. Princeps became the office that today we call emperor (from the Latin *imperator*, "commander"). Each new princeps was supposed to be designated only with the Senate's approval, but in practice each ruler chose his own successor. Augustus's arrangement thus made Rome into a monarchy—without the name.

This transformed political system brought stability for two hundred years, except for a few brief interludes of fighting between generals competing to become princeps. Worn out by war with each other, Romans welcomed this period of peace, which historians call the **Pax Romana** ("Roman peace"). In the early third century C.E., however, violent rivalries over rule reignited prolonged civil war that generated political and economic crisis. By the 280s C.E., Roman government desperately needed again to transform its political institutions to keep from disintegrating. The most pressing question remained how to retain the traditional values of citizen loyalty and public service by the wealthy. Coming to power in 284, C.E. the emperor Diocletian◆ began that transformation.

❖ Creating the Pax Romana

Inventing tradition takes time. Augustus founded his new political system gradually; as the biographer Suetonius◆ (c. 70–130) expressed it, Augustus "made haste slowly." He succeeded because he won the struggle for power, reinvented government, and built loyalty by communicating an image of himself as a dedicated leader. His professed respect for tradition and his reign's length decisively established monarchy as Rome's

---

◆*princeps:* PRIHN kehps

◆**Diocletian:** dy uh KLEE shuhn
◆**Suetonius:** swee TOH nee uhs

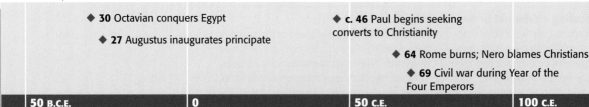

◆ **30** Octavian conquers Egypt

◆ **27** Augustus inaugurates principate

◆ **c. 46** Paul begins seeking converts to Christianity

◆ **64** Rome burns; Nero blames Christians

◆ **69** Civil war during Year of the Four Emperors

50 B.C.E.	0	50 C.E.	100 C.E.

◆ **c. 30** Jesus crucified

◆ **70** Titus destroys Jewish temple

◆ **c. 70–90** New Testament Gospels

◆ **80s** Domitian's campaigns against invaders

future political system and saved the state from anarchy. Succeeding where Caesar had failed, he did it by making the new look old.

From Republic to Principate, 44–27 B.C.E.

The gruesome infighting among those who hoped to fill the political vacuum created by Caesar's assassination in 44 B.C.E. transformed the republic into the principate. The main competitors for power were Caesar's close friend Mark Antony and Caesar's eighteen-year-old grandnephew and adopted son, Octavian (the future Augustus). Octavian won the support of Caesar's soldiers by promising them rewards from their murdered general's wealth, which he had inherited. Marching these troops to Rome, the teenager demanded that the Senate make him consul in 43 B.C.E. As with Pompey previously, fearful senators granted Octavian's demand, disregarding the rule that a man had to climb the ladder of offices before becoming consul. Once again, force trumped tradition.

Octavian, Antony, and a general named Lepidus joined forces to eliminate Caesar's assassins, their supporters, and anyone else they deemed dangerous. In late 43 B.C.E., the trio formed the so-called Second Triumvirate and forced the Senate to recognize them as an official panel for reconstituting the state. They then ruthlessly proscribed their enemies and confiscated their property. (See "Contrasting Views," page 194 in Chapter 5.)

Octavian and Antony, too ambitious to cooperate for long, forced Lepidus into retirement and began fighting each other. Antony based his forces in the eastern Mediterranean, allying with the Ptolemaic queen Cleopatra VII (69–30 B.C.E.), who had earlier allied with Caesar. Dazzled by her wit and intelligence, Antony, who was already married to Octavian's sister, fell deeply in love with Cleopatra. Octavian then rallied support by claiming that Antony planned to make this foreign woman their ruler. He made the residents of Italy and the western provinces his clients by having them swear a personal oath of allegiance to him. His victory in the naval battle of Actium in northwest Greece in 31 B.C.E. won the war. Cleopatra and Antony fled to Egypt, where they both committed suicide in 30 B.C.E. The general first stabbed himself, bleeding to death in his lover's embrace. The queen then ended her life by allowing a poisonous serpent, a symbol of Egyptian royal authority, to bite her. Octavian's capture of Egypt made him Rome's richest citizen and its unrivaled leader.

Augustus's Restoration, 27 B.C.E.–14 C.E.

Following up his victory by distributing land to army veterans and creating colonies in the provinces, Octavian formally announced in 27 B.C.E. that he had restored the republic. The Senate and the Roman people, he proclaimed, should decide how to preserve it. There followed a turning point in Roman history: recognizing that Octavian possessed overwhelming

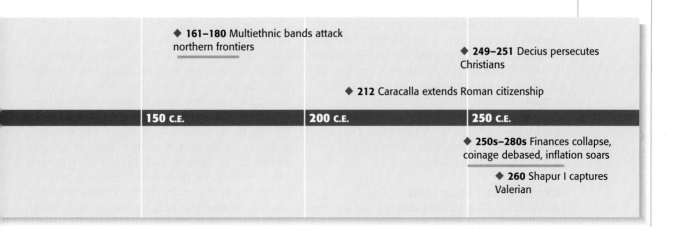

◆ **161–180** Multiethnic bands attack northern frontiers

◆ **249–251** Decius persecutes Christians

◆ **212** Caracalla extends Roman citizenship

150 C.E. | **200 C.E.** | **250 C.E.**

◆ **250s–280s** Finances collapse, coinage debased, inflation soars

◆ **260** Shapur I captures Valerian

Priests on the Altar of Augustan Peace
Augustus dedicated the Altar of Augustan Peace in northwest Rome on his wife's birthday in 9 B.C.E. The altar resided inside a four-walled enclosure, open to the sky, about thirty-four feet long, thirty-eight feet wide, and twenty-three feet high. Relief sculptures covered the marble walls. This section shows a religious procession, headed by the imperial family (out of the picture to the left) and completed by a representation of Rome's senators. The figures wearing leather caps with spikes are priests called *flamines*, whose special headgear was part of the complex ritual of their positions. The hooded man at the right, veiled for performing sacrifice, is probably Marcus Agrippa, Augustus's greatest general. Mythological figures were also sculpted on the walls, expressing the same message as the Prima Porta statue (page 217): Augustus, with his divine family origins, was the patron who brought peace and prosperity to Rome while respecting its republican traditions. The altar can be seen today in its original form because it was reconstructed by Benito Mussolini, Fascist dictator of Italy from 1926 to 1943, who wanted to appropriate Augustan glory for his regime. *Scala/Art Resource, NY.*

power, the senators implored him to safeguard the restored republic, granted him special civil and military powers, and bestowed on him the honorary name **Augustus**, meaning "divinely favored." Octavian had considered changing his name to Romulus, after Rome's legendary first king, but as the historian Cassius Dio (c. 164–230 C.E.) reported, "When he realized people thought this preference meant he longed to be their king, he accepted the other title instead, as if he were more than human; for everything that is most treasured and sacred is called *augustus*."

Inventing the Principate. The arrangements of 27 B.C.E. changed everything in reality, but Augustus, as everyone now called him, kept up the appearance of republican government. Consuls were elected every year, the Senate tendered its advice, and the assemblies still met. Augustus periodically served as consul, but mostly he let others have the honor of holding that revered office. To preserve the tradition that no official should hold more than one post at a time, he had the Senate grant him a tribune's powers without holding the office; that is, he possessed the authority to act and to veto as if he were a tribune protecting the rights of the people, but he left all the tribunates open for plebeians to occupy, just as under the republic. In truth, Augustus exercised supreme power because he controlled the army and the treasury. He knew, however, that symbols affect people's perception of reality, so he dressed and acted modestly, like a regular republican citizen, not a haughty monarch. Livia, his wife, played a prominent role under his regime as his very visible partner in upholding old-fashioned values.

Augustus's choice of princeps as his only official title was a brilliant symbolic move. In the republic, the princeps had guided Rome only by the respect and *auctoritas*♦ ("moral authority") he merited; he had no more *potestas*♦ ("formal power") than any other leader. By appropriating this title, Augustus claimed to carry on this valued tradition. He invented the principate to disguise a monarchy as a corrected and improved republic, headed by an emperor cloaked as a princeps ruling only by auctoritas. In reality, he revised the underlying power structure: no one previously could have exercised the powers of both consul and tribune simultaneously while also controlling the state's money and troops.

Augustus made the military the foundation of his moral authority by turning the republic's citizen militia into a full-time professional force. He established regular lengths of service for soldiers and a substantial retirement benefit, changes that made the princeps the soldiers' patron and solidified their loyalty to him. To pay the added costs, Augustus imposed Rome's first inheritance tax on citizens, angering the rich. His other major military innovation was to station troops in Rome for the first time ever. These soldiers—the **praetorian**♦ **guard**—would later play a crucial role in imperial politics by sometimes determining who the princeps should be. Augustus meant them to prevent rebellion in the capital by serving as a visible reminder that the princeps's superiority was grounded in the threat of force.

♦*auctoritas:* auk TORE ih tahs
♦*potestas:* poh TEHS tahs
♦*praetorian:* pree TAWR ee uhn

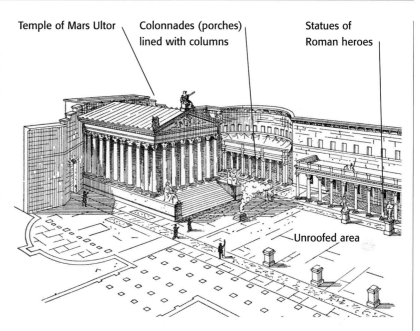

Temple of Mars Ultor   Colonnades (porches) lined with columns   Statues of Roman heroes

Unroofed area

FIGURE 6.1 Cutaway Reconstruction of the Forum of Augustus
Augustus built this large forum (120 x 90 yards) to commemorate his victory over the assassins of his adoptive father, Julius Caesar. Dedicated in 2 B.C.E., its centerpiece was a marble temple dedicated to the god Mars Ultor ("The Avenger"). Inside the temple he placed statues of Mars, Venus (the divine ancestor of Julius Caesar), and Julius Caesar (as a god), as well as Caesar's sword and works of art. The two apses flanking the temple featured statues of Aeneas and Romulus, Rome's founders. The porches stretching along the open courtyard housed other statues of Roman heroes. The ceremony marking teenaged boys' passage into adult status took place here, where they were surrounded by images of the valorous and glorious men whom they were expected to emulate. The high stone wall behind the temple was a barrier protecting it from fire, which was a constant threat in the crowded and poor neighborhood that lay just on the other side.

Communicating the Emperor's Image. In keeping with his policy of always complementing displays of force with displays of symbols, Augustus constantly communicated his image as patron and public benefactor (see "Augustus, *Res Gestae*," page 208). He used media as small as coins and as large as buildings. The only mass-produced medium for official messages, Roman coins functioned like modern political advertising. They proclaimed slogans such as "Father of His Country" to remind Romans of the princeps's moral authority or "Roads have been built" to emphasize his generosity in paying for highway construction.

Augustus also erected public buildings in Rome paid for by his personal fortune. The huge Forum of Augustus he dedicated in

Augustus, *Res Gestae* (My Accomplishments)

Augustus, the first Roman emperor, had stone inscriptions with an autobiographical report of his accomplishments displayed around the empire. These excerpts reveal his justifications for his rule. Many of the sections not included here list his numerous and expensive contributions to public works.

1. At the age of nineteen, on my own initiative and at my own expense, I raised an army, which I used to liberate the republic, which had been oppressed by the tyranny of a faction. For this reason the Senate passed honorary votes for me and made me a member [in 43 B.C.E.], at same time granting me the rank of a consul in its voting, and it gave me the power of military command [*imperium*]. It ordered me as propraetor to see to it, along with the consuls, that no harm came to the state. Moreover, in the same year, when both consuls had died in the war, the people elected me consul and a triumvir with the duty of establishing the republic. . . .

3. I waged many wars, civil and foreign, throughout the whole world by land and by sea, and as victor I spared all citizens who asked for pardons. Foreign peoples who could safely be pardoned I preferred to spare rather than destroy. Approximately 500,000 Roman citizens swore military oaths to me. A little more than 300,000 of these, when their terms of service were ended, I settled in colonies or sent back to their own municipalities; I allotted lands or granted money to all of them as rewards for military service. . . .

4. . . . At the time I wrote this, I had been consul thirteen times, and I was in the thirty-seventh year of my tribunician power [14 C.E.].

5. I refused to accept the dictatorship offered to me [in 22 B.C.E.] by the people and by the senate, both in my absence and my presence. During a severe scarcity of grain I accepted the supervision of the grain supply, which I so administered that within a few days I freed the whole people from imminent panic and danger by my expenditures and effort. The consulship, too, which was offered to me at that time as an annual office for life, I refused to accept.

2 B.C.E. best illustrates his skill at sending messages with bricks and stone. This public gathering space centered on a temple to Mars, the Roman god of war. Two-story colonnades extended from the temple like wings, sheltering statues of famous Roman heroes to serve as inspirations to future leaders. Augustus's forum provided space for religious rituals and the ceremonies marking the passage into adulthood of upper-class boys, but it also stressed the themes he wanted to communicate to justify his rule: peace restored through victory, the foundation of a new age, devotion to the gods who protected Rome, respect for tradition, and his unselfishness in spending money for public purposes.

Augustus's Motives.   Augustus never revealed his motives for establishing the principate. Was he a cynical despot suppressing the republic's freedoms? Or did he have to impose a veiled monarchy to stabilize a society crippled by anarchy? Or did his motives lie somewhere in between? Most likely he was a revolutionary bound by tradition. His problem was the one always facing a Roman leader—how to balance society's need for peace, its traditional commitment to its citizens' freedom of action, and his own ambitions. Augustus's solution was to employ traditional values in making changes, as with his inspired reinvention of the meaning of the word "princeps." Above all, he transferred the traditional paternalism of social relations—the patron-client system—to politics by making the princeps everyone's most important patron with the moral authority to guide their lives. This process culminated in 2 B.C.E. when the Senate joined the Roman people in formally proclaiming him "Father of His Country."

6. [In 19, 18, and 11 B.C.E.], although the Roman senate and people in unison agreed that I should be elected sole guardian of the laws and morals with supreme power, I refused to accept any office offered to me that was contrary to our ancestors' traditions [*mos maiorum*]. The measures that the senate desired me to take at that time I carried out under the tribunician power. While holding this power I five times voluntarily requested and was given a colleague by the senate.

7. . . . I have been ranking senator [*princeps senatus*] for forty years, up to the day on which I wrote this document. [There follows a list of priesthoods he held, including that of "the greatest priest," *pontifex maximus*.]

8. . . . By new legislation that I sponsored I restored many precedents from our ancestors that were becoming dead letters in our generation, and I myself handed down precedents in many spheres for posterity to imitate. . . .

34. In my sixth and seventh consulships [28 and 27 B.C.E.], after I had put an end to the civil wars, having gained possession of everything through the consent of everyone, I transferred the state from my own power [*potestas*] to the control of the Roman Senate and the people.

As reward for this meritorious service, I received the title of Augustus by vote of the senate, and the doorposts of my house were publicly decked with laurels, the civic crown was affixed over my doorway, and a golden shield was set up in the Julian senate house, which, as the inscription on this shield testifies, the Roman senate and people gave me in recognition of my valor, clemency, justice, and devotion. After that time I excelled all in authority [*auctoritas*], but I possessed no more power [*potestas*] than the others who were my colleagues in each magistracy.

35. When I held my thirteenth consulship [2 B.C.E.], the senate, the equestrian order, and the entire Roman people gave me the title of "father of the country" [*pater patriae*] and voted that this title should be inscribed in the vestibule of my house, in the Julian senate house, and in the Augustan Forum on the pedestal of the chariot which was set up in my honor by vote of the senate. At the time I wrote this document I was in my seventy-sixth year.

Source: Herbert W. Benario, ed. *Caesaris Augusti Res Gestae et Fragmenta*, 2nd ed. (1990). Translation by Thomas R. Martin.

Suetonius quotes Augustus as responding, "Fathers of the Senate, I have at last achieved my highest ambition. What more can I request from the immortal gods than that they will let me keep your approval until I die?" The title emphasized that the principate gave Romans a sole ruler who governed them like a father: stern but caring, expecting obedience and loyalty from his children, and obligated to nurture them in return. The goal of such an arrangement was a combination of stability and order, not political freedom.

Augustus ruled as emperor (to use the modern equivalent of the word "princeps") until his death at age seventy-five in 14 C.E. The length of his reign—forty-one years—solidified his transformation of Roman government. As the Roman historian Tacitus◆

◆**Tacitus:** TA suh tuhs

(c. 56–120) remarked, by the time Augustus died, "almost no one was still alive who had seen the republic." Through his longevity, command over the army, rapport with the capital's urban masses, and manipulation of the republic's political symbols and vocabulary to mask his power, Augustus restored stability to society and transformed republican Rome into imperial Rome.

Augustan Rome

A crucial factor in Augustus's success was his attention to citizens' everyday lives. The worst problems were in Rome, a metropolis teeming with a population approaching a million people, many of whom had no job and too little to eat. Archaeological and literary sources reveal a composite picture of life in Augustan Rome. Although some of the sources

Downtown Street in Herculaneum

Like Pompeii, the prosperous town of Herculaneum on the shore of the Bay of Naples was frozen in time by the massive eruption of the neighboring volcano, Mount Vesuvius, in 79 C.E. A flood of mud from the eruption buried the town and preserved its buildings until they were excavated beginning in the eighteenth century. Typical of a Roman town, it had straight roads paved with large, flat stones and flanked by sidewalks. Balconies jutted from the upper stories of houses, offering residents a shady viewing point for the lively traffic in the urban streets. Instead of having yards in front or back, houses often enclosed a garden courtyard open to the sky. Why do you think urban homes had this arrangement?
Scala/Art Resource, NY.

refer to times after Augustus and to cities other than Rome, they nevertheless help us understand this period, as economic and social conditions were essentially the same in Roman cities throughout the empire's early centuries.

Augustan Rome's population was vast for the ancient world. No European city would have this many people again until London in the 1700s. The streets were packed: "One man jabs me with his elbow, another whacks

me with a pole; my legs are smeared with mud, and big feet step on me from all sides" was how the poet Juvenal◆ described walking in Rome in the early second century. To ease congestion in the narrow streets, the city banned carts and wagons in the daytime. This regulation made nights noisy with the creaking of axles and the shouting of drivers caught in traffic jams.

The Precariousness of City Life.   Most urban residents lived in small apartments in multistoried buildings called *insulae*◆ ("islands," so named because in early times each building had an open strip around it). Outnumbering private houses by more than twenty to one, the apartment buildings' first floors housed shops, bars, and simple restaurants. Graffiti of all kinds—political endorsements, the posting of rewards, personal insults, and advertising—decorated the exterior walls. The higher the floor, the cheaper the rent. Well-off tenants occupied the lower stories, while the poorest people lived in single rooms rented by the day on the top floors. Aqueducts delivered a plentiful supply of fresh water to public fountains, but apartment dwellers had to lug jugs up the stairs. The wealthy few had piped-in water at ground level. Most tenants lacked bathrooms and had to use the public latrines or pots for toilets at home. Some buildings had cesspits, but most people had to carry buckets of excrement down to the streets to be emptied by sewage collectors. Lazy tenants flung these containers' foul-smelling contents out the window. Sanitation was an enormous problem because the city generated about sixty tons of human waste every day.

To keep clean, residents used public baths. Because admission fees were low, almost everyone could afford to go to the baths daily. Baths existed all over the city; like modern health clubs, they served as centers for exercising and socializing as well as washing (see "The Scene at a Roman Bath," page 211). Bath patrons progressed through a series of increasingly warm, humid areas until they reached a sauna-like room. Bathers swam naked in their choice of hot or

◆**Juvenal:** JOO vuh nuhl
◆*insulae*: IHN suh lie

The Scene at a Roman Bath

The Roman philosopher Seneca (4 B.C.E.–65 C.E.) wrote to a friend describing the commotion that he had to endure to keep up his studies while living in a rented apartment over a public bath. He offers a lively picture of the range of people using and working in and around the baths, which existed in every sizable community in the Roman Empire.

I am staying in an apartment directly above a public bath house. Imagine all the kinds of voices that I hear, enough to make me hate having ears! When the really strong guys are working out with heavy lead weights, when they are working hard or at least pretending to work hard, I hear their grunts; and whenever they exhale the breath they've been holding in, I hear them hissing and panting harshly. When I happen to notice some sluggish type getting a cheap rubdown, I hear the slap of the hand pounding his shoulders, changing its sound according to whether it's a blow with an open or a closed fist. If a serious ball-player comes along and starts keeping score out loud, then I'm done for. Add to this the bruiser who likes to pick fights, the pickpocket who's been caught, and the man who loves to hear the sound of his own voice in the bath. And there are those people who jump into the swimming pool with a tremendous splash and lots of noise. Besides all the ones who have awful voices, imagine the "armpit hair plucker-outer" with his high, shrill voice—so he'll be noticed—always chattering and never shutting up, except when he is plucking armpits and making his customer yell instead of yelling himself. And there are also all the different cries from the sausage seller, and the fellow hawking pastries, and all the food vendors screaming out what they have to sell, all of them with their own special tones.

Source: Seneca, *Moral Epistles*, 56.1–2. Translation by Thomas R. Martin.

---

cold pools. Women had full access to the public baths, but men and women bathed apart, either in separate rooms or at different times of the day. Since bathing was thought to be particularly valuable for sick people, communal baths contributed to the spread of communicable diseases.

Augustus did all he could to improve public health. By 33 B.C.E., his general Agrippa♦ had vastly improved the city's main sewer, but its contents still emptied untreated into the Tiber River in the city's midst. The technology for sanitary disposal of waste simply did not exist. People regularly left human and animal corpses in the streets, to be gnawed by vultures and dogs. The poor were not the only people affected by such conditions: a stray mutt once brought a human hand to the table where Vespasian,♦ who would be emperor from 69 to 79, was eating lunch. Flies buzzing everywhere and a lack of mechanical refrigeration contributed to frequent gastrointestinal ailments: the most popular jewelry of the time was supposed to ward off stomach trouble. Although the wealthy could not eliminate such discomforts, they made their lives more pleasant with luxuries such as snow rushed from the mountains to ice their drinks and slaves to clean their airy houses, which were built around courtyards and gardens.

City residents faced unpredictable hazards beyond infectious disease. Apartment dwellers often hurled broken pots and household debris out their windows, where it rained down like missiles on unwary pedestrians. "If you are walking to a dinner party in Rome," Juvenal warned, "you would be foolish not to make out your will first. For every open window is a source of potential disaster." The insulae could be dangerous to their inhabitants as well as to passersby because they were in constant danger of collapsing.

♦**Agrippa:** uh GRIH puh
♦**Vespasian:** veh SPAY zhee uhn

Roman engineers, despite their expertise in using concrete, brick, and stone as building materials, lacked the technology to calculate precisely how much stress their constructions could stand. Crooked builders cut costs by cheating on structural materials. Augustus tried to improve the situation by imposing a height limit of seventy feet on new apartment buildings. Fire presented the greater risk to city dwellers; one of Augustus's most important achievements was providing Rome with the first public fire department in Western history. He also established the first permanent police force, despite his reported fondness for stopping to watch the frequent brawls in Rome's crowded streets.

As Rome's patron, Augustus also worked to ensure an adequate food supply for the urban poor. He freely spent his personal fortune to pay for imported grain. Distributing subsidized or free grain to the capital's poor had long been a tradition, but the extent of his dole broke all precedents: 250,000 recipients. When we include the recipients' families, this statistic suggests that more than 700,000 people depended on the government for their dietary staple. Poor Romans cooked this grain into a watery porridge, which they washed down with cheap wine. If they were lucky, they might have some beans, leeks, or cheese on the side. The rich, as we learn from an ancient cookbook, ate more delectable dishes, such as spiced roast pork or crayfish, often flavored with sweet-and-sour sauce concocted from honey and vinegar.

More and more wealthy Romans spent money on luxuries and political careers instead of raising families. Fearing that a scarcity of children would destroy the elite on which Rome relied for public service, Augustus granted special legal privileges to the parents of three or more children. To strengthen marriages, he made adultery a criminal offense and supported this reform so strongly that he exiled his own daughter— his only child—and a granddaughter after sex scandals. His legislation had little effect, however, and the prestigious old families dwindled over the coming centuries. Recent research suggests that up to three-quarters of senatorial families either lost their official

status by spending all their money or died out every generation by failing to have children. Equestrians and provincials who won imperial favor took their places in the social hierarchy and the Senate.

Roman Slavery. Unlike other ancient states, Rome gave citizenship to freed slaves. All slaves could hope to acquire the rights of a free citizen, and their descendants, if they became wealthy, could become members of the social elite. This policy gave slaves reason to persevere and cooperate with their masters. It also meant that most Romans had slave ancestors.

The harshness of slaves' lives varied widely. Slaves in agriculture and manufacturing lived a grueling existence. Most such workers were men, although women might assist the foremen who managed gangs of rural laborers. The second-century novelist Apuleius◆ penned this grim description of slaves in a flour mill: "Through the holes in their ragged clothes you could see all over their bodies the scars from whippings. Some wore only loincloths. Letters had been branded on their foreheads and irons manacled their ankles." Worse than the mills were the mines, where the foremen constantly whipped the miners to keep them working in such a dangerous environment.

Household slaves lived better. Most Romans owned slaves as home servants; modestly well-off families had one or two, while rich houses and, above all, the imperial palace had hordes. Domestic slaves were often women, working as nurses, maids, kitchen helpers, and clothes makers. Some male slaves ran businesses for their masters, and they were often allowed to keep part of the profits as an incentive; they saved to purchase their freedom someday. Women had less opportunity to earn money, though masters sometimes granted tips for sexual favors. Many female prostitutes were slaves working for a master. Slaves with savings would sometimes buy other slaves, especially to have a mate. They could then live as a shadow family, barred from legal marriage because they and their children remained their master's property. Fortunate slaves

---

◆**Apuleius:** ahp you LAY uhs

could buy themselves from their masters or be freed in their masters' wills. Some tomb inscriptions record a master's affection for a slave, but even household slaves endured inhumane treatment if their masters were cruel. Slaves had no legal recourse, and if they attacked their owners, the punishment was death.

Violence in Public Entertainment. Potential violence defined slaves' lives; actual violence defined much Roman public entertainment. The emperors regularly provided spectacles featuring "hunters" killing fierce beasts, wild African animals of all kinds mangling condemned criminals, mock naval battles in flooded arenas, blood-drenched gladiatorial combats, and wreck-filled chariot races. Spectators packed arenas for these shows, seated according to their social rank and gender following an Augustan law; the emperor and senators sat close to the action, while women and the poor were relegated to the upper tiers. Roman spectacles had a political context, demonstrating that the ruler was generous in providing expensive entertainment, powerful enough to command life-and-death exhibitions, and dedicated to preserving the social hierarchy.

War captives, criminals, slaves, and free volunteers fought as gladiators; most were men, though women sometimes competed. Daughters trained by their gladiator fathers had first competed during the republic, and women continued to compete occasionally until the emperor Septimius Severus◆ (r. 193–211) banned their appearance. Gladiatorial shows had originated as part of extravagant funerals, but Augustus made them popular entertainment for tens of thousands of spectators. Gladiators were often wounded but rarely fought to the death, unless they were captives or criminals; professional fighters could have extended careers.

◆**Severus:** suh VEHR uhs

To make the fights more unpredictable, pairs of gladiators often competed with different weapons. One favorite bout pitted a lightly armored "net man," who used a net and a trident, against a more heavily armored "fish man," so named from the design of his helmet crest. Betting was popular, the crowds rowdy. As the Christian theologian Tertullian◆ (c. 160–240) complained: "Look at the mob coming to the show—already they're out of their minds! Aggressive, heedless, already in an uproar about their bets! They all share the same suspense, the same madness, the same voice."

Gladiatorial champions won riches and celebrity but not social respectability. Early in the first century C.E., the senators became alarmed when some members of the upper class became gladiators—they regarded this choice as a disgrace to the class. They therefore banned the elite and all freeborn women under twenty from appearing in gladiatorial shows.

Public festivals featuring gladiatorial shows, chariot races, and theater productions became a way for ordinary citizens to express their wishes to the emperors, who were expected to attend. Poorer Romans

◆**Tertullian:** tur TUHL yuhn

Gladiators Sculpted on a Tomb

This relief sculpture, which adorned a tomb near Rome dating to about 30–10 B.C.E., shows gladiators competing in games held to honor the person buried there. Gladiatorial combats originated as part of funeral ceremonies because they portrayed with dramatic energy the violent and inevitable struggle to avoid death. Hiring gladiators was very expensive, and only the very wealthy could afford to have them perform at their funerals or in spectacles meant to win the people's favor. These gladiators represent a traditional form of fighting called *provocator* ("challenger"). A challenger, who only fought gladiators of the same type, used a short sword (*gladius*), curved shield, greaves, a metal belt cinching up a loincloth, a forearm guard, a partial chest protector, and a plumed helmet. These men's muscular bodies show the great strength required to be a successful fighter.
© Alinari/Art Resource, NY.

Literacy and Social Status

This twenty-six-inch-high wall painting of a woman and her husband was found in an alcove off the central room of a comfortable house in Pompeii, the town in southern Italy buried by a volcanic explosion in 79 C.E. The couple may have owned the bakery that adjoined the house. Both are depicted with items meant to indicate that they were literate and therefore deserving of social status. She holds the notepad of the time, a hinged wooden tablet filled with wax for writing on with the stylus (thin stick) that she touches to her lips; he holds a scroll, the standard form for books in the early Roman Empire. Her hairstyle was one popular in the mid-first century C.E., which hints that this picture was painted not many years before Mount Vesuvius erupted and covered Pompeii in twelve feet of ash. *Erich Lessing/Art Resource, NY.*

rioted at festivals to protest shortfalls in the free grain supply. In this way, public entertainment served as two-way communication between ruler and ruled.

Arts and Letters Fit for an Emperor

Elite culture changed in the Augustan age to serve the same goal as public entertainment: legitimizing and strengthening the transformed political system. Oratory—the highest attainment of Roman arts and letters—lost its bite for this reason. Under the republic, the ability to make stirring speeches criticizing political opponents had been such a powerful weapon that it could catapult a "new man" like Cicero to a leadership role. Under the principate, the emperor's supremacy ruled out freewheeling political debate. Now ambitious men required rhetorical skills primarily to praise the emperor on the numerous public occasions that promoted his image as a competent and compassionate ruler. Political criticism was out.

Imperial Education. Education in oratory remained a privilege of the wealthy. Rome had no free public schools, so the poor received no formal education. Most people had time only for learning practical skills. A character in *Satyricon*,◆ a satirical literary work of the first century by Petronius,◆ expresses this utilitarian attitude: "I didn't study geometry and literary criticism and worthless junk like that. I just learned how to read the letters on signs and how to work out percentages, and I learned weights, measures, and the values of the different kinds of coins."

Servants looked after rich boys and girls, who attended private elementary schools from age seven to eleven to learn reading, writing, and basic arithmetic. Teachers used rote methods in the classroom, inflicting physical punishment for mistakes. Some children went on to the next three years of school, in which they studied literature, history, and grammar. Only a few boys then proceeded to the study of rhetoric.

Advanced studies concerned literature, history, ethical philosophy, law, and dialectic (reasoned argument). Mathematics and science were rarely studied as separate subjects, but engineers and architects became proficient at calculation despite the difficulty of using Roman numerals for complex math. Rich men and women employed slaves to read aloud to them. Books were continuous scrolls made from papyrus or animal skin. A reader had to unroll the scroll with one hand while rolling it up with the other.

◆***Satyricon:*** sa TIHR ih kahn
◆***Petronius:*** puh TROH nee uhs

Ideals in Literature and Sculpture. So much literature blossomed during Augustus's era that modern critics call it the Golden Age of Latin literature. The emperor, who himself composed verse and prose, supported the arts by serving as patron for writers and artists. His favorites were Horace (65–8 b.c.e.) and Virgil (70–19 b.c.e.). Horace entranced audiences with the rhythms and irony of his short poems on public and private subjects. His poem celebrating Augustus's victory at Actium became famous for its opening line: "Now we have to drink [a toast]!"

Virgil became the most famous Roman poet for his epic poem *The Aeneid,*♦ which both praised and criticized the emperor—very gently. He composed so painstakingly that he spent a decade writing it, and the poem remained unfinished at his death. He wanted it burned, but Augustus preserved it. Inspired by Homer's poetry, *The Aeneid* told the legend of the Trojan Aeneas, the legendary founder of the Roman people. Virgil tempered his praise for Rome with a profound recognition of the price in freedom to be paid for peace. *The Aeneid* therefore revealed the complex mix of gain and loss created by Augustus's transformation of Roman politics. Above all, it expressed a moral code for all Romans: no matter how tempting the emotional pull of revenge and pride, be merciful to the conquered but lay low the haughty.

Authors with a more independent streak had to be careful. The historian Livy (54 b.c.e.–17 c.e.) composed an enormous history of Rome in which he refused to hide Augustus's ruthlessness in the civil war after Caesar's murder. The emperor chided but did not punish Livy because the history did proclaim that success and stability depended on traditional values of loyalty and self-sacrifice. The poet Ovid♦ (43 b.c.e.–17 c.e.) fared worse.

An irreverent wit, in *Art of Love* and *Love Affairs* he implicitly mocked the emperor's moral legislation with tongue-in-cheek tips for conducting love affairs and picking up other men's wives at festivals. His book *Metamorphoses* undermined the idea of hierarchy as natural by telling bizarre stories of supernatural shape-changes, with people becoming animals and confusion between the human and the divine. In 8 b.c.e., after Ovid became embroiled in a scandal involving Augustus's daughter, the emperor exiled the poet to a bleak town on the Black Sea.

Public sculpture also reflected the emperor's influence. When Augustus was growing up, portraits were starkly realistic. The sculpture that Augustus commissioned displayed a more idealized style, reminiscent of classical Greek models. In renowned works such as the Prima Porta ("First Gate") statue

Marble Statue of Augustus from Prima Porta

At six feet eight inches high, this imposing sculpture of Rome's first emperor stood a foot taller than its subject. Found at his wife Livia's country villa at Prima Porta ("First Gate") just outside the capital, the marble statue was probably a copy of a bronze original sculpted about 20 b.c.e., when Augustus was in his early forties. The sculptor has depicted him as a younger man, using the idealizing techniques of classical Greek art. Compare his smooth face to Sulla's realistic wrinkles in the bust on page 191. The sculpture is crowded with symbols communicating the image Augustus wished to present: the bare feet hint he is a near-divine hero, the Cupid refers to the Julian family's descent from the goddess Venus, and the design on the breastplate shows a Parthian surrendering to a Roman soldier under the gaze of personified cosmic forces admiring the peace Augustus's regime has created. **For more help analyzing this image**, see the visual activity for this chapter in the Online Study Guide at **bedfordstmartins.com/hunt**. *Scala/Art Resource, NY.*

♦**Aeneid:** ih NEE ihd
♦**Ovid:** AH vihd

of him or the sculpted frieze on his Altar of Peace (finished in 9 B.C.E.), Augustus had himself portrayed as serene and dignified, not careworn and sick, as he often was. As with his monumental architecture, Augustus used sculpture to project a calm and competent image of himself as the "restorer of the world" and founder of a new age for Rome.

> **Review:** What were Augustus's most important actions in bringing peace to Rome and transforming its political system?

❖ Maintaining the Pax Romana

A serious problem confronted Augustus's restored republic: how to avoid a violent struggle for power when the emperor died, given that officially no successor could inherit power, only be awarded it by the Senate. Augustus's solution was to train an heir to take over as princeps after his death, with the Senate giving its blessing and awarding the same powers it had conferred on Augustus. This strategy kept rule in his family, called the Julio-Claudians,❖ until the death in 68 C.E. of Augustus's last descendent, the infamous Nero. It established the tradition that family dynasties ruled imperial Rome.

Under the Augustan system, the emperor's main goals were preventing unrest, building loyalty, and financing the administration while governing a vast territory of diverse provinces. Augustus set the pattern for effective imperial rule: taking special care of the army, communicating the emperor's image as a just and generous ruler, and promoting Roman law and culture as universal standards while allowing as much local freedom as possible. The citizens, in return for their loyalty, expected the emperors to be generous patrons—but, for better or worse, the difficulties of long-range communication imposed practical limits on imperial intervention in the lives of the residents of the provinces.

❖**Julio-Claudians:** JOOL yoh KLAW dee uhns

Making Monarchy Permanent, 14–180 c.e.

To avoid civil war, Augustus wanted to make his disguised monarchy Rome's permanent government, but his fiction that the republic continued meant that he needed the Senate's cooperation to give legitimacy to his successor. Already in the 20s B.C.E. he started looking for a relative to designate as the next princeps (he had no son), but one after another they died before he did. Finally, in 4 C.E., he adopted a relative who would survive him, Livia's son (by a previous marriage), Tiberius (42 B.C.E.–37 C.E.). Since Tiberius had a distinguished record as a general, the army supported Augustus's choice. The senators prudently recognized Tiberius as princeps when Augustus died in 14 C.E. The Julio-Claudian dynasty had begun.

The First Dynasty: The Julio-Claudians, 14–68. The stern and irascible Tiberius (r. 14–37) held power for twenty-three years because he had the most important qualification for succeeding as emperor: the army's respect. He built the praetorian guard a fortified camp in Rome so that its soldiers could better protect the emperor, which had the unintended consequence of guaranteeing them a de facto role in determining all future successions—no new emperor could succeed without their support.

Tiberius's long reign provided the stable transition period that the principate needed, establishing the compromise on power between the elite and the emperor on which imperial stability depended. On the one hand, the traditional offices of consul, senator, and so forth continued, with elite Romans filling them and basking in their prestige; on the other hand, the emperors decided who filled the offices and controlled law and government policy. In this way, everyone saved face by pretending that republican government's remaining traces still mattered.

Tiberius paid a bitter price for becoming emperor. To strengthen their family tie, Augustus forced Tiberius to divorce his beloved wife Vipsania to marry Augustus's daughter, Julia—and the marriage proved disastrously unhappy. Tiberius's reign revealed the problems that an unhappy emperor could create. When his personal torments led him to spend his reign's last decade in seclusion far from Rome, his neglect of routine governing permitted abuses by subordinates in Rome and kept him from grooming a decent successor.

Tiberius designated Gaius (r. 37–41), better known as Caligula,♦ to be the next emperor because Gaius was Augustus's great-grandson and Tiberius's fawning supporter, not because he exhibited the qualities a ruler needed or had any training for rule. Still, the third Julio-Claudian emperor might have been successful because he knew about soldiering: Caligula means "baby boots," the nickname the soldiers gave him as a child because he wore little leather shoes like theirs when he was growing up in the military garrisons his father commanded. Unfortunately, Gaius had feeble virtues but enormous appetites. Ruling with cruelty and violence, he bankrupted the treasury to humor his whims. Suetonius labeled him a monster for his murders and sexual crimes. He outraged social tradition by fighting in mock gladiatorial combats and appearing in public in women's clothing or costumes imitating gods. Two praetorian commanders murdered him in 41 to avenge personal insults.

The senators debated the idea of truly restoring the republic by refusing to choose a new emperor. They capitulated, however, when Claudius (r. 41–54), Augustus's grandnephew and Caligula's uncle, bribed the praetorian guard to back him. Claudius's succession made it clear that the soldiers would insist on there always being an emperor so that they would have a patron to pay them. It also revealed that senatorial yearnings for the republic's return would never be fulfilled.

Claudius opened the way for provincial elites to expand their participation in governing by enrolling men from Transalpine Gaul, a province outside Italy, in the Senate. In return for keeping their regions peaceful and paying taxes, they would receive offices at Rome and imperial patronage. Claudius also transformed imperial bureaucracy by employing freed slaves as powerful administrators; since they owed their great advancement to the emperor, they could be expected to be loyal.

Absolute power's temptations corrupted Claudius's teen-aged successor, Nero (r. 54–68). Emperor at sixteen, he loved music and acting, not governing. The lavish spectacles he sponsored and the cash he distributed kept him popular with Rome's poor. A giant fire in 64 (the incident that led to the legend that Nero fiddled while Rome burned), however, aroused suspicions that he ordered the conflagration to clear the way for a new palace. Nero scandalized the senatorial class by appearing onstage to sing to captive audiences, and he emptied the treasury by spending outrageous sums on a sumptuous palace (his Golden House) and a trip to perform in Greece. To raise money he faked treason charges against senators and equites to seize their property. When rebellious commanders in the provinces toppled his regime, Nero had a servant help him cut his own throat as he dug his grave, wailing, "I'm dying reduced to a laborer's status!"

The Flavian Dynasty and the Imperial Cult, 69–96.   Nero's fall sparked a year of civil war in which four generals vied for power (69, the Year of the Four Emperors). Vespasian (r. 69–79) won. His victory proved that the monarchy would continue because the ruling class and the army demanded it. To give his new dynasty—the Flavian,♦ from his family name—legitimacy, Vespasian had the Senate recognize him as ruler. Second, he encouraged the spread of the imperial cult (worship of the emperor as a living god and sacrifices for his household's welfare) in the provinces outside Italy, where most of the empire's population resided.

Vespasian built on local traditions to promote the imperial cult. In the eastern Mediterranean, the Hellenistic kingdoms had established the precedent of subjects worshiping their ruler; inhabitants of Roman provinces there had treated the emperor as a living god since Augustus's era. The imperial cult communicated the same image of the emperor to the provinces as the city's architecture and sculpture did in the capital: he was larger than life, deserved loyal respect,

---

♦**Caligula:** kuh LIH gyuh luh

♦**Flavian:** FLAY vee uhn

and provided benefactions. Because emperor worship was already well established in Greece and the ancient Near East, Vespasian promoted it in Spain, southern France, and North Africa. Traditional Romans scorned the imperial cult as a provincial aberration, and Vespasian evidently did not believe in his own divinity, to judge from the witty remark Suetonius reports he muttered as he lay dying in 79: "Oh me! I think I'm becoming a god." He allowed emperor worship in the provinces, however, because it was traditional there.

Following their father's lead, Titus (r. 79–81) and Domitian♦ (r. 81–96) conducted hardheaded fiscal policy, professional administration, and high-profile military campaigns. Titus, for example, suppressed a Jewish revolt in Judaea by capturing Jerusalem in 70. He sent relief to Pompeii and Herculaneum when in 79 Mount Vesuvius's massive volcanic eruption buried these towns. He also provided a state-of-the-art site for public entertainment by finishing Rome's **Colosseum**, outfitting the giant amphitheater with awnings to shade the crowd. The Colosseum was deliberately constructed on the site of the former fishpond in Nero's Golden House to demonstrate the new dynasty's public-spiritedness. Domitian balanced the budget and campaigned against Germanic tribes threatening the frontier regions along the Rhine and Danube Rivers.

In the end, Domitian failed because he alienated the Senate. His arrogance made the senators hate him; once he sent them a letter announcing, "Our lord god, myself, orders you to do this." Embittered by a general's rebellion in Germany, he executed numerous upper-class citizens as conspirators. Fearful that they, too, would become victims, his wife and members of his court murdered him in 96.

The Five "Good Emperors," 96–180. As Domitian's fate showed, the principate had not solved monarchy's inevitable weakness: rivalry for rule that could explode into murderous conspiracy. The danger of civil war persisted, whether generated by ambitious generals or the emperor's heirs. No one could predict whether a good ruler or bad would emerge from the struggle over succession. As Tacitus acidly commented, emperors were like the weather: "We just have to wait for bad ones to pass and hope for good ones to appear." Fortunately for Rome, fair weather dawned with the next five emperors—Nerva♦ (r. 96–98), Trajan♦ (r. 98–117), Hadrian♦ (r. 117–138), Antoninus Pius♦ (r. 138–161), and Marcus Aurelius♦ (r. 161–180). Following the influential eighteenth-century historian Edward Gibbon, historians dub these five emperors' period of rule the empire's Golden Age because it was marked by peaceful transfers of power for nearly a century. The period was, however, full of war and strife, as Roman history always was: Trajan fought fierce campaigns to expand Roman power northward across the Danube River into Dacia (today Romania) and eastward into Mesopotamia (Map 6.1); Hadrian earned the Senate's hatred by executing several senators as alleged conspirators and punished a Jewish revolt by turning Jerusalem into a military colony; and Marcus Aurelius spent miserable years on campaign protecting the Danube region from outside attacks.

Still, the five "good emperors" did preside over a political and economic Golden Age. They succeeded one another without murder or conspiracy—the first four, having no surviving sons, used adoption to find the best possible successor. Enough money came in through taxes to pay their expenses, and the army remained obedient. Their reigns marked Rome's longest stretch without a civil war since the second century B.C.E.

Life in the Golden Age, 96–180 C.E.

Peace and prosperity in Rome's Golden Age depended on defense by a loyal military, public-spiritedness by provincial elites in local administration and tax collection, common laws enforced throughout diverse territories, and a healthy population reproducing itself. The empire's size and the relatively

♦**Domitian:** duh MIH shuhn

♦**Nerva:** NUR vuh
♦**Trajan:** TRAY juhn
♦**Hadrian:** HAY dree uhn
♦**Antoninus Pius:** an tuh NY nuhs PY uhs
♦**Aurelius:** aw REEL i uhs

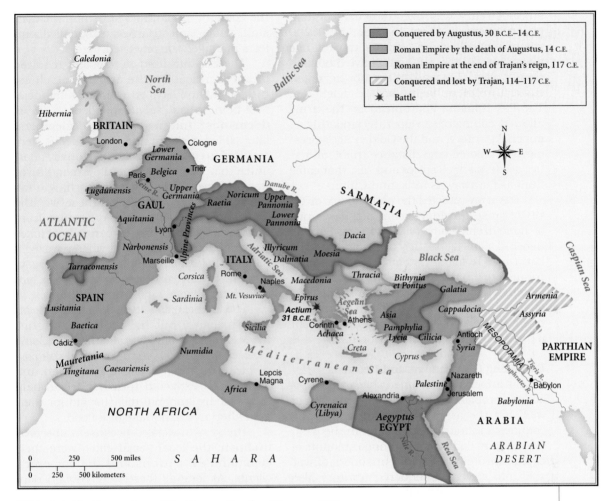

MAP 6.1 The Expansion of the Roman Empire, 30 b.c.e.–117 c.e.

When Octavian (the future Augustus) captured Egypt in 30 b.c.e. after the suicides of Mark Antony and Cleopatra, he greatly boosted Rome's economic strength. The land of the Nile yielded prodigious amounts of grain and gold, and Roman power now effectively encircled the Mediterranean Sea (indigenous kings ruled Mauretania with Roman approval until about 44 c.e. in the reign of Claudius). When the emperor Trajan took over the southern part of Mesopotamia in 114–117 c.e., imperial conquest reached its height; Rome's control had never extended so far east. Egypt remained part of the empire until the Arab conquest in 642 c.e., but Mesopotamia was immediately abandoned by Hadrian, Trajan's successor, probably because it seemed too distant to defend.

small numbers of soldiers and imperial officials in the provinces meant that emperors had only limited control over these factors.

Imperial Military Aims and the Army. In theory, Rome's military goal remained infinite expansion, because conquest brought glory. Virgil expressed this notion in *The Aeneid* by portraying Jupiter, the king of the gods, as promising Rome "imperial rule without limit."

In reality, the emperors were content to have other kingdoms and peoples recognize their authority and not disturb the frontier regions; imperial territory never expanded permanently much beyond what Augustus had controlled.

Most provinces were peaceful and had no need for garrisons, so soldiers were a rare sight in many places. Even Gaul, which had originally resisted imperial control with a suicidal frenzy, was, according to a contemporary witness, "kept in order by 1,200 troops—hardly more soldiers than it has towns." Most legions (a unit of five thousand troops) were stationed on the northern and eastern frontiers, facing hostile neighbors. The Pax Romana guaranteed by the army allowed commerce to operate smoothly in imperial territory, and the Golden Age's prosperity promoted long-distance trade for luxury goods, such as spices and silk, that came from as far away as India and China.

The army reflected the population's diversity because it included many auxiliary units of noncitizens from the provinces. Serving under Roman officers, they could pick up some Latin and Roman customs, and they contributed to improving life in the provinces by helping construct public works. Upon discharge, they received Roman citizenship. In this way the army served as an instrument for spreading a common way of life.

Financing Government and Defense. Paying for imperial government became an insoluble problem. The problem's deepest root was that the army was no longer making conquests to fund the treasury. In the past, foreign wars had brought in huge amounts of capital through booty and prisoners of war sold into slavery. Conquered territory also provided additional tax revenues. Now, there were no new sources of income, but the emperors' standing army had to be paid regularly to maintain discipline. To fulfill their obligations as the army's patrons, emperors at their accession and other special occasions supplemented soldiers' regular pay with substantial bonuses. These rewards made a soldier's career desirable.

A tax on agricultural land in the provinces (Italy was exempt) now provided the principal source of revenue for imperial government and defense. The administration required relatively little money because it was small compared with the size of the territory being governed: no more than several hundred top officials governed a population of about fifty million. Most locally collected taxes stayed in the provinces for expenditures there. Senatorial and equestrian governors with small staffs ran the provinces, which eventually numbered about forty. In Rome,

the emperor employed a substantial palace staff, while equestrian officials called prefects managed the city itself.

The decentralized tax system required public service by the provincial elites; the central and local governments' financial well-being absolutely depended on it. As **decurions**◆ (municipal senate members, later called *curiales*), the local officials were required to collect taxes and personally guarantee that their town's public expenditures were covered. If there was a shortfall in tax collection or local finances, these wealthy men had to make up the difference from their own pockets. Wise emperors kept taxes moderate. As Tiberius put it when refusing a request for tax increases from provincial governors, "I want you to shear my sheep, not skin them alive."

The financial liability could make civic office expensive, but the positions' prestige made the elite willing to take the risk. Some received priesthoods in the imperial cult as a reward, an honor open to both men and women. All expected their service to help them secure imperial disaster aid for their area after an earthquake or a flood.

The system worked because it observed tradition: the local social elites were their communities' patrons and the emperor's clients. As long as there were enough rich, public-spirited provincials participating in the system, the principate functioned by fostering the republican ideal of communal values.

The Impact of Roman Culture on the Provinces. The principate changed the Mediterranean world profoundly but unevenly. The provinces contained a wide diversity of peoples speaking different languages, observing different customs, dressing in different styles, and worshiping different divinities (Map 6.2). In the remote countryside, Roman conquest had only a modest effect on local customs. Where new cities sprang up around Roman forts or from settlements of army veterans, Roman influence prevailed. Roman culture had the greatest effect on western Europe, permanently rooting Latin (and the languages that would emerge from it) and Roman law and customs there. Modern cities

---

◆**decurions:** dih KYUR ee uhns

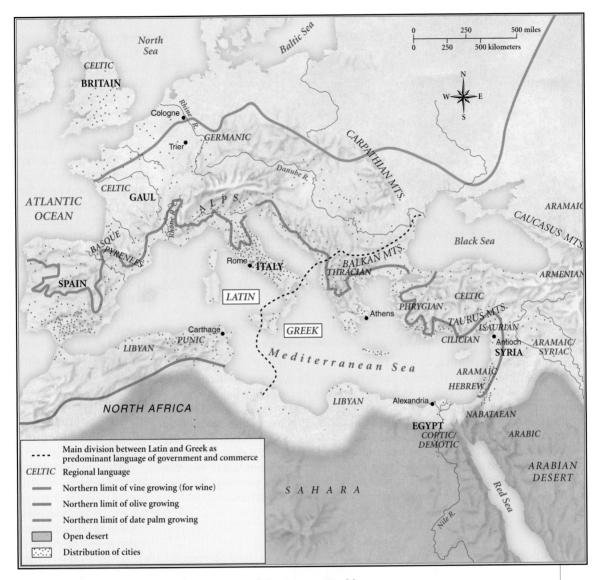

MAP 6.2 Natural Features and Languages of the Roman World

The environment of the Roman world included a large variety of topography, climate, and languages. The inhabitants of the Roman world, estimated to have numbered as many as 50 million, spoke dozens of different tongues, many of which survived well into the late empire. The two predominant languages were Latin in the western part of the empire and Greek in the eastern. Latin remained the language of law even in the eastern empire. Vineyards and olive groves were important agricultural resources because wine was regarded as an essential beverage, and olive oil was the principal source of fat for most people, as well as being used to make soap, perfume, and other products for daily life. Dates were a popular sweet in the Roman world, which had no sugar.

such as Trier♦ and Cologne♦ in Germany started as Roman towns. Over time, social and cultural distinctions lessened between the provinces and Italy. Eventually, emperors came from the provinces; Trajan, from Spain, was the first.

Romanization, as historians call the spread of Roman rule and culture in the provinces, raised the standard of living for

♦**Trier:** trihr
♦**Cologne:** kuh LOHN

Roman Architecture in North Africa

The Roman town of Thysdrus (today El Djem in Tunisia) built this massive amphitheater for public entertainment in the early third century C.E. Its design imitated that of the larger Colosseum in Rome and made it the seventh biggest such building in the empire. Its arched walls soared more than a hundred feet high; its storerooms under the arena floor had three elevators to lift wild animals to the surface; and its seats accommodated nearly 32,000 spectators. Since this seating capacity was several thousand more than the total population of the town, it is apparent that the citizens of Thysdrus planned to attract outside visitors to their spectacular sports facility; they also built a track for chariot racing and a smaller amphitheater for more intimate gatherings. Their big spending for public spectacle put them in the mainstream of Roman imperial culture. © *Erich Lessing/Art Resource.*

Romanization had less effect on the eastern provinces, which largely retained their Greek and Near Eastern character. In much of this region, daily life continued to follow traditional Greek models. When Romans had taken over these areas in the second and first centuries B.C.E., they encountered urban cultures that had flourished for thousands of years. Huge Hellenistic cities such as Alexandria in Egypt and Antioch♦ in Syria rivaled Rome in size and splendor. In fact, compared with Rome, they boasted more individual houses for the well-to-do, fewer blocks of high-rise tenements, and equally magnificent temples.

The eastern provincial elites readily accepted Roman governance. Hellenistic royal traditions had prepared them to see the emperor

many by providing roads and bridges, increasing trade, and establishing peaceful conditions for agriculture. The army's need for supplies meant business for farmers and merchants. The prosperity that provincials enjoyed under Roman rule made Romanization easier for them to take. In addition, Romanization was not a one-way street culturally. In western regions as diverse as Gaul, Britain, and North Africa, interaction between the local people and Romans produced new, mixed cultural traditions, especially in religion and art. Therefore, the process led to a gradual merging of Roman and local culture, not the unilateral imposition of the conquerors' way of life. (See the image, Roman Architecture in North Africa, above.)

as their patron and themselves as his clients, with the mutual obligations this ancient system required. Their willing cooperation in the task of governing the provinces was crucial for imperial stability and prosperity.

New Trends in Literature.   The continuing vitality of Greek language and culture contributed to a flourishing of Roman literature. New trends, often harking back to classical literature, blossomed. Authors of the second century C.E. such as Chariton and Achilles Tatius wrote romantic adventure novels in Greek. Lucian (c. 117–180) composed satirical dialogues fiercely mocking both stuffy people and superstitious reli-

♦**Antioch:** AN tee ahk

giosity. As part of his enormous and varied literary output, the essayist and philosopher Plutarch (c. 50–120) wrote *Parallel Lives*, biographies of matching Greek and Roman men. His keen moral sense and lively taste for anecdotes made him favorite reading for centuries; William Shakespeare (1564–1616) based several plays on Plutarch's work.

Latin literature thrived as well; in fact, scholars rank the late first and early-to-mid-second centuries C.E. as Rome's Silver Age, second only to the Augustan Golden Age. Its most famous authors wrote with acid wit, verve, and imagination. Tacitus (c. 56–120) composed his *Annals* as a biting narrative about the Julio-Claudians, laying bare Augustus's ruthlessness and his successors' crimes. The satiric poet Juvenal (c. 65–130) skewered pretentious Romans and grasping provincials while bemoaning the indignities of living broke in the capital. Apuleius (c. 125–170) scandalized readers with his *Golden Ass*, a lusty novel about a man turned into a donkey who then regains his body and his soul by the kindness of the Egyptian goddess Isis.

Law and Order through Equity. Unlike Augustus, second-century emperors never worried that scandalous literature posed a threat to the social order. They did, however, share his belief that law was crucial. Indeed, Romans prided themselves on their ability to order their society through law. As Virgil said, their mission was "to establish law and order within a framework of peace." Roman law influenced most systems of law in modern Europe. One distinctive characteristic was the recognition of the principle of equity, which meant accomplishing what was "good and fair" even if the letter of the law had to be ignored. This principle led legal thinkers to insist, for example, that people's intent in a contract outweighed the agreement's words, and that accusers should prove the accused guilty because it was often impossible for defendants to prove they had not committed the crime. The emperor Trajan ruled that no one should be convicted on the grounds of suspicion alone because it was better for a guilty person to go unpunished than for an innocent person to be condemned. (See "Contrasting Views," page 230.)

The Roman notion of hierarchy required formal distinctions among society's orders. The elites still constituted a tiny portion of the population. Only about one in every fifty thousand had enough money to qualify for the senatorial order, the highest-ranking class, while about one in a thousand belonged to the equestrian order, the second-ranking class. Different purple stripes on clothing identified these orders. The third-highest order consisted of decurions, the local officials in provincial towns.

Those outside the social elite faced greater disadvantages than snobbery. The republican distinction between "better people" and "humbler people" hardened under the principate, and by the third century C.E. it became a standard in Roman law. The legal class of "better people" included senators, equites, decurions, and retired army veterans. Everybody else—except slaves, who counted as property, not people—made up the vastly larger group of "humbler people." The latter faced their gravest disadvantage in court: the law imposed harsher penalties on them than on "better people" for the same crime. "Humbler people" convicted of capital crimes were regularly executed by being crucified or torn apart by wild animals before a crowd of spectators. "Better people" rarely suffered the death penalty; if they did, they received a quicker and more dignified execution by the sword. "Humbler people" could also be tortured in criminal investigations, even if they were citizens. Romans regarded these differences as fair on the grounds that an elite person's higher status required of him or her a higher level of responsibility for the common good. As one provincial governor expressed it, "Nothing is less equitable than mere equality itself."

Reproduction and Marriage. Nothing, not even law, mattered more to the stability and prosperity of the empire than steady population levels. Concern about reproduction therefore permeated Roman society. The upper-class government official Pliny,◆ for example, sent the following report to the grandfather of his third wife, Calpurnia: "You will be very sad to learn that your granddaughter has suffered

---

◆**Pliny:** PLIH nee

Midwife's Sign
Childbirth was dangerous for women because of the danger of bleeding to death from an internal hemorrhage. This terra-cotta sign from Ostia, the ancient port city of Rome, probably hung outside a midwife's room to announce her expertise in aiding women in giving birth. It shows a pregnant woman clutching the sides of her chair, with an assistant supporting her from behind and the midwife crouched in front to help deliver the baby. Why do you think the woman is seated for delivery instead of lying down? Such signs were especially effective for people who were illiterate; a person did not have to read to understand the services that the specialist inside could provide. *Scala/ Art Resource, NY.*

a miscarriage. She is a young girl and did not realize she was pregnant. As a result she was more active than she should have been and paid a high price."

Ancient medicine could do little to promote healthy childbirth and reduce infant mortality. Complications in childbirth could easily lead to the mother's death because doctors could not stop internal bleeding or cure infections. They possessed sturdy instruments for surgery and physical examinations, but they were badly mistaken about the process of reproduction. Gynecologists such as Soranus, who practiced in early second century Rome, erroneously recommended the days just after menstruation as the best time to become pregnant, when the woman's body was "not congested." As in Hellenistic medicine, treatments were mainly limited to potions, poultices, and bleeding; Soranus recommended treating exceptionally painful menstruation by drawing blood "from the bend of the arm." Many doctors were freedmen from Greece and other provinces, usually with only informal training. People considered their occupation of low status, unless they served the upper class.

As in earlier times, girls often wed in their early teens or even younger and thus had as many years as possible to bear children. Wealthier women hired wet nurses to breast-feed their babies for them. Because so many babies died young, families had to produce numerous offspring to keep from disappearing. The tombstone of Veturia,◆ a soldier's wife married at eleven, tells a typical story: "Here I lie, having lived for twenty-seven years. I was married to the same man for sixteen years and bore six children, five of whom died before I did." The propertied classes usually arranged marriages between spouses who hardly knew each other, although husband and wife could grow to love each other in a partnership devoted to family.

Marriage's emphasis on childbearing brought many health hazards to women, but to remain single and childless represented social failure for Romans. When Romans wanted to control family size, they practiced contraception by obstructing the female organs or by administering drugs to the female partner. They also exposed infant girls more frequently than boys because sons were considered more valuable than daughters as future supporters and protectors of their families.

The emperors did their best to support reproduction. They aided needy children to encourage larger families. Following the emperors' lead, wealthy people often adopted

◆**Veturia:** veh TOUR ee ah

children in their communities. One North African man supported three hundred boys and three hundred girls each year until they grew up. The differing value afforded male and female children was also evident in these humanitarian programs: boys often received more aid than girls.

> **Review:** What distinguished the rule of "bad" and "good" emperors?

❖ The Emergence of Christianity

Christianity began as a Jewish splinter group in Judaea, where, as elsewhere under Roman rule, Jews were allowed to practice their ancestral religion. The new faith was slow to attract believers; three centuries after the death of Jesus, Christians were still a small minority. Moreover, they faced constant suspicion and hostility; virtually every New Testament book decries the resistance the emerging faith encountered. It grew, if only gradually, because it had an appeal based on Jesus' charismatic career, its message of salvation, its early believers' sense of mission, and the strong bonds of community it inspired. Ultimately, Christianity's emergence proved the most significant development in Roman history.

Jesus of Nazareth and the Spread of His Teachings

The new religion sprang from the life and teachings of Jesus (c. 4 B.C.E.–30 C.E.), but its background lay in ancient Jewish history. Harsh Roman rule in Judaea had made the Jews restless and the provincial authorities anxious about rebellion. Jesus' career therefore developed in an unsettled environment. His execution reflected Roman readiness to eliminate perceived threats to peace and social order. In the two decades after his crucifixion, his devoted followers, particularly Paul of Tarsus, spread his teachings beyond Palestine's Jewish community into an unwelcoming wider world.

Jewish Apocalypticism and Christianity.

Christianity offered an answer to a difficult question about divine justice prompted by the Jews' long history of oppression under the kingdoms of the ancient and Hellenistic Near East: how could a just God allow the wicked to prosper and the righteous to suffer? Nearly two hundred years before Jesus's birth, persecution by the Seleucid king Antiochus IV (r. 175–164 B.C.E.) had provoked the Jews into a bloody revolt; this protracted struggle gave birth to apocalypticism (see page 51, Chapter 2). According to this religious idea, evil powers, divine and human, controlled the world. The regime of these powers would end, however, when God revealed his plan to conquer the forces of evil by sending a **Christ** (Greek for "anointed one"; in Hebrew *Mashiach*, or in English *Messiah*). A final judgment would soon follow, punishing the wicked and rewarding the righteous for eternity. Apocalypticism especially influenced the Jews living in Judaea under Roman rule. It later inspired Christians and Muslims.

Apocalyptic doctrines had special appeal around the time of Jesus' birth because most Judaean Jews detested the Romans and disagreed among themselves about what form Judaism should take in such troubled times. Some favored accommodation with their overlords, while others preached rejection of the non-Jewish world and its spiritual corruption. Their local ruler, installed by the Romans, was Herod the Great (r. 37–4 B.C.E.). His flamboyant taste for a Greek style of life, flouting Jewish law, made him unpopular with many locals, despite his magnificent rebuilding of the holiest Jewish shrine, the great temple in Jerusalem. When a decade of unrest followed Herod's death, Augustus responded to local petitions for help by installing provincial government to deal with squabbling dynasts and competing religious factions. Judaea had thus turned into a powder keg by Jesus' lifetime.

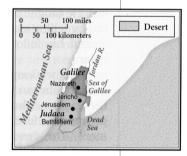

Palestine in the Time of Jesus, 30 C.E.

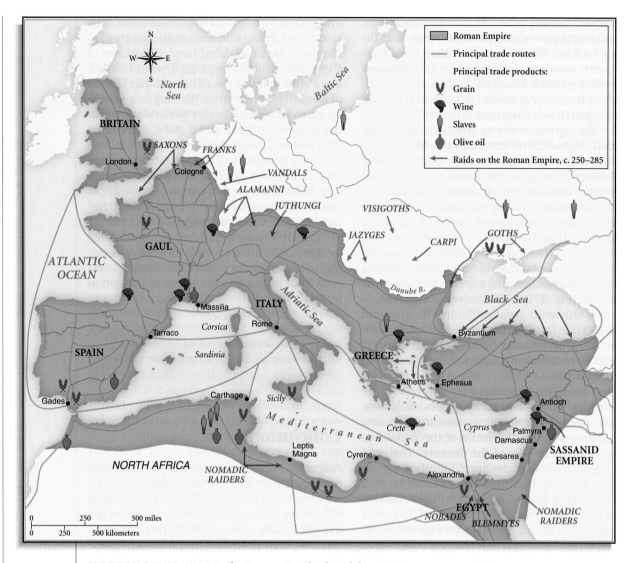

MAPPING THE WEST The Roman Empire in Crisis, c. 284 C.E.
By the 280s C.E., fifty years of civil war had torn the principate apart. Imperial territory retained the outlines inherited from the time of Augustus (compare Map 6.1 on page 219),
except for the loss of Dacia to the Goths during Aurelian's reign (270–275 C.E.). Attacks
from the north and east had repeatedly penetrated the frontiers, however. What do you
think would have been the greatest challenges in ruling such a vast empire in an age
without swift communications or fast travel?

army, now concentrating on defense, no
longer brought money into the treasury
through conquest. Severe inflation made the
situation desperate. Since the wealthy elites
could no longer meet the demand for
increased taxes without draining their fortunes, they lost their public-spiritedness and
avoided their communal responsibilities. Loyalty to the state became too expensive.

The emergence of Christians added to the
uncertainty because Roman officials doubted
their dedication to the state. Their new religion evolved from Jewish apocalypticism to
an increasingly hierarchical organization. Its
believers disputed with each other and with
the authorities; martyrs such as Vibia Perpetua impressed and worried the government
with the depth of their convictions. Citizens

placing loyalty to a divinity ahead of loyalty to the state was a new and inexplicable phenomenon for Roman officialdom.

When financial ruin, civil war, and natural disasters combined to weaken the imperial system in the mid-third century, the emperors lacked the money and the popular support to end the crisis. Not even persecutions of Christians could convince the gods to restore Rome's good fortunes. The empire instead had to be transformed politically and religiously. Against all expectations, that process began with Diocletian in 284.

Suggested References

Creating the Pax Romana

Whether scholars label Augustus tyrant or reformer, they agree that he was a brilliant visionary. Recent research on the ways Augustus and his successors communicated the meaning of empire to the public stresses the role of grandiose and often violent spectacles.

Barrett, Anthony A. *Livia: First Lady of Imperial Rome.* 2002.

Conlin, Diane Atnally. *The Artists of the Ara Pacis: The Process of Hellenization in Roman Relief Sculpture.* 1997.

Futrell, Alison. *Blood in the Arena: The Spectacle of Roman Power.* 1997.

Galinsky, Karl. *Augustan Culture.* 1996.

Horace's poetry and country house: http://www.humnet.ucla.edu/horaces-villa.

Potter, D. S., and D. J. Mattingly, eds. *Life, Death, and Entertainment in the Roman Empire.* 1999.

Roman emperors: http://www.roman-emperors.org.

Roman technology: http://www.unc.edu/courses/rometech/public/frames/art_set.html.

Southern, Pat. *Augustus.* 1998.

*Suetonius, *The Twelve Caesars.* Trans. Robert Graves. 1979.

*Virgil, *Aeneid.* Trans. Robert Fitzgerald. 1985.

Maintaining the Pax Romana

Research shows that the Pax Romana was made possible both by the devotion to duty of emperors such as Marcus Aurelius and by the general prosperity that emerged during the absence of war in imperial territory.

*Apuleius, *The Golden Ass.* Trans. P. G. Walsh. 1995.

Ball, Warwick. *Rome in the East: The Transformation of an Empire.* 2001.

Champlin, Edward. *Nero.* 2003.

Garnsey, Peter, and Richard Saller. *The Roman Empire: Economy, Society, and Culture.* 1987.

Mattern, Susan. *Rome and the Enemy: Imperial Strategy in the Principate.* 1999.

*Marcus Aurelius, *Meditations.* Trans. A. L. Farguharson. 1998.

Roman towns, monuments, and historical texts: http://www.ukans.edu/history/index/europe/ancient_rome/E/Roman/home.html.

Treggiari, Susan. *Roman Marriage: Iusti Coniuges from the Time of Cicero to the Time of Ulpian.* 1991.

Wiedemann, Thomas. *The Julio-Claudian Emperors, A.D. 14–70.* 1989.

The Emergence of Christianity

Scholarly debate concerning early Christianity remains energetic. The sources' meanings are hotly contested because both the ancient authors and their modern interpreters usually have particular points of view.

Brown, Peter. *The Rise of Western Christendom: A.D. 200–1000.* 2nd ed. 2003.

Crossan, John Dominic, and Jonathan L. Reed. *Excavating Jesus: Beneath the Stones, Behind the Texts.* 2001.

Early Christianity: http://www.wabashcenter.wabash.edu/internet/early.htm.

*Ehrman, Bart D. *The New Testament and Other Early Christian Writings: A Reader.* 1998.

Kraemer, Ross Shephard. *Her Share of the Blessings: Women's Religion among Pagans, Jews, and Christians in the Greco-Roman World.* 1992.

Nickelsburg, George W. E. *Ancient Judaism and Christian Origins. Diversity, Continuity, and Transformation.* 2003.

Schürer, Emil. *The History of the Jewish People in the Age of Jesus Christ (175 B.C.–A.D. 135).* Rev. ed. 4 vols. 1973–1987.

Stambaugh, John E., and David L. Balch. *The New Testament in Its Social Environment.* 1986.

*Primary source.

Torjesen, Karen Jo. *When Women Were Priests: Women's Leadership in the Early Church and the Scandal of Their Subordination in the Rise of Christianity.* 1993.

Turcan, Robert. *The Cults of the Roman Empire.* Trans. Antonia Nevill. 1996.

The Third-Century Crisis

The fundamental problem in the third century remained the same: the Roman monarchy's propensity to generate civil war and the inevitably disastrous effects on the economy. Hence, scholarly study of the crisis emphasizes military and political history.

Campbell, Brian. *Warfare and Society in Imperial Rome, 31 B.C.–A.D. 284.* 2002.

Decius, the persecutor of Christians: **http://www.roman-emperors.org/decius.htm**.

*Dodgeon, Michael H., and Samuel N. C. Lieu. *The Roman Eastern Frontier and the Persian Wars A.D. 226–363: A Documentary History.* 1994.

Elton, Hugh. *Frontiers of the Roman Empire.* 1996.

Grant, Michael. *The Collapse and Recovery of the Roman Empire.* 1999.

*Herodian, *The History (180 to 238 C.E.).* Trans. C. R. Whittaker, 1969.

Southern, Pat. *The Roman Empire from Severus to Constantine.* 2001.

CHAPTER REVIEW

IMPORTANT EVENTS

30 B.C.E.	Octavian (the future Augustus) conquers Ptolemaic Egypt
27 B.C.E.	Augustus inaugurates the principate
c. 30 C.E.	Jesus of Nazareth crucified in Jerusalem
c. 46 C.E.	Paul begins travels seeking converts to Christianity
64 C.E.	Much of Rome burns in mammoth fire; Nero blames Christians
69 C.E.	Civil war during the Year of the Four Emperors
70 C.E.	Titus captures Jerusalem and destroys the Jewish temple
c. 70–90 C.E.	New Testament Gospels are written
80s C.E.	Domitian leads campaigns against multiethnic invaders on northern frontiers
161–180 C.E.	Multiethnic bands attack the northern frontiers
212 C.E.	Caracalla extends Roman citizenship to almost all free inhabitants of the provinces
249–251 C.E.	Decius persecutes Christians
250s–280s C.E.	Imperial finances collapse from civil war, debased coinage, and massive inflation
260 C.E.	The Persian king Shapur I captures Emperor Valerian in battle in Syria

KEY TERMS

apostolic succession (228)

auctoritas (207)

Augustus (206)

Christ (226)

Colosseum (218)

debasement of coinage (235)

decurions (220)

martyr (228)

Neoplatonism (233)

orthodoxy (229)

Pax Romana (204)

praetorian guard (207)

principate (204)

Romanization (221)

REVIEW QUESTIONS

1. What were Augustus's most important actions in bringing peace to Rome and transforming its political system?
2. What distinguished the rule of "bad" and "good" emperors?
3. What beliefs and actions made Christians suspicious in the opinion of Roman officials?
4. What disasters provoked the crisis in Roman government and society in the third century C.E.?

MAKING CONNECTIONS

1. What were the similarities and differences between the crisis in the first century B.C.E. that undermined the republic and the crisis in the third century C.E. that undermined the principate?
2. If you had been a first-century Roman emperor under the principate, what would you have done about the Christians and why? What if you had been a third-century emperor?

FOR FURTHER EXPLORATION

To assess your mastery of the material in this chapter, see the Online Study Guide at **bedfordstmartins.com/hunt**.

To read additional primary-source material from this period, see Chapter 6 in *Sources of The Making of the West*, Second Edition.

INNOMINE
XPI·VINCAS
SEMPER·

DN·HONORIOSEMPAVG

DN·HONORIOSEMPER·AVG

PROBVS·FAMVLVSV·C·CONS·OR·D

PROBVS·FAMVLVSV·C·CONSORD

The Transformation of the Roman Empire, 284–c. 600 C.E.

A THIRD-CENTURY Egyptian woman named Isis sent a letter to her mother that archaeologists discovered while exploring a village near the Nile River. The letter, written in Greek on papyrus, hints at the anxiety that people in the Roman Empire felt during the turmoil of that century.

> *Every day I pray to the lord Sarapis and his fellow gods to watch over you. I want you to know that I have arrived in Alexandria safely after four days. I send affectionate greetings to my sister and the children and Elouath and his wife and Dioscorous and her husband and children and Tamalis and her husband and son and Heron and Ammonarion and...Sanpat and her children. And if Aion wants to be in the army, let him come—everybody is in the army!*

This letter raises tantalizing questions about Isis's life, such as her relationship with the people she mentions, who have a mixture of Greek and Semitic names. It also poses many other unanswered questions. Did Isis know how to write or, as was common, had she hired a scribe? Why did she go to Alexandria? Why did Aion◆ want to become a soldier? Why was "everybody" in the army?

The answers lie in the third-century crisis that nearly destroyed the empire. Perhaps economic troubles forced Isis to leave her home to look for work in the largest city in her area. Perhaps Aion wanted to join the army to better his prospects; the emperors, like

---

◆**Aion:** AYE uhn

Emperor Honorius as Christian Victor
Both leaves of this ivory diptych ("folding tablet") made in 406 C.E. depict Honorius, emperor of the western Roman empire, as a military victor attributing his success to Christ. Petronius Probus presented this gift to the emperor to signify his gratitude for being awarded the consulship, the empire's highest honor. On the left, Honorius holds a standard (a sign on a post) that says, "You will always conquer, in the name of Christ," and a statuette of Victory astride the globe offers him a victor's wreath. On the right, he holds a shield and a scepter. His clothing and armor identify him as a military leader; the inscription above his head and the diadem of pearls on it proclaim him "Our Master, Always Augustus," while the circle (nimbus) around his head testifies to his holiness. As this carving shows, Honorius, like other emperors, believed that he had divine backing for his army. In his case, it was not enough: the Goths sacked Rome only four years later.
Cathedral Treasury. Aosta, Italy. © Alinari/Art Resource, NY.

Honorius✦ (r. 395–423) shown in the chapter-opening illustration in his military garb, were always looking for more soldiers. No wonder, then, that it seemed everybody was in the army: the political turmoil during the third century had erupted into fifty years of civil war.

By 284 C.E., decades of bloodshed, with Roman armies fighting Roman armies over who should be emperor, had presented the imperial government with a desperate challenge: how to resume its fundamental role of guaranteeing peace, order, and prosperity. In that year, the empire was saved from falling apart when Diocletian became emperor (r. 284–305) and proved to be a leader tough enough to impose peace and flexible enough to reorganize the administration through subdivision of power.

Regaining social stability was difficult because religious tensions were growing between Christians and followers of traditional polytheistic cults like the letter writer Isis, whose faith was visible in her namesake, an Egyptian goddess. Diocletian, a follower of traditional Roman religion, blamed the Christians for angering the gods and thus bringing on the third-century crisis; he and his partners in rule therefore embarked on the worst persecutions of Christians yet. Diocletian's successor Constantine (r. 306–337) unexpectedly ended this brutality by converting to Christianity and supporting it with imperial funds and a

---

✦**Honorius:** ah NOHR ee uhs

Miniature Portrait of Emperor Constantine
This eight-inch-high bust of Constantine is carved from chalcedony, a crystalline mineral prized for its milky translucence. The first Christian emperor is depicted as gazing upward, to link himself to his hero and model Alexander the Great, who had ordered his portrait done in this posture. Constantine also appears without a beard, a style made popular by Alexander and imitated by Augustus and Trajan, successful emperors with whom Constantine also wished to be associated. The cross at the top center of Constantine's breastplate makes the statuette one of the relatively few pieces of fourth-century Roman art to display overtly Christian symbols. The position of this sign of the emperor's religious choice recalls the design on Augustus's breastplate depicted on page 215; like the founder of the principate, Constantine communicated his image through art. *Bibliothèque Nationale.*

250 C.E.	300 C.E.	350 C.E.	400 C.E.

✦ **293** Tetrarchy created

✦ **301** Edict on Maximum Prices

✦ **303** Diocletian launches Great Persecution of Christians

✦ **312** Battle of the Milvian Bridge; Constantine converts to Christianity

✦ **313** Edict of Milan

✦ **c. 323** Pachomius establishes first monasteries in Upper Egypt

✦ **324** Constantine wins civil war; Constantinople becomes "new Rome"

✦ **325** Council of Nicaea

✦ **361–363** Julian the Apostate tries to reinstate traditional religion

✦ **391** Theodosius I makes Christianity official religion

✦ **395** Empire divided into west and east

✦ **410** Visigoths sack Rome

policy of religious toleration. Even with official support, however, it took nearly a hundred years more for the new faith to become the state religion. The social and cultural transformations produced by the Christianization of the Roman Empire settled in even more slowly because many traditional Romans clung to their ancestral beliefs; even visibly Christian emperors such as Honorius had to employ non-Christians if they wanted to get the best possible administrators and generals.

The political rescue of the empire engineered by Diocletian only postponed the splintering of imperial territory: at the end of the fourth century, Honorius's father split the empire into two geographic divisions, with Honorius ruling the west and his brother Arcadius the east. The co-emperors were supposed to cooperate, but in the long run this system of divided rule could not cope with the different pressures that affected the two regions. In the western empire, a variety of non-Roman peoples from eastern Europe (sometimes referred to as barbarians) moved in, radically transforming the region's society, culture, and politics by displacing Roman provincial government with their own new kingdoms. There the newcomers lived side by side with Romans, the different groups keeping some traditional customs intact but merging other parts of their cultures. The growing strength of these new non-Roman regimes in western Europe and the consequent decentralization of authority there during the fifth century transformed the region in ways that foreshadowed its later political states. In the east, the Roman provinces remained econom-

ically vibrant and politically united, becoming (in modern terminology) the Byzantine Empire in the sixth century. Despite financial pressures and the gradual loss of territory, this continuation of the Roman imperial structure endured until Turkish invaders conquered it in 1453. In this way, the empire lived on in the eastern Mediterranean for a thousand years beyond its transformation in the west.

❖ Reorganizing the Empire, 284–395

Diocletian and Constantine pulled Roman government out of the third-century crisis by making the emperors' authority more blatant than ever before, reorganizing the empire's defense, restricting workers' freedom, and changing the tax system to try to raise the money to pay for all this. The two emperors also believed that they had to win back divine favor to make their people safe. This traditional duty, however, was now complicated by the thorny issue of a growing Christian church and the worry about the gods' goodwill that it provoked among followers of Rome's ancient religion.

Diocletian and Constantine believed that the best solution for the empire's problems was to strengthen their authority. Since for Romans strength had to be seen to be effective, they transformed their appearance as rulers to make their power seem awesome beyond compare, hoping that this display of supremacy would help keep the empire united.

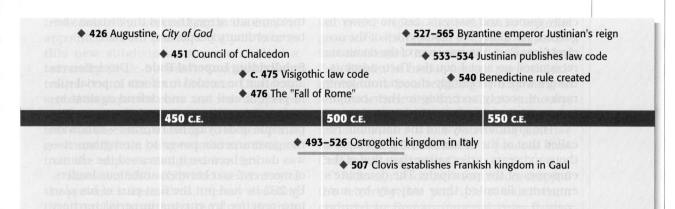

◆ **426** Augustine, *City of God*

◆ **451** Council of Chalcedon

◆ **c. 475** Visigothic law code

◆ **476** The "Fall of Rome"

◆ **527–565** Byzantine emperor Justinian's reign

◆ **533–534** Justinian publishes law code

◆ **540** Benedictine rule created

450 C.E.	500 C.E.	550 C.E.

◆ **493–526** Ostrogothic kingdom in Italy

◆ **507** Clovis establishes Frankish kingdom in Gaul

**Adam and Eve on
the Sarcophagus of Junius Bassus**
This scene of the biblical first man and woman in the Garden of Eden is one image on the most spectacular surviving Christian sarcophagus. Dated by an inscription to 359, it holds the remains of Junius Bassus, the son of a consul and himself prefect of Rome. Carved from marble in a classical style, the scenes are all taken from the Bible and center on the story of Christ. The exclusion of scenes from polytheistic mythology, which had been standard on Christian sarcophaguses, illustrates Christians' growing confidence in their religious traditions. What explains the position of Adam's and Eve's hands? (Consider the section on Augustine and sexual desire beginning on this page.) *Erich Lessing/Art Resource, NY.*

tion of slavery. While detesting slavery, he believed it was a lesser evil than the social disorder that he thought its abolition would create. To help maintain order, Christians had a duty to obey the emperor and participate in political life. Soldiers, too, had to follow their orders.

To make the *City of God* persuasive, Augustine argued that history has a divine purpose, even if people could not see it. All that Christians could know with certainty was that history progressed toward an ultimate goal, but only God could know the meaning of each day's events:

> To be truthful, I myself fail to understand why God created mice and frogs, flies and worms. Nevertheless, I recognize that each of these creatures is beautiful in its own way. For when I contemplate the body and limbs of any living creature, where do I not find proportion, number, and order exhibiting the unity of concord? Where one discovers proportion, number, and order, one should look for the craftsman.

The repeated *I* in this example indicates the intense personal engagement Augustine brought to matters of faith and doctrine. Many other Christians shared this intensity, a trait that energized their disagreements over orthodoxy and heresy.

Augustine and Sexual Desire.   Next to the nature of Christ, the question of how to understand and regulate sexual desire presented Christians with the thorniest problem in the search for religious truth. Augustine became the most influential source of the idea that sex enmeshed human beings in evil and that they should therefore strive for **asceticism**♦ (the practice of self-denial, from the Greek *askesis*, meaning "training"). Augustine knew from personal experience how difficult it was to accept this doctrine. In fact, he revealed in his autobiographical work *Confessions*, written about 397, that he felt a deep conflict between his sexual desire and his religious philosophy. Only after a long period of reflection and doubt, he explained, did he find the inner strength to pledge his future chastity as part of his conversion to Christianity.

least the second century—meant that people suffered from a hereditary moral disease that turned the human will into a disruptive force. This corruption necessitated governments that could suppress evil. The state therefore had a duty to compel people to remain united to the church, by force if necessary.

For Augustine, the purpose of secular authority was to maintain a social order based on a moral order. Order was so essential, Augustine argued, that it justified what he admitted was the unjust institu-

♦**asceticism:** uh SEH tuh sih zuhm

He advocated sexual abstinence as the highest course for Christians because he believed that Adam and Eve's disobedience had forever ruined the perfect harmony God created between the human will and human passions. According to Augustine, God punished his disobedient children by making sexual desire a disruptive force that human will would always struggle to control. He reaffirmed the value of marriage in God's plan, but he insisted that sexual intercourse even between loving spouses carried the melancholy reminder of humanity's fall from grace. A married couple should "descend with a certain sadness" to the task of procreation, the only acceptable reason for sex; sexual pleasure could never be a human good.

This doctrine ennobled virginity and sexual renunciation as the highest virtues; in the words of the ascetic biblical scholar Jerome, they counted as "daily martyrdom." By the end of the fourth century, the importance of virginity to Christians as an ascetic virtue had grown so great that congregations began to call for virgin priests and bishops.

The Beginning of Christian Monasticism

Christian asceticism reached its peak with the development of monasticism. Monks (from the Greek *monos*, for "single, solitary") were men and women who withdrew from everyday society to live a life of extreme self-denial imitating Jesus' suffering, while praying for divine mercy on the world. The first monks lived alone, but soon communities of monks formed for mutual support in the pursuit of holiness.

The Appeal of Monasticism. Polytheists and Jews also had strong ascetic traditions, but Christian monasticism was distinctive for the huge numbers of people drawn to it and the high status that they earned in the Christian population. Monks' renown came from their total disregard for ordinary pleasures and comforts. They left their families and congregations, renounced sex, worshiped almost constantly, wore rough clothes, and ate only enough to survive. To achieve inner peace detached from daily concerns, monks fought a constant spiritual battle against

fantasies of earthly delights—plentiful, tasty food and the joys of sex.

The earliest monks emerged in Egypt in the second half of the third century. Antony (c. 251–356), the son of a well-to-do family, was among the first to renounce regular existence. When he was eighteen he abruptly abandoned all his property after hearing a sermon stressing Jesus's command to a rich young man to sell his possessions and give the proceeds to the poor (Matt. 19:21). In about 285, Antony placed his sister in a home for unmarried women and fled alone into the desert for the rest of his life to worship God through extreme self-denial.

Antony achieved fame for his ascetic life, illustrating a principal appeal of monasticism: the chance to achieve excellence and recognition, a traditional ideal in the ancient Western world. This opportunity seemed especially valuable after the end of the Great Persecution. Becoming a monk—a living martyrdom—served as the substitute for dying a martyr's death and emulated the sacrifice of Christ. Individual, or eremitic,◆ monks (hence the word *hermit*) went to great lengths to secure fame for their dedication. In Syria, for example, "holy women" and "holy men" attracted great attention with feats of pious endurance; Symeon the Stylite (390–459), for one, lived atop a tall pillar (*stylos* in Greek) for thirty years, preaching to the people gathered at the foot of his perch. Egyptian Christians came to believe that their monks' supreme piety made them living heroes who ensured the annual flooding of the Nile, an event once associated with the pharaohs' religious power.

The influence of ascetics with reputations for exceptional holiness continued after their deaths. Their relics—body parts or clothing—became treasured sources of protection and healing. Projecting the enduring power of saints (people venerated after their deaths for their holiness), relics gave believers faith in divine favor. Christian reverence for relics continued a very long tradition: the fifth-century B.C.E. Athenians, for example, believed good fortune would follow from the recovery of bones identified as the remains of Theseus, their legendary founder.

◆**eremitic:** ehr uh MIH tihk

The Rise of Monastic Communities. In about 323, an Egyptian Christian named Pachomius◆ organized the first monastic community, establishing the tradition of single-sex settlements of male or female monks helping one another along the harsh path to holiness. This communal monasticism, called coenobitic (meaning "life in common"), dominated Christian asceticism ever after. Communities of men and women were often built close together to share labor, with women making clothing, for example, while men farmed.

All monastic groups imposed military-style discipline, but they differed in their degree of internal austerity and contact with the outside world (see Monastery of St. Catherine at Mount Sinai). Some strove for complete self-sufficiency to avoid transactions with outsiders. The most isolationist groups lived in the eastern empire, but the followers of Martin of Tours (c. 316–397), an ex-soldier famed for his pious deeds, founded communities in the west as austere as any. Basil of Caesarea◆ in Asia Minor (c. 330–379) started a competing tradition of monasteries in service to society. Basil (later dubbed "the Great") required monks to perform charitable deeds, especially ministering to the sick, a development that led to the foundation of the first hospitals, attached to monasteries.

A milder code of monastic conduct became the standard in the west, greatly influencing Catholic worship. It is called the Benedictine rule after its creator, Benedict of Nursia in central Italy (c. 480–553). Benedict created his code in about 540 to prescribe his monastery's daily routine of prayer, scriptural readings, and manual labor. The rule divided the day into seven parts, each with a compulsory service of prayers and lessons, called the office. Unlike the harsh regulations of other monastic communities, Benedict's code did not isolate the monks from the outside world or deprive them of sleep, adequate food, or warm clothing. Although it gave the abbot (the head monk) full authority, it instructed him to listen to what every member of the community had to say before deciding important matters. He was not allowed to beat disobedient monks, as sometimes happened under other systems. Communities of women, such as those founded by Basil's sister Macrina and Benedict's sister Scholastica, generally followed the rules of the male monasteries, with an emphasis on the decorum thought necessary for women.

The thousands upon thousands of Christians who joined monasteries from the fourth century onward abandoned the outside world for social as well as theological reasons. The glory of monastic piety held special appeal for women and the rich. Jerome wrote, "[As monks] we evaluate people's virtue not by their gender but by their character, and deem those to be worthy of the greatest glory who have renounced both status and riches." Some monks had not chosen their life; they had been given as babies to monasteries by parents who could not raise them or were fulfilling pious vows, a practice called oblation. Jerome once gave this advice to a mother who decided to send her young daughter to a monastery:

> Let her be brought up in a monastery, let her live among virgins, let her learn to avoid swearing, let her regard lying as an offense against God, let her be ignorant of the world, let her live the angelic life, while in the flesh let her be without the flesh, and let her suppose that all human beings are like herself.

When the girl reached adulthood as a virgin, he added, she should avoid the baths so she would not be seen naked or give her body pleasure by dipping in the warm pools. Jerome enunciated traditional values favoring males when he promised that God would reward the mother with the birth of sons in compensation for the dedication of her daughter.

Since monasteries were self-governing, they could find themselves in conflict with the church hierarchy. Bishops resented members of their congregations who withdrew into monasteries, especially because they then gave money and property to their new community instead of to their local churches. Moreover, monks represented a threat to bishops' authority because holy men and women earned their special status not by having it bestowed from the church hierarchy but through their own actions; strengthening

---

◆**Pachomius:** puh KOH mee uhs
◆**Basil of Caesarea:** BAAH zuhl (of) seh zuh REE uh

the bishops' right to discipline monks who resisted their authority was one of the goals of the Council of Chalcedon. At bottom, however, bishops and monks did share a spiritual goal—salvation and service to God. While polytheists had enjoyed immediate access to their gods, who were thought to visit the earth constantly, Christians worshiped a transcendent God removed from this world. Monks bridged the chasm between the human and the divine by interceding with God to ask mercy for the faithful.

Review: What were the major spiritual disputes among early Christians and why were they so fierce?

❖ Non-Roman Kingdoms in the West, c. 370–550s

The residents of the western empire had special reason to pray for God's help because their territory came under great pressure from the often violent incursion of non-Roman peoples that took place in the fourth and fifth centuries. Migrations and invasions of peoples from east of the Rhine River and north of the Danube River transformed politics, society, and economy in the western half of the Roman world. The multiethnic groups that forced their way into the empire from the northeast had two strong motivations to move westward: to flee attacks by the Huns, nomads from central Asia, and to

Monastery of St. Catherine at Mount Sinai
The Byzantine emperor Justinian (r. 527–565) built a wall to enclose the buildings of this monastery in the desert at the foot of Mount Sinai (on the peninsula between Egypt and Arabia). Justinian supported the monastery to promote orthodoxy in a region dominated by Monophysite Christians. The monastery gained its name in the ninth century when the story was circulated that angels had recently brought the body of Catherine of Alexandria there. Catherine was said to have been martyred in the fourth century for refusing to marry the emperor because, in her words, she was the bride of Christ, though no contemporary sources record her story.
Erich Lessing/ Art Resource, NY.

enjoy Roman prosperity. By the 370s this human tide had swollen to a flood, provoking violence and a loss of order in the western empire. Over the coming decades, the immigrants embarked on a remarkable transition, transforming themselves from loosely organized, multiethnic tribes into kingdoms with newly defined identities. By the 470s, one of their commanders ruled Italy—the political change that has been said to mark the so-called fall of the Roman Empire. In fact, the interactions of these non-Roman peoples with the empire's residents in western Europe and North Africa are better understood as causing a political, social, and cultural transformation that made them the heirs of the western Roman Empire and led to the formation of medieval Europe.

Non-Roman Migrations

The non-Roman peoples who flooded into the empire had diverse origins; scholars in the past referred to them generically as Germanic peoples, but this label misrepresents the variety of languages and customs among these multiethnic groups. Romans lumped them all together as barbarians, a term that some historians now use but whose negative implications impede fair-minded analysis. What we should remember is that they were a diverse population with no strongly established sense of ethnic identity; many of them had had previous contact with Romans through trade or employment as mercenary fighters. Fourth-century emperors at first encouraged the movement of non-Romans into imperial territory, recruiting the men to serve in the Roman army, as earlier emperors had done. By late in the century, these warriors' families had followed them into the empire. Hordes of men, women, and children crossed the Roman border as refugees. They came with no political or military unity and no clear plan. Loosely organized into tribes that often warred with one another, they shared only their terror of the Huns and their custom of conducting raids for a living.

The western government was fatally weakened by its inability to prevent the newcomers from crossing the border or to control them once they arrived. Persistent economic weakness rooted in the third-century crisis underlay this failure. Tenant farmers and landlords fleeing crushing taxes had left as much as 20 percent of arable territory unfarmed in the most seriously affected areas. The loss of revenue made the government unable to afford enough soldiers to control the situation. Over time the immigrating non-Roman peoples compelled Roman government to cede them territory in the empire. Remarkably, they then began to develop separate ethnic identities and formed new societies for themselves and the Romans living under their control.

Immigrant Traditions. The newcomers had to develop more tightly structured societies to govern the lands that the weak western government grudgingly granted them under threat of violence. The traditions they brought with them from their eastern homelands had ill prepared them for ruling others. There they had lived in small settlements whose economies depended on farming, herding, and ironworking; they had no experience with running kingdoms built on strong central authority.

Their original societies were chiefdoms, whose members could only be persuaded, not ordered, to follow the chief. The chiefs maintained their status by giving gifts to their followers and leading raids to capture cattle and slaves. They led clans—groups of households organized on kinship lines, following maternal as well as paternal descent. The members of a clan were supposed to keep peace among themselves, and violence against a fellow clan member was the worst possible offense. Clans in turn grouped themselves into tribes, very loose and fluctuating multiethnic coalitions that anyone could join. Tribes differentiated themselves by their clothing, hairstyles, jewelry, weapons, religious cults, and oral stories.

Family life was patriarchal: men headed households and held authority over women, children, and slaves. Warfare preoccupied men, as their ritual sacrifices of weapons preserved in northern European bogs have shown. Women were valued for their ability to bear children, and rich men could have more than one wife and perhaps concubines as well. A division of labor made women responsible for agriculture, pottery making, and the production of textiles, while men worked iron and herded cattle. Women enjoyed certain rights of inheritance and could control property, and married women received a dowry of one-third of their husband's property.

Assemblies of free male warriors provided the only traditional form of decision making among the tribes. Their leaders' authority was restricted mostly to religious and military matters. Tribes could be very unstable and prone to internal conflict— clans frequently feuded, with bloody consequences. Tribal law tried to determine what forms of violence were and were not acceptable in seeking revenge, but laws were oral, not written, and thus open to wide dispute.

Migrants Fleeing the Huns. The migrations avalanched when the Huns invaded eastern Europe in the fourth century. Distantly related to the Hiung-nu,◆ a central Asian people who had earlier attacked China and Persia, the Huns arrived on the Russian steppes shortly before 370 as the vanguard of Turkish-speaking nomads. Huns excelled as raiders, launching cavalry attacks far and wide. Their warriors' appearance terrified their victims, who reported skulls elongated from having been bound between boards in infancy, faces grooved with decorative scars, and arms fearsome with elaborate tattoos. Their prowess as horsemen made them legendary; they could shoot their powerful bows while riding full tilt and stay mounted for days, sleeping atop their horses and carrying snacks of raw meat between their thighs and the animal's back.

The Huns moved westward toward the Hungarian plain north of the Danube late in the fourth century, terrifying the peoples there and launching raids southward into the Balkans. The emperors in Constantinople began paying the Huns to spare their territory, so the most ambitious Hunnic leader, Attila (r. c. 440–453), pushed his domain westward toward the Alps. In 451, he led his forces as far west as central France, and in 452 into northern Italy. At Attila's death in 454, the Huns lost their fragile cohesiveness

and faded from history. By this time, however, the terror that they had inspired in the peoples living in eastern Europe had provoked the migrations that eventually transformed the western empire.

Visigoths: The First New Society. The first non-Roman group that coalesced to create a new society after entering imperial territory came to be called the Visigoths. Shredded by constant Hunnic raids, in 376 they obtained permission from the eastern emperor Valens◆ (r. 364–378) to move into the Balkans, so long as their warriors agreed to fight in the Roman army against the Huns (Map 7.3). Their history illustrates the pattern of the migrations: desperate people in barely organized groups seeking asylum from Roman government in return for service, being mistreated, and rebelling to form their own, new kingdom.

When greedy Roman officers charged with helping them instead extorted bribes, the refugees starved; the officials forced them to sell some of their own people into slavery to buy dogs to eat. The desperate band fought back. In 378, they defeated and killed Valens in the battle of Adrianople◆ in Thrace.◆ Theodosius I, Valens's successor, then had to agree to give them large annual payments, let them settle permanently inside the borders in a kingdom under their own laws, and designate them as federates (allies) helping protect the empire.

Realizing they could not afford to keep this agreement, the eastern emperors soon forced the newcomers to the west by cutting off the payments and threatening full-scale war unless the refugees left. The angry group moved violently into the western empire; neither they nor the western empire would ever be the same. In 410, they stunned the world by sacking Rome itself. For the first time since the Gauls eight hundred years before, a foreign force occupied the ancient capital. They terrorized the population: when their commander Alaric◆ demanded all the citizens' goods, the Romans asked, "What will be left to us?" "Your lives," he replied.

◆**Hiung-nu:** hee UNG new

◆**Valens:** VAL ehnz

◆**Adrianople:** ay dree uh NOH puhl

◆**Thrace:** thrays

◆**Alaric:** A luh rihk

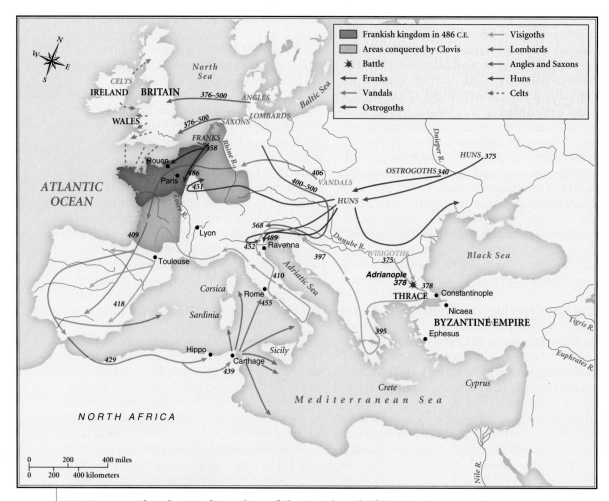

MAP 7.3   Migrations and Invasions of the Fourth and Fifth Centuries

The movements of non-Roman peoples into imperial territory transformed the Roman Empire. This phenomenon had begun as early as the reign of Domitian (r. 81-96), but in the fourth century it became a pressing problem for the emperors when the Huns' attacks pushed various multiethnic bands from their homelands in eastern Europe into the empire's northern provinces. Print maps can offer only a schematic representation of dynamic processes such as these migrations and invasions, but this map does convey a sense of the variety of peoples involved, the wide extent of imperial territory that they affected, and the concentration of their effects in the western section of the empire.

Too weak to fend off the invaders, the western emperor Honorius in 418 reluctantly agreed to settle the newcomers in south-western Gaul (present-day France), where they completed their unprecedented transition from tribe to kingdom, organizing a political state and establishing their ethnic identity as Visigoths. In this process of creation they followed the only model available: Roman tradition. For one thing, they estab-lished mutually beneficial relations with local Roman elites, who used time-tested ways of flattering their new superiors to gain advantages. Sidonius Apollinaris, for example, a well-connected noble from Lyon♦ (c. 430–479), once purposely lost a backgammon game to the Visigothic king as a way of winning a favor.

♦**Lyon:** ly OHN

How the new non-Roman kingdoms raised revenues has become a much-debated question. Did the newcomers become landed proprietors by forcing Roman landowners to redistribute a portion of their lands, slaves, and movable property to them? Or did Romans directly pay the expenses of the kingdom's soldiers, who lived mostly in urban garrisons? Whatever the new arrangements were, the Visigoths found them profitable enough to expand into Spain within a century of establishing themselves in southwestern Gaul.

The Vandals and the Spiral of Violence.

The western government's concessions to the Visigoths emboldened other groups to seize territory and create new kingdoms and identities. The violence spiraled to new levels in 406 when the Vandals, fleeing the Huns, crossed the Rhine into Roman territory. This huge group cut a swath through Gaul all the way to the Spanish coast. (The modern word *vandal*, meaning "destroyer of property," perpetuates their reputation for warlike ruthlessness.)

In 429, eighty thousand Vandals ferried to North Africa, where they soon broke their agreement to become federates and captured the region. They crippled the western empire by seizing North Africa's tax payments of grain and vegetable oil and disrupting the importation of food to Rome, and they frightened the eastern empire with their strong navy. In 455, they set the western government tottering by plundering Rome. The Vandals caused tremendous hardship for local Africans by confiscating property rather than (like the Visigoths) allowing owners to make regular payments to "ransom" their land.

The Anglo-Saxons at the Empire's Western Edge.

Small non-Roman groups took advantage of the disruption caused by bigger bands to break off distant pieces of the weakened western empire. The most significant group for later history was the Anglo-Saxons. Composed of Angles from what is now Denmark and Saxons from northwestern Germany, this mixed group invaded Britain in the 440s after the Roman army had been recalled from the province to defend Italy against the Visigoths. They established their kingdoms by wresting territory away from the indigenous Celtic peoples and the remaining Roman inhabitants. Gradually, their culture replaced the local traditions of the island's eastern regions; the Celts there lost most of their language, and Christianity gave way to Anglo-Saxon beliefs, surviving only in Wales and Ireland.

The Fall of Rome and the Ostrogoths.

Yet another non-Roman group, the Ostrogoths,♦ carved out a kingdom in Italy in the fifth century. By the time the Ostrogothic king Theodoric came to power (r. 493–526), there had not been a western Roman emperor for nearly twenty years, and there never would be again—the change that has traditionally, but simplistically, been called the fall of the Roman Empire. (See "New Sources, New Perspectives," page 268.) The story's details reveal the complexity of the political transformation of the western empire under the new kingdoms. The weakness of the western emperors' army had obliged them to hire foreign officers to lead the defense of Italy. By the middle of the fifth century, one non-Roman general after another decided who would serve as puppet emperor under his control. The employees were running the company.

The last such unfortunate puppet was only a child; his father, a former aide to Attila, tried to establish a royal house by proclaiming his young son as western emperor in 475. He gave the boy ruler the name Romulus Augustulus ("Romulus the Little Augustus") to match his tender age and recall both Rome's founder and its first emperor. In 476, following a dispute over pay, the emperor's non-Roman soldiers murdered his father and deposed him; pitied as an innocent child, Little Augustus was given safe refuge and a generous pension. The rebels' leader, Odoacer,♦ did not appoint another emperor, a move traditionally labeled the "fall of Rome." Instead, he had the Roman Senate petition Zeno, the eastern emperor, to recognize his leadership in return for his acknowledging Zeno as sole emperor over west and east. Odoacer thereafter oversaw Italy nominally as the eastern emperor's viceroy, but in fact he ruled as he liked.

♦**Ostrogoths:** AHS truh gahths
♦**Odoacer:** oh doh AH ker

NEW SOURCES, NEW PERSPECTIVES

Looking for the Decline and Fall of the Roman Empire

In 1776, the Englishman Edward Gibbon (1737–1794) became a celebrity by publishing the first installment of his best-selling, multi-volume work *The Decline and Fall of the Roman Empire*. The reading public loved his writing for its stinging style, though some people found Gibbon himself irritating for his flashy vanity and conceit.

Ironically, historians have found his title irritating for its enduring renown: the phrase grew so famous that, if there is anything commonly "known" about the Roman Empire, it is that it declined and fell. The trouble is that this idea is woefully misleading. Gibbon himself lived to regret his choice of a title because his work continued telling the empire's story far beyond 476 C.E., the year when a non-Roman general took over the western empire. His final volume (published in 1788) reached 1453, when the Turks toppled the Byzantine Empire by taking Constantinople.

Various sources of new information and analysis have revealed the inadequacies of the idea that the Roman Empire fell once and for all in 476. This is not to say that no disasters occurred in the fourth and fifth centuries: clearly some conditions of life—economic security and prosperity, opportunities for leisure and entertainment, and even nutrition—got worse for many people as non-Roman peoples entered the western empire and the center of power shifted to its eastern half. So, too, the Byzantine emperors regarded the political division of the old empire as a problem they wanted to remedy by conquering the new non-Roman kingdoms to reunite west and east. Still, these changes are far from the full story. To tell that entire story today, it is more accurate to describe the empire's fate as a complex transformation rather than as a simple decline and fall.

Art and archaeology have provided some of the most intriguing sources for this perspective, either looking at long-known objects in new ways or discovering new objects. Past scholars, for example, considered Gothic art inferior because, unlike classical art, its designs did not emphasize the human figure or symmetry. Instead, it focused on animal motifs and abstract patterns. This tendency did not mean that it could not communicate as powerfully as classical art; it just meant that observers had to be able to un-

In 488, Zeno plotted to rid himself of an ambitious non-Roman general then resident in Constantinople—Theodoric—by sending him to fight Odoacer, whom the emperor had found too independent. Successful in eliminating Odoacer by 493, Theodoric went on to establish his own Ostrogothic kingdom to rule Italy from the traditional capital at Ravenna.

Theodoric and his Ostrogothic nobles wanted to enjoy the luxurious life of the empire's elite, not destroy it, and to preserve the empire's prestige and status. They therefore left the Senate and consulships intact. An Arian Christian, Theodoric followed Constantine's example by announcing a policy of religious toleration: "No one can be forced to believe against his will." Like the other non-Romans, the Ostrogoths appropriated Roman traditions that supported the stability of their own rule. For these reasons, scholars consider it more accurate to speak of the western empire's "transformation" than of its "fall."

The Enduring Kingdom of the Franks. The Franks were the people who transformed Roman Gaul into Francia (from which the name France comes). Roman emperors had allowed some of the Franks to settle in a rough northern border region (now in the Netherlands) in the early fourth century; by the late fifth century they were a major pres-

Eagle Fibulae (Brooches) from Gothic Spain
Walters Art Gallery, Baltimore.

derstand the art's conventions and goals. Recent archaeological research has shown that Goths used everyday art objects to convey crucial meanings—in particular, assertions of the growing sense of ethnic identity that emerged during their migrations into the Roman Empire. When in the fifth century c.e. Visigoths took up permanent residence in Spain, the women expressed their identity by emphasizing an old custom from their traditional Danube region: wearing two artfully crafted brooches to fasten their clothes at the shoulders instead of just one. Previously,

this style had not served to identify separate groups; now it said, "I am a Visigothic woman."

Above all, Gothic art expressed the transformation of the empire. A clear example comes in the spectacular eagle pins that elite Goths favored. Dazzlingly fashioned in gold and semiprecious stones, these small works of art took their inspiration from the traditions of the Huns and the Romans, both of whom highlighted the eagle as a symbol of power. Goths had never previously used eagles this way, but now they adapted the traditions of others to express their own transformation into powerful members of imperial politics and society. From their perspective, the empire's fate was hardly a decline and fall.

Questions to Consider

1. How do historical and aesthetic appreciations of art differ? What are the advantages of each approach?
2. How do people determine whether art is "superior" or "inferior"? Are such judgments important to make?

Further Reading

Greene, K. "Gothic Material Culture." In Ian Hodder, ed. *Archaeology as Long-Term History.* 1987. 117–42.

Heather, Peter. *The Goths.* 1996. Chapter 10.

Hoxie, Albert. "Mutations in Art." In Lynn White Jr., ed. *The Transformation of the Roman World: Gibbon's Problem after Two Centuries.* 1966. 266–90.

ence in Gaul. Their king Clovis (r. 485–511) in 507 overthrew the Visigothic king in southern Gaul with support from the eastern Roman emperor. When the emperor named him an honorary consul, Clovis celebrated this ancient honor by having himself crowned with a diadem in the style of the emperors since Constantine. He carved out western Europe's largest new kingdom in what is today mostly France, overshadowing the neighboring and rival kingdoms of the Burgundians and Alemanni in eastern Gaul. Probably persuaded by his wife Clotilda, a Christian, to believe that God had helped him defeat the Alemanni, Clovis proclaimed himself an orthodox Christian and renounced Arianism,

which he had reportedly embraced previously. To build stability, he carefully fostered good relations with the bishops as the regime's intermediaries with the population.

Clovis's dynasty, called Merovingian♦ after the legendary Frankish ancestor Merovech, endured for another two hundred years, foreshadowing the kingdom that would emerge much later as the forerunner of modern France. The Merovingians survived so long because, better than any other kingdom, they created a workable symbiosis between their own traditions of military valor and Roman social and legal traditions, and because

♦**Merovingian:** mehr uh VIHN jee uhn

their location in far western Europe kept them out of the reach of the destructive invasions sent against Italy by the eastern emperor Justinian in the sixth century to reunite the Roman world.

Mixing Traditions

Western Europe's political transformation—the gradual replacement of imperial government by the new kingdoms—set in motion a social and cultural transformation (Map 7.4). The newcomers and their Roman subjects created novel ways of life by combining old traditions, as the Visigoth king Athaulf (r. 410–415) explained after marrying a Roman noblewoman:

> At the start I wanted to erase the Romans' name and turn their land into a Gothic empire, doing myself what Augustus had done. But I have learned that the Goths' freewheeling wildness will never accept the rule of law, and that state with no law is no state. Thus, I have more wisely chosen another path to glory: reviving the Roman name with Gothic vigor. I pray that future generations will remember me as the founder of a Roman restoration.

This process of social and cultural transformation promoted stability by producing new law codes but undermined long-term security by weakening the economic situation.

Visigothic and Frankish Law.   Roman law was the most influential precedent for the new kings in their efforts to construct stable states. Their original tribal societies never had written laws, but their new states required legal codes to create a sense of justice and keep order. The Visigothic kings were the first to issue a written law code. Published in Latin in about 475, it made fines and compensation the primary method for resolving disputes. Clovis also emphasized written law for the Merovingian kingdom. His code, also published in Latin between about 507 and 511, promoted social order through clear penalties for specific crimes. In particular, he formalized a system of fines intended to defuse feuds and vendettas between individuals and clans. The most prominent component of this system was **wergild**, the payment a murderer had to make as compensation for his crime. Most of the money was paid to the victim's kin, but the king received about one-third of the fine.

Since laws enshrine social values, the differing amounts of wergild in Clovis's code offer a glimpse of the relative values of different categories of people in his kingdom. Murdering a woman of childbearing age, a boy under twelve, or a man in the king's retinue incurred a massive fine of six hundred gold coins, enough to buy six hundred cattle. A woman past child-

Upper-Class Country Life

This fourth-century mosaic, fourteen by eighteen feet, covered a floor in a country villa at Carthage in North Africa. Like a set of cartoon strips, it portrays the life of an elite couple on their estate at different seasons of the year. Their home, resplendent with towers and a second-story colonnade, stands as a fortified retreat at the center. Above, the lady of the house sits in park-like surroundings while her servants and tenants tend to animals; winter activities are at the left, summer at the right. In the middle, hunters pursue game. Below left, the lady appears in springtime; below right, her husband in autumn. The servant to his left hands him a roll addressed "to the master Julius," revealing his name. Rural estates such as these provided prosperity and idyllic security for their owners in the western empire. They also made tempting targets for the Vandals during their invasion of North Africa; with the weakening of the provincial government in this period, these estates had to provide their own defense against raiders. *Le Musée du Bardo, Tunis.*

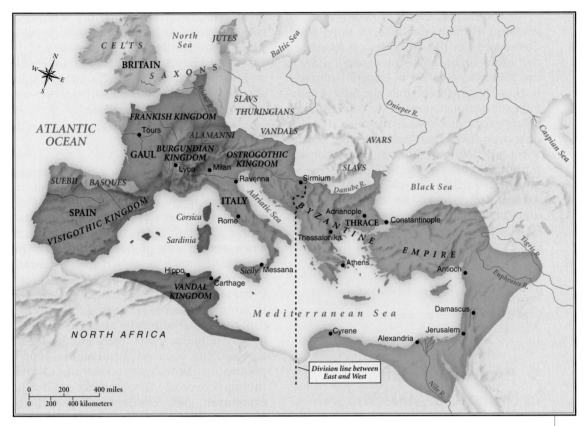

MAP 7.4 Peoples and Kingdoms of the Roman World, c. 526
The provinces of the Roman empire had always been home to a population diverse in language and ethnicity. By the early sixth century, the territory of the western empire had become a welter of diverse political units as well. Italy and most of the former western provinces were ruled by kingdoms organized by different non-Roman peoples, who had moved into former imperial territory over several centuries. The eastern empire, which we call the Byzantine Empire, remained under the political control of the emperor in Constantinople (formerly Byzantium until refounded by Constantine in 330).

bearing age (specified as sixty years), a young girl, or a freeborn man was valued at two hundred. Ordinary slaves rated thirty-five.

A Transformed Economic Landscape. The migrations that transformed the west harmed its already weakened economy. The Vandals' violent sweep severely damaged many towns in Gaul, hastening the decline of urban communities that had been growing for some time. In the countryside, now outside the control of any central government, wealthy Romans built sprawling villas on extensive estates, staffed by tenants bound to the land like slaves. These establishments strove to operate as self-sufficient units by producing all they needed, defending themselves against raids, and keeping their distance from any

authorities. Craving isolation, the owners shunned municipal offices and tax collection, the public services that had supplied the lifeblood of Roman administration. The vestiges of provincial government disappeared, and the new kingdoms never matured sufficiently to replace their services fully.

The situation only grew grimmer as the effects of these changes multiplied one another. The infrastructure of trade—roads and bridges—fell into disrepair with no public-spirited elite to maintain them. Nobles holed up on their estates could take care of themselves and their fortress-like households because they could be astonishingly rich. The very wealthiest boasted an annual income rivaling that of entire provinces in the old western empire.

In some cases, these fortunate few helped transmit Roman learning to later ages. Cassiodorus (c. 490–585), for one, founded a monastery on his ancestral estate in Italy in the 550s after a career in imperial administration. He gave the monks the task of copying manuscripts to keep their contents from disappearing as old ones disintegrated. His own book *Institutions* encapsulated the respect for tradition that kept classical traditions alive: listing the books a person of superior education should read, it included ancient secular texts as well as Scripture and Christian literature. The most strenuous effort to perpetuate the Roman past, however, came in the eastern empire.

> **Review:** What transformations took place in the society of the non-Romans who came into the Roman Empire from around 370 to the 550s?

❖ Byzantine Empire in the East, c. 500–565

The eastern empire avoided the massive transformations that reshaped western Europe. The east's trade and agriculture kept it from poverty, while its emperors employed force, diplomacy, and bribery to prevent invasions from the north and defeat attacks by the Sassanid kingdom in Persia, which was still making periodic attacks against the eastern empire. By about 500, the eastern empire had achieved such riches and ambition that historians have given it a new name, the **Byzantine empire**. Its emperors would rule in Constantinople until 1453, when a Turkish army finally captured the capital.

These rulers confidently saw themselves as perpetuating the Roman Empire and guarding its culture against barbarism; they regarded themselves as protectors of Constantine's "new Rome." The most famous early Byzantine emperor, Justinian (r. 527–565), took this mission so seriously that he waged war for decades against the non-Roman kingdoms in the west, aiming to reunite the empire and return it to its original scale as created by Augustus. Like Diocletian,

Justinian enlarged the authority of imperial rule and tried to purify religion to provide what he saw as the strong leadership and divine favor necessary in unsettled times. He and his successors in the Byzantine empire also contributed to later history by preserving much of classical literature.

Byzantine Society

The sixth-century Byzantine empire enjoyed a vitality that had vanished in the west. Its elite spent freely on silk, precious stones, and prized spices such as pepper imported from China and India. Markets in its large cities teemed with merchants from far and wide. Its churches' soaring domes testified to its confidence in God as its divine protector.

In keeping with Roman tradition, the Byzantine emperors sponsored religious festivals and entertainments on a massive scale to rally public support. Rich and poor alike crowded city squares, theaters, and hippodromes on these lively occasions. Chariot racing aroused the hottest passions. Constantinople's residents divided themselves into competitive factions called Blues and Greens after the racing colors of their favorite charioteers. These high-energy fans mixed religious competition with their sports rivalry: orthodox Christians joined the Blues, while Monophysites were Greens. They brawled with one another over theology as well as race results.

Preserving "Romanness." The Byzantine emperors ardently strove to maintain Roman tradition and identity, believing that "Romanness" was an important defense against what had happened to the western empire. They hired many foreign mercenaries, but they also tried to keep their subjects from adopting foreign ways. Styles of dress figured prominently in this struggle. Eastern emperors ordered Constantinople's residents not to wear barbarian-style clothing (especially heavy boots and clothing made from animal furs) instead of traditional Roman garb (sandals or light shoes and robes).

The quest for cultural unity was hopeless because Byzantine society was thoroughly multilingual and multiethnic. Byzantines regarded themselves as the heirs of ancient

Roman culture: they pointedly referred to themselves as Romans. At the same time, they spoke Greek as their native language and used Latin only for government and military communication. Many people retained their traditional languages, such as Phrygian and Cappadocian in western Asia Minor, Armenian farther east, and Syriac♦ and other Aramaic dialects along the eastern Mediterranean coast. The streets of Constantinople reportedly rang with seventy-two languages.

Romanness definitely included Christianity, but the Byzantines' theological diversity rivaled their ethnic complexity. Bitter controversies over doctrine divided eastern Christians; neither the emperors nor the bishops succeeded in imposing orthodoxy. Emperors used violence against heretics when persuasion failed. They had to resort to extreme measures, they believed, to save lost souls and preserve the empire's religious purity and divine goodwill. The persecution of Christian subjects by Christian emperors illustrates the disturbing consequences that the quest for a unitary identity required.

Women in Society and at Court. Most women in Byzantine society lived according to ancient Mediterranean tradition: they concentrated on the support of their households and minimized contact with men outside that circle. Law barred them from fulfilling many public functions, such as witnessing wills. Subject to the authority of their fathers and husbands, women veiled their heads (though not their faces) to show modesty. Since Christian theologians exceeded Roman tradition in restricting sexuality and reproduction, divorce became more difficult and remarriage was discouraged even for widows. Stiffer legal penalties for sexual offenses also were imposed. Female prostitution remained legal and common, but emperors raised the penalties for those who forced women under their control (children or slaves) into prostitution.

Women in the imperial family could achieve prominence unattainable for their workaday contemporaries. Theodora (d. 548), wife of the emperor Justinian, dramatically exhibited the influence women could achieve

in Byzantine monarchy. Uninhibited by her humble origins (she was the daughter of a bear trainer and had been an actress with a scandalous reputation), she came to rival anyone in influence and wealth (see the mosaic of Theodora on page 274). She had a hand in every aspect of Justinian's rule, advising him on personnel for his administration, pushing for her religious views in disputes over Christian doctrine, and rallying his courage at times of crisis. John Lydus, a contemporary government official and high-ranking administrator, judged her "superior in intelligence to any man."

Social Class and Government Services. Byzantine government aggravated social divisions because it provided services according to people's wealth. Officials demanded fees for countless activities, from commercial permits to legal grievances. Nothing got done without payment. People with money and status found this process easy: they relied on their social connections to get a hearing from the right official and on their wealth to pay bribes to move matters along quickly. Whether seeking preferential treatment or just spurring administrators to do what they were supposed to do, the rich could make the system work. The poor, by contrast, could not afford the hefty amounts that government officials extorted.

This fee-based system saved the emperors money to spend on other goals; they could pay their civil servants paltry salaries because the public paid them fees. John Lydus, for example, reported that he earned thirty times his annual salary in payments from petitioners during his first year in office. To keep the system from destroying itself through limitless extortion, the emperors published an official list of the maximum bribes that their employees could exact.

The Reign of Justinian, 527–565

Justinian, the most famous early Byzantine emperor, spent his regime's money trying to reverse the subdivision of the empire. Born in a small Balkan town, he rose rapidly in imperial service until 527, when he succeeded his uncle as emperor (see the mosaic of Justinian on page 275). During his reign he launched enormous military expeditions to

♦**Syriac:** SIHR ee ak

Theodora and Her Court in Ravenna
This resplendent mosaic shows the empress Theodora (c. 500–548) and members of her court presenting a gift to the church at San Vitale in Ravenna. It faced the matching scene of her husband Justinian and his attendants. Theodora wears the jewels, pearls, and rich robes characteristic of Byzantine monarchs. (Compare the style of the clothes in these two mosaics to those shown in the sculptural scene from Augustus's time on page 206. What were the different styles of dress meant to convey about the leaders in each period?) Theodora extends in her hands a gem-encrusted wine cup as her present; her gesture imitates the gift-giving of the Magi to the baby Jesus, the scene illustrated on the hem of her garment. The circle around her head, called a nimbus (Latin for "cloud"), indicates special holiness.
Scala/Art Resource, NY.

try to reunite the Roman Empire. His desire to perpetuate imperial glory also led him to embellish Constantinople with magnificent and costly architecture. The first intellectual on the throne since Julian in the 360s, Justinian was motivated by his deep interest in the law and theology to impose reforms with the same aims as all his predecessors: to preserve social order based on hierarchy and maintain divine goodwill. Unfortunately, the financial strains of his campaigns and programs instead led to social unrest.

Financial Distress and Social Unrest.
Justinian faced bitter resistance to his plans and their enormous cost. So unpopular were his taxes that they provoked a major riot in 532. Known as the Nika♦ Riot, it arose when the Blue and Green factions gathering to watch chariot races unexpectedly united against the emperor, shouting "Nika! Nika!" ("Win! Win!") as their battle cry. After nine days of violence that left much of Constantinople in ashes, Justinian was ready to abandon his throne and flee in panic. But Theodora sternly rebuked him: "Once born, no one can escape dying, but for one who has held im-

perial power it would be unbearable to be a fugitive. May I never take off my imperial robes of purple, nor live to see the day when those who meet me will not greet me as their ruler." Her husband then sent in troops, who quelled the disturbance by slaughtering thirty thousand rioters trapped in the racetrack.

Justinian's most ambitious goal was to restore the empire to a unified territory, religion, and culture. Invading the former western provinces, his brilliant generals Belisarius♦ and Narses♦ defeated the Vandals and Ostrogoths after campaigns that in some cases took decades to complete. With enormous effort and expense, imperial armies reoccupied Italy, the Dalmatian coast, Sicily, Sardinia, Corsica, part of southern Spain, and western North Africa by 562. These successes indeed restored the old empire's geography temporarily: Justinian's territory stretched from the Atlantic to the western edge of Mesopotamia.

These military triumphs came at a tragic cost: they destroyed the west's infrastructure and the east's finances. Italy endured the most physical damage; the war there against

♦**Nika:** NEE kah

♦**Belisarius:** beh luh SAWR ee uhs
♦**Narses:** NAHR seez

Justinian and His Court in Ravenna

This mosaic scene dominated by the Byzantine emperor Justinian (r. 527–565) stands across the chancel from Theodora's mosaic in San Vitale's church in Ravenna. The emperor is shown presenting a gift to the church. Justinian and Theodora finished building the church, which the Ostrogothic king Theodoric had started, to commemorate their successful campaign to restore Italy to the Roman Empire and reassert control of the western capital, Ravenna. The inclusion of the portrait of Maximianus, bishop of Ravenna, standing on Justinian's left and identified by name, stresses the theme of cooperation between bishops and emperors in ruling the world. What do you think the inclusion of the soldiers at the left is meant to indicate? *Scala/Art Resource, NY.*

the Goths spread death and destruction on a massive scale. The east suffered because Justinian squeezed even more taxes out of his already overburdened population to finance the western wars and bribe the Persian kingdom not to attack while his home defenses were depleted. The tax burden crippled the economy, leading to constant banditry in the countryside. Crowds poured into the capital from rural areas, seeking relief from poverty and robbers.

Natural disaster compounded Justinian's troubles. In the 540s, a horrific epidemic killed a third of his empire's inhabitants; a quarter of a million succumbed in Constantinople alone, half the capital's population. This was only the first of many pandemics that erased millions of people in the eastern empire over the next two centuries. Serious earthquakes, always a danger in this region, increased the death toll. The loss of so many people created a shortage of army recruits, requiring the hire of expensive mercenaries, and left countless farms vacant, reducing tax revenues.

Strengthening Monarchy. The threats to his regime made Justinian crave stability, which he sought by strengthening his authority in two ways: emphasizing his close-

ness to God and increasing the autocratic power of his rule. These traits became characteristic of Byzantine emperors. His artists brilliantly recast the symbols of his rule in a Christian context. A gleaming mosaic in his church at San Vitale♦ in Ravenna, for example, displayed a dramatic vision of the emperor's role: Justinian standing at the center of the cosmos shoulder to shoulder with both Christ and the ancient Hebrew patriarch Abraham. Moreover, Justinian proclaimed the emperor the "living law," recalling the Hellenistic royal doctrine that the ruler's decisions defined law.

His building program in Constantinople communicated his overpowering supremacy and religiosity. Most spectacular of all was his reconstruction of Constantine's Hagia Sophia♦ (Church of the Holy Wisdom). Creating a new design for churches, his architects erected a huge building on a square plan capped by a dome 107 feet across and soaring 160 feet above the floor. Its interior walls glowed like the sun from the light reflecting off their four acres of gold mosaics. Imported marble of every color added to the sparkling

---

♦**San Vitale:** sahn vee TAHL eh
♦**Hagia Sophia:** HAH gee uh so FEE uh

effect. When he first entered his masterpiece, dedicated in 538, Justinian exclaimed, "Solomon, I have outdone you," claiming to have bested the glorious temple that the ancient king built for the Hebrews.

His more autocratic monarchy reduced the autonomy of the empire's cities. Their councils ceased to govern; imperial officials took over instead. Provincial elites still had to ensure full payment of their area's taxes, but they lost the compensating reward of deciding local matters. Now the imperial government determined all aspects of decision making and social status. Men of property from the provinces who aspired to power and prestige knew they could satisfy their ambitions only by joining the imperial administration in the capital.

Constantinople during the Rule of Justinian

Law and Religion.   To solidify his authority, Justinian codified the laws of the empire to bring uniformity to the confusing mass of decisions that earlier emperors had announced. The final version of his *Codex* appeared in 534. A team of scholars also condensed millions of words of regulations to produce the *Digest* in 533, intended to expedite legal cases and provide a syllabus for law schools. This collection, like the *Codex* written in Latin and therefore readable in the western empire, influenced legal scholars for centuries. Justinian's legal experts also compiled a textbook for students, the *Institutes*, which appeared in 533 and remained on law school reading lists until modern times.

To fulfill the emperor's sacred duty to secure the welfare of his people, Justinian acted to enforce their religious purity. Like the polytheist and Christian emperors before him, he believed his world could not flourish if its divine protector became angered by the presence of religious offenders. As emperor, Justinian decided who the offenders were. Zealously enforcing laws against polytheists, he compelled them to be baptized or forfeit their lands and official positions. He also relentlessly purged heretical Christians who re-

jected his version of orthodoxy. In pursuit of sexual purity, his laws made male homosexual relations illegal for the first time in Roman history. Homosexual marriage, apparently not uncommon earlier, had been officially prohibited in 342, but civil sanctions had never before been imposed on men engaging in homosexual activity. All the previous emperors, for example, had simply taxed male prostitutes. The legal status of homosexual activity between women is less clear; it probably counted as adultery when married women were involved and thus constituted criminal behavior.

A brilliant theologian in his own right, Justinian labored mightily to reconcile orthodox and Monophysite Christians by having the creed of the Council of Chalcedon revised. But the church leaders in Rome and Constantinople had become too bitterly divided and too jealous of the others' prominence to agree on a unified church; the eastern and western churches were by now firmly launched on the diverging courses that would result in formal schism five hundred years later. Justinian's own ecumenical council in Constantinople ended in disaster in 553 when he jailed Rome's defiant Pope Vigilius while also managing to alienate Monophysite bishops. Probably no one could have done better, but his efforts to compel religious unity only drove Christians further apart and undermined his vision of a restored Roman world.

Preserving Classical Literature

Christianization of the empire put the survival of classical literature—plays, histories, poems, speeches, and novels alike—at risk because these works were polytheist and therefore potentially subversive of Christian belief. The real danger to the classical tradition, however, stemmed not so much from active censorship as simple neglect. As Christians became authors, which they did in great numbers, their works displaced the ancient texts of Greece and Rome as the most important literature of the age. Fortunately for later times, however, the Byzantine Empire played a crucial role in preserving the brilliant intellectual legacy of the past.

Classical texts survived because Christian education and literature depended on non-Christian models, Latin and Greek. In the eastern empire, the region's original Greek culture remained the dominant influence, but Latin literature continued to be read because the administration was bilingual, with official documents and laws published in Rome's ancient tongue along with Greek translations. Latin scholarship in the east received a boost when Justinian's Italian wars impelled Latin-speaking scholars to flee for safety to Constantinople. Their labors in the capital helped to conserve many works that might otherwise have disappeared in the violence in the western empire. Byzantine scholars preserved classical literature because they regarded it as a crucial part of a high-level education, an attitude reflecting their deep regard for elite tradition. Much of the classical literature available today survived because it served as schoolwork for Byzantine Christians. At least a rudimentary knowledge of some pre-Christian classics was required for a good career in government service, the goal of every ambitious student. In the words of an imperial decree from 360, "No person shall obtain a post of the first rank unless it shall be shown that he excels in long practice of liberal studies, and that he is so polished in literary matters that words flow from his pen faultlessly."

Another factor promoting the preservation of classical literature was that the principles of classical rhetoric provided the guidelines for the most effective presentation of Christian theology. When Ambrose, bishop of Milan from 374 to 397, composed the first systematic description of Christian ethics for young priests, he consciously imitated the great classical orator Cicero. Theologians refuted heretical Christian doctrines by employing the dialogue form pioneered by Plato, and polytheist traditions of laudatory biography inspired the hugely popular genre on saints' lives. Similarly, Christian artists incorporated polytheist traditions in communicating their beliefs and emotions in paintings, mosaics, and carved reliefs. A favorite artistic motif of Christ with a sunburst surrounding his head, for example, took its inspiration from polytheist depiction of the radiant Sun as a god.

The proliferation of Christian literature generated a technological innovation used

The Soaring Architecture of Hagia Sophia
Golden mosaics originally reflected a dazzling light from the interior of Hagia Sophia ("Holy Wisdom"), the enormous church that the Byzantine emperor Justinian built in the 530s c.e. near his palace in Constantinople. A central dome, 184 feet high and supported by four arches resting on massive piers, capped the church's vast interior; the ring of windows at the base of the dome is just visible at the top of the picture. Hagia Sophia became a mosque after the Turks captured the city in 1453; the large medallions contain religious quotations in Arabic. Now a museum, Hagia Sophia continues to host people offering prayers. © *Adam Woolfitt/Corbis.*

also to preserve classical literature. Polytheist scribes had written books on sheets of thin animal skin or paper made from papyrus. They then glued the sheets together and attached rods at both ends to form a scroll. Readers faced a cumbersome task in unrolling scrolls to read. For ease of use, Christians produced their literature in the form of the codex—a book with bound pages that was less susceptible to damage from rolling and unrolling and contained text more efficiently than scrolls. Eventually the codex became the standard form of book production in the Byzantine world.

Despite the continuing importance of classical Greek and Latin literature in Byzantine education and rhetoric, its survival remained precarious in a war-torn world dominated by Christians. Knowledge of Greek in the turbulent west faded so drastically that by the sixth century almost no one there could read the original versions of Homer's *Iliad* and *Odyssey*, the traditional foundations

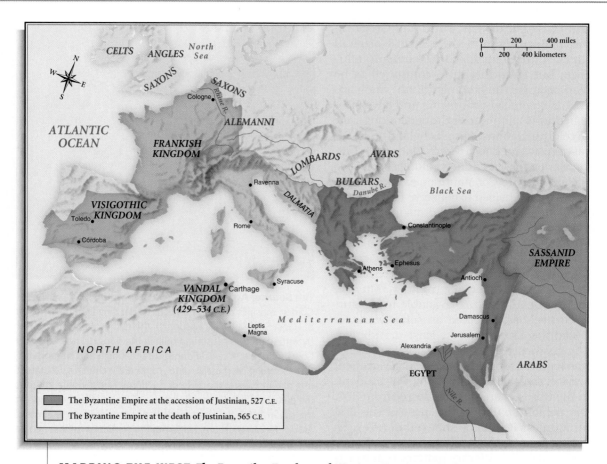

MAPPING THE WEST **The Byzantine Empire and Western Europe, c. 600**
The Byzantine emperor Justinian employed brilliant generals and expended huge sums of money to reconquer Italy, North Africa, and part of Spain to reunite the western and eastern halves of the former Roman Empire. His wars to regain Italy and North Africa eliminated the Ostrogothic and Vandal kingdoms, respectively, but at a huge cost in effort, time—the war in Italy took twenty years—and expense. The resources of the eastern empire were so depleted that his successors could not maintain the reunification. By the early seventh century, the Visigoths had taken back all of Spain. Africa, despite serious revolts by indigenous Berber tribes, remained under imperial control until the Arab conquest of the seventh century, but within five years of Justinian's death the Lombards had set up a new kingdom controlling a large section of Italy. Never again would anyone attempt to reestablish a universal Roman empire.

of a classical literary education. Latin fared better, and scholars such as Augustine and Jerome knew Rome's ancient literature extremely well. But they also saw its classics as potentially too seductive for a pious Christian because the pleasure that came from reading them could be a distraction from the worship of God. Jerome in fact once had a nightmare of being condemned on Judgment Day for having been a Ciceronian instead of a Christian.

The closing around 530 of the Academy founded in Athens by Plato more than nine

hundred years earlier vividly demonstrated the dangers for classical learning lurking in the Byzantine world. This most famous of classical schools finally went out of business when many of its scholars emigrated to Persia to escape harsher restrictions on polytheists and its revenues dwindled because the Athenian elite, its traditional supporters, were increasingly Christianized. The Neoplatonist school at Alexandria, by contrast, continued; its leader John Philoponus◆

◆**Philoponus:** fy luh POH nuhs

(his name means "loves to work," c. 490–570) was a Christian. In addition to Christian theology, Philoponus wrote commentaries on the works of Aristotle published from 517 to around 530; some of his ideas anticipated those of Galileo a thousand years later. With his work, he achieved the kind of synthesis of old and new that was one of the fruitful possibilities in the ferment of the late Roman world—he was a Christian subject of the Byzantine Empire in sixth-century Egypt, heading a school founded long before by polytheists, studying the works of an ancient Greek philosopher as the inspiration for his forward-looking scholarship. The strong possibility that present generations could learn from the past would continue as Western civilization once again remade itself in medieval times.

> **Review:** What role did the emperor Justinian see himself playing in Roman history?

Conclusion

The third-century civil wars brought the Roman Empire to a turning point. Military activity was so prominent that, as Isis wrote to her mother, it seemed as if everybody was in the army. Diocletian's creation of the dominate and reorganization of government delayed the empire's fragmentation, but his principle of subdivision opened the way to its separation in 395 into western and eastern halves. From this time on, Roman history increasingly divided into two regional streams, even though emperors as late as Justinian in the sixth century retained the dream of reuniting the empire and restoring it to the glory of its Golden Age.

Multiple disasters interacted to destroy the unity of the Roman world, beginning with the catastrophic losses of property and people during the third-century crisis, which hit the west harder than the east. In the late fourth century migrations of non-Roman peoples fleeing the Huns brought pressures on the central government. When the Roman authorities bungled the task of integrating the immigrant tribes into Roman society, the newcomers created kingdoms that eventually replaced imperial government in the west. This change transformed not only the west's politics, society, and economy but also the tribes themselves, as they developed a sense of ethnic identity while organizing themselves into kingdoms inside Roman territory. The economic deterioration accompanying these transformations drove a stake into the heart of the elite public-spiritedness that had been one of the foundations of imperial stability, as wealthy nobles retreated to self-sufficient country estates and shunned municipal office.

The eastern empire fared better economically and parried the worst violence of the migrations. As the Byzantine state, it self-consciously continued the empire both politically and culturally by working to preserve "Romanness." The financial drain of pursuing the goal of unity through war against the new kingdoms increased social discontent by driving tax rates to punitive levels, while the concentration of power in the capital weakened the local communities that had made the empire robust.

This period of increasing political and social division saw the official religious unification of the empire under the banner of Christianity. Constantine's conversion in 312 marked an epochal turning point in Western history. Christianization of the Roman world occurred gradually, and Christians disagreed among themselves, even to the point of violence, over fundamental doctrines of faith. The church developed a hierarchy to combat disunity, but believers proved remarkably recalcitrant in the face of authority. Many of them abandoned everyday society to live as monks attempting to come closer to God personally and praying daily for mercy for the world. Monastic life redefined the meaning of holiness by creating communities of God's heroes who withdrew from this world to devote their service to glorifying the next. In the end, then, the imperial vision of unity faded before the divisive forces of religious strife combined with the powerful dynamics of political and social transformation. Nevertheless, the memory of Roman power and culture remained potent and present, providing an influential inheritance to the peoples and states that would become Rome's heirs.

Suggested References

Reorganizing the Empire, 284–395

Scholars continue to debate the religious motives of Diocletian and Constantine. Understanding them is challenging because their religious sensibilities, markedly different from those of most modern believers, so deeply influenced their political actions.

Bowersock, G. W., Peter Brown, and Oleg Grabar, eds. *Late Antiquity: A Guide to the Postclassical World.* 1999.

Elsner, Jaś. *Imperial Rome and Christian Triumph: The Art of the Roman Empire* A.D. *100–450.* 1998.

*Grubbs, Judith Evans. *Women and Law in the Roman Empire: A Sourcebook on Marriage, Divorce, and Widowhood.* 2002.

Southern, Pat, and Karen R. Dixon. *The Late Roman Army.* 1996.

Christianizing the Empire, 312–c. 540

Recent research has deepened our appreciation of the emotional depths that the Christianization of the empire stirred for both polytheists and Christians. People's ideas about themselves changed as their ideas about divinity changed.

Brown, Peter. *Augustine of Hippo: A Biography.* Rev. ed. 2000.

Caner, Daniel. *Wandering, Begging Monks: Spiritual Authority and the Promotion of Monasticism in Late Antiquity.* 2002.

Curran, John. *Pagan City and Christian Capital: Rome in the Fourth Century.* 2000.

Drake, H. A. *Constantine and the Bishops: The Politics of Intolerance.* 2000.

*Early Christian literature: http://www.ocf .org/OrthodoxPage/reading/St.Pachomius/ Welcome.html.

Glancy, Jennifer A. *Slavery in Early Christianity.* 2002.

*Lee, A. D. *Pagans and Christians in Late Antiquity: A Sourcebook.* 2000.

*Maas, Michael. *Readings in Late Antiquity, A Sourcebook.* 2000.

MacMullen, Ramsay. *Christianity and Paganism in the Fourth to Eighth Centuries.* 1997.

Trombley, Frank R. *Hellenic Religion and Christianization c. 370–529.* Vol. 2. 2001.

---

*Primary source.

Non-Roman Kingdoms in the West, c. 370–550s

Debate still thrives over how to categorize the social and cultural transformation of the Roman world in the fourth and fifth centuries and the ethnogenesis (development of a separate ethnic identity) of the non-Roman peoples who created new kingdoms inside the empire's borders.

Burns, Thomas. *Rome and the Barbarians.* 2003.

Carr, Karen Eva. *Vandals to Visigoths: Rural Settlement Patterns in Early Medieval Spain.* 2002.

*Drew, Katherine Fischer. *The Laws of the Salian Franks.* 1991.

Effros, Bonnie. *Merovingian Mortuary Archaeology and the Making of the Middle Ages.* 2003.

Geary, Patrick J. *The Myth of Nations: The Medieval Origins of Europe.* 2001.

Goffart, Walter. *Barbarians and Romans,* A.D. *418–584.* 1987.

Heather, Peter. *The Goths and Romans.* 1996.

Lançon, Bertrand. *Rome in Late Antiquity: Everyday Life and Urban Change,* A.D. *312–609.* Trans. Antonia Nevill. 2001.

MacGeorge, Penny. *Late Roman Warlords.* 2002.

*Mathisen, Ralph W. *People, Personal Expression, and Social Relations in Late Antiquity.* 2 vols. 2002.

Byzantine Empire in the East, c. 500–565

Scholars today recognize the Byzantine Empire as the continuation of the eastern Roman Empire, emphasizing the challenge posed to its rulers in trying to maintain order and prosperity for their distinctly multicultural and multilingual population.

Byzantine civilization: http://www.fordham .edu/halsall/byzantium.

Cavallo, Guglielmo, ed. *The Byzantines.* 1997.

*Geanakoplos, Deno J. *Byzantium: Church, Society, and Civilization Seen Through Contemporary Eyes.* 1986.

Haldon, John. *The Byzantine Wars.* 2001.

Kalavrezou, Ioli. *Byzantine Women and Their World.* 2003.

Mango, Cyril, ed. *The Oxford History of Byzantium.* 2002.

Moorhead, John. *The Roman Empire Divided, 400–700.* 2001.

Women in Byzantine history, bibliography: http://www.wooster.edu/Art/wb.html.

CHAPTER REVIEW

IMPORTANT EVENTS

293	Diocletian creates the tetrarchy
301	Diocletian issues the Edict on Maximum Prices
303	Diocletian launches Great Persecution of Christians
312	Constantine wins the battle of the Milvian Bridge and converts to Christianity
313	Constantine and Licinius proclaim religious toleration in the Edict of Milan
c. 323	Pachomius in Upper Egypt establishes the first monasteries for men and women
324	Constantine wins the civil war and refounds Byzantium as Constantinople, the "new Rome"
325	Council of Nicaea
361–363	Julian the Apostate tries to reinstate traditional religion as official state religion
391	Theodosius I makes Christianity the official state religion
395	Theodosius I divides the empire into western and eastern halves
410	Visigoths sack Rome
426	Augustine publishes *City of God*
451	Council of Chalcedon
c. 475	Visigothic law code published
476	The "Fall of Rome" (German commander Odoacer deposes the final western emperor, the boy Romulus Augustulus)
493–526	Ostrogothic kingdom in Italy
507	Clovis establishes Frankish kingdom in Gaul
527–565	Reign of Byzantine emperor Justinian
533–534	Justinian publishes law code and handbooks
c. 540	Benedict devises his rule for monasteries

KEY TERMS

apostate (254)

Arianism (257)

asceticism (260)

Byzantine empire (272)

coloni (251)

curials (251)

dominate (246)

Edict of Milan (253)

Great Persecution (251)

tetrarchy (247)

wergild (270)

REVIEW QUESTIONS

1. What changes did Diocletian and his successors make in their reorganization of the empire and why?
2. What were the major spiritual disputes among early Christians and why were they so fierce?
3. What transformations took place in the society of the non-Romans who came into the Roman Empire from around 370 to the 550s?
4. What role did the emperor Justinian see himself playing in Roman history?

MAKING CONNECTIONS

1. What were the main similarities and differences between the political reality and the political appearance of the principate and the dominate?
2. What were the main similarities and differences between traditional Roman religion and Christianity as official state religion?

FOR FURTHER EXPLORATION

To assess your mastery of the material in this chapter, see the Online Study Guide at **bedfordstmartins.com/hunt**.

To read additional primary-source material from this period, see Chapter 7 in *Sources of The Making of the West*, Second Edition.

in interpreting it. The Arab world's religion, Islam, accepted the same one God that Christians did but considered Jesus one of God's prophets rather than his son.

The history of the seventh and eighth centuries is a story of adaptation and transformation. Historians consider the changes important enough to signal the end of one era—antiquity—and the beginning of another—the Middle Ages. (See "Terms of History," page 286.) During this period, all three heirs of the Roman Empire combined elements of their heritage with new values, interests, and conditions. The divergences among them resulted from disparities in geographical and climatic conditions, material and human resources, skills, and local traditions. But these differences should not obscure the fact that the Byzantine, Muslim, and western European worlds were sibling cultures.

❖ Byzantium: A Christian Empire under Siege

Emperor Justinian (r. 527–565) had tried to re-create the old Roman Empire. On the surface he succeeded. His empire once again included Italy, North Africa, and the Balkans. Vestiges of old Roman society persisted: an educated elite maintained its prestige, town governments continued to function, and old myths and legends were retold in poetry and depicted on silver plates and chests. By 600, however, the Byzantine Empire began to undergo a transformation as striking as the

one that had earlier remade the western half. Almost constant war beginning in the last third of the sixth century shrank Byzantium's territory drastically. Cultural and political change came as well. Cities decayed, and the countryside became the focus of governmental and military administration. In the wake of these shifts, the old elite largely disappeared and classical learning gave way to new forms of education, mainly religious in content. The traditional styles of urban life, dependent on public gathering places and community spirit, faded away.

Wars on the Frontiers, c. 570–750

From about 570 to 750, the Byzantine Empire waged war against invaders. One key challenge came from an old enemy, Persia. Another involved many new groups—Lombards, Slavs, Avars,◆ Bulgars, and Muslims. In the wake of these onslaughts, Byzantium was transformed.

Invasions from Persia.   The **Sassanid◆ Empire** of Persia was the superpower on the Byzantine doorstep. Since the third century, the Sassanid kings and Roman emperors had fought sporadically but never with decisive effect on either side. But in the middle of the sixth century, the Sassanids chose to concentrate their activities on their western half, Mesopotamia (today Iraq), nearer the Byzantine border (Map 8.1). They began to collect land taxes from the prosperous farmers of the

---

◆**Avars:** AY vahrz
◆**Sassanid:** suh SAH nihd

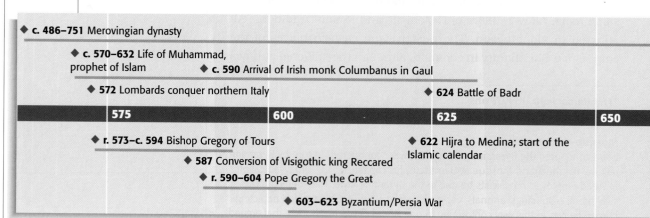

◆ **c. 486–751** Merovingian dynasty

◆ **c. 570–632** Life of Muhammad, prophet of Islam   ◆ **c. 590** Arrival of Irish monk Columbanus in Gaul

◆ **572** Lombards conquer northern Italy   ◆ **624** Battle of Badr

575   **600**   **625**   **650**

◆ **r. 573–c. 594** Bishop Gregory of Tours   ◆ **622** Hijra to Medina; start of the Islamic calendar

◆ **587** Conversion of Visigothic king Reccared

◆ **r. 590–604** Pope Gregory the Great

◆ **603–623** Byzantium/Persia War

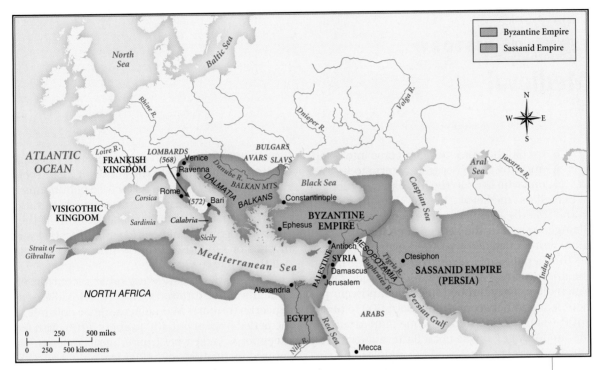

MAP 8.1 Byzantine and Sassanid Empires, c. 600
Justinian hoped to re-create the old Roman Empire, but just a century after his death Italy was largely conquered by the Lombards. Meanwhile, the Byzantine Empire had to contend with the Sassanid Empire to its east. In 600, these two major powers faced each other uneasily. Three years later, the Sassanid king attacked Byzantine territory. The resulting wars, which lasted until 627, exhausted both empires and left them open to invasion by the Arabs.

region, assuring their government of a steady, predictable income and turning Persia into a center of trade. Reforming the army, which previously had depended on nobles who could supply their own arms, the Sassanid kings began to pay and arm new warriors, drawn from the lower nobility.

The Sassanid rulers constructed their capital city at Ctesiphon♦ on the model of the great Byzantine city of Antioch (in fact, they gave it the title "Better-than-Antioch"). There they set up a bureaucracy of scribes tied to

♦**Ctesiphon:** TEH suh fahn

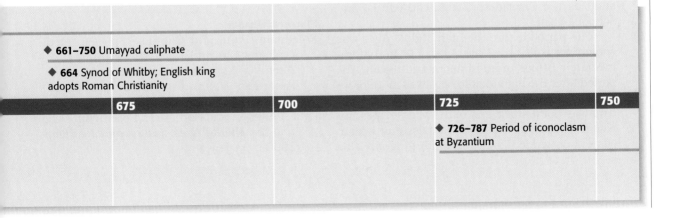

♦ **661–750** Umayyad caliphate

♦ **664** Synod of Whitby; English king adopts Roman Christianity

| 675 | 700 | 725 | 750 |

♦ **726–787** Period of iconoclasm at Byzantium

TERMS OF HISTORY

Medieval

How did the word *medieval* come into being, and why is it a derogatory term today? No one who lived in the Middle Ages thought of herself as "medieval." No one thought he lived in the "Middle Ages." The whole idea of the Middle Ages began in the sixteenth century. At that time, writers decided that their own age, known as the Renaissance (French for "rebirth"), and the ancient Greek and Roman civilizations were much alike. They dubbed the thousand-year period nearly in between—from about 600 to about 1400—with a Latin term: the *medium aevum*, or the "middle age." It was not a flattering term. Renaissance writers considered the middle age a single unfortunate, barbaric, and ignorant period.

Only with the Romantic movement of the nineteenth century and the advent of history as an academic discipline did writers begin to divide that middle age into several ages. Often, they divided it into three periods: early (c. 600–1100), high (c. 1100–1300), and late (c. 1300–1400). This categorization revealed a bias: the "high Middle Ages" was clearly considered more important—higher—than what came before or after. In the view of nineteenth-century historians, the high Middle Ages was important for two reasons. First, it saw the beginnings of modern institutions such as the common law, universities, and centralized states. Second, it fostered the development of typically medieval yet highly regarded institutions such as the Crusades, Gothic cathedrals, and scholasticism.

The period before the high Middle Ages was sometimes called the Dark Ages, a term that immediately brings to mind doom and gloom. The period after the high Middle Ages was more problematic for historians because the fourteenth century was not just the end of the Middle Ages but also the period in which the Renaissance began. Historians tended (and still tend) to ignore this fact. Instead, they fix on certain events, developments, and ideas within the period. If these seem modern and new—such as the rise of humanism and the development of diplomacy—historians call them part of the Renaissance. But if they seem retrograde or old—such as the ecstasies of mystics or knightly warfare—historians tend to call them late medieval.

One of the most remarkable recent developments in historians' view of the Middle Ages concerns the early Middle Ages. Since cultures in the period from about 400 to about 1100, with few exceptions, lacked centralized governments, organized institutions of higher learning, and well-developed legal systems, historians of the old school found little to praise in that time. However, in the 1960s some historians came to see the early Middle Ages differently. Rather than applaud the high Middle Ages for its bureaucratic states and its laws, they relished the variety of peoples, the informal methods of government, and the community involvement evident in the society of the early Middle Ages.

Today, newspaper reporters and others still sometimes use *medieval* as a pejorative term, for example, by calling a primitive prison system medieval. Little do they know that using the term in this way is as out-of-date as it was in the sixteenth century.

FURTHER READING

Freedman, Paul, and Gabrielle Spiegel. "Medievalisms Old and New: The Rediscovery of Alterity in North American Medieval Studies." *American Historical Review* 103 (1998): 677–704.

Little, Lester K., and Barbara H. Rosenwein. *Debating the Middle Ages: Issues and Readings.* 1998.

them by job and loyalty. They cultivated other writers and writings as well and thus opened their court to Byzantine and other Western influences and teachings. This openness accorded with their policy of maintaining good relations with the native population in Mesopotamia, many of whom were Nestorian Christians (see page 297), even though the Sassanid kings themselves still adhered to Zoroastrianism (see page 297).

These kings promoted an exalted view of themselves. They took the title "King of Kings" and gave the men at their court titles such as "priest of priests" and "scribe of scribes." (See A Sassanid King.) Royal glory was accompanied by military and imperial dreams. The Sassanid king Chosroes♦ II (r. 591–628) wanted to re-create the Persian empire of Xerxes and Darius, which had extended down through Syria all the way to Egypt. He began by invading the Byzantine Empire in 603, taking Damascus, Jerusalem, and even Egypt by 619. But the Byzantine emperor Heraclius reorganized his army and inspired his troops to avenge the sack of Jerusalem; by 627, the Byzantines had regained all their lost territory. The chief outcome of these fruitless confrontations was exhaustion on both sides.

Attack on All Fronts. Because Byzantium was preoccupied by war with the Sassanids, it was ill equipped to deal with other groups pushing into parts of the empire at about the same time (see Map 8.1). The Lombards, a Germanic people, arrived in northern Italy in 568 and by 572 were masters of the Po valley and some inland regions in Italy's south, leaving the Byzantines only Bari, Calabria, and Sicily as well as Rome and a narrow swath of land through the middle called the Exarchate♦ of Ravenna.

The Byzantine army could not contend any more successfully with the Slavs and other peoples just beyond the Danube River.

A Sassanid King

His head topped by a mighty horned headdress, this representation of a Sassanid ruler evokes the full majesty of a king of kings. A glance at "The Great King of Persia" on page 48 shows that traditional Persian sculpture was not, as here, in the round. The influence of Greek and Roman classical styles is evident in this sixth- or seventh-century bronze figure, despite the enmity between Sassanid Persia and Byzantium (heir of Greece and Rome) at the time. *Louvre/Agence Photographique de la réunion des musées nationaux.*

The Slavs conducted lightning raids on the Balkan countryside (part of Byzantium at the time); and, joined by the Avars, nomadic pastoralists and warriors, they attacked Byzantine cities as well. Meanwhile the Bulgars entered what is now Bulgaria in the 670s, defeating the Byzantine army and in 681 forcing the emperor to recognize their new state.

At the same time as the Byzantine Empire was being attacked on all fronts, its power was being whittled away by more peaceful means. For example, as Slavs and Avars, who were not subject to Byzantine rulers, settled in the Balkans, they often intermingled with the indigenous population, absorbing local agricultural techniques and burial practices while imposing their language and establishing religious cults.

Consequences of Constant Warfare. Byzantium's loss of control over the Balkans through both peaceful and military means meant the shrinking of its empire. More important over the long term was that the Balkans could no longer serve, as they had previously, as a major conduit between Byzantium and Europe. The loss of the Balkans exacerbated the increasing separation of the eastern and western parts of the former Roman Empire. The political division between the Greek-speaking and Latin-speaking halves had already begun in the fourth century. The events of the seventh century, however, made

---

♦**Chosroes:** KAHZ ruh eez
♦**Exarchate:** EHKS ar kate

the split both physical and cultural. Avar and Slavic control of the Balkans effectively cut off trade and travel between Constantinople and the cities of the Dalmatian coast, while the Bulgar state threw a political barrier across the Danube. Perhaps as a result of this physical separation, Byzantine historians ceased to be interested in Europe, and Byzantine scholars no longer bothered to learn Latin. The two halves of the former Roman Empire, once united, communicated very little in the seventh century.

The principal outcome of Byzantium's wars with the Sassanid Empire was the sap-ping of both Persian and Byzantine military strength. Exhausted, these empires were now vulnerable to attack by the Arabs, whose military prowess would create a new empire and spread a new religion, Islam. In the hundred years between 630 and 730, the Arabs succeeded in conquering much of the Byzantine Empire, at times attacking the very walls of Constantinople itself. No wonder the patriarch of Jerusalem saw in the Arab onslaught the impending end of the world: "Behold," he said, "the Abomination of Desolation, spoken of by the Prophet Daniel, that standeth in the Holy Place."

TAKING MEASURE

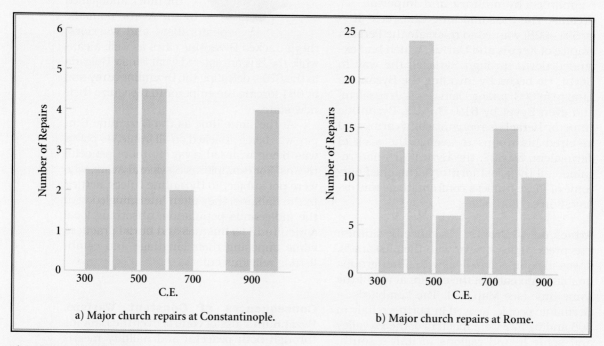

a) Major church repairs at Constantinople.

b) Major church repairs at Rome.

Church Repair, 600–900
The impoverishment of the period 600–750 is clear from graph (a), which shows a major slump in church repair at Constantinople during the period. If there had been any money to spend on building repairs, it would undoubtedly have gone to the churches first. By contrast, graph (b) shows that Rome was not so hard hit as Constantinople, even though it was part of the Byzantine Empire. There was, to be sure, a dramatic reduction in the number of church repairs in the period 500–600. But from 700 to 800, there was a clear, if small, increase. Taken together, the two graphs help show the toll taken by the invasions and financial hardships of the period 600–750. *Data adapted from Klavs Randsborg, "The Migration Period: Model History and Treasure," The Sixth Century: Production, Distribution and Demand, eds. Richard Hodges and William Bowden (Leiden: Brill, 1998).*

From an Urban to a Rural Way of Life

As their borders shrank, Byzantines had to contend with new rulers and learn to accommodate to them. When Byzantine subjects in Syria and Egypt found themselves under Arab rule, they adapted to the new conditions, paying a special tax to their conquerors and practicing their Christian and Jewish religions in peace. In the countryside they were permitted to keep and farm their lands, and their cities remained centers of government, scholarship, and business.

Ironically, the most radical transformations for seventh- and eighth-century Byzantines occurred not in the territories lost but in the shrunken empire itself. Under the ceaseless barrage of invaders, many towns, formerly bustling nodes of trade and centers of the imperial bureaucratic network, vanished or became unrecognizable in their changed way of life. The public activity of large, open marketplaces, theaters, and town squares largely ended. City baths, once places where people gossiped, made deals, and talked politics and philosophy, disappeared in most Byzantine towns—with the significant exception of Constantinople. Warfare reduced some cities to rubble, and the limited resources available for rebuilding went to construct thick city walls and solid churches instead of marketplaces and baths. Traders and craftspeople moved to overcrowded streets that looked much like the open-air bazaars of the modern Middle East. People under siege sought protection at home or in a church rather than in community pastimes. One example is the Byzantine city of Ephesus,♦ where the citizens who built the new walls in the seventh century enclosed not the old public edifices but rather their homes and churches (Map 8.2). Despite the new emphasis on church buildings, many cities were too impoverished even to repair their churches. (See Taking Measure on page 288)

The pressures of war against the Arabs brought a change in Byzantine society parallel to that in the western half of the empire a few centuries before. Above all the class of town councilors (the *curiales*), the elite that

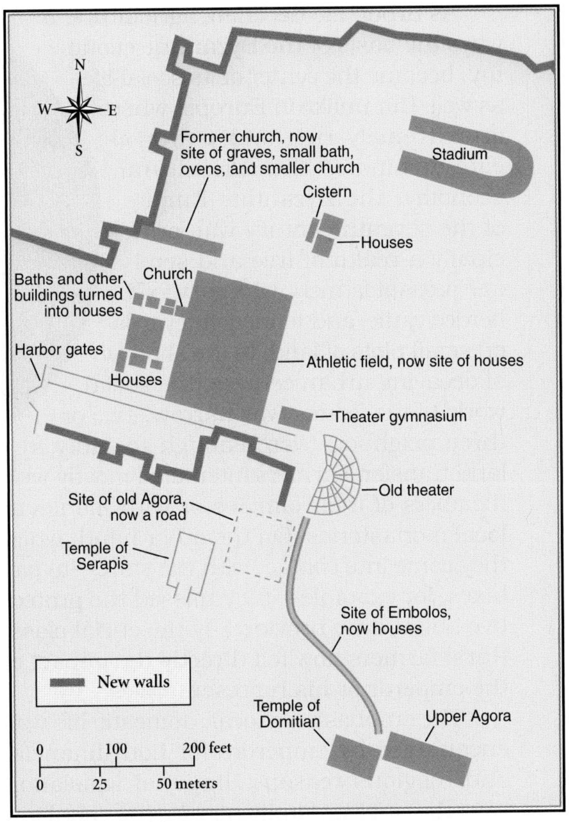

MAP 8.2 Diagram of the City of Ephesus
The center of classical Ephesus had been the agora and the embolos (a wide street paved with marble and rimmed by shops and monuments). After the seventh century, the city was partially destroyed, its population declined, and the rebuilt city—without agora or embolos—was located to the north and protected by walls.

for centuries had mediated between the emperor and the people, disappeared. But an upper class nevertheless remained: as in western Europe, bishops and their clergy continued to form a rich and powerful upper stratum even within declining cities.

Despite the general urban decay, the capital of Constantinople and a few other urban centers retained some of their old vitality. The manufacture and trade of fine silk textiles continued. Even though Byzantium's economic life became increasingly rural and barter-based in the seventh and eighth centuries, the skills, knowledge, and institutions of urban workers remained. The full use of these resources, however, had to await the end of centuries of debilitating wars.

♦**Ephesus:** EH fuh suhs

As urban life declined, agriculture, always the basis of the Byzantine economy, became the center of its social life as well. But unlike in Europe, where an extremely rich and powerful elite dominated the agricultural economy, the Byzantine Empire of the seventh century was principally a realm of free and semi-free peasant farmers, who grew food, herded cattle, and tended vineyards on small plots of land. In the shadow of decaying urban centers, the social world of the farmer was narrow. Two or three neighbors were enough to ratify a land transfer. Farmers interacted mostly with members of their families or with monks at local monasteries. On the other hand, when they came into contact with the state—to pay taxes, for example—they missed the protective buffer once provided by the curial class. Rural farmers now felt directly the impact of the emperor or his representatives.

The emphasis on local, domestic life was encouraged by emperors for both financial and religious reasons. Imperial legislation gave the nuclear family new institutional importance, narrowing the grounds for divorce and setting new punishments for marital infidelity. Husbands and wives who committed adultery were whipped and fined, and their noses were slit. Abortion was prohibited, and new protections were set in place against incest. Mothers were given equal power with fathers over their offspring and, if widowed, became the legal guardians of their minor children and controlled the household property.

New Military and Cultural Forms

The transformations of the countryside went hand in hand with military, political, and cultural changes. On the military front, the Byzantine navy found a potent weapon in "Greek fire," a combustible oil that floated on water and burst into flames upon hitting its target. Determined to win wars on land as well, the imperial government exercised greater autocratic control, hastening the decline of the curial class, wresting power from other elite families, and encouraging the formation of a middle class of farmer-soldiers.

David and Goliath
This large silver plate, nearly twenty inches in diameter, was made at Cyprus, a part of the Byzantine empire, in the first third of the seventh century. It formed part of a series of nine such plates, all showing scenes from the life of the biblical hero David. Here, in the center panel, armed only with his slingshot, David fights the champion of the Philistines, Goliath. In the bottom third, he cuts off Goliath's head. As the author of the Psalms, a king of Israel, and a victor in the battle against the Philistines, David was a particularly important figure for people whose education was largely religious. *Photograph © 2000 The Metropolitan Museum of Art.*

In the seventh century an emperor, possibly Heraclius, divided the empire into military districts called *themes* and put all civil as well as military matters in each district into the hands of one general, a *strategos* (plural, *strategoi*). Landless men were lured to join the army with the promise of land and low taxes; they fought side by side with local farmers, who provided their own weapons and horses. The new organization effectively countered frontier attacks.

The new emphasis on the rural world affected Byzantine education and culture. Whereas the old curial elite had cultivated the study of the pagan classics, sending their children (above all, their sons) to schools or tutors to learn to read the works of Greek poets and philosophers, eighth-century parents showed far more interest in giving their children, both sons and daughters, a religious education. Even with the decay of urban centers, cities and villages often retained an elementary school. There teachers used the Book of Psalms (the Psalter) as their primer. Throughout the seventh and eighth centuries, secular, classical learning remained decidedly out of favor, whereas dogmatic writings, biographies of saints, and devotional works took center stage.

Religion, Politics, and Iconoclasm

The importance placed on religious learning and piety complemented both the autocratic imperial ideal and the powers of the bishops in the seventh century. Since the spiritual and secular realms were understood to be inseparable, the bishops wielded political power in their cities, while Byzantine emperors ruled as both religious and political figures. In theory, imperial and church power were separate but interdependent. In fact, the emperor exercised considerable power over the church; he influenced the appointment of the chief religious official, the patriarch of Constantinople; he called church councils to determine dogma; and he regularly used bishops as local governors. Beginning with Heraclius, the emperors considered it one of their duties to baptize Jews forcibly, persecuting those who would not convert. In the view of the imperial court, this was part of the ruler's role in upholding orthodoxy.

Powerful Bishops and Monks. Bishops functioned as state administrators in their cities. They acted as judges and tax collectors. They distributed food in times of famine or siege, provisioned troops, and set up military fortifications. As part of their charitable work, they cared for the sick and the needy. Byzantine bishops were part of a three-tier system: they were appointed by metropolitans, bishops who headed an entire province; and the metropolitans, in turn, were appointed by the patriarchs, bishops with authority over whole regions.

Theoretically, monasteries were under the limited control of the local bishop, but in fact they were enormously powerful institutions that often defied the authority of bishops and even emperors. Because monks commanded immense prestige as the holiest of God's faithful, they could influence the many issues of church doctrine that racked the Byzantine church.

Conflict over Icons. The most important issue of the Byzantine church in this period revolved around icons. Icons are images of holy people—Christ, his mother (Mary), and the saints (see the image, Icon of Virgin and Child, on this page). To Byzantine Christians,

Icon of Virgin and Child
Surrounded by two angels in the back and two soldier-saints at either side, the Virgin Mary and the Christ Child are depicted with still, otherworldly dignity. Working with hot pigmented beeswax, the sixth-century artist gave the angels transparent halos to emphasize their spiritual natures, while depicting the saints as earthly men, with hair and beards, and feet planted firmly on the ground. Icons such as this were used in private worship as well as in the religious life of Byzantine monasteries. © *Copyright—All rights reserved by St. Catherine's Monastery at Sinai.*

icons were far more than mere representations. They were believed to possess holy power that directly affected people's daily lives as well as their chances for salvation.

Many seventh-century Byzantines made icons the focus of their religious devotion. To them, the images were like the incarnation of Christ: they turned spirit into material substance. Thus, an icon manifested in physical form the holy person it depicted. Some

Byzantines actually worshiped icons; others, particularly monks, considered icons a necessary part of Christian piety. As the monk St. John of Damascus put it in a vigorous defense of holy images, "I do not worship matter, I worship the God of matter, who became matter for my sake, and deigned to inhabit matter, who worked out my salvation through matter."

Other Byzantines abhorred icons. Most numerous of these were the soldiers on the frontiers. Shocked by Arab triumphs, they found the cause of their misfortunes in the biblical injunction against graven images. When they compared their defeats to Muslim successes, they could not help but notice that Islam prohibited all representations of the divine. To these soldiers and others who shared their view, icons revived pagan idolatry and desecrated Christian divinity. As iconoclastic (anti-icon or, literally, icon-breaking) feeling grew, some churchmen became outspoken in their opposition to icons.

Byzantine emperors shared these religious objections, and they also had important political reasons for opposing icons. In fact, the issue of icons became a test of their authority. Icons diffused loyalties, setting up intermediaries between worshipers and God that undermined the emperor's exclusive place in the divine and temporal order. In addition, the emphasis on icons in monastic communities made the monks potential threats to imperial power; the emperors hoped to use this issue to break the power of the monasteries. Above all, though, the emperors opposed icons because the army did, and they wanted to support their troops.

After Emperor Leo III the Isaurian (r. 717–741) had defeated the Arabs besieging Constantinople at the beginning of his reign, he turned his attention to consolidating his political position. Officers of the imperial court tore down the great golden icon of Christ at the gateway of the palace and replaced it with a cross, while a crowd of women protested by going on a furious rampage in support of icons. But Leo would not budge. In 726 he ordered all icons destroyed, a ban that remained in effect, despite much opposition, until 787. This is known as the period of **iconoclasm** in Byzantine history. A modified ban would be revived in 815 and last until 843.

Iconoclasm had an enormous impact on daily life. At home, where people had their own portable icons, it forced changes in private worship: the devout had to destroy their icons or worship them in secret. The ban on icons meant ferocious attacks on the monasteries: splendid collections of holy images were destroyed; vast properties were confiscated; and monks, who were staunch defenders of icons, were ordered to marry and give up their vocation. In this way iconoclasm destroyed communities that might otherwise have served as centers of resistance to imperial power. Reorganized and reoriented, the Byzantine rulers were able to maintain themselves against the onslaught of the Arabs, who attacked under the banner of Islam.

> **Review:** What stresses did the Byzantine Empire endure in the seventh and eighth centuries, and how was iconoclasm a response to those stresses?

❖ Islam: A New Religion and a New Empire

In the sixth century, Arabia, today Saudi Arabia, witnessed the rise of Islam, a religion that called on all to submit to the will of one God. Islam, which means "submission to God," emerged under Muhammad (c. 570–632), a merchant-turned-holy-man from the city of Mecca. While the great majority of people living in Arabia were polytheists, Muhammad recognized one God, the same one worshiped by the Jews and the Christians. He saw himself as God's last prophet—and thus he is called the Prophet—the person to receive and in turn repeat God's final words to humans. Invited by the disunited and pagan people of the city of Medina to come and act as a mediator for them, Muhammad exercised the powers of both a religious and a secular leader. This dual role became the model for his successors, known as caliphs.❖ Through a combination of persuasion and force, Muhammad and his co-

---

❖**caliph:** KAY luhf

religionists, the Muslims, converted most of the Arabian peninsula. By the time Muhammad died in 632, conquest and conversion had begun to move northward, into Byzantine and Persian territories. In the next generation, the Arabs conquered most of Persia and all of Egypt and were on their way across North Africa to Spain. Yet within the territories they conquered, daily life went on much as before.

The Desert and the Cities

Before the seventh century, the great deserts of the Arabian peninsula were sparsely populated by Bedouins.♦ These were nomads who lived in tribes—loose confederations of clans, or kin groups—herding flocks for meat and milk and trading (or raiding) for grain, dates, and slaves. Poor tribes herded sheep, whereas richer ones kept camels—extremely hardy animals, splendid beasts of burden, and good producers of milk and meat. (*Arab* was the name camel nomads called themselves.)

Tribal makeup shifted as kin groups joined or left. Though continually changing, these associations nevertheless saw outsiders as rivals, and tribes constantly fought with one another. Yet this very rivalry was itself an outgrowth of shared values. Bedouin men prized "manliness," which meant far more than sexual prowess. They strove to be brave in battle and feared being shamed. Manliness also entailed an obligation to be generous, to give away the booty that was the goal of intertribal warfare. Women were often part of this booty, for Bedouins practiced polygyny (having more than one wife at the same time). Bedouin wars rarely involved much bloodshed; their main purpose was to capture people and take belongings.

Tribal, nomadic existence produced its own culture, including an Arabic poetry of striking delicacy, precision, and beauty. In the absence of written language, the Bedouins used oral poetry and storytelling to transmit their traditions, simultaneously entertaining, reaffirming values, and teaching new generations.

Dotting the Bedouins' desert world were cities that arose around oases—fertile, green areas. Here more settled forms of life and trade took place. Mecca, near the Red Sea, was one such commercial center. Meccan caravans crisscrossed the peninsula, selling slaves and spices. More important, Mecca played an important religious role because it contained a shrine, the Ka'ba. Long before Muhammad was born, the Ka'ba, a great rock surrounded by the images of 360 gods, served as a sacred place within which war and violence were prohibited. The tribe that dominated Mecca, the Quraysh,♦ controlled access to the shrine and was able to tax the pilgrims who flocked there as well as sell them food and drink. In turn, plunder was transformed into trade as the visitors bartered with one another on the sacred grounds, assured of their security.

The Prophet Muhammad and the Faith of Islam

Mecca, the birthplace of Muhammad, was a center with two important traditions—one religious, the other commercial. Muhammad's early years were inauspicious: orphaned at the age of six, he spent two years with his grandfather and then came under the care of his uncle, a leader of the Quraysh tribe. Eventually, Muhammad became a trader. At the age of twenty-five, he married Khadija, a rich widow who had once employed him. They had at least four daughters and lived (to all appearances) happily and comfortably. Yet Muhammad sometimes left home and spent some time on the nearby Mount Hira, devoting himself to prayer and contemplation.

In about 610, on one of these retreats, Muhammad heard a voice and had a vision that summoned him to worship Allah, the God of the Jews and Christians. (*Allah* means "the God" in Arabic.) He accepted the call as coming from God. Over the next years he received messages that he understood to be divine revelation. Later, when they had been written down and arranged—a process that was completed in the seventh century, but after Muhammad's death—these messages

♦**Bedouins:** BEHD oo ihns

♦**Quraysh:** kur RAYSH

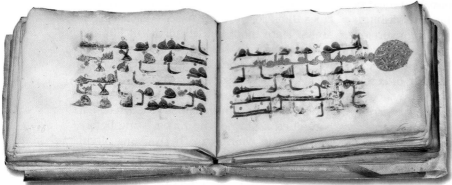

Qur'an
More than a holy book, the Qur'an represents for Muslims the very words of God that were dictated to Muhammad by the angel Gabriel. Generally the Qur'an was written on pages wider than long, perhaps to differentiate it from other books. This example dates from the seventh or eighth century. It is written in Kufic script, a formal and majestic form of Arabic that was used for the Qur'an until the eleventh century. The round floral decoration on the right-hand page marks a new section of the text. *Property of the Ambrosian Library. All rights reserved.*

became the Qur'an,◆ the holy book of Islam. (See pages of a Qur'an above.) *Qur'an* means "recitation"; each of its chapters, or *suras,* is understood to be God's revelation as told to Muhammad by the archangel Gabriel, then recited in turn by Muhammad to others. It begins with the Fatihah, frequently also said as an independent prayer, and continues with suras of gradually decreasing length, which cover the gamut of human experience and the life to come (see "The Fatihah of the Qur'an," page 295). For Muslims (literally, "those who submit to Islam") the Qur'an contains the foundations of history, prophecy, and the legal and moral code by which men and women should live: "Do not set up another god with God.... Do not worship anyone but Him, and be good to your parents.... Give to your relatives what is their due, and to those who are needy, and the wayfarers."

The Qur'an emphasizes the nuclear family—a man, his wife (or wives), and children—as the basic unit of Muslim society. Islam cuts its adherents adrift from the protection and particularism of the tribe but gives them in return an identity as part of the **ummah**, the community of believers, who share both a belief in one God and a set of religious practices. Islam stresses individual belief in God and adherence to the Qur'an. Thus, Muslims have no priests, no mass, and no intermediaries between the divine and the individual. However, Islam does rec-

ognize authorities whose interpretations of the Qur'an and related texts are considered decisive. The Ka'ba, with its many gods, had gathered together tribes from the surrounding vicinity. Muhammad, with his one God, forged an even more universal religion.

Growth of Islam, c. 610–632

First to convert to Muhammad's faith was his wife, Khadija; then a few friends and members of his immediate family joined him; and, as Muhammad preached the new faith, eventually some others became adherents. Soon, however, the new faith polarized Meccan society. Muhammad's insistence that the cults of all other gods be abandoned in favor of one brought him into conflict with leading clan members of the Quraysh tribe, whose control over the Ka'ba, a polytheistic shrine, had given them prestige and wealth. Lacking political means to expel him, they insulted Muhammad and harassed his adherents.

Hijra: Journey to Medina. Disillusioned with Mecca and angry with his own tribe, Muhammad tried to find a place and a population receptive to his message. Most important, he expected support from Jews, whose monotheism, in Muhammad's view, prepared them for his own faith. When a few of Muhammad's converts from Medina promised to protect him if he would join them there, he eagerly accepted the invitation, in part because Medina had a significant Jewish popu-

---

◆**Qur'an:** Kur AN/Koo RAHN

lation. In 622, Muhammad made the **Hijra**,♦ or emigration, to Medina, an oasis about two hundred miles north of Mecca. This journey proved a crucial event for the fledgling movement. At Medina, Muhammad found followers ready to listen to his religious message and to regard him as the leader of their community. They expected him to act as a neutral and impartial judge in their interclan disputes. Muhammad's political position in the community set the pattern by which Islamic society would be governed afterward; rather than adding a church to political and cultural life, Muslims made their political and religious institutions inseparable. After Muhammad's death, the year of the Hijra was named the first year of the Islamic calendar; it marked the beginning of the new Islamic era.[1]

Although successful at Medina, the Muslims felt threatened by the Quraysh at Mecca, who actively opposed the public practice of Islam. For this reason Muhammad led raids against them. At the battle of Badr♦ in 624, aided by their position near an oasis, Muhammad and his followers killed forty-nine of the Meccan enemy, took numerous prisoners, and confiscated rich booty. At the battle of Badr, Bedouin plundering was grafted onto the Muslim duty of jihad (literally, "striving").[2]

The battle of Badr was a great triumph for Muhammad, who was now able to consolidate his position at Medina, gaining new adherents and silencing all doubters, including the Jews. Muhammad had first seen the Jews of Medina as allies, but they had not converted to Islam as he had expected. Suspecting them of supporting his enemies, Muhammad expelled two Jewish tribes from Medina and killed the male members of another. Although Muslims had originally prayed in the direction of Jerusalem, the center of Jewish worship, Muhammad now had them turn in the direction of Mecca.

---

[1]Thus, 1 A.H. (1 *anno Hegirae*) on the Muslim calendar is equivalent to 622 C.E.

[2]*Jihad* means "striving" and is used in particular in the context of striving against unbelievers. In that sense, it is often translated as "holy war." But it can also mean striving against one's worst impulses.

♦**Hijra:** HID jruh
♦**Badr:** BAHD ihr

The Fatihah of the Qur'an

The Fatihah (or Prologue) is the prayer that begins the Qur'an. It emphasizes God's oneness and the believer's recourse to God alone, without intermediaries of any sort. The "path that is straight" is the path of right worship.

The Fatihah
In the name of Allah, most benevolent, ever-merciful
All praise be to Allah
Lord of all the worlds,
2. Most beneficent, ever-merciful,
3. King of the Day of Judgement.
4. You alone we worship, and to You alone turn for help.
5. Guide us (O Lord) to the path that is straight,
6. The path of those You have blessed,
7. Not of those who have earned Your anger, nor those who have gone astray.

Source: *Al-Qur'an: A Contemporary Translation*, trans. Ahmed Ali (Princeton: Princeton University Press, 1993), 11.

Defining the Faith. As Muhammad broke with the Jews, he instituted new practices to define Islam as a unique religion. Among these were the *zakat*, a tax on possessions to be used for alms; the fast of Ramadan, which took place during the ninth month of the Islamic year, the month in which the battle of Badr had been fought; the *hajj*, the pilgrimage to Mecca during the last month of the year, which each Muslim was to make once in his lifetime; and the *salat*, formal worship at least three times a day (later increased to five), which could include the *shahadah*, or profession of faith—"There is no divinity but God, and Muhammad is the messenger of God." Detailed regulations for these practices, sometimes called the five pillars of Islam, were worked out in the eighth and early ninth centuries.

Hijra and remained close to Muhammad. The first two caliphs ruled without serious opposition, but the third caliph, Uthman (r. 644–656), a member of the Umayyad♦ family and son-in-law (by marriage to two daughters) of Muhammad, aroused discontent among other clan members of the inner circle and soldiers unhappy with his distribution of high offices and revenues. Accusing Uthman of favoritism, they supported his rival, Ali, a member of the Hashim clan (to which Muhammad had belonged) and the husband of Muhammad's only surviving child, Fatimah. After a group of discontented soldiers murdered Uthman, civil war broke out between the Umayyads and Ali's faction. It ended when Ali was killed by one of his own erstwhile supporters, and the caliphate remained in Umayyad hands from 661 to 750.

Nevertheless, the *Shi'at Ali*, the faction of Ali, did not fade away. Ali's memory lived on among groups of Muslims (the Shi'ites) who saw in him a symbol of justice and righteousness. For them, Ali's death was the martyrdom of the only true successor to Muhammad. They remained faithful to his dynasty, shunning the mainstream caliphs of the other Muslims (Sunni Muslims, as they were later called, from *Sunna*, the practices of Muhammad). The Shi'ites awaited the arrival of the true leader—the imam—who in their view could come only from the house of Ali.

Under the **Umayyad caliphate**, which lasted from 661 to 750, the Muslim world became a state with its capital at Damascus, the historic capital of Syria—and today's as well. Borrowing from the institutions well known to the civilizations they had just conquered, the Muslims issued coins and hired former Byzantine and Persian officials. They made Arabic a tool of centralization, imposing it as the language of government on regions not previously united linguistically. For Byzantium, this period was one of unparalleled military crisis, the prelude to iconoclasm. For the Islamic world, now a multiethnic society of Muslim Arabs, Syrians, Egyptians, Iraqis, and other peoples, it was a period of settlement, new urbanism, and literary and artistic flowering.

♦**Umayyad:** oo MAH yuhd

Peace and Prosperity in Islamic Lands

Ironically, the Islamic warriors brought peace. While the conquerors stayed within their fortified cities or built magnificent hunting lodges in the deserts of Syria, the conquered went back to work, to study, to play, and—in the case of Christians and Jews, who were considered protected subjects—to worship as they pleased in return for the payment of a special tax. At Damascus, local artists and craftspeople worked on the lavish decorations for a mosque in a neoclassical style at the very moment Muslim armies were storming the walls of Constantinople. Leaving the Byzantine institutions in place, the Muslim conquerors allowed Christians and Jews to retain their posts and even protected dissidents.

During the seventh and eighth centuries, Muslim scholars wrote down the hitherto largely oral Arabic literature. They determined the definitive form for the Qur'an and compiled pious narratives about Muhammad (hadith literature). Scribes composed these works in exquisite handwriting; Arab calligraphy became an art form. A literate class, composed mainly of the old Persian and Syrian elite now converted to Islam, created new forms of prose writing in Arabic—official documents as well as essays on topics ranging from hunting to ruling. Umayyad poetry explored new worlds of thought and feeling. Patronized by the caliphs, who found in written poetry an important source of propaganda and a buttress for their power, the poets also reached a wider audience that delighted in their clever use of words, their satire, and their invocations of courage, piety, and sometimes erotic love:

> I spent the night as her bed-companion, each enamored of the other,
>
> And I made her laugh and cry, and stripped her of her clothes.
>
> I played with her and she vanquished me; I made her happy and I angered her.
>
> That was a night we spent, in my sleep, playing and joyful,
>
> But the caller to prayer woke me up.

Such poetry scandalized conservative Muslims, brought up on the ascetic tenets of the Qur'an. But this love poetry was a product of the new urban civilization of the Umayyad period, during which wealth, cultural mix, and the confidence born of conquest inspired diverse and experimental literary forms. By the close of the Umayyad period in 750, Islamic civilization was multiethnic, urban, and sophisticated, a true heir of Roman and Persian traditions.

> **Review:** How and why did the Muslims conquer so many lands in the very short period 632–750?

❖ Western Europe: A Medley of Kingdoms

With the demise of Roman imperial government in the western half of the empire, the region was divided into a number of kingdoms: various monarchs ruled in Spain, Italy, England, and Gaul. The primary foundations of power and stability in all of these kingdoms were kinship networks, church patronage, royal courts, and wealth derived from land and plunder. In contrast to Byzantium, where an emperor still ruled as the successor to Augustus and Constantine, drawing upon an unbroken chain of Roman legal and administrative traditions, political power in western Europe was more diffuse. There were kings, to be sure; but in some places churchmen and rich magnates were even more powerful than royalty. Power lodged too (as people believed) in the tombs and relics of saints, who represented and wielded the divine forces of God. Although the patterns of daily life and the procedures of government in western Europe remained recognizably Roman, they were also in the process of change,

borrowing from and adapting to local traditions and to the very powerful role of the Christian religion in every aspect of society.

Frankish Kingdoms with Roman Roots

The most important kingdoms in post-Roman Europe were Frankish. During the sixth century, the Franks had established themselves as dominant in Gaul, and by the seventh century the limits of their kingdoms roughly approximated the eastern borders of present-day France, Belgium, the Netherlands, and Luxembourg (Map 8.4). Moreover, the Frankish kings, known as the Merovingians◆ (the

◆**Merovingians:** Mehr oh VIN jians

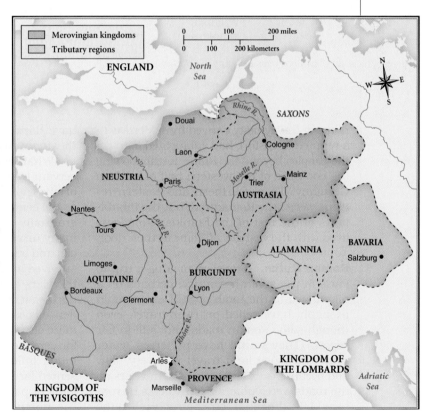

MAP 8.4 The Merovingian Kingdoms in the Seventh Century
By the seventh century, there were three powerful Merovingian kingdoms: Neustria, Austrasia, and Burgundy. The important cities of Aquitaine were assigned to one of these major kingdoms, while Aquitaine as a whole was assigned to a duke or other governor. Kings did not establish capital cities; they did not even stay in one place. Rather, they continually traveled throughout their kingdoms, making their power felt in person.

TABLE 8.1   The Three Monotheistic Religions, c. 750*

RELIGION	FOUNDER/ PROPHET	CHIEF RELIGIOUS HEAD(S)	PLACE OF WORSHIP	IMPORTANT ELEMENTS OF WORSHIP	KEY RELIGIOUS TEXTS	MATERIAL AIDS TO WORSHIP
CHRISTIANITY						
Roman Catholic	Jesus	Bishops, increasingly pope at Rome	Church	Mass, prayer, fasting	Bible, especially the Psalms	Relics
Byzantine	Jesus	Patriarch of Constantinople	Church	Mass, prayer, fasting	Bible, especially the Psalms	Icons
JUDAISM	Abraham	Rabbis	Synagogue	Prayer, fasting	Hebrew Scriptures and rabbinic legal literature (Talmud)	Torah (first five books of the Bible)
ISLAM	Muhammad	Caliphs or, increasingly, religious scholars	Mosque	Prayer, fasting	Qur'an and commentaries on it	Qur'an

*None of these religions fixed remained in the form they had in 750. See Chapter 15, in particular, for changes in Christianity.

name of the dynasty derived from Merovech, a reputed ancestor), had subjugated many of the peoples beyond the Rhine, foreshadowing the contours of the western half of modern Germany. These northern and eastern regions were little Romanized, but the inhabitants of the rest of the Frankish kingdoms lived with the vestiges of Rome at their door.

Roman Ruins.   Travelers making a trip to Paris in the seventh century, perhaps on a pilgrimage to the tomb of St. Denis, would probably have relied on river travel, even though some Roman roads were still in fair repair. (They would have preferred water routes because land travel was very slow and because even large groups of travelers on the roads were vulnerable to attacks by robbers.) Like the roads, other structures in the landscape would have seemed familiarly Roman. Coming up the Rhône River from the south, voyagers would have passed Roman amphitheaters and farmlands neatly and squarely laid out by Roman land surveyors. The great stone palaces of villas would still

have dotted the countryside. (See Amphitheater at Arles, page 301.)

What would have been missing, to observant travelers, were thriving cities. Hulks of cities remained, of course, and they served as the centers of church administration; but gradually during the late Roman period, many urban centers had lost their commercial and cultural vitality. Depopulated, many survived as mere skeletons. Moreover, if the travelers had approached Paris from the northeast, they would have passed through dense, nearly untouched forests and land more often used as pasture for animals than for cereal cultivation. These areas were not much influenced by Romans; they represented far more the farming and village settlement patterns of the Franks. Yet even on the northern and eastern fringes of the Merovingian kingdoms, some structures of the Roman Empire remained. Fortresses were still standing at Trier (near Bonn, Germany, today), and great stone villas, such as the one excavated by archaeologists near Douai (today in France, near the Belgian border), loomed over the more humble wooden dwellings of the countryside.

The Social Scale. In the south, gangs of slaves still might occasionally be found cultivating the extensive lands of wealthy estate owners, as they had done since the days of the late Roman Republic. Scattered here and there, independent peasants worked their own small plots as they had for centuries. But for the most part, seventh-century travelers would have found semifree peasant families settled on small holdings, their manses—including a house, a garden, and cultivable land—for which they paid dues and owed labor services to a landowner. Some of these peasants were descendants of the *coloni* (tenant farmers) of the late Roman Empire; others were the sons and daughters of slaves, now provided with a small plot of land; and a few were people of free Frankish origin who for various reasons had come down in the world. At the lower end of the social scale, the status of Franks and Romans had become identical.

Amphitheater at Arles
In what is today southern France, the ruins of an amphitheater built by the Romans still dwarfs the surrounding buildings of the modern city of Arles. This huge stadium must have been even more striking in the seventh century, when the city was impoverished and depopulated. Plague, war, and the dislocation of Roman trade networks meant that most people abandoned the cities to live on the land. Only the bishop and his clergy—and those who could make a living servicing them—remained in the cities. *Jean Dieuzaide.*

Romans (or, more precisely, Gallo-Romans) and Franks had also merged at the upper end of the social scale. Although people south of the Loire River continued to be called Romans and people to the north Franks, their cultures were strikingly similar: they shared language, settlement patterns, and religious sensibilities. (See "New Sources, New Perspectives," page 302.) There were many dialects in the Frankish kingdoms in the seventh century, but most were derived from Latin, though no longer the Latin of Cicero. "Though my speech is rude," Gregory, bishop of Tours♦ (r. 573–c. 594), wrote at the end of the sixth century,

I have been unable to be silent as to the struggles between the wicked and the upright; and I have been especially encouraged because, to my surprise, it has often been said by men of our day, that few understand the learned words of the rhetorician but many the rude language of the common people.

Thus Gregory began his *Histories*, a valuable source for the Merovingian period (c. 486–751). He was trying to evoke the sympathies of his readers, a traditional Roman rhetorical device; but he also expected that his "rude" Latin—the plain Latin of everyday speech—would be understood and welcomed by the general public.

Whereas the Gallo-Roman aristocrat of the fourth and fifth centuries had lived in

♦**Tours:** TOO ur

aristocratic families who had long controlled local affairs.

Both kings and aristocrats had good reason to want a powerful royal authority. The king acted as arbitrator and intermediary for the competing interests of the aristocrats while taking advantage of local opportunities to appoint favorites and garner prestige by giving out land and privileges to supporters and religious institutions. Gregory of Tours's history of the sixth century is filled with stories of bitter battles between Merovingian kings, as royal brothers fought continuously over territories, wives, and revenues. Yet what seemed to the bishop like royal weakness and violent chaos was in fact one way the kings focused local aristocratic enmities, preventing them from spinning out of royal control. By the beginning of the seventh century, three relatively stable Frankish kingdoms had emerged: Austrasia◆ to the northeast; Neustria to the west, with its capital city at Paris; and Burgundy, incorporating the southeast (see Map 8.4). These divisions were so useful to local aristocrats and the Merovingian dynasty alike that even when royal power was united in the hands of one king, Clothar II (r. 613–623), he made his son the independent king of Austrasia.

The very power of the kings in the seventh century, however, gave greater might to their chief court official, the mayor of the palace. In the following century, allied with the Austrasian aristocracy, one mayoral family would displace the Merovingian dynasty and establish a new royal line, the Carolingians.

Christianity and Classical Culture in the British Isles

The Merovingian kingdoms exemplify some of the ways in which Roman and non-Roman traditions combined. The British Isles show others. Ireland had never been part of the

◆**Austrasia:** aw STRAY zhuh

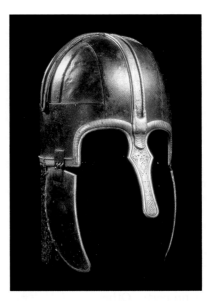

York Helmet
This fine helmet, once belonging to a very wealthy warrior living near York, England, in the second half of the eighth century, was intended for both display and real battle. The helmet, made of iron, and the back flap, made of flexible chain mail, gave excellent protection against sword blades. The cheek pieces were probably originally pulled close to the warrior's face by a leather tie. The nose piece, decorated with interlaced animals, protected his nose. Over the top, two bands of copper meet at the middle. They were inscribed "In the name of our Lord Jesus, the Holy Spirit, God, and with all, we pray. Amen. Oshere. Christ." *York Castle Museum/City of York Museum Services.*

Roman Empire, but it was early converted to Christianity, as were Roman Britain and parts of Scotland. Invasions by various Celtic and Germanic groups—particularly the Anglo-Saxons, who gave their name to England, "the land of the Angles"—redrew the religious boundaries. Ireland, largely free of invaders, remained Christian; Scotland, also relatively untouched by invaders, was slowly evangelized by the Irish from the west and the British from the south; England, which emerged from the invasions as a mosaic of about a dozen kingdoms ruled by separate Anglo-Saxon kings, became largely pagan.

Two Competing Forms of Christianity in Anglo-Saxon England. Christianity was introduced to **Anglo-Saxon England** from two directions. In the north of England, Irish monks brought their own brand of Christianity. Converted in the fifth century by St. Patrick and other missionaries, the Irish had rapidly evolved a church organization that corresponded to its rural clan organization. Abbots and abbesses, generally from powerful dynasties, headed monastic *familiae*, communities composed of blood relatives, servants, slaves, and of course monks or nuns. Bishops were often under the authority of abbots, since the monasteries rather than cities were the centers of population settlement in Ireland. The Irish missionaries to England were monks, and they set up monasteries on the model of those at home.

In the south of England, Christianity came via missionaries sent by Gregory the Great (r. 590–604) in 597. The missionaries, under the leadership of Augustine (not the same Augustine as the bishop of Hippo), intended to convert the king and people of Kent, the southernmost kingdom, and then work their way northward. But Augustine and his party brought with them Roman practices at odds with those of Irish Christianity, stressing ties to the pope and the organization of the church under bishops rather than abbots. Using the Roman model, they divided England into territorial units called dioceses headed by an archbishop and bishops. Augustine, for example, became archbishop of Canterbury. As he was a monk, he set up a monastery right next to his cathedral, and it became a peculiar characteristic of the English church to have a community of monks attached to the bishop's church. Later a second archbishopric was added at York.

A major bone of contention between the Roman and Irish churches involved the calculation of the date of Easter. The Roman church insisted that Easter fall on the first Sunday following the first full moon after the spring equinox. The Irish had a different method of determining when Easter should fall, and therefore they celebrated Easter on a different day. Because everyone agreed that believers could not be saved unless they observed Christ's resurrection properly and on the right date, the conflict was bitter. It was resolved by Oswy, king of Northumbria, who organized a meeting of churchmen, the Synod of Whitby in 664. Convinced by the synod that Rome spoke with the voice of St. Peter, who was said in the New Testament to hold the keys of the kingdom of heaven, Oswy chose the Roman date. His decision paved the way for the triumph of the Roman brand of Christianity in England.

Literary Culture. St. Peter was not the only reason for favoring Rome. To many English churchmen, Rome had great prestige because it was a treasure trove of knowledge, piety, and holy objects. Benedict Biscop♦ (c. 630–690), the founder of two important English monasteries, made many arduous trips to Rome, bringing back relics, liturgical vestments, and even a cantor to teach his monks the proper melodies in a time before written musical notation. Above all, he went to Rome to get books. At his monasteries in the north of England, he built up a grand library. In Anglo-Saxon England, as in Scotland and Ireland, all of which lacked a strong classical tradition from Roman times, a book was considered a precious object, to be decorated as finely as a garnet-studded brooch.

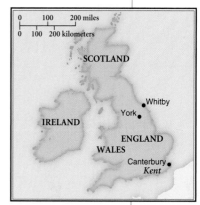

The British Isles

The Anglo-Saxons and Irish Celts had a thriving oral culture but extremely limited uses for writing. Books became valuable only when these societies converted to Christianity. Just as Islamic reliance on the Qur'an made possible a literary culture under the Umayyads, so Christian dependence on the Bible, liturgy, and the writings of the church fathers helped make England and Ireland centers of literature and learning in the seventh and eighth centuries. Archbishop Theodore (r. 669–690), who had studied at Athens and was one of the most learned men of his day, founded a school at Canterbury where students studied Latin and even some Greek manuscripts to comment on biblical texts. Men like Benedict Biscop soon sponsored other centers of learning, using the texts from the classical past. Although women did not establish famous schools, many abbesses ruled over monasteries that stressed Christian learning. Here as elsewhere, Latin writings, even pagan texts, were studied diligently, in part because Latin was

---

♦**Biscop:** BIS cup

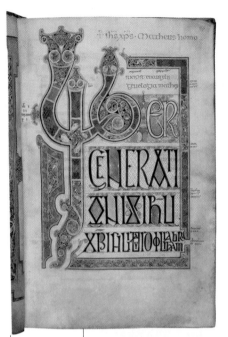

Lindisfarne Gospels
The lavishly illuminated manuscript known as the Lindisfarne Gospels, of which this is one page, was probably produced in the first third of the eighth century. For the monks at Lindisfarne and elsewhere in the British Isles, books were precious objects, to be decorated much like pieces of jewelry. To introduce each of the four Gospels, the artist—who was also the scribe—produced three elaborate pages: the first was a "portrait" of the evangelist, the second a decorative "carpet" page, and the third the beginning of the text. The page depicted here is the beginning of the Gospel according to St. Matthew, which begins with the words "Liber generationis." Note how elaborately the first letter, L, is treated and how the decoration gradually recedes, so that the last line, while still very embellished, is quite plain in comparison with the others. In this way the very layout of the book led the reader slowly and reverently into the text of the Gospels itself. *British Library.*

so foreign a language that mastering it required systematic and formal study. One of Benedict Biscop's pupils was Bede♦ (673–735), an Anglo-Saxon monk and a historian of extraordinary breadth. Bede in turn taught a new generation of monks who became advisers to eighth-century rulers.

The vigorous pagan Anglo-Saxon oral tradition was only partially suppressed; much of it was adapted to Christian culture. Bede encouraged and supported the use of Anglo-Saxon, urging Christian priests, for example, to use it when they instructed their flocks. In contrast to other European regions, where the vernacular was rarely written, Anglo-Saxon came to be a written language used in every aspect of English life, from government to entertainment.

♦**Bede:** beed

After the Synod of Whitby, the English church was tied by doctrine, friendship, and conviction to the church of Rome. An influential Anglo-Saxon monk and bishop, Wynfrith, even changed his name to the Latin Boniface to symbolize his loyalty to the Roman church. Preaching on the continent, Boniface (680–754) worked to set up churches in Germany and Gaul that, like those in England, looked to Rome for leadership and guidance. His zeal would give the papacy new importance in Europe.

Unity in Spain, Division in Italy

In contrast to the British Isles, southern Gaul, Spain, and Italy had long been part of the Roman Empire and preserved many of its traditions. Nevertheless, as they were settled and fought over by new peoples, their histories came to diverge dramatically. When the Merovingian king Clovis defeated the Visigoths in 507, their vast kingdom, which had sprawled across southern Gaul into Spain, was dismembered. By midcentury, the Franks came into possession of most of the Visigothic kingdom in southern Gaul.

In Spain the Visigothic king Leovigild (r. 569–586) established territorial control by military might. But no ruler could hope to maintain his position in **Visigothic Spain** without the support of the Hispano-Roman population, which included both the great landowners and leading bishops; and their backing was unattainable while the Visigoths remained Arian (see page 257). Leovigild's son Reccared (r. 586–601) took the necessary step in 587, converting to Catholic Christianity. Two years later, at the Third Council of Toledo, most of the Arian bishops followed their king by announcing their conversion to Catholicism.

Thereafter the bishops and kings of Spain cooperated to a degree unprecedented in other regions. While the king gave the churchmen free rein to set up their own hierarchy (with the bishop of Toledo at the top) and to meet regularly at synods to regulate and reform the church, the bishops in turn supported their Visigothic king, who ruled as a minister of the Christian people. Rebellion against him was tantamount to rebellion against Christ. The Spanish bishops reinforced this idea by anointing the king, daubing him with holy oil in a ritual that paralleled the ordination of priests and demonstrated divine favor. Toledo, the city where the highest bishop presided, was also where the kings were "made" through anointment. While the bishops in this way made the king's cause their own, their lay counterparts, the great landowners, helped supply the king with troops, allowing him to maintain internal order and repel his external enemies.

Ironically, it was precisely the centralization and unification of the Visigothic kingdom that proved its undoing. When the Arabs arrived in 711, they needed only to kill the king, defeat his army, and capture Toledo to deal the kingdom a crushing blow.

By contrast, in Italy the Lombard king constantly faced a hostile papacy in the center of the peninsula and virtually independent dukes in the south. Theoretically royal officers, in fact the dukes of Benevento and Spoleto ruled on their own behalf. Although many Lombards were Catholics, others, including important kings and dukes, were Arian. The "official" religion of **Lombard Italy** varied with the ruler in power. Rather than signal a major political event, the conversion of the Lombards to Catholic Christianity occurred gradually, ending only around the mid-seventh century. Partly as a result of this slow development, the Lombard kings, unlike the Visigoths, Franks, or even the Anglo-Saxons, never enlisted the wholehearted support of any particular group of churchmen.

Lacking strong and united ecclesiastical favor, Lombard royal power still had buttresses. Chief among these were the traditions of leadership associated with the royal dynasty, the kings' military ability and their control over large estates in northern Italy, and the Roman institutions that survived in Italy. Although the Italian peninsula had been devastated by the wars between the Ostrogoths and the Byzantine Empire, the Lombard kings took advantage of the still-urban organization of Italian society and economy, assigning dukes to city bases and setting up a royal capital at Pavia. Recalling emperors like Constantine and Justinian, the kings built churches, monasteries, and other places of worship in the royal capital, maintained the walls, issued laws, and minted coins. Revenues from tolls, sales taxes, port duties, and court fines filled their coffers, although their inability to revive the Roman land tax was a major weakness. The greatest challenge for the Lombard kings came not from their own institutions but from sharing the peninsula with Rome. As soon as the kings began to make serious headway into southern Italy against the duchies of Spoleto and Benevento, the pope began to fear for his own position and called on the Franks for help.

Lombard Italy, Early Eighth Century

Ruthwell Cross

Originally not a cross at all (the top was added later), the Ruthwell Cross is one of a number of monumental carved stone pillars constructed in the north of England in the eighth century. Nothing quite like it exists on the Continent. Containing a fascinating mixture of Latin and runic inscriptions, vine scrolls, and biblical scenes, the Ruthwell Cross includes the text of the poem "Dream of the Holy Rood," which purports to be the "dream" of the wood on which Christ was crucified. What purposes might have been served by monuments such as this? *Edwin Smith/ RIBA Library Photographs Collection, London.*

Political Tensions and Reorganization at Rome

By 600, the pope's position was ambiguous: he was both a ruler and a subordinate. On the one hand, believing he was the successor of St. Peter and head of the church, he wielded real secular power. Pope Gregory the Great in many ways laid the foundations for the papacy's spiritual and temporal ascendancy. (See A Portrait of Pope Gregory the Great, page 313.) During his tenure, the pope became the greatest landowner in Italy; he organized the defenses of Rome and paid for its army; he heard court cases, made treaties, and provided welfare services. The missionary expedition he sent to England was only a small part of his involvement in the rest of Europe. For example, Gregory maintained close ties with the church-men in Spain who were working to convert the Visigoths from Arianism to Catholicism. A prolific author of spiritual works and biblical commentaries, Gregory digested and simplified the ideas of church fathers like St. Augustine of Hippo, making them accessible to a wider audience. His practical handbook for the clergy, *Pastoral Rule*, was matched by practical reforms within the church: he tried to impose in Italy regular elections of bishops and to enforce clerical celibacy.

Yet the pope was not independent. He was only one of many bishops in the Roman Empire, which was now ruled from Constantinople, and he was therefore subordinate to the emperor and Byzantium. For a long time the emperor's views on dogma, discipline, and church administration prevailed at Rome. This authority began to unravel in the seventh

Mosaic at Santo Stefano Rotondo

The church of Santo Stefano, built by Pope Simplicius (r. 468–483), was round, like a classical temple. It made up part of the papal Lateran palace complex, in the southeastern zone of Rome. Later popes continued to beautify and adorn Santo Stefano, drawing on the artistic styles of their own time. Pope Theodore (r. 642–649) moved the relics of two Roman martyrs, Primus and Felician, from a small church outside of Rome to Santo Stefano. To celebrate the event, he commissioned the mosaic shown here, in which the figures of Primus and Felician flank a giant cross. The heavy outlines and gold surroundings echo mosaics done at Byzantium around the same time, attesting to political, cultural, and theological links between Rome and Constantinople. **For more help analyzing this image**, see the visual activity for this chapter in the Online Study Guide at **bedfordstmartins.com/hunt**. *Madeline Grimoldi.*

A Portrait of Pope Gregory the Great by Bishop Gregory of Tours

At the end of the sixth century, the pope at Rome had no jurisdiction over bishops outside of Italy, though Gregory's mission to England meant that his handpicked man would become archbishop there. Elsewhere the pope had no power to appoint or depose bishops; Gregory of Tours himself was named bishop by a Merovingian king and queen. Nevertheless, the bishop of Tours was well aware—and a great admirer—of the pope at Rome. This passage from his Histories *begins with a description of an attack of plague at Rome in 590 that resulted in the death of Pope Pelagius and many others.*

The people then unanimously chose as Pope the deacon Gregory,[1] for the Church could not be left without a leader. He was descended from one of the leading senatorial families. From his youth upwards had been devoted to God's service. He founded six monasteries in Sicily from his own re-sources, and he established a seventh inside the walls of the city of Rome. He endowed them with sufficient land to provide the monks with their daily sustenance; then he sold the rest of his possessions, including all his household goods, and he gave the proceeds to the poor. He who until then had been in the habit of processing through the city in silken robes sewn with glittering gems [when he was Prefect of the City] now served at the Lord's altar in a fustian gown. He was appointed as seventh among the deacons who served the Pope. His abstinence in taking food, his vigils and his prayers, the severity of his fasting, were such that his weakened stomach could scarce support his frame. He was so skilled in grammar, dialectic and rhetoric that he was held second to none in the entire city. He wanted very much to avoid the highest honor, lest as a result of his being elected the worldly pomp which he had renounced should invade once more his public life.

[1]The pope was served by seven deacons, one for each of the seven districts into which Rome was divided for church administration. Gregory, so soon to become Pope Gregory the Great, was the least of these.

Source: Excerpt from Gregory of Tours, *The History of the Franks*, trans. Lewis Thorpe (London: Penguin Books, 1974), 543–44. Some footnotes have been omitted, and the spellings have been Americanized.

century. In 691, Emperor Justinian II convened a council that determined 102 rules for the church, and he sent them to Rome for papal endorsement. Most of the rules were unobjectionable, but Pope Sergius I (r. 687 or 689–701) was unwilling to agree to the whole because it permitted priestly marriages (which the Roman church did not want to allow) and prohibited fasting on Saturdays in Lent (which the Roman church required). Outraged by Sergius's refusal, Justinian tried to arrest the pope, but Italian armies (theoretically under the emperor) came to the pontiff's aid, while Justinian's arresting officer cowered under the pope's bed. The incident reveals that some local forces were already willing to rally to the side of the pope against the emperor. By now Constantinople's influence and authority over Rome was tenuous at best. Sheer distance, as well as diminishing imperial power in Italy, meant that the popes were in effect the leaders of the parts of Italy not controlled by the Lombards.

The gap between Byzantium and the papacy widened in the early eighth century as Emperor Leo III tried to increase the taxes on papal property to pay for his all-consuming war against the Arab invaders. The pope responded by leading a general tax revolt. Meanwhile, Leo's fierce policy of iconoclasm collided with the pope's tolerance of images. In Italy, as in other European regions, Christian piety focused not so much on icons as on relics. Nevertheless, the papacy was not willing to allow sacred images and icons to be destroyed. The pope argued that holy images

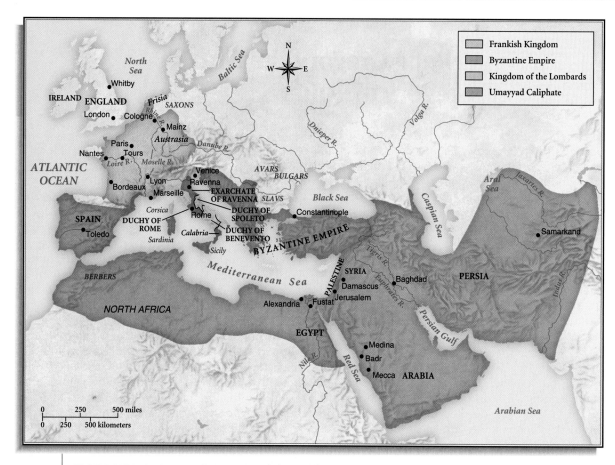

MAPPING THE WEST Europe and the Mediterranean, c. 750
The major political fact of the period 600–750 was the emergence of Islam and the creation of an Islamic state that reached from Spain to the Indus River. The Byzantine Empire, once a great power, was dwarfed—and half swallowed up—by its Islamic neighbor. To the west were fledgling barbarian kingdoms, mere trifles on the world stage. The next centuries, however, would prove their resourcefulness and durability.

could and should be venerated—but not worshiped. His support of images reflected popular opinion as well. A later commentator wrote that iconoclasm so infuriated the inhabitants of Ravenna and Venice that "if the pope had not prohibited the people, they would have attempted to set up a [different] emperor over themselves."

These difficulties with the emperor were matched by increasing friction between the pope and the Lombards. The Lombard kings had gradually managed to bring under their control the duchies of Spoleto and Benevento as well as part of the Exarchate of Ravenna. By the mid-eighth century, the popes feared that Rome would fall to the Lombards,

and Pope Zachary (r. 741–752) looked northward for friends. He created an ally by sanctioning the deposition of the last Merovingian king and his replacement by the first Carolingian king, Pippin III (r. 751–768). In 753, a subsequent pope, Stephen II (r. 752–757), called on Pippin to march to Italy with an army to fight the Lombards. Thus, events at Rome had a major impact on the history not only of Italy but of the Frankish kingdom as well.

Review: What were the roles, projects, and powers of the pope in early medieval Europe? On balance, how important was the papacy?

Conclusion

The three heirs of the Roman Empire—Byzantines, Muslims, and western Europeans—built on three distinct legacies. Byzantium directly inherited the central political institutions of Rome: its people called themselves Romans; its emperor was the Roman emperor; and its capital, Constantinople, was the new Rome. Sixth-century Byzantium also inherited the cities, laws, and religion—Christianity—of Rome. The changes of the seventh and eighth centuries—contraction of territory, urban decline, disappearance of the old elite, a ban on icons—whittled away at this Roman character. By 750, Byzantium was less Roman than it was a new, resilient political and cultural entity, a Christian polity on the borders of the new Muslim empire.

Muslims were the newcomers to the Roman world, but Islam was influenced by both Jewish and Christian monotheism, each with roots in Roman culture. Under the guidance of Muhammad (the Prophet), Islam became both a coherent theology and a tightly structured way of life. Once the Muslim Arabs embarked on military conquests, they too became heirs of Rome, preserving its cities, hiring its civil servants, and adopting its artistic styles. Drawing on Roman and Persian traditions, the Muslims created a powerful Islamic state, with a capital city in Syria, regional urban centers elsewhere, and a culture that generally tolerated a wide variety of economic, religious, and social institutions so long as the conquered paid taxes to their Muslim overlords.

Western Europe also inherited Roman institutions and transformed them with great diversity. Frankish Gaul built on Roman traditions that had long been transformed by provincial and Germanic custom. In England, however, once the far-flung northern outpost of the Roman Empire, the Roman legacy had to be reimported in the seventh century. In Spain, the Visigothic kings allied themselves with a Hispano-Roman elite that maintained elements of the organization and vigorous intellectual traditions of the late empire. In Italy and at Rome itself, the traditions of the classical past remained living parts of the fabric of life. The roads remained, the cities of Italy survived (although depopulated), and both the popes and the Lombard kings ruled in the traditions of Roman government.

All three heirs to Rome suffered the ravages of war. In all three societies, the social hierarchy became simpler, with the loss of "middle" groups like the *curiales* at Byzantium and the near-suppression of tribal affiliations among Muslims. As each of the three heirs shaped Roman institutions to its own uses and advantages, each also strove to create a religious polity. In Byzantium, the emperor was a religious force, presiding over the destruction of images. In the Islamic world, the caliph was the successor to Muhammad, a religious and political leader. In western Europe the kings allied with churchmen in order to rule. Despite their many differences, all these leaders had a common understanding of their place in a divine scheme: they were God's agents on earth, ruling over God's people.

Suggested References

Byzantium: A Christian Empire under Siege

While some scholars (Ousterhout and Brubaker, Weitzmann) concentrate on religion, culture, and the role of icons, others (Treadgold, Whittow) tend to stress politics and war.

*The Byzantine Studies Page: http://www.bway .net/~halsall/ byzantium.html.

*Geanakoplos, Deno John, ed. and trans. *Byzantium: Church, Society, and Civilization Seen through Contemporary Eyes.* 1986.

Haldon, J. F. *Byzantium in the Seventh Century: The Transformation of a Culture.* 1990.

Norwich, John Julius. *Byzantium: The Early Centuries.* 1989.

Ousterhout, Robert, and Leslie Brubaker. *The Sacred Image East and West.* 1995.

Treadgold, Warren. *A History of the Byzantine State and Society.* 1997.

Weitzmann, Kurt. *The Icon: Holy Images, Sixth to Fourteenth Century.* 1978.

Whittow, Mark. *The Making of Byzantium, 600–1025.* 1996.

*Primary sources.

Islam: A New Religion and a New Empire

The classic (and as yet unsurpassed) discussion is in Hodgson. Crone's book is considered highly controversial. Berkey's book is balanced and up-to-date.

Ahmed, Leila. *Women and Gender in Islam: Historical Roots of a Modern Debate.* 1992.

Berkey, Jonathan P. *The Formation of Islam: Religion and Society in the Near East, 600–1800.* 2003.

Crone, Patricia. *Meccan Trade and the Rise of Islam.* 1987.

Donner, Fred McGraw. *The Early Islamic Conquests.* 1981.

Hodgson, Marshall G. S. *The Venture of Islam: Conscience and History in a World Civilization.* Vol. 1, *The Classical Age of Islam.* 1974.

*Islamic Sourcebook: **http://www.fordham .edu/halsall/islam/islamsbook.html**.

Kennedy, Hugh. *The Prophet and the Age of the Caliphates: The Islamic Near East from the Sixth to the Eleventh Century.* 1986.

*Lewis, Bernard, ed. and trans. *Islam: From the Prophet Muhammad to the Capture of Constantinople.* 2 vols. 1987.

Waddy, Charis. *Women in Muslim History.* 1980.

Western Europe: A Medley of Kingdoms

Geary and Wood provide complementary guides to the Merovingian world. Recent keen historical interest in the role of the cults of the saints in early medieval society is reflected in Van Dam. While interest in Anglo-Saxon England has not diminished, other parts of the British Isles are receiving new attention, as Smyth demonstrates.

*Bede. *A History of the English Church and People.* Trans. Leo Sherley-Price. 1991.

Collins, Roger. *Early Medieval Spain: Unity in Diversity, 400–1000.* 1983.

*Fouracre, Paul, and Richard A. Gerberding. *Late Merovingian France: History and Hagiography, 640–720.* 1996.

Geary, Patrick. *Before France and Germany: The Creation and Transformation of the Merovingian World.* 1988.

*Gregory of Tours. *The History of the Franks.* Trans. Lewis Thorpe. 1976.

*Gregory of Tours: **http://www.unipissing.ca/ department/history/4505/show.htm**.

Heinzelmann, Martin, *Gregory of Tours: History and Society in the Sixth Century.* 2001.

Smyth, A. P. *Warlords and Holy Men: Scotland, AD 80–1000.* 1984.

Van Dam, Raymond. *Saints and Their Miracles in Late Antique Gaul.* 1993.

Wood, Ian. *The Merovingian Kingdoms, 450–751.* 1994.

Wickham, Chris. *Early Medieval Italy: Central Power and Local Society 400–1000.* 1981.

CHAPTER REVIEW

IMPORTANT EVENTS

c. 486–751	Merovingian dynasty
c. 570–632	Life of Muhammad, prophet of Islam
572	Lombards conquer northern Italy
r. 573–c. 594	Bishop Gregory of Tours
587	Conversion of Visigothic king Reccared
c. 590	Arrival of Irish monk Columbanus in Gaul
r. 590–604	Papacy of Pope Gregory the Great
603–623	War between Byzantium and Persia
622	Hijra to Medina; the beginning date of the Islamic calendar
624	Muhammad and Meccans fight Battle of Badr
661–750	Umayyad caliphate
664	Synod of Whitby; English king opts for Roman form of Christianity
726–787	Period of iconoclasm at Byzantium

KEY TERMS

Anglo-Saxon England (308)

Hijra (294)

iconoclasm (291)

Lombard Italy (311)

Merovingian dynasty (307)

Sassanid Empire (284)

Umayyad caliphate (298)

ummah (294)

Visigothic Spain (310)

REVIEW QUESTIONS

1. What stresses did the Byzantine Empire endure in the seventh and eighth centuries, and how was iconoclasm a response to those stresses?

2. How and why did the Muslims conquer so many lands in the very short period 632–750?

3. What were the roles, projects, and powers of the pope in early medieval Europe? On balance, how important was the papacy?

MAKING CONNECTIONS

1. What were the similarities and what were the differences between the three heirs of the Roman Empire?

2. Which of the heirs seemed most poised for success (economic, political, cultural) around the year 750, and why?

FOR FURTHER EXPLORATION

To assess your mastery of the material in this chapter, see the Online Study Guide at **bedfordstmartins.com/hunt**.

To read additional primary-source material from this period, see Chapter 8 in *Sources of The Making of the West*, Second Edition, Volume I.

Unity and Diversity in Three Societies, 750–1050

IN 841, A FIFTEEN-YEAR-OLD BOY NAMED WILLIAM went to serve at the court of the king of the Franks, Charles the Bald. William's father was Bernard, an extremely powerful noble. His mother was Dhuoda,◆ a well-educated, pious, and able woman; she administered the family's estates in the south of France while her husband occupied himself in court politics and royal administration. In 841, however, politics had become a dangerous business. King Charles, named after his grandfather Charlemagne,◆ was fighting with his brothers over his portion of the Carolingian Empire, and Bernard (who had been a supporter of Charles's father, Louis the Pious) held a precarious position at the young king's court. In fact, William was sent to Charles's court as a kind of hostage, to ensure Bernard's loyalty. Anxious about her son, Dhuoda wanted to educate and counsel him, so she wrote a handbook of advice for William, outlining what he ought to believe about God; about politics and society; about obligations to his family; and, above all, about his duties to his father, which she emphasized even over loyalty to the king:

> In the human understanding of things, royal and imperial appearance and power seem preeminent in the world, and the custom of men is to account those men's actions and their names ahead of all others. . . . But despite all this . . . I caution you to render first to him whose son you are special, faithful, steadfast loyalty as long as you shall live. . . . So I urge you again, most beloved son William, that first of all you love God. . . . Then love, fear, and cherish your father.

William heeded his mother's words, with tragic results: when Bernard ran afoul of Charles and was executed, William died in a failed attempt to avenge his father.

Dhuoda's handbook reveals the volatile political atmosphere of the mid-ninth century, and her advice to her son points to one of its

---

◆**Dhuoda:** doo OH duh
◆**Charlemagne:** SHAHR luh mayn

Carolingian Mother
This depiction of a nursing mother is a detail from a full-page illustration of the biblical story of the Creation and Fall in a Carolingian Bible manuscript made in the ninth century. The mother is Eve, cast out of the Garden of Eden and suckling her first born, Cain. Christian mothers had an important model in Mary, the mother of Jesus, and Eve's dignified placement within a bower of garlands may reflect this association. *By permission of the British Library.*

causes: a crisis of loyalty. Loyalty to emperors, caliphs, and kings—all of whom were symbols of unity cutting across regional and family ties—competed with allegiances to local authorities; and those, in turn, vied with family loyalties. The period 600–750 had seen the startling rise of Islam, the whittling away of Byzantium, and the beginnings of stable political and economic development in an impoverished Europe. The period 750–1050 would see all three societies contend with internal issues of diversity even as they became increasingly conscious of their unity and uniqueness. At the beginning of this period, rulers built up and dominated strong, united political communities. By the end, these realms had fragmented into smaller, more local units. While men and women continued to feel some loyalty toward faraway kings, caliphs, or emperors, their most powerful allegiances often focused on authorities closer to home.

At Byzantium, the military triumphs of the emperors brought them enormous prestige. A renaissance (that is, an important revival) of culture and art took place at Constantinople. Yet at the same time new elites began to dominate the Byzantine countryside. In the Islamic world, a dynastic revolution in 750 ousted the Umayyads from the caliphate and replaced them with a new family, the Abbasids. The new caliphs moved their capital east, away from Damascus, and they adopted some of the trappings of the Sassanid King of Kings. Yet their power too began to ebb as regional Islamic rulers came to the fore. In western Europe, Charlemagne—a Frankish king from a new dynasty, the Carolingians—forged a huge empire. Yet this newly unified kingdom was

fragile, disintegrating within a generation of Charlemagne's death. In western Europe, even more than in the Byzantine and Islamic worlds, power fell into the hands of local leaders.

All along the borders of these realms, new political entities began to develop, conditioned by the religion and culture of their more dominant neighbors. Russia grew up in the shadow of Byzantium, as did Bulgaria and Serbia. Western Europe was more crucial in the development of central Europe. By the year 1050, the contours of what were to become modern Europe and the Middle East were dimly visible.

❖ Byzantium: Renewed Strength and Influence

In the hundred years between 750 and 850, Byzantium staved off Muslim attacks in Asia Minor and began to rebuild. After 850, it went on the attack. Military victories brought new wealth and power to the imperial court, and the emperors supported a vast program of literary and artistic revival—the Macedonian renaissance—at Constantinople. But while the emperor dominated at the capital, a new landowning elite began to control the countryside. On its northern front, Byzantium helped create new Slavic realms.

Imperial Power

While the *themes,* with their territorial military organization, took care of attacks on Byzantine territory, new mobile armies made up of the best troops—*tagmata* (singular, *tagma*)—

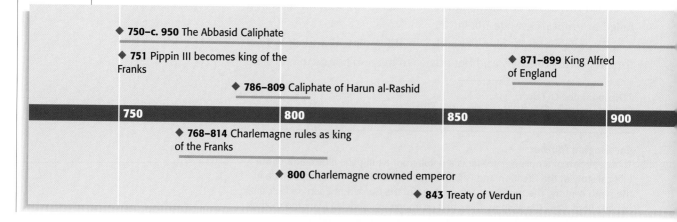

◆ **750–c. 950** The Abbasid Caliphate

◆ **751** Pippin III becomes king of the Franks

◆ **786–809** Caliphate of Harun al-Rashid

◆ **871–899** King Alfred of England

| 750 | 800 | 850 | 900 |

◆ **768–814** Charlemagne rules as king of the Franks

◆ **800** Charlemagne crowned emperor

◆ **843** Treaty of Verdun

moved aggressively outward, beginning around 850. By 1025, the empire had expanded to the Danube in the north and the Euphrates in the south (Map 9.1). The Byzantines had not controlled so much territory since their wars with the Sassanids four hundred years earlier.

Victories such as these gave new prestige and wealth to the army and to the imperial court. The emperors drew revenues from vast and growing imperial estates. They could tax and demand services from the general population at will—requiring citizens to build bridges and roads, to offer lodging to the emperor and his attendants, and to pay taxes in cash. Supported by their wealth, the emperors created a lavish court culture, surrounding themselves with servants, slaves, family members, and civil servants. Eunuchs, castrated men who could not pose a threat to the imperial line, were entrusted with some of the highest posts in government. From this powerful position, the emperors negotiated with other rulers, exchanging ambassadors and receiving and entertaining diplomats with elaborate ceremonies. One such diplomat, Liutprand, bishop of the northern Italian city of Cremona, reported on his audience with Emperor Constantine VII Porphyrogenitos♦ (r. 913–959) as follows:

> *Leaning upon the shoulders of two eunuchs I was brought into the emperor's presence. At my approach [mechanical] lions began to roar and birds to cry out, each according to its kind. . . . After I had three times [bowed] to the emperor with my face upon the ground, I lifted my head, and behold! the man whom just before I had seen sitting on a moderately elevated seat had now changed his [clothing] and was sitting on the level of the ceiling. How it was done I could not imagine, unless perhaps he was lifted up by some such sort of device as we use for raising the timbers of a wine press.*

Although Liutprand mocked this elaborate court ceremonial, it had a real function: to express the serious, sacred, concentrated power of imperial majesty.

The emperor's wealth relied on the prosperity of an agricultural economy organized for trade. State regulation and entrepreneurial enterprise were delicately balanced in Byzantine commerce. Although the emperor controlled craft and commercial guilds to ensure imperial revenues and a stable supply of valuable and useful commodities, entrepreneurs organized most of the markets held throughout the empire. Foreign merchants traded within the empire, either at Constantinople (where they were lodged at state expense) or in border cities. Because this international trade intertwined with foreign policy, the Byzantine government considered trade a political as well as an economic matter. Emperors issued privileges to certain "nations" (as, for example, the Venetians, Russians, and Jews were called), regulating the fees they were obliged to pay and the services they had to render. At the end of the tenth century, for example, the Venetians bargained to reduce their customs dues per ship from thirty *solidi*♦ (coins) to two; in return they promised to transport Byzantine soldiers to Italy whenever the emperor wished.

♦**Porphyrogenitos:** pohr fuh roh JEHN uht uhs

♦*solidi:* SAH luh dy

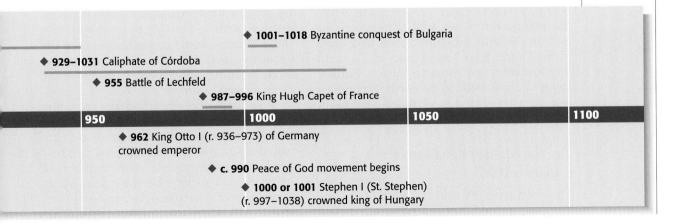

◆ **929–1031** Caliphate of Córdoba

◆ **1001–1018** Byzantine conquest of Bulgaria

◆ **955** Battle of Lechfeld

◆ **987–996** King Hugh Capet of France

| 950 | 1000 | 1050 | 1100 |

◆ **962** King Otto I (r. 936–973) of Germany crowned emperor

◆ **c. 990** Peace of God movement begins

◆ **1000 or 1001** Stephen I (St. Stephen) (r. 997–1038) crowned king of Hungary

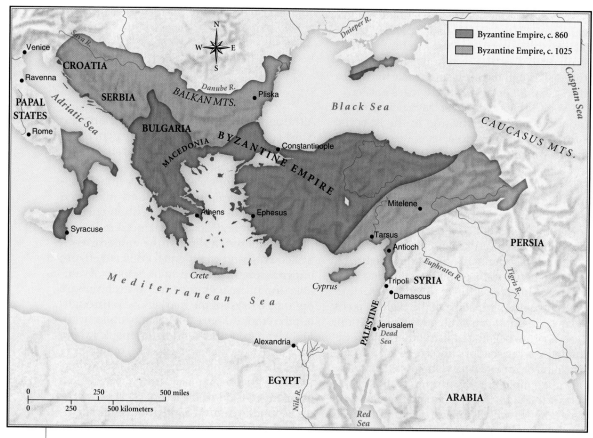

MAP 9.1 The Expansion of Byzantium, 860–1025
In 860, the Byzantine Empire was only a fraction of its former size. To the west, it had lost most of Italy, to the east, it held only part of Asia Minor. On its northern flank, the Bulgarians had set up an independent state. By 1025, however, it had ballooned, its western half embracing the whole Balkans, its eastern arm extending around the Black Sea, and its southern fringe reaching nearly to Tripoli. The year 1025 marked the Byzantine Empire's greatest size after the rise of Islam.

At the same time, the emperors negotiated privileges for their own traders in foreign lands. Byzantine merchants were guaranteed protection in Syria, for example, while the two governments split the income on sales taxes. Thus, Byzantine trade flourished in the Middle East and, thanks to Venetian intermediaries, with western Europe. Equally significant was trade to the north. Byzantines wore furs from Russia and imported Russian slaves, wax, and honey.

The Macedonian Renaissance, c. 870–c. 1025

Flush with victory and thinking of Byzantium's past glory, the emperors revived clas-sical intellectual pursuits. Basil I (r. 867–886) from Macedonia founded the imperial dynasty that presided over the so-called Macedonian renaissance. This renaissance (French for "rebirth") was made possible by an intellectual elite, who came from families that, even in the anxious years of the eighth century, had persisted in studying the classics in spite of the trend toward a simple religious education.

Now, with the empire slowly regaining its military eminence and with icons permanently restored in 843, this scholarly elite thrived again. Byzantine artists produced new works, and emperors and other members of the new court society, liberated from sober taboos against graven images, sponsored lavish artistic productions. Emperor Constantine

Porphyrogenitos (see the image on this page), wrote books of geography and history and financed the work of other scholars and artists. He even supervised the details of his craftspeople's products, insisting on exacting standards: "Who could enumerate how many artisans the Porphyrogenitos corrected? He

The Macedonian Renaissance

This manuscript illumination, made at Constantinople in the mid-ninth century, combines Christian and classical elements in a harmonious composition. David, author of the Psalms, sits in the center. Like the classical Orpheus, he plays music that attracts and tames the beasts. In the right-hand corner a figure labeled "Bethlehem" is modeled on a lounging river or mountain god. Compare this image of David with the one on the Cyprus plate on page 290. *Cliché Bibliotheque Nationale de France, Paris.*

The Crowning of Constantine Porphyrogenitos

The figures of this ivory relief were carved at Constantinople in the mid-tenth century. The artist wanted to emphasize hierarchy and symbolism, not nature. Christ is shown crowning Emperor Constantine Porphyrogenitos (r. 913–959). What message do you suppose the artist wanted to telegraph by making Christ higher than the emperor and by having the emperor slightly incline his head and upper torso to receive the crown? **For more help analyzing this image,** see the visual activity for this chapter in the Online Study Guide at **bedfordstmartins.com/hunt**. *Hirmer Fotoarchiv, München.*

corrected the stonemasons, the carpenters, the goldsmiths, the silversmiths, and the blacksmiths," wrote a historian supported by the same emperor's patronage.

The emperors were not alone. Other members of the imperial court also sponsored writers, philosophers, and historians. Scholars wrote summaries of classical literature, encyclopedias of ancient knowledge, and commentaries on classical authors. Some copied manuscripts of religious and theological commentaries, such as homilies, liturgical texts, Bibles, and Psalters. The merging of classical and Christian traditions is clearest in manuscript illuminations (painted illustrations or embellishments in hand-copied manuscripts). Both at Byzantium and in the West, artists chose their subjects by considering the texts they were to illustrate and the ways in which previous artists had handled particular themes. They drew on traditional models to make their subjects identifiable. Like modern illustrators of Santa Claus who rely on a tradition dictating a plump man with a bushy white beard—Santa's "iconography"—medieval artists depended on particular visual cues to alert viewers to the identity of their subjects. For example, to illustrate King David, the supposed poet of the Psalms, an artist illuminating a Psalter turned to a model of Orpheus, the enchanting musician of ancient Greek mythology.

The Dynatoi: A New Landowning Elite

At Constantinople the emperor reigned supreme. But outside the capital, especially in the border regions of Anatolia, where army leaders of the tagmata became famous as military heroes, extremely powerful military families established themselves and began to compete with imperial power. The **dynatoi,**♦ as this new hereditary elite was called, got rich on booty and new lands taken in the aggressive wars of the tenth century. They took over or bought up whole villages, turning the peasants' labor to their benefit. For the most part they exercised their power locally, but they also sometimes occupied the imperial throne.

The Phocas♦ family is a good example of the strengths as well as the weaknesses of the dynatoi. Probably originally from Armenia, they possessed military skills and exhibited loyalty to the emperor that together brought them high positions in both the army and at court in the last decades of the ninth century. But in the tenth century, with new successes in the east, the Phocas family gained independent power. In fact, after some particularly brilliant wars, Nicephorus♦ Phocas was declared emperor by his armies and ruled at Constantinople from 963 to 969. But opposing factions of the dynatoi brought him down. The mainstay of Phocas family power, as of that of all the dynatoi, was outside the capital, on the family's great estates.

With the development of the dynatoi, the social hierarchy of Byzantium began to resemble that of western Europe, where land owned by aristocrats was farmed by a subject peasantry whose tax and service obligations bound them to the fields they cultivated.

♦ **dynatoi:** DY nuh toy
♦**Phocas:** FOH kuhs
♦**Nicephorus:** ny SEH fuh ruhs

In Byzantium's Shadow: Bulgaria, Serbia, Russia

The shape of what was to become modern eastern Europe was created during the period 850–950. By 800, Slavic settlements dotted the area from the Danube River down to Greece and from the Black Sea to Croatia. The ruler of the Bulgarians, called a *khagan,*♦ presided over the largest realm, northwest of Constantinople. Under Khagan Krum♦ (r. c. 803–814) and his son, Bulgarian rule stretched west all the way to the Tisza♦ River in modern Hungary. At about the same time as Krum's triumphant expansion, however, the Byzantine Empire began its own campaigns to conquer, convert, and control these Slavic regions.

Bulgaria and Serbia. The Byzantine offensive to the north and west began under Emperor Nicephorus I (r. 802–811), who waged war against the Slavs of Greece in the Peloponnesus, set up a new Christian diocese there, organized it as a new military theme, and forcibly resettled Christians in the area to counteract Slavic paganism. The Byzantines followed this pattern of conquest as they pushed northward. By 900, Byzantium ruled all of Greece.

The Balkans, c. 850–950

Still under Nicephorus, the Byzantines launched a massive attack against the Bulgarians, took the chief city of Pliska,♦ plundered it, burned it to the ground, and then marched against Krum's encampment in the Balkan mountains. Krum, however, took advantage of his position, attacked the imperial troops, killed Nicephorus, and brought home the em-

♦**Khagan:** KAG an
♦**Khagan Krum:** KAG an kruhm
♦**Tisza:** TIH saw
♦**Pliska:** PLEE skah

peror's skull in triumph. Cleaned out and lined with silver, the skull served as the victorious Krum's drinking goblet. In 816, the two sides agreed to a peace that lasted for thirty years. But hostility remained, and the intermittent skirmishes between the Bulgarians and Byzantines gave way to longer wars throughout the tenth century. The Byzantines advanced in a slow, methodical conquest (1001–1018) led by Emperor Basil II (r. 976–1025). Aptly called the Bulgar-Slayer, Basil subjected the entire region to Byzantine control and forced its ruler to accept the Byzantine form of Christianity. Similarly, the Serbs, encouraged by Byzantium to oppose the Bulgarians, began to form the political community that would become Serbia, in the shadow of Byzantine interest and religion.

Religion played an important role in the Byzantine offensive. In 863, two brothers, Cyril♦ and Methodius,♦ were sent as Christian missionaries from the Byzantines to the Slavs. Well educated in both classical and religious texts, they spoke one Slavic dialect fluently and devised an alphabet for Slavic (until then an oral language) based on Greek forms. It was the ancestor of the modern Cyrillic♦ alphabet used in Bulgaria, Serbia, and Russia today.

Kievan Russia. Russia in the ninth and tenth centuries lay outside the sphere of direct Byzantine rule, but like Serbia and Bulgaria it came under increasingly strong Byzantine cultural and religious influence. In the ninth century the Vikings—Scandinavian adventurers who ranged over vast stretches of ninth-century Europe seeking trade, booty, and land—had penetrated Russia from the north and imposed their rule over the Slavs inhabiting the broad river valleys. Like the Bulgars in Bulgaria, the Scandinavian Vikings gradually blended into the larger Slavic population. At the end of the ninth century, one Dnieper♦ valley chief, Oleg, established control over most of the tribes in southwestern Russia and forced peoples far-

ther away to pay tribute money. The tribal association he created formed the nucleus of Kievan Russia, named for Kiev, the city that had become the commercial center of the region and today is the capital of Ukraine.

Kievan Russia and Byzantium began their relationship with war, developed it through trade agreements, and finally sustained it by religion. Around 905, Oleg launched a military expedition to Constantinople, forcing the Byzantines to pay him a large fee and open their doors to Russian traders in exchange for peace. At the time, only a few Christians lived in Russia, along with Jews and probably some Muslims. The Russians' conversion to Christianity was spearheaded by a Russian ruler later in the century. Vladimir (r. c. 980–1015), the grand prince of Kiev and all Russia, and the Byzantine emperor Basil II agreed that Vladimir should adopt the Byzantine form of Christianity. Vladimir took a variant of the name Basil in honor of the emperor and married the emperor's sister Anna; then he reportedly had all the people of his realm baptized in the Dnieper River.

Vladimir's conversion represented a wider pattern. Along with the Christianization of Slavic realms such as Old Moravia, Serbia, and Bulgaria under the Byzantine church, the rulers and peoples of Poland, Hungary, Denmark, and Norway were converted under the auspices of the Roman church. Russia's conversion to Christianity was especially significant, because Russia was geographically as close to the Islamic world as to the Christian and could conceivably have become an Islamic land. By converting to Byzantine Christianity, Russians made themselves heir to Byzantium and its church, customs, art, and political ideology. Adopting Christianity linked Russia to the Christian world, but choosing the Byzantine (Greek) form of Christianity, rather than the Roman Catholic, served later on to isolate Russia from western Europe, as in the course of the centuries the Greek and Roman churches became estranged.

Russian rulers at times sought to cement relations with central and western Europe, which were tied to Catholic Rome. Prince Iaroslav the Wise (r. 1019–1054) forged

♦**Cyril:** SIH ruhl
♦**Methodius:** meh THOH dee uhs
♦**Cyrillic:** suh RIH lihk
♦**Dnieper:** NEE pur

such links through his own marriage and those of his sons and daughters to rulers and princely families in France, Hungary, and Scandinavia. Iaroslav encouraged intellectual and artistic developments that would connect Russian culture to the classical past. At his own church of St. Sophia, at Kiev, which copied the one at Constantinople, Iaroslav created a major library.

When Iaroslav died, his kingdom was divided among his sons. Civil wars broke out between the brothers and eventually between cousins, shredding what unity Russia had known. Massive invasions by outsiders, particularly from the east, further weakened Kievan rulers, who were eventually displaced by princes from northern Russia. At the crossroads of East and West, Russia could meet and absorb a great variety of traditions; but its situation also opened it to unremitting military pressures.

> **Review:** What were the effects of expansion on the power of the Byzantine emperor?

❖ The Islamic World: From Unity to Fragmentation

A new dynasty of caliphs—the Abbasids—first brought unity and then, in their decline, fragmentation to the Islamic world. Caliphs continued to rule in name only as regional rulers took over the real business of government in Islamic lands. Local traditions based on religious and political differences played an increasingly important role in people's lives. Yet, even in the eleventh century, the Islamic world had a clear sense of its own unity, which came from language, commercial life, and vigorous intellectual debate across regional boundaries.

The Abbasid Caliphate, 750–c. 950

In 750, a civil war ousted the Umayyads and raised the **Abbasids**◆ to the caliphate. The Abbasids found support in an uneasy coalition of Shi'ites (the faction of Islam loyal to

Ali's memory) and non-Arabs who had been excluded from Umayyad government and now demanded a place in political life. The new regime signaled a revolution. The center of Islamic rule shifted from Damascus, with its roots in the Roman tradition, to Baghdad, a new capital city, built by the Abbasids right next to Ctesiphon, which had been the Sassanid capital. Here the Abbasid caliphs imitated the Persian King of Kings (whose image they knew from sculptures such as the one on page 287) and adopted the court ceremony of the Sassanids. Their administration grew more and more centralized: the caliph's staff grew, and he controlled the appointment of regional governors.

The Abbasid caliph Harun al-Rashid◆ (r. 786–809) presided over a flourishing empire from Baghdad. His contemporary Frankish ruler, Charlemagne, was very impressed with the elephant Harun sent him as a gift, along with monkeys, spices, and medicines. But these items were mainstays of everyday commerce in Harun's Iraq. For example, a mid-ninth-century list of imports inventoried "tigers, panthers, elephants, panther skins, rubies, white sandal, ebony, and coconuts" from India, as well as "silk, chinaware, paper, ink, peacocks, racing horses, saddles, felts [and] cinnamon" from China.

The Abbasid dynasty began to decline after Harun's death. Obliged to support a huge army and increasingly complex civil service, the Abbasids found their tax base inadequate. They needed to collect revenues from their provinces, such as Syria and Egypt, but the governors of those regions often refused to send the revenues. After Harun's caliphate, ex-soldiers seeking better salaries recognized different caliphs and fought for power in savage civil wars. The caliphs tried to bypass the regular army, made up largely of free Muslim foot soldiers, by turning to slaves, bought and armed to serve as mounted cavalry. This tactic failed, however, and in the tenth century the caliphs became figureheads only. Religious leadership was now in the hands of religious scholars. Political leadership fell into the hands of independent rulers, who established themselves in the various Islamic regions. To sup-

---

◆**Abbasids:** A buh suhds

◆**Harun al-Rashid:** huh ROON ahl ruh SHEED

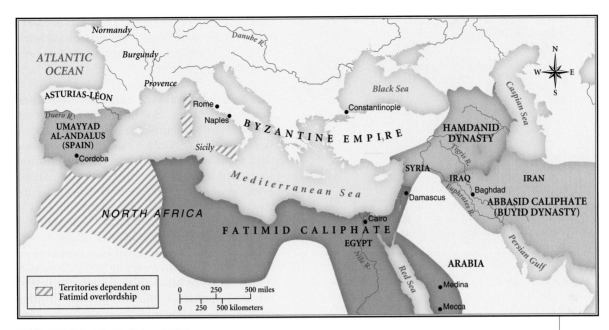

MAP 9.2 Islamic States, c. 1000
A glance back at Map 8.3 on page 296 will quickly demonstrate the fragmentation of the once united Islamic caliphate. In 750, one caliph ruled territory stretching from Spain to India. In 1000, there was more than one caliphate as well as several other ruling dynasties. The most important were the Fatimids, who began as organizers of a movement to overthrow the Abbasids. By 1000, they had conquered Egypt and claimed hegemony over all of North Africa.

port themselves militarily, many of these new rulers came to depend on independent military commanders who led armies of Mamluks◆—Turkish slaves or freedmen trained as professional mounted soldiers. Mamluks were well paid to maintain their mounts and arms, and many gained renown and high positions at the courts of regional rulers.

Thus, in the Islamic world, as in the Byzantine, a new military elite arose. But the Muslim and Byzantine elites differed in key ways. Whereas the Byzantine dynatoi were rooted in specific regions—tied to their estates and extended families—the Mamluks were highly mobile. They were not supported by land but rather were paid from taxes collected by local rulers. Organized into tightly knit companies bound together by devotion to a particular general and by a strong camaraderie, they easily changed employers, moving from ruler to ruler for pay.

Regional Diversity

A faraway caliph could not command sufficient allegiance from local leaders once he demanded more in taxes than he gave back in favors. The forces of fragmentation were strong in the Islamic world: it was, after all, based on the conquest of many diverse regions, each with its own deeply rooted traditions and culture. The Islamic religion, with its Sunni/Shi'ite split, also became a source of polarization. Western Europeans knew almost nothing about Muslims, calling all of them Saracens◆ (from the Latin for "Arabs") without distinction. But, in fact, Muslims were of different ethnicities, practiced different customs, and identified with different regions. With the fragmentation of political and religious unity, each of the tenth- and early-eleventh-century Islamic states built on local traditions under local rulers (Map 9.2).

◆**Mamluks:** MAM looks

◆**Saracens:** SAIR uh suhns

**Dome of the Mihrab of
the Great Mosque at Córdoba**
The mihrab is the prayer niche of the mosque, located so that the worshiper facing it is thereby facing Mecca. For the one at Córdoba, built between 961 and 976 by the Andalusian caliph al-Hakam, Byzantine mosaicists were imported to produce a decoration that would recall the mosaics of the Great Mosque at Damascus (see page 282). Why would this caliph, a Umayyad, be particularly interested in reminding Andalusians of the Damascus mosque? *Institut Amatller d'Art Hispanic, Barcelona.*

The Fatimid Dynasty.   In the tenth century, one group of Shi'ites, calling themselves the Fatimids◆ (after Fatimah, Muhammad's only surviving child and wife of Ali), began a successful political movement. Allying with the Berbers in North Africa, the Fatimids established themselves in 909 as rulers in the region now called Tunisia. The Fatimid Ubayd Allah◆ claimed to be not only the true imam,◆ descendant of Ali, but also the *mahdi,*◆ the "divinely guided" messiah, come to bring justice on earth. In 969, the Fatimids declared

themselves rulers of Egypt. Their dynasty lasted for about two hundred years. Fatimid leaders also controlled North Africa, Arabia, and even Syria for a time.

The Spanish Emirate.   Whereas the Shi'ites dominated Egypt, Sunni Muslims ruled al-Andalus,◆ the Islamic central and southern heart of Spain. Unlike the other independent Islamic states, which were forged during the ninth and tenth centuries, the Spanish emirate of Córdoba◆ (so called because its ruler took the secular title *emir,*◆ "commander," and fixed his capital at Córdoba) was created near the start of the Abbasid caliphate, in 756. During the Abbasid revolution, Abd al-Rahman—a member of the Umayyad family—fled to Morocco, gathered an army, invaded Spain, and was declared emir after only one battle. He and his successors ruled a broad range of peoples, including many Jews and Christians. After the initial Islamic conquest of Spain, the Christians adopted so much of the new language and so many of the customs that they were called Mozarabs,◆ that is, "like Arabs." The Arabs allowed them freedom of worship and let them live according to their own laws. Some Mozarabs were content with their status, others converted to Islam, and still others intermarried—most commonly, Christian women married Muslim men and raised their children as Muslims, since the religion of the father determined that of the children.

Abd al-Rahman◆ III (r. 912–961) was powerful enough to take the title of caliph; the caliphate of Córdoba that he created lasted from 929 to 1031. Under Abd al-Rahman's rule members of all religious groups in al-Andalus were given absolute freedom of worship and equal opportunity to rise in the civil service. The caliph also initiated important diplomatic contracts with Byzantine and European rulers, ignoring the weak and tiny Christian kingdoms squeezed into northern Spain. His successor, al-Hakam, built a splendid mihrab at Córdoba (see Dome of the

◆**Fatimids:** FAT ih mihds
◆**Ubayd Allah:** ub EYED a LAH
◆**imam:** ih MAHM
◆*mahdi:* MAH dee

◆**al-Andalus:** al AND uh loos
◆**Córdoba:** KAWR duh buh
◆*emir:* ih MIHR
◆**Mozarabs:** moh ZAR ruhbs
◆**Abd al-Rahman:** uhb dur rahk MAHN

Mihrab at Córdoba, page 328). Yet under later caliphs, al-Andalus, too, experienced the same political fragmentation that was occurring everywhere else. The caliphate of Córdoba broke up in 1031, and rulers of small, independent regions, called *taifas,*♦ took power.

Unity of Commerce and Language

Although the regions of the Islamic world were diverse culturally and politically, they maintained a measure of unity through trade networks and language. Their principal bond was Arabic, the language of the Qur'an. At once poetic and sacred, Arabic was also the language of commerce and government from Baghdad to Córdoba. Moreover, despite political differences, borders were open: an artisan could move from Córdoba to Cairo; a landowner in Morocco might very well own property in al-Andalus; a young man from North Africa would think nothing of going to Baghdad to find a wife; a young girl purchased as a slave in Mecca might become part of a prince's household in Baghdad. With few barriers to commerce (though every city and town had its own customs dues), traders regularly dealt in various, often exotic, goods.

Although the primary reason for these open borders was Islam itself, the openness extended to non-Muslims as well. We happen to know a good deal about the Tustari♦ brothers, Jewish merchants from southern Iran. The Tustaris' commercial activities were typical in the Arabic-speaking world. By 1026, they had established a flourishing business in Egypt. They did not have "branch offices," but informal contacts allowed them many of the same advantages and much flexibility: friends and family in Iran shipped the brothers fine textiles to sell in Egypt, and the Tustaris exported Egyptian fabrics to sell in Iran. Dealing in fabrics could yield fabulous wealth, for cloth was essential not only for clothing but also for home decoration: textiles covered walls; curtains separated rooms. The Tustari brothers held the highest rank in Jewish society and had contacts with Muslim rulers. The son of one of the brothers con-

verted to Islam and became **vizier** (chief minister) to the Fatimids in Egypt. But the sophisticated Islamic society of the tenth and eleventh centuries supported networks even more vast than those represented by the Tustari family. Muslim merchants brought tin from England; salt and gold from Timbuktu in west-central Africa; amber, gold, and copper from Russia; and slaves from every region.

The Islamic Renaissance, c. 790–c. 1050

The dissolution of the caliphate into separate political entities multiplied the centers of learning and intellectual productivity. Unlike the Macedonian renaissance, which was concentrated in Constantinople, a renaissance of Islam occurred throughout the Islamic world. It was particularly dazzling in capital cities such as Córdoba, where tenth-century rulers presided over a brilliant court culture, patronizing scholars, poets, and artists. The library at Córdoba contained the largest collection of books in Europe at that time.

Elsewhere, already in the eighth century, the Abbasid caliphs endowed research libraries and set up centers for translation where scholars culled the writings of the ancients, including the classics of Persia, India, and Greece. Many scholars read, translated, and commented on the works of ancient philosophers. Others worked on astronomy (see Andromeda C, page 330), and still others wrote on mathematical matters. Al-Khwarizmi's♦ book on equations, written around 825, became so well known in the West that the word *al-jabr* in the title of his book became the English word *algebra*. Muhammad ibn Musa♦ (d. 850) used numerals such as 1, 2, and 3, which had been created in India, in his treatise on arithmetical calculations. Inventing the crucial placeholder zero, Musa was for the first time able to manipulate very large numbers (something impossible with Roman numerals). When these numerals were introduced into western Europe in the twelfth century, they were known as Arabic, as they are still called today.

♦*taifas:* TY fuhs
♦**Tustari:** tus TAR ee

♦**Al-Khwarizmi:** al KWAHR ihz mee
♦**Muhammad ibn Musa:** moh HAM uhd

Andromeda C. (11th century)
The study of sciences such as medicine, physics, and astronomy flourished in the tenth and eleventh centuries in the cosmopolitan Islamic world. This whimsical depiction of Andromeda C, a constellation in the Northern Hemisphere, illustrates the *Book of Images of the Fixed Stars,* an astronomical treatise written around 965 by al-Sufi at the request of his "pupil," the ruler of Iran. Since the Muslim calendar was lunar and the times of Muslim prayer were calculated by the movement of the sun, astronomy was important for religious as well as secular purposes. Al-Sufi drew from classical treatises, particularly the *Almagest* by Ptolemy. This copy of his book, probably made by his son in 1009, also draws on classical models for the illustrations; but instead of Greek clothing, Andromeda wears the pantaloons and skirt of an Islamic dancer. *Reference (shelf-mark) MS Marsh 144. Bodleian Library. University of Oxford.*

The newly independent Islamic rulers supported science as well as mathematics. Ibn Sina◆ (980–1037), known in Christian Europe as Avicenna,◆ wrote books on logic, the natural sciences, and physics. His *Canon of Medicine* systematized earlier treatises and reconciled them with his own experience as a physician. Active in the centers of power, he served as vizier to various rulers. In his autobiography he spoke with pleasure and pride about his intellectual development:

> One day I asked permission [of the ruler] to go into [his doctors'] library, look at their books, and read the medical ones. He gave me permission, and I went into a palace of many rooms, each with trunks full of books, back-to-back. In one room there were books on Arabic and poetry, in another books on jurisprudence, and similarly in each room books on a single subject.... When I reached the age of eighteen, I had completed the study of all these sciences.

Long before there were universities in Europe, there were important institutions of higher learning in the Islamic world. Rich Muslims, often members of the ruling elite, demonstrated their piety and charity by establishing schools for professors and students. Each school, or **madrasa**,◆ was located within or attached to a mosque. Professors held classes throughout the day on the interpretation of the Qur'an and other literary or legal texts. Students, all male, attended the classes that suited their achievement level and interest. Most students paid a fee for learning, but there were also scholarship students. One tenth-century vizier was so solicitous of the welfare of all scholars that each day he set out iced refreshments, candles, and paper for them in his own kitchen.

The use of paper, made from flax and hemp or rags and vegetable fiber, points to a major difference among the Islamic, Byzantine, and (as we shall see) Carolingian renaissances. Byzantine scholars worked to enhance the prestige of the ruling classes. Their work, written on expensive parchment (made from animal skins), kept manuscripts out of the hands of all but the very rich. This was true of scholarship in Europe as well. By contrast, Islamic scholars had goals that cut

◆**Ibn Sina:** ihb uhn SEE nah
◆**Avicenna:** a vuh SEH nuh

◆**madrasa:** muh DRA suh

across all social classes: to be physicians to the rich, teachers to the young, and contributors to passionate religious debates. Their writings, on paper (less expensive than parchment), were widely available.

> **Review:** What forces led to the fragmentation of the Islamic world in the tenth and eleventh centuries?

❖ The Creation and Division of a New European Empire

Just as in the Byzantine and Islamic worlds, so too in Europe the period 750–1050 saw first the formation of a strong empire, ruled by one man, and then its fragmentation as local rulers took power into their own hands. A new dynasty, the Carolingians, came to rule in the Frankish kingdom at almost the very moment (c. 750) that the Abbasids gained the caliphate. Charlemagne, the most powerful Carolingian monarch, conquered new territory, took the title of emperor, and presided over a revival of Christian classical culture known as the Carolingian renaissance. He ruled at the local level through counts and other military men. Nevertheless, the unity of this empire—based largely on conquest, a measure of prosperity, and personal allegiance to Charlemagne—was shaky. Its weaknesses were exacerbated by attacks from invaders—Vikings, Muslims, and Magyars. Charlemagne's successors divided his empire among themselves and saw it divided further as local leaders took defense—and rule—into their own hands.

The Rise of the Carolingians

The Carolingians were among many aristocratic families on the rise during the Merovingian period, but they gained exceptional power by monopolizing the position of "palace mayor" under the Merovingian kings. Charles Martel, mayor 714–741, gave the name

Carolingian (from *Carolus*, the Latin for "Charles") to the dynasty. Renowned for defeating an invading army of Muslims from al-Andalus between Poitiers♦ and Tours in 732, he also contended vigorously against other aristocrats who were carving out independent lordships for themselves. Charles and his family turned aristocratic factions against one another, rewarded supporters, crushed enemies, and dominated whole regions by supporting monasteries that served as focal points for both religious piety and land donations.

The Carolingians also allied themselves with the Roman papacy and its adherents. They supported Anglo-Saxon missionaries like Boniface,♦ who went to areas on the fringes of the Carolingian realm as the pope's ambassador. Reforming the Christianity that these regions had adopted, Boniface set up a hierarchical church organization and founded monasteries dedicated to the Benedictine rule. His newly appointed bishops were loyal to Rome and the Carolingians. Pippin III (d. 768), Charles Martel's son, turned to the pope even more directly. When he deposed the Merovingian king in 751, taking over the kingship himself, Pippin petitioned Pope Zachary to legitimize the act. The pope agreed. The Carolingians readily returned the favor a few years later when the pope asked for their help in defense against hostile Lombards. That papal request signaled a major shift. Before 754, the papacy had been part of the Byzantine Empire; after that, it turned to Europe for protection. Pippin launched a successful campaign against the Lombard king that ended in 756 with the so-called Donation of Pippin, a peace accord between the Lombards and the pope. The treaty gave back to the pope cities that had been ruled by the Lombard king. The new arrangement recognized what the papacy had long ago created: a territorial "republic of St. Peter" ruled by the pope, not by the Byzantine emperor. Henceforth, the fate of Italy would be tied largely to the policies of the pope and the Frankish kings to the north, not to the emperors of the East.

♦**Poitiers:** pwah tee AY
♦**Boniface:** BAH nuh fuhs

The Carolingian partnership with the Roman church gave the dynasty a Christian aura, expressed in symbolic form by anointment. Bishops rubbed holy oil on the foreheads and shoulders of Carolingian kings during the coronation ceremony, imitating the Old Testament kings who had been anointed by God.

Charlemagne and His Kingdom, 768–814

The most famous Carolingian king was Charles (r. 768–814), called the Great (*le Magne* in Old French) by his contemporaries. Epic poems portrayed Charlemagne as a just, brave, wise, and warlike king. In a biography written by Einhard,◆ his friend and younger contemporary, and patterned closely on Suetonius's◆ *Lives of the Caesars*, Charlemagne appeared as the very model of a Roman emperor. Some scholars at his court described him as another David, the anointed Old Testament king. Modern historians are less dazzled than his contemporaries were, noting that Charlemagne was complex, contradictory, and sometimes brutal. He loved listening to St. Augustine's *City of God* as it was read aloud, and he supported major scholarly enterprises; yet he never learned to write. He was devout, building a beautiful chapel at his major residence at Aachen◆ (see Charlemagne's Throne on this page), yet he flouted the advice of churchmen when they told him to convert pagans rather than force baptism on them. He admired the pope, yet he was furious when a pope placed the imperial crown on his head. He waged many successful wars, yet he thereby destroyed the buffer states surrounding the Frankish kingdoms, unleashing a new round of invasions even before his death.

Behind these contradictions, however, lay a unifying vision. Charlemagne dreamed of an empire that would unite the martial and learned traditions of the Roman and Germanic worlds with the legacy of Christianity. This vision lay at the core of his

◆**Einhard:** EYN hard
◆**Suetonius:** swee TOH nee uhs
◆**Aachen:** AH kuhn

Charlemagne's Throne
Charlemagne was the first Frankish king to build a permanent capital city. The decision to do so was made in 789, and the king chose Aachen because of its natural warm springs. There he built a palace complex that included a grand living area for the king and his retinue and a church, still standing today, modeled on the Byzantine church of San Vitale in Ravenna. In the balcony above the altar of the church, Charlemagne placed his throne. Consider that Charlemagne had conquered northern Italy in 774. What aspirations might Charlemagne have been expressing by imitating a northern Italian Byzantine church? What idea of himself was he conveying by placing his own throne above the main altar? *Ann Munchow/Das Domkapital, Aachen.*

political activity, his building programs, and his active support of scholarship and education.

Territorial Expansion. Charlemagne spent the early years of his reign conquering lands in all directions and subjugating the conquered peoples (Map 9.3). He invaded Italy, seizing the crown of the Lombard kings and annexing northern Italy in 774. He then moved northward and began a long and dif-

MAP 9.3 Expansion of the Carolingian Empire under Charlemagne
The conquests of Charlemagne temporarily united almost all of western Europe under one ruler. Although this great empire broke apart (see the inset showing the divisions of the Treaty of Verdun), the legacy of that unity remained, even serving as one of the inspirations behind today's European Union.

ficult war against the Saxons, concluded only after more than thirty years of fighting, during which he forcibly annexed Saxon territory and converted the Saxon people to Christianity through mass baptisms at the point of the sword. To the southeast, Charlemagne waged a campaign against the Avars. Einhard exulted, "All the money and treasure that had been amassed over many years was seized, and no war in which the Franks have ever engaged within the memory of man brought them such riches and such booty." To the southwest, Charlemagne led an ex-

pedition to al-Andalus. Although suffering a notable but local defeat at Roncesvalles♦ in 778 (immortalized later in the medieval epic *The Song of Roland*), he did set up a march, or military buffer region, between al-Andalus and his own realm.

By the 790s, Charlemagne's kingdom stretched eastward to the Saale♦ River (today in eastern Germany), southeast to what is today Austria, and south to Spain and Italy.

♦**Roncesvalles:** rawn tsuhs VA Luh
♦**Saale:** ZAH luh

Such power in the West was unheard of since the time of the Roman Empire. Charlemagne began to follow the old Roman model: he sponsored building programs to symbolize his authority, standardized weights and measures, and acted as a patron of intellectual and artistic efforts. He built a capital city at Aachen, complete with a church patterned on one built by Justinian at Ravenna.

To discourage corruption, Charlemagne appointed special officials, called *missi dominici* ◆ (meaning "those sent out by the lord king"), to oversee his regional governors—the counts—on the king's behalf. The missi—lay aristocrats or bishops— traveled in pairs to make a circuit of regions of the kingdom. As one of Charlemagne's capitularies (summaries of royal decisions) put it, the missi "are to make diligent inquiry wherever people claim that someone has done them an injustice, so that the missi fully carry out the law and do justice for everyone everywhere, whether in the holy churches of God or among the poor, orphans, or widows."

Imperial Coronation. While Charlemagne was busy imitating Roman emperors through his conquests, his building programs, his legislation, and his efforts at church reform, the papacy was beginning to claim imperial power for itself. At some point, perhaps in the mid-750s, members of the papal chancery (writing office) created a document called the Donation of Constantine, which declared the pope the recipient of the fourth-century emperor Constantine's crown, cloak, and military rank along with "all provinces, palaces, and districts of the city of Rome and Italy and of the regions of the West." (The document was much later proved a forgery.) The tension between the imperial claims of the Carolingians and those of the pope was heightened by the existence of an emperor at Constantinople who also had rights in the West.

Pope Hadrian ◆ I (r. 772–795) maintained a balance among these three powers. But Hadrian's successor, Leo III (r. 795–816), tipped the balance. In 799, accused of adultery and perjury by a faction of the Roman aristocracy, Leo narrowly escaped being blinded and having his tongue cut out. He fled northward to seek Charlemagne's protection. Charlemagne had him escorted back to Rome under royal protection and arrived there himself to an imperial welcome orchestrated by Leo. On Christmas Day, 800, Leo put an imperial crown on Charlemagne's head and the clergy and nobles who were present acclaimed the king Augustus, the title of the first Roman emperor. The pope hoped in this way to exalt the king of the Franks, to downgrade the Byzantine ruler, and to enjoy the role of "emperor maker" himself.

About twenty years later, when Einhard wrote about this coronation, he said that the imperial title at first displeased Charlemagne "so much that he stated that, if he had known in advance of the pope's plan, he would not have entered the church that day." In fact, Charlemagne did not use any title but king for more than a year afterward. But it is unlikely that he was completely surprised by the imperial title; his advisers certainly had been thinking about it for him. He might have hesitated to adopt the title because he feared the reaction of the Byzantines, as Einhard went on to suggest, or he might have objected to the papal role in his crowning rather than to the crown itself. When Charlemagne finally did call himself emperor, after establishing a peace with the Byzantines, he used a long and revealing title: "Charles, the most serene Augustus, crowned by God, great and peaceful Emperor who governs the Roman Empire and who is, by the mercy of God, king of the Franks and the Lombards." According to this title, Charlemagne was not the Roman emperor crowned by the pope but rather God's emperor, who governed the Roman Empire along with his many other duties.

The Carolingian Renaissance, c. 790–c. 900

Charlemagne inaugurated—and his successors continued to support—a revival of learning designed to enhance the glory of the kings, educate their officials, reform the liturgy, and purify the faith. Like the renaissances of the Byzantine and Islamic worlds, the Carolingian renaissance resuscitated the learning of the past. Scholars studied Roman im-

---

◆ **missi dominici:** MEE si dom IN i kee
◆ **Hadrian:** HAY dree uhn

perial writers such as Suetonius and Virgil, read and commented on the works of the church fathers, and worked to establish complete and accurate texts of everything they read and prized.

The English scholar Alcuin♦ (c. 732–804), a member of the circle of scholars whom Charlemagne recruited to form a center of study, brought with him the traditions of Anglo-Saxon scholarship that had been developed by men such as Benedict Biscop and Bede. Invited to Aachen, Alcuin became Charlemagne's chief adviser, writing letters on the king's behalf, counseling him on royal policy, and tutoring the king's household, including the women and girls. He also prepared an improved edition of the Vulgate,♦ the Latin Bible read in all church services by the clergy.

The Carolingian renaissance depended on an elite staff of scholars such as Alcuin, yet its educational program had broader appeal. In one of his capitularies, Charlemagne ordered that the cathedrals and monasteries of his kingdom teach reading and writing to all who were able to learn. Some churchmen expressed the hope that schools for children (perhaps they were thinking of girls as well as boys) would be established even in small villages and hamlets. Although this dream was never realized, it shows that, at just about the same time as the Islamic world was organizing its madrasas, the Carolingians were thinking about the importance of religious education for more than a small elite.

Art, like scholarship, served Carolingian political and religious goals. Carolingian artists turned to models from Byzantium (perhaps some refugees from Byzantine iconoclasm joined them) and Italy to illustrate gospels, psalters, scientific treatises, and literary manuscripts.

The Carolingian program was ambitious and lasting, even after the Carolingian dynasty had faded to a memory. The work of locating, understanding, and transmitting models of the past continued in a number of monastic schools. In the materials they studied, the questions they asked, and the answers they suggested, the Carolingians offered a mode of inquiry fruitful for subse-

St. Matthew
The Carolingian renaissance produced art of extraordinary originality. Although the artist of this picture was inspired by classical models, his frenetic, emotional lines and uncanny colors are something new. This illustration, a depiction of St. Matthew writing (with an ink horn in his left hand and a quill in his right hand), precedes the text of St. Matthew's Gospel in a book of Gospels made around 820. Compare it to the Psalter illumination from Constantinople on page 323. What does this comparison tell you about the similarities and differences between the Macedonian and Carolingian renaissances?
La Médiathèque, Ville d'Epernay.

quent generations. In the twelfth century, scholars would build on the foundations laid by the Carolingian renaissance. The very print of this textbook depends on one achievement of the period: modern letter fonts are based on the clear and beautiful letter forms, called Caroline miniscule,♦

♦**Alcuin:** AL kwuhn
♦**Vulgate:** VUHL gayt

♦**Caroline miniscule:** KAR uh lyn MIHN his kyool

invented in the ninth century to standardize manuscript handwriting—and make it more readable—across the whole empire.

Charlemagne's Successors, 814–911

Charlemagne's son Louis the Pious (r. 814–840) took his role as leader of the Christian empire even more seriously than his father did. He brought the monastic reformer Benedict of Aniane♦ to court and issued a capitulary in 817 imposing a uniform way of life, based on the Benedictine rule, on all the monasteries of the empire. Although some monasteries opposed this legislation, and in the years to come the king was unable to impose his will directly, this moment marked the effective adoption of the Benedictine rule as the monastic standard in Europe.

In a new development of the coronation ritual, Louis's first wife, Ermengard♦, was crowned empress by the pope in 816. In 817, their firstborn son, Lothar, was given the title emperor and made co-ruler with Louis. Their other sons, Pippin and Louis (later called Louis the German), were made sub-kings under imperial rule. Louis the Pious hoped in this way to ensure the unity of the empire while satisfying the claims of all his sons. Should any son die, only his firstborn could succeed him, a measure intended to prevent further splintering. But Louis's hopes were thwarted by events. Ermengard died, and Louis married Judith, the daughter of one of the most powerful families in the kingdom. In 823, she and Louis had a son, Charles (later known as Charles the Bald, to whose court Dhuoda's son William was sent). The sons of Ermengard, bitter over the birth of another royal heir, rebelled against their father and fought one another for more than a decade. Finally, after Louis's death in 840, the Treaty of Verdun♦ (843) divided the empire among the three remaining brothers (Pippin had died in 838) in an arrangement that would roughly define the future political contours of western Europe (see Map 9.3). The western third, bequeathed to Charles the Bald (r. 843–877), would eventually become France; the eastern third, handed to Louis the German (r. 843–876), would become Germany. The "Middle Kingdom," which was given to Lothar (r. 840–855) along with the imperial title, had a different fate: parts of it were absorbed by France and Germany, and the rest eventually formed what were to become the modern states of the Netherlands, Belgium, Luxembourg, Switzerland, and Italy.

By 843, the European-wide empire of Charlemagne had dissolved. Forged by conquest, it had been supported by a small group of privileged aristocrats with lands and offices stretching across the whole of it. Their loyalty—based on shared values, real friendship, expectations of gain, and sometimes formal ties of vassalage♦ and fealty♦ (see page 342)—was crucial to the success of the Carolingians. The empire had also been supported by an ideal, shared by educated laymen and churchmen alike, of conquest and Christian belief working together to bring good order to the earthly state. But powerful forces operated against the Carolingian Empire. Once the empire's borders were fixed and conquests ceased, the aristocrats could not hope for new lands and offices. They put down roots in particular regions and began to gather their own followings. Powerful local traditions such as different languages also undermined imperial unity. Finally, as Dhuoda revealed, some people disagreed with the imperial ideal. Asking her son to put his father before the emperor, she demonstrated her belief in the primacy of the family and the personal ties that bound it together. Her ideal represented a new sensibility that saw real value in the breaking apart of Charlemagne's empire into smaller, more intimate local units. (See "Dhuoda's Handbook for Her Son on page 337")

Land and Power

The Carolingian economy, based on trade and agriculture, contributed to both the rise and the dissolution of the Carolingian Empire. At the onset, the empire's wealth came from land and plunder. After the booty from war

---

♦**Aniane:** ahn YAHN
♦**Ermengard:** EHR mehn gahrd
♦**Verdun:** vur DUHN

♦**vassalage:** VA suh lihj
♦**fealty:** FEE uhl tee

Dhuoda's Handbook for Her Son

Dhuoda's handbook, written in the mid-ninth century, is a rare example of writing by a woman from this period. Yet the excellent education that her handbook reveals cannot have been hers alone; it is likely that most of the female members of the aristocracy in the Carolingian period knew how to read and write. In the following passage she shows her concern for her son's moral character and religious faith.

It is I, Dhuoda, who give you direction, my son William. I wish that, as you grow patiently in worthy virtues among those who fight alongside you, you may always be "slow to speak, and slow to anger" [James 1:19]. If you grow angry, do so without sin. May it never happen that our merciful God grows angry in turn with you or—and may this also never befall—that you stray in your anger from the true path.

Therefore I direct you that, with gentleness, justice, and holiness, you perform your worldly service to him who, admonishing his faithful ones to shine with patience, says, "In your patience you shall possess your souls" [Luke 21:19]. If you are patient, and if you restrain your thoughts and your tongue, you will be blessed. . . .

If you encounter a poor man, offer him as much help as you can, not only in words but also in deeds. I direct you likewise to offer generous hospitality to pilgrims, widows and orphans, children and indigents and to be quick to lift your hand to help those who you see are in need. As Scripture says, "we are sojourners," immigrants and "strangers, as were all our fathers" [1 Par 29:5] who passed upon the earth. . . .

We know that poverty and want are found not only among the least of men but also frequently, for many reasons, among the great. So it is that a rich man too may be in need. Why? Because his soul is wretchedly needy. And then there is the poor man who gathers riches with great ease. Or the rich man who envies the poor man, or the poor man who wishes to become rich, just as an unlettered man wishing to become learned may desire this completely but never accomplish it.

Source: Dhuoda, Handbook for William: A Carolingian Woman's Counsel for Her Son, trans. Carol Neel (Washington, DC: Catholic University of America Press, 1991), 54–55.

---

ceased to pour in, the Carolingians still had access to money and goods. To the north, in Viking trading stations such as Haithabu♦ (today Hedeby, in northern Germany), archaeologists have found Carolingian glass and pots alongside Islamic coins and cloth, which tells us that the Carolingian economy intermingled with that of the Abbasid caliphate. Silver from the Islamic world probably came north up the Volga River through Russia to the Baltic Sea. There the coins were melted down, the silver traded to the Carolingians in return for wine, jugs, glasses, and other manufactured goods. The Carolingians turned the silver into coins of their own, to be used throughout the empire for small-scale local trade. The weakening of the Abbasid caliphate in the mid-ninth century, however, disrupted this far-flung trade network and contributed to the weakening of the Carolingians at about the same time.

Land provided the most important source of Carolingian wealth and power. Like the landholders of the late Roman Empire and the Merovingian period, Carolingian aristocrats held many estates, scattered throughout the Frankish empire. But in the Carolingian period these estates were reorganized and their productivity carefully calculated. Modern historians often call these estates **manors**.

Typical was the manor called Villeneuve♦ St.-Georges, which belonged to the monastery

---

♦**Haithabu:** HATH uh boo

♦**Villeneuve:** veel NUHV

of St.-Germain-des-Près◆ (today in Paris) in the ninth century. Villeneuve consisted of arable fields, vineyards, meadows where animals could roam, and woodland, all scattered about the countryside rather than connected in a compact unit. The land was not tilled by slave gangs, as had been the custom on great estates of the Roman Empire, but by peasant families, each one settled on its own manse, which consisted of a house, a garden, and small pieces of the arable land. The families farmed the land that belonged to them and also worked the demesne,◆ the very large manse of the lord (in this case the abbey of St.-Germain).

These peasant farms, cultivated by households, marked a major social and economic development. Slaves had not been allowed to live in family units. By contrast, the peasants on Villeneuve and on other Carolingian estates could not be separated involuntarily from their families or displaced from their manses. In this sense, the peasant household of the Carolingian period was the precursor of the modern nuclear family.

Peasants at Villeneuve practiced the most progressive sort of plowing, known as the three-field system, in which they farmed two-thirds of the arable land at one time. They planted one-third with winter wheat and one-third with summer crops and left one-third fallow, to restore its fertility. The crops sown and the fallow field then rotated so that land use was repeated only every three years. This method of organizing the land produced larger yields (because two-thirds of the land was cultivated each year) than the still prevalent two-field system, in which only half of the arable land was cultivated one year, the other half the next.

All the peasants at Villeneuve were dependents of the monastery and owed dues and services to St.-Germain. Their obligations varied enormously. One family, for example, owed four silver coins, wine, wood, three hens, and fifteen eggs every year, and the men had to plow the fields of the demesne land. Another family owed the intensive labor of working the vineyards. One woman was required to weave cloth and feed the chickens.

Peasant women spent much time at the lord's house in the *gynaeceum*◆—the women's workshop, where they made and dyed cloth and sewed garments—or in the kitchens, as cooks. Peasant men spent most of their time in the fields.

Estates organized on the model of Villeneuve were profitable. Like other lords, the Carolingians benefited from their extensive estates. Nevertheless, farming was still too primitive to return great surpluses, and as the lands belonging to the king were divided up in the wake of the partitioning of the empire and new invasions, Carolingian dependence on manors scattered throughout their kingdom proved to be a source of weakness.

Vikings, Muslims, and Magyars Invade, c. 790–955

Carolingian kings and counts confronted new groups—Vikings, Muslims, and Magyars—along their borders (Map 9.4). As royal sons fought one another and as counts and other powerful men sought to carve out their own principalities, some allied with the newcomers, helping to integrate them swiftly into European politics.

Vikings. About the same time as they made their forays into Russia, the Vikings moved westward as well. The Franks called them Northmen; the English called them Danes. They were, in fact, much less united than their victims thought. When they began their voyages at the end of the eighth century, they did so in independent bands. Merchants and pirates at the same time, Vikings followed a chief, seeking profit, prestige, and land. Many traveled as families: husbands, wives, children, and slaves.

The Vikings perfected the art of navigation. In their longships they crossed the Atlantic, settling Iceland and Greenland and (about 1000 C.E.) landing on the coast of North America. Other Viking bands navigated the rivers of Europe. The Vikings were pagans, and to them monasteries and churches—with their reliquaries, chalices, and crosses—were simply storehouses of booty.

◆**St.-Germain-des-Près:** san jair MAN duh PRAY
◆**demesne:** dih MAYN

◆*gynaeceum:* gy nuh SEE uhm

MAP 9.4 Muslim, Viking, and Magyar Invasions of the Ninth and Tenth Centuries

Bristling with multicolored arrows, this map suggests that western Europe was continually
and thoroughly pillaged by outside invaders for almost two centuries. That impression is only
partially true; it must be offset by several factors. First, not all the invaders came at once. The
Viking raids were nearly over when the Magyar attacks began. Second, the invaders were not
entirely unwelcome. The Magyars were for a time enlisted as mercenaries by the king of Italy,
and some Muslims were allied to local lords in Provence. Third, the invasions, though widespread, were local in effect. Note, for example, that the Viking raids were largely limited to
rivers or coastal areas.

TAKING MEASURE

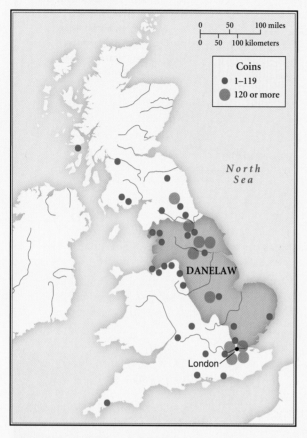

Viking Coin Hoards, c. 865–895

We know from chronicles and other written sources that the Vikings invaded and settled in parts of the British Isles. But where, exactly? And how many people were involved? Counting buried coins from the period can help answer these questions. Before safe-deposit boxes and banks, people buried their money in times of trouble. From Viking coin hoards in the British Isles archaeologists can see that the area called Danelaw was fairly thickly populated by Vikings, with a scattering in other regions as well. The Viking impact was not so much political—no Viking chief took it over—as demographic. After 900, England, in particular, was as much Scandinavian as it was Anglo-Saxon. The lack of Viking coin hoards in Ireland suggests that the Scandinavians did not settle there permanently. *From David Hill*, An Atlas of Anglo-Saxon England (Toronto, 1981).

Parts of the British Isles were especially hard hit. (See "Taking Measure," on this page.) In England, for example, the Vikings raided regularly in the 830s and 840s; by midcentury, they were spending winters there. The Vikings did not just destroy. In 876, they settled in the northeast of England, plowing the land and preparing to live on it. The region where they settled and imposed their own laws was later called the *Danelaw*.♦ (See the spot map England in the Age of King Alfred, on page 350.)

In Wessex, the southernmost kingdom of England, King Alfred the Great (r. 871–899) bought time and peace by paying tribute and giving hostages. Such tribute, later called *Danegeld*,♦ was collected as a tax that eventually became the basis of a relatively lucrative taxation system in England. Then in 878, Alfred led an army that, as his biographer put it, "gained the victory through God's will. He destroyed the Vikings with great slaughter and pursued those who fled . . . hacking them down." Thereafter the pressures of invasion eased as Alfred reorganized his army, set up strongholds, and deployed new warships.

On the continent, too, the invaders set up trading emporia and settled where originally they had raided. Beginning about 850, their attacks became well-organized expeditions for regional control. At the end of the ninth century, one contingent settled in the region of France that soon took the name Normandy, the land of the Northmen. The new inhabitants converted to Christianity during the tenth century. Rollo, the Viking leader in Normandy, accepted Christianity in 911; at the same time, Normandy was formally ceded to him by the Frankish king Charles the Simple.

Normandy was not the only new Christian polity created in the north during the tenth and eleventh centuries. Scandinavia itself was transformed with the creation of the powerful kingdom of Denmark. There had been kings in Scandinavia before the tenth century, but they had been weak, their power challenged by nearby chieftains. The Vikings had been led by these chieftains,

♦*Danelaw:* DAYN law
♦*Danegeld:* DAYN gehld

each competing for booty to win prestige, land, and power back home. During the course of their raids, they and their followers came into contact with new cultures and learned from them. Meanwhile the Carolingians and the English supported missionaries in Scandinavia. By the middle of the tenth century, the Danish kings and their people had become Christian. And, following the model of the Christian kings to their south, they built up an effective monarchy, with a royal mint and local agents who depended on them. By about 1000, the Danes had extended their control to parts of Sweden, Norway, and even England under King Cnut◆ (r. 1017–1035).

Muslims. The dynasty that preceded the Fatimids in Egypt developed a navy that, in the course of the ninth and tenth centuries, gradually conquered Sicily, which had formerly been under Byzantine rule. By the middle of the tenth century, independent Islamic princes ruled all of Sicily. Around the same time, other raiders from North Africa set up bases on other Mediterranean islands, while pirates from al-Andalus built a stronghold in Provence (in southern France). Liutprand◆ of Cremona was outraged:

> [Muslim pirates from al-Andalus], disembarking under cover of night, entered the manor house unobserved and murdered—O grievous tale!— the Christian inhabitants. They then took the place as their own...[fortified it and] started stealthy raids on all the neighboring country.... Meanwhile the people of Provence close by, swayed by envy and mutual jealousy, began to cut one another's throats, plunder each other's substance, and do every sort of conceivable mischief....[Furthermore, they called upon the Muslims] and in company with them proceeded to crush their neighbors.

In this way the Muslims, although outsiders, were drawn into local Provençal disputes.

Magyars. The Magyars,◆ a nomadic people and latecomers to Europe, arrived around 899 into the Danube basin. Until then the region

had been predominantly Slavic, but the Magyars came from the East and spoke a language unrelated to any other in Europe (except Finnish). Their entry drove a wedge between the Slavs near the Frankish kingdom and those bordering on Byzantium; the Bulgarians, Serbs, and Russians were driven into the Byzantine orbit, while the Slavs nearer the Frankish kingdom came under the influence of Germany.

From their bases in present-day Hungary, the Magyars raided far to the west, attacking Germany, Italy, and even southern Gaul frequently between 899 and 955. Then one marauding party of Magyars was met at the Lech River by the German king Otto I (r. 936–973), whose army defeated them in the battle of Lechfeld◆ in 955. Otto's victory, his subsequent military reorganization of his eastern frontiers, and the cessation of Magyar raids around this time made Otto a great hero to his contemporaries. However, histo-

◆**Lechfeld:** LEHK fehlt

Viking Picture Stone
Picture stones, some very elaborate, others with simple incisions, were made on the island of Gotland, today part of Sweden, from the fifth to the twelfth century. This one, dating from the eighth or ninth century, has four interrelated scenes. At the bottom is a battle between people defending a farm (note the cattle tied to the walls of the enclosure) and archers outside. Above is another enclosure with a woman at its wall. She is either Gudrun mourning her brother Gunnar, who was thrown into a snake pit, or Sigyn, the faithful wife of the god Loke, catching in a bowl the venom that a snake pours down on her chained husband. Next comes a ship, a typical motif on picture stones; it is the ship of death that takes heroes to heaven. At the very top is heaven, or Valhalla, itself, where the heroes hunt and feast for all eternity.
Photo: Raymond Hejdstrom.

◆**Cnut:** kuh NOOT
◆**Liutprand:** LEE ut
◆**Magyars:** MAH jahrs

rians today think the containment of the Magyars had more to do with their internal transformation from nomads to farmers than with their military defeat.

The Viking, Muslim, and Magyar invasions were the final onslaught western Europe experienced from outsiders. In some ways they were a continuation of the invasions that had rocked the Roman Empire in the fourth and fifth centuries. Loosely organized in warbands, the new groups entered western Europe looking for wealth but stayed on to become absorbed in the region's post-invasion society.

> **Review:** What were the strengths and weaknesses of Carolingian institutions of government, warfare, and defense?

❖ After the Carolingians: The Emergence of Local Rule

The Carolingian Empire was too diverse to cohere. Although Latin was the language of official documents and most literary and ecclesiastical text, few people spoke it; instead they used a wide variety of different languages and dialects. The king demanded loyalty from everyone, but most people knew only his representative, the local count. The king's power ultimately depended on the count's allegiance, but as the empire ceased to expand and was instead attacked by outsiders, the counts and other powerful men stopped looking to the king for new lands and offices and began to develop and exploit what they already had. They became powerful lords, commanding allegiance from vassals, building castles, setting up markets, collecting revenues, keeping the peace, and seeing themselves as independent regional rulers. They dominated the local peasantry. In this way, a new warrior class of lords and vassals came to dominate post-Carolingian society.

Yet it would be wrong to imagine that all of Europe came under the control of rural leaders. In northern and central Italy, where cities had never lost their importance, urban elites ruled over the surrounding countryside. Everywhere kings retained a certain amount of power; indeed, in some places, such as

Germany and England, they were extremely effective. Central European monarchies formed under the influence of Germany.[1]

Public Power and Private Relationships

The key way in which both kings and less powerful men commanded others was to ensure personal loyalty. In the ninth century, the Carolingian kings had their *fideles*,◆ their "faithful men." Among these were the counts. In addition to a share in the revenues of their administrative district, the county, the counts received benefices, later also called fiefs,◆ temporary grants of land given in return for service. These short-term arrangements often became permanent, however, once a count's son inherited the job and the fiefs of his father. By the end of the ninth century, fiefs were often properties that could be passed on to heirs.

Lords and Vassals. In the wake of the invasions, more and more warriors were drawn into similar networks of dependency, but not with the king: they became the faithful men—the vassals—of local lords. From the Latin word for fief comes the word *feudal*, and some historians use the term **feudalism** to describe the social and economic system created by the relationship among vassals, lords, and fiefs. (See "Terms of History," page 343.)

It was frequently said by medieval people that their society consisted of three groups: those who prayed, those who fought, and those who worked. All of these people were involved in a hierarchy of dependency and linked by personal bonds, but the upper classes—the prayers (monks) and the fighters (the knights)—were free. Their brand of dependency was prestigious, whether they were vassals, lords, or both. In fact, a typical warrior was lord of several vassals even while serving as the vassal of another lord. Monas-

---

[1] Terms such as *Germany*, *France*, and *Italy* are used here for the sake of convenience. They refer to regions, not the nation-states that would eventually become associated with those names.

◆ *fideles*: fee DAY lays
◆ **fiefs**: feefs

TERMS OF HISTORY

Feudalism

Feudalism is a modern word, like *capitalism* and *communism*. No one in the Middle Ages used it, or any of its related terms, such as *feudal system* or *feudal society*. Many historians today think that it is a misleading word and should be discarded. The term poses two serious problems. First, historians have used it to mean different things. Second, it implies that one way of life dominated the Middle Ages, when in fact there were numerous varieties of social, political, and economic arrangements.

Consider the many different meanings that *feudalism* has had. Historians influenced by Karl Marx's powerful communist theory used (and still use) *feudalism* to refer to an economic system in which nobles dominated subservient peasant cultivators. When they speak of feudalism, they are speaking of manors, lords, and serfs. Other historians, however, call that system *manorialism*. They reserve the term *feudalism* for a system consisting of vassals (who never did agricultural labor but only military service), lords, and fiefs. For example, in an influential book written in the mid-1940s, *Feudalism*, F. L. Ganshof considered the tenth to the thirteenth centuries to be the "classical age of feudalism" because during this period lords regularly granted fiefs to their vassals, who fought on their lord's behalf in return.

But, writing around the same time, Marc Bloch included in his definition of *feudalism* every aspect of the political and social life of the Middle Ages, including peasants, fiefs, knights, vassals, and the fragmentation of royal authority yet the survival of the state, which "was to acquire renewed strength" in the course of the feudal period. Some historians, reacting to this broad definition, have tried to narrow it by considering *feudalism* to be a political term that refers to the decline of the state and the dispersal of political power. Others, while also trying to narrow the definition, use *feudalism* to mean a system by which kings controlled their men. These definitions are opposites.

Whatever the definition, they all stress certain institutions that some recent historians argue were very peripheral to medieval life. The fief, for example, a word whose Latin form (*feodum*) gave rise to the word *feudalism*, was by no means important everywhere. And even where it was important, it did not necessarily have anything to do with lords, vassals, or military obligations. "Nobles and free men," writes the historian Susan Reynolds, "did not generally owe military service before the twelfth century because of the grant of anything like fiefs to them or their ancestors. . . . They owed whatever service they owed, not because they were vassals of a lord, but because they were subjects of a ruler." For Reynolds, feudalism is a myth.

Mythical or not, all these views, even that of Reynolds, have one thing in common: a stress on vertical hierarchies, such as lords over peasants or kings over their subjects. Some recent historians, however, point out that not all of medieval society was hierarchical. Horizontal relations—such as those that created peasant communities, urban corporations, and the comradeship of knightly troops—were equally, if not more, important.

For all of these reasons, many historians have stopped using the word *feudalism*, preferring to stress the variety of medieval social and political arrangements. How many times have you encountered the term in this history book?

FURTHER READING

Bloch, Marc. *Feudal Society.* 2 vols. Trans. L. A. Manyon, 1961.

Ganshof, F. L. *Feudalism.* Trans. Philip Grierson, 1961.

Reynolds, Susan. *Fiefs and Vassals: The Medieval Evidence Reinterpreted.* 1994.

Two Cities Besieged

In about 900, the monks of the monastery of St. Gall produced a Psalter with numerous illuminations. The illustration for Psalm 59, which tells of King David's victories, used four pages. This page was the fourth. On the top level, David's army besieges a fortified city from two directions. On the right are foot soldiers, one of whom holds a burning torch to set the city afire; on the left are horsemen—led by their standard-bearer—with lances and bows and arrows. Note their chain-mail coats and their horses' stirrups. Within the city, four soldiers protect themselves with shields, but another has fallen and hangs upside down from the city wall. The dead and wounded on the ground are bleeding. Four other men seem to be cowering behind the city. In the bottom register, a different city burns fiercely (note the towers on fire). This city lacks defenders; the people within it are unarmed. Although this illumination purports to show David's victories, in fact it nicely represents the equipment and strategies of ninth-century warfare. *Stiftsbibliothek St. Gallen, Switzerland.*

teries normally had vassals to fight for them, and their abbots in turn were often vassals of a king or other powerful lord (see Two Cities Beseiged, on this page).

Vassalage grew up as an alternative to public power and at the same time as a way to strengthen what little public power there was. Given the impoverished economic conditions of western Europe, its primitive methods of communication, and its lack of unifying traditions, kings came to rely on vassals personally loyal to them to muster troops, collect taxes, and administer justice. When in the ninth century the Frankish empire broke up politically and power fell into the hands of local lords, those lords, too, needed "faithful men" to protect them and carry out their orders. And vassals needed lords. At the low end of the social scale, poor vassals looked to their lords to feed, clothe, house, and arm them. They hoped that they would be rewarded for their service with a fief of their own, with which they could support themselves and a family. At the upper end of the social scale, vassals looked to lords to give them still more land. (For more on the mutual obligations of lords and vassals, see Fulbert of Chartres (c. 960–1028), "Letter to William of Aquitaine," page 345).

A few women were vassals, and some were lords (or, rather, ladies, the female counterpart); and many upper-class laywomen participated in the society of fighters and prayers as wives and mothers of vassals and lords. Other aristocratic women entered convents and became members of the social group that prayed. Through its abbess or a man standing in for her, convents often had vassals as well.

Becoming the vassal of a lord often involved both ritual gestures and verbal promises. In a ceremony witnessed by others, the vassal-to-be knelt and, placing his hands between the hands of his lord, said, "I promise to be your man." This act, known as homage,♦ was followed by the promise of fealty—fidelity, trust, and service—which the vassal swore with his hand on relics or a Bible. Then the vassal and the lord kissed. In an age when many people could not read, a public ceremony such as this represented a

♦**homage:** AH mihj

visual and verbal contract. Vassalage bound the lord and vassal to one another with reciprocal obligations, usually military. Knights, as the premier fighters of the day, were the most desirable vassals.

Lords and Peasants. At the bottom of the social scale were those who worked—the peasants. In the Carolingian period, many peasants were free; they did not live on a manor or, if they did, they owed very little to its lord. But as power fell into the hands of local rulers, fewer and fewer peasants remained free. Rather, they were made dependent on lords, not as vassals but as **serfs**. A serf's dependency was separate from and completely unlike that of a vassal. Serfdom was not voluntary but rather inherited. No serf did homage or fealty to his lord; no serf kissed his lord as an equal. And the serf's work as a laborer was not prestigious. Peasants constituted the majority of the population, but unlike knights, who were celebrated in song, they were barely noticed by the upper classes—except as a source of revenue.

New methods of cultivation and a burgeoning population helped transform the

Fulbert of Chartres, "Letter to William of Aquitaine" (1020)

Duke William of Aquitaine, a very powerful lord in France, often found himself in conflict with his vassals. To clarify his and their obligations, he asked Fulbert, bishop of Chartres, to advise him on the matter. Fulbert's letter, reproduced in full here, shows that many of the obligations were, like the Ten Commandments, negative ones.

Fulbert, bishop, to the glorious duke of the Aquitainians William

Invited to write something concerning the form of fealty, I have briefly noted for you the following things from the authority of books. He who swears fealty to his lord must always remember these six things: harmless, safe, honorable, useful, easy, possible. Harmless, that is, he must not harm his lord in his body. Safe, he must not harm him in his secrets or in the fortifications by which he is able to be safe. Honorable, so that he must not harm him in his justice or in other affairs which are seen to pertain to his honor. Useful, that he might not be harmful to him in his possessions. Easy or possible, so that he not make difficult any good which his lord could easily do nor make anything impossible that is difficult. It is just that the vassal avoid these evils, but he does not merit his holding [fief] for so doing, for it is not enough that he abstain from evil unless he does what is good.

Therefore it remains that he should give his lord counsel and aid in these same six above mentioned things if he wishes to be seen worthy of his benefice [fief] and to be safe in the fealty he has sworn. The lord should act toward his vassal reciprocally in all these things. If he does not do so, he deserves to be considered of bad faith, just as the vassal, if he were caught in collusion or in doing or in consenting to them, would be perfidious or perjured.

I would have written to you at greater length if I had not been occupied with many other things, both the restoration of our city and of our church which have recently been totally consumed by a horrendous fire. Although for a time we could not be turned away from this loss, through the hope in the consolation of God and of you we once more breathe.

Source: From Patrick J. Geary, *Readings in Medieval History*, 2nd ed. (Peterborough, Ontario: Broadview Press, 1998), 366.

Hard Work in January
During the cold month of January, peasants had to put on their warm clothes, harness their oxen to the plow, and turn over the heavy soil to loosen and aerate it for planting. This illustration of January's peasant labor comes from a calendar—a text useful to clergy because it listed the saints' feasts for each day of each month. In this case the artist was an Anglo-Saxon working in the second quarter of the eleventh century. Normally, medieval artists followed painted models rather than nature; nevertheless, this miniature probably represents contemporary reality fairly well. One peasant guides the heavy plow as it makes a deep furrow, another drives the animals, and a third drops the seeds. Farmwork was cooperative, and peasant solidarity was an important aspect of village life. *British Library.*

rural landscape and make it more productive. With a growing number of men and women to work the land, the lower classes now had more mouths to feed and faced the hardship of food shortage. Landlords began reorganizing their estates to run more efficiently. In the tenth century, the three-field system became more prevalent; heavy plows which could turn the heavy northern soils came into wider use; and horses (more effective than oxen) were harnessed to pull the plows. (See the image, Hard Work in January, on this page.) The result was surplus food and a better standard of living for nearly everyone.

In search of greater profits, some lords lightened the dues and services of peasants temporarily to allow them to open up new lands by draining marshes and cutting down forests. Some landlords converted dues and labor services into money payments, a boon for both lords and peasants. Lords now had money to spend on what they wanted rather than hens and eggs they might not need or want. Peasants benefited because their dues were fixed despite inflation. Thus, as the prices of their hens and eggs went up, they could sell them, reaping a profit in spite of the payments they owed their lords.

By the tenth century, many peasants lived in populous rural settlements, true villages. In the midst of a sea of arable land, meadow, wood, and wasteland, these villages developed a sense of community. Boundaries—sometimes real fortifications, sometimes simple markers—told nonresidents to keep out and to find shelter in huts located outside the village limits.

The church often formed the focal point of local activity. There people met, received the sacraments, drew up contracts, and buried their parents and children. Religious feasts and festivals joined the rituals of farming to mark the seasons. The church dominated the village in another way: men and women owed it a tax called a **tithe**◆ (equivalent to one-tenth of their crops or income, paid in money or in kind), which was first instituted on a regular basis by the Carolingians.

Village peasants developed a sense of common purpose based on their practical interdependence, as they shared oxen or horses for the teams that pulled the plow or turned to village craftsmen to fix their wheels or shoe their horses. A sense of solidarity sometimes encouraged people to band together to ask for privileges as a group. Near Verona, in northern Italy, for example, twenty-five men living around the castle of Nogara joined together in 920 to ask their lord, the abbot of Nonantola, to allow them to lease plots of land, houses, and pasturage there in return for a small yearly rent and the promise to defend the castle. The abbot granted their request.

Village solidarity could be compromised, however, by conflicting loyalties and obligations. A peasant in one village might very well have one piece of land connected with a certain manor and another bit of arable field on a different estate; and he or she might owe several lords different kinds of dues. Even peasants of one village working for one lord might owe him varied services and taxes.

Layers of obligations were even more striking across the regions of Europe than in particular villages. The principal distinction was between free peasants, such as small landowners in Saxony and other parts of Germany, and unfree peasants, who were especially common in France and England. In Italy, peasants ranged from small independent landowners to leaseholders (like the tenants at Nogara); most were both, owning a parcel in one place and leasing another nearby.

As the power of kings weakened, this system of peasant obligations became part of a larger system of local rule. When landlords consolidated their power over their manors, they collected not only dues and services but also fees for the use of their flour mills, bake houses, and breweries. Some built castles, fortified strongholds, and imposed the even wider powers of the **ban**: the rights to collect taxes, hear court cases, levy fines, and muster men for defense.

In France, for example, as the king's power waned, political control fell into the hands of counts and other princes. By 1000, castles had become the key to their power. In the south of France, power was so fragmented that each man who controlled a castle—a **castellan**◆—was a virtual ruler, although often with a very limited reach. In northwestern France, territorial princes, basing their rule on the control of *many* castles, dominated much broader regions. For example, Fulk Nera,◆ count of Anjou (987–1040), built more than thirteen castles and captured others from rival counts. By the end of his life, he controlled a region extending from Blois◆ to Nantes◆ along the Loire◆ valley.

Castellans extended their authority by subjecting everyone near their castle to their ban. Peasants, whether or not they worked on his estates, had to pay the castellan a variety of dues for his "protection" and judicial rights over them. Castellans also established links with the better-off landholders in the region, tempting or coercing them to become vassals. Lay castellans often supported local monasteries and controlled the appointment of local priests. But churchmen themselves sometimes held the position of territorial lord, as did, for example, the archbishop of Milan in the eleventh century.

The development of virtually independent local political units, dominated by a castle and controlled by a military elite, marks an important turning point in western Europe. Although this development did not occur everywhere simultaneously (and in some places it hardly occurred at all), the social, political, and cultural life of Europe was now dominated by landowners who saw themselves as military men and regional leaders.

◆**castellan:** KAS tuh luhn
◆**Fulk Nera:** FULK nehr rah
◆**Blois:** blwah
◆**Nantes:** naHnt
◆**Loire:** luh WAHR

◆**tithe:** tyth

Warriors and Warfare

Not all warriors were alike. At the top of the elite were the kings, counts, and dukes. Below them, but on the rise, were the castellans; and still further down the social scale were ordinary knights. Yet all shared in a common lifestyle.

Knights and their lords fought on horseback. High astride his steed, wearing a shirt of chain mail and a helmet of flat metal plates riveted together, the knight marked a military revolution. The war season started in May, when the grasses were high enough for horses to forage. Horseshoes allowed armies to move faster than ever before and to negotiate rough terrain previously unsuitable for battle. Stirrups, probably invented by Asiatic nomadic tribes, allowed the mounted warrior to hold his seat. This made it possible for knights to thrust at their enemy with heavy lances. The light javelin of ancient Roman warfare was abandoned.

Lords and their vassals often lived together. In the lord's great hall they ate, listened to entertainment, and bedded down for the night. They went out hunting together, competed with one another in military games, and went off to the battlefield as a group as well. Of course there were powerful vassals—counts, for example—who lived on their own fiefs. They hardly ever saw their lord (probably the king), except when doing homage and fealty—once in their lifetime—or serving him in battles, for perhaps forty days a year (as was the custom in eleventh-century France). But they themselves were lords of knightly vassals who were not married and who lived and ate and hunted with them.

No matter how old they might be, unmarried knights who lived with their lords were called youths by their contemporaries. Such perpetual bachelors were something new, the result of a profound transformation in the organization of families and inheritance. Before about 1000, noble families recognized all their children as heirs and had divided their estates accordingly. In the mid-ninth century, Count Everard◆ and his wife, for example, willed their large estates, scattered from Belgium to Italy, to their four sons and three daughters (although they gave the boys far more than the girls, and the oldest boy far more than the others).

By 1000, however, adapting to diminished opportunities for land and office, and wary of fragmenting the estates they had, French nobles changed both their conception of their family and the way property passed to the next generation. Recognizing the overriding claims of one son, often the eldest, they handed down their entire inheritance to him. (When the heir is indeed the eldest son, this system of inheritance is called **primogeniture.◆**) The heir, in turn, traced his lineage only through the male line, backward through his father and forward through his own eldest son. Such patrilineal◆ families left many younger sons without an inheritance and therefore without the prospect of marrying and founding a family; instead, the younger sons lived at the courts of the great as youths, or they joined the church as clerics or monks. The development of territorial rule and patrilineal families went hand in hand, as fathers passed down to one son undiminished not only manors but also titles, castles, and the authority of the ban.

Patrilineal inheritance tended to bypass daughters and so worked against aristocratic women, who lost the power that came with inherited wealth. In families without sons, however, widows and daughters did inherit property. And wives often acted as lords of estates when their husbands were at war. Moreover, all aristocratic women played an important role in this warrior society, whether in the monastery (where they prayed for the souls of their families) or through their marriages (where they produced children and helped forge alliances between their own natal families and the families of their husbands).

Efforts to Contain Violence

Warfare benefited territorial rulers in the short term, but in the long run their revenues suffered as armies plundered the countryside and sacked walled cities. Bishops, who were themselves from the class of lords and war-

---

◆**Everard:** EHV rahrd

◆**primogeniture:** Pry moh JEH nih chur
◆**patrilineal:** pa truh LIH nee uhl

riors, worried about the dangers to church property. Peasants cried out against wars that destroyed their crops or forced them to join regional infantries. Monks and religious thinkers were appalled at violence that was not in the service of an anointed king. By the end of the tenth century, all classes clamored for peace.

Sentiment against local violence was united in a movement called the **Peace of God**, which began in the south of France around 990 and by 1050 had spread over a wide region. Meetings of bishops, counts, and lords and often crowds of lower-class men and women set forth the provisions of this peace: "No man in the counties or bishoprics shall seize a horse, colt, ox, cow, ass, or the burdens which it carries.... No one shall seize a peasant, man or woman," ran the decree of one early council. Anyone who violated this peace was to be excommunicated: cut off from the community of the faithful, denied the services of the church and the hope of salvation.

The peace proclaimed at local councils like this limited some violence but did not address the problem of conflict between armed men. A second set of agreements, the Truce of God, soon supplemented the Peace of God. The truce prohibited fighting between warriors at certain times: on Sunday because it was the Lord's day, on Saturday because it was a reminder of Holy Saturday, on Friday because it symbolized Good Friday, and on Thursday because it stood for Holy Thursday. Enforcement of the truce fell to the local knights and nobles, who swore over saints' relics to uphold it and to fight anyone who broke it.

The Peace of God and Truce of God were only two of the mechanisms that attempted to contain or defuse violent confrontations in the tenth and eleventh centuries. At times, lords and their vassals mediated wars and feuds in assemblies called *placita*.◆ In other instances, monks or laymen tried to find solutions to disputes that would leave the honor of both parties intact. Rather than establishing guilt or innocence, winners or losers, these methods of adjudication often resulted in compromises on both sides.

Political Communities in Italy, England, and France

The political systems that emerged in the wake of the breakup of the Carolingian empire were as varied as the regions of Europe. In northern and central Italy, cities were the centers of power, still reflecting, if feebly, the political organization of ancient Rome. In England, strong kings came to the fore. In France, as we have seen, great lords dominated the countryside; there the king was relatively weak.

Urban Power in Northern and Central Italy. Unlike their counterparts in France, where great landlords built their castles in the countryside, Italian elites tended to construct their family seats within the walls of cities such as Milan and Lucca. Also built within the city walls were churches, as many as fifty or sixty, the proud work of rich laymen and laywomen or of bishops. From their perch within the cities, the great landholders, both lay and religious, dominated the countryside.

Italian cities also functioned as important marketplaces. Peasants sold their surplus goods there, artisans and merchants lived within the walls, and foreign traders offered their wares. These members of the lower classes were supported by the noble rich, who depended, here even more than elsewhere, on cash to satisfy their desires. In the course of the ninth and tenth centuries, both servile and free tenants became renters who paid in currency.

The social and political life in Italy was conducive to a familial organization somewhat different from the patrilineal families of France. To stave off the partitioning of their properties among heirs, families organized themselves by formal contract into *consorteria*,◆ in which all male members shared the profits of the family's inheritance and all women were excluded. The consorterial family became a kind of blood-related corporation, a social unit on which early Italian businesses and banks would later be modeled.

◆*placita*: PLAH kiht uh

◆*consorteria*: cohn sawr TEHR ee uh

Alfred and His Sucessors: Kings of All the English. Whereas much of Italy was urban, most of England was rural. In the face of the Viking invasions in England, King Alfred the Great of Wessex (r. 871–899) developed new mechanisms of royal government, instituting reforms that his successors continued. He fortified settlements throughout Wessex and divided the army into two parts, one with the duty of defending these fortifications (or *burhs*◆), the other operating as a mobile unit. Alfred also started a navy. These military innovations cost money, and the assessments fell on peasants' holdings.

Alfred sought to strengthen his kingdom's religious integrity as well as its regional fortifications. In the ninth century, people interpreted invasions as God's punishment for sin, the real culprit. Hence Alfred began a program of religious reform by bringing scholars to his court to write and to educate others. Above all, Alfred wanted to translate key religious works from Latin into Anglo-Saxon (or Old English). He was determined to "turn into the language that we can all understand certain books which are the most necessary for all men to know." Alfred and scholars under his guidance translated works by church fathers such as Gregory the Great and St. Augustine. Even the Psalms, until now sung only in Hebrew, Greek, and Latin, were rendered into Anglo-Saxon. In most of ninth- and tenth-century Europe, Latin remained the language of scholarship, government, and writing, separate from the language people spoke. In England, however, the vernacular—the common spoken language—was also a literary language. With Alfred's work giving it greater legitimacy, Anglo-Saxon came to be used alongside Latin for both literature and royal administration.

Kingdom of Alfred
Dependent on Wessex
To Alfred in 878

North Sea

Northumbria

DANELAW

Mercia *East Anglia*

Wales

Wessex

0   50   100 miles
0   50   100 kilometers

England in the Age of King Alfred, 871–899

◆*burhs:* Burhs

Alfred's reforms strengthened not only defense, education, and religion but also royal power. He consolidated his control over Wessex and fought the Danish kings, who by the mid-870s had taken Northumbria, northeastern Mercia, and East Anglia. Eventually, as he successfully fought the Danes who were pushing south and westward, he was recognized as king of all the English not under Danish rule. He issued a law code, the first by an English king since 695. Unlike earlier codes, drawn up for each separate kingdom of England, Alfred drew his laws from and for all of the English kingdoms. In this way Alfred became the first king of all the English.

Alfred's successors rolled back the Danish rule in England. "Then the Norsemen departed in their nailed ships, bloodstained survivors of spears," wrote one poet about a battle the Vikings lost in 937. But many Vikings remained. Converted to Christianity, their great men joined Anglo-Saxons in attending the English king at court. As peace returned, new administrative subdivisions were established throughout England: shires and hundreds, districts for judicial and taxation purposes. The powerful men of the kingdom swore fealty to the king, promising to be enemies of his enemies, friends of his friends. England was united and organized to support a strong ruler.

Alfred's grandson Edgar (r. 957–975) commanded all the possibilities early medieval kingship offered. He was the sworn lord of all the great men of the kingdom. He controlled appointments to the English church and sponsored monastic reform. In 973, following the continental fashion, he was anointed king. The fortifications of the kingdom were in his hands, as was the army, and he took responsibility for keeping the peace by proclaiming certain crimes—arson and theft—to be under his special jurisdiction and mobilizing the machinery of the shire and hundred to find and punish thieves.

Despite its apparent centralization, England was not a unified state in the modern sense, and the king's control was often tenuous. Many royal officials were great landowners who (as on the continent) worked for the king because it was in their best interest. When it was not, they allied with different claimants to the throne. This political fragility may have helped the Danish king Cnut (or Canute) to conquer England. King there from 1017 to 1035, Cnut reinforced the already strong connections between England and Scandinavia while keeping intact much of the administrative, ecclesiastical, and military apparatus already established in England by the Anglo-Saxons. By Cnut's time, Scandinavian traditions had largely merged with those of the rest of Europe and the Vikings were no longer an alien culture.

Capetian Kings of Franks: Weak but Prestigious.

French kings had a harder time than the English coping with the invasions because their realm was much larger. They had no chance to build up their defenses slowly from one powerful base. During most of the tenth century, Carolingian kings alternated on the throne with kings from a family that would later be called the Capetian.♦ As the Carolingian dynasty waned, the most powerful men of the kingdom — dukes, counts, and important bishops — came together to elect Hugh Capet (r. 987–996), a lord of considerable prestige yet relatively little power. His choice marked the end of Carolingian rule and the beginning of the new Capetian dynasty that would hand down the royal title from father to son until the fourteenth century.

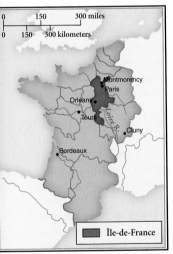

The Kingdom of the Franks under Hugh Capet, 987–996

In the eleventh century, the reach of the Capetian kings was limited by territorial lordships in the vicinity. The king's scattered but substantial estates lay in the north of France, in the region around Paris — the Île-de-France (literally, "island of France"). His castles and his vassals were there. Independent castellans, however, controlled areas nearby. In the sense that he was a neighbor of castellans and not much more powerful militarily than they, the king of the Franks — who would only later take the territorial title of king of France — was just another local leader. Yet the Capetian kings had considerable prestige. They were anointed with holy oil, and they represented the idea of unity inherited from Charlemagne. Most of the counts, at least in the north of France, became their vassals. They did not promise to obey the king, but they did vow not to try to kill or depose him.

Emperors and Kings in Central and Eastern Europe

In contrast with the development of territorial lordships in France, Germany's fragmentation hardly began before it was reversed. The Ottonian♦ kings of Germany consolidated their rule there; took the title emperor; and then, hand in hand with the papacy, fostered the emergence of new Christian monarchies. Aligned with the Roman church, these new kingdoms were the ancestors of today's Czech and Slovak Republics, Poland, and Hungary.

Ottonian Power in Germany. Five duchies♦ (regions dominated by dukes) emerged in Germany in the late Carolingian period, each much larger than the counties and castellanies of France. With the death in 911 of the last Carolingian king in Germany, Louis the Child, the dukes elected one of themselves as king. Then, as the Magyar invasions increased, the dukes gave the royal title to the duke of Saxony, Henry I (r. 919–936), who proceeded to set up fortifications and reorganize his army, crowning his efforts with a major defeat of a Magyar army in 933.

Otto I, the son of Henry I, was an even greater military hero. In 951, he marched into Italy and took the Lombard crown. His defeat of the Magyar forces in 955 at Lechfeld gave him prestige and helped solidify his dynasty. Against the Slavs, with whom the Germans shared a border, Otto set up marches from

---

♦**Capetian:** kuh PAY shuhn

♦**Ottonian:** ah TOH neean
♦**duchies:** DUH cheez

which he could make expeditions and stave off counterattacks. After the pope crowned him emperor in 962, Otto claimed the Middle Kingdom carved out by the Treaty of Verdun and cast himself as the agent of Roman imperial renewal.

Otto's victories brought tribute and plunder, ensuring him a following but also raising the German nobles' expectations for enrichment. He and his successors, Otto II (r. 973–983), Otto III (r. 983–1002)—for which reason the dynasty is called the Ottonian♦—and Henry II (r. 1002–1024), were not always able or willing to provide the gifts and inheritances their family members and followers expected. To maintain centralized rule, for example, the Ottonians did not divide their kingdom among their sons: like castellans in France, they created a patrilineal pattern of inheritance. But the consequence was that younger sons and other potential heirs felt cheated, and disgruntled royal kin led revolt after revolt against the Ottonian kings. The rebels found followers among the aristocracy, where the trend toward the patrilineal family prompted similar feuds and thwarted expectations.

Relations between the Ottonians and the German clergy were more harmonious. With a ribbon of new bishoprics along his eastern border, Otto I appointed bishops, gave them extensive lands, and subjected the local peasantry to their overlordship. Like Charlemagne, Otto believed that the well-being of the church in his kingdom depended on him. The Ottonians placed the churches and many monasteries of Germany under their control. They gave bishops the powers of the ban, allowing them to collect revenues and call men to arms. Answering to the king and furnishing him with troops, the bishops became royal officials, while also carrying out their pastoral and religious duties. German

The extent of the Empire under Otto I
The extent of the Empire under Otto III
Marcher regions
Dependent on Ottonians
✴ Battle

The Ottonian Empire, 936–1002

kings claimed the right to select bishops, even the pope at Rome, and to "invest" them by participating in the ceremony that installed them in office. The higher clergy joined royal court society. Most came to the court to be schooled; in turn, they taught the kings, princes, and noblewomen there.

Like all the strong rulers of the day, whether in Europe or the Byzantine and Islamic worlds, the Ottonians presided over a renaissance of learning. For example, the tutor of Otto III was Gerbert, the best-educated man of his time. Placed on the papal throne as Sylvester II (r. 999–1003), Gerbert knew how to use the abacus and to calculate with Arabic numerals. He spent "large sums of money to pay copyists and to acquire copies of authors," as he put it. He studied the Latin classics as models of rhetoric and argument, and he reveled in logic and debate. Not only did churchmen and kings support Ottonian scholarship, but to an unprecedented extent noblewomen in Germany also acquired an education and participated in the intellectual revival. Aristocratic women spent much of their wealth on learning. Living at home with their kinfolk and servants or in convents that provided them with comfortable private apartments, noblewomen wrote books and occasionally even Roman-style plays. They also supported other artists and scholars.

Despite their military and political strength, the kings of Germany faced resistance from dukes and other powerful princes, who hoped to become regional rulers themselves. The Salians,♦ the dynasty that succeeded the Ottonians, tried to balance the power among the German dukes but could not meld them into a corps of vassals the way the Capetian kings tamed their counts. In Germany vassalage was considered beneath the dignity of free men. Instead of relying on vassals, the Salian kings and their bishops used ministerials, men who were legally serfs, to collect taxes, administer justice, and fight on horseback. Ministerials retained their servile status even though they often rose to wealth and high position. Under the Salian kings, ministerials became the mainstay of the royal army and administration.

♦**Salians:** SAY leeans

Otto III Receiving Gifts

This triumphal image is in a book of Gospels made for Otto III. The crowned women on the left are personifications of the four parts of Otto's empire: Sclavinia (the Slavic lands), Germania (Germany), Gallia (Gaul), and Roma (Rome). Each offers a gift in tribute and homage to the emperor, who sits on a throne holding the symbols of his power (orb and scepter) and flanked by representatives of the church (on his right) and of the army (on his left). Why do you suppose that the artist separated the image of the emperor from that of the women? What does the body language of the women indicate about the relations Otto wanted to portray between himself and the parts of his empire? Can you relate this manuscript, which was made in 997–1000, to Otto's conquest over the Slavs in 997? *Pro Biblioteca Academiae Scientiarum, Hungaricae.*

Supported by their prestige, their churchmen, and their ministerials, the German kings expanded their influence eastward, into the region from the Elbe River to Russia. Otto I was so serious about expansion that he created an extraordinary "elastic" archbishopric: it had no eastern boundary, so it could increase as far as future conquests and conversions to Christianity would allow.

The Emergence of Catholic Bohemia, Poland, Hungary, and Croatia.

Hand in hand with the popes, German kings insisted on the creation of new, Catholic polities along their eastern frontier. The Czechs, who lived in the region of Bohemia, converted under the rule of Václav♦ (r. 920–929), who thereby gained recognition in Germany as the duke of Bohemia. He and his successors did not become kings, remaining politically within the German sphere. Václav's murder by his younger brother made him a martyr and the patron saint of Bohemia, a symbol around which later movements for independence rallied.

The Poles gained a greater measure of independence than the Czechs. In 966, Mieszko♦ I (r. 963–992), the leader of the Slavic tribe known as the Polanians, accepted baptism to forestall the attack that the

---

♦**Václav:** VAHT slahv
♦**Mieszko:** MYEHSH kaw

MAPPING THE WEST Europe and the Mediterranean, c. 1050
The clear borders and bright colors of the "states" on this map distort an essential truth: none of them had centralized governments that controlled whole territories, as in modern states. Instead, there were numerous regional rulers within each, and there were numerous overlapping claims of jurisdiction. The next centuries would show both the weaknesses and surprising strengths of this fragmentation.

Germans were already mounting against pagan Slavic peoples along the Baltic coast and east of the Elbe River. Busily engaged in bringing the other Slavic tribes of Poland under his control, he adroitly shifted his alliances with various German princes to suit his needs. In 991, Mieszko placed his realm under the protection of the pope, establishing a tradition of Polish loyalty to the Roman church. Mieszko's son Boleslaw◆ the Brave (r. 992–1025) greatly extended Poland's boundaries, at one time or another holding sway from the Bohemian border to Kiev. In 1000, he gained a royal crown with papal blessing.

◆**Boleslaw:** baw LEH slahf

Hungary's case is similar to that of Poland. The Magyars settled in the region known today as Hungary. They became landowners, using the native Slavs to till the soil and imposing their language. At the end of the tenth century, the Magyar ruler Stephen I (r. 997–1038) accepted Roman Christianity. In return, German knights and monks helped him consolidate his power and convert his people. According to legend, the crown placed on Stephen's head when he was crowned king (in late 1000 or early 1001) was sent to him by the pope. To this day, the crown of St. Stephen (Stephen was canonized in 1083) remains the most hallowed symbol of Hungarian nationhood.

Symbols of rulership such as crowns, consecrated by Christian priests and accorded a prestige almost akin to saints' relics, were among the most vital sources of royal power in central Europe. The economic basis for the power of central European rulers gradually shifted from slave raids to agriculture. This change encouraged a proliferation of regional centers of power that challenged monarchical rule. From the eleventh century onward, all the medieval Slavic realms faced the constant problem of internal division.

> **Review:** How and why did the different states of central and eastern Europe—Russia, Hungary, Serbia, Croatia, and so on—emerge?

Conclusion

In 800, the three heirs of the Roman Empire all appeared to be organized like their parent: centralized, monarchical, imperial. Byzantine emperors writing their learned books, Abbasid caliphs holding court in their new resplendent palace at Baghdad, and Carolingian emperors issuing their directives for reform to the *missi dominici* all mimicked the Roman emperors. Yet they confronted tensions and regional pressures that tended to decentralize political power. Byzantium felt this fragmentation least, yet even there the emergence of a new elite, the *dynatoi*, led to the emperor's loss of control over the countryside. In the Islamic world, economic crisis, religious tension, and the ambitions of powerful local rulers

decisively weakened the caliphate and opened the way to separate successor states. In Europe, powerful independent landowners strove with greater or lesser success (depending on the region) to establish themselves as effective rulers. By 1050, the states that would become those of modern Europe began to form.

In western Europe, local conditions determined political and economic organizations. Between 900 and 1000, for example, French society was transformed by the development of territorial lordships, patrilineal families, and ties of vassalage. These factors figured less prominently in Germany, where a central monarchy remained, buttressed by churchmen, ministerials, and conquests to the east.

After 1050, however, the German king would lose his supreme position as a storm of church reform whirled around him. The economy changed, becoming more commercial and urban, and new learning, new monarchies, and new forms of religious expression came to the fore.

Suggested References

Byzantium: Renewed Strength and Influence

Recent studies of Byzantium stress the revival in the arts and literature, but Whittow is excellent on political, social, and religious issues. Almost nothing was available in English on eastern Europe and Russia until the 1980s.

*Byzantine art: http://gallery.sjsu.edu/artH/byzantine/mainpage.html.

Fine, Jon V. A., Jr. *The Early Medieval Balkans: A Critical Survey from the Sixth to the Late Twelfth Century.* 1983.

Franklin, Simon, and Jonathan Shepard. *The Emergence of Rus, 750–1200.* 1996.

Garland, Lynda. *Byzantine Empresses: Women and Power in Byzantium, AD 527–1204.* 1999.

Maguire, Henry, ed. *Byzantine Court Culture from 829 to 1204.* 1997.

*Psellus, Michael. *Fourteen Byzantine Rulers: The Chronographia.* Trans. E. R. A. Sewter. 1966.

Whittow, Mark. *The Making of Byzantium, 600–1025.* 1996.

*Primary sources.

The Islamic World: From Unity to Fragmentation

The traditional approach to the Islamic world is political (Kennedy). Glick is unusual in taking a comparative approach. The newest issue for scholars is the role of women in medieval Islamic society (Spellberg).

Berkey, Jonathan P. *The Formation of Islam: Religion and Society in the Near East, 600–1800.* 2003.

Glick, Thomas. *Islamic and Christian Spain in the Early Middle Ages: Comparative Perspectives on Social and Cultural Formation.* 1979.

Kennedy, Hugh. *The Prophet and the Age of the Caliphates: The Islamic Near East from the Sixth to the Eleventh Century.* 1986.

Makdisi, George. *The Rise of Colleges.* 1981.

Spellberg, Denise. *Politics, Gender, and the Islamic Past.* 1994.

The Creation and Division of a New European Empire

Huge chunks of the primary sources for the Carolingian world are now available in English translation, thanks in large part to the work of Dutton. Hodges and Whitehouse provide the perspective of archaeologists. The Carolingian renaissance is increasingly recognized as a long-term development rather than simply the achievement of Charlemagne.

*Carolingian studies: **http://www.fordham.edu/halsall/sbooklh.html**.

*Dutton, Paul Edward. *Carolingian Civilization: A Reader.* 1993.

*———. *Charlemagne's Courtier: The Complete Einhard.* 1998.

*Einhard and Notker the Stammerer. *Two Lives of Charlemagne.* Trans. Lewis Thorpe. 1969.

Hodges, Richard, and David Whitehouse. *Mohammed, Charlemagne, and the Origins of Europe.* 1983.

McKitterick, Rosamond. *Carolingian Culture: Emulation and Innovation.* 1994.

Nelson, Janet. *Charles the Bald.* 1987.

Riche, Pierre. *Daily Life in the World of Charlemagne.* Trans. J. A. McNamara. 1978.

After the Carolingians : The Emergence of Local Rule

Historians used to lament the passing of the Carolingian Empire. More recently, however, they have come to appreciate the strengths and adaptive strategies of the post-Carolingian world. Duby speaks of the agricultural "takeoff" of the period, whereas Head and Landes explore new institutions of peace.

Duby, Georges. *The Early Growth of the European Economy: Warriors and Peasants from the Seventh to the Twelfth Century.* Trans. H. B. Clark. 1974.

Engel, Pál. *The Realm of St. Stephen: A History of Medieval Hungary, 895–1526.* Trans. Tamás Pálosfalvi. 2001.

Frantzen, Allen. *King Alfred.* 1986.

Head, Thomas, and Richard Landes, eds. *The Peace of God: Social Violence and Religious Response in France around the Year 1000.* 1992.

Jones, Gwyn. *A History of the Vikings.* Rev. ed. 1984.

*Medieval and Renaissance manuscripts: **http://www.columbia.edu/cu/libraries/indiv/rare/images**.

Reuter, Timothy. *Germany in the Early Middle Ages, c. 800–1056.* 1991.

Sweeney, Del, ed. *Agriculture in the Middle Ages: Technology, Practice, and Representation.* 1995.

*Whitelock, Dorothy, ed. *English Historical Documents*, Vol. 1. 2nd ed. 1979.

Wilson, David. *The Vikings and Their Origins: Scandinavia in the First Millennium.* 1970.

CHAPTER REVIEW

IMPORTANT EVENTS

750–c. 950	The Abbasid Caliphate
751	Pippin III becomes king of the Franks, establishing Carolingians on the throne
768–814	Charlemagne rules as king of the Franks
786–809	Caliphate of Harun al-Rashid
800	Charlemagne crowned emperor at Rome
843	Treaty of Verdun
871–899	King Alfred of England
929–1031	Caliphate of Córdoba
955	Battle of Lechfeld
962	King Otto I (r. 936–973) of Germany crowned emperor
987–996	Reign of King Hugh Capet of France
c. 990	Peace of God movement begins
1000 or 1001	Stephen I (St. Stephen) (r. 997–1038) crowned king of Hungary
1001–1018	Byzantine conquest of Bulgaria

KEY TERMS

Abbasids (326)

ban (347)

castellan (347)

dynatoi (324)

feudalism (343)

madrasa (330)

manor (337)

Peace of God (349)

primogeniture (348)

serfs (345)

tithe (347)

vassalage (344)

REVIEW QUESTIONS

1. What were the effects of expansion on the power of the Byzantine emperor?
2. What forces led to the fragmentation of the Islamic world in the tenth and eleventh centuries?
3. What were the strengths and weaknesses of Carolingian institutions of government, warfare, and defense?
4. How and why did the different states of central and eastern Europe—Russia, Hungary, Serbia, Croatia, and so on—emerge?

MAKING CONNECTIONS

1. How were the Byzantine, Islamic, and European economies similar? How did they differ? How did these economies interact?
2. How were the powers and ambitions of castellans similar to, and how were they different from, those of the dynatoi of Byzantium and of Muslim provincial rulers?
3. Compare the effects of the barbarian invasions into the Roman Empire with the effects of the Viking, Muslim, and Magyar invasions into Carolingian Europe.

FOR FURTHER EXPLORATION

To assess your mastery of the material in this chapter, see the Online Study Guide at bedfordstmartins.com/hunt.

To read additional primary-source material from this period, see Chapter 9 in *Sources of The Making of the West,* Second Edition, Volume I.

Renewal and Reform, 1050–1150

BRUNO OF COLOGNE WAS HEADED for a successful career in the church. An esteemed teacher at the prominent French cathedral school of Reims, he was a likely choice for promotion to bishop or even archbishop. But around 1084, he abandoned it all. He was disgusted with the new archbishop of Reims,♦ Manasses, who had purchased his office and was so uninterested in religious matters that he once reportedly said, "The archbishopric of Reims would be a good thing, if one did not have to sing Mass for it." Bruno quit his post at the school and left the city. But he did not do what ethical and morally outraged men of the time were expected to do—join a monastery. Rejecting both the worldly goals of secular clerics like Manasses and the communal goals of Benedictine monks, Bruno set up a hermitage—an isolated retreat—at Chartreuse,♦ high in the Alps. The hermits who gathered there lived in seclusion and poverty. One of Bruno's contemporaries marveled: "They do not take gold, silver, or ornaments for their church from anyone." This unworldliness was matched, however, with keen interest in learning: for all its poverty, Chartreuse had a rich library.

Thus began La Chartreuse, the chief house of the Carthusians, a monastic order still in existence. The Carthusian monks lived as hermits, eschewed material wealth, and emphasized learning. In some ways their style of life was a reaction against the monumental changes rumbling through their age: their solitude ran counter to the burgeoning cities, and their austerity contrasted sharply with the opulence and power of princely courts. Their reverence for the written word, however, reflected the growing interest in scholarship and learning.

The most salient feature of the period 1050–1150 was increasing wealth. Cities, trade, and agricultural production swelled. The resulting worldliness met with a wide variety of responses. Some

♦**Reims:** RANS
♦**Chartreuse:** shahr TROOZ

La Chartreuse
The impulse behind the foundation of La Chartreuse was withdrawal from the world. Yet the world came to the Carthusians' high perch. One of the abbots of Cluny made it his custom to visit every year. He said that the new monks reminded him of the desert hermits. He did not mean that the Alps looked like Egypt but rather that the monks, living in separate cells, practiced the heroically ascetic life of the first monks. *Photo © Gary Kleinschmidt.*

people, like Bruno, fled the world; others tried to reform it; and still others embraced, enjoyed, or tried to understand it.

Within one century, the development of a profit-based economy transformed western European communities. Many villages and fortifications became cities where traders, merchants, and artisans conducted business. Although most people still lived in less-populated, rural areas, their lives were touched in many ways by the new cash economy. Economic concerns drove changes within the church, where a movement for reform gathered steam. Money helped redefine the role of the clergy and, elaborating new political ideas, popes, kings, and princes came to exercise new forms of power.

At the same time, city dwellers began to demand their own governments. Monks and clerics reformulated the nature of their communities and, like Bruno of Cologne, sought intense spiritual lives. All of these developments inspired (and in turn were inspired by) new ideas, forms of scholarship, and methods of inquiry. The rapid pace of religious, political, and economic change was matched by new developments in thought, learning, and artistic expression.

❖ The Commercial Revolution

As the population of Europe continued to expand in the eleventh century, cities, long-distance trade networks, local markets, and new business arrangements meshed to create a profit-based economy. With improve- ments in agriculture and more land in cultivation, the great estates of the eleventh century produced surpluses that helped feed—and therefore make possible—a new urban population.

Commerce was not new to the history of western Europe, but the **commercial revolution** of the Middle Ages spawned the institutions that would be the direct ancestors of modern businesses: corporations, banks, accounting systems, and, above all, urban centers that thrived on economic vitality. Whereas ancient cities had primarily religious, social, and political functions, medieval cities were centers of production and economic activity. Wealth meant power: it allowed city dwellers to become self-governing.

Cities, Towns, and Fairs

The new commercial centers—cities and towns—developed around castles and monasteries and within the walls of ancient Roman towns. Great lords in the countryside—and this included monasteries—were eager to take advantage of the profits that their estates generated. In the late tenth century, they had reorganized their lands for greater productivity, encouraged their peasants to cultivate new land, and converted services and dues to money payments. Now with ready cash, they not only fostered the development of sporadic markets where they could sell their surpluses and buy luxury goods but even encouraged traders and craftspeople to settle down near them. The lords gained at each step: their purchases brought them an enhanced lifestyle and greater prestige, while

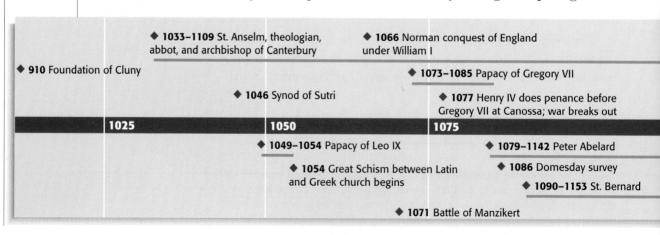

◆ **1033–1109** St. Anselm, theologian, abbot, and archbishop of Canterbury

◆ **1066** Norman conquest of England under William I

◆ **910** Foundation of Cluny

◆ **1073–1085** Papacy of Gregory VII

◆ **1046** Synod of Sutri

◆ **1077** Henry IV does penance before Gregory VII at Canossa; war breaks out

1025   **1050**   **1075**

◆ **1049–1054** Papacy of Leo IX

◆ **1079–1142** Peter Abelard

◆ **1054** Great Schism between Latin and Greek church begins

◆ **1086** Domesday survey

◆ **1090–1153** St. Bernard

◆ **1071** Battle of Manzikert

Medieval Besalú
The bridge leading to Besalú, a town in Catalonia (Spain), was constructed, like the town's walls and many of its other buildings, during the eleventh and twelfth centuries. The high fortified entrance was added in the fourteenth century. Already in the ninth century Besalú was the center of a county, and in the eleventh century it briefly became the seat of a bishopric. At the same time it was home to a thriving Jewish population, whose mikvah, or ritual bath house, still stands today.
AKG Images/Scheutze/Rodemann.

they charged merchants tolls and sales taxes, in this way profiting even more from trade.

Traders. At Bruges♦ (today in Belgium), the local lord's castle became the magnet around which a city formed. As a medieval chronicler observed:

♦**Bruges:** broozh

To satisfy the needs of the people in the castle at Bruges, first merchants with luxury articles began to surge around the gate: then the winesellers came; finally the innkeepers arrived to feed and lodge the people who had business with the prince. . . . So many houses were built that soon a great city was created.

Other commercial centers clustered around monasteries and churches. Still other markets

♦ **1095** Council of Clermont; Pope Urban II calls the First Crusade

♦ **1122** Concordat of Worms

♦ **1108–1137** Reign of Louis VI

♦ **c. 1140** Gratian, *Decretum*

♦ **1097** Establishment of commune at Milan

♦ **1151** Hildegard of Bingen, *Scivias*

| **1100** | **1125** | **1150** | |

♦ **1109** Establishment of the Crusader States

♦ **1096–1099** First Crusade

♦ **1147–1149** Second Crusade

♦ **1098** Foundation of Cîteaux

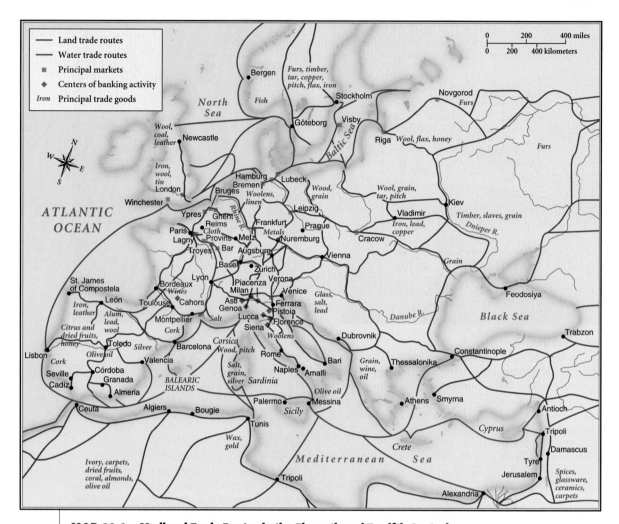

MAP 10.1   Medieval Trade Routes in the Eleventh and Twelfth Centuries
In the medieval world, bulk goods from the north (furs, fish, and wood) were traded for luxury goods from the south (ivory and spices, including medicines, perfumes, and dyes). Already regions were beginning to specialize. England, for example, supplied raw wool, but Flanders (Ypres, Ghent) specialized in turning that wool into cloth and shipping it farther south, to the fairs of Champagne (whose capital was Troyes) or Germany. Italian cities channeled goods from the Muslim and Byzantine worlds northward and exported European goods southward and eastward.

formed just outside the walls of older cities; these gradually merged into new and enlarged urban communities as town walls were built around them to protect their inhabitants. Sometimes informal country markets might eventually be housed in permanent structures. Along the Rhine and in other river valleys, cities sprang up to service the merchants who traversed the route between Italy and the north.

Many such long-distance traders were Jews and Italians. They supplied the fine

wines, spices, and fabrics beloved by lords and ladies, their families, and their vassals. Jews had often been involved at least part-time in long-distance trade as vintners; and as lords reorganized the countryside, driving out Jewish landowners, most Jews were forced to turn to commerce full-time. Italians took up long-distance trade because of their proximity to Byzantine and Islamic ports; their opportunities for plunder and trade on the high seas; and their never entirely extinguished urban traditions (Map 10.1).

Many other traders were local, like one Benedictine monk who supervised a manor twenty miles to the south of his monastery in France and sold its surplus horses and grain at a local market. At Reims, the city Bruno left, the middle of a forum dating back to the Roman Empire became a new commercial center. As early as 1067, the king of France was writing about the many fairs in his realm—great markets held at regular intervals that attracted large crowds. Around the marketplace at Reims grew a network of streets whose names (many of which still exist) revealed their essentially commercial functions: Street of the Butchers, Street of the Wool Market, Street of the Wheat Market. The shoemaker's sign on this page originally hung in a street full of other shoe stores.

The Building Boom. The look and feel of such developing cities varied enormously, but nearly all included a marketplace, a castle, and several churches. Most had to adapt to increasingly crowded conditions. Archaeologists have discovered that at the end of the eleventh century in Winchester, England, city plots were still large enough to accommodate houses parallel to the street; but the swelling population soon necessitated destroying these houses and building instead long, narrow, hall-like tenement houses, constructed at right angles to the thoroughfare. These were built on a frame made from strips of wood filled with wattle and daub—twigs woven together and covered with clay. If they were like the stone houses built in the late twelfth century (a period about which we know a good deal), they had two stories: a shop or warehouse on the lower floor and living quarters above. Behind this main building was the kitchen and perhaps also enclosures for livestock, as archaeologists have found at Southampton, England. Even city dwellers clung to rural pursuits, living largely off the food they raised themselves.

The construction of houses and markets was part of a building boom that began in the tenth century and continued at an accelerated pace through the thirteenth. Specialized buildings for trade and city government were put up—charitable houses for the sick and indigent, community houses, and warehouses. In addition, medieval cities surrounded them-

Shoemaker
By the twelfth century, a fortified village (a burg) had developed around the monastery of Cluny to cater to the monks' material needs. This carving of a shoemaker at his bench, which was displayed above his shop at Cluny, is an example of the sorts of signs that merchants used to advertise their services. *Musée d'Art et d' Archéologie (Musée Ochier), Cluny, France.*

selves with walls. By 1100, Speyer (today in Germany) had three: the first had been put up around its cathedral, the second went just beyond the parish church of St. Moritz, and the last was built still farther out to protect the marketplace. Within the walls lay a network of streets—often narrow, dirty, dark, and winding—made of packed clay or gravel. New bridges were built to span the rivers. Before the eleventh century, Europeans had depended on boats and waterways for bulky long-distance transport; now carts could haul items overland because new roads through the countryside linked the urban markets.

Although commercial centers developed throughout western Europe, they grew fastest and became most dense in regions along key waterways: the Mediterranean coasts of Italy, France, and Spain; northern Italy along the Po River; the river system of the Rhône-Saône-Meuse;◆ the Rhineland; the English Channel; the shores of the Baltic Sea. During the eleventh century these waterways became part of a single interdependent economy.

◆**Rhône-Saône-Meuse:** rohn / sohn / meyz

910 by the duke and duchess of Aquitaine, who endowed it with property but then gave it and its worldly possessions to Saints Peter and Paul. In this way they put control of the monastery into the hands of the two most powerful heavenly saints. They designated the pope, as the successor of St. Peter, to be the monastery's worldly protector if anyone should bother or threaten it. The whole notion of "freedom" at this point was very vague. But Cluny's prestige was great because of its status as St. Peter's property and the elaborate round of prayers that the monks carried out there with scrupulous devotion. The Cluniac monks fulfilled the role of "those who pray" in a way that dazzled their contemporaries. Through their prayers they seemed to guarantee the salvation of all Christians. Rulers, bishops, rich landowners, and even serfs (if they could) gave Cluny donations of land, joining their contributions to the land of St. Peter. Powerful men and women called on the Cluniac monks to reform other monasteries along the Cluniac model.

The abbots of Cluny came to see themselves as reformers of the world as well. They believed in clerical celibacy, arguing against the prevailing norm in which parish priests and even bishops were married. They also thought that the laity could be reformed, become more virtuous, and cease its oppression of the poor. In the eleventh century, the Cluniacs began to link their program of internal monastic and external worldly reform to the papacy. When their lands were encroached on by bishops and laypeople, they appealed to the popes to help them. At the same time the papacy itself was becoming interested in reform.

Church Reform in the Empire. Around the time the Cluniacs were joining their fate to that of the popes, a small group of clerics and monks in the empire began calling for systematic reform within the church. They buttressed their arguments with new interpretations of canon law—the laws decreed over the centuries at church councils and by bishops and popes. They concentrated on two breaches of those laws: clerical marriage and **simony**♦ (buying church offices).

Most of the men who promoted these ideas lived in the most commercialized regions of the empire—Italy and the regions along the northern half of the Rhine River. Their familiarity with the impersonal practices of a profit economy led them to interpret as crass purchases the gifts that churchmen were used to giving in return for their offices.

Emperor Henry III (r. 1039–1056) supported the reformers. Taking seriously his position as the anointed of God, Henry felt responsible for the well-being of the church in his empire. He denounced simony and personally refused to accept money or gifts when he appointed bishops to their posts. When in 1046 three men, each representing a different faction of the Roman aristocracy, claimed to be pope, Henry, as ruler of Rome, traveled to Italy to settle the matter. The Synod of Sutri (1046), over which he presided, deposed all three popes and elected another. In 1049, Henry appointed Leo IX (r. 1049–1054), a bishop from the Rhineland, to the papacy. But this appointment did not work out as Henry had expected, for Leo set out to reform the church under his own, not the emperor's, control.

Leo IX and the Expansion of Papal Power. During Leo's tenure, the pope's role expanded. (For one artist's image of Leo, see the picture on the next page.) He traveled to France and Germany, holding councils to condemn bishops guilty of simony. He sponsored the creation of a canon law textbook—the *Collection in 74 Titles*—which emphasized the pope's power. To the papal court Leo brought the most zealous reformers of his day: Humbert of Silva Candida, Peter Damian, and Hildebrand (later Gregory VII).

At first, Leo's claims to new power over the church hierarchy were complacently ignored by clergy and secular rulers alike. The Council of Reims, which Leo called in 1049, for example, was attended by only a few bishops and boycotted by the king of France. Nevertheless, the pope made it into a forum for exercising his authority. Placing the relics of St. Remegius♦ (the patron saint of Reims) on the altar of the church, he demanded that the attending bishops and ab-

---

♦**simony:** SY muh nee

♦**Remegius:** reh MEE gee uhs

Leo IX
This eleventh-century manuscript shows not so much a portrait of Leo IX as an idealized image of his power and position. What does the halo signify? Why do you suppose he stands at least three heads taller than the other figure in the picture, Warinus, the abbot of St. Arnulf of Metz? What is Leo doing with his right hand? With his left hand he holds a little church (symbol of a real one) that is being presented to him by Warinus. Compare these figures to those of emperor and Christ on page 323. What did the artist intend to convey about the relationship of this church to papal power? *Burgerbibliothek Bern cod. 292f.#72r.*

bots say whether or not they had purchased their offices. A few confessed they had, some did not respond, and others gave excuses. New and extraordinary was the fact that all present felt accountable to the pope and accepted his verdicts.

In his last year as pope, Leo sent Humbert of Silva Candida to Constantinople on a diplomatic mission to argue against the patriarch of Constantinople on behalf of the new, lofty claims of the pope. Furious at the contemptuous way he was treated by the patriarch, Humbert excommunicated him. In retaliation the patriarch excommunicated Humbert and his party, threatening them with eternal damnation. Clashes between the two churches had occurred before and had been patched up, but this one, called the **Great Schism** (1054), proved insurmountable.[1] Thereafter, the Roman Catholic and the Greek Orthodox churches were largely separate.

The popes who followed Leo continued his program to expand papal power. When military adventurers from Normandy began carving out states for themselves in southern Italy, the popes in nearby Rome felt threatened. After waging unsuccessful war against the interlopers, the papacy made the best of a bad situation by granting the Normans Sicily and parts of southern Italy as a fief, turning its former enemies into vassals.

As leader of the Christian people, the papacy also participated in wars in Spain, where it supported Christians against the dominant Muslims. The political fragmentation of al-Andalus into small and weak *taifas* (see page 329) made it fair game to the Christians to the north. Slowly the idea of the *reconquista,*♦ the Christian reconquest of Spain, took shape, fed by religious fervor as well as greed for land and power.

The Gregorian Reform and the Investiture Conflict, 1073–1122

The papal reform movement is above all associated with Pope Gregory VII (r. 1073–1085) and is therefore often called the **Gregorian reform**. He began as a lowly Roman cleric, named Hildebrand, with the job of administering the papal estates and rose slowly in the hierarchy. A passionate advocate of papal primacy (the theory that the pope was the head of the church), Gregory was not afraid to clash head-on with Emperor Henry IV (r. 1056–1106) over leadership of the church. In his view—and it was astonishing at the time, given

---

[1]Despite occasional thaws and liftings of the sentences, the mutual excommunications of pope and patriarch largely remained in effect until 1965, when Pope Paul VI and the Greek Orthodox patriarch, Anthanagoras I, publicly deplored them.

♦*reconquista:* ray con KEE stuh

the religious and spiritual roles associated with rulers—the emperor was just a layman who had no right to meddle in church affairs.

Gregory was and remains an extraordinarily controversial figure. He certainly thought that as pope he was acting as the vicar, or representative, of St. Peter on earth. Describing himself, he declared, "I have labored with all my power that Holy Church, the bride of God, our Lady Mother, might come again to her own splendor and might remain free, pure, and Catholic." He thought the reforms he advocated and the upheavals he precipitated were necessary to free the church from the Satanic rulers of the world. But his great nemesis, Henry IV, had a very different view of Gregory. He considered him an ambitious and evil man who "seduced the world far and wide and stained the Church with the blood of her sons." Not surprisingly, modern historians are only a bit less divided in their assessment of Gregory. Few deny his sincerity and deep religious devotion, but many speak of his pride, ambition, and single-mindedness. He was not an easy man.

Henry IV was less complex. He was brought up in the traditions of his father, Henry III, a pious church reformer who considered it part of his duty to appoint bishops and even popes to ensure the well-being of both church and state. The emperor believed that he and his bishops—who were, at the same time, his most valuable supporters and administrators—were the rightful leaders of the church. He had no intention of allowing the pope to become head of the church.

The Investiture Conflict.[2] The great confrontation between Gregory and Henry that

[2]This movement is also called the Investiture Controversy, Investiture Contest, or Investiture Struggle. The epithets all refer to the same thing: the disagreement between popes and emperors regarding the right to invest churchmen in particular and power over the church hierarchy in general.

The World of the Investiture Conflict, c. 1070–1122

historians call the **Investiture Conflict** began over the appointment of the archbishop of Milan. Gregory disputed Henry's right to "invest" churchmen. In the investiture ritual, the emperor or his representative symbolically gave the church and the land that went with it to the priest or bishop or archbishop chosen for the job. When, in 1075, Henry insisted on investing a new archbishop of Milan, the emperor and the pope began hurling denunciations at each other. The next year Henry called a council of German bishops who demanded that Gregory, that "false monk," resign. In reply, Gregory called a synod that both excommunicated and suspended Henry from office:

> I deprive King Henry, son of the emperor Henry, who has rebelled against [God's] Church with unheard-of audacity, of the government over the whole kingdom of Germany and Italy, and I release all Christian men from the allegiance which they have sworn or may swear to him, and I forbid anyone to serve him as king.

It was this part of the decree that made it politically explosive, because it authorized anyone in Henry's kingdom to rebel against him. Henry's enemies, mostly German princes (as German aristocrats were called), now threatened to elect another king. They were motivated partly by religious sentiments, as many had established links with the papacy through their support of reformed monasteries, and partly by political opportunism, as they had chafed under the strong German king, who had tried to keep their power in check. Some bishops joined forces with Gregory's supporters, however. This was a great blow to royal power because Henry desperately needed the troops supplied by his churchmen.

Attacked from all sides, Henry traveled to intercept Gregory, who was journeying northward to visit the rebellious princes. In early 1077, king and pope met at Canossa, high in central Italy's snowy Apennine◆ Mountains. Gregory was inside a fortress there; Henry stood outside as a penitent, begging forgiveness. Henry's move was astute, for no priest could refuse absolution to a penitent; Gregory had to lift the excommunication and receive Henry back into the church. But Gregory

◆**Apennine:** A puh nyn

Matilda of Tuscany
Matilda, countess of Tuscany and key supporter of
Pope Gregory VII, here sits on a throne. She is the
dominant figure in this picture, which was made
around 1115 to illustrate a book about her life. To her
right is Hugh, the abbot of Cluny. Beneath them both,
in a gesture of supplication, is Emperor Henry IV, who
asks them to intervene with the pope on his behalf.
© *Biblioteca Apostolica Vaticana (Vatican).*

now had the advantage of enjoying the king's
humiliation before the majesty of the pope.

Although Henry was technically back in
the church's fold, nothing of substance had
been resolved, and civil war began. The
princes elected an antiking (a king chosen illegally), and Henry and his supporters elected
an antipope. From 1077 until 1122, papal
and imperial armies and supporters waged
intermittent war in both Germany and Italy.

Outcome of the Investiture Conflict. The
Investiture Conflict was finally resolved long
after Henry IV and Gregory VII had died.
The Concordat of Worms♦ of 1122 ended the
fighting with a compromise that relied on a
conceptual distinction between two parts of
investiture—the spiritual (in which a man re-

♦**Worms:** vuhrms

ceived the symbols of his clerical office) and
the secular (in which he received the symbols
of the material goods that would allow him to
function). Under the terms of the concordat, the ring and staff, the symbols of church
office, were to be given by a churchman in
the first part of the ceremony. In the second
part, the emperor or his representative would
touch the bishop with a scepter, a symbolic
gesture that stood for the land and other
possessions that went with church office.
Elections of bishops in Germany would take
place "in the presence" of the emperor—that
is, under his influence. In Italy, the pope
would have a comparable role.

Superficially, nothing much had changed;
secular rulers would continue to have a part
in choosing and investing churchmen. In
fact, however, few people would now claim
that a king could act as head of the church.
Just as the new investiture ceremony broke
the ritual into spiritual and secular parts, so
too it implied a new notion of kingship that
separated it from priesthood. The Investiture Conflict did not produce the modern
distinction between church and state—that
would develop very slowly—but it set the
wheels in motion.

The most important changes brought
about by the Investiture Conflict, however,
were on the ground: the political landscape
in both Italy and Germany was irrevocably
transformed. In Germany, the princes consolidated their lands and their positions
at the expense of royal power. In Italy, the
emperor lost power to the cities. The northern and central Italian communes were
formed in the crucible of the war between the
pope and the emperor. In fierce communal
struggles, city factions, often created by local
grievances but claiming to fight on behalf of
the papal or the imperial cause, created their
own governing bodies. In the course of the
twelfth century, these Italian cities became
accustomed to self-government.

The Sweep of Reform

Church reform involved much more than the
clash of popes, emperors, and their supporters.
It penetrated into the daily lives of ordinary
Christians, inspired new forms of legal scholarship, and changed the way the church operated.

A Byzantine View of Papal Primacy

A continual source of friction between the Roman and Greek churches was the question of papal primacy (the pope's place at the head of the church). Even after the Great Schism of 1054, the two sides continued to argue over the matter. In 1136 a debate at Constantinople pitted a German bishop, Anselm of Havelburg—who argued that the pope had jurisdiction over the Greek church— against Nicetas, the Greek bishop of Nicomedia. In the following passage, Nicetas presents a moderate view.

I neither deny nor do I reject the Primacy of the Roman Church whose dignity you have extolled. As a matter of fact, we read in our ancient histories that there were three patriarchal sees closely linked in brotherhood, Rome, Alexandria, and Antioch, among which Rome, the highest see in the empire, received the primacy. . . .

But the Bishop of Rome himself ought not to be called the Prince of the Priesthood, nor the Supreme Priest nor anything of that kind, but only the Bishop of the first see. Thus it was that Boniface III [607], who was Roman by nationality, and the son of John, the Bishop of Rome, obtained from the Emperor Phocas confirmation of the fact that the apostolic see of Blessed Peter was the head of all the other Churches, since at that time, the Church of Constantinople was saying that it was the first see because of the transfer of the Empire. . . .

But the Roman Church to which we do not deny the Primacy among her sisters, and whom we recognize as holding the highest place in any general council, the first place of honor, that Church has separated herself from the rest by her pretensions. She has appropriated to herself the monarchy which is not contained in her office and which has divided the bishops and the churches of the East and the West since the partition of the Empire. When, as a result of these circumstances, she gathers a council of the Western bishops without making us (in the East) a part of it, it is fitting that her bishops should accept its decrees and observe them with the veneration that is due to them . . . but although we are not in disagreement with the Roman Church in the matter of the Catholic faith, how can we be expected to accept these decisions which were taken without our advice and of which we know nothing, since we were not at that same time gathered in council? If the Roman Pontiff, seated upon his sublime throne of glory, wishes to fulminate against us and to launch his orders from the height of his sublime dignity, if he wishes to sit in judgment on our Churches with a total disregard of our advice and solely according to his own will, as he seems to wish, what brotherhood and what fatherhood can we see in such a course of action? Who could ever accept such a situation? In such circumstances we could not be called nor would we really be any longer sons of the Church but truly its slaves.

Source: Deno John Geanakoplos, *Byzantium: Church, Society, and Civilization Seen through Contemporary Eyes* (Chicago: University of Chicago Press, 1984), 214–15, quoting in turn from F. Dvornik, *Byzantium and the Roman Primacy*, trans. Edwin A. Quain, S.J. (New York: Fordham University Press, 1966/1979), 145–46. Footnote omitted.

New Emphasis on the Sacraments. According to the Catholic church, the sacraments were the regular means by which God's heavenly grace infused mundane existence. But this did not mean that Christians were clear about how many sacraments there were, how they worked, or even what their significance was. Eleventh-century church reformers began the process—which would continue into the thirteenth century—of emphasizing the importance of the sacraments and the special nature of the priest, whose chief role was to administer them.

In the sacrament of marriage, for example, the effective involvement of the church in the wedding of husband and wife came only after the Gregorian reform. Before the twelfth century, priests had little to do with weddings, which were family affairs. After the twelfth century, however, priests were expected to consecrate the marriage. When the knight Arnulf of Ardres got married in 1194, for example, priests blessed and sprinkled him and his wife with holy water as the couple lay in their nuptial bed. Churchmen also began to assume jurisdiction over marital disputes, not simply in cases involving royalty (as they had always done) but also in those involving lesser aristocrats. The clergy's prohibition of marriage partners as distant as seventh cousins (marriage between such cousins was considered incest) had the potential to control dynastic alliances. Because many noble families kept their inheritance intact through a single male heir, the heirs' marriages took on great significance.

At the same time, churchmen began to stress the sanctity of marriage. Hugh of St. Victor, a twelfth-century scholar, dwelled on the sacramental meaning of marriage:

> Can you find anything else in marriage except conjugal society which makes it sacred and by which you can assert that it is holy? . . . Each shall be to the other as a same self in all sincere love, all careful solicitude, every kindness of affection, in constant compassion, unflagging consolation, and faithful devotedness.

Hugh saw marriage as a matter of Christian love.

The reformers also proclaimed the special importance of the sacrament of the Mass, holy communion through the body and blood of Christ. Gregory VII called the Mass "the greatest thing in the Christian religion." No layman, regardless of how powerful, and no woman of any class or status at all could perform anything equal to it, for the Mass was the key to salvation.

Clerical Celibacy. The new emphasis on the sacraments, which were now more thoroughly and carefully defined, along with the desire to set priests clearly apart from the laity, led to vigorous enforcement of an old element of church discipline: the celibacy of priests. The demand for a celibate clergy had far-reaching significance for the history of the church. It distanced western clerics even further from their eastern Orthodox counterparts (who did not practice celibacy), ex-

acerbating the Great Schism of 1054. It also broke with traditional local practices, as clerical marriage was customary in some places. Gregorian reformers exhorted every cleric in higher orders, from the humble parish priest to the exalted bishop, to refrain from marriage or to abandon his wife. Naturally many churchmen resisted. The historian Orderic Vitalis♦ (1075–c. 1142) reported that one zealous archbishop in Normandy

> fulfilled his duties as metropolitan with courage and thoroughness, continually striving to separate immoral priests from their mistresses [and wives]: on one occasion when he forbade them to keep concubines he was stoned out of the synod.

Undaunted, the reformers persisted, and in 1123 the pope proclaimed all clerical marriages invalid. With its new power, the papacy was largely able to enforce the rule.

The "Papal Monarchy." Part of the new powers of the papacy rested on its consolidation and imposition of canon law. These laws had begun simply as rules determined at church councils. Later they were supplemented with papal declarations. Several attempts to gather together and organize these laws had been made before the eleventh century. But the proliferation of rules during that century, along with the desire of Gregory's followers to clarify church law as they saw it, made a systematic collection of rules even more necessary. This was achieved around 1140 by a landmark synthesis, the *Decretum,*♦ written by a teacher of canon law named Gratian. Collecting nearly two thousand passages from the decrees of popes and councils as well as the writings of the church fathers, Gratian intended to demonstrate their essential agreement. In fact, the book's original title was *Harmony of Discordant Canons.* If he found any "discord" in his sources, Gratian usually imposed the harmony himself by arguing that the passages dealt with different situations. A bit later another legal scholar revised and expanded the *Decretum,* adding ancient Roman law to the mix.

♦**Orderic Vitalis:** awr duh REEK vy TAY luhs
♦***Decretum:*** duh KREET uhm

Already while Gratian was writing, the papal curia, or government, centered in Rome, resembled a court of law with its own collection agency. The papacy had developed a bureaucracy to hear cases and rule on petitions, such as disputed elections of bishops. Churchmen not involved in litigation went to Rome for other sorts of benefits: to petition for privileges for their monasteries or to be consecrated by the pope. All these services were also expensive, requiring lawyers, judges, hearing officers, notaries, and collectors. The lands owned by the papacy were not sufficient to support the growing cost of its administrative apparatus, and the petitioners and litigants themselves had to pay, a practice they resented. A satire written about 1100, in the style of the Gospels, made bitter fun of papal greed:

> There came to the court a certain wealthy clerk, fat and thick, and gross. . . . He first gave to the dispenser, second to the treasurer, third to the cardinals. But they thought among themselves that they should receive more. The Lord Pope, hearing that his cardinals had received many gifts, was sick, nigh unto death. But the rich man sent to him a couch of gold and silver and immediately he was made whole. Then the Lord Pope called his cardinals and ministers to him and said to them: "Brethren, look, lest anyone deceive you with vain words. For I have given you an example: as I have grasped, so you grasp also."

The pope, with his law courts, bureaucracy, and financial apparatus, had become a monarch.

Early Crusades and Crusader States

Asserting itself as head of the Christian church and leader of its reform, the papacy sometimes supported and proclaimed holy wars to advance the cause of Christianity. The most important of these were the crusades. Combinations of war and pilgrimage—the popular practice of making a pious voyage to a sacred shrine to petition for help or cure—the early crusades sent armed European Christians into battle against Muslims in the Holy Land, the place where Christ had lived and died. The crusaders established several tiny states along the coast of the eastern Mediterranean Sea, holding on to them precariously until 1291.

Although the crusades ultimately "failed" in the sense that the crusaders did not succeed in permanently retaining the Holy Land for Christendom, they were a pivotal episode in Western civilization. They marked the first stage of European overseas expansion, which would later become imperialism.

Calling the First Crusade. The First Crusade began with the entry of the Seljuk◆ Turks into Asia Minor (Map 10.2). In the 900s, the Muslim world had splintered into numerous small states; by the 1050s, the fierce, nomadic Sunni Muslim **Seljuk Turks** had captured Baghdad, subjugated the caliphate, and begun to threaten Byzantium. The difficulties the Byzantine emperor Romanus IV had in pulling together an army to attack the Turks in 1071 reveal how weak his position had become. Unable to muster Byzantine troops—which were either busy defending their own districts or led by *dynatoi* (see page 324) wary of sending support to the emperor—Romanus had to rely on a mercenary army made up of Normans, Franks, Slavs, and even Turks. This motley force met the Seljuks at Manzikert◆ in what is today eastern Turkey. The battle was a disaster for Romanus: the Seljuks, under Sultan Alp Arslan,◆ routed his army and captured him. The battle at Manzikert (1071) marked the end of Byzantine domination in the region.

The Turks, gradually settling in Asia Minor, extended their control across the empire and beyond, all the way to Jerusalem, which had been under Muslim control since the seventh century. In 1095, the Byzantine emperor Alexius Comnenus (Alexius I) appealed for help to Pope Urban II, hoping to get new mercenary troops for a fresh offensive.

Urban II chose to interpret the request in his own way. At the Council of Clermont (in France) in 1095, after finishing the usual business of proclaiming the Truce of God (prohibition of fighting on various days of the week for various reasons) and condemn-

---

◆**Seljuk:** SEL jook
◆**Manzikert:** MAN zuh kurt
◆**Alp Arslan:** ahlp ahr SLAHN

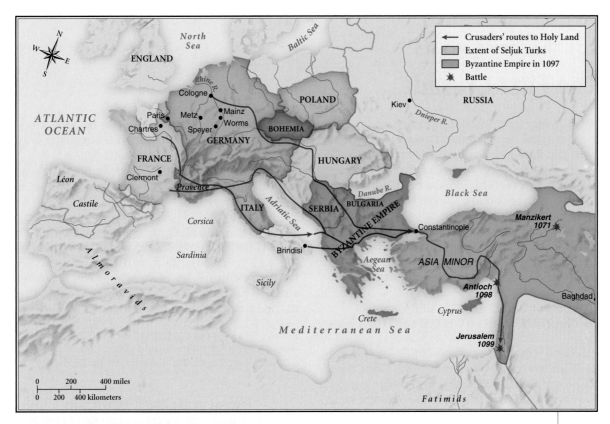

MAP 10.2   The First Crusade, 1096–1098

The First Crusade was a major military undertaking that required organization, movement over both land and sea, and enormous resources. Four main groups were responsible for the conquest of Jerusalem. One began at Cologne, in northern Germany; a second group started out from Blois, in France; the third originated just to the west of Provence; and the fourth launched ships from Brindisi, at the heel of Italy. All joined up at Constantinople, where their leaders negotiated with Alexius for help and supplies in return for a pledge of vassalage to the emperor.

ing simony among the clergy, Urban moved outside the church and addressed an already excited throng:

> Oh, race of Franks, race from across the mountains, race beloved and chosen by God. . . . Let hatred depart from among you, let your quarrels end, let wars cease, and let all dissensions and controversies slumber. Enter upon the road to the Holy Sepulcher; wrest that land from the wicked race, and subject it to yourselves.

The crowd reportedly responded with one voice: "God wills it." Historians remain divided over Urban's motives for his massive call to arms. Certainly he hoped to win Christian control of the Holy Land. He was also anxious to fulfill the goals of the Truce of God

by turning the entire "race of Franks" into a peace militia dedicated to holy purposes, an army of God. Just as the Truce of God mobilized whole communities to fight against anyone who broke the truce, so the First Crusade mobilized armed groups sworn to free the Holy Land of its enemies. Finally, Urban's call placed the papacy in a new position of leadership, one that complemented in a military arena the position the popes had gained in the church hierarchy.

Heeding the Call.   Both men and women, rich and poor, young and old heeded Urban's call to go on the First Crusade (1096–1099). They abandoned their homes and braved the rough journey to the Holy Land to fight for

CONTRASTING VIEWS

The First Crusade

When Urban II preached the First Crusade at Clermont in 1095, he unleashed a movement that was seen and interpreted in many different ways. Document 1 is an early and almost official account begun around 1100 by Fulcher of Chartres, who considered the crusade a wonderful historical movement and participated in it himself. Jews in the Rhineland who experienced the virulent attacks of some of the crusading forces had a very different view (Document 2). Document 3 presents an Arab view of the crusaders' capture of Jerusalem.

1. THE CHRONICLE OF FULCHER OF CHARTRES (EARLY TWELFTH CENTURY)

Fulcher of Chartres, a chaplain for one of the crusade leaders, wrote his account of the First Crusade for posterity. His chronicle is ordinarily very accurate, and he is careful to note the different experiences of different participants. It is all the more significant, therefore, that he expresses the public view of the First Crusade by making liberal use of biblical quotations and imagery to describe the event. He saw it as the fulfillment of God's plan for humanity.

In March of the year 1096 from the Lord's Incarnation, after Pope Urban had held the Council, which has been described, at Auvergne in November, some people, earlier prepared than others, hastened to begin the holy journey. Others followed in April or May, June or July, and also in August, September, or October, whenever the opportunity of securing expenses presented itself.

In that year, with God disposing, peace and a vast abundance of grain and wine overflowed through all the regions of the earth, so that they who chose to follow Him with their crosses according to His commands did not fail on the way for lack of bread. [Fulcher then names the "leaders of the pilgrims."] . . .

So, with such a great band proceeding from western parts, gradually from day to day on the way there grew armies of innumerable people coming together from everywhere. Thus a countless multitude speaking many languages and coming from many regions was to be seen. However, all were not assembled into one army until we arrived at the city of Nicaea.

What more shall I tell? The islands of the seas and all the kingdoms of the earth were so agitated that one believed that the prophecy of David was fulfilled, who said in his Psalm: "All nations whom Thou hast made shall come and worship before Thee O Lord" [Ps. 86:9]; and what those going all the way there later said with good reason: "We shall worship in the place where His feet have stood" [Ps. 132:7]. We have read much about this in the Prophets which it is tedious to repeat.

Source: Edward Peters, ed., *The First Crusade: The Chronicle of Fulcher of Chartres and Other Source Materials* (Philadelphia: University of Pennsylvania Press, 1971), 35–37.

2. THE JEWISH EXPERIENCE AS TOLD BY SOLOMON BAR SIMSON (MID-TWELFTH CENTURY)

Around 1140, Solomon Bar Simson, a Jew from Mainz, published a chronicle of the First Crusade. This excerpt shows that the Jewish community interpreted the coming of the crusaders as a punishment from God; hence their prayers and fasting and their conviction that those killed by the crusaders were martyrs for God.

At this time arrogant people, a people of strange speech, a nation bitter and impetuous, Frenchmen and Germans, set out for the Holy City, which had been desecrated by barbaric nations, there to seek their house of idolatry and banish the Ishmaelites [Muslims] and other denizens of the land and conquer the land for themselves. . . . Now it came to pass that as they passed through the towns where Jews dwelled, they said to one another: "Look now, we are going a long way to seek out the profane shrine and to avenge ourselves on the Ishmaelites, when here, in our very midst, are the Jews—they whose forefathers murdered and crucified [Christ] for no reason. Let us first avenge ourselves on them and exterminate them from among the nations so that the name of Israel will no longer be remembered, or let them adopt our faith and acknowledge the offspring of promiscuity."

When the Jewish communities became aware of their intentions, they resorted to the custom of our ancestors, repentance, prayer, and charity. The hands of the Holy Nation turned faint at this time, their hearts melted, and their strength flagged. They hid in their innermost rooms to escape the swirling sword. They subjected themselves to great endurance, abstaining from food and drink for three consecutive days and nights, and then fasting many days from sunrise to sunset, until their skin was shriveled and dry as wood upon their bones. And they cried out loudly and bitterly to God. . . .

On the eighth day of Iyar, on the Sabbath, the foe attacked the community of Speyer and murdered eleven holy souls who sanctified their Creator on the holy Sabbath and refused to defile themselves by adopting the faith of their foe. There was a distinguished, pious woman there who slaughtered herself in sanctification of God's name. She was the first among all the communities of those who were slaughtered. The remainder were saved by the local bishop without defilement [baptism], as described above.

On the twenty-third day of Iyar they attacked the community of Worms. The community was then divided into two groups; some remained in their homes and others fled to the local bishop seeking refuge. Those who remained in their homes were set upon by the steppe-wolves who pillaged men, women, and infants, children and old people. They pulled down the stairways and destroyed the houses, looting and plundering; and they took the Torah Scroll, trampled it in the mud, and tore and burned it.

Source: Patrick J. Geary, ed., *Readings in Medieval History* (Peterborough, Ontario, Canada: Broadview Press, 1989), 433–34.

3. THE SEIZURE OF JERUSALEM AS TOLD BY IBN AL-ATHIR (EARLY THIRTEENTH CENTURY)

Ibn Al-Athir (1160–1233) was an Arab historian who drew on earlier accounts for this recounting of the crusaders' conquest of Jerusalem. He stresses the greed and impiety of the crusaders, who pillaged Muslim holy places, and their pitiless slaughter.

After their vain attempt to take Acre by siege, the Franks moved on to Jerusalem and besieged it for more than six weeks. They built two towers, one of which, near Sion, the Muslims burnt down, killing everyone inside it. It had scarcely ceased to burn before a messenger arrived to ask for help and to bring the news that the other side of the city had fallen. In fact Jerusalem was taken from the north on the morning of Friday 22 sha'ban 492 [July 15, 1099]. The population was put to the sword by the Franks who pillaged the area for a week. A band of Muslims barricaded themselves into the Oratory of David and fought on for several days. They were granted their lives in return for surrendering.

The Franks honored their word, and the group left by night for Ascalon. In the Masjid al-Aqsa [a mosque] the Franks slaughtered more than 70,000 people, among them a large number of Imams and Muslim scholars, devout and ascetic men who had left their homelands to live lives of pious seclusion in the Holy Place. The Franks stripped the Dome of the Rock [a place holy to the Muslims, upon which was built the mosque that the Crusaders plundered] of more than forty silver candelabra, each of them weighing 3,600 drams, and a great silver lamp weighing forty-four Syrian pounds, as well as a hundred and fifty smaller silver candelabra and more than twenty gold ones, and a great deal more booty. Refugees from Syria reached Baghdad in ramadan [the month of fasting].

Source: Patrick J. Geary, ed., *Readings in Medieval History* (Peterborough, Ontario, Canada: Broadview Press, 1989), 443.

QUESTIONS TO CONSIDER

1. What commonalities, if any, do you detect between the religious ideas of the crusaders and those whom they attacked?
2. What were the similarities and what were the differences in the experiences of the Jews in Rhineland cities and the Arabs in Jerusalem.
3. What were the motives of the crusaders?

A Crusader and His Wife

How do we know that the man on the left is a crusader? On his shirt is a cross, the sign worn by all men going on the crusades. In his right hand is a pilgrim's staff, a useful reminder that the crusades were sometimes considered less a matter of war than of penance and piety. What does the crusader's wife's embrace imply about marital love in the twelfth century? *Musée Lorrain, Nancy/photo: P. Mignot.*

their God. They also went—especially younger sons of aristocrats, who could not expect an inheritance because of primogeniture— because they wanted land. Some knights took the cross because they were obligated to follow their lord. Others hoped for plunder. Although women were discouraged from going on the crusades (one, who begged permission from her bishop, was persuaded to stay home and spend her wealth on charity instead), some crusaders were accompanied by their wives. (See the image, A Crusader and His Wife, at left.) Other women went as servants; a few may have been fighters. Children and old men and women, not able to fight, made the cords for siege engines—giant machines used to hurl stones at enemy fortifications. As more crusades were undertaken during the twelfth century, the transport and supply of these armies became a lucrative business for the commercial classes of maritime Italian cities such as Venice, which was strategically located on the route eastward.

The armies of the First Crusade were organized not as one military force but rather as separate militias, each commanded by a different individual. Fulcher of Chartres♦ (c. 1059–c.1127), an eyewitness, reported: "There grew armies of innumerable people coming together from everywhere. Thus a countless multitude speaking many languages and coming from many regions was to be seen." Fulcher was speaking of the armies led by nobles and authorized by the pope.

Attacking the Jews. One band, not authorized by the pope, consisted of commoners. This People's (or Peasants') Crusade, which started out before the others under the leadership of an eloquent but militarily unprepared French preacher, Peter the Hermit, took a route through the Rhineland in Germany before going on to Asia Minor, where most of its participants were slaughtered.

The Rhineland route was no mistake. Peter went there because he meant to attack the Jews. By this time, most Jews—forced off the land by castellans and other landlords— lived in cities, many in the flourishing commercial region of the Rhineland. Under Henry IV,

♦**Chartres:** shahrt

the Jews in the empire gained a place within the political system by receiving protection from the local bishop (an imperial appointee) in return for paying a tax. Within these cities the Jews lived in their own neighborhoods, where their tightly knit communities focused around the synagogue, which was a school and community center as well as a place of worship. Nevertheless, Jews also participated in the life of the larger Christian community. Archbishop Anno of Cologne, for example, dealt with Jewish moneylenders, and other Jews in Cologne were allowed to trade their wares at the fairs there.

It was against such Jewish communities that Peter's group, joined by local nobles and militias, vented its fury. As one commentator put it, the crusaders considered it ridiculous to attack Muslims when other infidels lived in their own backyards: "That's doing our work backward." The Rhineland Jews faced either forced conversion or death. Some of their persecutors relented when the Jews paid them money; others, however, attacked. Jews sometimes found refuge with bishops or in the houses of Christian friends, but in many cities — Metz,♦ Speyer,♦ Worms, Mainz,♦ and Cologne♦ — they were massacred.

Reorganizing the Holy Land.

The main objective of the First Crusade—to wrest the Holy Land from the Muslims and subject it to Christian rule—was accomplished largely because of Muslim disunity. After nearly a year of ineffectual attacks, the crusaders took Antioch on June 28, 1098, killing every Turk in the city; on July 15, 1099, they seized Jerusalem. By 1109 they had carved out several tiny states in the Holy Land.

Because the crusader states were created by conquest, they were treated as lordships. The rulers granted fiefs to their own vassals, and some of these men in turn gave portions of their holdings as fiefs to some of their own vassals. Many other vassals simply lived in the households of their lords. Since most Europeans went home after the First Crusade, the rulers who remained learned to coexist with the indigenous population, which included Muslims, Jews, and Greek Orthodox Christians. They encouraged a lively trade at their ports, to which came merchants from Italy, Byzantium, and Islamic cities (see "Genoese Traders in Palestine," page 378).

Jewish Communities Attacked during the First Crusade

Adapted from Angus Mackay with David Ditchburn, eds., Atlas of Medieval Europe *(New York: Routledge, 1997).*

♦**Metz:** mets
♦**Speyer:** SHPY ur
♦**Mainz:** mynts
♦**Cologne:** kuh LOHN

Jewish Cemetery at Worms

There was a large Jewish community at Worms in the eleventh century, and Emperor Henry IV granted the Jews there the right to travel and trade within the empire. He also exempted them from various tolls and taxes. Lured by the size and wealth of its Jewish population, one crusading contingent massacred about eight hundred Jews at Worms in 1096. The slaughtered men, women, and children were no doubt buried in this cemetery, which dates to the completion of the synagogue in 1034. It contains about two thousand gravestones; the oldest one extant was put up in 1076. *Erich Lessing/Art Resource, NY.*

The main concern of these rulers, however, was military. They set up castles and recruited knights from Europe. So organized for war was this society that it produced a new and militant kind of monasticism: the Knights Templar. Like Bruno's Carthusians, the Templars vowed themselves to poverty and chastity. But rather than withdraw to a hermitage on a mountaintop, the Templars, whose name came from their living quarters in

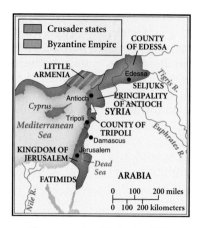

The Crusader States in 1109

the area of the former Jewish Temple at Jerusalem, devoted themselves to warfare. Their first mission—to protect the pilgrimage routes from Palestine to Jerusalem—soon diversified. They manned the town garrisons of the crusader states, and they transported money from Europe to the Holy Land. In this way, the Templars became enormously wealthy, with branch "banks" in major cities across Europe.

Genoese Traders in Palestine

The First Crusade yielded rich booty for the crusading armies and navies. In the entry for 1101 in the Annals of Genoa, *written by a chronicler named Caffaro, the Genoese, who sent a navy on the expedition, are shown fighting at Caesarea. Some of the officers and sailors later returned, turning their plunder into capital for trade or investment in land.*

The Genoese, wearing the cross on their right shoulders, climbed a palm tree leaning against the wall of the city and, calling Christ to their aid, at once crossed swords with the Saracens [the term that Europeans used for Muslims]. The Saracens, however, dropped their swords and other weapons on the spot and began to flee to their mosque. But before the Saracens could reach the mosque, the Genoese struck dead all men fighting on the walls, in the city [streets], and at every corner. And all the Christian [inhabitants of the city] in company with the patriarch [Daiberto, archbishop of Pisa] rushed without delay to the mosque. And a thousand wealthy merchants, who had gone up into the tower of the mosque, began to cry out to the patriarch: "Sir, sir, give us a safe conduct so that we shall not die, because

we hold to the rule of Christ, your God, and we shall give you everything we have." And the patriarch asked permission from the Genoese to grant the safe conduct. The Genoese then granted this permission to the patriarch. And immediately after the permission was granted [the Genoese] went through the city, seizing men and women and much money, and they took possession of everything that was inside. . . .

Later the Genoese with their galleys and the entire expeditionary force went to the beach of San Parlerio near Solino [probably al-Suwaydiyya, harbor of the ancient city of Antioch] and encamped there. First, they set aside from the money [pooled together] in the encampment one tenth and one fifth [which was due] to the [owners of the] galleys. But all the remaining money they divided among the eight thousand men. And they gave 48 solidi Poitevin and 2 pounds of pepper to each as his share.

Source: Robert S. Lopez and Irving W. Raymond, *Medieval Trade in the Mediterranean World: Illustrative Documents Translated with Introductions and Notes* (New York: W. W. Norton, n.d.), 88–89. Footnotes have been incorporated into the text itself in brackets.

Krak-des-Chevaliers
This imposing castle was built in 1142 on the site of a Muslim fortification in Syria by the Hospitallers, a religious military order much like the Knights Templar. A large community of perhaps fifty monk-knights and their hired mercenaries lived there. To the northeast (in back of the complex seen here) was a fortified village that in part served the needs of the castle. Peasants raised grain, which was ground by a windmill on one wall of the castle. For water, there were reservoirs to catch the rain, wells, and an aqueduct (on the right). Twelve toilets connected to a common drain. The monks worshiped in a chapel within the inner walls. The outer walls, built of masonry, completely enclosed the inner buildings, making Krak one of the most important places for refuge and defense in the crusader states. *Maynard Williams/NGS Image Collection.*

The Disastrous Second Crusade. The presence of the Knights Templar did not prevent a new Seljuk chieftain, Zengi, from taking one of the crusader states, Edessa, in 1144. The slow but steady shrinking of the crusader states began. The Second Crusade (1147–1149) came to a disastrous end. After only four days of besieging the walls of Damascus, the crusaders, whose leaders could not keep the peace among themselves, gave up and went home. Thereafter, despite numerous new crusades—fully eight major crusades were fought between the first in 1096 and the last at the end of the thirteenth century—most Europeans were simply not willing to commit the vast resources and personnel that would have been necessary to maintain the crusader states. They fell to the Muslims permanently in 1291.

Review: What were the causes and consequences of the Gregorian Reform?

❖ The Revival of Monarchies

Even as the papacy was exercising its new authority, kings and other rulers were enhancing and consolidating their own power. They created new ideologies and dusted off old theories to justify their hegemony, they hired officials to work for them, and they found vassals and churchmen to support them. Money gave them greater effectiveness, and the new commercial economy supplied them with increased revenues.

Reconstructing the Empire at Byzantium

In 1081, ten years after the disastrous battle at Manzikert, the energetic dynatoi Alexius Comnenus seized the Byzantine throne. It is no wonder that an artist of his times hopefully pictured him receiving Christ's blessing, for Alexius faced considerable unrest in Constantinople, whose populace suffered from a combination of high taxes and rising living costs. In addition, his empire was under attack on every side—from Normans in southern Italy, Seljuk Turks in Asia Minor, and new groups in the Balkans. But Alexius I (r. 1081–1118) managed to turn actual and potential enemies against one another, staving off immediate defeat.

Alexius Comnenus Stands before Christ
In this twelfth-century manuscript illumination, the Byzantine emperor Alexius is shown in the presence of Christ. Note that both are almost exactly the same height, and the halos around their heads are the same size. What do you suppose is the significance of Christ sitting on a throne while the emperor is standing? Compare this image of the emperor with that on page 323. What statement is the twelfth-century artist making about the relationship between Christ and Alexius? *Biblioteca Apostolica Vaticana.*

When Alexius asked Pope Urban II to supply him with some European troops to fight his enemies, he was shocked and disappointed to learn that crusaders rather than mercenaries were on the way. His daughter, Anna Comnena (1083–c. 1148), who wrote an account of the crusades from the Byzantine perspective in a book about her father, the *Alexiad*, considered the crusaders barbarians:

> The Latin race [the Europeans] at all times is unusually greedy for wealth, but when it plans to invade a country, neither reason nor force can restrain it. They set out helter-skelter, regardless of their individual companies. Near the Drakon [River] they fell into the Turkish [ambush] and were miserably slaughtered. . . . Some men of the same race as [those] slaughtered barbarians later . . . used the bones of the dead as pebbles to fill up the cracks [of a wall].

To wage all the wars he had to fight, Alexius relied on mercenaries and allied dynatoi, who were armed and mounted like European knights and accompanied by their own troops. In return for their services he gave these nobles lifetime possession of large imperial estates and their dependent peasants. Meanwhile, Alexius satisfied the urban elite by granting them new offices. He normally got on well with the patriarch and Byzantine clergy, for emperor and church depended on each other to suppress heresy and foster orthodoxy. The emperors of the Comnenian dynasty (1081–1185) thus gained a measure of increased power, but at the price of important concessions to the nobility.

In the eleventh and early twelfth centuries, Constantinople remained a rich, sophisticated, and highly cultured city. Sculptors and other artists strove to depict ideals of human beauty and elegance. Churches built during the period were decorated with elaborate depictions of the cosmos. Significant innovations occurred in the realm of Byzantine scholarship and literature. The neo-Platonic tradition of late antiquity had always influenced Byzantine religious and philosophical thought, but now scholars renewed their interest in the wellsprings of classical Greek philosophy, particularly Plato and Aristotle. The rediscovery of ancient culture inspired Byzantine writers to reintroduce old forms into the grammar, vocabulary, and rhetorical style of Greek literature. Anna Comnena wrote her *Alexiad* in this newly learned Greek and prided herself on "having read thoroughly the treatises of Aristotle and the dialogues of Plato." The revival of ancient Greek writings, especially Plato's, in eleventh- and twelfth-century Byzantium had profound consequences for both eastern and western European civilization in centuries to come, as their ideas slowly penetrated European culture.

England under Norman Rule

In the twelfth century the kings of England were the most powerful monarchs of Europe because they ruled their whole kingdom by right of conquest. When the Anglo-Saxon king Edward the Confessor (r. 1042–1066) died childless in 1066, three main contenders desired the English throne: Harold, earl of Wessex, an Englishman close to the king but not of royal blood; Harald Hardrada,♦ the king of Norway, who had unsuccessfully attempted to conquer the Danes and now turned hopefully to England; and William, duke of Normandy, who claimed that Edward had promised him the throne fifteen years earlier. On his deathbed, Edward had named Earl Harold to succeed him, and the witan, a royal advisory committee that had the right to choose the king, had confirmed the nomination.

The Norman Invasion, 1066. When he learned that Harold had been anointed and crowned, William (1027–1087) prepared for battle. Appealing to the pope, he received the banner of St. Peter, and with this symbol of God's approval William launched the invasion of England, filling his ships with warriors recruited from many parts of France. About a week before William's invasion force landed, Harold defeated Harald Hardrada at Stamford Bridge, near York, in the north of England. When he heard of William's arrival, Harold turned his forces south, marching them 250 miles and picking up new soldiers along the way to meet the Normans.

♦**Hardrada:** HAWR raw duh

The two armies clashed at Hastings on October 14, 1066, in one of history's rare decisive battles. Both armies had about seven or eight thousand men, Harold's in defensive position on a slope, William's attacking from below. All the men were crammed into a very small space as they began the fight. Most of Harold's men were on foot, armed with battle-axes and stones tied to sticks, which could be thrown with great force. William's army consisted of perhaps three thousand mounted knights, a thousand archers, and the rest infantry. At first William's knights broke rank, frightened by the deadly battle-axes thrown by the English; but then some of the English also broke rank as they pursued the knights. William removed his helmet so his men would know him, rallying them to surround and cut down the English who had broken away. Similar skirmishes lasted the entire afternoon, and gradually Harold's troops were worn down, particularly by William's archers, whose arrows flew a hundred yards, much farther than an Englishman could throw his battle-ax. (Some of the archers are depicted on the lower margin of the Bayeux "Tapestry" on the following page.) By dusk, King Harold was dead and his army utterly defeated. No other army gathered to oppose the successful claimant.

Some people in England gladly supported William, considering his victory a verdict from God and hoping to gain a place in the new order themselves. But William—known to posterity as William the Conqueror—wanted to replace, not assimilate, the Anglo-Saxons. In the course of William's reign, families from the continent almost totally supplanted the English aristocracy. And although the English peasantry remained—now with new lords—they were severely shaken. A twelfth-century historian claimed to record William's deathbed confession:

Legend:
- The Anglo-Norman realm
- William
- Harold

0   100   200 miles
0   100   200 kilometers

SCOTLAND

North Sea

York

ENGLAND

Hastings 1066
Wessex

Canterbury
Flanders

Normandy

Norman Conquest of England, 1066

Bayeux "Tapestry" (detail)
This famous "tapestry" is misnamed; it is really an embroidery, 231 feet long and 20 inches wide, that was made to tell the story of the Norman conquest of England from William's point of view. In this detail, the Norman archers are lined up along the lower margin, in a band below the armies. In the central band, the English warriors are on foot (the one at the farthest right holds a long battle-ax), while the Norman knights are on horseback. Who seems to be winning? Compare the armor and fighting gear shown here with that shown on page 344. **For more help analyzing this image**, see the visual activity for this chapter in the Online Study Guide at **bedfordstmartins .com/hunt**. *Tapisserie de Bayeux. By special permission of the City of Bayeux, France.*

> *I have persecuted [England's] native inhabitants beyond all reason. Whether gentle or simple, I have cruelly oppressed them; many I unjustly disinherited; innumerable multitudes, especially in the county of York, perished through me by famine or the sword.*

Modern historians estimate that one out of five people in England died as a result of the Norman conquest and its immediate aftermath.

Institutions of Norman Kingship. Although the Normans destroyed a generation of English men and women, they preserved and extended many Anglo-Saxon institutions. For example, the new kings used writs—terse written instructions—to communicate orders, and they retained the old administrative divisions and legal system of the shires (counties). The Norman kings also drew from continental institutions. They set up a graded political hierarchy, culminating in the king, whose strength was enforced by his castles and made visible to all. Because all of England was the king's by conquest, he could treat it as his booty; William kept about 20 percent of the land for himself and divided the rest, distributing it in large but scattered fiefs to a relatively small number of his barons and family members, lay and ecclesiastical, as well as to some lesser men, such as personal servants and soldiers. In turn these men maintained their own vassals; they owed the king military service (and the service of a fixed number of their vassals) along with certain dues, such as **reliefs** (money paid upon inheriting a fief) and **aids** (payments made on important occasions).

Domesday. Apart from the revenues and rights expected from the nobles, the king of England commanded the peasantry as well. Twenty years after his conquest, in 1086, William ordered a survey and census of England, popularly called Domesday because, like the records of people judged at doomsday, it provided facts that could not be appealed. It was the most extensive inventory of land, livestock, taxes, and population that had ever been compiled in Europe. (See "Taking Measure.") The king

> sent his men over all England into every shire and had them find out how many hundred hides [a measure of land] there were in the shire, or what land and cattle the king himself had in the country, or what dues he ought to receive every year from the shire. . . . So very narrowly did he have the survey to be made that there was not a single hide or yard of land, nor indeed . . . an ox or a cow or a pig left out.

The king's men conducted local surveys by consulting Anglo-Saxon tax lists and by taking testimony from local jurors, men sworn to answer a series of formal questions truthfully. From these inquests scribes wrote voluminous reports filled with facts and statements from villagers, sheriffs, priests, and barons. These reports were then summarized in Domesday itself, a concise record of England's resources that supplied the king and his officials with information such as how much and what sort of land England had, who held it, and what revenues—including the lucrative *Danegeld*, which was now in effect a royal tax—could be expected from it.

England and the Continent. The Norman conquest tied England to the languages, politics, institutions, and culture of the continent. Modern English is an amalgam of Anglo-Saxon and Norman French, the language the Normans spoke. English commerce was linked to the wool industry in Flanders. St. Anselm (1033–1109), the archbishop of Canterbury in England, had been born in Italy and served as the abbot of a monastery in Normandy before crossing the Channel to England.

The barons of England retained their estates in Normandy and elsewhere, and the kings of England often spent more time on the continent than they did on the island. When William's son Henry I (r. 1100–1135) died without male heirs, civil war soon erupted: the throne of England was fought over by two French counts, one married to Henry's daughter, the other to his sister. The story of England after 1066 was, in miniature, the story of Europe.

Praising the King of France

The twelfth-century kings of France were much less obviously powerful than their English and Byzantine counterparts. Yet they, too, took part in the monarchical revival. Louis VI, called Louis the Fat (r. 1108–1137), so heavy that he had to be hoisted onto his

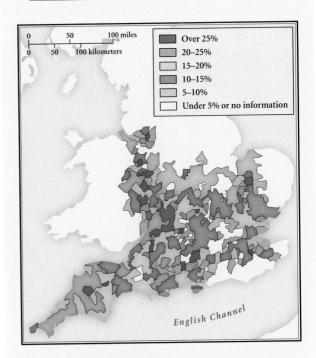

TAKING MEASURE

Slaves in England in 1086
Domesday provided important data for the English king in 1086, and those data remain important for historians today. We can see from this distribution map based on the data in Domesday, for example, that slavery was an important institution in eleventh-century England. The slaves, who were bought and sold, had no land of their own; they cultivated the land of their lord. Slavery was most important in the west of England, while free peasants dominated in the east. *Adapted from H. C. Darby,* Domesday England *(Cambridge: Cambridge University Press, 1977). Reprinted with the permission of Cambridge University Press.*

horse by a crane, was a tireless defender of royal power. We know a good deal about him and his reputation because a contemporary and close associate, Suger (1081–1152), abbot of St. Denis, wrote Louis's biography. Suger also tutored Louis's son Louis VII (r. 1137–1180) and acted as regent of France when Louis VII left to lead the Second Crusade in 1147.

Suger was a chronicler and propagandist for Louis the Fat. When Louis set himself the task of consolidating his rule in the Île-de-France,♦ Suger portrayed the king as a righteous hero. He thought of the king as the head of a political hierarchy in which Louis had rights over the French nobles because they were his vassals or because they broke the peace. Suger also believed that Louis had a religious role: to protect the church and the poor. He viewed Louis as another Charlemagne, a ruler for all society, not merely an overlord of the nobility. Louis waged war to keep God's peace. To be sure, the Gregorian reform had made its mark: Suger did not claim Louis was the head of the church, but he emphasized the royal dignity and its importance to the papacy. When a pope happened to arrive in France, Louis, not yet king, and his father, Philip I (r. 1052–1108), bowed low, but "the pope lifted them up and made them sit before him like devout sons of the apostles. In the manner of a wise man acting wisely, he conferred with them privately on the present condition of the church." Here the pope was shown needing royal advice. Meanwhile, Suger stressed Louis's piety and active defense of the faith:

> Helped by his powerful band of armed men, or rather by the hand of God, he abruptly seized the castle [of Crécy] and captured its very strong tower as if it were simply the hut of a peasant. Having startled those criminals, he piously slaughtered the impious.

When Louis VI died in 1137, Suger's notion of the might and right of the king of France reflected reality in an extremely small area. Nevertheless, Louis laid the groundwork for the gradual extension of royal power in France. As the lord of vassals, the king could call upon his men to aid him in times of war, though the most powerful among them sometimes disregarded his wishes and chose not to help. As a king and landlord, he could obtain many dues and taxes. He also drew revenues from Paris, a thriving city not only of commerce but also of scholarship. Officials, called provosts, enforced his royal laws and collected taxes. With money and land, Louis could dispense the favors and give the gifts that added to his prestige and his power. Louis VI and Suger together created the territorial core and royal ideal of the future French monarchy.

Review: Which ruler—Alexius, William the Conqueror, or Louis VI—was the strongest, which the feeblest, and why?

❖ New Forms of Scholarship and Religious Expression

The commercial revolution, the newly organized church, and the revived monarchies of the eleventh and twelfth centuries set the stage for the growth of schools and for new forms of scholarship. Money and career opportunities attracted unheard-of numbers of students to city schools. Worldly motivations were, however, equaled by spiritual ones. The movement for church reform stressed the importance of the church and its beliefs. Many students and teachers in the twelfth century sought knowledge to make their faith clearer and deeper.

Other people in the twelfth century, however, sought to avoid the cities and the schools. Some found refuge in the measured ceremonies and artistic splendor of Benedictine monasteries such as Cluny. Others considered these vast monastic complexes to be ostentatious and worldly. Rejecting the opulence of cities and the splendor of well-endowed monasteries alike, they pursued a monastic life of poverty.

But many people did not choose definitively one place or the other. Some shuttled back and forth between monasteries and city schools. Others, such as Bruno of

♦**Île-de-France:** eel duh FRAHNS

Cologne, imported the learning of the schools into their religious life. Others decidedly did not; yet the new learning, like the new commerce, had a way of seeping into the cracks and crannies of even the most resolutely separate institutions.

Schools and the Liberal Arts

Schools had been connected to monasteries and cathedrals since the Carolingian period. They served to train new recruits to become either monks or priests. Some were better endowed with books and masters (or teachers) than others; a few developed a reputation for a certain kind of theological approach or specialized in a branch of learning, such as literature, medicine, or law. By the end of the eleventh century, the best schools were generally in the larger cities: Reims, Paris, Bologna,♦ Montpellier.♦

Eager students sampled nearly all of them. The young monk Gilbert of Liège♦ was typical: "Instilled with an insatiable thirst for learning, whenever he heard of somebody excelling in the arts, he rushed immediately to that place and drank whatever delightful potion he could draw from the master there." For Gilbert and other students, a good lecture had the excitement of theater. Teachers at cathedral schools found themselves forced to find larger halls to accommodate the crush of students. Other teachers simply declared themselves "masters" and set up shop by renting a room. If they could prove their mettle in the classroom, they had no trouble finding paying students (see A Teacher and His Students, on this page).

"Wandering scholars" like Gilbert were probably all male, and because schools had hitherto been the training ground for clergymen, all students were considered clerics, whether or not they had been ordained. Wandering became a way of life as the consolidation of castellanies, counties, and kingdoms made violence against travelers less frequent. Urban centers soon responded to the needs of transients with markets, taverns, and lodgings.

♦**Bologna:** boh LOH nyuh
♦**Montpellier:** mohn peh LYAY
♦**Liège:** lee EHZH

A Teacher and His Students
This miniature expresses the hierarchical relationship between students and teachers in the twelfth century. But there is more. The miniature appears in a late-twelfth-century manuscript of a commentary written by Gilbert (d. 1154), bishop of Poitiers. Gilbert's ideas in this commentary provoked the ire of St. Bernard, who accused Gilbert of heresy. But Gilbert escaped condemnation. This artist asserts Gilbert's orthodoxy by depicting Gilbert with a halo, in the full dress of a bishop, speaking from his throne. Below Gilbert are three of his disciples, also with halos. The artist's positive view of Gilbert is echoed by modern historians, who recognize Gilbert as a pioneer in his approach to scriptural commentary. *Bibliothèque Municipale de Valenciennes*

Using Latin, Europe's common language, students could drift from, say, Italy to Spain, Germany, England, and France, wherever a noted master had settled. Along with crusaders, pilgrims, and merchants, students made the roads of Europe very crowded indeed.

What the students sought, above all, was knowledge of the seven liberal arts. Grammar, rhetoric, and logic (or dialectic) belonged to the "beginning" arts, the so-called **trivium.**♦ Logic, involving the technical analysis of texts as well as the application and manipulation of mental constructs, was a transitional subject leading to the second part of the liberal arts, the quadrivium. This comprised four areas of study that we might call theoretical math and science: arithmetic, geometry, music (theory rather than practice), and astronomy. Of all these arts, twelfth-century students were most interested in logic. Medieval students and masters were convinced that logic could bring together, order, and clarify every issue, even questions about the nature of God. Thus St. Anselm, who was a major theologian as well as an abbot and archbishop, saw logic as a way for faith to "seek understanding." Emptying his mind of all ideas except that of God, he used the tools of logic to prove God's existence.

After studying the trivium, students went on to schools of medicine, theology, or law. Paris was renowned for theology, Montpellier for medicine, and Bologna for law. All of these schools trained men for jobs. The law schools, for example, taught men who went on to serve popes, bishops, kings, princes, and communes. Scholars interested in the quadrivium, by contrast, tended to pursue those studies outside of the normal school curriculum, and few gained their living through such pursuits.

Scholars of the New Learning

The remarkable renewal of scholarship in the twelfth century had an unexpected benefit: we know a great deal about the men involved in it—and a few of the women—because they wrote so much, often about themselves. Three important figures typify the scholars of the period: Abelard and Heloise, who embraced the new learning wholeheartedly and retired to monasteries only when forced to do so; and Hildegard of Bingen, who happily spent most of her life in a cloister yet wrote knowingly about the world.

Abelard and Heloise. Born into a family of the petty (lesser) French Breton nobility and destined for a career as a warrior and lord, Peter Abelard (1079–1142) instead became one of the twelfth century's greatest thinkers. In his autobiographical account, *Historia calamitatum*♦ (*The Story of My Misfortunes*), Abelard describes his shift from the life of the warrior to the life of the scholar:

> I was so carried away by my love of learning, that I renounced the glory of a soldier's life, made over my inheritance and rights of the eldest son to my brothers, and withdrew from the court of Mars [war] in order to kneel at the feet of Minerva [learning].

Arriving eventually at Paris, Abelard studied with William of Champeaux♦ and then challenged his teacher's scholarship. He had nothing but scorn for William's position on "universals," one of the most controversial topics of the day. The question was whether a universal (something that can be said of more than one thing, such as *cat* may be said of Puffy and Fluffy) is real or just a mental category or manner of speaking. William taught that the species (such as *cat*) was indeed real. (We call such thinkers realists.) Others (people who were later called nominalists) claimed that the species was just a word. Abelard took a middle position, maintaining that the species did have a sort of reality, as the common "status" of Puffy and Fluffy.

Later in the twelfth century, scholars discovered that Aristotle had elaborated tools of logic to solve this and other problems. But until midcentury, very little of Aristotle's work was available in Europe because it had not been translated from Greek into Latin. By the end of the century, however, that situation had been rectified by translators who traveled to cities such as Córdoba in Spain and Syracuse in Sicily, where they found Islamic scholars who had already translated Aristotle's Greek into Arabic and could help them translate from Arabic to Latin. (See "Did You Know?," page 387.)

♦**trivium:** TRIH vee uhm

♦*Historia calamitatum:* hihs TAWR ee uh ka lam ih TAYT uhm
♦**Champeaux:** sham Poh

DID YOU KNOW?

Translations

Tlumaczenie! Do you know what that means? If you don't, it's easy enough to find out. Today there are many dictionaries, translators, and interpreters for almost every one of the world's three thousand languages. But for most of history, this has not been the case. In the Middle Ages, dictionaries and interpreters were very rare. The great writings of the three heirs of the Roman Empire—the Byzantine, Muslim, and European—were largely unavailable across cultures. This kept these societies from knowing about and benefiting from one another. And of the three, Europe was the most isolated.

In the twelfth century this began to change. The same Europeans who flocked to the city schools knew vaguely about Arabic philosophical learning, and they ached to know more. Some of them traveled to the peripheries of Europe, in particular, to Palermo, in Sicily, where Greek, Arabic, and Latin were all official languages. Palermo was unique as a European city that supported a diversity of languages and people who could read and write in a number of them. Some people from France, Germany, England, and northern Italy who wanted to read books in languages other than Latin went to Palermo to learn how to become translators or to find others to do the job.

Others headed to Spain, where they worked with Jewish converts to Christianity. Rather than learn Arabic, they relied on these converts to translate from Arabic into Spanish. Then the Europeans translated from Spanish into Latin. It was in this roundabout way that Aristotle's works were rediscovered in Arabic translation, that Arabic medical treatises were read, that the Qur'an became known outside of the Islamic world, that Arabic love poetry came to inspire medieval songwriters, and that Arabic mathematical breakthroughs, including the discovery of algebra and the use of Arabic numerals, came to Latin-speaking Europe.

By the way, the word *tlumaczenie* (pronounced "twoo-ma-CHAIN-yeh") means "translation" in Polish.

Translating the Qur'an into Latin (mid-twelfth century)
Those who originally translated the Qur'an into Latin wanted not so much to understand the Islamic religion better as to refute it more soundly. In 1142 the abbot of Cluny, Peter the Venerable, made a trip to Spain and commissioned some scholars there to make the first Latin translation of the Qur'an. In the prologue to his *Book Against the Sect or Heresy of the Saracens,* he explained why:

> *Because the Latin-speaking peoples, and most particularly those of recent times, losing their ancient zeal, according to the maxim of the Jews, have not known the various languages of the former wonderful Apostles, but only their own language into which they were born, in that condition they could not know what such an error [as Islam] was or, consequently, put up any resistance to it. For this reason "my heart glowed within me and a flame was enkindled in my meditation" (Ps. 38.4). I was indignant that the Latins did not know the cause of such perdition and, by that ignorance, could not be moved to put up any resistance; for there was no one who replied [to Islam] because there was simply no one who knew [about it].*

Source: Quoted and translated in James Kritzeck, *Peter the Venerable and Islam,* Princeton Oriental Studies 23 (Princeton, N.J., 1964), 30.

After his confrontation with William of Champeaux, Abelard began to lecture and to gather students of his own. Around 1122–1123, he composed a textbook for his students that consisted of opposing positions on 156 subjects, among them "That God is one and the contrary," "That all are permitted to marry and the contrary," "That it is permitted to kill men and the contrary." Arrayed on both sides of each question were passages from the Bible, the church fathers, the letters of popes, and other sources. The juxtaposition of authoritative sentences was nothing new; what was new was calling attention to their contradictions. Abelard's students loved the challenge: they were eager to find the origins of the quotes, consider the context of each one carefully, and seek a reconciliation of the opposing sides. Abelard wrote that his method "excite[d] young readers to the maximum of effort in inquiring into the truth." In fact, in Abelard's view the inquiring student followed the model of Christ himself, who as a boy sat among the rabbis, questioning them.

Abelard's fame as a teacher was such that a Parisian cleric named Fulbert gave Abelard room and board and engaged him as tutor for Heloise (c. 1100–c. 1163/1164), Fulbert's niece. Heloise is one of the few learned women of the period who left written traces. (Hildegard is another.) Brought up under Fulbert's guardianship, Heloise had been sent as a young girl to a convent school, where she received a thorough grounding in literary skills. Her uncle had hoped to continue her education at home by hiring Abelard. Abelard, however, became Heloise's lover as well as her tutor. "Our desires left no stage of love-making untried," wrote Abelard in his *Historia*. At first their love affair was secret. But Heloise became pregnant, and Abelard insisted they marry. They did so clandestinely to prevent damaging Abelard's career, for the new emphasis on clerical celibacy meant that Abelard's professional success and prestige would have been compromised if news of his marriage were made public. After they were married, Heloise and Abelard rarely saw one another; their child, Astrolabe, was raised by Abelarde's sister. Fulbert, suspecting foul play, plotted a cruel punishment: he paid a servant to castrate Abelard. Soon after, both husband and wife entered separate monasteries.

For Heloise, separation from Abelard was a lasting blow. Although she became a successful abbess, carefully tending to the physical and spiritual needs of her nuns, she continued to call on Abelard for "renewal of strength." In a series of letters addressed to him, she poured out her feelings as "his handmaid, or rather his daughter, wife, or rather sister":

You know, beloved, as the whole world knows, how much I have lost in you, how at one wretched stroke of fortune that supreme act of flagrant treachery robbed me of my very self in robbing me of you. . . . You alone have the power to make me sad, to bring me happiness or comfort.

For Abelard, however, the loss of Heloise and even his castration were not the worst disasters of his life. The cruelest blow came later, and it was directed at his intellect. He wrote a book that applied "human and logical reasons" (as he put it) to the Trinity; the book was condemned at the Council of Soissons in 1121, and he was forced to throw it, page by page, into the flames. Bitterly weeping at the injustice, Abelard lamented, "This open violence had come upon me only because of the purity of my intentions and love of our Faith, which had compelled me to write."

Hildegard of Bingen.   Unlike Abelard and Heloise, Hildegard (1098–1179) did not actively seek to become a scholar. Placed in a German convent at age eight, she received her schooling there and took vows as a nun. In 1136, she was elected abbess of the convent. Shortly thereafter, very abruptly, she began to write and to preach, an activity normally reserved for bishops. In addition, Hildegard addressed fearless letters of advice and admonition to the churchmen and rulers of her day.

Writing and preaching were the external manifestations of an inner life that had been extraordinary from the beginning. Even as a child, Hildegard had had visions—of invisible things, of the future, and (always) of a special kind of light. These visions were intermingled with pain and sickness. Only in her forties did Hildegard interpret her sickness and her visions as gifts from God; she thought her fragility made the visions possible. In her *Scivias*♦ ("Know the Ways of the Lord," 1151), Hildegard describes some of her visions and explains what they meant. She interprets them as containing nothing less than the full story of creation and redemption, a summa, or compendium, of church doctrine.

The *Scivias* was not just a text. Accompanying Hildegard's words were vivid

---

♦*Scivias:* SKIH Vee uhs

Hildegard of Bingen
The illustrations that Hildegard commissioned for her *Scivias* have been lost since the end of World War II, but a hand-drawn copy from 1920 has survived. This image from the copy shows Hildegard at the beginning of the book, where she writes, "Heaven was opened and a fiery light . . . came and permeated my whole brain. . . . And immediately I knew the meaning of the . . . Scriptures." In this miniature, the fiery light comes down in the form of giant red fingers to cover Hildegard's head, while she holds a wax tablet and stylus to write with. The monk peeking through the door is Volmar, who served as Hildegard's secretary.
Photograph by Erich Lessing/Art Resource.

illustrations—one of which is reproduced here—of her visions, probably painted by a nun under her supervision. For the final vision of the book, Hildegard added fourteen pieces of music. And at the conclusion of the entire *Scivias*, Hildegard appended a play, the leading roles taken by the Virtues, the Soul, and the Devil. She later expanded this and set it to music.

Hildegard's inventiveness was not confined to religious and artistic matters. During the 1150s, she wrote two scientific treatises, one focused on diseases and herbal remedies, the other on subjects ranging from animals and plants to gemstones and metallurgy. For Hildegard, knowledge of God made the world intelligible.

Benedictine Monks and Artistic Splendor

Hildegard's appreciation of worldly things as expressions of God's splendor was typical of Benedictine monks and nuns in the twelfth century. They spent nearly their entire day in large and magnificently outfitted churches singing an expanded and complex liturgy. Hildegard's music was added to the liturgical round at her convent, for example.

In the context of the new monastic movements stressing poverty, the Benedictines were old-fashioned. Yet the "black monks"—so called because they dyed their robes black—reached the height of their popularity in the eleventh century. Monasteries often housed hundreds of monks; convents for nuns were usually less populated. Cluny was one of the largest monasteries, with some four hundred brothers in the mid-eleventh century.

The chief occupation of the monks, as befitted (in their view) citizens of heaven, was prayer. The black monks and nuns devoted themselves to singing the Psalms and other prayers specified in the rule of St. Benedict, adding to them still more Psalms. The rule called for chanting the entire Psalter—150 psalms—over the course of a week, but some monks, like those at Cluny, chanted that number in a day.

Gregorian Chant.   Prayer was neither private nor silent. Black monks had to know not only the words but also the music that went with their prayers; they had to be musicians. The music of the Benedictine monastery was plainchant, also known as Gregorian chant, which consisted of melodies sung in unison and without instrumental accompaniment. Although chant was rhythmically free, lacking a regular beat, its melodies ranged from

empire. Musical notation was developed to help monks remember unfamiliar melodies and to ensure that the tunes were sung in approximately the same way in all parts of the Carolingian realm. The melodies were further mastered and organized at this time by fitting them into the Byzantine system of eight modes, or scales. This music survived the dissolution of the Carolingian Empire and remained the core of the music of the Catholic church into the twentieth century.

Romanesque Style.　The new emphasis on the liturgy meant that churches would echo throughout the day to the sounds of chanting monks. The building boom that gave towns their walls and houses extended to churches as well. The style of many of these buildings of the twelfth century was later called **Romanesque**. Although they varied greatly, most Romanesque churches had massive stone and masonry walls decorated on the interior with paintings in bright colors. (See the illustration of St.-Savin, on page 393) The various parts of the church—the chapels in the *chevet* (the east end), for example—were handled as discrete units, retaining the forms of cubes, cones, and cylinders (Figure 10.1). Inventive sculptural reliefs, both inside and outside the church, enlivened these pristine geometrical forms. Emotional and sometimes frenzied, Romanesque sculpture depicted themes ranging from the beauty of Eve (see the sinuous one from the monastery of Autun on this page) to the horrors of the Last Judgment.

In such a setting, gilded reliquaries and altars made of silver, precious gems, and pearls were the fitting accoutrements of worship. Prayer, liturgy, and music in this way complemented the gift economy of the early Middle Ages: richly clad in vestments of the finest materials, intoning the liturgy in the most splendid of churches, monks and priests offered up the gift of prayer to God; in return they begged for the gift of salvation of their souls and the souls of all the faithful.

New Monastic Orders of Poverty

But at the end of the eleventh century the old gift economy was being replaced by a new one, based on profit. Now many people con-

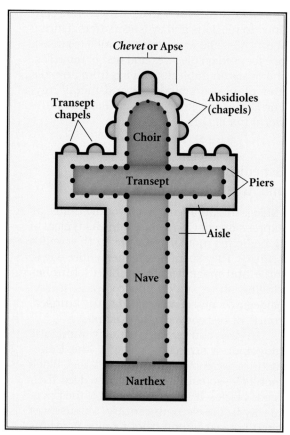

FIGURE 10.1　Floor Plan of a Romanesque Church
As churchgoers entered a Romanesque church, they passed through the narthex, an anteroom decorated with sculptures depicting important scenes from the Bible. Walking through the portal of the narthex, they entered the church's nave, at the east end of which—just after the crossing of the transept and in front of the choir—was the altar. Walking down the nave, they passed massive, tall piers leading up to the vaulting (the ceiling) of the nave. Each of these piers was decorated with sculpture, and the walls were brightly painted. Romanesque churches were both lively and colorful (because of their decoration) and solemn and somber (because of their heavy stones and massive scale).

extremely simple to highly ornate and embellished. By the twelfth century, a large repertoire of melodies had grown up, at first through oral composition and transmission and then in written notation, which first appeared in manuscripts of the ninth century.

The melodies preserved by this early notation probably originated in Rome and had been introduced into northern Europe at the command of Charlemagne, who wanted to standardize the liturgical practices of his

sidered opulence to be a sign of greed rather than honor. They rejected wealth and embraced poverty as a key element of religious life. The Carthusian order founded by Bruno of Cologne was one such group. Each monk took a vow of silence and lived as a hermit in his own small hut. Monks occasionally joined others for prayer in a common prayer room, or oratory. When not engaged in prayer or meditation, the Carthusians copied manuscripts. They considered this task part of their religious vocation, a way to preach God's word with their hands rather than their mouths.

Eve
The Romanesque sculptor of this depiction of Eve delighted in her sinuous curves, which he portrayed as a continuation of the snake from which Eve accepted the apple. Compare this seductive view of Eve with the motherly Eve on page 318. Sculptural figures such as this one, which once adorned the church at Autun, France and the shoemaker on page 363, were typical of the inventive variety of the Romanesque style. © Musée Rodin, Autun, France/Peter Willi/SuperStock.

The Carthusian order grew slowly. Each monastery was limited to only twelve monks, the number of the Apostles.

The Cistercians,♦ in contrast, expanded rapidly. The first Cistercian house, founded in 1098, was at Cîteaux♦ (in Latin, Cistercium) in France. But the guiding spirit and preeminent Cistercian abbot was St. Bernard (c. 1090–1153), who arrived at Cîteaux in 1112 along with about thirty friends and relatives. Soon he became abbot of Clairvaux, one of a cluster of Cistercian monasteries in Burgundy. By the mid-twelfth century, more than three hundred monasteries spread throughout Europe were following what they took to be the customs of Cîteaux. Nuns too—as eager as monks to live the life of simplicity and poverty that they believed the Apostles had enjoyed and endured—adopted Cistercian customs. By the end of the twelfth century, the Cistercians were an order: all of their houses followed rules determined at a General Chapter, a meeting at which the abbots met to hammer out legislation for the whole order.

Although they held up the rule of St. Benedict as the foundation of their monastic life, the Cistercians elaborated a style of life all their own, largely governed by the goal of simplicity. Rejecting even the conceit of blackening their robes, they left them undyed (hence their nickname, the "white monks").

Cistercian churches, though built of stone, were initially unlike the great Romanesque churches of the Benedictines. They were remarkably standardized; the church and the rest of the buildings of any Cistercian monastery were much like those of any other (Figure 10.2). The churches were small, made of smoothly hewn, undecorated stone. Wall paintings and sculpture were prohibited. St. Bernard wrote a scathing attack on Romanesque sculpture in which he acknowledged, in spite of himself, its exceptional allure:

What is the point of ridiculous monstrosities in the cloister where there are brethren reading—I mean those extraordinary deformed beauties and beautiful deformities? What are those lascivious apes doing, those fierce lions, monstrous centaurs, half-men and spotted leopards? . . . It is more diverting to decipher marble than the text before you.

♦**Cistercians:** sihs TUR shuhns
♦**Cîteaux:** see TOH

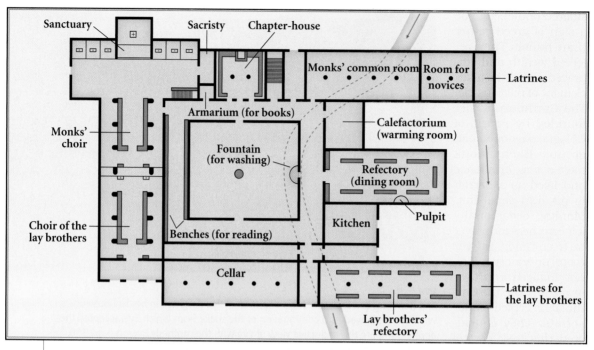

FIGURE 10.2 Floor Plan of a Cistercian Monastery

Cistercian monasteries seldom deviated much from this standard plan, which perfectly suited their double lifestyle—one half for the lay brothers, who worked in the fields, the other half for the monks, who performed the devotions. This plan shows the first floor. Above were the dormitories. The lay brothers slept above their cellar and refectory, the monks above their chapter house, common room, and room for novices. No one had a private bedroom, just as the rule of St. Benedict prescribed. *Adapted from Wolfgang Braunfels,* Monasteries of Western Europe *(Princeton, N.J.: Princeton University Press, 1972), 75.*

The Cistercians had no such visual diversions, but the simplicity of their buildings and of their clothing also had its beauty. Illuminated by the pure white light that came through clear glass windows, Cistercian houses like the one at Eberbech, illustrated on this page, were luminous, cool, and serene.

True to this emphasis on purity, the communal liturgy of the Cistercians was simplified and shorn of the many additions found in the houses of the black monks. Only the liturgy as prescribed in the rule of St. Benedict plus one daily Mass were allowed. Even the music for the chant was changed; the Cistercians rigorously suppressed the B-flat, even though doing so made the melody discordant, because of their insistence on strict simplicity.

With their time partly freed from the choir, the white monks dedicated themselves to private prayer and contemplation and to monastic administration. Each house had large and highly organized farms and grazing lands called granges. Cistercian monks spent much of their time managing their estates and flocks, both of which yielded handsome profits by the end of the twelfth century. Clearly part of the agricultural and commercial revolutions of the Middle Ages, the Cistercian order made managerial expertise a part of the monastic life.

At the same time, the Cistercians elaborated a spirituality of intense personal emotion. As St. Bernard said:

> *Often enough when we approach the altar to pray our hearts are dry and lukewarm. But if we persevere, there comes an unexpected infusion of grace, our breast expands as it were, and our interior is filled with an overflowing love.*

The Cistercians emphasized not only human emotion but also Christ's and Mary's humanity. While pilgrims continued to stream to the tombs and reliquaries of saints, the

St.-Savin-sur-Gartempe

The nave of the church of St.-Savin was built between 1095 and 1115. Its barrel (or tunnel) vault is typical of Romanesque churches, as is its sense of liveliness, variety, and color. The columns, decorated with striped or wavy patterns, are topped by carved capitals, each different from the next. The entire vault is covered with frescoes painted in shades of browns, ochers, and yellows depicting scenes from the Old Testament. Try to pick out the one that shows Noah's ark. Were such scenes meant to delight the worshipers? How would St. Bernard have answered this question? *Bridgeman–Giraudon/Art Resource, NY.*

Eberbech

Compare the nave of Eberbech, a Cistercian church built between 1170 and 1186, with that of St.-Savin. What at St.-Savin was full of variety and color is here subdued by order and calm. There are no wall paintings in a Cistercian church, no variegated columns, no distractions from the interior life of the worshiper. Yet, upon closer look, there are subtle points of interest. How has the architect played with angles, planes, and light in the vaulting? Are the walls utterly smooth? Can you see any decorative elements on the massive piers between the arches? *AKG London/ Stefan Drechsel.*

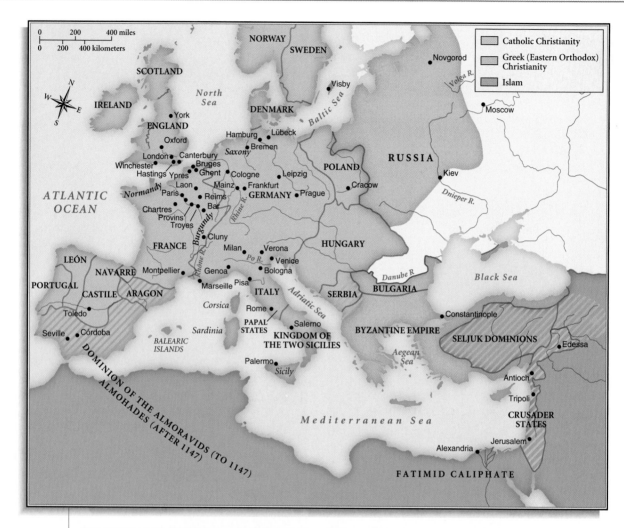

MAPPING THE WEST Major Religions in the West, c. 1150

The broad washes of color on this map tell a striking story: by 1150, there were three major religions, each corresponding to a broad region. To the west, north of the Mediterranean Sea, Catholic Christianity held sway; to the east, the Greek Orthodox Church was ascendent; all along the southern Mediterranean, Islam triumphed. Only a few places defied this logic: one was a tiny outpost of Catholic crusaders who ruled over a largely Muslim population. What this map does not show, however, are the details: Jewish communities in many cities, lively varieties of Islamic beliefs within the Muslim world, communities of Coptic Christians in Egypt, and scattered groups of heretics in Catholic lands.

Cistercians dedicated all their churches to the Virgin Mary (for whom they had no relics) because for them she signified the model of a loving mother. Indeed, the Cistercians regularly used maternal imagery (as St. Bernard's description invoking the metaphor of a flowing breast illustrates) to describe the nurturing care provided to humans by Jesus himself. The Cistercian Jesus was approachable, human, protective, even mothering.

Similar views of God were held by many who were not members of the Cistercian order; their spirituality signaled wider changes. For example, around 1099, St. Anselm wrote a theological treatise entitled *Why God Became Man* in which he argued that since man had sinned, only a sinless man could redeem him. St. Anselm's work represented a new theological emphasis on the redemptive power of human charity, including that of Jesus as a human being. The crusaders had trodden the very place of Christ's crucifixion, making his humanity both more real and more problematic to people who walked in the holy "place of God's humiliation and our redemption," as one chronicler put it. Yet this new stress on the loving bonds that tied Christians together also led to the persecution of others, like Jews and Muslims, who lived outside the Christian community.

> **Review:** To what degree and in what ways were religious life and thought influenced by the new learning of the schools?

Conclusion

The commercial revolution and the building boom it spurred profoundly changed Europe. New trade, wealth, and business institutions became common in its thriving cities. Merchants and artisans became important people. Mutual and fraternal organizations like the commune expressed and reinforced the solidarity and economic interest of city dwellers.

Political consolidation accompanied economic growth, as kings and popes exerted their authority and tested its limits. The Gregorian reform pitted the emperor against the pope, and two separate political hierarchies emerged, the secular and the ecclesiastical. The two might cooperate, as Suger and Louis VI did in mutual respect, admiration, and dependence; but they might also clash, as did Gregory VII and Henry IV. Secular and religious leaders developed new and largely separate systems of administration, reflecting in political life the new distinctions (such as clerical celibacy and allegiance to the pope) that differentiated clergy from laity. Although in some ways growing apart, the two groups never worked together so closely as in the crusades, military pilgrimages inspired by the pope and led by lay lords.

The commercial economy, political stability, and ecclesiastical needs fostered the growth of schools and the achievements of new scholarship. Young men like Abelard, who a generation before would have become knights, now sought education to enhance their careers and bring personal fulfillment.

Elite women like Heloise could gain an excellent basic education in a convent and then go on to higher studies. Logic fascinated students because it seemed to clarify what was real about themselves, the world, and God. Some churchmen, however, thought that faith could not be analyzed, and they forced Abelard to burn his book on the Trinity.

While Benedictine monks added to their hours of worship, built lavish churches, and devoted themselves to the music of the plainchant, a reformer such as St. Bernard insisted on an intense, interior spiritual life in a monastery austerely and directly based on the rule of St. Benedict. Other reformers, such as Bruno of Cologne, sought the high mountaintop for its isolation and hardship. These reformers repudiated urban society yet unintentionally reflected it: the Cistercians were as invested as any tradesman in the success of their granges, and the Carthusians were dedicated to their books.

The early twelfth century saw a period of renaissance and reform in the church, monarchies, and scholarship. The later twelfth century would be an age when people experimented with and rebelled against the various forms of authority.

Suggested References

The Commercial Revolution

The idea of a commercial revolution in the Middle Ages originated with Lopez. Little discusses some religious consequences. Hyde explores the society and government of the Italian communes.

Hyde, J. K. *Society and Politics in Medieval Italy: The Evolution of Civil Life, 1000–1350.* 1973.

Little, Lester K. *Religious Poverty and the Profit Economy in Medieval Europe.* 1978.

Lopez, Robert S. *The Commercial Revolution of the Middle Ages, 950–1350.* 1976.

*———, and Irving W. Raymond, *Medieval Trade in the Mediterranean World.* 1955.

Church Reform and Its Aftermath

The Investiture Conflict, which pitted the pope against the emperor, has been particularly important to German historians. Blumenthal gives

*Primary sources.

a useful overview. The consequences of church reform and the new papal monarchy included both the growth of canon law (see Brundage) and the crusades (see Riley-Smith).

Blumenthal, Uta-Renate. *The Investiture Controversy: Church & Monarchy from the 9th to the 12th Century.* 1991.

Brundage, James A. *Medieval Canon Law.* 1995.

Crusades: **http://www.medievalcrusades.com/**

*Peters, Edward, ed. *The First Crusade: The Chronicle of Fulcher of Chartres and Other Source Materials.* 1971.

Riley-Smith, Jonathan. *The Crusades. A Short History.* 1987.

———. *The First Crusaders, 1095–1131.* 1997.

Robinson, Ian S. *Henry IV of Germany.* 2000.

*Tierney, Brian, ed. *The Crisis of Church and State, 1050–1300.* 1964.

The Revival of Monarchies

The growth of monarchical power and the development of state institutions are topics of keen interest to historians. Clanchy points to the use of writing and recordkeeping in government. Suger shows the importance of the royal image. Douglas and Hallam discuss different aspects of the Norman conquest of England.

Chibnall, Marjorie. *Anglo-Norman England, 1066–1166.* 1986.

Clanchy, Michael. *From Memory to Written Record: England 1066–1307.* 2nd ed. 1993.

Douglas, David C. *William the Conqueror: The Norman Impact upon England.* 1967.

Dunbabin, Jean. *France in the Making, 843–1180.* 1985.

Grant, Lindy. *Abbot Suger of St-Denis: Church and State in Early Twelfth-Century France.* 1998.

Hallam, Elizabeth M. *Domesday Book through Nine Centuries.* 1986.

*Suger. *The Deeds of Louis the Fat.* Trans. Richard C. Cusimano and John Moorhead. 1992.

New Forms of Scholarship and Religious Expression

The new learning of the twelfth century was first called a renaissance by Haskins. Clanchy's more recent study looks less at the revival of the classics, stressing instead the social and political context of medieval teaching and learning. Recent research on religious developments include discussions of women in the new monastic movements of the twelfth century (Venarde), new views about the development of the Cistercian order (Berman), and new interpretations of the religious fervor of the period as a whole (Constable).

*Abelard's *The Story of My Misfortunes*: **http://www.fordham.edu/halsall/basis/abelard-histcal.html**.

Berman, Constance Hoffman. *The Cistercian Evolution: The Invention of a Religious Order in Twelfth-Century Europe.* 2000.

Bouchard, Constance Brittain. *"Every Valley Shall Be Exalted": The Discourse of Opposites in Twelfth-Century Thought.* 2003.

Clanchy, Michael. *Abelard: A Medieval Life.* 1997.

Constable, Giles. *The Reformation of the Twelfth Century.* 1996.

Haskins, Charles Homer. *The Renaissance of the Twelfth Century.* 1927.

Hildegard of Bingen: **http://www.hildegard.org/**

Hildegard von Bingen: Ordo virtutum, Deutsche Harmonia Mundi CD, 77394 (music from Hildegard's *Scivias* and the expanded play at its end).

The Letters of Abelard and Heloise. Trans. Betty Radice. 1974.

Venarde, Bruce L. *Women's Monasticism and Medieval Society: Nunneries in France and England, 890–1215.* 1997.

CHAPTER REVIEW

IMPORTANT EVENTS

910	Foundation of Cluny
1033–1109	St. Anselm, theologian, abbot, and archbishop of Canterbury
1046	Synod of Sutri
1049–1054	Papacy of Leo IX
1054	Great Schism between Latin and Greek church begins
1066	Norman conquest of England under William I
1071	Battle between Byzantines and Seljuk Turks at Manzikert
1073–1085	Papacy of Gregory VII
1077	Henry IV does penance before Gregory VII at Canossa; war breaks out
1079–1142	Peter Abelard
1086	Domesday survey
c. 1090–1153	St. Bernard
1095	Council of Clermont; Pope Urban II calls the First Crusade
1096–1099	First Crusade
1097	Establishment of commune at Milan
1098	Foundation of Cîteaux
1108–1137	Reign of Louis VI (Louis the Fat)
1109	Establishment of the Crusader States
1122	Concordat of Worms ends the Investiture Conflict
c. 1140	Gratian's *Decretum*, a systematic collection of canon law, published
1147–1149	Second Crusade
1151	*Scivias* written by Hildegard of Bingen

KEY TERMS

aids (382)

commercial revolution (360)

commune (364)

Great Schism (367)

Gregorian reform (367)

Investiture Conflict (368)

reconquista (367)

reliefs (382)

Romanesque (390)

Seljuk Turks (372)

simony (366)

trivium (386)

REVIEW QUESTIONS

1. What new professions and institutions arose as a result of the commercial revolution?
2. What were the causes and consequences of the Gregorian reform?
3. Which ruler—Alexius, William the Conqueror, or Louis VI—was the strongest, which the feeblest, and why?
4. To what degree and in what ways were religious life and thought influenced by the new learning of the schools?

MAKING CONNECTIONS

1. What were the similarities—and what were the differences—between the Carolingian renaissance and the twelfth-century schools?
2. What were the similarities—and what were the differences—between the powers wielded by the Carolingian kings and those wielded by twelfth-century rulers?

FOR FURTHER EXPLORATION

To assess your mastery of the material in this chapter, see the Online Study Guide at **bedfordstmartins.com/hunt**.

To read additional primary source material from this period, see Chapter 10 in *Sources of The Making of the West*, Second Edition, Volume I.

An Age of Confidence, 1150–1215

IN 1202, WITH THE MUSLIMS STILL OCCUPYING JERUSALEM, the pope called for a new crusade to the Holy Land. The Venetians fitted out a fine fleet of ships and galleys for the expedition, but when the crusaders arrived in Venice, there were far fewer fighters to pay for the transport than had been anticipated. To defray the costs of the ships and other expenses, the Venetians convinced the crusaders to do them some favors before taking off against the Muslims. First, they had the crusaders attack Zara,◆ a Christian city but Venice's competitor in the Adriatic. Then they had the army attack Constantinople itself, where the Venetians hoped to gain commercial advantage over their rivals. On April 12, 1204, Constantinople fell to the crusaders and the Byzantine Empire was reorganized under Western rule. The Venetians got just what they wanted: the harbor of Constantinople and new bases for an expanded maritime empire.

The planning, organization, assertiveness, and self-confidence of Venice in this episode was characteristic of the age. In the second half of the twelfth century, participants in government, commerce, and religion demanded—and created—permanent institutions and enhanced power. Kings, princes, popes, city dwellers, and even heretics were acutely conscious of themselves as individuals and as members of like-minded groups with identifiable objectives and plans to promote and perpetuate their aims. By about 1200, staffs of literate government officials were preserving both official documents and important papers; lords reckoned their profits with the help of accountants. Craft guilds and religious associations defined and regulated their memberships. The schools, which in the early

◆**Zara:** ZAH ruh

The Conquest of Constantinople in 1204
This mosaic, which was originally part of the sumptuous floor of the church of the Benedictine monastery of San Giovanni Evangelista in Ravenna (Italy), is one of several that illustrate episodes of the Fourth Crusade. Here the moment of capturing Constantinople is shown: the windowed tower symbolizes the gate of the city, and the man with the sword signifies a Western knight. The mosaic was produced less than ten years after the event, probably to celebrate the election of Francesco Morosini, the abbot of a monastery closely tied to San Giovanni, as Patriarch—the *Catholic* Patriarch—of Constantinople. *The Art Archive/Dagli Orti.*

twelfth century had crystallized around charismatic teachers like Peter Abelard, became permanent institutions—universities.

The period 1150–1215 was characterized by confidence buttressed by new organizations and institutions. Well-organized rulers exercised control over whole territories through institutions of government that could—if need be—function without them. In the cultural arena, new-style poets boldly used the common language of everyday life, rather than Latin, to write literature of astonishing beauty, humor, and emotional range. Laypeople and those who devoted themselves to religion participated in newly articulate and well-organized groups. But increased confidence and more clearly defined group and individual identities brought with them increased intolerance toward and aggression against those perceived as deviants.

❖ Governments as Institutions

By the end of the twelfth century, western Europeans for the first time spoke of their rulers not as kings of a people (for example, the king of the Franks) but as kings of a territory (for example, the king of France). This new designation reflected an important change in medieval rulership. However strong earlier rulers had been, their political power had been personal (depending on ties of kinship, friendship, and vassalage) rather than territorial (touching all who lived within the borders of their state). The new organization, along with renewed interest in Roman legal concepts, served as a foundation for strong, central rule. The process of state building began to encompass clearly delineated regions.

Western European rulers now began to employ professional administrators; sometimes, as in England, the system was so institutionalized that even when the king left England (as often happened, since he had continental possessions to attend to), his government ran smoothly under his subordinates and appointees. In other regions, such as Germany, bureaucratic administration did not develop so far. In eastern Europe it hardly existed at all.

Germany: The Revived Monarchy of Frederick Barbarossa

The Investiture Conflict and the civil war it generated (1075–1122) strengthened the German princes and weakened the kings, Henry IV and Henry V, who were also the emperors. For decades, the princes enjoyed near independence, building castles on their properties and establishing control over whole territories. To ensure that the emperors who succeeded Henry V (r. 1106–1125) would be weak, the princes supported only those rulers who agreed to give them new lands and powers. A ruler's success depended on balancing the many conflicting interests of his own royal and imperial offices, his family, and the German princes. He also had to contend with the increasing influence of the papacy and the Italian communes, which forged alliances with one another and

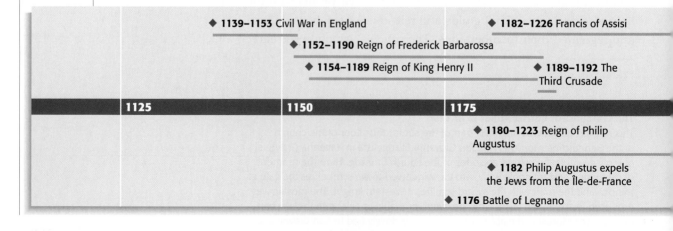

◆ **1139–1153** Civil War in England

◆ **1182–1226** Francis of Assisi

◆ **1152–1190** Reign of Frederick Barbarossa

◆ **1154–1189** Reign of King Henry II

◆ **1189–1192** The Third Crusade

1125	1150	1175

◆ **1180–1223** Reign of Philip Augustus

◆ **1182** Philip Augustus expels the Jews from the Île-de-France

◆ **1176** Battle of Legnano

with the German princes, preventing the consolidation of power under a strong German monarch during the first half of the twelfth century.

During the civil war in Germany, the two sides were represented by two noble families: leading the imperial party were the Staufer, or Hohenstaufen, clan; opposing them were the princely-papal party, the Welfs. (Two later Italian factions, the Ghibellines and the Guelphs, corresponded, respectively, to the Hohenstaufens and the Welfs.) The enmity between these families was legendary, and warfare between the groups raged even after the Concordat of Worms in 1122. Exhausted from constant battles, by 1152 all parties longed for peace. In an act of rare unanimity, they elected as king Frederick I (r. 1152–1190), who was called Barbarossa. In Frederick they seemed to have a candidate who could end the strife: his mother was a Welf, his father a Staufer. Contemporary accounts of the king's career represented Frederick in the image of Christ as the "cornerstone" that joined two houses and reconciled enemies.

New Foundations of Power.   Frederick's appearance impressed his contemporaries— the name *Barbarossa* referred to his red-blond hair and beard. But beyond appearances, Frederick impressed those around him by what they called his "firmness." He affirmed royal rights, even when he handed out duchies and allowed others to name bishops, because in return for these political powers Frederick required the princes to concede formally and publicly that they held their

Frederick Barbarossa
In a thirteenth-century manuscript about imperial honor, Frederick Barbarossa is remembered for his firmness. At the top Frederick takes leave of his sons before going on the Third Crusade. They bow in deference to his authority and dignity. At the bottom, Frederick mounts his horse, gesturing a command with his left hand. The caption in Latin reads, "Frederick orders his men to cut down the forest in Hungary." Did Frederick fear retaliation from the Hungarian king? What sort of vision of imperial might did the artist of this miniature want to suggest? *Burgerbibliothek Bern, Cod. 120, II, f. #143r.*

rights and territories from him as their lord. By making them his vassals, although with nearly royal rights within their principalities, Frederick defined the princes' relationship to

◆ **1202–1204** The Fourth Crusade

   ◆ **1204** Fall of Constantinople to Crusaders

      ◆ **1214** Battle of Bouvines

      ◆ **1215** Magna Carta

1200	**1225**	**1250**	**1275**

   ◆ **1204** Philip takes Normandy, Anjou, Maine, Touraine, and Poitou from John

      ◆ **1209–1229** Albigensian Crusade

         ◆ **1212** Battle of Las Navas de Tolosa; triumph of the reconquista

Frederick's Reply to the Romans

The confident claims of competing groups to the same rights and powers are well illustrated by Frederick Barbarossa's entry into Rome in 1155. The pope naturally considered it his right to confer the imperial crown on the king. But when Frederick came to Rome, envoys from the new city government that had been established there greeted him with their offer to give him the crown. Frederick reacted forcefully: the crown was not theirs to give; it was his by right. The gist of his reply to the Romans was recorded by his counselor and chronicler, Bishop Otto of Freising.

We have heard much heretofore concerning the wisdom and the valor of the Romans, yet more concerning their wisdom. Wherefore we cannot wonder enough at finding your words insipid with swollen pride rather than seasoned with the salt of wisdom. You set forth the ancient renown of your city. You extoll to the very stars the ancient status of your sacred republic. Granted, granted! To use the words of your own writer, "There was, *there was once*, virtue in this republic." "Once," I say. And O that we might truthfully and freely say "now"! Your Rome—nay, ours also—has experienced the vicissitudes of time. She could not be the only one to escape a fate ordained by the Author of all things for all that dwell beneath the orb of the moon. What shall I say? It is clear how first the strength of your nobility was transferred from this city of ours to the royal city of the East [Constantinople], and how for the course of many years the thirsty Greekling sucked the breasts of your delight. Then came the Frank, truly noble, in deed as in name, and forcibly possessed himself of whatever freedom was still left to you. Do you wish to know the ancient glory of your Rome? The worth of the senatorial dignity? The impregnable disposition of the camp? The virtue and the discipline of the equestrian order, its unmarred and unconquerable boldness when advancing to a conflict? Behold our state. All these things are to be found with us. All these have descended to us, together with the empire.

Source: Brian Tierney, *The Crisis of Church and State, 1050–1300: With Selected Documents* (Englewood Cliffs, NJ: Prentice Hall, 1964), 103–4.

the German king: they were powerful yet personally subordinate to him. In this way Frederick hoped to save the monarchy and to coordinate royal and princely rule, thus ending Germany's chronic civil wars. Frederick used the lord–vassal relationship to give him a free hand to rule while placating the princes.

As the king of Germany, Frederick had the traditional right to claim the imperial crown. When, in 1155, he marched to Rome to be crowned emperor, the fledgling commune there protested that it alone had the right to give him the crown. Frederick interrupted them, asserting that the glory of Rome, together with its crown, came to him by right of conquest. To the pope he was equally insistent: when Hadrian IV (r. 1154–1159) wrote to say that Rome belonged to "St. Peter,"

Frederick replied that his imperial title gave him rights over the city. In part, Frederick was influenced by the revival of knowledge about Roman law—the laws of Theodosius and Justinian—that was taking place in the schools of Italy. In part, too, he was convinced of the sacred—not just secular—origins of the imperial office. Frederick called his empire *sacer*, "sacred," asserting that it was in its own way as precious, worthwhile, and God-given as the church.

Frederick buttressed this high view of his imperial right with worldly power. He married Beatrice of Burgundy, whose vast estates in Burgundy and Provence enabled Frederick to establish a powerful political and territorial base centered in Swabia (today southwestern Germany).

Frederick and Italy.

Frederick then looked south to Italy. Its flourishing commercial cities could make him rich. Taxes on agricultural production there alone yielded thirty thousand silver talents annually, an incredible sum equal to the annual income of the richest ruler of the day, the king of England. Finally, Swabia and northern Italy together would give Frederick a compact and centrally located territory.

Furthermore, no emperor could leave Italy alone. The very title came from the Roman emperor, who had controlled the city of Rome and all of Italy. It would have seemed laughable to be "emperor" without holding at least some of this territory. Some historians have faulted Frederick for "entangling" himself in Italy. But Frederick's title demanded he intervene in Italy. To blame him for not concentrating on Germany is to accuse him of lacking modern wisdom, which knows only from hindsight that European polities developed into nation-states, such as France, Germany, and Italy. There was nothing inevitable about the development of nation-states, and Frederick should not be criticized simply because he did not see into the future.

Nevertheless, Frederick's ambitions in Italy were problematic. Since the Investiture Conflict, the emperor had ruled Italy in name only. The communes of the northern cities guarded their liberties jealously, while the pope considered Italy his own sphere of influence. Frederick's territorial base just north of Italy threatened those interests (Map 11.1). In 1157, soon after Frederick's imperial coronation, Hadrian's envoys arrived at a meeting called by the emperor with a letter detailing

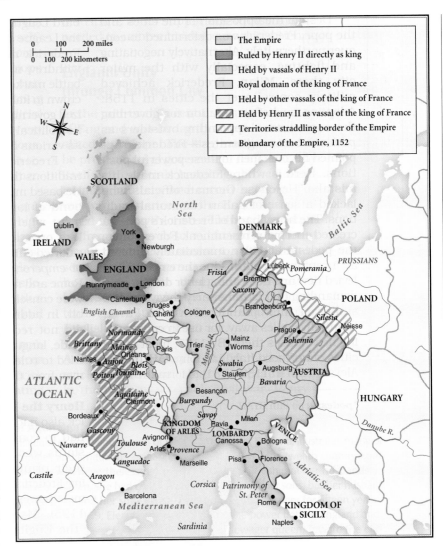

MAP 11.1 Europe in the Age of Frederick Barbarossa and Henry II, 1150–1190
The second half of the twelfth century was dominated by two men, Emperor Frederick Barbarossa and King Henry II. Of the two, Frederick seemed to control more land, but this was deceptive. Although he was emperor, he had great difficulty ruling the territory that was theoretically part of the empire. Frederick's base was in central Germany, and even there he had to contend with very powerful vassals. Henry II's territory was more compact but also more surely under his control.

the dignities, honors, and other *beneficia* the pope had showered on Frederick. The word *beneficia* incensed Frederick's supporters because it meant not only "benefits" but also "fiefs," casting Frederick as the pope's vassal. The incident opened old wounds from the Investiture Conflict and revealed the gulf between papal and imperial conceptions of worldly authority.

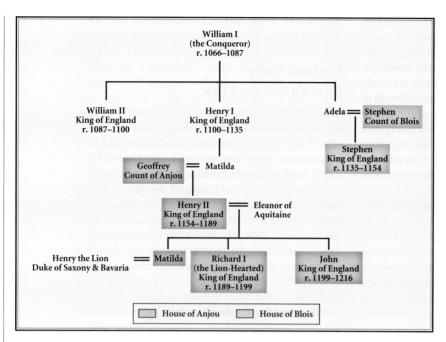

FIGURE 11.1 Genealogy of Henry II
King William I of England was succeeded by his sons William II and Henry I. When Henry died, the succession was disputed by two women and their husbands. One was William I's daughter Adela, married to the count of Blois; the other was Henry's daughter Matilda, wife of the count of Anjou. Although the English crown first went to the house of Blois, it reverted in midcentury to the house of Anjou, headed by Matilda's son Henry. Henry II thus began the Angevin dynasty in England.

(r. 1100–1135), son of William the Conqueror, had no male heir. Before he died, he called on the great barons to swear that his daughter Matilda would rule after him. The effort failed; the Norman barons could not imagine a woman ruling them, and they feared her husband, Geoffrey of Anjou, their perennial enemy on the continent. Many were glad to see Stephen of Blois (r. 1135–1154), the son of Henry's sister Adela, take the throne. With Matilda's son, the future Henry II, only two years old when Stephen took the crown, the struggle for control of England during Stephen's reign became part of a larger territorial contest between the house of Anjou◆ (Henry's family) and the house of Blois (Stephen's family) (Figure 11.1). Continual civil war (1139–1153) in England, as in Germany, benefited the English barons and high churchmen, who gained new privileges and powers as the monarch's authority waned.

Newly built private castles, already familiar on the continent, now appeared in England as symbols of the rising power of the English barons. But Stephen's coalition of barons, high clergymen, and townsmen eventually fell apart, causing him to agree to the accession of Matilda's son, Henry of Anjou. Thus began what would be known as the **Angevin**◆ (from *Anjou*) dynasty.[1]

Henry's marriage to Eleanor of Aquitaine in 1152 brought the enormous inheritance of the duchy of Aquitaine to the English crown (see Eleanor's tomb effigy). Although he remained the vassal of the king of France for his continental lands, Henry in effect ruled a territory that stretched from England to southern France.

Not only did Eleanor bring to Henry the duchy of Aquitaine, but she also bore him sons to maintain his dynasty. Before her marriage to Henry, Eleanor had been married to King Louis VII of France; Louis had the marriage annulled because Eleanor had borne him only daughters. Nevertheless, as queen of France, Eleanor had enjoyed an important position: she disputed with St. Bernard, the Cistercian abbot who was the most renowned churchman of the day, and she accompanied her husband on the Second Crusade, bringing more troops than he did. She had determined to separate from her husband even before he considered leaving her. But she lost much of her power under her English husband, for Henry dominated her just as he came to dominate his barons. Turning

---

[1]Henry's father, Geoffrey of Anjou, was nicknamed "Plantagenet" from the *genet*, a shrub he liked. Historians sometimes use the name to refer to the entire dynasty, so Henry II was the first Plantagenet as well as the first Angevin king of England.

◆**Anjou:** AN joo

◆**Angevin:** AN juh vihn

to her offspring in 1173, Eleanor, disguised as a man, tried to join her eldest son, Henry the Younger, in a plot against his father. But the rebellion was put down, and she spent most of her years thereafter, until her husband's death in 1189, confined under guard at Winchester Castle.

Royal Authority and Common Law. When Henry II became king of England, he immediately set to work to undo the damage to the monarchy caused by the civil war. He destroyed or confiscated the new castles and regained crown land. Then he proceeded to extend monarchical power, above all by imposing royal justice.

Henry's judicial reforms built on an already well-developed English system. The Anglo-Saxon kings had royal district courts: the king appointed sheriffs to police the shires, muster military levies, and haul criminals into court. The Norman kings retained these courts, which all the free men of the shire were summoned to attend. To these established institutions, Henry II added a system of judicial visitations called eyres◆ (from the Latin *iter*, "journey"). Under this system, royal justices made regular trips to every locality in England. Henry declared that some crimes, such as murder, arson, and rape, were so heinous as to violate the "king's peace," no matter where they were committed. The king required local representatives of the knightly class to meet during each eyre and either give the sheriff the names of those suspected of committing crimes in the vicinity or arrest the suspects themselves and hand them over to the royal justices.

During the eyres, the justices also heard cases between individuals, today called civil cases. Free men and women (that is, people of the knightly class or above) could bring their disputes over such matters as inheritance, dowries, and property claims to the king's justices. Earlier courts had generally relied on duels between litigants to determine verdicts. Henry's new system offered a different option, an inquest under royal supervision.

The new system of **common law**—law that applied to all of England—was praised

◆**eyres:** ayrs

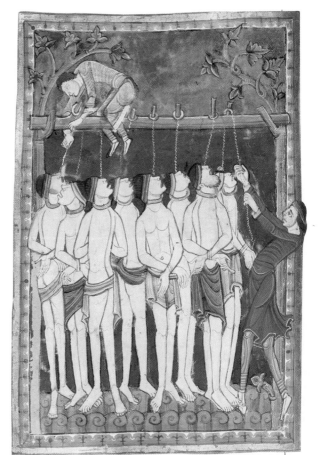

Hanging Thieves
The development of common law in England meant mobilizing royal agents to bring charges and arrest people throughout the land. In 1124, the royal justice Ralph Basset hanged forty-four thieves. It could not have been very shocking in that context to see, in this miniature from around 1130, eight thieves hanged for breaking into the shrine of St. Edmund. Under Henry II all cases of murder, arson, and rape were considered crimes against the king himself. The result was not just the enhancement of the king's power but also new definitions of crime, more thorough policing, and more systematic punishments. Even so, hanging was probably no more frequent than it had been before.
Pierpont Morgan Library/Art Resource, NY.

for its efficiency, speed, and conclusiveness by a twelfth-century legal treatise known as *Glanvill* (after its presumed author): "This legal institution emanates from perfect equity. For justice, which after many and long delays is scarcely ever demonstrated by the duel, is advantageously and speedily attained

The Murder of Thomas Becket
Almost immediately after King Henry II's knights murdered Archbishop Thomas Becket in his church at Canterbury, Becket was viewed as a martyr. In this early depiction of the event, one of the murderers knocks off Becket's cap, while another hits the arm of Becket's supporter, who holds the bishop's cross-staff. *British Library, London, UK/Bridgeman Art Library.*

The stiffest opposition to Henry's extension of royal courts came from the church, where a separate system of trial and punishment had long been available to the clergy and to others who enjoyed church protection. The punishments for crimes meted out by these courts were generally quite mild. Jealous of their prerogatives, churchmen refused to submit to the jurisdiction of Henry's courts, and the ensuing contest between Henry II and his appointed archbishop, Thomas Becket (1118–1170), became the greatest battle between the church and the state in the twelfth century. The conflict simmered for six years, until Henry's henchmen murdered Thomas, unintentionally turning him into a martyr. Although Henry's role in the murder remained ambiguous, he was forced by the general outcry to do public penance for the deed. In the end both church and royal courts expanded to address the concerns of an increasingly litigious society. (See The Murder of Thomas Becket on this page.)

Henry II was an English king with an imperial reach. He was lord over almost half of France, though much of this territory was in the hands of his vassals, and he was, at least theoretically, vassal to the French king. In England, he made the king's presence felt everywhere through his system of royal courts that traveled the length and breadth of the country. On the continent, he maintained his position through a combination of war and negotiation, but rebellions begun by his own sons with help from the king of France dogged him throughout his life.

Henry's Successors. Under Henry and his sons Richard I (r. 1189–1199) and John (r. 1199–1216), the English monarchy was omnipresent and rich. Its omnipresence derived largely from its eyre system of justice and its administrative apparatus. Its wealth came from court fees, income from numerous royal estates both in England and on the continent, taxes from cities, and customary feudal dues (reliefs and aids) collected from barons and knights. These dues were paid on such occasions as the knighting of the king's eldest son and the marriage of the king's eldest daughter. Enriched by the commercial economy of the late twelfth century, the English

through this institution." *Glanvill* might have added that the king also speedily gained a large treasury. The exchequer, as the financial bureau of England was called, recorded all the fines paid for judgments and the sums collected for writs. The amounts, entered on parchment sewn together and stored as rolls, became the Receipt Rolls and Pipe Rolls, the first of many such records of the English monarchy and an indication that writing had become a mechanism for institutionalizing royal power in England.

kings encouraged their knights and barons not to serve them personally in battle but instead to pay the king a tax called **scutage** in lieu of service. The monarchs preferred to hire mercenaries both as troops to fight external enemies and as police to enforce the king's will at home.

Richard I was known as the Lion-Hearted for his boldness. But historians have often criticized him for being an "absentee" king. Yet it is hard to see what he might have done differently. He went on the Third Crusade the very year he was crowned; on his way home, he was captured and held for a long time for ransom by political enemies; and he died defending his possessions on the continent. Richard's real tragedy was that he died young.

Richard's successor, John, has also been widely faulted. Even in his own day, he was accused of asserting his will in a high-handed way. But to understand John, it is necessary to appreciate how desperate he was to keep his continental possessions. In 1204, the king of France, Philip II (r. 1180–1223), confiscated the northern French territories held by John. Between 1204 and 1214, John did everything he could to add to the crown revenues so he could pay for an army to win back the territories. He forced his vassals to pay ever-increasing scutages and extorted money in the form of new feudal dues. He compelled the widows of his vassals to marry men of his choosing or pay him a hefty fee if they refused. Yet despite John's heavy investment in this war effort, his army was defeated in 1214 at the battle of Bouvines. The defeat caused discontented English barons to rebel openly against the king. At Runnymede in June 1215, John was forced to agree to the charter of baronial liberties that has come to be called Magna Carta, or "Great Charter."

Magna Carta, 1215. The English barons intended Magna Carta (so named to distinguish it from a smaller charter issued around the same time concerning the royal forests) to be a conservative document defining the "customary" obligations and rights of the nobility and forbidding the king to break from these customs without consulting his barons. It also maintained that all free men in the land had certain rights that the king was obligated to uphold. (See "Contrasting Views," page 410.) In this way, Magna Carta implied that the king was not above the law. The growing royal power was matched by the self-confidence of the English barons, certain of their rights and eager to articulate them. In time, as the definition of *free men* expanded to include all the king's subjects, Magna Carta came to be seen as a guarantee of the rights of Englishmen in general.

France: Consolidation and Conquest

Whereas the power of the English king led to a baronial movement to curb it, the weakness of the French monarchy ironically led to its expansion. In 1180, the French crown passed from the Capetian king Louis VII (first husband of Eleanor of Aquitaine) to his young son, Philip II. When the new king came to the throne, the royal domain, the Île-de-France, was sandwiched between territory controlled by the counts of Flanders, Champagne, and Anjou. By far the most powerful ruler on the continent was King Henry II of England. He was the count of Anjou and the duke of Normandy, and he held the duchy of Aquitaine through his wife. He also controlled Poitou♦ and Brittany.

Henry and the counts of Flanders and Champagne vied to control the newly crowned fourteen-year-old king of France. Philip, however, quickly learned to play them off against one another, in particular by setting the sons of Henry II against their father. Contemporaries were astounded when Philip successfully gained territory: he wrested Vermandois and Artois from Flanders in the 1190s and Normandy, Anjou, Maine, Touraine, and Poitou from King John of England in 1204. After these

The Consolidation of France under Philip Augustus, 1180–1223

♦**Poitou:** pwah TOO

Magna Carta

Magna Carta, today considered a landmark of constitutional government, began as a demand by English barons and churchmen for specific rights and privileges. Reacting to King John's "abuses," they forced him in 1215 to affix his seal to a "charter of liberties," the "Great Charter" (Magna Carta, Document 1). It set forth the customs that the king was expected to observe and, in its sixty-first clause, in effect allowed the king's subjects to declare war against him if he failed to carry out the charter's provisions.

In 1225, Henry III, John's son, issued a definitive version of the charter. By then it had become more important as a symbol of liberty than for its specific provisions. It was, for example, invoked by the barons in 1242 when they were summoned to one of the first Parliaments (Document 2).

1. MAGNA CARTA, 1215

In these excerpts, the provisions that were dropped in the definitive version of 1225 are starred. Explanatory notes are in brackets. The original charter had sixty-three clauses. In every clause John refers to himself by the royal "we."

1. First of all [we, i.e., John] have granted to God, and by this our present charter confirmed for us and our heirs for ever that the English church shall be free, and shall have its rights undiminished and its liberties unimpaired....

8. No widow shall be forced to marry so long as she wishes to live without a husband, provided that she gives security [a pledge or deposit] not to marry without our consent if she holds [her land] from us, or without the consent of her lord of whom she holds, if she holds of another.

9. Neither we nor our bailiffs will seize for any debt any land or rent, so long as the chattels [property] of the debtor are sufficient to repay the debt....

*10. If anyone who has borrowed from the Jews any sum, great or small, dies before it is repaid, the debt shall not bear interest as long as the heir is under age, of whomsoever [lord] he holds [his land]; and if the debt falls into our hands [which might happen, as Jews were serfs of the crown], we will not take anything except the principal mentioned in the bond.

*12. No scutage or aid [money payments owed by a vassal to his lord] shall be imposed in our kingdom unless by common counsel of our kingdom, except for ransoming our person, for making our eldest son a knight, and for once marrying our eldest daughter; and for these only a reasonable aid shall be levied....

30. No sheriff, or bailiff of ours, or anyone else shall take the horses or carts of any free man [for the most part, a member of the elite] for transport work save with the agreement of that freeman.

31. Neither we nor our bailiffs will take, for castles or other works of ours, timber which is not ours, except with the agreement of him whose timber it is....

39. No free man shall be arrested or imprisoned or disseised [deprived of his land] or outlawed or exiled or in any way victimized, neither will we attack him or send anyone to attack him, except by the lawful judgment of his peers or by the law of the land....

*61. Since... we have granted all these things aforesaid... we give and grant [the barons] the under-written security, namely, that the barons shall choose any twenty-five barons of the kingdom they wish, who must with all their might observe, hold, and cause to be observed, the peace and liberties which we have granted and confirmed to them by this present charter of ours, so that if we, or our justiciar [the king's chief minister], or our bailiffs or any one of our servants offend in any way against anyone or transgress any of the articles of the peace or the security..., [the barons] shall come to us ... and laying the transgression before us, shall petition us to have that transgression corrected without delay. And if we do not correct the transgression... within forty days ... those twenty-five barons together with the community of the whole land shall distrain and distress us in every way they can, namely, by seizing castles, lands, possessions, and in such other ways as they can, saving [not harming] our person.

Source: *English Historical Documents*, vol. 3, ed. Harry Rothwell (London: Eyre & Spottiswoode, 1975), 317–23.

2. THE BARONS AT PARLIAMENT REFUSE TO GIVE THE KING AN AID, 1242

Henry III convoked the barons to a meeting (parliament), expecting them to ratify his request for money to wage war for his French possessions. As this document makes clear, the barons considered his request an excessive imposition. Magna Carta thus became a justification for their flat rejection of the king's request.

Since he had been their ruler they had many times, at his request, given him aid, namely, a thirteenth of their movable property, and afterwards a fifteenth and a sixteenth and a fortieth.... Scarcely, however, had four years or so elapsed from that time, when he again asked them for aid, and, at length, by dint of great entreaties, he obtained a thirtieth, which they granted him on the condition that neither that exaction nor the others before it should in the future be made a precedent of. And regarding that he gave them his charter. Furthermore, he then [at that earlier time] granted them that all the liberties contained in Magna Carta should thence-

John's Seal on Magna Carta
When the rebels at Runnymede got John to assent to their charter, later known as Magna Carta, he did not sign it; he sealed it. From the thirteenth through the fifteenth century, seals were used by kings, queens, aristocrats, guilds, communes, and many other individuals and groups at all levels of society to authenticate their charters— what we would call "legal documents." The seal itself was made out of wax or lead, melted and pressed with a matrix of hard metal, such as gold or brass, that was carved with an image in the negative, designed to produce a raised image. These seals reminded the public of the status as well as the name of the sealer. What image did John wish to project? *British Museum.*

forward be fully observed throughout the whole of his kingdom....

Furthermore, from the time of their giving the said thirtieth, itinerant justices have been continually going on eyre [moving from place to place] through all parts of England, alike for pleas of the forest [to enforce the king's monopoly on forests] and all other pleas, so that all the counties, hundreds, cities, boroughs, and nearly all the vills of England are heavily amerced [fined]; wherefore, from that eyre alone the king has, or ought to have, a very large sum of money, if it were paid, and properly collected. They therefore say with truth that all in the kingdom are so oppressed and impoverished by these amercements and by the other aids given before that they have little or no goods left. And because the king had never, after the granting of the thirtieth, abided by his charter of liberties, nay had since then oppressed them more than usual...they told the king flatly that for the present they would not give him an aid.

Source: *English Historical Documents*, 3:355–56.

QUESTIONS TO CONSIDER
1. From the clauses of Magna Carta that say what will henceforth *not* be done, speculate about what the king *had been* doing.
2. How did the barons of 1242 use Magna Carta as a symbol of liberty?

feats a contemporary chronicler dubbed him Philip Augustus, the "augmenter."

After Philip's army confirmed its triumph over most of John's continental territories in 1214, the French monarch could boast that he was the richest and most powerful ruler in France. Unlike Frederick I Barbarossa, who was compelled to divide the territory he had seized from Henry the Lion among the German princes, Philip had sufficient support and resources to keep a tight hold on Normandy.[2] He received homage and fealty from most of the Norman aristocracy; his officers carefully carried out their work there in accordance with Norman customs. For ordinary Normans, the shift from duke to king brought few changes.

Wherever he ruled, Philip instituted a new kind of French administration, run by officials who kept accounts and files. Before Philip's day most French royal arrangements were committed to memory rather than to writing. If decrees were recorded at all, they were saved by the recipient, not by the government. The king did keep some documents, which generally followed him in his travels like personal possessions. But in 1194, in a battle with the king of England, Philip lost his meager cache of documents along with much treasure when he had to abandon his baggage train. After 1194, the king had all his decrees written down, and he established permanent repositories in which to keep them.

Whereas German rulers employed ministerials to do the daily work of government, Philip, like the English king, relied largely on members of the lesser nobility—knights and clerics, many of whom were "masters" educated in the city schools of France. They served as officers of his court, tax collectors, and overseers of the royal estates, making the king's power felt locally as never before.

Eastern Europe and Byzantium: Fragmenting Realms

The importance of institutions such as those developed in England and France is made clear by the experience of regions where they

were not established. In eastern Europe the characteristic pattern was for states to form under the leadership of one great ruler and then to fragment under his successor. For example, King Béla III of Hungary (r. 1172–1196) built up a state that looked superficially like a western European kingdom. He married a French princess, employed at least one scholar from Paris, and built his palace in the French Romanesque style. He enjoyed an annual income from his estates, tolls, dues, and taxes equal to that of the richest western monarchs. But he did not set up enduring government institutions, and in the decades that fol-

Eastern Europe and Byzantium, c. 1200

lowed his death, wars between Béla's sons splintered his monarchical holdings, and aristocratic supporters divided the wealth.

Russia underwent a similar process. Although twelfth-century Kiev was politically fragmented, autocratic princes to the north constructed Suzdal,♦ the nucleus of the later Muscovite state. The borders of Suzdal were clearly defined, well-to-do towns prospered, monasteries and churches dotted the countryside, and the other princes of Russia recognized its ruler as the "grand prince." Yet in 1212 this nascent state began to crumble as the sons of Grand Prince Vsevolod♦ III (r. 1176–1212) fought one another for territory, much as Béla's sons had done in Hungary.

Although the Byzantine Empire was already a consolidated, bureaucratic state, after the mid-twelfth century it gradually began to show weakness. Traders from the west—the Venetians especially—dominated its commerce. The Byzantine emperors who ruled during the last half of the twelfth century down-

---

[2]Philip was particularly successful in imposing royal control in Normandy; later French kings gave most of the other territories to collateral members of the royal family.

♦**Suzdal:** SOO zduhl
♦**Vsevolod:** TSEV a lid

graded the old civil servants, elevated their relatives to high offices, and favored the military elite. As Byzantine rule grew more personal and European rule became more bureaucratic, the two gradually became more like one another. The final blow came when the crusaders took Constantinople in 1204, parceling out most of the empire among themselves.

Review: What new sources and institutions of power became available to rulers in the twelfth century?

❖ The Growth of a Vernacular High Culture

With their consolidation of territory, wealth, and power in the last half of the twelfth century, kings, barons, princes, and their wives and daughters supported new kinds of literature and music. For the first time on the continent, though long true in England, poems and songs were written in the vernacular, the spoken language, rather than in Latin. They celebrated the lives of the nobility and were meant to be read or sung aloud, sometimes with accompanying musical instruments. They provided a common experience for aristocrats at court. Whether in the cities of Italy or the more isolated courts of northern Europe, patrons and patronesses, enriched by their estates and commerce, now spent their profits on the arts. Their support helped develop and enrich the spoken language while it heightened their prestige as aristocrats.

The Troubadours: Poets of Love and Play

Already at the beginning of the twelfth century, Duke William IX of Aquitaine (1071–1126), the grandfather of Eleanor, had written lyric poems in Occitan, the vernacular of southern France. Perhaps influenced by Arabic and Hebrew love poetry from al-Andalus, his own poetry in turn provided a model for poetic forms that gained popularity through repeated performances. The final four-line stanza of one such poem demonstrates the composer's skill with words:

> Per aquesta fri e tremble,
>
> quar de tan bon' amor l'am;
> qu'anc no cug qu'en nasques semble
>
> en semblan de gran linh n'Adam.

> For this one I shiver and tremble,
> I love her with such a good love;
> I do not think the like of her was ever born
> in the long line of Lord Adam.

The rhyme scheme of this poem appears to be simple—*tremble* goes with *semble*, *l'am* with *n'Adam*—but the entire poem has five earlier verses, all six lines long and all containing the *-am,-am* rhyme in the fourth and sixth lines, while every other line within each verse rhymes as well.

Troubadours, lyric poets who wrote in Occitan, varied their rhymes and meters endlessly to dazzle their audiences with brilliant originality. Most of their rhymes and meters resemble Latin religious poetry of the same time, indicating that the vernacular and Latin religious cultures overlapped. Such similarity is also evident in the troubadours' choice of subjects. The most common topic, love, echoed the twelfth-century church's emphasis on the emotional relationship between God and humans.

The troubadours invented new meanings for old images. When William IX sang of his "good love" for a woman unlike any other born in the line of Adam, the words could be interpreted in two ways. They reminded listeners of the Virgin Mary, a woman unlike any other, but they also referred to William's lover, recalled in another part of the poem, where he had complained

> If I do not get help soon
> and my lady does not give me love,
> by Saint Gregory's holy head I'll die
> if she doesn't kiss me in a chamber or under a tree.

His lady's character is ambiguous: she is like the Virgin Mary, but she is also his mistress.

Troubadours, both male and female, expressed prevalent views of love much as popular singers do today. The Contessa de Dia (flourished c. 1160) wrote about her unrequited love for a man:

> So bitter do I feel toward him
> whom I love more than anything.
> With him my mercy and fine manners [cortesia] are in vain.

FIGURE 11.2 Troubadour Song: "I Never Died for Love"
This music is the first part of a song that the troubadour poet Peire Vidal wrote sometime between 1175 and 1205. It has been adapted here for the treble clef. There is no time signature, but the music may easily be played by calculating one beat for each note, except for the two-note slurs, which fit into one beat together, a half-beat for each note.
From Samuel N. Rosenberg, Margaret Switten, and Gerard Le Vot, eds., Songs of the Troubadours and Trouvères. Copyright © 1997 by Samuel N. Rosenberg, Margaret Switten, and Gerard Le Vot. Reprinted by permission of Taylor & Francis/Garland Publishing, http://www.taylorandfrancis.com.

The key to troubadour verse is the idea of *cortesia*. It refers to courtesy, the refinement of people living at court, and to their struggle to achieve an ideal of virtue.

Historians and literary critics used to use the term *courtly love* to emphasize one of the themes of courtly literature: overwhelming love for a beautiful married noblewoman who is far above the poet in status and utterly unattainable. But this was only one of many aspects of love that the troubadours sang about: some boasted of sexual conquests, others played with the notion of equality between lovers, and still others preached that love was the source of virtue. The real overall theme of this literature is not courtly love; it is the power of women. No wonder Eleanor of

Aquitaine and other aristocratic women patronized the troubadours: they enjoyed the image that it gave them of themselves. Until recently historians thought that the image was a delusion and that twelfth-century aristocratic women were valuable mainly as heiresses to marry and as mothers of sons. But new research reveals that there were many powerful female lords in southern France. They owned property, had vassals, led battles, decided disputes, and entered into and broke political alliances as their advantage dictated. Both men and women appreciated troubadour poetry, which recognized and praised women's power even as it eroticized it.

Music was part of troubadour poetry, which was always sung, typically by a *jongleur*◆ (musician). Unfortunately, no written troubadour music exists from before the thirteenth century, and even then we have music for only a fraction of the poems. By the thirteenth century, music was written on four- and five-line staves, so scholars can at least determine relative pitches, and modern musicians can sing some troubadour songs with the hope of sounding reasonably like the original. This is the earliest popular music that can be re-created authentically (Figure 11.2).

From southern France the troubadours' songs spread to Italy, northern France, England, and Germany. Similar poetry appeared in other vernacular languages: the *minnesingers*◆ (literally, "love singers") sang in German; the *trouvères*◆ sang in the Old French of northern France. One trouvère was the English king Richard the Lion-Hearted. Taken

◆*jongleur:* zhon GLUR
◆*minnesinger:* MIH nuh sihn gur
◆*trouvère:* troo VEHR

prisoner on his return from the Third Crusade, Richard wrote a poem expressing his longing not for a lady but for the good companions of war, the knightly "youths" he had joined in battle:

> They know well, the men of Anjou and Touraine, those bachelors, now so magnificent and safe, that I am arrested, far from them, in another's hands.
> They used to love me much, now they love me not at all.
> There's no lordly fighting now on the barren plains,
> because I am a prisoner.

The Literature of Epic and Romance

The yearning for the battlefield was not as common a topic in lyric poetry as love, but long narrative poems about heroic deeds **(chansons de geste)**♦ appeared frequently in vernacular writing. Such poems followed a long oral tradition and appeared at about the same time as love poems. Like the songs of the troubadours, these epic poems implied a code of behavior for aristocrats, in this case on the battlefield.

By the end of the twelfth century, warriors wanted a guide for conduct and a common class identity. Nobles and knights had begun to merge into one class because they felt threatened from below by newly rich merchants and from above by newly powerful kings. Their ascendancy on the battlefield, where they unhorsed one another with lances and long swords and took prisoners rather than kill their opponents, was also beginning to wane in the face of mercenary infantrymen who wielded long hooks and knives that ripped easily through chain mail. A knightly ethos and sense of group solidarity emerged in the face of these social, political, and military changes.

Thus, the protagonists of heroic poems yearned not for love but for battle:

> The armies are in sight of one another. . . . The cowards tremble as they march, but the brave hearts rejoice for the battle.

Examining the moral issues that made war both tragic and inevitable, poets played on the contradictory values of their society, such as the conflicting loyalties of friendship and vassalage or a vassal's right to a fief versus a son's right to his father's land.

These vernacular narrative poems, later called epics, focused on war. Other long poems, later called romances, explored the relationships between men and women. Romances reached their zenith of popularity during the late twelfth and early thirteenth centuries. The legend of King Arthur inspired a romance by Chrétien de Troyes♦ (c. 1150–1190) in which a heroic knight, Lancelot, in love with Queen Guinevere, the wife of his lord, comes across a comb bearing some strands of her radiant hair:

> Never will the eye of man see anything receive such honour as when [Lancelot] begins to adore these tresses. . . . Even for St. Martin and St. James he has no need.

Chrétien is evoking the familiar imagery of relics, such as bits of hair or the bones of saints, as items of devotion. Making Guinevere's hair an object of adoration not only conveys the depth of Lancelot's feeling but also pokes a bit of fun at him. Like the troubadours, the romantic poets delighted in the interplay between religious and amorous feelings. Just as the ideal monk merged his will in God's will, Chrétien's Lancelot loses his will to Guinevere. When she sees Lancelot—the greatest knight in Christendom—fighting in a tournament, she tests him by asking him to do his "worst." The poor knight is obliged to lose all his battles until she changes her mind.

Lancelot was the perfect chivalric knight. The word **chivalry** derives from the French word *cheval* ("horse"); the fact that the knight was a horseman marked him as a warrior of the most prestigious sort. Perched high on his horse, his heavy lance couched in his right arm, the knight was an imposing and menacing figure. Chivalry made him gentle—except to his enemies on the battlefield. The chivalric hero was a knight constrained by a code of refinement, fair play, piety, and devotion to an ideal. Historians debate whether real knights lived up to the codes implicit in epics and romances. But there is no doubt that knights saw themselves mirrored in the codes. They were the poets' audience; sometimes they were the poets' subject as well.

♦**chansons de geste:** shahn SOHN duh ZHEST

♦**Chrétien de Troyes:** kray TYAN duh TWAH

For example, when the knight William the Marshal died, his son commissioned a poet to write his biography. In it, William was depicted as a model knight, courteous with the ladies and brave on the battlefield.

> **Review:** What does the work of the troubadours and vernacular poets reveal about the nature of entertainment—its themes, its audience, its performers—in the twelfth century?

❖ New Lay and Religious Associations

The new vernacular culture was merely one reflection of the growing wealth, sophistication, and self-confidence of twelfth-century society. At every level, people were creating new and well-defined institutions to implement their goals. Great lords hired estate managers; townspeople joined guilds that regulated their lives according to impersonal rules; and students and teachers came together to form universities. Many of these associations reflected the developing commercialization of the economy.

The Commercial Revolution Penetrates the Countryside

The earlier commercial revolution had created cities and networks of trade. Now the countryside itself was caught in the web. By 1150, rural life was increasingly organized for the marketplace. The commercialization of the countryside opened up opportunities for both peasants and lords, but it also burdened some with unwelcome obligations.

Great lords hired trained, literate agents to administer their estates, calculate profits and losses, and make marketing decisions. Aristocrats needed money not only because they relished luxuries but also because their honor and authority continued to depend on their personal generosity, patronage, and displays of wealth. In the late twelfth century, when some townsmen could boast fortunes that rivaled the riches of the landed aristocracy, the economic pressures on the nobles increased as their extravagance exceeded their income. Most went into debt.

The lord's need for money changed peasant life, as peasants too became more integrated into the developing commercial economy. The population continued to increase in the twelfth century, and the greater demand for food required more farmland. By the middle of the century, isolated and sporadic attempts to cultivate new land had become a regular and coordinated activity. Great lords offered special privileges to peasants who would do the backbreaking work of plowing marginal land. In 1154, the bishop of Neisse◆ (today in Germany) called for settlers from Flanders and established a village for them. Experts in drainage, these new settlers got rights to the land they reclaimed and owed only light monetary obligations to the bishop, who nevertheless expected to reap a profit from their tolls and tithes. Similar encouragement came from lords throughout Europe, especially in northern Italy, England, Flanders, and Germany. In Flanders, where land was regularly inundated by seawater, the great monasteries sponsored drainage projects. Canals linking the cities to the agricultural districts let boats ply the waters to virtually every nook and cranny of the region. With its dense population, Flanders provided not only a natural meeting ground for long-distance traders from England and France but also numerous markets for local traders.

Sometimes free peasants acted on their own to clear land and relieve the pressure of overpopulation, as when the small freeholders in England's Fenland region cooperated to build banks and dikes to reclaim the land that led out to the North Sea. Villages were founded on the drained land, and villagers shared responsibility for repairing and maintaining the dikes even as each peasant family farmed its new holding individually.

On old estates the rise in population strained to the breaking point the manse organization that had developed in Carolingian Europe, where each household was settled on the land that supported it. Now in the twelfth century, twenty peasant families might live on what had been, in the tenth century, the manse of one family. With the manse supporting so many more people,

◆**Neisse:** NY suh

labor services and dues had to be recalculated, and peasants and their lords often turned services and dues into money rents, payable once a year. With this change, peasant men gained more control over their plots—they could sell them, will them to their sons, or even designate a small portion for their daughters. However, for these privileges, they had either to pay extra taxes or, like communes, to join together to buy their collective liberty for a high price, paid out over many years to their lord. Peasants, like town citizens, gained a new sense of identity and solidarity as they bargained with a lord keen to increase his income at their expense.

Peasants now owed more taxes to support the new administrative apparatuses of monarchs and princes. Kings' demands for money from their subjects filtered to the lowest classes either directly or indirectly. In northern Italy the cities themselves often imposed and enforced dues on the peasants, normally tenant farmers who leased their plots in the countryside surrounding each city. In the mid-twelfth century the urban officials at Florence, working closely with the bishop, dominated the countryside, collecting taxes from its cultivators, calling up its men to fight, and importing its food into the city. Therefore, peasants' gains from rising prices, access to markets, greater productivity, and increased personal freedom were partially canceled out by their cash burdens. Peasants of the late twelfth century ate better than their forebears, but they also had more responsibilities.

Guilds for Commerce and Scholarship

Many **guilds**—associations of craftspeople, merchants, or professionals—began as religious associations. In Ferrara, Italy, for example, the shoemakers' guild started as a prayer confraternity, an association whose members gathered and prayed for one another. But in the second half of the twelfth century, guilds became professional corporations defined by statutes and rules. They negotiated with lords and town governments, set the standards of their trade, and controlled their membership. Universities were also a special kind of guild, defined by statutes and devoted to setting standards

and controlling membership. But in the case of the universities, the standards concerned scholarship, and the members consisted of masters (teachers) and students.

Trade Guilds. As guilds became formally organized, they drew up statutes to determine dues, working hours, wages, and standards for materials and products. Sometimes they came into conflict with town government, as for example in northern Italy, where some communes considered bread too important a commodity to allow bakers to form a guild. At other times the communes supported guild efforts to control wages, reinforcing guild regulations with statutes of their own. When great lords rather than communes governed

A Weaving Workshop

A series of pen-and-ink drawings of various crafts was made in an early-thirteenth-century manuscript produced at Cistercian monastery of Reun, in Austria. In this depiction of a weavers' workshop, a woman (at left) works a carpet loom. She holds a spindle in her left hand and a beater in her right. Two men nearby use other implements of the weaver's trade: shuttles, scissors, and a beater. *Österreichische National-bibliothek, Vienna.*

a city, they too tried to control and protect the guilds. King Henry II of England, for example, eagerly gave some guilds in his Norman duchy special privileges so that they would depend on him.

The manufacture of finished products often required the cooperation of several guilds. Producing wool cloth involved numerous guilds—shearers, weavers, fullers (who thickened the cloth), dyers—generally working under the supervision of the merchant guild that imported the raw wool (see the illustration of weavers on the previous page). Some guilds were more prestigious than others: in Florence, for example, professional guilds of notaries and judges ranked above craft guilds. Within each guild of artisans or merchants existed another kind of hierarchy. Apprentices were at the bottom, journeymen and journeywomen in the middle, and masters at the top. Apprentices were boys and occasionally girls placed under the tutelage of a master for a number of years to learn a trade. At Paris, it took four years of apprenticeship to become a baker; at Genoa, it took ten to become a silversmith. Learning a trade was not the same as becoming a master. A young person would spend many years as a day laborer hired by a master who needed extra help. Unlike apprentices, these journeymen and journeywomen did not live with their masters; they worked for them for a wage. This marked an important stage in the economic history of the West. For the first time, many workers were neither slaves nor dependents but free and independent wage earners. At least a few day workers were female; invariably they received wages far lower than those of their male counterparts. Sometimes a married couple worked at the same trade and hired themselves out as a team. Often journeymen and journeywomen were required to be guild members—so that they would pay dues and so their masters could keep tabs on them.

Masters occupied the top of the guild hierarchy, dominating the offices and policies of the guild. They drew up the guild regulations and served as its chief overseers, inspectors, and treasurers. Because the number of masters was few and the turnover of official posts frequent, most masters eventually had a chance to serve as guild officers.

Occasionally they were elected, but more often they were appointed from among the masters of the craft by the ruler—whether a prince or a commune—of the city.

During the late twelfth century, women's labor in some trades gradually declined in importance. In Flanders, for example, as the manufacture of woolen cloth shifted from rural areas to cities, women participated less in the process. Only isolated manors still needed a *gynaeceum*, the women's quarter where female dependents spun, wove, and sewed garments. Instead, large, new-style looms in cities like Ypres◆ and Ghent were run by men working in pairs. They produced a heavy-weight cloth superior to the fabric made on the lighter looms that women had worked. Similarly, water mills and animal-powered mills gradually took the place of female labor in grinding flour by hand. Some women were certainly artisans and traders, and their names occasionally appeared in guild memberships. But they rarely became guild officers.

Universities. Guilds of masters and students developed at the beginning of the thirteenth century at places such as Paris, Bologna, and Oxford. Each guild (*universitas* in Latin) was so tightly connected to the schools at which the masters taught and the students learned that eventually the term *university* came to include the school as well as the guild.

The universities regulated student discipline, scholastic proficiency, and housing while determining the masters' behavior in equal detail. For example, at the University of Paris the masters were required to wear long black gowns, follow a particular order in their lectures, and set the standards by which students could become masters themselves. The University of Bologna was unique in having two guilds, one of students and one of masters. At Bologna, the students participated in the appointment of masters and paid their salaries.

The University of Bologna was unusual because it was principally a school of law, where the students were often older men, well along in their careers and used to wielding power. The University of Paris, however, at-

◆**Ypres:** EEP ruh

tracted younger students, drawn particularly by its renown in the liberal arts and theology. The Universities of Salerno and Montpellier specialized in medicine. Oxford, once a sleepy town where students clustered around one or two masters, became a center of royal administration, and its university soon developed a reputation for teaching the liberal arts, theology and—very extraordinarily—science.

University curricula differed in content and duration. At the University of Paris in the early thirteenth century, for example, a student had to spend at least six years studying the liberal arts before he could begin to teach. If he wanted to continue his studies with theology, he had to attend lectures on the subject for at least another five years. Lectures were clearly the most important way in which material was conveyed to students. Books were very expensive and not readily available, so students committed their teachers' lectures to memory. The lectures were organized around important texts: the master read an excerpt aloud, delivered his commentary on it, and disputed any contrary commentaries that rival masters might have proposed.

Within the larger association of the university, students found more intimate groups with which to live. These groups, called nations, were linked to the students' place of origin. At Bologna, for example, students incorporated themselves into two nations, the Italians and the non-Italians. Each nation protected its members, wrote statutes, and elected officers.

With few exceptions, masters and students were considered clerics. This had two important consequences. First, it meant that there were no university women. And second, it ensured that university men would be subject to church courts rather than the secular jurisdiction of towns or lords. Many universities could also boast generous privileges from popes and kings, who valued the services of scholars. The combination of clerical status and special privileges made universities virtually self-governing corporations within the towns. This sometimes led to friction. For example, when a student at Oxford was suspected of killing his mistress and the townspeople tried to punish him, the masters protested by refusing to teach and leaving town. Incidents such as this explain why historians speak of the hostility between

"town" and "gown." Yet university towns depended on scholars to patronize local restaurants, shops, and hostels. Town and gown normally learned to negotiate with each other to their mutual advantage.

Religious Fervor and Dissent

Around the same time as universities were forming, renewed religious fervor led to the formation of new religious movements that galvanized individual piety and involved great numbers of laypeople. Unlike the reformed orders of the early twelfth century, which had fled the cities, the new religious groups of the late twelfth century embraced (and were embraced by) urban populations. Rich and poor, male and female joined these movements. They criticized the existing church as too wealthy, impersonal, and spiritually superficial. Intensely focused on the life of Christ, men and women in the late twelfth century made his childhood, agony, death, and presence in the Eucharist—the bread and wine that became the body and blood of Christ in the Mass—the most important experiences of their own lives.

For women in particular, common involvement in new sorts of piety was unprecedented, even in the monasteries of the past. Now beckoning to women of every age and every walk of life, the new piety spread beyond the convent, punctuating the routines of daily life with scriptural reading, fasting, and charity. Some of this intense religious response developed into official, orthodox movements within the church; other religious movements so threatened established doctrine that church leaders declared them heretical.

Francis and the Franciscans. St. Francis (c. 1182–1226) founded the most famous orthodox religious movement—the Franciscans. Francis was a child of city life and commerce. Although expected to follow his well-to-do father in the cloth trade at Assisi in Italy, Francis began to experience doubts, dreams, and illnesses, which spurred him to religious self-examination. Eventually he renounced his family's wealth, dramatically marking the decision by casting off all his clothes and standing naked before his father, a crowd of spectators, and the bishop of

NEW SOURCES, NEW PERSPECTIVES

The Cairo Geniza

What do historians know about the daily life of ordinary people in the Middle Ages? Generally speaking, very little. We have writings from the intellectual elite and administrative documents from monasteries, churches, and courts. But these rarely mention ordinary folk, and if they do, it is always from the standpoint of those who are not ordinary themselves. Glimpsing the concerns, occupations, and family relations of medieval people as they went about their daily lives is very difficult—except at old Cairo (now called Fustat), in Egypt.

Cairo is exceptional because of a cache of unusual sources that were discovered in the *geniza*, or "depository" of the Jewish synagogue near the city. Because their writings might include the name of God, members of the Jewish community left everything that they wrote, including their notes, letters, and even shopping lists, in the geniza to await ceremonial burial. Cairo was not the only place where this was the practice. But by chance at Cairo, the papers were left untouched in the depository and not buried. In 1890, when the synagogue was remodeled, workers tore down the walls of the geniza and discovered literally heaps of documents.

Many of these documents were purchased by American and English collectors and ended up in libraries in New York, Philadelphia, and Cambridge, England, where they remain. As is often the case in historical research, the questions that scholars ask are just as important as the sources themselves. At first, historians did not ask what the documents could tell them about everyday life. They wanted to know how to transcribe and read them; they wanted to study the evolution of their writing style (a dicipline called paleography). They also needed to organize the material. Dispersed among various libraries, the documents were a hodgepodge of lists, books, pages, and fragments. For example, the first page of a personal letter might be in one library, the second page in a completely different location. For decades, scholars were busy simply transcribing the documents with a view to printing and publishing their contents. Not until 1964 was a bibliography of these published materials made available.

Only then, when they knew where to find the sources and how to piece them together, did historians, most notably S. D. Goitein, begin to work through the papers for their historical interest. What Goitein learned through the remains of the

---

theless, heavily taxed. (See "New Sources, New Perspectives," above.) In western Europe, scholars had elaborated objections against Jewish doctrine in the twelfth century. Socially isolated and branded as outcasts, Jews served as scapegoats who helped define the larger western society as orthodox. Like lepers, whose disease cut them off from ordinary communities, Jews were believed to threaten the health of those around them. Lepers had to wear a special costume, were forbidden to touch children, could not eat with those not afflicted, and were housed in

hospices called leprosaria.◆ Jews were similarly segregated from emerging Christian institutions, though they were not confined to hospices.

Forced off their lands during the eleventh century, most Jews ended up in the cities as craftsmen, merchants, or moneylenders, providing capital for the developing commercial society, whose Christian members were prohibited from charging interest, considering it to be usury, which was forbidden by the

---

◆**leprosaria:** leh pruh SAIR ee uh

geniza amplified historians' understanding of the everyday life of much of the Mediterranean world. He discovered a cosmopolitan community occupied with trade, schooling, marriages, divorces, poetry, litigation—all the common issues and activities of a middle-class society. For example, some documents showed that middle-class Jewish women disposed of their own property and that widows often reared and educated their children on their own.

The documents from the Cairo geniza also challenged accepted ideas. For example, historians tended to think that the special tax Christians and Jews were obliged to pay under Muslim rule was paltry, but that was because they did not realize how many Jews and Christians lived on the edge of poverty. This financial hardship is revealed in a letter found in the Cairo geniza, written on behalf of a man named Isaac by Moses Maimonides, who is best known as a major Jewish philosopher but was also a very down-to-earth leader of the Jews in Egypt, 1165–1204. Isaac seems not to have been registered as a taxpayer in any particular place, and Moses is here trying to get him registered in Minyat Ziftā, a provincial town where the rates were lower than elsewhere.

Kindly assist the bearer of this letter, Isaac of Der'a [a town in Morocco], for he is an acquaintance of mine. Ask the hāvēr [the local spiritual leader] to make the community care for him, so that he will get the money for his poll tax in your place. He has to pay two [poll taxes], one for himself and one for his son. If possible, enable him to pay the tax in your town, Minyat Ziftā. For he is a newcomer and thus far has not paid anywhere. He is now on his way to Damietta on an errand important for me. On his way back, action should be taken for him according to your means.

So think twice the next time you throw away a piece of paper. If a historian of the year 3000 were to read your notes, lists, or letters, what would he or she learn about your culture?

QUESTIONS TO CONSIDER

1. Why do the documents in the geniza tell us about Muslim as well as Jewish life in medieval Cairo?
2. Why was it impossible for historians to begin to write about daily life in medieval Cairo immediately after the discovery of the geniza?

FURTHER READING

Constable, Olivia Remie. *Trade and Traders in Muslim Spain: The Commercial Realignment of the Iberian Peninsula, 900–1500.* 1994.

Goitein, S. D. *A Mediterranean Society: The Jewish Communities of the Arab World as Portrayed in the Documents of the Cairo Geniza.* 6 vols. 1967–1983.

Source: Quoted in S. D. Goitein, *A Mediterranean Society: The Jewish Communities of the Arab World as Portrayed in the Documents of the Cairo Geniza*, vol. 2: *The Community* (Berkeley: University of California Press, 1971), 382.

Gospel. The growing monopoly of the guilds, which prohibited Jewish members, pushed Jews out of the crafts and trades: in effect, Jews were compelled to become "usurers" because other fields were closed to them. Even with Christian moneylenders available (for some existed despite the prohibitions), lords, especially kings, borrowed from Jews and encouraged others to do so because, along with their newly asserted powers, European rulers claimed the Jews as their serfs and Jewish property as their own. In England a special royal exchequer of the Jews created in 1194 collected unpaid debts due after the death of a Jewish creditor.

Even before 1194, Henry II had imposed new and arbitrary taxes on the Jewish community. Similarly in France, persecuting Jews and confiscating their property benefited both the treasury and the authoritative image of the king. For example, early in his reign Philip Augustus's agents surprised Jews at Sabbath worship in their synagogues and seized their goods, demanding that they redeem their own property for a large sum of money. Shortly thereafter, Philip declared forfeit 80 percent of all debts owed to Jews; the remaining 20 percent was to be paid directly to the king. About a year later, in 1182, Philip expelled the Jews from the Île-de-France:

> The king gave them leave to sell each his movable goods. . . . But their real estate, that is, houses, fields, vineyards, barns, winepresses, and such like, he reserved for himself and his successors, the kings of the French.

When he allowed the Jews to return, in 1198, he intended for them to be moneylenders or money changers exclusively, and their activities were to be taxed and monitored by officials.

Limiting Jews to moneylending in an increasingly commercial economy also served the interests of lords in debt to Jewish creditors. For example, in 1190, local nobles orchestrated a brutal attack on the Jews of York (in England) to rid themselves of their debts and of the Jews to whom they owed money. Churchmen too used credit in a money economy but resented the fiscal obligations it imposed. With their drive to create centralized territorial states and their desire to make their authority known and felt, powerful rulers of Europe—churchmen and laymen alike—exploited and coerced the Jews while drawing on and encouraging a wellspring of elite and popular anti-Jewish feeling. Although they must have looked exactly like Christians in reality, Jews now became clearly identified in sculpture and in drawings by markers such as conical hats and, increasingly, by demeaning features (see the illustration "Jews as the Other," on this page).

Attacks against Jews were inspired by more than resentment against Jewish money and the desire for power and control. They also, ironically, grew out of the codification of Christian religious doctrine and Christians' anxiety about their own institutions. For example, in the twelfth century, a newly rigorous definition of the Eucharist was promulgated. This held that when the bread and wine were blessed by the priest during Mass, they became the true body and blood of Christ. For some this meant, in effect, that Christ, wounded and bleeding, lay upon the altar. Reflecting Christian anxi-

Jews as the Other

In medieval art, people were often portrayed not as individuals but rather as "types" who could be identified by physical markers. In the second half of the twelfth century, Jews were increasingly portrayed as looking different from Christians. In this illustration, clerics are shown borrowing money from a Jew. What physical features do all the clerics have in common? (Be sure to look at the clothes as well as the hairstyles.) What distinguishes the laymen from the clerics? How do you know who is meant to be the Jew? In fact, Jews did not regularly wear this type of pointed hat until they were forced to do so in some regions of Europe in the late thirteenth century. *Bayerische Staatsbibliothek.*

eties about real flesh upon the altar, sensational stories, originating in clerical circles but soon widely circulated, told of Jews who secretly sacrificed Christian children in a morbid revisiting of the crucifixion of Jesus. This charge, called blood libel by historians, led to massacres of Jews in cities in England, France, Spain, and Germany. Jews had no rituals involving blood sacrifice at all, but they were convenient and vulnerable scapegoats for Christian guilt and anxiety.

Persecuting Heretics

Attacks against Jews coincided with campaigns against heretics those who deviated from the orthodox teachings of the Catholic Church. Heretical beliefs spread in regions where political control was less centralized, as, for example, in southern France. By the end of the twelfth century, church and secular powers combined to stamp out heresies.

Papal missions to Languedoc to address the heretical Albigensians led to the establishment of the Dominican order. Its founder, St. Dominic (1170–1221), recognized that preachers of Christ's word who came on horseback, followed by a crowd of servants and wearing fine clothes, had no moral leverage with their audience. Dominic and his followers, like their adversaries the Albigensians, rejected material riches and instead went about on foot, preaching and begging. They resembled the Franciscans both organizationally and spiritually and were also called friars.

Sometimes the church resorted to armed force in its campaign against heretics. In 1208, the murder of a papal legate in southern

Blood Libel Charges in France and England, c. 1100–1300

Adapted from Angus Mackay with David Ditchburn, eds., Atlas of Medieval Europe (New York: Routledge, 1997).

France prompted the pope to demand that northern princes take up the sword, invade Languedoc, wrest the land from the heretics, and populate it with orthodox Christians. This Albigensian Crusade (1209–1229) marked the first time the pope offered warriors fighting an enemy in Christian Europe all the spiritual and temporal benefits of a crusade to the Holy Land. The crusaders' monetary debts were suspended, and they were promised that their sins would be forgiven after forty days' service. Like all crusades, the Albigensian Crusade had political as well as religious dimensions. It pitted southern French princes who often had heretical sympathies against northern leaders eager to demonstrate their piety and win new possessions. After twenty years of fighting, leadership of the crusade was taken over in 1229 by the Capetian kings of France. Southern resistance was broken, and Languedoc was brought under the French crown.

The Albigensian Crusade, 1209–1229

Disastrous Crusades to the Holy Land

The second half of the twelfth century saw new crusades aimed at the Holy Land (Map 11.2). Following the crushing defeat of the crusaders in the Second Crusade, the Muslim hero Nur al-Din united Syria and presided over a renewal of Sunni Islam. His successor, Saladin (1138–1193), fought the Christian king of Jerusalem over Egypt, which Saladin ruled, together with Syria, by 1186. Caught in a pincer, Jerusalem fell to Saladin's armies in 1187. The Third Crusade was called to retake Jerusalem, and it marked a military and political watershed for the crusader states. The European outpost survived, but it was reduced to a narrow strip of land. Christians could continue to enter Jerusalem as pilgrims, but Islamic hegemony over the Holy Land would remain a fact of life for centuries.

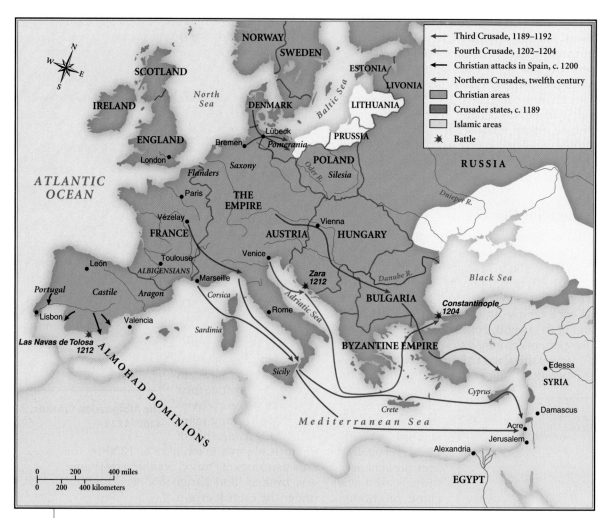

Third Crusade, 1189–1192
Fourth Crusade, 1202–1204
Christian attacks in Spain, c. 1200
Northern Crusades, twelfth century
Christian areas
Crusader states, c. 1189
Islamic areas
Battle

MAP 11.2 Crusades and Anti-Heretic Campaigns, 1150–1204

Europeans aggressively expanded their territory during the second half of the twelfth century. To the north, German knights pushed into Pomerania; to the south, Spanish warriors moved into the remaining strip of Islamic Iberia; to the east, new crusades were undertaken to shore up the tiny European outpost in the Holy Land. Although most of these aggressive activities had the establishment of Christianity as at least one motive, the conquest of Constantinople in 1204 had no such justification. It grew in part out of general European hostility toward Byzantium but mainly out of Venice's commercial ambitions.

The Third Crusade, 1189–1192.   Called by the pope and led by the greatest rulers of Europe—Emperor Frederick I Barbarossa, Philip II of France, Leopold of Austria, and Richard I of England—the Third Crusade reflected political tensions among the European ruling class. Richard in particular seemed to cultivate enemies. The most serious of these was Leopold, whom he offended at the siege of Acre. But the apparent personal tensions indicated a broader hostility between the kings of England and France. Leopold, for example, was Philip's ally. On his return home, Richard was captured by Leopold and held for a huge ransom. He had good reason to write his plaintive poem bemoaning his captivity and the lost "love" of former friends.

The Third Crusade accomplished little and exacerbated tensions with Byzantium.

Frederick I went overland on the crusade, passing through Hungary and Bulgaria and descending into the Byzantine Empire. Before his untimely death by drowning in Turkey, he spent most of his time harassing the Byzantines.

The Fourth Crusade, 1202–1204. The hostilities that surfaced during the Third Crusade made it a dress rehearsal for the Fourth. Prejudice, religious zeal, and self-confidence had become characteristic of western European attitudes toward the Byzantine Greeks. The capture of Constantinople by the crusading army, recounted at the beginning of this chapter, was the logical outcome of these attitudes. Convinced of the rightness of their cause, the crusaders plundered, killed, and ransacked the city for treasure and relics. "Never," wrote a contemporary, "was so great an enterprise undertaken by any people since the creation of the world." When one crusader discovered a cache of relics, a chronicler recalled, "he plunged both hands in and, girding up his loins, he filled the folds of his gown with the holy booty of the Church." The Byzantines, naturally enough, saw the same events as a great tragedy. The bishop of Ephesus wrote:

> And so the streets, squares, houses of two and three stores, sacred places, nunneries, houses for nuns and monks, sacred churches, even the Great Church of God and the imperial palace, were filled with men of the enemy, all of them maddened by war and murderous in spirit. . . . [T]hey tore children from their mothers and mothers from their children, and they defiled the virgins in the holy chapels, fearing neither God's anger nor man's vengeance.

The pope decried the sacking of Constantinople, but he also took advantage of it, ordering the crusaders to stay there for a year to consolidate their gains. Plans to go on to the Holy Land were never carried out. The crusade leaders chose one of themselves—Baldwin of Flanders—to be Byzantine emperor, and he, the other princes, and the Venetians divided the empire among themselves. The new Latin empire of Constantinople lasted until 1261, when the Byzantines recaptured the city and some of its outlying territory.

Popes continued to call crusades to the Holy Land until the mid-fifteenth century, but the Fourth Crusade marked the last major mobilization of men and leaders for such an enterprise. Working against these expeditions were the new values of the late twelfth century, which placed a premium on the interior pilgrimage of the soul and valued rulers who stayed home to care for their people. The crusades served as an outlet for religious

Reconquista
In the north of Spain, the Christians adopted the figure of St. James, considered the Apostle to Spain, as the supernatural leader of their armies against the Muslims to the south. On this tympanum from the cathedral of St. James (Santiago) at Compostela, James is shown as a knight on horseback, holding a flag and a sword. He was known as "the Moor-slayer"—slayer of Muslims. Was the reconquista a holy war? How was it like the crusades, and how was it different? *Institut Amatller d'Art Hispanic, Barcelona.*

The Children's Crusade (1212)

In some regions intense lay piety led uncoordinated groups of young people to attempt making a pilgrimage to or capturing the Holy Land. Chroniclers recorded their activities, some with dismay, others with amusement or admiration. The account below comes from the Ebersheim Chronicle, *written in Germany.*

Unheard-of events appeal to us from their outset, challenging us to preserve their memory. A certain little boy named Nicholas, who came from the region of Cologne, spurred on a great gathering of children through some unknown counsel, claiming that he could walk across the waves of the sea without wetting his feet and could provide sufficient provisions for those following him. The rumor of such a marvelous deed resounded through the cities and towns, and however many heard him, boys or girls, they abandoned their parents, marked themselves as crusaders, and prepared to cross the sea. And so throughout all Germany and France an infinite number of serving-boys, handmaids, and maidens followed their leader and came to Vienne, which is a city by the sea [*sic*]. There they were taken on board some ships, carried off by pirates, and sold to the Saracens. Some who tried to return home wasted away with hunger; and many girls who were virgins when they left were pregnant when they returned. Thus, one can clearly see that this journey issued from the deception of the devil because it caused so much loss.

Source: *Medieval Popular Religion 1000–1500: A Reader,* ed. John Shinners (Peterborough, Ontario: Broadview Press, 1997), 398.

---

fervor, self-confidence, ambition, prejudice, and aggression and were a dress rehearsal for the next wave of European colonization, which began in the sixteenth century. But they had in themselves very little lasting positive effect. They marginally stimulated the European economy, taught Europeans about the importance of stone fortifications, and inspired a vast literature of songs and chronicles. Such achievements must be weighed against the lives lost (on both sides) and the religious polarization and prejudices that the crusades fed on and fortified.

Victorious Crusades on the Borders of Europe

Armed expeditions against those perceived as infidels were launched not only against the Holy Land but also much nearer to home. In the second half of the twelfth century, the Spanish reconquista continued with increasing success and virulence while new wars of conquest were waged at the northern edge of Europe.

The Reconquista Triumphs, 1212.   In the second half of the twelfth century, Christian Spain achieved the political configuration that would last for centuries, dominated to the east by the kingdom of Aragon; in the middle by Castile, whose ruler styled himself emperor; and in the west by Portugal, whose ruler similarly transformed his title from prince to king. The three leaders competed for territory and power, but above all they sought an advantage against the Muslims to the south (Map 11.3).

Muslim disunity aided the Christian conquest of Spain. The Muslims of al-Andalus were themselves beset from the south by a new group of Muslims from North Africa, the Almohades.◆ Claiming religious purity, the Almohades declared their own holy war against the Andalusians. These simultaneous threats caused alliances in Spain to be based on political as well as religious considerations. The Muslim ruler of Valencia, for example, declared himself a vassal of the king of

---

◆**Almohades:** AL moh hadz

Castile and bitterly opposed the Almohades' expansion.

But the crusading ideal held no room for such subtleties. During the 1140s, armies under the command of the kings of Portugal, Castile, and Aragon scored resounding victories against Muslim cities. Enlisting the aid of crusaders on their way to the Holy Land in 1147, the king of Portugal promised land, plunder, and protection to all who would help him attack Lisbon. His efforts succeeded, and Lisbon's Muslim inhabitants fled or were slain. Its Mozarabic bishop (the bishop of the Christians under Muslim rule) was killed, and a crusader from England was put in his place. In the 1170s, when the Almohades conquered the Muslim south and advanced toward the cities taken by the Christians, their exertions had no lasting effect. In 1212, a Christian crusading army of Spaniards led by the kings of Aragon and Castile defeated the Almohades decisively at Las Navas de Tolosa.◆ "On their side 100,000 armed men or more fell in the battle," the king of Castile wrote afterward, "but of the army of the Lord . . . incredible though it may be, unless it be a miracle, hardly 25 or 30 Christians of our whole army fell. O what happiness! O what thanksgiving!" The decisive turning point in the reconquista was reached, though all of Spain came under Christian control only in 1492.

The Northern Crusades. Christians flexed their military muscle along Europe's northern frontiers as well. By the twelfth century, the peoples living along the Baltic coast—partly pagan, mostly Slavic- or Baltic-speaking—had learned to glean a living and a profit

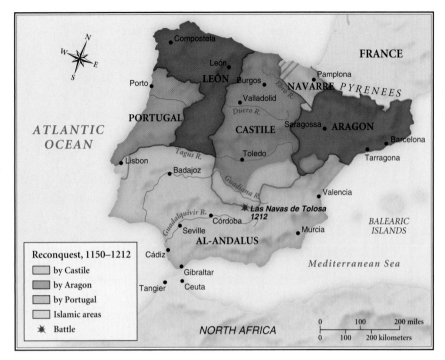

MAP 11.3 The Reconquista, 1150–1212
Slowly but surely the Christian kingdoms of Spain encroached on al-Andalus, taking Las Navas de Tolosa, deep in Islamic territory, in 1212. At the center of this activity was Castile. It had originally been a tributary of León, but in the course of the twelfth century it became a power in its own right. (In 1230, León and Castile merged into one kingdom.) Meanwhile, the ruler of Portugal, who had also been dependent on León, began to claim the title of king, which was recognized officially in 1179, when he put Portugal under the protection of the papacy. Navarre was joined to Aragon until 1134, when it became, briefly, an independent kingdom. (In 1234 the count of Champagne came to the throne of Navarre, and thereafter its history was as much tied to France as to Spain.)

from the inhospitable soil and climate. Through fishing and trading, they supplied the rest of Europe and Russia with slaves, furs, amber, wax, and dried fish. Like the earlier Vikings, they combined commercial competition with outright raiding, so that the Danes and the Germans of Saxony both benefited and suffered from their presence. When St. Bernard began to preach the Second Crusade in Germany, he discovered that the Germans were indeed eager to attack the infidels—the ones right next door, that is. St. Bernard pressed the pope to add these northern heathens to the list of those against whom holy war should be launched and urged their conversion or extermination. Thus began the Northern Crusades, which continued intermittently until the early fifteenth century.

◆**Las Navas de Tolosa:** lahs NAH vahs zay toh LOH suh

MAPPING THE WEST Europe and Byzantium, c. 1215
The major transformation in the map of the West between 1150 and 1215 was the conquest of Constantinople and the setting up of European rule there until 1261. The Byzantine Empire was now a mere shell. A new state, Epirus, emerged in the power vacuum to dominate Thrace. Bulgaria once again gained its independence. If Venice had hoped to control the Adriatic by conquering Constantinople, it must have been disappointed, for Hungary became its rival over the ports of the Dalmatian coast.

The Danish king Valdemar I (r. 1157–1182) and the Saxon duke Henry the Lion led the first phase of the Northern Crusades. Their initial attacks on the Slavs were uncoordinated—in some instances they even fought each other. But in key raids in the 1160s and 1170s, the two leaders worked together briefly to bring much of the region west of the Oder River under their control. They took some land outright—Henry the Lion apportioned conquered territory to his followers, for example—but more often the Slavic princes surrendered and had their territories reinstated once they became vassals of the Christian rulers. Meanwhile,

churchmen arrived: the Cistercians came long before the first phase of fighting had ended, confidently building their monasteries to the very banks of the Oder River. Slavic peasants surely suffered from the conquerors' fire and pillage, but the Slavic ruling classes ultimately benefited from the crusades. Once converted to Christianity, they found it advantageous for both their eternal salvation and their worldly profit to join new crusades to areas still farther east.

Meanwhile German traders, craftspeople, and colonists poured in, populating new towns and cities along the Baltic coast and dominating the shipping that had once been controlled by non-Christians. The leaders of the crusades gave these townsmen some political independence but demanded a large share of the cities' wealth in return.

Although less well known than the crusades to the Holy Land, the Northern Crusades had far more lasting effects: they settled the Baltic region with German-speaking lords and peasants and forged a permanent relationship between northeastern Europe and its neighbors to the south and west. With the Baltic dotted with churches and monasteries and its peoples dipped into baptismal waters, the region would gradually adopt the institutions of western medieval society—cities, guilds, universities, castles, and manors. The Livs (whose region was eventually known as Livonia) were conquered by 1208, and their bishop sent knights northward to conquer the Estonians. The Prussians would be conquered with the cooperation between the Polish and German aristocracy; German peasants eventually settled Prussia. Only the Lithuanians managed to successfully resist western conquest, settlement, and conversion.

Review: In what ways was Europe's increasing hostility toward the Jews linked to its crusading movements?

Conclusion

In the second half of the twelfth century, Christian Europe expanded from the Baltic Sea to the southern Iberian peninsula. European settlements in the Holy Land, by contrast, were nearly obliterated. When western Europeans sacked Constantinople in 1204, Europe and the Islamic world became the dominant political forces in the West.

Powerful territorial kings and princes expressed their new self-confidence by supporting a lay vernacular culture that celebrated their achievements and power. They also began to establish institutions of bureaucratic authority. They hired staffs to handle their accounts, record acts, collect taxes, issue writs, and preside over courts. Flourishing cities, a growing money economy, and trade and manufacturing provided the finances necessary to support the personnel now hired by medieval governments. Clerical schools and, by the end of the twelfth century, universities became the training grounds for the new administrators.

Rulers were not alone in their quest to document, define, and institutionalize their power. The second half of the twelfth and the early thirteenth centuries were a great age of organization. Craft guilds and universities drew up statutes providing clearly specified rights, obligations, and privileges to their members. Developing out of the commercial revolution, such organizations in turn made commercial activities a permanent part of medieval life.

Religious associations also formed. Franciscans, Dominicans, and heretics—however dissimilar their beliefs—all rejected wealth and material possessions, revealing how deeply the commercial revolution had affected the moral life of some Europeans, who could not accept the profit motive inherent in a money economy. In emphasizing preaching, these religious associations showed that a lay population, already Christian, now yearned for a more intense and personal spirituality.

New piety, new exclusivity, and new power arose in a society both more confident and less tolerant. Crusaders fought more often and against an increasing variety of foes, not only in the Holy Land but also in Spain, in southern France, and on Europe's northern frontiers. With heretics voicing criticisms and maintaining their beliefs, the church, led by the papacy, now defined orthodoxy and declared dissenters its enemies. The Jews, who had once been fairly well integrated into the Christian community, were treated ambivalently, alternately used and abused. The Slavs and Balts became targets for new evangelical zeal; the Greeks became the butt of envy, hostility, and finally enmity. European Christians still considered Muslims arrogant heathens, and the deflection of the Fourth Crusade did not stem the zeal of popes to call for new crusades to the Holy Land.

Confident and aggressive, the leaders of Christian Europe in the thirteenth century would attempt to impose their rule, legislate morality, and create a unified worldview impregnable to attack. But this drive for order would be countered by unexpected varieties of thought and action, by political and social tensions, and by intensely personal religious quests.

Suggested References

Governments as Institutions

The medieval origins of modern state institutions is a traditional interest of historians studying the medieval period. Hudson explores the growth of royal institutions of justice. Baldwin gives a carefully focused account of the French experience. Bartlett, however, insists on the differences between medieval and modern politics.

Baldwin, John W. *The Government of Philip Augustus: Foundations of French Royal Power in the Middle Ages.* 1986.

Bartlett, Robert. *England under the Norman and Angevin Kings, 1075–1225.* 2000.

Evergates, Theodore, ed. *Aristocratic Women in Medieval France.* 1999.

Fuhrmann, Horst. *Germany in the High Middle Ages, c. 1050–1200.* Trans. T. Reuter. 1986.

Hudson, John. *The Formation of the English Common Law: Law and Society in England from the Norman Conquest to Magna Carta.* 1996.

Jordan, Karl. *Henry the Lion: A Biography.* Trans. P. S. Falla. 1986.

*Otto of Freising. *The Deeds of Frederick Barbarossa.* Trans. C. C. Mierow. 1953.

The Growth of a Vernacular High Culture

Chrétien de Troyes's *Yvain* is a good example of a twelfth-century romance, while troubadour poetry is collected in Goldin's anthology. Cheyette gives an illuminating account of one southern French ruler and her world, and Wheeler and Parsons's collection sheds light on another.

Bouchard, Constance B. *"Strong of Body, Brave and Noble": Chivalry and Society in Medieval France.* 1998.

Cheyette, Fredric L. *Ermengard of Narbonne and the World of the Troubadours.* 2001.

*Chrétien de Troyes. *Yvain: The Knight of the Lion.* Trans. Burton Raffel. 1987.

Crouch, David. *William Marshal: Court, Career, and Chivalry in the Angevin Empire, 1147–1219.* 1990.

*Goldin, Frederick. *Lyrics of the Troubadors and Trouvères: Original Texts, with Translations.* 1973.

The Song of Roland. Trans. P. Terry. 1965.

Wheeler, Bonnie and John Carmi Parsons, ed. *Eleanor of Aquitaine: Lord and Lady.* 2003.

New Lay and Religious Associations

The Little Flowers of Saint Francis gives a good idea of Franciscan spirituality, while the Franciscans are explored as part of wider religious, social, and economic movements in Little's study. Audisio's study looks sympathetically at one heretical group.

Audisio, Gabriel. *The Waldensian Dissent: Persecution and Survival, c. 1170–c. 1570.* Trans. Claire Davison. 1999.

Epstein, Steven. *Wage Labor and Guilds in Medieval Europe.* 1991.

Ferruolo, Stephen C. *The Origins of the University: The Schools of Paris and Their Critics, 1100–1215.* 1985.

The Little Flowers of Saint Francis. Trans. L. Sherley-Price. 1959.

Little, Lester K. *Religious Poverty and the Profit Economy in Medieval Europe.* 1978.

European Aggression Within and Without

Bartlett looks at expansion on all the frontiers of Europe, connecting movement outward with the creation of internal identity. Christiansen's book is the essential source for the Northern Crusades, Wakefield's for the Albigensian Crusade. There are numerous books on the crusades to the east; Riley-Smith gives a good overview. Tolan considers attitudes and prejudices.

Bartlett, Robert. *The Making of Europe: Conquest, Colonization, and Cultural Change, 950–1350.* 1993.

*Blood libel: http://www.fordham.edu/halsall/source/1173williamnorwich.html.

Christiansen, Eric. *The Northern Crusades.* 2nd ed. 1998.

Queller, Donald E., and Thomas F. Madden. *The Fourth Crusade: The Conquest of Constantinople, 1201–1204.* 2nd ed. 1999.

Riley-Smith, Jonathan. *The Crusades: A Short History.* 1987.

Tolan, John V. *Saracens: Islam in the Medieval European Imagination.* 2002.

Wakefield, Walter L. *Heresy, Crusade, and Inquisition in Southern France, 1100–1250.* 1974.

*Primary sources.

CHAPTER REVIEW

IMPORTANT EVENTS

1139–1153	Civil War in England
1152–1190	Reign of Frederick Barbarossa
1154–1189	Reign of King Henry II
1176	Battle of Legnano
1180–1223	Reign of Philip II Augustus
1182	Philip Augustus expels the Jews from the Île-de-France
1182–1226	Francis of Assisi
1189–1192	The Third Crusade
1202–1204	The Fourth Crusade
1204	Fall of Constantinople to Crusaders
1204	Philip takes Normandy, Anjou, Maine, Touraine, and Poitou from John
1209–1229	Albigensian Crusade
1212	Battle of Las Navas de Tolosa; triumph of the reconquista
1214	Battle of Bouvines
1215	Magna Carta

KEY TERMS

Albigensians (420)

Angevin (406)

Beguines (420)

chansons de geste (415)

chivalry (415)

common law (407)

friars (420)

guilds (417)

jongleur (414)

scutage (409)

troubadours (413)

REVIEW QUESTIONS

1. What new sources and institutions of power became available to rulers in the twelfth century?
2. What does the work of the troubadours and vernacular poets reveal about the nature of entertainment—its themes, its audience, its performers—in the twelfth century?
3. Why did guilds develop in medieval European cities?
4. In what ways was Europe's increasing hostility toward the Jews linked to its crusading movements?

MAKING CONNECTIONS

1. What were the chief differences that separated the ideals of the religious life in the period 1150–1215 from those of the period 1050–1150?
2. How did commercial interests enter into the crusading movements of the thirteenth century?

FOR FURTHER EXPLORATION

To assess your mastery of the material in this chapter, see the Online Study Guide at bedfordstmartins.com/hunt.

To read additional primary-source material from this period, see Chapter 11 in *Sources of The Making of the West*, Second Edition, Volume I.

The Medieval Search for Order and Harmony,
1215–1320

IN THE SECOND half of the thirteenth century, a wealthy patron asked a Parisian workshop specializing in manuscript illuminations to decorate Aristotle's *On the Length and Shortness of Life*. Most Parisian illuminators knew very well how to illustrate the Bible, liturgical books, and patristic writings. But Aristotle was a Greek who had lived before the time of Christ, and he was skeptical about the possibility of an afterlife. His treatise on the length of life ended with death. The workshop's artists did not care about this fact. They proceeded to illustrate Aristotle's work as if he had been a Christian and had believed in the immortal soul. As may be seen in the illustration opposite this page, for the first initial of the book (the large, highly decorated letter that opened the text), the artists depicted the Christian Mass for the dead, a rite that is performed for the eternal salvation of Christians. In this way, the artists subtly but surely forced Aristotle's treatise into the prevailing system of Christian belief and practice.

In the period 1215 to 1320, people at all levels, from workshop artisans to kings and popes, expected to find harmony, order, and unity in a world they believed was created by God. Sometimes, as in the case of the illumination made for Aristotle's work or in the Gothic cathedrals built in the cities, such harmony was made manifest. Because of this, historians sometimes speak of the "medieval synthesis." But often unity was a delusion. For example, kings and popes debated the limits of their power, while theologians fought over the place of reason in matters of faith. Discord continually threatened expectations of unity, harmony, and synthesis.

Christianizing Aristotle
This illumination was created for a thirteenth-century Latin translation of Aristotle's book *On the Length and Shortness of Life.* Although Aristotle did not believe in the eternity of the soul, the artists nevertheless placed a depiction of the Christian Mass for the dead in one of the book's initials, in this way revealing their conviction that the ancient teachings of Aristotle and Christian practice were harmonious. *Biblioteca Apostolica Vaticana.*

New institutions of power and control were created to ensure unity. The church set up tribunals to root out religious dissidents, and kings and other rulers extended their influence over their subjects. Yet these tribunals did not end heresy, and kings did not gain all the power that they wanted. Diversity and opposition continually threatened attempts at control from above.

❖ The Church's Mission of Reform

The church had long sought to reform the secular world. In the eleventh century, during the Gregorian reform, that effort had focused on the king. In the thirteenth century,

however, the church focused on purifying all of society. It looked to strengthened institutions of justice to combat heresy and heretics, and it supported preachers who would bring the official views of the church to the streets. In this way, the church attempted to reorder the world in the image of heaven, with everyone following one rule of God in order and harmony. To some degree, the church succeeded in this endeavor; but it also came up against the limits of control, as dissident voices and forces clashed with its vision.

Innocent III and the Fourth Lateran Council, 1215

Innocent III (r. 1198–1216), whose portrait appears on this page, was the most powerful, respected, and prestigious of medieval popes.

Innocent III
Pope Innocent III appears young, aristocratic, and impassive in this thirteenth-century fresco in the lower church of Sacro Speco, Subiaco, about thirty miles east of Rome and not far from Innocent's birthplace. Innocent claimed full power over the whole church, in any region. Moreover, he thought the pope had the right to intervene in any issue where sin might be involved—and that meant most matters. While these were only theoretical claims, difficult to put into practice given his meager resources and inefficient staff, Innocent was a major force in his day. *Scala/Art Resource, NY.*

1175	1200	1225

♦ **1188** King Alfonso IX summons townsmen to the *cortes*

♦ **1240** Mongols capture Kiev

♦ **1212–1250** Reign of Frederick II

♦ **1215** Fourth Lateran Council

♦ **1226–1270** Reign of Louis IX (St. Louis)

♦ **1232** Frederick II, "Statute in Favor of the Princes"

♦ **1233** First permanent Inquisition

He was the pope who allowed St. Francis's group of impoverished followers to become a new church order, and he was the pope who called the Fourth Crusade, the last to mobilize a large force drawn from every level of European society. The first pope to be trained at universities, Innocent studied theology at Paris and law at Bologna. From theology, he learned to tease new meaning out of canonical writings to magnify papal authority: he thought of himself as ruling in the place of Christ the King, with kings and emperors existing to help the pope. From law, Innocent gained his conception of the pope as lawmaker and of law as an instrument of moral reformation.

Innocent utilized the traditional method of declaring church law: a council. Presided over by Innocent, the Fourth Lateran Council (1215) attempted to regulate all aspects of Christian life. The comprehensive legislation it produced in only three days—the pope and his committees had prepared almost all the provisions beforehand—aimed at reforming both the clergy and the laity. Innocent and the other members of the council hoped in this way to create a society united under the authority of the church and its priesthood. They expected that Christians, lay and clerical alike, would work together harmoniously to achieve the common goal of salvation. They

Host Mold
One of the most important decisions of the Fourth Lateran Council was to declare that the body and blood of Christ were "transubstantiated" in the Eucharist: that is, they were transformed into the actual body and blood of Christ. Veneration of the host began to supplant veneration of saints, and increasingly people desired to gaze at the host. Albertus Magnus wrote: "Showing the host to good people impels them to the good." Molds such as the one shown here, made in the fourteenth century, impressed inspiring images into the bread, in this case the image of Christ surrounded by the twelve apostles.

did not anticipate either the sheer variety of responses to their message or the persistence of those who defied it altogether.

The Laity and the Sacraments.   For laymen and laywomen, perhaps the most important canons of the Fourth Lateran Council concerned the sacraments, the rites the church believed Jesus had instituted to confer sanctifying grace. Building on the reforms of the eleventh century, the council made the obligations that the sacraments imposed on the laity more precise and detailed. One canon required Christians to attend Mass and to confess their sins to a priest at

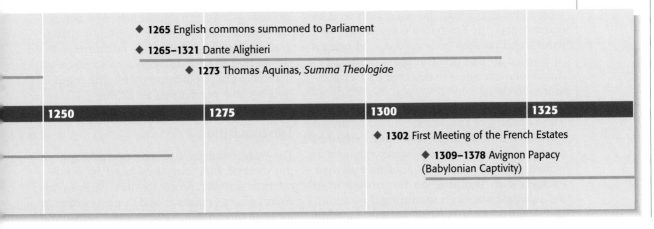

◆ **1265** English commons summoned to Parliament

◆ **1265–1321** Dante Alighieri

◆ **1273** Thomas Aquinas, *Summa Theologiae*

| 1250 | 1275 | 1300 | 1325 |

◆ **1302** First Meeting of the French Estates

◆ **1309–1378** Avignon Papacy (Babylonian Captivity)

least once a year. The increasing importance of the Eucharist as God's potent salvific instrument was reinforced by the council's definition:

> [Christ's] body and blood are truly contained in the sacrament of the altar under the forms of bread and wine, the bread and wine having been changed in substance [transubstantiated], by God's power, into his body and blood, so that in order to achieve this mystery of unity we receive from God what he received from us. Nobody can effect this sacrament except a priest who has been properly ordained according to the church's keys, which Jesus Christ himself gave to the apostles and their successors.

The Council's emphasis on this moment of transformation strengthened the role of the priest, for only he could celebrate this mystery.

Other canons of the Fourth Lateran Council codified the traditions of marriage. The church declared that it had the right to discover any impediments to a union, and it claimed jurisdiction over any marital disputes. The canons further insisted that children conceived within clandestine or forbidden marriages be declared illegitimate; they were not to inherit from their parents or become priests.

The impact of these provisions was perhaps less dramatic than church leaders hoped. Well-to-do London fathers included their bastard children in their wills. On English manors, sons conceived out of wedlock regularly took over their parents' land. Men and women continued to marry in secret, and even churchmen had to admit that the consent of both parties made any marriage valid. Nevertheless, many men and women took to heart the obligation to take communion (the Eucharist consecrated by a priest) and confess once a year, and priests proceeded to call out the bans (announcements of marriages) to discover any impediments to them.

The Labeling of the Jews. Innocent III had wanted the council to condemn Christian men who had sexual intercourse with Jewish women and then claimed ignorance as their excuse. But, building on the anti-Jewish feelings that had been mounting throughout the twelfth century, the Fourth Lateran Council went even further, requiring all Jews to advertise their religion by some outward sign: "We decree that [Jews] of either sex in every Christian province at all times shall be distinguished from other people by the character of their dress in public."

As with all church rules, these took effect only when local rulers enforced them. In many instances, they did so with zeal, not so much because they were eager to humiliate Jews but rather because they could make money selling exemptions to Jews who were willing to pay to avoid the requirements. Nonetheless, sooner or later Jews almost everywhere had to wear a badge as a sign of their second-class status.

In southern France and in a few places in Spain, Jews were supposed to wear round badges. In England, Oxford required a badge, while Salisbury demanded that Jews wear special clothing. In Vienna they were told to put on pointed hats (see the illustration on page 424).

The Suppression of Heretics. The Fourth Lateran Council's longest decree blasted heretics: "Those condemned as heretics shall be handed over to the secular authorities for punishment." If the secular authority did not "purge his or her lands of heretical filth," the heretic was to be excommunicated. If he or she had vassals, they were to be released from their oaths of fealty. The land of heretics were to be taken over by orthodox Christians.

Rulers heeded these declarations. Already some had taken up arms against heretics in the Albigensian Crusade (1209–1229). As a result of this crusade, southern France, which had been the home of most Albigensians, came under French royal control. The continuing presence of heretics there and elsewhere led church authorities inspired by the Fourth Lateran Council to set up a court of papal inquisitors. The Inquisition became permanent in 1233.

The Inquisition

The word *inquisition* simply means "inquiry"; the method had long been used by secular rulers to summon people together, either to discover facts or to uncover and punish crimes. In its zeal to end heresy and save souls, the thirteenth-century church used the **Inquisition** to ferret out "heretical depravity." Calling suspects to testify, inquisitors, aided by secular authorities, rounded up virtually entire villages and interrogated everyone. (See "New Sources, New Perspectives," page 440.)

First the inquisitors typically called the people of a district to a "preaching," where they gave a sermon and promised clemency to those who confessed their heresy promptly. Then, at a general inquest, they questioned each man and woman who seemed to know something about heresy: "Have you ever seen any heretics . . . ? Have you heard them preach? Attended any of their ceremonies? Adored heretics?" The judges assigned relatively lenient penalties to those who were not aware that they held heretical beliefs and to heretics who quickly recanted. But unrepentant heretics were punished severely because the church believed that such people threatened the salvation of all. (See "Taking Measure," on this page.)

In the thirteenth century, for the first time, long-term imprisonment became a tool to repress heresy, even if the heretic confessed. "It is our will," wrote one tribunal, "that [Raymond Maurin and Arnalda, his wife,] because they have rashly transgressed against God and holy church . . . be thrust into perpetual prison to do [appropriate] penance, and we command them to remain there in perpetuity." The inquisitors also used imprisonment to force people to recant, to give the names of other heretics, or to admit a plot. As the quest for religious control spawned wild fantasies of conspiracy, the inquisitors pinned their fears on real people.

Lay Piety

The church's zeal to reform the laity was matched by the desire of many laypeople to become more involved in their religion. They flocked to hear the preaching of friars and took what they heard to heart. Some women found new outlets for their piety by focusing on the Eucharist.

Preaching Friars and Receptive Townspeople. The friars made themselves a permanent feature of the towns. At night they slept in their convents, but they spent their

TAKING MEASURE

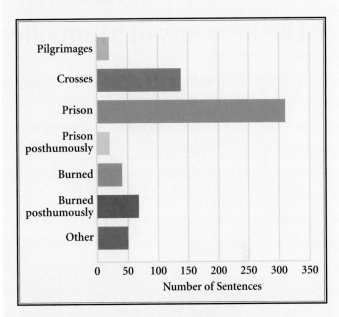

Sentences Imposed by an Inquisitor, 1308–1323
How harsh was the Inquisition? Did its agents regularly burn people alive? How frequently did they imprison people, or order them to go on pilgrimage or wear crosses on their clothing? Statistical data to answer these sorts of questions are normally lacking for the medieval period. But there are exceptions. One comes from a register of offenses and punishments kept by Bernard Gui, an inquisitor in Languedoc from 1308 to 1323. Of 633 punishments handed down by Gui's tribunal, only a relatively small number of people were burned alive. (Those "burned posthumously" would have been burned alive but died beforehand.) Nearly half of the guilty were sentenced to prison, usually for life. (Some were sent to prison posthumously; that is, they would have gone to prison had they not died in the meantime.) Many historians conclude that the Inquisition was not particularly harsh, for capital punishment at the time was regularly meted out to criminals under secular law. *From J. Given, "A Medieval Inquisitor at Work," in* Portraits of Medieval and Renaissance Living, *ed. S. K. Cohn and S. A. Epstein (Ann Arbor: University of Michigan Press, 1996), 215.*

days preaching. So too did other men, often trained in the universities and willing to take to the road to speak to throngs of townsfolk. When Berthold,♦ a Franciscan who traveled the length and breadth of Germany giving

♦**Berthold:** BEHR tohlt

NEW SOURCES, NEW PERSPECTIVES

The Peasants of Montaillou

While historians can know from material evidence how medieval peasants lived and worked, it is nearly impossible to find out what peasants thought. Almost all of our written sources come from the elite classes who, if they noticed peasants at all, certainly did not care about their ideas. How, then, can historians hear and record the voices of peasants themselves? Until the 1960s, historians did not much care to hear those voices. They wanted to know about economic structures rather than peasant mentalities.

That is why historians did not notice an extremely important source of peasant voices, the Inquisition register made at the command of Bishop Fournier of Pamiers in the years 1318–1325. Fournier was a zealous anti-heretic, and when he became bishop of a diocese that harbored many Albigensians, he put the full weight of his office behind rounding them up. He concentrated on one particularly "heretic-infested" village, Montaillou, in the south of France near the Spanish border. Interrogating a total of 114 people, including 48 women, over seven years, he committed their confessions and testimony to parchment with a view to punishing those who were heretics. Fournier was not interested in the peasants' "voices": he wanted to know their religious beliefs and every other detail of their lives and thoughts. However, the long-term result of Fournier's zealous inquest—though he would not be happy to hear it—was to preserve the words of a whole village of peasants, shepherds, artisans, and shopkeepers.

Fournier's register sat in the Vatican archives for centuries, gathering dust, until it was transcribed and published in 1965. Only in 1975 was its great potential for peasant history made clear; in that year, Emmanuel Le Roy Ladurie published *Montaillou: The Promised Land of Error,* which for the first time made a medieval peasant village come to life.

Le Roy Ladurie's book reveals the myths, beliefs, rivalries, tensions, love affairs, tendernesses, and duplicities of a small peasant community where all the people, even those who were better off, worked with their hands; where wealth was calculated by the size of a family's herd of livestock; and where the church's demands for tithes seemed outrageously unfair.

The register shows a community torn apart by the opportunities the Inquisition gave to informers. The village priest, from a well-off family, was very clear about why he was denouncing his parishioners. He liked the Albigensians, he said (he was probably one himself), but "I want to be revenged on the peasants of Montaillou, who have done me harm, and I will avenge myself in every possible way." But the register also shows a community united by love: parents cared about their children, husbands and wives loved one another, and illicit lovers were caught up in passion. One affair took place between the village priest and Béatrice, a woman of somewhat higher rank. The priest courted her for half a year, and after she gave in, they met two or three nights a week. In the end, though, Béatrice decided to marry someone else and left the village.

Béatrice was not the only independent-minded person in Montaillou. Many people there were indeed heretics in the sense that their beliefs defied the teachings of the church. But they called themselves "good Christians." Other villagers re-

sermons, came to a town, a high tower was set up for him outside the city walls. A pennant advertised his presence and let people know which way the wind would blow his voice. St. Anthony of Padua preached in Italian to huge audiences that had lined up hours in advance to be sure they would have a place to hear him.

Townspeople flocked to such preachers because they wanted to know how the Christian message applied to their daily lives. They were concerned, for example, about

mained in the Catholic fold. And still others in the region had their own ideas, as may be seen from Raimond de l'Aire's testimony.

Fournier's register became a "new" source because Le Roy Ladurie had new questions and sought a way to answer them, treating his evidence the way ethnographers treat reports by native peoples they have interviewed. Today some historians question Le Roy Ladurie's approach, arguing that an Inquisition record cannot be handled in the same way that ethnographers consider information from their informants. For example, they point out that the words of the peasants were translated from Occitan, the language they spoke, to Latin for the official record. What readers hear are not the voices of the peasants but rather their ideas filtered through the vocabulary and summaries of the elite. Moreover, the peasants called before the tribunal were held in prison, feared for their lives, and were forced to talk about events that had taken place ten or more years earlier. In light of these circumstances, to what extent is their testimony a direct window onto their lives? Nevertheless, the register remains a precious source for learning at least something about what ordinary people thought and felt in a small village about seven hundred years ago.

Raimond de l'Aire's Testimony   One of the witnesses recorded by Jacques Fournier was Raimond de l'Aire. He was not from Montaillou but rather from Tignac, a small town in Fournier's diocese. In this testimony he reports on the beliefs of one of his acquaintances.

An older man told [Raimond de l'Aire] that a mule has a soul as good as a man's; "and from this belief he had by himself deduced that his own soul and those of other men are nothing but blood, because when a person's blood is taken away, he dies. He also believed that a dead person's soul and body both die, and that after death nothing human remains. . . . From this he believed that the human soul after death [is] neither good nor evil, and that there is no hell or paradise in another world where human souls are rewarded or punished."

QUESTIONS TO CONSIDER

1. In what ways are modern court cases like the Inquisition register of Fournier? In what ways are they unlike such a source? Could you use modern court cases to reconstruct the life of a community?
2. What are the advantages and the pitfalls of using a source such as the register for historical research?
3. Do you think that Raimond might have made up his testimony? Why or why not?
4. What does this testimony suggest about the impact of church doctrines in the French countryside?

FURTHER READING

Boyle, Leonard. "Montaillou Revisited: Mentalité and Methodology." In J. A. Raftis, ed., *Pathways to Medieval Peasants*. 1981.

Le Roy Ladurie, Emmanuel. *Montaillou: The Promised Land of Error*. 1978. The original French version was published in 1975.

Resaldo, Renato. "From the Door of His Tent: The Fieldworker and the Inquisitor." In James Clifford and George E. Marcus, eds., *Writing Culture: The Poetics and Politics of Ethnography*. 1986.

Source: *Heresy and Authority in Medieval Europe: Documents in Translation*, ed. Edward Peters (Philadelphia: University of Pennsylvania Press, 1980), 253.

the ethics of moneymaking, sex in marriage, and family life. In turn, the preachers represented the front line of the church. They met the laity on their own turf and taught them to shape their behaviors to church teachings.

Laypeople further tied their lives to the mendicants, particularly the Franciscans, by becoming **tertiaries**.♦ They adopted the practices of the friars—prayer and works of

---

♦**tertiaries:** Tur shee eh reez

Friars and Usurers

As the illustration on page 424 reveals, clerics sometimes borrowed money. The friars had a different attitude. St. Francis, son of a merchant, refused to touch money altogether. Instead, he and his friars begged for food and shelter. Even when their numbers grew and they began forming communities and living in monasteries, the friars still insisted on personal poverty, while ministering to city dwellers, who had to deal with money in some way to make a living. In this illumination from about 1250, a Franciscan (in light-colored robes) and a Dominican (in black) reject offers from two usurers, whose profession they are thus shown to condemn. Other friars, including Thomas Aquinas, worked out justifications for some kinds of moneymaking professions, though not usury.

Bibliothèque Nationale, Paris.

charity, for example—while continuing to live in the world, raising families and tending to the normal tasks of daily life, whatever their occupation. Even kings and queens became tertiaries.

The Piety of Women. All across Europe, women in the thirteenth century sought outlets for their intense piety. As in previous centuries, powerful families founded new nunneries, especially within towns and cities. On the whole, these were set up for the daughters of the very wealthy. Ordinary women found different modes of religious expression. Some sought the lives of quiet activity and rapturous mysticism of the Beguines, others the lives of charity and service of women's mendicant orders, and still others domestic lives of marriage and family punctuated by religious devotions. Elisabeth of Hungary, who married a German prince at the age of fourteen, raised three children. At the same time, she devoted her life to fasting, prayer, and service to the poor.

Many women were not as devout as Elisabeth. In the countryside, they cooked their porridge, brewed their ale, and raised their children. They attended church regularly, but only on major feast days or for

churching—the ritual of purification after a pregnancy. In the cities, working women scratched out a meager living. They sometimes made pilgrimages to relic shrines to seek help or cures. Religion was a part of these women's lives, but it did not dominate them.

For some urban women, however, religion was the focus of life, and the church's attempt to define and control the Eucharist had some unintended results. The new emphasis on the holiness of the transformed wine and bread induced some of these pious women to eat nothing but the Eucharist. One such woman, Angela of Foligno,♦ reported that the consecrated bread swelled in her mouth, tasting sweeter than any other food. For these women, eating the Eucharist was truly eating God. This is how they understood the church's teaching that the consecrated bread was actually Christ's body. In the minds of these holy women, Christ's crucifixion was the literal sacrifice of his body, to be eaten by sinful men and women as the way to redeem themselves and others. Renouncing all other foods became part of a life of service, because many of these devout women gave the poor the food that they refused to eat.

These women both accepted and challenged the pronouncements of the Fourth Lateran Council about the meaning of the Eucharist. They agreed that only priests could say Mass, but some of them bypassed their own priests, receiving the Eucharist (as they explained) directly from Christ in the form of a vision. Although men dominated the institutions that governed political, religious, and economic affairs, these women found ways to control their own lives and to some extent the lives of those around them, both those whom they served and those they

---

♦**Angela of Foligno:** AN jehl uh (of) foh LEE nyoh

A Lady and Her Loving Falcon
This sumptuous velvet-and-silk pouch, made by an embroideress in about 1320, shows a lady in the position of falconer. The falcon—a bird ordinarily used as an aid in hunting—is here depicted as her lover. He is flying toward her to place a crown of greenery on her head, while she touches him tenderly on the shoulder. In her other hand she holds the leash with which she trained him. © *Musée de Tissus, Lyon.*

lived with. Typically involved with meal preparation and feeding, like other women of the time, these holy women found a way to use their control over ordinary food to gain new kinds of social and religious power that could force the clergy to confront female piety.

Review: How did people respond to the teachings and laws of the church in the early thirteenth century?

❖ Cultural Harmonies

Just as the church saw itself as regulating worldly life in accordance with God's plan for salvation, so contemporary thinkers, writers, musicians, and artists sought to harmonize the secular with the sacred. Scholars wrote treatises that reconciled faith with reason, poets and musicians sang of the links between heaven and human life on earth, and artists expressed the same ideas in stone and sculpture. Even in the face of many contradictions, all of these groups were largely successful in communicating a harmonious image of the world.

Scholasticism: Harmonizing Faith and Reason

Scholasticism was the method of logical inquiry and exposition pioneered by Peter Abelard and other twelfth-century teachers. In the thirteenth century, the method was used to summarize and reconcile all knowledge. Many of the thirteenth-century scholastics (the name given to the scholars who used this method) were members of the Dominican and Franciscan orders and taught in the universities. On the whole, they were confident that knowledge obtained through the senses and reason was compatible with the knowledge derived from faith and revelation. One of their goals was to demonstrate this harmony. The scholastic **summa**, or summary of knowledge, was a systematic exposition of the answer to every possible question about human morality, the physical world, society, belief, action, and theology. Another goal of the scholastics was to preach the conclusions of these treatises. As one scholastic put it, "First the bow is bent in study, then the arrow is released in preaching": first you study the summa and then you hit your mark—convert people—by preaching. Many of the preachers who came to the towns were students and disciples of scholastic university teachers.

The method of the summa borrowed much of the vocabulary and many of the rules of logic long ago outlined by Aristotle. Even though Aristotle was a pagan, scholastics considered his coherent and rational body of thought the most perfect that human reason alone could devise. Because they had the benefit of Christ's revelations, the scholastics considered themselves able to take Aristotle's philosophy one necessary step further and reconcile human reason with Christian faith. Full of confidence in their method and conclusions, scholastics embraced the world and its issues.

Some scholastics considered questions about the natural world. Albertus Magnus

The Debate between Reason and the Lover

Jean de Meun's portion of the Romance of the Rose *is organized as a dialogue between the Lover and various figures he meets on his quest for the rose. Reason gives this jaundiced definition of love:*

If I know anything of love, it is
Imaginary illness freely spread
Between two persons of opposing sex,
Originating from disordered sight,
Producing great desire to hug and kiss
And see enjoyment in a mutual lust.
To which the lover responds:
Madam, you would betray me; should I scorn
All folk because the God of Love now frowns?
Shall I no more experience true love,
But live in hate? Truly, so help me God,
Then were I moral sinner worse than thief!

Source: Guillaume de Lorris and Jean de Meun, *The Romance of the Rose*, trans. Harry W. Robbins (New York: Dutton, 1962), 97, 102.

French *mot*, meaning "word"). The motet is an example of **polyphony**,♦ music that consists of two or more melodies performed simultaneously. Before about 1215, most polyphony was sacred; purely secular polyphony was not common before the fourteenth century. The motet, a unique merging of the sacred and the secular, evidently originated in Paris, the center of scholastic culture as well.

The typical thirteenth-century motet has two or three melody lines (or "voices"). The lowest, usually from a liturgical chant melody, has only one or two words; it may have been played on an instrument rather than sung. The remaining melodies have different texts, either Latin or French (or one of each), which are sung simultaneously. Latin texts are usually sacred, whereas French

---

♦**polyphony:** puh LIH fuh nee

---

ones are secular, dealing with themes such as love and springtime. The motet thus weaves the sacred (the chant melody in the lowest voice) and the secular (the French texts in the upper voices) into a sophisticated tapestry of words and music. Like the scholastic summae, the motets were written by and for a clerical elite. Yet they incorporated the music of ordinary people, such as the calls of street vendors and the boisterous songs of students. In turn they touched the lives of everyone, for polyphony influenced every form of music, from the Mass to popular songs that entertained and diverted laypeople and churchmen alike.

Complementing the motet's complexity was the development of a new notation for rhythm. By the eleventh century, musical notation could indicate pitch but had no way to denote the duration of the notes. Music theorists of the thirteenth century, however, developed increasingly precise methods to indicate rhythm. Franco of Cologne, for example, in his *Art of Measurable Song* (c. 1280), used different shapes to mark the number of beats each note should be held. His system became the basis of modern musical notation. Because each note could now be allotted a specific duration, written music could express new and complicated rhythms. The music of the thirteenth century reflected both the melding of the secular and the sacred and the possibilities of greater order and control.

The Gothic Revolution in Art and Architecture

Just as polyphonic music united the sacred with the secular, so **Gothic** architecture, sculpture, and painting expressed the order and harmony of the universe.[1] This new style, which was popular from the twelfth to fifteenth centuries, was characterized by pointed arches. These began as architectural motifs but were soon adopted in every art form. Gothic churches appealed to the senses the way that scholastic argument appealed to human reason: both were designed

---

[1]*Gothic* is a modern term. It was originally meant to denigrate the style's "barbarity," but most contemporary observers now use the word admiringly.

to lead people to knowledge that touched the divine. Being in a Gothic church was a foretaste of heaven.

Architecture. Gothic architecture began around 1135, with the project of Abbot Suger, the close associate of King Louis the Fat of France (see page 384), to remodel portions of the church of St. Denis. Suger's rebuilding of St. Denis was part of the fruitful melding of royal and ecclesiastical interests and ideals in the north of France. At the west end of his church, the point where the faithful entered, Suger decorated the portals with figures of Old Testament kings, queens, and patriarchs, signaling the links between the present king and his illustrious predecessors. Within the church, Suger rebuilt the *chevet,* or choir area, using pointed arches and stained glass to let in light, which Suger believed would transport the worshiper from the "slime of earth" to the "purity of Heaven." Suger said that the Father of lights, God himself, "illuminated" the minds of the beholders through the light that filtered through the stained-glass windows.

Soon the style that Suger pioneered was taken up all across France and Europe. Gothic was an urban architecture, reflecting—in its grand size, jewel-like windows, and bright ornaments—the aspirations, pride, and confidence of rich and powerful merchants, artisans, and bishops. A Gothic church, usually a cathedral (the bishop's principal church), was the religious, social, and commercial focal point of a city. Building Gothic cathedrals was a community project, enlisting the labor and support of an entire urban center. New cathedrals required a small army of quarrymen, builders, carpenters, and glass cutters. Bishops, papal legates, and clerics planned and helped pay for these grand churches, but townspeople also generously financed them and filled them to attend Mass and visit relics. Guilds raised money to pay for stained-glass windows that depicted and celebrated their own patron saints. In turn, towns made money when pilgrims came to visit relics and sightseers arrived to marvel at their great churches.

The technologies making Gothic churches possible were all known before the twelfth century. But Suger's church showed how they could be used together to achieve a particularly dazzling effect. Gothic techniques included ribbed vaulting, which gave a sense of precision and order; the pointed arch, which produced a feeling of soaring height; and flying buttresses, which took the weight of the vault off the walls (Figure 12.1 on page 448). The buttresses permitted much of the wall to be cut away and the open spaces to be filled with glass.

Unlike Romanesque churches, whose exteriors prepare visitors for what they will see within them, Gothic cathedrals surprise. The exterior of a Gothic church has an opaque, bristling, and forbidding look owing to the dark surface of its stained glass and its flying buttresses. The interior, however, is just the opposite. All is soaring lightness, harmony, and order, as the photograph of Ste.-Chapelle illustrates. Just as a scholastic presented his

French Gothic: Ste.-Chapelle
Gothic architecture opened up the walls of the church to windows. Filled with "stained" glass—actually the colors were added to the ingredients of the glass before they were heated, melted, and blown—the windows glowed like jewels. Moreover, each had a story to tell: the life of Christ, major events from the Old Testament, the lives of saints. Ste.-Chapelle, commissioned by King Louis IX (St. Louis) and consecrated in 1248, was built to house Christ's crown of thorns and other relics of the Passion. Compare the use of windows, walls, vault, and piers here to that of a Romanesque church such as St.-Savin (see page 393). *Bridgeman-Giraudon/Art Resource, NY.*

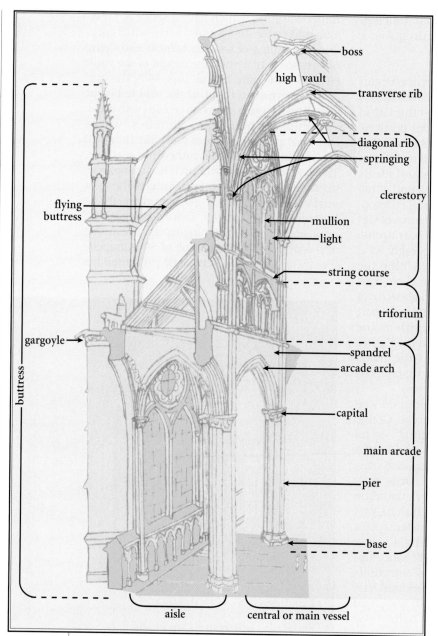

boss
high vault
transverse rib
diagonal rib
springing
clerestory
mullion
light
string course
triforium
spandrel
arcade arch
capital
main arcade
pier
base
flying buttress
gargoyle
buttress
aisle
central or main vessel

FIGURE 12.1 Elements of a Gothic Cathedral
Bristling on the outside with stone flying buttresses, Gothic cathedrals were lofty and serene on the inside. The buttresses, which held the weight of the vault, allowed Gothic architects to pierce the walls with windows running the full length of the church. Within, thick piers anchored on sturdy bases became thin columns as they mounted over the triforium and clerestory, blossoming into ribs at the top. Whether plain or ornate, the ribs gave definition and drew attention to the high pointed vault. *Figure adapted from Michael Camille,* Gothic Art: Glorious Visions *(New York: Abrams, 1996).*

At Sant'Andrea in Vercelli, shown on the next page, for example, there are only two stories, and light filters in from small windows. Yet this is considered a Gothic church, for it uses pointed arches and ribbed vaulting. With no flying buttresses and relatively little portal sculpture, the Italian version of Gothic conveys a spirit of austerity.

Art. Gothic art, both painting and sculpture, decorated the Gothic cathedral. Liberated from their background and sculpted in the round, Gothic figures turned, moved, and interacted with one another. Taken together, they were often meant to be "read" like a scholastic summa. The south portal complex of Chartres cathedral is a good example. Each massive doorway tells a separate story through sculpture: the left depicts the martyrs, the right the confessors, and the center the Last Judgment. Like Dante's *Divine Comedy,* these portals taken together show the soul's pilgrimage from the suffering of this world to eternal life.

argument with utter clarity, so the interior of a Gothic church revealed its structure through its skeleton of ribbed vaults and piers. And just as a scholastic bridged the gap between earthly and celestial realms, so the cathedral elicited a response beyond reason, evoking a sense of awe.

By the mid-thirteenth century, Gothic architecture had spread from France to other European countries. Yet the style varied by region, most dramatically in Italy.

Sant'Andrea
The church of Sant'Andrea at Vercelli was begun about twenty years before Ste.-Chapelle (see page 447). It suggests that Italian church architects and patrons adopted what they liked of French Gothic, particularly its pointed arches, while remaining uninterested in soaring heights and grand stained-glass windows. The real interest of the interior of Sant'Andrea is its inventive and lively use of contrasting light and dark stone. *Scala/Art Resource, NY.*

Giotto's *Last Judgment*
The theme of the Last Judgment fills the west wall of the Arena Chapel in Padua, painted by Giotto between 1304 and 1313. In the center is Christ, surrounded by angels and saints. Beneath him is the cross, symbol of his passion and triumph. Under the cross, to Christ's right, is the donor of church, Enrico Scrovegni, kneeling as he offers a scale model of the chapel to the Virgin Mary, mother of Jesus. Behind and above him are the blessed of heaven. The funnel-like space to Christ's left shows hell, with the devil contentedly munching on the souls of the damned. *Cameraphoto Arte, Venice/Art Resource, NY.*

Like architecture, Gothic sculpture began in France and was adopted, with many variations, elsewhere in Europe during the thirteenth century. The Italian sculptor Nicola Pisano (c. 1220–1278?), for example, crafted dignified figures inspired by classical forms. German sculptors, in contrast, created excited, emotional figures that sometimes gestured dramatically to one another. (See page 450 for an example of German Gothic.)

By the early fourteenth century, the expansive sculptures so prominent in architecture were reflected in painting as well. This new style is evident in the work of Giotto♦ (1266–1337), a Florentine artist who changed the emphasis of painting, which had been predominantly symbolic, decorative, and intellectual. When Giotto filled the walls of a private chapel at Padua with paintings de-

♦**Giotto:** JAHT toh

German Gothic: Strasbourg
The Virgin is mourned in this tympanum over the portal of the Strasbourg cathedral's south transept (the arm that crosses the church from north to south). Here, in German Gothic, the emphasis is on emotion and expressivity. Why do you suppose that Christ stands in the center of the tympanum, as if he is one of the mourners? What is he holding in the crook of his arm? (Hint: The souls of the dead are often shown as miniature people.)
Foto Marburg/Art Resource, NY.

picting scenes of Christ's life, he experimented with the illusion of depth. Giotto's figures, appearing weighty and voluminous, express a range of emotions as they seem to move across interior and exterior spaces. In bringing sculptural naturalism to a flat surface, Giotto stressed three-dimensionality, illusional space, and human emotion. By fusing earthly forms with religious meaning, Giotto found yet another way to bring together the natural and divine realms.

> **Review:** How did artists, architects, musicians, and scholastics try to link this world with the divine?

❖ The Politics of Control

The quest for order, control, and harmony also became part of the political agendas of princes, popes, and cities. These rulers and institutions imposed—or tried to impose—their authority ever more fully and systematically through taxes, courts, and sometimes representative institutions. The ancestors of modern European parliaments and of the U.S. Congress can be traced to this era.

The Weakening of the Empire

During the thirteenth century, both popes and emperors sought to dominate Italy. In the end, the emperor lost control not only of Italy but of Germany as well.

The clash of the emperor and papacy had its origins in Frederick Barbarossa's failure to control northern Italy, which was crucial to imperial policy. The model of Charlemagne required his imperial successors to exercise hegemony there. Moreover, Italy's prosperous cities beckoned as rich sources of income. When Barbarossa failed in the north, his son Henry VI (r. 1190–1197) tried a new approach to gain Italy: he married the heiress of Sicily, Constance. From this base near the southern tip of Italy, Henry hoped to make good his imperial title. But Henry died suddenly, leaving a three-year-old son, Frederick II, to take up his plan. It was a perilous moment.

While Frederick was a child, the imperial office became the plaything of the German princes and the papacy. Both wanted an emperor, but a virtually powerless one. Thus, when Frederick's uncle Duke Philip of Swabia♦ attempted to become interim king until Frederick reached his majority, many princes and the papacy blocked the move. They supported Otto of Brunswick, the son of Henry the Lion and an implacable foe of Frederick's Staufer family. Otto promised the pope that he would not intervene in Italy, and Pope Innocent III, revealing yet another side of his policy, crowned him emperor in return.

♦**Swabia:** SWAY bee uh

But Innocent had miscalculated. No emperor worthy of the name could leave Italy alone. Almost immediately after his coronation, Otto invaded Sicily, and Innocent excommunicated him in 1211. In 1212, Innocent gave the imperial crown to Frederick II (r. 1212–1250), now a young man ready to take up the reins of power.

Frederick was an amazing ruler: *stupor mundi*—"wonder of the world"—his contemporaries called him. Heir to two cultures, Sicilian on his mother's side and German on his father's, he cut a worldly and sophisticated figure. In Sicily he moved easily within a diverse culture of Jews, Muslims, and Christians. Here he could play the role of all-powerful ruler. In Germany he was less at home. There

Christian princes, often churchmen with ministerial retinues, were acutely aware of their crucial role in royal elections and jealously guarded their rights and privileges.

Both emperor and pope needed to dominate Italy to maintain their power and position (Map 12.1). The papacy under Innocent III was expansionist, gathering money and troops to make good its claim to the Papal States. From this region the pope expected dues and taxes, military service, and the profits of justice. To ensure its survival, the pope refused to tolerate any imperial claims to Italy.

Frederick, in turn, could not imagine ruling as an emperor unless he controlled Italy. He attempted to do this throughout his life, as

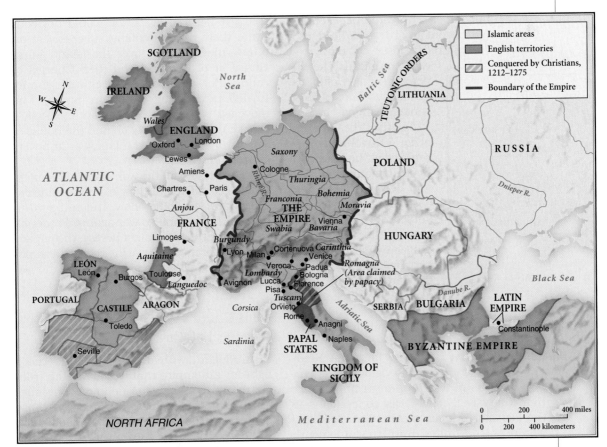

MAP 12.1 Europe in the Time of Frederick II, r. 1212–1250
King of Sicily and Germany and emperor as well, Frederick ruled over territory that encircled—and threatened—the papacy. Excommunicated several times, Frederick spent much of his career fighting the pope's forces. In the process he conceded so many powers to the German princes that the emperor thenceforth had little power in Germany. Meanwhile rulers of smaller states, such as England, France, and León-Castile, were increasing their power and authority.

did his heirs. Frederick had a three-pronged strategy. First, he revamped the government of Sicily to give him more control and yield greater profits. His *Constitutions of Melfi* (1231), an eclectic body of laws, set up a system of salaried governors who worked according to uniform procedures. The *Constitutions* called for nearly all court cases to be heard by royal courts, regularized commercial privileges, and set up a system of taxation. Second, to ensure that he would not be hounded by opponents in Germany, Frederick granted them important concessions in his "Statute in Favor of the Princes," finalized in 1232. These privileges allowed the German princes to turn their principalities into virtually independent states. Third, Frederick sought to enter Italy through Lombardy, as his grandfather had done.

The four popes who came between the deaths of Innocent (1216) and Frederick (1250) followed Frederick's every move and excommunicated the emperor a number of times. The most serious of these condemnations came in 1245, when the pope and other churchmen, assembled at the Council of Lyon, excommunicated and deposed Frederick, absolving his vassals and subjects of their fealty to him and, indeed, forbidding anyone to support him. By 1248 papal legates were preaching a crusade against Frederick and all his followers. Frederick's death soon after ensured their triumph.

Italy at the End of the Thirteenth Century

The fact that Frederick's vision of the empire failed is of less long-term importance than the way it failed. His concessions to the German princes meant that Germany would not be united until the nineteenth century. The political entity now called Germany was simply a geographical expression, divided under many independent princes. Between 1254 and 1273, the princes kept the German throne empty. Splintered into factions, they elected two different foreigners, who spent their time fighting each other. In one of history's great ironies, it was during this low point of the German monarchy that the term *Holy Roman Empire* was coined. In 1273, the princes at last united and elected a German, Rudolph (r. 1273–1291), whose family, the Habsburgs, was new to imperial power. Rudolf used the imperial title to help him consolidate control over his own principality, Swabia, but he did not try to fulfill the meaning of the imperial title elsewhere. For the first time, the word *emperor* was freed from its association with Italy and Rome. For the Habsburgs, the title Holy Roman Emperor was a prestigious but otherwise meaningless honorific.

The Staufer failure in Italy meant that the Italian cities would continue their independent course. In Sicily, the papacy ensured that the heirs of Frederick would not continue their rule by calling successively on other rulers to take over the island—first Henry III of England and then Charles of Anjou. Forces loyal to the Staufer family turned to the king of Aragon (Spain). The move left two enduring claimants to Sicily's crown: the kings of Aragon and the house of Anjou. And it spawned a long war impoverishing the region.

The popes won the war against Frederick, but at a cost. Even the king of France criticized the popes for doing "new and unheard-of things." By making its war against Frederick part of its crusade against heresy, the papacy came under attack for using religion as a political tool. (See Municipal Legislation at Pisa, on page 455.)

Louis IX and a New Ideal of Kingship

In hindsight, we can see that Frederick's fight for an empire that would stretch from Germany to Sicily was doomed. The successful rulers of medieval Europe were those content with smaller, more compact, more united polities. The future was reserved for "national" states, like France and England. (Of course, that too may just be one phase of Western civilization.) In France the new ideal of a "stay-at-home" monarch started in the thirteenth century with the reign of Louis IX (r. 1226–1270). His two crusades to the Holy

Land made clear to his subjects just how much they needed him in France, even though his place was ably filled the first time by his mother, Blanche of Castile. The two are pictured on this page.

Louis was revered not because he was a military leader but because he was an administrator, judge, and "just father" of his people. On warm summer days, he would sit under a tree in the woods near his castle at Vincennes on the outskirts of Paris, hearing disputes and dispensing justice personally. Through his administrators, he vigorously imposed his laws and justice over much of France. At Paris he appointed a salaried chief magistrate, who could be supervised and fired if necessary. During his reign the influence of the parlement of Paris, the royal court of justice, increased significantly. Originally a changeable

Louis IX and Blanche of Castile
This miniature probably shows St. Louis, portrayed as a young boy, sitting opposite his mother, Blanche of Castile. Blanche served as regent twice in Louis's lifetime, once when he was too young to rule and a second time when he was away on crusade. The emphasis on the equality of queen and king may be evidence of Blanche's influence on and patronage of the artist. Note that the artist has set both royal figures in a Gothic windowlike setting. **For more help analyzing this image,** see the visual activity for this chapter in the Online Study Guide at **bedfordstmartins.com/hunt**. *The Pierpont Morgan Library/ Art Resource, NY.*

and movable body, part of the king's personal entourage when he dealt with litigation, it was now permanently housed in Paris and staffed by professional judges who heard cases and recorded their decisions.

Unlike his grandfather Philip Augustus, Louis did not try to expand his territory. He inherited a large kingdom that included Poitou and Languedoc (Map 12.2 on page 454), and he was content. Although Henry III, the king of England, attacked him continually to try to regain territory lost under Philip Augustus, Louis remained unprovoked. Rather than prolong the fighting, he conceded a bit and made peace in 1259. At the same time, Louis was a zealous crusader. He took seriously the need to defend

the Holy Land when most of his contemporaries were weary of the idea.

Louis was respectful of the church and the pope; he accepted limits on his power in relation to the church and never claimed power over spiritual matters. Nevertheless, he vigorously maintained the dignity of the king and his rights. He expected royal and ecclesiastical power to work in harmony, and he refused to let the church dictate how he should use his temporal authority. For example, French bishops wanted royal officers to support the church's sentences of excommunication. But Louis declared that he would authorize his officials to do so only if he were able to judge each case for himself, to see if the excommunication had been

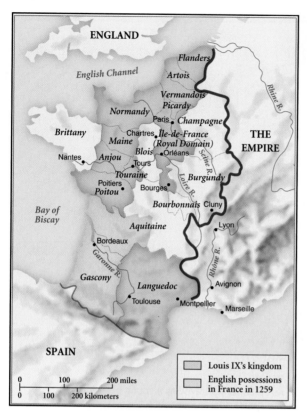

MAP 12.2 France under Louis IX, r. 1226–1270
Louis IX did not expand his kingdom as dramatically as his grandfather Philip Augustus had done. He was greatly admired nevertheless, for he was seen by contemporaries as a model of Christian piety and justice. After his death, he was recognized as a saint and thus posthumously enhanced the prestige of the French monarchy.

justly pronounced or not. The bishops refused, and Louis held his ground. Royal and ecclesiastical power would work side by side, neither subservient to the other.

Many modern historians fault Louis for his policies toward the Jews. His hatred of them was well known. He did not exactly advocate violence against them, but he sometimes subjected them to arrest, canceling the debts owed to them (but collecting part into the royal treasury), and confiscating their belongings. In 1253, he ordered them to live "by the labor of their hands" or leave France. He meant that they should no longer lend money, in effect taking away their one means of livelihood. Louis's contemporaries

did not criticize him for his Jewish policies. If anything, his hatred of Jews enhanced his reputation.

In fact, many of Louis's contemporaries considered him a saint, praising his care for the poor and sick, the pains and penances he inflicted on himself, and his regular participation in church services. In 1297 Pope Boniface VIII canonized him as St. Louis. The result was enormous prestige for the French monarchy. This prestige, joined with the renown of Paris as the center of scholarship and the repute of French courts as the hubs of chivalry, made France the cultural model of Europe.

The Birth of Representative Institutions

As thirteenth-century monarchs and princes expanded their powers, they devised a new political tool to enlist more broadly based support: all across Europe, from Spain to Poland, from England to Hungary, rulers summoned parliaments. These grew out of the ad hoc advisory sessions kings had held in the past with men from the two most powerful classes, or "orders," of medieval society—the nobility and the clergy. In the thirteenth century, the advisory sessions turned into solemn, formal meetings of representatives of the orders to the kings' chief councils—the precursor of parliamentary sessions. Eventually these bodies became organs through which people not ordinarily present at court could articulate their wishes.

In practice, thirteenth-century kings did not so much command representatives of the orders to come to court as they simply summoned the most powerful members of their realm—whether clerics, nobles, or important townsmen—to support their policies. In thirteenth-century León (part of present-day Spain), for example, the king sometimes called only the clergy and nobles; sometimes he sent for representatives of the towns, especially when he wanted the help of town militias. As townsmen gradually began to participate regularly in advisory sessions, kings came to depend on them and their support. In turn, commoners became more fully integrated into the work of royal government.

Municipal Legislation at Pisa (1286)

Large and prosperous cities like Pisa were concerned with controlling the sexual activities of their inhabitants. They prohibited prostitution in the "better" parts of the city, though they allowed it in the medieval version of a red-light district. Sometimes, as at Pisa, homosexuality was seen as a form of heresy.

III. Concerning apostolic regulations against heretics and sodomites:

We will take heed of apostolic regulations which have been laid down against heretics, will observe them to the letter, and will have others do likewise during the entire period of our governance. We and others will harass and threaten sodomites, buggers, and other persons found guilty of the depravity of heresy, proceeding against them in accordance with the form of the law. . . .

IV. Concerning prostitutes and men of ill-fame:

We will not allow any public prostitute or female go-between, or one who receives prostitutes, or pimps, male or female to remain within the walls of the city of Pisa, in "good" public places, from which we will have them expelled in accordance with the desires of the local residents, or at least three of them, who are of good reputation, neither near, inside or outside the walls of the city of Pisa[1] . . . and they are not to stay or dwell in any street or public square. The podestà and captains [local officials charged with prosecuting criminals] are to do and observe this. If they don't they are to forfeit one hundred *denarii*. . . .

Persons may expel such prostitutes by force if necessary from the aforementioned places without incurring any punishment. No prostitute may presume to enter a bathhouse, except on Wednesday, under penalty of a fine of fifty *solidi*, to be paid every time they break the law. The bathhouse attendants (or owners) are to pay the same fine, and this is to be announced throughout the city. No public prostitute may wear a cloak, under penalty of the same fine; this is to be overseen by the police. Any Pisan who allows his home to serve as a dwelling for a prostitute or for any of the aforementioned persons, male or female, that is, persons of ill fame, reputation, class or conduct; who received thieves, buggers, sodomites, gamblers, dice throwers or other persons of ill fame, should be condemned to pay one hundred *denarii*.

---

[1]This is followed by a very detailed list of the boundaries of those parts of the city of Pisa from which they are excluded.

Source: Michael Goodich, ed., *Other Middle Ages: Witnesses at the Margins of Medieval Society*, (Philadelphia: University of Pennsylvania Press, 1998), 116–17.

Spanish Cortes. The *cortes*♦ of Castile-León were among the earliest representative assemblies called to the king's court and the first to include townsmen. Enriched by plunder, fledgling villages soon burgeoned into major commercial centers. Like the cities of Italy, Spanish towns dominated the countryside. Their leaders—called *caballeros*♦ *villanos,* or "city horsemen," because they were rich enough to fight on horseback—monopolized municipal offices. In 1188, when King Alfonso IX (r. 1188–1230) summoned townsmen to the cortes for the first time on record, the city caballeros served as

---

♦*cortes:* kawr TEHZ

♦*caballeros:* ka buh YEHR os

their representatives, agreeing to Alfonso's plea for military and financial support and for help in consolidating his rule. Once convened at court, these wealthy townsmen joined bishops and noblemen in formally counseling the king and assenting to royal decisions. Beginning with Alfonso X (r. 1252–1284), Castilian monarchs regularly called on the cortes to participate in major political and military decisions and to assent to new taxes to finance them.

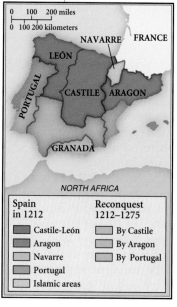

Spain in the Thirteenth Century

Spain in 1212 / Reconquest 1212–1275
- Castile-León
- Aragon
- Navarre
- Portugal
- Islamic areas
- By Castile
- By Aragon
- By Portugal

English Parliament. The English Parliament also developed as a new tool of royal government.[2] In this case, however, the king's control was complicated by the power of the barons, manifested, for example, in Magna Carta. In the twelfth century, King Henry II had consulted prelates and barons at Great Councils, using these parliaments as his tool to ratify and gain support for his policies. Although Magna Carta had nothing to do with such councils, the barons thought the document gave them an important and permanent role in royal government as the king's advisers and a solid guarantee of their customary rights and privileges. Henry III (r. 1216–1272) was crowned at the age of nine and therefore was king in name only for the first sixteen years of his reign. Instead, England was governed by a council consisting of a few barons, university-trained administrators, and a papal legate. Although not quite "government by

---

[2]Although *Parlement* and *Parliament* are similar words, both deriving from the French word *parler* ("to speak"), the institutions they named were very different. The Parlement of France was a law court, whereas the English Parliament, although beginning as a court to redress grievances, had by 1327 become above all a representative institution. The major French representative assembly, the Estates General, first convened at the beginning of the fourteenth century.

Parliament," this council set a precedent for baronial participation in government.

A parliament that included commoners came only in the midst of war and as a result of political weakness. Henry so alienated nobles and commoners alike by his wars, debts, choice of advisers, and demands for money that the barons threatened to rebel. At a meeting at Oxford in 1258, they forced Henry to dismiss his foreign advisers, rule with the advice of a Council of Fifteen chosen jointly by the barons and the king, and limit the terms of his chief officers. However, this new government was itself riven by strife among the barons, and civil war erupted in 1264. At the battle of Lewes in the same year, the leader of the baronial opposition, Simon de Montfort (c. 1208–1265), routed the king's forces, captured the king, and became England's de facto ruler. Because only a minority of the barons followed Simon, he sought new support by convening a parliament in 1265, to which he summoned not only the earls, barons, and churchmen who backed him but also representatives from the towns, the "commons"—and he appealed for their help. Thus, for the first time the commons were given a voice in government. Even though Simon's brief rule ended that very year and Henry's son Edward I (r. 1272–1307) became a rallying point for royalists, the idea of representative government in England had emerged, born out of the interplay between royal initiatives and baronial revolts.

The Weakening of the Papacy

In France, the development of representative institutions originated in the conflict between Pope Boniface VIII (r. 1294–1303) and King Philip IV (r. 1285–1314), known as Philip the Fair. At the time, this confrontation seemed to be just one more episode in the ongoing struggle between medieval popes and rulers for power and authority. But in fact, at the end of the thirteenth century kings had more power, and the standoff between Boniface and Philip became a turning point that weakened the papacy and strengthened the monarchy.

Taxing the Clergy. For centuries the clergy had maintained a special status within the medieval state. Since the twelfth century

popes had declared the clergy under their jurisdiction. Clerics were not taxed except in the case of religious wars; they were not tried except in clerical courts. At the end of the thirteenth century, royal challenges to these principles were met by angry papal responses. The clashes began over taxing the clergy. Philip the Fair and the English king Edward I both financed their wars (mainly against one another) by taxing the clergy along with everyone else. The new principle of national sovereignty that they were claiming led them to assert jurisdiction over all people, even churchmen, who lived within their borders. For the pope, however, the principle at stake was his role as head of the clergy. Thus, Pope Boniface VIII, whose heavy, dignified image is illustrated on this page, declared that only the pope could authorize taxes on clerics. Threatening to excommunicate kings who taxed prelates without papal permission, he called on clerics to disobey any such royal orders.

Edward and Philip reacted swiftly. Taking advantage of the important role English courts played in protecting the peace, Edward declared that all clerics who refused to pay his taxes would be considered outlaws—literally "outside the law." Clergymen who were robbed, for example, would have no recourse against their attackers; if accused of crimes, they would have no defense in court. Relying on a different strategy, Philip forbade the exportation of precious metals, money, or jewels, effectively sealing French borders. Immediately the English clergy cried out for legal protection, while the papacy itself cried out for the revenues it had long enjoyed from French pilgrims, litigants, and travelers. Boniface was forced to back down, conceding in 1297 that kings had the right to tax their clergy in emergencies. But this did not end the confrontation.

The King's New Tools: Propaganda and Popular Opinion. In 1301, Philip the Fair tested his jurisdiction in southern France by arresting Bernard Saisset,♦ the bishop of Pamiers, on a charge of treason for slandering the king by comparing him to an owl, "the handsomest of birds which is worth absolutely nothing." Saisset's imprisonment violated the principle, maintained both by the pope and by French law, that a clergyman was not subject to lay justice. Boniface reacted angrily, and Philip seized the opportunity to deride and humiliate him, orchestrating a public relations campaign against Boniface. He convened representatives of the clergy, nobles, and townspeople to explain, justify, and propagandize his position. This new assembly, which met in 1302, was the ancestor of the French representative institution, the Estates General. The pope's reply, the

Boniface VIII
For the sculptor who depicted Pope Boniface VIII, Arnolfo di Cambio (d. 1302), not much had changed since the time of Innocent III. Look at the picture of Innocent on page 436 and compare the two popes: both are depicted as young, majestic, authoritative, sober, and calm. Yet Boniface could not have been very calm, for his authority was challenged at every turn. He was forced to withdraw his opposition to royal taxation of the clergy. He tried to placate the French king, Philip the Fair, by canonizing Philip's grandfather, St. Louis. Even so, Philip arrested the bishop of Pamiers and brought him to trial. When Boniface protested, he was proclaimed a heretic by the French. A few months later he was dead. *Scala/Art Resource, NY.*

♦**Bernard Saisset:** bair NAHR say SAY

bull[3] *Unam Sanctam*◆ (1302), intensified the situation to fever pitch by declaring bluntly "that it is altogether necessary to salvation for every human creature to be subject to the Roman Pontiff." At meetings of the king's inner circle, Philip's agents declared Boniface a false pope, accusing him of sexual perversion, various crimes, and heresy.

Papal Defeat. In 1303, royal agents, acting under Philip's orders, invaded Boniface's palace at Anagni (southeast of Rome) to capture the pope, bring him to France, and try him. Fearing for the pope's life, however, the people of Anagni joined forces and drove the French agents out of town. Yet even after such public support for the pope, the king made his power felt. Boniface died very shortly thereafter, and the next two popes quickly pardoned Philip and his agents for their actions.

Just as Frederick II's defeat showed the weakness of the empire, so Boniface's humiliation showed the limits of papal control. The two powers that claimed "universal" authority had very little weight in the face of new, limited, but tightly controlled national states such as France and England. After 1303, popes continued to fulminate against kings and emperors, but henceforth their words had less and less impact. In the face of newly powerful medieval states—undergirded by vast revenues, judicial apparatuses, representative institutions, and even the loyalty of churchmen—the papacy could make little headway. The delicate balance between church and state, a hallmark of the years of St. Louis that reflected a search for harmony as well as a drive for power, had broken down by the end of the thirteenth century. The quest for control led not to harmony but to confrontation and extremism.

In 1309, forced from Rome by civil strife, the papacy settled at Avignon, a city technically in the Holy Roman Empire but very close to, and influenced by, France. Here the popes remained until 1378. The period 1309–1378 came to be called the Babylonian Captivity by Europeans sensitive to having the popes live far from Rome, on the Rhône River.[4] The Avignon popes, many of them French, established a sober and efficient organization that took in regular revenues and gave the papacy more say than ever before in the appointment of churchmen. They would, however, slowly abandon the idea of leading all of Christendom and would tacitly recognize the growing power of the secular states to regulate their internal affairs.

The Road to the Signori

In the course of the thirteenth century, new groups, generally made up of the non-noble classes—the *popolo*, the "people," who fought on foot—attempted to take over the reins of power in many Italian communes. The popolo incorporated members of city associations such as craft and merchant guilds, parishes, and the commune itself. In fact, the popolo was a kind of alternative commune. Armed and militant, the popolo demanded a share in city government, particularly to gain a voice in matters of taxation. In 1222 at Piacenza, for example, the popolo's members won half the government offices; a year later they and the nobles worked out a plan to share the election of their city's government. Such power sharing was a typical result of the popolo's struggle. In some cities, however, nobles overcame and dissolved the popolo, while in others the popolo virtually excluded the nobles from government. Constantly confronting one another, quarreling, feuding, and compromising, such factions turned northern Italian cities into centers of civil discord.

Weakened by this constant friction, the communes were tempting prey for great regional nobles who, allying with one or another faction, often succeeded in establishing themselves as *signori*◆ (singular *signore*, "lord") of the cities, keeping the peace at the

---

[3]An official papal document is called a bull, from the *bulla*, or seal, that was used to authenticate it.

◆*Unam Sanctam:* UN ahm SANKT ahm

---

[4]The term *Babylonian Captivity* refers to the biblical story of the forced deportation of the people of Judea to Babylon and their long exile there. See 2 Kings 24–25.

◆*signori:* see noh REE ah

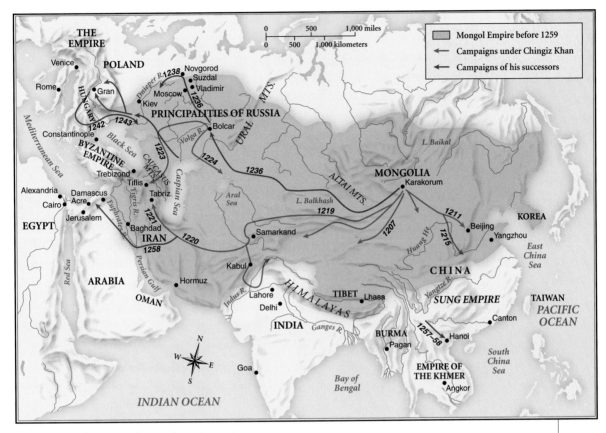

MAP 12.3 The Mongol Invasions to 1259
The Mongols were the first people to tie the eastern world to the west. Their conquest of China, which took place at about the same time as their invasions of Russia and Iran, created a Eurasian economy, opening up trade relations across regions that had long been separated by language, religion, and political regimes.

price of repression. In these circumstances, many communes gave way to lordships, with one family dominating the government. The fate of Piacenza over the course of the thirteenth century was typical: first dominated by nobles, its commune granted the popolo a voice by 1225; but then by midcentury both the nobles and the popolo were eclipsed by the power of a signore.

The Mongol Takeover

Europeans were not the only warring society in the thirteenth century: to the east the Mongols (sometimes called Tatars or Tartars) created an aggressive army under the leadership of Chingiz (or Genghis) Khan

(c. 1162–1227) and his sons. In part, economic necessity drove them out of Mongolia: climatic changes had reduced the grasslands that sustained their animals and their nomadic way of life. But they were also inspired by Chingiz's hope of conquering the world. By 1215, the Mongols held Beijing and most of northern China. Some years later they moved through central Asia and skirted the Caspian Sea (Map 12.3).

The Golden Horde in Russia. In the 1230s, the Mongols began concerted attacks in Europe—in Russia, Poland, and Hungary, where weak native princes were no match for the Mongols' formidable armies and tactics. Only the death of their Great Khan, Chingiz's

MAPPING THE WEST Europe, c. 1320

The empire, now called the Holy Roman Empire, still dominated the map of Europe in 1320, but the emperor himself had little power. Each principality—often each city—was ruled separately and independently. To the east, the Ottoman Turks were just beginning to make themselves felt. In the course of the next century they would disrupt the Mongol hegemony and become a great power.

son Ogodei (1186–1241)—styled the *khagan,* or khan of khans—and disputes over his succession prevented a concentrated assault on Germany. In the 1250s, the Mongols took Iran, Iraq, and Syria.

The Mongols' sophisticated and devastating military tactics contributed to their overwhelming success. They devised two- and three-flank operations. The invasion of Hungary, for example, was two-pronged: one division of their army arrived from Russia while the other moved through Poland and Germany. Many Hungarians perished

in the assault as the Mongols, fighting mainly on horseback, with heavy lances and powerful bows and arrows whose shots traveled far and penetrated deeply, crushed the Hungarian army of mixed infantry and cavalry.

In the West, the Mongol rule in Russia lasted the longest. At Vladimir in the north, they broke through the defensive walls of the city and burned the populace huddled for protection inside the cathedral. Their most important victory in Russia was the capture of Kiev in 1240. Making the mouth of the

Volga River the center of their power in Russia, the Mongols dominated all of Russia's principalities for about two hundred years.

The Mongol Empire in Russia, later called the **Golden Horde** (*golden* probably from the color of their leader's tent; *horde* from a Turkish word meaning "camp"), adopted much of the local government apparatus and left many of the old institutions in place. They allowed Russian princes to continue ruling as long as they paid homage and tribute to the khan, and they tolerated the Russian church, exempting it from taxes. The Mongol's chief undertaking was a series of population censuses on the basis of which they recalculated taxes and recruited troops.

Opening of China to Europeans. The Mongol invasion changed the political configuration of Europe and Asia. Because the Mongols were willing to deal with westerners, one effect of their conquests was to open China to European travelers for the first time. Some missionaries, diplomats, and merchants went to China by overland routes; others set sail from the Persian Gulf (controlled by the Mongols) and rounded India before arriving in China. Some of these voyagers hoped to enlist the aid of the Mongols against the Muslims; others expected to make new converts to Christianity; still others dreamed of lucrative trade routes.

The most famous of these travelers was Marco Polo (1254–1324), son of a merchant family from Venice. Marco's father and uncle had already been to China once and returned when Marco joined them on a second expedition. He stayed in China for nearly two years, as did other westerners. In fact, evidence suggests that an entire community of Venetian traders—women, men, and children—lived in the city of Yangzhou in the mid-fourteenth century.

Merchants paved the way for missionaries. Friars, preachers to the cities of Europe, became missionaries to new continents as well. In 1289, the pope made the Franciscan John of Monte Corvino his envoy to China. Preaching in India along the way, John arrived in China four or five years after setting out, converting one local ruler, and building a church. A few years later, now at Beijing, he

boasted that he had converted six thousand people, constructed two churches, and translated the New Testament and Psalms into the native language.

The long-term effect of the Mongols on the West was to open up new land routes to the East that helped bind the two halves of the known world together. Travel stories such as Marco Polo's stimulated others to seek out the fabulous riches—textiles, ginger, ceramics, copper—of China and other regions of the East. In a sense, the Mongols initiated the search for exotic goods and missionary opportunities that culminated in the European "discovery" of a new world, the Americas.

> **Review:** In what ways did the secular rulers of the period 1215–1320 cooperate with the church; in what ways did they not—and why?

Conclusion

The thirteenth century sought harmony but discovered how elusive it could be. Theoretically, the universal papacy and empire were supposed to work together; instead they clashed in bitter warfare, leaving the government of Germany to the princes and northern Italy to its communes and *signori*. Theoretically, faith and reason were supposed to arrive at the same truths. In the hands of scholastics they sometimes did so, but not always. Theoretically, all Christians were expected to practice the same rites and follow the teachings of the church. In fact, local enforcement determined which church laws took effect—and to what extent. Moreover, the quest for harmony was never able to bring together all the diverse peoples, ideas, and interests of thirteenth-century society. Far from integrating, Jews found themselves set apart from everyone else through legislation and visible markers. Heretics were pursued with zeal; there was no question here of unity.

The quest for harmony worked more surely in the arts. Artists and architects integrated sculpture, stone, and glass to depict religious themes and fill the light-infused space of Gothic churches. Musicians wove together disparate melodic and poetic lines into motets. Writers melded heroic and romantic themes with theological truths and mystical visions.

Political leaders also aimed at order and control: to increase their revenues, expand their territories, and enhance their prestige. The kings of England and France and the governments of northern and central Italian cities partially succeeded in achieving these goals, while the king of Germany (who was also the emperor) failed miserably. Germany remained fragmented until the nineteenth century. Within the new, compact governments, however, the quest for harmony succeeded to a degree. Kings and representative institutions worked well together on the whole, and clergy and laymen came to feel that they were part of the same political entity, whether that entity was France or a German principality. Ironically, the Mongols, who began as invaders in the west, helped unify areas that were far apart through opening trade routes.

The harmonies became even more discordant toward the end of the thirteenth century. The balance between church and state achieved under St. Louis in France, for example, disintegrated into irreconcilable claims to power in the time of Pope Boniface and Philip the Fair. The carefully constructed tapestry of St. Thomas's summae, which wove together Aristotle's secular philosophy and divine Scripture, began to unravel in the teachings of John Duns Scotus. The eclectic Italian Gothic style, which gathered indigenous as well as northern elements, gave way to a new style, that of Giotto, whose work, rooted in the medieval search for harmony, also heralded the Renaissance art of the fourteenth century.

Suggested References

The Church's Mission of Reform

While historians continue to explore the traditional and important political figures behind the thirteenth-century church (Sayers), other scholars have begun to trace the impact of new church doctrine on the laity and the way the laity actively interpreted it (Bynum).

Bynum, Caroline Walker. *Holy Feast and Holy Fast: The Religious Significance of Food to Medieval Women.* 1987.

*Fourth Lateran Council: http://abbey.apana .org.au/councils/ecum12.htm.

Logan, F. Donald. *A History of the Church in the Middle Ages.* 2002.

Sayers, Jane. *Innocent III: Leader of Europe, 1198–1216.* 1994.

Cultural Harmonies

Most studies of the art and thought of the period specialize in one or the other, but the pioneering synthesis by Panofsky demonstrates that a wider view is possible. Duby attempts to place Gothic architecture in the context of the culture and society that produced it.

*Amiens cathedral: http://www.learn.columbia .edu/MCAHweb/index-frame.html.

*Dante. *The Divine Comedy.* Many editions; recommended are translations by Mark Musa and John Ciardi. The *Inferno* has been particularly well translated by Robert Pinsky and, most recently, by Robert Hollander and Jean Hollander.

Duby, Georges. *The Age of the Cathedrals: Art and Society, 980–1420.* Trans. Eleanor Levieux and Barbara Thompson. 1981.

Katzenellenbogen, Adolf. *The Sculptural Programs of Chartres Cathedral.* 1959.

Panofsky, Erwin. *Gothic Architecture and Scholasticism.* 1951.

Sargent, Steven D., ed. and trans. *On the Threshold of Exact Science: Selected Writings of Anneliese Maier on Late Medieval Natural Philosophy.* 1982.

Smart, Alastair. *The Dawn of Italian Painting, 1250–1400.* 1978.

*Thomas Aquinas: http://www.newadvent.org/ summa.

The Politics of Control

Thirteenth-century states used to be seen as harbingers of modern ones, but the newest history suggests that this is anachronistic. Thus, Abulafia argues that Frederick II followed models of medieval rulership, and O'Callaghan shows how far different medieval representative institutions were from their modern counterparts.

---

*Primary sources.

Only in the last ten or so years have historians studied the prelude to Columbus's voyages by looking at medieval precedents.

Abulafia, David. *Frederick II: A Medieval Emperor.* 1988.

Campbell, Mary B. *The Witness and the Other World: Exotic European Travel Writing, 400–1600.* 1989.

Farmer, Sharon. *Surviving Poverty in Medieval Paris: Gender, Ideology, and the Daily Lives of the Poor.* 2002.

Fernández-Armesto, Felipe. *Before Columbus: Exploration and Colonization from the Mediterranean to the Atlantic, 1229–1492.* 1987.

*Joinville, Jean de, and Geoffroy de Villehardouin. *Chronicles of the Crusades.* Trans. M. R. B. Shaw. 1963.

Jordan, William Chester. *The French Monarchy and the Jews: From Philip Augustus to the Late Capetians.* 1989.

Morgan, David. *The Mongols.* 1986.

O'Callaghan, Joseph F. *The Cortes of Castille-León, 1188–1350.* 1989.

Richard, Jean. *Saint Louis: Crusader King of France.* Trans. Jean Birrell. 1992.

Strayer, Joseph R. *The Reign of Philip the Fair.* 1980.

*Wood, Charles T. *Philip the Fair and Boniface VIII: State vs. Papacy.* 2nd ed. 1971.

CHAPTER REVIEW

IMPORTANT EVENTS

1188	King Alfonso IX summons townsmen to the *cortes*
1212–1250	Reign of Frederick II
1215	Fourth Lateran Council
1273	Thomas Aquinas publishes the *Summa Theologiae*
1226–1270	Reign of Louis IX (St. Louis)
1232	"Statute in Favor of the Princes"
1233	First permanent Inquisition
1240	Mongols capture Kiev
1265	English commons summoned to Parliament
1265–1321	Dante Alighieri
1302	First Meeting of the French Estates
1309–1378	Avignon Papacy (Babylonian Captivity)

KEY TERMS

Golden Horde (461)

Gothic (446)

Inquisition (438)

motet (445)

polyphony (446)

scholasticism (443)

summa (443)

tertiaries (441)

REVIEW QUESTIONS

1. How did people respond to the teachings and laws of the church in the early thirteenth century?
2. How did artists, architects, musicians, and scholastics try to link this world with the divine?

3. In what ways did the secular rulers of the period 1215–1320 cooperate with the church; in what ways did they not—and why?

MAKING CONNECTIONS

1. Why was Innocent III more successful than Boniface VIII in carrying out his objectives?
2. What impact did the Mongolian invasions have on the medieval economy?

FOR FURTHER EXPLORATION

To assess your mastery of the material in this chapter, see the Online Study Guide at **bedfordstmartins.com/hunt**.

To read additional primary-source material from this period, see Chapter 12 in *Sources of The Making of the West*, Second Edition, Volume I.

The Crisis of Late Medieval Society, 1320–1430

"IN THE YEAR OF OUR LORD 1349," begins the chronicle kept by the Nuremberg citizen Ulman Stromer, "the Jews resided in the middle of the square, and their houses lined its sides as well as a street behind where Our Lady's now stands. And the Jews were burned on the evening of St. Nicholas's as it has been described." These terse words belie the horror experienced by the Jewish community. Robbed of their belongings in an uprising, the Jews of Nuremberg were later rounded up by the city magistrates and required to convert to Christianity. Those who refused were burned at the stake. The new church of Our Lady went up on the site where the Jewish synagogue was razed.

Nuremberg, in central Germany, was but one of numerous sites of anti-Jewish furor in 1349. After decades in which religious and political institutions had gained control, the violence of 1349 represented the breakdown of authority in the face of widespread warfare, catastrophic losses of population from disease, and unprecedented challenges to religious authority. The coming together of these political, demographic, and religious developments resulted in a general crisis of late medieval society.

The political aspect of the crisis centered on the conflict between the English and the French that came to be called the Hundred Years' War (1337–1453). High taxes and widespread devastation also led to popular revolts that shook political establishments. But the loss of life in war paled in comparison to deaths by disease and famine.

In the mid-fourteenth century a series of disasters—famine, climatic changes, and disease—scourged a society already weakened by overpopulation, economic stagnation, social conflicts, and war.

The Burning of Jews
While townspeople watch, an executioner carries more firewood to the pyre of Jews, an example of the horrible persecutions against Jewish communities during the plague years of 1348–1350. This religious violence, arising out of the confrontation between Christianity and Judaism, had the opposite effect to that intended by Christians. Instead of converting, most Jews honored their martyrs and felt less incentive to accept the faith of their oppressors. © Brussels, Royal Library of Belgium.

Siege Warfare
Siege warfare during the Hundred Years' War pitted cannons against fortifications. As cannons grew in caliber, walls became thicker, and protruding battlements and gun emplacements were added to provide counter-firepower. Late-medieval sieges were time-consuming affairs that often lasted for years. *Bibliothèque Nationale de France.*

hostages, and tales of bloody slaughter and amorous conquests. War became its own engine. Mercenary companies came to replace freemen in the English army. These companies remained in France during the long intervals of armistice between short, destructive campaigns punctuated by a few spectacular battles.

Elaborate chivalric behavior, savage brutality, and unabashed profiteering permeated the fighting in the Hundred Years' War. This warfare involved definite rules whose application depended on social status. English and French knights took one another prisoner and showed all the formal courtesy

required by chivalry—but they slaughtered captured common soldiers like cattle. Overall the war consisted not of pitched battles but rather of a series of raids in which English fighters plundered cities and villages, causing terrible destruction. English knights financed their own campaigns, and war was expected to turn a profit either in captured booty or in ransom paid to free captured nobles.

Ruling over a more populous realm and commanding far larger armies, the French kings were nevertheless hindered in the war by the independent actions of their powerful barons. Against the accurate and deadly English freemen archers, the French knights met repeated defeats. Yet perhaps even more than they despised their English adversaries, the French nobles feared their own peasants and the urban middle classes. Their fears of peasant rebellion were not unfounded, for a deep chasm separated the warrior class from their social inferiors in medieval Europe.

The Course of the War. Historians divide the Hundred Years' War into three periods: the first marked by English triumphs, the second in which France slowly gained the upper hand, and the third ending in the English expulsion from France (Map 13.1). The final, most important phase saw two key developments: the rise of Burgundy, a hodgepodge of territories held together only by the political machinations of its dukes, and the rise of France as a distinct nation.

The final phase began when the English king Henry V (r. 1413–1422) launched a full-scale invasion of France and crushed the French at Agincourt (1415). Three parties then struggled for domination in France. Henry occupied Normandy and claimed the French throne; the dauphin (heir apparent to the French throne), later Charles VII (r. 1422–1461), ruled central France;[1] and the duke of Burgundy held a vast territory in the northeast that included the Low Countries. Burgundy was thus able to broker war or peace by shifting support first to the

_____

[1]Although the dauphin was not crowned until 1429, he assumed the title Charles VII in 1422, following the death of his father.

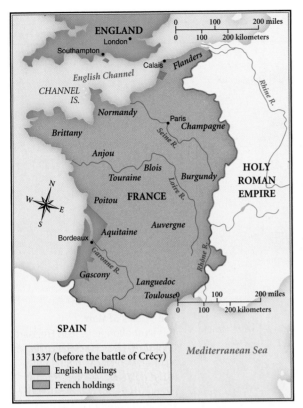

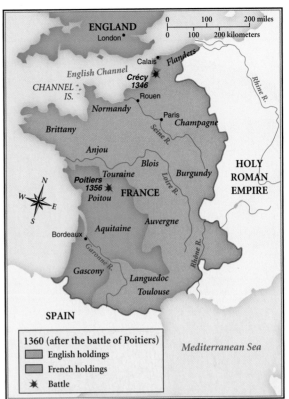

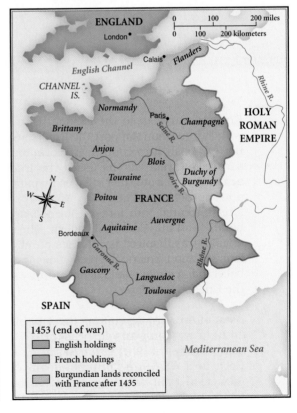

MAP 13.1 The Hundred Years' War, 1337–1453
As rulers of Aquitaine, English kings contested the French monarchy for the domination of France. Squeezed between England and Burgundy, the effective possession of the French kings was vastly reduced after the battle of Poitiers.

The Spoils of War
This illustration from Jean Froissart's *Chronicles* depicts soldiers pillaging a conquered city. Looting in the Hundred Years' War became the main income for mercenary troops and contributed to the general misery of late-medieval society. Food, furniture, and even everyday household items were looted. War had come to feed on itself. *Bibliothèque Nationale de France.*

English and then to the French. But even with Burgundian support the English could not establish firm control. In Normandy, a savage guerrilla war harassed the English army. Driven from their villages by pillaging and murdering soldiers, the Norman peasants retreated into forests, formed armed bands, and attacked the English. The miseries of war inspired prophecies of miraculous salvation; among the predictions was the belief that a virgin would deliver France from the English invaders.

Joan of Arc.   At the court of the dauphin, in 1429, a sixteen-year-old peasant girl presented herself and her vision to save France. Born in a village in Lorraine, Joan of Arc grew up in a war-ravaged country that longed for divine deliverance. (See "Contrasting Views," page 474.) The young maid had first presented herself as God's messenger to the local noble, who was sufficiently impressed to equip Joan with a horse, armor, and a ret-

inue to send her to the dauphin's court. (According to her later testimony, Joan ran away from home when her father threatened to drown her because she refused an arranged marriage.) Joan of Arc's extraordinary appearance inspired the beleaguered French to trust in divine providence. In that same year, she accompanied the French army that laid a prolonged but successful siege on Orléans, was wounded, and showed great courage in battle. Upon her urging, the dauphin traveled deep into hostile Burgundian territory to be anointed King Charles VII of France at the cathedral in Reims, thus strengthening his legitimacy by following the traditional ritual of coronation.

Joan's fortunes declined after Reims. She promised to capture Paris, but the Anglo-Burgundian defenders drove back her troops and the French began to lose faith in the Maid, as she was known. When the Burgundians captured Joan in 1430, Charles and his forces did little to save her. Still, Joan was a powerful symbol, and the English were determined to undermine her claim to divine guidance. In a trial conducted by French theologians in Anglo-Burgundian service, Joan was accused of false prophecy and witchcraft because she wore men's clothes and led armies (see Joan of Arc, on this page). Tricked into recanting her prophetic mission, she retracted her confessions, returned the female attire given her after an English soldier had raped her in prison, and reaffirmed her divine mission. The English then burned her at the stake as a relapsed heretic in 1431.

After Joan's death, the English position slowly crumbled and their alliance with the Burgundians fell apart in 1435. The duke of Burgundy then recognized Charles VII as king of France. Skirmish by skirmish, the English were driven from French soil, retaining only the port of Calais when hostilities ceased in 1453. Two years later, the French church rescinded the 1431 verdict that had condemned Joan of Arc as a heretic. Some five centuries later, she was canonized and declared the patron saint of France.

Consequences of the War. The Hundred Years' War had four major impacts. First, the long years of warfare aggravated the demographic and economic crises of the fourteenth century. Recurrent plagues (discussed later in this chapter) and pillage further ravaged the population. Constant insecurity caused by marauding bands of soldiers prevented farmers from cultivating fields even in times of truce. In Normandy, perhaps up to half the population had perished by the end of the war, victims of disease, famine, and warfare.

Second, the war prevented a quick resolution of the crisis in spiritual authority. As we will see, the collapse of papal authority known as the Great Schism owed much to the fact that rival popes could call on the respective belligerents to support their own claims. Locked in combat, the French, English, and Burgundian rulers could not agree to restore papal authority.

Third, the political landscape of western Europe changed. The necessity of mobilization strengthened the hand of the French mon-

Joan of Arc, c. 1420
Painted in the style of the French-Flemish school, this manuscript illustration contrasts the metallic hardness of Joan's armor and sword with the soft fluttering banner depicting God and two angels. With her right arm upturned clasping a sword and her left turned down to support the banner, Joan strikes a perfect pose as a messenger of God, similar to the angels depicted above. © *AKG-Images, London.*

archy. Under Charles VII, a standing army was established to supplement the feudal noble levies, financed by increased taxation and expanded royal judicial claims. By 1500, the French monarchy would emerge as one of the leading powers of Europe, ready to battle Burgundy and the empire for the domination of Europe. Burgundy also emerged as a strong power from the Hundred Years' War. By absorbing the Low Countries, this French duchy was evolving into an independent state, a rich power situated between France and Germany and commanding the fabulous wealth of Flemish cities. The Burgundian dukes became

Joan of Arc: Who Was "the Maid"?

The figure of Joan of Arc looms above the confused events and personalities of the Hundred Years' War. But who was this slender young woman from the Lorraine? Calling herself La Pucelle♦ ("the Maid"), Joan left home after she was instructed in a vision to present herself as God's messenger at the court of Charles, the dauphin of France (Document 1). Either captivated by her piety and bravery or threatened by her power and actions, contemporaries labeled Joan everything from a divine symbol to a relapsed heretic (Documents 2–3). Her capture and her year-long imprisonment, torture, interrogation, and subsequent execution generated documentation and ensured her immortality (Document 4).

1. JOAN'S VISION

Joan first spoke of her visions at length after her capture by her enemies, who were eager to prove that she was inspired by the devil. This document is the only information we have from Joan herself about her childhood. Notice three things: first, the references to light and voice, a standard representation by medieval visionaries; second, the instruction not to tell her father about her mission, which implied that she left home without his consent; and third, the reference to the siege of Orléans, which might have been an addition to her memory after the momentous events of her career. It was likely that she first thought of her mission in a more general way of saving France.

When I was thirteen years old, I had a voice from God to help me govern my conduct. And the first time I was very fearful. And came this voice, about the hour of noon, in the summer-time, in my father's garden; I had not fasted on the eve preceding that day. I heard the voice on the right-hand side, towards the church; and rarely do I hear it without a brightness. This brightness

comes from the same side as the voice is heard. It is usually a great light. When I came to France, often I heard this voice....The voice was sent to me by God and, after I had thrice heard this voice, I knew that it was the voice of an angel. This voice has always guarded me well and I have always understood it clearly....

It has taught me to conduct myself well, to go habitually to church. It told me that I, Joan, should come into France....This voice told me, twice or thrice a week, that I, Joan, must go away and that I must come to France and that my father must know nothing of my leaving. The voice told me that I should go to France and I could not bear to stay where I was. The voice told me that I should raise the siege laid to the city of Orléans....And me, I answered it that I was a poor girl who knew not how to ride nor lead in war.

Source: Régine Pernoud, ed., Joan of Arc: By Herself and Her Witnesses (Lanham, Md.: Scarborough House, 1994), 30.

2. MESSENGER OF GOD?

When Joan appeared at the court of the dauphin, her reputation as the messenger of God had preceded her. The French court received her with a mixture of wonder, curiosity, and outright skepticism. The political and military situation looked so desperate that many had been hoping for a divine deliverance when Joan made her arrival in history. There was debate among the dauphin's counselors whether Joan should be taken seriously, however, and the dauphin referred the case to a panel of theologians to determine whether Joan's mission was of divine origin. The following account of Joan's first visit to the dauphin was recorded by Simon Charles, president of the Chamber of Accounts.

I know that, when Joan arrived in [the castle and town of] Chinon, there was deliberation in counsel to decide whether the King should hear her or not. To start with they sent to ask her why she was

---

♦ *La Pucelle:* lah poo SEHL

come and what she was asking for. She was unwilling to say anything without having spoken to the King, yet was she constrained by the King to say the reasons for her mission. She said that she had two [reasons] for which she had a mandate from the King of Heaven; one, to raise the siege of Orléans, the other to lead the King to Rheims for his [coronation]. Which being heard, some of the King's counsellors said that the King should on no account have faith in Joan, and the others that since she said that she was sent by God, and that she had something to say to the King, the King should at least hear her.

Source: Pernoud, 48–49.

3. NORMAL GIRL?

This memoir, written by Marguerite la Touroulde, one of the women who lived with Joan and took care of her after the dauphin had accepted Joan's services to save France, testifies to Joan's ordinariness. The messenger of God appears in these words as a normal, devout young girl whose only remarkable quality seems to be her physical and martial prowess.

Joan was then brought to Bourges and, by command of the lord d'Albret, she was lodged in my house....She was in my house for a period of three weeks, sleeping, drinking and eating, and almost every day I slept with Joan and I neither saw in her nor perceived anything of any kind of unquietness, but she behaved herself as an honest and Catholic woman, for she went very often to confession, willingly heard mass and often asked me to go to Matins. And at her instance I went, and took her with me several times.

Sometimes we talked together and some said to Joan that doubtless she was not afraid to go into battle because she knew well that she would not be killed. She answered that she was no safer than any other combatant....Joan was very simple and ignorant and knew absolutely nothing, it seems to me, excepting in the matter of war....She was open-handed in almsgiving and most willingly gave to the indigent and to the poor, saying that she had been sent for the consolation of the poor and the indigent.

And several times I saw her at the bath and in the bath-houses, and so far as I was able to see, she was a virgin, and from all that I know she was all innocence, excepting in arms, for I saw her riding on horseback and bearing a lance as the best of soldiers would have done it, and at that the men-at-arms marvelled.

Source: Pernoud, 64–65.

4. SACRED MARTYR?

After her capture, Joan was condemned to burn at the stake. She went to her death in 1431 clutching a crucifix and uttering the name of Christ. Her actions and demeanor moved many to remember the event. Their testimonies ten years later provided the evidence for judges to overturn her conviction. Her good name restored, Joan would live on in the memory of France as its greatest heroine. Pierre Cusquel, a stonemason from Orléans, offered the following testimony.

I heard say that Master Jean Tressard, secretary to the King of England, returning from Joan's execution afflicted and groaning, wept lamentably over what he had seen in that place and said indeed: "We are all lost, for we have burnt a good and holy person," and that he believed that her soul was in God's hands and that, when she was in the midst of the flames, she had still declaimed the name of the Lord Jesus. That was common repute and more or less all the people murmured that a great wrong and injustice had been done to Joan....After Joan's death the English had the ashes gathered up and thrown into the Seine because they feared lest she escape or lest some say she had escaped.

Source: Pernoud, 233.

QUESTIONS TO CONSIDER
1. What was Joan's vision? Was her vision understood differently by the French king or by herself during her trial?
2. What was the source of Joan's charisma? Why did she inspire such a wide range of responses?

rivals of French kings after about 1450 and established a brilliant court culture. As for England, defeat abroad spread discontent at home. The English monarchy suffered through decades of disunity and strife, and from the 1460s to 1485, England was torn by civil war—the War of the Roses (described in Chapter 14).

Further, the heavy financial burden of warfare also destabilized the banking system. Default on war loans by England's Edward III precipitated the collapse of several of the largest banks in Europe, all based in Italy. The political crisis of the Hundred Years' War thus had a direct impact on the economic crisis of the fourteenth century.

Popular Uprisings

English and French knights waged war at the expense of the common people. While French peasants and townsfolk were taxed, robbed, raped, and murdered by marauding bands of mercenaries, their English counterparts had to pay ever higher taxes to support the wars. Widespread resentment fueled popular uprisings, which contributed to the general disintegration of political and social order. In 1358, a short but savage rebellion erupted in the area around Paris, shocking the nobility. And in 1381, a more widespread and broadly based revolt broke out in England. In the cities, the social and economic dislocations of the war deepened the general crisis of mid-century and sparked insurrections in the cities of France, Flanders, and Italy.

Jacquerie Uprising in Paris. Historians traditionally described the 1358 rebellion—named the Jacquerie◆ after the jacket (*jacque*) worn by serfs—as a "peasant fury," implying that it represented simply a spontaneous outburst of aimless violence. More recent research, however, has revealed the complex social origins of the movement. The revolt broke out after the English captured King John at the battle of Poitiers,◆ when the estates of France (the representatives of the clergy, nobility, and the cities) met in Paris to discuss monarchical reform and national defense. Unhappy with the heavy war taxes, the incompetence of the warrior nobility, and the brutality of marauding mercenaries, the townspeople sought greater political influence. Political conflict between commoner and nobles soon turned into a massive uprising.

The rebels, under Étienne Marcel, the leader of the merchants of Paris, began to destroy manor houses and castles near the city, massacring entire noble families in a savage class war. Contemporaries were astonished at the intensity and violence of the Jacquerie. The chronicler Jean Froissart, sympathetic to the nobility, said the rebels aimed "to destroy all the nobles and gentry in the world." Repression by nobles was even more savage, however, as thousands of rebels died in battles or were executed. In Paris the rebel leader Marcel was killed in factional strife, but urban rebellions continued to flicker.

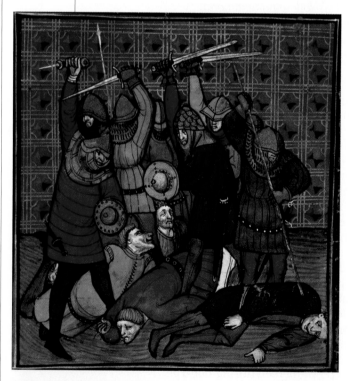

Outbreak of the Jacquerie
Soldiers massacre unarmed peasants during the 1358 Jacquerie, or peasant insurrection, in this illustration from Jean Froissart's *Chronicles*. Wielding swords, spears, and daggers, the soldiers brutally repress the peasantry. © *The British Library/Topham-HIP/The Image Works.*

English Peasant Revolt. In England, rural and urban discontent intensified as land-

◆**Jacquerie:** zhah kuh REE
◆**Poitiers:** pwah TYAY

lords, peasants, and workers pursued increasingly opposing interests. The trigger for outright rebellion was the imposition of a poll tax (per capita tax) passed by Parliament in 1377 to raise money for the war against France. In May 1381, a revolt broke out. Rebels in Essex and Kent joined bands in London to confront the king. A famous couplet by the radical preacher John Ball, who was executed after the revolt, expresses the rebels' egalitarian, antinoble sentiment:

> When Adam delved [dug] and Eve span [spun]
> Who was then a gentleman?

Forced to address the rebels, young King Richard II agreed to abolish serfdom and impose a ceiling on land rent, concessions immediately rescinded after the rebels' defeat in a suppression as bloody as that in France.

Unrest in Flanders. Popular uprisings also took place in the Low Countries, especially in the cities of Flanders, the most densely populated and urbanized region of Europe. For more than a century, Flanders had been Europe's industrial and financial heartland, importing raw wool from England, manufacturing fine cloth, and exporting woolen goods to all parts of Europe.

Because the region depended on trade for food and goods, Flanders was especially sensitive to the larger political and economic changes. The Hundred Years' War undermined the woolen industry as Edward III of England declared a trade embargo, thus halting shipments of raw materials to Flemish industries. Although Flanders was a French fief, weavers and other artisans opposed their count's pro-French policy because they depended on English wool. From 1338 to 1345, the citizens of the large industrial city of Ghent rebelled against their prince. In the late 1370s, the townspeople of Ghent sought an alliance with the people of Paris and fielded an army to battle the count. Though they suffered a disastrous defeat in 1382, they were not completely subdued until the fifteenth century.

Urban Insurrections in Italy. Revolts in Rome and Florence resulted in part from the long absence of the popes during the Avignon papacy, which had been established in 1309 after civil strife forced the pope out of Rome. Factional violence between powerful noble families in Rome fueled popular hatred of local magnates and provided the background for a popular revolt. The Florentine chronicler Giovanni Villani wrote that "on May 20, 1347....a certain Cola di Rienzo had just returned to Rome from a mission on behalf of the Roman people to the court of the Pope, to beg him to come and live, with his court, in the bishopric of St. Peter, as he should do." Although unsuccessful in his mission to Avignon, Rienzo so impressed the Romans with his speech that they proclaimed him "tribune of the people," a title harking back to the plebeians' representatives in the ancient Roman republic. "Certain of the Orsini and the Colonna [families]," continued Villani, "as well as other nobles, fled from the city to their lands and castles to escape the fury of the tribune and the people." Rienzo and his followers took advantage of the nobles' flight and tried to remake their city in the image of classical Roman republicanism. But like the revolts in Paris and Ghent, the Roman uprising (1347–1354) was suppressed by the nobility.

The pattern of social conflict behind these urban revolts is best exemplified by the Ciompi♦ uprising in Florence. One of the largest European cities in the fourteenth century, Florence was a center of banking and the woolen industry in southern Europe. As the wool industry declined because of falling demand, unemployment became an explosive social problem. During the summer of 1378, the lower classes, many of them woolworkers, rose against the regime. Joined by artisans and merchants, they demanded more equitable power sharing with the bankers and wealthy merchants who controlled city government. By midsummer, crowds thronged the streets, and woolworkers set fire to the palaces of the rich and demanded the right to form their own guild. The insurrection was subsequently called the Ciompi uprising (meaning "uprising by the little people"). Alarmed by the radical turn of events, the guild artisans turned against their worker allies and defeated them in fierce street battles. The revolt ended

♦**Ciompi:** CHAHM pee

MAP 13.2 Central and Eastern Europe, c. 1400
Through the Holy Roman Empire and the Teutonic Knights, Germanic influence extended far into eastern Europe including Bohemia, Moravia, and the Baltic coast. The Polish-Lithuanian Commonwealth, united in 1386, and the Kingdom of Hungary were the other great powers in eastern Europe.

Europe, nor did they significantly alter the distribution of power. Instead they were subsumed by larger political transformations, from which the princely states would emerge as the major political forces in European civilization in the next centuries.

Imperial Fragmentation and Eastern European State Building

While England and France struggled for domination in western Europe, the Holy Roman Empire, unified in name only, became an arena in which princes and cities assumed more power in their own hands. This political fragmentation, together with a stronger orientation toward the Slavic lands of eastern Europe, signified a growing separation between central and western Europe (see Map 13.2 on this page). Within the empire, the four most significant developments were the shift of political focus from the south and west to the east, the changing balance of power between the emperor and the princes, the development of cities, and the rise of self-governing communes in the Alps.

Three of the five Holy Roman Emperors in the period from 1350 to 1450 belonged to the House of Luxembourg: Charles IV (r. 1355–1378), Wenceslas (r. 1378–1400), and Sigismund (r. 1410–1437). Having obtained Bohemia by marriage, the Luxembourg dynasty based its power in the east, and Prague became the imperial capital. This move initiated a shift of power within the Holy Roman Empire away from the Rhineland and Swabia toward east-central Europe. Except for a continuous involvement with northern Italy, theoretically a part of the Holy

with a restoration of the patrician regime, although Ciompi exiles continued to plot worker revolts into the 1380s.

The Ciompi rebellion, like the uprisings in Paris, Ghent, and Rome, were part of a larger set of changes in late medieval Europe. The rebels were motivated by social and economic depression, which in turn was caused by the general crisis of warfare, economic stagnation, and disease. But as significant as their motivations was their failure. Urban revolts did not redraw the political map of

Roman Empire, German institutions became more closely allied with eastern rather than western Europe. For example, the Holy Roman Empire's first university, Charles University (named after its royal founder, Charles IV), was established in 1348 in Prague. Bohemians and Hungarians also began to exert more influence in imperial politics.

Another development that separated central from western Europe was the fragmentation of political authority in the Holy Roman Empire at a time when French, English, and Castilian monarchs were consolidating their power. Charles IV's coronation as emperor in 1355 did not translate into more power at home. The Bohemian nobility refused to recognize his supreme authority, and the German princes secured from him a constitutional guarantee for their own sovereignty. In 1356, Charles was forced to agree to the Golden Bull, a document that required the German king to be chosen by seven electors: the archbishops of Mainz, Cologne, and Trier, the king of Bohemia, the elector of Saxony, the count of the Palatinate, and the margrave of Brandenburg. The imperial electoral college also guaranteed the existence of numerous local and regional power centers, a distinctive feature in German history that continued into the modern age.

Although no single German city rivaled Paris, London, Florence, or Ghent in population, its large number of cities made Germany an economic power. But rivalry among powerful princes prevented the cities from evolving into republics like those in Italy. Nevertheless, the cities were at the forefront of economic growth. Nuremberg and Augsburg became centers of the north–south trade, linking Poland, Bohemia, and the German lands with the Mediterranean. In northern Germany, the Hanseatic League (from *Hansa*, a German merchant guild or trading association), under the leadership of Lübeck, united the many towns trading between the Baltic and the North Sea. At its zenith in the fifteenth century, the Hanseatic fleet controlled the Baltic, and the league was a power to be reckoned with by kings and princes.

Another sign of political fragmentation was the growth of self-governing peasant and town communes in the high Alpine valleys that united in the Swiss Confederation. In 1291, the peasants of Uri, Schwyz, and Unterwalden had sworn a perpetual alliance against their oppressive Habsburg overlord. After defeating a Habsburg army in 1315, these free peasants took the name Confederates and developed a new alliance that would become Switzerland. In the process, the Swiss enshrined their freedom in the legend of William Tell, their national hero who was forced by a Habsburg official to prove his archery skills by successfully shooting an arrow through an apple placed on the head of his own son. This challenge so outraged the citizens that they rose up in arms against the Habsburg rule. By 1353, Lucerne, Zurich, and Bern had joined the confederation. The Swiss Confederation continued to acquire new members into the sixteenth century, defeating armies sent by different princes.

Growth of the Swiss Confederation to 1353

Also in the mid-fourteenth century, two large monarchies took shape in northeastern Europe—Poland and Lithuania. In the early twelfth century, Poland had splintered into petty duchies, and the Mongol invasion of the 1240s had caused frightful devastation. But recovery was under way by 1300, and unlike almost every other part of Europe, Poland experienced an era of demographic and economic expansion in the fourteenth century. Both Jewish and German settlers, for example, helped build thriving towns like Cracow. Monarchical consolidation followed. King Casimir◆ III (r. 1333–1370) won recognition in most of the country's regions for his royal authority, embodied in comprehensive law codes. A problem that persisted throughout his reign, however, was conflict with the neighboring princes of Lithuania, Europe's last pagan rulers, who for centuries fiercely resisted Christianization by the German crusading order, the Teutonic Knights. After the Mongols overran Russia, Lithuania extended its rule southward, offering western Russian princes protection against Mongol and Musco-

---

◆**Casimir:** KAH zuh mihr

vite rule. By the late fourteenth century, a vast Lithuanian principality had arisen, embracing modern Lithuania, Belarus, and Ukraine.

Casimir III died in 1370 without a son; the failure of a new dynasty to take hold opened the way for the unification of Poland and Lithuania. In 1386, the Lithuanian prince Jogailo accepted Roman Catholic baptism, married the young queen of Poland, and later assumed the Polish crown. Under the Jagiellonian dynasty, Poland and Lithuania kept separate legal systems. Catholicism and Polish culture prevailed among the principality's upper class, while most native Lithuanian village folk remained pagan for several centuries. With only a few interruptions, the Polish-Lithuanian federation would last for five centuries.

Multiethnic States on the Frontiers

While some Christian princes were battling one another, others were fighting Muslim foes at the frontiers of Christian Europe. Two regions at opposite ends of the Mediterranean—Spain and the Ottoman Empire—were unusual in medieval Europe for their religious and ethnic diversity. As a result of the Spanish **reconquista** of the twelfth and thirteenth centuries, the Iberian Christian kingdoms contained large religious and ethnic minorities. In Castile, where historians estimate the population before the outbreak of the plague in 1348 at four to five million, 7 percent of the inhabitants were Muslims or Jews. In Aragon, of the approximately one million people at midcentury, perhaps 3 to 4 percent belonged to these two religious minorities. In the Iberian peninsula, the Christian kingdoms consolidated their gains against Muslim Granada, bringing sizable minority populations into newly Christian regions. At the same time, the orthodox Byzantine Empire, hardly recovered from the Fourth Crusade, fought for survival against the Ottoman

Christian Territory in Iberia, c. 1350

Turks. In the Balkans and Anatolia, the Ottomans created a multiethnic state, but one different from the Iberian kingdoms.

The Iberian Peninsula. In the mid-fourteenth century, the Iberian peninsula encompassed six areas: Portugal, Castile, Navarre, Aragon, and Catalonia—all Christian—and Muslim Granada. Among these territories, Castile and Aragon were the most important, both politically and economically. The Muslim population was concentrated in the south. Initially, the Iberian Muslims, called **Moors**, under Christian rule could own property, practice their religion, and elect their own judges, but conditions worsened for them in the fifteenth century as fears of rebellions and religious prejudices intensified among Christians. As Christian conquerors and settlers advanced, most Muslims were driven out of the cities or confined to specific neighborhoods. Many Muslims were captured and enslaved by Christian armies. These slaves worked in Christian households or on large estates called **latifundia**, which were granted by the Castilian kings to the crusading orders, the church, and powerful noble families. Slavery existed on a fairly large scale in Mediterranean areas where Christian and Muslim civilizations confronted one another: in Iberia, North Africa, Anatolia, and in the Balkans.

Jews congregated mostly in cities, where they practiced many professions and encountered few social obstacles to advancement. Jewish physicians and tax collectors made up part of the administration of Castile, but the Christian populace resented their social prominence and wealth. Moreover, the religious fervor and sense of crisis in the later fourteenth century intensified the ever-present intolerance toward Jews. In June 1391, incited by the sermons of the priest Fernando Martínez, a mob attacked the Jewish community in Seville, plundering, burning, and killing all who refused baptism. The anti-Semitic violence spread to other cities in the peninsula. Sometimes the authorities tried to protect the Jews, who were legally the king's property. About half of the 200,000 Castilian Jews converted to Christianity to save themselves; another 25,000 were murdered or fled to

Portugal and Granada. The survivors were to face even more discrimination and violence in the fifteenth century.

The Ottoman and Byzantine Empires.

The fourteenth century also saw a great power rise at the other end of the Mediterranean. Under Osman I (r. 1280–1324) and his son Orhan Gazi (r. 1324–1359), the Ottoman dynasty became a formidable force in Anatolia and the Balkans, where political disunity opened the door for Ottoman advances (Map 13.3). The Ottomans were one of several Turkish tribal confederations in central Asia. As converts to Islam and as warriors, the Ottoman cavalry raided Byzantine territory in an Islamic jihad, or holy war.

Under Murat I (r. 1360–1389), the Ottomans reduced the Byzantine Empire to the city of Constantinople and the status of a vassal state. In 1364, Murat defeated a joint Hungarian-Serbian army at the Maritsa River, alerting Europe for the first time to the new threat of an Islamic invasion. Pope Urban V called for a crusade, but the Christian kingdoms in the west were already fighting in the Hundred Years' War. In the Balkans, the Ottomans skillfully exploited Christian disunity, playing

Janissaries in the Ottoman Army
Janissaries (literally "new infantry") were recruited from among Christian boys raised by the sultan. They were distinguished by their high ornamental headgear and their use of firearms, which made them a particularly effective component of the Ottoman forces. Here a squad of Janissaries is shown on parade, with a model of a Turkish war galley. *Österreichische National bibliothek.*

Serbian, Albanian, Wallachian,◆ Bulgarian, and Byzantine interests against one another. Moreover, Venice, Genoa, and Ragusa each pursued separate commercial interests. Thus, an Ottoman army allied not only with the Bulgarians but even with some Serbian princes won the battle of Kosovo (1389), destroying the last organized Christian resistance south of the Danube. The Ottomans secured control of southeastern Europe after 1396, when at Nicopolis they crushed a crusading army.

The Ottoman invasion was more than a continuation of the struggle between Christendom and Islam. The battle for territory transcended the boundaries of faith. Christian princes also served the Ottoman Empire as vassals to the sultan. The **Janissaries** (above), Christian slave children raised by the sultan

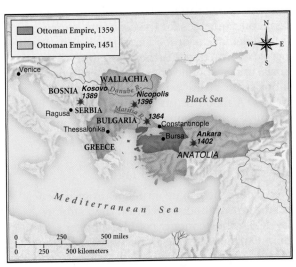

MAP 13.3 Ottoman Expansion in the Fourteenth and Fifteenth Centuries
The Balkans were the major theater of expansion for the Ottoman Empire, whose conquests also included Egypt and the North African coast. The Byzantine Empire was long reduced to the city of Constantinople and surrounded by the Ottomans before its final fall in 1453.

◆**Wallachian:** wah LAY kee uhn

as Muslims, constituted the fundamental backbone of the Ottoman army. They formed a service class, the *devshirme*, which was both dependent on and loyal to the ruler. At the sultan's court, Christian women were prominent in the harem; thus, many Ottoman princes had Greek or Serbian mothers. In addition to the Janissaries, Christian princes and converts to Islam served in the emerging Ottoman administration. In conquered areas, existing religious and social structures remained intact when local people accepted Ottoman overlordship and paid taxes. Only in areas of persistent resistance did the Ottomans drive out or massacre the inhabitants, settling Turkish tribes in their place. A distinctive pattern of Balkan history was thus established at the beginning of the Ottoman conquest: extremely diverse ethnic and religious communities were woven together into the fabric of an efficient central state.

By the mid-fourteenth century, the territory of the Byzantine Empire consisted of only Constantinople, Thessalonika, and a narrow strip of land in modern-day Greece. During the century, the Black Death, three civil wars between rivals to the throne, and numerous Ottoman incursions devastated Byzantine land and population. Constantinople was saved in 1402 from a five-year Ottoman siege only when Mongol invaders crushed another Ottoman army near Ankara in Anatolia. Although the empire's fortunes declined, Byzantium experienced a religious and cultural ferment, as the elites compensated for their loss of power in a search for past glory. The majority asserted the superiority of the Greek Orthodox faith and opposed the reunion of the Roman and Greek churches, the political price for western European military aid. Many adhered to tradition, attacking any departures from ancient literary models and Byzantine institutions. A handful, such as the scholar George Gemistos (1353–1452), abandoned Christianity and embraced Platonic philosophy. Gemistos even changed his name (meaning "full" in Greek) to Plethon, its classical equivalent. The scholar Manuel Chrysoloras♦ became professor of Greek in Florence in 1397, thus establishing the study of ancient Greece in

♦**Chrysoloras:** krihs uh LOHR uhs

western Europe. This revival of interest in Greek antiquity eventually became part of the broad cultural movement known as the Renaissance.

> **Review:** How were dynastic warfare and popular uprisings related in the fourteenth century?

❖ The Plague and Society

Confronted with the rise of the Ottoman Empire, Latin Christendom faced a series of internal crises that wrought havoc on its population and economy. In the fifty years after 1348, Europe lost one-third of its population to repeated outbreaks of the bubonic plague, which originated in central Asia. A healthy population could have resisted the plague, but Europeans were far from healthy: they had been suffering from famines and hunger for two generations before the first outbreak. In the face of massive deaths, a new climate of fear settled on the landscape. Some people tried to avert the "scourge of God" in rituals of religious fanaticism; others searched out scapegoats, killing Jews and burning synagogues.

The demographic crisis also had important consequences for the economy, causing falling demands for food and goods and economic contraction. Further symptoms of this social and economic crisis were social unrest, labor strife, rising wages, and falling investments. A mood of uncertainty prevailed in business, and women were excluded more and more from the urban economy.

Rise and Spread of the Plague

Well before the plague struck, European economic growth had slowed and then stopped. By 1300, the economy could no longer support Europe's swollen population. Having cleared forests and drained swamps, the peasant masses now farmed marginal lands and divided their plots into ever smaller parcels; as a result, their income and the quality of their diet eroded. In the great urban centers, where thousands depended on steady employment and cheap bread, a bad harvest, always followed by sharply rising food prices, meant hunger and eventual famine. A cooling of the European climate also contributed to the crisis in the food supply. Modern studies of tree rings indicate that fourteenth-century Europe entered a colder period, with a succession of severe winters beginning in 1315. The extreme cold upset an ecological system already overtaxed by human civilization. Crop failures were widespread. In many cities of northwestern Europe, the price of bread tripled in a month, and thousands starved to death. Some Flemish cities, for example, lost 10 percent of their population. But the Great Famine of 1315–1317 was only the first in a series of catastrophes confronting the overpopulated and undernourished society of fourteenth-century Europe. In midcentury, death mowed down masses of weakened bodies.

From its breeding ground in central Asia, the bubonic plague passed eastward into China, where it decimated the population and wiped out the remnants of the tiny Italian merchant community in Yangzhou. Bacteria-carrying fleas, living on black rats, transmitted the disease. The disease traveled back to Europe alongside valuable cargoes of silk, porcelain, and spices. In 1347, the Genoese colony in Caffa in the Crimea contracted the plague from the Mongols. Fleeing by ship in a desperate but futile attempt to escape the disease, the Genoese in turn communicated the plague to other Mediterranean seaports. By January 1348, the plague had infected Sicily, Sardinia, Corsica, and Marseilles. Six months later, it had spread to Aragon, all of Italy, the Balkans, and most of France. The disease then crept northward to Germany, England, and Scandinavia, reaching the Russian city of Novgorod in 1350 (Map 13.4 on page 484).

Nothing like the Black Death (1348–1350), as this epidemic came to be called, had struck Europe since the great plague of the sixth century. The Italian writer Giovanni Boccaccio♦ (1313–1375) reported that the plague

> first betrayed itself by the emergence of certain tumors in the groin or the armpits, some of which grew as large as a common apple, others as an egg. . . . From the two said parts of the

Death Strangling a Plague Victim
In this graphic and terrifying illustration from a fourteenth-century Czech manuscript, the plague is personified as Death choking a sick man to death in his bed. Note the black running sore on the side of the body under the right armpit, which corresponds to contemporary descriptions of symptoms of the plague. *Werner Forman/Art Resource, NY.*

> body this . . . began to propagate and spread itself in all directions indifferently; after which the form of the malady began to change, black spots or livid making their appearance in many cases on the arm or the thigh or elsewhere, now few and large, now minute and numerous.

Most cities, where crowding and filth increased the chances of contagion, lost roughly half their population in less than a year. Florence lost almost two-thirds of its population of ninety thousand; Siena lost half its people. Paris, the largest city of western Europe, came off relatively well, losing only a quarter of its 200,000 inhabitants. Rural areas seem to have suffered fewer deaths, but regional differences were pronounced. (See "Taking Measure," page 485.)

♦**Giovanni Boccaccio:** joh VAHN nee bohk KAHT choh

Flagellants

The penitential brothers of the cross carried a banner depicting the instruments of Christ's torture and a crucifix as they scourged themselves on their exposed backs with whips (shown in their right hands), chanting for God's forgiveness and an end to the plague. The Latin text beneath this illustration (not shown) explained the flagellant procession in 1349 in Tournai: "The preceding year on the day of the Assumption of the Virgin, some two hundred men came from the town of Bruges, and almost every hour they whipped themselves and called on God to bestow grace on their penance." Both Tournai and Bruges are in today's Belgium. © ARPL/Topham/The Image Works.

obtained approval from Emperor Charles IV before organizing the 1349 persecution directed by the city government. Thousands of German Jews were slaughtered. Many fled to Poland, where incidence of the plague was low and where the authorities welcomed Jews as productive taxpayers. In western and central Europe, however, the persecutions destroyed the financial power of the Jews.

Consequences of the Plague

Although the Black Death took a horrible human toll, some people profited from the disaster. In an overpopulated society with limited resources, massive death opened the ranks for advancement. For example, after 1350, landlords had difficulty acquiring new tenant farmers without

fueled anti-Semitism as those in debt turned on creditors, often Jews who had become rich from the commercial revolution of the thirteenth century. Perhaps most cynical were the nobility of Alsace, heavily indebted to Jewish bankers, who sanctioned the murder of Jews to avoid repaying their debts.

Many anti-Semitic incidents were spontaneous, with mobs plundering Jewish quarters and killing anyone who refused baptism. Authorities seeking a focus for the widespread anger and fear orchestrated some of the violence. Relying on chronicles, historians have long linked the arrival of the Black Death with anti-Jewish violence. More recent historical research shows that in some cities the anti-Semitic violence actually preceded the epidemic. This revised chronology of events demonstrates official complicity and even careful premeditation in the destruction of some Jewish communities, exploiting popular hysteria about the plague. For example, the magistrates of Nuremberg

making concessions in land contracts; fewer priests now competed for the same number of **benefices** (ecclesiastical offices funded by an endowment), and workers received much higher wages because the supply of laborers had plummeted. The Black Death and the resulting decline in urban population meant a lower demand for grain relative to the supply and thus a drop in cereal prices. All across Europe noble landlords, whose revenues dropped as prices dropped, had to adjust to these new circumstances. Some revived feudal demands for labor services; others looked to their central government for legislation to regulate wages; and still others granted favorable terms to peasant proprietors, often after bloody peasant revolts. Many noblemen lost a portion of their wealth and a measure of their autonomy and political influence. Consequently, European nobles became more dependent on their monarchs and on war to supplement their incomes and enhance their power.

For the peasantry and the urban working population, the higher wages generally meant an improvement in living standards. To compensate for the lower demand and price for grain, many peasants and landlords turned to stock breeding and grape and barley cultivation. As European agriculture diversified, peasants and artisans consumed more beer, wine, meat, cheese, and vegetables—a better and more varied diet than their thirteenth-century forebears had eaten. The reduced cereal prices also stimulated sheep raising in place of farming, and thus a portion of the settled population, especially in the English Midlands and in Castile, became migratory.

Because of the shrinking population and decreased demand for food, cultivating marginal fields was no longer profitable and many settlements were simply abandoned. By 1450, for example, some 450 large English villages and many smaller hamlets had disappeared. In central Europe east of the Elbe River, where German peasants had migrated, large tracts of cultivated land reverted to forest. Estimates suggest that some 80 percent of all villages in parts of Thuringia♦ (Germany) vanished.

Also as a result of the plague, the focus of manufacturing shifted from a mass market to a highly lucrative, if small, luxury market. The drastic loss in urban population had reduced the demand for such mass-manufactured goods as cloth, one of the causes for the Ciompi uprising in Florence. Fewer people now possessed proportionately greater concentrations of wealth. In the southern French city of Albi, for example, the proportion of citizens with possessions worth more than a hundred French pounds doubled between 1343 and 1357, while the number of poor people, those with less than ten pounds, declined by half.

Faced with the possibility of imminent and untimely death, some of the urban populace sought immediate gratification. The Florentine Matteo Villani described the newfound desire for luxury in his native city in 1351: "The common people . . . wanted the dearest and most delicate foods . . . while children and common women clad themselves in all the fair and costly garments of the illustrious who had died." Those with means increased their consumption of luxuries: silk clothing, hats, doublets (snug-fitting men's jackets), and boots from Italy as well as expensive jewelry and spices from Asia became fashionable in northwestern Europe. Whereas agricultural prices continued to decline, prices of manufactured goods, particularly luxury items, remained constant and even rose as demand for them outstripped supply.

The long-term consequences of this new consumption pattern spelled the end for the traditional woolen industry that had produced for a mass market. Diminishing demand for wool caused hardships for woolworkers, and social and political unrest shook many older industrial centers dependent on the cloth industry. In the Flemish clothing center of Ypres,♦ for example, production figures fell from a high of ninety thousand pieces of cloth in 1320 to fewer than twenty-five thousand by 1390. In Ghent, where 44 percent of all households were woolworkers and where some 60 percent of the working population depended on the textile industry, the woolen market's slump meant constant labor unrest.

Much more difficult to measure was the sense of economic insecurity. One trend, however, seemed clear: the increasingly restrictive labor market for women in the urban economy in this age of crisis. In the German city of Cologne, for example, more and more artisan guilds excluded women from their ranks. By the late fifteenth century, the independent women's guilds had become a relic of the past. Everywhere, fathers favored sons and sons-in-law to succeed them in their crafts. Daughters and widows, however, resisted this patriarchal regime in the urban economy. They were most successful in industries with the least regulations, such as in beer brewing—where in Munich, for example, women held productive positions amid the economic recession.

Review: What were the demographic, economic, and psychological consequences of the plague?

♦**Thuringia:** thu RIHN jee uh

♦**Ypres:** EEP ruh

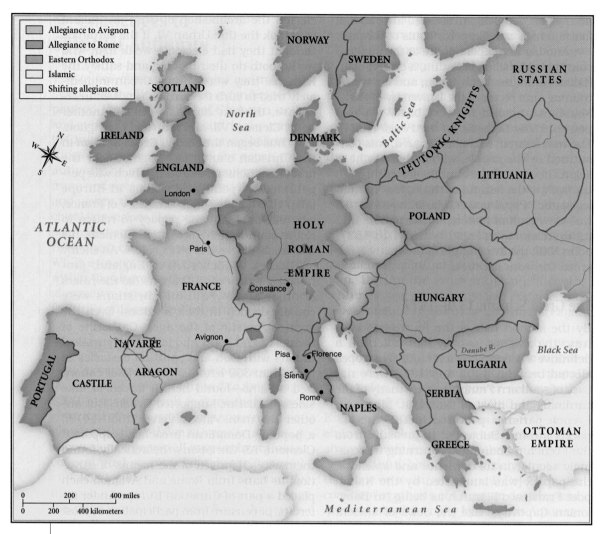

MAP 13.5 The Great Schism, 1378–1417

The allegiances to Roman and Avignon popes followed the political divisions between the European monarchs. The Great Schism weakened the Latin West during a period of Islamic expansion through the Ottoman Empire.

that "normally a council is not legally... celebrated without papal calling....But, as in grammar and in morals, general rules have exceptions."

The first attempt to resolve the question of church authority came in 1409, at the Council of Pisa, attended by cardinals who had defected from the two popes. The council asserted its supremacy by declaring both popes deposed and electing a new pontiff, Alexander V. When the popes at Rome and Avignon refused to yield to the authority of the council, Christian Europe found itself in the embarrassing position of choosing among three popes. Pressure to hold another council then came from central Europe, where a new heretical movement, ultimately known as Hussitism, undermined orthodoxy from Bohemia to central Germany. Threatened politically by challenges to church authority, Emperor Sigismund pressed Pope John XXIII, the successor to Alexander (who had died ten months after being elected), to convene a church council at Constance in 1414–1417.

The cardinals, bishops, and theologians assembled in Constance felt compelled to combat heresy and heal the schism. As described later in this chapter, they ordered Jan Hus, leader of the Hussite movement, burned at the stake. They deposed John XXIII, the "Pisan pope," because of tyrannical behavior, condemning him as an antipope. The Roman pope, Gregory XII, accepted the council's authority and resigned in 1415 (having been elected in 1406). At its closing in 1417, the council also deposed Benedict XIII (Clement's successor), who refused to abdicate the Avignon papacy. The rest of Christendom, however, hailed Martin V, the council's appointment, as the new pope, thus ending the Great Schism.

Dissenters and Heretics

Religious conflict in the late Middle Ages took a variety of forms. The papacy struggled with its critics within the church but found religious dissension outside the church even more threatening.

Free Spirits, Beguines, and Beghards. The Free Spirits, found mostly in northern Europe, practiced an extreme form of **mysticism**. They asserted that humans and God were of the same essence and that individual believers could attain salvation, even sanctity, without the church and its sacraments. In the fourteenth century, the Free Spirits found converts among the Beguines,◆ pious laywomen who lived together, and the Beghards, men who did not belong to a particular religious order but who led pious lives and begged for their sustenance. Living in community houses (*beguinages*), the Beguines imitated the convent lives of nuns but did not submit to clerical control. First prevalent in northern Europe, beguinages sprang up rapidly in the Low Countries and the Rhineland, regions of heavy urbanization. This essentially urban development represented the desire by many urban women to achieve salvation through piety and good works, as many began to feel that the clergy did not adequately address their spiritual needs.

For the church, the existence of Free Spirits among the Beghards and Beguines raised the larger question of ecclesiastical control, for this development threatened to eliminate the boundary between the laity and the

◆**Beguines:** bay GEENS

Burning of a Heretic
Execution by fire was the usual method of killing heretics. This illustration shows the burning of a Lollard, a follower of the teachings of Wycliffe, who opposed the established church. While heretics were condemned by the church, their executions were at the hands of secular authorities, who are present here.
Hulton Getty/Liaison Agency.

clergy. In the 1360s, Emperor Charles IV and Pope Urban V extended the Inquisition to Germany in a move to crush this heresy. In the cities of the Rhineland, fifteen mass trials took place, most around the turn of the fifteenth century. By condemning the heretics and requiring beguinages to be under the control of the mendicant orders, the church contained potential dissent. Throughout the fifteenth century the number of beguinages continued to drop.

Lollards. In England, intellectual dissent, social unrest, and nationalist sentiment combined to create a powerful anticlerical movement that the church hierarchy labeled Lollardy (from *lollar*, meaning "idler"). John Wycliffe (c. 1330–1384), who inspired the movement, was an Oxford professor. Initially employed as a royal apologist in the struggle between state and church, Wycliffe gradually developed ideas that challenged the very foundations of the Roman church. His treatise *On the Church*, composed in 1378, advanced the view that the true church was a community of believers rather than a clerical hierarchy. In other writings, Wycliffe repudiated monasticism, excommunication, the Mass, and the priesthood, substituting reliance on Bible reading and individual conscience in place of the official church as the path to salvation. Responsibility for church reform, Wycliffe believed, rested with the king, whose authority he claimed exceeded that of the pope.

At Oxford, Wycliffe gathered around him like-minded intellectuals, and together they influenced and reflected a widespread anticlericalism in late medieval England. Wycliffe actively promoted the use of English in religious writing. His supporters included members of the gentry, but most were artisans and other humbler people who had some literacy. Religious dissent was key in motivating the 1381 peasant uprising in England, and the radical preacher John Ball was only one of the many common priests who supported the revolt. Real income for parish priests had fallen steadily after the Black Death, and as a result the sympathy of the impoverished clergy lay with the common folk against the great bishops, abbots, and lords of the realm.

After Wycliffe's death, the English bishops suppressed intellectual dissent at Oxford. But in spite of persistent persecutions, Lollard ideas, such as clandestine English Bibles, survived underground during the fifteenth century, to resurface during the convulsive religious conflict of the early sixteenth century known as the Reformation.

The Hussite Revolution

The most profound challenge to papal authority in the late Middle Ages came from Bohemia. Here the spiritual, intellectual, political, and economic criticisms of the papacy that sprang up in other countries fused in one explosive spark. Religious dissent quickly became the vehicle for a nationalist uprising and a social revolution.

Under Emperor Charles IV the pace of economic development and social change in the Holy Roman Empire had quickened in the mid-fourteenth century. Prague, the capital, became one of Europe's great cities: the new silver mine at Kutná Hora boosted Prague's economic growth, and the first uni-

versity in the empire was founded there in 1348. Prague was located in Bohemia, a part of the Holy Roman Empire settled by a Slavic people, the Czechs, since the early Middle Ages. Later, many German merchants and artisans migrated to Bohemian cities, and Czech peasants, uprooted from the land, flocked to the cities in search of employment. This diverse society became a potentially explosive mass when heightened expectations of commercial and intellectual growth collided with the grim realities of the plague and economic problems in the late fourteenth century. Tax protests, urban riots, and ethnic conflicts signaled growing unrest, but it was religious discontent that became the focus for popular revolt.

Critics of the clergy, often clergy themselves, decried the moral conduct of priests and prelates who held multiple benefices, led dissolute lives, and ignored their pastoral duties. Critics asked how the clergy, living in a state of mortal sin, could legitimately perform the sacraments. Advocating greater lay participation in the Mass and in the reading of Scripture, religious dissenters drew some of their ideas from the writings of Wycliffe. Among those influenced by Wycliffe's ideas were Jan Hus (d. 1415) and his follower Jerome of Prague (d. 1416), both Prague professors, ethnic Czechs, and leaders of a group of reformers. Although the reform party attracted adherents from all Czech-speaking social groups, the German minority, who dominated the university and urban elites in Prague, opposed it out of ethnic rivalry. The Bohemian nobility protected Hus; the common clergy rebelled against the bishops; and the artisans and workers in Prague were ready to back the reform party by force. These disparate social interests all focused on one symbolic but passionately felt religious demand: the ability to receive the Eucharist as both bread and wine at Mass. In traditional Roman liturgy, the chalice was reserved for the clergy; the Utraquists, as their opponents called them (from *utraque*, Latin for "both"), also wanted to drink wine from the chalice, to achieve a measure of equality between laity and clergy.

Despite a guarantee of safety from Emperor Sigismund, Hus was burned at the stake while attending the Council of Constance in 1415. Hus's death caused a national uproar, and the reform movement, which had thus far focused only on religious issues, burst forth as a national revolution.

Sigismund's initial repression of the revolt in the provinces was brutal, and many dissenters were massacred. To organize their defense, Hussites gathered at a mountain in southern Bohemia, which they called Mount Tabor after the mountain in the New Testament where the transfiguration of Christ took place. Now called Taborites, they began to restructure their community according to biblical injunctions. Like the first Christian church, they initially practiced communal ownership of goods and thought of themselves as the only true Christians awaiting the return of Christ and the end of the world. As their influence spread, the Taborites compromised with the surrounding social order, collecting tithes from peasants and retaining magistrates in towns under their control. Taborite leaders were radical priests who ministered to the community in the Czech language, exercised moral and judicial leadership, and even led the people into battle.

Modeling themselves after the Israelites of the Old Testament and the first Christians of the New Testament, the Taborites impressed even their enemies. Aeneas Sylvius Piccolomini, the future Pope Pius II (r. 1458–1464), observed that "among the Taborites you will hardly find a woman who cannot demonstrate familiarity with the Old and New Testaments." The Taborite army, drawn from many social classes and led by priests, repelled five attacks by the "crusader" armies from neighboring Germany, triumphing over their enemies using a mixture of religious fervor and military technology, such as a wagon train to protect the infantry from cavalry charges. Resisting all attempts to crush them, the Czech revolu-

The Hussite Revolution, 1415–1436

Map legend: Areas under Hussite control. 0–400 miles / 0–400 kilometers. HOLY ROMAN EMPIRE, POLAND, TEUTONIC KNIGHTS, HUNGARY, Bohemia. Cities: Nuremberg, Prague, Kutná Hora, Tabor, Constance.

tionaries eventually gained the right from the papacy to receive the Eucharist as both bread and wine, a practice that continued until the sixteenth century.

Review: How did the papacy lose and then recover authority in the late Middle Ages?

❖ The Social Order and Cultural Change

An abundance of written and visual records documenting the lives of all social groups has survived from the fourteenth century. Sources ranging from chronicles of dynastic conflicts and noble chivalry to police records of criminality paint a vivid picture of late medieval society, showing the changed relations between town and country, noble and commoner, and men and women. These sources reveal Europeans' struggles to adjust to uncertainties and changes related to the plague, war, and religious dissent (see "Piers the Ploughman" page 494). New material wealth allowed some to enjoy more comfortable lives, but the disruptions and dislocations caused by various crises forced many on the margins of society—the poor, beggars, and prostitutes—into a violent underworld of criminality.

One response to the upheavals of the later Middle Ages was the blossoming of a broad cultural movement. As the Byzantines recovered their appreciation of Greek antiquity, so did Italians revive ancient Roman culture. This movement focused initially on imitating classical Latin rhetoric, but it later extended to other disciplines, such as the study of history. The brilliant achievements in the visual arts and vernacular literature realized at this time were the beginnings of the great movement known as the Renaissance (French for "rebirth").

The Household

Family life and the household economy formed the fabric of late medieval society. Most Europeans lived in a confined social world, surrounded by families and neighbors. The focus of their lives was the house, where parents and children, and occasionally a grandparent or other relative, lived together. This pattern generally characterized both urban and rural society. In some peasant societies, such as in Languedoc (southern France), brothers and their families shared the same roof; but the nuclear family was by far the norm.

For artisans and peasants of medium wealth, the family dwelling usually consisted of a two- or three-story building in the city and a single farmhouse in the countryside. For these social groups the household generally served as both work and private space; shopkeepers and craftspeople used their ground floors as workshops and storefronts, reserving the upper stories for family life. By today's standards, late medieval urban life was intolerably crowded, with little privacy. Neighbors could easily spy on each other from adjoining windows. In rural areas the family house served a variety of purposes, not least to shelter the farm animals during the winter.

In a society with an unequal distribution of power between women and men, the worlds of commerce and agriculture were those in which women came closest to partnership with their husbands. Even though women were excluded from privileged guilds in some cities such as Cologne, many women worked in the unorganized retail trade. They sold dairy products, meat, cloth, salt, flour, and fish; brewed beer; spun and wove cloth; and often acted informally as their husbands' business partners. Fourteenth-century women played a crucial role in the urban economy.

Piers the Ploughman

In Piers the Ploughman, *English cleric William Langland blends prophecy and satirical comedy in his fourteenth-century poem about the failures of society to live up to Christianity's ideals. This selection from the prologue describes the narrator's dream in which unscrupulous clergy appear prominently. His observations on the state of the Church reflect the mood of discontent in an age that gave rise to the English Peasants Uprising as well as the Great Schism.*

I saw the Friars there too—all four Orders of them—preaching to the people for what they could get. In their greed for fine clothes, they interpreted the Scriptures to suit themselves and their patrons. Many of these Doctors of Divinity can dress as handsomely as they please, for as their trade advances, so their profits increase. And now that Charity has gone into business, and become confessor-in-chief to wealthy lords, many strange things have happened in the last few years; unless the Friars and Holy Church mend their quarrel, the worst evil in the world will soon be upon us.

There was also a Pardoner,[1] preaching like a priest. He produced a document covered with Bishops' seals, and claimed to have power to absolve all the people from broken fasts and vows of every kind. The ignorant folk believed him and were delighted. They came up and knelt to kiss his documents, while he, blinding them with letters of indulgence[2] thrust in their faces, raked in their rings and jewellery with his roll of parchment!—So the people give their gold to support these gluttons, and put their trust in dirty-minded scoundrels. If the Bishop were worthy of the name, if he kept his ears open to what went on around him, his seal would not be sent out like this to deceive the people. But it is not by the Bishop's leave that this rogue preaches; for the parish priest is in league with the Pardoner, and they divide the proceeds between them—money which, but for them, would go to the poor of the parish.

---

[1] Church official who raised money by selling waivers to absolve sins.
[2] Means by which a person could perform certain religious tasks or pay fees to avoid purgatory after death.

Source: William Langland, *Piers the Ploughman* (New York: Penguin Classics, 1986), 26–27.

June

Real farmwork in fourteenth-century France was never as genteel as in this miniature painting, part of a series illustrating the months of the year in the beautiful devotional book, the *Book of Hours* of the Duke de Berry. Nevertheless, the scene does faithfully represent haying and suggests the gendered division of village labor, as the men swing their scythes and the women wield rakes. **For more help analyzing this image**, please see the visual activity for this chapter in the Online Study Guide at **bedfordstmartins.com/hunt**. *Bridgeman-Giraudon/Art Resource, NY.*

February

As in all the miniatures in the Duke de Berry's prayer book, this cozy scene shows that the late-medieval nobility liked to imagine their peasants and livestock securely housed in warm, separate shelters, while the customary work of rural society goes on peacefully. But in reality, peasants led a hard life, faced with the uncertainties of weather and the depredations of war. *Bridgeman-Giraudon/Art Resource, NY.*

The degree to which women participated in public life, however, varied with class and region. Women in Mediterranean Europe, especially in upper-class families, lived more circumscribed lives than their counterparts in northern Europe. In the southern regions, for example, women could not dispose of personal property without the consent of males, be they fathers, husbands, or grown sons. In the north, women regularly represented themselves in legal transactions and testified in court.

Partnership characterized the peasant marriage. Although men and women performed different tasks, such as plowing and spinning, many chores required mutual effort. During harvests, all family members were mobilized. The men usually reaped with sickles, while the women picked the fields. Viticulture (the cultivation of grapes for wine-making) called for full cooperation between the sexes: both men and women worked equally in picking grapes and trampling them to make wine.

Because the rural household constituted the basic unit of agricultural production, most men and women remarried quickly after a spouse died. The incidence of households headed by a single person, usually a poor widow, was much lower in villages than in cities. Studies of court records for fourteenth-century English villages show relatively few reports of domestic violence, a result perhaps of the economic dependency between the sexes. Violence against women was more visible in urban societies, where many women worked as servants and prostitutes.

The improved material life of the middle classes was represented in many visual images of the later Middle Ages. Italian and Flemish paintings of the late fourteenth and early fifteenth centuries depict the new comforts of urban life such as fireplaces and private latrines and show an interest in material objects: beds, chests, rooms, curtains, and buildings provide the ubiquitous background of Italian paintings of the period.

The Underclass

If family life and the household economy formed the fabric of late medieval society, the world of poverty and criminality represented its torn fringes. Fourteenth-century society rested on a broad base of underclass—poor peasants and laborers in the countryside, workers and servants in the cities. Lower still were the marginal elements of society, straddling the line between legality and criminality.

Organized gangs prowled the larger cities. In Paris, a city teeming with thieves, thugs, beggars, prostitutes, and vagabonds, the Hundred Years' War led to a sharp rise in crime. Gang members were mostly artisans who vacillated between work and crime. Sometimes disguised as clerics, they robbed, murdered, and extorted from prostitutes. Many soldiers, having been initiated into a life of plunder and killing, turned to crime.

Those on society's fringes were mostly young people who lacked stable families; they wandered extensively, begging and stealing. Criminals were even present among the clergy. Some clerics turned to crime to make ends meet during an age of steadily declining clerical income. "Decent society" treated these marginal elements with suspicion and hatred. New laws restricted vagabonds and begging clerics, although cities and guilds also began building hospitals and almshouses to deal with these social problems.

Women featured prominently in the underclass, reflecting the unequal distribution of power between the sexes. In Mediterranean Europe, some 90 percent of slaves were women in domestic servitude. Their actual numbers were small—several hundred in fourteenth-century Florence, for example—because only rich households could afford slaves. The women came from Muslim or Greek Orthodox countries and usually served in upper-class households in the great commercial city republics of Venice, Florence, and Ragusa. Urban domestic service was also the major employment for girls from the countryside, who worked to save money for their dowries. In addition to the usual household chores, women also worked as wet nurses.

Given their exclusion from many professions and their powerlessness, many poor women found prostitution the only way to make a living. Male violence also forced some women into prostitution: rape stripped away their social respectability and any prospects for marriage. Though condemned by the church, prostitutes were tolerated throughout the Middle Ages. In the fourteenth and fifteenth centuries, however, governments intensified their attempts to control sexuality by institutionalizing prostitution. Restricted to particular quarters in cities, supervised by officials, sometimes under direct government management, prostitutes found themselves confined to brothels, increasingly controlled by males. In legalizing and controlling prostitution, officials aimed to maintain the public order.

Hard Times for Trade

Compared with the commercial prosperity of the twelfth and thirteenth centuries, the later Middle Ages was an age of retrenchment for business. As the fourteenth-century crises afflicted the business community, a climate of pessimism and caution permeated commerce, especially during the second half of the century.

The first major crisis that undermined Italian banks was caused by the Hundred Years' War, during which England's Edward III borrowed heavily from the largest Italian banking houses, the Bardi and Peruzzi of Florence. In the early 1340s, however, Edward defaulted. Adding to their problems, the Florentine bankers were forced to make war loans to their own government. The once-powerful banks could not rebound from the losses they incurred, and both of them fell.

This breakdown in the most advanced economic sector reflected the general recession in the European economy. Merchants were less likely to take risks and more willing to invest their money in government bonds than in production and commerce. Fewer merchants traveled to Asia, partly because of the danger of attack by Ottoman Turks on the overland routes that had once been protected by the Mongols. The Medici of Florence, who would dominate Florentine politics in the next century, stuck close to home, investing part of their banking profits in art and politics and relying mostly on business agents to conduct their affairs in other European cities.

Historians have argued that this fourteenth-century economic depression diverted capital away from manufacturing and into investments in the arts and luxuries for immediate consumption. Instead of plowing their profits back into their businesses, merchants acquired land, built sumptuous townhouses, purchased luxury items, and invested in bonds.

The most important trade axis continued to link Italy with the Low Countries. Italian cities produced silk, wool, jewelry, and other luxury goods that northern Europeans desired, and Italian merchants also imported spices, gold, and other coveted products from Asia and Africa. Traveling either by land through Lyon or by sea around Gibraltar, these products reached Bruges, Ghent, and Antwerp, where they were shipped to England, northern Germany, Poland, and Scandinavia. The reverse flow carried raw materials and silver, the latter to help balance the trade between northern Europe and the Mediter-ranean. Diminished production and trade eventually caused turmoil in northern Europe and a crisis for financiers in the Low Countries. Bruges, the financial center for northwestern Europe, saw its power fade during the fifteenth century when a succession of its money changers went bankrupt. The Burgundian dukes eventually enacted a series of monetary laws that undermined Bruges's financial and banking community and, by extension, the city's political autonomy as well.

The Flourishing of Vernacular Literature and the Birth of Humanism

Vernacular literature blossomed in the fourteenth century. Poetry, stories, and chronicles composed in Italian, French, English, and other national languages helped articulate a new sense of aesthetics. No longer did Latin and church culture dominate the intellectual life of Europe, and no longer were writers principally clerics or aristocrats. Also located in the cities, a new intellectual movement, humanisme, a return to the study of Greek and Roman texts, and an emulation of the civic values expressed by authors of classical antiquity.

Middle-Class Writers and Noble Patrons. The great writers of late medieval Europe were of urban middle-class origins, from families that had done well in government or church service or commercial enterprises, unlike the medieval troubadours, who had aristocratic backgrounds. The audience of these new writers was the literate laity. Francesco Petrarch (1304–1374), the poet laureate of Italy's vernacular literature, and his younger contemporary and friend Giovanni Boccaccio (1313–1375) were both Florentine. Petrarch was born in Arezzo, where his father, a notary, lived in political exile from Florence. Boccaccio's father worked for the Florentine banking firm of Bardi in Paris, where Boccaccio was born. Geoffrey Chaucer (c. 1342–1400) was the first great vernacular poet of medieval England. His father was a wealthy wine merchant; Chaucer worked as a servant to the king and controller of customs in London. Even writers who celebrated the life of the nobility were children of commoners. Although born in Valenciennes to a family of moneylenders and merchants, Jean Froissart (1333?–c. 1405), whose chronicle vividly describes the events of the Hundred Years' War, was an ardent admirer of chivalry. Christine de Pizan (1364–c. 1430), the official biographer of the French king, was the daughter of a Venetian municipal councilor.

Life in all its facets found expression in the flourishing vernacular literature, as writers told of love, greed, and salvation. Boccaccio's *Decameron* popularized the short story, as the characters in this novella tell sensual and bizarre tales in the shadow of the Black Death. Members of different social orders parade themselves in Chaucer's *Can-*terbury Tales*, journeying together on a pilgrimage. Chaucer describes a merchant on horseback as follows:

> A marchant was ther with a forked berd
> In mottelee, and hye on horse he sat
> up-on his heed a Flaundrish bever hat
> his botes clasped faire and fetisly....
> For sothe he was a worthy man withalle
> but sooth to seyn, I noot how men him calle.

Chaucer also vividly portrayed other social classes—yeomen, London guildsmen, and minor officials.

Noble patronage was crucial to the growth of vernacular literature, a fact reflected in the careers of the most famous writers. Perhaps closest to the model of an

The Book of the City of Ladies (1405)

In The Book of the City of Ladies, *Christine de Pizan confronts a long tradition of misogyny by male writers. Each chapter recounts the accomplishments and capabilities of remarkable women—both mythical and historic—who reside within her fictional city. In this section from the book's opening, de Pizan expresses her distress at widespread works that disparage women's abilities, which prompts her to write her own account.*

...given that I could scarcely find a moral work by any author which didn't devote some chapter or paragraph to attacking the female sex, I had to accept their unfavourable opinion of women since it was unlikely that so many learned men, who seemed to be endowed with such great intelligence and insight into all things, could possibly have lied on so many different occasions. It was on the basis of this one simple argument that I was forced to conclude that, although my understanding was too crude and ill-informed to recognize the great flaws in myself and other women, these men had to be in the right. Thus I preferred to give more weight to what others said than to trust my own judgement and experience.

I dwelt on these thoughts at such length that it was as if I had sunk into a deep trance. My mind became flooded with an endless stream of names as I recalled all the authors who had written on this subject. I came to the conclusion that God had surely created a vile thing when He created woman. Indeed, I was astounded that such a fine craftsman could have wished to make such an appalling object which, as these writers would have it, is like a vessel in which all the sin and evil of the world has been collected and preserved. This thought inspired such a great sense of disgust and sadness in me that I began to despise myself and the whole of my sex as an aberration in nature.

With a deep sigh, I called out to God: 'Oh Lord, how can this be? Unless I commit an error of faith, I cannot doubt that you, in your infinite wisdom and perfect goodness, could make anything that wasn't good. Didn't you yourself create woman especially and then endow her with all the qualities that you wished her to have? How could you possibly have made a mistake in anything? Yet here stand women not simply accused, but already judged, sentenced and condemned! I just cannot understand this contradiction.

Source: Christine de Pizan, *The Book of the City of Ladies* (London: Penguin Classics, 1999), 6–7.

independent man of letters, Petrarch nonetheless relied on powerful patrons at various times. His early career began at the papal court in Avignon, where his father worked; during the 1350s, he enjoyed the protection and patronage of the duke of Milan. For Boccaccio, who started out in the world of commerce, the court of King Robert of Naples initiated him into the world of letters. Chaucer served the English crown in administrative posts and on many diplomatic missions, during which he met his two Italian counterparts. Noble patronage also shaped the literary creations of Froissart and Christine de Pizan. Commissioned to write the official biography of King Charles V, Christine would have been unable to produce most of her writings without the patronage of women in the royal household. She presented her most famous work, *The Book of the City of Ladies* (1405), a defense of women's reputation and virtue, to Isabella of Bavaria, the queen of France and wife of Charles VI (see excerpt on page 498).

Classical Revival. Vernacular literature blossomed not at the expense of Latin but alongside a classical revival. In spite of the renown of their Italian writings, Petrarch and Boccaccio, for example, took great pride in their Latin works. Latin represented the language of salvation and was also the international language of learning. Professors taught and wrote in Latin; students spoke it as best they could; priests celebrated Mass and dispensed sacraments in Latin; and theologians composed learned treatises in Latin. Church Latin was very different from the Latin of the ancient Romans, both in syntax and in vocabulary. In the second half of the fourteenth century, writers began to imitate the "classical" Latin of Roman literature. In the forefront of this literary and intellectual movement, Petrarch traveled to many monasteries in search of long-ignored Latin manuscripts. For writers like Petrarch, medieval church Latin was an artificial, awkward language, whereas classical Latin and, after its revival, Greek were the mother tongues of the ancients. Thus the classical writings of Rome and Greece represented true vernacular literature, only more authentic, vivid, and glorious than the poetry

Poet and Queen
Christine de Pizan, kneeling, presents a manuscript of her poems to Isabelle of Bavaria, the queen of France. Isabelle's royal status is marked by the French coat of arms, the fleur-de-lis that decorates the bedroom walls. The sumptuous interior (chairs, cushions, tapestry, paneled ceiling, glazed and shuttered windows) was typical of aristocratic domestic architecture. Even in the intimacy of her bedroom, Queen Isabelle, like all royal personages, was constantly attended and almost never alone (note her ladies-in-waiting). *The British Library Picture Library, London.*

and prose written in Italian and other contemporary European languages. Classical allusions and literary influences abound in the works of Boccaccio, Chaucer, Christine de Pizan, and others. The new intellectual fascination with the ancient past also stimulated translations of classical works into the vernacular.

This attempt to emulate the virtues and learning of the ancients gave rise to a new intellectual movement: humanism. For humanists the study of history and literature was the chief means of identifying with the glories of the ancient world. By the early fifteenth century, the study of classical Latin had become fashionable among a small intellectual elite, first in Italy and gradually throughout Europe. Reacting against the painstaking logic and abstract language of the scholastic philosophy that predominated in the medieval period, the humanists of the Renaissance preferred eloquence and style in their discourse, imitating the writings of Cicero and other great Roman authors.

Paradise Lost
This fourteenth-century painting by the Sienese Giovanni di Paolo depicts the expulsion of Adam and Eve from the Garden of Eden. At right, an angel chases away the ancestors of humanity. At left, Paradise is the core around which the seven celestial spheres rotate, propelled by the action of God. By positioning Adam and Eve to the right-hand side of the panel, Paolo dramatically represents their expulsion. *The Metropolitan Museum of Art, Robert Lehman Collection, 1975. (1975.1.31) Photograph © 1981 the Metropolitan Museum of Art.*

Italian lawyers and notaries had a long-standing interest in classical rhetoric because eloquence was a skill essential to their professions. Gradually the imitation of ancient Roman rhetoric led to the absorption of ancient ideas. In the writings of Roman historians such as Livy and Tacitus, fifteenth-century Italian civic elites (many of them lawyers) found echoes of their own devout patriotism. Between 1400 and 1430 in Florence, a time of war and crisis, the study of the humanities evolved into a republican ideology that historians call "civic humanism." In the early fifteenth century, the Florentines waged a highly successful propaganda war on behalf of virtuous republican Florence against tyrannical Milan, invoking the memory of the overthrow of Etruscan tyrants by the first Romans. Thus the study of ancient civilization was not only an antiquarian quest but also a call to public service and political action.

Review: What were examples of the new secular culture of the fourteenth century?

Conclusion

Between 1320 and 1430, European civilization was in crisis. The traditional order, achieved during the optimism and growth of the High Middle Ages, was undercut first—and most severely—by the Hundred Years' War and the Black Death, which combined to cause a drastic reduction in population and contraction of the economy. Faced with massive death and destruction, some people sought escape in rituals of religious fanaticism. Others searched out scapegoats, spawning a wave of anti-Jewish persecutions that reached from southern France throughout the Holy Roman Empire; the Nuremberg pogrom of 1349 was only one example. Empire and papacy, long symbols of unity, collapsed into political disintegration and spiritual malaise.

The disintegration of European order hastened the consolidation of some states, such as France. Other areas, such as Spain and the Ottoman Empire, included different linguistic and religious groups under one political authority. Still other regions, principally central Europe and Italy, remained divided into competing principalities and city-states characterized more by the sense of local differences than by their linguistic similarity.

In the eastern Mediterranean, European civilization retreated in the face of Ottoman Turk advances. Christian Europe continued to grow, however, in the Iberian peninsula; for the next three centuries the Mediterranean would be the arena for struggles between Christian and Islamic empires. The papacy called for new crusades, but divisions among European powers largely thwarted this effort.

The conciliar movement, although instrumental in ending the Great Schism, failed to limit supreme papal power, identified by its critics as the source of spiritual discontent. Successful in repressing or compromising

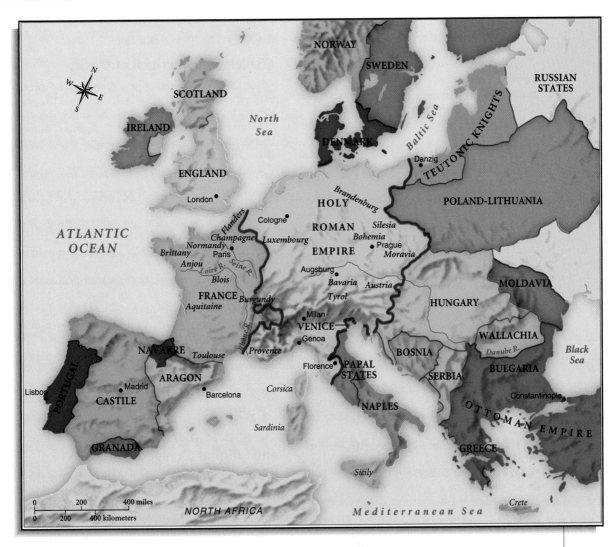

MAPPING THE WEST Europe, c. 1430
Two of the dynamic regions of expansion lie in the southeastern and southwestern sectors of this map: the Ottoman Empire, which continued its attacks into central Europe and the Mediterranean, and the Iberian countries that opposed Muslim advances by their own crusades and maritime expansions. While England, France, Iberia, and the Balkans were consolidated into large political entities, central Europe and Italy remained fragmented. Yet it was these two fragmented regions that gave Europe the cultural and technological innovations of the age.

with the Lollard, Hussite, and other heretical movements, the church survived the crisis of the later Middle Ages but left unresolved issues of spiritual authority.

In the world of letters, vernacular literature and humanism prepared the ground for a golden age of culture that would spread from the Italian cities to other areas of Europe.

Suggested References

Political Crises across Europe

The scholarship on the political conflicts of late medieval Europe has shifted from narrative of military campaigns and diplomacy to focus on peasant uprisings, urban revolts, and their relationship to the larger struggles between dynasties and countries. In addition to the Hundred

Years' War, southeastern Europe and Iberia have also come into focus.

Allmand, Christopher. *The Hundred Years' War: England and France at War, c. 1300–1450.* 1988.

*Froissart: http://www.nipissings.ca/department/history/muhlberger/froissart/tales.htm.

*Froissart, Jean. *Chronicles.* Trans. Geoffrey Brereton. 1968.

Hilton, R. H., and T. H. Aston, eds. *The English Rising of 1381.* 1984.

Index of Late Medieval Maps: http://www.henry-davis.com/MAPS/LMwebpages/LML.html.

Leuschner, Joachim. *Germany in the Late Middle Ages.* 1980.

Mollat, Michel, and Philippe Wolff. *The Popular Revolutions of the Late Middle Ages.* 1973.

Nichols, David. *The van Arteveldes of Ghent: The Varieties of Vendetta and the Hero in History.* 1988.

O'Callaghan, Joseph F. *A History of Medieval Spain.* 1975.

*Pernoud, Régine ed. *Joan of Arc: By Herself and Her Witnesses.* 1966.

Shaw, Stanford J. *History of the Ottoman Empire and Modern Turkey.* Vol. 1, *Empire of the Gazia: The Rise and Decline of the Ottoman Empire, 1280–1808.* 1976.

Vale, Malcolm. *War and Chivalry: Warfare and Aristocratic Culture in England, France, and Burgundy at the End of the Middle Ages.* 1981.

Warner, Marina. *Joan of Arc: The Image of Female Heroism.* 1981.

The Plague and Society

Recent scholarship stresses the social, economic, and cultural impact of the plague. One particularly exciting direction of research focuses on the persecution of religious minorities as a result of the Black Death.

Bois, Guy. *The Crisis of Feudalism: Economy and Society in Eastern Normandy, c. 1300–1550.* 1984.

Cohn, Samuel K. "The Black Death: End of a Paradigm." *American Historical Review* 107, no. 3 (2002), pp. 703–38.

Herlihy, David. *The Black Death and the Transformation of the West.* 1997.

Nicholas, David. *The Later Medieval City 1300–1500.* 1997.

Nirenberg, David. *Communities of Violence: Persecution of Minorities in the Middle Ages.* 1996.

Plague and public health in Renaissance Europe: http://jefferson.village.virginia.edu/osheim/intro.html.

Rörig, Fritz. *The Medieval Town.* 1967.

Ziegler, Philip. *The Black Death.* 1970.

Challenges to Spiritual Authority

While there continues to be a great deal of interest in dissident thinkers who challenged the authority of the medieval church, much recent scholarship is devoted to the popular movements of dissent against papal and ecclesiastical authority.

Ashton, Margaret. *Lollards and Reformers.* 1989.

———. *Lollardy and the Gentry in the Later Middle Ages.* 1997.

Fudge, Thomas A. *The Magnificent Ride: The First Reformation in Hussite Bohemia.* 1998.

Kaminsky, Howard. *A History of the Hussite Revolution.* 1967.

Leff, Gordon. *Heresy in the Later Middle Ages: The Relation of Heterodoxy to Dissent, c. 1250–1450.* 1967.

Oakley, Francis. *Council over Pope? Towards a Provisional Ecclesiology.* 1969.

Ozment, Steven. *The Age of Reform, 1250–1550: An Intellectual and Religious History of Late Medieval and Reformation Europe.* 1980.

Renouard, Yves. *The Avignon Papacy, 1305–1403.* 1970.

The Social Order and Cultural Change

In addition to the importance of Italy, other research examines the household, gender, and women's work during this period. Literary scholarship continues to explore the relationship between vernacular literature and humanism.

Duby, Georges. *A History of Private Life.* Vol. 2, *Revelations of the Medieval World.* 1988.

Fubini, Riccardo. *Humanism and Secularization: From Petrarch to Valla.* 2003.

Geremek, Bronislaw. *The Margins of Society in Late Medieval Paris.* 1987.

Gersh, Stephen, and Bert Roest, eds. *Medieval and Renaissance Humanism: Rhetoric, Representation and Reform.* 2003.

Hanawalt, Barbara A., ed. *Women and Work in Preindustrial Europe.* 1986.

Herlihy, David. *Women, Family, and Society in Medieval Europe.* 1995.

———. *Opera muliebria. Women and Work in Medieval Europe.* 1990.

Miskimim, Harry A. *The Economy of Early Renaissance Europe, 1300–1460.* 1975.

*Primary source.

CHAPTER REVIEW

IMPORTANT EVENTS

1315–1317	Great Famine in Europe
1324	Marsilius of Padua denies the legitimacy of papal supremacy in *The Defender of the Peace*
1328	Pope John XXII imprisons the English theologian William of Ockham for criticizing papal power
1337–1453	Hundred Years' War between the English and French
1347–1354	Rebellion in Rome
1348–1350	First outbreak in Europe of the Black Death
1349–1351	Anti-Jewish persecutions in the empire
1356	Charles IV agrees to Golden Bull document requiring imperial electors to select the German king
1358	Jacquerie uprising in France
1378	Ciompi rebellion in Florence; John Wycliffe's treatise *On the Church* asserts that the true church is a community of believers
1378–1417	Great Schism divides papacy
1381	English peasant uprising
1386	Union of Poland and Lithuania
1389	Ottomans defeat Serbs at Kosovo
1391	Attack on Jews and forced conversion in Spain
1414–1417	Council of Constance ends the Great Schism
1415	Execution of Jan Hus; Hussite revolution begins
1429	Joan of Arc leads French to victory at siege of Orléans

KEY TERMS

benefices (486)

flagellants (485)

Great Schism (489)

Janissaries (481)

latifundia (480)

mercenary (469)

Moors (480)

mysticism (491)

nominalism (488)

reconquista (480)

vernacular literature (497)

REVIEW QUESTIONS

1. How were dynastic warfare and popular uprisings related in the fourteenth century?
2. What were the demographic, economic, and psychological consequences of the plague?
3. How did the papacy lose and then recover authority in the late Middle Ages?
4. What were examples of the new secular culture of the fourteenth century?

MAKING CONNECTIONS

1. Is it reasonable to say that the late Middle Ages experienced a general crisis in society? Why or why not?
2. To what extent was Christendom less tolerant and open in the fourteenth century than in the high Middle Ages?

FOR FURTHER EXPLORATION

To assess your mastery of the material in this chapter, see the Online Study Guide at **bedfordstmartins.com/hunt**.

To read additional primary-source material from this period, see Chapter 13 in *Sources of The Making of the West*, Second Edition.

Renaissance Europe, 1400–1500

IN 1461, THE OTTOMAN RULER MEHMED II sent a letter to Sigismondo Malatesta, the lord of the Italian city-state of Rimini, asking the Italian prince to lend him court painter and architect Matteo de Pasti. The Ottoman sultan was planning to build a new palace in the recently conquered capital, Constantinople (modern Istanbul), as a fitting symbol of his imperial dominion, and he had heard of de Pasti's reputation. The Rimini painter had not only produced illuminated manuscripts and portrait medals of Sigismondo's mistress but also designed a monument to the prince's military glory, which was modeled after the principles described in Vitruvius's treatise *On Architecture* (first century B.C.E.). This was a work rediscovered in Italy in 1414.

Armed with a letter from Sigismondo, maps, and gifts, de Pasti set out for Constantinople, ready to court favors for his patron, who was eager to form an alliance with the Turkish ruler. Venetian authorities, however, intercepted the artist in Crete. Anxious to prevent a political connection between another Italian power and the sultan, the Venetians confiscated the gifts and sent de Pasti back to Rimini. Thus, Mehmed's new palace was constructed without de Pasti's help—but with the aid of several Venetian painters instead. The palace came to be called the Topkapi Saray and still stands today looking across the Bosporus, the strait that divides European and Asian Turkey.

The story of Matteo de Pasti's failed mission illustrates the central theme of the Renaissance: the connection among power, culture, and fame in an age that was rediscovering the arts and the worldview of classical antiquity. This rediscovery, which scholars in the sixteenth century labeled the **Renaissance** (French for "rebirth"),

Sacred and Social Body
The fifteenth-century Venetian state used lavish, dignified ceremony to impress citizens and visitors with its grandeur and to symbolize its divine protection. Here the great Venetian Renaissance painter Gentile Bellini depicts one such scene, a procession of the Eucharist across the Piazza San Marco uniting in common purpose the clergy and the Venetian governing elite.
Scala/Art Resource, NY.

505

signified the revival of forms of classical learning and the arts following the long interval they characterized as the Middle Ages. (See "Terms of History," page 508.) After the crisis of the fourteenth century, European civilization seemed to rise in the fifteenth like a phoenix from the ashes of the Black Death. The Renaissance had two main trajectories: a revolution in culture that originated in Italy and gradually expanded north to other countries of Europe, and (even more profound and far-reaching) the expansion of European control to the non-European world.

The story of de Pasti's mission further illustrates three secondary themes: First, it shows how specific Renaissance artistic practices were based on the revival of classical learning. Second, it reflects the competition among Italian city-states set against a larger backdrop of changing relations between Christian Europe and the non-Christian world. Third, it demonstrates the significance of culture in the political representation of power.

The rebirth of culture took many forms: in learning, in the visual arts, in architecture, and in music. Portraits, palaces, and poetry commemorated the glory of the rich and powerful, while a new philosophy called humanism advocated classical learning and argued for the active participation of the individual in civic affairs. Family, honor, social status, and individual distinction—these were the goals that fueled the ambitions of Renaissance men and women.

A new feeling of power characterized the spirit of the Renaissance, as Europeans recovered their sense of control over the world after the crisis of the fourteenth century. The quest for power by families and individuals duplicated on a smaller scale the enhanced power of the state. Like individuals, the Renaissance states competed for wealth, glory, and honor. While warfare and diplomacy channeled the restless energy of the Italian states, monarchies and empires outside of Italy also expanded their power through conquests and institutional reforms. The European world changed drastically as new powers such as the Ottoman Empire and Muscovy rose to prominence in the east, while the Iberian kingdoms of Portugal and Spain expanded European domination to Africa, Asia, and the Americas.

❖ Widening Intellectual Horizons

A revolution in the arts and learning was in the making. Europeans' rediscovery of Greek and Roman writers reflected an expanded interest in human achievements and glory. New secular voices celebrating human glory were added to the old prayers for salvation in the afterlife. While the intense study of Latin and Greek writings focused on rhetoric and eloquence in learning, revolutionary techniques in bookmaking, painting, architecture, and music created original forms and expressed a new excitement with the beauty of nature. In the center of this fascinating nature was humanity.

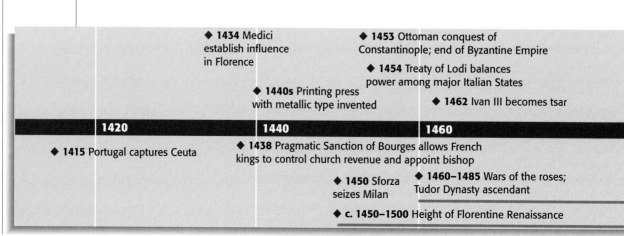

◆ **1434** Medici establish influence in Florence

◆ **1453** Ottoman conquest of Constantinople; end of Byzantine Empire

◆ **1454** Treaty of Lodi balances power among major Italian States

◆ **1440s** Printing press with metallic type invented

◆ **1462** Ivan III becomes tsar

1420   **1440**   **1460**

◆ **1415** Portugal captures Ceuta

◆ **1438** Pragmatic Sanction of Bourges allows French kings to control church revenue and appoint bishop

◆ **1450** Sforza seizes Milan

◆ **1460–1485** Wars of the roses; Tudor Dynasty ascendant

◆ **c. 1450–1500** Height of Florentine Renaissance

The Humanist Renewal

Europeans' fascination with the ancient past in turn gave rise to a new intellectual movement: **humanism**, so called because its practitioners studied and supported the liberal arts, or humanities. As a group, the humanists were far from homogeneous: some were professional scholars, others high-ranking civil servants; some worked as notaries, and still others were rich patricians who had acquired a taste for learning. Nonetheless, all humanists focused on classical history and literature in their attempt to emulate the glories of the ancient world.

By the early fifteenth century the study of classical Latin (which had begun in the late fourteenth century) as well as classical and biblical Greek had become fashionable among a small intellectual elite, first in Italy and gradually throughout Europe. The fall of Constantinople in 1453 sent Greek scholars to Italy for refuge, giving extra impetus to the revival of Greek learning in the West. Venice and Florence assumed leadership in this new field—the former by virtue of its commercial and political ties to the eastern Mediterranean, the latter thanks to the patronage of Cosimo de' Medici,♦ who sponsored the Platonic Academy, a discussion group dedicated to the study of Plato and his followers under the intellectual leadership of Marsilio Ficino (1433–1499). Thinkers of the second half of the fifteenth century had more curiosity about Platonic and various mystical neo-Platonic ideas—particularly alchemy, numerology, and natural magic—than about the serious study of natural phenomena and universal principles.

Most humanists did not consider the study of ancient cultures a conflict with their Christian faith. In "returning to the sources"—a famous slogan of the time—philosophers attempted to harmonize the disciplines of Christian faith and ancient learning. Ficino, the foremost Platonic scholar of the Renaissance, was deeply attracted to natural magic and was also a priest. He argued that the immortality of the soul, a Platonic idea, was perfectly compatible with Christian doctrine and that much of ancient wisdom actually foreshadowed later Christian teachings.

In Latin learning, the fifteenth century continued in the tradition of Petrarch. Reacting against the painstaking logic and abstract language of scholastic philosophy, the humanists of the Renaissance advocated eloquence and style in their discourse, imitating the writings of Cicero and other great Roman authors (see Chapter 13). Through their activities as educators and civil servants, professional humanists gave new vigor to the humanist curriculum of grammar, rhetoric, poetry, history, and moral philosophy. By the end of the fifteenth century, European intellectuals considered a good command of classical Latin, with perhaps some knowledge of Greek, as one of the requirements of an educated man. This humanist revolution would influence school curricula up to the middle of the nineteenth century and even beyond.

♦**Cosimo de' Medici:** KAW zee moh day MEH dih chee

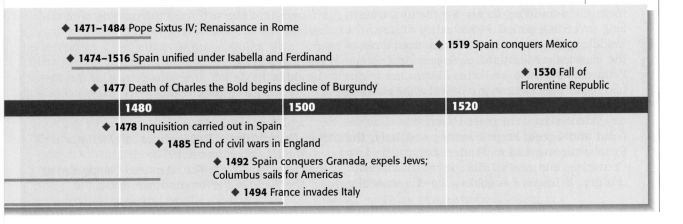

♦ **1471–1484** Pope Sixtus IV; Renaissance in Rome

♦ **1474–1516** Spain unified under Isabella and Ferdinand

♦ **1477** Death of Charles the Bold begins decline of Burgundy

♦ **1519** Spain conquers Mexico

♦ **1530** Fall of Florentine Republic

| 1480 | 1500 | 1520 |

♦ **1478** Inquisition carried out in Spain

♦ **1485** End of civil wars in England

♦ **1492** Spain conquers Granada, expels Jews; Columbus sails for Americas

♦ **1494** France invades Italy

MAP 14.1 The Spread of Printing in the Fifteenth Century
The Holy Roman Empire formed the center of printing. Presses in other countries were often established by migrant German printers, especially in Italy. Printing did not reach Muscovy until the sixteenth century.

one of the most expensive books in history, for both its rarity and its exquisite crafting.

Some historians argue that the invention of mechanical printing gave rise to a communications revolution as significant as, for example, the widespread use of the personal computer today. The multiplication of standardized texts altered the thinking habits of Europeans by freeing individuals from having to memorize everything they learned; it certainly made possible the relatively speedy and inexpensive dissemination of knowledge, and it created a wider community of scholars, no longer dependent on personal patronage or church sponsorship for texts. Printing facilitated the free expression and exchange of ideas, and its disruptive potential did not go unnoticed by political and ecclesiastical au-

thorities. Emperors and bishops in Germany, the homeland of the printing industry, moved quickly to issue censorship regulations.

Review: How did humanism and the printing press influence learning in the Renaissance?

❖ Revolution in the Arts

The Renaissance was one of the most creative periods in the European arts. New techniques in painting, architecture, and musical performance fostered original styles and new subjects. Three transformations were particularly significant. First, artists, previously seen as artisans, acquired a more prominent social status, as individual talent and genius were recognized by a society hungry for culture. Second, sculptors and painters developed a more naturalistic style, especially in representing the human body. And finally, the use of perspective in Renaissance art reflected a new mathematical and scientific basis for artistic creation, which was manifest not only in the visual arts but also in architecture and musical composition.

From Artisan to Artist

The artist was a new social type in the Renaissance. Leonardo da Vinci (1452–1519)— a painter, architect, and inventor trained in the artisanal tradition—described his freedom to create as a gentleman of leisure: "The painter sits at his ease in front of his work, dresses as he pleases, and moves his light brush with the beautiful colors... often accompanied by musicians or readers of various beautiful works." If this picture fits with today's image of the creative genius, so do the stories about Renaissance painters and their eccentricities: some were violent, others absentminded; some worked as hermits, while others cared little for money.

The point of stories about "genius," often told by Renaissance artists themselves, was to convince society that the artists' works were unique and their talents priceless. The artist, as opposed to the artisan, was an individual with innate talents who created works of art according to his imagination rather than following the blueprints of a patron. Of course, the reality was that most artists still relied on wealthy patrons for support. And although they wished to create as their genius dictated, not all patrons of the arts allowed artists to work without restrictions. While the duke of Milan appreciated Leonardo's genius, the duke of Ferrara paid for his art by the square foot. For every successful artist—such as the painter Andrea Mantegna (1431–1506), who was exalted by Pope Innocent VIII—there were many others who painted marriage chests and look-alike Madonnas for middle-class homes.

A successful artist who did fit the new vision of unfettered genius was the Florentine sculptor Donatello (1386–1466), one of the heroes Giorgio Vasari described in his *Lives of the Artists,* a seventeenth-century book of biographies of the greatest artists of the Renaissance. Not only did Donatello's sculptures evoke classical Greek and Roman models, but the grace and movement of his work inspired Cosimo de' Medici, the ruler of Florence, to excavate antique works of art. Moreover, Donatello transcended material preoccupations. According to Vasari:

> Donatello was free, affectionate, and courteous ... and more so to his friends than to himself. He thought nothing of money, keeping it in a basket suspended by a rope from the ceiling, so that all his workmen and friends took what they wanted without saying anything to him.

A favorite artist of the most powerful man in fifteenth-century Florence, Donatello owed his ability to be generous in large part to Medici patronage.

Renaissance artists worked under any of three conditions: long-term service in princely courts, commissioned piecework, and production for the market. Mantegna, for example, worked from 1460 until his death in 1506 for the princes of Mantua. In return for a monthly salary and other gifts, he promised to paint panels and frescoes (paintings on a wet plaster surface). His masterpieces— fresco scenes of courtly life with vivid and accurate portraits of members of the princely family—decorated the walls of the palace. In practice, however, Mantegna sometimes was treated more as a skilled worker than as an independent artist: he was once asked to adorn his majestic tapestries with life sketches of farm animals.

The workshop—the norm of artistic production in Renaissance Florence and in northern European cities such as Nuremberg and Antwerp—afforded the artist greater autonomy. As heads of workshops, artists trained apprentices and negotiated contracts with clients. Famous artists developed followings, and wealthy consumers came to pay a premium for work done by a master instead of apprentices. Studies of art contracts show that in the course of the fifteenth century artists gained greater control over their work. Early in the century clients routinely stipulated detailed conditions for works of art. Clients might also determine the arrangement of figures in a picture, leaving the artist little more than the execution. After mid-century, however, such specific directions became less common. In 1487, for example, the Florentine painter Filippo Lippi (1457–1504), in his contract to paint frescoes in the Strozzi chapel, specified that the work should be "all from his own hand and particularly the figures." The shift underscores the increasing recognition of the unique skills of individual artists.

In the fifteenth century, most large-scale work was commissioned by specific patrons, but the art market, for which artists produced works without prior arrangement for sale, developed initially in the Low Countries.

Limited at first to smaller altarpieces, woodcuts, engravings, sculpture, and pottery paintings, this market began to extend to larger panel paintings. The commercialization of art celebrated the new context of artistic creation itself: artists working in an open, competitive, urban civilization.

The Human Figure

If the individual artist is a man of genius, what greater subject for the expression of beauty is there than the human body itelf? From the fourteenth-century Florentine painter Giotto (see Chapter 12), Renais-

Masaccio's *Trembling Man*
Renaissance paintings differ from medieval paintings in many ways, one of which is their use of naturalism, in which subjects—human and nature—are depicted in a realistic rather than a symbolic way. Here, the important subject is baptism, but Masaccio's representation emphasizes the feeling of cold water, a naturalistic treatment intended to connect the subject of the painting and the viewer. *Erich Lessing/Art Resource, NY.*

St. Ivo by Rogier van der Weyden
This painting of St. Ivo of Chartres (c.1040–1116) by Rogier van der Weyden (1400?–64) exemplifies the Flemish School style of detailed realistic human portraits shown against the backdrop of a landscape or city scene. Born in Tournai, Weyden spent most of his life as the official city painter of Brussels. The Flemish School exerted a significant influence on painting in France, Portugal, and Castile in the 15th century. © *National Gallery Collection; by kind permission of the Trustees of the National Gallery/CORBIS.*

Madonna and Child
Raphael's *Madonna and Child* flows with natural grace: Jesus and the Virgin Mary are unfrozen from their static representations in Byzantine and medieval art. This naturalistic portrayal reflects how religious feelings were permeated by the everyday in the Renaissance. *Scala/Art Resource, NY.*

Botticelli's *Spring*
This detail from Botticelli's *Spring* depicts the graceful movements of dance and the beauty of the female body through the naturalistic technique of Renaissance art. Note the contrast between the stillness of the formal composition, with the figures anchored by the trees in the background, and the movement conveyed by the gently flowing robes and the swirling motion of the dancing figures. *Scala/Art Resource, NY.*

sance artists learned to depict ever more expressive human emotions and movements. The work of the short-lived but brilliant painter Masaccio♦ (1401–1428) exemplifies this development. His painting *Expulsion from Paradise* shows Adam and Eve grieving in shame and despair.

Feminine beauty also found many masterpiece representations in Renaissance art. These representations range from the graceful movements of classical pagan figures and allegories, as in Sandro Botticelli's (c. 1445–1510) *The Birth of Venus* and *Springtime*, to Raphael's (1483–1520) numerous tender depictions of the Virgin Mary and the infant Jesus. In addition to rendering homage to classical and biblical figures, Renaissance artists painted portraits of their contemporaries. The increasing number of portraits in Renaissance painting illustrates the new, elevated view of human existence. Initially limited to representations of pontiffs, monarchs, princes, and patricians, portraiture of the middle classes became more widespread as the century advanced. Painters from the Low Countries such as Jan van Eyck♦ (1390?–1441) distinguished themselves in this genre; their portraits achieved a sense of detail and reality unsurpassed until the advent of photography.

♦**Masaccio:** muh ZAH chee oh

♦**Jan van Eyck:** yahn vahn EYEK

The ideal of a universal man was elaborated in the writings of Giovanni Pico della Mirandola (1463–1494). Born to a noble family, Pico avidly studied Latin and Greek philosophy. He befriended Ficino, Florence's leading Platonic philosopher, and enjoyed the patronage of Lorenzo de' Medici (1449–1492), who provided him with a villa after the papacy condemned some of his writings. Pico's oration *On the Dignity of Man* embodied the optimism of Renaissance philosophy. To express his marvel at the human species, Pico imagined God's words at his creation of Adam: "In conformity with your free judgment, in whose hands I have placed them, you are confined by no bounds, and you will fix limits of nature for yourself." Pico's construct placed mankind at the center of the universe as the measure of all things and "the molder and maker of himself." In his efforts to reconcile Platonic and Christian philosophy, Pico stressed both the classical emphasis on human responsibility in shaping society and the religious trust in God's divine plan.

For the first time after classical antiquity, sculptors again cast the human body in bronze, in life-size or larger freestanding statues. Donatello's equestrian statue of a Venetian general, one of the finest examples of this new endeavor, was consciously based on Roman statues of mounted emperors. Free from fabric and armor, the human body was idealized in the eighteen-foot-tall marble sculpture *David*, the work of the great Michelangelo Buonarroti◆ (1475–1564).

Order through Perspective

Renaissance art was distinguished from that of earlier eras by its depiction of the world as the eye perceives it. The use of visual perspective—an illusory three-dimensional space on a two-dimensional surface and the ordered arrangement of painted objects from one viewpoint—became one of the distinctive features of Western art. Neither Persian, Chinese, Byzantine, nor medieval Western art—all of which had been more concerned with conveying symbolism than reality—expressed this aesthetic for order through the use of perspective. Underlying the idea of perspective was a new Renaissance worldview: humans asserting themselves over nature in painting and design by controlling space. Optics became the organizing principle of the natural world in that it detected the "objective" order in nature. The Italian painters were keenly aware of their new technique, and they criticized the Byzantine and the northern Gothic stylists for "flat" depiction of the human body and the natural world. The highest accolade for a Renaissance artist was to be described as an "imitator of nature": the artist's teacher was nature, not design books or master painters. Leonardo described how "painting...compels the mind of the painter to transform itself into the mind of nature itself and to translate between nature and art, setting out, with nature, the causes of nature's phenomena regulated by nature's laws."

◆**Buonarroti:** bwoh nahr RAW tee

Michelangelo's *David*

Commissioned of the great Florentine artist when he was twenty-six, *David* (1501–1504) represents a masterpiece of sculpture that equaled the glory of ancient human sculpture. This huge marble figure—the earliest monumental statue of the Renaissance—depicts David larger than life-size in the full beauty and strength of the male body. *Nimatallah/Art Resource, NY.*

The perspectival representation that now dominated art is illustrated aptly by the work of three artists: Lorenzo Ghiberti♦ (c. 1378–1455), Andrea Mantegna, and Piero della Francesca (1420–1492). In 1401, the sculptor and goldsmith Ghiberti won a contest to design bronze doors for the San Giovanni Baptistry in Florence, a project that would occupy <u>him</u> the rest of his life. Choosing stories from the Old and New Testaments as his themes, Ghiberti used linear perspective to create a sense of depth and space in his bronze panels. His doors were so moving that Michelangelo in the sixteenth century described them as "the Gates of Paradise."

The Sacrifice of Isaac
Ghiberti's brilliant work (1401–1402) forms one of the panels on the door of the San Giovanni Baptistry in Florence. Technically difficult to execute, this bronze relief captures the violence of movement when the angel intervenes as Abraham prepares to slit the throat of Isaac, a story told in the Hebrew Scriptures.
Scala/Art Resource, NY.

Mantegna's most brilliant achievement, his frescoes in the bridal chamber of the Gonzaga Palace, completed between 1465 and 1474, created an illusory extension of reality, a three-dimensional representation of life, as the actual living space in the chamber "opened out" to the painted landscape on the walls. By contrast, the painter Piero della Francesca set his detached and expressionless figures in a geometrical world of columns and tiles, framed by intersecting lines and angles. Human existence, if della Francesca's painting can be taken as a reflection of his times, was shaped by human design, in accordance with the faculties of reason and observation. Thus, the artificially constructed urban society of the Renaissance was the ideal context in which to understand the ordered universe.

Perhaps even more than the visual artists, fifteenth-century architects embodied the Renaissance ideals of uniting artistic creativity and scientific knowledge. Among the greatest talents of the day was Filippo Brunelleschi♦ (1377–1446), a Florentine architect whose designs included the dome of the city's cathedral, modeled after ancient Roman ruins; the Ospedale degli Innocenti (a hospital for orphans); and the interiors of several Florentine churches.

One of the first buildings designed by the Florentine architect Leon Battista Alberti (1404–1472), the Rucellai Palace in Florence, shows a strong classical influence and inaugurated a trend in the construction of urban palaces for the Florentine ruling elite. Although Alberti undertook architectural designs for many princes, his significance lies more in his theoretical works, which strongly influenced his contemporaries. In a book on painting dedicated to Brunelleschi, Alberti analyzed the technique of perspective as the method of imitating nature. In *On Architecture* (1415), modeled after the Roman Vitruvius, Alberti argued for large-scale urban planning, with monumental buildings set on open squares, harmonious and beautiful in their proportions. His ideas were put into action by Pope Sixtus IV (r. 1471–1484) and his successors in the urban renewal of Rome, and they

♦**Lorenzo Ghiberti:** loh REHNT soh gee BEHR tee

♦**Brunelleschi:** broo nuhl EHS kee

Frescoes of the Camera degli Sposi
Andrea Mantegna's frescoes in the ducal palace depict members of the Gonzaga family, together with their court and animals, in various festive scenes. In masterly use of the perspective techniques, four painted walls lead to a vaulted ceiling decorated as heaven. The landscape view to the left of the door reflects the Renaissance idea of a painting as a window to the real world. *Scala/Art Resource, NY.*

Piero della Francesca, *The Flagellation of Christ*
Active in Urbino in the mid-fifteenth century, the Tuscan artist Piero della Francesca was a master of dramatic perspective design, as exemplified in this small panel painting. His use of cool colors and his imaginative manipulation of geometric space have led many art historians to regard Piero as the earliest forebear of the abstract artists of our own time. *Scala/Art Resource, NY.*

served to transform that unruly medieval town into a geometrically constructed monument to architectural brilliance by recalling the grandeur of its ancient origins.

New Musical Harmonies

Italy set the standards for the visual arts in Europe, but in musical styles it was more influenced by the northern countries. Around 1430, a new style of music appeared in the Low Countries that would dominate composition for the next two centuries. Instead of writing pieces with one major melodic line, composers wrote for three or four instrumental or human voices, each equally important in expressing a melody in harmony with the others.

The leader of this new style, known as polyphonic ("many sounds") music, was Guillaume Dufay (1400–1474), whose musical training began in the cathedral choir of his hometown, Cambrai in the Low Countries. His successful career took him to all the cultural centers of the Renaissance, where nobles sponsored new compositions and maintained a corps of musicians for court and religious functions. In 1438, Dufay composed festive music to celebrate the completion of the cathedral dome in Florence designed by Brunelleschi. Dufay expressed the harmonic relationship among four voices in ratios that matched the mathematically precise dimensions of Brunelleschi's architecture. After a period of employment at the papal court, Dufay returned to his native north and composed music for the Burgundian and French courts.

Although his younger counterpart Johannes Ockeghem♦ (c. 1420–1495), whose influence rivaled Dufay's, worked almost exclusively at the French court, Dufay's mobile career was typical. Josquin des Prez♦ (1440–1521), another Netherlander, wrote music in Milan, Ferrara, Florence, and Paris and at the papal court. The new style of music was beloved by the elites.

Within Renaissance polyphony were three main musical genres: the canon (central texts) of the Catholic Mass; the motet, which used both sacred and secular texts; and the secular chanson, often using the tunes of folk dances. Composers often adapted familiar folk melodies for sacred music, expressing religious feeling primarily through human voices instead of instruments. The tambourine and the lute were indispensable for dances, however, and small ensembles of wind and string instruments with contrasting sounds performed with singers in the fashionable courts of Europe. Also in use in the fifteenth century were new keyboard instruments—the harpsichord and clavichord—which could play several harmonic lines at once.

> **Review:** How did the shift from artisan to artist, a new naturalistic style, and the use of perspective in art reflect and influence a Renaissance mentality?

♦**Johannes Ockeghem:** yoh HAHN uhs OH kuh gehm
♦**Josquin des Prez:** zhaw SKAN deh PRAY

❖ The Intersection of Private and Public Lives

Lineage and descent shaped political power in dynastic states. In the fourteenth century, the state itself, through its institutions and laws, attempted to shape private life. Nowhere was this process more evident than in Florence. Considerations of state power intruded into the most intimate personal concerns: sexual intimacy, marriage, and childbirth could not be separated from the values of the ruling classes. With a society dominated by upper-class, patriarchal households, Renaissance Italy specified rigid roles for men and women, subordinating women and making marriage a vehicle for consolidating social hierarchy.

Renaissance Social Hierarchy

To deal with a mounting fiscal crisis, in 1427 the government of Florence ordered that a comprehensive tax record of households in the city and territory be compiled. Completed in 1430, this survey represented the most detailed population census then taken in European history. From this mass of data, historians have been able to reconstruct a picture of the Florentine state, particularly its capital.

The state of Florence, roughly the size of Massachusetts, had a population of more than 260,000. Tuscany, the area in which the Florentine state was located, was one of the most urbanized regions of Europe. With 38,000 inhabitants, the capital city of Florence claimed 14 percent of the total population and an enormous 67 percent of the state's wealth. Straddling the Arno River, Florence was a beautiful, thriving city with a defined social hierarchy. Some 60 percent of all households belonged to what the Florentines called the "little people"—workers, artisans, small merchants. The Florentines' "fat people" (roughly our middle class) made up 30 percent of the urban population and included the wealthier merchants, the leading artisans, notaries, doctors, and other professionals (see "A Merchant's Advice to His Sons" on the next page). At the very bottom of the hierarchy were slaves and servants,

A Merchant's Advice to His Sons

Giovanni Rucellai, one of the most successful merchants of fifteenth-century Florence, kept an extensive diary that reveals life among the city's urban elite. In this selection, Rucellai warns his sons against pursuing political power for self-serving reasons. Rucellai's comments on political office reflect a strong sentiment of support for the Florentine Republic and an implicit critique of the Medici, who dominated the city by means of their enormous wealth.

I do not deny that participation in the republic's affairs is not a most worthy enterprise, nor do I castigate him who, because of his excellence and his good works, honours his country by being just and honest. In fact, I say that a true honour is one which is appreciated by all citizens. But to do as they do: submit to this one, line up behind that one, form alliances, factions and conspiracies in order to surpass the most sagacious citizens; to desire to administer the state as if it were one's shop, appropriating its wealth and considering it as dowry for one's daughters, competing with one group of citizens while despising another; all these are dishonest things in a city. Therefore, my sons, I wish that you never desire an important political position in order to convert the treasure of the state into your own, for such an action is not good and I shall not approve it. He who aspires to a political position with this goal in mind has always been destroyed by the state itself regardless of the power of ingenuity which he might command. Everyone who has tried to ride this horse has always fallen from it, and the higher his position, the greater his blow and the more complete his ruin....

Let me repeat that the act of governing is notable and praiseworthy. He is a true citizen who assumes office not of his own will, not for his own advancement or grandeur, but when guided by reason, justice, prudence and has the approval of the good citizens–not with a view to becoming an overlord and superior to others, but in order to be of greater service. The good citizen wishes the good of all, he loves peace, equality, honesty, humility, the tranquility of the entire city, is happy in the pursuit of his own affairs, scorns avarice and uncontrollable passions and seeks to advance good understanding in his household and even more in his country.

Source: Anthony Molho, ed., *Social and Economic Foundations of the Italian Renaissance* (New York: John Wiley, 1969), 197–98.

largely women from the surrounding countryside employed in domestic service. At the top, a tiny elite of very wealthy patricians, bankers, and wool merchants controlled the state. In fact, the richest 1 percent of urban households (approximately one hundred families) owned more than one-quarter of the city's wealth and one-sixth of Tuscany's total wealth. The patricians in particular owned almost all government bonds, a lucrative investment guaranteed by a state they dominated.

Surprisingly, men seem to have outnumbered women in the 1427 survey. For every 100 women there were 110 men, unlike most past and present populations, in which women are the majority. In addition to female infanticide, which was occasionally practiced, the persistent underreporting of women probably explains the statistical abnormality.

Most people, men and women alike, lived in households with at least six inhabitants, although the form of family unit—nuclear or extended—varied, depending mainly on wealth, with poor people rarely able to support extended families. Among urban patricians and landowning peasants, the extended family held sway. The number of children in a family, it seems, reflected class differences as well. Wealthier families had more children; childless couples existed almost exclusively among the poor, who were also more likely to abandon the infants they could not feed.

Family Alliances

Wealth and class clearly determined family structure and the pattern of marriage and childbearing. In a letter to her eldest son, Filippo, dated 1447, Alessandra Strozzi announced the marriage of her daughter Caterina to the son of Parente Parenti. She described the young groom, Marco Parenti, as "a worthy and virtuous young man, and... the only son, and rich, 25 years old, and keeps a silk workshop; and they have a little political standing." The dowry was set at one thousand florins, a substantial sum—but for four to five hundred florins more, Alessandra admitted to Filippo, Caterina would have fetched a husband from a more prominent family.

The Strozzi belonged to one of Florence's most distinguished traditional families, but at the time of Caterina's betrothal the family had fallen into political disgrace. Alessandra's husband, an enemy of the Medici, was exiled in 1434; Filippo, a rich merchant in Naples, lived under the same political ban. Although Caterina was clearly marrying beneath her social station, the marriage represented an alliance in which money, political status, and family standing all balanced out. More an alliance between families than the consummation of love, an Italian Renaissance marriage was usually orchestrated by the male head of a household. In this case, Alessandra, as a widow, shared the matchmaking responsibility with her eldest son and other male relatives. Eighteen years later, when it came time to find a wife for Filippo, who had by then accumulated enough wealth to start his own household, Marco Parenti, his brother-in-law, would serve as matchmaker.

The upper-class Florentine family traced descent and determined inheritance through the male line. Because the distribution of wealth depended on this patriarchal system, women occupied an ambivalent position in the household. A daughter could claim inheritance only through her dowry, and she often disappeared from family records after her marriage. A wife seldom emerged from the shadow of her husband, and consequently the lives of many women have been lost to history.

In the course of a woman's life, her family often pressured her to conform to conventional expectations. At the birth of a daughter, most wealthy Florentine fathers opened an account at the Dowry Fund, a public fund established in 1425 to raise state revenues and a major investment instrument for the upper classes. In 1433, the fund paid annual interest of between 15 and 21 percent, and fathers could hope to raise handsome dowries to marry their daughters to more prominent men when the daughters reached their late teens. The Dowry Fund supported the structure of the marriage market, in which the circulation of wealth and women consolidated the social coherence of the ruling classes. (See "Taking Measure," on the next page.)

Women's subordination in marriage often reflected the age differences between spouses. The Italian marriage pattern, in which young women married older men, contrasted sharply with the northern European model, in which partners were much closer in age. Significant age disparity also left many women widowed in their twenties and thirties, and remarriage often created hard choices. A widow's father and brothers frequently pressed her to remarry to form a new family alliance. A widow, however, could not bring her children into her new marriage because they belonged to her first husband's family. Faced with the choice between her children and her paternal family, not to mention the question of her own happiness, a widow could hope to gain greater autonomy only in her old age, when, like Alessandra, she might assume matchmaking responsibilities to advance her family's fortunes.

In northern Europe, however, women enjoyed a relatively more secure position. In England, the Low Countries, and Germany, for example, women played a significant role in the economy—not only in the peasant household, in which everyone worked, but especially in the town, serving as peddlers, weavers, seamstresses, shopkeepers, midwives, and brewers. In Cologne, for example, women could join one of several artisans' guilds, and in Munich they ranked among some of the richest brewers. Women in northern Europe shared inheritances with their brothers, retained control of their dowries, and had the right to

TAKING MEASURE

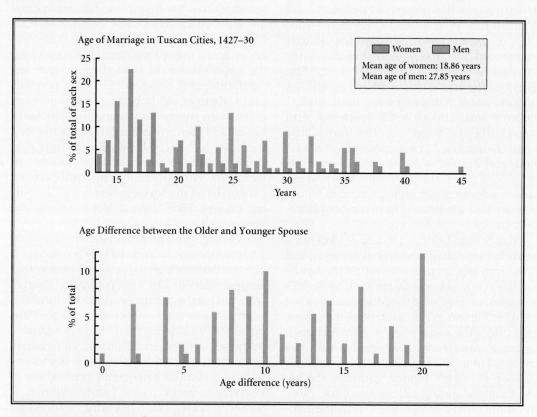

TAKING MEASURE Age of Marriage in Tuscan Cities, 1427–1430
The 1427–1430 Florentine tax and census records indicate two distinctly different marriage patterns for men and women. While the mean marriage age for women was 18.86 years, that for men was 27.85 years. This difference reflected the considerable difficulty for young men to amass enough wealth to start a household. More revealing is the chart showing the differences in age between the spouses. Some 12 percent of all spouses had a difference of twenty years. While the great majority of these marriages involved older, wealthier, established males, often in second marriages after the death of their first spouses, a small number involved younger men marrying up in the social ladder to widows of guild members to acquire a position. Together these charts give important information on gender relations and reflect the underlying class and gender inequalities in Renaissance society. *From David Herlihy and Christiane Klapisch-Zuber,* Tuscans and Their Families: A Study of Florentine Catasto of 1427 *(New Haven: Yale University Press, 1985), 205. Reprinted by permission of Yale University Press.*

represent themselves before the law. Italian men who traveled to the north were appalled at the differences in gender relations, criticizing English women as violent and brazen and disapproving of the mixing of the sexes in German public baths.

The Regulation of Sexuality

Along with marriage patterns, child care and attitudes toward sexuality also reflected class differences in Renaissance life. Florentine middle- and upper-class fathers arranged business contracts with wet nurses to breast-feed their infants; babies thus spent pro-longed periods of time away from their families. Such elaborate child care was beyond the reach of the poor, who often abandoned their children to strangers or to public charity.

By the beginning of the fifteenth century, Florence's two hospitals were accepting large numbers of abandoned children in addition to the sick and infirm. In 1445, the government opened the Ospedale degli Innocenti to deal with the large number of abandoned children. These unfortunate children came from two sources: poor families who were unable to feed another mouth, especially in times of famine, war, and economic depression; and women who had given birth out of wedlock. A large number of the latter were domestic slaves or servants who had been impregnated by their masters; in 1445, one-third of the first hundred foundlings at the new hospital were children of such liaisons. For some women the foundling hospital provided an alternative to infanticide. More than two-thirds of abandoned infants were girls, a clear indicator of the inequality between the sexes. The large number of abandoned infants overtaxed the hospital's limited resources—the death rate for infants there was much higher than the already high infant mortality rate of the time.

Illegitimacy in itself did not necessarily carry a social stigma in fifteenth-century Europe. Most upper-class men acknowledged and supported their illegitimate children as a sign of virility, and illegitimate children of noble lineage often rose to social and political prominence. Any social stigma was borne primarily by the woman, whose ability to marry became compromised. Shame and guilt drove some poor single mothers to kill their infants, a crime for which they paid with their own lives if discovered.

In addition to prosecuting infanticide, the public regulation of sexuality focused on prostitution and homosexuality. Intended "to eliminate a worse evil by a lesser one," a 1415 statute established government brothels in Florence. Concurrent with its higher tolerance of prostitution, the Renaissance state had a low tolerance of homosexuality. In 1432, the Florentine state appointed magistrates "to discover—whether by means of secret denunciation, accusations, notification, or any other method—those who commit the vice of sodomy, whether actively or passively." The government set fines for homosexual acts and carried out death sentences against pederasts (men who have sex with boys).

Fifteenth-century European magistrates took violence against women less seriously than illegal male sexual behavior, as the different punishments indicate. In Renaissance Venice, for example, the typical jail sentence for rape or attempted rape was only six months. Magistrates often treated noblemen with great leniency and handled rape cases according to class distinctions. For example, Agneta, a young girl living with a government official, was abducted and raped by two millers, who were sentenced to five years in prison; several servants who abducted and raped a slave woman were sentenced to three to four months in jail; and a nobleman who abducted and raped Anna, a slave woman, was freed. The brilliant civilization of the Renaissance was experienced very differently by men and women.

> **Review:** In what ways did the Renaissance state shape the private sphere?

❖ The Renaissance State and the Art of Politics

Among the achievements of the Renaissance, the state seemed to represent a work of art. For the Florentine political theorist Niccolò Machiavelli◆ (1469–1527), the state was an artifice of human creation to be conquered, shaped, and administered by princes according to the principles of power politics. Machiavelli laid out these principles in *The Prince*: "It can be observed that men use various methods in pursuing their own personal objectives, that is glory and riches.... I believe that... fortune is the arbiter of half the things we do,

---

◆**Niccolò Machiavelli:** neek koh LOH mah kee uh VEHL ee

MAP 14.2 Italy, c. 1450
The political divisions of Italy reflected powerful city-centered republics and duchies in the north and the larger but economically more backward south. Local and regional identities remained strong into the modern age.

leaving the other half or so to be controlled by ourselves." *The Prince* was the first treatment of the science of politics to discuss the acquisition and exercise of power without reference to an ultimate moral or ethical end. Machiavelli's keen observations of power, scandalous to his contemporaries, were based on a careful study of Italian politics during the Renaissance. Though a republican at heart, Machiavelli recognized the necessity of power in founding a state, whose survival ultimately rested on republican virtue. Outside of Italy, other European states also furnished many examples to illustrate the ruthless nature of power politics and the artifice of state building. In general, a mid-century period of turmoil gave way to the restructuring of central monarchical power in the last decades of the fifteenth century.

Many states developed stronger, institutionally more complex central governments in which middle-class lawyers played an increasingly prominent role. The expanded Renaissance state paved the way for the development of the nation-state in later centuries.

Republics and Principalities in Italy

The Italian states of the Renaissance can be divided into two broad categories: republics, which preserved the traditional institutions of the medieval commune by allowing a civic elite to control political and economic life, and principalities, which were ruled by a dynasty. The most powerful and influential states were the republics of Venice and Florence and the principalities of Milan and Naples. In addition to these four, a handful of smaller states, such as Siena, Ferrara, and Mantua stood out as important cultural centers during the Renaissance (Map 14.2).

Venice. Venice, a city built on a lagoon, ruled an extensive colonial empire that extended from the Adriatic to the Aegean Sea. Venetian merchant ships sailed the Mediterranean, the Atlantic coast, and the Black Sea; Christian pilgrims to Palestine booked passage on Venetian ships; in 1430, the Venetian navy numbered more than three thousand ships. Symbolizing their intimacy with and dominion over the sea, the Venetians celebrated an annual "Wedding of the Sea." Amid throngs of spectators and foreign dignitaries, the Venetian doge (the elected duke) sailed out to the Adriatic, threw a golden ring into its waters to renew the union, and intoned, "Hear us with favor, O Lord. We worthily entreat Thee to grant that this sea be tranquil and quiet for our men and all others who sail upon it."

In the early fifteenth century, however, Venetians faced threats on both sides. From 1425 to 1454, Venice fought expanding Milan on land. The second, and greater, danger came from the eastern Mediterranean, where the Ottoman Turks finally captured Byzantine Constantinople in 1453. Faced by these external threats, Venice drew strength from its internal social cohesion. Under the rule of an oligarchy of aristocratic merchants,

Venice enjoyed stability; and its maritime empire benefited citizens of all social classes, who joined efforts to defend the interests of the "Most Serene Republic," a contemporary name that reflected Venice's lack of social strife.

Florence. Compared with serene Venice, the republic of Florence was in constant agitation, responsive to political conflicts, new ideas, and artistic styles. Like Venice, Florence described its government in the humanist language of ancient Roman republicanism. Unlike Venice, Florentine society was turbulent as social classes and political factions engaged in constant civic strife. By 1434, a single family had emerged dominant in this fractious city: the Medici. Cosimo de' Medici (1388–1464), the head of the family, was ruthless. His contemporary Pope Pius II did not mince words in describing Medici power: "Cosimo, having thus disposed of his rivals, proceeded to administer the state at his pleasure and amassed wealth." Even though he did not hold any formal political office, Cosimo wielded influence in government through business associates and clients who were indebted to him for loans, political appointments, and other favors.

The Medici Bank handled papal finances and established branch offices in many Italian cities and the major northern European financial centers. Backed by immense private wealth, Cosimo became the arbiter of war and peace, the regulator of law, more master than citizen. Yet the prosperity and security that Florence enjoyed made him popular as well. At his death, Cosimo was lauded as the "father of his country."

Cosimo's grandson Lorenzo ("the Magnificent"), who assumed power in 1467, bolstered the regime's legitimacy with his lavish patronage of the arts. But opponents were not lacking. In 1478, Lorenzo narrowly escaped an assassination attempt. Two years after Lorenzo's death in 1494, partisans who opposed the Medici drove them from Florence. The Medici returned to power in 1512, only to be driven out again in 1527. In 1530, the republic fell and the Medici once again seized control, declaring Florence a **duchy** (a state ruled by dukes) and naming themselves its dukes.

Milan. Unlike Florence, with its republican aspirations, the duchy of Milan had been under dynastic rule since the fourteenth century. The most powerful Italian principality, Milan was a military state; it was relatively uninterested in the support of the arts but had first-class armaments and textile industries in the capital city and rich farmlands in Lombardy. Until 1447, the duchy was ruled by the Visconti dynasty, a group of powerful lords whose plans to unify all of northern and central Italy failed because of combined opposition from Venice, Florence, and other Italian powers. In 1447, the last Visconti duke died without a male heir, and the nobility proclaimed Milan to be a republic.

For three years the new republic struggled to maintain Milan's political and military strength. Cities that the Visconti family had subdued rebelled against Milan, and the two great republics of Venice and Florence plotted its downfall. Milan's ruling nobility, seeking further defense, appointed Francesco Sforza,♦ who had married the illegitimate daughter of the last Visconti duke, to the post of general. Sforza promptly turned against his employers, claiming the duchy as his own. A bitter struggle between the nobility and the townspeople in Milan further undermined the republican cause, and in 1450 Sforza entered Milan in triumph.

The power of the Sforza dynasty reached its height during the 1490s. In 1493, Duke Ludovico married his niece Bianca Maria to Maximilian, the newly elected Holy Roman Emperor, promising an immense dowry in exchange for the emperor's recognition of his rule. But the newfound Milanese glory was soon swept aside by France's invasion of Italy in 1494, and the duchy itself eventually came under Spanish rule.

The Papal States. In the violent arena of Italian politics, the papacy, an uneasy mixture of worldly splendor and religious authority, was a player like the other states. The vicars of Christ negotiated treaties, made war, and built palaces; a few led scandalous lives. Pope Alexander VI (r. 1492–1503), the most notorious pontiff, kept a mistress and

♦**Francesco Sforza:** frahn CHEHS kaw SFAWR tsah

fathered children, one of whom, Cesare Borgia, served as Machiavelli's model for a ruthless ruler in *The Prince*.

The popes' concern with politics stemmed from their desire to restore papal authority, greatly undermined by the Great Schism of 1378–1417 and the conciliar movement. To that end, the popes used both politics and culture to enhance their authority. Politically, they curbed local power, expanded papal government, increased taxation, enlarged the papal army and navy, and extended papal diplomacy. Culturally, the popes renovated churches, created the Vatican Library, sponsored artists, and patronized writers to glorify their role and power as St. Peter's successors. In undertaking these measures, the Renaissance papacy merely exemplified the larger trend toward the centralization of power evident in the development of monarchies and empires outside of Italy as well.

Naples. After a struggle for succession between Alfonso of Aragon and René d'Anjou, a cousin of the king of France, the kingdoms of Naples and Sicily came under Aragonese rule between 1435 and 1494. Unlike the northern Italian states, Naples was dominated by powerful feudal barons who retained jurisdiction and taxation over their own vast estates. Alfonso I (r. 1435–1458), called Alfonso the Magnanimous for his generous patronage of the arts, promoted the urban middle class to counter baronial rule, using as his base Naples, the only large city in a relatively rural kingdom. Alfonso's son Ferante I (r. 1458–1494) continued his father's policies: two of his chief ministers hailed from humble backgrounds. With their private armies and estates intact, however, the barons constantly threatened royal power, and in 1462 many rebelled against Ferante. More ruthless than his father, Ferante handily crushed the opposition.

Embroiled in Italian politics, Alfonso and Ferante shifted their alliances among the papacy, Milan, and Florence. But the greater threat to Neapolitan security was external. In 1480, Ottoman forces captured the Adriatic port of Otranto, where they massacred the entire male population. And in 1494, a French invasion ended the Aragonese dynasty in Naples, although, as in Milan, France's claim would eventually be superseded by that of Spain.

Renaissance Diplomacy

Many features of diplomacy characteristic of today's nation-states first appeared in fifteenth-century Europe. By midcentury, competition between states and the extension of warfare raised the practice of diplomacy to nearly an art form. The first diplomatic handbook, composed in 1436 by Frenchman Bernard du Rosier, later archbishop of Toulouse, declared that the business of the diplomat was "to pay honor to religion... and the Imperial crown, to protect the rights of kingdoms, to offer obedience... to confirm friendships... make peace... to arrange past disputes and remove the cause for future unpleasantness."

The emphasis on ceremonies, elegance, and eloquence (Italians referred to ambassadors as orators) masked the complex game of diplomatic intrigue and spying. In the fifteenth century, a resident ambassador was expected to keep a continuous stream of foreign political news flowing to the home government, not just to conduct temporary diplomatic missions, as earlier ambassadors had done. In some cases the presence of semiofficial agents developed into full-fledged ambassadorships: the Venetian embassy to the sultan's court in Constantinople developed out of the merchant-consulate that had represented all Venetian merchants, and Medici Bank branch managers eventually acted as political agents for the Florentine republic.

Foremost in the development of diplomacy was Milan, a state with political ambition and military might. Under the Visconti dukes, Milan sent ambassadors to Aragon, Burgundy, the Holy Roman Empire, and the Ottoman Empire. Under the Sforza dynasty, Milanese diplomacy continued to function. For generations Milanese diplomats at the French court sent home an incessant flow of information on the rivalry between France and Burgundy. Francesco Sforza also used his diplomatic corps to extend his political patronage. In letters of recommendation to the papacy, Francesco commented on the political desirability of potential ecclesiastical candidates by using code words, sometimes supplemented with instructions to his ambassador to indicate his true intent regardless of the coded letter of recommendation. In more sensitive diplomatic reports, ciphers (codes) were used to prevent the messages from being understood by hostile powers if they were captured.

As the center of Christendom, Rome became the diplomatic hub of Europe. During the 1490s, well over two hundred diplomats were stationed in Rome. The papacy sent out far fewer envoys than it received; only at the end of the fifteenth century were papal nuncios, or envoys, permanently established in the European states.

The most outstanding achievement of Italy's Renaissance diplomacy was the negotiation of a general peace treaty that settled the decades of warfare engendered by Milanese expansion and civil war. The Treaty of Lodi (1454) established a complex balance of power among the major Italian states and maintained relative stability in the peninsula for half a century. Renaissance diplomacy eventually failed, however, when France invaded in 1494, leading to the collapse of the whole Italian state system.

Monarchies and Empires

Locked in fierce competition among themselves, the Italian states paid little attention to the large territorial states emerging in the rest of Europe that would soon overshadow Italy with their military power and economic resources. Whether in Burgundy, England, Spain, France, the Ottoman Empire, or Muscovy, rulers employed various stratagems to expand or enhance their power. In central Europe, by contrast, rulers failed to centralize power.

Burgundy. The expansion of Burgundy during the fifteenth century was a result of military might and careful statecraft. The spectacular success of the Burgundian dukes and their equally dramatic demise both bear testimony to the artful creation of the Renaissance state, paving the way for the development of the European nation-state.

Part of the French royal house, the Burgundian dynasty expanded its power rapidly by acquiring land, primarily in the Netherlands. Between 1384 and 1476, the Burgundian state filled the territorial gap between France and Germany, extending from the Swiss border in the south to Friesland (Germany) in the north. Through purchases, inheritance, and conquests, the dukes ruled over French-, Dutch-, and German-speaking subjects, creating a state that resembled a patchwork of provinces and regions, each jealously guarding its laws and traditions. The Low Countries, with their flourishing cities, constituted the state's economic heartland, and the region of Burgundy itself, which gave the state its name, offered rich farmlands and vineyards. Unlike England, whose island geography made it a natural political unit; or France, whose borders were forged in the national experience of repelling English invaders; or Castile, whose national identity came from centuries of warfare against Islam, Burgundy was an artificial creation whose coherence depended entirely on the skillful exercise of statecraft.

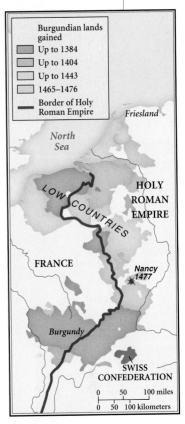

Expansion of Burgundy, 1384–1476

At the heart of Burgundian politics was the personal cult of its dukes. Philip the Good (r. 1418–1467) and his son Charles the Bold (r. 1467–1477) were very different kinds of rulers, but both were devoted to enhancing the prestige of their dynasty and the security of their dominion. A bon vivant who fathered many illegitimate children, Philip was a lavish patron of the arts who commissioned numerous illuminated manuscripts, chronicles, tapestries, paintings, and music in his efforts to glorify Burgundy. Charles, by contrast, spent more time on war than at court. Renowned for his courage

The Burgundian Court

The ideals of late-medieval courtly style found fullest expression in fifteenth-century Burgundy. This painting of the wedding of Philip the Good and Isabella of Portugal was executed in the workshop of the Flemish master Jan van Eyck. It conveys the atmosphere of chivalric fantasy in which the Burgundian dynasty enveloped itself. *Bridgeman-Giraudon/Art Resource, NY.*

another, they also staged elaborate ceremonies to enhance their power and promote their legitimacy (see The Burgundian Court, on this page). Their entries into cities and their presence at weddings, births, and funerals became the centerpieces of a "theater" state in which the dynasty provided the only link among very diverse territories. New rituals became propaganda tools. Philip's revival of chivalry at court transformed the semi-independent nobility into courtiers closely tied to the prince.

In addition to sponsoring political propaganda, the Burgundian rulers controlled their geographically dispersed state by developing a financial bureaucracy and a standing army. But maintaining the army, one of the largest in Europe, left the dukes chronically short of money. They were forced to sell political offices to raise funds, a practice that led to an inefficient and corrupt bureaucracy. The demise of the Burgundian state had two sources: the loss of Charles the Bold, who died without a male heir, and an alliance between France and the Holy Roman Empire. When Charles fell in battle in 1477, France seized the duchy of Burgundy. The Netherlands remained loyal to Mary, Charles's daughter, and through her husband, the future Holy Roman Emperor Maximilian, some of the Burgundian lands and the dynasty's political and artistic legacy passed on to the Habsburgs.

(hence his nickname), he died in 1477 when his army was routed by the Swiss at Nancy, a loss that began the decline of Burgundian power.

The Burgundians' success depended in large part on their personal relationship with their subjects. Not only did the dukes travel constantly from one part of their dominion to

England. In England, defeat in the Hundred Years' War was followed by civil war at home. Henry VI (r. 1422–1461), who ascended to the throne as a child, proved in maturity to be a weak and, on occasion, mentally unstable monarch. He was unable to control the great lords of the realm, who wrought anarchy with their numerous private feuds. In 1460, Richard of York rebelled;

his son defeated Henry and was then crowned Edward IV (r. 1461–1483). England's intermittent civil wars, later called the Wars of the Roses continued until 1485, fueled at home by factions among nobles and regional discontent and abroad by Franco-Burgundian intervention. The ultimate victor was Henry Tudor, who took the title of Henry VII (r. 1485–1509).

The Wars of the Roses did relatively little damage to England's soil. The battles were generally short and, in the words of the French chronicler Philippe de Commynes (c. 1447–1511), "England enjoyed this peculiar mercy above all other kingdoms, that neither the country, nor the people nor the houses, were wasted, destroyed or demolished, but the calamities and misfortunes of the war fell only upon the soldiers, and especially on the nobility." As a result, the English economy continued to grow during the fifteenth century. The cloth industry expanded considerably, and the English now used much of the raw wool that they had been exporting to the Low Countries to manufacture goods at home. London merchants, taking a vigorous role in trade, also assumed greater political prominence not only in governing London but also as bankers to kings and members of Parliament. In the countryside the landed classes—the nobility, the gentry (a kind of lesser nobility), and the yeomanry (free farmers)—benefited from rising farm and land-rent income as the population increased slowly but steadily.

Spain.   In the Iberian monarchies, decades of civil war over the royal successions began to wane only in 1469, when Isabella of Castile and Ferdinand of Aragon married. Retaining their separate titles, the two monarchs ruled jointly over their dominions, each of which adhered to its traditional laws and privileges. Their union represented the first step toward the creation of a unified Spain. Isabella and Ferdinand limited the privileges of the nobility and allied themselves with the cities, relying on the Hermandad (civic militia) to enforce justice and on lawyers to staff the royal council.

The united strength of Castile and Aragon brought the reconquista to a close with a final crusade against the Muslims.

Isabella I of Spain, c. 1500
In 1474 Isabella became queen of Castile, and in 1479 her husband Ferdinand took control of the kingdom of Aragon. The union of these crowns would lead to the creation of a unified Spain under "Catholic monarchs." This detail from the retable in a Spanish church (the ledge raised above the back of altars) shows her in pious devotion with her hands clasped next to a prayer book. *The Granger Collection, NY.*

After more than a century of peace, war broke out in 1478 between Granada, the last Iberian Muslim state, and the Catholic royal forces. Weakened by internal strife, Granada finally fell in 1492. Two years later, in recognition of the crusade, Pope Alexander VI bestowed the title "Catholic monarchs" on Isabella and Ferdinand, ringing in an era in which militant Catholicism became an instrument of state authority and shaped the national consciousness.

The relative religious tolerance of the Middle Ages in Iberia, in which Muslims, Jews, and Christians had generally lived side by side, now yielded to the demand for religious conformity. The practice of Catholicism became a test of one's loyalty to the church and to the Spanish monarchy. In 1478, royal jurisdiction introduced the Inquisition to Spain, primarily as a means to control the **conversos** (Jewish converts to Christianity), whose elevated positions in the economy and the government aroused widespread resentment from the so-called Old Christians. Conversos often were suspected of practicing their ancestral religion in secret while pretending to adhere to their new Christian faith. Appointed by the monarchs, the clergy (called inquisitors) presided over tribunals set up to investigate those suspected of religious lapses. The accused could defend themselves but not confront their accusers, who were often anonymous. The wide spectrum of punishments ranged from monetary fines to the ritual of public confession called **auto da fé**♦ (literally, "demonstration of faith") to burning at the stake. After the fall of Granada, many Moors were forced to convert or resettle in Castile, and in 1492 Ferdinand and Isabella ordered all Jews in their kingdoms to choose between exile or conversion.

The single most dramatic event for the Jews of Renaissance Europe was their expulsion from Spain, the country with the largest and most vibrant Jewish communities, and their subsequent dispersion throughout the Mediterranean world. On the eve of the expulsion, approximately 200,000 Jews and 300,000 conversos were living in Castile and Aragon. Well over 100,000 Jews chose exile. The priest Andrés Bernáldez described the expulsion:

> Just as with a strong hand and outstretched arm, and much honor and riches, God through Moses had miraculously taken the other people of Israel from Egypt, so in these parts of Spain they had... to go out with much honor and riches, without losing any of their goods, to possess the holy promised land, which they confessed to have lost through their great and abominable sins which their ancestors had committed against God.

France. France, too, was recovering from war. Although France won the Hundred Years' War, it emerged from that conflict in the shadow of the brilliant Burgundian court. Under Charles VII (r. 1422–1461) and Louis XI (r. 1461–1483), the French monarchy began the slow process of expansion and recovery. Abroad, Louis fomented rebellion in England. At home, however, lay the more dangerous enemy, Burgundy. In 1477, with the death of Charles the Bold, Louis seized large tracts of Burgundian territory. France's horizons expanded even more when Louis inherited most of southern France after the Anjou dynasty died out. By the end of the century, France had doubled its territory, assuming close to its modern-day boundaries.

To strengthen royal power at home, Louis promoted industry and commerce, imposed permanent salt and land taxes, maintained western Europe's first standing army (created by his predecessor), and dispensed with the meeting of the Estates General, which included the clergy, the nobility, and representatives from the major towns of France. The French kings further increased their power with important concessions from the papacy. With the 1438 Pragmatic Sanction of Bourges, Charles asserted the superiority of a general church council over the pope. Harking back to a long tradition of the high Middle Ages, the Sanction of Bourges established what would come to be known as **Gallicanism** (after Gaul, the ancient Roman name for France), in which the French king would effectively control ecclesiastical revenues and the appointment of French bishops.

Spain Just before Unification, Late Fifteenth Century

♦**auto da fé:** ow toh duh FAY

Central and Eastern Europe. The rise of strong, new monarchies in western Europe contrasted sharply with the weakness of state authority in central and eastern Europe, where developments in Hungary, Bohemia, and Poland resembled the Burgundian model of personal dynastic authority (Map 14.3). Under Matthias Corvinus (r. 1456–1490), the Hungarian king who briefly united the Bohemian and Hungarian crowns, an east-central European empire seemed to be emerging. A patron of the arts and a humanist, Matthias created a great library in Hungary. He repeatedly defeated the encroaching Austrian Habsburgs and even occupied Vienna in 1485. His empire did not outlast his death in 1490, however. The powerful Hungarian magnates, who enjoyed the constitutional right to elect the king, ended it by refusing to acknowledge his son's claim to the throne.

In Poland, the nobility preserved their power under the monarchy by maintaining their right to elect kings. By selecting weak monarchs and fiercely defending noble liberties, the Polish nobility ruled a land of serfs and frustrated any attempt at the centralization of power and state building. Only in 1506 would Poland and Lithuania again form a loosely united "commonwealth" under a single king.

The Ottoman Empire. In the Balkans, the Ottoman Empire, under Sultan Mehmed II (r. 1451–1481), became a serious threat to all of Christian Europe. After Mehmed ascended the throne, he proclaimed a holy war and laid siege to Constantinople in 1453. A city of 100,000, the Byzantine capital could muster only 6,000 defenders (including a small contingent of Genoese) against an Ottoman force estimated at between 200,000 and 400,000 men. The city's fortifications, many of which dated from Emperor Justinian's rule in the sixth century, were no match for fifteenth-century cannons. The defenders held out for fifty-three days: while the Christians confessed their sins and prayed for divine deliverance, in desperate anticipation of the Second Coming, the Muslim besiegers pressed forward, urged on by the certainty of rich spoils and Allah's promise of a final victory over the infidel Rome. Finally the de-

MAP 14.3 Eastern Europe in the Fifteenth Century
The rise of Muscovy and the Ottomans shaped the map of eastern Europe. Some Christian monarchies such as Serbia lost their independence. Others, such as Hungary, held off the Ottomans until the early sixteenth century.

fenders were overwhelmed, and the last Byzantine emperor, Constantine Palaeologus,♦ died in battle. Some sixty thousand residents were carried off in slavery, and the city was sacked. Mehmed entered Constantinople in triumph, rendered thanks to Allah in Justinian's Church of St. Sophia, which became a mosque, and was remembered as "the Conqueror."

♦**Palaeologus:** pay lee AHL uh guhs

Muscovy. North of the Black Sea and east of Poland-Lithuania, a very different polity was taking shape. In the second half of the fifteenth century, the princes of Muscovy embarked on a spectacular path of success that would make their state the largest on earth. Subservient to the Mongols in the fourteenth century, the Muscovite princes began to assert their independence with the collapse of Mongol power. Ivan III (r. 1462–1505) was the first Muscovite prince to claim an imperial title, referring to himself as **tsar** (or czar, from the name Caesar). In 1471, Ivan defeated the city-state of Novgorod, whose territories encompassed a vast region in northern Russia. Six years later he abolished the local civic government of this proudly independent city, which had enjoyed trade with the thriving cities of central Europe. To consolidate his autocratic rule and wipe out memories of past freedoms, in 1484 and 1489 Ivan forcibly relocated thousands of leading Novgorod families to lands around Moscow. He also expanded his territory to the south and east when his forces pushed back the Mongols to the Volga River.

Unlike other European monarchies, whose powers were bound by collective rights and laws, Ivan's Russian monarchy claimed absolute property rights over all lands and subjects. The expansionist Muscovite state was shaped by two traditions: religion and service. After the fall of the Byzantine Empire, the tsar was the Russian Orthodox church's only defender of the faith against Islam and Catholicism. Orthodox propaganda thus legitimized the tsar's rule by proclaiming Moscow the "Third Rome" (the first two being Rome itself and Constantinople) and praising the tsar's autocratic power as the best protector of the faith. The Mongol system of service to rulers, by which the prince's subjects were bound to him by life and blood and not by a contract of loyalty, also deeply informed Muscovite statecraft. In their conception of the state as private dominion,

The Medieval Royal Castle of Visegrad
King Matthias Corvinus made Visegrad the political and cultural center of Hungary before it was destroyed in the Ottoman conquests. Situated on top of a hill commanding a strategic position over the road and the Danube River, Visegrad—shown here in a present-day reconstruction—was above all a fortification.
Szabolcs Hámor/ MTI/Eastfoto.

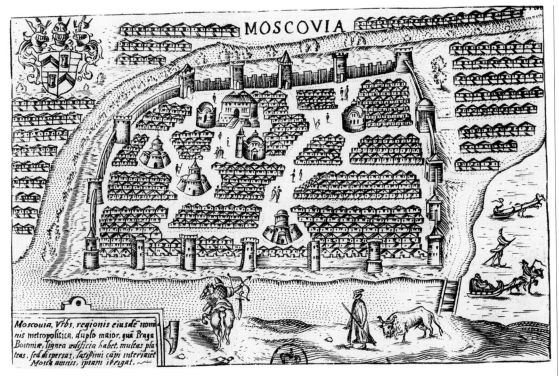

A View of Moscow

This image comes from the travel book of the Habsburg ambassador to Moscow, Sigismund von Herberstein, who engraved it himself in 1547. Note the representation of Muscovite soldiers with bows and arrows, weapons long since outdated in western Europe. Note also the domination of the Kremlin (in the middle) over a city that consisted mostly of modest wooden houses.

Bridgeman-Giraudon/Art Resource, NY.

their emphasis on autocratic power, and their division of the populace into a land-holding elite in service to the tsar and a vast majority of taxpaying subjects, the Muscovite princes created a state more in the despotic political tradition of the central Asian steppes and the Ottoman Empire than of western Europe.

In state building, Muscovy joined England, France, and Spain as examples of success, in sharp contrast to Burgundy and Poland. Yet far more significant was the expansion of the boundary of Europe itself, as maritime explorations brought Europeans into contact with indigenous civilizations in Africa, the Americas, and Asia.

Review: How did Renaissance princes increase their power at the expense of the nobility and their subjects?

❖ On the Threshold of World History: Widening Geographic Horizons

The fifteenth century constituted the first era of world history. The significance of the century lies not so much in the European "discovery" of Africa and the Americas as in the breakdown of cultural frontiers inaugurated by European colonial expansion. Before the maritime explorations of Portugal and Spain, Europe had remained at the periphery of world history. Fourteenth-century Mongols had been more interested in conquering China and Persia—lands with sophisticated cultures—than in invading Europe; Persian historians of the early fifteenth century dismissed Europeans as "barbaric Franks"; and China's Ming dynasty rulers, who sent maritime expeditions to Southeast Asia and East

Africa around 1400, seemed unaware of the Europeans, even though Marco Polo and other Italian merchants had appeared at the court of the preceding Mongol Yuan dynasty. In the fifteenth century, the Portuguese and Spanish, inspired by the search for profit (from spices and gold) and by a crusading spirit against Islam, sailed across the Atlantic, Indian, and Pacific Oceans; they were followed a century later by the English, French, and Dutch, bringing people, merchandise, crops, and diseases in a global exchange that would shape the modern world. For the first time the people of the Americas were brought into contact with a larger historical force that threatened to destroy not only their culture but their existence as well. European exploitation, conquest, and racism defined this historical era of transition from the medieval to the modern world.

The Divided Mediterranean

In the second half of the fifteenth century, the Mediterranean Sea, which had dominated medieval maritime trade, began to lose its preeminence to the Atlantic Ocean. To win control over the Mediterranean, the Ottomans embarked on an ambitious naval program to transform their empire into a major maritime power. War and piracy disrupted the flow of Christian trade: the Venetians mobilized all their resources to fight off Turkish advances, and the Genoese largely abandoned the eastern Mediterranean for trade opportunities presented by the Atlantic voyage.

The Mediterranean states used ships made with relatively backward naval technology, compared with that of Portugal and Spain. The most common ship, the galley—a flat-bottomed vessel propelled by sails and oars—dated from the time of ancient Rome. Most galleys could not withstand open-ocean voyages, although Florentine and Genoese galleys still made long journeys to Flanders and England, hugging the coast for protection. The galley's dependence on human labor was a more serious handicap. Because prisoners of war and convicted criminals toiled as oarsmen in both Christian and Muslim ships, victory in war or the enforcement of criminal penalties was crucial to a state's ability to float

Engraving of Katharina, an African Woman
Like other artists in early-sixteenth-century Europe, Albrecht Dürer would have seen in person Africans who went to Portugal and Spain as students, servants, and slaves. Note Katharina's noble expression and dignified attire. Before the rise of the slave trade in the seventeenth century, most Africans in Europe were household servants of the aristocracy. Considered prestigious symbols, such servants were not employed primarily for economic production. *Foto Marburg/Art Resource, NY.*

large numbers of galleys. Slavery, too, a traditional Mediterranean institution, sometimes provided the necessary labor.

Although the Mediterranean was divided into Muslim and Christian zones, it still offered a significant opportunity for exchange. Sugarcane was transported to the western Mediterranean from western Asia. From the Balearic Islands off Spain (under Aragonese rule), the crop then traveled to the Canary Islands in the Atlantic, where the Spanish enslaved the native population to work the new sugar plantations. Eventually sugar—and slavery—were exported to the Americas.

Different ethnic groups also moved across the maritime frontier. After Granada fell in 1492, many Muslims fled to North Africa and continued to raid the Spanish coast. When Castile expelled the Jews, some of them settled in North Africa, more in Italy, and many in the Ottoman Empire, Greek-speaking Thessalonika, and Palestine. Conversant in two or three languages, Spanish Jews often served as intermediaries between the Christian West and Muslim East. Greeks occupied a similar position. Most Greeks in the homeland adhered to the Greek Orthodox church under Ottoman protection, but some converted to Islam and entered imperial service, making up a large part of the Ottoman navy. The Greeks on Crete, Chios, and other Aegean islands, however, lived under Italian rule, some of them converting to Roman Catholicism and entering Venetian, Genoese, and Spanish service. A region with warring 0states and competing religions, the Mediterranean remained a divided zone as more and more Europeans turned instead to the unknown oceans.

Portuguese Explorations

The first phase of European overseas expansion began in 1433 with Portugal's systematic exploration of the West African coast and culminated in 1519–1522 with Spain's circumnavigation of the globe (Map 14.4, page 537). Looking back, the sixteenth-century Spanish historian Francisco López de Gómora described the Iberian maritime voyages to the East and West Indies as "the greatest event since the creation of the world, apart from the incarnation and death of him who created it." (See "New Sources, New Perspectives," page 534.)

In many ways a continuation of the struggle against Muslims in the Iberian peninsula, Portugal's maritime voyages displayed that country's mixed motives of piety, glory, and greed. The Atlantic explorations depended for their success on several technological breakthroughs, such as the lateen sail adapted from the Arabs (it permitted a ship to tack against headwinds), new types of sailing vessels, and better charts and instruments. What motivated these explorers was a combination of crusading zeal against Muslims and medieval adventure stories, such as the tales of the Venetian traveler Marco Polo (1254–1324). Behind the spirit of the crusade lurked vistas of vast gold mines in West Africa (the trade across the Sahara was controlled by Arabs) and a mysterious Christian kingdom established by Prester John (actually the Coptic Christian kingdom of Abyssinia, or Ethiopia, in East Africa). The Portuguese hoped to reach the spice-producing lands of South and Southeast Asia by sea to bypass the Ottoman Turks, who controlled the traditional land routes between Europe and Asia.

By 1415, the Portuguese had captured Ceuta on the Moroccan coast, thus establishing a foothold in Africa. Thereafter, Portuguese voyages sailed farther and farther down the West African coast. By midcentury, the Portuguese chain of forts had reached Guinea and could protect the gold and slave trades. At home the royal house of Portugal financed the fleets, with crucial roles played by Prince Peter, regent of the throne between 1440 and 1448; his more famous younger brother, Prince Henry the Navigator; and King John II (r. 1481–1495). Henry financed many voyages out of the revenues of a noble crusading order. Private monies also helped; leading Lisbon merchants participated in financing the gold and slave trades off the Guinea coast.

In 1455, Pope Nicholas V (r. 1447–1455) sanctioned Portuguese overseas expansion, commending King John II's crusading spirit and granting him and his successors the monopoly on trade with inhabitants of the newly "discovered" regions. In 1487–1488, Bartholomeu Dias took advantage of the prevailing winds in the South Atlantic to reach the Cape of Good Hope. A mere ten years later (1497–1499), under the captainship of Vasco da Gama, a Portuguese fleet rounded the cape and reached Calicut, India, the center of the spice trade. Twenty-three years later, in 1512, Ferdinand Magellan, a Portuguese sailor in Spanish service, led the first expedition to circumnavigate the globe. By 1517, a chain of Portuguese forts dotted the Indian Ocean: at Mozambique, Hormuz (at the mouth of the Persian Gulf), Goa (in India), Colombo (in modern Sri Lanka), and Malacca (modern Malaysia).

NEW SOURCES, NEW PERSPECTIVES

Portuguese Voyages of Discovery

The quincentennial celebration of Vasco da Gama's 1499 voyage to India took place in the same year (1998) that Lisbon staged a World Exposition—thus inspiring the theme of "Discoveries of the Oceans" in Portugal's presentation of its past and its contributions to civilization. The celebration of Portugal and the oceans strengthened interest in Portuguese maritime history and traditions, but it also inspired examination and criticism of that country's history. The result has been a rich mix of new sources and perspectives, presented in publications and exhibitions.

The traditional historical approach emphasizes the technical innovations of Portuguese seamanship. Inventions of new sailing vessels, such as the caravel, a high-sided ship capable of carrying a large load and maintaining balance in rough seas, enabled Portuguese sailors to venture ever farther into the oceans. Other nautical instruments reflected a cumulative knowledge of seamanship and geography that reduced the risks of long-distance travel. Sailors compiled nautical guides showing the time of tides (see A Nautical Tide Calendar) and the position of the sun in the sky at different latitudes at different seasons (see A Nautical Solar Guide). Most valuable of all were the pilots' books, or *roteiros* (books of sailing directions), often accompanied by detailed maps of maritime regions and coasts. These books of routes and maritime charts lessened but did not eliminate

Portuguese Ships
Maritime voyagers in Portugal were sponsored by the highest authorities in the land, the best known of whom was Prince Henry, nicknamed "the Navigator." This detail from the altarpiece of Santa Ana depicts monarchs, noblemen, and bishops against a backdrop of different types of sailing vessels. The caravel, the largest ship in the background, was the main type of vessel for Portuguese voyages in the fifteenth and sixteenth centuries.

A Nautical Tide Calendar

dias dalua	oras	quito
0	3	0
1	3	4
2	4	3
3	5	2
4	6	1
5	7	0
6	7	4
7	8	3
8	9	2
9	10	1
10	11	0
11	11	4
12	12	3
13	13	2
14	14	1
15	15	0

A high-tide chart, showing at which hour and at which fifth (the hour is divided into twelve-minute segments) high tide will recur from the day of the new moon. The left column in black starts with the date of the new moon and day. The red columns indicate first the hour and then the fifth of high tide.

A Nautical Solar Guide

Abrill			Mayo			Junho		
dias	g.	m.	dias	g.	m.	dias	g.	m.
1	8	20	1	17	52	1	23	8
2	8	41	2	18	8	2	23	12
3	9	2	3	18	23	3	23	16
4	9	24	4	18	39	4	23	20
5	9	47	5	18	53	5	23	23
6	10	7	6	19	7	6	23	26
7	10	29	7	19	21	7	23	28
8	10	51	8	19	33	8	23	30
9	11	12	9	19	47	9	23	32
10	11	32	10	19	56	10	23	33
11	11	52	11	20	11	11	23	33
12	12	12	12	20	24	12	23	33
13	12	31	13	20	35	13	23	32
14	12	49	14	20	46	14	23	31
15	13	8	15	20	58	15	23	30
16	13	28	16	21	10	16	23	28
17	13	48	17	21	20	17	23	26
18	14	8	18	21	30	18	23	24
19	14	28	19	21	40	19	23	22
20	14	47	20	21	48	20	23	19
21	15	7	21	21	57	21	23	15
22	15	24	22	22	5	22	23	11
23	15	43	23	22	13	23	23	7
24	16	0	24	22	21	24	23	2
25	16	16	25	22	28	25	22	57
26	16	31	26	22	36	26	22	52
27	16	48	27	22	41	27	22	47
28	17	4	28	22	48	28	22	41
29	17	20	29	22	54	29	22	34
30	17	36	30	23	0	30	22	26
0	0	0	31	23	4	0	0	0

From the codex of Bastiao Lopes (c. 1568), this guide shows the declination angle of the sun for different days in the months of April, May, and June.

the dangers of the oceans. The roteiro of Diogo Alfonso (1535), for example, gave these directions for the voyage to India:

> Setting forth from Lisbon you steer to the southwest until you catch sight of the island of Porto Santo or the island of Madeira. And from thence go southward in search of the Canaries; and as soon as you pass the Canaries set course southwest and south until you reach 15 degrees, that is 50 leagues from Cape Verde.

After passing through the mid-Atlantic, Alfonso advised the pilots to seek the most important landmark of all:

> If you come 35 degrees more or less, seeking the Cape of Good Hope, when you come upon cliff-faces, you may know that they are those of the Cape of Good Hope. . . . From hence you should set course northeast by north to 19 1/4 degrees. Then north-northeast, until you reach the latitude of 16 3/4 degrees.

(Continued)

Columbus Describes His First Voyage, 1493

In this famous letter to Raphael Sanchez, treasurer to his patrons, Ferdinand and Isabella, Columbus recounts his initial journey to the Bahamas, Cuba, and Hispaniola (today Haiti and the Dominican Republic), and tells of his achievements. This passage reflects the first contact between Native Americans and Europeans; already the themes of trade, subjugation, gold, and conversion all emerge in Columbus's own words.

Indians would give whatever the seller required; ...Thus they bartered, like idiots, cotton and gold for fragments of bows, glasses, bottles, and jars; which I forbad as being unjust, and myself gave them many beautiful and acceptable articles which I had brought with me, taking nothing from them in return; I did this in order that I might the more easily conciliate them, that they might be led to become Christians, and be inclined to entertain a regard for the King and Queen, our Princes and all Spaniards, and that I might induce them to take an interest in seeking out, and collecting, and delivering to us such things as they possessed in abundance, but which we greatly needed. They practise no kind of idolatry, but have a firm belief that all strength and power, and indeed all good things, are in heaven, and that I had descended from thence with these ships and sailors, and under this impression was I received after they had thrown aside their fears. Nor are they slow or stupid, but of very clear understanding; and those men who have crossed to the neighbouring islands give an admirable description of everything they observed; but they never saw any people clothed, nor any ships like ours. On my arrival at that sea, I had taken some Indians by force from the first island that I came to, in order that they might learn our language, and communicate to us what they know respecting the country; which plan succeeded excellently, and was a great advantage to us, for in a short time, either by gestures and signs, or by words, we were enabled to understand each other. These men are still travelling with me, and although they have been with us now a long time, they continue to entertain the idea that I have descended from heaven.

Source: Christopher Columbus, *Four Voyages to the New World.* Translated by R. H. Major (New York: Corinth Books, 1961), 8–9.

difficulty of the venture.) But after the Portuguese and French monarchs rejected his proposal, Columbus found royal patronage with Isabella of Castile and Ferdinand of Aragon.

In August 1492, equipped with a modest fleet of three ships and about ninety men, Columbus set sail across the Atlantic. His contract stipulated that he would claim Castilian sovereignty over any new land and inhabitants and share any profits with the crown. Reaching what is today the Bahamas on October 12, Columbus mistook the islands to be part of the East Indies, not far from Japan and "the lands of the Great Khan." As the Castilians explored the Caribbean islands, they encountered communities of peaceful Indians, the Arawaks, who were awed by the Europeans' military technology, not to mention their appearance. Exchanging gifts of beads and broken glass for Arawak gold—an exchange that convinced Columbus of the trusting nature of the Indians—the crew established peaceful relationships with many communities. Yet in spite of many positive entries in the ship's log referring to Columbus's personal goodwill toward the Indians, the Europeans' objectives were clear: find gold, subjugate the Indians, and propagate Christianity. (See "Columbus Describes His First Voyage," above.)

Excited by the prospect of easy riches, many flocked to join Columbus's second voyage. When Columbus departed Cádiz in September 1493, he commanded seventeen ships that carried between 1,200 and 1,500 men, many believing that all they had to do was "to load the gold into the ships." Failing to find the imaginary gold mines and spices, however, the colonial enterprise quickly switched its focus to finding slaves. Columbus and his crew first enslaved the Caribs, enemies of the Arawaks; in 1494, Columbus proposed a regular slave trade based in Hispaniola. The Spaniards exported enslaved Indians to Spain, and slave traders sold them in Seville. Soon the Spaniards began importing sugarcane from Madeira, forcing large numbers of Indians to work on plantations to produce enough sugar for export to Europe. Columbus himself was edged out of this new enterprise. When the Spanish monarchs realized the vast potential for material gain that lay in their new dominions, they asserted direct royal authority by sending officials and priests to the Americas, which were named after the Italian Amerigo Vespucci, who led a voyage across the Atlantic in 1499–1502.

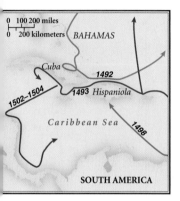

Columbus in the Caribbean

Columbus's place in history embodies the fundamental transformations of his age. A Genoese in the service of Portuguese and Spanish employers, Columbus had a career illustrating the changing balance between the Mediterranean and the Atlantic. As the fifteenth-century Ottomans drove Genoese merchants out of the eastern Mediterranean, the Genoese turned to the Iberian peninsula. Columbus was one of many such adventurers who served the Spanish and Portuguese crowns.

A New Era in Slavery

The European voyages of discovery initiated a new era in slavery, both in expanding the economic scale of slave labor and in attaching race and color to servitude. Slavery had existed since antiquity. During the Renaissance, slavery was practiced in many

diverse forms. Nearly all slaves arrived as strangers in the Mediterranean ports of Barcelona, Marseille, Venice, and Genoa. Some were captured in war or by piracy; others—Africans—were sold by other Africans and Bedouin traders to Christian buyers; in western Asia, parents sold their children into servitude out of poverty; and many in the Balkans became slaves when their land was devastated by Ottoman invasions. Slaves were Greek, Slav, European, African, and Turk. Many served as domestic slaves in the leading European cities of the Mediterranean. Others sweated as galley slaves in Ottoman and Christian fleets. Still others worked as agricultural laborers on Mediterranean islands. In the Ottoman army, slaves even formed an important elite contingent.

The Portuguese maritime voyages changed this picture. From the fifteenth century, Africans increasingly filled the ranks of slaves. Exploiting warfare in West Africa, the Portuguese traded in gold and "pieces," as African slaves were called, a practice condemned at home by some conscientious clergy. One, Manoel Severim de Faria, observed that "one cannot yet see any good effect resulting from so much butchery; for this is not the way in which commerce can flourish and the preaching of the gospel progress." Critical voices, however, could not deny the enormous profits that the slave trade brought to Portugal. Most slaves toiled in the sugar plantations of the Portuguese Atlantic islands and in Brazil. A fortunate few labored as domestic servants in Portugal, where African freedmen and slaves, some 35,000 in the early sixteenth century, constituted almost 3 percent of the population, a percentage that was much higher than in other European countries. In the Americas, slavery would truly flourish as an institution of exploitation.

Europeans in the New World

In 1500, on the eve of European invasion, the native peoples of the Americas were divided into many societies, both sedentary and nomadic. Among the settled peoples, the largest political and social organizations centered in the Mexican and Peruvian highlands. The

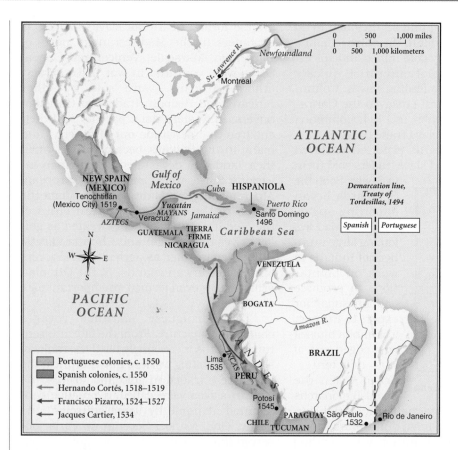

MAP 14.5 European Explorations in the Americas in the Sixteenth Century
While Spanish and Portuguese explorers claimed Central and South America for the
Iberian crowns, there were relatively few voyages to North America. The discovery of
precious metals fueled the explorations and settlements of Central and South America,
establishing the foundations of European colonial empires in the New World.

Aztecs and the Incas ruled over subjugated
Indian populations in their respective empires. With an elaborate religious culture
and a rigid social and political hierarchy,
the Aztecs and Incas based their civilizations in large urban capitals.

The Spanish explorers organized their
expeditions to the mainland from a base in
the Caribbean (Map 14.5). Two prominent
leaders, Hernán Cortés (1485–1547) and
Francisco Pizarro (c. 1475–1541), gathered
men and arms and set off in search of gold.
Catholic priests accompanied the fortune
hunters to bring Christianity to allegedly
uncivilized peoples and thus to justify brutal
conquests. His small band swelled by peoples who had been subjugated by the
Aztecs, Cortés captured the Aztec capital,
Tenochtitlán, in 1519. Two years later

Mexico, then named New Spain, was added
to Charles V's empire. To the south, Pizarro
conquered the Andean highlands, exploiting a civil war between rival Incan kings.

By the mid-sixteenth century the Spanish empire, built on greed and justified by its
self-proclaimed Catholic mission, stretched
unbroken from Mexico to Chile. In addition
to the Aztecs and Incas, the Spaniards also
subdued the Mayas on the Yucatán peninsula, a people with a sophisticated knowledge
of cosmology and arithmetic. The gold and
silver mines in Mexico proved a treasure
trove for the Spanish crown, but the real
prize was the discovery of vast silver deposits
in Potosí (today in Bolivia).

Not to be outdone by the Spaniards,
other European powers joined the scramble
for gold in the New World. In North America,

the French went in search of a "northwest passage" to China. By 1504, French fishermen had appeared in Newfoundland. Thirty years later Jacques Cartier led three voyages that explored the St. Lawrence River as far as Montreal. An early attempt in 1541 to settle Canada failed because of the harsh winter and Indian hostility, and John Cabot's 1497 voyage to find a northern route to Asia also failed. More permanent settlements in Canada and the present-day United States would succeed only in the seventeenth century.

> **Review:** What European countries led the way in maritime expansion and what were their motives?

Conclusion

During the Renaissance, Western civilization expanded in several important aspects: in the intellectual horizons of Europeans through the rediscovery of classical civilization and a renewed appreciation of human potential and achievement; in the greater centralization and institutionalization of expanded power of the state; and, finally, in the widened geographic horizons of an age of maritime exploration. Above all, the Renaissance was one of the most brilliant periods in artistic activity, one that glorified both God and humanity. A new spirit of confidence spurred Renaissance artists to develop a new appreciation for the

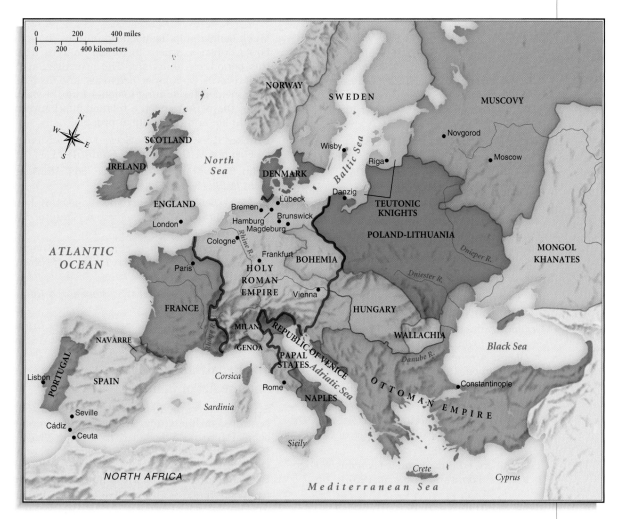

MAPPING THE WEST Renaissance Europe, c. 1500
By 1500, the shape of early modern Europe was largely consolidated and would remain stable until the eighteenth century. The only exception was the disappearance of an independent Hungarian kingdom after 1529.

human body and a new visual perspective in art and to apply mathematics and science to architecture, music, and artistic composition.

Highlighting the intensity of cultural production was the competition between burgeoning states and between Christian Europe and the Muslim Ottoman Empire. That competition fostered an expansion of the frontiers of Europe first to Africa and then across the Atlantic Ocean to the Americas. While centered in Italy, the Renaissance spread throughout Europe—in fact, historians view it as the first global movement in history—eventually shifting the center of European civilization from the Mediterranean to the Atlantic seaboard. But while Europeans of the Renaissance recovered from the deprivations of the late Middle Ages, they would soon enter yet another period of turmoil, one brought about not by demographic and economic collapse but by a profound crisis of conscience that the brilliance of Renaissance civilization had tended to obscure.

Suggested References

Widening Intellectual Horizons

In addition to the study of great artists and writers, recent scholarship has turned its attention to the "consumption" of cultural goods. Its focus has been on issues of education, art markets, and the different habits of reading and seeing in the past.

Burke, Peter. *The Italian Renaissance: Culture and Society in Italy.* 1986.

Eisenstein, Elizabeth. *The Printing Revolution in Early Modern Europe.* 1993.

Grafton, Anthony, and Lisa Jardine. *From Humanism to the Humanities: Education and the Liberal Arts in Fifteenth and Sixteenth Century Europe.* 1986.

Hankins, James, ed. *Renaissance Civic Humanism: Reappraisals and Reflections.* 2000.

Martin, Henri-Jean, and Lucien Febvre. *The Coming of the Book: The Impact of Printing, 1450–1800.* 1976.

Rabil, Albert, ed. *Renaissance Humanism: Foundations, Forms, and Legacy.* 1997.

Revolution in the Arts

Scholarship in Renaissance art history advances along two time-honored axes of research: studies of individual artists that focus heavily on Italy, and interpretations of art history within the larger cultural history of the period, with themes such as cross-cultural comparisons, patronage, and markets.

Baxandall, Michael. *Painting and Experience in Fifteenth Century Italy: A Primer in the Social History of Pictorial Style.* 1972.

Goffen, Rona. *Renaissance Rivals: Michelangelo, Leonardo, Raphael.* 2002.

Jardine, Lisa, and Jerry Brotton. *Global Interests: Renaissance Art between East and West.* 2000.

Mulryne, J. R., and Elizabeth Goldring, eds. *Court Festivals of the European Renaissance: Art, Politics, and Performance.* 2002.

The Intersection of Private and Public Lives

Much scholarship has focused on Italy and the Low Countries, where historical sources from this period are abundant. The investigation of legal records, population censuses, and tax rolls have yielded fascinating insights into the daily life of the period and the relationship between private life and the political process.

Brucker, Gene A., ed. *The Society of Renaissance Florence: A Documentary Study.* 1971.

Dean, Trevor, and K. J. P. Lowe, eds. *Marriage in Italy, 1300–1650.* 1998.

Herlihy, David, and Christiane Klapisch-Zuber. *Tuscans and Their Families: A Study of the Florentine Catasto of 1427.* 1978.

Pitkin, Hanna Fenichel. *Fortune Is a Woman: Gender and Politics in the Thought of Niccolò Machiavelli.* 1984.

Po-chia Hsia, R. *Trent 1475: Stories of a Ritual Murder Trial.* 1992.

Ruggiero, Guido. *Boundaries of Eros: Sex Crime and Sexuality in Renaissance Venice.* 1985.

The Renaissance State and the Art of Politics

Scholarship on the Renaissance state had concentrated on the study of Florence, but recent scholarship has broadened to include Venice, Milan, and smaller Italian city-states as well. Outside of Italian history, research on the Burgundian state gives a valuable comparative perspective.

Blockmans, Wim. *A History of Power in Europe: Peoples, Markets, States.* 1997.

Goffman, Daniel. *The Ottoman Empire and Early Modern Europe.* 2001.

Imber, Colin. *The Ottoman Empire 1300–1650: The Structure of Power.* 2002.

Kollmann, Nancy. *Kinship and Politics: The Making of the Muscovite Political System, 1345–1547.* 1987.

Liss, Peggy K. *Isabel the Queen: Life and Times.* 1992.

Lowe, Kate J. P., ed. *Cultural Links between Portugal and Italy in the Renaissance.* 2000.

Martines, Lauro. *Power and Imagination: City-States in Renaissance Italy.* 1979.

Prevenier, Walter, and Wim Blockmans. *The Burgundian Netherlands.* 1986.

On the Threshold of World History: Widening Geographic Horizons

The recent celebrations of the overseas voyages of Christopher Columbus and Vasco da Gama have inspired studies with new perspectives. The traditional view of "Europe discovers the world" has been replaced by a more nuanced and complex picture that takes in non-European views and uses Asian, African, and Mesoamerican sources.

Boxer, Charles R. *Four Centuries of Portuguese Expansion, 1415–1826.* 1969.

*Fuson, Robert H., ed. *The Log of Christopher Columbus.* 1987.

Russell-Wood, A. J. R. *A World on the Move: The Portuguese in Africa, Asia, and America, 1415–1808.* 1992.

Subrahmanyam, Sanjay. *The Career and Legend of Vasco da Gama.* 1997.

———

*Primary source.

CHAPTER REVIEW

IMPORTANT EVENTS

1415	Portugal captures Ceuta, establishing foothold in Africa
1434	Medici establish influence in Florence
1438	Pragmatic Sanction of Bourges allows French kings to control church revenue and appoint bishops
1440s	Printing press invented
1450	General Francesco Sforza seizes Milan
c. 1450–1500	Height of Florentine Renaissance
1453	Ottoman conquest of Constantinople; end of Byzantine Empire
1454	Treaty of Lodi balances power among major Italian states
1460–1485	Wars of the Roses; Tudor dynasty ascendant
1462	Ivan III becomes tsar
1471–1484	Pope Sixtus IV; Renaissance in Rome
1474–1516	Spain unified under Isabella and Ferdinand
1477	Death of Charles the Bold begins decline of Burgundy
1478	Inquisition carried out in Spain
1485	End of civil wars in England
1492	Spain conquers Granada, expels Jews; Columbus sails for Americas
1494	France invades Italy, beginning of more than fifty years of Habsburg-Valois conflict
1519	Spain conquers Mexico
1531	Fall of Florentine Republic

KEY TERMS

auto da fé (528)

conversos (528)

duchy (523)

Gallicanism (528)

humanism (507)

Renaissance (505)

tsar (530)

REVIEW QUESTIONS

1. How did humanism and the printing press influence learning in the Renaissance?

2. How did the shift from artisan to artist, a new naturalistic style, and the use of perspective in art reflect and influence a Renaissance mentality?

3. In what ways did the Renaissance state shape the private sphere?

4. How did Renaissance princes increase their power at the expense of the nobility and their subjects?

5. What European countries led the way in maritime expansion and what were their motives?

MAKING CONNECTIONS

1. Where were the centers of Renaissance creativity and why did this movement arise in those places?

2. How did Renaissance and medieval culture and society differ? How were they similar?

3. Compare the relative strengths of economic and religious motives in European voyages of exploration.

FOR FURTHER EXPLORATION

To assess your mastery of the material in this chapter, see the Online Study Guide at **bedfordstmartins.com/hunt**.

To read additional primary-source material from this period, see Chapter 14 in *Sources of The Making of the West*, Second Edition.

H...
16...
to...
he...
W...
by...
th...
an... bəyət, god murder. Homeyer...
bə...ved to set her but after he had told...
sh...ed to behead his head, reducing the request...
to... versions inspired by this story, Helle bri...
a...ed to terminate the commander of the besieging...
h... to the enemy promising to reveal to him how to...
th... city without further fighting. Judar unable, a delic...
Helle and betrayed her. She was beheaded.

Salic Helle and the other martyrs in Münster were par...
known as Anabaptists, whose members believed th...
ni...ty of sinful amid a hopeless, sinful world. The Anaba...
efforts to form a separate holy community free at the worst...
o... social order, and subject to intense persecution from bo...
io...l and religious authorities. Anabaptism became one dire...
o... the Protestant Reformation, which had been launched by th...
German reformer Martin Luther in 1517. As a widespread dis...
ing movement to reform the Catholic church from within grew m...
to...nger. When Luther a...
o... the Catholic church to re...
As the breach widened, Luth...

Münster Celebs, Italia

Erasmus Writes to Martin Luther (1519)

Prior to Luther's formal excommunication by Pope Leo X in January 1521, it was still possible for the Christian humanist Erasmus to see the fierce critic of Rome as a kindred spirit. Erasmus wrote from Leuven in the Spanish Netherlands (today in Belgium), the site of a university whose theologians were among the first to condemn the opinions of Luther.

Leuven, May 30, 1519
Greetings, dearest brother in Christ. Your letter was most delightful, revealing as it did the clarity of your intellect and breathing as it did a Christian spirit. No words of mine could make clear the tragedies which your books are causing here. These people cannot even rid their minds of the completely false supposition that your reflections were written with my assistance, and that I am the standard-bearer of your party, as they call it. They believe they have a handle to destroy humane letters, which they mortally detest, as being likely to infringe upon the supremacy of theology, which to them is far more important than Christ. They also think they can destroy me, whom they regard as having contributed some impetus to the revival of interest in studies. The whole business is carried in with ranting, impertinence, tricks, insults, and deceit. If I had not seen it with my own eyes, or rather felt it, I would never have believed anyone who told me that theologians could rave in such fashion. You might say it is a plague sent by fate. And yet this poison, which originated among a few, has spread among many others, so that a great part of this academy may be said to be infected with the contagion of the common disease.

I have sworn that you are completely unknown to me, that I have not even read your books; hence that I neither approve nor disapprove. But I did warn them not to heap such public opprobrium on your books before they had read them. I added that this was of particular importance for them, whose judgment ought to be carefully weighed. They should, I said, consider whether it was right to vilify before the common herd matters which should rather be refuted in published books and discussed among learned men, especially when the life of the author is unanimously praised. It was all to no purpose. They still rave with their hostile, indeed slanderous discussions. How often we have met to agree on peace! How often they have started new trouble as the result of baseless suspicions! And these people claim to be theologians.

Source: W. T. H. Jackson, ed., *Essential Works of Erasmus* (New York: Bantam, 1965), 317.

Huldrych Zwingli and the Swiss Confederation

While Luther provided the religious leadership for northern Germany, the south came under the strong influence of a reform movement that had emerged in Switzerland. In the late fifteenth and early sixteenth centuries, Switzerland's chief source of income was the export of soldiers; hardy Swiss peasants fought as mercenaries in papal, French, and imperial armies, earning respect as fierce pikemen. Many young Swiss men died in battle, and many others returned maimed for life. In 1520, the chief preacher of the Swiss city of Zurich, Huldrych Zwingli (1484–1531), criticized his superior, Cardinal Matthew Schinner, for sending the country's young men off to serve in papal armies.

The son of a Swiss village leader, Zwingli became a reformer independent of Martin Luther. After completing his university studies, Zwingli was ordained a priest and served as an army chaplain for several years. Deeply influenced by Erasmus, whom he met in 1515, Zwingli adopted the Dutch humanist's vision of social renewal through education. In 1520, he openly declared himself a reformer and attacked not only corruption among the ecclesiastical (church) hierarchy but also the church rituals of fasting and clerical celibacy.

Under Zwingli's leadership, Zurich served as the center for the Swiss reform movement.

Guided by his vision of a theocratic (church-directed) society that would unite religion, politics, and morality, Zwingli refused to draw any distinction between the ideal citizen and the perfect Christian—an idea radically different from Luther's—and rooted out internal dissent. Theologically, Luther insisted that Christ was both truly and symbolically present in the Eucharist, the central Christian sacrament; Zwingli, however, viewed the Eucharist as simply a ceremony symbolizing Christ's union with believers.

In 1529, troubled by these differences and other disagreements, Evangelical princes and magistrates assembled the major reformers in the Colloquy of Marburg, in central Germany. After several days of intense discussions, the North German and Swiss reformers managed to resolve many differences over doctrine, but Luther and Zwingli failed to agree on the meaning of the Eucharist. Thus, the German and Swiss reform movements continued on separate paths. The issue of the Eucharist would later divide Lutherans and Calvinists as well.

John Calvin and Christian Discipline

Under the leadership of John Calvin (1509–1564), another wave of reform pounded at the gates of Rome. Born in Picardy, in northern France, to the secretary of the bishop of Noyon, Calvin studied in Paris and Orléans, where he took a law degree. A gifted intellectual who was attracted to humanism, Calvin could have enjoyed a brilliant career in government or the church. Instead, experiencing a crisis of faith, like Luther, he sought salvation through intense theological study.

Calvin read the works of the leading French humanists who sought to reform the church from within and gradually came to question fundamental Catholic teachings. Unlike Luther, who described his life in vivid detail, Calvin generally revealed nothing about the personal struggle that brought him to this point.

During Calvin's long religious development, the Reformation steadily gained adherents in France. On Sunday, October 18, 1534, Parisians found church doors posted with ribald broadsheets denouncing the Catholic Mass. Smuggled into France from the Protestant and French-speaking parts of Switzerland, the broadsheets unleashed a wave of royal repression in the capital. This so-called Affair of the Placards provoked a national crackdown on church dissenters, who had until then been left alone. Hundreds of French Protestants were arrested, scores were executed, and many more, including Calvin, fled abroad.

On his way to Strasbourg, Germany, a haven for religious dissidents, Calvin detoured to Geneva—the French-speaking city-republic where he would find his life's work. Geneva had renounced allegiance to its bishop, and the local reformer Guillaume Farel threatened Calvin with God's curse if he did not stay and labor there. This frightening appeal succeeded. Under Calvin and Farel, the reform party became embroiled in a political struggle between two civic factions: their supporters, many of whom were

THE PROGRESS OF THE REFORMATION

1517	Martin Luther disseminates ninety-five theses attacking the sale of indulgences and other church practices
1520	Reformer Huldrych Zwingli breaks with Rome
1525	Radical reformer Thomas Müntzer killed in Peasants' War
1529	Lutheran German princes protest the condemnation of religious reform by Charles V; genesis of the term *Protestants*
1534	The English Parliament establishes King Henry VIII as head of the Anglican church, severing ties to Rome
1534–1535	Anabaptists control the city of Münster, Germany, in a failed experiment to create a holy community
1541	John Calvin establishes himself permanently in Geneva, making that city a model of Christian reform and discipline

Calvin's World in the Mid-Sixteenth Century

MAP 15.1 scale: 0 200 400 miles / 0 200 400 kilometers

Map labels: FINLAND, NORWAY, SWEDEN, ESTONIA, LIVONIA, COURLAND, Baltic Sea, DENMARK, SCOTLAND, North Sea, IRELAND, TEUTONIC KNIGHTS, Elbe R., Brandenburg, ENGLAND, Wittenberg, Saxony, POLAND, Canterbury, Cologne, English Channel, Rhine R., Frankfurt, Bohemia, Worms, Nuremberg, Paris, Strasbourg, Vienna, HUNGARY, Danube R., Münster, SWISS CONFED., Loire R., FRANCE, Geneva, Milan, OTTOMAN EMPIRE, Po R., Navarre, PAPAL STATES, Adriatic Sea, Castile, Catalonia, Corsica, Rome, NAPLES, SPAIN, Tyrrhenian Sea, Sardinia, Mediterranean Sea, Sicily

Legend:
- Reformed faith dominant, c. 1560
- Reformed faith growing, c. 1560
- Considerable local reformed faith, c. 1560
- Calvinist influenced
- Some penetration of reform, c. 1560
- Boundary of the Holy Roman Empire

MAP 15.1 Spread of Protestantism in the Sixteenth Century
The Protestant Reformation divided northern and southern Europe. From its heartland in the Holy Roman Empire, the Reformation won the allegiance of Scandinavia, England, and Scotland and made considerable inroads in the Low Countries, France, eastern Europe, Switzerland, and even parts of northern Italy. While the Mediterranean countries remained loyal to Rome, a vast zone of confessional divisions and strife characterized the religious landscape of Europe from Britain in the west to Poland in the east.

Geneva, but Calvin returned in 1541, after his supporters triumphed. He remained there until his death in 1564.

Under Calvin's inspiration and moral authority, Geneva became a disciplined Christian republic, modeled after the ideas in his *The Institutes of the Christian Religion*, first published in 1536. No reformer prior to Calvin had expounded on the doctrines, organization, history, and practices of Christianity in such a systematic, logical, and coherent manner. Calvin followed Luther's doctrine of salvation to its ultimate logical conclusion: if God is almighty and humans cannot earn their salvation by good works, then no Christian can be certain of salvation. Developing the doctrine of **predestination**, Calvin argued that God had ordained every man, woman, and child to salvation or damnation—even before the creation of the world. Thus, the "elect," in Calvinist theology, were known only to God. In practice, however, Calvinist doctrine demanded rigorous discipline: the knowledge that only the elect, a small group, would be saved should guide the actions of the godly in an uncertain world. Fusing church and society into what followers named the Reformed church, Geneva became a single moral community, as reflected in its very low rate of extramarital births in the sixteenth century. The community was praised by advocates as less troubled by crime and sin than other cities and attacked by critics as despotic.

This charge of despotism came from Calvin's treatment of dissenters. Like Zwingli, he did not tolerate them. While passing through

French refugees, and the opposition, represented by the leading old Genevan families, who resented the strict moral regulations of the new, foreign-born clerical regime. A political setback in 1538 drove Calvin and Farel from

Geneva in 1553, the Spanish physician Michael Servetus was arrested because he had published books attacking Calvin and questioning the doctrine of the Trinity, the belief that God exists in three persons—the Father, Son (Christ), and Holy Spirit. Upon Calvin's advice, Servetus was executed by the authorities. (Calvin did not approve, however, of the method of execution: burning at the stake.) Although Calvin came under criticism for Servetus's death, Geneva became the new center of the Reformation, the place where pastors trained for mission work and from which books expressing Calvinist doctrines were exported. The Calvinist movement spread to France, the Netherlands, England, Scotland, Germany, Poland, Hungary, and eventually New England, becoming the established form of the Reformation in many of these countries (Map 15.1 on page 558).

> **Review:** In what ways did Luther, Zwingli, and Calvin challenge the Roman Catholic church?

❖ Reshaping Society through Religion

The religious upheavals of the sixteenth century affected European society in two major ways. First, those who challenged the social order were crushed by the political and religious authorities. Such was the fate of the Anabaptists and peasant rebels in the Holy Roman Empire, who tried in vain to establish new, biblically inspired social orders. As a result of these radical movements, both Protestant and Catholic authorities became alarmed by the subversive potential of religious reforms. They viewed religious reforms, instead, as ways of instilling greater discipline in Christian worship and in social behavior. Hence, the second and most lasting impact of the Reformation was in the realm of church discipline and piety. Protestant reformers and their supporters worked to create a God-fearing, pious, and disciplined Christian.

Challenging the Social Order

The freedom of the Christian proclaimed by Luther resonated with those who suffered oppression, and the corruption of sin decried by the reformers inspired others to seek Christian perfection. During the early 1520s, two movements emerged in the Holy Roman Empire to challenge the foundations of religious and political order. While peasants and urban artisans staged massive revolts against church and nobility, the Anabaptists attempted to re-create the perfect Christian community on earth.

The Peasants' War of 1525.   Between 1520 and 1525, many city governments, often under intense popular pressure and sometimes in sympathy with the Evangelicals, allowed the reform movement to sweep away church authority. Local officials appointed new clerics who were committed to reforming Christian doctrine and ritual. The turning point came in 1525, when the crisis of church authority exploded in the Peasants' War, a massive rural uprising that threatened the entire social order (Map 15.2 on the next page).

German Peasants' War of 1525
This colored woodcut depicts peasants attacking the pope, a monk, and a nobleman during the massive rural uprisings against the church that took place in southern and central Germany in 1525. Even the heavens show signs of trouble: a comet and clouds in the shape of a goat signify bloodshed and sin. *The Granger Collection, NY.*

The church was the largest landowner in the Holy Roman Empire: about one-seventh of the empire's territory consisted of ecclesiastical principalities in which bishops and abbots exercised both secular and churchly power. Luther's anticlerical message struck home with peasants who were paying taxes to both their lord and the church. In the spring of 1525, many peasants in southern and central Germany rose in rebellion, sometimes inspired by wandering preachers. Some urban workers and artisans joined the peasant bands, which plundered monasteries, refused to pay church taxes, and demanded village autonomy, the abolition of serfdom, and the right to appoint their own pastors. The more radical rebels called for the destruction of the entire ruling class. In Thuringia, the rebels were led by an ex-priest, Thomas Müntzer (1468?–1525), who promised to chastise the wicked and thus clear the way for the Last Judgment.

The Peasants' War split the reform movement. Princes and city authorities turned against the rebels. The Catholic and evangelical princes of Thuringia joined hands to crush Müntzer and his supporters. All over the empire, princes defeated peasant armies, hunted down their leaders, and uprooted all opposition. By the end of the year, more than 100,000 rebels had been killed and many others maimed, imprisoned, or exiled. Luther had tried to mediate the conflict initially, criticizing the princes for their brutality toward the peasants but also warning the rebels against mixing religion and social protest. Luther believed that rulers were ordained by God and thus must be obeyed even if they were tyrants. The Kingdom of God belonged not to this world but to the next, he insisted. Luther considered Müntzer's mixing of religion and politics the greatest danger to the Reformation, nothing less than "the devil's work." When the rebels ignored Luther's appeal and continued to follow more radical preachers, Luther called on the princes to restore the divinely ordained social order and slaughter the rebels. Fundamentally conservative in its political philosophy, the Lutheran church would henceforth depend on established political authority for its protection.

Emerging as the champions of an orderly religious reform, many German princes eventually confronted Emperor Charles V, who supported Rome. In 1529, Charles declared the Roman Catholic faith the empire's only legitimate religion.

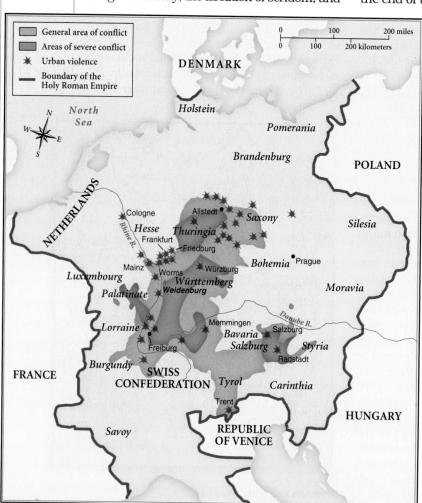

MAP 15.2 The Peasants' War of 1525

The centers of uprisings clustered in southern and central Germany, where the density of cities encouraged the spread of discontent and allowed for alliances between urban masses and rural rebels. The proximity to the Swiss Confederation, a stronghold of the Reformation movement, also inspired antiestablishment uprisings.

Proclaiming their allegiance to the reform cause, the Lutheran German princes protested, and thus came to be called Protestants.

Anabaptists. While Zwingli was challenging the Roman Catholic church, some laypeople in Zurich were secretly pursuing their own path to reform. Taking their cue from the New Testament's descriptions of the first Christian community, these men and women believed that true faith was based on reason and free will. How could a baby knowingly choose Christ? Only adults could believe and accept baptism; hence the invalidity of Catholic infant baptism and the need for a new rite. These people came to be called **Anabaptists**—those who were rebaptized. As pacifists, they rejected the authority of courts and considered themselves a community of true Christians unblemished by sin. The Anabaptist movement drew its leadership primarily from the artisan class and its members from the middle and lower classes— men and women attracted by a simple message of peace and salvation.

Persecution of the Anabaptists
A large number of the more than one thousand martyrs killed for their faith in the Low Countries were Anabaptists. Until persecutions stopped in the 1580s, the authorities executed hundreds of Anabaptist men by beheading and women by drowning. This drawing is from the 1685 Dutch Anabaptist martyrology (a collection of books dedicated to the study and remembrance of martyrs) titled *The Bloody Theater,* compiled by Tilleman van Bracht. *Beinecke Rare Book and Manuscript Library, Yale University.*

Zwingli immediately attacked the Anabaptists for their refusal to bear arms and swear oaths of allegiance, sensing accurately that they were repudiating his theocratic order. When persuasion failed to convince the Anabaptists, Zwingli urged Zurich magistrates to impose the death sentence. Thus, the Reformation's first martyrs of conscience were victims of its evangelical reformers.

Nevertheless, Anabaptism spread quickly from Zurich to many cities in southern Germany, despite the Holy Roman Empire's general condemnation of the movement in 1529. In 1534, one Anabaptist group, believing that the end of the world was imminent, seized control of the northwestern city of Münster. Proclaiming themselves a community of saints and imitating the ancient Israelites, the Münster Anabaptists abolished private property in imitation of the early Christian church and dissolved traditional marriages, allowing men, like Old Testament patriarchs, to have multiple wives, to the consternation of many women. Besieged by a combined Protestant and Catholic army,

the city fell in June 1535. The leaders died in battle or were horribly executed. The Anabaptist movement in northwestern Europe nonetheless survived under the determined pacifist leadership of the Dutch reformer Menno Simons (1469–1561), whose followers were eventually named Mennonites. Defeated in their bid for revolution, the common people became the subject of religious reforms and discipline. The Reformation strengthened rather than loosened social control in a vast effort to instill religious conformity and moral behavior orchestrated by secular rulers and a new clerical elite.

New Forms of Discipline

The emergence of a new urban, middle-class culture was one result of the religious cataclysms of the sixteenth century. Appearing first in Protestant Europe, it included an emphasis on literacy, a new educational agenda, and a new work ethic, all of which came together as a watershed in European civilization. Other changes, although sparked by the Protestant

The Court

At the center of this politics of dynasty and religion was the court, the focus of princely power and intrigue. European princes used the institution of the royal court to bind their nobility and impress their subjects. Briefly defined, the court was the prince's household. Around the ruling family, however, coalesced a small community of household servants, noble attendants, councilors, officials, artists, and soldiers. During the sixteenth century, this political elite developed a sophisticated culture.

The French court of Francis I (r. 1515–1547) became the largest in Europe after the demise of the Burgundian dukes. In addition to the prince's household, the royal family set up households for other members: the queen and the queen mother each had her own staff of maids and chefs, as did each of the royal children. The royal household employed officials to handle finances, guard duty, clothing, and food; in addition, physicians, librarians, musicians, dwarfs, animal trainers, and a multitude of hangers-on bloated its size. By 1535, the French court numbered 1,622 members.

Although Francis built many palaces (the most magnificent at Fontainebleau), the French court was often on the move. It took no fewer than eighteen thousand horses to transport the people, furniture, and documents—not to mention the dogs and falcons for the royal hunt. Hunting, in fact, was a passion for the men at court; it represented a form of mock combat, essential in the training of a military elite. Francis himself loved war games and almost lost his own life when, storming a house during one mock battle, he was hit on the head by a burning log.

Two writers, both Italian, were the most eloquent spokesmen for the culture of courtesy, or proper court behavior: Ludovico Ariosto (1474–1533), in service at the Este court in Ferrara, and Baldassare Castiglione (1478–1529), a servant of the duke of Urbino and the pope. Considered one of the greatest Renaissance poets, Ariosto composed a long epic poem, *Orlando Furioso*, which represented court culture as the highest synthesis of Christian and classical values. Set against the historic struggle between Charlemagne and the Arabs, the poem tells the love story of Bradamante and Ruggiero. Before the separated lovers are reunited, the reader meets scores of characters who have hundreds of adventures. Modeled after Greek and Roman epics, *Orlando Furioso* also followed the tradition of the medieval chivalric romance. The tales of combat, valor, love, and magic captivated the court's noble readers, who, through this highly idealized fantasy, enjoyed a glorified view of their own world.

Equally popular was *The Courtier* by the suave diplomat Castiglione. Like Ariosto, Castiglione tried to represent court culture as a synthesis of military virtues and literary and artistic cultivation. Speaking in eloquent dialogues, Castiglione's characters debate the qualities of an ideal courtier. The true courtier, Castiglione asserts, is a gentleman who speaks in a refined language and carries himself with nobility and dignity in the service of his prince and his lady. Clothing assumes a significant symbolism in *The Courtier*; in the words of one character, "I am not saying that clothes provide the basis for making hard and fast judgments about a man's character. . . . But I do maintain that a man's attire is also no small evidence for what kind of personality he has." All the formalities of court culture, however, could not mask the smoldering religious passions within, and the chivalry of Ariosto's *Orlando Furioso* had its real-life counterpart in the savage wars between Christianity and Islam in the sixteenth century.

Art and the Christian Knight

Through their patronage of artists, the Habsburg emperors and the Catholic popes created idealized self-images, representations of their era's hopes. The use of art for political glorification was nothing new, but below the surface of sixteenth-century art flowed an undercurrent of idealism. For all his political limitations, Emperor Maximilian I (r. 1493–1519), for example, was a visionary who dreamed of restoring Christian chivalry and even toyed with the idea of ruling as pope and emperor. He appointed the Nuremberg artist Albrecht Dürer (1471–1528) as court painter, to represent the Habsburg vision of universal Christian emperorship. Dürer's design for Maximilian's triumphal carriage in

1518 positioned the figures of Justice, Temperance, Prudence, and Fortitude at a level above the seated emperor, with other important allegorical figures—Reason, Nobility, and Power—also in attendance.

For many artists and humanists, such as Erasmus, Emperor Charles V embodied the ideal Christian knight. The Venetian painter Titian (1477–1576) captured the emperor's life on canvas four times (see the illustrations on this page). His 1532 portrait depicts a grand prince in his early thirties. Two portraits from 1548 and 1550 show him victorious over Protestants. Charles's favorite was the final portrait, *Gloria*, one of two Titians he took with him to his monastic retirement: it shows the kneeling emperor wrapped in a white death shroud joining the throng of the saved to worship the Trinity.

The Habsburg dynasty did not monopolize artistic self-glorification, however. The Florentine Michelangelo Buonarroti (1475–1564) matured his multiple talents in the service of the Medici family. After the overthrow of the Medici, Michelangelo became Pope Julius II's favorite artist, painting with furious energy the Sistine Chapel and working on a never-finished tomb and sculpture for the warrior-pope. Later Michelangelo was commissioned by Pope Paul III to design palaces in Rome; in 1547, he became the chief architect of St. Peter's Basilica. Michelangelo's work signified the transition from the Renaissance to the age of religious conflicts. His artistic talents served to glorify a papacy under siege, just as Titian lent his hand in defending the Habsburg cause against **infidels** (unbelievers) and heretics.

Titian, *Charles V at Mühlberg* and *Gloria*
The Venetian artist Titian was commissioned by Charles V to paint a series of portraits of the emperor at four stages of his career to show events in his long life for which he wished to be remembered. In the first painting, Titian captures the emperor's sense of victory at having finally crushed the German Protestant princes in battle in 1547. In the detail from *Gloria* (right), Titian vividly shows that all military glory and earthly power is doomed to fade away. Emperor Charles V, dressed in a white robe, turns to the Trinity in the heavens. Painted after his abdication in 1556, *Gloria* is a reminder to Charles of the transience of earthly glory. Compare these two very different images of Charles V. What impression does his attire in each convey? *Scala/Art Resource, NY/Institut Amatller d'Art Hispanic.*

Wars Among Habsburgs, Valois, and Ottomans

While the Reformation was taking hold in Germany, the great powers of Spain and France fought each other for the domination of Europe (Map 15.3). French claims over Italian territories provided the fuse for this conflict. The Italian Wars, started in 1494, escalated into a general conflict that involved most Christian monarchs and the Muslim Ottoman sultan as well. From 1494 to 1559 the Valois and Habsburg dynasties remained implacable enemies; only in 1559 did the French king acknowledge defeat and sign the Treaty of Cateau-Cambrésis◆ that established peace. This basic Franco-Spanish (Valois-Habsburg) struggle drew in many other belligerents, who fought on one side or the other for their own benefits. Some acted purely out of power considerations, such as England, first siding

◆**Cateau-Cambrésis:** ka TOH kahn bray ZEE

with France and then with Spain. Others fought for their independence, such as the papacy and the Italian states, who did not want any one power, particularly Spain, to dominate Italy. Still others chose sides for religious reasons, such as the Protestant princes in Germany, who exploited the Valois-Habsburg conflict to extract religious liberties from the emperor in 1555. Finally, the Ottoman Turks saw in this fight an opportunity to further their territorial expanse.

The Ottoman Empire reached its height of power under Sultan Suleiman I, known as Suleiman the Magnificent (r. 1520–1566). In 1526, a Turkish expedition destroyed the Hungarian army at Mohács (see the illustration on page 570). Three years later, the Ottoman army laid siege to Vienna; though unsuccessful, the siege sent shock waves throughout Christian Europe. In 1535, Charles V led a campaign to capture Tunis, the lair of North African pirates loyal to the Ottomans. Desperate to overcome Charles's

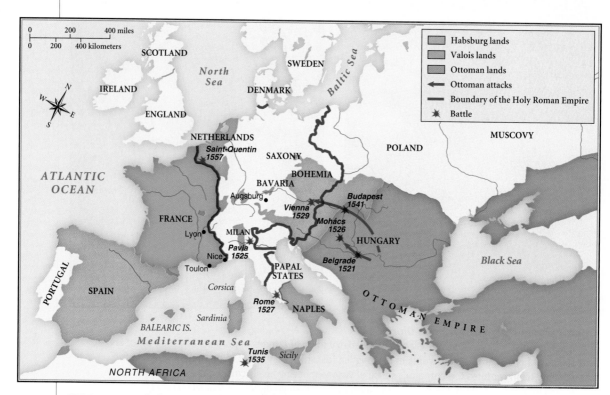

MAP 15.3 Habsburg-Valois-Ottoman Wars, 1494–1559

As the dominant European power, the Habsburg dynasty fought on two fronts: a religious war against the Islamic Ottoman Empire and a political war against the French Valois, who challenged Habsburg hegemony. The Mediterranean, the Balkans, and the Low Countries all became theaters of war.

superior forces, Francis I eagerly forged an alliance with the Turkish sultan. Coming to the aid of the French, the Turkish fleet besieged the imperial troops holding Nice, on the southern coast of France. Francis even ordered all inhabitants of nearby Toulon to vacate the town so that he could turn it into a Muslim colony for eight months, complete with a mosque and slave market.

Many Christians were scandalized that France would ally itself with the Turks to make war on another Christian king. This brief Franco-Turkish alliance, however, reflected the spirit of the times: the age-old idea of the Christian crusade against Islam was in competition with a new political strategy that saw religion as but one factor in power politics.

While the Mediterranean served as the theater of war between Habsburgs and Ottomans, most Habsburg-Valois battles were fought in Italy and the Low Countries. There were spectacular and bloody victories, but none led to a speedy and decisive end to the war. During the 1520s, the Habsburgs seemed triumphant. In 1525, the troops of Charles V crushed the French army at Pavia, Italy, counting among their captives the French king, Francis I. Treated with great honor by Charles, Francis was kept in Spain until he agreed to a treaty renouncing all claims to Italy. Furious at this humiliation, Francis repudiated the treaty the moment he reached France, reigniting the conflict. In 1527, Charles's troops captured Rome because the pope had allied with the French. Many of the imperial troops were German Protestant mercenaries, who pillaged Catholic churches and tortured the Catholic clergy. Protestants and Catholics alike interpreted the sack of Rome by imperial forces as a punishment of God; this disaster spurred the Catholic church to enact reforms.

The 1530s and 1540s saw more indecisive battles. Constantly distracted by the challenges of the Ottomans and the German Protestants, Charles V could not crush France

The Field of the Cloth of Gold
This painting by an unknown artist shows the meeting of Henry VIII of England and Francis I of France near Calais for the sealing of an Anglo-French alliance. Note the prominent figure of Henry on horseback among his entourage. The meeting was a scene of ritual display of power and pomp, with tents and canopies laid out over a vast area for the royal receptions, hence the name of the painting, *The Field of the Cloth of Gold*. *The Royal Collection © 2004 Her Majesty Queen Elizabeth II.*

The Battle at Mohács
This Ottoman painting shows the 1529 victory of the sultan's army over the Hungarians at Mohács. The battle resulted in the end of the Hungarian kingdom, which would be divided into three realms under Ottoman, Habsburg, and Transylvanian rule. Note the prominence of artillery and the Janissaries with muskets. The Ottomans commanded a vast army with modern equipment, a key to their military prowess in the sixteenth century. *Topkapi Palace Museum.*

in one swift blow. Years of conflict drained the treasuries of all monarchs because warfare was becoming more expensive.

The Finance and Technologies of War

The sixteenth century marked the beginning of superior Western military technology. All armies grew in size and their firepower became ever more deadly, increasing the cost of war. For example, heavier artillery pieces meant that the rectangular walls of medieval cities had to be transformed into fortresses

with jutting forts and gun emplacements. England had a war expenditure more than double its royal revenues in the 1540s. To pay these bills, the government devalued its coinage (the sixteenth-century equivalent of printing more paper money), causing prices to rise rapidly.

Other European powers fell into similar predicaments. Charles V boasted the largest army in Europe—but he also sank deeper into debt. Between 1520 and 1532, Charles borrowed 5.4 million ducats, primarily to pay his troops; from 1552 to 1556, his war loans soared to 9.6 million ducats. On his death in 1547, Francis I owed the bankers of Lyon almost 7 million French pounds—approximately the entire royal income for that year. The European powers literally fought themselves into bankruptcy. Taxation, the sale of offices, and outright confiscation failed to bring in enough money to satisfy the war machine. Both the Habsburg and the Valois kings looked to the leading bankers to finance their costly wars.

Foremost among these financiers was the Fugger bank, the largest such enterprise in sixteenth-century Europe. Based in the southern German imperial city of Augsburg, the Fugger family and their associates built an international financial empire that helped to make kings. The enterprise began with Jakob Fugger (1459–1525), who became personal banker to Charles V's grandfather Maximilian I. Constantly short of cash, Maximilian had granted the Fugger family numerous mining and minting concessions. The Fugger enterprise reaped handsome profits from its Habsburg connections. To pay for the service of providing and accepting bills of exchange, the Fuggers charged substantial fees. By the end of his life, Maximilian was so deeply in debt to Jakob Fugger that he had to pawn the royal jewels.

In 1519, Fugger assembled a consortium of German and Italian bankers to secure the election of Charles V as Holy Roman Emperor. For the next three decades, the alliance between Europe's largest international bank and its largest empire tightened. Between 1527 and 1547, the Fugger bank's assets grew from three million guldens (German currency) to over seven million; roughly 55 percent of the assets were from loans to the Habsburgs, with the Spanish branch taking the lion's share.

Charles barely stayed one step ahead of his creditors, and his successor in Spain gradually lost control of the Spanish state finances. To service debts, European monarchs sought revenues in war and tax increases. But paying for troops and crushing rebellions took more money and more loans. Debt forced Spain and France to sign the Treaty of Cateau-Cambrésis in 1559, thus ending more than sixty years of warfare, but the cycle of financial crises and warfare persisted until the late eighteenth century.

Divided Realms

Throughout Europe, rulers viewed religious divisions as a dangerous challenge to the unity of their realms and the stability of their rule. A subject could very well swear greater allegiance to God than to his lord. Moreover, the Peasants' War of 1525 showed that religious dissent could lead to rebellion. In addition, religious differences intensified the formation of noble factions, which exploited the situation when weak monarchs or children ruled.

France.   In France, Francis I tolerated Protestants until the Affair of the Placards in 1534. Persecutions of Huguenots—as Protestants were called in France—were only sporadic, however, and the Reformed church grew steadily. During the 1540s and 1550s, many French noble families—including some of the most powerful—converted to Calvinism. Under their protection, the Reformed church was able to organize openly and hold synods (church meetings), especially in southern and western France. Francis and his successor, Henry II (r. 1547–1559), succeeded in maintaining a balance of power between Catholic and Huguenot and between hostile noble factions. But after Henry's death the weakened monarchy could no longer hold together the fragile realm. The real drama of the Reformation in France took place after 1560, when the country plunged into decades of religious wars, whose savagery was unparalleled elsewhere in Europe.

England.   The English monarchy played the central role in shaping that country's religious reform. During the 1520s, English Protestants were few in number. King Henry VIII (r. 1509–1547) changed all that.

In the first eighteen years of his reign, Henry firmly opposed the Reformation, even receiving the title "Defender of the Faith" from Pope Leo X for a treatise Henry wrote against Luther. A robust, ambitious, and well-educated man, Henry wanted to make his mark on history and, with the aid of his chancellors Cardinal Thomas Wolsey and Thomas More, he vigorously suppressed Protestantism and executed its leaders.

But by 1527, the king wanted to divorce his wife, Catherine of Aragon (d. 1536), the daughter of Ferdinand and Isabella of Spain and the aunt of Charles V. The eighteen-year marriage had produced a daughter, Princess Mary (known as Mary Tudor), but Henry desperately needed a male heir to consolidate the rule of the still-new Tudor dynasty. Moreover, he was in love with Anne Boleyn, a lady at court and a strong supporter of the Reformation. Henry claimed that his marriage to Catherine had never been valid because she was the widow of his older brother, Arthur. Arthur and Catherine's marriage, which apparently was never consummated, had been annulled by Pope Julius II to allow the marriage between Henry and Catherine to take place. Now Henry asked the reigning pope, Clement VII, to declare his marriage to Catherine invalid.

Around "the king's great matter" unfolded a struggle for political and religious control. When Henry failed to secure papal approval of his divorce, he chose two Protestants as his new loyal servants: Thomas Cromwell (1485–1540) as chancellor and Thomas Cranmer (1489–1556) as archbishop of Canterbury. Under their leadership the English Parliament passed a number of acts between 1529 and 1536 that severed ties between the English church and Rome. The Act of Supremacy of 1529 made Henry the head of the so-called Anglican church (the Church of England), invalidated the claims of Catherine's daughter, Princess Mary, to the throne, recognized Henry's marriage to Anne Boleyn, and allowed the English crown to confiscate the properties of the monasteries.

By 1536, Henry had grown tired of Anne Boleyn, who had given birth to the future

Queen Elizabeth I but had produced no sons. The king, who would go on to marry four other wives but father only one son, Edward, had Anne beheaded on the charge of adultery, an act that he defined as treason. Thomas More also had gone to the block in 1535 for treason—in his case, for refusing to recognize Henry as "the only supreme head on earth of the Church of England"—and Cromwell suffered the same fate in 1540 when he lost favor. When Henry died in 1547, the Anglican church, nominally Protestant, still retained much traditional Catholic doctrine and ritual. But the principle of royal supremacy in religious matters would remain a lasting feature of Henry's reforms.

The boy king Edward VI (r. 1547–1553) furthered the Reformation by welcoming prominent religious refugees from the continent. With the accession of Mary Tudor (r. 1553–1558), however, Catholicism was restored and Protestants persecuted. Close to three hundred Protestants perished at the stake, and more than eight hundred fled to Germany and Switzerland. Finally, after Anne Boleyn's daughter, Elizabeth, succeeded her half-sister Mary to the throne in 1558, the Anglican cause again gained momentum; it eventually defined the character of the English nation, and Catholic missionaries were ruthlessly hunted down and executed as traitors to a Protestant nation.

Scotland. Still another pattern of religious politics unfolded in Scotland, where powerful noble clans directly challenged royal power. Until the 1550s, Protestants had been a small minority in Scotland. The most prominent Scottish reformer, John Knox (1514–1572), spent many of his early years in exile in England and on the continent. For Knox, God's cause was obstructed by a woman, who became his greatest enemy.

The queen regent Mary of Guise (d. 1560) stood at the center of Scotland's conflict. After the death of her husband, James V, in 1542, Mary of Guise, a Catholic, cultivated the support of her native France. Her daughter and heir to the throne, Mary Stuart (also a Catholic), had been educated in France and was married to the French dauphin Francis, son of Henry II. The queen regent surrounded herself with French advisers and soldiers.

Alienated by this pro-French atmosphere, many Scottish noblemen had joined the pro-English, anti-French Protestant cause.

The era's suspicion of female rulers and regents also played a part in Protestant propaganda. In 1558, John Knox published *The First Blast of the Trumpet against the Monstrous Regiment [Rule] of Women*, a diatribe against both Mary Tudor of England and Mary of Guise. Knox declared that "to promote a woman to bear rule, superiority, dominion, or empire above any realm, nation, or city is repugnant to nature, contumely to God, a thing most contrary to his revealed will and approved ordinance and, finally, it is the subversion of good order, of all equality and justice." In 1560, the Protestants assumed control of the Scottish Parliament, and dethroned the regent Mary of Guise. They later forced her daughter, Mary, queen of Scots, to flee to England, and installed Mary's infant son James as king.

The German States. In the German states, the Protestant princes and cities formed the Schmalkaldic♦ League in 1531. Headed by the elector of Saxony and Philip of Hesse (the two leading Protestant princes), the league included most of the imperial cities, the chief source of the empire's wealth. On the other side, allied with Emperor Charles V, were the bishops and the few remaining Catholic princes. Although Charles had to concentrate on fighting the French and the Turks during the 1530s, he had by now temporarily secured the western Mediterranean; thus, he turned to central Europe to try to resolve the growing religious differences there.

In 1541, Charles convened an Imperial Diet at Regensburg to patch up the theological differences between Protestants and Catholics, only to see negotiations between the two sides break down rapidly. The schism threatened to become permanent. Vowing to crush the Schmalkaldic League, the emperor secured French neutrality in 1544 and papal support in 1545. Luther died in 1546. In the following year, war broke out. Using seasoned Spanish veterans and German allies, Charles occupied the German imperial cities in the south, restoring Catholic elites and

---

♦**Schmalkaldic:** shmahl KAHL dihk

suppressing the Reformation. In 1547, he defeated the Schmalkaldic League armies at Mühlberg and captured the leading Lutheran princes. Jubilant, Charles proclaimed a decree, the "Interim," which restored Catholics' right to worship in Protestant lands while permitting Lutherans to keep their own rites. Protestant resistance to the Interim was deep and widespread: many pastors went into exile, and riots broke out in many cities.

For Charles V, the reaction of his former allies proved far more alarming than Protestant resistance. His success frightened some Catholic powers. With Spanish troops controlling Milan and Naples, Pope Julius III (r. 1550–1552) feared that papal authority would be subjugated by imperial might. In the Holy Roman Empire, Protestant princes spoke out against "imperial tyranny." Jealously defending their traditional liberties against an over-mighty emperor, the Protestant princes, led by Duke Maurice of Saxony, a former ally, raised arms against Charles. The princes declared war in 1552, chasing a surprised, unprepared, and practically bankrupt emperor back to Italy.

Forced to construct an accord, Charles V agreed to the Peace of Augsburg in 1555. The settlement recognized the Lutheran church in the empire, accepted the secularization of church lands but "reserved" the remaining ecclesiastical territories (mainly the bishoprics) for Catholics, and, most important, established the principle that all princes, whether Catholic or Lutheran, enjoyed the sole right to determine the religion of their lands and subjects. Significantly, Calvinist, Anabaptist, and other dissenting groups were excluded from the settlement. The religious revolt of the common people had culminated in a princes' Reformation. As the constitutional framework for the Holy Roman Empire, the Augsburg settlement preserved a fragile peace in central Europe until 1618, but the exclusion of Calvinists would plant the seed for future conflict.

Exhausted by decades of war and disappointed by the disunity in Christian Europe, Emperor Charles V resigned his many thrones in 1555 and 1556, leaving his Netherlandish-Burgundian and Spanish dominions to his son, Philip II, and his Austrian lands to his brother, Ferdinand (who was also elected Holy Roman Emperor to succeed Charles). Retiring to a monastery in southern Spain, the most powerful of the Christian monarchs spent his last years quietly seeking salvation (Figure 15.1).

> **Review:** How did European rulers attempt to stabilize their territories in the face of religious divisions?

❖ A Continuing Reformation

Reacting to the waves of Protestant challenge, the Catholic church mobilized for defense. Drawing on traditions from before the Reformation, Catholicism offered hopes of renewal in the 1540s and 1550s. The Council of Trent defined the beliefs and practices of the Catholic church and condemned Protestant beliefs, while new religious orders, most notably the Society of Jesus, began a vigorous campaign for the reclamation of souls. Christian Europe was transformed. Not only had the old religious unity passed

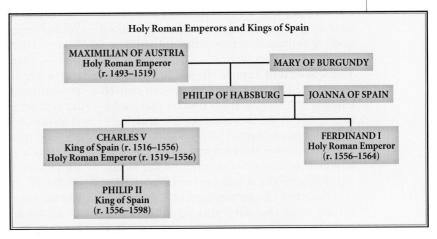

FIGURE 15.1 The Habsburg Succession, 1493–1556
The reign of Charles V ended with the splintering of the largest empire in Europe. Saddled with debts inherited from his grandfather and accrued from perpetual warfare, Charles ceded the Holy Roman Empire to his brother Ferdinand and gave Spain to his son Philip.

forever, but a new earth emerged under the canopy of a new heaven, as missionaries from Catholic Europe traveled to other parts of the world to win converts who might compensate for the millions lost to the Protestant Reformation.

Catholic Renewal

Many voices for reform had echoed within the Catholic church long before Luther, but the papacy had failed to sponsor any significant change in the decades before the Reformation. Nevertheless, a Catholic reform movement gathered momentum in Italy during the 1530s and 1540s. Drawn from the elite, especially the Venetian upper class, the Catholic reformers stressed biblical ethics and moral discipline. Gian Matteo Giberti, bishop of Verona from 1524 to 1543, resigned his position in the Roman curia to concentrate on his pastoral duties. Gasparo Contarini♦ (1483–1542), who was descended from a Venetian noble family and had served the republic as ambassador to Charles V, subsequently was elevated to cardinal, in which position he labored to heal the schism within the church.

Under Pope Paul III (r. 1534–1549) and his successors, the papacy finally took the lead in church reform. The Italian nobility also played a leading role, and Spaniards and Italians of all classes provided the backbone for this movement, sometimes called the Catholic Reform. Its crowning achievements were the calling of a general church council and the founding of new religious orders.

The Council of Trent.   In 1545, Pope Paul III and Charles V convened a general church council at Trent, a town on the border between the Holy Roman Empire and Italy. The Council of Trent, 1545–1563, which met sporadically over the next seventeen years before completing its work, shaped the essential character of Catholicism until the 1960s. It reasserted the supremacy of clerical authority over the laity and stipulated that bishops reside in their dioceses and that seminaries be established in each diocese to train priests. The council also confirmed

and clarified church doctrine and sacraments. On the sacrament of the Eucharist, the council reaffirmed that the bread actually becomes Christ's body—a rejection of all Protestant positions on this issue sufficiently emphatic as to preclude compromise. For the sacrament of marriage, the council specified that all weddings must henceforth take place in churches and be registered by the parish clergy; it further rejected the Protestant allowance for divorce.

The Council of Trent marked a watershed; henceforth, the schism between Protestant and Catholic remained permanent, and all hopes of reconciliation faded. The focus of the Catholic church turned now to rolling back the tide of dissent.

The Society of Jesus.   The energy of the Catholic renewal expressed itself most vigorously in the founding of new religious orders. The most important of these, the Society of Jesus, or Jesuits, was established by a Spanish nobleman, Ignatius of Loyola (1491–1556). Imbued with tales of chivalric romances and the national glory of the *reconquista,* Ignatius eagerly sought to prove his mettle as a soldier. In 1521, while defending a Spanish border fortress against French attack, he sustained a severe injury. During his convalescence, Ignatius read lives of the saints; once he recovered, he abandoned his quest for military glory in favor of serving the church.

Attracted by his austerity and piety, young men gravitated to this charismatic figure. Thanks to his noble birth and a cardinal's intercession, Ignatius gained a hearing before the pope, and in 1540 the church recognized his small band. With Ignatius as its first general, the Jesuits became the most vigorous defenders of papal authority. The society quickly expanded; by the time of Ignatius's death in 1556, Europe had one thousand Jesuits. Jesuits established hundreds of colleges throughout the Catholic world, educating future generations of Catholic leaders. Jesuit missionaries played a key role in the global Portuguese maritime empire and brought Roman Catholicism to Africans, Asians, and native Americans. Together with other new religious orders, the Jesuits restored the confidence of the faith-

---

♦**Gasparo Contarini:** GAHS pahr oh kohn tah REE nee

ful in the dedication and power of the Catholic church.

Missionary Zeal

To win new souls, Catholic missionaries set sail throughout the globe. They saw their effort as proof of the truth of Roman Catholicism and the success of their missions as a sign of divine favor, both particularly important in the face of Protestant challenge. But the missionary zeal of Catholics brought different messages to indigenous peoples: for some the message of a repressive and coercive alien religion, for others a sweet sign of reason and faith. Frustrated in his efforts to convert Brazilian Indians, a Jesuit missionary wrote to his superior in Rome in 1563 that "for this kind of people it is better to be preaching with the sword and rod of

The Portuguese in Japan
In this sixteenth-century Japanese black-lacquer screen painting of Portuguese missionaries, the Jesuits are dressed in black and the Franciscans in brown. At the lower right corner is a Portuguese nobleman depicted with exaggerated "Western" features. The Japanese considered themselves lighter in skin color than the Portuguese, whom they classified as "barbarians." In turn, the Portuguese classified Japanese (and Chinese) as "whites." The perception of ethnic differences in the sixteenth century depended less on skin color than on clothing, eating habits, and other cultural signals. Color classifications were unstable and changed over time: by the late seventeenth century, Europeans no longer regarded Asians as "whites." *Laurie Platt Winfrey, Inc.*

iron." This attitude was common among Christian missionaries in the Americas and Africa, despite the isolated missionary voices that condemned Europeans' abuse of native populations.

The Dominican Bartolomé de Las Casas (1474–1566) was perhaps the most severe critic of colonial brutality in Spanish America, yet even he argued that Africans were constitutionally more suitable for labor than native Americans and should be imported to the plantations in the Americas to relieve the indigenous peoples, who were being worked to death. Under the influence of Las Casas and his followers, the Spanish crown tried to protect the indigenous peoples against exploitation by European settlers, a policy whose success was

determined by the struggle among missionaries, conquistadores (Spanish conquerors in the Americas), and royal officials for the bodies and souls of native populations.

To ensure rapid Christianization, European missionaries focused initially on winning over local elites. The recommendation of a Spanish royal official in Mexico City was typical. He wrote to the crown in 1525:

In order that the sons of caciques [chiefs] and native lords may be instructed in the faith, Your Majesty must command that a college be founded wherein they may be taught . . . to the end that they may be ordained priests. For he who shall become such among them, will be of greater profit in attracting others to the faith than will fifty [European] Christians.

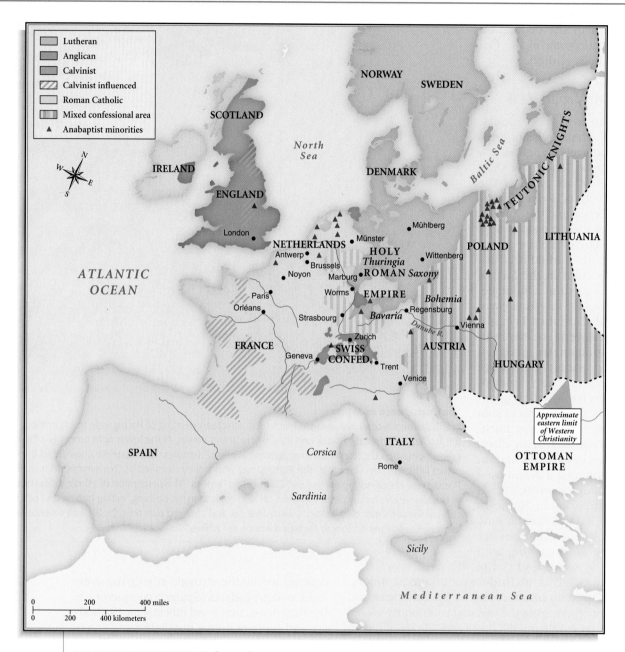

MAPPING THE WEST Reformation Europe, c. 1560
The fortunes of Roman Catholicism were at their lowest point around 1560. Northern Germany and Scandinavia owed allegiance to the Lutheran church, England broke away under a national church headed by its monarchs, and the Calvinist Reformation would extend across large areas of western, central, and eastern Europe. Southern Europe remained solidly Catholic.

Nevertheless, this recommendation was not adopted and the Catholic clergy in Spanish America remained overwhelmingly European.

The Portuguese were more willing than the Spanish to train indigenous peoples as missionaries. A number of young African

nobles went to Portugal to be trained in theology, among them Dom Henry, a son of King Afonso I of Kongo, a Portuguese ally. In East Asia, Christian missionaries under Portuguese protection concentrated their efforts on the elites, preaching the Gospel to

Confucian scholar-officials in China and to the samurai (the warrior aristocracy) in Japan. The missionary enterprise seemed highly successful: by the second half of the sixteenth century, vast multitudes of native Americans had become nominal Christians, and thirty years after Francis Xavier's 1549 landing in Japan the Jesuits could claim more than 100,000 Japanese converts.

After an initial period of relatively little racial discrimination, the Catholic church in the Americas and Africa adopted strict rules based on color. For example, the first Mexican Ecclesiastical Provincial Council in 1555 declared that holy orders were not to be conferred on Indians, mestizos (people of mixed European-Indian parentage), and mulattoes (people of mixed European-African heritage); along with descendants of Moors, Jews, and persons who had been sentenced by the Spanish Inquisition, these groups were deemed "inherently unworthy of the sacerdotal [priestly] office." Europeans reinforced their sense of racial superiority with their perception of the "treachery" that native Americans and Africans exhibited whenever they resisted domination.

A different conversion tactic applied to Asia. There, European missionaries, who admired Chinese and Japanese civilization and were not backed by military power, used the sermon rather than the sword to win converts (see the illustration on page 575). The Jesuit Francis Xavier preached in India and Japan, his work vastly assisted by a network of Portuguese trading stations. He died in 1552, awaiting permission to travel to China. A pioneer missionary in Asia, Xavier had prepared the ground for future missionary successes in Japan and China.

> **Review:** How did the Catholic church maintain and, in the wake of the Reformation, regain its influence?

Conclusion

Mocking the warlike popes, the Dutch humanist Erasmus compared his times to those of the early Christian church. In *The* *Praise of Folly,* he satirized Christian prelates and princes, who "continued to shed Christian blood," the same blood as that of the martyrs who had built the foundations of Christianity. Turning from the papacy to the empire, Erasmus and many intellectuals and artists of his generation saw in Emperor Charles V the model Christian prince. As the most powerful ruler in all Europe, Charles was hailed as the harbinger of peace, the protector of justice, and the foe of the infidel Turks. For the generation that came of age before the Reformation, Christian humanism—and its imperial embodiment—represented an ideal for political and moral reform that would save Christendom from corruption and strife.

The Reformation changed this dream of peace, justice, and unity. Instead of leading a crusade against Islam, Charles V wore himself out in ceaseless struggle against Francis I of France and the German Protestants. Instead of the Christian faith of charity and learning that Erasmus had envisioned, Christianity split into a number of hostile camps that battled one another with words and swords. Instead of the intellectual unity of the generation of Erasmus and Thomas More, the mid-sixteenth-century cultural landscape erupted in a burst of conflicting doctrinal statements and left in its wake a climate of censorship, repression, division, and inflexibility.

After the brutal suppression of popular revolts in the 1520s and 1530s, religious persecution became a Christian institution: Luther called on the princes to kill rebellious peasants in 1525, Zwingli advocated the drowning of Anabaptists, and Calvin supported the death sentence for Michael Servetus. Meanwhile, persecutions and executions in Catholic lands provided Protestants with a steady stream of martyrs. The two peace settlements in the 1550s failed to provide long-term solutions: the Peace of Augsburg gradually disintegrated as the religious struggles in the empire intensified, and the Treaty of Cateau-Cambrésis was but a brief respite in a century of crisis. In the following generations, civil war and national conflicts would set Catholics against Protestants in numerous futile attempts to restore a single faith.

Suggested References

A New Heaven and a New Earth

Recent scholarship on the Reformation era has emphasized the connected nature of religious, political, social, economic, and cultural history. Another new direction is to connect the study of Christian reform movements with Christian-Jewish relations prior to the Reformation.

Brady, Thomas A. *Turning Swiss: Cities and Empire, 1450–1550.* 1985.

Essential Works of Erasmus. Ed. W. T. H. Jackson. 1965.

Hsia, R. Po-chia. *The Myth of Ritual Murder: Jews and Magic in the Reformation.* 1988.

Jardine, Lisa. *Erasmus: Man of Letters.* 1993.

Protestant Reformers

While continuing to refine our understanding of the leading Protestant reformers, recent scholars have also offered new interpretations that take into consideration the popular impact of the reformers' teachings.

Bouwsma, William J. *John Calvin: A Sixteenth-Century Portrait.* 1988.

Haigh, Christopher. *English Reformations: Religion, Politics, and Society under the Tudors.* 1993.

*Hillerbrand, Hans J., ed. *The Protestant Reformation.* 1969.

Martin Luther's life and thought: http://www.wsu.edu/~dee/REFORM/LUTHER.htm.

Oberman, Heiko A. *Luther: Man between God and Devil.* 1990.

Puritan and Reformed sermons and other writings: http://www.puritansermons.com/poetry.htm.

Scribner, R. W. *For the Sake of Simple Folk: Popular Propaganda for the German Reformation.* 1981.

Scribner, R. W., et al., eds. *The Reformation in a National Context.* 1994.

Reshaping Society through Religion

The most important trend in recent scholarship has been the consideration of the impact of the Reformation on society and culture. Many studies have shown the limited influence of the ideas of reformers; others document the persistence of traditional religious habits and practices well past the sixteenth century.

*Primary source.

Bainton, Roland. *Women of the Reformation in Germany and Italy.* 1971.

Blickle, Peter. *The Revolution of 1525.* 1981.

Elton, G. R. *Reformation Europe, 1517–1559.* 1963.

Hsia, R. Po-chia. *The German People and the Reformation.* 1988.

Ozment, Steven E. *The Reformation in the Cities.* 1975.

Strauss, Gerald. *Luther's House of Learning: Indoctrination of the Young in the German Reformation.* 1978.

Wiesner, Merry. *Christianity and the Regulation of Sexuality in the Early Modern World.* 2000.

A Struggle for Mastery

Still focused on the struggle between the Habsburg and Valois dynasties, historical scholarship has also moved out in the direction of cultural and military history. Recent works have studied military innovations and artistic representations of the sixteenth-century monarchs.

Elliott, J. H. *The Old World and the New, 1492–1650.* 1970.

*Guicciardini, Francesco. *The History of Italy.* Trans. Sidney Alexander. 1969.

Knecht, R. J. *Francis I.* 1982.

Parker, Geoffrey. *The Military Revolution: Military Innovation and the Rise of the West, 1500–1800.* 1988.

Partridge, Loren, and Randolph Starn. *A Renaissance Likeness: Art and Culture in Raphael's Julius II.* 1980.

Trevor-Roper, Hugh. *Princes and Artists: Patronage and Ideology at Four Habsburg Courts, 1517–1633.* 1976.

A Continuing Reformation

Current scholarship suggests that by comparing the Protestant Reformation and the Catholic Reforms, we can gain insight into the underlying social and cultural changes that affected all of Christian Europe. Another new direction of research brings the study of Christianity into the non-European realm by focusing on missions.

Crosby, Alfred W. *The Colombian Exchange: Biological and Cultural Consequences of 1492.* 1972.

Evennet, Henry Outram. *The Spirit of the Counter-Reformation.* 1968.

Hsia, R. Po-chia. *The World of the Catholic Renewal.* 1997.

O'Malley, John W. *Trent and All That.* 2000.

Prodi, Paolo. *The Papal Prince, One Body and Two Souls: The Papal Monarchy in Early Modern Europe.* 1982.

CHAPTER REVIEW

IMPORTANT EVENTS

1494   Italian Wars begin

1516   Erasmus publishes Greek edition of the New Testament; More writes *Utopia*

1517   Martin Luther composes ninety-five theses to challenge church profiteering

1520   Luther publishes three treatises; Zwingli breaks from Rome

1525   German Peasants' War

1527   Charles V's imperial troops sack Rome

1529   German Protestants; Colloquy of Marburg assembles to address disagreements between German and Swiss church reformers

1534   Act of Supremacy Henry VIII breaks with Rome; Affair of the Placards in France

1536   Calvin publishes first edition of *Institutes*

1540   Jesuits established as new Catholic order

1541   Calvin installed in Geneva

1545–1563   Catholic Council of Trent condemns Protestant beliefs and confirms church doctrine and sacraments

1547   Charles V defeats Protestants at Mühlberg

1555   Peace of Augsburg ends religious wars in Germany and recognizes Lutherans

1559   Treaty of Cateau-Cambrésis ends conflict between Habsburg and Valois

KEY TERMS

Anabaptist (561)

Christian humanists (550)

Evangelicals (548)

indulgence (549)

infidel (567)

parish (563)

predestination (558)

Protestants (548)

Vulgate (562)

REVIEW QUESTIONS

1. How did the Christian humanists combine classical learning with their goals of Christian renewal?

2. In what ways did Luther, Zwingli, and Calvin challenge the Roman Catholic Church?

3. How did the forces for radical change unleashed by the Protestant Reformation interact with the urge for social order and stability?

4. How did European rulers attempt to stabilize their territories in the face of religious divisions?

5. How did the Catholic church maintain and, in the wake of the Reformation, regain its influence?

MAKING CONNECTIONS

1. Contrast the ways in which the Christian humanists and the Protestant reformers tried to change society.

2. How were the religious and political conflicts of the early sixteenth century related?

FOR FURTHER EXPLORATION

To assess your mastery of the material in this chapter, see the Online Study Guide at **bedfordstmartins.com/hunt**.

To read additional primary-source material from this period, see Chapter 15 in *Sources of The Making of the West*, Second Edition.

A Century of Crisis, 1560–1648

IN MAY 1618, PROTESTANTS IN THE KINGDOM of Bohemia furiously protested the Holy Roman Emperor's attempts to curtail their hard-won religious freedoms. Protestants wanted to build new churches; the Catholic emperor wanted to stop them. Tensions boiled over when two Catholic deputy governors tried to dissolve the meetings of Protestants. On May 23, a crowd of angry Protestants surged up the stairs of the royal castle in Prague, trapped the two Catholic deputies, dragged them screaming for mercy to the windows, and hurled them to the pavement below. One of the rebels jeered: "We will see if your [Virgin] Mary can help you!" But because they landed in a dung heap, the Catholic deputies survived. One of the two limped off on his own; the other was carried away by his servants to safety. Although no one died, this "defenestration" (from the French for "window," *la fenêtre*) of Prague touched off the Thirty Years' War (1618–1648), which eventually involved almost every major power in Europe. Before it ended, the fighting had devastated the lands of central Europe and produced permanent changes in European politics and culture.

The Thirty Years' War grew out of the religious conflicts initiated by the Reformation. When Martin Luther began the Protestant Reformation in 1517, he had no idea that he would be unleashing such dangerous forces, but religious turmoil and warfare followed almost immediately upon his break with the Catholic church. Until the early 1600s, the Peace of Augsburg of 1555 maintained relative calm in the lands of the Holy Roman Empire by granting each ruler the right to determine the religion of his territory. But in western Europe, religious strife increased dramatically after 1560 as Protestants made inroads in France, the Spanish-ruled Netherlands, and England. All in all, nearly constant warfare marked the century between 1560 and 1648. These struggles most often began as religious conflicts, but religion was never the sole motive; political power entered into every equation and raised the stakes of conflict.

The Defenestration of Prague, 1618
In this detail from a copper-plate engraving by Swiss artist Matthäus Merian (1593–1650), Czech Protestants attack the Catholic deputies sent to disband their meeting. The attackers are about to throw the two Catholics out of the windows of the royal castle (that is, the Catholics are about to suffer "defenestration"). The defenestration touched off the Thirty Years' War. *Mary Evans Picture Library.*

The Bohemian Protestants, for example, wanted both freedom to practice their religion as Protestants and national independence for the Czechs, the largest ethnic group in Bohemia. Since Bohemia had many Catholics, religious and political aims inevitably came into conflict.

Although particularly dramatic and deadly, the church-state crisis was only one of a series of upheavals that shaped this era. In the early seventeenth century, a major economic downturn led to food shortages, famine, and disease in much of Europe. These hit especially hard in the central European lands devastated by the fighting of the Thirty Years' War and helped shift the balance of economic power to northwestern Europe, away from the Mediterranean and central Europe. The deepening sense of crisis prompted some to seek new, nonreligious grounds for all forms of authority, whether artistic, political, or philosophical. A clash of worldviews was in the making. The development of new scientific methods of research would ultimately reshape Western attitudes over the long term.

❖ Religious Conflicts and State Power, 1560–1618

The Peace of Augsburg of 1555 made Lutheranism a legal religion in the predominantly Catholic Holy Roman Empire, but it did not extend recognition to Calvinists. Although the followers of Martin Luther (Lutherans) and those of John Calvin (Calvinists) similarly refused the authority of the Catholic church, they disagreed with each other about religious doctrine and church organization. The rapid expansion of Calvinism after 1560 threatened to alter the religious balance of power in much of Europe. Calvinists challenged Catholic dominance in France, the Spanish-ruled Netherlands, Scotland, and Poland-Lithuania. In England they sought to influence the new Protestant monarch, Elizabeth I. Calvinists were not the only source of religious contention, however. Philip II of Spain also fought the Muslim Ottoman Turks in the Mediterranean and expelled the remnants of the Muslim population in Spain. To the east, the Russian tsar Ivan IV fought to make Muscovy the center of an empire based on Russian Orthodox Christianity. He had to compete with Lutheran Sweden and Poland-Lithuania, itself divided by conflicts among Catholics, Lutherans, and Calvinists.

French Wars of Religion, 1562–1598

Calvinist inroads in France had begun in 1555, when the Genevan Company of Pastors took charge of missionary work. Supplied with false passports and often disguised as merchants, the Calvinist pastors moved rapidly among their growing congregations, which gathered in secret in towns near Paris or in the south. Calvinist nobles provided military protection to local congregations and helped set up a national organization for the French Calvinist—or **Huguenot**❖—church. In 1562, rival Huguenot and Catholic armies

❖**Huguenot:** HYOO guh no

◆ **1562** French Wars of Religion

◆ **1566** Calvinist revolt against Spain

◆ **1569** Poland-Lithuania formed

◆ **1571** Battle of Lepanto

◆ **1618** Thirty Years' War

◆ **1598** Edict of Nantes

1560	1580	1600

◆ **1572** St. Bartholomew's Day Massacre

◆ **1588** England defeats Spanish Armada

◆ **1601** Shakespeare, *Hamlet*

began fighting a series of wars that threatened to tear the French nation into shreds (Map 16.1).

Religious Division in the Nobility. Conversion to Calvinism in French noble families often began with the noblewomen, some of whom sought intellectual independence as well as spiritual renewal in the new faith. Charlotte de Bourbon, for example, fled from a Catholic convent and eventually married William of Orange, the leader of the anti-Spanish resistance in the Netherlands. Calvinist noblewomen protected pastors, provided money and advice, and helped found schools and establish relief for the poor.

Religious divisions in France often reflected political disputes among noble families. At least one-third of the nobles—a much larger proportion than in the general population—joined the Huguenots, who usually followed the lead of the Bourbon family. The Bourbons were close relatives of the French king and stood first in line to inherit the throne if the Valois♦ kings failed to produce a male heir. The most militantly Catholic nobles took their cues from the Guise♦ family, who aimed to block Bourbon ambitions. The Catholic Valois were caught between these two powerful factions, each with its own military organization. The situation grew even more volatile when King Henry II was accidentally killed during a jousting tournament in 1559 and his fifteen-year-old son, Francis, died soon after. Ten-

year-old Charles IX (r. 1560–1574) became king, with his mother, Catherine de Médicis, as regent. An ambassador commented on the weakness of Catherine's hold: "It is sufficient to say that she is a woman, a foreigner, and a Florentine to boot, born of a simple house, altogether beneath the dignity of the Kingdom of France." The Bourbon and Guise factions consolidated their forces, and civil war erupted in 1562. Both sides committed terrible atrocities. Priests and pastors were murdered, and massacres of whole congregations became frighteningly commonplace.

St. Bartholomew's Day Massacre, 1572. Although a Catholic herself, Catherine aimed to preserve the throne for her son by playing the Guise and Bourbon factions off each other. To this end she arranged the marriage of the king's Catholic sister, Marguerite de Valois, to Henry of Navarre,♦ a Huguenot and Bourbon. Just four days after the wedding in August 1572, assassins tried but failed to kill one of the Huguenot nobles allied with the Bourbons, Gaspard de Coligny. Panicked at the thought of Huguenot revenge and perhaps herself implicated in the botched plot, Catherine convinced her son to order the killing of leading Huguenots. On St. Bartholomew's Day, August 24, a bloodbath began, fueled by years of growing animosity between Catholics and Protestants. (See Massacre Motivated by Religion page 585.) The duke of Guise himself killed Coligny. Each side viewed the other as less than human, as a source of moral pollution

♦**Valois:** VAL wah
♦**Guise:** geez

♦**Navarre:** nuh VAHR

♦ **1625** Grotius, *The Laws of War and Peace*

♦ **1629** Puritans begin colonizing New England

♦ **1648** Peace of Westphalia

| 1620 | 1640 | 1660 | 1680 |

♦ **1633** Galilieo forced to recant

♦ **1635** French declare war on Spain

MAP 16.1 Protestant Churches in France, 1562

Calvinist missionaries took their message from their headquarters in Geneva across the border into France. The strongest concentration of Protestants was in southern France. The Bourbons, leaders of the Protestants in France, had their family lands in Navarre, a region in southwestern France that had been divided between France and Spain.

right of resistance was linked to a notion of contract; upholding the true religion was part of the contract imagined as binding the ruler to his subjects. Both the right of resistance and the idea of a contract fed into the larger doctrine of constitutionalism—that a government's legitimacy rested on its upholding a constitution or contract between ruler and ruled. Constitutionalism justified resistance movements from the sixteenth century onward. Protestants and Catholics alike now saw the conflict as an international struggle for survival that required aid to coreligionists in other countries. In this way, the French Wars of Religion paved the way for wider international conflicts over religion in the decades to come.

Henry IV and the Edict of Nantes. The religious division in France grew even more dangerous when Charles IX died and his brother Henry III (r. 1574–1589) became king. Like his brothers before him, Henry III failed to produce an heir. Next in line to the throne was none other than the Protestant Bourbon leader Henry of Navarre. Convinced that Henry III lacked the will to root out Protestantism, the Guises formed the Catholic League, which requested help from Spanish king Philip II. Henry III responded with a fatal trick: in 1588 he summoned the two Guise leaders to a meeting and had his men kill them. A few months later a fanatical monk stabbed Henry III to death, and Henry of Navarre became Henry IV (r. 1589–1610), despite Philip II's attempt to block his way with military intervention.

The new king soon concluded that to establish control over the war-weary country he had to place the interests of the French state

that had to be eradicated. In three days, Catholic mobs murdered three thousand Huguenots in Paris. Ten thousand died in the provinces over the next six weeks. The pope joyfully ordered the church bells rung throughout Catholic Europe; Spain's Philip II wrote Catherine that it was "the best and most cheerful news which at present could come to me."

The massacre settled nothing. Huguenot pamphleteers now proclaimed their right to resist a tyrant who worshiped idols (a practice that Calvinists equated with Catholicism). This

Massacre Motivated by Religion

The Italian artist Giorgio Vasari painted *St. Bartholomew's Night: The Massacre of the Huguenots* for a public room in Pope Gregory XIII's residence. In what ways did the artist celebrate what he saw as a Catholic victory over Protestant heresy? *Scala/Art Resource.*

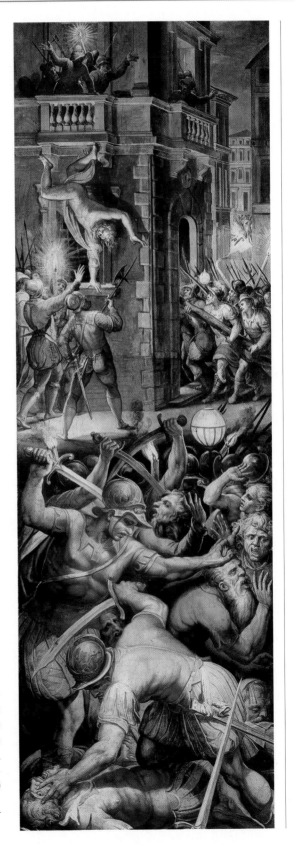

ahead of his Protestant faith. In 1593, Henry IV publicly embraced Catholicism, reputedly explaining his conversion with the statement "Paris is worth a Mass." Within a few years he defeated the ultra-Catholic opposition and drove out the Spanish. In 1598, he made peace with Spain and issued the Edict of Nantes, in which he granted the Huguenots a large measure of religious toleration. The approximately 1.25 million Huguenots became a legally protected minority within an officially Catholic kingdom of some 20 million people. Protestants were free to worship in specified towns and were allowed their own troops, fortresses, and even courts. Few believed in religious toleration, but Henry IV followed the advice of those neutral Catholics and Calvinists called ***politiques***◆ who urged him to give priority to the development of a durable state. Although their opponents hated them for their compromising spirit, the politiques believed that religious disputes could be resolved only in the peace provided by strong government.

The Edict of Nantes ended the French Wars of Religion, but Henry still needed to reestablish monarchical authority. He used court festivities and royal processions to rally subjects around him, and he developed a new class of royal officials to counterbalance the fractious nobility. In exchange for an annual payment, officials who had purchased their offices could pass them on to heirs or sell them to someone else. By buying offices that eventually ennobled their holders, rich middle-class merchants and lawyers could become part of a new social elite known as the "nobility of the robe" (named after the robes that magistrates wore, much like those judges wear today). New income raised by the increased sale of offices reduced the state debt and helped Henry build the base for a strong monarchy. His efforts did not, however, prevent his own assassination in 1610 after nineteen unsuccessful attempts.

◆***politiques:*** paw LUH teek

Challenges to Spanish Power

Although he failed to prevent Henry IV from taking the French throne, Philip II of Spain (r. 1556–1598) was the most powerful ruler in Europe (Map 16.2). In addition to the western Habsburg lands in Spain and the Netherlands, he had inherited from his father, Charles V, all the Spanish colonies recently settled in the New World of the Americas. Gold and silver funneled from the colonies supported his campaigns against the Ottoman Turks and French and English Protestants. But all of the money of the New World could not prevent Philip's eventual defeat in the Netherlands, where Calvinist rebels established an independent Dutch Republic that soon vied with Spain, France, and England for commercial supremacy.

Philip II, the Catholic King. A deeply devout Catholic, Philip II came to the Spanish throne at age twenty-eight determined to restore Catholic unity in Europe and lead the Christian defense against the Muslims. In his quest Philip benefited from a series of misfortunes. His four wives all died, but through them he became part of four royal families:

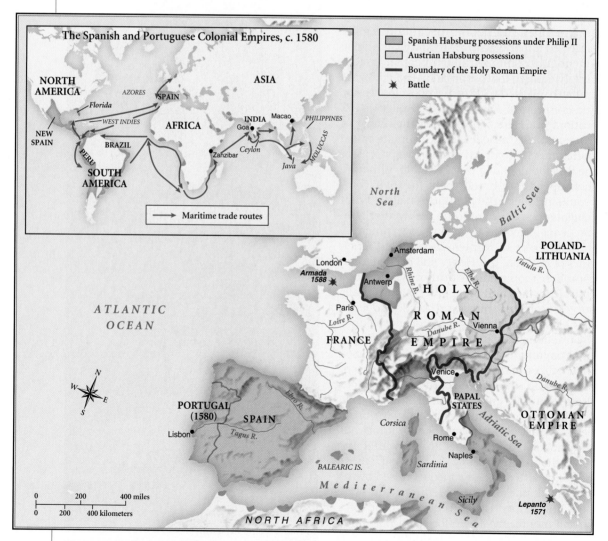

MAP 16.2 The Empire of Philip II, r. 1556–1598
Spanish king Philip II drew revenues from a truly worldwide empire. In 1580 he was the richest European ruler, but the demands of governing such far-flung territories eventually drained many of his resources.

Portuguese, English, French, and Austrian. His brief marriage to Mary Tudor (Mary I of England) did not produce an heir, but it and his subsequent marriage to Elisabeth de Valois, the sister of Charles IX and Henry III of France, gave him reason enough for involvement in English and French affairs. In 1580, when the king of Portugal died without a direct heir, Philip took over this neighboring realm with its rich empire in Africa, India, and the Americas.

Philip insisted on Catholic unity in his own possessions and worked to forge an international Christian coalition against the Ottoman Turks. In 1571, he achieved the single greatest military victory of his reign when he joined with Venice and the papacy to defeat the Turks in a great sea battle off the Greek coast at Lepanto.♦ Fifty thousand sailors and soldiers fought on the allied side, and eight thousand died. Spain now controlled the western Mediterranean. But Philip could not rest on his laurels. Between 1568 and 1570, the **Moriscos**♦—Muslim converts to Christianity who remained secretly faithful to Islam—had revolted in the south of Spain, killing 90 priests and 1,500 Christians. The victory at Lepanto destroyed any prospect that the Turks might come to their aid, yet Philip took stern measures against the Moriscos. He forced 50,000 to leave their villages and resettle in other regions. In 1609, his successor, Philip III, ordered their expulsion, and by 1614 some 300,000 Moriscos had been forced to relocate to North Africa.

The Revolt of the Netherlands. The Calvinists of the Netherlands were less easily intimidated than the Moriscos: they were far from Spain and accustomed to being left alone. In 1566, Calvinists in the Netherlands attacked Catholic churches, smashing stained-glass windows and statues of the Virgin Mary. Philip sent an army, which executed more than 1,100 people during the next six years. Prince William of Orange (whose name came from the lands he owned in southern France) took the lead of the anti-Spanish resistance. He encouraged adventurers and pirates known as the Sea Beggars

to invade the northern ports. The Spanish responded with more force, culminating in November 1576 when Philip's long-unpaid mercenary armies sacked Antwerp, then Europe's wealthiest commercial city. In eleven days of horror known as the Spanish Fury, the Spanish soldiers slaughtered seven thousand people. Shocked into response, the Netherlands' ten largely Catholic southern provinces formally allied with the seven largely Protestant northern provinces and expelled the Spaniards.

Important religious, ethnic, and linguistic differences promoted a federation rather than a union of Dutch states. The southern provinces remained Catholic, French-speaking in parts, and suspicious of the increasingly strict Calvinism in the north. In 1579, the southern provinces returned to the Spanish fold. Despite the assassination in 1584 of William of Orange, Spanish troops never regained control in the north. Spain would not formally recognize Dutch independence until

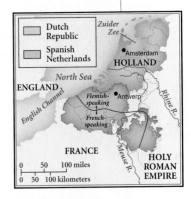

The Netherlands during the Revolt, c. 1580

1648, but by the end of the sixteenth century the Dutch Republic was a self-governing state sheltering a variety of religious groups.

The Dutch Republic. The princes of Orange resembled a ruling family in the Dutch Republic (sometimes incorrectly called Holland after the most populous of the seven provinces), but their powers paled next to those of local elites. Urban merchant and professional families known as regents controlled the towns and provinces. In the absence of a national bureaucracy, a single legal system, or a central court, each province governed itself and sent delegates to the one common institution, the States General, which carried out the wishes of the strongest individual provinces and their ruling families.

Well situated for maritime commerce, the Dutch Republic developed a thriving economy based on shipping and shipbuilding. Whereas elites in other countries focused on their landholdings, the Dutch looked for

♦**Lepanto:** lee PAHN toh
♦**Moriscos:** muh RIHS kohs

Rembrandt van Rijn's⁺ Depiction of Dutch Life

Rembrandt's painting known as *The Night Watch* (1642) shows members of a voluntary militia company in action. In fact, it is a group portrait, probably commissioned by the guardsmen themselves. Once responsible for defending the city, the militia companies had become eating and drinking clubs for prosperous businessmen. The painting demonstrates Rembrandt's interest in every aspect of daily life in the Dutch Republic. *Rijksmuseum, Amsterdam.*

investments in trade. After the Dutch gained independence, Amsterdam became the main European money market for two centuries. The city was also a primary commodities market and a chief supplier of arms—to allies, neutrals, and even enemies. Dutch entrepreneurs produced goods at lower prices than anyone else and marketed them more efficiently. Dutch merchants favored free trade in Europe because they could compete at an advantage. They controlled many

overseas markets thanks to their preeminence in seaborne commerce: by 1670, the Dutch commercial fleet was larger than the English, French, Spanish, Portuguese, and Austrian fleets combined.

Since the Dutch traded with anyone anywhere, it is perhaps not surprising that Dutch society tolerated more religious diversity than the other European states. One-third of the Dutch population remained Catholic, and the secular authorities allowed them to worship as they chose in private. Because Protestant sects could generally count

---

⁺**Rembrandt van Rijn:** REHM brant van ryn

on toleration from local regents, they remained peaceful. The Dutch Republic also had a relatively large Jewish population because many Jews had settled there after being driven out of Spain and Portugal; from 1597, Jews could worship openly in their synagogues. This openness to various religions helped make the Dutch Republic one of Europe's chief intellectual and scientific centers in the seventeenth and eighteenth centuries.

Elizabeth I's Defense of English Protestantism

As the Dutch revolt unfolded, Philip II became increasingly infuriated with Elizabeth I (r. 1558–1603), who had succeeded her half-sister Mary Tudor as queen of England. Philip had been married to Mary and had enthusiastically seconded Mary's efforts to return England to Catholicism. When Mary died in 1558, Elizabeth rejected Philip's proposal of marriage and promptly brought Protestantism back to England. Eventually she provided funds and troops to the Dutch Protestant cause. As Elizabeth moved to solidify her personal power and the authority of the Anglican church (Church of England), she had to squash uprisings by Catholics in the north and at least two serious plots against her life. In the long run, however, her greater challenges came from the Calvinist Puritans and Philip II.

Puritanism and the Church of England. The **Puritans** were strict Calvinists who opposed all vestiges of Catholic ritual in the Church of England. After Elizabeth became queen, many Puritans returned from exile abroad, but Elizabeth resisted their demands for drastic changes in church ritual and governance. The Church of England's Thirty-Nine Articles of Religion, issued under her authority in 1563, incorporated elements of Catholic ritual along with Calvinist doctrines. Puritan ministers angrily denounced the Church of England's "popish attire and foolish disguising, . . . tithings, holy days, and a thousand more abominations." To accomplish their reforms, Puritans tried to undercut the crown-appointed bishops' authority by placing control of church administration in the hands of a local presbytery made up of the minister

and the elders of the congregation. Elizabeth rejected this Calvinist "presbyterianism."

The Puritans nonetheless steadily gained influence. Known for their emphasis on strict moral lives, the Puritans tried to close England's theaters and Sunday fairs. Every Puritan father—with the help of his wife—was to "make his house a little church" by teaching the children to read the Bible. At Puritan urging, a new translation of the Bible, known as the King James Bible after Elizabeth's successor, James I, was authorized in 1604. Believing themselves God's elect and England an "elect nation," the Puritans also pushed Elizabeth to help Protestants on the continent.

Queen Elizabeth I of England
The Anglican (Church of England) Prayerbook of 1569 included a handcolored print of Queen Elizabeth saying her prayers. As queen, Elizabeth was also official head of the Church of England (the scepter or sword at her feet symbolizes her power). She named bishops and made final decisions about every aspect of church governance. *Bridgeman Art Library.*

Triumph over Spain. Although enraged by Elizabeth's aid to the Dutch rebels, Philip II bided his time as long as Elizabeth remained unmarried and her Catholic cousin Mary Stuart, better known as Mary, Queen of Scots, stood next in line to inherit the English throne. In 1568, Scottish Calvinists forced Mary to abdicate the throne of Scotland in favor of her year-old son James (eventually James I of England), who was then raised as a Protestant. After her abdication, Mary spent nearly twenty years under house arrest in England, fomenting plots against Elizabeth. In 1587, when a letter from Mary offering her succession rights to Philip was discovered, Elizabeth overcame her reluctance to execute a fellow monarch and ordered Mary's beheading.

In response, Pope Sixtus V decided to subsidize a Catholic crusade under Philip's leadership against the heretical queen, "the English Jezebel." At the end of May 1588, Philip II sent his armada (Spanish for "fleet") of 130 ships from Lisbon toward the English Channel. The English scattered the Spanish Armada by sending blazing fire ships into its midst. A great gale then forced the Spanish to flee around Scotland. When the armada limped home in September, half the ships had been lost and thousands of sailors were dead or starving. Protestants throughout Europe rejoiced. In his play *King John* a few years later (1596), William Shakespeare wrote, "This England never did, nor never shall,/Lie at the proud foot of a conqueror." Philip and Catholic Spain suffered a crushing psychological blow. A Spanish monk lamented, "Almost the whole of Spain went into mourning."

By the time Philip II died in 1598, his great empire had begun to lose its luster. The costs of fighting the Dutch, the English, and the French had mounted, and an overbur-

Retreat of the Spanish Armada, 1588

dened peasantry could no longer pay the taxes required to meet rising expenses. In his novel *Don Quixote*♦ (1605), the Spanish writer Miguel de Cervantes captured the sadness of Spain's loss of grandeur. Cervantes himself had been wounded at Lepanto, been held captive in Algiers, and then served as a royal tax collector. His novel's hero, a minor nobleman, wants to understand "this thing they call reason of state," but he reads so many romances and books of chivalry that he loses his wits and wanders the countryside hoping to re-create the heroic deeds of times past. Don Quixote's futile adventures incarnated the thwarted ambitions of a declining military aristocracy.

England could never have defeated Spain in a head-to-head battle on land, but Elizabeth made the most of her limited means and consolidated the country's position as a Protestant power. In her early years, she held out the prospect of marriage to many political suitors; but in order to maintain her—and England's—independence, she never married. She cajoled Parliament with references to her female weaknesses, but she showed steely-eyed determination in protecting the monarchy's interests. Her chosen successor, James I (r. 1603–1625), came to the throne as king of both Scotland and England. Shakespeare's tragedies *Hamlet* (1601), *King Lear* (1605), and *Macbeth* (1606), written around the time of James's succession, might all be read as commentaries on the uncertainties faced by Elizabeth and James. But Elizabeth's story, unlike those of Shakespeare's tragedies, had a happy ending; she left James secure in a kingdom of growing weight in world politics.

The Clash of Faiths and Empires in Eastern Europe

In the east, the most contentious border divided Christian Europe from the Islamic realm of the Ottoman Turks. After their defeat at Lepanto in 1571, the Ottomans were down but far from out. They continued their attacks, seizing Venetian-held Cyprus in 1573. In the Balkans, the Turks allowed their Christian subjects to cling to the

♦**Don Quixote:** dahn kee HOH tee

Orthodox faith rather than forcibly converting them to Islam. They also tolerated many prosperous Jewish communities, which grew with the influx of Jews expelled from Spain.

The Muscovite tsars officially protected the Russian Orthodox church, which faced no competition within Russian lands. Building on the base laid by his grandfather Ivan III, Tsar Ivan IV (r. 1533–1584) stopped at nothing in his endeavor to make Muscovy the center of a mighty Russian empire. Given to unpredictable fits of rage, Ivan tortured priests, killed numerous *boyars* (nobles), and murdered his own son with an iron rod during a quarrel. His epithet "the Terrible" reflects not only the terror he unleashed but also the awesome impression he evoked. Cunning, intelligent, morbidly suspicious, and cruel, Ivan came to embody barbarism in the eyes of westerners. An English visitor wrote that Ivan's actions had bred "a general hatred, distreccion [distraction], fear and discontentment throw [throughout] his kingdom. . . . God has a great plague in store for this people." Such warnings did not keep away the many westerners drawn to Moscow by opportunities to buy furs and sell western cloth and military hardware.

Ivan brought the entire Volga valley under Muscovite control and initiated Russian expansion eastward into Siberia. In 1558, he struck out to the west, vainly attempting to seize the decaying state of the German crusader (Teutonic) knights in present-day Estonia and Latvia to provide Russia direct access to the Baltic Sea. Two formidable foes blocked Ivan's plans for expansion: Sweden (which then included much of present-day Finland) and Poland-Lithuania. Their rulers hoped to annex the eastern Baltic provinces themselves. Poland and the grand duchy of Lithuania united into a single commonwealth in 1569 and controlled territory stretching from the Baltic Sea to deep within present-day Ukraine and Belarus.♦ It was the largest state lying wholly within the boundaries of Europe.

Poland-Lithuania, like the Dutch Republic, constituted one of the great exceptions to the general trend in early modern Europe

toward greater monarchical authority; the Polish and Lithuanian nobles elected their king and severely circumscribed his authority. Noble converts to Lutheranism or Calvinism feared religious persecution by the Catholic majority, so the Polish-Lithuanian nobility insisted that their kings accept the principle of religious toleration as a prerequisite for election. The numerous Jewish communities prospered under the protection of the king and nobles.

Poland-Lithuania threatened the rule of Ivan's successors in Russia. After Ivan IV died in 1584, a terrible period of chaos known as the Time of Troubles ensued, during which the king of Poland-Lithuania tried to put his son on the Russian throne. In 1613, an army of nobles, townspeople, and peasants finally drove out the intruders and put on the throne a nobleman, Michael Romanov (r. 1613–1645), who established an enduring new dynasty. With the return of peace, Muscovite Russia resumed the process of state building.

Russia, Poland-Lithuania, and Sweden in the Late 1500s

Review: In what ways did the power of states depend on unity in religion?

❖ The Thirty Years' War and the Balance of Power, 1618–1648

Although the eastern states managed to avoid civil wars over religion, the rest of Europe was drawn into the final and most deadly of the wars of religion, the Thirty Years' War. It began in 1618 with conflicts between Catholics and Protestants within the Holy Roman Empire and eventually involved most European states. By its end in 1648, many central European lands lay in ruins and the balance of power had shifted away

♦**Belarus:** bee luh ROOS

The Horrors of the Thirty Years' War

Hans Grimmelshausen experienced the Thirty Years' War firsthand and then wrote about it in his novel, The Adventures of a Simpleton *(published in 1669). He had been a Lutheran schoolboy when soldiers from an unidentified army looted his town. Later he served as a musketeer in the Catholic imperial armies and converted to Catholicism. In the novel, he writes from the point of view of a "simpleton," a naive peasant who does not understand what is happening around him as a group of cavalrymen ransack the village.*

What they did not intend to take along they broke and spoiled. Some ran their swords into the hay and straw, as if there hadn't been hogs enough to stick. Some shook the feathers out of beds and put bacon slabs, hams, and other stuff in the ticking, as if they might sleep better on these. Others knocked down the hearth and broke the windows, as if announcing an everlasting summer. They flattened out copper and pewter dishes and baled the ruined goods. They burned up bedsteads, tables, chairs, and benches, though there were yards of dry firewood outside the kitchen. Jars and crocks, pots and casseroles all were broken, either because they preferred their meat broiled or because they thought they'd eat only one meal with us. In the barn, the hired girl was handled so roughly that she was unable to walk away, I am ashamed to report. They stretched the hired man out flat on the ground, stuck a wooden wedge in his mouth to keep it open, and emptied a milk bucket full of stinking manure drippings down his throat; they called it a Swedish cocktail. He didn't relish it and made a very wry face. . . . Then they used thumbscrews, which they cleverly made out of their pistols, to torture the peasants, as if they wanted to burn witches. Though he had confessed to nothing as yet, they put one of the captured hayseeds in the bake-oven and lighted a fire in it. They put a rope around someone else's head and tightened it like a tourniquet until blood came out of his mouth, nose, and ears. In short, every soldier had his favorite method of making life miserable for peasants, and every peasant had his own misery.

Source: *The Adventures of Simplicius Simpliccissimus*, 2nd ed. Trans. George Schulz-Behrend (Columbia, S.C.: Camden House, 1993), 6–7.

by Hans Grimmelshausen,♦ recounts the horror of the war in detail (see excerpt above). In one scene, the boy Simplicius has to watch while unidentified enemy cavalrymen ransack the house; rape the maid, his mother, and his sister; and hold the feet of his father to the fire until he tells where he hid his gold and jewels. Peasants fled their villages, which were often burned down. At times, desperate peasants revolted and attacked nearby castles and monasteries. War and intermittent outbreaks of plague cost some German towns one-third or more of their population. One-third of the inhabitants of Bohemia also perished.

Soldiers did not fare all that much better. An Englishman who fought for the Dutch army in 1633 described how he slept on the wet ground, got his boots full of water, and "at peep of day looked like a drowned ratt." Governments increasingly short of funds often failed to pay the troops, and frequent mutinies, looting, and pillaging resulted. Armies attracted all sorts of displaced people desperately in need of provisions. In the last year of the Thirty Years' War, the Imperial-Bavarian Army had 40,000 men entitled to draw rations—and more than 100,000 wives, prostitutes, servants, children, maids, and other camp followers forced to scrounge for their own food. The result was scenes like those witnessed by Simplicius.

Although foreign mercenaries still predominated in many armies, rulers began to recruit more of their own subjects. Volunteers proved easiest to find in hard times, when the threat of starvation induced men to accept the bonus offered for signing up. A Venetian general

♦**Grimmelshausen:** GRIHM uhls how zuhn

explained the motives for enlisting: "To escape from being craftsmen [or] working in a shop; to avoid a criminal sentence; to see new things; to pursue honour (though these are very few) ... all in the hope of having enough to live on and a bit over for shoes, or some other trifle."

The Peace of Westphalia, 1648

The comprehensive settlement provided by the Peace of Westphalia♦—named after the German province where negotiations took place—would serve as a model for resolving conflict among warring European states.

♦**Westphalia:** wehst FAYL yuh

For the first time, a diplomatic congress addressed international disputes, and the signatories to the treaties guaranteed the resulting settlement. A method still in use, the congress was the first to bring *all* parties together, rather than two or three at a time.

The Winners and Losers. France and Sweden gained most from the Peace of Westphalia. Although France and Spain continued fighting until 1659, France acquired parts of Alsace and replaced Spain as the prevailing power on the continent. Baltic conflicts would not be resolved until 1661, but Sweden took several northern territories from the Holy Roman Empire (Map 16.3).

MAP 16.3 The Thirty Years' War and the Peace of Westphalia, 1648
The Thirty Years' War involved many of the major continental European powers. The arrows marking invasion routes show that most of the fighting took place in central Europe in the lands of the Holy Roman Empire. The German states and Bohemia sustained the greatest damage during the fighting. None of the combatants emerged unscathed because even ultimate winners such as Sweden and France depleted their resources of men and money.

The Arts and State Power
Diego Velázquez painted King Philip IV of Spain and many members of his court. This painting of 1634–1635 shows Philip on horseback. In the seventeenth century, many rulers hired court painters to embellish the image of royal majesty. Philip IV commissioned this painting for his new palace called Buen Retiro. *All rights reserved.* © *Museo Nacional del Prado–Madrid.*

the west, the Austrian Habsburgs turned eastward to concentrate on restoring Catholicism to Bohemia and wresting Hungary from the Turks.

The Peace of Westphalia permanently settled the distributions of the main religions in the Holy Roman Empire: Lutheranism would dominate in the north, Calvinism in the area of the Rhine River, and Catholicism in the south. Most of the territorial changes in Europe remained intact until the nineteenth century. In the future, international warfare would be undertaken for reasons of national security, commercial ambition, or dynastic pride rather than to enforce religious uniformity. As the *politiques* of the late sixteenth century had hoped, state interests now outweighed motivations of faith in political affairs.

Growth of State Authority. Warfare increased the reach of states: as the size of armies increased, governments needed more men, more money, and more supervisory officials. Most armies in the 1550s had fewer than 50,000 men, but Gustavus Adolphus had 100,000 men under arms in 1631. In France the rate of land tax paid by peasants doubled in the eight years after France joined the war. In addition to raising taxes, governments deliberately depreciated the value of the currency, which often resulted in inflation and soaring prices. Rulers also sold new offices and manipulated the embryonic stock and bond markets. When all else failed, they declared bankruptcy. The Spanish government, for example, did so three times in the first half of the seventeenth century. From Portugal to Muscovy, ordinary people resisted new taxes by forming makeshift armies and battling royal forces. With their colorful banners, unlikely leaders, strange names (the Nu-Pieds, or "Barefooted," in

The Habsburgs lost the most. The Spanish Habsburgs recognized Dutch independence after eighty years of war. The Swiss Confederation and the German princes demanded autonomy from the Austrian Habsburg rulers of the Holy Roman Empire. Each German prince gained the right to establish Lutheranism, Catholicism, or Calvinism in his state, a right denied to Calvinist rulers by the Peace of Augsburg in 1555. The independence ceded to German princes sustained political divisions that would remain until the nineteenth century and prepared the way for the emergence of a new power, the Hohenzollern♦ Elector of Brandenburg, who increased his territories and developed a small but effective standing army. After losing considerable territory in

♦**Hohenzollern:** hoh uhn ZOH lurn

France, for instance), and crude weapons, the rebels usually proved no match for state armies, but they did keep officials worried and troops occupied.

As the demand for soldiers and for the money to supply them rose, the number of state employees multiplied, paperwork proliferated, and appointment to office began to depend on university education in the law. Monarchs relied on advisers who now took on the role of modern prime ministers. Axel Oxenstierna,♦ for example, played a central part in Swedish governments between 1611 and 1654; continuity in Swedish affairs, especially after the death of Gustavus Adolphus, largely depended on him. As Louis XIII's chief minister, Richelieu arranged support for the Lutheran Gustavus even though Richelieu was a cardinal of the Catholic church. His priority was **raison d'état**♦ ("reason of state"), that is, the state's interest above all else. He silenced Protestants within France because they had become too independent and crushed noble and popular resistance to Louis's policies. He set up intendants—delegates from the king's council dispatched to the provinces—to oversee police, army, and financial affairs.

To justify the growth of state authority and the expansion of government bureaucracies, rulers carefully cultivated their royal images. (See The Arts and State Power, left.) James I of England explicitly argued that he ruled by divine right and was accountable only to God: "The state of monarchy is the supremest thing on earth; for kings are not only God's lieutenant on earth, but even by God himself they are called gods." He advised his son to maintain a manly appearance (his own well-known homosexual liaisons did not make him seem less manly to his subjects): "Eschew to be effeminate in your clothes, in perfuming, preening, or such like, and fail never in time of wars to be galliardest and bravest, both in clothes and countenance." Clothes counted for so much that most rulers regulated who could wear which kinds of cloth and decoration, reserving the richest and rarest such as ermine and gold for themselves.

♦**Axel Oxenstierna:** AK suhl OOK sehn stehr nah
♦**raison d'état:** ray zohn DAY TAH

Just as soldiers had to learn new drills for combat, courtiers had to learn to follow precise rituals at court. In Spain, court regulations set the wages, duties, and ceremonial functions of every official. Hundreds, even thousands, of people made up such a court. The court of Philip IV (r. 1621–1665), for example, numbered seventeen hundred. In the 1630s Philip built a new palace near Madrid. There the courtiers lived amid extensive parks and formal gardens, artificial ponds and grottoes, an iron aviary (which led some critics to call the whole thing a chicken coop), a wild animal cage, a courtyard for bullfights, and rooms filled with sculptures and paintings. State funerals, public festivities, and court display, like the acquisition of art and the building of sumptuous palaces, served to underline the power and glory of the ruler.

> **Review:** Why did a war fought over religious differences result in stronger states?

❖ Economic Crisis and Realignment

The devastation caused by the Thirty Years' War deepened an economic crisis that was already under way. After a century of rising prices, caused partly by massive transfers of gold and silver from the New World and partly by population growth, in the early 1600s prices began to level off and even to drop, and in most places population growth slowed. With fewer goods being produced, international trade fell into recession. Agricultural yields also declined. Just when states attempted to field ever-expanding standing armies, peasants and townspeople alike were less able to pay the escalating taxes needed to finance the wars. Famine and disease trailed grimly behind economic crisis and war, in some areas causing large-scale uprisings and revolts. Behind the scenes, the economic balance of power gradually shifted as northwestern Europe began to dominate international trade and broke the stranglehold of Spain and Portugal in the New World.

From Growth to Recession

Population grew and prices rose in the second half of the sixteenth century. Even though religious and political turbulence led to population decline in some cities, such as war-torn Antwerp, overall rates of growth remained impressive: in the sixteenth century, parts of Spain doubled in population and England's population grew by 70 percent. The supply of precious metals swelled too. Improvements in mining techniques in central Europe raised the output of silver and copper mines, and in the 1540s new silver mines had been discovered in Mexico and Peru. Spanish gold imports peaked in the 1550s, silver in the 1590s. (See "Taking Measure," below.) This flood of precious metals combined with population growth to fuel an astounding inflation in food prices in western Europe—400 percent in the sixteenth century—and a more moderate rise in the cost of manufactured goods. Wages rose much more slowly, at about half the rate of the increase in food prices. Governments always overspent revenues and by the end of the century most of Europe's rulers faced deep deficits.

Recession did not strike everywhere at the same time, but the warning signs were unmistakable. From the Baltic to the East Indies, foreign trade slumped as war and an uncertain money supply made business riskier. After 1625, silver imports to Spain declined, in part because so many of the native Americans who worked in Spanish colonial mines died from disease and in part because the ready supply of precious metals was progressively exhausted. Textile production fell in many countries and in some places nearly collapsed, largely because of decreased demand and a shrinking labor force. Even the relatively limited trade in African slaves stagnated, though its growth would resume after 1650 and skyrocket after 1700. African slaves were first transported to the new colony of Virginia in 1619, foreshadowing a major transformation of economic life in the New World colonies.

Demographic slowdown also signaled economic trouble. Overall, Europe's population may actually have declined, from 85 million in 1550 to 80 million in 1650. In the Mediterranean, growth apparently stopped in the 1570s. The most sudden reversal occurred in central Europe as a result of the Thirty Years' War: one-fourth of the inhabitants of the Holy Roman Empire perished in the 1630s and 1640s. The population continued to increase only in England and Wales, the Dutch Republic and the Spanish Netherlands, and Scandinavia.

Where the population stagnated or declined, agricultural prices dropped because of less demand, and farmers who produced for the market suffered. The price of grain fell most precipitously, causing many farmers to convert grain-growing land to pasture or vineyards.

TAKING MEASURE

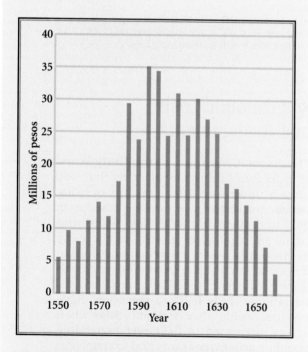

The Rise and Fall of Silver Imports to Spain, 1550–1660
Gold and silver from the New World enabled the king of Spain to pursue aggressive policies in Europe and around the world. At what point did silver imports reach their highest level? Was the fall in silver imports precipitous or gradual? What can we conclude about the resources available to the Spanish king? *From Earl J. Hamilton,* American Revolution and the Price Revolution in Spain, 1501–1650 *(Cambridge, MA: Harvard University Press, 1934).*

Interest in improvement of the land diminished. In some places, peasants abandoned their villages and left land to waste, as had happened during the plague epidemic of the late fourteenth century. The only country that emerged unscathed from this downturn was the Dutch Republic, principally because it had long excelled in agricultural innovation. Inhabiting Europe's most densely populated area, the Dutch developed systems of field drainage, crop rotation, and animal husbandry that provided high yields of grain for both people and animals. Their foreign trade, textile industry, crop production, and population all grew. After the Dutch, the English fared best; unlike the Spanish, the English never depended on New World gold and silver, and unlike most continental European countries, England escaped the direct impact of the Thirty Years' War.

Historians have long disagreed about the causes of the early-seventeenth-century recession. Some cite the inability of agriculture to support a growing population by the end of the sixteenth century; others blame the Thirty Years' War, the states' demands for more taxes, the irregularities in money supply resulting from rudimentary banking practices, or the waste caused by middle-class expenditures in the desire to emulate the nobility. To this list of causes, recent researchers have added climatic changes. (See "New Sources, New Perspectives," page 600.) Cold winters and wet summers meant bad harvests, and these natural disasters ushered in a host of social catastrophes. When the harvest was bad, prices shot back up and many could not afford to feed themselves.

Consequences for Daily Life

The recession of the early 1600s had both short-term and long-term effects. In the short term it aggravated the threat of food shortages and increased the outbreaks of famine and disease. In the long term it deepened the division between prosperous and poor peasants and fostered the development of a new pattern of late marriages and smaller families.

Famine and Disease. When grain harvests fell short, peasants immediately suffered because, outside of England and the Dutch Republic, grain had replaced more expensive meat as the essential staple of most Europeans' diets. The average adult European now ate more than four hundred pounds of grain per year. Peasants lived on bread, soup with a little fat or oil, peas or lentils, garden vegetables in season, and only occasionally a piece of meat or fish. Usually the adverse years differed from place to place, but from 1594 to 1597 most of Europe suffered from shortages; the resulting famine triggered revolts from

The Life of the Poor

This mid-seventeenth-century painting by the Dutch artist Adriaen Pietersz van de Venne depicts the poor peasant weighed down by his wife and child. An empty food bowl signifies their hunger. In retrospect, this painting seems unfair to the wife of the family; she is shown in clothes that are not nearly as tattered as her husband's and is portrayed entirely as a burden, rather than as a help in getting by in hard times. In reality, many poor men abandoned their homes in search of work, leaving their wives behind to cope with hungry children and what remained of the family farm. *Allen Memorial Art Museum, Oberlin College, Oberlin, Ohio, Mrs. F. F. Prentiss Fund, 1960.*

NEW SOURCES, NEW PERSPECTIVES
Tree Rings and the Little Ice Age

Global cooling helped bring about the economic crisis of the seventeenth century. Glaciers advanced, average temperatures fell, and winters were often exceptionally severe. Canals and rivers essential to markets froze over. Great storms disrupted ocean traffic (one storm changed the escape route of the Spanish Armada). Even in the valleys far from the mountain glaciers, cooler weather meant lower crop yields, which quickly translated into hunger and greater susceptibility to disease, leading in turn to population decline. Some historians of climate refer to the entire period 1600–1850 as the little ice age because glaciers advanced during this time and retreated only after 1850; others argue for the period 1550–1700 as the coldest, but either time frame includes the seventeenth century. Since systematic records of European temperatures were kept only from the 1700s onward, how do historians know that the weather was cooler? Given the current debates about global warming, how can we sift through the evidence to come up with a reliable interpretation?

Information about climate comes from various sources. The advance of glaciers can be seen in letters complaining to the authorities. In 1601, for example, panic-stricken villagers in Savoy (in the French Alps) wrote, "We are terrified of the glaciers . . .

which are moving forward all the time and have just buried two of our villages." Yearly temperature fluctuations can be determined from the dates of wine harvests; growers harvested their grapes earliest when the weather was warmest and latest when it was coolest. Scientists study ice cores taken from Greenland to determine temperature variations; such studies seem to indicate that the coolest times were the periods 1160–1300; the 1600s; and 1820–1850. The period 1730–1800 appears to have been warmer. Recently, scientists have developed techniques for sampling corals in the tropics and sediments on oceanic shelves.

But the most striking are data gathered from tree rings (the science is called dendrochronology or dendroclimatology). Timber samples have been taken from very old oak trees and also from ancient beams in buildings and archaeological digs and from logs left long undisturbed in northern bogs and riverbeds. In cold summers, trees lay down thinner growth rings; in warm ones, thicker rings. Information about tree rings confirms the conclusions drawn from wine harvest and ice core samples: the seventeenth century was relatively cold. Recent tree ring studies have shown that some of the coldest summers were caused by volcanic eruptions; according to a study of more

Ireland to Muscovy. To head off social disorder, the English government drew up a new Poor Law in 1597 that required each community to support its poor. Many other governments also increased relief efforts.

Most people, however, did not respond to their dismal circumstances by rebelling or mounting insurrections. They simply left their huts and hovels and took to the road in search of food and charity. Overwhelmed officials recorded pitiful tales of suffering. Women and children died while waiting in line for food at convents or churches. Husbands left their wives and families to search

for better conditions in other parishes or even other countries. Those left behind might be reduced to eating chestnuts, roots, bark, and grass. In eastern France in 1637, a witness reported, "The roads were paved with people. . . . Finally it came to cannibalism." Eventually compassion gave way to fear as these hungry vagabonds, who sometimes banded together to beg for bread, became more aggressive, occasionally threatening to burn a barn if they were not given food.

Successive bad harvests led to malnutrition, which weakened people and made them more susceptible to such epidemic

The Frozen Thames
This painting by Abraham Hondius of the frozen Thames River in London dates to 1677. In the 1670s and 1680s the Thames froze several times. Hondius himself depicted another such view in 1684. Diarists recorded that shopkeepers even set up their stalls on the ice. In other words, the expected routines of daily life changed during the cooling down of the seventeenth century. Contemporaries were shocked enough by the changes to record them for posterity. *Museum of London.*

than one hundred sites in North America and Europe, the five coldest summers in the past four hundred years were in 1601, 1641, 1669, 1699, and 1912 (four out of five in the seventeenth century), and all but the summer of 1699 came in years following recorded eruptions.

QUESTIONS TO CONSIDER
1. What were the historical consequences of global cooling in the seventeenth century?

2. Why would trees be especially valuable sources of information about climate?

FURTHER READING
Galloway, Patrick R. "Long-Term Fluctuations in Climate and Population in the Preindustrial Era." *Population and Development Review* 12 (1986): 1–24.
Lamb, H. H. *Climate, History and the Modern World,* 2nd ed. 1995.

diseases as the plague, typhoid fever, typhus, dysentery, smallpox, and influenza. Disease did not spare the rich, although many epidemics hit the poor hardest. The plague was feared most: in one year it could cause the death of up to half of a town's or village's population, and it struck with no discernible pattern. Nearly 5 percent of France's entire population died just in the plague of 1628–1632.

The Changing Status of the Peasantry.
Economic crisis heightened the contrast between prosperity and poverty. Peasants

faced many obligations, including rent and various fees for inheriting or selling land and tolls for using mills, wine presses, or ovens. States collected direct taxes on land and sales taxes on such consumer goods as salt, an essential preservative. Protestant and Catholic churches alike exacted a **tithe**♦ (a tax equivalent to one-tenth of the parishioner's annual income); often the clergy took their tithe in the form of crops and collected it directly during the harvest. Any reversal of fortune could force peasants into the home-

♦**tithe:** tyth

The Figure Explained:

Being a Diffection of the WOMB, with the ufual manner how the CHILD lies therein near the time of its Birth.

B B. The inner parts of the *Chorion* extended and branched out.

C. The *Amnios* extended.

D D. The Membrane of the Womb extended and branched.

E. The Flefhy fubftance call'd the *Cake* or *Placenta*, which nourifhes the Infant, it is full of Veffels.

F. The Veffels appointed for the Navel ftring.

G. The Navel ftring carrying nourifhment from the *Placenta* to the Navel.

H H H. The manner how the Infant lieth in the Womb near the time of its Birth.

I. The Navel ftring how it enters into the Navel.

The *Midwives Book* (1671)
The English woman Jane Sharp wrote the first book on midwifery by a woman. She endeavored to provide as much scientific information about the female body as was available at the time. *British Library.*

less world of vagrants and beggars, who numbered as much as 1 to 2 percent of the total population.

In England, the Dutch Republic, northern France, and northwestern Germany, the peasantry was disappearing: improvements gave some peasants the means to become farmers who rented substantial holdings, produced for the market, and in good times enjoyed relative comfort and higher status. Those who could not afford to plant new crops such as maize (American corn) or buckwheat or to use techniques that ensured higher yields became simple laborers with little or no land of their own. One-half to four-fifths of the peasants did not have enough land to support a family. They descended deeper into debt during difficult times and often lost their land to wealthier farmers or to city officials intent on developing rural estates.

As the recession deepened, women lost some of their economic opportunities. Widows who had been able to take over their late husbands' trade now found themselves excluded by the urban guilds or limited to short tenures. Many women went into domestic service until they married, some for their entire lives. When town governments began to fear the effects of increased mobility from country to town and town to town,

they carefully regulated the work of female servants, requiring women to stay in their positions unless they could prove mistreatment by a master.

Effects on Marriage and Childbearing.
Demographic historians have shown that European families reacted almost immediately to economic crisis. During bad harvests they postponed marriages and had fewer children. When hard times passed, more people married and had more children. But even in the best of times, one-fifth to one-quarter of all children died in their first year, and half died before age twenty. In 1636, an Englishman described his grief when his twenty-one-month-old son died: "We both found the sorrow for the loss of this child, on whom we had bestowed so much care and affection . . . far to surpass our grief for the decease of his three elder brothers, who dying almost as soon as they were born, were not so endeared to us as this [one] was."

Childbirth still carried great risks for women, about 10 percent of whom died in the process. Even in the richest and most enlightened homes, childbirth often occasioned an atmosphere of panic. To allay their fears, women sometimes depended on magic stones and special pilgrimages and prayers. Midwives delivered most babies; physicians were scarce, and even if they did attend a birth they were generally less helpful than the midwife. The Englishwoman Alice Thornton described in her diary how a doctor bled her to prevent a miscarriage after a fall (bloodletting, often by the application of leeches, was a common medical treatment); her son died anyway in a breech birth that almost killed her too.

It might be assumed that families would have more children to compensate for high death rates, but beginning in the early seventeenth century and continuing until the end of the eighteenth, families in all ranks of society started to limit the number of children. Because methods of contraception were not widely known, they did this for the most part by marrying later; the average age at marriage during the seventeenth century rose from the early twenties to the late twenties. The average family had about four children. Poorer families seem to have had fewer children, wealthier ones more. Peasant couples, especially in eastern and southeastern Europe, had more children than urban couples because cultivation still required intensive manual labor—and having children was the most economical means of securing enough laborers.

The consequences of late marriage were profound. Young men and women were expected to put off marriage (and sexual intercourse) until their mid to late twenties—if they were among the lucky 50 percent who lived that long and not among the 10 percent who never married. Because both the Reformation and the Counter-Reformation had stressed sexual fidelity and abstinence before marriage, the number of births out of wedlock was relatively small (2–5 percent of births); premarital intercourse was generally tolerated only after a couple had announced their engagement.

The Economic Balance of Power

Just as the recession produced winners and losers among ordinary people, so too it created winners and losers among the competing states of Europe. The economies of southern Europe declined, whereas those of the northwest emerged stronger. Competition in the New World reflected and reinforced

this shift as the English, Dutch, and French rushed to establish trading outposts and permanent settlements to compete with the Spanish and Portuguese.

Regional Differences.   The crisis of the seventeenth century ended the dominance of Mediterranean economies, which had endured since the time of the Greeks and Romans, and ushered in the new powers of northwestern Europe with their growing Atlantic economies. With expanding populations and geographical positions that promoted Atlantic trade, England and the Dutch Republic vied with France to become the leading mercantile powers. Northern Italian industries were eclipsed; Spanish commerce with the New World dropped. Amsterdam replaced Seville, Venice, Genoa, and Antwerp as the center of European trade and commerce. The plague also had differing effects. Whereas central Europe and the Mediterranean countries took generations to recover from its ravages, northwestern Europe quickly replaced its lost population, no doubt because this area's people had suffered less from the effects of the Thirty Years' War and from the malnutrition related to the economic crisis.

All but the remnants of serfdom had disappeared in western Europe, yet in eastern Europe nobles reinforced their dominance over peasants, and the burden of serfdom increased. The price rise of the sixteenth century prompted Polish and eastern German nobles to increase their holdings and step up their production of grain for western markets. To raise production, they demanded more rent and dues from their peasants, whom the government decreed must stay in their villages. Although noble landlords lost income in the economic downturn of the first half of the seventeenth century, their peasants gained nothing. Those who were already dependent became serfs—completely tied to the land. A local official might complain of "this barbaric and as it were Egyptian servitude," but he had no power to fight the nobles. In Muscovy the complete enserfment of the peasantry would eventually be recognized in the Code of Laws in 1649. Although enserfment produced short-term profits for landlords, in the long run it

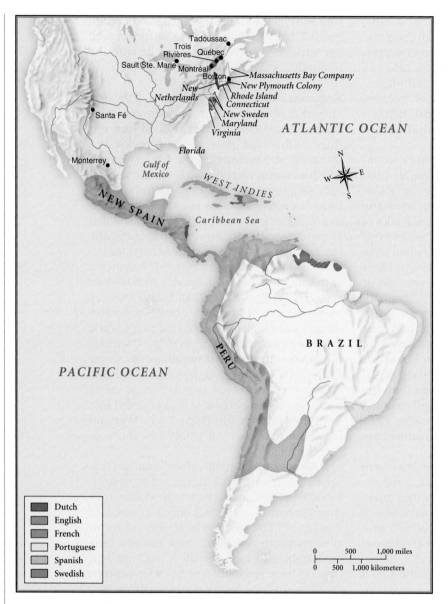

MAP 16.4 European Colonization of the Americas, c. 1640
Europeans established themselves first in coastal areas. The English, French, and Dutch set up most of their colonies in the Caribbean and North America because the Spanish and Portuguese had already colonized the easily accessible regions in South America. Vast inland areas still remained unexplored and uncolonized in 1640.

petition as a way of increasing national wealth. To this end, they chartered private joint-stock companies to enrich investors by importing fish, furs, tobacco, and precious metals, if they could be found, and to develop new markets for European products. Because Spain and Portugal had divided among themselves the rich spoils of South America, other prospective colonizers had to carve niches in seemingly less hospitable places, especially North America and the Caribbean (Map 16.4). Eventually the English, French, and Dutch would dominate commerce with these colonies.

In establishing permanent colonies, the Europeans created whole new communities across the Atlantic. Careful plans often fell afoul of the hazards of transatlantic shipping, however. Originally, the warm climate of Virginia made it an attractive destination for the Pilgrims, a small English sect that, unlike the Puritans, attempted to separate from the Church of England. But the *Mayflower*, which had sailed for Virginia with Pilgrim emigrants, landed far to the north in Massachusetts, where in 1620 the settlers founded New Plymouth Colony. As the religious situation for English Puritans worsened, wealthier people became willing to emigrate, and in 1629 a prominent group of Puritans incorporated themselves as the Massachusetts Bay Company. They founded a virtually self-governing colony headquartered in Boston.

Colonization in North America grew steadily. By the 1640s, the British North American colonies had more than fifty thousand people—not including the Indians, whose numbers had been decimated in epi-

retarded economic development in eastern Europe and kept most of the population in a stranglehold of illiteracy and hardship.

Competition in the New World. Many European states, including Sweden and Denmark, rushed to join the colonial com-

demics and wars—and the foundations of representative government in locally chosen colonial assemblies. By contrast, French Canada had only about three thousand European inhabitants by 1640. Because the French government refused to let Protestants emigrate from France and establish a foothold in the New World, it denied itself a ready population for the settling of permanent colonies abroad. Both England and France turned their attention to the Caribbean in the 1620s and 1630s when they occupied the islands of the West Indies after driving off the native Caribs. These islands would prove ideal for a plantation economy of tobacco and sugarcane.

Some colonists justified their mission by promising to convert the native population to Christianity. As the English colonizer John Smith told his followers in Virginia, "The growing provinces addeth to the King's Crown; but the reducing heathen people to civility and true religion bringeth honour to the King of Heaven." Catholic France and Spain were more successful, however, than Protestant England in their efforts to convert American natives. Protestantism did not mesh well with native American cultures because it demanded an individual conversion experience based on a Christian notion of sin. Catholicism, in contrast, stressed shared rituals, which were more accessible to the native populations.

Spain did not stand still while the British and French moved into North America and the Caribbean. Even while developing silver mines in Mexico and South America with compulsory Indian labor, the Spanish explored the Pacific coast up to northern California and pushed as far north as New Mexico. On the other side of the world, in the Philippines, they competed with local Muslim rulers and indigenous tribal leaders to extend their control. Catholic missionaries printed tracts in Spanish and the island's native Tagalog and established a university in 1611. Spanish officials worked closely with the missionaries to rule over a colony composed of indigenous peoples, Spaniards, and some Chinese merchants. By 1600 they had gained control of much of the area.

Review: What were the consequences of economic recession in the early 1600s?

"Savages" of the New World

The half-dressed savage appears much like a noble Italian in Paolo Farinati's 1595 painting *America;* he holds a crucifix in his right hand, signifying his conversion to Christianity. But to his left his comrades are roasting human flesh. Europeans were convinced that many native peoples were cannibals. What can we conclude from this painting about European attitudes toward peoples of the New World? *Villa della Torre, Mezzane de Sotto, Verona.*

❖ A Clash of Worldviews

The countries that moved ahead economically in this period—England, the Dutch Republic, and to some extent France—turned out to be the most receptive to new secular worldviews. In the long-term process known as **secularization**, religion became a matter of private conscience rather than public policy. Secularization did not entail a loss of religious faith, but it did prompt a search for nonreligious explanations for political authority and natural phenomena. During the late sixteenth and early seventeenth centuries, art, political theory, and science all began to break some of their bonds with religion. The visual arts, for example, more frequently depicted secular subjects. Scientists and scholars sought laws in nature to explain politics as well as movements in the heavens and on earth. A scientific revolution was in the making. Yet traditional attitudes did not disappear. Belief in magic and witchcraft pervaded every level of society. People of all classes accepted supernatural explanations for natural phenomena, a view only gradually and partially undermined by new ideas.

The Arts in an Age of Crisis

Two new forms of artistic expression—professional theater and opera—developed to express secular values in an age of conflict over religious beliefs. The greatest playwright of the English language, William Shakespeare, never referred to religious disputes in his plays, and he always set his most personal reflections on political turmoil and uncertainty in faraway times or places. Religion played an important role in the new mannerist and baroque styles of painting, however, even though many rulers commissioned paintings on secular subjects for their own uses.

Theater in the Age of Shakespeare. Permanent professional theater companies appeared for the first time in Europe in the last quarter of the sixteenth century. In previous centuries, traveling companies made their living by playing at major religious festivals and by repeating their performances in small towns and villages along the way. In London, Seville, and Madrid, the first professional acting companies performed before paying audiences in the 1570s. A huge outpouring of playwriting followed. The Spanish playwright Lope de Vega♦ (1562–1635) alone wrote more than fifteen hundred plays. Between 1580 and 1640, three hundred English playwrights produced works for a hundred different acting companies. Theaters did a banner business despite Puritan opposition in England and Catholic objections in Spain. Shopkeepers, apprentices, lawyers, and court nobles crowded into open-air theaters to see everything from bawdy farces to profound tragedies.

The most enduring and influential playwright of the time was the Englishman William Shakespeare (1564–1616), son of a glovemaker, who wrote three dozen plays and acted in one of the chief troupes. Although Shakespeare's plays were not set in contemporary England, they reflected the concerns of his age: the nature of power and the crisis of authority. As noted earlier in this chapter, three of his greatest tragedies—*Hamlet* (1601), *King Lear* (1605), and *Macbeth* (1606)—show the uncertainty and even chaos that result when power is misappropriated or misused. In each play, family relationships are linked to questions about the legitimacy of government, just as they were for Elizabeth I herself. Hamlet's mother marries the man who murdered his royal father and usurped the crown; two of Lear's daughters betray him when he tries to divide his kingdom; Macbeth's wife persuades him to murder the king and seize the throne. One character in the final act describes the tragic story of Prince Hamlet as one "Of carnal, bloody, and unnatural acts; / Of accidental judgments, casual slaughters; / Of deaths put on by cunning and forced cause." Like many real-life people, Shakespeare's tragic characters found little peace in the turmoil of their times.

Mannerism and the Baroque in Art. New styles of painting departed abruptly from Renaissance perspective, which had emphasized precise and harmonious lines. In the late sixteenth century the artistic style

♦**Lope de Vega:** LOH pay day VAY gah

known as **mannerism** emerged in the Italian states and soon spread across Europe. Mannerism was an almost theatrical style that allowed painters to distort perspective to convey a message or emphasize a theme. The most famous mannerist painter, called El Greco because he was of Greek origin, trained in Venice and Rome before he moved to Spain in the 1570s. His paintings encapsulated the mannerist style: he crowded figures or objects into every available space, used larger-than-life or elongated figures, and created new and often bizarre visual effects. The religious intensity of El Greco's pictures shows that faith still motivated many artists, as it did much political conflict. (See Mannerist Painting, right column.)

The most important new style was the **baroque,**♦ which, like mannerism, originated in the Italian states. Like many historical categories, the word *baroque* was not used as a label by people living at the time; in the eighteenth century, art critics coined the word to mean shockingly bizarre, confused, and extravagant, and until the late nineteenth century, art historians and collectors largely disdained the baroque. In place of the Renaissance emphasis on harmonious design, unity, and clarity, the baroque featured curves, exaggerated lighting, intense emotions, release from restraint, and even a kind of artistic sensationalism.

Closely tied to the Counter-Reformation, the baroque melodramatically reaffirmed the emotional depths of the Catholic faith and glorified both church and monarchy. The style spread from Rome to other Italian states and then into central Europe. The Catholic Habsburg territories, including Spain and the Spanish Netherlands, embraced the style. The Spanish built baroque churches in their American colonies as part of their massive conversion campaign. Within Europe, Protestant countries largely resisted the baroque, as we can see by comparing Flemish painters from the Spanish Netherlands with Dutch artists. The first great baroque painter was an Italian-trained Fleming, Peter Paul Rubens (1577–1640). A devout Catholic, Rubens painted vivid, exuberant pictures on religious themes, packed with figures. His style

♦**baroque:** buh ROHK

Mannerist Painting
With its distortion of perspective, crowding of figures, and mysterious allusions, El Greco's painting *The Dream of Philip II* (1577) is a typical mannerist painting. What can we conclude about Philip II's character from the way he is depicted here? © *National Gallery, London.*

was an extension of the theatrical baroque style, conveying ideas through broad gestures and dramatic poses. (See Baroque Style of Painting, on the next page.) The great Dutch Protestant painters of the next generation, such as Rembrandt van Rijn (1606–1669), sometimes used biblical subjects, but their pictures were more realistic and focused on everyday scenes. Many of them

Baroque Style of Painting
Although the subject matter here is secular and not religious, *The Hippo Hunt* (1615–1616) by the Flemish painter Peter Paul Rubens displays many of the elements that define the baroque style: dramatic action, intense emotions, and an emphasis on curves and violent contrasts. Rubens painted this scene for Duke Maximilian of Bavaria. The picture also shows European interest in exotic places; the Turks are hunting animals not seen in Europe. *Alte Pinakothek, Munich/Giraudon, Paris/SuperStock.*

suggested the Protestant concern for an inner life and personal faith rather than the public expression of religiosity.

Opera. A new secular musical form, the opera, grew up parallel to the baroque style in the visual arts. First influential in the Italian states, opera combined music, drama, dance, and scenery in a grand sensual display, often with themes chosen to please the ruler and the aristocracy. Operas could be based on typically baroque sacred subjects or on traditional stories. Like Shakespeare, opera composers often turned to familiar stories their audiences would recognize and readily follow. One of the most innovative composers of opera was Claudio Monteverdi (1567–1643), whose work contributed to the development of both opera and the orchestra. His earliest operatic production, *Orfeo* (1607), was the first to require an orchestra of about forty instruments and to include instrumental as well as vocal sections.

The Natural Laws of Politics

In reaction to the religious wars, jurists and scholars not only began to defend the primacy of state interests over those of religious conformity but also insisted on secular explanations for politics. Machiavelli had pointed in this direction with his prescriptions for

Renaissance princes in the early sixteenth century, but the intellectual movement gathered steam in the aftermath of the religious violence unleashed by the Reformation. Religious toleration could not take hold until government could be organized on some principle other than one king, one faith. The French politiques Michel de Montaigne and Jean Bodin started the search for those principles, and the Dutch jurist Hugo Grotius developed ideas on government that would influence John Locke and the American revolutionaries of the eighteenth century.

Montaigne and Bodin. Michel de Montaigne♦ (1533–1592) was a French magistrate who resigned his office in the midst of the wars of religion to write about the need for tolerance and open-mindedness. Although himself a Catholic, Montaigne painted on the beams of his study the statement "All that is certain is that nothing is certain." To capture this need for personal reflection in a tumultuous age of religious discord, he invented the essay as a short and pithy form of expression. He revived the ancient doctrine of skepticism, which held that total certainty is never attainable—a doctrine, like toleration of religious differences, that was repugnant to Protestants and Catholics alike, both of whom were certain that their religion was the right one. He also questioned the common European habit of calling newly discovered peoples in the New World barbarous and savage: "Everyone gives the title of barbarism to everything that is not in use in his own country."

The French Catholic lawyer Jean Bodin♦ (1530–1596) sought systematic secular answers to the problem of disorder in *The Six Books of the Republic* (1576). Comparing the different forms of government throughout history, he concluded that there were three basic types of sovereignty: monarchy, aristocracy, and democracy. Only strong monarchical power offered hope for maintaining order, he insisted. Bodin rejected any doctrine of the right to resist tyrannical authority: "I denied that it was the function of a good man or of a good citizen to offer violence to his prince for any reason, however great a

tyrant he might be" (and, it might be added, whatever his ideas on religion). Bodin's ideas helped lay the foundation for absolutism, the idea that the monarch should be the sole and uncontested source of power. Nonetheless, the very discussion of types of governments in the abstract implied that they might be subject to choice rather than simply being God-given, as most rulers maintained.

Grotius and Natural Law. During the Dutch revolt against Spain, the jurist Hugo Grotius♦ (1583–1645) gave new meaning to the notion of "natural law"—laws of nature that give legitimacy to government and stand above the actions of any particular ruler or religious group. Grotius argued that natural law stood beyond the reach of either secular or divine authority; it would be valid even if God did not exist. By this account, natural law, not Scripture, religious authority, or tradition, should govern politics. Such ideas got Grotius into trouble with both Catholics and Protestants. His work, *The Laws of War and Peace* (1625), was condemned by the Catholic church. The Dutch Protestant government arrested him for his part in religious controversies; his wife helped him escape prison by hiding him in a chest of books. He fled to Paris, where he got a small pension from Louis XIII and served as his ambassador to Sweden. The Swedish king Gustavus Adolphus claimed that he kept Grotius's book under his pillow even while at battle. Grotius was one of the first to argue that international conventions should govern the treatment of prisoners of war and the making of peace treaties.

At the same time that Grotius expanded the principles of natural law, most jurists worked on codifying the huge amount of legislation and jurisprudence devoted to legal forms of torture. Most states and the courts of the Catholic church used torture when the crime was very serious and the evidence seemed to point to a particular defendant but no definitive proof had been established. The judges ordered torture—hanging the accused by the hands with a rope thrown over a beam, pressing the legs in a leg screw, or just tying the hands very tightly—to extract

♦**Montaigne:** mahn TAYN
♦**Bodin:** baw DAN

♦**Grotius:** GROH shee uhs

DID YOU KNOW?

The Gregorian Calendar: 1582

The Catholic church relied on the work of astronomers when it undertook a major reform of the calendar in 1582. Every culture has some kind of calendar by which it groups days to mark time, but the length of the day, the week, and the month have varied throughout human history. At different moments in the past, West Africans, for example, used four-day weeks, central Asians five-day weeks, and Egyptians ten-day weeks. These different systems became uniform when most of the world's countries adopted the Gregorian calendar. The spread of the use of the Gregorian calendar, which happened only very gradually after its introduction in 1582, marked the extension of Western influence in the world.

The Gregorian calendar got its name from Pope Gregory XIII, who ordered calendar reform to compute more accurately the exact date on which Easter—the Christian holiday commemorating the resurrection of Jesus—should fall. Easter was supposed to fall on the first Sunday after the first full moon after the vernal equinox. But over the years the dates had become confused because no one had been able to calculate the exact length of a solar year (365.242199 days). As a result, the calendar had become increasingly out of phase with the seasons; by 1545, the vernal (spring) equinox had moved ten days from its proper date. In 1582, when the reform took effect, October 5 became October 15, thus omitting ten days and setting the vernal equinox straight—but causing any number of legal complications.

Although the Gregorian calendar was based on a truer calculation of the length of a year and thus required less adjustment than previous calendars, it was not immediately adopted, even in Christian Europe, in part because any change would have been difficult to enforce given the state of communications at the time. Because the pope had sponsored the reform, the Catholic countries embraced it first; Protestant countries used it only after 1700. England accepted it in 1752. Adoption followed in Japan in 1873, Egypt in 1875, Russia in 1918, and Greece in 1923. The Greek Orthodox church never accepted it, so Easter in that church is about one week later than elsewhere in Christianity.

Even though the Gregorian calendar is astronomically correct, it still has bothersome

a confession, which had to be given with a medical expert and notary present and had to be repeated without torture. Children, pregnant women, the elderly, aristocrats, kings, and even professors were exempt.

Grotius's conception of natural law directly challenged the use of torture. To be in accord with natural law, Grotius argued, governments had to defend natural rights, which he defined as life, body, freedom, and honor. Grotius did not encourage rebellion in the name of natural law or rights, but he did hope that someday all governments would adhere to these principles and stop killing their own and one another's subjects in the name of religion. Natural law and natural rights would play an important role in the founding of constitutional governments from the 1640s forward and in the establishment of various charters of human rights in our own time.

Origins of the Scientific Revolution

Although the Catholic and Protestant churches encouraged the study of science and many prominent scientists were themselves clerics, the search for a secular, scientific method of determining the laws of nature eventually challenged the traditional accounts of natural phenomena. (See "Did You Know?", above.) Christian doctrine had incorporated the scientific teachings of ancient philosophers, especially Ptolemy and Aristotle; now these came into question. A

Calendar
This painting by Aldo Durazzi shows Gregory XIII presiding over the council of 1582 that reformed the calendar. The Catholic church sponsored the work of many astronomers and other scientists.
Archivio di Stato, Siena. Photo Lensini Fabrio.

defects: the months are different in length, and holidays do not fall on the same day in each year. Two other calendars have been proposed. The International Fixed Calendar would divide the year into thirteen months of twenty-eight days with an additional day at the end. The World Calendar would divide the year into four quarters of ninety-one days, each with an additional day at the end of the year; the first month in each quarter would have thirty-one days, and the second and third thirty days each. Neither has been adopted. Logic does not always win this kind of argument, for changing the length of the months seems almost equivalent to changing which side of the road you drive on; once a system is learned, no one really wants to give it up and start all over again. The same is true for the numbering of the years, which was set by the Council of Nicaea in 325. The year 1 was designated as the year it was believed Jesus was born. Today scholars have determined that the date was wrong by several years, and many object in any case to the use of a calendar based on the birth of Jesus. But if that dating system were eliminated, what would replace it? Where should a common calendar begin?

revolution in astronomy challenged the Ptolemaic view, endorsed by the Catholic church, which held that the sun revolved around the earth. Startling breakthroughs took place in medicine, too, which laid the foundations for modern anatomy and pharmacology. By the early seventeenth century, a new **scientific method** had been established based on a combination of experimental observation and mathematical deduction. Conflicts between the new science and religion followed almost immediately.

The Revolution in Astronomy. The traditional account of the movement of the heavens derived from the second-century Greek astronomer Ptolemy, who put the earth at the center of the cosmos. Above the earth were fixed the moon, the stars, and the planets in concentric crystalline spheres; beyond these fixed spheres dwelt God and the angels. The planets revolved around the earth at the command of God. In this view, the sun revolved around the earth; the heavens were perfect and unchanging, and the earth was "corrupted." Ptolemy insisted that the planets revolved in perfectly circular orbits (because circles were more "perfect" than other figures). To account for the actual elliptical paths that could be observed and calculated, he posited orbits within orbits, or epicycles.

In 1543, the Polish clergyman Nicolaus Copernicus (1473–1543) began the revolution in astronomy by publishing his treatise *On the Revolution of the Celestial Spheres.* Copernicus attacked the Ptolemaic account, arguing that the earth and planets revolved around the sun, a view known as **heliocentrism** (a sun-centered universe). He discovered that by placing the sun instead of the earth at the center of the system of spheres, he could eliminate many epicycles from the calculations. In other words, he claimed that the heliocentric view simplified the mathematics. Copernicus died soon after publishing his theories, but when the Italian monk Giordano Bruno (1548–1600) taught heliocentrism, perhaps with the aim of establishing a new religion, the Catholic Inquisition (set up to seek out heretics) arrested him and burned him at the stake.

Copernicus's views began to attract widespread attention in the early seventeenth century, when astronomers systematically collected evidence that undermined the Ptolemaic view. A leader among them was the Danish astronomer Tycho Brahe◆ (1546–1601). While at university he lost part of his nose in a duel and for the rest of his life he wore a metal insert to replace the missing part. Brahe designed and built new instruments for observing the heavens and trained a whole generation of astronomers. His observation of a new star in 1572 and a comet in 1577 called into question the Aristotelian view that the universe was unchanging. Brahe still rejected heliocentrism, but the assistant he employed when he moved to Prague in 1599, Johannes Kepler (1571–1630), was converted to the Copernican view. Kepler continued Brahe's collection of planetary observations and used the evidence to develop his three laws of planetary motion, published between 1609 and 1619. Kepler's laws provided mathematical backing for heliocentrism and directly challenged the claim long held, even by Copernicus, that planetary motion was circular. Kepler's first law stated that the orbits of the planets are ellipses, with the sun always at one focus of the ellipse.

The Italian Galileo Galilei (1564–1642) provided more evidence to support the heliocentric view and also challenged the doctrine that the heavens were perfect and unchanging. In 1609, he learned that two Dutch astronomers had built a telescope. He quickly invented a better one and observed the earth's moon, four satellites of Jupiter, the phases of Venus (a cycle of changing physical appearances), and sunspots. The moon, the planets, and the sun were no more perfect than the earth, he insisted, and the shadows he could see on the moon could only be the product of hills and valleys like those on earth. Galileo portrayed the earth as a moving part of a larger system, only one of

The Trial of Galileo
In this anonymous painting of the trial held in 1633, Galileo appears seated on a chair in the center facing the church officials who accused him of heresy for insisting that the sun, not the earth, was the center of the universe (heliocentrism). Catholic officials forced him to recant or suffer the death penalty. What do you think the painter thought of Galileo? *Private collection, New York. © Photograph by Erich Lessing/Art Resource.*

◆**Brahe:** BRAH hee

Galileo Writes to Kepler about Their Common Interests in Astronomy

Galileo Galilei and Johannes Kepler were two of the pioneers of the scientific revolution. In this letter, written before either of them became famous, Galileo writes to Kepler about his interest in the German astronomer's work. It shows that experimenters knew of each other's work even across considerable distances. Galileo expresses his worries about embracing Copernicanism, worries that turned out to be well founded when the Inquisition sentenced him in 1633 to house arrest for his views.

Padua, August 4, 1597

I received your book, most learned sir, which you sent me by Paulus Amberger, not some days since, but only a few hours ago. And as this Paulus has notified me of his return to Germany, I would consider myself ungrateful if I did not now send you my thanks in the present letter. I thank you, therefore, and most especially because you have judged me worthy of such a token of your friendship. So far I have read only the introduction of your work, but I have to some extent gathered your plan from it, and I congratulate myself on the exceptional good fortune of having such a man as a comrade in the pursuit of truth. For it is too bad that there are so few who seek the truth and so few who do not follow a mistaken method in philosophy. This is not, however, the place to lament the misery of our century, but to rejoice with you over such beautiful ideas for proving the truth. So I add only, and I promise, that I shall read your book at leisure; for I am certain that I shall find the noblest things in it. And this I shall do the more gladly, because I accepted the view of Copernicus many years ago, and from this standpoint I have discovered from their origins many natural phenomena, which doubtless cannot be explained on the basis of the more commonly accepted hypothesis. I have written many direct and indirect arguments for the Copernican view, but until now I have not dared to publish them, alarmed by the fate of Copernicus himself, our master. He has won for himself undying fame in the eyes of a few, but he has been mocked and hooted at by an infinite multitude (for so large is the number of fools). I would dare to come forward publicly with my ideas if there were more people of your way of thinking. As this is not the case, I shall refrain. The shortness of time and my eager desire to read your book compel me to close, but I assure you of my sympathy, and I shall always gladly be at your service. Farewell and do not neglect to send me further good news of yourself.

many planets revolving around the sun, not as the fixed center of a single, closed universe. (See Galileo Writes to Kepler, above.)

Because he recognized the utility of the new science for everyday projects, Galileo published his work in Italian, rather than Latin, to appeal to a lay audience of merchants and aristocrats. But he meant only to instruct an educated elite. The new science, he claimed, suited "the minds of the wise," not "the shallow minds of the common people." After all, his discoveries challenged the commonsensical view that it is the sun that rises and sets while the earth stands still. If the Bible were wrong about motion in the universe, as Galileo's position implied, the error came from the Bible's use of common language to appeal to the lower orders. The Catholic church was not mollified by this explanation. In 1616 the church forbade Galileo to teach that the earth moves, and in 1633 accused him of not obeying the earlier order. Forced to appear before the Inquisition, he agreed to publicly recant his assertion about the movement of the earth to save himself from torture and death. (See the Trial of Galileo, on page 612.) Afterward he lived under house arrest and could publish his work only in the Dutch Republic, which had become a haven for iconoclastic scientists and thinkers.

Breakthroughs in Medicine. Until the mid-sixteenth century, medical knowledge in Europe had been based on the writings of the second-century Greek physician Galen, who was a contemporary of Ptolemy. Galen derived his knowledge of the anatomy of the human body from partial dissections. In the same year that Copernicus challenged the traditional account in astronomy (1543), the Flemish scientist Andreas Vesalius♦ (1514–1564) did the same for anatomy. Drawing on public dissections in the medical faculties of European universities, Vesalius eventually refuted Galen's work in his illustrated anatomical text, *On the Construction of the Human Body.* Theophrastus Bombastus von Hohenheim, better known as Paracelsus♦ (1493–1541), went even further than Vesalius. He burned Galen's text at the University of Basel, where he was a professor of medicine. Paracelsus experimented with new drugs; performed operations (at the time, most academic physicians taught medical theory, not practice); and pursued his interests in magic, alchemy, and astrology. He helped establish the modern science of pharmacology.

The Englishman William Harvey (1578–1657) also used dissection to examine the circulation of blood within the body, demonstrating how the heart worked as a pump. The heart and its valves were "a piece of machinery," Harvey insisted. They obeyed mechanical laws just as the planets and earth revolved around the sun in a mechanical universe. Nature could be understood by experiment and rational deduction, not by following traditional authorities.

Scientific Method: Bacon and Descartes. In the 1630s, the European intellectual elite began to accept the new scientific views. Ancient learning, the churches and their

theologians, and even cherished popular beliefs seemed to be undermined by a new standard of truth—the scientific method, which was based on systematic experiments and rational deduction. Two men were chiefly responsible for spreading the prestige of scientific method: the English politician Sir Francis Bacon (1561–1626) and the French mathematician and philosopher René Descartes♦ (1596–1650). They represented the two essential halves of scientific method: respectively, inductive reasoning through observation and experimental research and deductive reasoning from self-evident principles.

In *The Advancement of Learning* (1605), Bacon attacked reliance on ancient writers and optimistically predicted that scientific method would lead to social progress. The minds of the medieval scholars, he said, had been "shut up in the cells of a few authors (chiefly Aristotle, their dictator) as their persons were shut up in the cells of monasteries and colleges," and they could therefore produce only "cobwebs of learning" that were "of no substance or profit." Advancement would take place only through the collection, comparison, and analysis of information. Knowledge, in Bacon's view, must be empirically based (that is, gained by observation and experiment). Bacon ardently supported the scientific method over popular beliefs, which he rejected as "fables and popular errors." Claiming that God had called the Catholic church "to account for their degenerate manners and ceremonies," Bacon looked to the Protestant English state, which he served as lord chancellor, for leadership on the road to scientific advancement.

Although Descartes agreed with Bacon's denunciation of traditional learning, he saw that the attack on tradition might only replace the dogmatism of the churches with the skepticism of Montaigne—that nothing at all was certain. A Catholic who served in the Thirty Years' War, Descartes aimed to establish the new science on more secure philosophical foundations, those of mathematics and logic (Descartes invented analytic geometry). In his *Discourse on Method* (1637), he argued that mathematical and mechanical principles provided the key to under-

♦**Vesalius:** vuh SAY lee uhs
♦**Paracelsus:** pa ruh SEHL suhs

♦**Descartes:** day KAHRT

standing all of nature, including the actions of people and states. All prior assumptions must be repudiated in favor of one elementary principle: "I think, therefore I am." Everything else could—and should—be doubted, but even doubt showed the certain existence of someone thinking. Begin with the simple and go on to the complex, he asserted, and believe only those ideas that present themselves "clearly and distinctly." Descartes believed that rational individuals would see the necessity of strong state power and that only "meddling and restless spirits" would plot against it. He insisted that human reason could not only unravel the secrets of nature but also prove the existence of God. Although he hoped to secure the authority of both church and state, his reliance on human reason alone irritated authorities, and his books were banned in many places. He moved to the Dutch Republic to work in peace. Scientific research, like economic growth, became centered in the northern, Protestant countries, where it was less constrained by church control than in the Catholic south.

Magic and Witchcraft

Despite the new emphasis on clear reasoning, observation, and independence from past authorities, science had not yet become separate from magic. Many scholars, like Paracelsus, studied alchemy alongside other scientific pursuits. Elizabeth I maintained a court astrologer who was also a serious mathematician, and many writers distinguished between "natural magic," which was close to experimental science, and demonic "black magic." The astronomer Tycho Brahe defended his studies of alchemy and astrology as part of natural magic. For many of the greatest minds, magic and science were still closely linked.

In a world in which most people believed in astrology, magical healing, prophecy, and ghosts, it is hardly surprising that many of Europe's learned people also firmly believed in witchcraft, the exercise of magical powers gained by a pact with the devil. The same Jean Bodin who argued against religious fanaticism insisted on death for witches—and for those magistrates who would not prosecute them. In France alone, 345 books and

The Witches' Sabbath
This English woodcut from about 1600 shows witches dining with the devil and his demons. Many believed that witches made a pact with the devil to carry out his evil deeds. It is hard to tell whether or not all the witches in this picture are women. *Mary Evans Picture Library.*

pamphlets on witchcraft appeared between 1550 and 1650. Trials of witches peaked in Europe between 1560 and 1640, the very time of the celebrated breakthroughs of the new science. Montaigne was one of the few to speak out against executing accused witches: "It is taking one's conjectures rather seriously to roast someone alive for them," he wrote in 1580.

Belief in witches was not new in the sixteenth century. Witches had long been thought capable of almost anything: passing through walls, flying through the air, destroying crops, and causing personal catastrophes from miscarriage to demonic possession. What was new was the official persecution, justified by the notion that witches were agents of Satan whom the righteous must oppose. In a time of economic crisis, plague, warfare, and the clash of religious differences, witchcraft trials provided an outlet for social stress and anxiety, legitimated by state power. Denunciation and persecution of witches coincided with the spread of reform, both Protestant and Catholic. The

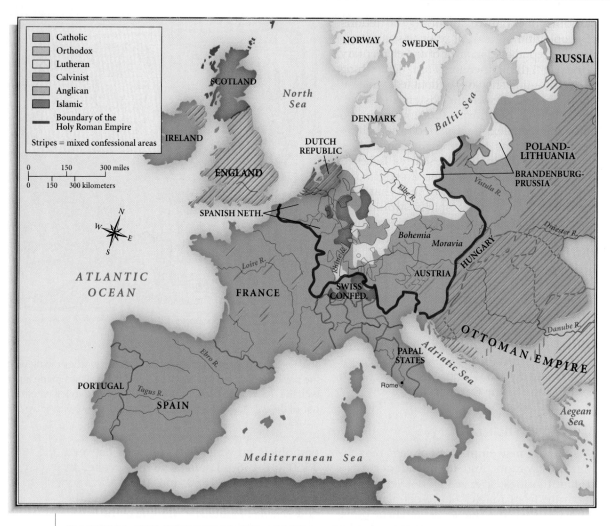

MAPPING THE WEST The Religious Divisions of Europe, c. 1648
The Peace of Westphalia recognized major religious divisions within Europe that have endured for the most part to the present day. Catholicism dominated in southern Europe, Lutheranism had its stronghold in northern Europe, and Calvinism flourished along the Rhine River. In southeastern Europe, the Islamic Ottoman Turks accommodated the Greek Orthodox Christians under their rule but bitterly fought the Catholic Austrian Habsburgs for control of Hungary.

trials concentrated especially in the German lands of the Holy Roman Empire, the boiling cauldron of the Thirty Years' War.

The victims of the persecution were overwhelmingly female: women accounted for 80 percent of the accused witches in about 100,000 trials in Europe and North America during the sixteenth and seventeenth centuries. About one-third were sentenced to death. Before 1400, when witchcraft trials were rare, nearly half of those accused had been men. Explanations for this gender difference have raised many controversies.

Some historians argue that the trials expressed a fundamental hatred of women that came to a head during conflicts over the Reformation. Official descriptions of witchcraft oozed lurid details of sexual orgies, incest, homosexuality, and cannibalism, in which women acted as the devil's sexual slaves. In this view, Catholic and Protestant reforming clergy attacked the presumably wild and undisciplined sexuality of women as the most obvious manifestation of popular unruliness and heretical tendencies. Lawyers and judges followed their lead.

Other historians point to a social dimension that helps explain the prominence of women among the accused. Accusers were almost always better off than those they accused. The poorest and most socially marginal people in most communities were elderly spinsters and widows. Because they were thought likely to hanker after revenge on those more fortunate, they were singled out as witches. Another commonly accused woman was the midwife, who was a prime target for suspicion when a baby or mother died in childbirth. Although sometimes venerated for their special skill, midwives also numbered among the thousands of largely powerless women persecuted for their supposed consorting with the devil.

Witchcraft trials declined when scientific thinking about causes and effects raised questions about the evidence used in court: how could judges or jurors be certain that someone was a witch? The tide turned everywhere at about the same time, as physicians, lawyers, judges, and even clergy came to suspect that accusations were based on popular superstition and peasant untrustworthiness. As early as the 1640s, French courts ordered the arrest of witch-hunters and released suspected witches. In 1682, a French royal decree treated witchcraft as fraud and imposture, meaning that the law did not recognize anyone as a witch. In 1693, the jurors who had convicted twenty witches in Salem, Massachusetts, recanted, claiming: "We confess that we ourselves were not capable to understand. . . . We justly fear that we were sadly deluded and mistaken." The Salem jurors had not stopped believing in witches; they had simply lost confidence in their ability to identify them. This was a general pattern. Popular attitudes had not changed; what had changed was the attitudes of the elites. When physicians and judges had believed in witches and carried out official persecutions, with torture, those accused of witchcraft had gone to their deaths in record numbers. But when the same groups distanced themselves from popular beliefs, the trials and the executions stopped.

Review: How could belief in witchcraft and the rising prestige of scientific method coexist?

Conclusion

The witchcraft persecutions of the late sixteenth and early seventeenth centuries reflected the traumas of these times of religious war, economic decline, and crises of political authority. Faced with new threats, some people blamed the poor widow or upstart midwife for their problems; others joined desperate revolts, and still others emigrated to the New World to seek a better life. Even rulers confronted frightening choices: forced abdication, death in battle, or assassination often accompanied their religious decisions, and economic shocks could threaten the stability of their governments.

Religious conflicts shaped the destinies of every European power in this period. These conflicts came to a head in the Thirty Years' War (1618–1648), which cut a path of destruction through central Europe and involved most of the European powers. Repulsed by the effects of religious violence on international relations, European rulers agreed to a peace that effectively removed disputes between Catholics and Protestants from the international arena. The growing separation of political motives from religious ones did not mean that violence or conflict had ended, however. Struggles for religious uniformity within states would continue, though on a smaller scale. Bigger armies required more state involvement, and almost everywhere rulers emerged from these decades of conflict with expanded powers. The growth of state power directly changed the lives of ordinary people: more men went into the armies, and most families paid higher taxes. The constant extension of state power is one of the defining themes of modern history; religious warfare gave it a jump-start.

For all their power, rulers could not control economic, social, or intellectual trends, much as they often tried. The economic downturn of the seventeenth century produced unexpected consequences for European states even while it made life miserable for many ordinary people; economic power and vibrancy shifted from the Mediterranean world to the northwest because the countries of northwestern Europe—England, France, and the Dutch Republic especially—suffered less from the fighting of the Thirty Years' War and recovered more quickly from the loss of population and production during bad times.

In the face of violence and uncertainty, some began to look for secular alternatives in art, politics, and science. Although it would be foolish to claim that everyone's mental universe changed because of the clash between religious and secular worldviews, a truly monumental shift in attitudes had begun. Secularization combined a growing interest in nonreligious forms of art, such as theater and opera, the search for nonreligious foundations of political authority, and the establishment of scientific method as the standard of truth. Proponents of these changes did not renounce their religious beliefs or even hold them less fervently, but they did insist that attention to state interests and scientific knowledge could serve as a brake on religious violence and popular superstitions.

Suggested References

Religious Conflicts and State Power, 1560–1618

The personalities of rulers such as Elizabeth I of England and Philip II of Spain remain central to the religious and political conflicts of this period.

Benedict, Philip. *Christ's Churches Purely Reformed: A Social History of Calvinism.* 2002.

Holt, Mack P. *The French Wars of Religion, 1562–1629.* 1995.

Israel, Jonathan. *The Dutch Republic: Its Rise, Greatness, and Fall, 1477–1806.* 1995.

Kamen, Henry. *Philip of Spain.* 1997.

*Marcus, Leah S., Janel Mueller, and Mary Beth Rose. *Elizabeth I: Collected Works.* 2000.

Mattingly, Garrett. *The Defeat of the Spanish Armada.* 2nd ed. 1988.

Philip II: http://www.historylearningsite.co.uk/Phillip.htm.

The Thirty Years' War and the Balance of Power, 1618–1648

As ethnic conflicts erupt again in eastern Europe, historians have traced their roots back to the intertwined religious, ethnic, and dynastic struggles of the Thirty Years' War.

*Primary sources.

Asch, Ronald G. *The Thirty Years' War: The Holy Roman Empire and Europe, 1618–1648.* 1997.

Osborne, Toby. *Dynasty and Diplomacy in the Court of Savoy: Political Culture and the Thirty Years' War.* 2002.

Parker, Geoffrey. *The Military Revolution: Military Innovation and the Rise of the West, 1500–1800.* 1988.

Parrott, David. *Richelieu's Army: War, Government and Society in France, 1624–1642.* 2001.

Economic Crisis and Realignment

Painstaking archival research has enabled historians to reconstruct the demographic, economic, and social history of the period discussed in this chapter. Recently, attention has focused more specifically on women, the family, and the early history of slavery.

Ashton, Trevor H., ed. *Crisis in Europe.* 1965.

Braudel, Fernand. *The Mediterranean and the Mediterranean World in the Age of Philip the Second.* 2 vols. Trans. Siân Reynolds. 1972–1973.

Ringrose, David R. *Expansion and Global Interaction, 1200–1700.* 2001.

Rublack, Ulinka. *The Crimes of Women in Early Modern Germany.* 1999.

Wiesner, Merry E. *Women and Gender in Early Modern Europe*, 2nd ed. 2000.

A Clash of Worldviews

The transformation of intellectual and cultural life has long fascinated scholars. Recent works have developed a new kind of study called microhistory, which focuses on one person (like Ginzburg's Italian miller).

Butterfield, Sir Herbert. *The Origins of Modern Science: 1300–1800.* Rev. ed. 1965.

Clark, Stuart, ed. *Languages of Witchcraft: Narrative, Ideology, and Meaning in Early Modern Culture.* 2001.

The Galileo Project: http://riceinfo.rice.edu/Galileo.

Ginzburg, Carlo. *The Cheese and the Worms: The Cosmos of a Sixteenth-Century Miller.* Trans. John Tedeschi and Anne Tedeschi. 1992.

Jacob, James. *The Scientific Revolution.* 1998.

Thomas, Keith. *Religion and the Decline of Magic.* 1971.

CHAPTER REVIEW

IMPORTANT EVENTS

1562 French Wars of Religion begin

1566 Revolt of Calvinists in the Netherlands against Spain begins

1569 Formation of commonwealth of Poland-Lithuania

1571 Battle of Lepanto marks victory of West over Ottomans at sea

1572 St. Bartholomew's Day Massacre of French Protestants

1588 Defeat of the Spanish Armada by England

1598 French Wars of Religion end with Edict of Nantes

1601 William Shakespeare, *Hamlet*

1618 Thirty Years' War begins

1625 Hugo Grotius publishes *The Laws of War and Peace*

1629 English Puritans set up the Massachusetts Bay Company and begin to colonize New England

1633 Galileo Galilei is forced to recant his support of heliocentrism

1635 French join the Thirty Years' War by declaring war on Spain

1648 Peace of Westphalia ends the Thirty Years' War

KEY TERMS

baroque (607)

heliocentrism (612)

Huguenot (582)

mannerism (607)

Moriscos (587)

politiques (585)

Puritans (589)

raison d'état (597)

scientific method (611)

secularization (606)

tithe (601)

REVIEW QUESTIONS

1. In what ways did the power of states depend on unity in religion?

2. Why did a war fought over religious differences result in stronger states?

3. What were the consequences of economic recession in the early 1600s?

4. How could belief in witchcraft and the rising prestige of scientific method coexist?

MAKING CONNECTIONS

1. How did the balance of power shift in Europe between 1560 and 1648? What were the main reasons for the shift?

2. Relate the new developments in the arts and sciences to the political and economic changes of this period of crisis.

FOR FURTHER EXPLORATION

To assess your mastery of the material in this chapter, see the Online Study Guide at **bedfordstmartins.com/hunt**.

To read additional primary-source material from this period, see Chapter 16 in *Sources of The Making of the West*, Second Edition.

Louis XIV, Conqueror of the Fronde
In this painting of 1654, Louis XIV is depicted as the Roman god Jupiter, who crushes the discord of the Fronde (represented on the shield by the Medusa's head made up of snakes). When the Fronde began, Louis was only ten years old; at the time of this painting, he was sixteen. The propaganda about his divine qualities had already begun. *Réunion des Musées Nationaux/Art Resource, NY. Photo: Gérard Blot.*

Neither the nobles nor the judges of the parlements really wanted to overthrow the king; they simply wanted a greater share in power. But Louis XIV never forgot the humiliation and uncertainty that marred his childhood. Years later he recalled an incident in which a band of Parisians invaded his bedchamber to determine whether he had fled the city, and he declared the event an affront not only to himself but also to the state. His own policies as ruler would be designed to prevent the repetition of any such revolts.

Court Culture as an Element of Absolutism

When Cardinal Mazarin died in 1661, Louis XIV decided to rule without a first minister. He described the dangers of his situation in the memoirs he wrote later for his son's instruction: "Everywhere was disorder. My Court as a whole was still very far removed from the sentiments in which I trust you will find it." Louis listed many other problems in the kingdom, but none occupied him more than his attempts to control France's leading nobles, some of whom came from families that had opposed him militarily during the Fronde.

Typically quarrelsome, the French nobles had long exercised local authority by maintaining their own fighting forces, meting out justice on their estates, arranging jobs for underlings, and resolving their own conflicts through dueling. Louis set out to domesticate the warrior nobles by replacing violence with court ritual, such as the three-day festival described by Marie de Sévigné. Using a systematic policy of bestowing pensions, offices, honors, gifts, and the threat of disfavor or punishment, Louis induced the nobles to cooperate with him and made himself the center of French power and culture. The aristocracy vied for his favor, attended the ballets and theatricals he put on, and learned the rules of etiquette he supervised—in short, became his clients, dependent on him for advancement. Great nobles competed for the honor of holding his shirt when he dressed, foreign ambassadors squabbled for places near him, and royal mistresses basked in the glow of his personal favor.

Participation at court required constant study. The preferred styles changed without notice, and the tiniest lapse in attention to etiquette could lead to ruin. Madame de Lafayette described the court in her novel *The Princess of Clèves* (1678): "The Court gravitated around ambition. Nobody was tranquil or indifferent—everybody was busily trying to better his or her position by pleasing, by helping, or by hindering somebody else." Occasionally the results were tragic, as in the suicide of Vatel recounted by Marie de Sévigné. Elisabeth Charlotte, duchess of Orléans, the German-born sister-in-law of Louis, complained that "everything here is pure self-interest and deviousness."

Politics and the Arts. Louis XIV appreciated the political uses of every form of art. Mock battles, extravaganzas, theatrical performances, even the king's dinner—Louis's daily life was a public performance designed to enhance his prestige. Calling himself the Sun King, after Apollo, Greek god of the sun, Louis stopped at nothing to burnish this radiant image. He played Apollo in ballets performed at court; posed for portraits with the emblems of Apollo (laurel, lyre, and tripod); and adorned his palaces with statues of the god. He also emulated the style and methods of ancient Roman emperors. At a celebration for the birth of his first son in 1662, Louis dressed in Roman attire, and many engravings and paintings showed him as a Roman emperor. Commissioned histories vaunted his achievements, and coins and medals spread his likeness throughout the realm.

The king's officials treated the arts as a branch of government. The king gave pensions to artists who worked for him and sometimes protected writers from clerical critics. The most famous of these was the playwright Molière,♦ whose comedy *Tartuffe* (1664) made fun of religious hypocrites and was loudly condemned by church leaders. Louis forced Molière to delay public performances of the play but resisted calls for his dismissal. Louis's ministers set up royal academies of dance, painting, architecture, music, and science and took control of the Académie française (French Academy), which to this day decides on correct usage of the French language. Louis's government also regulated the number and locations of theaters and closely censored all forms of publication.

Music and theater enjoyed special prominence. Louis commissioned operas to celebrate royal marriages, baptisms, and military victories. His favorite composer, Jean-Baptiste Lully, an Italian who began as a cook's assistant and rose to be virtual dictator of French musical taste, wrote sixteen operas for court performances as well

♦**Molière:** mohl YEHR

as many ballets. Louis himself danced in the ballets if a role seemed especially important. Playwrights presented their new plays directly to the court. Pierre Corneille and Jean-Baptiste Racine wrote tragedies set in Greece or Rome that celebrated the new aristocratic virtues that Louis aimed to inculcate: a reverence for order and self-control. All the characters were regal or noble, all the language lofty, all the behavior aristocratic.

The Palace of Versailles.   Louis glorified his image as well through massive public works projects. Veterans' hospitals and new fortified towns on the frontiers represented his military might. Urban improvements, such as the reconstruction of the Louvre palace in Paris, proved his wealth. But his most ambitious project was the construction of a new palace at Versailles,♦ twelve miles from the turbulent capital (see illustration on the next page).

Building began in the 1660s. By 1685, the frenzied effort engaged 36,000 workers, not including the thousands of troops who diverted a local river to supply water for pools

♦**Versailles:** vur SY

Louis XIV Visits the Royal Tapestry Workshop
This tapestry was woven at the Gobelins tapestry workshop between 1673 and 1680. It shows Louis XIV (wearing a red hat) and his minister Colbert (dressed in black, holding his hat) visiting the workshop on the outskirts of Paris. The workshop artisans scurry to show Louis all the luxury objects they manufacture. Louis bought the workshop in 1662 and made it a national enterprise for making tapestries and furniture. *Bridgeman-Giraudon/Art Resource, NY.*

The Palace of Versailles
This view of the palace from 1675 shows the central section of the newly reconstructed palace. The entire building was still not complete at this date, but some sense of King Louis XIV's emphasis on majesty and order is already apparent. *Réunion des Musées Nationaux/Art Resource, NY. Photo: Gérard Blot.*

and fountains. The gardens designed by landscape architect André Le Nôtre reflected the spirit of Louis XIV's rule: their geometrical arrangements and clear lines showed that art and design could tame nature and that order and control defined the exercise of power. Le Nôtre's geometrical landscapes were imitated in places as far away as St. Petersburg in Russia and Washington, D.C. Versailles symbolized Louis's success in reining in the nobility and dominating Europe, and other monarchs eagerly mimicked French fashion and often conducted their business in French.

Yet for all its apparent luxury and frivolity, life at Versailles was often cramped and cold. Fifteen thousand people crowded into the palace's apartments, including all the highest military officers, the ministers of state, and the separate households of each member of the royal family. Refuse collected in the corridors during the incessant building, and thieves and prostitutes overran the grounds.

By the time Louis actually moved from the Louvre to Versailles in 1682, he had reigned as monarch for thirty-nine years. After his wife's death in 1683, he secretly married his mistress, Françoise d'Aubigné, marquise de Maintenon, and conducted most state affairs from her apartments at the palace. Her opponents at court complained that she controlled all the appointments, but her efforts focused on her own projects, including her favorite: the founding in 1686 of a royal school for girls from impoverished noble families. She also inspired Louis XIV to increase his devotion to Catholicism.

Enforcing Religious Orthodoxy

Louis believed that he ruled by divine right. As Bishop Jacques-Benigne Bossuet♦ (1627–1704) explained, "We have seen that kings

---

♦**Bossuet:** baw SWAY

take the place of God, who is the true father of the human species. We have also seen that the first idea of power which exists among men is that of the paternal power; and that kings are modeled on fathers." The king, like a father, should instruct his subjects in the true religion, or at least make sure that others did so.

Louis's campaign for religious conformity first focused on the Jansenists, Catholics whose doctrines and practices resembled some aspects of Protestantism. Following the posthumous publication of the book *Augustinus* (1640) by the Flemish theologian Cornelius Jansen (1585–1638), the Jansenists stressed the need for God's grace in achieving salvation. They emphasized the importance of original sin and, in their austere religious practice, resembled the English Puritans. Prominent among the Jansenists was Blaise Pascal (1623–1662), a mathematician of genius, who wrote his *Provincial Letters* (1656–1657) to defend Jansenism against charges of heresy. Many judges in the parlements likewise endorsed Jansenist doctrine.

Some questioned Louis's understanding of the finer points of doctrine: according to his sister-in-law, Louis himself "has never read anything about religion, nor the Bible either, and just goes along believing whatever he is told." But Louis rejected any doctrine that gave priority to considerations of individual conscience over the demands of the official church hierarchy, especially when that doctrine had been embraced by some noble supporters of the Fronde. Louis preferred teachings that stressed obedience to authority. Therefore, in 1660 he began enforcing various papal bulls (decrees) against Jansenism and closed down Jansenist theological centers. Jansenists were forced underground for the rest of his reign.

After many years of escalating pressure on the Calvinist Huguenots, Louis revoked the Edict of Nantes in 1685 and eliminated all of the Calvinists' rights. Louis considered the Edict (1598), by which his grandfather Henry IV granted the Protestants religious freedom and a degree of political independence, a temporary measure, and he fervently hoped to reconvert the Huguenots to Catholicism. He closed their churches and schools, banned all their public activities, and exiled those who refused to embrace the state religion. Thousands of Huguenots emigrated to England, Brandenburg-Prussia, the Dutch Republic, or North America. Many now wrote for publications attacking Louis XIV's absolutism. Protestant European countries were shocked by this crackdown on religious dissent and would cite it in justification of their wars against Louis.

> **Review:** How "absolute" was the power of Louis XIV?

Extending State Authority at Home and Abroad

Louis XIV could not have enforced his religious policies without the services of a nationwide bureaucracy. **Bureaucracy**—a network of state officials carrying out orders according to a regular and routine line of authority—comes from the French word *bureau*, for "desk," which came to mean "office," both in the sense of a physical space and a position of authority. Louis personally supervised the activities of his bureaucrats and worked to ensure his supremacy in all matters. But he always had to negotiate with nobles and local officials in order to achieve his ends.

Bureaucracy and Mercantilism.   Louis extended the bureaucratic forms his predecessors had developed, especially the use of intendants, officials who held their positions directly from the king rather than owning their offices, as crown officials had traditionally done. Louis handpicked an intendant for each region to represent his will against entrenched local interests such as the parlements, provincial estates, and noble governors; they supervised the collection of taxes, the financing of public works, and the provisioning of the army. In 1673 Louis decreed that the parlements could no longer vote against his proposed laws or even speak against them. His intendants reduced local powers over finances and insisted on more efficient tax collection. Despite the doubling of taxes in Louis's reign, the local rebellions that had so beset the crown from the 1620s to the 1640s subsided in the face of these better-organized state forces.

Louis's success in consolidating his authority depended on hard work, an eye for detail, and an ear to the ground. In his memoirs he described the tasks he set for himself:

> to learn each hour the news concerning every province and every nation, the secrets of every court, the mood and weaknesses of each Prince and of every foreign minister; to be well-informed on an infinite number of matters about which we are supposed to know nothing; to elicit from our subjects what they hide from us with the greatest care; to discover the most remote opinions of our courtiers and the most hidden interests of those who come to us with quite contrary professions [claims].

To gather all this information, Louis relied on a series of talented ministers, usually of modest origins, who gained fame, fortune, and even noble status from serving the king. Most important among them was Jean-Baptiste Colbert (1619–1683), the son of a wool merchant turned royal official. Colbert had managed Mazarin's personal finances and worked his way up under Louis XIV to become head of royal finances, public works, and the navy. He founded a family dynasty that eventually produced five ministers of state, an archbishop, two bishops, and three generals.

Colbert used the bureaucracy to establish a new economic doctrine, **mercantilism**. According to mercantilist policy, governments must intervene to increase national wealth by whatever means possible. Such government intervention inevitably increased the role and eventually the number of bureaucrats needed. Under Colbert, the French government established overseas trading companies, granted manufacturing monopolies, and standardized production methods for textiles, paper, and soap. A government inspection system regulated the quality of finished goods and compelled all craftsmen to organize into guilds, in which masters could supervise the work of the journeymen and apprentices. To protect French production, Colbert rescinded many internal customs fees but enacted high foreign tariffs, which cut imports of competing goods. To compete more effectively with England and the Dutch Republic, Colbert also subsidized shipbuilding, a policy that dramatically expanded the number of seaworthy vessels. Such mercan-

tilist measures aimed to ensure France's prominence in world markets and to provide the resources needed to fight wars against the increasingly long list of enemies. Although later economists questioned the value of this state intervention in the economy, virtually every government in Europe embraced mercantilism.

Colbert's mercantilist projects extended to Canada, where in 1663 he took control of the trading company that had founded New France. He transplanted several thousand peasants from western France to the present-day province of Quebec, which France had claimed since 1608. To guard his investment, Colbert sent fifteen hundred soldiers to join the settlers. Of particular concern to the French government were the Iroquois, who regularly interrupted French fur-trading convoys. Shows of French military force, including the burning of Indian villages and winter food supplies, forced the Iroquois to make peace with New France; and from 1666 to 1680, French traders moved westward with minimal interference. In 1672, fur trader Louis Jolliet and Jesuit missionary Jacques Marquette reached the upper Mississippi River and traveled downstream as far as Arkansas. In 1684, French explorer Sieur de La Salle went all the way down to the Gulf of Mexico, claiming a vast territory for Louis XIV and calling it Louisiana after him. Louis and Colbert encouraged colonial settlement as part of their rivalry with the English and the Dutch in the New World.

The Army and War. Colonial settlement occupied only a small portion of Louis XIV's attention, however, for his main foreign policy goal was to extend French power in Europe. In pursuing this purpose, he inevitably came up against the Spanish and Austrian Habsburgs, whose lands encircled his. To expand French power, Louis needed the biggest possible army. His powerful ministry of war centralized the organization of French troops. Barracks built in major towns received supplies from a central distribution system. The state began to provide uniforms for the soldiers and to offer veterans some hospital care. A militia draft instituted in 1688 supplemented the army in times of war and enrolled a hundred thousand men. Louis's wartime army could field a force as large as that of all his enemies combined.

Absolutist governments always tried to increase their territorial holdings, and as Louis extended his reach, he gained new enemies. In 1667–1668, in the War of Devolution (so called because Louis claimed that lands in the Spanish Netherlands should devolve to him because the Spanish king had failed to pay the dowry of Louis's Spanish bride), Louis defeated the Spanish armies but had to make peace when England, Sweden, and the Dutch Republic joined the war. In the Treaty of Aix-la-Chapelle♦ in 1668, he gained control of a few towns on the border of the Spanish Netherlands. Pamphlets sponsored by the Habsburgs accused Louis of aiming for "universal monarchy," or domination of Europe. The chorus of denunciation would only grow over the years.

In 1672, Louis XIV opened hostilities against the Dutch because they stood in the way of his acquisition of more territory in the Spanish Netherlands. He declared war again on Spain in 1673. By now the Dutch had allied themselves with their former Spanish masters to hold off the French. Louis also marched his troops into territories of the Holy Roman Empire, provoking many of the German princes to join with the emperor, the Spanish, and the Dutch in an alliance against Louis, now denounced as a "Christian Turk" for his imperialist ambitions. But the French armies more than held their own. Faced with bloody but inconclusive results on the battlefield, the parties agreed to the Treaty of Nijmegen♦ of 1678–1679, which ceded several Flemish towns and Franche-Comté to Louis, linking Alsace to the rest of France. French government deficits soared, and in 1675 increases in taxes touched off the most serious antitax revolt of Louis's reign.

Louis had no intention of standing still. Heartened by the Habsburgs' seeming weakness, he pushed eastward, seizing the city of Strasbourg in 1681 and invading the province of Lorraine in 1684. In 1688, he attacked some of the small German cities of the Holy

WARS OF LOUIS XIV

1667–1668	**War of Devolution**
	Enemies: Spain, Dutch Republic, England, Sweden
	Ended by Treaty of Aix-la-Chapelle in 1668, with France gaining towns in Spanish Netherlands (Flanders)
1672–1678	**Dutch War**
	Enemies: Dutch Republic, Spain, Holy Roman Empire
	Ended by Treaty of Nijmegen, 1678–1679, which gave several towns in Spanish Netherlands and Franche-Comté to France
1688–1697	**War of the League of Augsburg**
	Enemies: Holy Roman Empire, Sweden, Spain, England
	Ended by Peace of Rijswijk, 1697, with Louis returning all his conquests made since 1678 except Strasbourg

Roman Empire. As Louis's own mental powers diminished with age, he seems to have lost all sense of measure. His armies laid waste to German cities such as Mannheim; his government ordered the local military commander to "kill all those who would still wish to build houses there." Between 1689 and 1697, a coalition known as the League of Augsburg—made up of England, Spain, Sweden, the Dutch Republic, the Austrian emperor, and various German princes—fought Louis XIV to a stalemate. When hostilities ended in the Peace of Rijswijk♦ in 1697, Louis returned many of his conquests made since 1678 with the exception of Strasbourg (Map 17.1). Louis never lost his taste for war, but his allies learned how to set limits on his ambitions.

Louis was the last French ruler before Napoleon to accompany his troops to the battlefield. In later generations, as the military became more professional, French rulers left the fighting to their generals. Although Louis had eliminated the private armies of his noble courtiers, he constantly promoted his own military prowess in order to keep his noble officers under his sway. He had minia-

---

♦**Aix-la-Chapelle:** ayks lah shah PEHL
♦**Nijmegen:** NY may guhn

♦**Rijswijk:** RYS vyk

France in 1667
Acquisitions to 1668
Treaty of Nijmegen, 1678
Treaty of Rijswijk, 1697

MAP 17.1 Louis XIV's Acquisitions, 1668–1697

Every ruler in Europe hoped to extend his or her territorial control, and war was often the result. Louis XIV steadily encroached on the Spanish Netherlands to the north and the lands of the Holy Roman Empire to the east. Although coalitions of European powers reined in Louis's grander ambitions, he nonetheless incorporated many neighboring territories into the French crown.

ture battle scenes painted on his high heels and commissioned tapestries showing his military processions into cities, even those he did not take by force. He seized every occasion to assert his supremacy, insisting that other fleets salute his ships first.

War required money and men, which Louis obtained by expanding state control over finances, conscription, and military supply. Thus, absolutism and warfare fed each other as the bureaucracy created new ways to raise and maintain an army and the army's success in war justified further expansion of state power. But constant warfare also eroded the state's resources. Further administrative and legal reform, the elimination of the buying and selling of offices, and the lowering of taxes—all were made impossible by the need for more money.

The playwright Corneille wrote, no doubt optimistically, "The people are very happy when they die for their kings." What is certain is that the wars touched many peasant and urban families. The people who lived on the routes leading to the battlefields had to house and feed soldiers; only nobles were exempt from this requirement. Everyone, moreover, paid the higher taxes that were necessary to support the army. By the end of Louis's reign, one in six Frenchmen had served in the military.

❖ Absolutism in Central and Eastern Europe

Central and eastern European rulers saw in Louis XIV a powerful model of absolutist state building, yet they did not blindly emulate the Sun King, in part because they confronted conditions peculiar to their regions. The ruler of Brandenburg-Prussia had to rebuild lands ravaged by the Thirty Years' War and unite far-flung territories. The Austrian Habsburgs needed to govern a mosaic of ethnic and religious groups while fighting off the Ottoman Turks. The Russian tsars wanted to extend their power over an extensive but relatively impoverished empire. The great exception to absolutism in eastern Europe was Poland-Lithuania, where a long crisis virtually destroyed central authority and pulled much of eastern Europe into its turbulent wake.

Brandenburg-Prussia and Sweden: Militaristic Absolutism

Brandenburg-Prussia began as a puny state on the Elbe River, but it had a remarkable future. In the nineteenth century, it would unify the disparate German states into modern-day Germany. The ruler of Brandenburg was an elector, one of the seven German princes entitled to select the Holy Roman Emperor. Since the sixteenth century the ruler of Brandenburg had also controlled the duchy of East Prussia; after 1618 the state was called Brandenburg-Prussia. Despite meager resources, Frederick William of Hohenzollern, the Great Elector of Brandenburg-Prussia (r. 1640–1688), succeeded in welding his scattered lands into an absolutist state.

Pressured first by the necessities of fighting the Thirty Years' War and then by the demands of reconstruction, Frederick William determined to force his territories' estates (representative assemblies) to grant him a dependable income. The Great Elector struck a deal with the Junkers◆ (nobles) of each province: in exchange for allowing him to collect taxes, he gave them complete control over their enserfed peasants and exempted them from taxation. The tactic worked. By the end of his reign, the estates met only on ceremonial occasions.

Supplied with a steady income, Frederick William could devote his attention to military and bureaucratic consolidation. Over

forty years he expanded his army from eight thousand to thirty thousand men. (See "Taking Measure" below.) The army mirrored the rigid domination of nobles over peasants that characterized Brandenburg-Prussian society: peasants filled the ranks, and Junkers became officers. Nobles also took positions as bureaucratic officials, but military needs always had priority. The elector named special war commissars to take charge not only of military affairs but also of tax collection. To hasten military dispatches, he also established one of Europe's first state postal systems.

As a Calvinist ruler, Frederick William avoided the ostentation of the French court, even while following the absolutist model of centralizing state power. He boldly rebuffed Louis XIV by welcoming twenty thousand French Huguenot refugees after Louis's revocation of the Edict of Nantes. In pursuing foreign and domestic policies that promoted state power and prestige, Frederick William adroitly switched sides in Louis's wars and would stop at almost nothing to crush resistance at home.

TAKING MEASURE

State	Soldiers	Population	Ratio of soldiers/ total population
France	300,000	20 million	1:66
Russia	220,000	14 million	1:64
Austria	100,000	8 million	1:80
Sweden	40,000	1 million	1:25
Brandenburg-Prussia	30,000	2 million	1:66
England	24,000	10 million	1:410

*Figures for the end of the seventeenth century, ranging from 1688 for Prussia to 1710 for France

The Seventeenth-Century Army
The figures in this chart are only approximate, but they tell an important story. What conclusions can be drawn about the relative weight of the military in the different European states? Why would England have such a smaller army than the others? Is the absolute or the relative size of the military the most important indicator? *From André Corvisier, Armées et sociétés en Europe de 1494 à 1789 (Paris: Presses Universitaires de France, 1976), 126.*

◆**Junkers:** YUN kurs

In 1701, his son Frederick I (r. 1688–1713) persuaded Holy Roman Emperor Leopold I to grant him the title "king in Prussia." Prussia had arrived as an important power.

Across the Baltic, Sweden also stood out as an example of absolutist consolidation. In the Thirty Years' War, King Gustavus Adolphus's superb generalship and highly trained army had made Sweden the supreme power of northern Europe. The huge but sparsely populated state included not only most of present-day Sweden but also Finland, Estonia, half of Latvia, and much of the Baltic coastline of modern Poland and Germany. The Baltic, in short, was a Swedish lake. After Gustavus Adolphus died, his daughter Queen Christina (r. 1632–1654) conceded much authority to the estates. Absorbed by religion and philosophy, Christina eventually abdicated and converted to Catholicism. Her successors temporarily made Sweden an absolute monarchy.

In Sweden (as in neighboring Denmark-Norway), absolutism meant the estates standing aside while the king led the army in lucrative foreign campaigns. The aristocracy went along because it staffed the bureaucracy and reaped war profits. Intrigued by French culture, Swedes also gleamed with national pride. In 1668, the nobility demanded the introduction of a distinctive national costume: should we Swedes, they asked, "who are so glorious and renowned a nation. . . . let ourselves be led by the nose by a parcel of French dancing-masters"? Sweden spent the forty years after 1654 continuously warring with its neighbors. By the 1690s, war expenses began to outrun the small Swedish population's ability to pay, threatening the continuation of absolutism.

An Uneasy Balance: Austrian Habsburgs and Ottoman Turks

Holy Roman Emperor Leopold I (r. 1658–1705) ruled over a variety of territories of different ethnicities, languages, and religions, yet in ways similar to his French and Prussian counterparts, he gradually consolidated his power. Like all the Holy Roman emperors since 1438, Leopold was an Austrian Habsburg. He was simultaneously duke of Upper and Lower Silesia,♦ count of Tyrol,

archduke of Upper and Lower Austria, king of Bohemia, king of Hungary and Croatia, and ruler of Styria♦ and Moravia (Map 17.2). Some of these territories were provinces in the Holy Roman Empire; others were simply ruled from Vienna as Habsburg family holdings.

The Austrian Version of Absolutism. Leopold needed to build up his armies and state authority in order to defend the Holy Roman Empire's international position, which had been weakened by the Thirty Years' War. The emperor and his closest officials took control over recruiting, provisioning, and strategic planning and worked to replace the mercenaries hired during the Thirty Years' War with a permanent standing army that promoted professional discipline. To pay for the army and staff his growing bureaucracy, Leopold had to gain the support of local aristocrats and chip away at provincial institutions' powers.

Intent on replacing Bohemian nobles who had supported the 1618 revolt against Austrian authority, the Habsburgs promoted a new nobility made up of Czechs, Germans, Italians, Spaniards, and even Irish who used German as their common tongue, professed Catholicism, and loyally served the Austrian dynasty. Bohemia became a virtual Austrian colony. "You have utterly destroyed our home, our ancient kingdom, and have built us no new one in its place," lamented a Czech Jesuit in 1670, addressing Leopold. "Woe to you!. . . The nobles you have oppressed, great cities made small. Of smiling towns you have made straggling villages." Austrian censors prohibited publication of this protest for over a century.

Battle for Hungary. In addition to holding Louis XIV in check on his western frontiers, Leopold had to confront the ever-present challenge of the Ottoman Turks to his east. Hungary was the chief battle zone between Austria and the Turks for more than 150 years. In 1682, when war broke out again, Austria controlled the northwest section of Hungary; the Turks occupied the center; and in the east, the Turks demanded tribute from the Hungarian princes who ruled Transylvania. In 1683, the Turks pushed all the way to the gates of Vienna and laid siege to the Austrian

---

♦**Silesia:** sy LEE zhee uh

♦**Styria:** STIHR ee uh

MAP 17.2 State Building in Central and Eastern Europe, 1648–1699
The Austrian Habsburgs had long contested the Ottoman Turks for dominance of eastern Europe, and by 1699 they had pushed the Turks out of Hungary. In central Europe, the Austrian Habsburgs confronted the growing power of Brandenburg-Prussia, which had emerged from relative obscurity after the Thirty Years' War to begin an aggressive program of expanding its military and its territorial base. As emperor of the Holy Roman Empire, the Austrian Habsburg ruler governed a huge expanse of territory, but the emperor's control was in fact only partial because of guarantees of local autonomy.

capital; after reaching this high-water mark, however, Turkish power ebbed. With the help of Polish cavalry, the Austrians finally broke the siege and turned the tide in a major counteroffensive (see illustration on the next page). By the Treaty of Karlowitz✦ of 1699, the Ottoman Turks surrendered almost all of Hungary to the Austrians.

Hungary's "liberation" from the Turks came at a high price. The fighting laid waste vast stretches of Hungary's central plain, and the population may have declined by as much as 65 percent after 1600. Once the Turks had been beaten back, Austrian rule over Hungary tightened. In 1687, the Habsburg dynasty's hereditary right to

the Hungarian crown was acknowledged by the Hungarian diet, a parliament revived by Leopold in 1681 to gain the support of Hungarian nobles. The diet was dominated by nobles who had amassed huge holdings in the liberated territories. They formed the core of a pro-Habsburg Hungarian aristocracy that would buttress the dynasty until it fell in 1918; Austrians and Hungarians dominated the other ethnic groups such as Croats and Romanians who had enjoyed considerable autonomy under the Ottoman Turks. To root out remaining Turkish influence and assert Austrian superiority, Leopold systematically destroyed Turkish buildings and rebuilt Catholic churches, monasteries, roadside shrines, and monuments in the flamboyant Austrian baroque style.

✦**Karlowitz:** KAHR luh vihts

The Siege of Vienna, 1683
This detail from a painting by Franz Geffels shows the camp of the Ottoman Turks. The Turkish armies had surrounded Vienna since July 14, 1683. Jan Sobieski led an army of Poles which joined with Austrians and Germans to beat back the Turks on September 12, 1683. © *Archivo Iconografico, S.A./CORBIS.*

Ottoman State Authority. The Ottoman Turks also pursued state consolidation, but in a very different fashion from the Europeans. The Ottoman state extended its authority through a combination of settlement and military control. Hundreds of thousands of Turkish families moved with Turkish soldiers into the Balkan peninsula in the 1400s and 1500s. As locals converted to Islam, administration passed gradually into their hands. To this day, the Croatian language, for example, includes many Turkish words. In the Ottoman homeland of Anatolia, the sultans, the Ottoman rulers, were often challenged by mutinous army officers. Despite frequent palace coups and assassinations of sultans, the Ottoman state survived. Un-

like its European counterparts, it rarely faced peasant revolts. Rather than resisting state authorities, Ottoman peasants periodically worked for the state as mercenaries. Similarly, the Ottomans played the elites off each other, absorbing some into the state bureaucracy and pitting one level of authority against another. This constantly shifting social and political system explains how the coup-ridden Ottoman state could appear weak in Western eyes and still pose a massive military threat on Europe's southeastern borders. In the end, the Ottoman state lasted longer than Louis XIV's absolute monarchy. Nevertheless, the seventeenth century marked a period of cultural decline in the eyes of the Turks themselves; they looked back to the sixteenth century as their golden age in poetry and architecture.

Russia: Foundations of Bureaucratic Absolutism

Seventeenth-century Russia seemed a world apart from the Europe of Louis XIV. Straddling Europe and Asia, it stretched across Siberia to the Pacific Ocean. Western visitors either sneered or shuddered at the "barbarism" of Russian life, and Russians reciprocated by nursing deep suspicions of everything foreign. But under the surface, Russia was evolving along paths much like the rest of absolutist Europe; the tsars wanted to claim unlimited autocratic power, but they had to surmount internal disorder and come to an accommodation with noble landlords.

Serfdom and the Code of 1649. When Tsar Alexei (r. 1645–1676) tried to extend state authority by imposing new administrative structures and taxes in 1648, Moscow and other cities erupted in bloody rioting. The government immediately doused the fire. In 1649, Alexei convoked the Assembly of the Land (consisting of noble delegates from the provinces) to consult on a sweeping law code to organize Russian society in a strict social hierarchy that would last for nearly two centuries. The code of 1649 assigned all subjects to a hereditary class according to their current occupation or state needs. Slaves and free peasants were merged into a serf class. As serfs they could not change occupations or move; they were tightly tied to the soil and to their noble masters. To prevent tax evasion, the code also forbade townspeople to move from the community where they resided. Nobles owed absolute obedience to the tsar and were required to serve in the army, but in return no other group could own estates worked by serfs. Serfs became the chattel of their lord, who could sell them like horses or land. Their conditions of life differed little from those of the slaves on the plantations in the Americas.

Some peasants resisted enserfment. In 1667, Stenka Razin, a Cossack from the Don region in southern Russia, led a rebellion that promised liberation from "the traitors and bloodsuckers of the peasant communes"—the great noble landowners, local governors, and Moscow courtiers. Captured four years later by the tsar's army, Razin was dismembered, his head and limbs publicly displayed, and his body thrown to the dogs (see the illustration on this page). Thousands of his followers also suffered grisly deaths, but his memory lived on in folk songs and legends. Landlords successfully petitioned for the abolition of the statute of limitations on runaway serfs, the use of state agents in searching for runaways, and harsh penalties against those who harbored runaways. The increase in Russian state authority went hand in hand with the enforcement of serfdom.

The Tsar's Absolute Powers. To extend his power and emulate his western rivals, Tsar Alexei wanted a bigger army, exclusive control over state policy, and a greater say in religious matters. The size of the army increased dramatically from 35,000 in the 1630s to 220,000 by the end of the century. The Assembly of the Land, once an important source of noble consultation, never met again after 1653. Alexei also imposed firm control over the Russian Orthodox church. In 1666, a church council reaffirmed the tsar's role as God's direct representative on earth. The state-dominated church took action against a religious group called the **Old Believers**, who rejected church efforts to bring Russian worship in line with Byzantine tradition. Old Believer leaders, including the noblewoman Fedosia Morozova, endured exile, prison, and torture; whole communities of

Stenka Razin in Captivity
After leading a revolt of thousands of serfs, peasants, and members of non-Russian tribes of the middle and lower Volga region, Stenka Razin was captured by Russian forces and led off to Moscow, as shown here, where he was executed in 1671. He has been the subject of songs, legends, and poems ever since. *Novosti Photo Library (London).*

Old Believers starved or burned themselves to death rather than submit. Religious schism opened a gulf between the Russian people and the crown.

Nevertheless, modernizing trends prevailed. As the state bureaucracy expanded, adding more officials and establishing regulations and routines, the government intervened more and more in daily life. Decrees regulated tobacco smoking, card playing, and alcohol consumption and even dictated how people should leash and fence their pet dogs. Nobles and ordinary citizens commissioned portraits of themselves instead of only buying religious icons. Tsar Alexei set up the first Western-style theater in the Kremlin, and his daughter Sophia translated French plays. The most adventurous nobles began to wear German-style clothing. Some even argued that service and not just birth should determine rank. A long struggle over Western influences had begun.

Poland-Lithuania Overwhelmed

Unlike the other eastern European powers, Poland-Lithuania did not follow the absolutist model. Decades of war weakened the monarchy and made the great nobles into virtually autonomous warlords. They used the parliament and demands for constitutionalism

its consent. Charles hoped to avoid further interference with his plans by simply refusing to call Parliament into session between 1629 and 1640. Without it, the king's ministers had to find every loophole possible to raise revenues. They tried to turn "ship money," a levy on seaports in times of emergency, into an annual tax collected everywhere in the country. The crown won the ensuing court case, but many subjects still refused to pay what they considered to be an illegal tax.

Religious tensions brought conflicts over the king's authority to a head. The Puritans had long agitated for the removal of any vestiges of Catholicism, but Charles, married to a French Catholic, moved in the opposite direction. With Charles's encouragement, the archbishop of Canterbury, William Laud (1573–1645), imposed increasingly elaborate ceremonies on the Anglican church. Angered by these moves toward "popery," the Puritans poured forth reproving pamphlets and sermons. In response Laud hauled them before the feared Court of Star Chamber, which the king personally controlled. The court ordered harsh sentences for Laud's Puritan critics; they were whipped, pilloried, branded, and even had their ears cut off and their noses split. When Laud tried to apply his policies to Scotland, however, they backfired completely: the stubborn Presbyterian Scots rioted against the imposition of the Anglican prayer book—the Book of Common Prayer—and in 1640 they invaded the north of England. To raise money to fight the war, Charles called Parliament into session and unwittingly opened the door to a constitutional and religious crisis.

The Parliament of 1640 did not intend revolution, but reformers in the House of Commons (the lower house of Parliament) wanted to undo what they saw as the royal tyranny of the 1630s. Parliament removed Laud from office, ordered the execution of an unpopular royal commander, abolished the Court of Star Chamber, repealed recently levied taxes, and provided for a parliamentary assembly at least once every three years, thus establishing a constitutional check on royal authority. Moderate reformers expected to stop there and resisted Puritan pressure to abolish bishops and eliminate the Anglican prayer book. But their hand was forced in

January 1642, when Charles and his soldiers invaded Parliament and tried unsuccessfully to arrest those leaders who had moved to curb his power. Faced with mounting opposition within London, Charles quickly withdrew from the city and organized an army.

Civil War and the Challenge to All Authorities. The ensuing civil war between king and Parliament lasted four years (1642–1646) and divided the country. The king's army of royalists, known as Cavaliers, enjoyed the most support in northern and western England. The parliamentary forces, called Roundheads because they cut their hair short, had their stronghold in the southeast, including London. Although Puritans dominated on the parliamentary side, they were divided among themselves about the proper form of church government: the Presbyterians wanted a Calvinist church with some central authority, whereas the Independents favored entirely autonomous congregations free from other church government (hence the term *congregationalism,* often associated with the Independents). Putting aside their differences for the sake of military unity, the Puritans united under an obscure member of the House of Commons, the country gentleman Oliver Cromwell (1599–1658), who sympathized with the Independents. After Cromwell skillfully reorganized the parliamentary troops, his New Model Army defeated the Cavaliers at the battle of Naseby in 1645. Charles surrendered in 1646.

Although the civil war between king and Parliament had ended in victory for Parliament, divisions within the Puritan

England during the Civil War

ranks now came to the fore: the Presbyterians dominated Parliament, but the Independents controlled the army. The disputes between elites drew lower-class groups into the debate. (See "Contrasting Views," page 640.) When Parliament tried to disband the New Model Army in 1647, disgruntled soldiers protested. Called **Levellers** because of their insistence on leveling social differences, the soldiers took on their officers in a series of debates about the nature of political authority. The Levellers demanded that Parliament meet annually, that members be paid so as to allow common people to participate, and that all male heads of households be allowed to vote. Their ideal of political participation excluded servants, the propertyless, and women but offered access to artisans, shopkeepers, and modest farmers. Cromwell and other army leaders rejected the Levellers' demands as threatening to property owners. Cromwell insisted, "You have no other way to deal with these men but to break them in pieces.... If you do not break them they will break you."

Just as political differences between Presbyterians and Independents helped spark new political movements, so too their conflicts over church organization fostered the emergence of new religious doctrines. The new sects had in common only their emphasis on the "inner light" of individual religious inspiration and a disdain for hierarchical authority (see the illustration). Their emphasis on equality before God and greater participation in church governance appealed to the middle and lower classes. The Baptists, for example, insisted on adult baptism because they believed

that Christians should choose their own church and that every child should not automatically become a member of the Church of England. The Quakers demonstrated their beliefs in equality and the inner light by refusing to doff their hats to men in authority. Manifesting their religious experience by trembling, or "quaking," the Quakers believed that anyone—man or woman—inspired by a direct experience of God could preach.

Parliamentary leaders feared that the new sects would overturn the whole social hierarchy. Rumors abounded, for example, of naked Quakers running through the streets waiting

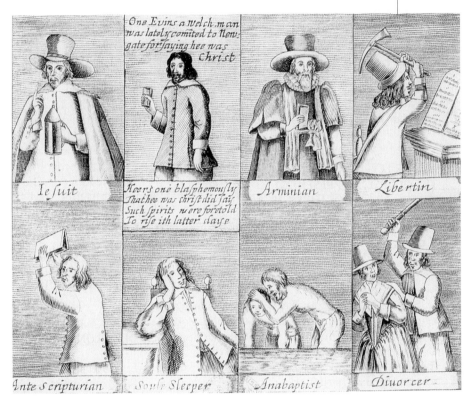

Religious Radicals

The Puritans in Parliament had opposed the Catholic leanings of the Church of England (shown as the Arminian here) and worried that Catholic missionary groups, such as the Jesuits (top left), might gain access to England. But they also detested the nonconformist Protestant sects that sprang up during the civil war: some individuals, called Ranters or Seekers, supposedly claimed they were Jesus come again; Arians rejected the doctrine of the Trinity; libertines attacked all sacramental objects of religion; anti-scripturians rejected the authority of the Bible; soul sleepers believed that souls of the dead remained "asleep" until the Second Coming; Anabaptists refused infant baptism; the family of love did not keep the sabbath; and some advocated easier divorce. It should be remembered that pamphlets such as the one from which this illustration was taken represented the views of those who opposed these tendencies. It is questionable, for example, whether Arians believed in free love, libertines attacked religious objects, or those in favor of easier divorce beat their wives. *British Library.*

CONTRASTING VIEWS

The English Civil War

The civil war between Charles I and Parliament (1642–1646) excited furious debates about the proper forms of political authority, debates that influenced political thought for two centuries or more. The Levellers, who served in the parliamentary army, wanted Parliament to be more accountable to ordinary men like themselves (Document 1). After the restoration of the monarchy in 1660, Lucy Hutchinson wrote a memoir in which she complained that Puritan *had become a term of political slander. Her memoir shows how religious terms had been politicized by the upheaval (Document 2). Thomas Hobbes, in his famous political treatise* Leviathan *(1651), develops the consequences of the civil war for political theory (Document 3).*

1. THE LEVELLERS, "THE AGREEMENT OF THE PEOPLE, AS PRESENTED TO THE COUNCIL OF THE ARMY" (OCTOBER 28, 1647)

Note especially two things about this document: (1) it focuses on Parliament as the chief instrument of reform, and (2) it claims that government depends on the consent of the people.

. . . Since, therefore, our former oppressions and scarce-yet-ended troubles have been occasioned, either by want of frequent national meetings in Council [Parliament], or by rendering those meetings ineffectual, we are fully agreed and resolved to provide that hereafter our representatives be neither left to an uncertainty for the time nor made useless to the ends for which they are intended. In order whereunto we declare:— That the people of England, being at this day very unequally distributed by Counties, Cities, and Borough for the election of their deputies in Parliament, ought to be more indifferently [equally] proportioned according to the number of the inhabitants. . . . That the power of this, and all future Representatives of this Nation, is inferior only to theirs who choose them, and doth extend, without the consent or concurrence of any other person or persons [the king], to the enacting, altering, and repealing of laws, to the erecting and abolishing of offices and courts, to the appointing, removing, and calling to account magistrates and officers of all degrees, to the making of war and peace, to the treating with foreign States [in other words, Parliament is the supreme power, not the king]. . . . These things we declare to be our native rights, and therefore are agreed and resolved to maintain them with our utmost possibilities against all opposition whatsoever. . . .

Source: Samuel Rawson Gardiner, ed., *The Constitutional Documents of the Puritan Revolution, 1625–1660* (Oxford: Clarendon Press, 1906), 333–35.

2. LUCY HUTCHINSON, MEMOIRS OF THE LIFE OF COLONEL HUTCHINSON (1664–1671)

Lucy Hutchinson wrote her memoir to defend her Puritan husband, who had been imprisoned upon the restoration of the monarchy.

for "a sign." Some sects did advocate sweeping change. The Diggers promoted rural communism—collective ownership of all property. Seekers and Ranters questioned just about everything. One notorious Ranter, John Robins, even claimed to be God. A few men advocated free love. These developments convinced the political elite that tolerating the new sects would lead to skepticism, anarchism, and debauchery.

In keeping with their notions of equality and individual inspiration, many of the new sects provided opportunities for women to become preachers and prophets. The Quakers thought women especially capable of prophecy. One prophet, Anna Trapnel, explained her vocation: "For in all that was said by me, I was nothing, the Lord put all in my mouth, and told me what I should say." Women pre-

If any were grieved at the dishonour of the kingdom, or the griping of the poor, or the unjust oppressions of the subject by a thousand ways invented to maintain the riots of the courtiers and the swarms of needy Scots the king had brought in to devour like locusts the plenty of this land, he was a puritan; if any showed favour to any godly, honest person, kept them company, relieved them in want, or protected them against violent and unjust oppression, he was a puritan. . . . In short, all that crossed the views of the needy courtiers, the proud encroaching priests, the thievish projectors, the lewd nobility and gentry . . . all these were puritans; and if puritans, then enemies to the king and his government, seditious, factious hypocrites, ambitious disturbers of the public peace, and finally the pest of the kingdom.

Source: Christopher Hill and Edmund Dell, eds., *The Good Old Cause: The English Revolution of 1640–1660, Its Causes, Course and Consequences* (London: Lawrence and Wishart, 1949), 179–80.

3. THOMAS HOBBES, *LEVIATHAN* (1651)

In this excerpt, Hobbes depicts the anarchy of a society without a strong central authority, but he leaves open the question of whether that authority should be vested in "one Man" or "one Assembly of men," that is, a king or a parliament.

During the time men live without a common Power to keep them all in awe, they are in that condition which is called Warre; and such a warre, as is of every man, against every man. . . . In such condition, there is no place for Industry; because the fruit thereof is uncertain: and consequently no

Culture of the Earth; no Navigation, nor use of the commodities that may be imported by Sea; no commodious Building; no Instrument of moving, and removing such things as require much force; no Knowledge of the face of the Earth; no account of Time; no Arts; no Letters; no Society; and which is worst of all, continuall feare, and danger of violent death; and the life of man, solitary, poore, nasty, brutish, and short.

The only way to erect such a Common Power, as may be able to defend them from the invasion of Forraigners, and the injuries of one another, and thereby to secure them in such sort, as that by their owne industrie, and by the Fruites of the Earth, they may nourish themselves and live contentedly; is, to conferre all their power and strength upon one Man, or upon one Assembly of men, that may reduce all their wills, by plurality of voices, unto one Will. . . . This is more than Consent, or Concord; it is a reall Unitie of them all, in one and the same Person, made by Covenant of every man with every man. . . . This done, the Multitude so united in one Person, is called a COMMON-WEALTH, in latine CIVITAS. This is the Generation of that great LEVIATHAN, or rather (to speake more reverently) of that *Mortall God*, to which wee owe under the *Immortall God*, our peace and defence.

Source: Thomas Hobbes, *Leviathan*, ed. Richard E. Flathman and David Johnston (New York: Norton, 1997), 70, 95.

QUESTIONS TO CONSIDER
1. Why would both the king and the parliamentary leaders find the Levellers' views disturbing?
2. Why did Hobbes's arguments about political authority upset supporters of both monarchy and Parliament?

sented petitions, participated prominently in street demonstrations, distributed tracts, and occasionally even dressed as men, wearing swords and joining armies. The duchess of Newcastle complained in 1650 that women were "affecting a Masculinacy . . . practicing the behaviour . . . of men." The outspoken women in new sects like the Quakers underscored the threat of a social order turning upside down.

Oliver Cromwell. At the heart of the continuing political struggle was the question of what to do with the king, who tried to negotiate with the Presbyterians in Parliament. In late 1648, Independents in the army purged the Presbyterians from Parliament, leaving a "rump" of about seventy members. This Rump Parliament then created a high court to try Charles I. The court found him guilty

Oliver Cromwell
In this painting of 1649, Robert Walker deliberately evokes previous portraits of English kings. Cromwell is shown preparing for battle in Ireland (note the shore and sea on Cromwell's right); he holds the baton of military command, and a young page is tying on a sash, symbol of his rank. Cromwell lived an austere life; he is depicted here without any sign of luxury. When he died, he was buried in Westminster Abbey, but in 1661 his body was exhumed and hanged in its shroud. His head was cut off and displayed outside Westminster Hall for nearly twenty years. *Courtesy of the National Portrait Gallery, London.*

of attempting to establish "an unlimited and tyrannical power" and pronounced a death sentence. On January 30, 1649, Charles was beheaded before an enormous crowd, which reportedly groaned as one when the axe fell. Although many had objected to Charles's autocratic rule, few had wanted him killed. For royalists, Charles immediately became a martyr, and reports of miracles, such as the curing of blindness by the touch of a handkerchief soaked in his blood, soon circulated.

The Rump Parliament abolished the monarchy and the House of Lords (the upper house of Parliament) and set up a Puritan republic with Oliver Cromwell (see the illustration on this page) as chairman of the Council of State. Cromwell did not tolerate

dissent from his policies. He saw the hand of God in events and himself as God's agent. Pamphleteers and songwriters ridiculed his red nose and accused him of wanting to be king, but few challenged his leadership. When his agents discovered plans for mutiny within the army, they executed the perpetrators; new decrees silenced the Levellers. Although Cromwell allowed the various Puritan sects to worship rather freely and permitted Jews with needed skills to return to England for the first time since the thirteenth century, Catholics could not worship publicly, nor could Anglicans use the Book of Common Prayer. The elites—many of them were still Anglican—were troubled by Cromwell's religious policies but pleased to see some social order reestablished.

The new regime aimed to extend state power just as Charles I had before. Cromwell laid the foundation for a Great Britain made up of England, Ireland, and Scotland by reconquering Scotland and subduing Ireland. Anti-English rebels in Ireland had seized the occasion of troubles between king and Parliament to revolt in 1641. When his position was secured in 1649, Cromwell went to Ireland with a large force and easily defeated the rebels, massacring whole garrisons and their priests. He encouraged expropriating the lands of the Irish "barbarous wretches," and Scottish immigrants resettled the northern county of Ulster. This seventeenth-century English conquest left a legacy of bitterness that the Irish even today call "the curse of Cromwell." In 1651, Parliament turned its attention overseas, putting mercantilist ideas into practice in the first Navigation Act, which allowed imports only if they were carried on English ships or came directly from the producers of goods. The Navigation Act was aimed at the Dutch, who dominated world trade; Cromwell tried to carry the policy further by waging naval war on the Dutch from 1652 to 1654.

At home, however, Cromwell faced growing resistance. His wars required a budget twice the size of Charles I's, and his increases in property taxes and customs duties alienated landowners and merchants. The conflict reached a crisis in 1653: Parliament considered disbanding the army, whereupon Cromwell abolished the Rump Parliament in a military coup and made himself Lord

Protector. He now silenced his critics by banning newspapers and using networks of spies and mail readers to keep tabs on his enemies. When Cromwell died in 1658, the diarist John Evelyn claimed, "There were none that cried but dogs." Cromwell intended that his son should succeed him, but his death only revived the prospect of civil war and political chaos. In 1660, a newly elected, staunchly Anglican Parliament invited Charles II, the son of the executed king, to return from exile.

The Glorious Revolution of 1688

The traditional monarchical form of government was reinstated in 1660, restoring the king to full partnership with Parliament. Charles II (r. 1660–1685) promised "a liberty to tender consciences" in an attempt to extend religious toleration, especially to Catholics, with whom he sympathized. Yet in the first years of his reign more than a thousand Puritan ministers lost their positions, and after 1664, attending a service other than one conforming with the Anglican prayer book was illegal. Natural disasters also marred the early years of Charles II's reign. The plague stalked London's rat-infested streets in May 1665 and claimed more than thirty thousand victims by September. Then in 1666, the Great Fire (see the illustration below) swept the city. The crown now had a city as well as a monarchy to rebuild.

The Restored Monarchy. The restoration of monarchy made some in Parliament fear that the English government would come to resemble French absolutism. This fear was

Great Fire of London, 1666
This view of London shows the three-day fire at its height. The writer John Evelyn described the scene in his diary: "All the sky was of a fiery aspect, like the top of a burning oven, and the light seen above 40 miles round about for many nights. God grant mine eyes may never behold the like, who now saw above 10,000 houses all in one flame; the noise and cracking and thunder of people, the fall of towers, houses, and churches, was like an hideous storm." Everyone in London at the time felt overwhelmed by the catastrophe, and many attributed it to God's punishment for the upheavals of the 1640s and 1650s. *Museum of London Photographic Library.*

not unfounded. In 1670, Charles II made a secret agreement, soon leaked, with Louis XIV in which he promised to announce his conversion to Catholicism in exchange for money for a war against the Dutch. Charles never proclaimed himself a Catholic, but in his Declaration of Indulgence (1673) he did suspend all laws against Catholics and Protestant dissenters. Parliament refused to continue funding the Dutch war unless Charles rescinded his Declaration of Indulgence. Asserting its authority further, Parliament passed the Test Act in 1673, requiring all government officials to profess allegiance to the Church of England and in effect disavow Catholic doctrine. Then in 1678, Parliament precipitated the so-called Exclusion Crisis by explicitly denying the throne to a Roman Catholic. This action was aimed at the king's brother and heir, James, an open convert to Catholicism. Charles refused to allow it to become law.

The dynastic crisis over the succession of a Catholic gave rise to two distinct factions in Parliament: the Tories, who supported a strong, hereditary monarchy and the restored ceremony of the Anglican church, and the Whigs, who advocated parliamentary supremacy and toleration for Protestant dissenters such as Presbyterians. Both labels were originally derogatory: *Tory* meant an Irish Catholic bandit; *Whig* was the Irish Catholic designation for a Presbyterian Scot. The Tories favored James's succession despite his Catholicism, whereas the Whigs opposed a Catholic monarch. The loose moral atmosphere of Charles's court also offended some Whigs, who complained tongue in cheek that Charles was father of his country in much too literal a fashion (he had fathered more than one child by his mistresses but produced no legitimate heir).

Parliament's Revolt against James II. Upon Charles's death, James succeeded to the throne as James II (r. 1685–1688). James pursued pro-Catholic and absolutist policies even more aggressively than his brother. When a male heir—who would take precedence over James's two adult Protestant daughters—was born to James's second wife, an Italian Catholic, Tories and Whigs banded together. They invited the

Dutch ruler William, prince of Orange, and his wife, James's older daughter Mary, to invade England. Mary was brought up as a Protestant and willing to act with her husband against her father's pro-Catholic policies. James fled to France and hardly any blood was shed. Parliament offered the throne jointly to William (r. 1689–1702) and Mary (r. 1689–1694) on the condition that they accept a bill of rights guaranteeing Parliament's full partnership in a constitutional government.

In the Bill of Rights (1689), William and Mary agreed not to raise a standing army or to levy taxes without Parliament's consent. They also agreed to call meetings of Parliament at least every three years, to guarantee free elections to parliamentary seats, and to abide by Parliament's decisions and not suspend duly passed laws. The agreement gave England's constitutional government a written, legal basis by formally recognizing Parliament as a self-contained, independent body that shared power with the rulers. Victorious supporters of the coup declared it the **Glorious Revolution**. Constitutionalism had triumphed over absolutism in England.

The propertied classes who controlled Parliament prevented any resurgence of the popular turmoil of the 1640s. The Toleration Act of 1689 granted all Protestants freedom of worship, though non-Anglicans were still excluded from the universities; Catholics got no rights but were more often left alone to worship privately. When the Catholics in Ireland rose to defend James II, William and Mary's troops brutally suppressed them. With the Whigs in power and the Tories in opposition, wealthy landowners now controlled political life throughout the realm. The factions' differences, however, were minor; essentially, the Tories had less access to the king's patronage. A contemporary reported that King William had said "that if he had good places [honors and land] enough to bestow, he should soon unite the two parties."

Review: What differences over religion and politics caused the conflict between king and Parliament in England?

❖ Constitutionalism in the Dutch Republic and the Overseas Colonies

When William and Mary came to the throne in England in 1689, the Dutch and the English put aside the rivalries that had brought them to war against each other in 1652–1654, 1665–1667, and 1672–1674. Under William, the Dutch and the English together led the coalition that blocked Louis XIV's efforts to dominate continental Europe. The English and Dutch had much in common: oriented toward commerce, especially overseas, they were the successful exceptions to absolutism in Europe. Also among the few outposts of constitutionalism in the seventeenth century were the British North American colonies, which developed representative government while the English were preoccupied with their revolutions at home. Constitutionalism was not the only factor shaping this Atlantic world; as constitutionalism developed in the colonies, so too did the enslavement of black Africans as a new labor force.

The Dutch Republic

When the Dutch Republic gained formal independence from Spain in 1648, it had already established a decentralized, constitutional state. Rich merchants called regents effectively controlled the internal affairs of each province and through the Estates General named the *stadholder,*◆ the executive officer responsible for defense and for representing the state at all ceremonial occasions. They almost always chose one of the princes of the house of Orange, but the prince of Orange resembled a president more than a king.

The decentralized state encouraged and protected trade, and the Dutch Republic soon became Europe's financial capital. The Bank of Amsterdam offered interest rates less than half those available in England and France. Praised for their industriousness, thrift, and cleanliness—and maligned as greedy, dull "butter-boxes"—the Dutch dominated overseas commerce with their

shipping (Map 17.3). They imported products from all over the world: spices, tea, and silk from Asia; sugar and tobacco from the Americas; wool from England and Spain; timber and furs from Scandinavia; grain from eastern Europe. (See "Did You Know?" on page 647.) A widely reprinted history of Amsterdam that appeared in 1662 described the city as "risen through the hand of God to the peak of prosperity and greatness....The whole world stands amazed at its riches and from east and west, north and south they come to behold it."

The Dutch rapidly became the most prosperous and best-educated people in Europe. Middle-class people supported the visual arts, especially painting, to an unprecedented degree. Artists and engravers produced thousands of works, and Dutch artists were among the first to sell to a mass market. Whereas in other countries kings, nobles, and churches bought art, Dutch buyers were merchants, artisans, and shopkeepers. Engravings, illustrated histories, and oil paintings, even those of Rembrandt van Rijn (1606–1669), were all relatively inexpensive. One foreigner commented that "pictures are very common here, there being scarce an ordinary tradesman whose house is not decorated with them." Dutch artists focused on familiar daily details (see the illustration on page 648) because for them ordinary people had religious as well as political significance; even children at play could be infused with radiant beauty. The family household, not the royal court, determined the moral character of this intensely commercial society. Relative prosperity decreased the need for married women to work, so Dutch society developed the clear contrast between middle-class male and female roles that would become prevalent elsewhere in Europe and in America more than a century later. As one contemporary Dutch writer explained, "The husband must be on the street to practice his trade; the wife must stay at home to be in the kitchen."

Extraordinarily high levels of urbanization and literacy created a large reading public. Dutch presses printed books censored elsewhere (printers or authors censored in one province simply shifted operations to another), and the University of Leiden attracted students

---

◆*stadholder:* STAT hohl dur

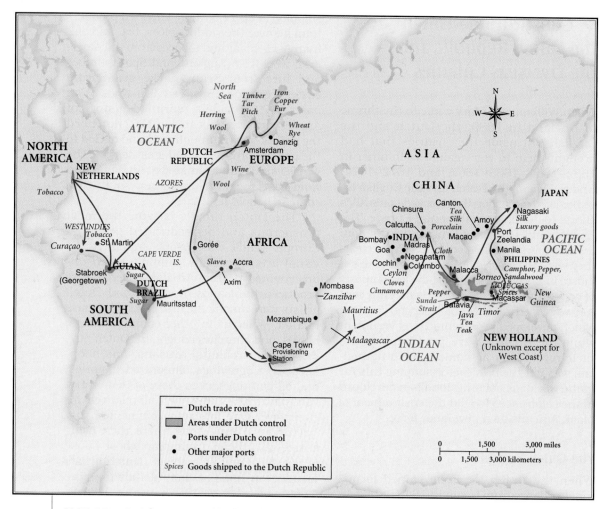

MAP 17.3 Dutch Commerce in the Seventeenth Century

Even before gaining formal independence from the Spanish in 1648, the Dutch had begun to compete with the Spanish and Portuguese all over the world. In 1602, a group of merchants established the Dutch East India Company, which soon offered investors an annual rate of return of 35 percent on the trade in spices with countries located on the Indian Ocean. Global commerce gave the Dutch the highest standard of living in Europe and soon attracted the envy of the French and the English.

and professors from all over Europe. Dutch tolerance extended to the works of Benedict Spinoza (1633–1677), a Jewish philosopher and biblical scholar who was expelled by his synagogue for alleged atheism but left alone by the Dutch authorities. Spinoza strove to reconcile religion with science and mathematics, but his work scandalized many Christians and Jews because he seemed to equate God and nature. Like nature, Spinoza's God followed unchangeable laws and could not be influenced by human actions, prayers, or faith.

Dutch learning, painting, and commerce all enjoyed wide renown in the seventeenth century, but this luster proved hard to maintain. The Dutch lived in a world of international rivalries in which strong central authority gave their enemies an advantage. Though inconclusive, the naval wars with England drained the state's revenues. Even more dangerous were the land wars with France, which continued into the eighteenth century. The Dutch survived these challenges but increasingly depended on alliances with other powers, especially England. At

DID YOU KNOW?

Tobacco and the Invention of "Smoking"

In the early seventeenth century, a "new astonishing fashion," wrote a German ambassador, came to the Dutch Republic from the New World. The term *smoking* gradually evolved in the seventeenth century out of "a fog-drinking bout," "drinking smoke," or "drinking tobacco." One Jesuit preacher called it "dry drunkenness." The analogy to inebriation is not entirely far-fetched, for nicotine (named after the French ambassador to Portugal, Jean Nicot, who brought tobacco to France in the mid-sixteenth century) does have an effect more comparable to alcohol than to caffeine; nicotine is a nerve toxin that dulls the nervous system. It is not known exactly where in the Americas tobacco had its birthplace, but its use was widespread by the time the Europeans arrived. Mayans and Aztecs smoked ceremonial pipes, Incas used tobacco as a medicine, and Indians in Brazil took snuff.

Spain began exporting tobacco to other European countries in the sixteenth century. The Spanish did not exploit the possibilities of producing tobacco on plantations; tobacco growing began in earnest in the seventeenth century only with the spread of black slavery. Virginia and Maryland expanded their exports of tobacco sixfold between 1663 and 1699. Until 1700, Amsterdam dominated the curing process; half the tobacco factories in Amsterdam were owned by Jewish merchants of Spanish or Portuguese descent.

Smoking spread geographically from western to eastern Europe, socially from the upper classes downward, and from men to women. At first the Spanish preferred cigars, the British pipes, and the French snuff. In the eighteenth century, both upper- and middle-class women took snuff, which was considered an aristocratic taste. Before the end of the nineteenth century, women did not regularly take tobacco in any form other than snuff. A woman smoking a pipe or cigar was a favorite target of cartoonists in the eighteenth and nineteenth centuries. This changed with the Russian invention of the cigarette in the mid-nineteenth century. Women began to smoke cigarettes in the late 1800s as a sign of emancipation.

Source: Wolfgang Schivelbusch, *Tastes of Paradise: A Social History of Spices, Stimulants, and Intoxicants*, trans. David Jacobson (New York: Vintage Books, 1992).

The Vice of Tobacco
In this engraving of 1628, *The Vice of Tobacco,* the Dutch artist Gillis van Scheyndel portrays smoking as similar to excessive drinking, a habit that makes people sick and leads them astray. Pipes often symbolized the folly and futility of a life given over to materialistic pleasures. The company of revelers is led on by a pipe-smoking ape who has features like a devil. *Koninklijke Bibliotheek.*

A Typical Dutch Scene from Daily Life
Jan Steen painted *The Baker Arent Oostward and His Wife* in 1658. Steen ran a brewery and tavern in addition to painting, and he was known for his interest in the details of daily life. Dutch artists popularized this kind of "genre" painting, which showed ordinary people at work and play. How does this typically Dutch approach differ from Baroque painting as seen in Chapter 16, page 608? **For more help analyzing this image**, see the visual activity for this chapter in the Online Study Guide at **bedfordstmartins.com/hunt**. *Rijksmuseum, Amsterdam.*

the end of the seventeenth century, the regent elite became more exclusive, more preoccupied with ostentation, less tolerant of deviations from strict Calvinism, and more concerned with imitating French styles than with encouraging their own.

> **Review:** What social factors explain Dutch willingness to tolerate religious differences?

Freedom and Slavery in the New World

The French and English also increasingly overshadowed the Dutch in the New World colonies. While the Dutch concentrated on shipping, including the slave trade, the seventeenth-century French and English es-

tablished settler colonies that would eventually provide fabulous revenues to the home countries. Many European governments encouraged private companies to vie for their share of the slave trade, and slavery began to take clear institutional form in the New World in this period. Even as slavery offered only a degrading form of despotism to black Africans, whites found in the colonies greater political and religious freedom than in Europe.

The Rise of the Slave Trade. After the Spanish and Portuguese had shown that African slaves could be transported and forced to labor in South and Central America, the English and French endeavored to set up similar labor systems in their new Caribbean island colonies. White planters with large tracts of land bought African slaves to work fields of sugarcane; and as they gradually built up their holdings, the planters displaced most of the original white settlers, who moved to mainland North American colonies. After 1661, when Barbados instituted a slave code that stripped all Africans of rights under English law, slavery became codified as an inherited status that applied only to blacks. The result was a society of extremes: the very wealthy whites, about 7 percent of the population in Barbados; and the enslaved, powerless black majority. The English brought few of their religious or constitutional practices to the Caribbean. Other Caribbean colonies followed a similar pattern of development. Louis XIV promulgated a "black code" in 1685 to regulate the legal status of slaves in the French colonies. Although one of his aims was to prevent non-Catholics from owning slaves in the French colonies, the code had much the same effect as the English codes on the slaves themselves: they had no legal rights.

The highest church and government authorities in Catholic and Protestant countries alike condoned the gradually expanding slave trade; the governments of England, France, Spain, Portugal, the Dutch Republic, and Denmark all encouraged private companies to traffic in black Africans. The Dutch West India Company was the most successful of them. In 1600, about 9,500 Africans were exported from Africa to the New World every year; by 1700, this number had increased nearly fourfold to 36,000 annually. Historians advance several different ideas about which factors increased the slave trade: some claim that improvements in muskets made European slavers more formidable; others cite the rising price for slaves, which made their sale more attractive for Africans; still others focus on factors internal to Africa such as the increasing size of African armies and their use of muskets in fighting and capturing other Africans for sale as slaves. Whatever the reason, the way had been prepared for the development of an Atlantic economy based on slavery.

Constitutional Freedoms in the English Colonies. Virtually left to themselves during the upheavals in England, the fledgling English colonies in North America developed representative government on their own. Almost every colony had a governor and a two-house legislature. The colonial legislatures constantly sought to increase their power and resisted the efforts of Charles II and James II to reaffirm royal control. William and Mary reluctantly allowed emerging colonial elites more control over local affairs. The social and political elite among the settlers hoped to impose an English social hierarchy dominated by rich landowners. Ordinary immigrants to the colonies, however, took advantage of plentiful land to carve out their own farms using white servants and, later, in some colonies, African slaves.

For native Americans, the expanding European presence meant something else altogether. They faced death through disease and warfare and the accelerating loss of their homelands. Unlike white settlers, many native Americans believed that land was a divine gift provided for their collective use and not subject to individual ownership. Europeans' claims that they owned exclusive land rights consequently resulted in frequent skirmishes. In 1675–1676, for instance, three tribes allied under Metacomet♦ (called King Philip by the English) threatened the survival of New England settlers, who savagely repulsed the attacks and sold their captives as slaves. Whites could portray native Americans as "noble savages," but when threatened they often depicted them as conspiring villains and sneaky heathens who were akin to Africans in their savagery.

♦**Metacomet:** MEH TAH caw MEHT

❖ The Search for Order in Elite and Popular Culture

The early success of constitutionalism in England, the Dutch Republic, and the English North American colonies would help to shape a distinctive Atlantic world in the eighteenth century. Just how constitutionalism was linked to the growing commerce with the colonies remains open to debate, however, since the constitutional governments, like the absolutist ones, avidly pursued profits in the burgeoning slave trade. Freedom did not mean liberty for everyone. One of the great debates of the time—and thereafter—concerned the meaning of freedom: for whom, under what conditions, with what justifiable limitations could freedom be claimed?

There was no freedom without order to sustain it, and most Europeans feared disorder above all else. In 1669, the English writer Margaret Cavendish, duchess of Newcastle, cataloged some of the sources of disorder in her time: "I wish Men were as Harmless as most Beasts are, then surely the World would be more Quiet and Happy than it is, for then there would not be such Pride, Vanity, Ambition, Covetousness, Faction, Treachery, and Treason, as is now." Cavendish wrote not long after the restoration of the monarchy in England, and her thoughts echoed the titanic struggles that had taken place over the nature of authority, not only in England but throughout Europe. Political theories, science, poetry, painting, and architecture all reflectedin some measure the attempts to ground authority—to define the relation between freedom and order—in new ways. Authority concerned not just rulers and subjects but also the hierarchy of groups in society. As European states consolidated their powers, elites worked to distinguish themselves from the lower classes. They developed new codes of correct behavior for themselves and tried to teach order and discipline to their social inferiors.

Social Contract Theory: Hobbes and Locke

The turmoil of the times prompted a major rethinking of the foundations of all authority. Two figures stood out prominently amid the cacophony of voices: Thomas Hobbes and John Locke. Their writings fundamentally shaped the modern subject of political science. Hobbes justified absolute authority; Locke provided the rationale for constitutionalism. Yet both argued that all authority came not from divine right but from a **social contract** among citizens.

Hobbes. Thomas Hobbes (1588–1679) was a royalist who sat out the English civil war of the 1640s in France, where he tutored the future king Charles II. Returning to England in 1651, he published his masterpiece, *Leviathan* (1651), in which he argued for unlimited authority in a ruler. Absolute authority could be vested in either a king or a parliament; it had to be absolute, he insisted, in order to overcome the defects of human nature. Believing that people are essentially self-centered and driven by the "right to self-preservation," Hobbes made his case by referring to science, not religion. To Hobbes, human life in a state of nature—that is, any situation without firm authority— was "solitary, poor, nasty, brutish, and short." He believed that the desire for power and natural greed would inevitably lead to unfettered competition. Only the assurance of social order could make people secure enough to act according to law; consequently, giving up personal liberty, he maintained, was the price of collective security. Rulers derived their power, he concluded, from a contract in which absolute authority protects people's rights.

Hobbes's notion of rule by an absolute authority left no room for political dissent or nonconformity, and it infuriated both royalists and supporters of Parliament. He enraged royalists by arguing that authority came not from divine right but from the social contract. Parliamentary supporters resisted Hobbes's claim that rulers must possess absolute authority to prevent the greater evil of anarchy; they believed that a constitution should guarantee shared power between king and parliament and protect individual rights under the law. Like Machiavelli before him, Hobbes became associated with a cynical, pessimistic view of human nature, and future political theorists often began their arguments by refuting Hobbes.

Locke. Rejecting both Hobbes and the more traditional royalist defenses of absolute authority, John Locke (1632–1704) used the notion of a social contract to provide a foundation for constitutionalism. Locke experienced political life firsthand as physician, secretary, and intellectual companion to the earl of Shaftesbury, a leading English Whig. In 1683, during the Exclusion Crisis, Locke fled with Shaftesbury to the Dutch Republic. There he continued work on his *Two Treatises of Government*, which, when published in 1690, served to justify the Glorious Revolution of 1688. Locke's position was thoroughly anti-absolutist. He denied the divine right of kings and ridiculed the common royalist idea that political power in the state mirrored the father's authority in the family. Like Hobbes, he posited a state of nature that applied to all people. Unlike Hobbes, however, he thought people were reasonable and the state of nature peaceful.

Locke insisted that government's only purpose was to protect life, liberty, and property, a notion that linked economic and political freedom. Ultimate authority rested in the will of a majority of men who owned property, and government should be limited to its basic purpose of protection. A ruler who failed to uphold his part of the social contract between the ruler and the populace could be justifiably resisted, an idea that would become crucial for the leaders of the American Revolution a century later. For England's landowners, however, Locke helped validate a revolution that consolidated their interests and ensured their privileges in the social hierarchy. Although Locke himself owned shares in the Royal African Company and justified slavery, his writings were later used by abolitionists in their campaign against slavery.

Locke defended his optimistic view of human nature in the immensely influential *Essay Concerning Human Understanding* (1690). He denied the existence of any innate ideas and asserted instead that each human is born with a mind that is a tabula rasa (blank slate). Everything humans know, he claimed, comes from sensory experience, not from anything inherent in human nature. Locke's views promoted the belief that "all men are created equal," a belief that challenged absolutist forms of rule and ultimately raised questions about women's roles as well. Not surprisingly, Locke devoted considerable energy to rethinking educational practices; he believed that education crucially shaped the human personality by channeling all sensory experience.

Newton and the Consolidation of the Scientific Revolution

New breakthroughs in science lent support to Locke's optimistic view of human potential. Building on the work of Copernicus, Kepler, and Galileo (see Chapter 16), the English natural philosopher Isaac Newton finally synthesized the laws of movement found among bodies on earth and related them to planetary motion. He united the mechanics of heavenly motion in a single **law of universal gravitation**, and in a stroke further enhanced the prestige of the new science. Almost immediately, upper-class men and women realized that being truly educated required a knowledge of the new science, while monarchs spied in science a new form of power that should not be ignored.

Newton. A Cambridge University student at the time of Charles II's restoration, Isaac Newton (1642–1727) learned mathematics and natural philosophy from his tutors and through his extraordinary application of his own mind. Sent home to weather the plague in 1665 and 1666, he attacked various problems in mathematics and established the basis for the new mathematics of moving bodies, the infinitesimal calculus. Over the next twenty years, he labored on an astounding variety of problems in mechanics and optics. In 1687 he finally brought his most significant mathematical and mechanical discoveries together in his masterwork, *Principia Mathematica*. Newton united celestial and terrestrial mechanics with his law of universal gravitation. According to Newton, the planets as well as the earth's moon move

Isaac Newton Analyzing the Nature of Light
To study the refraction of light, Newton made a hole in a window shutter, darkened the room, and let in a column of light, which he passed through a prism. In this way, he discovered that light is not homogeneous; violet refracts more light than any of the other colors, while red refracts less than orange, and orange refracts less than yellow. Newton used this knowledge to construct a reflecting telescope, which used mirrors to eliminate the distortion introduced by the spectrum of colors in light. © *The Image Works Archive.*

at uniform speeds proportional to their weight and to their distance from the sun. His law held that every body in the universe exerts over every other body an attractive force directly proportional to the product of their masses and inversely proportional to the square of the distance between them. The law of universal gravitation explained Kepler's elliptical planetary orbits just as it accounted for the motion of ordinary objects as they descend toward the earth.

Newton proved that a universal force acts at a distance between the sun and all the planets and that the same mathematical formula applies to all the movements at all times. To establish his law of universal gravitation, Newton first applied mathematical principles to formulate three fundamental physical laws: (1) in the absence of force, motion continues in a straight line; (2) the rate of change in the motion of an object is a result of the forces acting on it; and (3) the action and reaction between two objects are equal and opposite. Newtonian physics thus combined mass, inertia, force, velocity, and acceleration—all key concepts in modern science—and made them quantifiable. Newton showed that these laws of motion explained the orbiting of the planets as well as the fall of an apple to the ground: "From the same principles [of motion] I now demonstrate the frame of the System of the World."

Once set in motion, in Newton's view, the universe operated like a masterpiece made possible by the ingenuity of God. Others, less devout than Newton, could see it as a clockwork, with no need for God's continuing intervention. Gravity, although a mysterious force, could be expressed mathematically. Newton saw no conflict between faith and science. He believed that by demonstrating that the physical universe followed rational principles, natural philosophers could prove the existence of God and so liberate humans from doubt and the fear of chaos. The English poet Alexander Pope later valorized Newton, as did many others among his contemporaries:

> Nature and Nature's laws lay hid in night
> God said, Let Newton be! and all was light.

Even while laying the foundation for modern physics, optics and mechanics, Newton carried out alchemical experiments in his rooms at Cambridge University and spent long hours trying to calculate the date of the beginning of the world and its end with the second coming of Jesus. Not all scientists accepted Newton's planetary theories immediately, especially on the continent; the Dutch scientist Christian Huygens, for example, declared the concept of attraction (action at a distance) "absurd." But within a couple of generations Newton's work gained widespread assent, partly because of experimental verification.

Public Interest in Science. Despite the initial controversies about the possibility of universal gravitation at a distance, absolutist rulers quickly saw the potential of the new science for enhancing their prestige and glory. Frederick William, the Great Elector of

Brandenburg-Prussia, for example, set up agricultural experiments in front of his Berlin palace, and various German princes supported the work of Gottfried Wilhelm Leibniz♦ (1646–1716), who claimed that he, and not Newton, had invented the calculus. A lawyer, diplomat, mathematician, and scholar who wrote about metaphysics, cosmology, and history, Leibniz also helped establish scientific societies in the German states. Government involvement in science was greatest in France, where it became an arm of mercantilist policy; in 1666, Colbert founded the Royal Academy of Sciences, which supplied fifteen scientists with government stipends. It met in the King's Library in Paris, where for the first years the members devoted themselves to alchemical experiments and the study of mechanical devices.

Constitutional states supported science informally but provided an environment that encouraged its spread. The Royal Society of London, the counterpart to the one in Paris, grew out of informal meetings of scientists at London and Oxford rather than direct government involvement. It received a royal charter in 1662 but maintained complete independence; its members arranged for the publication of Newton's *Principia*. The society's secretary described its business to be "in the first place, to scrutinize the whole of Nature and to investigate its activity and powers by means of observations and experiments; and then in course of time to hammer out a more solid philosophy and more ample amenities of civilization." Whether the state paid for the work or not, thinkers of the day now tied science explicitly to social progress.

Because of their exclusion from most universities, women only rarely participated in the new scientific discoveries. In 1667, nonetheless, the Royal Society of London invited Margaret Cavendish, a writer of poems, essays, letters, and philosophical treatises, to attend a meeting to watch the exhibition of experiments. Labeled "mad" by her peers, she attacked the use of telescopes and microscopes because she detected in the new experimentalism a mechanistic view of the world that exalted masculine prowess and challenged the Christian belief in freedom of

♦**Leibniz:** LYB nits

the will. Yet she urged the formal education of women, complaining that "we are kept like birds in cages to hop up and down in our houses." "Many of our Sex may have as much wit, and be capable of Learning as well as men," she insisted, "but since they want Instructions [lack education], it is not possible they should attain to it."

Freedom and Order in the Arts

Like Newton, Locke, and Hobbes, most artists and intellectuals had experienced enough of the upheavals of the seventeenth century to fear the prospect of chaos and disintegration. The French mathematician Blaise Pascal vividly captured their worries in his *Pensées*♦ (Thoughts) of 1660: "I look on all sides, and I see only darkness everywhere." But Pascal was more skeptical than most about man's ability to forge order out of chaos: "Nature presents to me nothing which is not a matter of doubt and concern....It is incomprehensible that God should exist, and incomprehensible that He should not exist." Poets, painters, and architects all tried to make sense of the individual's place within what Pascal called "the eternal silence of these infinite spaces."

Milton. The English Puritan poet John Milton (1608–1674) gave priority to individual liberty. In 1643, in the midst of the civil war between king and Parliament, he published writings in favor of divorce. When Parliament enacted a censorship law aimed at such literature, Milton responded in 1644 with one of the first defenses of freedom of the press, *Areopagitica.*♦ (See the excerpt on page 654.) Milton served as secretary to the Council of State during Cromwell's rule and earned the enmity of Charles II by writing a justification for the execution of his father, Charles I.

Forced into retirement after the restoration of the monarchy, Milton published in 1667 his epic poem *Paradise Lost.* He used Adam and Eve's Fall to meditate on human freedom and the tragedies of rebellion. Although Milton wanted to "justify the ways of God to man," his Satan, the proud angel who challenges God, is so compelling as to be heroic. In the

end, Adam and Eve learn to accept moral responsibility. Individuals learn the limits to their freedom, yet personal liberty remains essential to their definition as human.

The Varieties of Artistic Style. The dominant artistic styles of the time—the baroque and the classical—both submerged the ordinary individual in a grander design. The baroque style proved to be especially suitable for public displays of faith and power that overawed individual beholders. The combination of religious and political purposes in baroque art is best exemplified in the architecture and sculpture of Gian Lorenzo Bernini (1598–1680), the papacy's official

Gian Lorenzo Bernini, *Ecstasy of St. Teresa of Ávila* (c. 1650)
This ultimate statement of baroque sculpture captures all the drama and even sensationalism of a mystical religious faith. Bernini based his figures on a vision reported by St. Teresa in which she saw an angel: "In his hands I saw a great golden spear, and at the iron tip there appeared to be a point of fire. This he plunged into my heart several times so that it penetrated my entrails. When he pulled it out I felt that he took them with it, and left me utterly consumed by the great love of God." *Scala/Art Resource, NY.*

♦*Pensées:* pahn SAYS
♦*Areopagitica:* ar ee oh puh JIHT ih kuh

John Milton's Defense of Freedom of the Press

In Areopagitica (1644), the English poet John Milton rebuked Parliament for passing a bill to restrict freedom of the press by requiring licensing of every publication. The title came from Areopagus, the name of a court in ancient Athens. Milton argued that freedom of thought was essential to human dignity.

I deny not but that it is of greatest concernment in the church and commonwealth to have a vigilant eye how books demean themselves as well as men; and thereafter to confine, imprison, and do sharpest justice on them as malefactors. For books are not absolutely dead things, but do contain a potency of life in them to be as active as that soul was whose progeny they are; nay, they do preserve as in a vial the purest efficacy and extraction of that living intellect that bred them. I know they are as lively and as vigorously productive as those fabulous dragon's teeth; and being sown up and down, may chance to spring up armed men. And yet, on the other hand, unless wariness be used, as good almost kill a man as kill a good book: who kills a man kills a reasonable creature, God's image; but he who destroys a good book, kills reason itself, kills the image of God, as it were, in the eye. Many a man lives a burden to the earth; but a good book is the precious lifeblood of a master spirit, embalmed and treasured up on purpose to a life beyond life. 'Tis true, no age can restore a life, whereof perhaps there is no great loss; and revolutions of ages do not oft recover the loss of a rejected truth, for the want of which whole nations fare the worse. We should be wary, therefore, what persecution we raise against the living labors of public

men, how we spill that seasoned life of man preserved and stored up in books; since we see a kind of homicide may be thus committed, sometimes a martyrdom; and if it extend to the whole impression, a kind of massacre, whereof the execution ends not in the slaying of an elemental life, but strikes at that ethereal and fifth essence, the breath of reason itself, slays an immortality rather than a life. But lest I should be condemned of introducing license, while I oppose licensing, I refuse not the pains to be so much historical as will serve to show what hath been done by ancient and famous commonwealths against this disorder, till the very time that this project of licensing crept out of the Inquisition, was caught up by our prelates, and hath caught some of our presbyters. [...]

As therefore the state of man now is, what wisdom can there be to choose, what continence to forbear without the knowledge of evil? He that can apprehend and consider vice with all her baits and seeming pleasures, and yet abstain, and yet distinguish, and yet prefer that which is truly better, he is the true warfaring Christian. I cannot praise a fugitive and cloistered virtue, unexercised and unbreathed, that never sallies out and sees her adversary, but slinks out of the race where that immortal garland is to be run for, not without dust and heat. Assuredly we bring not innocence into the world, we bring impurity much rather: that which purifies us is trial, and trial is by what is contrary.

Source: John Milton, *Milton's Prose Writing* (London: J.M. Dant, 1961), 149–50, 158.

---

artist. His architectural masterpiece was the gigantic square facing St. Peter's Basilica in Rome (1656–1671). His use of freestanding colonnades and a huge open space is meant to impress the individual observer with the power of the popes and the Catholic religion. Bernini also sculpted tombs for the popes and a large statue of Constantine, the first Christian emperor of Rome—perfect ex-

amples of the marriage of power and religion. In 1665, Louis XIV hired Bernini to plan the rebuilding of the Louvre palace in Paris but then rejected his ideas as incompatible with French tastes.

Although France was a Catholic country, French painters, sculptors, and architects, like their patron Louis XIV, preferred the standards of **classicism** to those of the

French Classicism
This painting by Nicolas Poussin, *Discovery of Achilles on Skyros* (1649–1650), shows the French interest in classical themes and ideals. In the Greek story, Thetis dressed her son Achilles as a young woman and hid him on the island of Skyros so he would not have to fight in the Trojan War. When a chest of treasures is offered to the women, Achilles reveals himself (he is the figure on the far right) because he cannot resist the sword. In telling the story, Poussin emphasizes harmony and almost a sedateness of composition, avoiding the exuberance and emotionalism of the baroque style. *Photograph © 2003 Museum of Fine Arts, Boston.*

baroque. French artists developed classicism to be a French national style, distinct from the baroque style that was closely associated with France's enemies, the Austrian and Spanish Habsburgs. As its name suggests, classicism reflected the ideals of the art of antiquity: geometric shapes, order, and harmony of lines took precedence over the sensuous, exuberant, and emotional forms of the baroque. Rather than being overshadowed by the sheer power of emotional display, in classicism the individual could be found at the intersection of converging, symmetrical, straight lines (see illustration above). These influences were apparent in the work of the leading French painters of the period, Nicolas Poussin (1594–1665) and Claude Lorrain (1600–1682), both of whom worked in Rome and tried to re-create classical Roman values in their mythological scenes and Roman landscapes.

Dutch painters found the baroque and classical styles less suited to their private market, where buyers sought smaller-scale works with ordinary subjects. Dutch artists came from common stock themselves—Rembrandt's father was a miller, and the father of Jan Vermeer (1632–1675) was a silk worker. Their clients were people like themselves who purchased paintings much as they bought tables and chairs. Although he occasionally worked on commission for the prince of Orange, even Rembrandt painted ordinary people, suffusing his canvases with a radiant, otherworldly light that made the plainest people and objects appear deeply spiritual. Vermeer's best-known paintings show women working at home; like Rembrandt, Vermeer made ordinary activities seem precious and beautiful.

Art might also serve the interests of science. One of the most skilled illustrators of insects and flowers was Maria Sibylla Merian (1646–1717), a German-born painter-scholar whose engravings were widely celebrated for their brilliant realism and microscopic clarity. Merian eventually separated from her husband and joined a sect called the Labadists (after its French founder, Jean de Labadie), whose members did not believe in formal marriage ties. After moving with her daughters to the Labadists' community in the northern Dutch province of Friesland, Merian went with missionaries from the sect to the Dutch colony of Surinam in South America and painted watercolors (see the illustration on page 656) of the exotic flowers, birds, and insects she found in the jungle around the cocoa and sugarcane plantations. In the seventeenth century, many women became known for their still lifes and

Dutch Art

Dutch artists went their own way, following neither the baroque nor the classical style. *Officer with a Laughing Girl* (1657) by Jan Vermeer shows a scene that captures the Dutch fascination with the details of ordinary life. Note for example the richness of the texture of the girl's clothing, the delicacy of the glass in the window, and the presence of a map as decoration on the wall. As worldwide traders, the Dutch gave great value to maps. *Copyright © The Frick Collection, New York.*

European Fascination with Products of the New World

In this painting of a banana plant, Maria Sibylla Merian offers a scientific study of one of the many exotic plants and animals found by Europeans who traveled to the colonies overseas. Merian was fifty-one when she traveled to the Dutch South American colony of Surinam with her daughter. *Courtesy of Hunt Institute for Botanical Documentation, Carnegie Mellon University, Pittsburgh, PA.*

especially their paintings of flowers. Paintings by the Dutch artist Rachel Ruysch, for example, fetched higher prices than those received by Rembrandt.

Women and Manners

Poetry and painting imaginatively explored the place of the individual within a larger whole, but real-life individuals had to learn to navigate their own social worlds. Manners—which involved individual self-discipline—were essential skills of social navigation, and women usually took the lead in teaching them. Women's importance in refining social relationships quickly became a subject of controversy.

The Cultivation of Manners. The court had long been a central arena for the development of manners. Under the tutelage of their mothers and wives, nobles learned to hide all that was crass and to maintain a fine sense of social distinction. In some ways, aristocratic men were expected to act more like women; just as women had long been expected to please men, now aristocratic men had to please their monarch or patron by displaying proper manners and conversing with elegance and wit. The art of pleasing included foreign languages (especially French), dance, a taste for fine music, and attention to dress.

As part of the evolution of new aristocratic ideals, nobles learned to disdain all that was lowly. The upper classes began to reject popular festivals and fairs in favor of private theaters, where seats were relatively expensive and behavior was formal. Clowns and buffoons now seemed vulgar; the last king of England to keep a court fool was Charles I. Chivalric romances that had entranced the nobility down to the time of Cervantes's *Don Quixote* (1605) now passed into popular literature.

The greatest French playwright of the seventeenth century, Molière (the pen name of Jean-Baptiste Poquelin, 1622–1673), wrote sparkling comedies of manners that revealed much about the new aristocratic behavior. His play *The Middle-Class Gentleman*, first performed for Louis XIV in 1670, revolves around the yearning of a rich, middle-class Frenchman, Monsieur Jourdain, to learn to act like a *gentilhomme*♦ (meaning both "gentleman" and "nobleman"). Monsieur Jourdain buys fancy clothes; hires private instructors in dancing, music, fencing, and philosophy; and lends money to a debt-ridden noble in hopes that the noble will marry his daughter. Only his sensible wife and his daughter's love for a worthier commoner stand in his way. The message for the king's courtiers seemed to be a reassuring one: only true nobles by blood can hope to act like nobles. But the play also showed how the middle classes were learning to emulate the nobility; if one could learn to act nobly through self-discipline, could not anyone with some education and money pass himself off as noble?

As Molière's play demonstrated, new attention to manners trickled down from the court to the middle class. A French treatise on manners written in 1672 explained proper behavior:

> *If everyone is eating from the same dish, you should take care not to put your hand into it before those of higher rank have done so.... Formerly one was permitted ... to dip one's bread into the sauce, provided only that one had not already bitten it. Nowadays that would be a kind of rusticity. Formerly one was allowed to take from one's mouth what one could not eat and drop it on the floor, provided it was done skillfully. Now that would be very disgusting.*

The key words *rusticity* and *disgusting* reveal the association of unacceptable social behavior with the peasantry, dirt, and repulsion. Similar rules governed spitting and blowing one's nose in public. Once the elite had successfully distinguished itself from the lower classes through manners, scholars became more interested in studying popular expressions. They avidly collected proverbs, folktales, and songs—all of these now curiosities. In fact, many nobles at Louis XIV's court read fairy tales.

Debates about Women's Roles. Courtly manners often permeated the upper reaches of society by means of the salon,♦ an informal gathering held regularly in private homes and presided over by a socially eminent woman. In 1661, one French author claimed to have identified 251 Parisian women as hostesses of salons. Although the French government occasionally worried that these gatherings might challenge its authority, the three main topics of conversation were love, literature, and philosophy. Hostesses often worked hard to encourage the careers of budding authors. Before publishing a manuscript, many authors would read their compositions to a salon gathering. Corneille, Racine, and even Bishop Bossuet sought women's approval for their writings.

Some women went beyond encouraging male authors and began to write on their own, but they faced many obstacles. Marie-Madeleine de La Vergne, known as Madame de Lafayette, wrote several short novels that were published anonymously because it was considered inappropriate for aristocratic women to appear in print. Following the publication of *The Princess of Clèves* in 1678, she denied having written it. Hannah Wooley, the English author of many books on domestic conduct, published under the name of her first husband. Women were known for writing wonderful letters (Marie de Sévigné was a prime example), but the correspondence circulated only in handwritten form. In the 1650s, despite these limitations, French women began to turn out best sellers in a new type of literature, the novel. Their success prompted the philosopher Pierre

♦*gentilhomme:* ZHOHN tee ohm

♦*salon:* SA lahn

Bayle to remark in 1697 that "our best French novels for a long time have been written by women."

The new importance of women in the world of manners and letters did not sit well with everyone. Although the French writer François Poulain de la Barre (1647–1723), in a series of works published in the 1670s, used the new science to assert the equality of women's minds, most men resisted the idea. Clergy, lawyers, scholars, and playwrights attacked women's growing public influence. Women, they complained, were corrupting forces and needed restraint. Only marriage, "this salutary yoke," could control their passions and weaknesses. Women were accused of raising "the banner of prostitution in the salons, in the promenades, and in the streets." Molière wrote plays denouncing women's pretension to judge literary merit. English playwrights derided learned women by creating characters with names such as Lady Knowall, Lady Meanwell, and Mrs. Lovewit.

A real-life target of the English playwrights was Aphra Behn (1640–1689), one of the first professional woman authors, who supported herself by journalism and wrote plays and poetry. She also translated scientific works and defended Copernicanism. Her short novel *Oroonoko*♦ (1688) told the story of an African prince wrongly sold into slavery. (See the excerpt on the next page.) The story was so successful that it was adapted by playwrights and performed repeatedly in England and France for the next hundred years. Behn responded to her critics by arguing that there was "no reason why women should not write as well as men." Women also played important roles in the new colonies. In order to establish more permanent and settled colonies, governments promoted the emigration of women so that male colonists would set up orderly Christian white households rather than pursuing sexual relations with native or slave women.

Reforming Popular Culture

The illiterate peasants who made up most of Europe's population had little or no knowledge of the law of gravitation, upper-class

♦*Oroonoko:* OH roo noh koh

manners, or novels, no matter who authored them. Their culture had three main elements: the knowledge needed to work at farming or in a trade; popular forms of entertainment such as village fairs and dances; and their religion, which shaped every aspect of life and death. What changed most noticeably in the seventeenth century was the social elites' attitude toward lower-class culture. The division between elite and popular culture widened as elites insisted on their difference from the lower orders and tried to instill new forms of discipline in their social inferiors.

Popular Religion. In the seventeenth century, Protestant and Catholic churches alike pushed hard to change popular religious practices. Their campaigns against popular "paganism" began during the sixteenth-century Protestant Reformation and Catholic Counter-Reformation but reached much of rural Europe only in the seventeenth century. Puritans in England tried to root out maypole dances, Sunday village fairs, gambling, taverns, and bawdy ballads because they interfered with sober observance of the Sabbath. In Lutheran Norway, pastors denounced a widespread belief in the miracle-working powers of St. Olaf. The word *superstition* previously meant "false religion" (Protestantism was a superstition for Catholics, Catholicism for Protestants); in the seventeenth century it took on its modern meaning of irrational fears, beliefs, and practices, which anyone educated or refined would avoid.

The Catholic campaign against superstitious practices found a ready ally in Louis XIV. While the Sun King reformed the nobles at court through etiquette and manners, Catholic bishops in the French provinces trained parish priests to reform their flocks by using catechisms in local dialects and insisting that parishioners attend Mass. The church faced a formidable challenge. One bishop in France complained in 1671, "Can you believe that there are in this diocese entire villages where no one has even heard of Jesus Christ?" In some places, believers sacrificed animals to the Virgin, prayed to the new moon, and worshiped at the sources of streams as in pre-Christian times.

Like its Protestant counterpart, the Catholic campaign against ignorance and

Aphra Behn, *Oroonoko*

Aphra Behn wrote poetry, plays, and novels—though writing was denounced by some men as an indecent activity for women. Behn also traveled to Surinam, where she set her novel Oroonoko *(1688). In this passage, she describes the "royal slave" (an African prince tricked into slavery) as very much like a European aristocrat. His physical appearance made him seem like an ancient Roman rather than a seventeenth-century African slave.*

I have often seen and conversed with this great man, and been a witness to many of his mighty actions; and do assure my reader, the most illustrious courts could not have produced a braver man, both for greatness of courage and mind, a judgment more solid, a wit more quick, and a conversation more sweet and diverting. He knew almost as much as if he had read much: he had heard of, and admired the Romans; he had heard of the late Civil Wars in England, and the deplorable death of our great monarch, and would discourse of it with all the sense and abhorrence of the injustice imaginable. He had an extreme good and graceful mien, and all the civility of a well-bred great man. He had nothing of barbarity in his nature, but in all points addressed himself as if his education had been in some European court.

This great and just character of Oroonoko gave me an extreme curiosity to see him, especially when I knew he spoke French and English, and that I could talk with him. But though I had heard so much of him, I was as greatly surprised when I saw him as if I had heard nothing of him, so beyond all report I found him. He came into the room, and addressed himself to me, and some other women, with the best grace in the world. He was pretty tall, but of a shape the most exact that can be fancied; the most famous statuary could not form the figure of a man more admirably turned from head to foot. His face was not of that brown, rusty black which most of that nation are, but a perfect ebony, or polished jet. His eyes were the most awful that could be seen, and very piercing; the white of them being like snow, as were his teeth. His nose was rising and Roman, instead of African and flat. His mouth, the finest shaped that could be seen; far from those great turned lips, which are so natural to the rest of the Negroes. The whole proportion and air of his face was so noble, and exactly formed, that, bating his colour, there could be nothing in nature more beautiful, agreeable, and handsome.

Source: Aphra Behn, *Oroonoko, The Rover, and Other Works* (New York: Penguin, 1992), 80–81.

---

superstition helped extend state power. Clergy, officials, and local police worked together to limit carnival celebrations, to regulate pilgrimages to shrines, and to replace "indecent" images of saints with more restrained and decorous ones. In Catholicism, the cult of the Virgin Mary and devotions closely connected with Jesus, such as the Holy Sacrament and the Sacred Heart, took precedence over the celebration of popular saints who seemed to have pagan origins or were credited with unverified miracles. Reformers everywhere tried to limit the number of feast days on the grounds that they encouraged lewd behavior.

New Attitudes toward Poverty. The campaign for more disciplined religious practices helped generate a new attitude toward the poor. Poverty previously had been closely linked with charity and virtue in Christianity; it was a Christian duty to give alms to the poor, and Jesus and many of the saints had purposely chosen lives of poverty. In the sixteenth and seventeenth centuries, the upper classes, the church, and the state increasingly regarded the poor as dangerous, deceitful, and lacking in character. "Criminal laziness is the source of all their vices," wrote a Jesuit expert on the poor. The courts had previously expelled beggars from cities; now local leaders,

MAPPING THE WEST Europe at the End of the Seventeenth Century
A map can be deceiving. Although Poland-Lithuania looks like a large country on this map, it had been fatally weakened by internal conflicts. In the next century it would disappear entirely. The Ottoman Empire still controlled an extensive territory, but outside of Anatolia its rule depended on intermediaries. The Austrian Habsburgs had pushed the Turks out of Hungary and back into the Balkans. At the other end of the scale, the very small Dutch Republic had become very rich through international commerce. Size did not always prove to be an advantage.

both Catholic and Protestant, tried to reform their character. Municipal magistrates collected taxes for poor relief, and local notables organized charities; together they transformed hospitals into houses of confinement for beggars. In Catholic France, upper-class women's religious associations, known as confraternities, set up asylums that confined prostitutes (by arrest if necessary) and rehabilitated them. Confraternities also

founded hospices where orphans learned order and respect. Such groups advocated harsh discipline as the cure for poverty.

As hard times increased the numbers of the poor and the rates of violent crime as well, attitudes toward the poor hardened. The elites wanted to separate the very poor from society either to change them or to keep them from contaminating others. Hospitals became holding pens for society's unwanted members; in them, the poor joined the disabled, the incurably diseased, and the insane. The founding of hospitals demonstrates the connection between elites' attitudes and state building. In 1676, Louis XIV ordered every French city to establish a hospital, and his government took charge of the finances. Other rulers soon followed the same path.

> **Review:** In what ways did elite and popular culture become more separate in this period?

Conclusion

The search for order took place on various levels, from the reform of the disorderly poor to the establishment of more regular bureaucratic routines in government. The absolutist government of Louis XIV served as a model for all those who aimed to increase the power of the central state. Even Louis's rivals—such as the Holy Roman Emperor Leopold I and Frederick William, the Great Elector of Brandenburg-Prussia—followed his lead in centralizing authority and building up their armies. Whether absolutist or constitutionalist in form, seventeenth-century states aimed to penetrate more deeply into the lives of their subjects. They wanted more men for their armed forces; higher taxes to support their projects; and more control over foreign trade, religious dissent, and society's unwanted.

Some tears had begun to appear, however, in the seamless fabric of state power. The civil war between Charles I and Parliament in England in the 1640s opened the way to new demands for political participation. When Parliament overthrew James II in 1688, it also insisted that the new king and queen, William and Mary, agree to a Bill of Rights. Left on their own during the turmoil in England, the English North American colonies developed distinctive forms of representative government. In the eighteenth century, new levels of economic growth and the appearance of new social groups would exert pressures on the European state system. The success of seventeenth-century rulers created the political and economic conditions in which their critics would flourish.

Suggested References

Louis XIV: Model of Absolutism

Recent studies have insisted that absolutism could never be entirely absolute because the king depended on collaboration and cooperation to enforce his policies. Some of the best sources for Louis XIV's reign are the letters written by important noblewomen. The Web site of the Château of Versailles includes views of rooms in the castle.

*Beik, William. *Louis XIV and Absolutism: A Brief Study with Documents.* 2000.

*Forster, Elborg, trans. *A Woman's Life in the Court of the Sun King: Elisabeth Charlotte, Duchesse d'Orléans.* 1984.

Hurt, John J. *Louis XIV and the Parlements.* 2002.

*Sévigné, Madame de. *Selected Letters.* Trans. Leonard Tancock. 1982.

Treasure, Geoffrey. *Louis XIV.* 2001.

Versailles: **http://www.chateauversailles.fr**.

Absolutism in Central and Eastern Europe

Too often central and eastern European forms of state development have been characterized as backward in comparison with those of western Europe. Now historians emphasize the patterns of ruler-elite cooperation shared with western Europe, but they also underscore the weight of serfdom in eastern economies and political systems.

Barkey, Karen. *The Ottoman Route to State Centralization.* 1994.

Çiçek, Kemal, ed. *The Great Ottoman-Turkish Civilisation,* 4 vols. 2000.

Kivelson, Valerie A. *Autocracy in the Provinces: The Muscovite Gentry and Political Culture in the Seventeenth Century.* 1996.

Vierhaus, Rudolf. *Germany in the Age of Absolutism.* Trans. Jonathan B. Knudsen. 1988.

Wilson, Peter H. *German Armies: War and German Politics, 1648–1806.* 1998.

Constitutionalism in England

Though recent interpretations of the English revolutions emphasize the limits on radical change, Hill's portrayal of the radical ferment of ideas remains fundamental.

Cromwell: **http://www.cromwell.org**.

*Primary sources.

*Graham, Elspeth, et al., eds. *Her Own Life: Autobiographical Writings by Seventeenth-Century English Women.* 1989.

*Haller, William, and Godfrey Davies, eds. *The Leveller Tracts, 1647–1653.* 1944.

Hill, Christopher. *The World Turned Upside Down: Radical Ideas during the English Revolution.* 1972.

Israel, Jonathan, ed. *The Anglo-Dutch Moment: Essays on the Glorious Revolution and Its World Impact.* 1991.

Knoppers, Laura Lunger. *Constructing Cromwell: Ceremony, Portrait, and Print, 1645–1661.* 2000.

Constitutionalism in the Dutch Republic and the Overseas Colonies

Studies of the Dutch Republic emphasize the importance of trade and consumerism. Recent work on the colonies has begun to explore the intersecting experiences of settlers, native Americans, and African slaves.

*Campbell, P. F. *Some Early Barbadian History.* 1993.

Israel, Jonathan. *Dutch Primacy in World Trade, 1585–1740.* 1989.

Price, J. L. *The Dutch Republic in the Seventeenth Century.* 1998.

Schama, Simon. *The Embarrassment of Riches: An Interpretation of Dutch Culture in the Golden Age.* 1988.

Taylor, Alan. *American Colonies.* 2002.

Thornton, John. *Africa and Africans in the Making of the Atlantic World, 1400–1800.* 1992.

The Search for Order in Elite and Popular Culture

Historians do not always agree about the meaning of popular culture: Was it something widely shared by all social classes or a set of activities increasingly identified with the lower classes, as Burke argues? The central Web site for Dutch museums allows the visitor to tour rooms and see paintings in scores of Dutch museums, many of which have important holdings of paintings by Rembrandt and Vermeer. The Web site on Isaac Newton links to many other sites on his scientific and mathematical discoveries.

Burke, Peter. *Popular Culture in Early Modern Europe.* 1978.

Davis, Natalie Zemon. *Women on the Margins: Three Seventeenth-Century Lives.* 1995.

Dutch Museums: **http://www.hollandmuseums.nl**.

*Fitzmaurice, James, ed. *Margaret Cavendish: Sociable Letters.* 1997.

Jardine, Lisa. *On a Grander Scale: The Outstanding Life of Sir Christopher Wren.* 2003.

Newton: **http://www-history.mcs.st-andrews.ac.uk/history/Mathematicians/Newton.html**.

Westfall, Richard S. *The Life of Isaac Newton.* 1993.

*Primary sources.

CHAPTER REVIEW

IMPORTANT EVENTS

1642–1646 Civil war between King Charles I and Parliament in England

1648 Peace of Westphalia ends Thirty Years' War; the Fronde revolt challenges royal authority in France; Ukrainian Cossack warriors rebel against the king of Poland-Lithuania; Spain formally recognizes independence of the Dutch Republic

1649 Execution of Charles I of England; new Russian legal code

1651 Thomas Hobbes publishes *Leviathan*

1660 Monarchy restored in England

1661 Slave code set up in Barbados

1667 Louis XIV begins first of many wars that continue throughout his reign

1670 Molière's play, *The Middle-Class Gentleman*

1678 Marie-Madeline de La Vergne (Madame de Lafayette) anonymously publishes her novel *The Princess of Clèves*

1683 Austrian Habsburgs break the Turkish siege of Vienna

1685 Louis XIV revokes toleration for French Protestants granted by the Edict of Nantes

1687 Isaac Newton publishes *Principia Mathematica*

1688 Parliament deposes James II and invites his daughter, Mary, and her husband, William of Orange, to take the throne

1690 John Locke's *Two Treatises of Government*, *Essay Concerning Human Understanding*

KEY TERMS

absolutism (621)

bureaucracy (627)

classicism (654)

constitutionalism (622)

Fronde (623)

Glorious Revolution (644)

law of universal gravitation (651)

Levellers (639)

mercantilism (628)

Old Believers (635)

parlements (623)

social contract (650)

REVIEW QUESTIONS

1. How "absolute" was the power of Louis XIV?

2. Why did absolutism succeed everywhere in eastern Europe except Poland-Lithuania?

3. What differences over religion and politics caused the conflict between king and Parliament in England?

4. What social factors explain Dutch willingness to tolerate religious differences?

5. In what ways did elite and popular culture become more separate in this period?

MAKING CONNECTIONS

1. What are the most important differences between absolutism and constitutionalism as political systems?

2. In what ways did religious differences still cause political conflict?

3. Why was the search for order a major theme in science, politics, and the arts?

FOR FURTHER EXPLORATION

To assess your mastery of the material in this chapter, see the Online Study Guide at **bedfordstmartins.com/hunt**.

To read additional primary-source material from this period, see Chapter 17 in *Sources of The Making of the West*, Second Edition.

The Atlantic System and Its Consequences, 1690–1740

JOHANN SEBASTIAN BACH (1685–1750), composer of mighty organ fugues◆ and church cantatas, was not above amusing his Leipzig audiences, many of them university students. In 1732 he produced a cantata about a young woman in love—with coffee. Her old-fashioned father rages that he won't find her a husband unless she gives up the fad. She agrees, secretly vowing to admit no suitor who will not promise in the marriage contract to let her brew coffee whenever she wants. Bach offers this conclusion:

> *The cat won't give up its mouse,*
> *Girls stay faithful coffee-sisters*
> *Mother loves her coffee habit,*
> *Grandma sips it gladly too—*
> *Why then shout at the daughters?*

Bach's era might well be called the age of coffee. European travelers at the end of the sixteenth century had noticed Middle Eastern people drinking a "black drink," *kavah*, and the Turks took coffee beans with them on their military campaigns in eastern Europe. Few Europeans sampled the drink at first, and the Arab monopoly on its production kept prices high. This changed around 1700 when the Dutch East India Company introduced coffee plants to Java and other Indonesian islands. Coffee production then spread to the French Caribbean, where African slaves provided the plantation labor. In Europe, imported coffee spurred the development of a new kind of meeting place: the first coffeehouse opened in London in 1652, and the idea spread quickly to other European cities. The coffeehouses became gathering places for men to drink, read

---

◆**fugues:** fyoogs

London Coffeehouse
This gouache (a variant on watercolor painting) from about 1725 depicts a scene from a London coffeehouse located in the courtyard of the Royal Exchange (merchants' bank). Middle-class men (wearing wigs) read newspapers, drink coffee, smoke pipes, and discuss the news of the day. The coffeehouse draws them out of their homes into a new public space. *British Museum, Bridgeman Art Library, NY.*

newspapers, and talk politics. As a London newspaper commented in 1737, "There's scarce an Alley in City and Suburbs but has a Coffeehouse in it, which may be called the School of Public Spirit, where every Man over Daily and Weekly Journals, a Mug, or a Dram . . . devotes himself to that glorious one, his Country."

European consumption of coffee, tea, chocolate, and other novelties increased dramatically as European nations forged worldwide economic links. At the center of this new global economy was the **Atlantic system**, the triangular pattern of trade that bound together western Europe, Africa, and the Americas. Europeans bought slaves in western Africa, transported and sold them in their colonies in North and South America and the Caribbean, bought the commodities such as coffee and sugar that were produced by the new colonial plantations, and then sold the goods in European ports for refining and reshipment. This Atlantic system first took clear shape in the early eighteenth century; it was the hub of European expansion all over the world.

Coffee drinking was one example among many of the new social and cultural patterns that took root between 1690 and 1740. Improvements in agricultural production at home reinforced the effects of trade overseas; Europeans now had more disposable income for extras, and they spent their money not only in the new coffeehouses and cafés that sprang up all over Europe but also on newspapers, musical concerts, paintings, and novels. A new middle-class public began to make its presence felt in every domain of culture and social life.

Although the rise of the Atlantic system gave Europe new prominence in the global context, European rulers still focused most of their political, diplomatic, and military energies on their rivalries within Europe. A coalition of countries succeeded in containing French aggression, and a more balanced diplomatic system emerged. In eastern Europe, Prussia and Austria had to contend with the rising power of Russia under Peter the Great. In western Europe, both Spain and the Dutch Republic declined in influence but continued to vie with Britain and France for colonial spoils in the Atlantic. The more evenly matched competition among the great powers encouraged the development of diplomatic skills and drew attention to public health as a way of encouraging population growth.

In the aftermath of Louis XIV's revocation of the Edict of Nantes in 1685, a new intellectual movement known as the Enlightenment began to germinate. An initial impetus came from French Protestant refugees who published works critical of absolutism in politics and religion. Increased prosperity, the growth of a middle-class public, and the decline in warfare after Louis XIV's death in 1715 helped fuel this new critical spirit. Fed by the popularization of science and the growing interest in travel literature, the Enlightenment encouraged greater skepticism about religious and state authority. Eventually the movement would question almost every aspect of social and political life in

◆ **1690s** Development of Caribbean plantations

◆ **1694** Bank of England established; Astell, *A Serious Proposal to the Ladies*

◆ **1697** Bayle, *Historical and Critical Dictionary*

◆ **1714–1727** King George I of England

◆ **1715** Death of Louis XIV

◆ **1719** Defoe, *Robinson Crusoe*

1690	1700	1710

◆ **1699** Turks forced to recognize Austrian rule over Hungary, Transylvania

◆ **1703** Building of St. Petersburg begins; first Russian newspaper

◆ **1713–1714** Peace of Utrecht

Europe. The Enlightenment began in western Europe in those countries—Britain, France, and the Dutch Republic—most affected by the new Atlantic system. It too was a product of the age of coffee.

❖ The Atlantic System and the World Economy

Although their ships had been circling the globe since the early 1500s, Europeans did not draw most of the world into their economic orbit until the 1700s. Western European trading nations sent ships loaded with goods to buy slaves from local rulers on the western coast of Africa; then transported the slaves to the colonies in North and South America and the Caribbean and sold them to the owners of plantations producing coffee, sugar, cotton, and tobacco; and bought the raw commodities produced in the colonies and shipped them back to Europe, where they were refined or processed and then sold to other parts of Europe and the world. The Atlantic system and the growth of international trade helped create a new consumer society.

Slavery and the Atlantic System

Spain and Portugal dominated Atlantic trade in the sixteenth and seventeenth centuries, but in the eighteenth century European trade in the Atlantic rapidly expanded and became more systematically interconnected

(Map 18.1, page 668). By 1630, Portugal had already sent 60,000 African slaves to Brazil to work on the new **plantations** (large tracts of lands producing staple crops, farmed by slave labor, and owned by colonial settlers from western Europe), which were producing some 15,000 tons of sugar a year. Realizing that plantations producing staples for Europeans could bring fabulous wealth, the European powers grew less interested in the dwindling trade in precious metals and more eager to colonize. In the 1690s large-scale planters of sugar, tobacco, and coffee began displacing small farmers who relied on one or two servants. Planters and their plantations won out because cheap slave labor allowed them to produce mass quantities of commodities at low prices.

State-chartered private companies from Portugal, France, Britain, the Dutch Republic, Prussia, and even Denmark exploited the 3,500-mile coastline of West Africa for slaves. Before 1675, most blacks taken from Africa had been sent to Brazil, but by 1700 half of the African slaves landed in the Caribbean (Figure 18.1). Thereafter, the plantation economy began to expand on the North American mainland. The numbers stagger the imagination. Before 1650, slave traders transported about 7,000 Africans each year across the Atlantic; this rate doubled between 1650 and 1675, nearly doubled again in the next twenty-five years, and kept going until the 1780s (Figure 18.2, page 670). In all, more than 11 million Africans, not counting those who died at sea or in Africa, were transported to the Americas before the slave trade

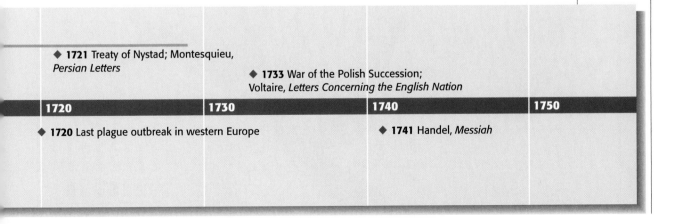

◆ **1721** Treaty of Nystad; Montesquieu, *Persian Letters*

◆ **1733** War of the Polish Succession; Voltaire, *Letters Concerning the English Nation*

| 1720 | 1730 | 1740 | 1750 |

◆ **1720** Last plague outbreak in western Europe

◆ **1741** Handel, *Messiah*

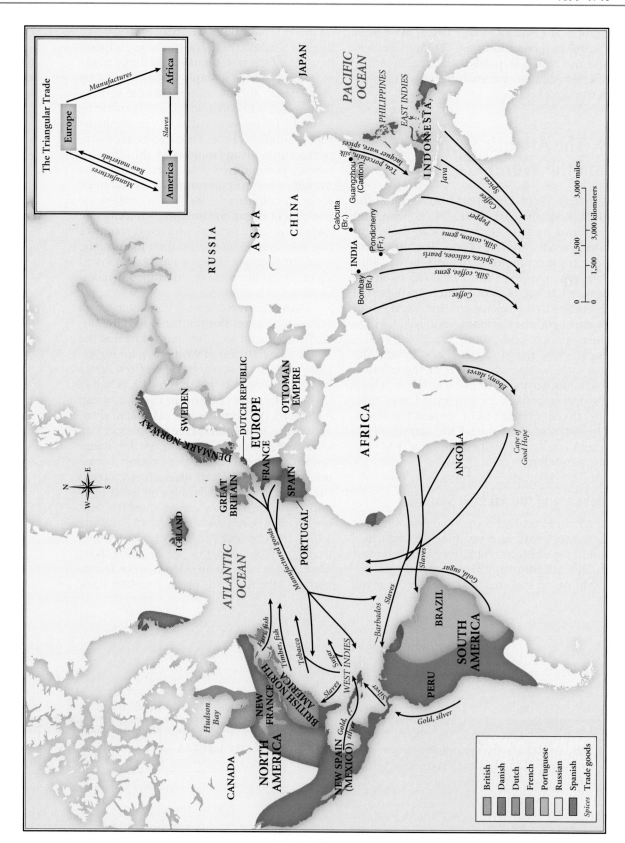

◄ MAP 18.1 European Trade Patterns, c. 1740

By 1740, the European powers had colonized much of North and South America and incorporated their colonies there into a worldwide system of commerce centered on the slave trade and plantation production of staple crops. Europeans still sought spices and luxury goods in China and the East Indies, but outside of Java, few Europeans had settled permanently in these areas. How did control over colonies determine dominance in international trade in this period?

began to wind down after 1850. Many traders gained spectacular wealth, but companies did not always make profits. The English Royal African Company, for example, delivered 100,000 slaves to the Caribbean, imported 30,000 tons of sugar to Britain, yet lost money after the few profitable years following its founding in 1672.

The Life of the Slaves. The balance of white and black populations in the New World colonies was determined by the staples produced. Because they did not own plantations, New England merchants and farmers bought few slaves. Blacks—both slave and free—made up only 3 percent of the population in eighteenth-century New England, compared with 60 percent in South Carolina. On the whole, the British North American colonies contained a higher proportion of African Americans from 1730 to 1765 than at any other time in American history. The imbalance of whites and blacks was even more extreme in the Caribbean; by 1713, the French Caribbean colony of Saint Domingue had four times as many black slaves as whites,

and by 1754 slaves outnumbered whites more than ten to one. Most indigenous people had died fighting Europeans or the diseases brought by them.

Enslaved women and men suffered terribly. Most had been sold to European traders by Africans from the west coast who acquired them through warfare or kidnapping. The vast majority were between fourteen and thirty-five years old. Before they were crammed onto the ships for the three-month trip, their heads were shaved, they were stripped naked, and some were branded with red-hot irons. Men and women were separated. Men were shackled with leg irons. Sailors and officers raped the women whenever they wished and beat those who refused their advances. In the cramped and appalling conditions of the voyage, as many as one-fourth of the slaves died.

Those who survived the transit were forced into degrading and oppressive conditions. As soon as masters bought slaves, they gave them new names, often only first names, and in some colonies branded them as personal property. Slaves had no social

FIGURE 18.1 African Slaves Imported into American Territories, 1701–1810

During the eighteenth century, planters in the newly established Caribbean colonies imported millions of African slaves to work the new plantations that produced sugar, coffee, indigo, and cotton for the European market. The vast majority of African slaves transported to the Americas ended up in either the Caribbean or Brazil. Why were so many slaves transported to the Caribbean islands, which are relatively small compared to Spanish or British North America? *Adapted from Philip D. Curtin,* The Atlantic Slave Trade: A Census *(Madison: University of Wisconsin Press, 1969).*

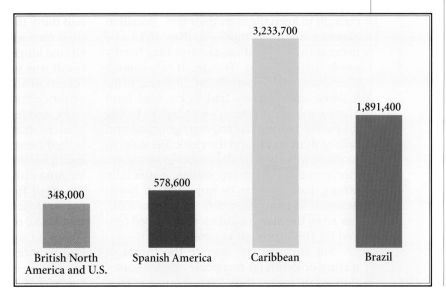

NEW SOURCES, NEW PERSPECTIVES

Oral History and the Life of Slaves

Historians have found it difficult to reconstruct slave life from the point of view of the slaves themselves, in part because slaves newly imported from Africa to the New World did not speak the language of their captors. Scholars have attempted to fill in this blank by using a variety of overlapping sources. The most interesting and controversial of these sources are oral histories taken from descendants of slaves. In some former slave societies, these descendants still tell stories about their ancestors' first days under slavery. The controversy comes from using present-day memories to get at eighteenth-century lives.

One of the regions most intensively studied in this fashion is Dutch Surinam, on the northeast coast of South America between present-day Guyana and French Guiana. This region is a good source of oral histories because 10 percent of the African slaves transported there between the 1680s and the 1750s escaped from the plantations and fled into the nearby rain forests. There they set up their own societies and developed their own language, in which they carried on the oral traditions of the first runaway slaves. The descendants of the runaway slaves recount:

In slavery, there was hardly anything to eat. It was at the place called Providence Plantation. They whipped you there till your ass was burning. Then they would give you a bit of plain rice in a calabash [a bowl made from the tropical American tree known as calabash]. . . . And the gods told them that this is no way for human beings to live. They would help them. Let each person go where he could. So they ran.

Slaves of Surinam in the 1770s
John Gabriel Stedman published an account of his participation in a five-year expedition against the runaway slaves of Surinam that took place in the 1770s. He provided drawings such as the one reproduced here, which shows Africans who have just come off a slave ship. *Schomburg Center for Research in Black Culture/New York Public Library/Art Resource, NY.*

enslaved Africans. White Europeans and colonists sometimes described black slaves as animal-like, akin to apes. A leading New England Puritan asserted about the slaves: "Indeed their *Stupidity* is a *Discouragement*. It may seem, unto as little purpose, to *Teach*, as to *wash an Aethiopian* [Ethiopian]." One of the great paradoxes of this time was that

talk of liberty and self-evident rights, especially prevalent in Britain and its North American colonies, coexisted with the belief that some people were meant to be slaves. Although Christians believed in principle in a kind of spiritual equality between blacks and whites, the churches often defended or at least did not oppose the inequities of slavery.

From other sources, historians have learned that there was a major slave rebellion at Providence Plantation in Surinam, in 1693.

By comparing such oral histories to written accounts of plantation owners, missionaries, and Dutch colonial officials, historians have been able to paint a richly detailed picture not only of slavery but also of runaway slave societies, which were especially numerous in South America. At the end of the eighteenth century, a Portuguese-speaking Jew wrote his own history of plantation life based on records from the local Jewish community that are now lost. Because the Dutch, unlike most other Europeans, allowed Jews to own slaves, Portuguese-speaking Jews from Brazil owned about one-third of the plantations and slaves in Surinam. This eighteenth-century chronicler, David de Ishak Cohen Nassy, wrote his version of Surinam's first slave revolt:

> There was in the year 1690 a revolt on a plantation situated on the Cassewinica Creek, behind Jews Savannah, belonging to a Jew named Imanuël Machado, where, having killed their master, they fled, carrying away with them everything that was there. . . . The Jews . . . in an expedition which they undertook against the rebels, killed many of them and brought back several who were punished by death on the very spot.

The oral histories told about the revolt from the runaway slaves' perspective:

> There had been a great council meeting [of runaway slaves] in the forest. . . . They decided to burn a different one of his plantations from the place where he had whipped Lanu [one of the runaway slaves] because they would find more tools there. This was the Cassewinica Plantation, which had many slaves. They knew all about this plantation from slavery times. So, they attacked. It was at night. They killed

> the head of the plantation, a white man. They took all the things, everything they needed.

The runaway slaves saw the attack as part of their ongoing effort to build a life in the rain forest, away from the whites.

Over the next decades, the runaway slaves fought a constant series of battles with plantation owners and Dutch officials. Finally in 1762, the Dutch granted the runaway slaves their freedom in a peace agreement and allowed them to trade in the main town of the colony in exchange for agreeing to return all future runaways. The runaways had not destroyed the slave system, but they had gained their own independence alongside it. From their oral histories it is possible to retrace their efforts to build new lives in a strange place, in which they combined African practices with New World experiences.

Source: Richard Price, *Alabi's World* (Baltimore: Johns Hopkins University Press, 1990), 17, 9.

QUESTIONS TO CONSIDER
1. What did runaway slaves aim to accomplish when they attacked plantations?
2. Why would runaway slaves make an agreement with the Dutch colonial officials to return future runaways?
3. Can oral histories recorded in the twentieth century be considered accurate versions of events that took place in the eighteenth century? How can they be tested?

FURTHER READING
Price, Richard. *Alabi's World.* 1990.
Stedman, John Gabriel. *Narrative of a Five Years' Expedition Against the Revolted Negroes of Surinam.* Edited, and with an introduction and notes, by Richard Price and Sally Price. 1988.

World Trade and Settlement

The Atlantic system helped extend European trade relations across the globe. The textiles that Atlantic shippers exchanged for slaves on the west coast of Africa, for example, were manufactured in India and exported by the British and French East India Companies. As much as one-quarter of the British exports to Africa in the eighteenth century were actually re-exports from India. To expand its trade in the rest of the world, Europeans seized territories and tried to establish permanent settlements. The eighteenth-century extension of European power prepared the way for western global domination in the nineteenth and twentieth centuries.

The Americas.   In contrast to the sparsely inhabited trading outposts in Asia and Africa, the colonies in the Americas bulged with settlers. The British North American colonies, for example, contained about 1.5 million nonnative (that is, white settler and black slave) residents by 1750. While the Spanish competed with the Portuguese for control of South America, the French competed with the British for control of North America. Spanish and British settlers came to blows over the boundary between the British colonies and Florida, which was held by Spain.

Local economies shaped colonial social relations; men in French trapper communities in Canada, for example, had little in common with the men and women of the plantation societies in Barbados or Brazil. Racial attitudes also differed from place to place. The Spanish and Portuguese tolerated intermarriage with the native populations in both America and Asia. Sexual contact, both inside and outside marriage, fostered greater racial variety in the Spanish and Portuguese colonies than in the French or the English territories (though mixed-race people could be found everywhere). By 1800, **mestizos**, children of Spanish men and Indian women, accounted for more than a quarter of the population in the Spanish colonies, and many of them aspired to join the local elite. Greater racial diversity seems not to have improved the treatment of slaves.

Where intermarriage between colonizers and natives was common, conversion to Christianity proved most successful. Although the Indians maintained many of their native religious beliefs, many Indians in the Spanish colonies had come to consider themselves devout Catholics by 1700. Indian carpenters and artisans in the villages produced innumerable altars, retables (painted panels), and sculpted images to adorn their local churches, and individual families put up domestic shrines. Yet the clergy remained overwhelmingly Spanish: the church hierarchy concluded that the Indians' humility and innocence made them unsuitable for the priesthood.

In the early years of American colonization, many more men than women emigrated from Europe. Although the sex imbalance began to decline at the end of the seventeenth century, it remained substantial; two and a half times as many men as women were among the immigrants leaving Liverpool, England, between 1697 and 1707, for example. Women who emigrated as indentured servants ran great risks: if they did not die of disease during the voyage, they were likely to give birth to illegitimate children (the fate of at least one in five servant women) or be virtually sold into marriage. Many upper-class women were kept in seclusion, especially in the Spanish and Portuguese colonies.

The uncertainties of life in the American colonies provided new opportunities for European women and men willing to live outside the law, however. In the 1500s and 1600s, the English and Dutch governments had routinely authorized pirates to prey on the ships of their rivals, the Spanish and Portuguese. Then, in the late 1600s, English, French, and Dutch bands made up of deserters and crews from wrecked vessels began to form their own associations of pirates, especially in the Caribbean. Called **buccaneers** from their custom of curing strips of beef, called *boucan* by the native Caribs of the islands, the pirates governed themselves and preyed on everyone's shipping without regard to national origin. In 1720, the trial of buccaneers associated with Calico Jack Rackham in Jamaica revealed that two women had dressed as men and joined the pirates in looting and plundering English ships. Mary Read and Anne Bonny escaped death by hanging only because they were pregnant. After 1700, the colonial governments tried to stamp out piracy. As one British judge argued in 1705, "A pirate is in perpetual war with every individual and every state. . . . They are worse than ravenous beasts."

Africa and Asia.   White settlements in Africa and Asia remained small and almost insignificant, except for their long-term potential. Europeans had little contact with East Africa and almost none with Africa's vast interior. A few Portuguese trading posts in Angola and Dutch farms on the Cape of Good Hope provided the only toeholds for future expansion. In China the emperors had welcomed Catholic missionaries at court in the seventeenth century, but the priests' credibility diminished as they squabbled among themselves and associated with

European merchants, whom the Chinese considered pirates. "The barbarians [Europeans] are like wild beasts," one Chinese official concluded. In 1720, only one thousand Europeans resided in Guangzhou (Canton), the sole place where foreigners could legally trade for spices, tea, and silk (see Map 18.1 page 668).

Europeans exercised more influence in Java (in what was then called the East Indies) and in India. Dutch coffee production in Java and nearby islands increased phenomenally in the early 1700s, and many Dutch settled there to oversee production and trade. Dutch, English, French, Portuguese, and Danish companies competed in India for spices, cotton, and silk; by the 1740s the English and French had become the leading rivals in India, just as they were in North America. Both countries extended their power as India's Muslim rulers lost control to local Hindu princes, rebellious Sikhs, invading Persians, and their own provincial governors. A few thousand Europeans lived in India, though many thousand more soldiers were stationed there to protect them. The staple of trade with India in the early 1700s was calico—lightweight, brightly colored cotton cloth that caught on as a fashion in Europe (see the image on this page).

Europeans who visited India were especially struck by what they viewed as exotic religious practices. In a book published in 1696 of his travels to western India, an Anglican minister described the fakirs♦ (religious mendicants or beggars of alms), "some of whom show their devotion by a shameless appearance, walking naked, without the least rag of clothes to cover them." Such writings increased European interest in the outside world but also fed a European sense of superiority that helped excuse the more violent forms of colonial domination (see The Exotic as Consumer Item on the next page).

♦**fakirs:** fuh KEER

India Cottons and Trade with the East
This colored cotton cloth (now faded with age) was painted and embroidered in Madras in southern India sometime in the late 1600s. The male figure with a mustache may be a European, but the female figures are clearly Asian. Europeans—especially the British—discovered that they could make big profits on the export of Indian cotton cloth to Europe. They also traded Indian cottons in Africa for slaves and sold large quantities in the colonies. *Victoria and Albert Museum, London.*

The Birth of Consumer Society

As worldwide colonization produced new supplies of goods, from coffee to calico, population growth in Europe fueled demand for them. Beginning first in Britain, then in France and the Italian states, and finally in eastern Europe, population surged, growing by about 20 percent between 1700 and 1750. The gap between a fast-growing northwest and a more stagnant south and central Europe now diminished as regions that had lost population during the seventeenth-century downturn recovered. Cities, in particular, grew. Between 1600 and 1750, London's population more than tripled and Paris's more than doubled.

Although contemporaries could not have realized it then, this was the start of the modern population explosion. It appears that a decline in the death rate, rather than a rise in the birthrate, explains the turnaround. Three main factors contributed to increased longevity: better weather and hence more bountiful harvests,

Contrary to the fears of contemporaries, small farmers and cottagers (those with little or no property) were not forced off the land all at once. But most villagers could not afford the litigation involved in resisting enclosure, and small landholders consequently had to sell out to landlords or farmers with larger plots. Landlords with large holdings leased their estates to tenant farmers at constantly increasing rents, and the tenant farmers in turn employed the cottagers as salaried agricultural workers. In this way the English peasantry largely disappeared, replaced by a more hierarchical society of big landlords, enterprising tenant farmers, and poor agricultural laborers.

Treatment of Serfs in Russia
Visitors from western Europe often remarked on the cruel treatment of serfs in Russia. This drawing by one such visitor shows the punishment that could be inflicted by landowners. Serfs could be whipped for almost any reason, even for making a soup too salty or neglecting to bow when the lord's family passed by. Their condition actually deteriorated in the 1700s, as landowners began to sell serfs much like slaves. New decrees made it illegal for serfs to contract loans, enter into leases, or work for anyone other than their lord. Some landlords kept harems of serf girls. Although the Russian landlords' treatment of serfs was even more brutal than that in the German states and Poland, upper classes in every country regarded the serfs as dirty, deceitful, brutish, and superstitious. *New York Public Library Slavonic Division/Art Resource, NY.*

The new agricultural techniques spread slowly from Britain and the Low Countries (the Dutch Republic and the Austrian Netherlands) to the rest of western Europe. Outside a few pockets in northern France and the western German states, however, subsistence agriculture (producing just enough to get by rather than surpluses for the market) continued to dominate farming in western Europe and Scandinavia. In southwestern Germany, for example, 80 percent of the peasants produced no surplus because their plots were too small. Unlike the populations of the highly urbanized Low Countries (where half the people lived in towns and cities), most Europeans, western and eastern, eked out their existence in the countryside.

In eastern Europe, the condition of peasants worsened in the areas where landlords tried hardest to improve crop yields. To produce more for the Baltic grain market, aristocratic landholders in Prussia, Poland, and parts of Russia drained wetlands, cultivated moors, and built dikes. They also forced peasants off lands that the peasants had worked for themselves, increased compulsory labor services (the critical element in serfdom), and began to manage their estates directly. Some eastern landowners grew fabulously wealthy. The Potocki family in the Polish Ukraine, for example, owned three million acres of land and had 130,000 serfs. In parts of Poland and Russia the serfs hardly differed from slaves in status, and their "masters" ran their huge estates much like American plantations (see the image on this page).

Social Life in the Cities

Because of emigration from the countryside, cities grew in population and consequently exercised more influence on culture and social life. Between 1650 and 1750, cities with at least ten thousand inhabitants increased in population by 44 percent. From the eighteenth century onward, urban growth would be continuous. Along with the general growth of cities, an important south-to-north shift occurred in the pattern of urbanization. Around 1500, half of the people in cities of at least ten thousand residents could be found in the Italian states, Spain, or Portugal; by 1700, the urbanization of northwestern and southern Europe was roughly equal. Eastern Europe, despite the huge cities of Istanbul and Moscow, was still less urban than western Europe. London was by far the most populous European city, with 675,000 inhabitants in 1750; Berlin had 90,000 people, Warsaw only 23,000.

Urban Social Classes.   Many landowners kept a residence in town, so the separation between rural and city life was not as extreme as might be imagined, at least not for the very rich. At the top of the ladder in the big cities were the landed nobles. Some of them filled their lives only with conspicuous consumption of fine food, extravagant clothing, coaches, books, and opera; others held key political, administrative, or judicial offices. However they spent their time, these rich families employed thousands of artisans, shopkeepers, and domestic servants. Many English peers (highest-ranking nobles) had thirty or forty servants at each of their homes.

The middle classes of officials, merchants, professionals, and landowners occupied the next rung down on the social ladder. London's population, for example, included about 20,000 middle-class families (constituting, at most, one-sixth of the city's population). In this period the middle classes began to develop distinctive ways of life that set them apart from both the rich noble landowners and the lower classes. Unlike the rich nobles, the middle classes lived primarily in the cities and towns, even if they owned small country estates. They ate more moderately than nobles but much better than peasants or laborers. For breakfast the British middle classes ate toast and rolls and, after 1700, drank tea. Dinner, served midday, consisted of roasted or boiled beef or mutton, poultry or pork, and vegetables. Supper was a light meal of bread and cheese with cake or pie. Beer was the main drink in London, and many families brewed their own. Even children drank beer because of the lack of fresh water.

In contrast to the gigantic and sprawling country seats of the richest English peers, middle-class houses in town had about seven rooms, including four or five bedrooms and one or two living rooms, still many more than the poor agricultural worker. New household items reflected society's increasing wealth

and its exposure to colonial imports: by 1700, a middle-class house in London typically had mirrors in every room, a coffeepot and coffee mill, numerous pictures and ornaments, a china collection, and several clocks. Life for the middle classes on the continent was quite similar, though wine replaced beer in France.

Below the middle classes came the artisans and shopkeepers (most of whom were organized in professional guilds), then the journeymen, apprentices, servants, and laborers. At the bottom of the social scale were the unemployed poor, who survived by intermittent work and charity. Women married to artisans and shopkeepers often kept the accounts, supervised employees, and ran the household as well. Every middle-class and upper-class family employed servants; artisans and shopkeepers frequently hired them too. Women from poorer families usually worked as domestic servants until they married. Four out of five domestic servants in the city were female. In large cities such as London, the servant population grew faster than the population of the city as a whole.

Signs of Social Distinction.   Social status in the cities was readily visible. Wide, spacious streets graced rich districts; the houses had gardens, and the air was relatively fresh. In poor districts the streets were narrow, dirty, dark, humid, and smelly, and the houses were damp and crowded. The poorest people were homeless, sleeping under bridges or in abandoned homes. A Neapolitan prince described his homeless neighbors as "lying like filthy animals, with no distinction of age or sex." In some districts, rich and poor lived in the same buildings; the poor clambered up to shabby, cramped apartments on the top floors.

Like shelter, clothing was a reliable social indicator. The poorest workingwomen in Paris wore woolen skirts and blouses of dark colors over petticoats, a bodice, and a corset. They also donned caps of various sorts, cotton stockings, and shoes (probably their only pair). Workingmen dressed even more drably. Many occupations could be recognized by their dress: no one could confuse lawyers in their dark robes with masons or butchers in their special aprons, for example. People higher on the social ladder were more likely to sport a variety of fabrics, colors, and unusual designs in their clothing

Gin Lane, London

The English painter and engraver William Hogarth chronicled every aspect of social life in London. In this engraving from 1751, he shows the appalling effects of cheap gin on lower-class London families. In the front center, a drunken woman is taking snuff while her unwatched baby falls to his death. Everywhere violence and mayhem reign. The only buildings of substance are the pawnbroker and the gin shop. In the same year, Parliament passed a gin act regulating the sale of alcohol. Hogarth's depiction reveals as much about middle-class fears as it does of actual lower-class behavior. © *Archivo Iconografico, S.A./CORBIS.*

and to own many different outfits. Social status was not an abstract idea; it permeated every detail of daily life.

The Growth of a Literate Public

The ability to read and write also reflected social differences. People in the upper classes were more literate than those in the lower classes; city people were more literate than peasants. Protestant countries appear to have been more successful at promoting education and literacy than Catholic countries, perhaps because of the Protestant emphasis on Bible reading. Widespread literacy among the lower classes was first achieved in the Protes-

tant areas of Switzerland and in Presbyterian Scotland, and rates were also very high in the New England colonies and the Scandinavian countries. In France, literacy doubled in the eighteenth century thanks to the spread of parish schools, but still only one in two men and one in four women could read and write. Most peasants remained illiterate. Despite the efforts of some Protestant German states to encourage primary education, primary schooling remained woefully inadequate almost everywhere in Europe: few schools existed, teachers received low wages, and no country had yet established a national system of control or supervision.

Despite the deficiencies of primary education, a new literate public arose especially among the middle classes of the cities. More books and periodicals were published than ever before. Britain and the Dutch Republic led the way in this powerful outpouring of printed words. The trend began in the 1690s and gradually accelerated. In 1695, the British government allowed the licensing system, through which it controlled publications, to lapse, and new newspapers and magazines appeared almost immediately. The first London daily newspaper came out in 1702, and in 1709 Joseph Addison and Richard Steele published the first literary magazine, *The Spectator*. They devoted their magazine to the cultural improvement of the increasingly influential middle class. By the 1720s, twenty-four provincial newspapers were published in England. In the London coffeehouses, an edition of a single newspaper might reach ten thousand male readers. Women did their reading at home. Newspapers on the continent lagged behind and often consisted mainly of advertising with little critical commentary. France, for example, had no daily paper until 1777.

Review: What were the social and cultural consequences of the agricultural revolution?

New Tastes in the Arts

The new literate public did not just read newspapers; its members now pursued an interest in painting, attended concerts, and besieged booksellers in search of popular

Rococo Painting

Painted originally as a shop sign for an art merchant, *Gersaint's Shopsign* (1721) by Antoine Watteau demonstrates the new rococo style. The colors are muted and the atmosphere is light and airy. The subject matter—the sale of art, gilded mirrors, and toiletries to the new urban aristocrats and middle classes—is entirely secular and even commercial. The canvas reflects the new urban market for art and slyly notes the passing of a era: a portrait of the recently deceased Louis XIV is being packed away on the left-hand side of the painting. Watteau painted the sign in eight days while suffering from the tuberculosis that would kill him just a few months later. *Scala/Art Resource, NY.*

novels. Because increased trade and prosperity put money into the hands of the growing middle classes, a new urban audience began to compete with the churches, rulers, and courtiers as chief patrons for new work. As the public for the arts expanded, printed commentary on them emerged, setting the stage for the appearance of political and social criticism. New artistic tastes thus had effects far beyond the realm of the arts.

Rococo Painting. Developments in painting reflected the tastes of the new public, as the **rococo**♦ style challenged the hold of the baroque and classical schools, especially in France. Like the baroque, the rococo emphasized irregularity and asymmetry, movement and curvature, but it did so on a much smaller, subtler scale. Many rococo paintings depicted scenes of intimate sensuality rather than the monumental, emotional grandeur favored by classical and baroque painters.

Personal portraits and pastoral paintings took the place of heroic landscapes and grand, ceremonial canvases. Rococo paintings adorned homes as well as palaces and served as a form of interior decoration rather than as a statement of piety. (See the painting above for an example of a painting of a shop sign.) Its decorative quality made rococo art an ideal complement to newly discovered materials such as stucco and porcelain, especially the porcelain vases now imported from China.

Rococo, like *baroque*, was an invented word (from the French word *rocaille*, meaning "shellwork") and originally a derogatory label, meaning "frivolous decoration." But the great French rococo painters, such as Antoine Watteau♦ (1684–1721) and François Boucher♦ (1703–1770), were much more than mere decorators. Although both emphasized the erotic in their depictions, Watteau

♦**rococo:** ruh KOH koh

♦**Watteau:** vah TOH
♦**Boucher:** boo SHAY

captured the melancholy side of a passing aristocratic style of life, and Boucher painted middle-class people at home during their daily activities. Both painters thereby contributed to the emergence of new sensibilities in art that increasingly attracted a middle-class public.

Music for the Public. The first public music concerts were performed in England in the 1670s, becoming much more regular and frequent in the 1690s. City concert halls typically seated about two hundred, but the relatively high price of tickets limited attendance to the better-off. Music clubs provided entertainment in smaller towns and villages. On the continent, Frankfurt organized the first regular public concerts in 1712; Hamburg and Paris began holding them within a few years. Opera continued to spread in the eighteenth century; Venice had sixteen public opera houses by 1700, and in 1732 Covent Garden opera house opened in London.

The growth of a public that appreciated and supported music had much the same effect as the extension of the reading public: like authors, composers could now begin to liberate themselves from court patronage and work for a paying audience. This development took time to solidify, however, and court or church patrons still commissioned much eighteenth-century music. Bach, a German Lutheran, wrote his *St. Matthew Passion* for Good Friday services in 1729 while he was organist and choirmaster for the leading church in Leipzig. He composed secular works (like the "Coffee Cantata") for the public and a variety of private patrons.

The composer George Frederick Handel (1685–1759) was among the first to grasp the new directions in music. A German by birth, he wrote operas in Italy and then moved in 1710 to Britain, where he wrote music for the court and began composing oratorios, a form he introduced in Britain. The oratorio combined the drama of opera with the majesty of religious and ceremonial music and featured the chorus over the soloists. The "Hallelujah Chorus" from Handel's oratorio *Messiah* (1741) is perhaps the single best-known piece of Western classical music. It reflected the composer's personal, deeply felt piety but also his willingness to combine musical materials

into a dramatic form that captured the enthusiasm of the new public. In 1740, a poem about Handel published in the *Gentleman's Magazine* exulted: "His art so modulates the sounds in all, / Our passions, as he pleases, rise and fall." Music had become an integral part of the new middle-class public's culture.

Novels. Nothing captured the imagination of the new public more than the novel, the literary genre whose very name underscored the eighteenth-century taste for novelty. More than three hundred French novels appeared between 1700 and 1730. During this unprecedented explosion, the novel took on its modern form and became more concerned with individual psychology and social description than with the adventure tales popular earlier (such as Cervantes's *Don Quixote*). The novel's popularity was closely tied to the expansion of the reading public, and novels were available in serial form in periodicals or from the many booksellers who popped up to serve the new market.

Women figured prominently in novels as characters, and women writers abounded. The English novel *Love in Excess* (1719) quickly reached a sixth printing, and its author, Eliza Haywood (1693?–1756), earned her living turning out a stream of novels with titles such as *Persecuted Virtue, Constancy Rewarded,* and *The History of Betsy Thoughtless*—all showing a concern for the proper place of women as models of virtue in a changing world. When her husband deserted her and her two children, Haywood first worked as an actress but soon turned to writing plays and novels. In the 1740s, she began publishing a magazine, *The Female Spectator,* which argued in favor of higher education for women.

Haywood's male counterpart was Daniel Defoe (1660–1731), a merchant's son who had a diverse and colorful career as a manufacturer, political spy, novelist, and social commentator. Defoe wrote about schemes for national improvement, the state of English trade, the economic condition of the countryside, the effects of the plague, and the history of pirates; he is most well known, however, for his novels *Robinson Crusoe* (1719) and *Moll Flanders* (1722). The story of the adventures of a shipwrecked sailor,

Robinson Crusoe portrayed the new values of the time: to survive, Crusoe had to employ fearless entrepreneurial ingenuity. He had to be ready for the unexpected and be able to improvise in every situation. He was, in short, the model for the new man in an expanding economy. Crusoe's patronizing attitude toward the black man Friday now draws much critical attention, but his discovery of Friday shows how the fate of blacks and whites had become intertwined in the new colonial environment.

Religious Revivals

Despite the novel's growing popularity, religious books and pamphlets still sold in huge numbers, and most Europeans remained devout, even as their religions were changing. In this period, a Protestant revivalist movement known as **Pietism**♦ rocked the complacency of the established churches in the German Lutheran states, the Dutch Republic, and Scandinavia. Pietists believed in a mystical religion of the heart; they wanted a deeply emotional, even ecstatic religion. They urged intense Bible study, which in turn promoted popular education and contributed to the increase in literacy. Many Pietists attended catechism instruction every day and also went to morning and evening prayer meetings in addition to regular Sunday services.

As a grassroots movement, Pietism appealed to both Lutherans and Calvinists, some of whom left their churches to form new sects. One of the most remarkable disciples of Pietism was the Englishwoman Jane Leade (1623–1704), who founded the sect of Philadelphians (from the Greek for "brotherly love"), which soon spread to the Dutch Republic and the German states. Leade's visions and studies of mysticism led her to advocate a universal, nondogmatic church that would be open to all Christians. Philadelphic societies maintained only loose ties to one another, however, and despite Leade's organizational aims they soon went off in different directions.

Catholicism also had its versions of religious revival, especially in France. A Frenchwoman, Jeanne Marie Guyon♦ (1648–1717),

attracted many noblewomen and a few leading clergymen to her own Catholic brand of Pietism, known as Quietism. Claiming miraculous visions and astounding prophecies, she urged a mystical union with God through prayer and simple devotion. Despite papal condemnation and intense controversy within Catholic circles in France, Guyon had followers all over Europe.

Even more influential were the Jansenists, who gained many new adherents to their austere form of Catholicism despite Louis XIV's harassment and repeated condemnation by the papacy. Under the pressure of religious and political persecution, Jansenism took a revivalist turn in the 1720s. At the funeral of a Jansenist priest in Paris in 1727, the crowd who flocked to the grave claimed to witness a series of miraculous healings. Within a few years a cult formed around the priest's tomb, and clandestine Jansenist presses reported new miracles to the reading public. When the French government tried to suppress the cult, one enraged wit placed a sign at the tomb that read, "By order of the king, God is forbidden to work miracles here." Some believers fell into frenzied convulsions, claiming to be inspired by the Holy Spirit through the intercession of the dead priest. After midcentury, Jansenism became even more politically active as its adherents joined in opposition to crown policies on religion.

❖ Consolidation of the European State System

The spread of Pietism and Jansenism reflected the emergence of a middle-class public that now participated in every new development, including religion. The middle classes could pursue these interests because the European state system gradually stabilized despite the increasing competition for wealth in the Atlantic system. Warfare settled three main issues between 1690 and 1740: a coalition of powers held Louis XIV's France in check on the continent, Great Britain emerged from the wars against Louis as the preeminent maritime power, and Russia defeated Sweden in the contest for supremacy in the Baltic. After

---

♦**Pietism:** PY uh tih zuhm
♦**Guyon:** gwee yohn

Louis XIV's death in 1715, Europe enjoyed the fruits of a more balanced diplomatic system, in which warfare became less frequent and less widespread. States could then spend their resources establishing and expanding control over their own populations, both at home and in their colonies.

The Limits of French Absolutism

Lying on his deathbed in 1715, the seventy-six-year-old Louis XIV watched helplessly as his accomplishments began to unravel. Not only had his plans for territorial expansion been thwarted, but his incessant wars had exhausted the treasury, despite new taxes. In 1689, Louis's rival, William III, prince of Orange and king of England and Scotland (r. 1689–1702), had set out to forge a European alliance that eventually included Britain, the Dutch Republic, Sweden, Austria, and Spain. The allies fought Louis to a stalemate in the War of the League of Augsburg, sometimes called the Nine Years' War (1689–1697), and when hostilities resumed four years later, they finally put an end to Louis's expansionist ambitions.

The War of the Spanish Succession, 1701–1713. When the mentally and physically feeble Charles II (r. 1665–1700) of Spain died without a direct heir, all of Europe poised for a fight over the spoils. The Spanish succession could not help but be a burning issue. Even though Spanish power had declined since Spain's golden age in the sixteenth century, Spain still had extensive territories in Italy and the Netherlands as well as colonies overseas. Before Charles died, he named Louis XIV's second grandson, Philip, duke of Anjou, as his heir, but the Austrian emperor Leopold I refused to accept Charles's deathbed will.

In the ensuing war, the French lost several major battles and had to accept disadvantageous terms in the Peace of Utrecht◆ of 1713–1714 (Map 18.2). Although Philip was recognized as king of Spain, he had to renounce any future claim to the French crown, thus barring unification of the two kingdoms. Spain surrendered its territories in Italy and the Netherlands to the Austrians and Gibraltar

to the British; France ceded possessions in North America (Newfoundland, the Hudson Bay area, and most of Nova Scotia) to Britain. France no longer threatened to dominate European power politics.

The Death of Louis XIV and the Regency. At home, Louis's policy of absolutism had fomented bitter hostility. Nobles fiercely resented his promotions of commoners to high office. The duke of Saint-Simon◆ complained that "falseness, servility, admiring glances, combined with a dependent and cringing attitude, above all, an appearance of being nothing without him, were the only ways of pleasing him." Archbishop Fénelon,◆ who tutored the king's grandson, called for reform. An admirer of Guyon's Quietism, Fénelon severely criticized the "steady stream of extravagant adulation, which reaches the point of idolatry"; the constant, bloody wars; and the misery of the people.

On his deathbed, Louis XIV offered sound advice to his five-year-old great-grandson and successor, Louis XV (r. 1715–1774): "Do not imitate my love of building nor my liking for war." After being named regent, the duke of Orléans (1674–1723), nephew of the dead king, revived some of the parlements' powers and tried to give leading nobles a greater say in political affairs. To raise much-needed funds, in 1719 the regent encouraged the Scottish financier John Law to set up an official trading company for North America and a state bank that issued paper money and stock (without them, trade depended on the available supply of gold and silver). The bank was supposed to offer lower interest rates to the state, thus cutting the cost of financing the government's debts. The value of the stock rose rapidly in a frenzy of speculation, only to crash a few months later. With it vanished any hope of establishing a state bank or issuing paper money for nearly a century.

France finally achieved a measure of financial stability under the leadership of Cardinal Hercule de Fleury (1653–1743), the most powerful member of the government after the death of the regent. Fleury aimed to avoid adventure abroad and keep social

◆**Utrecht:** OO trehkt

◆**Saint-Simon:** san see MOHN
◆**Fénelon:** fehn LOHN

Inset (upper left):

English and French Claims
after the Peace of Utrecht, 1714

Hudson Bay

Newfoundland

English claim

French claim

Nova Scotia

English claim

0 500 1000 miles
0 500 1000 kilometers

Main map labels:

0 200 400 miles
0 200 400 kilometers

SWEDEN

St. Petersburg

Moscow

DENMARK–NORWAY

Baltic Sea

POLAND-LITHUANIA

RUSSIA

North Sea

Warsaw

SCOTLAND

Edinburgh

IRELAND

Dublin

Kiev

GREAT BRITAIN

ENGLAND

London

Utrecht

Hanover

BRANDENBURG-PRUSSIA

Berlin

Elbe R.

Vistula R.

English Channel

Austrian Neth.

Cologne

HOLY ROMAN EMPIRE

Rhine R.

ATLANTIC OCEAN

Paris

AUSTRIA

Vienna

HUNGARY

Pest

Buda

Loire R.

FRANCE

SWISS CONFED.

SAVOY

MILAN VENICE

Danube R.

GENOA

Marseille

TUSCANY PAPAL STATES

Black Sea

OTTOMAN EMPIRE

Constantinople

PORTUGAL

Madrid

Corsica

Rome

Lisbon

SPAIN

Minorca (Gr. Br.)

Sardinia

KINGDOM OF NAPLES

BALEARIC IS.

Gibraltar (Gr. Br.)

Sicily

Mediterranean Sea

Legend:

French Bourbon lands
Spanish Bourbon lands
Austrian Habsburg lands
Prussian lands
Great Britain

Territories gained after the Peace of Utrecht, 1714
To Great Britain
To the Austrian Empire
The Jacobite rising of 1715
Main areas of fighting during the War of the Spanish Succession, 1701–1713
Boundary of the Holy Roman Empire

MAP 18.2 Europe, c. 1715

Although Louis XIV succeeded in putting his grandson Philip on the Spanish throne, France emerged considerably weakened from the War of Spanish Succession. France ceded large territories in Canada to Britain, which also gained key Mediterranean outposts from Spain, as well as a monopoly on providing slaves to the Spanish colonies. Spanish losses were catastrophic. Philip had to renounce any future claim to the French crown and give up considerable territories in the Netherlands and Italy to the Austrians. How did the competing English and French claims in North America around 1715 create potential conflicts for the future?

peace at home; he balanced the budget and carried out a large project for road and canal construction. Colonial trade boomed. Peace and the acceptance of limits on territorial expansion inaugurated a century of French prosperity.

British Rise and Dutch Decline

The British and the Dutch had formed a coalition against Louis XIV under their joint ruler William III, who was simultaneously stadholder (elected head) of the Dutch Republic and, with his English wife, Mary (d. 1694), ruler of England, Wales, and Scotland. After William's death in 1702, the British and Dutch went their separate ways. Over the next decades, England incorporated Scotland and subjugated Ireland, becoming "Great Britain." At the same time Dutch imperial power declined; by 1700, Great Britain dominated the seas and the Dutch, with their small population of less than two million, came to depend on alliances with bigger powers.

From England to Great Britain.   English relations with Scotland and Ireland were complicated by the problem of succession: William and Mary had no children. To ensure a Protestant succession, Parliament ruled that Mary's sister, Anne, would succeed William and Mary and that the Protestant House of Hanover in Germany would succeed Anne if she had no surviving heirs. Catholics were excluded. When Queen Anne (r. 1702–1714) died leaving no children, the elector of Hanover, a Protestant great-grandson of James I, consequently became King George I (r. 1714–1727). The House of Hanover—renamed the House of Windsor during World War I—still occupies the British throne.

Support from the Scots and Irish for this solution did not come easily because many in Scotland and Ireland supported the claims to the throne of the deposed Catholic king, James II, and, after his death in 1701, his son James Edward. Out of fear of this **Jacobitism** (from the Latin *Jacobus* for "James"), Scottish Protestant leaders agreed to the Act of Union of 1707, which abolished the Scottish Parliament and affirmed the Scots' recognition of the Protestant Hanoverian succession. The Scots agreed to obey the Parliament of Great Britain, which would include Scottish members in the House of Commons and the House of Lords. A Jacobite rebellion in Scotland in 1715, aiming to restore the Stuart line, was suppressed. The threat of Jacobitism nonetheless continued into the 1740s (see Map 18.2 on page 685).

The Irish—90 percent of whom were Catholic—proved even more difficult to subdue. When James II had gone to Ireland in 1689 to raise a Catholic rebellion against the new monarchs of England, William III responded by taking command of the joint English and Dutch forces and defeating James's Irish supporters. James fled to France, and the Catholics in Ireland faced yet more confiscation and legal restrictions. By 1700, Irish Catholics, who in 1640 had owned 60 percent of the land in Ireland, owned just 14 percent. The Protestant-controlled Irish Parliament passed a series of laws limiting the rights of the Catholic majority: Catholics could not bear arms, send their children abroad for education, establish Catholic schools at home, or marry Protestants. Catholics could not sit in Parliament, nor could they vote for its members unless they took an oath renouncing Catholic doctrine. These and a host of other laws reduced Catholic Ireland to the status of a colony; one English official commented in 1745, "The poor people of Ireland are used worse than negroes." Most of the Irish were peasants who lived in primitive housing and subsisted on a meager diet that included no meat.

The Parliament of Great Britain was soon dominated by the Whigs. In Britain's constitutional system, the monarch ruled with Parliament. The crown chose the ministers, directed policy, and supervised administration, while Parliament raised revenue, passed laws, and represented the interests of the people to the crown. The powers of Parliament were reaffirmed by the Triennial Act in 1694, which provided that Parliaments meet at least once every three years (this was extended to seven years in 1716, after the Whigs had established their ascendancy). Only 200,000 propertied men could vote, out of a population of more than 5 million, and, not surprisingly, most members of Parliament came from the landed gentry. In fact, a few hundred families controlled all the important political offices.

George I and George II (r. 1727–1760) relied on one man, Sir Robert Walpole (1676–1745), to help them manage their relations with Parliament. From his position as First Lord of the Treasury, Walpole made himself into the first, or "prime," minister, leading the House of Commons from 1721 to 1742 (see the illustration on this page). Although appointed initially by the king, Walpole established an enduring pattern of parliamentary government in which a prime minister from the leading party guided legislation through the House of Commons. Walpole also built a vast patronage machine that dispensed government jobs to win support for the crown's policies. Walpole's successors relied more and more on the patronage system and eventually alienated not only the Tories but also the middle classes in London and even the North American colonies.

The partisan division between the Whigs, who supported the Hanoverian succession and the rights of dissenting Protestants, and the Tories, who had backed the Stuart line and the Anglican church, did not hamper Great Britain's pursuit of economic, military, and colonial power. In this period, Great Britain became a great power on the world stage by virtue of its navy and its ability to finance major military involvement in the wars against Louis XIV. The founding in 1694 of the Bank of England—which, unlike the French bank, endured—enabled the government to raise money at low interest for foreign wars. By the 1740s, the government could borrow more than four times what it could in the 1690s.

The Dutch Eclipse. When William of Orange (William III of England) died in 1702, he left no heirs, and for forty-five years the Dutch lived without a stadholder. The merchant ruling class of some two thousand families dominated the Dutch Republic more than ever, but they presided over a country that counted for less in international power politics. In some areas, Dutch decline was only relative: the Dutch population was not growing as fast as others, for example, and the Dutch share of the Baltic trade decreased from 50 percent in 1720 to less than 30 percent by the 1770s. After 1720, the Baltic countries—Prussia, Russia, Denmark, and

Sir Robert Walpole at a Cabinet Meeting
Sir Robert Walpole and George II developed the institution of a cabinet, which brought together the important heads of departments. The cabinet included Walpole as first lord of the treasury, the two secretaries of state, the lord chancellor, the chancellor of the exchequer, the lord privy seal, and the lord president of the council. Walpole's cabinet was the ancestor of modern cabinets in both Great Britain and the United States. Its similarities to modern forms should not be overstated, however. The entire staff of the two secretaries of state, who had charge of all foreign and domestic affairs other than taxation, numbered twenty-four in 1726. How would discussions in the new coffeehouses (shown in the opening illustration to this chapter) influence the kinds of decisions made by Walpole and his cabinets?
The Fotomas Index, U.K.

Sweden—began to ban imports of manufactured goods to protect their own industries, and Dutch trade in particular suffered. The output of Leiden textiles dropped to one-third of its 1700 level by 1740. Shipbuilding, paper manufacturing, tobacco processing, salt refining, and pottery production all dwindled as well. The Dutch East India Company saw its political and military grip loosened in India, Ceylon, and Java.

The biggest exception to the downward trend was trade with the New World, which increased with escalating demands for sugar and tobacco. The Dutch shifted their interest away from great power rivalries toward those areas of international trade and finance where they could establish an enduring presence.

Russia's Emergence as a European Power

The commerce and shipbuilding of the Dutch and British so impressed Russian tsar Peter I (r. 1689–1725) that he traveled incognito to their shipyards in 1697 to learn their methods firsthand. Known to history as Peter the Great, he dragged Russia kicking and screaming all the way to great-power status. Although he came to the throne while still a minor (on the eve of his tenth birthday), grew up under the threat of a palace coup, and enjoyed little formal education, his accomplishments soon matched his seven-foot-tall stature. Peter transformed public life in Russia and established an absolutist state on the western model. His attempts to create a society that resembled western Europe known as **Westernization**, ignited an enduring controversy: did Peter set Russia on a course of inevitable Westernization required to compete with the West, or did he forever and fatally disrupt Russia's natural evolution into a distinctive Slavic society?

Westernization.   To pursue his goal of Westernizing Russian culture, Peter set up the first greenhouses, laboratories, and technical schools and founded the Russian Academy of Sciences. He ordered translations of western classics and hired a German theater company to perform the French plays of Molière. He replaced the traditional Russian calendar with the western one,* introduced Arabic numerals, and brought out the first public newspaper. He ordered his

---

*Peter introduced the Julian calendar, then still used in Protestant but not Catholic countries. Later in the eighteenth century, Protestant Europe abandoned the Julian for the Gregorian calendar. Not until 1918 was the Julian calendar abolished in Russia, at which point it had fallen thirteen days behind Europe's Gregorian calendar.

Peter the Great Modernizes Russia
In this popular print, a barber forces a protesting noble to conform to western fashions. (The barber is sometimes erroneously identified as Peter himself.) Peter ordered all nobles, merchants, and middle-class professionals to cut off their beards or pay a huge tax to keep them. An early biographer of Peter, the French writer Jean Rousset de Missy (1730), claimed that those who lost their beards saved them to put in their coffins, in fear that they would not enter heaven without them. Most western Europeans applauded these attempts to change Russian customs, but many Russians deeply resented the attack on traditional ways. Why was everyday dress such a contested issue in Russia? *Carole Frohlich Archive.*

officials and the nobles to shave their beards (see the illustration above) and dress in western fashion, and he even issued precise regulations about the suitable style of jacket, boots, and cap (generally French or German). He published a book on manners for young noblemen and experimented with dentistry on his courtiers.

Peter encouraged foreigners to move to Russia to offer their advice and skills, especially for building the capital city. Named St. Petersburg after the tsar, the new capital symbolized Russia's opening to the West. Construction began in 1703 in a Baltic province that had been recently conquered from Sweden. By the end of 1709, forty thousand recruits a year found themselves assigned to the work. Peter ordered skilled workers to move to the new city and commanded all landowners possessing more than forty serf households to build houses there. In the 1720s, a German minister described St. Petersburg "as a wonder of the world, considering its magnificent palaces, . . . and the short time that was employed in the building of it." By 1710, the permanent population of the capital reached eight thousand. At Peter's death in 1725, it had forty thousand residents.

As a new city far from the Russian heartland around Moscow, St. Petersburg represented a decisive break with Russia's past. Peter widened that gap by every means possible. At his new capital he tried to improve the traditionally denigrated, secluded status of women by ordering them to dress in European styles and appear publicly at his dinners for diplomatic representatives. Imitating French manners, he decreed that women attend his new social salons of officials, officers, and merchants for conversation and dancing. A foreigner headed every one of Peter's new technical and vocational schools, and for its first eight years the new Academy of Sciences included no Russians. Every ministry was assigned a foreign adviser. Upper-class Russians learned French or German, which they spoke even at home. Such changes affected only the very top of Russian society, however; the mass of the population had no contact with the new ideas and ended up paying for the innovations either in ruinous new taxation or by building St. Petersburg, a project that cost the lives of thousands of workers. Serfs remained tied to the land, completely dominated by their noble lords.

The Great Peterhof Palace
Peter the Great wanted a residence that could compete with the palace at Versailles, and in 1714 work began at a site 18 miles from Saint Petersburg. Peter's daughter Elizabeth replaced the original building with this more elaborate one in the late 1740s. Peter built the canal in front as a way of linking the palace to the nearby Gulf of Finland. He also ordered the installation of a hydraulic system to feed water to the fountains whose statuary is much like that of western palaces. © *Didier Roland/Imapress/The Image Works.*

Peter the Great's Brand of Absolutism.
Peter also reorganized government and finance on western models and, like other absolute rulers, strengthened his army. With ruthless recruiting methods, which included branding a cross on every recruit's left hand to prevent desertion, he forged an army of 200,000 men and equipped it with modern weapons. He created schools for artillery, engineering, and military medicine and built the first navy in Russian history. Not surprisingly, taxes tripled.

The tsar allowed nothing to stand in his way. He did not hesitate to use torture, and he executed thousands. He allowed a special guards regiment unprecedented power to expedite cases against those suspected of rebellion, espionage, pretensions to the throne, or just "unseemly utterances" against him. Opposition to his policies reached into his own family: because his only son, Alexei, had allied himself with Peter's critics, the tsar threw him into prison, where the young man mysteriously died.

To control the often restive nobility, Peter insisted that all noblemen engage in state service. A Table of Ranks (1722) classified them into military, administrative, and court categories, a codification of social and legal relationships in Russia that would last for nearly two centuries. All social and material advantages now depended on serving the crown. Because the nobles lacked a secure independent status, Peter could command them to a degree that was unimaginable in western Europe. State service was not only compulsory but also permanent. Moreover, the male children of those in service had to be registered by the age of ten and begin serving at fifteen. To increase his authority over the Russian Orthodox church, Peter allowed the office of patriarch (supreme head) to remain vacant, and in 1721 he replaced it with the Holy Synod, a bureaucracy of laymen under his supervision. To many Russians, Peter was the devil incarnate.

Peter's achievements could not ensure his succession. In the thirty-seven years after his death in 1725, Russia endured six different rulers, none of whom established firm control. Recurrent palace coups weakened the monarchy and enabled the nobility to loosen Peter's rigid code of state service. In the process the serfs' status only worsened. Serfs ceased to be counted as legal subjects; the criminal code of 1754 listed them as property. They not only were bought and sold like cattle but also had become legally indistinguishable from them. Westernization had not yet touched their lives.

> **Review:** How did Peter the Great's government compare to those of Britain and France?

The Balance of Power in the East

Peter the Great's success in building up state power changed the balance of power in eastern Europe. Overcoming initial military setbacks, Russia eventually defeated Sweden and took its place as the leading power in the Baltic region. Russia could then turn its attention to eastern Europe, where it competed with Austria and Prussia. Once-mighty Poland-Lithuania became the playground for great power rivalries.

The Decline of Sweden. Sweden had dominated the Baltic region since the Thirty Years' War (1618–1648) and did not easily give up its preeminence. When Peter the Great joined an anti-Swedish coalition in 1700 with Denmark, Saxony, and Poland, Sweden's Charles XII (r. 1697–1718) stood up to the test. Still in his teens at the beginning of the Great Northern War, Charles first defeated Denmark, then destroyed the new Russian army, and quickly marched into Poland and Saxony. After defeating the Poles and occupying Saxony, Charles invaded Russia. Here Peter's rebuilt army finally defeated him at the battle of Poltava (1709).

The Russian victory resounded everywhere. The Russian ambassador to Vienna reported, "It is commonly said that the tsar will be formidable to all Europe, that he will be a kind of northern Turk." Prussia and other German states joined the anti-Swedish alliance, and war resumed. Charles XII died in battle in 1718, and complex negotiations finally ended the Great Northern War. By the terms of the Treaty of Nystad (1721), Sweden ceded its eastern Baltic provinces—Livonia, Estonia, Ingria, and southern Karelia—to Russia. Sweden also lost territories on the north German coast to Prussia and the other allied German states (Map 18.3). An aristocratic reaction against Charles XII's incessant demands for war supplies swept away Sweden's absolutist regime, essentially removing Sweden from great power competition.

Prussian Militarization. Prussia had to make the most of every military opportunity, as it did in the Great Northern War, because it was much smaller in size and population than Russia, Austria, or France. King Frederick William I (r. 1713–1740) doubled the size of the Prussian army; though much smaller than those of his rivals, it was the best-trained and most up-to-date force in Europe. By 1740, Prussia had Europe's highest proportion of men at arms (1 of every 28 people, versus 1 in 157 in France and 1 in 64 in Russia) and the highest proportion of nobles in the military (1 in 7 noblemen, as compared with 1 in 33 in France and 1 in 50 in Russia).

The army so dominated life in Prussia that the country earned the label "a large army with a small state attached." So obsessed was Frederick William with his soldiers that the five-foot-five-inch-tall king formed a regiment of "giants," the Grenadiers, composed exclusively of men over six

feet tall. Royal agents scoured Europe trying to find such men and sometimes kidnapped them right off the street. Frederick William, the "Sergeant King," was one of the first rulers to wear a military uniform as his everyday dress. He subordinated the entire domestic administration to the army's needs. He also installed a system for recruiting soldiers by local district quotas. He financed the army's growth by subjecting all the provinces to an excise tax on food, drink, and manufactured goods and by increasing rents on crown lands. Prussia was now poised to become one of the major players on the continent.

The War of Polish Succession, 1733–1735. Prussia did not enter into military conflict foolishly. During the War of Polish Succession it stood on the sidelines, content to watch the bigger powers fight each other. The war showed how the balance of power had changed since the heyday of Louis XIV: France had to maneuver within a complex great-power system that now included Russia, and Poland-Lithuania no longer controlled its own destiny. When the king of Poland-Lithuania died in 1733, France, Spain, and Sardinia went to war against Austria and Russia, each side supporting rival claimants to the Polish throne. After Russia

MAP 18.3 Russia and Sweden after the Great Northern War, 1721
After the Great Northern War, Russia supplanted Sweden as the major power in the north. Although Russia had a much larger population from which to draw its armies, Sweden made the most of its advantages and gave way only after a great military struggle.

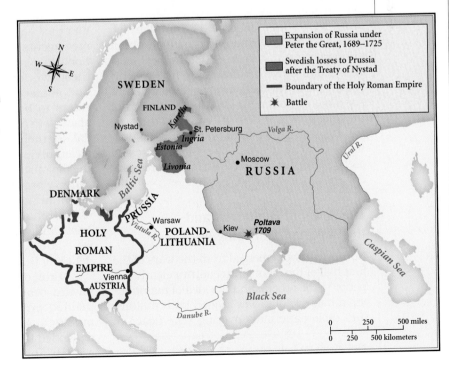

drove the French candidate out of Poland-Lithuania, France agreed to accept the Austrian candidate; in exchange, Austria gave the province of Lorraine to the French candidate, the father-in-law of Louis XV, with the promise that the province would pass to France on his death. France and Britain went back to pursuing their colonial rivalries. Prussia and Russia concentrated on shoring up their influence within Poland-Lithuania.

Austria did not want to become mired in a long struggle in Poland-Lithuania because its armies still faced the Turks on its southeastern border. Even though the Austrians had forced the Turks to recognize their rule over all of Hungary and Transylvania in 1699 and occupied Belgrade in 1717, the Turks did not stop fighting. In the 1730s, the Turks retook Belgrade, and Russia now claimed a role in the struggle against the Turks. Moreover, Hungary, though "liberated" from Turkish rule, proved less than enthusiastic about submitting to Austria. In 1703, the wealthiest Hungarian noble landlord, Ferenc Rákóczi♦ (1676–1735), raised an army of seventy thousand men who fought for "God, Fatherland, and Liberty" until 1711. They forced the Austrians to recognize local Hungarian institutions, grant amnesty, and restore confiscated estates in exchange for confirming hereditary Austrian rule.

Legend:
- Habsburg dominions, 1657
- Habsburg Hungary, 1657
- Expansion to 1699
- Expansion to 1718
- Regained by Ottoman Empire
- ✳ Battle

POLAND-LITHUANIA

AUSTRIA
HUNGARY
Vienna 1683
Transylvania
Belgrade 1717
Adriatic Sea
OTTOMAN EMPIRE

0   250   500 miles
0   250   500 kilometers

Austrian Conquest of Hungary, 1657–1730

The Power of Diplomacy and the Importance of Numbers

No single power emerged from the wars of the first half of the eighteenth century clearly superior to the others, and the idea of maintaining a balance of power guided both military and diplomatic maneuvering. The Peace of

♦**Rákóczi:** RA koht see

Utrecht had explicitly declared that such a balance was crucial to maintaining peace in Europe, and in 1720 a British pamphleteer wrote, "There is not, I believe, any doctrine in the law of nations, of more certain truth... than this of the balance of power." This system of equilibrium often rested on military force, such as the leagues formed against Louis XIV or the coalition against Sweden. All states counted on diplomacy, however, to resolve issues even after fighting had begun.

To meet the new demands placed on it, the diplomatic service, like the military and financial bureaucracies before it, had to develop regular procedures. The French set a pattern of diplomatic service that the other European states soon imitated. By 1685, France had embassies in all the important capitals. Nobles of ancient families served as ambassadors to Rome, Madrid, Vienna, and London, whereas royal officials were chosen for Switzerland, the Dutch Republic, and Venice. The ambassador selected and paid for his own staff. This practice could make the journey to a new post very cumbersome, because the staff might be as large as eighty people, and they brought along all their own furniture, pictures, silverware, and tapestries. It took one French ambassador ten weeks to get from Paris to Stockholm.

Despite a new emphasis on honest and informed negotiation, rulers still employed secret agents and often sent secret instructions that negated the official ones sent by their own foreign offices. Secret diplomacy had some advantages because it allowed rulers to break with past alliances, but it also led to confusion and, sometimes, scandal, for the rulers often employed unreliable adventurers as their confidential agents. Still, the diplomatic system in the early eighteenth century proved successful enough to ensure a continuation of the principles of the Peace of Westphalia (1648); in the midst of every crisis and war, the great powers would convene and hammer out a written agreement detailing the requirements for peace.

Adroit diplomacy could smooth the road toward peace, but success in war still depended on sheer numbers—of men and muskets. Because each state's strength depended largely on the size of its army, the growth and health of the population increasingly entered into government calculations. The publication in 1690 of the Englishman William Petty's *Political Arithmetick* quickened the interest of government officials everywhere. Petty offered statistical estimates of human capital—that is, of population and wages—to determine Britain's national wealth. A large, growing population could be as vital to a state's future as access to silver mines or overseas trade, so government officials devoted increased effort to the statistical estimation of total population and rates of births, deaths, marriages, and fertility. In 1727, Frederick William I of Prussia founded two university chairs to encourage population studies, and textbooks and handbooks advocated state intervention to improve the population's health and welfare.

Public Hygiene and Health Care

Physicians used the new population statistics to explain the environmental causes of disease, another new preoccupation in this period. Petty devised a quantitative scale that distinguished healthy from unhealthy places largely on the basis of air quality, an early precursor of modern environmental studies. Cities were the unhealthiest places because excrement (animal and human) and garbage accumulated where people lived densely packed together. Paris seemed to a visitor "so detestable that it is impossible to remain there" because of the smell; even the facade of the Louvre palace in Paris was soiled by the contents of night commodes that servants routinely dumped out of windows. Only the wealthy could escape walking in mucky streets, by hiring men to carry them in sedan chairs or to drive them in coaches.

After investigating specific cities, medical geographers urged government campaigns to improve public sanitation. Everywhere, environmentalists gathered and analyzed data on climate, disease, and population, searching for correlations to help direct policy. As a result of these efforts, local governments undertook such measures as draining low-lying areas, burying refuse, and cleaning wells, all of which eventually helped lower the death rates from epidemic diseases.

Hospitals and medical care underwent lasting transformations. Founded originally as charities concerned foremost with the moral worthiness of the poor, hospitals gradually evolved into medical institutions that defined patients by their diseases. The process of diagnosis changed as physicians began to use specialized Latin terms for illnesses. The gap between medical experts and their patients increased, as physicians now also relied on postmortem dissections in the hospital to gain better knowledge, a practice most patients' families resented. Press reports of body snatching and grave robbing by surgeons and their apprentices outraged the public well into the 1800s.

Despite the change in hospitals, individual health care remained something of a free-for-all in which physicians competed with bloodletters, itinerant venereal-disease doctors, bonesetters, druggists, midwives, and "cunning women," who specialized in home remedies. The medical profession, with nationwide organizations and licensing, had not yet emerged, and no clear line separated trained physicians from quacks. Physicians often followed popular prescriptions for illnesses because they had nothing better to offer. Patients were as likely to die of diseases caught in the hospital as to be cured there. Antiseptics were virtually unknown.

The various "medical" opinions about childbirth highlight the confusion people faced. Midwives delivered most babies, though they sometimes encountered criticism, even from within their own ranks. One consulting midwife complained that ordinary midwives in Bristol, England, made women in labor drink a mixture of their husband's urine and leek juice. By the 1730s, female midwives faced competition from male midwives, who were known for using instruments such as forceps to pull the baby out of the birth canal. Women rarely sought a physician's help in giving birth, however; they preferred the advice and assistance of trusted local midwives. In any case, trained physicians were few in number and almost nonexistent outside cities.

Insanity was treated as a physical rather than an emotional ailment. Doctors believed most madness was caused by "melancholia,"♦ a condition they attributed to disorders in the

---

♦**melancholia:** meh luhn KOH lee uh

Lady Mary Wortley Montagu, Smallpox Inoculation in the Ottoman Empire

In this letter of 1718 Lady Mary described the Turkish practice of deliberately stimulating a mild form of smallpox in order to confer immunity to the disease. Lady Mary had herself suffered the disfiguring ravages of the disease in 1715, and her brother had died of it. She was so impressed by the Turkish example that she inoculated her own children. Her letters show her to be an astute observer of foreign customs. They also reflect the growing interest in foreign travel in the eighteenth century.

A propos of distempers, I am going to tell you a thing, that will make you wish yourself here. The small-pox, so fatal, and so general amongst us, is here entirely harmless, by the invention of engrafting, which is the term they give it. There is a set of old women, who make it their business to perform the operation, every autumn, in the month of September, when the great heat is abated. People send to one another to know if any of their family has a mind to have the small-pox; they make parties for this purpose, and when they are met (commonly fifteen or sixteen together) the old woman comes with a nut-shell full of the matter of the best sort of small-pox, and asks what vein you please to have opened. She immediately rips open that you offer to her, with a large needle (which gives you no more pain than a common scratch) and puts into the vein as much matter as can ly [lie] upon the head of her needle, and after that, binds up the little wound with a hollow bit of shell, and in this manner opens four or five veins. The Grecians have commonly the superstition of opening one in the middle of the forehead, one in each arm, and one on the breast, to mark the sign of the Cross; but this

has a very ill effect, all these wounds leaving little scars, and is not done by those that are not superstitious, who chuse [choose] to have them in the legs, or that part of the arm that is concealed. The children or young patients play together all the rest of the day, and are in perfect health to the eighth. Then the fever begins to seize them, and they keep their beds two days, very seldom three. They have very rarely above twenty or thirty in their faces, which never mark, and in eight days time they are as well as before their illness. Where they are wounded, there remains running sores during the distemper, which I don't doubt is a great relief to it. Every year, thousands undergo this operation, and the French Ambassador says pleasantly, that they take the small-pox here by way of diversion, as they take the waters in other countries. There is no example of any one that has died in it, and you may believe I am well satisfied of the safety of this experiment, since I intend to try it on my dear little son. I am patriot enough to take the pains to bring this useful invention into fashion in England, and I should not fail to write to some of our doctors very particularly about it, if I knew any one of them that I thought had virtue enough to destroy such a considerable branch of their revenue, for the good of mankind. But that distemper is too beneficial to them, not to expose to all their resentment, the hardy wight that should undertake to put an end to it. Perhaps if I live to return, I may, however, have courage to war with them. Upon this occasion, admire the heroism in the heart of . . .

Source: From letter 31, to Mrs. S. C. from Adrianople, April 1, 1718, in *Letters of the Right Honourable Lady M—y W—y M—e: Written During her Travels in Europe, Asia and Africa* . . . (London: A. Homer, 1764), 113–16.

system of bodily "humors." Their prescribed treatments included blood transfusions; ingestion of bitter substances such as coffee, quinine, and even soap; immersion in water; various forms of exercise; and burning or cauterizing the body to allow black vapors to escape.

Hardly any infectious diseases could be cured, though inoculation against smallpox spread from the Middle East to Europe in the early eighteenth century, thanks largely to the efforts of Lady Mary Wortley Montagu (1689–1762). In 1716 Montagu accompanied her husband to Constantinople, where he took up a post as British ambassador to the Ottoman Empire. She returned in 1718, after witnessing firsthand the Turkish use of inoculation (see "Lady Mary Wortley Montagu, Smallpox Inoculation in the Ottoman Empire", opposite). When a new smallpox epidemic threatened England in 1721, she called on her physician to inoculate her daughter. Two patients died after inoculation in the following months, prompting clergymen and physicians to attack the practice, which remained in dispute for decades. Inoculation against smallpox began to spread more widely after 1796 when the English physician Edward Jenner developed a serum based on cowpox, a milder disease. Many other diseases spread quickly in the unsanitary conditions of urban life. Ordinary people washed or changed clothes rarely, lived in overcrowded housing with poor ventilation, and got their water from contaminated sources such as refuse-filled rivers.

Until the mid-1700s, most people considered bathing dangerous. Public bathhouses had disappeared from cities in the sixteenth and seventeenth centuries because they seemed a source of disorderly behavior and epidemic illness. In the eighteenth century, even private bathing came into disfavor because people feared the effects of contact with water. Fewer than one in ten newly built private mansions in Paris had baths. Bathing was hazardous, physicians insisted, because it opened the body to disease. One manners manual of 1736 admonished, "It is correct to clean the face every morning by using a white cloth to cleanse it. It is less good to wash with water, because it renders the face susceptible to cold in winter and sun in summer." The upper classes associated cleanliness not with baths but with frequently changed linens, powdered hair, and perfume, which was thought to strengthen the body and refresh the brain by counteracting corrupt and foul air.

❖ The Birth of the Enlightenment

Economic expansion, the emergence of a new consumer society, and the stabilization of the European state system all generated optimism about the future. The intellectual corollary was the **Enlightenment**, a term used later in the eighteenth century to describe the loosely knit group of writers and scholars who believed that human beings could apply a critical, reasoning spirit to every problem they encountered in this world. The new secular, scientific, and critical attitude first emerged in the 1690s, scrutinizing everything from the absolutism of Louis XIV to the traditional role of women in society. After 1740, criticism took a more systematic turn as writers provided new theories for the organization of society and politics; but as early as the 1720s, established authorities realized they faced a new set of challenges. Even while slavery expanded in the Atlantic system, Enlightenment writers began to insist on the need for new freedoms in Europe.

Popularization of Science and Challenges to Religion

The writers of the Enlightenment glorified the geniuses of the new science and championed the scientific method as the solution for all social problems. (See "Terms of History," page 696.) One of the most influential popularizations was the French writer Bernard de Fontenelle's *Conversations on the Plurality of Worlds* (1686). Presented as a dialogue between an aristocratic woman and a man of the world, the book made the Copernican, heliocentric view of the universe available to the literate public. By 1700, mathematics and science had become fashionable pastimes in high society, and the public flocked to lectures explaining scientific discoveries. Journals complained that scientific learning had become the

TERMS OF HISTORY

Progress

Believing as they did in the possibilities of improvement, many Enlightenment writers preached a new doctrine about the meaning of human history. They challenged the traditional Christian belief that the original sin of Adam and Eve condemned human beings to unhappiness in this world and offered instead an optimistic vision: human nature, they claimed, was inherently good, and progress would be continuous if education developed human capacities to the utmost. Science and reason could bring happiness in this world. The idea of novelty or newness itself now seemed positive rather than threatening. Europeans began to imagine that they could surpass all those who preceded them in history, and they began to think of themselves as more "advanced" than the "backward" cultures they encountered in other parts of the world.

More than an intellectual concept, the idea of progress included a new conception of historical time and of Europeans' place within world history. Europeans stopped looking back, whether to a lost Garden of Eden or to the writings of Greek and Roman antiquity. Growing prosperity, European dominance overseas, and the scientific revolution oriented them toward the future. Europeans began to apply the word *modern* to their epoch, to distinguish it from the Middle Ages (a new term), and they considered their modern period superior in achievement. Consequently, Europeans took it as their mission to bring their modern, enlightened ways of progress to the areas they colonized.

The economic and ecological catastrophes, destructive wars, and genocides of the twentieth century cast much doubt on this rosy vision of continuing progress. As the philosopher George Santayana (1863–1952) complained, "The cry was for vacant freedom and indeterminate progress: *Vorwarts! Avanti! Onward! Full Speed Ahead!*, without asking whether directly before you was a bottomless pit." In the movement toward postmodernism, which began in the 1970s, critics argued that we should no longer be satisfied with the modern; the modern brought us calamity and disaster, not reason and freedom. They wanted to go beyond the modern, hence the term *postmodernism*. The most influential postmodern historian, the Frenchman Michel Foucault, argued in the 1970s and 1980s that history did not reveal a steady progress toward enlightenment, freedom, and humanitarianism but rather a descent into greater and greater social control, what he called a "carceral [prisonlike] society." He analyzed the replacement of torture with the prison, the birth of the medical clinic, and the movements for sexual liberation and declared that all simply ended up teaching people to watch themselves more closely and to cooperate in the state's efforts to control their lives.

Historians are now chastened in their claims about progress. They would no longer side with the German philosopher Georg W. F. Hegel, who proclaimed in 1832, "The history of the world is none other than the progress of the consciousness of freedom." They worry about the nationalistic claims inherent, for example, in the English historian Thomas Babington Macaulay's insistence that "the history of England is emphatically the history of progress" (1843). But most would not go so far as Foucault in denouncing modern developments. As with many other historical questions, the final word is not yet in: Is there a direction in human history that can correctly be called progress? Or is history, as many in ancient times thought, a set of repeating cycles?

FURTHER READING

Bury, J. B. *The Idea of Progress: An Inquiry into Its Origin and Growth.* 1932.

Foucault, Michel. *Discipline and Punish: The Birth of the Prison.* Trans. Alan Sheridan. 1977.

passport to female affection: "There were two young ladies in Paris whose heads had been so turned by this branch of learning that one of them declined to listen to a proposal of marriage unless the candidate for her hand undertook to learn how to make telescopes." Such writings poked fun at women with intellectual interests, but they also demonstrated that women now participated in discussions of science.

The New Skepticism.   Interest in science spread in literate circles because it offered a model for all forms of knowledge. As the prestige of science increased, some developed a skeptical attitude toward attempts to enforce religious conformity. A French Huguenot refugee from Louis XIV's persecutions, Pierre Bayle (1647–1706), launched an internationally influential campaign against religious intolerance from his safe haven in the Dutch Republic. His *News from the Republic of Letters* (first published in 1684) bitterly criticized the policies of Louis XIV and was quickly banned in Paris and condemned in Rome. After attacking Louis XIV's anti-Protestant policies, Bayle took a more general stand in favor of religious toleration. No state in Europe officially offered complete tolerance, though the Dutch Republic came closest with its tacit acceptance of Catholics, dissident Protestant groups, and open Jewish communities. In 1697, Bayle published the *Historical and Critical Dictionary*, which cited all the errors and delusions that he could find in past and present writers of all religions. Even religion must meet the test of reasonableness: "Any particular dogma, whatever it may be, whether it is advanced on the authority of the Scriptures, or whatever else may be its origins, is to be regarded as false if it clashes with the clear and definite conclusions of the natural understanding [reason]."

Although Bayle claimed to be a believer himself, his insistence on rational investigation seemed to challenge the authority of faith. As one critic complained, "It is notorious that the works of M. Bayle have unsettled a large number of readers, and cast doubt on some of the most widely accepted principles of morality and religion." Bayle asserted, for example, that atheists might possess moral codes as effective as those

A Budding Scientist
In this engraving, *Astrologia,* by the Dutch artist Jacob Gole (c. 1660–1723), an upper-class woman looks through a telescope to do her own astronomical investigations. Women with intellectual interests were often disparaged by men, yet some middle- and upper-class women managed to pursue serious interests in science. One of the best known of these was the Italian Laura Bassi (1711–1778), who was a professor of physics at the University of Bologna. Such a position was all but impossible to attain since women were not allowed to attend university classes in any European country. Yet because many astronomical observatories were set up in private homes rather than public buildings or universities, wives and daughters of scientists could make observations and even publish their own findings. *Bibliotèque Nationale de France.*

of the devout. Bayle's *Dictionary* became a model of critical thought in the West.

Other scholars challenged the authority of the Bible by subjecting it to historical criticism. Discoveries in geology in the early eighteenth century showed that marine fossils dated immensely further back than the biblical flood. Investigations of miracles, comets, and oracles, like the growing literature against belief in witchcraft, urged the use of reason to combat superstition and prejudice. Comets, for example, should not be considered evil omens just because earlier generations had passed down such a belief. Defenders of church and state published books warning of the new skepticism's dangers. The spokesman for Louis XIV's absolutism, Bishop Bossuet, warned that "reason is the guide of their choice, but reason only brings them face to face with vague conjectures and baffling perplexities." Human beings, the traditionalists held, were simply incapable of subjecting everything to reason, especially in the realm of religion.

State authorities found religious skepticism particularly unsettling because it threatened to undermine state power too. The extensive literature of criticism was not limited to France, but much of it was published in French, and the French government took the lead in suppressing the more outspoken works. Forbidden books were then often published in the Dutch Republic, Britain, or Switzerland and smuggled back across the border to a public whose appetite was only whetted by censorship.

The Young Voltaire. The most influential writer of the early Enlightenment was a Frenchman born into the upper middle class, François-Marie Arouet,♦ known by his pen name, Voltaire (1694–1778). Voltaire took inspiration from Bayle: "He gives facts with such odious fidelity, he exposes the arguments for and against with such dastardly impartiality, he is so intolerably intelligible, that he leads people of only ordinary common sense to judge and even to doubt." In his early years Voltaire suffered arrest, imprisonment, and exile, but he eventually achieved wealth and acclaim. His tangles with church and state began in the early 1730s, when he published his *Letters Concerning the English Nation* (the English version appeared in 1733), in which he devoted several chapters to Newton and Locke and used the virtues of the British as a way to attack Catholic bigotry and government rigidity in France (see the extract on page 699). Impressed by British toleration of religious dissent (at least among

♦**Arouet:** ahr WEH

Protestants), Voltaire spent two years in exile in Britain when the French state responded to his book with yet another order for his arrest.

Voltaire also popularized Newton's scientific discoveries in his *Elements of the Philosophy of Newton* (1738). The French state and many European theologians considered Newtonianism threatening because it glorified the human mind and seemed to reduce God to an abstract, external, rationalistic force. So sensational was the success of Voltaire's book on Newton that a hostile Jesuit reported, "The great Newton, was, it is said, buried in the abyss, in the shop of the first publisher who dared to print him. . . . M. de Voltaire finally appeared, and at once Newton is understood or is in the process of being understood; all Paris resounds with Newton, all Paris stammers Newton, all Paris studies and learns Newton." The success was international too. Before long, Voltaire was elected a fellow of the Royal Society in London and in Edinburgh, as well as to twenty other scientific academies. Voltaire's fame continued to grow, reaching truly astounding proportions in the 1750s and 1760s (see Chapter 19).

Travel Literature and the Challenge to Custom and Tradition

Just as scientific method could be used to question religious and even state authority, a more general skepticism also emerged from the expanding knowledge about the world outside of Europe. During the seventeenth and eighteenth centuries, the number of travel accounts dramatically increased as travel writers used the contrast between their home societies and other cultures to criticize the customs of European society.

Visitors to the new colonies sought something resembling "the state of nature," that is, ways of life that preceded sophisticated social and political organization—although they often misinterpreted different forms of society and politics as having no organization at all. Travelers to the Americas found "noble savages" (native peoples) who appeared to live in conditions of great freedom and equality; they were "naturally good" and "happy" without taxes, lawsuits, or much organized government. In China, in contrast, travelers

Voltaire, *Letters Concerning the English Nation* (1733)

In the 1720s, Voltaire (1694–1778) visited both the Dutch Republic and England. He learned English and came to admire English political institutions and customs, using comparison with them to criticize religious intolerance and Catholic censorship in France. In this selection from a letter on Locke, Voltaire develops the argument that religion should be considered a matter of faith and conscience and be separated from arguments concerning philosophy. He also shows his disdain for the common people.

We must not be apprehensive that any philosophical opinion will ever prejudice the religion of a country. Though our demonstrations clash directly with our mysteries, that's nothing to the purpose, for the latter are not less revered upon that account by our Christian philosophers, who know very well that objects of reason and those of faith are of a very different nature. Philosophers will never form a religious sect, the reason of which is, their writings are not calculated for the vulgar, and they themselves are free from enthusiasm. If we divide mankind into twenty parts, it will be found that nineteen of these consist of persons employed in manual labour, who will never know that such a man as Mr. Locke existed. In the remaining twentieth part how few are readers? And among such as are so, twenty amuse themselves with romances to one who studies philosophy. The thinking part of mankind are confined to a very small number, and these will never disturb the peace and tranquillity of the world.

Neither Montaigne, Locke, Bayle, Spinoza, Hobbes, Lord Shaftesbury, Collins nor Toland lightened up the firebrand of discord in their countries; this has generally been the work of divines, who, being at first puffed up with the ambition of becoming chiefs of a sect, soon grew very desirous of being at the head of a party. But what do I say? All the works of the modern philosophers put together will never make so much noise as even the dispute which arose among the Franciscans [a Catholic religious order] merely about the fashion of their sleeves and of their cowls.

Source: Peter Gay, ed., *The Enlightenment: A Comprehensive Anthology* (New York: Simon & Schuster, 1973), 166.

---

found a people who enjoyed prosperity and an ancient civilization. Christian missionaries made little headway in China, and visitors had to admit that China's religious systems had flourished for four or five thousand years with no input from Europe or from Christianity. The basic lesson of travel literature in the 1700s, then, was that customs varied: justice, freedom, property, good government, religion, and morality all were relative to the place. One critic complained that travel encouraged free thinking and the destruction of religion: "Some complete their demoralization by extensive travel, and lose whatever shreds of religion remained to them. Every day they see a new religion, new customs, new rites."

Travel literature turned explicitly political in Montesquieu's *Persian Letters* (1721). Charles-Louis de Secondat, baron of Montesquieu◆ (1689–1755), the son of an eminent judicial family, was a high-ranking judge in a French court. He published *Persian Letters* anonymously in the Dutch Republic, and the book went into ten printings in just one year—a best seller for the times. Montesquieu tells the story of two Persians, Rica and Usbek, who leave their country "for love

---

◆**Montesquieu:** mahn thus KYOO

of knowledge" and travel to Europe. They visit France in the last years of Louis XIV's reign, writing of the king: "He has a minister who is only eighteen years old, and a mistress of eighty. . . . Although he avoids the bustle of towns, and is rarely seen in company, his one concern, from morning till night, is to get himself talked about." Other passages ridicule the pope. Beneath the satire, however, was a serious investigation into the foundation of good government and morality. Montesquieu chose Persians for his travelers because they came from what was widely considered the most despotic of all governments, in which rulers had life-and-death powers over their subjects. In the book, the Persians constantly compare France to Persia, suggesting that the French monarchy might verge on despotism.

The paradox of a judge publishing an anonymous work attacking the regime that employed him demonstrates the complications of the intellectual scene in this period. Montesquieu's anonymity did not last long, and soon Parisian society lionized him. In the late 1720s, he sold his judgeship and traveled extensively in Europe, staying eighteen months in Britain. In 1748, he published a widely influential work on comparative government, *The Spirit of Laws*. The Vatican soon listed both *Persian Letters* and *The Spirit of Laws* on its index of forbidden books.

Raising the Woman Question

Many of the letters exchanged in *Persian Letters* focused on women, marriage, and the family because Montesquieu considered the position of women a sure indicator of the nature of government and morality. Although Montesquieu was not a feminist, his depiction of Roxana, the favorite wife in Usbek's harem, struck a chord with many women. Roxana revolts against the authority of Usbek's eunuchs and writes a final letter to her husband announcing her impending suicide: "I may have lived in servitude, but I have always been free, I have amended your laws according to the laws of nature, and my mind has always remained independent." Women writers used the same language of tyranny and freedom to argue for concrete changes in their status. Feminist ideas were not entirely new, but they were presented systematically for the first time during the Enlightenment and represented a fundamental challenge to the ways of traditional societies.

The most systematic of these women writers was the English author Mary Astell (1666–1731), the daughter of a businessman and herself a supporter of the Tory party and the Anglican religious establishment. In 1694, she published *A Serious Proposal to the Ladies*, in which she advocated founding a private women's college to remedy women's lack of education. Addressing women, she asked, "How can you be content to be in the World like Tulips in a Garden, to make a fine *shew* [show] and be good for nothing?" Astell argued for intellectual training based on Descartes's principles, in which reason, debate, and careful consideration of the issues took priority over custom or tradition. Her book was an immediate success: five printings appeared by 1701. In later works such as *Reflections upon Marriage* (1706), Astell criticized the relationship between the sexes within marriage: "If absolute sovereignty be not necessary in a state, how comes it to be so in a family? . . . *If all men are born free*, how is it that all women are born slaves?" Her critics accused her of promoting subversive ideas and of contradicting the Scriptures.

Astell's work inspired other women to write in a similar vein. The anonymous *Essay in Defence of the Female Sex* (1696) attacked "the Usurpation of Men; and the Tyranny of Custom," which prevented women from getting an education. In 1709, Elizabeth Elstob published a detailed account of the prominent role women played in promoting Christianity in English history. She criticized men who "would declare openly they hated any Woman who knew more than themselves." In the introduction to the work of one of the best-known female poets, Elizabeth Singer Rowe, a friend of the author, complained of the "notorious Violations on the Liberties of Freeborn English Women" that came from "a plain and an open design to render us meer [mere] Slaves, perfect Turkish Wives."

Most male writers unequivocally stuck to the traditional view of women, which held that women were less capable of reasoning than men and therefore did not need

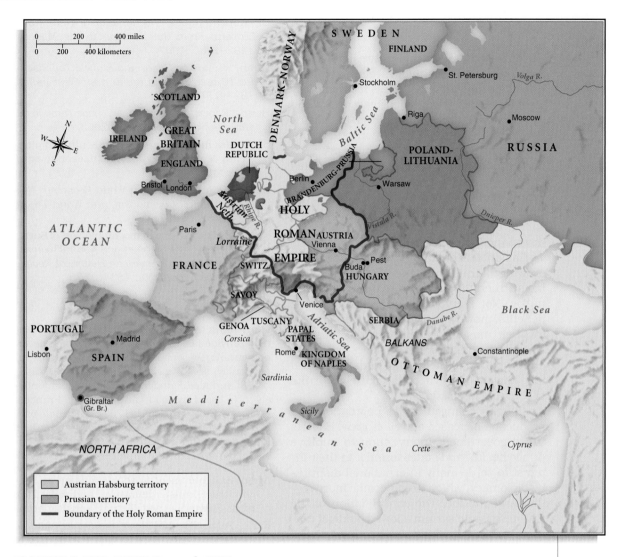

MAPPING THE WEST Europe in 1740

By 1740, Europe had achieved a kind of diplomatic equilibrium in which no one power predominated. But the relative balance should not deflect attention from important underlying
changes: Spain, the Dutch Republic, Poland-Lithuania, and Sweden had all declined in power
and influence while Great Britain, Russia, Prussia, and Austria had solidified their positions,
each in a different way. France's ambitions had been thwarted, but its combination of a big
army and rich overseas possessions made it a major player for a long time to come.

systematic education. Such opinions often
rested on biological suppositions. The long-
dominant Aristotelian view of reproduction
held that only the male seed carried spirit
and individuality. At the beginning of the
eighteenth century, however, scientists began
to undermine this belief. Physicians and surgeons began to champion the doctrine of
ovism—that the female egg was essential in

making new humans. During the decades
that followed, male Enlightenment writers
would continue to debate women's nature
and appropriate social roles.

Review: What were the major issues in the
early decades of the Enlightenment?

Conclusion

Europeans crossed a major threshold in the first half of the eighteenth century. They moved silently but nonetheless momentously from an economy governed by scarcity and the threat of famine to one of ever-increasing growth and the prospect of continuing improvement. Expansion of colonies overseas and economic development at home created greater wealth, longer life spans, and higher expectations for the future. In these better times for many, a spirit of optimism prevailed. People could now spend money on newspapers, novels, and travel literature as well as on coffee, tea, and cotton cloth. The growing literate public avidly followed the latest trends in religious debates, art, and music. Not everyone shared equally in the benefits, however: slaves toiled in misery for their masters in the Americas, eastern European serfs found themselves ever more closely bound to their noble lords, and rural folk almost everywhere tasted fewer fruits of consumer society.

Politics changed too as population and production increased and cities grew. Experts urged government intervention to improve public health, and states found it in their interest to settle many international disputes by diplomacy, which itself became more regular and routine. The consolidation of the European state system allowed a tide of criticism and new thinking about society to swell in Great Britain and France and begin to spill throughout Europe. Ultimately, the combination of the Atlantic system and the Enlightenment would give rise to a series of Atlantic revolutions.

Suggested References

The Atlantic System and the World Economy

It is easier to find sources on individual parts of the system than on the workings of the interlocking trade as a whole, but work has been rapidly increasing in this area. The Dunn book remains one of the classic studies of how the plantation system took root.

Blackburn, Robin. *The Making of New World Slavery: From the Baroque to the Modern, 1492–1800.* 1997.

Dunn, Richard S. *Sugar and Slaves: The Rise of the Planter Class in the English West Indies, 1624–1713.* 1972.

Harms, Robert. *The Diligent: A Voyage Through the Worlds of the Slave Trade.* 2003.

Slave movement during the eighteenth and nineteenth centuries: http://dpls.dacc.wisc.edu/slavedata.

Smith, Alan K. *Creating a World Economy: Merchant Capital, Colonialism, and World Trade, 1400–1825.* 1991.

Tadman, Michael. "The Demographic Cost of Sugar: Debates on Slave Societies and Natural Increase in the Americas," *American Historical Review* 105 (December 2000): 1534–1575.

New Social and Cultural Patterns

Many of the novels of the early eighteenth century provide fascinating insights into the development of new social attitudes and customs. In particular, see Daniel Defoe's *Robinson Crusoe* (1719) and *Moll Flanders* (1722); the many novels of Eliza Haywood; and Antoine François Prévost's *Manon Lescaut* (1731), a French psychological novel about a nobleman's fatal love for an unfaithful woman, which became the basis for an opera in the nineteenth century.

Age of Enlightenment (with sections on art, architecture, music, literature, and daily life): http://history.evansville.net/enlighte.html.

Earle, Peter. *The Making of the English Middle Class: Business, Society, and Family Life in London, 1660–1730.* 1989.

Handel's Messiah: The New Interactive Edition (CD-ROM). 1997.

Roche, Daniel. *The People of Paris: An Essay in Popular Culture in the Eighteenth Century.* Trans. Marie Evans. 1987.

Consolidation of the European State System

Studies of rulers and states can be supplemented by work on "political arithmetic" and public health.

Aspromourgos, Tony. *On the Origins of Classical Economics: Distribution and Value from William Petty to Adam Smith.* 1996.

Brewer, John. *The Sinews of Power: War, Money, and the English State, 1688–1783.* 1990.

Brockliss, Laurence, and Colin Jones. *The Medical World of Early Modern France.* 1997.

Frey, Linda, and Marsha Frey. *Societies in Upheaval: Insurrections in France, Hungary, and Spain in the Early Eighteenth Century.* 1987.

Hughes, Lindsey. *Peter the Great: A Biography.* 2002.

Porter, Roy. *Madness: A Brief History.* 2002.

Raeff, Marc. *Understanding Imperial Russia: State and Society in the Old Regime.* Trans. Arthur Goldhammer. 1984.

The Birth of the Enlightenment

The definitive study of the early Enlightenment is the book by Hazard, but many others have contributed biographies of individual figures or, more recently, studies of women writers.

Besterman, Theodore. *Voltaire.* 1969.

Grendy, Isobel. *Lady Mary Wortley Montagu.* 1999.

Hazard, Paul. *The European Mind: The Critical Years, 1680–1715.* 1990.

*Hill, Bridget, ed. *The First English Feminist: Reflections upon Marriage and Other Writings by Mary Astell.* 1986.

Israel, Jonathan I. *Radical Enlightenment: Philosophy and the Making of Modernity, 1650–1750.* 2001.

*Jacob, Margaret C. *The Enlightenment: A Brief History with Selected Readings.* 2000.

---

*Primary sources.

CHAPTER REVIEW

IMPORTANT EVENTS

1690s   Beginning of rapid development of plantations in Caribbean

1694   Bank of England established; Mary Astell's
A Serious Proposal to the Ladies argues for
the founding of a private women's college

1697   Pierre Bayle publishes *Historical and Critical Dictionary,* detailing errors of religious
writers

1699   Turks forced to recognize Habsburg rule
over Hungary and Transylvania

1703   Peter the Great of Russia begins construction of St. Petersburg, founds first Russian
newspaper

1713–1714   Peace of Utrecht

1714   Elector of Hanover becomes King George I
of England

1715   Death of Louis XIV

1719   Daniel Defoe publishes *Robinson Crusoe*

1720   Last outbreak of bubonic plague in western Europe

1721   Treaty of Nystad; Montesquieu publishes
Persian Letters anonymously in the Dutch
Republic

1733   War of the Polish Succession; Voltaire's
Letters Concerning the English Nation
attacks French intolerance and narrow-
mindedness

1741   George Frederick Handel composes the
Messiah

KEY TERMS

agricultural revolution (676)

Atlantic system (666)

buccaneers (674)

consumer revolution (676)

Enlightenment (695)

Jacobitism (686)

mestizo (674)

Pietism (683)

plantation (667)

rococo (681)

Westernization (688)

REVIEW QUESTIONS

1. How is consumerism related to slavery?
2. What were the social and cultural consequences
of the agricultural revolution?
3. How did Peter the Great's government compare
to those of Britain and France?
4. What were the major issues in the early decades
of the Enlightenment?

MAKING CONNECTIONS

1. In what ways did the rise of slavery and the
plantation system change European politics
and society?
2. Why was the Enlightenment born just at the
moment that the Atlantic system took shape?
3. What were the major differences between the
wars of the first half of the eighteenth century
and those of the seventeenth century? (Refer
to Chapters 16 and 17.)

FOR FURTHER EXPLORATION

**For additional help mastering the material in
this chapter**, see the Online Study Guide at
bedfordstmartins.com/hunt.

**For additional primary-sources material from
this period**, see Chapter 18 in *Sources of The
Making of the West*, Second Edition.

The Promise of Enlightenment, 1740–1789

IN THE SUMMER OF 1766, Empress Catherine II ("the Great") of Russia wrote to Voltaire, one of the leaders of the Enlightenment:

> It is a way of immortalizing oneself to be the advocate of humanity, the defender of oppressed innocence. . . . You have entered into combat against the enemies of mankind: superstition, fanaticism, ignorance, quibbling, evil judges, and the powers that rest in their hands. Great virtues and qualities are needed to surmount these obstacles. You have shown that you have them: you have triumphed.

Over a fifteen-year period Catherine corresponded regularly with Voltaire, a writer who, at home in France, found himself in constant conflict with authorities of church and state. Her admiring letter shows how influential Enlightenment ideals had become by the middle of the eighteenth century. Even an absolutist ruler such as Catherine endorsed many aspects of the Enlightenment call for reform; she too wanted to be an "advocate of humanity."

Catherine's letter aptly summed up Enlightenment ideals: progress for humanity could be achieved only by rooting out the wrongs left by superstition, religious fanaticism, ignorance, and outmoded forms of justice. Enlightenment writers used every means at their disposal—from encyclopedias to novels to personal interaction with rulers—to argue for reform. Everything had to be examined in the cold light of reason, and anything that did not promote the improvement of humanity was to be jettisoned. As a result, Enlightenment writers attacked the legal use of torture to extract confessions, supported religious toleration, favored the spread of education to eliminate ignorance, and criticized censorship by state or church. The book trade and new places for urban socializing, such as coffeehouses and learned societies, spread these ideas within a new elite of middle- and upper-class men and women.

Catherine the Great
In this portrait by the Danish painter Vigilius Eriksen, the Russian empress Catherine the Great is shown on horseback (c.1752), much like any male ruler of the time. Born Sophia Augusta Frederika of Anhalt-Zerbst in 1729, Catherine was the daughter of a minor German prince. When she married the future tsar Peter III in 1745, she promptly learned Russian and adopted Russian Orthodoxy. Peter, physically and mentally frail, proved no match for her; in 1762 she staged a coup against him and took his place when he was killed. *Bridgeman–Giraudon/Art Resource, NY.*

The lower classes had little contact with Enlightenment ideas. Their lives were shaped more profoundly by the continuing rise in population, the development of factories to produce cotton cloth, and wars among the great powers. States had to balance conflicting social pressures: rulers pursued Enlightenment reforms that they believed might enhance state power, but they feared changes that might unleash popular discontent. For example, Catherine aimed to bring Western ideas, culture, and reforms to Russia, but when faced with a massive uprising of the serfs, she not only suppressed the revolt but also increased the powers of the nobles over their serfs. All reform-minded rulers faced similar potential challenges to their authority.

Even if the movement for reform had its limits, governments now needed to respond to a new force: "public opinion." Rulers wanted to portray themselves as modern, open to change, and responsive to the segment of the public that was reading newspapers and closely following political developments. Enlightenment writers appealed to public opinion, but they still looked to rulers to effect reform. Writers such as Voltaire expressed little interest in the future of peasants or lower classes; they favored neither revolution nor political upheaval. Yet their ideas paved the way for something much more radical and unexpected. The American Declaration of Independence in 1776 showed how Enlightenment ideals could be translated into democratic political practice. After 1789, democracy would come to Europe as well.

❖ The Enlightenment at Its Height

The Enlightenment emerged as an intellectual movement before 1740 but reached its peak only in the second half of the eighteenth century. The writers of the Enlightenment called themselves **philosophes**◆ (French for "philosophers"), but that term is somewhat misleading. Whereas philosophers concern themselves with abstract theories, the philosophes were public intellectuals dedicated to solving the real problems of the world. They wrote on subjects ranging from current affairs to art criticism, and they wrote in every conceivable format. The Swiss philosophe Jean-Jacques Rousseau,◆ for example, wrote a political tract, a treatise on education, a constitution for Poland, an analysis of the effects of the theater on public morals, a best-selling novel, an opera, and a notorious autobiography. The philosophes wrote for a broad educated public of readers who snatched up every Enlightenment book they could find at their local booksellers, even when rulers or churches tried to forbid such books. Between 1740 and 1789, the Enlightenment acquired its name and, despite heated conflicts between the philosophes and state and religious authorities, gained support in the highest reaches of government. (See "Terms of History," page 710.)

◆**philosophes:** fee luh ZAWFS
◆**Jean-Jacques Rousseau:** zhahn zhawk roo SOH

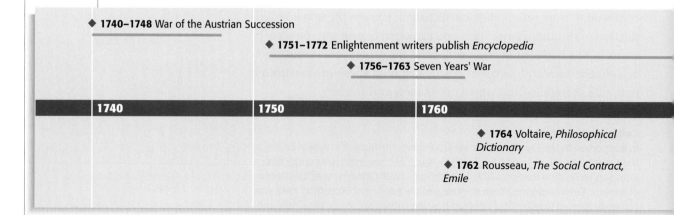

◆ **1740–1748** War of the Austrian Succession

◆ **1751–1772** Enlightenment writers publish *Encyclopedia*

◆ **1756–1763** Seven Years' War

| 1740 | 1750 | 1760 |

◆ **1764** Voltaire, *Philosophical Dictionary*

◆ **1762** Rousseau, *The Social Contract, Emile*

Men and Women of the Republic of Letters

Although *philosophe* is a French word, the Enlightenment was distinctly cosmopolitan; philosophes could be found from Philadelphia to Moscow. The philosophes considered themselves part of a grand "republic of letters" that transcended national political boundaries. They were not republicans in the usual sense, that is, people who supported representative government and opposed monarchy. What united them were the ideals of reason, reform, and freedom. In 1784, the German philosopher Immanuel Kant summed up the program of the Enlightenment in two Latin words: *sapere aude*, "dare to know"—have the courage to think for yourself.

Bookbinding
In this plate from the *Encyclopedia*, the various stages in bookbinding are laid out from left to right. Binding was not included in the sale of books; owners had to order leather bindings from a special shop. The man at (a) is pounding the pages to be bound on a marble block. The woman at (b) is stitching the pages with a special frame. The worker at (c) cuts the pages, and at (d) the volumes are pressed to prevent warping. In what ways is this illustration representative of the aims of the *Encyclopedia*?

The philosophes used reason to attack superstition, bigotry, and religious fanaticism, which they considered the chief obstacles to free thought and social reform. Voltaire took religious fanaticism as his chief target: "Once fanaticism has corrupted a mind, the malady is almost incurable. . . . The only remedy for this epidemic malady is the philosophical spirit." Enlightenment writers did not necessarily oppose organized religion, but they strenuously objected to religious intolerance. They believed that the systematic application of reason could do what religious belief could not: improve the human condition by pointing to needed reforms. Reason meant critical, informed, scientific thinking about social issues and problems. Many Enlightenment writers collaborated on a new multivolume *Encyclopedia* (published 1751–1772) that aimed to gather together knowledge about science, religion, industry, and society (see the illustration on this page). The chief editor of the

◆ **1770** Louis XV's legal reform fails

◆ **1772** First partition of Poland

◆ **1773** Pugachev rebellion

◆ **1776** American Declaration of Independence; Watt's steam engine; Smith, *Wealth of Nations*

1770	1780	1790	1800

◆ **1780** Joseph II's reforms

◆ **1781** Kant, *The Critique of Pure Reason*

◆ **1785** Charter of the Nobility

◆ **1787** U.S. Constitution

TERMS OF HISTORY

Enlightenment

In 1784, in an essay titled "What Is Enlightenment?" the German philosopher Immanuel Kant gave widespread currency to a term that had been in the making for several decades. The term *enlightened century* had become common in the 1760s. Closely related to Enlightenment was the French term *philosophe*, which was first used to mean "proponent of Enlightenment" in the 1740s. A clandestine tract of 1743 titled *Le Philosophe* explained that the philosophe was the man who saw through popular errors.

The Enlightenment gave itself its own name, and the name clearly had propaganda value. The philosophes associated Enlightenment with philosophy, reason, and humanity; religious tolerance; natural rights; and criticism of outmoded customs and prejudices. They tied Enlightenment to "progress" and to the "modern," and it came into question, just as these other terms did, when events cast doubt on the benefits of progress and the virtues of modernity. Although some opposed the Enlightenment from the very beginning as antireligious, undermining of authority, and even atheistic and immoral, the French Revolution of 1789 galvanized the critics of Enlightenment who blamed every excess of revolution on Enlightenment principles.

For most of the nineteenth century, condemnation of the Enlightenment came from right-wing sources. Some of the more extreme of these critics denounced a supposed "Jewish-Masonic conspiracy," believing that Jews and Freemasons benefited most from the spread of Enlightenment principles and worked secretly to jointly undermine Christianity and established monarchical authorities. Adolf Hitler and his followers shared these suspicions, and during World War II the Germans confiscated the records of Masonic lodges in every country they occupied. They sent the documents back to Berlin so that a special office could trace the links of this supposed conspiracy. They found nothing.

After the catastrophes of World War II, the Enlightenment came under attack for the first time from left-wing critics. In a book published right after World War II, *Dialectic of Enlightenment*, Max Horkheimer and Theodor W. Adorno, two German Jewish refugees from Hitler's regime who had fled to the United States, denounced the Enlightenment as "self-destructive" and even "totalitarian" because its belief in reason led not to freedom but to greater bureaucratic control. They asked "why mankind, instead of entering into a truly human condition, is sinking into a new kind of barbarism," and they answered, because we have trusted too much in the Enlightenment and its belief in reason and science. Reason provided the technology to transport millions of Jews to their deaths in scientifically sound gas chambers. Reason invented the atomic bomb and gave us the factories that pollute the atmosphere. The masses did not rise up against these uses of reason because they were distracted by a mass culture that emphasized entertainment rather than reflection. These criticisms of the Enlightenment, however extreme and sometimes outlandish, show how central the Enlightenment remains to the very definition of modern history.

Sources: Max Horkheimer and Theodor W. Adorno, *Dialectic of Enlightenment*, trans. John Cumming (New York: Continuum, 1993; first published 1947), xi, 6.

Encyclopedia, Denis Diderot♦ (1713–1784), explained the goal: "All things must be examined, debated, investigated without exception and without regard for anyone's feelings."

♦**Diderot:** deed ROH

The philosophes believed that the spread of knowledge would encourage reform in every aspect of life, from the grain trade to the penal system. Chief among their desired reforms was intellectual freedom, the freedom to use one's own reason and to publish the results. The philosophes wanted freedom of

Madame Geoffrin's Salon in 1755
This 1812 painting by Anicet Charles Lemonnier claims to depict the best-known Parisian salon of the 1750s. Lemonnier was only twelve years old in 1755 and so could not have based his rendition on firsthand knowledge. Madame Geoffrin is the figure in blue on the right facing the viewer. The bust is of Voltaire. Rousseau is the fifth person to the left of the bust (facing right) and behind him (facing left) is Raynal. *Bridgeman–Giraudon/Art Resource, NY.*

the press and freedom of religion, which they considered "natural rights" guaranteed by "natural law." In their view, progress depended on these freedoms. As Voltaire asserted, "I quite understand that the fanatics of one sect slaughter the enthusiasts of another sect . . . [but] that Descartes should have been forced to flee to Holland to escape the fury of the ignorant . . . these things are a nation's eternal shame."

Most philosophes, like Voltaire, came from the upper classes, yet Rousseau's father was a modest watchmaker in Geneva, and Diderot was the son of a cutlery maker. Although it was a rare phenomenon, some women were philosophes, such as the French noblewoman Émilie du Châtelet◆ (1706–1749), who wrote extensively about the mathematics and physics of Gottfried Wilhelm Leibniz◆ and Isaac Newton. (Her lover Voltaire learned much of his science from her.) Few of the leading writers held university positions, except those who were German or Scottish. Universities in France were dominated by the Catholic clergy and unreceptive to Enlightenment ideals.

Enlightenment ideas developed instead through personal contacts; through letters that were hand-copied, circulated, and sometimes published; through informal readings of manuscripts; and through letters to the editor and book reviews in periodicals. **Salons◆**—informal gatherings, usually sponsored by middle-class or aristocratic women, that provided a forum for new ideas—gave intellectual life an anchor outside the royal court and the church-controlled universities. (*Salon* is French for "living room.") Best known was the Parisian salon of Madame Marie-Thérèse Geoffrin◆ (1699–1777), a wealthy middle-class widow who had been raised by her grandmother and married off at fourteen to a much older man (see Madame Geoffrin's Salon on this page). Creating a salon was her way of educating herself and participating directly in the movement for reform. She brought together the most exciting thinkers and artists of the time; her social gatherings provided a forum for new ideas and an opportunity to establish new intellectual contacts. In the salon the philosophes could discuss ideas they might hesitate to put into print, testing public opinion and even pushing it in new directions. Madame Geoffrin corresponded extensively with influential people across Europe, including

---

◆**Émilie du Châtelet:** AY mee lee du SHAHT leh
◆**Leibniz:** LYB nuhts

◆**Salons:** suh LAHNS
◆**Marie-Thérèse Geoffrin:** ma ree tay rehz zhaw FRAN

❖ Society and Culture in an Age of Enlightenment

Religious revivals and the first stirrings of romanticism show that not all intellectual currents of the eighteenth century were flowing in the same channel. Some social and cultural developments, too, manifested the influence of Enlightenment ideas, but others did not. The traditional leaders of European societies—the nobles—responded to Enlightenment ideals in contradictory fashion: many simply reasserted their privileges and resisted the influence of the Enlightenment, but an important minority embraced change and actively participated in reform efforts. The expanding middle classes saw in the Enlightenment a chance to make their claim for joining society's governing elite. They bought Enlightenment books, joined Masonic lodges, and patronized new styles in art, music, and literature. The lower classes were more affected by economic growth than by ideas. Population increases contributed to a rise in prices for basic goods, but the mechanization of textile manufacturing, which began in this period, made cotton clothing more accessible to those at the bottom of the social scale.

The Nobility's Reassertion of Privilege

Nobles made up about 3 percent of the European population, but their numbers and ways of life varied greatly from country to country. At least 10 percent of the population in Poland and 7 to 8 percent in Spain was noble, in contrast to only 2 percent in Russia and between 1 and 2 percent in the rest of western Europe. Many Polish and Spanish nobles lived in poverty; titles did not guarantee wealth. Still, the wealthiest European nobles luxuriated in almost unimaginable opulence. Many of the English peers, for example, owned more than ten thousand acres of land; invested widely in government bonds and trading companies; kept several country residences with scores of servants, as well as houses in London; and occasionally even had their own private orchestras to complement libraries of expensive books, greenhouses for exotic plants, kennels of pedigreed dogs, and collections of antiques, firearms, and scientific instruments.

To support an increasingly expensive lifestyle in a period of inflation, European aristocrats sought to cash in on their remaining legal rights (called seigneurial dues, from the French *seigneur*, for "lord"). Peasants felt the squeeze as a result. French landlords required their peasants to pay dues to grind grain at the lord's mill, bake bread in his oven, press grapes at his winepress, or even pass on their own land as inheritance. In addition, peasants had to work without compensation for a specified number of days every year on the public roads. They also paid taxes to the government on salt, an essential preservative, and on the value of their land; customs duties if they sold produce or wine in town; and the tithe on their grain (one-tenth of the crop) to the church.

In Britain, the landed gentry could not claim these same onerous dues from their tenants, but they tenaciously defended their exclusive right to hunt game. The game laws kept the poor from eating meat and helped protect the social status of the rich. The gentry enforced the game laws themselves by hiring gamekeepers who hunted down poachers and even set traps for them in the forests. According to the law, anyone who poached deer or rabbits while armed or disguised could be sentenced to death. After 1760, the number of arrests for breaking the game laws increased dramatically. In most other countries, too, hunting was the special right of the nobility, a cause of deep popular resentment.

Even though Enlightenment writers sharply criticized nobles' insistence on special privileges, most aristocrats maintained their marks of distinction. The male court nobility continued to sport swords, plumed hats, makeup, and powdered hair, while middle-class men wore simpler and more somber clothing. Aristocrats had their own seats in church and their own quarters in the universities. Frederick II ("the Great") of Prussia (r. 1740–1786) made sure that nobles dominated both the army officer corps and the civil bureaucracy. Catherine II of Russia (r. 1762–1796) granted the nobility vast tracts of land, the exclusive right to own serfs, and exemption from personal taxes and corporal punishment. Her Charter of the Nobility of 1785 codified these privileges in exchange for the nobles' political subservience to the state. In Austria, Spain, the Italian states, Poland-Lithuania, and Russia, most nobles consequently cared little about Enlightenment ideas; they did not read the books of the philosophes and feared reforms that might challenge their dominance of rural society.

In France, Britain, and the western German states, however, the nobility proved more open to the new ideas. Among those who personally corresponded with Rousseau, for example, half were nobles, as were 20 percent of the 160 contributors to the *Encyclopedia*. It had not escaped their notice that Rousseau had denounced inequality. In his view, it was "manifestly contrary to the law of nature . . . that a handful of people should gorge themselves with superfluities while the hungry multitude goes in want of necessities." The nobles of western Europe sometimes married into middle-class families and formed with them a new mixed elite, united by common interests in reform and new cultural tastes.

The Middle Class and the Making of a New Elite

The Enlightenment offered middle-class people an intellectual and cultural route to social improvement. The term *middle class* referred to the middle position on the social ladder; middle-class families did not have legal titles like the nobility above them, but neither did they work with their hands like the peasants, artisans, or workers below them. Most middle-class people lived in towns or cities and earned their living in the professions—as doctors, lawyers, or lower-level officials—or through investment in land, trade, or manufacturing. In the eighteenth century, the ranks of the middle class—also known as the bourgeoisie♦ after *bourgeois*, the French word for "city dweller"—grew steadily in western Europe as a result of economic expansion. In France, for example, the overall population grew by about one-third in the 1700s, but the bourgeoisie nearly tripled in size. Although middle-class people had many reasons to resent the nobles, they also aspired to be like them.

♦**bourgeoisie:** bawrzh wah ZEE

Lodges and Learned Societies. Nobles and middle-class professionals mingled in Enlightenment salons and joined the new Masonic lodges and local learned societies. The Masonic lodges began as social clubs organized around elaborate secret rituals of stonemasons' guilds. They called their members **Freemasons** because that was the term given to apprentice masons when they were deemed "free" to practice as masters of their guild. Although not explicitly political in aim, the lodges encouraged equality among members, and both aristocrats and middle-class men could join. Members wrote constitutions for their lodges and elected their own officers, thus promoting a direct experience of constitutional government.

Freemasonry arose in Great Britain and spread eastward: the first French and Italian lodges opened in 1726; Frederick II of Prussia founded a lodge in 1740; and after 1750, Freemasonry spread in Poland, Russia, and British North America. In France, women set up their own Masonic lodges. Despite the papacy's condemnation of Freemasonry in 1738 as subversive of religious and civil authority, lodges continued to multiply throughout the eighteenth century because they offered a place for socializing outside of the traditional channels and a way of declaring one's interest in the Enlightenment and reform. In short, Freemasonry offered a kind of secular religion. After 1789 and the outbreak of the French Revolution, conservatives would blame the lodges for every kind of political upheaval, but in the 1700s many high-ranking nobles became active members and saw no conflict with their privileged status.

Nobles and middle-class professionals also met in local learned societies, which greatly increased in number in this period. They gathered to discuss such practical issues as new scientific innovations or methods to eliminate poverty. The societies, sometimes called academies, brought the Enlightenment down from the realm of books and ideas to the level of concrete reforms. They sponsored essay contests, such as the one won by Rousseau in 1749, or the one set by the society in Metz in 1785 on the question "Are there means for making the Jews happier and more useful in France?" The Metz society approved essays that argued for granting civil rights to Jews.

New Cultural Styles. Shared tastes in travel, architecture, the arts, and even reading helped strengthen the links between nobles and members of the middle class. "Grand tours" of Europe often led upper-class youths to recently discovered Greek and Roman ruins at Pompeii, Herculaneum, and Paestum in Italy. These excavations aroused enthusiasm for the neoclassical style in architecture and painting, which began pushing aside the rococo and the long dominant baroque. Urban residences, government buildings, furniture, fabrics, wallpaper, and even pottery soon reflected the neoclassical emphasis on purity and clarity of forms. As one German writer noted, with considerable exaggeration, "Everything in Paris is in the Greek style." Employing neoclassical motifs, the English potter Josiah Wedgwood (1730–1795) almost single-handedly created a mass market for domestic crockery and appealed to middle-class desires to emulate the rich and royal. His designs of special tea sets for the British queen, for Catherine the Great of Russia, and for leading aristocrats allowed him to advertise his wares as fashionable. By 1767, he claimed that his Queens-ware pottery had "spread over the whole Globe," and indeed by then his pottery was being marketed in France, Russia, Venice, the Ottoman Empire, and British North America.

This period also supported artistic styles other than neoclassicism. Frederick II of Prussia built himself a palace in the earlier rococo style, gave it a French name, Sans-souci◆ ("worry-free"), and filled it with the works of French masters of the rococo. A growing taste for moralistic family scenes in painting reflected the same middle-class preoccupation with the emotions of ordinary private life that could be seen in novels. The middle-class public now attended the official painting exhibitions in France that were held regularly every other year after 1737. Court painting nonetheless remained much in demand. Marie-Louise-Elizabeth Vigée-Lebrun◆ (1755–1842), who painted portraits at the French court, reported that in the 1780s "it was difficult to get a place on my waiting list. . . . I was the fashion."

Although wealthy nobles still patronized Europe's leading musicians, music too began to reflect the broadening of the elite and the spread of Enlightenment ideals as classical forms replaced the baroque style. Complex polyphony gave way to melody, which made the music more accessible to ordinary listeners. Large sections of string instruments became the backbone of professional orchestras, which now played to large audiences of well-to-do listeners in sizable concert halls. The public concert gradually displaced the private recital, and a new attitude toward "the classics" developed: for the first time in the 1770s and 1780s, concert groups began to play older music rather than simply playing the latest commissioned works.

This laid the foundation for what we still call classical music today, that is, a repertory of the greatest music of the eighteenth and early nineteenth centuries. Because composers

Neoclassical Style

In this Georgian interior of Syon House on the outskirts of London, various neoclassical motifs are readily apparent: Greek columns, Greek-style statuary on top of the columns, and Roman-style mosaics in the floor. The Scottish architect Robert Adam created this room for the duke of Northumberland in the 1760s. Adam had spent four years in Italy and returned in 1758 to London to decorate homes in the "Adam style," meaning the neoclassical manner. *Fotomas Index, UK.*

◆**Sans-souci:** SAHN soo SEE
◆**Vigée-Lebrun:** vee ZHAY luh BRUHN

now created works that would be performed over and over again as part of a classical repertory, rather than occasional pieces for the court or noble patrons, they deliberately attempted to write lasting works. As a result, the major composers began to produce fewer symphonies: the Austrian composer Franz Joseph Haydn (1732–1809) wrote more than one hundred symphonies, but his successor Ludwig van Beethoven (1770–1827) would create only nine.

The two supreme masters of the new musical style of the eighteenth century show that the transition from noble patronage to classical concerts was far from complete. Haydn and his fellow Austrian Wolfgang Amadeus Mozart (1756–1791) both wrote for noble patrons, but by the early 1800s their compositions had been incorporated into the canon of concert classics all over Europe. Incredibly prolific, both excelled in combining lightness, clarity, and profound emotion. Both also wrote numerous Italian operas, a genre whose popularity continued to grow: in the 1780s, the Papal States alone boasted forty opera houses. Haydn spent most of his career working for a Hungarian noble family, the Eszterházys.♦ Asked why he had written no string quintets (at which Mozart excelled), he responded simply: "No one has ordered any."

Interest in reading, like attending public concerts, took hold of the middle classes and fed a frenzied increase in publication. By the end of the eighteenth century, six times as many books were being published in the German states, for instance, as at the beginning. One Parisian author commented that "people are certainly reading ten times

Jean-Baptiste Greuze, *Broken Eggs* (1756)
Greuze made his reputation as a painter of moralistic family scenes. In this one, an old woman (perhaps the mother) confronts the lover of a young girl and points to the eggs that have fallen out of a basket. The broken eggs are a symbol of lost virginity. Diderot praised Greuze's work as "morality in paint," but the paintings often had an erotic subtext. **For more help analyzing this image**, see the visual activity for this chapter in the Online Study Guide at **bedfordstmartins.com/hunt**. © *Francis G. Mayer/CORBIS.*

as much in Paris as they did a hundred years ago." Provincial towns in western Europe published their own newspapers; by 1780, thirty-seven English towns had local newspapers. Lending libraries and book clubs multiplied. Despite the limitations of women's education, which emphasized domestic skills, women benefited as much as men from the spread of print. As one Englishman observed, "By far the greatest part of ladies now have a taste for books." Women also wrote them. Catherine Macaulay (1731–1791) published best-selling histories of Britain, and in France Stéphanie de Genlis (1746–1830) wrote children's books—a genre that was growing in importance as middle-class parents became more interested in education. The universities had little impact on these new tastes. An Austrian reformer complained about the universities in his country: "Critical history, natural sciences—which

♦**Eszterházys:** EHS tur hah zees

TAKING MEASURE

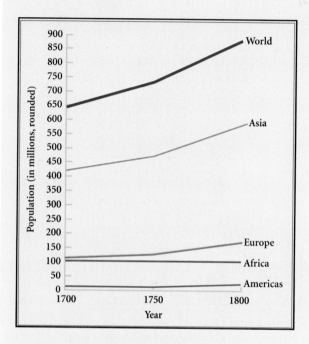

World Population Growth, 1700–1800
This graph gives a very crude comparison of regional population growth in the 1700s. Precise statistical data are impossible to develop for this period on a worldwide scale. Asia had many more people than Europe, and both Asia and Europe were growing much more rapidly in the 1700s than Africa or the Americas. The population stagnation in Africa has been the subject of much scholarly controversy; it seems likely that it was the result of the slave trade, which transported millions across the ocean to the Americas. The native population in the Americas died because of disease and was only partially replaced by the import of African slaves. What are the advantages of a growing population? What are the disadvantages? *Adapted from Andre Gundar Frank,* Reorient: Global Economy in the Asian Age *(Berkeley: University of California Press), 1998.*

are supposed to make enlightenment general and combat prejudice—were neglected or wholly unknown."

Life on the Margins

Booming foreign trade fueled a dramatic economic expansion—French colonial trade increased tenfold in the 1700s—but the results did not necessarily trickle all the way down

the social scale. The population of Europe grew by nearly 30 percent, with especially striking gains in England, Ireland, Prussia, and Hungary. (See "Taking Measure," on this page.) Even though food production increased, shortages and crises still occurred periodically. Prices went up in many countries after the 1730s and continued to rise gradually until the early nineteenth century; wages in many trades rose as well, but less quickly than prices. Some people prospered—for example, peasants who produced surpluses to sell in local markets and shopkeepers and artisans who could increase their sales to meet growing demand. But those at the bottom of the social ladder—day laborers in the cities and peasants with small holdings—lived on the edge of dire poverty, and when they lost their land or work, they either migrated to the cities or wandered the roads in search of food and work. In France alone, 200,000 workers left their homes every year in search of seasonal employment elsewhere. At least 10 percent of Europe's urban population depended on some form of charity.

The growing numbers of poor overwhelmed local governments. In some countries, beggars and vagabonds had been locked up in workhouses since the mid-1600s. The expenses for running these overcrowded institutions increased by 60 percent in England between 1760 and 1785. After 1740, most German towns created workhouses that were part workshop, part hospital, and part prison. Such institutions also appeared for the first time in Boston, New York, and Philadelphia. To supplement the inadequate system of religious charity, offices for the poor, public workshops, and workhouse-hospitals, the French government created *dépôts de mendicité,*♦ or beggar houses, in 1767. The government sent people to these new workhouses to labor in manufacturing, but most were too weak or sick to work, and 20 percent of them died within a few months of incarceration. The ballooning number of poor people created fears about rising crime. To officials, beggars seemed more aggressive than ever. The handful of police assigned to keep

♦*dépôts de mendicité:* day POH duh mehn dee see TAY

order in each town or district found themselves confronted with increasing incidents of rural banditry and crimes against property.

The Persistence of Popular Culture. Those who were able to work or keep their land fared better: an increase in literacy, especially in the cities, allowed some lower-class people to participate in new tastes and ideas. One French observer insisted, "These days, you see a waiting-maid in her backroom, a lackey in an ante-room reading pamphlets. People can read in almost all classes of society." In France, however, only 50 percent of men and 27 percent of women could read and write in the 1780s (although that was twice the rate of a century earlier). Literacy rates were higher in England and the Dutch Republic, much lower in eastern Europe. About one in four Parisians owned books, but the lower classes overwhelmingly read religious books, as they had in the past.

Whereas the new elite might attend salons, concerts, or art exhibitions, peasants enjoyed their traditional forms of popular entertainment, such as fairs and festivals, and the urban lower classes relaxed in cabarets and taverns. Sometimes pleasures were cruel. In Britain, bullbaiting, bearbaiting, dogfighting, and cockfighting were all common forms of entertainment that provided opportunities for organized gambling. Even "gentle" sports frequented by the upper classes had their violent side, showing that the upper classes had not become so different as they sometimes thought. Cricket matches, whose rules were first laid down in 1744, were often accompanied by brawls among fans (not unlike soccer matches today, though on a much smaller scale). Many Englishmen enjoyed what one observer called a "battle royal with sticks, pebbles and hog's dung."

Changes in Sexual Behavior. As population increased and villagers began to move to cities to better their prospects, sexual behavior changed too. The rates of births out of wedlock soared, from less than 5 percent of all births in the seventeenth century to nearly 20 percent at the end of the eighteenth. Historians have disagreed about the causes and meaning of this change. Some detect in this pattern a sign of sexual liberation and the beginnings of a modern sexual revolution: as women moved out of the control of their families, they began to seek their own sexual fulfillment. Others view this change more bleakly, as a story of seduction and betrayal: family and community pressure had once forced a man to marry a woman pregnant with his child, but now a man could abandon a pregnant lover by simply moving away.

Increased mobility brought freedom for some women, but it also aggravated the vulnerability of those newly arrived in cities from the countryside. Desperation, not reason, often ruled their choices. Women who came to the city as domestic servants had little recourse against masters or fellow servants who seduced or raped them. The result was a startling rise in abandoned babies. Most European cities established foundling hospitals in the 1700s, but infant and child mortality was 50 percent higher in such institutions than for children brought up at home. Some women tried herbs, laxatives, or crude surgical means of abortion; a few, usually servants who would lose their jobs if their employers discovered they had borne a child, resorted to infanticide.

European states had long tried to regulate sexual behavior; every country had laws against prostitution, adultery, fornication, sodomy, and infanticide. Reformers criticized the harshness of laws against infanticide, but they showed no mercy for "sodomites" (as male homosexuals were called), who in some places, in particular the Dutch Republic, were systematically persecuted and imprisoned or even executed. Male homosexuals attracted the attention of authorities because they had begun to develop networks and special meeting places. The stereotype of the effeminate, exclusively homosexual male seems to have appeared for the first time in the eighteenth century, perhaps as part of a growing emphasis on separate roles for men and women.

The Enlightenment's emphasis on reason, self-control, and childhood innocence made parents increasingly anxious about their children's sexuality. Moralists and physicians wrote books about the evils of masturbation, "proving" that it led to physical and mental degeneration and even madness. One English writer linked masturbation to debility of body and of mind; infertility;

the Great's admiring relationship with Voltaire showed how even the most absolutist rulers championed reform when it suited their own goals. Implementation of reforms was directly affected by success or failure in the competition for trade and territory. French losses in the Seven Years' War, for example, prompted the French crown to introduce far-reaching reforms that provoked violent resistance and helped pave the way for the French Revolution of 1789. Reform proved to be a two-edged sword.

War and Diplomacy

Europeans no longer fought devastating wars over religion that killed hundreds of thousands of civilians; instead, professional armies and navies battled for control of overseas empires and for dominance on the European continent. Rulers continued to expand their armies: the Prussian army, for example, nearly tripled in size between 1740 and 1789. Widespread use of flintlock mus-

kets required deployment in long lines, usually three men deep, with each line in turn loading and firing on command. Military strategy became cautious and calculating, but this did not prevent the outbreak of hostilities. The instability of the European balance of power resulted in two major wars, a diplomatic reversal of alliances, and the partition of Poland-Lithuania among Russia, Austria, and Prussia.

War of the Austrian Succession, 1740–1748. The difficulties over the succession to the Austrian throne typified the dynastic complications that repeatedly threatened the European balance of power. In 1740, Holy Roman Emperor Charles VI died without a male heir. Most European rulers recognized the emperor's chosen heiress, his daughter Maria Theresa, because Charles's Pragmatic Sanction of 1713 had given a woman the right to inherit the Habsburg crown lands. The new king of Prussia, Frederick II, who had just succeeded his father a few months

Maria Theresa and Her Family
In this portrait by Martin van Meytens (1695–1770), Austrian empress Maria Theresa is shown with her husband, Francis I, and twelve of their sixteen children. Their eldest son eventually succeeded to the Austrian throne as Joseph II, and their youngest daughter, Maria Antonia, or Marie-Antoinette, became the queen of France. *Bridgeman–Giraudon/Art Resource, NY.*

earlier in 1740, saw his chance to grab territory and immediately invaded the rich Austrian province of Silesia. France joined Prussia in an attempt to further humiliate its traditional enemy Austria, and Great Britain allied with Austria to prevent the French from taking the Austrian Netherlands (Map 19.2). The War of the Austrian Succession (1740–1748) soon expanded to the overseas colonies of Great Britain and France as well. French and British colonials in North America fought each other all along their boundaries, enlisting native American auxiliaries. Britain tried but failed to isolate the French Caribbean colonies during the war, and hostilities broke out in India too.

Maria Theresa (r. 1740–1780) survived only by conceding Silesia to Prussia in order to split the Prussians off from France. The Peace of Aix-la-Chapelle of 1748 recognized Maria Theresa as the heiress to the Austrian lands, and her husband, Francis I, became Holy Roman Emperor, thus reasserting the integrity of the Austrian Empire. The peace of 1748 failed to resolve the colonial conflicts between Britain and France, and fighting for domination continued unofficially.

MAP 19.2 War of the Austrian Succession, 1740–1748
The accession of a twenty-three-year-old woman, Maria Theresa, to the Austrian throne gave the new king of Prussia, Frederick II, an opportunity to invade the province of Silesia. France joined on Prussia's side, Great Britain on Austria's. In 1745, the French defeated the British in the Austrian Netherlands and helped instigate a Jacobite uprising in Scotland. The rebellion failed and British attacks on French overseas shipping forced the French to negotiate. The peace treaties guaranteed Frederick's conquest of Silesia, which soon became the wealthiest province of Prussia. France came to terms with Great Britain to protect its overseas possessions; Austria had to accept the peace settlement after a formal public protest.

Seven Years' War, 1756–1763. In 1756, a major reversal of alliances—what historians call the Diplomatic Revolution—reshaped relations among the great powers. Prussia and Great Britain signed a defensive alliance, prompting Austria to overlook two centuries of hostility and ally with France. Russia and Sweden soon joined the Franco-Austrian alliance. When Frederick II invaded Saxony, an ally of Austria, with his bigger and better-disciplined army, the long-simmering hostilities between Great Britain and France over colonial boundaries flared into a general war that became known as the Seven Years' War (1756–1763).

Fighting soon raged around the world (Map 19.3 on the next page). The French and British battled on land and sea in North America (where the conflict was called the French and Indian War), the West Indies, and India. The two coalitions also fought each other in central Europe. At first, in 1757, Frederick the Great surprised Europe with a spectacular victory at Rossbach in Saxony over a much larger Franco-Austrian

drove his officials, boasted, "I am the first servant of the state."

Legal reform, both of the judicial system and of the often disorganized and irregular law codes, was central to the work of many reform-minded monarchs. Although Frederick II favored all things French in culture—he insisted on speaking French in his court and prided himself on his personal friendship with Voltaire—he made Prussian justice the envy of Europe. His institution of a uniform civil justice system created the most consistently administered laws and efficient judiciary of the time. Joseph II of Austria (r. 1780–1790) also ordered the compilation of a unified law code, a project that required many years for completion. Catherine II of Russia began such an undertaking even more ambitiously. In 1767, she called together a legislative commission of 564 deputies and asked them to consider a long document called the *Instruction*, which represented her hopes for legal reform based on the ideas of Montesquieu and the Italian writer Cesare Beccaria. Montesquieu had insisted that punishment should fit the crime; he criticized the use of torture and brutal corporal punishment. In his influential book *On Crimes and Punishments* (1764), Beccaria argued that laws should be printed for everyone to read and administered in rational procedures, that torture should be abolished as inhumane, and that the accused should be presumed innocent until proven guilty. Despite much discussion and hundreds of petitions and documents about local problems, little came of Catherine's commission because the monarch herself—despite her regard for Voltaire and his fellow philosophes—proved ultimately unwilling to see through far-reaching legal reform.

The Church, Education, and Religious Toleration. Rulers everywhere wanted more control over church affairs, and they used Enlightenment criticisms of the organized churches to get their way. In Catholic countries, many government officials resented the influence of the Jesuits, the major Catholic teaching order. The Jesuits trained the Catholic intellectual elite, ran a worldwide missionary network, enjoyed close ties to the papacy, and amassed great wealth.

Critics mounted campaigns against the Jesuits in many countries, and by the early 1770s the Society of Jesus had been dissolved in Portugal, France, and Spain. In 1773, Pope Clement XIV (r. 1769–1774) agreed under pressure to disband the order, an edict that held until a reinvigorated papacy restored the society in 1814. Joseph II of Austria not only applauded the suppression of the Jesuits but also required Austrian bishops to swear fidelity and submission to him. Joseph had become Holy Roman Emperor and co-regent with his mother, Maria Theresa, in 1765. After her death in 1780 he initiated a wide-ranging program of reform. Under him, the Austrian state supervised Catholic seminaries, abolished comtemplative monastic orders, and confiscated monastic property to pay for education and poor relief.

Joseph II launched the most ambitious educational reforms of the period. In 1774, once the Jesuits had been disbanded, a General School Ordinance in Austria ordered state subsidies for local schools, which the state would regulate. By 1789, one-quarter of the school-age children attended school. In Prussia the school code of 1763 required all children between the ages of five and thirteen to attend school. Although not enforced uniformly, the Prussian law demonstrated Frederick II's belief that modernization depended on education. Catherine II of Russia also tried to expand elementary education—and the education of women in particular—and founded engineering schools.

No ruler pushed the principle of religious toleration as far as Joseph II of Austria, who in 1781 granted freedom of religious worship to Protestants, Orthodox Christians, and Jews. For the first time these groups were allowed to own property, build schools, enter the professions, and hold political and military offices. The efforts of other rulers to extend religious toleration proved more limited. Louis XVI signed an edict in 1787 restoring French Protestants' civil rights—but still they could not hold political office. Great Britain continued to deny Catholics freedom of open worship and the right to sit in Parliament. Most European states limited the rights and opportunities available to Jews. In Russia, only wealthy Jews could hold municipal office, and in the Papal

States, the pope encouraged forced baptism. Even in Austria, where Joseph encouraged toleration, the laws forced Jews to take German-sounding names. The leading philosophes opposed persecution of the Jews in theory but often treated them with undisguised contempt. Diderot's comment was all too typical: the Jews, he said, bore "all the defects peculiar to an ignorant and superstitious nation."

Limits of Reform

When enlightened absolutist leaders introduced reforms, they often ran into resistance from groups threatened by the proposed changes. The most contentious area of reform was agricultural policy. Whereas Frederick II and Catherine II reinforced the authority of nobles over their serfs, Joseph II tried to remove the burdens of serfdom in the Habsburg lands. In 1781, he abolished the personal aspects of serfdom: serfs could now move freely, enter trades, or marry without their lords' permission. Joseph abolished the tithe to the church, shifted more of the tax burden to the nobility, and converted peasants' labor services into cash payments.

The Austrian nobility furiously resisted these far-reaching reforms. When Joseph died in 1790, his brother Leopold II had to revoke most reforms to appease the nobles. On his deathbed, Joseph recognized the futility of many of his efforts; as his epitaph he suggested, "Here lies Joseph II, who was unfortunate in all his enterprises." Prussia's Frederick II, like Joseph, encouraged such agricultural innovations as planting potatoes and turnips (new crops that could help feed a growing population), experimenting with cattle breeding, draining swamplands, and clearing forests. But Prussia's noble landlords, the Junkers, continued to expand their estates at the expense of poorer peasants, and Frederick did nothing to ameliorate serfdom except on his own domains.

Reforming ministers also tried to stimulate agricultural improvement in France. Unlike most other western European countries, France still had about a hundred thousand serfs; though their burdens weighed less heavily than those in eastern Europe, serf-

Dividing Poland, 1772
In this contemporary depiction, Catherine the Great, Joseph II, and Frederick II point on the map to the portion of Poland-Lithuania each plans to take. The artist makes it clear that Poland's fate rested in the hands of neighboring rulers, not its own people. Can you infer the sentiments of the artist from the content of this engraving? *Mansell/Time Life Pictures/Getty Images.*

dom did not entirely disappear until 1789. A group of economists called the physiocrats urged the French government to deregulate the grain trade and make the tax system more equitable to encourage agricultural productivity. In the interest of establishing a free market, they also insisted that urban guilds be abolished because the guilds prevented free entry into the trades. Their proposed reforms applied the Enlightenment emphasis on individual liberties to the economy; Adam Smith took up many of the physiocrats' ideas in his writing in favor of free markets. The French government heeded some of this advice and gave up its system of price controls on grain in 1763, but it had to reverse the decision in 1770 when grain shortages caused a famine.

French reform efforts did not end there. In 1770 Louis XV tried to replace the parlements, the thirteen high courts of law, with courts in which the judges no longer owned their offices and thus could not sell them or pass them on as an inheritance. Justice would then be more impartial. Nevertheless, the judges of the displaced parlements aroused widespread opposition to what they portrayed as tyrannical royal policy. The furor calmed down only when Louis XV died in 1774 and his successor, Louis XVI (r. 1774–1792), yielded to aristocratic demands and restored the old parlements. Louis XV died one of the most despised kings in French history, resented both for his high-handed reforms and his private vices. Underground pamphlets lampooned him, describing his final mistress, Madame Du Barry, as a prostitute who pandered to the elderly king's well-known taste for young girls. This often pornographic literature linked despotism to the supposedly excessive influence of women at court.

Louis XVI tried to carry out part of the program suggested by the physiocrats, and he chose one of their disciples, Jacques Turgot (1727–1781), as his chief minister. A contributor to the *Encyclopedia*, Turgot pushed through several edicts that again freed the grain trade, suppressed guilds, converted the peasants' forced labor on roads into a money tax payable by all landowners, and reduced court expenses. He also began making plans to introduce a system of elected local assemblies, which would have made government much more representative. Faced with broad-based resistance led by the parlements and his own courtiers, as well as with riots against rising grain prices, Louis XVI dismissed Turgot, and one of the last possibilities to overhaul France's government collapsed.

The failure of reform in France paradoxically reflected the power of Enlightenment thinkers; everyone now endorsed Enlightenment ideas but used them for different ends. The nobles in the parlements blocked the French monarchy's reform efforts using the very same Enlightenment language spoken by the crown's ministers. But unlike Austria, the other great power that faced persistent aristocratic resistance to reform,

France had a large middle-class public that was increasingly frustrated by the failure to institute social change, a failure that ultimately helped undermine the monarchy itself. Where Frederick II, Catherine II, and even Joseph II used reform to bolster the efficiency of absolutist government, attempts at change in France backfired. French kings found that their ambitious programs for reform succeeded only in arousing unrealistic hopes.

> **Review:** What prompted enlightened absolutists to undertake reforms in the second half of the eighteenth century?

❖ Rebellions against State Power

Although traditional forms of popular discontent had not disappeared, Enlightenment ideals and reforms changed the rules of the game in politics. Governments had become accountable for their actions to a much wider range of people than ever before. In Britain and France, ordinary people rioted when they perceived government as failing to protect them against food shortages. The growth of informed public opinion had its most dramatic consequences in the North American colonies, where a struggle over the British Parliament's right to tax turned into a full-scale war for independence. The American War of Independence showed that once put into practice, Enlightenment ideals could have revolutionary implications.

Food Riots and Peasant Uprisings

Population growth, inflation, and the extension of the market system put added pressure on the already beleaguered poorest classes of people. Seventeenth-century peasants and townspeople had rioted to protest new taxes. In the last half of the eighteenth century, the food supply became the focus of political and social conflict. Poor people in the villages and the towns believed that it was the government's responsibility to ensure they had enough food, and many governments did stockpile grain to make up for the occa-

A Cossack
Pugachev and many of his followers were Cossacks, Ukrainians who set up nomadic communities of horsemen to resist outside control, whether from Turks, Poles, or Russians. This eighteenth-century engraving captures the common view of Cossacks as horsemen always ready for battle but with a fondness for music too. *Bridgeman Art Library.*

sional bad harvest. At the same time, in keeping with Adam Smith's and the French physiocrats' free-market proposals, governments wanted to allow grain prices to rise with market demand, because higher profits would motivate producers to increase the overall supply of food.

Free trade in grain meant selling to the highest bidder even if that bidder was a foreign merchant. In the short run, in times of scarcity, big landowners and farmers could make huge profits by selling grain outside their hometowns or villages. This practice enraged poor farmers, agricultural workers, and city wage workers, who could not afford the higher prices. Lacking the political means to affect policy, they could enforce

their desire for old-fashioned price regulation only by rioting. Most did not pillage or steal grain but rather forced the sale of grain or flour at a "just" price and blocked the shipment of grain out of their villages to other markets. Women often led these "popular price fixings," as they were called in France, in desperate attempts to protect the food supply for their children.

Such food riots occurred regularly in Britain and France in the last half of the eighteenth century. One of the most turbulent was the so-called Flour War in France in 1775. Turgot's deregulation of the grain trade in 1774 caused prices to rise in several provincial cities. Rioting spread from there to the Paris region, where villagers attacked grain convoys heading to the capital city. Local officials often ordered merchants and bakers to sell at the price the rioters demanded, only to find themselves arrested by the central government for overriding free trade. The government brought in troops to restore order and introduced the death penalty for rioting.

Frustrations with serfdom and hopes for a miraculous transformation provoked the Pugachev rebellion in Russia beginning in 1773. An army deserter from the southeast frontier region, Emelian Pugachev◆ (1742–1775) claimed to be Tsar Peter III, the dead husband of Catherine II. Pugachev's appearance seemed to confirm peasant hopes for a "redeemer tsar" who would save the people from oppression. He rallied around him Cossacks like himself who resented the loss of their old tribal independence. Now increasingly enserfed or forced to pay taxes and endure army service, these nomadic bands joined with other serfs, rebellious mineworkers, and Muslim minorities. Catherine dispatched a large army to squelch

The Pugachev Rebellion, 1773

◆**Emelian Pugachev:** yihm yihl YAN poo guh CHAWF

the uprising, but Pugachev eluded them and the fighting spread. Nearly three million people eventually participated, making this the largest single rebellion in the history of tsarist Russia. When Pugachev urged the peasants to attack the nobility and seize their estates, hundreds of noble families perished. Foreign newspapers called it "the revolution in southern Russia" and offered fantastic stories about Pugachev's life history. Finally, the army captured the rebel leader and brought him in an iron cage to Moscow, where he was tortured and executed. In the aftermath, Catherine tightened the nobles' control over their serfs and harshly punished those who dared to criticize serfdom.

Public Opinion and Political Opposition

Peasant uprisings might briefly shake even a powerful monarchy, but the rise of public opinion as a force independent of court society caused more enduring changes in European politics. Across much of Europe and in the North American colonies, demands for broader political participation reflected Enlightenment notions about individual rights. Aristocratic bodies such as the French parlements, which had no legislative role like that of the British Parliament, insisted that the monarch consult them on the nation's affairs, and the new educated elite wanted more influence too. Newspapers began to cover daily political affairs, and the public learned the basics of political life, despite the strict limits on political participation in most countries. Monarchs turned to public opinion to seek support against aristocratic groups that opposed reform. Gustavus III of Sweden (r. 1771–1792) called himself "the first citizen of a free people" and promised to deliver the country from "insufferable aristocratic despotism." Shortly after coming to the throne, Gustavus proclaimed a new constitution that divided power between the king and the legislature, abolished the use of torture in the judicial process, and assured some freedom of the press.

In France both the parlements and the monarch appealed to the public through the printed word. The crown hired writers to make its case; the magistrates of the parle-

ments wrote their own rejoinders. French-language newspapers published in the Dutch Republic provided many people in France with detailed accounts of political news and also gave voice to pro-parlement positions. One of the new French-language newspapers printed inside France, *Le Journal des Dames* (The Ladies' Journal), was published by women and mixed short stories and reviews of books and plays with demands for more women's rights.

The Wilkes affair in Great Britain showed that public opinion could be mobilized to challenge a government. In 1763, during the reign of George III (r. 1760–1820), John Wilkes, a member of Parliament, attacked the government in his newspaper, *North Briton*, and sued the crown when he was arrested. He won his release as well as damages. When he was reelected, Parliament denied him his seat, not once but three times.

The Wilkes episode soon escalated into a major campaign against the corruption and social exclusiveness of Parliament, complaints the Levellers had first raised during the English Revolution of the late 1640s. Newspapers, magazines, pamphlets, handbills, and cheap editions of Wilkes's collected works all helped promote his cause. Those who could not vote demonstrated for Wilkes. In one incident eleven people died when soldiers broke up a huge gathering of his supporters. The slogan "Wilkes and Liberty" appeared on walls all over London. Middle-class voters formed a Society of Supporters of the Bill of Rights, which circulated petitions for Wilkes; they gained the support of about one-fourth of all the voters. The more determined Wilkesites proposed sweeping reforms of Parliament, including more frequent elections, more representation for the counties, elimination of "rotten boroughs" (election districts so small that they could be controlled by one big patron), and restrictions of pensions used by the crown to gain support. These demands would be at the heart of agitation for parliamentary reform in Britain for decades to come.

Popular demonstrations did not always support reforms. In 1780, the Gordon riots devastated London. They were named after the fanatical anti-Catholic crusader Lord George Gordon, who helped organize huge marches and petition campaigns against a bill the House of Commons passed to grant limited toleration to Catholics. The demonstrations culminated in a seven-day riot that left fifty buildings destroyed and three hundred people dead. Despite the continuing limitation on voting rights in Great Britain, British politicians were learning that they could ignore public opinion only at their peril.

Political opposition also took artistic forms, particularly in countries where governments restricted organized political activity. A striking example of a play with a political message was *The Marriage of Figaro* (1784) by Pierre-Augustin Caron de Beaumarchais◆ (1732–1799), a watchmaker, a judge, a gunrunner in the American War of Independence, and a French spy in Britain. *The Marriage of Figaro* was first a hit at court, when Queen Marie-Antoinette had it read for her friends. But when her husband, Louis XVI, read it, he forbade its production on the grounds that "this man mocks at everything that should be respected in government." When finally performed publicly, the play caused a sensation. The chief character, Figaro, is a clever servant who gets the better of his noble employer. When speaking of the count, he cries, "What have you done to deserve so many rewards? You went to the trouble of being born, and nothing more." Two years later, Mozart based an equally famous but somewhat tamer opera on Beaumarchais's story.

Revolution in North America

Oppositional forms of public opinion came to a head in Great Britain's North American colonies, where the result was American independence and the establishment of a republican constitution that stood in stark contrast to most European regimes. The successful revolution was the only blow to Britain's increasing dominance in world affairs in the eighteenth century, and as such it was another aspect of the power rivalries existing at that time. Yet many Europeans saw the American War of Independence, or the American Revolution, as a triumph for Enlightenment ideas. As one

German writer exclaimed in 1777, American victory would give "greater scope to the Enlightenment, new keenness to the thinking of peoples and new life to the spirit of liberty."

The American revolutionary leaders had been influenced by a common Atlantic civilization; they participated in the Enlightenment and shared political ideas with the opposition Whigs in Britain. Supporters demonstrated for Wilkes in South Carolina and Boston, and the South Carolina legislature donated a substantial sum to the Society of Supporters of the Bill of Rights. In the 1760s and 1770s, both British and American opposition leaders became convinced that the British government was growing increasingly corrupt and despotic. British radicals wanted to reform Parliament so that the voices of a broader, more representative segment of the population would be heard. The colonies had no representatives in Parliament, and colonists claimed that "no taxation without representation" should be allowed. Indeed, they denied that Parliament had any jurisdiction over the colonies, insisting that the king govern them through colonial legislatures and recognize their traditional British liberties. The failure of the "Wilkes and Liberty" campaign to produce concrete results convinced many Americans that Parliament was hopelessly tainted and that they would have to stand up for their rights as British subjects.

The British colonies remained loyal to the crown until Parliament's encroachment on their autonomy and the elimination of the French threat at the end of the Seven Years' War transformed colonial attitudes. Unconsciously, perhaps, the colonies had begun to form a separate nation; their economies generally flourished in the eighteenth century, and between 1750 and 1776 their population almost doubled. With the British clamoring for lower taxes and the colonists paying only a fraction of the tax rate paid by the Britons at home, Parliament passed new taxes, including the Stamp Act in 1765, which required a special tax stamp on all legal documents and publications. After violent rioting in the colonies, the tax was repealed, but in 1773 a new Tea Act revived colonial resistance, which culminated in the so-called Boston Tea Party of 1773. Colonists dressed

◆**Beaumarchais:** boh mahr SHAY

Thomas Jefferson, Declaration of Independence (July 4, 1776)

Although others helped revise the Declaration of Independence of the thirteen North American colonies from Great Britain, Jefferson wrote the original draft himself. A Virginia planter and lawyer, Jefferson went on to become governor of Virginia, minister to France, Secretary of State, vice president and president of the United States (1801–1809). The Declaration begins with a stirring expression of the belief in natural or human rights.

When in the Course of human events, it becomes necessary for one people to dissolve the political bands which have connected them with another, and to assume among the powers of the earth, the separate and equal station to which the Laws of Nature and of Nature's God entitle them, a decent respect to the opinions of mankind requires that they should declare the causes which impel them to the separation.

We hold these truths to be self-evident, that all men are created equal, that they are endowed by their Creator with certain unalienable Rights, that among these are Life, Liberty and the pursuit of Happiness.—That to secure these rights, Governments are instituted among Men, deriving their just powers from the consent of the governed,—That whenever any Form of Government becomes destructive of these ends, it is the Right of the People to alter or to abolish it, and to institute new Government, laying its foundation on such principles and organizing its powers in such form, as to them shall seem most likely to effect their Safety and Happiness. Prudence, indeed, will dictate that Governments long established should not be changed for light and transient causes; and accordingly all experience hath shewn, that mankind are more disposed to suffer, while evils are sufferable, than to right themselves by abolishing the forms to which they are accustomed. But when a long train of abuses and usurpations, pursuing invariably the same Object evinces a design to reduce them under absolute Despotism, it is their right, it is their duty, to throw off such Government, and to provide new Guards for their future security.—Such has been the patient sufferance of these Colonies; and such is now the necessity which constrains them to alter their former Systems of Government. The history of the present King of Great Britain is a history of repeated injuries and usurpations, all having in direct object the establishment of an absolute Tyranny over these States. . . .

Source: U.S. National Archives and Records Administration, Washington, D.C.

as Indians boarded British ships and dumped the imported tea (by this time an enormously popular beverage) into Boston's harbor. The British government tried to clamp down on the unrest, but British troops in the colonies soon found themselves fighting locally organized militias.

Political opposition in the American colonies turned belligerent when Britain threatened to use force to maintain control. In 1774, the First Continental Congress convened, composed of delegates from all the colonies, and unsuccessfully petitioned the crown for redress. The next year the Second Continental Congress organized an army with George Washington in command. After actual fighting had begun, in 1776, the congress proclaimed the Declaration of Independence. An eloquent statement of the American cause written by Thomas Jefferson, the Declaration of Independence was couched in the language of universal human rights, which enlightened Europeans could be expected to understand. (See

"Declaration of Independence," opposite.) George III denounced the American "traitors and rebels." But European newspapers enthusiastically reported on every American response to "the cruel acts of oppression they have been made to suffer." In 1778 France boosted the American cause by entering on the colonists' side. Spain, too, saw an opportunity to check the growing power of Britain, though without actually endorsing American independence out of fear of the response of its Latin American colonies. Spain declared war on Britain in 1779; in 1780, Great Britain declared war on the Dutch Republic in retaliation for Dutch support of the rebels. The worldwide conflict that resulted was more than Britain could handle. The American colonies achieved their independence in the peace treaty of 1783.

The newly independent states still faced the challenge of republican self-government. The Articles of Confederation, drawn up in 1777 as a provisional constitution, proved weak because they gave the central government few powers. In 1787, a constitutional convention met in Philadelphia to draft a new constitution. It established a two-house legislature, an indirectly elected president, and an independent judiciary. The U.S. Constitution's preamble insisted explicitly, for the first time in history, that government derived its power solely from the people and did not depend on divine right or on the tradition of royalty or aristocracy. The new educated elite of the eighteenth century had now created government based on a "social contract" among male, property-owning, white citizens. It was by no means a complete democracy (women and slaves were excluded from political participation), but the new government represented a radical departure from European models. In 1791, the Bill of

Overthrowing British Authority
The uncompromising attitude of the British government went a long way toward dissolving long-standing loyalties to the home country. During the American War of Independence, residents of New York City pulled down the statue of the hated George III. *Lafayette College Art Collection, Easton, Pennsylvania.*

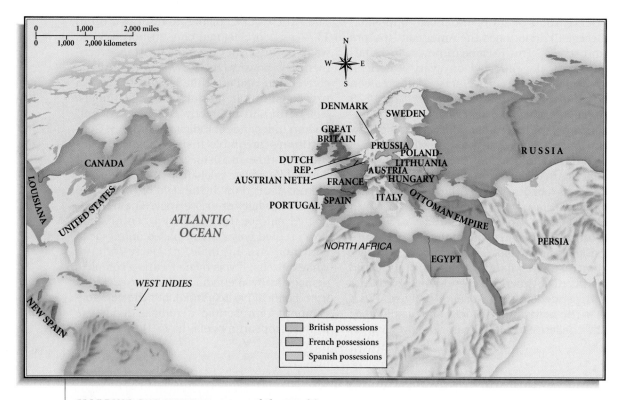

MAPPING THE WEST **Europe and the World, c. 1780**
Although Great Britain lost control over the British North American colonies, which became the new United States, European influence on the rest of the world grew dramatically in the eighteenth century. The slave trade linked European ports to African slave-trading outposts and to plantations in the Caribbean, South America, and North America. The European countries on the Atlantic Ocean benefited most from this trade. Yet almost all of Africa, China, Japan, and large parts of India still resisted European incursion, and the Ottoman Empire, with its massive territories, still presented Europe with a formidable military challenge.

Rights was appended to the Constitution outlining the essential rights (such as freedom of speech) that the government could never overturn. Although slavery continued in the American republic, the new emphasis on rights helped fuel the movement for its abolition in both Britain and the United States.

Interest in the new republic was greatest in France. The U.S. Constitution and various state constitutions were published in French with commentary by leading thinkers. Even more important in the long run were the effects of the American war. Dutch losses to Great Britain aroused a widespread movement for political reform in the Dutch Republic, and debts incurred by France in supporting the American colonies would soon

force the French monarchy to the edge of bankruptcy and then to revolution. Ultimately, the entire European system of royal rule would be challenged.

Review: Why did public opinion become a new factor in politics in the second half of the eighteenth century?

Conclusion

When Thomas Jefferson looked back many years later on the Declaration of Independence, he said he hoped it would be "the signal of arousing men to burst the chains under which monkish ignorance and superstition had persuaded them to bind themselves." What began as a cosmopolitan movement of a few intellectuals in the first half of the eighteenth century had reached a relatively wide audience among the educated elite of men and women by the 1770s and 1780s. The spirit of Enlightenment swept from the coffeehouses and Masonic lodges into the halls of government from Philadelphia to Vienna. Reasoned, scientific inquiry into the causes of social misery and laws defending individual rights and freedoms gained adherents even among the rulers and ministers responsible for censoring Enlightenment works.

For most Europeans, however, the promise of the Enlightenment did not become a reality. Rulers such as Catherine the Great had every intention of retaining their full, often unchecked, powers, even as they corresponded with leading philosophes and entertained them at their courts. Moreover, would-be reformers often found themselves thwarted by the resistance of nobles, by the priorities rulers gave to waging wars, or by popular resistance to deregulation of trade that increased the uncertainties of the market. Yet even the failure of reform contributed to the ferment in Europe after 1770. Peasant rebellions in eastern Europe, the "Wilkes and Liberty" campaign in Great Britain, the struggle over reform in France, and the revolution in America all occurred around the same time, and their conjunction convinced many Europeans that change was brewing. Just how much could change, and whether change made life better or worse, would come into question in the next ten years.

Suggested References

The Enlightenment at Its Height

The interpretive study by Gay remains useful even though it is over thirty years old, but the Kors volumes give the most up-to-date views. Equiano, a freed slave, offers one of the earliest firsthand views of the experience of slavery, but some scholars now question whether he was born in Africa (and not the New World).

*Equiano, Olaudah. *The Interesting Narrative and Other Writings.* Ed. Vincent Carretta. 1995.

Gay, Peter. *The Enlightenment: An Interpretation.* 2 vols. 1966, 1969.

Goodman, Dena. *The Republic of Letters: A Cultural History of the French Enlightenment.* 1994.

Jacob, Margaret C. *Living the Enlightenment: Freemasonry and Politics in Eighteenth-Century Europe.* 1991.

Kors, Alan Charles, ed. *Encyclopedia of the Enlightenment.* 4 vols. 2003.

Porter, Roy. *The Creation of the Modern World: The Untold Story of the British Enlightenment.* 2000.

*Voltaire. *Candide.* Ed. and trans. Daniel Gordon. 1999.

Voltaire Foundation: http://www.voltaire.ox.ac.uk.

Society and Culture in an Age of Enlightenment

Recent work has drawn attention to the lives of ordinary people. The personal journal of the French glassworker Ménétra is a rarity: it offers extensive documentation of the inner life of an ordinary person during the Enlightenment. Ménétra claimed to have met Rousseau. Even if not true, the claim shows that Rousseau's fame was not limited to the upper classes.

Adams, Christine. *A Taste for Comfort and Status: A Bourgeois Family in Eighteenth-Century France.* 2000.

Darnton, Robert. *The Great Cat Massacre and Other Episodes in French Cultural History.* 1984.

Hull, Isabel V. *Sexuality, State, and Civil Society in Germany, 1700–1815.* 1996.

*Ménétra, Jacques Louis. *Journal of My Life.* Trans. Arthur Goldhammer. Intro. Daniel Roche. 1986.

Mozart Project: http://www.mozartproject.org.

Smith, Douglas. *Working the Rough Stone: Freemasonry and Society in Eighteenth-Century Russia.* 1999.

Stone, Lawrence. *The Family, Sex, and Marriage in England, 1500–1800.* Abridged ed. 1979.

State Power in an Era of Reform

Biographies and general histories of this period tend to overemphasize the individual decisions of rulers. Although these decisions are incontestably important, side-by-side reading of Büsch,

*Primary source.

Frederick II's writings on war, and Showalter's book on the wars themselves offers a broader view that puts Frederick II's policies into the context of military growth and its impact on society.

Blanning, T. C. W. *Joseph II and Enlightened Despotism.* 1994.

Büsch, Otto. *Military System and Social Life in Old Regime Prussia, 1713–1807: The Beginnings of the Social Militarization of Prusso-German Society.* Trans. John G. Gagliardo. 1997.

Crankshaw, Edward. *Maria Theresa.* 1996.

Dixon, Simon. *Catherine the Great.* 2001.

*Frederick II, King of Prussia. *Frederick the Great on the Art of War.* Ed. and trans. Jay Luvaas. 1999.

Showalter, Dennis E. *The Wars of Frederick the Great.* 1996.

Venturi, Franco. *The End of the Old Regime in Europe, 1768–1776: The First Crisis.* Trans. R. Burr Litchfield. 1989.

Rebellions against State Power

Historians have recently shown great interest in the riots and rebellions of this era, but most have focused on one national case. Palmer's overview of political movements therefore remains valuable for its comparative aspects.

Alexander, John T. *Autocratic Politics in a National Crisis: The Imperial Russian Government and Pugachev's Revolt, 1773–1775.* 1969.

Palmer, R. R. *The Age of Democratic Revolution: A Political History of Europe and America, 1760–1800.* Vol. 1, *The Challenge.* 1959.

*Rakove, Jack N. *Declaring Rights: A Brief History with Documents.* 1998.

Thomas, P. D. G. *John Wilkes: A Friend to Liberty.* 1996.

Thompson, E. P. *Whigs and Hunters: The Origin of the Black Act.* 1975.

Wood, Gordon S. *The Radicalism of the American Revolution.* 1992.

CHAPTER REVIEW

IMPORTANT EVENTS

1740–1748	War of the Austrian Succession: France, Spain, and Prussia versus Austria and Great Britain
1751–1772	*Encyclopedia* published in France
1756–1763	Seven Years' War fought in Europe, India, and the American colonies
1762	Jean-Jacques Rousseau, *The Social Contract* and *Emile*
1764	Voltaire, *Philosophical Dictionary*
1770	Louis XV of France fails to break the power of the French law courts
1772	First partition of Poland
1773	Pugachev rebellion of Russian peasants
1776	American Declaration of Independence from Great Britain; James Watt improves the steam engine, making it suitable for new industrial projects; Adam Smith, *The Wealth of Nations*
1780	Joseph II of Austria undertakes a wide-reaching reform program
1781	Immanuel Kant, *The Critique of Pure Reason*
1785	Catherine the Great's Charter of the Nobility grants nobles exclusive control over their serfs in exchange for subservience to the state
1787	Delegates from the states draft the U.S. Constitution

KEY TERMS

abolitionists (713)

atheist (712)

deist (712)

enlightened despots (or enlightened absolutists) (729)

Freemasons (723)

Hasidim (721)

industrialization (728)

laissez-faire (716)

Methodism (721)

philosophes (708)

romanticism (720)

salons (711)

REVIEW QUESTIONS

1. Why was France the center of the Enlightenment?

2. What were the major differences in the impact of the Enlightenment on nobles, middle classes, and lower classes?

3. What prompted enlightened absolutists to undertake reforms in the second half of the eighteenth century?

4. Why did public opinion become a new factor in politics in the second half of the eighteenth century?

MAKING CONNECTIONS

1. Why would rulers feel ambivalent about the Enlightenment, supporting reform on the one hand, while clamping down on political dissidents on the other hand?

2. Which major developments in this period ran counter to the influence of the Enlightenment?

3. In what ways had politics changed, and in what ways did they remain the same during the Enlightenment?

FOR FURTHER EXPLORATION

To assess your mastery of the material in this chapter, see the Online Study Guide at **bedfordstmartins.com/hunt**.

To read additional primary-source material from this period, see Chapter 19 in *Sources of The Making of the West*, Second Edition.

The Cataclysm of Revolution, 1789–1800

ON OCTOBER 5, 1789, a crowd of several thousand women marched in a drenching rain twelve miles from the center of Paris to Versailles. They demanded the king's help in securing more grain for the hungry and his reassurance that he did not intend to resist the emerging revolutionary movement. Joined by thousands of men who came from Paris to reinforce them, the next morning they broke into the royal family's private apartments. To prevent further bloodshed— two of the royal bodyguards had already been killed and their heads paraded on pikes—the king agreed to move his family and his government to Paris. A dramatic procession guarded by thousands of ordinary men and women made its slow way back to the capital. The people's proud display of cannons and pikes underlined the fundamental transformation that was occurring. Ordinary people had forced the king of France to respond to their grievances. The French monarchy was in danger, and if such a powerful and long-lasting institution could come under fire, then could any monarch of Europe rest easy?

Although even the keenest political observer did not predict its eruption in 1789, the French Revolution had its immediate origins in a constitutional crisis provoked by a growing government deficit, traceable to French involvement in the American War of Independence. The constitutional crisis came to a head on July 14, 1789, when armed Parisians captured the Bastille,♦ a royal fortress and symbol of monarchical authority in the center of the capital. The fall of the Bastille, like the women's march to Versailles three months later, showed the determination of the common people to put their mark on events.

The French Revolution first grabbed the attention of the entire world because it seemed to promise universal human rights, constitutional

♦**Bastille:** ba STEEL

Women's March to Versailles
Thousands of prints broadcast the events of the French Revolution to the public in France and elsewhere. They varied from fine art engravings signed by the artist to anonymous simple woodblock prints. This colored etching shows a crowd of armed women marching to Versailles on October 5, 1789, to confront the king. The sight of armed women frightened many observers and demonstrated that the Revolution was not only a men's affair. *AKG-Images.*

government, and broad-based political participation. Its most famous slogan pledged "Liberty, Equality, and Fraternity" for all. An enthusiastic German wrote, "One of the greatest nations in the world, the greatest in general culture, has at last thrown off the yoke of tyranny." The revolutionaries used a blueprint based on the Enlightenment idea of reason to remake all of society and politics: they executed the king and queen, established a republic for the first time in French history, abolished nobility, and gave the vote to all adult men. Even as the Revolution promised democracy, however, it also inaugurated a cycle of violence and intimidation. When the revolutionaries encountered resistance to their programs, they set up a government of terror to compel obedience. Some historians therefore see in the French Revolution the origins of modern totalitarianism—that is, governments that try to control every aspect of life, including daily activities, while limiting all forms of political dissent. As events unfolded after 1789, the French Revolution became the model of modern revolution; republicanism, democracy, terrorism, nationalism, and military dictatorship all took their modern forms during the French Revolution.

The Revolution might have remained a strictly French affair if war had not involved the rest of Europe. After 1792, huge French republican armies, fueled by patriotic nationalism, marched across Europe, promising liberation from traditional monarchies but often delivering old-fashioned conquest and annexation. French victories spread revolutionary ideas far and wide, from the colonies in the Caribbean, where the first successful slave revolt established the republic of Haiti, to Poland and Egypt. The army's success ultimately undermined the republic and made possible the rise of Napoleon Bonaparte, a remarkable young general from Corsica, an island off Italy, who brought France more wars, more conquests, and a form of military dictatorship.

The breathtaking succession of regimes in France between 1789 and 1799 and the failure of the republican experiment after ten years of upheaval raised disturbing questions about the relationship between rapid political change and violence. Do all revolutions inevitably degenerate into terror or wars of conquest? Is a regime democratic if it does not allow poor men, women, or blacks to vote? The French Revolution raised these questions and many more. The questions resonated in many countries because the French Revolution seemed to be only the most extreme example of a much broader political and social movement at the end of the eighteenth century.

❖ The Revolutionary Wave, 1787–1789

Between 1787 and 1789, revolts in the name of liberty broke out in the Dutch Republic, the Austrian Netherlands (present-day Belgium and Luxembourg), and Poland, as well as in France. At the same time, the

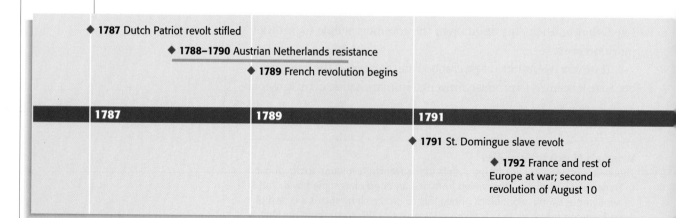

◆ **1787** Dutch Patriot revolt stifled

◆ **1788–1790** Austrian Netherlands resistance

◆ **1789** French revolution begins

| 1787 | 1789 | 1791 |

◆ **1791** St. Domingue slave revolt

◆ **1792** France and rest of Europe at war; second revolution of August 10

newly independent United States of America prepared a new federal constitution. Historians have sometimes referred to these revolts as the **Atlantic revolutions** because so many protest movements arose in countries on both shores of the North Atlantic in the late 1700s. These revolutions were the product of long-term prosperity and high expectations: Europeans in general were wealthier, healthier, more numerous, and better educated than they had ever been before; and the Dutch, Belgian, and French societies were among the wealthiest and best educated within Europe. Most scholars agree, however, that the French Revolution differed greatly from the others. Not only was France the richest, most powerful, and most populous state in western Europe, but its revolution was also more violent, more long-lasting, and ultimately more influential. (See "Terms of History," page 750.)

Protesters in the Low Countries and Poland

Political protests in the Dutch Republic attracted European attention because Dutch banks still controlled a hefty portion of the world's capital at the end of the eighteenth century, even though the Dutch Republic's role in international politics had diminished. Revolts also broke out in the neighboring Austrian Netherlands and Poland. Although none of these movements ultimately succeeded, they showed how quickly political discontent could boil over in this era of rising economic and political expectations.

The Dutch Patriot Revolt, 1787. The Dutch Patriots, as they chose to call themselves, wanted to reduce the powers of the prince of Orange, the kinglike stadholder who favored close ties with Great Britain. Government-sponsored Dutch banks owned 40 percent of the British national debt, and by 1796 they held the entire foreign debt of the United States. Relations with the British deteriorated during the American War of Independence, however, and by the middle of the 1780s, agitation in favor of the Americans had boiled over into an attack on the stadholder.

Building on support among middle-class bankers, merchants, and writers who sympathized with the American cause, the Patriots soon gained a more popular audience by demanding political reforms and organizing armed citizen militias of men, called Free Corps. Parading under banners that read "Liberty or Death," the Free Corps forced local officials to set up new elections to replace councils that had been packed with Orangist supporters through patronage or family connections. The future American president John Adams happened to be visiting Utrecht when such a revolt occurred. He wrote admiringly to Thomas Jefferson that "in no instance, of ancient or modern History, have the People ever asserted more unequivocally their own inherent and unalienable Sovereignty."

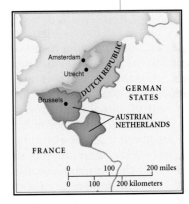

The Low Countries in 1787

◆ **1793** Second Partition of Poland; Louis XVI executed

◆ **1794** French abolish slavery; Robespierre falls

◆ **1797–1798** "Sister" republics established in Italian states and Switzerland

1793	1795	1797	1799

◆ **1795** Third Partition of Poland; France annexes Austrian Netherlands

◆ **1799** Bonaparte comes to power

TERMS OF HISTORY

Revolution

Revolution had previously meant cyclical change that brought life back to a starting point, as a planet makes a revolution around the sun. Revolutions could come and go, by this definition, and change nothing fundamental in the structure of society. After 1789, *revolution* came to mean a self-conscious attempt to leap into the future by reshaping society and politics and even the human personality. A revolutionary official analyzed the meaning of the word in 1793: "A revolution is never made by halves; it must either be total or it will abort. . . . *Revolutionary* means outside of all forms and all rules; *revolutionary* means that which affirms, consolidates the revolution, that which removes all the obstacles which impede its progress." In short, *revolution* soon had an all-or-nothing meaning; you were either for the revolution or against it. There could be no in between.

Revolution still has the same meaning given it by the French revolutionaries, but it is now an even more contested term because of its association with communist theory. In the nineteenth century, Karl Marx incorporated the French Revolution into his new doctrine of communism. In his view, the middle-class French revolutionaries had overthrown the monarchy and the "feudal" aristocracy to pave the way for capitalist development. In the future, the proletariat (industrial workers) would overthrow the capitalist middle class to install a communist government that would abolish private property. Since Marxists claimed the French Revolution as the forerunner of the communist revolution in the nineteenth and twentieth centuries, it was perhaps inevitable that those who opposed communism would also criticize the French Revolution.

The most influential example of this view is that of the French scholar François Furet. An ex-communist, Furet argued that the French Revolution can be seen as the origin of totalitarianism: "Today the Gulag [the Soviet system of prison camps for dissidents] is leading to a rethinking of the Terror precisely because the two undertakings are seen as identical." The Soviet Gulag and the Terror were identical systems for repressing all avenues of dissent. The French Revolution ended up in totalitarianism during the Terror because it incarnated what Furet calls "the illusion of politics," that is, the belief that people can transform social and economic relationships through political revolution. However, the French revolutionaries became totalitarian, in Furet's view, because they wanted to establish a kind of political and social utopia (a perfect society), in which reason alone determined the shape of political and social life. Because this dream was impossible given human resistance to rapid change, the revolutionaries had to use force to achieve their goals. In other words, revolution itself was a problematic idea, according to Furet.

Controversy about the relationship between the French Revolution and totalitarianism continues. *Revolution* as a term remains as contested as the events that gave rise to it.

FURTHER READING

Furet, François. *Interpreting the French Revolution.* Trans. Elborg Forster. 1981.

Hunt, Lynn. *Politics, Culture, and Class in the French Revolution.* 1984.

In 1787, the protesters demanded "the true republican form of government in our commonwealth," that is, the reduction of stadholder powers. The Free Corps took on the troops of the prince of Orange and got the upper hand. In response, Frederick William II of Prussia, whose sister had married the stadholder, intervened with tacit British support. Thousands of Prussian troops soon occupied Utrecht and Amsterdam, and the House of Orange regained its former position.

Internal social divisions paved the way for successful outside intervention. Many of the Patriots from the richest merchant families feared the growing power of the Free Corps. The Free Corps wanted a more democratic form of government, and to get it they encouraged the publication of pamphlets and cartoons attacking the prince and his wife, promoted the rapid spread of clubs and societies made up of common people, and organized crowd-pleasing public ceremonies, such as parades and bonfires, that sometimes turned into riots. In the aftermath of the Prussian invasion in September 1787, the Orangists got their revenge: lower-class mobs pillaged the houses of prosperous Patriot leaders, forcing many to flee to the United States, France, or the Austrian Netherlands. Those Patriots who remained nursed their grievances until the French republican armies invaded in 1795.

The Belgian Independence Movement.

If Austrian emperor Joseph II had not tried to introduce Enlightenment-inspired reforms, the Belgians of the ten provinces of the Austrian Netherlands might have remained tranquil. Joseph abolished torture, decreed toleration for Jews and Protestants (in this resolutely Catholic area), and suppressed monasteries. His reorganization of the administrative and judicial systems eliminated many offices that belonged to nobles and lawyers, sparking resistance among the upper classes in 1788. The countess of Yves,♦ for example, wrote pamphlets against Joseph's reforms and provided meeting places for the rebels.

Upper-class protesters intended only to defend historic local liberties against an overbearing government. Nonetheless, their resistance galvanized democrats, who wanted a more representative government and organized clubs to give voice to their demands. At the end of 1788, a secret society formed armed companies to prepare an uprising. By late 1789, each province had separately declared its independence, and the Austrian administration had collapsed. Delegates from the various provinces declared themselves the United States of Belgium, a clear reference to the American precedent.

Once again, however, social divisions doomed the rebels. Emboldened by the revolt's success, the democrats began to challenge aristocratic authority. "The nobles have no acquired right over the people," one writer proclaimed. In the face of increasing democratic ferment, aristocratic leaders drew to their side the Catholic clergy and peasants, who had little sympathy for the democrats of the cities. Every Sunday in May and June 1790, thousands of peasant men and women, led by their priests, streamed into Brussels carrying crucifixes, nooses, and pitchforks to intimidate the democrats and defend the church. Faced with the choice between the Austrian emperor and "our current tyrants," the democrats chose to support the return of the Austrians under Emperor Leopold II (r. 1790–1792), who had succeeded his brother.

Polish Patriots. A reform party calling itself the Patriots also emerged in Poland, which had been shocked by the loss of a third of its territory in the First Partition of 1772. The Patriots sought to overhaul the weak commonwealth along modern western European lines and looked to King Stanislaw August Poniatowski♦ (r. 1764–1795) to lead them. A nobleman who owed his crown solely to the dubious honor of being Catherine the Great's discarded lover but who was also a favorite correspondent of the Parisian salon hostess Madame Geoffrin, Poniatowski saw in moderate reform the only chance for his country to escape the consequences of a century's misgovernment and cultural decline. Ranged against the Patriots stood most of the aristocrats and the formidable Catherine the Great, determined to uphold imperial Russian influence.

Watchful but not displeased to see Russian influence waning in Poland, Austria and Prussia allowed the reform movement to proceed. In 1788, the Patriots got their golden chance. Bogged down in war with the Ottoman Turks, Catherine could not block the summoning of a reform-minded parliament, which with King Stanislaw's aid outmaneuvered the antireform aristocrats. Amid much oratory denouncing Russian overlordship, the parliament enacted the constitution of May 3, 1791, which established a hereditary monarchy with somewhat strengthened authority, at last freed the two-house legislature from the individual veto power of every aristocrat, granted townspeople

♦**Yves:** eev

♦**Poniatowski:** PAWN ya TAWF skee

limited political rights, and vaguely promised future Jewish emancipation. Abolishing serfdom was hardly mentioned. Modest though they were, the Polish reforms did not endure. Catherine II could not countenance the spread of revolution into eastern Europe and within a year engineered the downfall of the Patriots and further weakened the Polish state.

Origins of the French Revolution, 1787–1789

Many French enthusiastically greeted the American experiment in republican government and supported the Dutch, Belgian, and Polish patriots. But they did not expect the United States and the Dutch Republic to provide them a model. Montesquieu and Rousseau, the leading political theorists of the Enlightenment, taught that republics suited only small countries, not big ones like France. After suffering humiliation at the hands of the British in the Seven Years' War (1756–1763), the French had regained international prestige by supporting the victorious Americans, and the monarchy had shown its eagerness to promote reforms. In 1787, for example, the French crown granted civil rights to Protestants. Yet by the late 1780s, the French monarchy faced a serious fiscal crisis caused by a mounting deficit. It soon provoked a constitutional crisis of epic proportions.

Fiscal Crisis.   France's fiscal problems stemmed from its support of the Americans against the British in the American War of Independence. About half of the French national budget went to paying interest on the debt that had accumulated. In contrast to Great Britain, which had a national bank to help raise loans for the government, the French government lived off relatively short-term, high-interest loans from private sources including Swiss banks, government annuities, and advances from tax collectors.

For years the French government had been trying unsuccessfully to modernize the tax system to make it more equitable. The peasants bore the greatest burden of taxes, whereas the nobles and clergy were largely exempt. Tax collection was also far from systematic: private contractors collected many taxes and pocketed a large share of the proceeds. With the growing support of public

Queen Marie-Antoinette
Painted in 1789 by Marie-Louise-Elizabeth Vigée-Lebrun, this portrait of the French queen shows her with her three children. Her eldest son Louis died in 1789. When he died, her second son, also called Louis, became heir to the throne. Known to supporters of the monarch as Louis XVII, he died in prison in 1795 and never ruled. Vigée-Lebrun fled France in 1789 and only returned in 1805. *Réunion des Musées Nationaux/Art Resource, NY. Photo: J. Schormanns Arnaudet.*

opinion, the bond and annuity holders from the middle and upper classes now demanded a clearer system of fiscal accountability. Declaring bankruptcy, as many rulers had in the past, was no longer an option.

In a monarchy the ruler's character is always crucial. Louis XVI (r. 1774–1792) was the model of a virtuous husband and father, but he took a limited view of his responsibilities in this time of crisis. Many complained that he showed more interest in hunting or in his hobby of making locks than in the problems of government. His wife, Marie-Antoinette, was blond, beautiful, and much criticized for her extravagant taste in clothes, elaborate hairdos, and supposed indifference to popular misery. "The Austrian bitch," as underground writers called her, had been the target of an increasingly nasty pamphlet campaign in the 1780s. By 1789, the queen had become an object of popular hatred; when confronted by the inability of the poor to buy bread, she was mistakenly reported to have replied, "Let them eat cake." The king's ineffectiveness and the queen's growing unpopularity helped undermine the monarchy as an institution.

Faced with a mounting deficit, in 1787 Louis submitted a package of reforms to the Assembly of Notables, a group of handpicked nobles, clergymen, and officials. When this group refused to cooperate, the king presented his proposals for a more uniform land tax to his old rival the parlement of Paris. When it too refused, he ordered the parlement judges into exile in the provinces. Overnight, the judges (members of the nobility because of the offices they held) became popular heroes for resisting the king's "tyranny"; in reality, however, the judges, like the notables, wanted reform only on their own terms. Louis finally gave in to demands that he call a meeting of the Estates General,♦ which had last met 175 years before.

The Estates General. The calling of the Estates General electrified public opinion. Who would determine the fate of the nation? The **Estates General** was a body of deputies from the three estates, or orders, of France. The deputies in the First Estate represented some 100,000 clergy of the Catholic church, which owned about 10 percent of the land and collected a 10 percent tax (the tithe) on peasants. The deputies of the Second Estate represented the nobility, about 400,000 men and women who owned about 25 percent of the land, enjoyed many tax exemptions, and collected seigneurial dues and rents from their peasant tenants. The deputies of the Third Estate represented everyone else, at least 95 percent of the nation. In 1614, at the last meeting of the Estates General, each order had voted separately, and either the clergy or the nobility could therefore veto any decision of the Third Estate. Before the elections to the Estates General in 1789, the king agreed to double the number of deputies for the Third Estate (making them equal in number to the other two combined), but he refused to order voting by individual head rather than by order. Voting by order (each order would have one vote) would conserve the traditional powers of the clergy and nobility; voting by head (each

deputy would have one vote) would give the Third Estate an advantage since many clergymen and even some nobles sympathized with the Third Estate.

As the state's censorship apparatus broke down, pamphleteers by the hundreds denounced the traditional privileges of the nobility and clergy and called for voting by head rather than by order. In the most vitriolic of all the pamphlets, *What Is the Third Estate?*, the middle-class clergyman Abbé (Abbot) Emmanuel-Joseph Sieyès♦ charged that the nobility contributed nothing at all to the nation's well-being; they were "a malignant disease which preys upon and tortures the body of a sick man." In the winter and spring of 1789, thousands of men (and a few women by proxy) held meetings to elect deputies and write down their grievances. The effect was immediate. Although educated men dominated the meetings at the regional level, the humblest peasants also voted in their villages and burst forth with complaints, especially about taxes. As one villager lamented, "The last crust

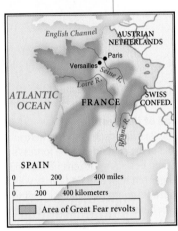

The Great Fear, 1789

of bread has been taken from us." The long series of meetings raised expectations that the Estates General would help the king solve all the nation's ills.

These new hopes soared just at the moment France experienced an increasingly rare but always dangerous food shortage. Bad weather damaged the harvest of 1788, causing bread prices to soar in many places in the spring and summer of 1789 and threatening starvation for the poorest people. A serious slump in textile production had been causing massive unemployment since 1786. Hundreds of thousands of textile workers were out of work and hungry, adding another volatile element to an already tense situation.

When some twelve hundred deputies journeyed to the king's palace of Versailles for

---

♦**Estates General:** uh STAYTS JEHN uh ruhl

♦**Emmanuel-Joseph Sieyès:** ay ma nwehl zhoh zehf syay YEHS

Fall of the Bastille

The Bastille prison is shown here in all its imposing grandeur. The moment depicted is that of the surrender of the fortress's governor, Bernard René de Launay. Because so many of the besieging citizens had been killed (only one of the defenders died), popular anger ran high and de Launay was to be the sacrificial victim. As the hastily formed citizens' guard marched him off to city hall, huge crowds taunted and spat at him. When he lashed out at one of the men nearest him, he was immediately stabbed and shot. A pastry cook cut off the governor's head, which was promptly displayed as a trophy on a pike held high above the crowd. Royal authority had been successfully challenged and even humiliated. *Château de Versailles, France/Giraudon/Bridgeman Art Library.*

the Third Estate to carry through a constitutional revolution.

July 14, 1789: The Fall of the Bastille. At first Louis appeared to agree to the new National Assembly, but he also ordered thousands of soldiers to march to Paris. The deputies who supported the Assembly feared a plot by the king and high-ranking nobles to arrest them and disperse the Assembly. "Everyone is convinced that the approach of the troops covers some violent design," one deputy wrote home. Their fears were confirmed when on July 11 the king fired Jacques Necker, the Swiss Protestant finance minister and the one high official regarded as sympathetic to the deputies' cause.

The popular reaction in Paris to Necker's dismissal and the threat of military force changed the course of the French Revolution. When the news spread, the common people in Paris began to arm themselves and attack places where either grain or arms were thought to be stored (Map 20.1). A deputy in Versailles reported home: "Today all of the evils overwhelm France, and we are between despotism, carnage, and famine." On July 14, 1789, an armed crowd marched on the Bastille, a fortified prison that symbolized royal authority. After a chaotic battle in which a hundred armed citizens died, the prison officials surrendered. The angry crowd killed the governor of the prison and flaunted his head on a pike.

The fall of the Bastille (an event now commemorated as the French national holiday) set an important precedent. The common people showed themselves willing to intervene violently at a crucial political moment (see The Third Estate Awakens). All over France, food riots turned into local revolts. The officials in one city wrote of their plight: "Yesterday afternoon [July 19] more than seven or eight thousand people, men

the opening of the Estates General in May 1789, many readers avidly followed the developments in newspapers that sprouted overnight. Although most nobles insisted on voting by order, the deputies of the Third Estate refused to proceed on that basis. After six weeks of stalemate, on June 17, 1789, the deputies of the Third Estate took unilateral action and declared themselves and whoever would join them the National Assembly, in which each deputy would vote as an individual. Two days later the clergy voted by a narrow margin to join them. Tensions rose. Denied access to their meeting hall on June 20, the deputies met on a nearby tennis court and swore an oath not to disband until they had given France a constitution that reflected their newly declared authority. This "tennis court oath" expressed the determination of

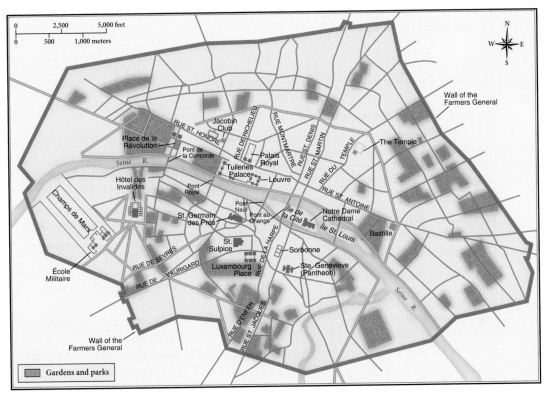

MAP 20.1 Revolutionary Paris, 1789

The French Revolution began with the fall of the Bastille prison on July 14, 1789. The huge fortified prison was located on the eastern side of the city in a neighborhood of working people. Before attacking the Bastille, crowds had torn down many of the customs booths located in the wall of the Farmers General (the private company in charge of tax collection), and taken the arms stored in the Hôtel des Invalides, a veterans' hospital on the western side of the city where the upper classes lived. In other words, the crowds had roamed throughout the city.

The Third Estate Awakens

This print, produced after the fall of the Bastille (note the heads on pikes outside the prison), shows a clergyman (First Estate) and a noble (Second Estate) alarmed by the awakening of the commoners (Third Estate). The Third Estate breaks the chains of oppression and arms itself to battle for its rights. In what ways does this print draw attention to the social conflicts that lay behind the political struggles in the Estates General? **For more help analyzing this image**, see the visual activity for this chapter in the Online Study Guide at **bedfordstmartins.com/hunt**. *Musée Carnavalet/Photo Bulloz.*

MAJOR EVENTS OF THE FRENCH REVOLUTION

1789

May 5	The Estates General opens at Versailles
June 17	The Third Estate decides to call itself the National Assembly
June 20	"Tennis court oath" shows determination of deputies to carry out a constitutional revolution
July 14	Fall of the Bastille
August 4	Night session of the National Assembly abolishes "feudalism"
August 26	National Assembly passes Declaration of the Rights of Man and Citizen
October 5–6	Women march to Versailles and join with men in bringing the royal family back to Paris

1790

July 12	Civil Constitution of the Clergy

1791

June 20	Louis and Marie-Antoinette attempt to flee in disguise and are captured at Varennes

1792

April 20	Declaration of war on Austria
August 10	Insurrection in Paris and attack on Tuileries palace lead to suspension of the king
September 2–6	Murder of prisoners in "September massacres" in Paris
September 22	Establishment of the republic

1793

January 21	Execution of Louis XVI
March 11	Beginning of uprising in the Vendée
May 31–June 2	Insurrection leading to arrest of the Girondins
July 27	Robespierre named to the Committee of Public Safety
September 29	Convention establishes General Maximum on prices and wages
October 16	Execution of Marie-Antoinette

1794

February 4	Slavery abolished in the French colonies
March 13–24	Arrest, trial, and executions of so-called ultrarevolutionaries
March 30–April 5	Arrest, trial, and executions of Danton and his followers
July 27	"The Ninth of Thermidor" arrest of Robespierre and his supporters (executed July 28–29)

1795

October 26	Directory government takes office
April 1796–October 1797	Succession of Italian victories by Bonaparte
May 1798–October 1799	Bonaparte in Egypt and Middle East

1799

November 9	Bonaparte's coup of 18 Brumaire

and women, assembled in front of the two gates to the city hall. . . . We were forced to negotiate with them and to promise to give them wheat . . . and to reduce the price of bread." Local governments were forced out of power and replaced by committees of "patriots" loyal to the revolutionary cause. To restore order, the patriots relied on newly formed National Guard units composed of civilians. The king's government began to crumble. One of Louis XVI's brothers and many other leading aristocrats fled into exile. In Paris, the marquis de Lafayette, a hero of the American War of Independence and a noble deputy in the National Assembly, became commander of the new National Guard. The Revolution thus had its first heroes, its first victims, and its first enemies.

> **Review:** In what ways did the beginning of the French Revolution resemble the other revolutions of 1787–1789?

❖ From Monarchy to Republic, 1789–1793

Until July 1789, the French Revolution followed a course much like that of the protest movements in the Low Countries. Unlike the Dutch and Belgian uprisings, however, the French Revolution did not come to a quick end. The French revolutionaries first tried to establish a constitutional monarchy based on the Enlightenment principles of human rights and rational government. This effort failed when the king attempted to raise a counter-revolutionary army. When war broke out in 1792, new tensions culminated in a second revolution on August 10, 1792, that deposed the king and established a republic in which all power rested in an elected legislature.

The Revolution of Rights and Reason

Before drafting a constitution, the deputies of the National Assembly had to confront growing violence in the countryside. Peasants made up 80 percent of the French population but owned only about 50 percent of the land. Most could barely make ends meet but still had to pay taxes to the state, the tithe to the Catholic church, and a host of seigneurial dues to their lords, whether for using the lords' mills to grind wheat or to ensure their ability to give their land as inheritance to their children. Peasants greeted the news of events in 1789 with a mixture of hope and anxiety. As food shortages spread, they feared that the beggars and vagrants crowding the roads might be part of an aristocratic plot to starve the people by burning crops or barns. In some places, the **Great Fear** (the term used by historians to describe this rural panic) turned into peasant attacks on aristocrats or on seigneurial records of peasants' dues kept in the lord's château. Peasants now refused to pay seigneurial dues to their lords, and the persistence of peasant violence raised alarms about the potential for a general peasant insurrection.

"The End of Feudalism." In response to peasant unrest, the National Assembly decided to make sweeping changes. On the night of August 4, 1789, noble deputies announced their willingness to give up their tax exemptions and seigneurial dues. By the end of the night, amid wild enthusiasm, dozens of deputies had come to the podium to relinquish the tax exemptions of their own professional groups, towns, or provinces. The National Assembly decreed the abolition of what it called "the feudal regime"—that is, it freed the few remaining serfs and eliminated all special privileges in matters of taxation, including all seigneurial dues on land. (A few days later the deputies insisted on financial compensation for some of these dues, but most peasants refused to pay.) Peasants had achieved their goals. The Assembly also mandated equality of opportunity in access to official posts. Talent, rather than birth, was to be the key to success. Enlightenment principles were beginning to become law.

The Declaration of the Rights of Man and Citizen. Three weeks later, the deputies drew up the **Declaration of the Rights of Man and Citizen** as a preamble to the Constitution. In words reminiscent of the American Declaration of Independence, whose author, Thomas Jefferson, was in Paris at the time, it proclaimed, "Men are born and remain free and equal in rights." The Declaration granted freedom of religion, freedom of the press, equality of taxation, and equality before the law. It established the principle of national sovereignty: since "all sovereignty rests essentially in the nation," the king derived his authority henceforth from the nation rather than from tradition or divine right.

By pronouncing all "men" free and equal, the Declaration immediately created new dilemmas. Did women have equal rights with men? What about free blacks in the colonies? How could slavery be justified if all men were born free? Did religious toleration of Protestants and Jews include equal political rights? Women never received the right to vote during the French Revolution, though Protestant and Jewish men did. Women were theoretically citizens under civil law but without the right to full political participation. (See "The Rights of Minorities," on page 758.)

Some women did not accept their exclusion, viewing it as a betrayal of the promised new order. In addition to joining demonstrations, such as the march to Versailles in

The Rights of Minorities

When the National Assembly passed the Declaration of the Rights of Man and Citizen on August 26, 1789, it opened the way to discussion of the rights of various groups, from actors (considered ineligible for voting under the monarchy because they impersonated other people as part of their profession) to women, free blacks, mulattoes, and slaves. A nobleman, Count Stanislas de Clermont Tonnerre, gave a speech on December 23, 1789, in which he advocated giving full political rights to actors, executioners, Protestants, and Jews (he did not mention women, free blacks, mulattoes, or slaves).

Sirs, in the declaration that you believed you should put at the head of the French constitution you have established, consecrated, the rights of man and citizen. In the constitutional work that you have decreed relative to the organization of the municipalities, a work accepted by the King, you have fixed the conditions of eligibility that can be required of citizens. It would seem, Sirs, that there is nothing else left to do and that prejudices should be silent in the face of the language of the law; but an honorable member has explained to us that the *non-Catholics* of some provinces still experience harassment based on former laws, and seeing them excluded from the elections and public posts, another honorable member has protested against the effect of prejudice that persecutes some professions. This prejudice, these laws, force you to make your position clear. I have the honor to present you with the draft of a decree, and it is this draft that I defend here. I establish in it the principle that professions and religious creed can never become reasons for ineligibility. . . .

Every creed has only one test to pass in regard to the social body: it has only one examination to which it must submit, that of its morals. It is here that the adversaries of the Jewish people attack me. This people, they say, is not sociable. They are commanded to loan at usurious rates; they cannot be joined with us either in marriage or by the bonds of social interchange; our food is forbidden to them; our tables prohibited; our armies will never have Jews serving in the defense of the fatherland. The worst of these reproaches is unjust; the others are only specious. Usury is not commanded by their laws; loans at interest are forbidden between them and permitted with foreigners. . . .

But, they say to me, the Jews have their own judges and laws. I respond that is your fault and you should not allow it. We must refuse everything to the Jews as a nation and accord everything to Jews as individuals. We must withdraw recognition from their judges; they should only have our judges. We must refuse legal protection to the maintenance of the so-called laws of their Judaic organization; they should not be allowed to form in the state either a political body or an order. They must be citizens individually. But, some will say to me, they do not want to be citizens. Well then! If they do not want to be citizens, they should say so, and then, we should banish them. It is repugnant to have in the state an association of non-citizens, and a nation within the nation. . . . In short, Sirs, the presumed status of every man resident in a country is to be a citizen.

Source: *Archives parlementaires*, 10 (Paris, 1878): 754–57. Translation by Lynn Hunt.

October 1789, women wrote petitions, published tracts, and organized political clubs to demand more participation (see A Women's Club, opposite). In her Declaration of the Rights of Women of 1791, Olympe de Gouges◆ (1748–1793) played on the language of the official Declaration to make the point that women should also be included. In Article I, she announced, "Woman is born free and lives equal to man in her rights." She also insisted that since "woman has the right to mount the scaffold," she must "equally have the right to mount the rostrum." De Gouges linked her complaints to a program of social reform in which women would have equal rights to property and

◆**de Gouges:** duh GOOJ

public office and equal responsibilities in taxes and criminal punishment.

The Constitution and the Church.

Unresponsive to calls for women's equality, the National Assembly turned to preparing France's first written constitution. The deputies gave voting rights only to white men who passed a test of wealth. The Constitution defined them as the "active citizens"; all others were "passive." Despite these limitations, France became a constitutional monarchy in which the king served as the leading state functionary. A one-house legislature was responsible for making laws. The king could hold up enactment of laws but could not veto them absolutely. The deputies abolished all the old administrative divisions of the provinces and replaced them with a national system of eighty-three *départements* (literally "departments") with identical administrative and legal structures (Map 20.2 on page 760). All officials were elected; no offices could be bought or sold. The deputies also abolished the old taxes and replaced them with new ones that were supposed to be uniformly levied. The National Assembly had difficulty collecting taxes, however, because many people had expected a substantial cut in the tax rate. The new administrative system survived, nonetheless, and the departments are still the basic units of the French state today.

When the deputies turned to reforming the Catholic church, they created enduring conflicts. Motivated partly by the ongoing financial crisis, the National Assembly confiscated all the church's property and promised to pay clerical salaries in return. A Civil Constitution of the Clergy passed in July 1790 set pay scales for the clergy and provided that the voters elect their own parish priests and bishops just as they elected other officials. The impounded property served as a guarantee for the new paper money, called assignats,♦

♦**assignats:** a seen YAH

A Women's Club

In this gouache by the Lesueur brothers, *The Patriotic Women's Club,* the club president urges the members to contribute funds for poor patriot families. Women's clubs focused on philanthropic work but also discussed revolutionary legislation and the debates in the legislature. The colorful but sober dress indicates that the women are middle class. *Musée de la Ville de Paris/Musée Carnavalet, Paris/ Bridgeman-Giraudon/Art Resource, NY.*

issued by the government. The assignats soon became subject to inflation because the government began to sell the church lands to the highest bidders in state auctions. The sales increased the landholdings of wealthy city dwellers and prosperous peasants but cut the ground out from under the assignats.

Convinced that monastic life encouraged idleness and a decline in the nation's population, the deputies outlawed any future monastic vows and encouraged monks and nuns to return to private life on state pensions. Many monks took the opportunity, but few nuns did. For nuns, the convent was all they knew. As the Carmelite nuns of Paris responded, "If there is true happiness on earth, we enjoy it in the shelter of the sanctuary."

Faced with resistance to these changes, in November 1790, the National Assembly required all clergy to swear an oath of loyalty to the Civil Constitution of the Clergy. Pope Pius VI in Rome condemned the constitution, and half of the French clergy refused to take the oath. The oath of allegiance permanently divided the Catholic population, which had to choose between loyalty to the old church and

The Execution of King Louis XVI
Louis XVI was executed by order of the National Convention on January 21, 1793. In this print, the executioner shows the severed head to the crowd, which stands in orderly silence around the scaffold. Note the empty pedestal on the right. It had held a statue of Louis XV after whom the square was named. The revolutionaries renamed it the Square of the Revolution and later put a statue of Liberty on the pedestal. *The Art Archive/Musée Carnavalet, Paris/Dagli Orti.*

one of the queen's favorites, was hacked to pieces and her mutilated body displayed beneath the windows where the royal family was kept under guard. These "September massacres" showed the dark side of popular revolution, in which the common people demanded instant revenge on supposed enemies and conspirators.

Republican Rivals and the Execution of the King. The National Convention faced a dire situation. It needed to write a new constitution for the republic while fighting a war with external enemies and confronting increasing resistance at home. The Revolution had divided the population: for some, it had not gone far enough toward providing food, land, and retribution against enemies; for others, it had gone too far by dismantling the church and the monarchy. The French people had never known any government other than monarchy. Only half the population could read and write at even a basic level. In this situation, symbolic actions became very important. Any public sign of monarchy was at risk, and revolutionaries soon pulled down statues of kings and burned reminders of the former regime.

The fate of Louis XVI and the future direction of the republic divided the deputies elected to the National Convention. Most of the deputies were middle-class lawyers and professionals who had developed their ardent republican beliefs in the network of Jacobin Clubs. After the fall of the monarchy in August 1792, however, the Jacobins divided into two factions. The Girondins◆ (named after a department in southwestern France, the Gironde, which provided some of its leading orators) met regularly at the salon of Jeanne Roland, the wife of a minister. They resented the growing power of Parisian militants and tried to appeal to the departments outside of Paris. The Mountain (so called because its

the sans-culottes organized an insurrection and attacked the Tuileries palace, the residence of the king. The king and his family had to seek refuge in the meeting room of the Legislative Assembly, where the frightened deputies ordered new elections. They abolished the property qualifications for voting required by the constitution of 1791; the voters chose the National Convention by universal male suffrage.

When it met, the National Convention abolished the monarchy and on September 22, 1792, established the first republic in French history. The republic would answer only to the people, not to any royal authority. Lafayette and other liberal aristocrats who had supported the constitutional monarchy fled into exile. Violence soon exploded again when early in September 1792 the Prussians approached Paris. Hastily gathered mobs stormed the overflowing prisons to seek out traitors who might help the enemy. In an atmosphere of near hysteria, eleven hundred inmates were killed, including many ordinary and completely innocent people. The princess of Lamballe,

---

◆**Girondins:** juh RAHN dihns

deputies sat in the highest seats of the National Convention), in contrast, was closely allied with the Paris militants.

The first showdown between the Girondins and the Mountain occurred during the trial of the king in December 1792. Although the Girondins agreed that the king was guilty of treason, many of them argued for clemency, exile, or a popular referendum on his fate. After a long and difficult debate, the National Convention supported the Mountain and voted by a very narrow majority to execute the king. Louis XVI went to the guillotine♦ on January 21, 1793, sharing the fate of Charles I of England in 1649. "We have just convinced ourselves that a king is only a man," wrote one newspaper, "and that no man is above the law."

Review: Why did the French Revolution turn in an increasingly radical direction after 1789?

❖ Terror and Resistance

The execution of the king did not end the new regime's problems. The continuing war required even more men and money, and the introduction of a national draft provoked massive resistance in some parts of France. In response to growing pressures, the National Convention named the Committee of Public Safety to supervise food distribution, direct the war effort, and root out counter-revolutionaries. The leader of the committee, Maximilien Robespierre,♦ wanted to go beyond these stopgap measures and create a "republic of virtue," in which the government would teach, or force, citizens to become virtuous republicans through a massive program of political reeducation. Thus began the **Terror**, in which the guillotine became the most terrifying instrument of a government that suppressed almost every form of dissent (see The Guillotine, shown here). These policies only in-

♦**guillotine:** GIH luh teen
♦**Robespierre:** roh behs PYEHR

creased divisions, which ultimately led to Robespierre's fall from power and to a dismantling of government by terror.

Robespierre and the Committee of Public Safety

The conflict between the Girondins and the Mountain did not end with the execution of Louis XVI. Militants in Paris agitated for the removal of the deputies who had proposed a referendum on the king, and in retaliation the Girondins engineered the arrest of Jean-Paul Marat, a deputy who had urged violent measures in his newspaper *The Friend of the People*. When Marat was acquitted, the Girondins set up a special commission to

The Guillotine

Before 1789 only nobles were decapitated if condemned to death; commoners were usually hanged. Equalization of the death penalty was first proposed by J. I. Guillotin, a professor of anatomy and a deputy for the Third Estate in the National Assembly. He also suggested that a mechanical device be constructed for decapitation, leading to the instrument's association with his name. The Assembly decreed decapitation as the death penalty in June 1791 and another physician, A. Louis, actually invented the guillotine. The executioner pulled up the blade by a cord and then released it. Use of the guillotine began in April 1792 and did not end until 1981, when the French government abolished the death penalty. The guillotine fascinated as much as it repelled. Reproduced in miniature, painted onto snuffboxes and china, worn as jewelry, and even serving as a toy, the guillotine became a part of popular culture. How could the guillotine be simultaneously celebrated as the people's avenger by supporters of the Revolution and vilified as the preeminent symbol of the Terror by opponents? *Musée Carnavalet/ Photo Bulloz.*

investigate the situation in Paris, ordering the arrest of various local leaders. In response, Parisian militants organized an armed demonstration and invaded the National Convention on June 2, 1793, forcing the deputies to decree the arrest of their twenty-nine Girondin colleagues. The Convention consented to the establishment of paramilitary bands called "revolutionary armies" to hunt down political suspects and hoarders of grain. The deputies also agreed to speed up the operation of special revolutionary courts.

Setting the course for government and the war increasingly fell to the twelve-member Committee of Public Safety, set up by the National Convention on April 6, 1793. When Robespierre (1758–1794) was elected to the committee three months later, he became in effect its guiding spirit and the chief spokesman of the Revolution. A lawyer from northern France known as "the incorruptible" for his stern honesty and fierce dedication to democratic ideals, Robespierre remains one of the most controversial figures in world history because of his association with the Terror. In September 1793, in response to popular pressure, the deputies of the Convention voted to "put Terror on the agenda." Robespierre took the lead in implementing this decision. Although he originally opposed the death penalty and the war, he was convinced that the emergency situation of 1793 required severe measures, including death for those, such as the Girondins, who opposed the committee's policies.

Like many other educated eighteenth-century men, Robespierre had read the classics of republicanism from the ancient Roman writers Tacitus and Plutarch to the Enlightenment thinkers Montesquieu and Rousseau. But he took them a step further. He spoke eloquently about "the theory of revolutionary government" as "the war of liberty against its enemies." He defended the people's right to democratic government, while in practice he supported many emergency measures that restricted their liberties. He personally favored a free-market economy, as did almost all middle-class deputies, but in this time of crisis he was willing to enact price controls and requisitioning. In an effort to stabilize prices, the National Convention established the General Maximum on September 29,

1793, which set limits on the prices of thirty-nine essential commodities and on wages. In a speech to the Convention, Robespierre explained the necessity of government by terror: "The first maxim of your policies must be to lead the people by reason and the people's enemies by terror. . . . Without virtue, terror is deadly; without terror, virtue is impotent." *Terror* was not an idle term; it seemed to imply that the goal of democracy justified what we now call totalitarian means, that is, the suppression of all dissent.

Through a series of desperate measures, the Committee of Public Safety set the machinery of the Terror in motion. It sent deputies out "on mission" to purge unreliable officials and organize the war effort. In the first universal draft of men in history, every unmarried man and childless widower between the ages of eighteen and twenty-five was declared eligible for conscription. Revolutionary tribunals set up in Paris and provincial centers tried political suspects. In October 1793, the Revolutionary Tribunal in Paris convicted Marie-Antoinette of treason and sent her to the guillotine. The Girondin leaders and Madame Roland were also guillotined, as was Olympe de Gouges. The government confiscated all the property of convicted traitors.

The Terror won its greatest success on the battlefield. As of April 1793, France faced war with Austria, Prussia, Great Britain, Spain, Sardinia, and the Dutch Republic—all fearful of the impact of revolutionary ideals on their own populations. The execution of Louis XVI, in particular, galvanized European governments; according to William Pitt, the British prime minister, it was "the foulest and most atrocious act the world has ever seen." To face this daunting coalition of forces, the French republic tapped a new and potent source of power—nationalist pride—in decrees mobilizing young and old alike:

> The young men will go to battle; married men will forge arms and transport provisions; women will make tents and clothing and serve in hospitals; children will make bandages; old men will get themselves carried to public places to arouse the courage of warriors and preach hatred of kings and unity of the republic.

Forges were set up in the parks and gardens of Paris to produce thousands of guns, and citizens everywhere helped collect saltpeter, a rock salt used to make gunpowder. By the end of 1793, the French nation in arms had stopped the advance of the allied powers, and in the summer of 1794 it invaded the Austrian Netherlands and crossed the Rhine River. The army was ready to carry the gospel of revolution and republicanism to the rest of Europe.

The Republic of Virtue, 1793–1794

The program of the Terror went beyond pragmatic measures to fight the war and internal enemies to include efforts to "republicanize everything"—in other words, to effect a cultural revolution. While censoring writings deemed counterrevolutionary, the government encouraged republican art, set up civic festivals, and in some places directly attacked the churches in a campaign known as de-Christianization. In addition to drawing up plans for a new program of elementary education, the republic set about politicizing every aspect of daily life, from the naming of babies to the measurement of space and time.

Republican Culture. Refusing to tolerate opposition, the republic left no stone unturned in its endeavor to get its message across. Songs—especially the new national anthem, "La Marseillaise"—placards, posters, pamphlets, books, engravings, paintings, sculpture, even everyday crockery, chamberpots, and playing cards conveyed revolutionary slogans and symbols. Foremost among them was the figure of Liberty (an early version of the Statue of Liberty now in New York harbor), which appeared on coins and bills, letterheads and seals, and as statues in festivals (see Representing Liberty, shown here). Hundreds of new plays were produced and old classics revised. To encourage the production of patriotic and republican works, the government sponsored state competitions for artists. Works of art were supposed to "awaken the public spirit and make clear how atrocious and ridiculous were the enemies of liberty and of the Republic."

At the center of this elaborate cultural campaign were the revolutionary festivals modeled on Rousseau's plans for a civic religion. The festivals first emerged in 1789

Representing Liberty

Liberty was represented by a female figure because in French the noun is feminine (*la liberté*). This painting from 1793–1794, by Jeanne-Louise Vallain, captures the usual attributes of Liberty: she is soberly seated, wearing a Roman-style toga, and holding a pike with a Roman liberty cap on top. Her Roman appearance signals that she is the representation of an abstract quality. The fact that she holds an instrument of battle suggests that women might be active participants. Liberty is holding the Declaration of the Rights of Man and Citizen as it was revised in 1793. This painting was most likely hung in a central location in the Paris Jacobin Club. *Musée de la Revolution Française, Vizille.*

with the spontaneous planting of liberty trees in villages and towns. The Festival of Federation on July 14, 1790, marked the first anniversary of the fall of the Bastille. Under the National Convention, the well-known painter Jacques-Louis David (1748–1825), who was a deputy and associate of Robespierre, took over festival planning. David aimed to destroy the mystique of monarchy and to make the republic sacred. His Festival of Unity on August 10, 1793, for example, celebrated the first anniversary of the overthrow of the monarchy. In front of the statue of Liberty built for the occasion, a bonfire consumed the crowns and scepters of royalty while a cloud of three thousand white doves rose into the sky. This was all part of preaching the "moral order of the Republic . . . that will make us a people of brothers, a people of philosophers."

De-Christianization. Some revolutionaries hoped the festival system would replace the Catholic church altogether. They initiated a campaign of **de-Christianization** that included closing churches (Protestant as well as Catholic), selling many church buildings to the highest bidder, and trying to force even those clergy who had taken the oath of loyalty to abandon their clerical vocations and marry. Great churches became storehouses for arms or grain, or their stones were sold off to contractors. The medieval statues of kings on the facade of Notre Dame cathedral were beheaded. Church bells were dismantled and church treasures melted down for government use.

In the ultimate step in de-Christianization, extremists tried to establish what they called the Cult of Reason to supplant Christianity. In Paris in the fall of 1793, a goddess of Liberty, played by an actress, presided over the Festival of Reason in Notre Dame cathedral. Local militants in other cities staged similar festivals, which alarmed deputies in the National Convention, who were wary of turning rural, devout populations against the republic. The Committee of Public Safety halted the de-Christianization campaign, and Robespierre, with David's help, tried to institute an alternative, the Cult of the Supreme Being, in June 1794. Robespierre objected to the de-Christianization campaign's atheism; he favored a Rousseau-inspired deistic religion without the supposedly superstitious trappings of Catholicism. Neither cult attracted many followers, but both show the depth of the commitment to overturning the old order and all its traditional institutions.

Politicizing Daily Life. In principle the best way to ensure the future of the republic was through the education of the young. The deputy Georges-Jacques Danton (1759–1794), Robespierre's main competitor as theorist of the Revolution, maintained that "after bread, the first need of the people is education." The National Convention voted to make primary schooling free and compulsory for both boys and girls. It took control of education away from the Catholic church and tried to set up a system of state schools at both the primary and secondary levels, but it lacked trained teachers to replace those the Catholic religious orders provided. As a result, opportunities for learning how to read and write may have diminished. In 1799, only one-fifth as many boys enrolled in the state secondary schools as had studied in church schools ten years earlier.

Although many of the ambitious republican programs failed, almost all aspects of daily life became politicized, even colors. The tricolor—the combination of red, white, and blue that was to become the flag of France—was devised in July 1789, and by 1793 everyone had to wear a cockade (a badge made of ribbons) with the colors. Using the formal forms of speech—*vous* for "you"—or the title *monsieur* or *madame* might identify someone as an aristocrat; true patriots used the informal *tu* and *citoyen*♦ or *citoyenne* ("citizen") instead. Some people changed their names or gave their children new kinds of names. Biblical and saints' names such as Jean, Pierre, Joseph, and Marie gave way to names recalling heroes of the ancient Roman republic (Brutus, Gracchus, Cornelia), revolutionary heroes, or flowers and plants. Such changes symbolized adherence to the republic and to Enlightenment ideals rather than to Catholicism.

Even the measures of time and space were revolutionized. In October 1793, the National Convention introduced a new calendar to replace the Christian one. Its bases were reason and republican principles. Year I dated from the beginning of the republic on September 22, 1792. Twelve months of exactly thirty days each received new names

---

♦*citoyen:* sih twoy en

derived from nature—for example, Pluviôse♦ (roughly equivalent to February) recalled the rain (*la pluie*) of late winter. Instead of seven-day weeks, ten-day *décades* provided only one day of rest every ten days and pointedly eliminated the Sunday of the Christian calendar. The five days left at the end of the calendar year were devoted to special festivals called *sans-culottides*.♦ The calendar remained in force for twelve years despite continuing resistance to it. More enduring was the new metric system based on units of ten that was invented to replace the hundreds of local variations in weights and measures. Other countries in Europe and throughout the world eventually adopted the metric system.

Successive revolutionary legislatures had also changed the rules of family life. The state took responsibility for all family matters away from the Catholic church: birth, death, and marriage registration now happened at city hall, not the parish church. Marriage became a civil contract and as such could be broken and thereby nullified. The new divorce law of September 1792 was the most far-reaching in Europe: a couple could divorce by mutual consent or for reasons such as insanity, abandonment, battering, or criminal conviction. Thousands of men and women took advantage of the law to dissolve unhappy marriages, even though the pope had condemned the measure. (In 1816, the government revoked the right to divorce, and not until the 1970s did French divorce laws return to the principles of the 1792 legislation.) In one of its most influential actions, the National Convention passed a series of laws that created equal inheritance among all children in the family, including girls. The father's right to favor one child, especially the oldest male, was considered aristocratic and hence antirepublican.

Resisting the Revolution

By intruding into religion, culture, and daily life, the republic inevitably provoked resistance. Shouting curses against the republic, uprooting liberty trees, carrying statues of the Virgin Mary in procession, hiding a priest who would not take the oath, singing a royalist song—all these expressed dissent with the new symbols, rituals, and policies. Resistance also took more violent forms, from riots over food shortages or religious policies to assassination and full-scale civil war.

Women's Resistance. Many women, in particular, suffered from the hard conditions of life that persisted in this time of war, and they had their own ways of voicing discontent. Long bread lines in the cities exhausted the patience of women, and police spies reported their constant grumbling, which occasionally turned into spontaneous demonstrations or riots over high prices or food shortages. Women also took the lead in protesting against changes forced on the Catholic church; they organized their fellow parishioners to refuse to hear mass offered by the "constitutional" priests, and they protected the priests who would not sign the oath of loyalty.

Other forms of resistance were more individual. One young woman, Charlotte Corday, assassinated the outspoken deputy Jean-Paul Marat in July 1793. Corday fervently supported the Girondins, and she considered it her patriotic duty to kill the deputy who, in the columns of his paper, had constantly demanded more heads and more blood. Marat was immediately eulogized as a great martyr, and Corday went to the guillotine vilified as a monster but confident that she had "avenged many innocent victims."

Rebellion and Civil War. Organized resistance broke out in many parts of France. The arrest of the Girondin deputies in June 1793 sparked insurrections in several departments. After the government retook the city of Lyon, one of the centers of the revolt, the deputy on mission ordered sixteen hundred houses demolished. Special courts sentenced almost two thousand people to death. Thereafter, the name of the city was changed to Ville Affranchie♦ (Liberated Town).

♦**Pluviôse:** PLOO vee ohs
♦*sans-culottides:* sahn ku law TEED

♦**Ville Affranchie:** veel uh FRAHNSH ee

In the Vendée region of western France, resistance turned into full-scale civil war. Between March and December 1793, peasants, artisans, and weavers joined under noble leadership to form a "Catholic and Royal Army." One rebel group explained its motives: "They [the republicans] have killed our king, chased away our priests, sold the goods of our church, eaten everything we have and now they want to take our bodies [in the draft]." The uprising took two different forms: in the Vendée itself, a counterrevolutionary army organized to fight the republic; in nearby Brittany, resistance took the form of guerrilla bands, which united to attack a target and then quickly melted into the countryside. Great Britain provided money and underground contacts for these attacks, which were almost always aimed at towns. Town officials sold church lands, enforced measures against the clergy, and supervised conscription. In many ways this was a civil war between town and country, for the townspeople were the ones who supported the Revolution and bought church lands for themselves. The peasants had gained most of what they wanted in 1789 with the abolition of seigneurial dues, and they resented the government's demands for money and manpower and actions taken against their local clergy.

For several months in 1793, the Vendée rebels stormed the largest towns in the region. Both sides committed horrible atrocities. At the small town of Machecoul, for example, the rebels massacred five hundred republicans, including administrators and National Guard members; many were tied together, shoved into freshly dug graves, and shot. By the fall, however, republican soldiers had turned back the rebels. A republican general wrote to the Committee of Public Safety claiming, "There is no more Vendée, citizens, it has perished under our free sword along with its women and children. . . . Fol-

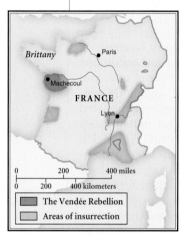

The Vendée Rebellion, 1793

lowing the orders that you gave me I have crushed children under the feet of horses, massacred women who at least . . . will engender no more brigands."

"Infernal columns" of republican troops marched through the region to restore control, military courts ordered thousands executed, and republican soldiers massacred thousands of others. In one especially gruesome incident, the deputy Jean-Baptiste Carrier supervised the drowning of some two thousand Vendée rebels, including a number of priests. Barges loaded with prisoners were floated into the Loire River near Nantes and then sunk. Controversy still rages about the rebellion's death toll. Estimates of rebel deaths alone range from about 20,000 to 250,000 and higher. Many thousands of republican soldiers and civilians also lost their lives. Even the low estimates reveal the carnage of this catastrophic confrontation between the republic and its opponents.

The Fall of Robespierre and the End of the Terror, 1794–1799

In an atmosphere of fear of conspiracy that these outbreaks fueled, Robespierre tried simultaneously to exert the National Convention's control over popular political activities and to weed out opposition among the deputies. As a result, the Terror intensified until July 1794, when a group of deputies joined within the Convention to order the arrest and execution of Robespierre and his followers. The Convention then ordered elections and drew up a new republican constitution that gave executive power to five directors. This "Directory government" maintained power during four years of seesaw battles between royalists and former Jacobins. Ultimately it gave way to Napoleon Bonaparte.

The Revolution Devours Its Own. In the fall of 1793, the National Convention cracked down on popular clubs and societies. First to be suppressed were women's political clubs. Founded in early 1793, the Society of Revolutionary Republican Women played a very active part in sans-culottes politics. The society urged harsher measures against the republic's enemies and insisted that women have a voice in politics even if they did not have the vote. Women had set up their own clubs in many provincial towns and also attended the meetings of local men's organizations. The closing of women's clubs marked an important turning point in the Revolution. From then on the sans-culottes and their political organizations came increasingly under the thumb of the Jacobin deputies in the National Convention.

The National Convention abolished women's political clubs in order to limit agitation in the streets. As one deputy stated, women's clubs consisted of "adventuresses, knights-errant, emancipated women, amazons." The deputies called on biological arguments about natural differences between the sexes to bolster their case. As one argued, "Women are ill suited for elevated thoughts and serious meditations." In subsequent years physicians, priests, and philosophers amplified such opinions by formulating explanations for women's "natural" differences from men to justify their inferior status.

In the spring of 1794, the Committee of Public Safety moved against its critics among leaders in Paris and deputies in the National Convention itself. First a handful of "ultrarevolutionaries"—in fact a motley collection of local Parisian politicians—were arrested and executed. Next came the other side, the "indulgents," so called because they favored a moderation of the Terror. Included among them was the deputy Danton, himself once a member of the Committee of Public Safety and a friend of Robespierre, despite the striking contrast in their personalities. Danton was the Revolution's most flamboyant orator and, unlike Robespierre, a high-living, high-spending, excitable politician. At every critical turning point in national politics, his booming voice had swayed opinion in the National Convention. Now, under government pressure, the Revolutionary Tribunal convicted him and his friends of treason and sentenced them to death.

With the arrest and execution of these leaders in Paris, the prophecies of doom for the Revolution seemed about to be realized. "The Revolution," as one of the Girondin victims of 1793 had remarked, "was devouring its own children." Even after the major threats to the Committee of Public Safety's power had been eliminated, the Terror continued and even worsened. A law passed in June 1794 denied the accused the right of legal counsel, reduced the number of jurors necessary for conviction, and allowed only two judgments: acquittal or death. The category of political crimes expanded to include "slandering patriotism" and "seeking to inspire discouragement." Ordinary people risked the guillotine if they expressed any discontent. The rate of executions in Paris rose from five a day in the spring of 1794 to twenty-six a day in the summer. The political atmosphere darkened even though the military situation improved. At the end of June, the French armies decisively defeated the main Austrian army and advanced through the Austrian Netherlands to Brussels and Antwerp. The emergency measures for fighting the war were working, yet Robespierre and his inner circle had made so many enemies that they could not afford to loosen the grip of the Terror.

The Terror hardly touched many parts of France, but overall the experience was undeniably traumatic. Across the country the official Terror cost the lives of at least forty thousand French people, most of them living in the regions of major insurrections or near the borders with foreign enemies, where suspicion of collaboration ran high. As many as 300,000 people—one out of every fifty French people—went to prison as suspects between March 1793 and August 1794. The toll for the aristocracy and the clergy was especially high. Many leading nobles perished under the guillotine, and thousands emigrated. Thirty thousand to forty thousand clergy who refused the oath emigrated, at least two thousand (including many nuns) were executed, and thousands were imprisoned. The clergy were singled out in particular in the civil war zones: 135 priests were massacred at Lyon in November 1793, and 83 were shot in one day during the Vendée revolt. Yet many victims of the Terror were peasants or ordinary working people.

The final crisis of the Terror came in July 1794. Conflicts within the Committee of Public Safety and the National Convention left Robespierre isolated. On July 27, 1794 (the ninth of Thermidor, Year II, according to the revolutionary calendar), Robespierre appeared before the Convention with yet another list of deputies to be arrested. Many feared they would be named, and they shouted him down and ordered him arrested along with his followers on the committee, the president of the Revolutionary Tribunal in Paris, and the commander of the Parisian National Guard. An armed uprising led by the Paris city government failed to save Robespierre when most of the National Guard took the side of the Convention. Robespierre tried to kill himself with a pistol but only broke his jaw. The next day he and scores of followers went to the guillotine.

The Thermidorian Reaction and the Directory, 1794–1799. The men who led the attack on Robespierre in Thermidor (July 1794) did not intend to reverse all his policies, but that happened nonetheless because of a violent backlash known as the **Thermidorian Reaction**. As most of the instruments of terror were dismantled, newspapers attacked the Robespierrists as "tigers thirsting for human blood." The new government released hundreds of suspects and arranged a temporary truce in the Vendée. It purged Jacobins from local bodies and replaced them with their opponents. It arrested some of the most notorious "terrorists" in the National Convention, such as Carrier, and put them to death. Within the year the new leaders abolished the Revolutionary Tribunal and closed the Jacobin Club in Paris. Popular demonstrations met severe repression. In southeastern France, in particular, the "White Terror" replaced the Jacobins' "Red Terror." Former officials and local Jacobin leaders were harassed, beaten, and often murdered by paramilitary bands who had tacit support from the new authorities. Those who remained in the National Convention prepared yet another constitution in 1795, setting up a two-house legislature and an executive body—the Directory, headed by five directors.

The Directory regime tenuously held on to power for four years, all the while trying to fend off challenges from the remaining Jacobins and the resurgent royalists. The puritanical atmosphere of the Terror gave way to the pursuit of pleasure—low-cut dresses of transparent materials, the reappearance of prostitutes in the streets, fancy dinner parties, and "victims' balls" where guests wore red ribbons around their necks as reminders of the guillotine. Bands of young men dressed in knee breeches and rich fabrics picked fights with known Jacobins and disrupted theater performances with loud antirevolutionary songs. All over France people banded together and petitioned to reopen churches closed during the Terror. If necessary they broke into a church to hold services with a priest who had been in hiding or a lay schoolteacher who was willing to say Mass.

Although the Terror had ended, the revolution had not. In 1794, the most democratic and most repressive phases of the Revolution both ended at once. Between 1795 and 1799, the republic endured in France, but it directed a war effort abroad that would ultimately bring to power the man who would dismantle the republic itself.

> **Review:** What factors can explain the Terror? To what extent was it simply a response to a national emergency or a reflection of deeper problems within the French Revolution?

❖ Revolution on the March

Beginning in 1792, war raged almost constantly until 1815. At one time or another, and sometimes all at once, France faced every principal power in Europe. The French republic—and later the French Empire under its supreme commander, Emperor Napoleon Bonaparte—proved an even more formidable opponent than the France of Louis XIV. New means of mobilizing and organizing soldiers enabled the French to dominate Europe for a generation. The influence of the Revolution as a political model and the threat of French military conquest combined to challenge the traditional order in Europe.

Arms and Conquests

The powers allied against France squandered their best chance to triumph in early 1793, when the French armies verged on chaos because of the emigration of noble army officers and the problems of integrating new draftees. By the end of 1793, once the new national draft had gone into effect, the French had a huge and powerful fighting force of 700,000 men. But the army still faced many problems in the field. As many as a third of the recent draftees deserted before or during battle. Uniforms fashioned out of rough cloth constricted movements, tore easily, and retained the damp of muddy battlefields, exposing the soldiers to the elements and the spread of disease. At times the soldiers were fed only moldy bread, and if their pay was late, they sometimes resorted to pillaging and looting. Generals might pay with their lives if they lost a key battle and their loyalty to the Revolution came under suspicion.

France nevertheless had one overwhelming advantage: its soldiers, drawn largely from the peasantry and the lower classes of the cities, fought for a revolution that they and their brothers and sisters had helped make. The republic was their government, and the army was in large measure theirs too; many officers had risen through the ranks by skill and talent rather than by inheriting or purchasing their positions. One young peasant boy wrote to his parents, "Either you will see me return bathed in glory, or you will have a son who is a worthy citizen of France who knows how to die for the defense of his country."

When the French armies invaded the Austrian Netherlands and crossed the Rhine in the summer of 1794, they proclaimed a war of liberation. But as they annexed more and more territory, "liberated" people in many

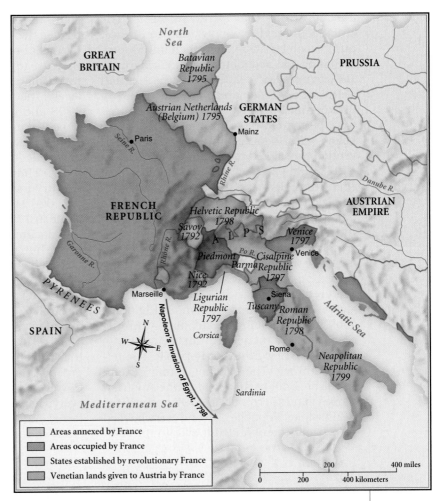

MAP 20.3 French Expansion, 1791–1799
The influence of the French Revolution on neighboring territories is dramatically evident in this map. The French directly annexed the papal territories in southern France in 1791, Nice and Savoy in 1792, and the Austrian Netherlands in 1795. They set up a series of sister republics in the former Dutch Republic and in various Italian states. Local people did not always welcome these changes. For example, the French made the Dutch pay a huge war indemnity, support a French occupying army of 25,000 soldiers, and give up some southern territories. One of the generals who invaded the Dutch Republic wrote, "Holland has done nothing to avoid being classed among the general order of our conquests. . . . It follows from this that there can be no reason to treat her any differently from a conquered country." The sister republics faced a future of subordination to French national interests.

places began to view them as an army of occupation (Map 20.3). Middle-class people near the northern and eastern borders of France reacted most positively to the French invasion. In the Austrian Netherlands, Mainz, Savoy, and Nice, French officers organized

Jacobin Clubs that attracted locals. The clubs petitioned for annexation to France, and French legislation was then introduced, including the abolition of seigneurial dues. Despite resistance, especially in the Austrian Netherlands, these areas remained part of France until 1815, and the legal changes were permanent. Like Louis XIV a century before, most deputies in the National Convention considered the territories annexed in 1794 within France's "natural frontiers"—the Rhine, the Alps, and the Pyrenees.

The Directory government that came to power in 1795 was torn between defending the new frontiers and launching a more aggressive policy of creating semi-independent "sister republics" wherever the armies succeeded. Aggression won out. When Prussia declared neutrality in 1795, the French armies swarmed into the Dutch Republic, abolished the stadholderate, and—with the revolutionary penchant for renaming—created the new Batavian Republic, a satellite of France. The brilliant young general Napoleon Bonaparte defeated the Austrian armies in northern Italy in 1797 and created the Cisalpine Republic. Next he overwhelmed Venice and then handed it over to the Aus-

trians in exchange for a peace agreement that lasted less than two years. After the French attacked the Swiss cantons in 1798, they set up the Helvetic Republic and curtailed many of the Catholic church's privileges. They conquered the Papal States in 1798 and installed a Roman Republic; the pope fled to Siena.

The revolutionary wars had an immediate impact on European life at all levels of society. Thousands of men died in every country involved, with perhaps as many as 200,000 casualties in the French armies alone in 1794 and 1795. No accurate statistics documenting casualties in these wars exist, but we do know that more soldiers died in hospitals as a result of their wounds than on the battlefields. Constant warfare hampered world commerce and especially disrupted French overseas shipping. (The abolition of slavery in the French colonies in 1794 also cut off one lucrative market for the French port cities.) In contrast to the prosperous times that preceded the French Revolution, times were now hard almost everywhere, because the dislocations of internal and external commerce provoked constant shortages.

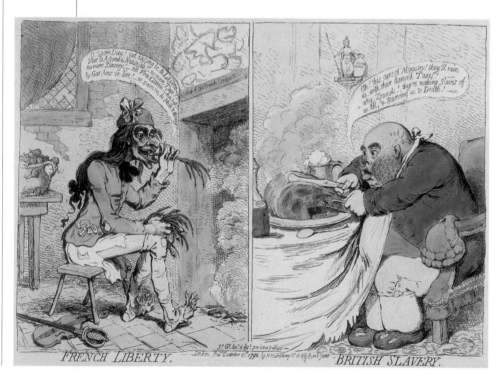

FRENCH LIBERTY.   BRITISH SLAVERY.

The English Rebuttal In this caricature, James Gillray satirizes the French version of liberty. Gillray, a supporter of the Tories in Britain, produced thousands of political caricatures. How would you interpret the message of this print? *British Museum.*

European Reactions to Revolutionary Change

The French Revolution profoundly transformed European politics and social relations. (See "Contrasting Views," page 774.) In 1789, many had greeted events with unabashed enthusiasm. The English Unitarian minister Richard Price had exulted, "Behold, the light . . . after setting AMERICA free, reflected to FRANCE, and there kindled into a blaze that lays despotism in ashes, and warms and illuminates EUROPE." Democrats and reformers from many countries flooded to Paris to witness events firsthand. Supporters of the French Revolution in Great Britain, like the earlier reformers of the 1760s and 1770s, joined constitutional and reform societies that sprang up in many cities. The most important of these societies, the London Corresponding Society, founded in 1792, corresponded with the Paris Jacobin Club and served as a center for reform agitation in England. Pro-French feeling ran even stronger in Ireland. Catholics and Presbyterians, both excluded from the vote, came together in 1791 in the Society of United Irishmen, which eventually pressed for secession from England.

European elites became alarmed when the French abolished monarchy and nobility and encouraged popular participation in politics. The British government, for example, quickly suppressed the corresponding societies and harassed their leaders, charging that their ideas and their contacts with the French were seditious (see the illustration opposite for a negative English view). When the Society of United Irishmen timed a rebellion to coincide with an attempted French invasion in 1798, the British mercilessly repressed them, killing thirty thousand rebels. Twice as many regular British troops (seventy thousand) as fought in any of the major continental battles were required to put down the rebellion.

Those countries near France with a substantial middle class and access to newspapers and other publications generally sympathized the most with French ideas. Yet even countries close to France sometimes fiercely resisted French occupation, often in the form of banditry. Because the French offered the

Jews religious toleration and civil and political rights wherever they conquered, anti-French groups sometimes attacked Jews. One German traveler reported, "It is characteristic of the region in which the bandits are based that these two nations [the French and the Jews] are hated. So crimes against them are motivated not just by a wish to rob them but also by a variety of fanaticism which is partly political and partly religious."

Many leading intellectuals in the German states, including the philosopher Immanuel Kant, initially supported the revolutionary cause, but after 1793 most of them turned against the popular violence and military aggressiveness of the Revolution. One of the greatest writers of the age, Friedrich Schiller (1759–1805), typified the turn in sentiment against revolutionary politics:

Freedom is only in the realm of dreams
And the beautiful blooms only in song.

The German states, still run by many separate rulers, experienced a profound artistic and intellectual revival, which eventually connected with anti-French nationalism. This renaissance included a resurgence of intellectual life in the universities, a thriving press (1,225 journals were launched in the 1780s alone), and the multiplication of Masonic lodges and literary clubs.

Not surprisingly, the areas farthest from France—Russia, the Ottoman Empire, the Balkans, Austria, Hungary, and the Scandinavian states—were generally least affected by the French Revolution. One exception was the United States, where opinion fiercely divided on the virtues of the French Revolution. Sweden was a second exception. Gustavus III (r. 1771–1792) was assassinated in Stockholm by a nobleman who claimed that "the king has violated his oath . . . and declared himself an enemy of the realm." The king's murder changed little in Sweden's power structure, however; his son Gustavus IV (r. 1792–1809) was convinced that the French Jacobins had sanctioned his father's assassination, and he insisted on avoiding "licentious liberty." Even though it was just across the border, Spain's royal government suppressed all news from France, fearing that it might ignite the spirit

Consequences of the French Revolution

Contemporaries instantly grasped the cataclysmic significance of the French Revolution and began to argue about its lessons for their own countries. A member of the British Parliament, Edmund Burke, ignited a firestorm of controversy with his Reflections on the Revolution in France *(Document 1). He condemned the French revolutionaries for attempting to build a government on abstract reasoning rather than taking historical traditions and customs into account; his book provided a foundation for the doctrine known as conservatism, which argued for "conserving" the traditional foundations of society and avoiding the pitfalls of radical or revolutionary change. Burke's views provoked a strong response from the English political agitator Thomas Paine. Paine's pamphlet* Common Sense *(1776) helped inspire the British North American colonies to demand independence from Great Britain. In* The Rights of Man *(Document 2), written fifteen years later, Paine attacked the traditional order as fundamentally unjust and defended the idea of a revolution to uphold rights. Joseph de Maistre, an aristocratic opponent of both the Enlightenment and the French Revolution, put the conservative attack on the French Revolution into a deeply religious and absolutist framework (Document 3). In contrast, Anne-Louise-Germaine de Staël, an opponent of Napoleon and one of the most influential intellectuals of the early nineteenth century, took the view that the violence of the Revolution had been the product of generations of superstition and arbitrary rule, that is, rule by an absolutist Catholic church and monarchical government (Document 4).*

1. EDMUND BURKE, *REFLECTIONS ON THE REVOLUTION IN FRANCE* (1790)

Born in Ireland and a supporter of the American colonists in their opposition to the British Parliament, Edmund Burke (1729–1797) opposed the French Revolution. He argued the case for tradition, continuity, and gradual reform based on practical experience— what he called "a sure principle of conservation."

Can I now congratulate the same nation [France] upon its freedom? Is it because liberty in the abstract may be classed amongst the blessings of mankind, that I am seriously to felicitate a madman, who has escaped from the protecting restraint and wholesome darkness of his cell, on his restoration to the enjoyment of light and liberty? Am I to congratulate an highwayman and murderer, who has broke prison, upon the recovery of his natural rights? . . .

Government is not made in virtue of natural rights, which may and do exist in total independence of it; and exist in much greater clearness, and in a much greater degree of abstract perfection: but their abstract perfection is their practical defect. By having a right to every thing they want every thing. . . . The science of constructing a commonwealth, or renovating it, or reforming it, is, like every other experimental science, not to be taught *a priori* [based on theory rather than on experience]. Nor is it a short experience that can instruct us in that practical science; because the real effects of moral causes are not always immediate; but that which in the first instance is prejudicial may be excellent in its remoter operation; and its excellence may arise even from the ill effects it produces in the beginning. . . .

In the groves of *their* academy, at the end of every visto [vista], you see nothing but the gallows. Nothing is left which engages the affections on the part of the commonwealth. . . . To make us love our country, our country ought to be lovely.

Source: Two Classics of the French Revolution: Reflections on the Revolution in France *(Edmund Burke) and* The Rights of Man *(Thomas Paine) (New York: Doubleday Anchor Books, 1973), 19, 71–74, 90–91.*

2. THOMAS PAINE, *THE RIGHTS OF MAN* (1791)

In his reply to Burke, The Rights of Man, *which sold 200,000 copies in two years, Thomas Paine (1737–1809) defended the idea of reform based on reason, advocated a concept of universal human rights, and attacked the excesses of privilege and tradition in Great Britain. Elected as a deputy to the French National Convention in 1793 in recognition of his writings in favor of the French Revolution, Paine narrowly escaped condemnation as an associate of the Girondins.*

Before anything can be reasoned upon to a conclusion, certain facts, principles, or data, to reason from, must be established, admitted, or denied. Mr. Burke, with his usual outrage, abuses the *Declaration of the Rights of Man*, published by the National Assembly of France, as the basis on which the Constitution of France is built. This he calls "paltry and blurred sheets of paper about the rights of man."

Does Mr. Burke mean to deny that *man* has any rights? If he does, then he must mean that there are no such things as rights any where, and that he has none himself; for who is there in the world but man? . . .

Hitherto we have spoken only (and that but in part) of the natural rights of man. We have now to consider the civil rights of man, and to show how the one originates from the other. Man did not enter into society to become *worse* than he was before, nor to have fewer rights than he had before, but to have those rights better secured. His natural rights are the foundation of all his civil rights. . . .

A constitution is not a thing in name only, but in fact. It has not an ideal, but a real existence; and wherever it cannot be produced in a visible form, there is none. A constitution is a thing *antecedent* to a government, and a government is only the creature of a constitution. The constitution of a country is not the act of its government, but of the people constituting a government. . . .

Can then Mr. Burke produce the English Constitution? If he cannot, we may fairly conclude, that though it has been so much talked about, no such thing as a constitution exists, or ever did exist, and consequently that the people have yet a constitution to form.

Source: *Two Classics of the French Revolution*: Reflections on the Revolution in France (*Edmund Burke*) *and* The Rights of Man (*Thomas Paine*) (New York: Doubleday Anchor Books, 1973), 302, 305–306, 309.

3. JOSEPH DE MAISTRE, *CONSIDERATIONS ON FRANCE* (1797)

An aristocrat born in Savoy, Joseph de Maistre (1753–1821) believed in reform but he passionately opposed both the Enlightenment and the French Revolution as destructive to good order. He believed that Protestants, Jews, lawyers, journalists, and scientists all threatened the social order because they questioned the need for absolute obedience to authority in matters both religious and political. De Maistre set the foundations for reactionary conservatism, a conservatism that defended throne and altar.

This consideration especially makes me think that the French Revolution is a great epoch and that its consequences, in all kinds of ways, will be felt far beyond the time of its explosion and the limits of its birthplace. . . .

There is a satanic quality to the French Revolution that distinguishes it from everything we have ever seen or anything we are ever likely to see in the future. Recall the great assemblies, Robespierre's speech against the priesthood, the solemn apostasy [renunciation of vows] of the clergy, the desecration of objects of worship, the installation of the goddess of reason, and that multitude of extraordinary actions by which the provinces sought to outdo Paris. All this goes beyond the ordinary circle of crime and seems to belong to another world.

Source: Joseph de Maistre, *Considerations on France*, trans. Richard A. Lebrun (Cambridge: Cambridge University Press, 1994), 21, 41.

4. ANNE-LOUISE-GERMAINE DE STAËL, *CONSIDERATIONS ON THE MAIN EVENTS OF THE FRENCH REVOLUTION* (1818)

De Staël published her views long after the Revolution was over, but she had lived through the events herself. She was the daughter of Jacques Necker, Louis XVI's Swiss Protestant finance minister. Necker's dismissal in July 1789 had sparked the attack on the Bastille. De Staël published novels, literary tracts, and memoirs and became one of the

(Continued)

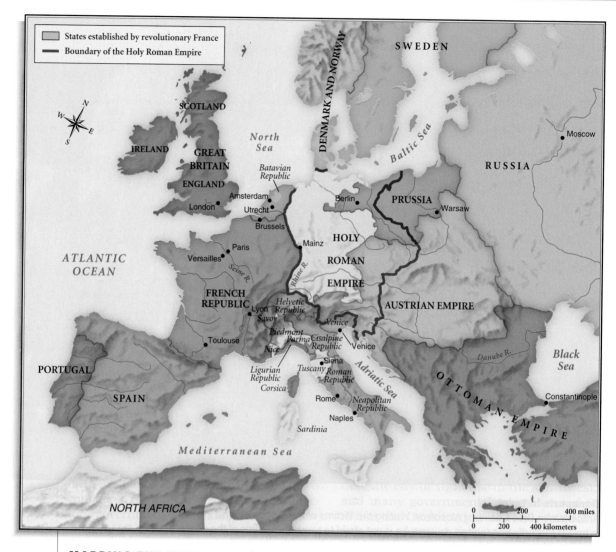

MAPPING THE WEST Europe in 1800

France's expansion during the revolutionary wars threatened to upset the balance of power in Europe. A century earlier the English and Dutch had allied and formed a Europe-wide coalition to check the territorial ambitions of Louis XIV. Thwarting French ambitions after 1800 would prove to be even more of a challenge to the other European powers. The Dutch had been reduced to satellite status, as had most of the Italian states. After 1800, even Austria and Prussia would suffer devastating losses to the French on the battlefield. Only a new coalition of European powers could stop France in the future.

ashes of the republic, and the French armies would recover from their reverses of 1799 to push the frontiers of French influence even farther eastward.

Review: Why did some groups outside of France embrace the French Revolution while others resisted it?

Conclusion

In 1799, no one knew what course Napoleon Bonaparte would follow. Everyone sensed, however, that the political landscape in Europe had been permanently altered by the revolutionary cataclysm. Between 1789 and 1799, monarchy as a form of government had given way to a republic whose leaders were elected. Aristocracy based on rank and birth had been undermined in favor of civil equality and the promotion of merit. The people who marched in demonstrations, met in clubs, and, in the case of men, voted in national elections for the first time had insisted that government respond to them. Thousands of men had held elective office. A revolutionary government had tried to teach new values with a refashioned calendar, state festivals, and a civic religion. Its example would inspire future revolutionaries.

But the French Revolution also had its darker side. The divisions created by the Revolution within France endured in many cases until after World War II. Even now, French public-opinion surveys ask if it was right to execute the king in 1793 (most believe Louis XVI was guilty of treason but should not have been executed). The revolutionaries proclaimed human rights and democratic government as a universal goal, but they also explicitly excluded women, even though they admitted Protestant, Jewish, and eventually black men. They used the new spirit of national pride to inspire armies that conquered other peoples. Their ideals of universal education, religious toleration, and democratic participation could not prevent the institution of new forms of government terror to persecute, imprison, and kill dissidents. These paradoxes created an opening for Napoleon Bonaparte, who rushed in with his remarkable military and political skills to push France—and with it all of Europe—in new directions.

Suggested References

The Revolutionary Wave, 1787–1789

In the 1950s and 1960s, historians debated vehemently about whether the French Revolution should be considered part of a more general phenomenon of Atlantic revolutions, as R. R. Palmer argues. The most influential book on the meaning of the French Revolution is still the classic study by Tocqueville, who insisted that the Revolution continued the process of state centralization undertaken by the monarchy.

*Censer, Jack R., and Lynn Hunt. *Liberty, Equality, Fraternity: Exploring the French Revolution.* 2001. (Includes a CD-ROM with images, songs, and documents.) See also the accompanying Web site: http://www.chnm.gmu.edu/revolution.

Lefebvre, Georges. *The Coming of the French Revolution.* Trans. with a new preface, R. R. Palmer. 1989.

Palmer, R. R. *The Age of the Democratic Revolution: A Political History of Europe and America, 1760–1800.* Vol. 2, *The Struggle.* 1964.

Polasky, Janet L. *Revolution in Brussels, 1787–1793.* 1987.

Te Brake, Wayne. *Regents and Rebels: The Revolutionary World of an Eighteenth-Century Dutch City.* 1989.

Tocqueville, Alexis de. *The Old Regime and the French Revolution.* Trans. Stuart Gilbert. 1955. Originally published 1856.

From Monarchy to Republic, 1789–1793

From 1789 onward, commentators on the French Revolution have differed over its meaning: Was it a revolution for human rights and democracy or a dangerous experiment in implementing reason and destroying religion and tradition? Among the most important additions to the debate have been new works on women, Jews, Protestants, and slaves.

*Hunt, Lynn, ed. *The French Revolution and Human Rights: A Brief Documentary History.* 1996.

*Levy, Darline Gay, Harriet Branson Applewhite, and Mary Durham Johnson, eds. *Women in Revolutionary Paris, 1789–1795.* 1979.

Schama, Simon. *Citizens: A Chronicle of the French Revolution.* 1989.

Schechter, Ronald. *The French Revolution: The Essential Readings.* 2001.

Two Classics of the French Revolution: Reflections on the Revolution in France (Edmund Burke) and The Rights of Man (Thomas Paine). 1973.

*Wollstonecraft, Mary. *A Vindication of the Rights of Woman.* Ed. Miriam Brody. 1992.

Terror and Resistance

The most controversial episode in the French Revolution has not surprisingly provoked con-

*Primary source.

flicting interpretations. Soboul offers the Marxist interpretation, which Furet specifically opposes. Very recently interest has shifted from these broader interpretive issues back to the principal actors themselves: Robespierre, the Jacobins, and women's clubs have all attracted scholarly attention.

Desan, Suzanne. *Reclaiming the Sacred: Lay Religion and Popular Politics in Revolutionary France.* 1990.

Furet, François. *Interpreting the French Revolution.* Trans. Elborg Forster. 1981.

Godineau, Dominique. *The Women of Paris and Their French Revolution.* Trans. Katherine Streip. 1998.

Haydon, Colin, and William Doyle, eds. *Robespierre.* 1999.

Hunt, Lynn. *Politics, Culture, and Class in the French Revolution.* 1984.

Palmer, R. R. *Twelve Who Ruled: The Year of the Terror in the French Revolution.* 1989.

Soboul, Albert. *The Sans-Culottes: The Popular Movement and Revolutionary Government, 1793–1794.* Trans. Remy Inglis Hall. 1980.

Revolution on the March

In the past, controversy about the Revolution in France raged while its influence on other places was relatively neglected. This imbalance is now being redressed in studies of the colonies and the impact of the revolutionary wars on areas from Egypt to Ireland.

Beaucour, Fernand Emile, Yves Laissus, and Chantal Orgogozo. *The Discovery of Egypt.* Trans. Bambi Ballard. 1990.

Blackburn, Robin. *The Overthrow of Colonial Slavery, 1776–1848.* 1988.

Blanning, T. C. W. *The French Revolutionary Wars, 1787–1802.* 1996.

Elliot, Marianne. *Partners in Revolution: The United Irishmen and France.* 1982.

Forrest, Alan I. *The Soldiers of the French Revolution.* 1990.

Geggus, David Patrick. *Haitian Revolutionary Studies.* 2002.

Irish rebellion of 1798: http://www.bbc.co.uk/history/timelines/ni/rebellion_1798.shtml.

Moiret, Joseph-Marie, ed. *Memoirs of Napoleon's Egyptian Expedition, 1798–1801.* Trans. Rosemary Brindle. 2001.

CHAPTER REVIEW

IMPORTANT EVENTS

1787 Dutch Patriot revolt is stifled by Prussian invasion

1788 Beginning of resistance of Austrian Netherlands against reforms of Joseph II; opening of reform parliament in Poland

1789 French Revolution begins

1790 Internal divisions lead to collapse of resistance in Austrian Netherlands

1791 Beginning of slave revolt in St. Domingue (Haiti)

1792 Beginning of war between France and the rest of Europe; second revolution of August 10 overthrows monarchy

1793 Second Partition of Poland by Austria and Russia; Louis XVI of France executed for treason

1794 Abolition of slavery in French colonies; Robespierre's government by terror falls

1795 Third (final) Partition of Poland; France annexes the Austrian Netherlands

1797–1798 Creation of "sister republics" in Italian states and Switzerland

1799 Napoleon Bonaparte comes to power in a coup that effectively ends the French Revolution

KEY TERMS

Atlantic revolutions (749)

de-Christianization (766)

Declaration of the Rights of Man and Citizen (757)

Estates General (753)

First Consul (781)

Great Fear (757)

Jacobin Club (761)

sans-culottes (761)

Terror (763)

Thermidorian Reaction (770)

REVIEW QUESTIONS

1. In what ways did the beginning of the French Revolution resemble the other revolutions of 1787–1789?

2. Why did the French Revolution turn in an increasingly radical direction after 1789?

3. What factors can explain the Terror? To what extent was it simply a response to a national emergency or a reflection of deeper problems within the French Revolution?

4. Why did some groups outside of France embrace the French Revolution while others resisted it?

MAKING CONNECTIONS

1. Should the French Revolution be viewed as the origin of democracy or the origin of totalitarianism (a government in which no dissent is allowed)? Explain.

2. Why did the other rulers of Europe find the French Revolution so threatening?

FOR FURTHER EXPLORATION

To assess your mastery of the material in this chapter, see the Online Study Guide at **bedfordstmartins.com/hunt**.

To read additional primary-source material from this period, see Chapter 20 in *Sources of The Making of the West*, Second Edition.

BONAPARTE

DAVID·L·AN·IX

Napoleon and the Revolutionary Legacy, 1800–1830

IN HER NOVEL *FRANKENSTEIN* (1818), the prototype for modern thrillers, Mary Shelley tells the story of a Swiss technological genius who creates a humanlike monster in his pursuit of scientific knowledge. The monster, "so scaring and unearthly in his ugliness," terrifies all who encounter him and ends by destroying Dr. Frankenstein's own loved ones. Despite desperate chases across deserts and frozen landscapes, Frankenstein never manages to trap the monster, who is last seen hunched over his creator's deathbed.

Frankenstein's monster can be taken as a particularly horrifying incarnation of the fears of the postrevolutionary era, but just what did Shelley intend? Did the monster represent the French Revolution, which had devoured its own children in the Terror? Shelley was the daughter of Mary Wollstonecraft, an English feminist who had defended the French Revolution and died in childbirth when Mary was born. Did the monster stand for the dangerous possibilities that might be unleashed by science and industry in the new age of industrial growth? Mary Shelley was also the wife of the romantic poet Percy Bysshe Shelley, who often wrote against the ugliness of contemporary life and celebrated nature and the "beautiful idealisms of moral excellence." Whatever the meaning—and Mary Shelley may well have intended more than one—*Frankenstein* makes the forceful point that humans cannot always control their own creations. The Enlightenment and the French Revolution had celebrated the virtues of human creativity, but Shelley shows that innovation often has a dark and uncontrollable side.

Those who witnessed Napoleon Bonaparte's stunning rise to European dominance after 1800 might have cast him as either Frankenstein or his monster. Like the scientist Frankenstein, Bonaparte created something dramatically new: the French Empire with himself as emperor. Like the former kings of France, he ruled under

Napoleon as Military Hero
In this painting from 1800–1801, *Napoleon Crossing the Alps at St. Bernard*, Jacques-Louis David reminds the French of Napoleon's heroic military exploits. Napoleon is a picture of calm and composure while his horse shows the fright and energy of the moment. David painted this propagandistic image shortly after one of his former students went to the guillotine on a trumped-up charge of plotting to assassinate the new French leader. The former organizer of republican festivals during the Terror had become a kind of court painter for the new regime. © *Photo RMN-Daniel Arraudet.*

his first name. This Corsican artillery officer who spoke French with an Italian accent ended the French Revolution even while maintaining some of its most important innovations. Bonaparte transformed France from a democratically elected republic to an empire with a new aristocracy based on military service. But he kept the revolutionary administration and most of its laws that ensured equal treatment of all citizens. Although he tolerated no opposition at home, he prided himself on bringing French-style changes to peoples elsewhere.

Bonaparte continued the revolutionary policy of conquest and annexation until it reached grotesque dimensions. His foreign policies made many see him as a monster hungry for dominion; he turned the sister republics of the revolutionary era into kingdoms personally ruled by his relatives, and he exacted tribute from subject peoples wherever he triumphed. Eventually resistance to the French armies and the ever-mounting costs of military glory toppled Napoleon. The powers allied against him met and agreed to restore the monarchical governments that had been overthrown by the French, shrink France back to its pre-revolutionary boundaries, and maintain this settlement against future demands for change.

Although the people of Europe longed for peace and stability in the aftermath of the Napoleonic whirlwind, they lived in a world that was deeply unsettled by two parallel revolutions: the Industrial Revolution and the French Revolution. The Industrial Revolution spread from Great Britain to the continent in the early 1800s in the form of factories and railroads. Even those who resisted the impact of the French Revolution with its Napoleonic sequel had to confront the underlying changes in social and economic structures that resulted from industrialization. These changes inevitably reinforced the legacy of the French Revolution, which included equality before the law, religious toleration, and, eventually, nationalism.

Profoundly affected by French military occupation, many peoples organized to demand ethnic and cultural autonomy, first from Napoleon and then from the restored governments after 1815. Alongside nationalism, other new ideologies such as liberalism and socialism emerged under the impact of the Industrial and French Revolutions. These offered their adherents a doctrine that explained social change and advocated political transformation. In 1830, the development of liberalism, socialism, and nationalism shocked Europe with a new round of revolutions in France, Belgium, Poland, and some of the Italian states. By then the spread of industry, the growing awareness of social problems, and aspirations for national self-determination had reinvigorated the force of the revolutionary legacy.

❖ Napoleon's Authoritarian State

When Napoleon Bonaparte came to power in 1799, his coup d'état appeared to be just the latest in a long line of upheavals in revolutionary France. Within the year, how-

◆ **1799** Coup against Directory; Napoleon named First Consul

◆ **1801** Napoleon signs concordat with pope

◆ **1804** Napoleon crowned emperor; issues new civil code

1800	1805	1810

◆ **1805** Battle of Trafalgar; battle of Austerlitz

◆ **1812** Napoleon invades Russia

◆ **1814–1815** Congress of Vienna

ever, he had effectively ended the French Revolution and set France on a new course toward an authoritarian state. As emperor after 1804, he dreamed of European integration in the tradition of Augustus and Charlemagne, but he also mastered the details of practical administration. To achieve his goals, he compromised with the Catholic church and with exiled aristocrats willing to return to France. His most enduring accomplishment, the new Civil Code, tempered the principles of the Enlightenment and the Revolution with an insistence on the powers of fathers over children, husbands over wives, and employers over workers. His influence spread into many spheres as he personally patronized scientific inquiry and encouraged artistic styles in line with his vision of imperial greatness.

From Republic to Empire

Napoleon had no long-range plans to establish himself as emperor and conquer most of Europe. The deputies of the legislature who engineered the coup d'état of November 1799 picked him as one of three provisional **consuls** (the title drew on the ancient Roman precedent) only because he was a famous general. Napoleon immediately asserted his leadership over the other two consuls in the process of drafting another constitution—the fourth since 1789 and the third for the republic established in 1792.

The End of the Republic. The constitution of 1799 made Napoleon the First Consul with the right to pick the Council of State,

which drew up all laws. He quickly exerted control by choosing men loyal to him. Government was no longer representative in any real sense: the new constitution eliminated direct elections for deputies and granted no independent powers to the three houses of the legislature. Napoleon and his advisers chose the legislature's members out of a small pool of "notables." Almost all men over twenty-one could vote in the plebiscite (referendum) to approve the constitution, but their only option was to choose Yes or No.

Napoleon's most urgent task was to reconcile to his regime Catholics who had been alienated by revolutionary policies. Although nominally Catholic, Napoleon held no deep religious convictions. "How can there be order in the state without religion?" he asked cynically. "When a man is dying of hunger beside another who is stuffing himself, he cannot accept this difference if there is not an authority who tells him: 'God wishes it so.'" In 1801, a concordat with Pope Pius VII (r. 1800–1823) ended a decade of church-state conflict. The pope validated all sales of church lands, and the government agreed to pay the salaries of bishops and priests who would swear loyalty to the state. Catholicism was officially recognized as the religion of "the great majority of French citizens." (The state also paid Protestant pastors' salaries.) The pope thus brought the huge French Catholic population back into the fold and Napoleon gained the pope's support for his regime.

Napoleon continued the centralization of state power that had begun under the

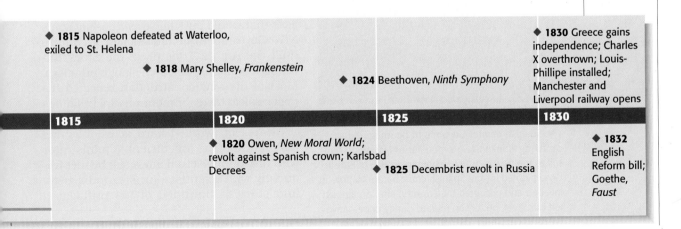

◆ **1815** Napoleon defeated at Waterloo, exiled to St. Helena

◆ **1818** Mary Shelley, *Frankenstein*

◆ **1824** Beethoven, *Ninth Symphony*

◆ **1830** Greece gains independence; Charles X overthrown; Louis-Phillipe installed; Manchester and Liverpool railway opens

| 1815 | 1820 | 1825 | 1830 |

◆ **1820** Owen, *New Moral World*; revolt against Spanish crown; Karlsbad Decrees

◆ **1825** Decembrist revolt in Russia

◆ **1832** English Reform bill; Goethe, *Faust*

absolutist monarchy of Louis XIV and resumed under the Terror. As First Consul he appointed prefects who directly supervised local affairs in every *département*, or region. He created the Bank of France to facilitate government borrowing and relied on gold and silver coinage rather than paper money. He made good use of budgets and improved tax collection, but he also frequently made ends meet by exacting tribute from the territories he conquered.

Napoleon promised order and an end to the upheavals of ten years of revolutionary turmoil, but his regime severely limited political expression. He never relied on mass executions to achieve control, but he refused to allow those who opposed him to meet in clubs, influence elections, or publish news-

Francisco de Goya, *The Colossus* (1808–1812)
The Spanish painter Goya might be imagined as capturing Frankenstein's monster or Napoleon himself as the new giant overwhelming much of Europe. Goya painted for the Spanish court before Napoleon invaded and occupied the country; after an illness left him deaf, he turned toward darkly imaginative works such as this one. *Museo del Prado, Madrid.*

papers. A decree reduced the number of newspapers in Paris from seventy-three to thirteen (and then finally to four), and the newspapers that remained became government organs. Government censors had to approve all operas and plays, and they banned "offensive" artistic works even more frequently than their royal predecessors had. The minister of police, Joseph Fouché, once a leading figure in the Terror of 1793–1794, could impose house arrest, arbitrary imprisonment, and surveillance of political dissidents. Political contest and debate shriveled to almost nothing. When a bomb attack on Napoleon's carriage failed in 1800, Fouché suppressed the evidence of a royalist plot and instead arrested hundreds of former Jacobins. More than one hundred of them were deported, and seven hundred imprisoned.

Napoleon feared the influence of fervent supporters of the republic more than that of supporters of the monarchy. In 1802, his intentions became clear: he planned to eliminate the republic. He named himself First Consul for life, and in 1804, with the pope's blessing, he crowned himself emperor. Once again, plebiscites approved his decisions, but no alternatives were offered.

Imperial Rule. Napoleon's charismatic personality dominated the new regime. His face and name adorned coins, engravings, histories, paintings, and public monuments. His favorite painters embellished his legend by depicting him as a warrior-hero of mythic proportions even though he was short and physically unimpressive in person. Believing that "what is big is always beautiful," Napoleon embarked on ostentatious building projects that would outshine even those of Louis XIV. Government-commissioned architects built the Arc de Triomphe,♦ the Stock Exchange, fountains, and even slaughterhouses. Most of his new construction reflected his neoclassical taste for monumental buildings set in vast empty spaces.

Napoleon worked hard at establishing his reputation as an efficient administrator with broad intellectual interests: he met frequently with scientists, jurists, and artists, and stories abounded of his unflagging

♦**Arc de Triomphe:** AHRK duh tre OHNF

Napoleon's Coronation as Emperor
In *The Coronation of Napoleon and Josephine* (1805–1807), Jacques-Louis David shows Napoleon crowning his wife at the ceremony of 1804. Napoleon orchestrated the entire event and took the only active role in it: Pope Pius VII gave his blessing to the ceremony (he can be seen seated behind Napoleon), but Napoleon crowned himself. What is the significance of Napoleon crowning himself? **For more help analyzing this image**, see the visual activity for this chapter in the Online Study Guide at **bedfordstmartins.com/hunt**. *Scala/Art Resource, NY.*

energy. When not on military campaigns, he worked on state affairs, usually until 10:00 P.M., taking only a few minutes for each meal. "Authority," declared his adviser Abbé Emmanuel-Joseph Sieyès, "must come from above and confidence from below." To establish his authority, Napoleon relied on men who had served with him in the army. His chief of staff Alexandre Berthier,♦ for example, became minister of war, and the chemist Claude Berthollet,♦ who had organized the scientific part of the expedition to Egypt, became vice president of the Senate in 1804. Napoleon's bureaucracy was based on a patron-client relationship, with Napoleon as the ultimate patron. Some of Napoleon's closest associates married into his family.

Combining aristocratic and revolutionary values in a new social hierarchy that rewarded merit and talent, Napoleon personally chose as senators the nation's most illustrious generals, ministers, prefects, scientists, rich men, and former nobles. Intending to replace both the old nobility of birth and the republic's strict emphasis on equality, in 1802 he took the first step toward creating a new nobility by founding a Legion of Honor. (Members of the legion received lifetime pensions along with their titles.) Napoleon usually equated honor with military success. By 1814, the legion had thirty-two thousand members, only 5 percent of them civilians.

In 1808, Napoleon introduced a complete hierarchy of noble titles, ranging from princes down to barons and chevaliers. All Napoleonic nobles had served the state. Titles could be inherited but had to be supported by wealth—a man could not be a duke without

---

♦**Berthier:** behr TYAY
♦**Berthollet:** behr taw leh

Medal of the Legion of Honor
"Men are led through baubles," Napoleon once remarked, but "a little cash does not hurt." He gave this medal to members of the Legion of Honor and added a small pension. Never missing an occasion to glorify his own image, Napoleon had his portrait installed in the center of the star and garland. © *Photo Musée de L'Armée, Paris.*

a fortune of 200,000 francs, or a chevalier without 3,000 francs. To go along with their new titles, Napoleon gave his favorite generals huge fortunes, often in the form of estates in the conquered territories.

Napoleon's own family reaped the greatest benefits. He made his older brother, Joseph, ruler of the newly established kingdom of Naples in 1806, the same year he installed his younger brother Louis as king of Holland. He proclaimed his twenty-three-year-old stepson Eugène de Beauharnais viceroy of Italy in 1805 and established his sister Caroline and brother-in-law General Joachim Murat as king and queen of Naples in 1808 when he moved Joseph to the throne of Spain. Napoleon wanted to establish an imperial succession, but he lacked an heir. In thirteen years of marriage, his wife Josephine had borne no children, so in 1809 he divorced her and in 1810 married the eighteen-year-old princess Marie-Louise of Austria. The next year she gave birth to a son, to whom Napoleon immediately gave the title king of Rome.

The New Paternalism: The Civil Code

Because Napoleon shared the rewards of rule with his own family, it is perhaps not surprising that he brought a paternalist model of power to his state. Previous governments had tried to unify and standardize France's multiple legal codes, but only Napoleon successfully established a new one, partly because he personally presided over the commission that drafted the new **Civil Code**,

completed in 1804. Called the Napoleonic Code as a way of further exalting his image, it defined and assured property rights, guaranteed religious liberty, and established a uniform system of law that provided equal treatment for all adult males and affirmed the right of men to choose their professions. It also reasserted the Old Regime's patriarchal system of male domination over women and insisted on a father's control over his children, which revolutionary legislation had limited. For example, if children under age sixteen refused to follow their fathers' commands, they could be sent to prison for up to a month with no hearing of any sort. At the same time, the code required fathers to provide for their children's welfare. Napoleon himself encouraged the foundation of private charities to help indigent mothers, and one of his decrees made it easier for women to abandon their children anonymously to a government foundling hospital. Napoleon hoped that such measures would discourage abortion and infanticide, especially among the poorest classes in the fast-growing urban areas.

The code sharply curtailed women's rights in almost every aspect of public and private life. Napoleon wanted to restrict women to the private sphere of the home. One of his leading jurists remarked, "There have been many discussions on the equality and superiority of the sexes. Nothing is more useless than such disputes. . . . Women need protection because they are weaker; men are free because they are stronger." The law obligated a husband to support his wife, but he alone controlled any property held in common; a wife could not sue in court, sell or mortgage her own property, or contract a debt without her husband's consent.

The Civil Code modified even those few revolutionary laws that had been favorable to women and in some instances denied women rights they had had under the monarchy. Divorce was still possible but severely restricted. Adultery was an acceptable grounds for divorce, but the law considered a wife's infidelity more reprehensible than a husband's. A wife could petition for divorce only if her husband brought his mistress to live in the family home. In contrast, a wife convicted of adultery could be imprisoned for up to two years. The code's framers saw these discrepancies as a way to reinforce the family and make women responsible for private virtue, while leaving public decisions to men. The French code was imitated in many European and Latin American countries and the French colony of Louisiana, where it had a similar negative effect on women's rights. Not until 1965 did French wives gain legal status equal to that of their husbands.

Napoleon took little interest in girls' education, believing that girls should spend most of their time at home learning religion, manners, and such "female occupations" as sewing and music. For boys, by contrast, the government set up a new system of lycées,♦ state-run secondary schools in which boys wore military uniforms and drumrolls signaled the beginning and end of classes. (Without the military trappings, the lycées are now coeducational and still the heart of the French educational system.)

The new paternalism extended to relations between employers and employees. The state required all workers to carry a work card attesting to their good conduct, and it prohibited all workers' organizations. The police considered workers without cards as vagrants or criminals and could send them to workhouses or prison. After 1806, arbitration boards settled labor disputes, but they took employers at their word while treating workers as minors, demanding that foremen and shop superintendents represent them. Occasionally strikes broke out, led by secret, illegal journeymen's associations, yet many employers laid off employees when times were hard, deducted fines from their wages, and dismissed them without appeal for being absent or making errors. These limitations on workers' rights won Napoleon the support of French business.

Patronage of Science and Intellectual Life

Napoleon did everything possible to promote French scientific inquiry, especially that which could serve practical ends. (See "Did You Know?," page 794.) He closely monitored the research institutes established during the Revolution, sometimes intervening personally to achieve political conformity. An impressive outpouring of new theoretical and practical scientific work rewarded the state's efforts. Experiments with balloons led to the discovery of laws about the expansion of gases, and research on fossil shells prepared the way for new theories of evolutionary change later in the nineteenth century. The surgeon Dominique-Jean Larrey developed new techniques of battlefield amputation and medical care during Napoleon's wars, winning an appointment as an officer in the Legion of Honor and becoming a baron with a pension.

Napoleon aimed to modernize French society through science, but he could not tolerate criticism. Napoleon considered most writers useless or dangerous, "good for nothing under any government." Some of the most talented French writers of the time had to live in exile. The best-known expatriate was Germaine de Staël♦ (1766–1817), known as Madame de Staël, the daughter of Louis XVI's chief minister Jacques Necker. When explaining his desire to banish her, Napoleon exclaimed, "She is a machine in motion who stirs up the salons." While exiled in the German states, Madame de Staël wrote a novel, *Corinne* (1807), whose heroine is a brilliant woman thwarted by a patriarchal system, and *On Germany* (1810), an account of the important new literary currents east of the Rhine. Her books were banned in France.

Although Napoleon restored the strong authority of state and religion in France, many royalists and Catholics still criticized him as an impious usurper. (See "Contrasting Views," page 796.) François-René de Chateaubriand (1768–1848) admired Napoleon as "the strong man who has saved us from the abyss," but he preferred monarchy. In his view, Napoleon

♦**lycées:** lee SAY

♦**Germaine de Staël:** zhehr mehn duh STAL

DID YOU KNOW?

How the Orient Became Oriental

Eugène Delacroix, *The Death of Sardanapalus* (1826–1827)
All of the exoticism, violence, and erotic imagery of the East are on view in this romantic painting that aims to recapture a moment in ancient history when the Assyrian king Sardanapalus first killed his harem before killing himself. Delacroix was presumably influenced by a play by Byron on the subject, though Delacroix's rendition is much less favorable to the king than Byron's.
© *Photo RMN/Herve Lewandowski.*

As a result of Napoleon's expedition to conquer Egypt in 1798, Europeans began to study systematically what they named the Orient (from *orins*, Latin for "rising sun"), meaning the lands east of Europe. Napoleon took with him 151 French scientific experts in everything from architecture to mineralogy. Their mission was to discover and record the natural and human history of Egypt. While some set up the Institute of Egypt in Cairo to conduct scientific experiments, others traveled with army units, collecting information and data on Egypt.

Of course, Europeans had visited the Middle East before, but they had never so rigorously studied its cultures. Although Napoleon's occupation of Egypt eventually failed, enthusiasm for so-called Orientalism spread far and wide; scholarly societies set up professorships and periodicals dedicated to Oriental studies, and before long romantic poets, novelists, and painters flocked to North Africa and the Middle East in search of new themes for their work.

Europeans viewed the Orient as exotic but also backward. In the introduction to the twenty-three-volume *Description of Egypt* published by French scholars of the Institute of Egypt between 1809 and 1828, Jean-Baptiste Fourier wrote, "Napoleon wanted to offer a useful European example to the Orient, and finally also to make the inhabitants' lives more pleasant, as well as to procure for them all the advantages of a perfect civilization." According to Fourier, "This country [Egypt], which has transmitted its knowledge to so many nations, today is plunged into barbarism." Civilization versus barbarism; advancement versus backwardness; science versus superstition: before long Europeans had set up a series of mutually reinforcing categories to distinguish their culture from that of the Orient. It is probably fair to say that Orientalism led to much new knowledge but also to many unpleasant stereotypes of non-Western peoples and cultures.

It is important to remember, moreover, that *West* and *East* are relative terms; they can be defined only in relation to each other. Americans sometimes call Japan, for instance, the Far East, following European usage, but it is closest to the western, not the eastern, half of the United States. For Japan, in fact, the United States is the "Far East."

Source: Edward W. Said, *Orientalism* (New York: Pantheon Books, 1978), quote from page 85.

Germaine de Staël
One of the most fascinating intellectuals of her time, Anne-Louise-Germaine de Staël seemed to irritate Napoleon more than any other person did. Daughter of Louis XVI's Swiss Protestant finance minister, Jacques Necker, and wife of a Swedish diplomat, Madame de Staël frequently criticized Napoleon's regime. She published best-selling novels and influential literary criticism, and whenever allowed to reside in Paris she encouraged the intellectual and political dissidents from Napoleon's regime. *Photographie Bulloz.*

had not properly understood the need to defend Christian values against the Enlightenment's excessive reliance on reason. Chateaubriand wrote his *Genius of Christianity* (1802) to draw attention to the power and mystery of faith. He warned, "It is to the vanity of knowledge that we owe almost all our misfortunes.... The learned ages have always been followed by ages of destruction."

> **Review:** In what ways did Napoleon continue the French Revolution; in what ways did he break with it?

❖ "Europe Was at My Feet": Napoleon's Conquests

Building on innovations introduced by the republican governments before him, Napoleon revolutionized the art of war with tactics and strategy based on a highly mobile army. By 1812, he ruled an empire more extensive than any since the time of ancient Rome (Map 21.1 on page 798). Yet that empire had already begun to crumble, and with it went Napoleon's power at home. Napoleon's empire failed because it was based on a contradiction: Napoleon tried to reduce virtually all of Europe to the status of colonial dependents when Europe had long consisted of independent states. The result, inevitably, was a great upsurge in nationalist feeling that has dominated European politics to the present.

The Grand Army and Its Victories, 1800–1807

Napoleon attributed his military success "three-quarters to morale" and the rest to leadership and superiority of numbers at the point of attack. Conscription provided the large numbers: 1.3 million men ages twenty to twenty-four were drafted between 1800 and 1812, another million in 1813–1814. So many willingly served because the republic had taught them to identify the army with the nation. Military service was both a patriotic duty and a means of social mobility. The men who rose through the ranks to become officers were young, ambitious, and accustomed to the new ways of war. Consequently, the French army had higher morale than the armies of other powers, most of which rejected conscription as too democratic and continued to restrict their officer corps to the nobility. Only in 1813–1814 did French morale plummet, as the military tide turned against Napoleon.

When Napoleon came to power in 1799, desertion was rampant, and the generals competed with one another for predominance. Napoleon ended this squabbling by uniting all the armies into one Grand Army under his personal command. By 1812, he commanded 700,000 troops; while 250,000 soldiers fought in Spain, others remained

CONTRASTING VIEWS

Napoleon: For and Against

After his final exile, Napoleon presented himself as a martyr to the cause of liberty whose goal was to create a European "federation of free people." Few were convinced by this "gospel according to St. Helena" (Document 1). Followers such as Emmanuel de Las Cases burnished the Napoleonic legend, but detractors such as Benjamin Constant viewed him as a tyrant (Document 2). For all his defects, Napoleon fascinated even those who were too young to understand his rise and fall. The French romantic poet Victor Hugo celebrated both the glory and the tragedy of Napoleonic ambitions (Document 3).

1. NAPOLEON'S OWN VIEW FROM EXILE

As might be expected, Napoleon put the most positive possible construction on his plans for France. In exile he wrote letters and talked at length to Emmanuel de Las Cases (1766–1842), an aristocratic officer in the royal navy who rallied to Napoleon in 1802, served in the Council of State, and later accompanied him to St. Helena. Much of what we know about Napoleon's views comes from a book published by Las Cases in 1821.

March 3, 1817:

In spite of all the libels, I have no fear whatever about my fame. Posterity will do me justice. The truth will be known; and the good I have done will be compared with the faults I have committed. I am not uneasy as to the result. Had I succeeded, I would have died with the reputation of the greatest man that ever existed. As it is, although I have failed, I shall be considered as an extraordinary man: my elevation was unparalleled, because unaccompanied by crime. I have fought fifty pitched battles, almost all of which I have won. I have framed and carried into effect a code of laws that will bear my name to the most distant posterity. I raised myself from nothing to be the most powerful monarch in the world. Europe was at my feet. I have always been of the opinion that the sovereignty lay in the people. In fact, the imperial government was a kind of republic. Called to the

head of it by the voice of the nation, my maxim was, *la carrière est ouverte aux talents* ["careers open to talent"] without distinction of birth or fortune, and this system of equality is the reason that your oligarchy hates me so much.

Source: R. M. Johnston, *The Corsican: A Diary of Napoleon's Life in His Own Words* (Boston: Houghton Mifflin, 1921), 492.

2. BENJAMIN CONSTANT, SPOKESMAN FOR THE LIBERAL OPPOSITION TO NAPOLEON

Benjamin Constant (1767–1830) came from an old French Calvinist family that had fled to Switzerland to escape persecution. Constant spent the early years of the French Revolution in a minor post at a minor German court. He moved to Paris in 1795 and became active in French politics during the Directory. Under Napoleon he went into exile, where he published a romantic novel, Adolphe (1806), and pamphlets like this one attacking Napoleon. He reconciled to Napoleon during the Hundred Days and then opposed the restored Bourbon monarchy. In this selection, written during his exile, he expresses his hostility to Napoleon as a usurper dependent on war to maintain himself in power.

Surely, Bonaparte is a thousand times more guilty than those barbarous conquerors who, ruling over barbarians, were by no means at odds with their age. Unlike them, he has chosen barbarism; he has preferred it. In the midst of enlightenment, he has sought to bring back the night. He has chosen to transform into greedy and bloodthirsty nomads a mild and polite people: his crime lies in this premeditated intention, in his obstinate effort to rob us of the heritage of all the enlightened generations who have preceded us on this earth. But why have we given him the right to conceive such a project?

When he first arrived here, alone, out of poverty and obscurity, and until he was twenty-four, his greedy gaze wandering over the country around him, why did we show him a country in which any religious idea was the object of irony?

[Constant refers here to de-Christianization during the French Revolution.] When he listened to what was professed in our circles, why did serious thinkers tell him that man had no other motivation than his own interest?...

Because immediate usurpation was easy, he believed it could be durable, and once he became a usurper, he did all that usurpation condemns a usurper to do in our century.

It was necessary to stifle inside the country all intellectual life: he banished discussion and proscribed the freedom of the press.

The nation might have been stunned by that silence: he provided, extorted or paid for acclamation which sounded like the national voice.... War flung onto distant shores that part of the French nation that still had some real energy. It prompted the police harassment of the timid, whom it could not force abroad. It struck terror into men's hearts, and left there a certain hope that chance would take responsibility for their deliverance: a hope agreeable to fear and convenient to inertia. How many times have I heard men who were pressed to resist tyranny postponing this, during wartime till the coming of peace, and in peacetime until war commences!

I am right therefore in claiming that a usurper's sole resource is uninterrupted war. Some object: what if Bonaparte had been pacific? Had he been pacific, he would never have lasted for twelve years. Peace would have re-established communication among the different countries of Europe. These communications would have restored to thought its means of expression. Works published abroad would have been smuggled into the country. The French would have seen that they did not enjoy the approval of the majority of Europe.

Source: Benjamin Constant, "Further Reflections on Usurpation," in *Political Writings*, trans. Biancamaria Fontana (Cambridge: Cambridge University Press, 1988), 161–63.

3. VICTOR HUGO, "THE TWO ISLANDS" (1825)

Victor Hugo (1802–1885) was France's greatest romantic poet and novelist, author of The Hunchback of Notre Dame *and* Les Misérables. *His father was a Napoleonic general, but his mother was an equally ardent royalist. In this early poem, Hugo compares Napoleon to one of Napoleon's favorite*

icons, the eagle, symbol of empire. The two islands of the title are Corsica, Napoleon's birthplace, and St. Helena, his place of final exile and death.

These Isles, where Ocean's shattered spray
Upon the ruthless rocks is cast,
Seem like two treacherous ships of prey,
Made by eternal anchors fast.
The hand that settled bleak and black
Those shores on their unpeopled rack,
And clad in fear and mystery,
Perchance thus made them tempest-torn,
That Bonaparte might there be born,
And that Napoleon there might die....
He his imperial nest hath built so far and high,
He seems to us to dwell within that tranquil sky,
Where you shall never see the angry tempest
    break.
'Tis but beneath his feet the growling storms
    are sped,
And thunders to assault his head
Must to their highest source go back.
The bolt flew upwards: from his eyrie [nest]
    riven,
Blazing he falls beneath the stroke of heaven;
Then kings their tyrant foe reward—
They chain him, living, on that lonely shore;
And earth captive giant handed o'er
To ocean's more resistless guard....
Shame, hate, misfortune, vengeance, curses
    sore,
On him let heaven and earth together pour:
Now, see we dashed the vast Colossus low.
May he forever rue, alive and dead,
All tears he caused mankind to shed,
And all the blood he caused to flow.

Source: Henry Carrington, *Translations from the Poems of Victor Hugo* (London: Walter Scott, 1885), 34–41.

QUESTIONS TO CONSIDER

1. Which of these views of Napoleon has the most lasting value as opposed to immediate dramatic effect?

2. According to these selections, what was Napoleon's greatest accomplishment? His greatest failure?

3. Victor Hugo called Napoleon "the vast Colossus." Why did he pick this larger-than-life metaphor even when writing lines critical of Napoleon's legacy of tears and bloodshed?

garrisoned in France. In any given battle, between 70,000 and 180,000 men, not all of them French, fought for France. Life on campaign was no picnic—ordinary soldiers slept in the rain, mud, and snow and often had to forage for food—but Napoleon nonetheless inspired almost fanatical loyalty. A brilliant strategist who carefully studied the demands of war, he outmaneuvered virtually all his opponents. He fought alongside his soldiers in some sixty battles and had nineteen horses shot from under him. One opponent said that Napoleon's presence alone was worth 50,000 men.

Napoleon had a pragmatic and direct approach to strategy: he went for the main body of the opposing army and tried to crush it in a lightning campaign. He gathered the largest possible army for one great and decisive battle and then followed with a relentless pursuit to break enemy morale altogether. His military command, like his domestic role, was personal and highly centralized. He essentially served as his own

MAP 21.1 Napoleon's Empire at Its Height, 1812
In 1812, Napoleon had at least nominal control of almost all of western Europe. Even before he made his fatal mistake of invading Russia, however, his authority had been undermined in Spain and seriously weakened in the Italian and German states. His efforts to extend French power sparked resistance almost everywhere: as Napoleon insisted on French domination, local people began to think of themselves as Italian, German, or Dutch. Thus Napoleon inadvertently laid the foundations for the nineteenth-century spread of nationalism.

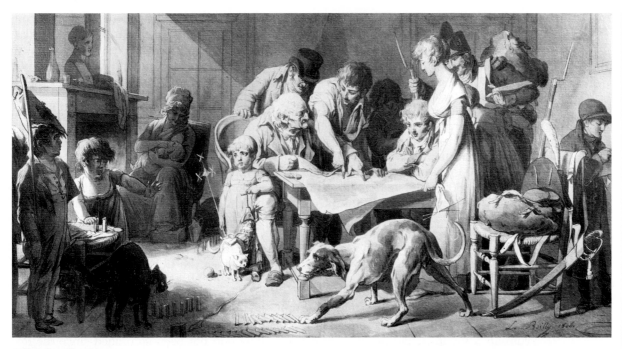

Following the Wars
Louis-Léopold Boilly's *Reading of the XIth and XIIth Bulletins of the Grand Army* shows ordinary people on the home front eagerly reading Napoleon's own bulletins of the army's progress.
Collection Privée/Photographic Bulloz.

operations officer: "I alone know what I have to do," he insisted. This style worked as long as Napoleon could be on the battlefield, but he failed to train independent subordinates to take over in his absence. He also faced constant difficulties in supplying a rapidly moving army, which could not always live off the land.

One of Napoleon's greatest advantages was the lack of coordination among his enemies. Britain dominated the seas but did not want to field huge land armies. On the continent, the French republic had already set up satellites in the Netherlands and Italy, which served as a buffer against the big powers to the east, Austria, Prussia, and Russia. By maneuvering diplomatically and militarily, Napoleon could usually take these on one by one. After reorganizing the French armies in 1799, for example, Napoleon won striking victories against the Austrians at Marengo and Hohenlinden♦ in 1800, forcing them to agree to peace terms. Once the Aus-

♦**Hohenlinden:** HOH uhn lihn duhn

trians had withdrawn, Britain agreed to the Treaty of Amiens in 1802, effectively ending hostilities on the continent. Napoleon considered the peace with Great Britain merely a truce, however, and it lasted only until 1803.

Napoleon used the breathing space not only to consolidate his position before taking up arms again but also to send an expeditionary force to St. Domingue to regain control of the island. Continuing resistance among the black population and an epidemic of yellow fever forced Napoleon to withdraw his troops from St. Domingue and abandon his plans to extend his empire to the Western Hemisphere. As part of his retreat, he sold the Louisiana Territory to the United States in 1803.

When war resumed in Europe, the British navy once more proved its superiority by

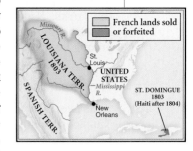

France's Retreat from America

blocking an attempted French invasion and by defeating the French and their Spanish allies in a huge naval battle at Trafalgar in 1805. France lost many ships; the British lost no vessels, but their renowned admiral Lord Horatio Nelson died in the battle. On land, Napoleon remained invincible. In 1805, Austria took up arms again when Napoleon demanded that it declare neutrality in the conflict with Britain. Napoleon promptly captured 25,000 Austrian soldiers at Ulm in Bavaria in 1805. After marching on to Vienna, he again trounced the Austrians, who had been joined by their new ally, Russia. The battle of Austerlitz,♦ often considered Napoleon's greatest victory, was fought on December 2, 1805, the first anniversary of his coronation.

After maintaining neutrality for a decade, Prussia now declared war on France. In 1806, the French promptly destroyed the Prussian army at Jena and Auerstadt.♦ In 1807, Napoleon defeated the Russians at Friedland. Personal negotiations between Napoleon and the young tsar Alexander I (r. 1801–1825) resulted in a humiliating settlement imposed on Prussia, which paid the price for temporary reconciliation between France and Russia; the Treaties of Tilsit turned Prussian lands west of the Elbe River into the kingdom of Westphalia♦ under Napoleon's brother Jerome, and Prussia's Polish provinces became the duchy of Warsaw. Alexander recognized Napoleon's conquests in central and western Europe and promised to help him against the British in exchange for Napoleon's support against the Turks. Neither party kept the bargain. Napoleon once again had turned the divisions among his enemies in his favor.

The Impact of French Victories

Wherever the Grand Army conquered, Napoleon's influence soon followed. By annexing some territories and setting up others as satellite kingdoms with much reduced autonomy, Napoleon attempted to colonize large parts of Europe (see Map 21.1 on page 798). But even where he did not rule directly or through his relatives, his startling string of victories forced the other powers to reconsider their own methods of rule.

Rule in the Colonized Territories. Napoleon brought the disparate German and Italian states together to rule them more effectively and to exploit their resources for his own ends. In 1803, he consolidated the tiny German states by abolishing some of them and attaching them to larger units. In July 1806, he established the Confederation of the Rhine, which soon included almost all the German states except Austria and Prussia. The Holy Roman Emperor gave up his title, held since the thirteenth century, and became simply the emperor of Austria. Napoleon established three units in Italy: the territories directly annexed to France and the satellite kingdoms of Italy and Naples. Italy had not been so unified since the Roman Empire.

Napoleon forced French-style reforms on both the annexed territories, which were ruled directly from France, and the satellite kingdoms, which were usually ruled by one or another of Napoleon's relatives but with a certain autonomy. French reforms included abolishing serfdom, eliminating seigneurial dues, introducing the Napoleonic Code, suppressing monasteries, and subordinating church to state, as well as extending civil rights to Jews and other religious minorities. The experience in the kingdom of Westphalia was typical of a French satellite. When Jerome Bonaparte and his wife, Catherine, arrived as king and queen in 1807, they relied on French experts who worked with a handpicked committee of Germans to write a constitution and install legal reforms. The Westphalian army had the first Jewish officers in the German states, and the army, administration, and judiciary were all opened to the middle classes. As time passed, however, the German subjects began to chafe under French rule. German officials enforced French decrees only halfheartedly, and the French army had to forbid its soldiers to frequent local taverns and shops because their presence often started fights.

As the example of Westphalia shows, reactions to Napoleonic innovations were mixed.

♦**Austerlitz:** AW stur lihts
♦**Auerstadt:** OW ur shteht
♦**Westphalia:** wehst FAYL yuh

Napoleon's chosen rulers often made real improvements in roads, public works, law codes, and education. The removal of internal tariffs fostered economic growth by opening up the domestic market for goods, especially textiles. By 1814, Bologna had five hundred factories and Modena four hundred. Yet almost everyone had some cause for complaint. Republicans regretted Napoleon's conversion of the sister republics into kingdoms after his coronation. Tax increases and everrising conscription quotas fomented discontent as well. The annexed territories and satellite kingdoms paid half of the French war expenses.

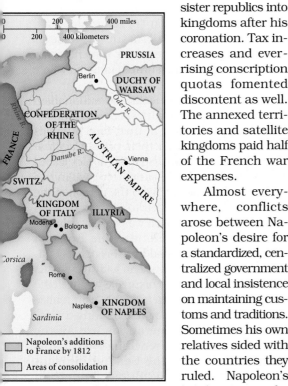

Consolidation of German and Italian States, 1812

Almost everywhere, conflicts arose between Napoleon's desire for a standardized, centralized government and local insistence on maintaining customs and traditions. Sometimes his own relatives sided with the countries they ruled. Napoleon's brother Louis, for instance, would not allow conscription in the Netherlands because the Dutch had never had compulsory military service. When Napoleon tried to introduce an economic policy banning trade with Great Britain, Louis's lax enforcement prompted the frustrated emperor to complain that "Holland [the leading province in the Netherlands] is an English province." In 1810, Napoleon annexed the satellite kingdom because his brother had become too sympathetic to Dutch interests.

Pressure for Reform in Prussia and Russia.
Napoleon's victories forced defeated rulers to rethink their political and cultural assumptions. After the crushing defeat of Prussia in 1806 left his country much reduced in terri-

tory, Frederick William III (r. 1797–1840) appointed a reform commission, and on its recommendation he abolished serfdom and allowed nonnobles to buy and enclose land. Peasants gained their personal independence from their noble landlords, who could no longer sell them to pay gambling debts, for example, or refuse them permission to marry. Yet the lives of the former serfs remained bleak; they were left without land and their landlords no longer had to care for them in hard times. The king's advisers also overhauled the army to make the high command more efficient and to open the way to the appointment of middle-class officers. Prussia instituted these reforms to try to compete with the French, not to promote democracy. As one reformer wrote to Frederick William, "We must do from above what the French have done from below."

Reform received lip service in Russia. Tsar Alexander I had gained his throne after an aristocratic coup deposed and killed his autocratic and capricious father, Paul (r. 1796–1801), and in the early years of his reign the remorseful young ruler created Western-style ministries, lifted restrictions on importing foreign books, and founded six new universities; reform commissions studied abuses; nobles were encouraged voluntarily to free their serfs (a few actually did so); and there was even talk of drafting a constitution. But none of these efforts reached beneath the surface of Russian life, and by the second decade of his reign Alexander began to reject the Enlightenment spirit that his grandmother Catherine the Great had instilled in him.

The Continental System. The one power always standing between Napoleon and total dominance of Europe was Great Britain. The British ruled the seas and financed anyone who would oppose Napoleon. In an effort to bankrupt this "nation of shopkeepers" by choking its trade, Napoleon inaugurated the **Continental System** in 1806. It prohibited all commerce between Great Britain and France, as well as between Great Britain and France's dependent states and allies. At first the system worked: British exports dropped by 20 percent in 1807–1808, and industrial production declined by 10 percent;

unemployment and a strike of 60,000 workers in northern England resulted. The British retaliated by confiscating merchandise on ships, even those of powers neutral in the wars, that sailed to or from ports from which the British were excluded by the Continental System.

In the midst of continuing wars, moreover, the system proved impossible to enforce, and widespread smuggling brought British goods into the European market. British industrial growth continued, despite some setbacks; calico-printing works, for example, quadrupled their production, and imports of raw cotton increased by 40 percent. At the same time, French and other continental industries benefited from the temporary protection from British competition.

Resistance to French Rule, 1807–1812. Smuggling British goods was only one way of opposing the French. Almost everywhere in Europe, resistance began as local opposition to French demands for money or draftees, but it eventually prompted a more nationalistic patriotic defense. In southern Italy, gangs of bandits harassed the French army and local officials; 33,000 Italian bandits were arrested in 1809 alone. But resistance continued via a network of secret societies, called the *carbonari* ("charcoalburners"), which got its name from the practice of marking each new member's forehead with a charcoal mark. Throughout the nineteenth century the carbonari played a leading role in Italian nationalism. In the German states, intellectuals wrote passionate defenses of the virtues of the German nation and of the superiority of German literature.

The Spanish War for Independence, 1807–1813

No nations bucked under Napoleon's reins more than Spain and Portugal. In 1807, Napoleon sent 100,000 troops through Spain to invade Portugal, Great Britain's ally. The royal family fled to the Portuguese colony of Brazil, but fighting continued, aided by a British army. When Napoleon got his brother Joseph named king of Spain in place of the senile Charles IV (r. 1788–1808), the Spanish clergy and nobles raised bands of peasants to fight the French occupiers. Even Napoleon's taking personal command of the French forces failed to quell the Spanish, who for six years fought a war of national independence that pinned down thousands of French soldiers. Germaine de Staël commented that Napoleon "never understood that a war might be a crusade. . . . He never reckoned with the one power that no arms could overcome—the enthusiasm of a whole people."

More than a new feeling of nationalism was aroused in Spain. Peasants hated French requisitioning of their food supplies and sought to defend their priests against French anticlericalism. Spanish nobles feared revolutionary reforms and were willing to defend the old monarchy in the person of the young Ferdinand VII, heir to Charles IV, even while Ferdinand himself was congratulating Napoleon on his victories. The Spanish Catholic church spread anti-French propaganda that equated Napoleon with heresy. As the former archbishop of Seville wrote to the archbishop of Granada in 1808, "You realize that we must not recognize as king a freemason, heretic, Lutheran, as are all the Bonapartes and the French nation." In this tense atmosphere, the Spanish peasant rebels, assisted by the British, countered every French massacre with atrocities of their own. They tortured their French prisoners (boiling one general alive) and lynched collaborators.

From Russian Winter to Final Defeat, 1812–1815

Despite opposition, Napoleon ruled over an extensive empire by 1812. He controlled more territory than any European ruler had since Roman times. Only two major European states remained fully independent—Great Britain and Russia—but once allied they would successfully challenge his dominion and draw many other states to their side. Britain sent aid to the Portuguese and Spanish rebels, while Russia once again prepared for war. Tsar Alexander I made peace with

Napoleon's Mamelukes Massacre the Spanish
In one of the paintings he produced to criticize Napoleon's occupation of Spain, *Second of May 1808 at the Puerta del Sol* (1814), Goya depicts the brutal suppression of the Spanish revolt in Madrid against Napoleon. Napoleon used Mamelukes, Egyptian soldiers descended from freed Turkish slaves. Why would the portrayal of these foreign mercenaries make the event seem even more horrifying to Spanish and European viewers? *Museo del Prado, Madrid.*

Turkey and allied himself with Great Britain and Sweden. In 1812, Napoleon invaded Russia with 250,000 horses and 600,000 men, including contingents of Italians, Poles, Swiss, Dutch, and Germans. This daring move proved to be his undoing.

Invasion of Russia, 1812. Napoleon followed his usual strategy of trying to strike quickly, but the Russian generals avoided confrontation and retreated eastward, destroying anything that might be useful to the invaders (see "An Ordinary Soldier on Campaign with Napoleon" on page 804). In September, on the road to Moscow, Napoleon finally engaged the main Russian force in the gigantic battle of Borodino (see Map 21.1 on page 798). French casualties were 30,000 men, including 47 generals; the Russians lost 45,000. The French soldiers had nothing

to celebrate around their campfires: as one soldier wrote, "Everyone...wept for some dead friend." Once again the Russians retreated, leaving Moscow undefended. Napoleon entered the deserted city, but the victory turned hollow because the departing Russians had set the wooden city on fire. Within a week, three-fourths of it had burned to the ground. Still Alexander refused to negotiate, and French morale plunged with worsening problems of supply. Weeks of constant marching in the dirt and heat had worn down the foot soldiers, who were dying of disease or deserting in large numbers.

In October Napoleon began his retreat; in November came the cold. Napoleon himself reported that on November 14 the temperature fell to 24 degrees Fahrenheit. A German soldier in the Grand Army described trying to cook fistfuls of raw bran with snow to make

Congress of Vienna
An unknown French engraver caricatured the efforts of the diplomats at the Congress of Vienna, complaining that they used the occasion to divide the spoils of European territory. At the far left is Metternich preparing to take Venice and Lombardy (northern Italy). What elements in this engraving make it a caricature? *Historisches Museum der Stadt Wien.*

status of smaller states. The revolutionary and Napoleonic wars had produced a host of potentially divisive issues. In addition to determining the boundaries of France, the congress had to decide the fate of Napoleon's duchy of Warsaw, the German province of Saxony, the Netherlands, the states once part of the confederation of the Rhine, and various Italian territories. All had either changed hands or been created during the wars. These issues were resolved by face-to-face negotiations among representatives of the five major powers: Austria, Russia, Prussia, Britain, and France. With its aim to establish a long-lasting, negotiated peace endorsed by all parties, both winners and losers, the Congress of Vienna provided a model for the twentieth-century League of Nations and United Nations.

Austria's chief negotiator, Prince Klemens von Metternich♦ (1773–1859), took the lead in devising the settlement. A well-educated

♦**Klemens von Metternich:** KLAY mehnts fawn MEH tur nihk

nobleman who spoke five languages, Metternich served as a minister in the Austrian cabinet from 1809 to 1848. More than anyone else, he shaped the post-Napoleonic order. Although his penchant for womanizing made him a security risk in the eyes of the British Foreign Office (he even had an affair with Napoleon's younger sister), he worked with the British prime minister Robert Castlereagh (1769–1822) to ensure a moderate agreement that would check French aggression and yet maintain France's great-power status. Metternich and Castlereagh believed that French aggression must be contained because it had threatened the European peace since the days of Louis XIV but also that France must remain a major player precisely so that no one European power might dominate the others. In this way France could help Austria and Britain counter the ambitions of Prussia and Russia. Castlereagh hoped to make Britain the arbiter of European affairs, but he knew this could be accomplished only through adroit diplomacy because the British constitutional monarchy had little in common with most of its more absolutist continental counterparts.

The task of ensuring France's status at the congress fell to Prince Charles Maurice de Talleyrand (1754–1838), an aristocrat and former bishop who had embraced the French Revolution, served as Napoleon's foreign minister, and ended as foreign minister to Louis XVIII after helping to arrange the emperor's overthrow. Informed of Talleyrand's betrayal, Napoleon called him "excrement in silk stockings." When the French army failed to oppose Napoleon's return to power in the Hundred Days, the allies took away all territory conquered since 1790 and required France to pay an indemnity and support an army of occupation until it had paid. Talleyrand nonetheless successfully argued that the restored French monarchy could succeed only if it retained its great-power status and participated fully in the negotiations. The goal of the congress was to achieve postwar stability by establishing secure states with guaranteed borders (Map 21.2). Because the congress aimed to "restore" as many regimes as possible to their former rulers, this epoch is

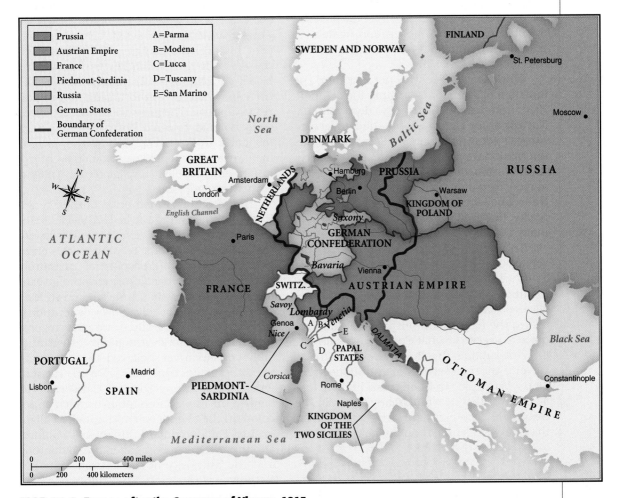

MAP 21.2 Europe after the Congress of Vienna, 1815
The Congress of Vienna forced France to return to its 1789 borders. The Austrian Netherlands and the Dutch Republic were united in a new kingdom of the Netherlands, the German states were joined in a Germanic Confederation that built upon Napoleon's Confederation of the Rhine, and Napoleon's Grand Duchy of Warsaw became the kingdom of Poland with the tsar of Russia as king. To compensate for its losses in Poland, Prussia gained territory in Saxony and on the left bank of the Rhine. Austria reclaimed the Italian provinces of Lombardy and Venetia and the Dalmatian coast.

sometimes labeled the **restoration**. Some of the returning rulers so detested French innovations that they tore French plants out of their gardens and threw French furniture out of their palaces. But simple restoration was not always feasible, and in those cases the congress rearranged territory to balance the competing interests of the great powers. Thus the congress turned the duchy of Warsaw into a new Polish kingdom but made the tsar of Russia its king. (Poland would not regain its independence until 1918.) The former Dutch Republic and the Austrian Netherlands, both annexed to France, now united as the new kingdom of the Netherlands under the restored stadholder. Austria now presided over the German Confederation, which replaced the defunct Holy Roman Empire and also included Prussia.

The lesser powers were not forgotten. The kingdom of Piedmont-Sardinia took Genoa, Nice, and part of Savoy. Sweden obtained Norway from Denmark but had to accept Russia's conquest of Finland. Finally, various international trade issues were also resolved. At the urging of Great Britain, the congress agreed to condemn in principle the slave trade, abolished by Great Britain in 1807. In reality, however, the slave trade continued in many places until the 1840s.

To impart spiritual substance to this very calculated settlement of political affairs, Tsar Alexander proposed a Holy Alliance calling upon divine assistance in upholding religion, peace, and justice. Prussia and Austria signed the agreement, but Great Britain refused to accede to what Castlereagh called "a piece of sublime mysticism and nonsense." Despite the reassertion of traditional religious principle, the congress had in fact given birth to a new diplomatic order: in the future, the legitimacy of states depended on the treaty system, not on divine right.

The Emergence of Conservatism

The French Revolution and Napoleonic domination of Europe had shown contemporaries that government could be changed overnight, that the old hierarchies could be overthrown in the name of reason, and that even Christianity could be written off or at least profoundly altered with the stroke of a pen. The potential for rapid change raised many questions about the proper sources of authority. Kings and churches could be restored and former revolutionaries locked up or silenced, but the old order no longer commanded automatic obedience. The old order was now merely *old*, no longer "natural" and "timeless." It had been ousted once and therefore might fall again. People insisted on having reasons to believe in their "restored" governments. The political doctrine that justified the restoration was **conservatism**.

Conservatives benefited from the disillusionment that permeated Europe after 1815. In the eyes of most Europeans, Napoleon had become a tyrant who ruled in his own interests. Conservatives saw a logical progression in recent history: the Enlightenment based on reason led to the French Revolution, with its bloody guillotine and horrifying Terror, which in turn spawned the authoritarian and militaristic Napoleon. Therefore, those who espoused conservatism rejected both the Enlightenment and the French Revolution. They favored monarchies over republics, tradition over revolution, and established religion over Enlightenment skepticism.

The original British critic of the French Revolution, Edmund Burke (1729–1799), inspired many of the conservatives that followed. He had argued that the revolutionaries erred in thinking they could construct an entirely new government based on reason. Government, Burke said, had to be rooted in long experience, which evolved over generations. All change must be gradual and must respect national and historical traditions. Like Burke, later conservatives believed that religious and other major traditions were an essential foundation for any society. Conservatives blamed the French Revolution's attack on religion on the skepticism and anticlericalism of such Enlightenment thinkers as Voltaire, and they defended both hereditary monarchy and the authority of the church, whether Catholic or Protestant. The "rights of man," according to conservatives, could not stand alone as doctrine based simply on nature and reason. The community too had its rights, more important than those of any individual, and established institutions best represented those rights. The church, the state, and the patriarchal family would provide an enduring social order for everyone. Faith, sentiment, history, and tradition must fill the vacuum left by the failures of reason and excessive belief in individual rights. Across Europe these views were taken up and elaborated by government advisers, professors, and writers. Not surprisingly, they had their strongest appeal in ruling circles and guided the politics of men such as Metternich in Austria and Alexander I in Russia.

The restored monarchy in France provided a major test for conservatism because the returning Bourbons had to confront the legacy of twenty-five years of upheaval. Louis XVIII tried to ensure a measure of continuity by maintaining Napoleon's Civil Code. He also guaranteed the rights of ownership to church lands sold during the revolutionary period and created a parliament composed of a Chamber of Peers nominated by the king and a Chamber of Deputies elected by very restricted suffrage (fewer than 100,000 voters in a population of 30 million, or about 3 percent). In making these concessions, the king tried to follow a moderate course of compromise, but the Ultras (ultraroyalists) pushed for complete repudiation of the revolutionary past. When Louis returned to power after Napoleon's final defeat, armed royalist bands attacked and murdered hundreds of Bonapartists and former revolutionaries. In 1816, the Ultras insisted on abolishing divorce and set up special courts to punish opponents of the regime. When an assassin killed Louis XVIII's nephew in 1820, the Ultras demanded even more extreme measures.

The Revival of Religion

The experience of revolutionary upheaval and nearly constant warfare prompted many to renew their religious faith once peace returned. In France, the Catholic church sent missionaries to hold open-air "ceremonies of reparation" to express repentance for the outrages of revolution. In Rome, the papacy reestablished the Jesuit order, which had been disbanded during the Enlightenment. In the Italian states and Spain, governments used religious societies of laypeople to combat the influence of reformers and nationalists such as the Italian carbonari.

Revivalist movements, especially in Protestant countries, could on occasion challenge the status quo rather than supporting it. In parts of Protestant Germany and Britain, religious revival had begun in the eighteenth century with the rise of Pietism and Methodism, movements that stressed individual religious experience rather than reason as the true path to moral and social reform. The English Methodists followed John Wesley (1703–1791), who had preached an emotional, morally austere, and very personal "method" of gaining salvation. The Methodists, or Wesleyans, gradually separated from the Church of England and in the early decades of the nineteenth century attracted thousands of members in huge revival meetings that lasted for days.

Shopkeepers, artisans, agricultural laborers, miners, and workers in cottage industry, both male and female, flocked to the new denomination, even though at first Methodism seemed to emphasize conservative political views: Methodist statutes of 1792 had insisted that "none of us shall either in writing or in conversation speak lightly or irreverently of the government." In their hostility to rigid doctrine and elaborate ritual and their encouragement of popular preaching, however, the Methodists fostered a sense of democratic community and even a rudimentary sexual equality. From the beginning, women preachers traveled on horseback to preach in barns, town halls, and textile dye houses. The Methodist Sunday schools that taught thousands of poor children to read and write eventually helped create greater demands for working-class political participation.

The religious revival was not limited to Europe. In the United States, the second Great Awakening began around 1790 with huge camp meetings that brought together thousands of worshipers and scores of evangelical preachers, many of them Methodist. (The original Great Awakening took place in the 1730s and 1740s, sparked by the preaching of George Whitefield, a young English evangelist and follower of John Wesley.) Men and women danced to exhaustion, fell into trances, and spoke in tongues. During this period, Protestant sects began systematic missionary activity in other parts of the world, with British and American missionary societies taking the lead in the 1790s and early 1800s. In the British colony of India, for example, Protestant missionaries argued for the reform of Hindu customs. *Sati*◆—the burning of widows on the funeral pyres of their husbands—was abolished by the British administration of India in 1829. Missionary activity by Protestants and Catholics would become one of the arms of European imperialism and cultural influence in the nineteenth century.

Review: To what extent was the old order restored by the Congress of Vienna?

❖ Forces for Social and Cultural Change

Conservatives hoped to clamp a lid on European affairs, but the lid kept threatening to fly off. Rapid urban growth and the spread of industry created new social tensions and inspired new political doctrines to explain the meaning of economic and social changes. These doctrines soon galvanized opponents of the conservative Vienna settlement. Both cutting across and drawing on the turmoil in society and politics was romanticism, a new international movement in the arts and literature that originated in reaction to the Enlightenment in the eighteenth century and dominated artistic expression in the first half of the nineteenth.

Industrial and Urban Growth in Britain

Historians today use the term *Industrial Revolution* to describe the set of changes that brought steam-driven machinery, large factories, and a new working class first to Britain, then to the rest of Europe, and eventually to the rest of the world. French and English writers of the 1820s introduced the term to capture the drama of contemporary change and to draw a parallel with the French Revolution. But we should not take the comparison too literally. Unlike the

◆*sati:* suh TEE

French upheaval, the Industrial Revolution was not over in a decade. From Great Britain in the second half of the eighteenth century it spread slowly; even by the 1830s it had little effect on the continent outside of northern France, Belgium, and the Rhineland. Most Europeans were still peasants working in the old ways.

Factories and Workers. Steam-driven machines first brought workers together in factories in the textile industry. By 1830, more than a million people in Britain depended on the cotton industry for employment, and cotton cloth constituted 50 percent of the country's exports. Factories quickly sprang up in urban areas, where the growing population provided a ready source of labor. The rapid expansion of the British textile industry had as its colonial corollary the destruction of the hand manufacture of textiles in India. The British put high import duties on Indian cloth entering Britain and kept such duties very low for British cloth entering India. The figures are dramatic: in 1813, the Indian city of Calcutta exported to England £2,000,000 of cotton cloth; by 1830, Calcutta was importing from England £2,000,000 of cotton cloth. When Britain abolished slavery in its Caribbean colonies in 1833, British manufacturers began to buy raw cotton in the southern United States, where slavery still flourished.

Factories drew workers from the urban population surge, which had begun in the eighteenth century and now accelerated. The reasons for urban growth are not entirely clear. The population of such new industrial cities as Manchester and Leeds increased by 40 percent in the 1820s alone. Historians long thought that factory workers came from the countryside, pushed off the land by the field enclosures of the 1700s. But recent studies have shown that the number of agricultural laborers actually increased during industrialization in Britain, suggesting that a growing birthrate created a larger population and fed workers into the new factory system.

The new workers came from several sources: families of farmers who could not provide land for all their children, soldiers demobilized after the Napoleonic wars, artisans displaced by the new machinery, and children of the earliest workers who had moved to the factory towns. A system of employment that resembled family labor on farms or in cottage industry also developed in the new factories. Entire families came to toil for a single wage, although family members performed different tasks. Workdays of twelve to seventeen hours were typical, even for children, and the work was grueling. Community ties remained important as workers migrated from rural to urban areas to join friends and family from their original villages.

As urban factories grew, their workers gradually came to constitute a new socioeconomic class with a distinctive culture and traditions. Like middle class, the term **working class** came into use for the first time in the early nineteenth century. It referred to the laborers in the new factories. In the past, workers had labored in isolated trades: water and wood carrying, gardening, laundry, and building. In contrast, factories brought working people together with machines, under close supervision by their employers. They soon developed a sense of common interests and organized societies for mutual help and political reform. From these would come the first labor unions.

Fearing displacement by machines, in 1811 and 1812 bands of handloom weavers wrecked factory machinery and burned mills in the Midlands, Yorkshire, and Lancashire. To restore order and protect industry, the government sent in an army of twelve thousand regular soldiers and made machine wrecking punishable by death. The rioters were called Luddites♦ after the fictitious figure Ned Ludd, whose signature appeared on their manifestos. (The term is still used to describe those who resist new technology.)

Other British workers focused their organizing efforts on reforming Parliament, whose members were chosen in elections dominated by the landowning elite. One reformer complained that the members of the House of Commons were nothing but "toadeaters, gamblers, public plunderers, and hirelings." Reform clubs held large open-air meetings, and ordinary people eagerly bought cheap newspapers that clamored for change. In August 1819, sixty thousand people attended an illegal meeting held in St. Peter's Fields in Manchester. When the local authorities sent the cavalry to arrest the speaker, panic resulted; eleven people were killed and many hundreds injured. Punsters called it the Battle of Peterloo or the Peterloo Massacre. An alarmed government passed the Six Acts, which forbade large political meetings and restricted press criticism, suppressing the reform movement in Britain for a decade.

The Rise of the Railroad. Steam-driven engines took on a dramatic new form in the 1820s when the English engineer George Stephenson perfected an engine to pull wagons along rail tracks. (See "Taking Measure," page 812.) The idea of a railroad was not new: iron tracks had been used since the seventeenth century to haul coal from mines in wagons pulled by horses. A railroad system as a mode of transport, however, developed only after Stephenson's invention of a steam-powered locomotive. In 1830, the Liverpool and Manchester Railway line opened to the cheers of crowds and the congratulations of government officials, including the duke of Wellington, the hero of Waterloo and now prime minister. In the excitement, some of the dignitaries gathered on a parallel track. Another engine, George Stephenson's famous Rocket, approached at high speed. Most of the gentlemen scattered to safety, but former cabinet minister William Huskisson fell and was hit. In a few hours he died, the first official casualty of the newfangled railroad.

Railroads were dramatic and expensive—the most striking symbol of the new industrial age. Placed on the new tracks, steam-driven carriages could transport people and goods to the cities and link coal and iron deposits to the new factories. They gave industrialization a big push forward as every European country soon tried to set up its own railroad system. One German entrepreneur confidently predicted, "The locomotive is the hearse which will carry absolutism and feudalism to the graveyard."

The New Ideologies

Although traditional ways of life still prevailed in much of Europe, new modes of thinking about the changes in the social

♦**Luddites:** LUH dyts

TAKING MEASURE

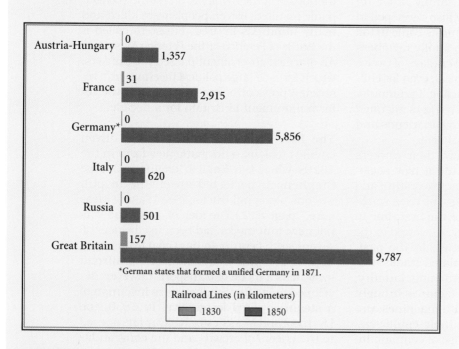

*German states that formed a unified Germany in 1871.

Railroad Lines (in kilometers)
▧ 1830 ■ 1850

Railroad Lines, 1830–1850
Great Britain quickly extended its lead in the building of railroads. The extension of commerce and, before long, the ability to wage war would depend on the development of effective railroad networks. These statistics might be taken as predicting a realignment of power within Europe after 1850. What do the numbers say about the relative position of Germany (the German states, including Prussia but excluding Austria) and Austria-Hungary and France? *From B. R. Mitchell,* European Historical Statistics 1750–1970 *(New York: Columbia University Press, 1975), F1.*

and political order arose in direct response to what some have called the dual revolution of the French Revolution and the Industrial Revolution. The French Revolution had caused people to ask questions about the best possible form of government, and its effects had made clear that people acting together could change their political system. Similarly, the Industrial Revolution, first in Britain and then in western Europe, posed fundamental questions about changes in society and social relations: How did the new social order differ from the earlier one, which was less urban and less driven by commercial concerns? Who should control this new order? Should governments try to moderate

or accelerate the pace of change? Answers to these questions about the social and political order were called ideologies. A word coined during the French Revolution, **ideology** refers to a coherent set of beliefs about the way a society's social and political order should be organized. The 1820s and 1830s were, indeed, an era of "isms" — conservatism, liberalism, nationalism, romanticism, and, newest on the scene, socialism. In the 1830s and 1840s, new political and social movements organized themselves around these ideologies.

Liberalism. As an ideology, liberalism traced its origins to the writings of John Locke in the seventeenth century and the Enlightenment philosophy of the eighteenth. The adherents of **liberalism** defined themselves in opposition to conservatives on one end of the political spectrum and revolutionaries on the other. Unlike conservatives, liberals supported the Enlightenment ideals of constitutional guarantees of personal liberty and free trade in economics, believing that greater liberty in politics and economic matters would promote social improvement and economic growth. For that reason, they also generally applauded the social and economic changes produced by the Industrial Revolution, while opposing the violence and excessive state power promoted by the French Revolution. The leaders of the rapidly expanding middle class composed of manufacturers, merchants, and professionals favored liberalism.

The foremost proponent of early-nineteenth-century liberalism was the English philosopher and jurist Jeremy Bentham (1748–1832). He called his brand of liberalism utilitarianism because he held that the best policy is the one that produces "the greatest good for the greatest number" and is thus the most useful, or utilitarian. Bentham's criticisms spared no institution; he railed against the injustices of the British parliamentary process, the abuses of the prisons and the penal code, and the educational system. In his zeal for social engineering, he proposed elaborate schemes for managing the poor and model prisons that would emphasize rehabilitation through close supervision rather than corporal punishment. British liberals like Bentham wanted government involvement, including deregulation of trade, but they shied away from any association with revolutionary violence.

Bentham and many other liberals joined the abolitionist, antislavery movement that intensified between the 1790s and 1820s. One English abolitionist put the matter in these terms: "[God] has given to us an unexampled portion of civil liberty; and we in return drag his rational creatures into a most severe and perpetual bondage." The contradiction between calling for more liberty at home and maintaining slavery in the West Indies seemed intolerable to British liberals and to many religious groups, especially the Quakers, who since the 1780s had taken the lead in forming antislavery societies in both the United States and Great Britain. Agitation by such groups as the London Society for Effecting the Abolition of the Slave Trade succeeded in gaining a first victory in 1807 when the British House of Lords voted to abolish the slave trade. Throughout the 1820s, antislavery activism expanded in the United States, Great Britain, and France because the slave trade still continued in some countries and because slavery itself had not been abolished. As one disappointed British abolitionist explained in 1830:

We supposed that when by the abolition of the slave trade the planters could get no more slaves, they would not only treat better those whom they then had in their power, but that they would gradually find it to their advantage to emancipate them. . . . We did not sufficiently take into account the effect of unlimited power.

The abolitionists' efforts would bear fruit in 1833 when Britain abolished slavery in all its colonies.

Socialism. The newest ideology of the 1820s, **socialism**, took up where liberalism left off: socialists believed that the liberties advocated by liberals benefited only the middle class—the owners of factories and businesses, not the workers. They sought to reorganize society totally rather than to reform it piecemeal through political measures. Many were utopians who believed that ideal communities are based on cooperation rather than competition. Like Thomas More, whose book *Utopia* (1516) gave the movement its name, the utopian socialists believed that society would benefit all its members only if private property did not exist.

Socialists criticized the new industrial order for dividing society into two classes: the new middle class, or capitalists, who owned the wealth; and the working class, their downtrodden and impoverished employees. Such divisions tore the social fabric, and, as their name suggests, the socialists aimed to restore harmony and cooperation through social reorganization. Robert Owen (1771–1858), a successful Welsh-born manufacturer, founded British socialism. In 1800, he bought a cotton mill in New Lanark, Scotland, and began to set up a model factory town, where workers labored only ten hours a day (instead of seventeen, as was common) and children between the ages of five and ten attended school rather than working in the factory. Owen moved to the United States in the 1820s to put his principles once more into action in the community in Indiana he named New Harmony. The experiment collapsed after three years, a victim of internal squabbling. But out of Owen's experiments and writings, such as *The Book of the New Moral World* (1820), would come the movement for producer cooperatives (businesses owned and controlled by their workers), consumers' cooperatives (stores in which consumers owned shares), and a national trade union.

Claude Henri de Saint-Simon (1760–1825) and Charles Fourier◆ (1772–1837) were

◆**Fourier:** FOOR ee ay

Owen's counterparts in France. Saint-Simon was a noble who had served as an officer in the War of American Independence and lost a fortune speculating in national property during the French Revolution. Fourier traveled as a salesman for a Lyon cloth merchant. Both shared Owen's alarm about the effects of industrialization on social relations. Saint-Simon—who coined the terms *industrialism* and *industrialist* to define the new economic order and its chief animators—believed that work was the central element in the new society and that it should be controlled not by politicians but by scientists, engineers, artists, and industrialists themselves. To correct the abuses of the new industrial order, Fourier urged the establishment of utopian communities that were part garden city and part agricultural commune; all jobs would be rotated to maximize happiness. Fourier hoped that a network of small, decentralized communities would replace the state. The emancipation of women was essential to Fourier's vision of a harmonious community: "The extension of the privileges of women is the fundamental cause of all social progress." Fourier's projects sometimes included outlandish predictions; he envisioned a world in which the oceans would turn into lemonade and the population would include 37 million poets equal to Homer, 37 million mathematicians equal to Newton, and 37 million dramatists equal to Molière.

After Saint-Simon's death in 1825, some of his followers established a quasi-religious cult with elaborate rituals and a "he-pope" and "she-pope," or ruling father and mother. Saint-Simonians lived and worked together in cooperative arrangements and scandalized some by advocating free love. They set up branches in the United States and Egypt. In 1832, Saint-Simonian women founded a feminist newspaper, *The Free Woman*, asserting that "with the emancipation of woman will come the emancipation of the worker." These early utopian socialists were lonely voices. Their emphasis on community and cooperation gained more adherents after 1830.

Nationalism. Nationalists could be liberals, socialists, or even conservatives. **Nationalism** holds that all peoples derive their identities from their nations, which are defined by common language, shared cultural traditions, and sometimes religion. When such nations do not coincide with state boundaries, as they often did not in the nineteenth and twentieth centuries, nationalism can produce violence and warfare as different national groups compete for control over territory.

The French showed the power of national feeling in their revolutionary and Napoleonic wars, but they also provoked nationalism in the people they conquered. Once Napoleon and his satellite rulers departed, nationalist sentiment turned against other outside rulers—the Ottoman Turks in the Balkans, the Russians in Poland, and the Austrians in Italy. Intellectuals took the lead in demanding unity and freedom for their peoples. They collected folktales, poems, and histories and prepared grammars and dictionaries of their native languages. Students, middle-class professionals, and army officers formed secret societies to promote national independence and constitutional reform.

Nationalist aspirations were especially explosive for the Austrian Empire, which included a variety of peoples united only by their enforced allegiance to the Habsburg emperor. The empire included three main national groups: the Germans, who made up one-fourth of the population; the Magyars of Hungary (which included Transylvania and Croatia); and the Slavs, who together formed the largest group in the population but were divided into different nationalities such as Poles, Czechs, Croats, and Serbs. The empire also included Italians in Lombardy and Venetia and Romanians in Transylvania. Efforts to govern such diverse peoples preoccupied Metternich, chief minister to the weak Habsburg emperor Francis I (r. 1792–1835). Metternich's domestic policy aimed to restrain nationalist impulses, and it largely succeeded until the 1840s. He set up a secret police on the Napoleonic model that opened letters of even the highest officials. Censorship in the Italian provinces was so strict that even the works of Dante were expurgated, and Metternich announced that "the Lombards must forget that they are Italians."

In reaction, novelists, playwrights, and poets used their pens to arouse nationalist sentiment. Membership grew in secret societies such as the carbonari; before the fall of Napoleon, many had been anti-French, but now the societies turned anti-Austrian and supported political rights and national self-determination. The societies had no common program across Italy and no central organization, but they attracted tens of thousands of members, including physicians, lawyers, officers, and students.

The new Germanic Confederation set up by the Congress of Vienna had a federal assembly, but it largely functioned as a tool of Metternich's policies. The only sign of resistance came from university students, who formed nationalist student societies, or *Burschenschaften*.◆ In 1817, they held a mass rally at which they burned books they did not like, including Napoleon's Civil Code. One of their leaders, Friedrich Ludwig Jahn, spouted such xenophobic◆ (antiforeign) slogans as "If you let your daughter learn French, you might just as well train her to become a whore." Metternich was convinced that the Burschenschaften in the German states and the carbonari in Italy were linked in an international conspiracy; in 1820, when a student assassinated the playwright August Kotzebue◆ because he ridiculed the student movement, Metternich convinced the leaders of the biggest German states to pass the Karlsbad Decrees dissolving the student societies and more strictly censoring the press. No evidence for a conspiracy was found.

Tsar Alexander faced similar problems in Poland, his congress kingdom (so called because the Congress of Vienna had created it), which in 1815 was one of Europe's most liberal states. The tsar reigned in Poland as a limited monarch, having bestowed a constitution that provided for an elected parliament, a national army, and guarantees of free speech and a free press. But by 1818, Alexander had begun retracting his concessions. Polish students and military officers responded by forming secret nationalist societies to plot for change by illegal means. The government then cracked down, arresting student leaders and dismissing professors

who promoted reforms. By the 1820s, Polish nationalists and the Russian imperial government were on a collision course.

Romanticism

More of an artistic movement than a true ideology, **romanticism** glorified nature, emotion, genius, and imagination. It proclaimed these as antidotes to the Enlightenment and to classicism in the arts, challenging the reliance on reason, symmetry, and cool geometric spaces. Classicism idealized models

Lord Byron
George Gordon, Lord Byron (1788–1824), lived a short, tumultuous life, wrote enduring romantic poetry, loved both women and young men, and died a heroic death fighting for Greek independence. In the midst of the Napoleonic wars, he left Britain in 1809 for a two-year trip through Spain and Portugal, Greece, Turkey, and Turkish-controlled Albania. He visited the Turkish rulers in Greece and Albania and collected souvenir costumes, such as that worn in this portrait by Thomas Philips (1813). As a result of this trip, he became passionately involved in things Greek; when the Greek rebellion broke out, he promptly joined the British Committee that gathered aid for the Greeks. He died of a fever in Greece, where he had gone to distribute funds. How would viewers have reacted to the costume Byron is wearing? *National Portrait Gallery, London.*

◆*Burschenschaften:* bur shen shaaf ten
◆**xenophobic:** zeh nuh FOH bihk
◆**Kotzebue:** KAHT suh boo

Wordsworth's Poetry

The son of a lawyer, William Wordsworth (1770–1850) studied at Cambridge University and then traveled to France during the early years of the French Revolution. He returned to England and began publishing the poetry that for many scholars marks the beginning of romanticism with its emphasis on the sublime beauties of nature. This excerpt from "Lines Composed a Few Miles above Tintern Abbey" (1798) shows the influence of his extensive walking tours through the English countryside. But the passage also captures the melancholy and nostalgia that characterized much of Romantic poetry.

> And now, with gleams of half-extinguished
>   thought,
> With many recognitions dim and faint,
> And somewhat of a sad perplexity,
> The picture of the mind revives again:
> While here I stand, not only with the sense
> Of present pleasure, but with pleasing
>   thoughts
> That in this moment there is life and food
> For future years. And so I dare to hope,
> Though changed, no doubt, from what I was
>   when first

> I came among these hills; when like a roe
> I bounded o'er the mountains, by the sides
> Of the deep rivers, and the lonely streams,
> Wherever nature led: more like a man
> Flying from something that he dreads, than
>   one
> Who sought the thing he loved. For nature
>   then
> (The coarser pleasures of my boyish days,
> And their glad animal movements all gone by)
> To me was all in all.—I cannot paint
> What then I was. The sounding cataract
> Haunted me like a passion: the tall rock,
> The mountain, and the deep and gloomy
>   wood,
> Their colours and their forms, were then to
>   me
> An appetite; a feeling and a love,
> That had no need of a remoter charm,
> By thought supplied, nor any interest
> Unborrowed from the eye.—That time is past.

Source: Paul Davis, ed., *Bedford Anthology of World Literature.* Book 5: *The Nineteenth Century, 1800–1900* (Boston: Bedford/St. Martin's, 2003), 246–47.

from Roman history; romanticism turned to folklore and medieval legends. Classicism celebrated orderly, crisp lines; romantics sought out all that was wild, fevered, and disorderly. Chief among the arts of romanticism were poetry, music, and painting, which captured the deep-seated emotion characteristic of romantic expression. Romantics might take any political position, but they exerted the most political influence when they expressed nationalist feelings.

Romantic Poetry.   Romantic poetry celebrated overwhelming emotion and creative imagination. George Gordon, Lord Byron (1788–1824), explained his aims in writing poetry:

> For what is Poesy but to create
> From overfeeling, Good and Ill, and aim
> At an external life beyond our fate,
> And be the new Prometheus of new man.

Prometheus was the mythological figure who brought fire from the Greek gods to human beings. Byron did not seek the new Prometheus among the men of industry; he sought him within his own "overfeeling," his own intense emotions. Byron became a romantic hero himself when he rushed off to act on his emotions by fighting and dying in the Greek war for independence from the Turks. An English aristocrat, Byron nonetheless claimed, "I have simplified my politics into a detestation of all existing governments."

Romantic poetry elevated the wonders of nature almost to the supernatural. In a poem that became one of the most beloved exemplars of romanticism, "Tintern Abbey" (1798), the English poet William Wordsworth (1770–1850) compared himself to a deer even while making nature seem filled with human emotions (see "Wordsworth's Poetry", opposite page). Like many poets of his time, Wordsworth greeted the French Revolution with joy; in his poem "French Revolution" (1809), he remembered his early enthusiasm: "Bliss was it in that dawn to be alive." But gradually he became disenchanted with the revolutionary experiment and celebrated British nationalism instead; in 1816, he published a poem to commemorate the "intrepid sons of Albion [England]" who died at the battle of Waterloo.

Their emphasis on authentic self-expression at times drew romantics to exotic, mystical, or even reckless experiences. Such transports drove one leading German poet to the madhouse and another to suicide. Some romantics depicted the artist as possessed by demons and obsessed with hallucinations. This more nightmarish side was captured, and perhaps criticized, by Mary Shelley in *Frankenstein*. The aged German poet Johann Wolfgang von Goethe (1749–1832) likewise denounced the extremes of romanticism, calling it "everything that is sick." In his epic poem *Faust* (1832), he seemed to warn of the same dangers Shelley portrayed in her novel. In Goethe's retelling of a sixteenth-century legend, Faust offers his soul to the devil in return for a chance to taste all human experience—from passionate love to the heights of power—in his effort to reshape nature for humanity's benefit. Faust's striving, like Frankenstein's, leaves a wake of suffering and destruction. Goethe did not make the target of his warn-

ing explicit, but the French revolutionary legacy and industrialization both seemed to be releasing Faustian energies that could turn destructive.

Romantic Painting and Music. Romanticism in painting often expressed anxiety about the coming industrial order while idealizing nature. These concerns came together in an emphasis on natural landscape. The German romantic painter Caspar David Friedrich (1774–1840) depicted scenes—often in the mountains, far from any factory—that captured the romantic fascination with the sublime power of nature (see page 818). His melancholy individual figures looked lost in the vastness of an overpowering nature. Friedrich hated the new modern world and considered industrialization a disaster. His landscapes often had religious meaning as well, as in his controversial painting *The Cross in the Mountains* (1808), which showed a Christian cross standing alone in a

William Blake, *The Circle of the Lustful* (1824)
An English romantic poet, painter, engraver, and printmaker, Blake always sought his own way. Self-taught, he began writing poetry at age twelve and apprenticed to an engraver at fourteen. His works incorporate many otherworldly attributes; they are quite literally visionary—imagining other worlds. In this engraving of hell, the figures twist and turn and are caught up in a kind of spiritual ether. Can you find elements in this engraving that reflect a criticism of Enlightenment ideals? *Blake, "The Circle of the Lustful"/ Birmingham Museums and Art Gallery.*

Caspar David Friedrich,
Wanderer above the Sea of Fog **(1818)**
Friedrich, a German romantic painter, captured many of the themes most dear to romanticism: melancholy, isolation, and individual communion with nature. He painted trees reaching for the sky and mountains stretching into the distance. Nature to him seemed awesome, powerful, and overshadowing of human perspectives. The French sculptor David d'Angers said of Friedrich, "Here is a man who has discovered the tragedy of landscape." *Hamburg Kunsthalle, Hamburg/Bridgeman Art Library.*

mountain scene. It symbolized the steadfastness of faith but seemed to separate religion from the churches and attach it to mystical experience.

Many other artists developed similar themes. The English painter Joseph M. W. Turner (1775–1851) depicted his vision of nature in mysterious, misty seascapes, anticipating later artists by blurring the outlines of objects. The French painter Eugène Delacroix♦

♦**Delacroix:** deh luh KWAH

(1798–1863) chose contemporary as well as medieval scenes of great turbulence to emphasize light and color and break away from what he saw as "the servile copies repeated *ad nauseum* in academies of art." Critics denounced the new techniques as "painting with a drunken broom." To broaden his experience of light and color, Delacroix traveled in the 1830s to North Africa and painted many exotic scenes in Morocco and Algeria.

The towering presence of the German composer Ludwig van Beethoven (1770–1827) in early nineteenth-century music helped establish the direction for musical romanticism. His music, according to one leading German romantic, "sets in motion the lever of fear, of awe, of horror, of suffering, and awakens just that infinite longing which is the essence of Romanticism." Beethoven transformed the symphony into a connected work with recurring and evolving musical themes. Romantic symphonies conveyed the impression of growth, a metaphor for the organic process with an emphasis on the natural that was dear to the romantics. For example, Beethoven's Sixth Symphony, the *Pastoral* (1808), used a variety of instruments to represent sounds heard in the country. Beethoven's work showed remarkable diversity ranging from religious works to symphonies, sonatas, and concertos. Some of his work was explicitly political; his Ninth Symphony (1824) employed a chorus to sing the German poet Friedrich Schiller's verses in praise of universal human solidarity.

Romantic Nationalism. If romantics had any common political thread, it was the support of nationalist aspirations, especially through the search for the historical origins of national identity. In the German states, the Austrian Empire, Russia and other Slavic lands, and Scandinavia, romantic poets and writers collected old legends and folktales that expressed a shared cultural and linguistic heritage stretching back to the Middle Ages. These collections showed that Germany, for example, had always existed even if it did not currently take the form of a single unified state. Romantic nationalism permeated *The Betrothed* (1825–1827), a novel by Alessandro Manzoni (1785–

1873) that constituted a kind of bible for Italian nationalists.

The career of Sir Walter Scott (1771–1832) incorporates many of the strands of romanticism. He translated Goethe and published Scottish ballads that he heard as a child. After achieving immediate success with his poetry, he switched to historical novels, but he also wrote a nine-volume life of Napoleon and edited historical memoirs. His novels are almost all renditions of historical events, from *Rob Roy* (1817), with its account of Scottish resistance to the English in the early eighteenth century, to *Ivanhoe* (1819), with its tales of medieval England. The influence of Scott's historical novels was immense. One contemporary critic claimed that *Ivanhoe* was more historically true than any scholarly work: "There is more history in the novels of Walter Scott than in half of the historians."

> **Review:** In what ways did ideologies reflect the economic and social changes of the early nineteenth century?

❖ Political Challenges to the Conservative Order

In many places, discontent with the conservative Vienna settlement threatened to rise over its banks as liberals, nationalists, and socialists expressed their exasperation. The revolutionary legacy kept coming to the surface to challenge Europe's rulers. Isolated revolts threatened the hold of some conservative governments in the 1820s, but most of them were quickly bottled up. Then in 1830, successive uprisings briefly overwhelmed the established order. Across Europe, angry protesters sought constitutional guarantees of individual liberties and national unity and autonomy.

Political Revolts in the 1820s

The restoration of regimes after Napoleon's fall disappointed those who dreamed of constitutional freedoms and national independence. Revolts broke out in the 1820s in Spain and Italy, Russia, Greece (Map 21.3),

MAP 21.3 Revolutionary Movements of the 1820s
The revolts of the 1820s took place on the periphery of Europe, in Spain, Italy, Greece, Russia, and in the Spanish and Portuguese colonies of Latin America. Rebels in Spain and Russia wanted constitutional reforms. Although the Italian revolts failed, as did the uprisings in Spain and Russia, the Greek and Latin American independence movements succeeded.

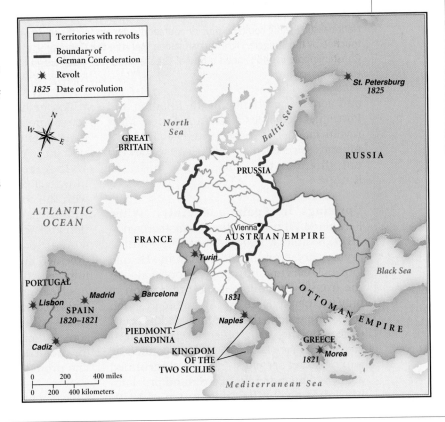

Greek Independence

From 1836 to 1839 the Greek painter Panagiotis Zographos worked with his two sons on a series of scenes from the Greek struggle for independence from the Turks. Response was so favorable that one Greek general ordered lithographic reproductions for popular distribution. Nationalistic feeling could be thus encouraged even among those who were not directly touched by the struggle. Here Turkish sultan Mehmet the Conqueror, exulting over the fall of Constantinople in 1453, views a row of Greeks under the yoke, a sign of submission. *Collection, Visual Connection.*

and across the Atlantic in the Spanish and Portuguese colonies of Latin America. Most revolts failed, but those in Greece and Latin America succeeded, largely because they did not threaten the conservative order in Europe.

Uprisings in Spain and Italy. When Ferdinand VII regained the Spanish crown in 1814, he quickly restored the prerevolutionary nobility, church, and monarchy. He had foreign books and newspapers confiscated at the frontier and allowed the publication of only two newspapers. Not surprisingly, such repressive policies disturbed the middle class, especially the army officers who had encountered French ideas. Many responded by joining secret societies. In 1820, disgruntled soldiers demanded that Ferdinand proclaim his adherence to the Constitution of 1812,

which he had abolished in 1814. When the revolt spread, Ferdinand convened the *cortes*♦ (parliament), which could agree on virtually nothing. Ferdinand bided his time, and in 1823 a French army invaded and restored him to absolute power. The French acted with the consent of the other great powers, who had met to discuss the Spanish situation and agree on a course of action. The restored Spanish government tortured and executed hundreds of rebels; thousands were imprisoned or forced into exile.

Hearing of the Spanish uprising, rebellious soldiers in the kingdom of Naples joined forces with the carbonari and demanded a constitution. When a new parliament met, it too broke down over internal disagreements. The promise of reform sparked rebellion in

♦*cortes:* KAWR tays

the northern Italian kingdom of Piedmont-Sardinia, where rebels urged Charles Albert, the young heir to the Piedmont throne, to fight the Austrians for Italian unification. He vacillated; but in 1821, after the rulers of Austria, Prussia, and Russia met and agreed on intervention, the Austrians defeated the rebels in Naples and Piedmont. Liberals were arrested in many Italian states, and the pope condemned the secret societies as "at heart only devouring wolves." Despite the opposition of Great Britain, which condemned the indiscriminate suppression of revolutionary movements, Metternich convinced the other powers to agree to his muffling of the Italian opposition to Austrian rule.

The Decembrist Revolt in Russia.

Aspirations for constitutional government surfaced in Russia when Alexander I died suddenly in 1825. On the December day that the troops assembled in St. Petersburg to take an oath of loyalty to Alexander's brother Nicholas as the new tsar, rebel officers insisted that the crown belonged to another brother, Constantine, whom they hoped would be more favorable to constitutional reform. Constantine, though next in the line of succession after Alexander, had refused the crown. The soldiers nonetheless raised the cry "Long live Constantine, long live the Constitution." (Some troops apparently thought that "the Constitution" was Constantine's wife.) Soldiers loyal to Nicholas easily suppressed the Decembrists (so called after the month of their uprising), who were so outnumbered that they had no realistic chance to succeed. The subsequent trial, however, made the rebels into legendary heroes. Of their imprisonment at hard labor, the Russian poet Alexander Pushkin (1799–1837) wrote:

> The heavy-hanging chains will fall,
> The walls will crumble at a word,
> And Freedom greet you in the light,
> And brothers give you back the sword.

Pushkin would not live to see this freedom. For the next thirty years, Nicholas I (r. 1825–1855) used a new political police, the Third Section, to spy on potential opponents and stamp out rebelliousness.

Greek Independence from the Turks.

The Ottoman Turks faced growing nationalist challenges in the Balkans, but the European powers feared that supporting such opposition would encourage a rebellious spirit at home. The Serbs revolted against Turkish rule and won virtual independence by 1817. A Greek general in the Russian army, Prince Alexander Ypsilanti,◆ tried to lead a revolt against the Turks in 1820 but failed when the tsar, urged on by Metternich, disavowed him. Metternich feared rebellion even by Christians against their Turkish rulers. A second revolt, this time by Greek peasants, sparked a wave of atrocities in 1821 and 1822. The Greeks killed every Turk who did not escape; in retaliation the Turks hanged the Greek patriarch of Constantinople, and in the areas they still controlled they pillaged churches, massacred thousands of men, and sold the women into slavery.

Nationalistic Movements in the Balkans, 1815–1830

Western opinion turned against the Turks; Greece, after all, was the home of Western civilization. While the great powers negotiated, Greeks and pro-Greece committees around the world sent food and military supplies; like the English poet Byron, a few enthusiastic European and American volunteers joined the Greeks. The Greeks held on until the great powers were willing to intervene. In 1827, a combined force of British, French, and Russian ships destroyed the Turkish fleet at Navarino Bay; and in 1828, Russia declared war on Turkey and advanced close to Istanbul. The Treaty of Adrianople of 1829 gave Russia a protectorate over the Danubian principalities in the Balkans and provided for a conference among representatives of Britain, Russia, and France, all of whom had broken with Austria in support of the Greeks. In 1830,

◆**Ypsilanti:** ihp suh LAN tee

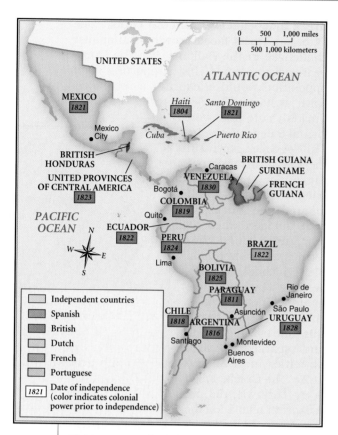

MAP 21.4 Latin American Independence, 1804–1830

Napoleon's occupation of Spain and Portugal seriously weakened those countries' hold on their Latin American colonies. Despite the restoration of the Spanish and Portuguese rulers in 1814, most of their colonies successfully broke away in a wave of rebellions between 1811 and 1830.

Simon Bolívar

Known as "the Liberator," Simon Bolívar (1783–1830) is shown in this chalk lithograph near the end of his life. He is the figure on the white horse in the front. Bolívar led the armies that gained independence from Spain in Venezuela, Colombia, Ecuador, Peru, and Bolivia. He had dreamed of creating a United States of Latin America but died of tuberculosis as factional fighting kept the various states separate from each other. *AKG-Images, London.*

Greece was declared an independent kingdom under the guarantee of the three powers; in 1833, the son of King Ludwig of Bavaria became Otto I of Greece. Nationalism, with the support of European public opinion, had made its first breach in Metternich's system.

Wars of Independence in Latin America.
Across the Atlantic, national revolts also succeeded after a series of bloody wars of independence. Taking advantage of the upheavals in Spain and Portugal that began under Napoleon, restive colonists from Mexico to Argentina rebelled. Their leader was Simon

Bolívar, son of a slave owner, who was educated in Europe on the works of Voltaire and Rousseau. Although Bolívar fancied himself a Latin American Napoleon, he had to acquiesce to the formation of a series of independent republics between 1821 and 1823, even in Bolivia, which is named after him. At the same time, Brazil (then still a monarchy) separated from Portugal (Map 21.4). The United States recognized the new states, and in 1823 President James Monroe announced his Monroe Doctrine, closing the Americas to European intervention—a prohibition that depended on British naval power and British willingness to declare neutrality. Great Britain dominated the Latin American economies, which had suffered great losses during the wars for independence.

Revolution and Reform, 1830–1832

In 1830 a new wave of liberal and nationalist revolts broke against the bulwark of conservatism. The revolts of the 1820s served as warning shots, but the earlier uprisings had been largely confined to the peripheries of Europe. Now revolution once again threatened the established order in western Europe.

The French Revolution of 1830. Louis XVIII's younger brother and successor, Charles X (r. 1824–1830), brought about his own downfall by steering the monarchy in an increasingly repressive direction. In 1825, a Law of Indemnity compensated nobles who had emigrated during the Revolution for the loss of their estates, and a Law of Sacrilege in the same year imposed the death penalty for such offenses as stealing religious objects from churches. Charles enraged liberals when he dissolved the legislature, removed many wealthy and powerful voters from the rolls, and imposed strict censorship. Spontaneous demonstrations in Paris led to fighting on July 26, 1830. After three days of street battles in which 500 citizens and 150 soldiers died, a group of moderate liberal leaders, fearing the reestablishment of a republic, agreed to give the crown to Charles X's cousin Louis-Philippe, duke of Orléans.

Charles X went into exile in England, and the new king extended political liberties and voting rights. Although the number of voting men nearly doubled, it remained minuscule—approximately 170,000 in a country of 30 million, between 5 and 6 percent. Such reforms did little for the poor and working classes, who had manned the barricades in July. Dissatisfaction with the 1830 settlement boiled over in Lyon in 1831, when a silk-workers' strike over wages turned into a rebellion that died down only when the army arrived. Revolution had broken the hold of those who wanted to restore the pre-1789 monarchy and nobility, but it had gone no further this time than installing a more liberal, constitutional monarchy.

Belgian Independence from the Dutch. The success of the July Revolution in Paris ignited the Belgians, whose country had been annexed to the kingdom of the Netherlands in 1815. Differences in traditions, language, and religion separated the largely Catholic Belgians from the Dutch. An opera about a seventeenth-century insurrection in Naples provided the spark, and students in Brussels rioted, shouting "Down with the Dutch."

The riot turned into revolt. King William of the Netherlands appealed to the great powers to intervene; after all, the Congress of Vienna had established his kingdom. But Great Britain and France opposed intervention and invited Russia, Austria, and Prussia to a conference that guaranteed Belgium independence in exchange for its neutrality in international affairs. Belgian neutrality would remain a cornerstone of European diplomacy for a century. After much maneuvering, the crown of the new kingdom of Belgium was offered to a German prince, Leopold of Saxe-Coburg, in 1831. Belgium, like France and Britain, now had a constitutional monarchy.

Revolts in Italy and Poland. The Russian tsar and the Austrian emperor would have supported intervention in Belgium had they not been preoccupied with their own revolts. Anti-Austrian uprisings erupted in a handful of Italian states, but they fizzled without the hoped-for French aid. The Polish revolt was more serious. Once again, in response to news of revolution in France, students raised the banner of rebellion, this time in Warsaw in November 1830. Polish aristocrats soon formed a provisional government. Despite some victories on the battlefield, the provisional government got no support from Britain or France and was defeated. In reprisal, Nicholas abolished the Polish constitution that Alexander had granted and ordered thousands of Poles executed or banished.

The British Reform Bill of 1832. The British had long been preoccupied with two subjects: the royal family and elections for control of Parliament. In 1820, the domestic quarrels between the new king George IV (r. 1820–1830) and his German wife, Caroline, seemed to threaten the future of the monarchy.

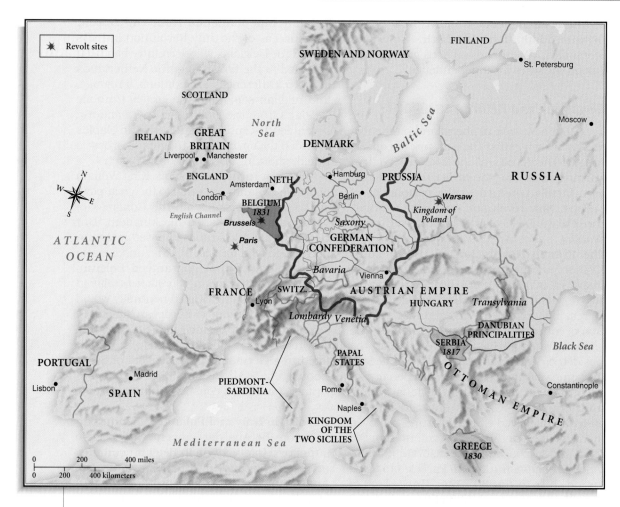

MAPPING THE WEST Europe in 1830

By 1830, the fragilities of the Congress of Vienna settlement had become apparent. Rebellion in Poland failed, but Belgium won its independence from the kingdom of the Netherlands, and a French revolution chased out the Bourbon ruler and installed Louis-Philippe, who promised constitutional reform. Most European rulers held on to their positions in this period of ferment, but they had to accommodate the new demands created by industrialization, desires for constitutional guarantees of rights, and growing nationalist sentiment.

When George IV came to the throne, he tried to divorce Caroline, and he refused to have her crowned queen. He hoped to use rumors of her love affairs on the continent to win his case, but the divorce trial provoked massive demonstrations in support of Caroline. Women's groups gathered thousands of signatures on petitions supporting her, and popular songs and satires portrayed George as a fat, drunken libertine. Caroline's death a few months after George's coronation ended the Queen Caroline Affair. The monarchy survived but with a tarnished reputation.

The 1820s had brought into British government new men who were open to change. Sir Robert Peel (1788–1850), the secretary for home affairs, revised the criminal code to reduce the number of crimes punishable by death and introduced a municipal police force in London, called the Bobbies after him. In 1824, the laws prohibiting labor unions were repealed, and though restrictions on strikes remained, workers could now organize themselves legally to confront their employers collectively. In 1828, the appointment of the duke of Wellington, the hero of Waterloo, as prime minister kept the Tories in power, and his government pushed through a bill in 1829 allowing Catholics to sit in Parliament and hold most public offices.

When in 1830, and again in 1831, the Whigs in Parliament proposed an extension of the right to vote, Tory diehards, principally in the House of Lords, dug in their heels and predicted that even the most modest proposals would doom civilization itself. Even though the proposed law would not grant universal male suffrage, mass demonstrations in favor of it took place in many cities. One supporter of reform described the scene: "Meetings of almost every description of persons were held in cities, towns, and parishes; by journeymen tradesmen in their clubs, and by common workmen who had no trade clubs or associations of any kind." In this "state of diseased and feverish excitement" (according to its opponents), the Reform Bill of 1832 passed, after the king threatened to create enough new peers to obtain its passage in the House of Lords.

Although the Reform Bill altered Britain's political structure in significant ways, the gains were not revolutionary. One of the bill's foremost backers, historian and member of Parliament Thomas Macaulay, explained, "I am opposed to Universal Suffrage, because I think that it would produce a destructive revolution. I support this plan, because I am sure that it is our best security against a revolution." Although the number of male voters increased by about 50 percent, only one in five Britons could now vote, and voting still depended on holding property. Nevertheless, the bill gave representation to new cities in the industrial north for the first time and set a precedent for further widening suffrage. Exclusive aristocratic politics now gave way to a mixed middle-class and aristocratic structure that would prove more responsive to the problems of a fast-growing industrial society. Those disappointed with the outcome would organize with renewed vigor in the 1830s and 1840s.

Review: Why were Austria and Russia able to thwart independence movements in Italy and Poland but not in Greece, Belgium, and Latin America?

Conclusion

The agitations and uprisings of the 1820s and early 1830s showed that the revolutionary legacy still smoldered and might erupt into flames again at any moment. Napoleon Bonaparte had kept the legacy alive by insisting on fundamental reforms wherever his armies triumphed. His imperial rule galvanized supporters and opponents alike; no one could be indifferent to his impact on European and even world affairs. The powers who eventually defeated him tried to maintain the European peace by shoring up monarchical governments and damping down aspirations for constitutional freedoms and national autonomy. They sometimes fell short. Belgium separated from the Netherlands, Greece achieved independence from the Turks, Latin American countries shook off the rule of Spain and Portugal, and the French installed a more liberal monarchy than the one envisioned by the Congress of Vienna. Yet Metternich's vision of a conservative Europe still held, and most efforts at revolt failed.

In her novel *Frankenstein*, Mary Shelley had captured some of the deepest worries of the age; human creativity might have an unpredictably destructive side in spite of every good intention. Although she did not intend her novel as a brief in support of political conservatism—she hated what Metternich stood for—she did tap into European fears about the changes taking place. The French and Industrial Revolutions promised to transform European life, for better or worse. Napoleon Bonaparte had built upon the French revolutionary legacy to reform institutions in France and elsewhere, but he also attempted to colonize much of Europe. New ideologies such as conservatism, liberalism, and socialism all took off from an analysis of the revolutionary legacy, some opposing it, others supporting parts of it. The machines of industrialization seemed to some Europeans just as horrible as Frankenstein's monster; others welcomed them as promising a brighter future. In the years to come industrialization would proceed even faster, and revolution would return to shatter the order so carefully nurtured by Metternich and his colleagues.

Suggested References

Napoleon's Authoritarian State

Much has been written about Napoleon as a military leader, but only recently has his regime within France attracted interest. Historians now emphasize the mixed quality of Napoleon's rule. He carried forward some revolutionary innovations and halted others.

*Arnold, Eric A., Jr., ed. *A Documentary Survey of Napoleonic France*. 1994.

Ellis, Geoffrey James. *Napoleon*. 1996.

Kafker, Frank A., and James M. Laux. *Napoleon and His Times: Selected Interpretations*. 1989.

Napoleon Foundation: http://www.napoleon.org.

Wilson-Smith, Timothy. *Napoleon and His Artists*. 1996.

Woloch, Isser. *Napoleon and His Collaborators: The Making of a Dictatorship*. 2001.

"Europe Was at My Feet": Napoleon's Conquests

Recent work shows how powerfully Napoleon's armies affected every European state. Whether annexed, allied, or simply defeated, every nation had to come to terms with this dynamo of activity.

*Brunn, Geoffrey. *Napoleon and His Empire*. 1972.

Connelly, Owen. *Napoleon's Satellite Kingdoms*. 1965.

Forrest, Alan. *Napoleon's Men: The Soldiers of the Revolution and Empire*. 2002.

Simms, Brendan. *The Impact of Napoleon: Prussian High Politics, Foreign Policy, and the Crisis of the Executive, 1797–1806*. 1997.

The "Restoration" of Europe

Diplomatic historians have shown how events in this period shaped European affairs for decades. Domestic politics have been relatively understudied, and as a consequence, Artz's book is still a good introduction.

Artz, Frederick B. *Reaction and Revolution, 1814–1832*. 1934.

*Primary source.

Johnson, Paul. *The Birth of the Modern: World Society, 1815–1830*. 1991.

Schroeder, Paul W. *The Transformation of European Politics, 1763–1848*. 1994.

Seward, Desmond. *Metternich: The First European*. 1991.

Forces for Social and Cultural Change

The new ideologies have been the subject of a steady stream of excellent work, ranging from individual figures such as Fourier to the antislavery movement and the origins of working-class activism. The Web site Romantic Chronology provides access to a wealth of information about every aspect of romanticism.

Beecher, Jonathan. *Charles Fourier: The Visionary and His World*. 1986.

Berlin, Sir Isaiah. *The Roots of Romanticism*. 1999.

Davis, David Brion. *The Problem of Slavery in the Age of Revolution, 1770–1823*. 1975.

*Leader, Zachary, and Ian Haywood, eds. *Romantic Period Writings, 1798–1832: An Anthology*. 1998.

Romantic Chronology: http://english.ucsb.edu:591/rchrono.

Thompson, E. P. *The Making of the English Working Class*. 1964.

Political Challenges to the Conservative Order

In general, the early nineteenth century is an understudied period of European history. Unsuccessful revolts attract less attention than successful ones, but even the Greek, Latin American, and Belgian independence movements need to be better integrated into European history.

Colley, Linda. *Britons: Forging the Nation, 1707–1837*. 1992.

Di Scala, Spencer. *Italy: From Revolution to Republic, 1700 to the Present*. 2nd ed. 1998.

Gallant, Thomas W. *Experiencing Dominion: Culture, Identity, and Power in the British Mediterranean*. 2002.

Spitzer, Alan B. *The French Generation of 1820*. 1987.

CHAPTER REVIEW

IMPORTANT EVENTS

1799	Coup against Directory government in France; Napoleon Bonaparte named First Consul
1801	Napoleon signs a concordat with the pope
1804	Napoleon crowned as emperor of France; issues new Civil Code
1805	British naval forces defeat the French at the battle of Trafalgar; Napoleon wins his greatest victory at the battle of Austerlitz
1812	Napoleon invades Russia
1814–1815	Congress of Vienna
1815	Napoleon defeated at Waterloo and exiled to island of St. Helena, where he dies in 1821
1818	Mary Shelley, *Frankenstein*
1820	Robert Owen, *The Book of the New Moral World*; revolt of liberal army officers against the Spanish crown; the Karlsbad Decrees abolish German student societies and tighten press censorship
1824	Ludwig van Beethoven, Ninth Symphony
1825	Russian army officers demand constitutional reform in the Decembrist Revolt
1830	The Manchester and Liverpool Railway opens in England; Greece gains its independence from Ottoman Turks; rebels overthrow Charles X of France and install Louis-Philippe
1832	English Parliament passes Reform Bill; Johann Wolfgang von Goethe, *Faust*

KEY TERMS

Civil Code (792)

conservatism (808)

consuls (789)

Continental System (801)

ideology (812)

liberalism (812)

nationalism (814)

restoration (808)

romanticism (815)

socialism (813)

working class (811)

REVIEW QUESTIONS

1. In what ways did Napoleon continue the French Revolution; in what ways did he break with it?
2. Why was Napoleon able to gain control over so much of Europe's territory?
3. To what extent was the old order restored by the Congress of Vienna?
4. In what ways did ideologies reflect the economic and social changes of the early nineteenth century?
5. Why were Austria and Russia able to thwart independence movements in Italy and Poland but not in Greece, Belgium, and Latin America?

MAKING CONNECTIONS

1. What was the long-term significance of Napoleon for Europe?
2. In what ways did Metternich succeed in holding back the tide of forces for change? In what ways did he fail? And which of those forces for change made the most difference?

FOR FURTHER EXPLORATION

To assess your mastery of the material in this chapter, see the Online Study Guide at bedfordstmartins.com/hunt.

To read additional primary-source material from this period, see Chapter 21 in *Sources of The Making of the West, Second Edition*.

Industrialization, Urbanization, and Revolution, 1830–1850

IN 1830–1832 AND AGAIN in 1847–1851, devastating outbreaks of **cholera** swept across Asia and Europe, touching the United States as well in 1849–1850. Today we know that a waterborne bacterium causes cholera, but at the time no one understood the disease and everyone feared it. The usually fatal illness induced violent vomiting and diarrhea and left the skin blue, eyes sunken and dull, and hands and feet ice cold. While cholera particularly ravaged the crowded, filthy neighborhoods of rapidly growing cities, it also claimed many rural and some well-to-do victims. In Paris, 18,000 people died in the 1832 epidemic and 20,000 in that of 1849; in London, 7,000 died in each epidemic; and in Russia, the epidemic was catastrophic, claiming 250,000 victims in 1831–1832 and 1 million in 1847–1851.

Rapid industrial and urban growth in the early to mid-nineteenth century created unprecedented social problems as peasants and workers streamed into the cities. The population of London grew by 130,000 people in the 1830s alone. Berlin more than doubled between 1819 and 1849, and Paris expanded by 120,000 just between 1841 and 1846. Disease, overcrowding, prostitution, crime, and drinking all seemed to be on the increase. The lithograph, on the facing page, is one of countless that artists produced to capture the swirl of social change. A mass-produced print from inked stone, the **lithograph** played a key role in social commentary and political

---

The Threat of Cholera
In this lithograph from 1831 by the British artist Robert Seymour, Cholera appears as a kind of monster that tramples everyone in its path. Lithography (from the Greek *lithos*, "stone") was invented by a German engraver in 1798, but, like the steam engine perfected in 1776, its use spread across Europe only in the nineteenth century. In lithography, an artist uses a greasy crayon to trace an image on a flat stone; the grease attracts the ink while the blank areas repel it. The inked stone is embedded in a printing press that can produce thousands of identical images. Designed for a mass audience, nineteenth-century lithographs helped ordinary people make sense of the changes taking place around them. *Courtesy of the National Library of Medicine, Bethesda / Visual Image Presentations.*

discussion in this period. By publishing their work in daily and weekly newspapers, artists enlightened a mass audience about the social and political problems created by the startling industrial and urban growth of the 1830s and 1840s. The French artist Honoré Daumier,♦ for example, published no fewer than four thousand prints and caricatures criticizing the social inequalities exacerbated by economic development.

The shock of industrial and urban growth generated an outpouring of commentary on the need for social reforms. Painters, poets, and especially novelists joined in the chorus warning about rising tensions. Many who wrote on social issues expected middle-class women to organize their homes as a domestic haven from the heartless process of upheaval. Yet despite the emphasis on domesticity, middle-class women participated in public issues too: they set up reform societies that fought prostitution and helped poor mothers, and they agitated for temperance (abstention from alcohol) and joined the campaigns to abolish slavery. Middle-class men and women frequently denounced the lower classes' appetites for drink, tobacco, and cockfighting, but they remained largely silent when British traders received government support in forcing the Chinese to accept imports of **opium**, an addictive drug derived from the heads of poppy plants.

Social and economic changes kept the ideological pots boiling. Nationalists, liberals, socialists, and communists offered compet-

---

♦**Honoré Daumier:** aw naw RAY dohm YAY

ing visions of the new social order: they all agreed that change was necessary, but they disagreed about both the means and the ends of change. Their contest came to a head in 1848 when the rapid transformation of European society provided the combustible material for a new set of revolutionary outbreaks, more consuming than any since 1789. As in 1789, food shortages and constitutional crises fueled the rebellion, but now class tensions and nationalist impulses sparked outbreaks in capitals across Europe, not only in Paris. Some revolutionaries, such as Karl Marx, the theorist of communism, saw this as the beginning of a new age of class warfare. Because of internal quarrels and conflicts, however, the revolutionaries of 1848 eventually went down to defeat.

❖ The Advance of Industrialization and Urbanization

Industrialization and urbanization transformed Europe and eventually most of the world in the nineteenth and twentieth centuries. Because they are not single events but rather long-term processes that continue to the present, it is impossible to give them precise beginning and ending dates. Nevertheless, historians have shown that both processes accelerated quite suddenly in the first half of the nineteenth century and that their effects touched off loud complaints. Great Britain

---

♦ **1830–1832** Cholera epidemic

♦ **1830** France invades Algeria

♦ **1831** British and Foreign Temperance Society established

♦ **1832** George Sand, *Indiana*

♦ **1839** Opium War begins; invention of photography

♦ **1841** Dickens, *The Old Curiosity Shop*

1830	1835	1840

♦ **1833** British Factory Act; abolition of slavery

♦ **1834** *Zollverein* established

♦ **1835** Belgium opens first continental railway

led the way in both industrialization and urbanization, but contemporaries did not fully
understand their linkage; even today, scholars
debate the connection between industrial and
urban growth. Rulers quickly saw the advantages in industrialization, and in the 1830s
and 1840s many of them encouraged railroad
construction and the mechanization of manufacturing. States exercised little control over
the consequences of industrial and urban
growth, and many officials, preachers, and
intellectuals worried that unchecked growth
would destroy traditional social relationships
and create disorder. Some held out the constancy of rural life as an antidote to the ravages of industrialization and urbanization,
but population growth produced new tensions in the countryside too.

Engines of Change

Great Britain had led the way in the development of factories and railroads since the
late eighteenth century. In the 1830s and
1840s, industrialization spread to continental Europe, first to Belgium, northern France,
and northern Italy and then eastward to
Prussia, Austria, and eventually Russia. Although the new industries employed only a
small percentage of workers, the working
class that took shape in them immediately attracted the attention of social commentators
and government officials.

Railroads and Steam.   In the 1840s alone,
railroad track mileage more than doubled
in Great Britain, and British investment in

railways jumped tenfold. The British also
began to build railroads in India. Canal building waned in the 1840s: the railroad had
won out. Britain's success with rail transportation led other countries to develop their
own projects. Railroads grew spectacularly in
the United States in the 1830s and 1840s.
Belgium, newly independent in 1830, opened
the first continental European railroad with
state bonds backed by British capital in 1835.
By 1850, France had 2,000 miles of railroad
and the German states nearly twice as many;
Great Britain had 6,000 miles and the United
States 9,000 miles. In all, the world had
23,500 miles of track by midcentury.

Railroad building spurred both industrial
development and state power (Map 22.1).
Governments everywhere participated in the
construction of railroads, which depended on
private and state funds to pay for the massive
amounts of iron, coal, heavy machinery, and
human labor required to build and run them.
Demand for iron products accelerated industrial development. Until the 1840s, cotton had
led industrial production; between 1816 and
1840, cotton output more than quadrupled in
Great Britain. But from 1830 to 1850, Britain's
output of iron and coal doubled (Table 22.1).
Similarly, Austrian output of iron doubled between the 1820s and the 1840s. One-third of
all investment in the German states in the
1840s went into railroads.

Steam-powered engines made Britain
the world leader in manufacturing. By midcentury, more than half of Britain's national
income came from manufacturing and trade.
The number of steamboats in Great Britain

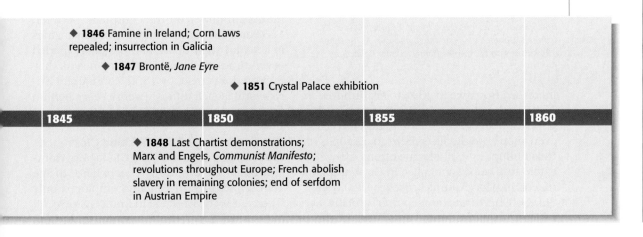

◆ **1846** Famine in Ireland; Corn Laws
repealed; insurrection in Galicia

◆ **1847** Brontë, *Jane Eyre*

◆ **1851** Crystal Palace exhibition

| 1845 | 1850 | 1855 | 1860 |

◆ **1848** Last Chartist demonstrations;
Marx and Engels, *Communist Manifesto*;
revolutions throughout Europe; French abolish
slavery in remaining colonies; end of serfdom
in Austrian Empire

The Limits of Charity

In this lithograph from 1844, Daumier shows a middle-class philanthropist refusing to give aid to a poor mother and her children. The caption below explains his refusal: "I'm sorry, my good woman, I cannot do anything for you. I am a member of the Society of Philanthropists of the Nord [a region in northern France] . . . I only give to the poor of Kamchatka!" (That is, the faraway poor rather than those at home.) Daumier spared no one in his satires, even King Louis-Philippe himself. In the early 1830s, the artist's political cartoons landed him in prison with a six-month sentence. His work always took the side of the lowly and downcast and made most fun of the high and mighty in society. His massive output of caricatures typifies an era of preoccupation with the consequences of rapid social change. *Robert D. Farber University Archives and Special Collections Department, Brandeis University Libraries. Donated by Benjamin A. and Julia M. Trustman, 1959. Forms part of the Trustman Daumier Collection.*

increased from two in 1812 to six hundred in 1840. Between 1840 and 1850, steam-engine power doubled in Great Britain and increased even more rapidly elsewhere in Europe, as those adopting British inventions strove to catch up. The power applied in German manufacturing, for example, rose from 60,000 to 360,000 hp (units horsepower) during the 1840s but still amounted to only a little more than a quarter of the British figure. German coal and iron outputs were only 6 or 7 percent of the British outputs.

Industrialization Moves Eastward. Industrialization spread slowly east from key areas in Prussia (near Berlin), in Saxony, and in Bohemia. The Austrian Empire, with industrialization centered in Bohemia, produced more cotton cloth than either Prussia or Saxony. Cotton production in the Austrian Empire tripled between 1831 and 1845. By 1847, coal production, also concentrated in Bohemia, had increased fourfold in just over twenty years.

The advance of industrialization in eastern Europe was slow, in large part because serfdom still survived there, hindering labor mobility and tying up investment capital: as long as peasants were legally tied to the land as serfs, they could not migrate to the new factory towns, and landlords felt little incentive to invest their income in manufacturing. The problem was worst in Russia, where industrialization had hardly begun and would not take off until the end of the nineteenth century. Nevertheless, even in Russia signs of industrialization could be detected: raw cotton imports (a sign of a growing textile industry) increased sevenfold between 1831 and 1848, and the number of factories doubled along with the size of the industrial workforce.

Although Great Britain consciously strove to protect its industrial supremacy, thousands of British engineers defied laws against the export of machinery or the emigration of artisans. Only slowly, thanks to the pirating of British methods and to new technical schools, did most continental countries begin closing the gap. Belgium became the fastest-growing industrial power on the continent: between 1830 and 1844, the number of steam engines in Belgium quadrupled, and Belgians exported seven times as many steam engines as they imported. Even so, by 1850, continental Europe still lagged almost twenty years behind Great Britain in industrial development.

The Formation of the Working Class. Despite striking industrial growth, factory workers remained a minority everywhere. In the 1840s, factories in England employed only 5 percent of the workers; in France, 3 percent; in Prussia, 2 percent. Many peasants kept

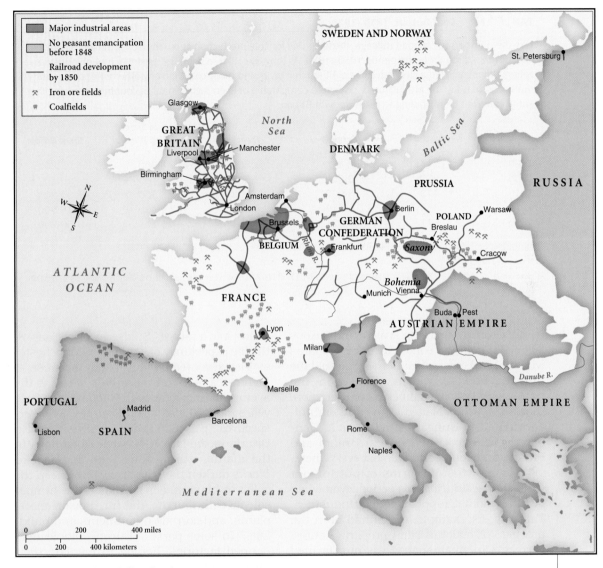

MAP 22.1 Industrialization in Europe, c. 1850
Industrialization first spread in a band across northern Europe that included Great Britain, northern France, Belgium, the northern German states, the region around Milan in northern Italy, and Bohemia. Much of Scandinavia and southern and eastern Europe were left out of this first phase of industrial development. Although railroads were not the only factor in promoting industrialization, the map makes clear the interrelationship between railroad building and the development of new industrial sites of coal mining and textile production.

their options open by combining factory work with agricultural labor. From Switzerland to Russia, people worked in agriculture during the spring and summer and in manufacturing in the fall and winter. Unstable industrial wages made such arrangements essential. Some new industries idled periodically: for example, iron forges stopped for several months when the water level in streams dropped, and blast furnaces shut down for repairs several weeks every year. In hard times, factory owners simply closed their doors until demand for their goods improved.

In addition, workers continued to toil at home in putting-out, or cottage, industries. In the 1840s, for example, two-thirds of the

TABLE 22.1   Coal Output, 1830–1850

Like the numbers for railroad mileage, these figures for coal production show the economic dominance of Great Britain throughout the period 1830–1850. As long as coal remained the essential fuel of industrialization, Britain enjoyed a clear advantage. Although it produced more coal than any other European country, rates of increase in the production of coal were comparable or even higher in other countries, showing that some countries were starting to catch up with Britain.

	Austria	Belgium	France	German States (including Prussia)	Great Britain
1830	214	*	1,863	1,800	22,800
1835	251	2,639	2,506	2,100	28,100
1840	473	3,930	3,003	3,200	34,200
1845	689	4,919	4,202	4,400	46,600
1850	877	5,821	4,434	5,100	50,200

Output of coal (in thousands of metric tons).

*Data not available.

Source: B. R. Mitchell, *European Historical Statistics, 1750–1970* (New York: Columbia University Press, 1975), D2.

manufacturing workers in Prussia and Saxony labored at home for contractors or merchants who supplied raw materials and then sold the finished goods. Women worked in the putting-out system as much as or even more than men—they plaited straw and embroidered cloth in Hungary, made pots in Denmark, fashioned lace in Great Britain and France, and spun cotton almost everywhere.

Some of the old forms of putting-out work changed during this period, even when factories did not supplant cottage industries. Tailoring, for example, which had been the province of male artisans preparing entire garments in small shops, was now farmed out to women working at home for much lower "piece rates." Even though factories employed only a small percentage of the population, they attracted much attention. Factories produced wealth without regard to the pollution they caused or the exhausted state of their workers; industry created unheard-of riches and new forms of poverty all at once. "From this foul drain the greatest stream of human industry flows out to fertilize the whole world," wrote the French aristocrat Alexis de Tocqueville after visiting the new English industrial city of Manchester in the 1830s. "From this filthy sewer pure gold flows. Here humanity attains its most complete development and its most brutish, here civilization works its miracles and civilized man is turned almost into a savage." Studies by physicians set the life expectancy of workers in Manchester at just seventeen years (partly because of high rates of infant mortality), whereas the average life expectancy in England was forty years in 1840. (See "New Sources, New Perspectives," page 836.) One American visitor in Britain in the late 1840s described how "in the manufacturing town, the fine soot or *blacks* darken the day, give white sheep the color of black sheep, discolor the human saliva, contaminate the air, poison many plants, and corrode monuments and buildings." In some parts of Europe, city leaders banned factories, hoping to insulate their towns from the effects of industrial growth.

As factory production expanded, local and national governments collected information about the workers. Investigators detailed their pitiful condition. A French physician in the eastern town of Mulhouse described the "pale, emaciated women who walk barefooted through the dirt" to reach the factory. The young children who worked in the factory appeared "clothed in rags which are greasy with the oil from the looms and frames." A report to the city government in Lille, France, in 1832 described "dark cellars" where the cotton workers lived: "the air is never renewed, it is infected; the walls are plastered with garbage." In the Prussian town of Breslau (population 111,000 in

1850), a doctor reported that in working-class districts "several persons live in one room in a single bed, or perhaps a whole family, and use the room for all domestic duties. . . . Their diet consists largely of bread and potatoes. These are clearly the two main reasons for the scrofula [a disease related to tuberculosis] which is so widespread here; the diet is also the cause of the common malformation of limbs."

Government inquiries often focused on women and children. In Great Britain, the Factory Act of 1833 outlawed the employment of children under the age of nine in textile mills (except in the lace and silk industries) and limited the workdays of children ages nine to thirteen to nine hours a day and those ages thirteen to eighteen to twelve hours. Adults worked even longer hours. When investigating commissions showed that women and young children, sometimes under age six, were hauling coal trucks through low, cramped passageways in coal mines, the British Parliament passed a Mines Act in 1842 prohibiting the employment of women and girls underground. One nine-year-old girl, Margaret Gomley, had described her typical day in the mines as beginning at 7:00 A.M. and ending at 6:00 P.M.: "I get my dinner at 12 o'clock, which is a dry muffin, and sometimes butter on, but have no time allowed to stop to eat it, I eat it while I am thrusting the load. . . . They flog us down in the pit, sometimes with their hand upon my bottom, which hurts me very much." In 1847, the Central Short Time Committee, one of Britain's many social reform organizations, successfully pressured Parliament to limit the workday of women and children to ten hours. The continental countries followed the British lead, but since most did not insist on government inspection, enforcement was lax.

Urbanization and Its Consequences

Industrial development spurred urban growth wherever factories were located in or near cities, yet cities grew even with little industry. Here, too, Great Britain led the way: half the population of England and Wales lived in towns by 1850, while in France and the German states the urban population was only about a quarter of the total. Both old and new cities teemed with growing population in the 1830s and 1840s; the population of Vienna grew by 125,000 between 1827 and 1847, and the new industrial city Manchester grew by 70,000 just in the 1830s. (See "Taking Measure," page 838.)

Massive rural emigration, rather than births to women already living in cities, accounted for this remarkable increase. Agricultural improvements had increased the food supply and hence the rural population, but the land could no longer support the people living on it. City life and new factories beckoned those faced with hunger and poverty, including emigrants from other lands: thousands of Irish emigrated to English cities, Italians went to French cities, and Poles flocked to German cities. Settlements sprang up outside the old city limits but gradually became part of the urban area. As cities grew, their medieval walls came down. At the same time, cities incorporated parks, cemeteries, zoos, and greenways, all imitations of the countryside, which itself was being industrialized by railroads and factories. "One can't even go to one's land for the slightest bit of gardening," grumbled a French citizen, annoyed by new industrial potteries in town, "without being covered with a black powder that spoils every plant that it touches."

Overcrowding and Disease.   The rapid influx of people caused serious overcrowding in the cities because the housing stock expanded much more slowly than population growth. In Paris, 30,000 workers lived in lodging houses, eight or nine to a room, with no separation of the sexes. One contemporary observed: "The difficulty of finding lodgings is for the worker a constant ordeal and a perpetual cause of misery." In 1847 in St. Giles, the Irish quarter of London, 461 people lived in just twelve houses. Men, women, and children huddled together on piles of filthy rotting straw or potato peels because they had no money for fuel to keep warm.

Severe crowding worsened already dire sanitation conditions. Residents dumped refuse into streets or courtyards, and human excrement collected in cesspools under apartment houses. At midcentury, London's approximately 250,000 cesspools were emptied only once or twice a year. Water was scarce

NEW SOURCES, NEW PERSPECTIVES

Statistics and the Standard of Living of the Working Class

From the very beginning of industrialization, experts argued about whether industrialization improved or worsened the standard of living of the working class. For every claim, there was a counterclaim, and most often these claims came in the form of statistics. Some experts argued that factories offered higher-paying jobs to workers; others countered that factories took work away from artisans such as handloom weavers and left them on the verge of starvation. Supporters of industrialization maintained that factories gave women paying work; opponents insisted that factories destroyed the family by taking women away from the home. Through mass production, industrialization made goods cheaper and therefore more available; by polluting the air, it destroyed health, lowered life expectancy, and ruined the environment. Karl Marx and Friedrich Engels would give the debate even more of an edge by tying it to the ideology of communism. In 1844, Engels described to Marx his aim in writing *The Condition of the Working Class in England:* "I shall present the English with a fine bill of indictment. At the bar of world opinion I charge the English middle classes with mass murder, wholesale robbery and all the other crimes in the calendar."* The stakes of the argument were not small.

The controversy about the benefits and costs of industrialization has continued in different forms right down to the present, in part because

*Quoted in R. M. Hartwell et al., *The Long Debate on Poverty* (Surrey, England: Institute of Economic Affairs, 1972), 185.

it is an argument directly inspired by the ideologies—liberalism, socialism, communism—that emerged as explanations of and blueprints for economic and social change. In the 1830s and 1840s, liberals insisted that industrialization would promote greater prosperity for everyone, whereas conservatives complained that it destroyed traditional ways of life and socialists warned that it exaggerated inequality and class division. In the 1950s and 1960s, defenders of capitalist free enterprise still advanced the argument about prosperity, but now they were opposed by communists who argued that state control of production could sidestep the horrors of early capitalist exploitation. Newly developing countries looked to the history of the 1830s and 1840s for lessons about the likely impact of industrialization on their countries in the 1950s and beyond. The scholarly debates therefore attracted worldwide attention, and all sides called on statistics to make their competing cases.

Unfortunately, the statistics can be interpreted in many different ways. Did it matter more that wages for factory workers went up or that life expectancy went down? If an increase in sugar consumption in Great Britain from 207,000 tons in 1844 to 290,000 tons in 1847 meant an overall increase in the standard of living, how does that square with the hundreds of thousands of deaths in Ireland at the same time or the increasing disparity throughout Great Britain between rich and poor? Some convergence of opinion has taken place, however. Most now agree that by sometime between 1820 and 1845 (the exact date depending on the scholar), conditions

and had to be fetched daily from nearby fountains. Despite the diversion of water from provincial rivers to Paris and a tripling of the number of public fountains, Parisians had enough water for only two baths annually per person (the upper classes enjoyed more baths, of course; the lower classes, fewer). In London, private companies that supplied water turned on pumps in the poorer sections for only a few hours three days a week. In rapidly growing British industrial cities such as Manchester, one-third

in Great Britain had become better than before the Industrial Revolution. And there is no doubt that the debate itself has had one major positive effect: since making one's point depends on having statistics to prove it, the debate itself has encouraged a staggering amount of research into quantitative measures of just about everything imaginable, from measures of wages and prices to rates of mortality and even average heights (height being correlated, it is thought, to economic well-being). British soldiers in the nineteenth century were taller on average than those in any other country except the United States, and people who believe that industrialization improved the standard of living are happy to seize on this as evidence for their case.

Trends in the British Nominal-Wage Gap, 1797–1851

Year	Index	Year	Index
1797	100	1827	132.4
1805	86.6	1835	134.7
1810	96.7	1851	148.3
1815	105.1		

The gap is calculated as the difference between the weighted average of nonfarm unskilled earnings (common laborers, porters, police, guards, watchmen, coal miners, and so on) and the farm-earnings rate, divided by the farm-earnings rate. Thus, it is the percentage differential by which nonfarm unskilled wages exceeded farm wages.

Source: Jeffrey G. Williamson, "Leaving the Farm to Go to the City: Did They Leave Quickly Enough?" in John A. James and Mark Thomas, *Capitalism in Context: Essays on Economic Development and Cultural Change in Honor of R. M. Hartwell* (Chicago: University of Chicago Press, 1994), 159–83; table on page 182.

One example of a recently developed statistic shows both how powerful and how debatable such sources can be. This table, adapted from a re-

cent study by Jeffrey G. Williamson, provides a simple measure—based on complex calculations—of the gap in wages between British farm and nonfarm laborers for the period 1797 to 1851. The index measures the attractiveness of nonfarm (basically city, mining, and factory) work. It shows that nonfarm wages rose faster than farm wages, but only after 1820 or so. By 1851, nonfarm wages had far outstripped those on the farm. What can we conclude? Although these data seem to support the view that the standard of living of workers improved sometime in the 1820s and continued to do so afterward, Williamson does not conclude that factory workers were better off than farmers; instead, he argues that the gap indicates that farm people did not migrate quickly enough to the city to satisfy urban labor demands. In short, he seems to consider the gap between farm and nonfarm wages to be a problem of "labor-market disequilibrium." The lesson to be learned is that all historians' conclusions depend on the questions they ask and the sources they use—and few other sources are as open to different interpretations as statistics.

QUESTIONS TO CONSIDER

1. What is a good measure of the standard of living in the first half of the nineteenth century? How would you measure the standard of living today?
2. How do you explain the initial decline in nonfarm wages relative to farm wages and the subsequent rise?
3. What are the virtues of using statistical measures to determine the standard of living? What are the defects?

FURTHER READING

Morgan, Kenneth. *The Birth of Industrial Britain: Economic Change 1750–1850.* 1999.

Thompson, Noel W. *The Real Rights of Man: Political Economies for the Working Class, 1775–1850.* 1998.

of the houses contained no latrines. Human waste ended up in the rivers that supplied drinking water. The horses that provided transportation inside the cities left droppings everywhere, and city dwellers often kept chickens, ducks, goats, pigs, geese, and even

cattle, as well as dogs and cats, in their houses. The result was a "universal atmosphere of filth and stink."

Such conditions made cities prime breeding grounds for disease; those with 50,000 people or more had twice the death rates of

TAKING MEASURE

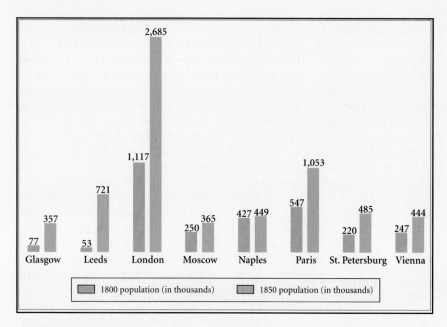

Population of Major European Cities, 1800–1850
Although London was by far the biggest city in mid-nineteenth-century Europe, it was not the fastest growing. According to these figures for population in 1800 and 1850, which city was the fastest growing? To what extent was population growth in these cities due to industrialization? What problems might have been created by especially rapid growth? *From B. R. Mitchell,* European Historical Statistics, 1750–1970 *(New York: Columbia University Press, 1975), B4.*

In Great Britain, the reports on sanitation conditions among the working class led to the passage of new public health laws.

Middle-Class Fears. Government intervention did little to ease the social tensions inspired by rapid urban growth. The middle and upper classes lived in large, well-appointed apartments or houses with more light, more air, and more water than in lower-class dwellings. But the lower classes lived nearby, sometimes in the cramped upper floors of the same apartment houses. Middle-class reformers often considered the poor to be morally degenerate because of the circumstances of urban life. In their view, overcrowding led to sexual promiscuity and illegitimacy. They depicted the lower classes

rural areas. Rumors and panic followed in the wakes of epidemics such as cholera (Map 22.2). Everywhere the downtrodden imagined conspiracies: in Paris in April 1832, a crowd of workers attacked a central hospital, believing the doctors were poisoning the poor but using cholera as a hoax to cover up the conspiracy. Eastern European peasants burned estates and killed physicians and officials. Although devastating, cholera did not kill as many people as tuberculosis, Europe's number-one deadly disease. But tuberculosis took its victims one by one and therefore had less impact on social relations.

Raging epidemics spurred a growing concern for public health. When news of the cholera outbreak in eastern Europe reached Paris in 1831, the city set up commissions in each municipal district to collect information about lower-class housing and sanitation.

as dangerously lacking in sexual self-control. A physician visiting Lille, France, in 1835 wrote of "individuals of both sexes and of very different ages lying together, most of them without nightshirts and repulsively dirty. . . . The reader will complete the picture. . . . His imagination must not recoil before any of the disgusting mysteries performed on these impure beds, in the midst of obscurity and drunkenness."

Officials collected statistics on illegitimacy that seemed to bear out these fears: one-quarter to one-half of the babies born in the big European cities in the 1830s and 1840s were illegitimate, and alarmed medical men wrote about thousands of infanticides. Between 1815 and the mid-1830s in France, 33,000 babies were abandoned at foundling hospitals every year; 27 percent of births in Paris in 1850 were illegitimate, compared with only 4 percent of rural births.

By collecting such statistics, physicians and administrators in the new public health movement hoped to promote legislation to better the living conditions for workers, but at the same time they helped stereotype workers as helpless and out of control.

Sexual disorder seemed to go hand in hand with drinking and crime. Beer halls and pubs dotted the urban landscape. By the 1830s, Hungary's twin cities of Buda and Pest had eight hundred beer and wine houses for the working classes. One London street boasted twenty-three pubs in three hundred yards. Police officials estimated that London had 70,000 thieves and 80,000 prostitutes. In many cities, nearly half the urban population lived at the level of bare subsistence, and increasing numbers depended on public welfare, charity, or criminality to make ends meet.

Everywhere reformers warned of a widening separation between rich and poor and a growing sense of hostility between the classes. The French poet Amédée Pommier wrote of "These leagues of laborers who have no work,/These far too many arms, these starving mobs." Clergy joined the chorus of physi-cians and humanitarians in making dire predictions. A Swiss pastor noted: "A new spirit has arisen among the workers. Their hearts seethe with hatred of the well-to-do; their eyes lust for a share of the wealth about them; their mouths speak unblushingly of a coming day of retribution." In 1848 it would seem that that day of retribution had arrived.

Agricultural Perils and Prosperity

Rising population created increased demand for food and spurred changes in life in the countryside too. Peasants and farmers planted fallow land, chopped down forests, and drained marshes to increase their farming capacity. Still, Europe's ability to feed its expanding population remained questionable: although agricultural yields increased by 30 to 50 percent in the first half of the nineteenth century, population grew by nearly 100 percent. Railroads and canals improved food distribution, but much of Europe—particularly in the east—remained isolated from markets and vulnerable to famines.

Most people still lived on the land, and the upper classes still dominated rural society. Successful businessmen bought land avidly, seeing it not only as the ticket to respectability but also as a hedge against hard times. Hardworking, crafty, or lucky commoners sometimes saved enough to purchase holdings that they had formerly rented or slowly acquired slivers of land from less fortunate neighbors. In France at midcentury, almost two million economically independent peasants tended their own small properties. But in England, southern Italy, Prussia, and eastern Europe, large landowners, usually noblemen, consolidated and expanded their estates by buying up the land of less successful nobles or peasants. As agricultural prices rose, the big landowners pushed for legislation to allow them to continue converting common land to private property.

Wringing a living from the soil under such conditions put pressure on traditional family life. For example, men often migrated seasonally to earn cash in factories or as village artisans, while their wives, sisters, and daughters did the traditional "men's work" of tending crops. The threat of subdivision of the land encouraged rudimentary forms of birth control.

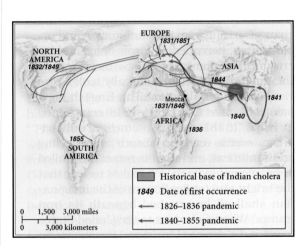

MAP 22.2 The Spread of Cholera, 1826–1855
Contemporaries did not understand the causes of the cholera epidemics in the 1830s and the 1840s in Europe. Western Europeans knew only that the disease marched progressively from east to west across Europe. Nothing seemed able to stop it. It appeared and died out for reasons that could not be grasped at the time. Nevertheless, the cholera epidemics prompted authorities in most European countries to set up public health agencies to coordinate the response and study sanitation conditions in the cities.

Joseph M. W. Turner, *The Fighting "Téméraire"*
***Tugged to Her Last Berth to Be Broken Up* (1838)**
In this painting a steamer belching smoke tows a wooden sailing ship to its last berth, where it will be destroyed. Turner muses about the passing of old ways but also displays his mastery of color in the final blaze of sunset, itself another sign of the passing of time. Turner considered painting to be closely related to poetry; he was an avid reader of the romantic poets, especially Byron. How does the painting capture the clash of old and new? **For more help in analyzing this image,** see the visual activity for this chapter in the Online Study Guide at **bedfordstmartins.com/hunt**. *National Gallery, London.*

rooms and lending libraries, and serialization in newspapers and journals, novels reached a large reading public. Unlike the fiction of the eighteenth century, which had focused on individual personalities, the great novels of the 1830s and 1840s specialized in the portrayal of social life in all its varieties. Manufacturers, financiers, starving students, workers, bureaucrats, prostitutes, underworld figures, thieves, and aristocratic men and women filled the pages of works by popular writers. Pushing himself to exhaustion and a premature death to get out of debt, the French writer Honoré de Balzac (1799–1850) cranked out ninety-five novels and many short stories. He aimed to catalog the social types that could be found in French society. Many

of his characters, like himself, were driven by the desire to climb higher in the social order.

The English author Charles Dickens (1812–1870) worked with a similar frenetic energy and for much the same reasons. When his father was imprisoned for debt in 1824, the young Dickens took a job in a shoe-polish factory. In 1836, he published a series of literary sketches of daily life in London to accompany a volume of caricatures by the artist George Cruikshank. Dickens then produced a series of novels that appeared in monthly installments and attracted thousands of readers. In them, he paid close attention to the distressing effects of industrialization and urbanization. In *The Old Curiosity Shop* (1841), for example, he depicts the Black Country, the manufacturing region west and northwest of Birmingham, as a "cheerless region," a "mournful place," in which tall chimneys "made foul the melancholy air." In addition to publishing such enduring favorites as *Oliver Twist* (1838) and *A Christmas Carol* (1843), he ran charitable organizations and pressed for social reforms. For Charles Dickens, the ability to portray the problems of the poor went hand in hand with a personal commitment to reform.

Novels by women often revealed the bleaker side of women's situations. *Jane Eyre* (1847), a novel by Charlotte Brontë, describes the difficult life of an orphaned girl who becomes a governess, the only occupation open to most single middle-class women. Although in an economically weak position, Jane Eyre refuses to achieve respectability and security through marriage, the usual option for women. The French novelist George Sand (Amandine-Aurore Dupin, 1804–1876) took her social criticism a step further. She announced her independence in the 1830s by dressing like a man and smoking cigars. Like many other women writers of the time, she published her work under a male pseudonym while creating female characters who prevail in difficult circumstances through romantic love and moral idealism. Sand's novel *Indiana* (1832), about an unhappily married woman, was read all over Europe. Her notoriety—she became the lover of the Polish pianist Frédéric Chopin, among others, and threw herself into socialist politics—made the term *George-Sandism* a common expression of disdain for independent women.

The Explosion of Culture. As artists became more interested in society and social relations, ordinary citizens crowded cultural

George Sand
In this lithograph by Alcide Lorentz of 1842, George Sand is shown in one of her notorious male costumes. Sand published numerous works, including novels, plays, essays, travel writing, and an autobiography. She actively participated in the revolution of 1848 in France, writing pamphlets in support of the new republic. Disillusioned by the rise to power of Louis-Napoleon Bonaparte, she withdrew to her country estate and devoted herself exclusively to her writing. *The Granger Collection.*

events. Museums opened to the public across Europe, and the middle classes began collecting art. Popular theaters in big cities drew thousands from the lower and middle classes every night; in London, for example, some 24,000 people attended eighty "penny theaters" nightly. The audience for print culture also multiplied. In the German states, for example, the production of new literary works doubled between 1830 and 1843, as did the number of periodicals and newspapers and the number of booksellers. Thirty or forty private lending libraries offered books in Berlin in the 1830s, and reading rooms in pastry shops stocked political newspapers and satirical journals. Young children and ragpickers sold cheap prints and books door to door or in taverns.

The advent of photography in 1839 provided an amazing new medium for artists. The **daguerreotype**,◆ named after its inventor, French painter Jacques Daguerre (1787–1851), prompted one artist to claim that "from today, painting is dead." Although this prediction was highly exaggerated, photography did open up new ways of portraying reality. Visual images, whether in painting, on the stage, or in photography, heightened the public's awareness of the effects of industrialization and urbanization.

◆**daguerreotype:** duh GEH roh type

Daguerreotype of Paris
Daguerre experimented extensively with producing an image on a metal plate before he came up with a viable photographic process in 1837. In 1839, the French government bought the rights and made the process freely available. This picture of the Louvre and the Tuileries garden in Paris (c. 1850) seems almost empty of people because with the long exposure required to capture the image, moving objects did not register. The image is also reversed (as if seen in a mirror). Because of these technical problems, the early photographic process proved most suitable for portraits. *Bridgeman Art Library/ Archives Charmet.*

The Varieties of Social Reform

Lithographs, novels, even joke booklets helped drive home the need for social reform, but religious conviction also inspired efforts to help the poor. Moral reform societies, Bible groups, Sunday schools, and temperance groups all aimed to turn the poor into respectable people. In 1844, for example, 450 different relief organizations operated in London alone. States supported these efforts by encouraging education and enforcing laws against the vagrant poor.

The Religious Impulse for Social Reform. Religiously motivated reformers first had to overcome the perceived indifference of the working classes. Protestant and Catholic clergy complained that workers had no interest in religion; less than 10 percent of the workers in the cities attended religious services. In a report on the state of religion in England and Wales in 1851, the head of the census Horace Mann commented that "the masses of our working population . . . are *unconscious secularists*. . . . These are never, or but seldom seen in our religious congregations." To combat such indifference, British religious groups launched the Sunday school movement, which reached its zenith in the 1840s. By 1851, more than half of all working-class children ages five to fifteen were attending Sunday school, even though very few of their parents regularly went to religious services. The Sunday schools taught children how to read at a time when few working-class children could go to school during the week.

Women took a more prominent role than ever before in charitable work. Catholic religious orders, which by 1850 enrolled many more women than men, ran schools, hospitals, leper colonies, insane asylums, and old-age

The number of artists and writers swelled. Estimates suggest that the number of painters and sculptors in France, the undisputed center of European art at the time, grew sixfold between 1789 and 1838. Not everyone could succeed in this hothouse atmosphere, in which writers and artists furiously competed for public attention. Their own troubles made some of them more keenly aware of the hardships faced by the poor. In one of many bitingly critical journals and booklets published in Berlin appeared the following "Lies Chronicle": "In Ipswich in England a mechanical genius has invented a stomach, whose extraordinary efficient construction is remarkable. This artificial stomach is intended for factory workers there and is adjusted so that it is fully satisfied with three lentils or peas; one potato is enough for an entire week."

homes. New Catholic orders, especially for women, were established, and Catholic missionary activity overseas increased. Protestant women in Great Britain and the United States established Bible, missionary, and female reform societies by the hundreds. Chief among their concerns was prostitution, and many societies dedicated themselves to reforming "fallen women" and castigating men who visited prostitutes. As a pamphlet of the Boston Female Moral Reform Society explained, "Our mothers, our sisters, our daughters are sacrificed by the thousands every year on the altar of sin, and who are the agents in this work of destruction: Why, our fathers, our brothers, and our sons." Elizabeth Fry, an English Quaker minister, toured Europe in the 1830s helping set up institutions for female prisoners modeled on the school and manufacturing shop she had organized at Newgate Prison in London.

Catholics and Protestants alike promoted the **temperance movement**. In Ireland, England, the German states, and the United States, temperance societies organized to fight the "pestilence of hard liquor." The first societies had appeared in the United States as early as 1813, and by 1835 the American Temperance Society claimed 1.5 million members. The London-based British and Foreign Temperance Society, established in 1831, matched its American counterpart in its opposition to all alcohol. In the northern German states, temperance societies drew in the middle and working classes, Catholic as well as Protestant. Temperance advocates saw drunkenness as a sign of moral weakness and a threat to social order. Industrialists pointed to the loss of worker productivity, and efforts to promote temperance often reflected middle- and upper-class fears of the lower classes' lack of discipline. One German temperance advocate insisted, "One need not be a prophet to know that all efforts to combat the widespread and rapidly spreading pauperism will be unsuccessful as long as the common man fails to realize that the principal source of his degradation and misery is his fondness of drink." Yet temperance societies also attracted working-class people who shared the desire for respectability.

Education and Reform of the Poor. Social reformers saw education as one of the main prospects for uplifting the poor and the working class. In addition to setting up Sunday schools, British churches founded organizations such as the National Society for the Education of the Poor in the Principles of the Established Church and the British and Foreign

The Temperance Movement

This 1847 engraving by George Cruikshank was fifth in a series of eight prints that told the story of a family ruined by drink. The caption to this engraving—"Cold misery and want destroy their youngest child: they console themselves with the bottle"—makes the artist's message clear. Alcohol only made the miserable lives of the working poor even more miserable. *Bridgeman Art Library. The Stapleton Collection.*

Bearbaiting

This colored engraving from 1821 of Charley's Theater in London shows that bearbaiting did not attract only the lower classes, as reformers often implied. Top hats were most often worn by middle-class men, who seem to be enjoying the spectacle of dogs taunting the bear as much as the working-class men present. At this time, bearbaiting, like bullbaiting, began to come under fire as cruel to animals. *Mary Evans Picture Library.*

School Society. Most of these emphasized Bible reading. More secular in intent were the Mechanics Institutes, which provided education for workers in the big cities.

In 1833, the French government passed an education law that required every town to maintain a primary school, pay a teacher, and provide free education to poor boys. As the law's author, François Guizot, argued, "Ignorance renders the masses turbulent and ferocious." Girls' schools were optional, although hundreds of women taught at the primary level, most of them in private, often religious schools. Despite these efforts, only one out of every thirty children went to school in France, many fewer than in Protestant states such as Prussia, where 75 percent of children were in primary school by 1835. Popular education remained woefully undeveloped in most of eastern Europe. Peasants were specifically excluded from the few primary schools in Russia, where Tsar Nicholas I blamed the Decembrist Revolt of 1825 on education.

Above all else, the elite sought to impose discipline and order on working people. Popular sports, especially blood sports such as cockfighting and bearbaiting, suggested a lack of control, and long-standing efforts in Great Britain to eliminate these recreations now gained momentum through organizations such as the Society for the Prevention of Cruelty to Animals. By the end of the 1830s, bullbaiting had been abandoned in Great Britain. "This useful animal," rejoiced one reformer in 1839, "is no longer tortured amidst the exulting yells of those who are a disgrace to our common form and nature." The other blood sports died out more slowly, and efforts in other countries generally lagged behind those of the British.

When private charities failed to meet the needs of the poor, governments often intervened. Great Britain sought to control the costs of public welfare by passing a new poor law in 1834, called by its critics the "Starvation Act." The law required that all able-bodied persons receiving relief be housed together in workhouses, with husbands separated from wives and parents from children. Workhouse life was designed to be as unpleasant as possible so that poor people would move on to regions of higher employment. British women from all social classes organized anti–poor law societies to protest the separation of mothers from their children in the workhouses.

Domesticity and the Subordination of Women. Many women viewed charitable work as the extension of their domestic roles: they promoted virtuous behavior and morality and thus improved society. In one widely read advice book, Englishwoman Sarah Lewis suggested in 1839 that "women may be the prime agents in the regeneration of mankind." But women's social reform activities concealed a paradox. According to the set of beliefs, or ideology, that historians call **domesticity**, women should live their lives entirely within the domestic sphere; they should devote themselves to the home. The English poet Alfred, Lord Tennyson, captured this view in a popular poem published in 1847: "Man for the field and woman for the hearth; / Man for the sword and for the needle she. . . . All else confusion." Many believed that maintaining proper and distinct roles for men and women was critically important to maintaining social order in general.

Most women had little hope of economic independence. The notion of a separate, domestic sphere for women prevented them from pursuing higher education, work in professional careers, or participation in politics through voting or holding office—all activities deemed appropriate only to men. Laws everywhere codified the subordination of women. Many countries followed the model of Napoleon's Civil Code, which classified married women as legal incompetents along with children, the insane, and criminals. In Great Britain, which had no national law code, the courts upheld the legality of a husband's complete control. For example, in 1840 a court ruled that "there can be no doubt of the general dominion which the law of England attributes to the husband over the wife." In some countries, such as France and Austria, unmarried women enjoyed some rights over property, but elsewhere laws explicitly defined them as perpetual minors under paternal control.

Distinctions between men and women were most noticeable in the privileged classes. Whereas boys attended secondary schools, most middle- and upper-class girls still received their education at home or in church schools, where they were taught to be religious, obedient, and accomplished in music and languages. As men began to wear practical clothing—long trousers and short jackets of solid, often dark colors, no makeup (previously common for aristocratic men), and simply cut hair—women continued to dress for decorative effect, now with tightly corseted waists that emphasized the differences between female and male bodies. Middle- and upper-class women had long hair that required hours of brushing and pinning up, and they wore long, cumbersome skirts. Advice books written by women detailed the tasks that such women undertook in the home: maintaining household accounts, supervising servants, and organizing social events.

Scientists reinforced stereotypes. Once considered sexually insatiable, women were now described as incapacitated by menstruation and largely uninterested in sex, an attitude that many equated with moral superiority. Thus was born the "Victorian woman," a figment of the largely male medical imagination. Physicians and scholars considered women mentally inferior. In 1839, Auguste Comte, an influential early French sociologist, wrote, "As for any functions of government, the radical inaptitude of the female sex is there yet more marked . . . and limited to the guidance of the mere family."

Some women denounced the ideology of domesticity; according to the English writer Ann Lamb, for example, "the duty of a wife *means* the obedience of a Turkish slave." Middle-class women who did not marry, however, had few options for earning a living; they often worked as governesses or ladies' companions for the well-to-do. Most lower-class women worked because of financial necessity; as the wives of peasants, workers, or shopkeepers, they had to supplement the family's meager income by working on the farm, in a factory, or in a shop. For them, domesticity might have been an ideal but rarely was it a reality. Families crammed into small spaces had no time or energy for separate spheres.

Abuses and Reforms Overseas

Like the ideal of domesticity, the ideal of colonialism often conflicted with the reality of economic interests. In the first half of the nineteenth century, those economic interests changed as European colonialism underwent a subtle but momentous transformation.

Colonialism became **imperialism**—a word coined only in the mid-nineteenth century—as Europeans turned their interest away from the plantation colonies of the Caribbean toward the new colonies in Asia and Africa. Whereas colonialism most often led to the establishment of settler colonies, direct rule by Europeans, the introduction of slave labor from Africa, and the wholesale destruction of indigenous peoples, imperialism usually meant more indirect forms of economic exploitation and political rule. Europeans still profited from their colonies, but now they also aimed to reform colonial peoples in their own image—when it did not conflict too much with their economic interests to do so.

Abolition of Slavery. Colonialism—as opposed to imperialism—rose and fell with the enslavement of black Africans. The antislavery movement spread slowly but decisively following the British withdrawal from the slave trade in 1807. The new Latin American republics abolished slavery in the 1820s and 1830s after they defeated the Spanish with armies that included many slaves. British missionary and evangelical groups condemned the conquest, enslavement, and exploitation of native African populations and successfully blocked British annexations in central and southern Africa in the 1830s. British reformers finally obtained the abolition of slavery in the British Empire in 1833. Antislavery petitions to Parliament bore 1.5 million signatures, including those of 350,000 women on one petition alone. In France, the new government of Louis-Philippe took strong measures against clandestine slave traffic, virtually ending French participation during the 1830s. Slavery was abolished in the remaining French Caribbean colonies in 1848.

Slavery did not disappear immediately just because the major European powers had given it up. The transatlantic trade in slaves actually reached its peak numbers in the early 1840s. Human bondage continued unabated in Brazil, Cuba (still a Spanish colony), and the United States. Some American reformers supported abolition, but they remained a minority. Like serfdom in Russia, slavery in the Americas involved a quagmire of economic, political, and moral problems that worsened over time.

Historians debate the causes of the end of the African slave trade and of African slavery as a form of labor in the New World. Some argue that industrialization made slavery superfluous because with steam-driven machinery free labor proved itself more productive in the long run. Yet the British textile manufacturers relied heavily on imports of cotton from the southern slave states of the United States. Others place more emphasis on the antislavery campaign itself, arguing that slavery was incompatible with the humanitarian values of a reforming era. This explanation, however, does not account for the fact that the French and Dutch governments also abolished slavery even though neither faced major public reform campaigns. Whatever the reason for abolition, slavery, and with it the old-style colonialism, was on the wane.

Economic and Political Imperialism. Despite the abolition of slavery, Britain and France had not lost interest in overseas colonies. Using the pretext of an insult to its envoy, France invaded Algeria in 1830 and after a long military campaign established political control over most of the country in the next two decades. By 1850, more than seventy thousand French, Italian, and Maltese colonists had settled there, often confiscating the lands of native peoples. The new French administration of the colony made efforts to balance native and settler interests, however, and eventually France would not only incorporate Algeria into France but also try to assimilate its native population to French culture. France also imposed a protectorate government over the South Pacific island of Tahiti.

Although the British granted Canada greater self-determination in 1839, they extended their dominion elsewhere by annexing Singapore (1819), an island off the Malay peninsula, and New Zealand (1840). They also increased their control in India through the administration of the East India Company, a private group of merchants chartered by the British crown. The British educated a native elite to take over much of the day-to-day business of administering the country and used native soldiers to augment their military control. By 1850, only one in six soldiers serving Britain in India was European.

The East India Company also tried to establish a regular trade with China in opium, a drug long known for its medicinal uses but increasingly bought in China as a recreational drug. (See "Did You Know?," page 850.) The Chinese government did its best to keep the highly addictive drug away from its people, both by forbidding Western merchants to venture outside the southern city of Guangzhou◆ (Canton) and by banning the export of precious metals and the import of opium. These measures failed. By smuggling opium into China and bribing local officials, British traders built up a flourishing market, and by the mid-1830s they were pressuring the British government to force an expanded opium trade on the Chinese. When in 1839 the Chinese authorities expelled British merchants from southern China, Britain retaliated by bombarding Chinese coastal cities. The Opium War ended in 1842, when Britain dictated to a defeated China the Treaty of Nanking, by which four more Chinese ports were opened to Europeans and the British took sovereignty over the island of Hong Kong, received a substantial war indemnity, and were assured of a continuation of the opium trade. In this case, reform took a backseat to economic interest, despite the complaints of religious groups in Britain.

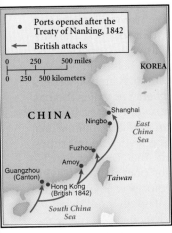

**The Opium War,
1839–1842**

> **Review:** How did reformers try to address the social problems created by industrialization and urbanization? In which areas did they succeed, and in which did they fail?

❖ The Ferment of Ideologies

Although reform organizations grew rapidly in the 1830s and 1840s, many Europeans found them insufficient to solve the problems created by industrialization and urbanization. They turned to movements inspired by the new political ideologies that had taken shape in the aftermath of the French Revolution. Liberals sought constitutional guarantees of rights and economic growth through free trade. Socialists developed new organizations to speak for the working classes and demand changes in the nature of work itself. But the most potent ideology—nationalism—looked past social problems to concentrate on achieving political autonomy and self-determination for groups identified by common languages and cultures rather than by class.

The Spell of Nationalism

Nationalists sought political autonomy for their ethnic group—a people linked by language and shared traditions. Although nationalism was still nascent in the first half of the nineteenth century among the peasants and workers of most countries, ethnic heritage was increasingly a major determinant of personal and political identity. Poles, Italians, Germans, Irish, and Russians all pursued nationalist goals (Map 22.3, page 852).

Polish nationalism became more self-conscious after the collapse of the revolt in 1830 against Russian domination. Ten thousand Poles, mostly noble army officers and intellectuals, fled Poland in 1830 and 1831. Most of them took up residence in western European capitals, especially Paris, where they mounted a successful public relations campaign for worldwide support. Their intellectual hero was the poet Adam Mickiewicz◆ (1798–1855), whose mystical writings portrayed the Polish exiles as martyrs of a crucified nation with an international Christian mission: "Your endeavors are for all men, not only for yourselves. You will achieve a new Christian civilization."

Mickiewicz formed the Polish Legion to fight for national restoration, but rivalries and divisions among the Polish nationalists

◆**Guangzhou:** GWAHN JOH

◆**Mickiewicz:** mihts KYAY vihch

DID YOU KNOW?

Opium Addiction in Nineteenth-Century Britain

Great Britain fought two opium wars with China (1839–1842 and 1856–1858) that drew world attention to the problem of Chinese drug addiction. In Great Britain itself, the government did not regulate or restrict opium use until 1868. Pharmacists and grocers sold pills, lozenges, enemas, vinegars, and wines prepared with opium, which came from the heads of poppy plants imported first from the Ottoman Empire and, after 1750, from India. A tincture of opium (opium dissolved in alcohol) known as laudanum was widely used as a sedative, and even children's opiates could be bought almost anywhere. Laudanum mixed with egg yolk was sold as a cure for hemorrhoids, and opiates were a popular remedy for toothache and diarrhea. Most doctors considered opium a good cure for delirium tremens, caused by alcohol abuse.

Death by overdose was a well-known phenomenon, but public opinion turned against the drug only when it became associated with abuse by the lower classes. Parliamentary inquiries in the 1830s denounced the use of opiates by working-class mothers, who gave their children Godfrey's Cordial or Street's Infant Quietness to make them sleep while they worked. Officials also worried that workers took opium and laudanum as a cheap substitute for alcohol, whose use was widely and loudly denounced by temperance societies. The concern about opiates followed from the general trend toward "reforming" lower-class behavior.

Well-known cases of addiction among writers and poets also attracted attention. The writer Thomas De Quincey stirred up controversy when he published his *Confessions of an English Opium-Eater* in 1821, but the book was reissued many times during the nineteenth century. In it, De Quincey discusses his and the romantic poet Samuel Taylor Coleridge's addiction. De Quincey calls himself the "pope" of the "true church" of opium and describes weaning himself from the drug in 1819 to escape the hallucinatory dreams that haunted him. He had terrifying nightmares of living in China in houses in which tables and sofas turned into crocodiles multiplied ten thousand times. But he relapsed and soon took bigger and bigger doses right into the 1840s. De Quincey and Coleridge were only the best-known cases of opium addiction: Lord Byron, Percy Bysshe Shelley, Elizabeth Barrett Browning, Walter Scott, and Charles Dickens all took opiates at one time or another, as did many leading doctors and preachers.

The history of opium use in the nineteenth century raises significant questions: Why did

prevented united action until 1846, when Polish exiles in Paris tried to launch a coordinated insurrection for Polish independence. Plans for an uprising in the Polish province of Galicia in the Austrian Empire collapsed when peasants instead revolted against their noble Polish masters. Slaughtering some two thousand aristocrats, a desperate rural population served the Austrian government's end by defusing the nationalist challenge. Class interests and national identity were not always the same.

One of those most touched by Mickiewicz's vision was Giuseppe Mazzini (1805–1872), a fiery Italian nationalist and republican journalist. Exiled in 1831 for his opposition to Austrian rule in northern Italy, Mazzini founded Young Italy, a secret society that attracted thousands with its message that Italy would touch off a European-wide revolutionary movement. The conservative order throughout Europe felt threatened by Mazzini's charismatic leadership and conspiratorial scheming, but he lacked both European allies against Austria and widespread support among the Italian masses.

Nationalism was an especially volatile issue in the Austrian Empire because Austria

Opium Den in London (c. 1870)
This woodcut by Gustave Doré shows that opium smoking persisted in Britain at least to the 1870s. Doré was a French book illustrator who came to London in 1869–1871 and produced illustrations of the poorer neighborhoods in the city. His taste for the grotesque is apparent in the figures watching the smokers. Doré also illustrated a book of Coleridge's poetry. *Print Collection, Miriam and Ira D. Wallach Division of Arts, Prints and Photographs. New York Public Library. Astor, Lenox and Tilden Foundation/Art Resource, NY.*

British authorities condemn its use at home even while forcing opium on the Chinese? Why was lower-class use of opiates especially disturbing to officials? Why did so many writers experiment with the drug? The history of opium is a fascinating example of the West's interaction with the rest of the world: the drug was first cultivated by ancient Sumerians and passed on to the Assyrians, Babylonians, Egyptians, and then Greeks; the Portuguese brought it to Europe in the sixteenth century as part of their trade with China; and its modern derivative heroin is now the subject of worldwide smuggling and official regulation.

Sources: Virginia Berridge and Griffith Edwards, *Opium and the People: Opiate Use in Nineteenth-Century England* (New York: St. Martin's Press, 1981); Thomas De Quincey, *The Confessions of an English Opium-Eater and Other Essays* (London: Macmillan, 1924).

ruled over so many different nationalities (see Map 22.3). The 1830s and 1840s saw the spread of nationalism among Magyars, Czechs, Slovaks, Serbs, Slovenes, Croats, and Romanians, in addition to Poles and Italians, all ethnic groups within the empire. Each of these peoples produced leaders who called for a cultural revival in language, literature, and education, as well as political rights. Scholars compiled dictionaries and created standard literary languages to replace peasant dialects; writers used the rediscovered vernacular instead of Latin or German; and historians glorified the national past. During the revolutions of 1848, however, it would become evident that these different ethnic groups disliked each other as much as they disliked their Austrian masters.

Economic unification in the German states took a step forward with the foundation in 1834, under Prussian leadership, of the *Zollverein,*♦ or "customs union." Economist Friedrich List argued for external tariffs that would promote industrialization and cooperation across the boundaries of the German states so that an economically united

─────────────

♦*Zollverein:* TSAWL vehr eyen

In the 1840s, however, Széchenyi's efforts paled before those of the flamboyant Magyar nationalist Lajos Kossuth◆ (1802–1894). After spending four years in prison for sedition, Kossuth grabbed every opportunity to publicize American democracy and British political liberalism, all in a fervent nationalist spirit. In 1844, he founded the Protective Association, whose members bought only Hungarian products; to Kossuth, boycotting Austrian goods was crucial to ending "colonial dependence" on Austria. Born of a lesser landowning family without a noble title, Kossuth did not hesitate to attack "the cowardly selfishness of the landowner class."

Even in Russia, signs of liberal, even socialist, opposition appeared in the 1830s and 1840s. Small circles of young noblemen serving in the army or bureaucracy met in cities, especially Moscow, to discuss the latest Western ideas and to criticize the Russian state: "The world is undergoing a transformation, while we vegetate in our hovels of wood and clay," wrote one. Out of these groups came such future revolutionaries as Alexander Herzen (1812–1870), described by the police as "a daring free-thinker, extremely dangerous to society." Tsar Nicholas I (r. 1825–1855) banned Western liberal writings as well as all books about the United States. He sent nearly ten thousand people a year into exile in Siberia as punishment for their political activities.

Socialism and the Early Labor Movement

Socialists railed against the inequalities caused by industrialization and considered liberalism an inadequate response. They envisioned a future society in which workers would share a harmonious, cooperative, and prosperous life. Building on the theoretical and practical ideas laid out in the early nineteenth century by Count Henri de Saint-Simon, Charles Fourier, and Robert Owen, the socialists of the 1830s and 1840s hoped that economic planning and working-class organization would solve the problems caused by industrial growth, including the threat of increasingly mechanical, unfeeling social relations.

◆**Lajos Kossuth:** LAW yohsh KAW shut

Socialism and Women. Women participated actively in the socialist movements of the day, even though socialist men often shared the widespread prejudice against women's political activism. In Great Britain many women joined the Owenites and helped form cooperative societies and unions. They defended women's working-class organizations against the complaints of men in the new societies and trade unions. As one woman wrote, "Do not say the unions are only for men. . . . 'Tis a wrong impression, forced on our minds to keep us slaves!" As women became more active, Owenites agitated for women's rights, marriage reform, and popular education. Rousing speakers such as Emma Martin (1812–1851) forcefully put the case: "One great evil is the depraved and ignorant condition of woman; this evil can only be removed by Socialism." Martin's speeches often stirred turbulent opposition as clergymen urged their congregations to shout her down. Occasionally, she was jeered, chased, and even stoned by mobs, so much did her ideas and very presence challenge conventional expectations.

The French activist Flora Tristan (1801–1844) devoted herself to reconciling the interests of male and female workers. She had seen the "frightful reality" of London's poverty and made a reputation reporting on British working conditions. Tristan published a stream of books and pamphlets urging male workers to address women's unequal status, arguing that "the emancipation of male workers is *impossible* so long as women remain in a degraded state." She advocated a Universal Union of Men and Women Workers. Despite political harassment, she traveled around France speaking out for her beliefs and attempting to organize workers.

Collectivists and Communists. Even though most male socialists ignored Tristan's plea for women's participation, like her they also strove to found working-class associations. The French socialist Louis Blanc (1811–1882) explained the importance of working-class associations in *Organization of Labor* (1840), which deeply influenced the French labor movement. Similarly, Pierre-Joseph Proudhon (1809–1865) urged workers to form producers' associations so that the workers could control the work process and eliminate profits made by capitalists. His 1840 book *What Is Property?* argues that property is theft: labor alone is productive, and rent, interest, and profit unjust.

After 1840, some socialists began to call themselves **communists**, emphasizing their desire to replace private property by communal, collective ownership. The Frenchman Étienne Cabet (1788–1856) first used the word *communist*. In 1840, he published *Travels in Icaria*, a novel describing a communist utopia in which a popularly elected dictatorship efficiently organized work, reduced the workday to seven hours, and made work tasks "short, easy, and attractive."

French socialist ideas circulated throughout Europe, from Belgium and the German states to Russia. They evoked most response in areas of incipient industrialization where artisans and workers felt intensely threatened by the prospect of change. The German tailor Wilhelm Weitling (1808–1871) developed an influential variant of socialism that had deeply religious overtones. His book *Guarantees of Harmony and Freedom* (1842) argues for a communal society but also emphasizes faith as necessary to life. In his view, "Jesus, too, was a communist." Weitling made a profound impression on workers' societies in the western German states.

Out of the churning of socialist ideas of the 1840s emerged two men whose collaboration would change the definition of socialism and remake it into an ideology that would shake the world for the next 150 years. Karl Marx (1818–1883) had studied philosophy at the University of Berlin, edited a liberal newspaper until the Prussian government suppressed it, and then left for Paris, where he met Friedrich Engels (1820–1895). While working in the offices of his wealthy family's cotton manufacturing interests in Manchester, England, Engels had been shocked into writing *The Condition of the Working Class in England in 1844* (1845), a sympathetic depiction of industrial workers' dismal lives. In Paris, where German and eastern European intellectuals could pursue their political interests more freely than at home, Marx and Engels organized the Communist League, in whose name they published *The Communist Manifesto* in 1848 (see the excerpt, page 856). It eventually became the touchstone of Marxist and communist revolution all over the world. Marx and Engels embraced industrialization because they believed it would eventually bring on the proletarian revolution and lead inevitably to the abolition of exploitation, private property, and class society. Communists, the *Manifesto* declared, must aim for "the downfall of the bourgeoisie [capitalist class] and the ascendancy of the proletariat [working class], the abolition of the old society based on class conflicts and the foundation of a new society without classes and without private property."

Working-Class Organization. Socialism accompanied, and in some places incited, an upsurge in working-class organization in western Europe. British workers founded cooperative societies, local trade unions, and so-called friendly societies for mutual aid, associations that frightened the middle classes. A newspaper exclaimed in 1834, "The trade unions are, we have no doubt, the most dangerous institutions that were ever permitted to take root."

Many British workers joined in **Chartism**, which aimed to transform Britain into a democracy. In 1838, political radicals drew up the People's Charter, which demanded universal manhood suffrage, vote by secret ballot, equal electoral districts, annual elections, and the elimination of property qualifications for and the payment of stipends to members of Parliament. Chartists denounced their opponents as seeking "to keep the people in social slavery and political degradation." Many women took part by founding female political unions, setting up Chartist Sunday schools, organizing boycotts of unsympathetic shopkeepers, and joining Chartist temperance associations. Nevertheless, the People's Charter refrained from calling for woman suffrage because the movement's leaders feared that doing so would alienate potential supporters.

The Chartists organized a massive campaign during 1838 and 1839, with large public meetings, fiery speeches, and torchlight parades. Presented with petitions for the People's Charter signed by more than a million people,

Marx and Engels, *The Communist Manifesto*

Karl Marx (1818–1883) and Friedrich Engels (1820–1895) were both sons of prosperous German-Jewish families that had converted to Christianity. In the manifesto for the Communist League, they laid out many of the central principles that would guide Marxist revolution in the future: they insisted that all history is shaped by class struggle and that in future revolutions the working class would overthrow the bourgeoisie, or middle class, and replace capitalism and private property with a communist state in which all property is collectively rather than individually owned. As this selection shows, Marx and Engels always placed more emphasis on class struggle than on the state that would result from the ensuing revolution.

The history of all hitherto existing society is the history of class struggles.

Freeman and slave, patrician and plebeian, lord and serf, guild-master and journeyman, in a word, oppressor and oppressed, stood in constant opposition to one another, carried on an uninterrupted, now hidden, now open fight, a fight that each time ended, either in a revolutionary reconstitution of society at large, or in the common ruin of the contending classes. . . .

The modern bourgeois society that has sprouted from the ruins of feudal society has not done away with class antagonisms. It has but established new classes, new conditions of oppression, new forms of struggle in place of the old ones.

Our epoch, the epoch of the bourgeoisie, possesses, however, this distinctive feature: It has simplified the class antagonisms: Society as a whole is more and more splitting up into two great hostile camps, into two great classes directly facing each other: Bourgeoisie [middle class] and Proletariat [working class]. . . .

The weapons with which the bourgeoisie felled feudalism to the ground are now turned against the bourgeoisie itself.

But not only has the bourgeoisie forged the weapons that bring death to itself; it has also called into existence the men who are to wield those weapons—the modern working class—the proletarians. . . .

The essential condition for the existence, and for the sway of the bourgeois class, is the formation and augmentation of capital; the condition for capital is wage-labour. Wage-labour rests exclusively on competition between labourers. The advance of industry, whose involuntary promoter is the bourgeoisie, replaces the isolation of the labourers, due to competition, by their revolutionary combination, due to association. The development of Modern Industry, therefore, cuts from under its feet the very foundation on which the bourgeoisie produces and appropriates products. What the bourgeoisie, therefore, produces, above all, is its own gravediggers. Its fall and the victory of the proletariat are equally inevitable.

Source: Karl Marx and Friedrich Engels, *The Communist Manifesto.* Translated by Samuel Moore (New York: Penguin, 1985), 79–80, 87, 93–94.

the House of Commons refused to act. In response to this rebuff from middle-class liberals, the Chartists allied themselves in the 1840s with working-class strike movements in the manufacturing districts and associated with various European revolutionary movements. But at the same time they—like their British and continental allies—distanced themselves from women workers. Chartists complained that working women undermined men's manhood, taking men's jobs and turning the men into "women-men" or "eunuchs." Continuing agitation and organization prepared the way for a last wave of Chartist demonstrations in 1848.

Continental workers were less well organized because trade unions and strikes were illegal everywhere except Great Britain. Nevertheless, artisans and skilled workers in France formed mutual aid societies that provided insurance, death benefits, and education. Workers in new factories rarely organized, but artisans in the old trades, such as the silk workers of Lyon, France, created societies to resist mechanization and wage cuts.

The new workers' press, such as the Saint-Simonian *People's Beehive* (1839), spread the ideas of socialist harmony and economic reform among the working classes. In eastern and central Europe, however, socialism and labor organization—like liberalism—had less impact than in western Europe. Guild-based organizations survived in the German states, for example, but cooperative societies and workers' newspapers did not appear until 1848. Farther east, the working classes were even smaller, and labor organizing reached few people.

The New Historical Imagination

In an age of competing ideologies, every ideology offered its own reading of history. Nationalism, in particular, fostered an enthusiasm for history, because history substantiated claims for a common national identity. German nationalists, for example, avidly read such massive books as Friedrich C. Schlosser's eighteen-volume *General History for the German People* (1844–1856). In Great Britain the equally famous histories by Thomas Macaulay described the British people as "the greatest and most highly civilized people that the world ever saw." Macaulay aimed to broaden history to include everyday life as well as politics, war, and diplomacy.

History entered the lifeblood of literature and painting as well. Romanticism had given history a special glamour, opening the way for a commercially successful genre, the historical novel. Readers devoured novels like Alexandre Dumas's *The Three Musketeers* (1844), set in the reign of Louis XIII in the 1620s. Dumas, the grandson of a Haitian slave, recounts the adventures of four soldiers who valiantly serve the queen of France and foil the plots of Cardinal Richelieu. Governments appreciated the value of paintings with a historical theme in reinforcing their own legitimacy. To link himself to the growing cult of Napoleon, for example, Louis-Philippe commissioned four paintings of the emperor's victories for the new Gallery of Battles at Versailles, now transformed into a museum. This effort culminated in 1840 when the government, led by the new prime minister Adolphe Thiers◆ (himself a noted historian of the French Revolution), arranged to return Napoleon's ashes to the Invalides◆ church in Paris. Although the spectacular public funeral showed Louis-Philippe's eagerness to establish his connections to Napoleonic history, it would not succeed in its goal of stifling demands for reform.

Nationalism and the new historical imagination also influenced musical romanticism. The Polish composer and pianist Frédéric Chopin (1810–1849) became a powerful champion in the West for the cause of his native land, with music that incorporated Polish folk rhythms and melodies. Opera, long a favorite with the public, experienced an abrupt transformation about 1830. Before this time, operatic plots had generally derived from classical mythology or had been contemporary social satires; now the public demanded passionate tragedy, usually with a picturesque medieval or Renaissance setting. The operatic portrayal of heroines as tragic victims who were sexually pure, noble-minded, and emotionally vulnerable mirrored the redefinition of women's character in contemporary middle-class opinion.

Alongside the burst of interest in the political and artistic uses of history came a new trend in historical writing that valued professional training above literary skill. The foremost practitioner of this new scholarship was Leopold von Ranke (1795–1886), a professor at the University of Berlin who taught many of the leading German historians of the nineteenth century. Ranke tried to understand the past objectively, on its own terms, rather than as lessons for present-day purposes. He organized small seminars of young men for the close study of documents. His reliance on source materials instead of legend or tradition helped reshape the study of history into a discipline based on critical methods. The most immediate response to this approach came in the history of religion. In 1835, the German scholar David Friedrich Strauss published the two-volume

◆**Thiers:** tee EHR
◆**Invalides:** an vahl EED

MAP 22.4
The Revolutions of 1848
The attempts of rulers to hold back the forces of change collapsed suddenly in 1848 when once again the French staged a revolution that inspired many others in Europe. This time, cities all over central and eastern Europe joined in as the spirit of revolt inflamed one capital after another. Although all of these revolutions eventually failed because of social and political divisions, the sheer scale of rebellion forced rulers to reconsider their policies.

Life of Jesus, in which he argues that the Gospels were not history but only imaginative stories that reflected Jewish myths in Roman times. Widely reprinted, Strauss's book caused a storm of controversy. In the 1840s, a series of new books followed Strauss's lead; some of them ended with proclamations that Jesus never existed.

The study of geology prompted the examination of other religious doctrines. A three-volume work published in 1830–1833 by the British geologist Charles Lyell (1797–1875) with the bland title *Principles of Geology* ignited debate. Lyell argues that the earth is much older than the dating of the biblical story of creation (assumed by many to be 4004 B.C.E.). Questioning religious assumptions enraged those whose beliefs rested on biblical certainty. Under Lyell's influence, Charles Darwin (1809–1882) would begin to sketch out the essentials of his theory of evolution by natural selection. Geology, the arts, nationalist histories, and historical novels all helped foster new forms of histor-

ical sensibility. But a sense of history did nothing to quiet the storm of ideological discontent. Liberals, socialists, and nationalists all vied for public support for their answers to the political and social questions raised by industrialization, urbanization, and the demand for national self-determination.

Review: Why did ideologies have such a powerful appeal in the 1830s and 1840s?

❖ The Revolutions of 1848

Food shortage, overpopulation, and unemployment helped turn ideological turmoil into revolution. In 1848, demonstrations and uprisings toppled governments, forced rulers and ministers to flee, and offered revolutionaries an opportunity to put liberal, socialist, and nationalist ideals into practice (Map 22.4). Of the major powers, only Great

The Potato Blight and Irish Famine

In this painting by Daniel McDonald, *The Discovery of the Potato Blight* (1852), a family is shown digging up its potato crop only to find that the potatoes had rotted from blight. This discovery spelled disaster for this family and thousands like it. The blight spores were airborne. After landing on potato plants, they killed the leaves, which fell to the ground. The spores were washed into the earth, where they infected the underground tubers. The crop could even look normal but still be infected.

Britain and Russia remained untouched, the former because it already had constitutional government and the latter because its autocratic government had stamped out all signs of dissent. In the end, all the revolutions failed because liberal, socialist, and nationalist movements quarreled with one another, leaving an opening for rulers and their armies to return to power.

The Hungry Forties

Beginning in 1845, crop failures across Europe caused food prices to shoot skyward. In the best of times urban workers paid 50 to 80 percent of their income for a diet consisting largely of bread; now even bread was beyond their means. An aristocrat from Silesia, a province in Prussia, described the political consequences: "As long as there was a sure, and honest livelihood, none of the Silesian weavers paid any attention to communistic agitation. . . . Despair was aroused among them by hunger."

Overpopulation hastened famine in some places, especially Ireland, where an airborne blight destroyed the staple crop, potatoes, first in 1846, and again in 1848 and 1851. Irish peasants had planted potatoes because a family of four might live off one acre of potatoes but would require at least two acres of grain. As potato cultivation increased, greater food production spurred population growth as peasants, assured of a food supply, had more children. Irish peasants often sought security in large families, trusting that their children might help work the land and care for them in old age. Thus Irish population growth surpassed that of the rest of Europe. By the 1840s, Ireland was especially vulnerable to the potato blight. Out of a population of eight million, as many as one million people died of starvation and disease. Corpses lay unburied on the sides of roads, and whole families were found dead in their cottages, half-eaten by dogs. Hundreds of thousands emigrated to England, the United States, and Canada.

REVOLUTIONS OF 1848

1848

January Uprising in Palermo, Sicily

February Revolution in Paris; proclamation of republic

March Insurrections in Vienna, German cities, Milan, and Venice; autonomy movement in Hungary; Charles Albert of Piedmont-Sardinia declares war on Austrian Empire

May Frankfurt parliament opens

June Austrian army crushes revolutionary movement in Prague; June Days end in defeat of workers in Paris

July Austrians defeat Charles Albert and Italian forces

November Insurrection in Rome

December Francis Joseph becomes Austrian emperor; Louis-Napoleon elected president in France

1849

February Rome declared a republic

April Frederick William of Prussia rejects crown of united Germany offered by Frankfurt parliament

July Roman republic overthrown by French intervention

August Russian and Austrian armies combine to defeat Hungarian forces

them; a "Professors Parliament" was the common sneer. These delegates had no access to an army, and they dreaded the demands of the lower classes for social reforms. Unemployed artisans and workers smashed machines; peasants burned landlords' records and occasionally attacked Jewish moneylenders; women set up clubs and newspapers to demand their emancipation from "perfumed slavery."

The advantage lay with the princes, who retained legal authority and control over the armed forces. The most powerful German states, Prussia and Austria, expected to determine whether and how Germany should unite. While the Frankfurt parliament laboriously prepared a liberal constitution for a united Germany—one that denied self-determination to Czechs, Poles, and Danes within its proposed German borders—the Prussian king Frederick William IV (r. 1840–1860) recovered his confidence. First his army crushed the revolution in Berlin in the fall of 1848. Prussian troops then intervened to help other local rulers put down the last wave of democratic and nationalist insurrections in the spring of 1849. When the Frankfurt parliament finally concluded its work, offering the emperorship of a constitutional, federal Germany to the king of Prussia, Frederick William contemptuously refused this "crown from the gutter."

Ethnic Divisions in the Austrian Empire.

By the summer of 1848, the Austrian Empire, too, had reached the verge of complete collapse. Just as Italians were driving the Austrians out of their lands in northern Italy and Magyar nationalists were demanding political autonomy for Hungary, on March 13, 1848, in Vienna, a student-led demonstration for political reform turned into rioting, looting, and machine-breaking. Metternich resigned, escaping to England in disguise. Emperor Ferdinand promised a constitution, an elected parliament, and the end of censorship. The beleaguered authorities in Vienna could not refuse Magyar demands for home rule, and Széchenyi and Kossuth both became ministers in the new Hungarian government. The Magyars were the largest ethnic group in Hungary but still did not make up 50 percent of the population, which included Romanians, Slovaks, Croats, and Slovenes who preferred Austrian rule to domination by local Magyars.

The ethnic divisions in Hungary foreshadowed the many political and social divisions that would doom the revolutionaries. Fears of peasant insurrection prompted the Magyar nationalists around Kossuth to abolish serfdom. This measure alienated the largest noble landowners. In Prague, Czech nationalists convened a Slav congress as a counter to the Germans' Frankfurt parliament and called for a reorganization of the Austrian Empire that would recognize the rights of ethnic minorities. Such assertiveness by non-German peoples provoked German nationalists to protest on behalf of German-speaking people in areas with a Czech or Magyar majority.

Revolution of 1848 in Eastern Europe
This painting by an unknown artist shows Ana Ipatescu leading a group of Romanian revolutionaries in Transylvania in opposition to Russian rule. The Transylvanian provinces of Moldavia and
Walachia had been under Russian domination since the 1770s and occupied directly since 1829.
In April 1848, local landowners began to organize meetings. Paris-educated nationalists spearheaded the movement, which demanded the end of Russian control and various legal and political reforms. By August, the movement had split between those who wanted independence only
and those who pushed for the end of serfdom and for universal manhood suffrage. In response,
the Russians invaded Moldavia and the Turks moved into Walachia. By October, the uprising was
over. Russia and Turkey agreed to control the provinces jointly. *The Art Archive.*

The Austrian government slowly took advantage of these divisions. To quell peasant discontent and appease liberal reformers, it abolished all remaining peasant obligations to the nobility in March 1848. Rejoicing country folk soon lost interest in the revolution. Class conflicts flared in Vienna, where the middle classes had little sympathy for the starving artisans and workers. The new Hungarian government alienated the other nationalities when it imposed the Magyar language on them. Similar divisions sapped national unity in the Polish and Czech lands of the empire.

Military force finally broke up the revolutionary movements. The first blow fell in Prague in June 1848; General Prince Alfred von Windischgrätz,♦ the military governor, bombarded the city into submission when a demonstration led to violence (including the shooting death of his wife, watching from a window). After another uprising in Vienna a few months later, Windischgrätz marched seventy thousand soldiers into the capital and set up direct military rule. In December the Austrian monarchy came back to life when the eighteen-year-old Francis Joseph (r. 1848–1916), unencumbered by promises extracted by the revolutionaries from his now feeble uncle Ferdinand, assumed the

---

♦**Windischgrätz:** vihn dihsh GREHTS

imperial crown after intervention by leading court officials. In the spring of 1849, General Count Joseph Radetsky defeated the last Italian challenges to Austrian power in northern Italy, and his army moved east, joining with Croats and Serbs to take on the Hungarian rebels. The Austrian army teamed up with Tsar Nicholas I, who marched into Hungary with more than 300,000 Russian troops. Hungary was put under brutal martial law. Széchenyi went mad, and Kossuth found refuge in the United States. Social conflicts and ethnic divisions weakened the revolutionary movements from the inside and gave the Austrian government the opening it needed to restore its position.

Aftermath to 1848

Although the revolutionaries of 1848 failed to achieve most of their goals, their efforts left a profound mark on the political and social landscape. Between 1848 and 1851, the French served a kind of republican apprenticeship that prepared the population for another, more lasting republic after 1870. No French government could henceforth rule without extensive popular consultation. In Italy, the failure of unification did not stop the spread of nationalist ideas and the rooting of demands for democratic participation. In the German states, the revolutionaries of 1848 turned nationalism from an idea of professors and writers into a popular enthusiasm and even practical reality. The initiation of artisans, workers, and journeymen into democratic clubs increased political awareness in the lower classes and helped prepare them for broader political participation. Almost all the German states had a constitution and a parliament after 1850. The spectacular failures of 1848 thus hid some important underlying successes.

The absence of revolution in 1848 was just as significant as its presence. No revolution occurred in Great Britain, the Netherlands, or Belgium, three places where industrialization and urbanization had developed most rapidly. In Great Britain the prospects for revolution actually seemed quite good: the Chartist movement took inspiration from the European revolutions in 1848 and mounted several gigantic demonstrations to force Parliament into granting all

adult males the vote. But Parliament refused and no uprising occurred, in part because the government had already proved its responsiveness. The middle classes in Britain had been co-opted into the established order by the Reform Bill of 1832, and the working classes had won parliamentary regulation of children's and women's work.

The other notable exception to revolution among the great powers was Russia, where Tsar Nicholas I maintained a tight grip through police surveillance and censorship. The Russian schools, limited to the upper classes, taught Nicholas's three most cherished principles: autocracy (the unlimited power of the tsar), orthodoxy (obedience to the church in religion and morality), and nationality (devotion to Russian traditions). These provided no space for political dissent. Social conditions also fostered political passivity: serfdom continued in force and the slow rate of industrial and urban growth created little discontent.

For all the differences between countries, some developments touched them all. European states continued to expand their bureaucracies. For example, in 1750 the Russian government employed approximately 10,500 functionaries; a century later it needed almost 114,000. In Great Britain a swelling army of civil servants produced parliamentary studies on industrialization, foreign trade, and colonial profits, while new agencies such as the British urban police forces (ten thousand strong in the 1840s) intruded increasingly in ordinary people's lives. States wanted to take children out of the fields and factories where they worked with their families and educate them. In some German cities the police reported people who cleared snow off their roofs after the permitted hour or smoked in the street. A few governments even prescribed the length of sermons.

Although much had changed, the aristocracy remained the dominant power almost everywhere. As army officers, aristocrats put down revolutionary forces. As landlords, they continued to dominate the rural scene and control parliamentary bodies. They also held many official positions in the state bureaucracies. One Italian princess explained, "There are doubtless men capable of leading the nation . . . but their names are unknown to the people, whereas those of noble families . . .

The Crystal Palace, 1851

George Baxter's lithograph (above) shows the exterior of the main building for the Exhibition of the Works of Industry of All Nations in London. It was designed by Sir Joseph Paxton to gigantic dimensions: 1,848 feet long by 456 feet wide; 135 feet high; 772,784 square feet of ground floor area covering no less than 18 acres. The second view, a lithograph by Peter Mabuse, offers a view of one of the colonial displays at the exhibition. The tented room and ivory carved throne are meant to recall India, Britain's premier colony. In a sermon given at the opening of the exhibition, Reverend George Clayton attributed Britain's national greatness to its colonial presence: *"Great she [Britain] truly is—great in her trade and commerce—great in her laws and constitution—great in her freedom, both civil and religious—great in the power, the character, and the virtues of her queen . . . great in the resources of her wealth, in the number and extent of her colonial possessions—great in the multitude of her subjects—great in the moral and Christian bearing of a large proportion of her people—great in the cultivation of the mind and morals of the rising population of her inhabitants—great in the distribution of her Bibles, in her mission to the heathen, in the emancipation of the slave, and in the circulation of her countless tracts for the instruction of universal man."* Top: Maidstone Museum and Art Gallery, Kent, UK/ Bridgeman Art Library. At right: From Dickinson's Comprehensive Pictures, The Stapleton Collection / Bridgeman Art Library.

are in every memory." Aristocrats kept their authority by adapting to change: they entered the bureaucracy and professions, turned their estates into moneymaking enterprises, and learned how to invest shrewdly.

The reassertion of conservative rule hardened gender definitions. Women everywhere had participated in the revolutions, especially in the Italian states, where they joined armies in the tens of thousands and applied household skills toward making bandages, clothing, and food. Schoolgirls in Prague had thrown desks and chairs out of windows and helped build students' barricades. Many

MAPPING THE WEST Europe in 1850

This map of population growth between 1800 and 1850 reveals important trends that would not otherwise be evident. Although population growth correlated for the most part with industrialization, population also grew in more agricultural regions such as East Prussia, Poland, and Ireland. Ireland's rapid population growth does not appear on this map because by 1850 more than a million people had died or emigrated because of the famine of 1846–1851. Compare this map to Map 22.1: Which areas experienced both industrialization and population increase?

women in Paris had supported the new republic and seized the occasion of greater political openness to demand women's rights, only to experience isolation as their claims were denied by most republican men. Men in the revolutions of 1848 almost always defined universal suffrage as a male right. When workingmen gained the vote and women did not, the notion of separate spheres penetrated even into working-class life: political participation became one more way to distinguish masculinity from femininity. As conservatives returned to power, all signs of women's political activism disappeared. The French feminist movement, the most advanced in Europe, fell apart after the June

Days when the increasingly conservative republican government forbade women to form political clubs and arrested and imprisoned two of the most outspoken women leaders for their socialist activities.

In May 1851, Europe's most important female monarch presided over a midcentury celebration of peace and industrial growth that helped dampen the still-smoldering fires of revolutionary passion. Queen Victoria (r. 1837–1901), who herself promoted the notion of domesticity as women's sphere, opened the international Exhibition of the Works of Industry of All Nations in London on May 1. A monument of modern iron and glass architecture had been built to house the display; the building was more than a third of a mile long and so tall that it was built over the trees of its Hyde Park site. Soon people referred to it as the Crystal Palace; its nine hundred tons of glass created an aura of fantasy, and the abundant goods from all nations inspired satisfaction and pride. One German visitor described it as "this miracle which has so suddenly appeared to dazzle the inhabitants of our globe." In the place of revolutionary fervor, the Crystal Palace offered a government-sponsored spectacle of what industry, hard work, and technological imagination could produce.

Review: Why did the revolutions of 1848 fail?

Conclusion

Many of the six million people who visited the Crystal Palace display had not forgotten the specter of cholera, fears of overpopulation, popular resentments, and political upheavals that had been so prominent in the 1830s and 1840s. Even though industrial growth brought railroads, cheaper clothing, and access to exhibitions like the Crystal Palace, it also brought in its train urban overcrowding and miserable working conditions. The Crystal Palace presented the rosy view, but the housing shortages, inadequacy of water supplies, and recurrent epidemic diseases had not disappeared. Social reform organizations still drew attention to prosti-

tution, child abandonment, alcohol abuse, and other problems associated with burgeoning cities.

Although the revolutions of 1848 brought to the surface the profound tensions within a European society in transition toward industrialization and modernization, they did not definitively resolve those tensions. Industrialization and urbanization continued, workers developed more extensive organizations, and liberals and socialists fought over the pace of reform. The revolutions produced their most striking impact negatively rather than positively: confronted with the menace of revolution, elites now sought alternatives that would be less threatening to the established order and still permit some change. This search for alternatives became immediately evident in the question of national unification in Germany and Italy. National unification would hereafter depend on what the Prussian leader Otto von Bismarck would call "blood and iron," and not on speeches and parliamentary resolutions.

Suggested References

The Advance of Industrialization and Urbanization

The spread of industrialization has elicited much more historical interest than the process of urbanization because the analysis of industrialization occupied a central role in Marxism.

Hobsbawm, E. J. *The Age of Revolution, 1789–1848.* 1996.

Kudlick, Catherine J. *Cholera in Post-Revolutionary Paris: A Cultural History.* 1996.

Mokyr, Joel, ed. *The British Industrial Revolution: An Economic Perspective.* 2nd ed. 1999.

Pinkney, David H. *Decisive Years in France, 1840–1847.* 1986.

*Pollard, S., and C. Holmes. *Documents of European Economic History.* Vol. 1, *The Process of Industrialization, 1750–1870.* 1968.

Spartacus Internet Encyclopedia, British History 1700–1950: http://www.spartacus.schoolnet.co.uk/Britain.html.

*Primary source.

Reforming the Social Order

Although romanticism remains a focus of interest for cultural historians, the history of women and the origins of feminism have also attracted attention in recent years. The Web site Gallica, produced by the National Library of France, offers a wealth of imagery and information on French cultural history.

Davidoff, Leonore, and Catherine Hall. *Family Fortunes: Men and Women of the English Middle Class, 1780–1850*. 1987.

The Dickens Project: http://humwww.ucsc .edu/dickens/index.html.

Gallica: Images and Texts from Nineteenth-Century French-Speaking Culture: http:// gallica.bnf.fr.

Kerr, David S. *Caricature and French Political Culture, 1830–1848*. 2000.

*Murray, Janet Horowitz. *Strong-Minded Women and Other Lost Voices from Nineteenth-Century England*. 1982.

Rendall, Jane. *The Origins of Modern Feminism: Women in Britain, France, and the United States, 1780–1860*. 1990.

Townsend, Mary Lee. *Forbidden Laughter: Popular Humor and the Limits of Repression in Nineteenth-Century Prussia*. 1992.

The Ferment of Ideologies

Ideologies are too often studied in an exclusively national context, so broader generalizations are difficult. The important exception to this national focus is the wide-ranging study by Anderson.

Anderson, Benedict. *Imagined Communities: Reflections on the Origin and Spread of Nationalism*. 1983.

Clark, Anna. *The Struggle for the Breeches: Gender and the Making of the British Working Class*. 1995.

*Mather, F. C., ed. *Chartism and Society: An Anthology of Documents*. 1980.

Sewell, William H., Jr. *Work and Revolution in France: The Language of Labor from the Old Regime to 1848*. 1980.

Taylor, Barbara. *Eve and the New Jerusalem: Socialism and Feminism in the Nineteenth Century*. 1983.

The Revolutions of 1848

Interest in the revolutions of 1848 has revived of late, perhaps because the recent upsurge of ethnic violence in the Balkans has prompted scholars to look again at this critical period.

Dowe, Dieter, ed. *Europe in 1848: Revolution and Reform*. Trans. David Higgins. 2001.

Evans, Robert, and Hartmut Pogge von Strandmann, eds. *The Revolutions in Europe, 1848–1849*. 2000.

Lincoln, W. Bruce. *Nicholas I: Emperor and Autocrat of All the Russias*. 1978.

O'Grada, Cormac. *The Great Irish Famine*. 1989.

Sperber, Jonathan. *The European Revolutions, 1848–1851*. 1994.

*Walker, Mack. *Metternich's Europe*. 1968.

––––––––––

*Primary source.

CHAPTER REVIEW

IMPORTANT EVENTS

1830–1832	Cholera epidemic sweeps across Europe
1830	France invades and begins conquest of Algeria
1831	British and Foreign Temperance Society established
1832	George Sand, *Indiana*
1833	Factory Act regulates work of children in Great Britain; abolition of slavery in the British Empire
1834	German *Zollverein* ("customs union") established under Prussian leadership
1835	Belgium opens first continental railway built with state funds
1839	Beginning of Opium War between Britain and China; invention of photography
1841	Charles Dickens, *The Old Curiosity Shop*
1846	Famine strikes Ireland; Corn Laws repealed in England; peasant insurrection in Austrian province of Galicia
1847	Charlotte Brontë, *Jane Eyre*
1848	Revolutions of 1848 throughout Europe; last great wave of Chartist demonstrations in Britain; Karl Marx and Friedrich Engels, *The Communist Manifesto*; abolition of slavery in French colonies; end of serfdom in Austrian Empire
1851	Crystal Palace exhibition in London

KEY TERMS

Chartism (855)
cholera (829)
communists (855)
Corn Laws (853)
daguerreotype (843)
domesticity (847)
imperialism (848)
lithograph (829)
opium (830)
social question (840)
temperance movement (845)

REVIEW QUESTIONS

1. Why were cities seen as dangerous places?
2. How did reformers try to address the social problems created by industrialization and urbanization? In which areas did they succeed, and in which did they fail?
3. Why did ideologies have such a powerful appeal in the 1830s and 1840s?
4. Why did the revolutions of 1848 fail?

MAKING CONNECTIONS

1. Which of the ideologies of this period had the greatest impact on political events? How can you explain this?
2. In what ways might industrialization be considered a force for peaceful change rather than a revolution? (Hint: Think about the situation in Great Britain.)

FOR FURTHER EXPLORATION

To assess your mastery of the material in this chapter, see the Online Study Guide at **bedfordstmartins.com/hunt**.

To read additional primary-source material from this period, see Chapter 22 in *Sources of The Making of the West*, Second Edition.

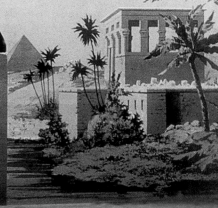

Politics and Culture of the Nation-State, c. 1850–1870

IN 1859, THE NAME "VERDI" suddenly appeared scrawled on walls across the disunited cities of the Italian peninsula. The graffiti seemed to celebrate the composer Giuseppe Verdi, whose operas thrilled crowds of Europeans. Verdi was a hero among Italians, however, for his stories of downtrodden groups struggling against tyrannical government seemed to refer specifically to their plight. As his operatic choruses thundered out calls to rebellion in the name of the nation, Italian audiences were sure that Verdi meant for them to throw off Austrian and papal rule and unite in a new version of the ancient Roman Empire. Yet the graffiti was doubly political: A call to arms in the days before mass media, VERDI also formed an acronym for *Vittorio Emmanuele Re* ("king") *d'Italia*, and in 1859 it summoned Italians to unite immediately under Victor Emmanuel II, king of Sardinia and Piedmont—the one Italian leader with a nationalist, modernizing profile. The graffiti did its work, and the very next year Italy united as a result of warfare, popular uprisings, and hard bargaining by political realists.

In the wake of the failed revolutions of 1848, European statesmen and the politically conscious public increasingly rejected the politics of idealism in favor of **Realpolitik**◆—a politics of tough-minded realism aimed at strengthening the state and tightening social order. Claiming to distrust the romanticism and high-minded ideologies of the revolutionaries and hoping to control nationalism and other movements for reform, Realpolitikers believed in playing power

◆**Realpolitik:** ray AHL poh lih teek
◆***Aïda:*** ah EE duh

Aïda◆ Poster
Aïda (1871), Giuseppe Verdi's opera of human passion and state power among people of different nations, became a staple of Western culture, bringing people across Europe into a common cultural orbit. Written to celebrate the opening of the Suez Canal, *Aïda* also celebrated the improvement of Europe's access to Asian resources provided by the new waterway. As the poster shows, the opera ushered in a wave of Egyptomania in which Egyptian styles and objects were of great interest in the West. What images from Egypt were popular in Western culture in the nineteenth century? What do you think the images shown here represented for Europeans? *Madeline Grimoldi.*

politics and even using violence to attain their goals. Two particularly skilled practitioners of Realpolitik, the Italian Camillo di Cavour and the Prussian Otto von Bismarck, succeeded in unifying Italy and Germany, respectively, not by consensus but by war and diplomacy. Most leading figures of the decades 1850–1870, enmeshed like Verdi's operatic heroes in violent political maneuverings, advanced state power by harnessing the forces of nationalism and liberalism that had led to earlier romantic revolts. Their achievements changed the face of Europe.

Nation building was the order of the day, and it occurred in a variety of ways during these momentous decades. Continued economic development was crucial, as was a growing sense of national identity and common purpose forged by both culture and government policy. As productivity and wealth increased, governments took vigorous steps to improve the urban environment, monitor public health, and promote national sentiment. State support for cultural developments ranging from public schools to public health programs helped establish a common fund of knowledge and even shared political beliefs. Authoritarian leaders such as Bismarck and the new French emperor Napoleon III believed that a better quality of life would not only calm revolutionary impulses and build state power but also keep political liberals at bay.

Shared culture built a sense of shared identity. Reading novels, attending art exhibitions, keeping up-to-date at the newly fashionable world's fairs, and attending theater and opera gave ordinary people a stronger sense not only of being French or German or British but also of being European. The public consumed cultural works that increasingly rejected romanticism, featuring instead harsher, more realistic aspects of everyday life. Artists painted nudes in shockingly blunt ways, eliminating romantic hues and poses. Verdi's celebrated opera *La Traviata* showed a frolicking courtesan menacing a middle-class family. The Russian author Leo Tolstoy depicted the bleak life of soldiers in the Crimean♦ War, which erupted in 1853 between the Russian and Ottoman Empires, while his countryman Fyodor Dostoevsky♦ wrote of ordinary people turning to crime in urban neighborhoods.

Advocates of Realpolitik cared less for the costs than for the outcomes of state building. Advancing state power entailed stamping out resistance to global expansion. At home, Realpolitikers uprooted neighborhoods to construct public buildings, roads, and parks. The process of nation building was often brutal, bringing war, arrests, protests, and outright civil war—all of these the centerpieces of Verdi's operas as well. As the wars of German unification drew to a close in 1871, an uprising of Parisians threw the new terms of national and industrial growth into question as citizens challenged the central government's intrusion into everyday life and its failure to count

---

♦**Crimean:** kry MEE uhn
♦**Dostoevsky:** dahs tuh YEHF skee

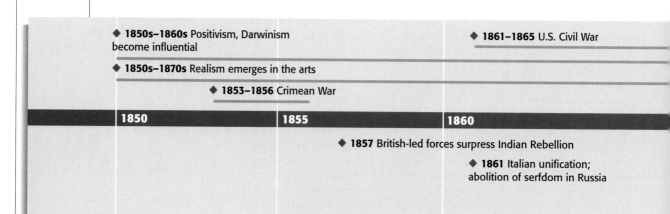

♦ **1850s–1860s** Positivism, Darwinism become influential

♦ **1850s–1870s** Realism emerges in the arts

♦ **1853–1856** Crimean War

♦ **1861–1865** U.S. Civil War

| 1850 | 1855 | 1860 |

♦ **1857** British-led forces surpress Indian Rebellion

♦ **1861** Italian unification; abolition of serfdom in Russia

the costs. For the most part, the powerful Western state did not take shape automatically. Instead, its growth occasioned warfare, dislocation, new inroads on the lives of people around the world, shrewd policy, and heated debate. The Realpolitik approach to nation building that produced all of these outcomes also created a general climate of modern opinion that valued realism and hard facts.

❖ The End of the Concert of Europe

The revolutions of 1848 had weakened the concert of Europe, driving out its architect Klemens von Metternich and allowing the forces of nationalism to flourish. It became more difficult for countries to control their competing ambitions and act together. In addition, the dreaded resurgence of Bonapartism in the person of Napoleon III added to the volatility in international politics as France sought to reassert itself. One of Napoleon's targets was Russia, formerly a mainstay of the concert of Europe. Taking advantage of Russia's continuing drive to expand, France helped engineer the Crimean War. The war took a huge toll in human life and weakened Russia and Austria. Not only did Russia's defeat lead to substantial reforms in the country, but it also made way for a massive shift in the distribution of European power.

Napoleon III and the Quest for French Glory

Louis-Napoleon Bonaparte (Napoleon III) encouraged the resurgence of French grandeur and the cult of his famous uncle as part of nation building. "There are certain men who are born to serve as a means for the march of the human race," he wrote. "I consider myself to be one of these." Napoleon III acted as Europe's schoolmaster, showing its leaders how to combine economic liberalism and nationalism with authoritarian rule. Cafés where men might discuss politics were closed, and a rubber-stamp legislature (the Corps législatif) reduced representative government to a facade. Imperial style replaced republican rituals (see the illustration on the next page). Napoleon's opulent court dazzled the public, and the emperor (like his namesake) cultivated a masculine image of strength and majesty by wearing military uniforms and by conspicuously maintaining mistresses. Napoleon's wife, Empress Eugénie,◆ however, followed middle-class conventions such as separate spheres for men and women by serving as a devoted mother to her only son and supporting many volunteer charities. The authoritarian, apparently old-fashioned order imposed by Napoleon satisfied the many peasants who opposed urban radicalism as they went to the polls.

Yet Napoleon III was simultaneously a modernizer, and he promoted a strong economy, public works programs, and jobs,

◆**Eugénie:** oo jay NEE

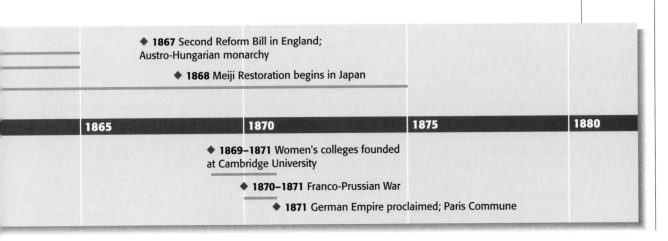

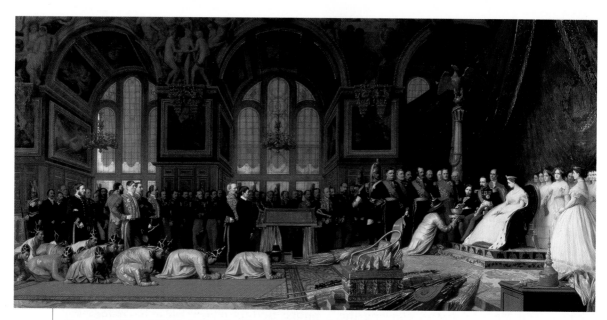

Napoleon III and Eugénie Receive the Siamese Ambassadors, 1864
At a splendid gathering of their court, the emperor Napoleon III, his consort Eugénie, and their son and heir greet ambassadors from Siam, whose exoticism and servility before the imperial family are the centerpiece of this depiction by Jean-Léon Gerome. Amid the grandeur of the Napoleonic dynasty, the West towers above the East. How might a middle-class French grocer react to this scene? *Bridgeman-Giraudon/Art Resource, NY.*

which lured the middle and working classes away from radical politics. International trade fairs, artistic expositions, and the magnificent rebuilding of Paris helped sustain French prosperity as Europe recovered from the hard times of the late 1840s. Empress Eugénie wore lavish gowns, encouraging French silk production and keeping Paris at the center of the lucrative fashion trade. The regime also reached a free-trade agreement with Britain and backed the establishment of innovative investment banks. Such new institutions led the way in financing railroad expansion, and railway mileage increased fivefold during Napoleon III's reign. During the economic downturn of the late 1850s, he wooed support by allowing working-class organizations to form and introducing democratic features into his governing methods. Although some historians have judged Napoleon III to be enigmatic and shifty because of these abrupt changes, his maneuvers were pragmatic responses to the fluid conditions.

On the international scene, Napoleon III's main goals were to overcome the containment of France imposed by the Congress of Vienna, realign continental politics to benefit France, and acquire international glory like a true Bonaparte. To realign European politics, Napoleon pitted France first against Russia in the Crimean War, then against Austria in the War of Italian Unification, and finally against Prussia in the Franco-Prussian War of 1870. Beyond Europe, Napoleon's army continued to enforce French rule in Algeria and Southeast Asia and tried to install Habsburg emperor Francis Joseph's brother Maximilian as ruler of Mexico and ultimately of all Central America—an assault that brought on rebellion and Maximilian's execution in 1867. Napoleon's foreign policy transformed relations among the great powers by causing a breakdown in the international system of peaceful diplomacy established at the Congress of Vienna. While his encouragement of projects like the Suez Canal to connect the Mediterranean and the Red Seas proved visionary, this push for worldwide influence eventually destroyed him: the French overthrew him after Prussia easily defeated his army in 1870.

The Crimean War, 1853–1856: Turning Point in European Affairs

Napoleon first flexed his diplomatic muscle in the Crimean War (1853–1856), which began as a conflict between the Russian and Ottoman Empires but ended as a war with long-lasting consequences for much of Europe. While professing to uphold the concert of Europe, Russia continued to build state power by making further inroads into Asia and the Middle East. In particular, Tsar Nicholas I wanted to absorb much of the Ottoman Empire, fast becoming known as "the sick man of Europe" because of its disintegrating authority. Napoleon III maneuvered Nicholas to be more aggressive in his expansionism, and amid this increasing belligerence war erupted in October 1853 between the two eastern empires (Map 23.1). The war disrupted the united Austrian and Russian front that kept France—and Napoleon III—in check.

The war drew in other states, because behind it lay the question of Europe's balance of power. To protect its Mediterranean routes to East Asia, Britain prodded the Ottomans to stand up to Russia. The Austrian government still resented its dependence on Russia in putting down Hungarian revolutionaries in 1849 and felt threatened by continuing Russian expansion into the Balkans. This anxiety helped Napoleon III gain a promise of Austrian neutrality during the war, thus fracturing the conservative Russian-Austrian coalition that had quashed French ambitions since 1815. In the fall of 1853, the Russians blasted the wooden Turkish ships to bits at the Ottoman port of Sinope♦ on the Black Sea; in 1854, France and Great Britain, enemies in war for more than a century, declared war on Russia to defend the Ottoman Empire's sovereignty and territories.

Faced with attacking the massive Russian Empire, the allies settled for limited military goals focused on capturing the Russian naval base at Sevastopol on the Black Sea in the Crimea. Even so, the Crimean War was spectacularly bloody. British and French troops landed in the Crimea in September 1854 and waged a long siege of the fortified city,

MAP 23.1 The Crimean War, 1853–1856
The most destructive war in Europe between the Napoleonic Wars and World War I, the Crimean War drew attention to the conflicting ambitions around territories of the declining Ottoman Empire. Importantly for state building in these decades, the war fractured the alliance of conservative forces from the Congress of Vienna, allowing Italy and Germany to come into being as unified states and permitting Napoleon III to pursue his ambitions for France. Why were Britain and France interested in so distant an area as the Crimea? What were Russia's interests?

but it fell only after a year of savage and costly combat. Generals on both sides demonstrated their incompetence, and governments failed to provide combatants with even minimal supplies, sanitation, or medical care. Hospitals had no beds, no dishes, and no water. As a result, the war claimed a massive toll. Of the three-quarters of a million deaths, more than two-thirds were from disease and starvation.

In the midst of this unfolding catastrophe, Alexander II (r. 1855–1881) ascended the Russian throne following the death of his father, Nicholas I. With casualties mounting, the new tsar asked for peace. As a result of the Peace of Paris, signed in March 1856, Russia lost the right to base its navy in the Straits of Dardanelles and the Black Sea, which were declared neutral waters. Moldavia and Walachia♦ (which soon merged to form

♦**Sinope:** suh NOH pee

♦**Walachia:** wah LAY kee uh

Romania) became autonomous Turkish provinces under the victors' protection.

Some historians have called the Crimean War one of the most senseless conflicts in modern history because competing claims in southeastern Europe could have been settled by diplomacy had it not been for Napoleon III's driving ambition to disrupt the peace. Yet the war was full of consequence. New technologies were introduced into warfare: the railroad, shell-firing cannon, breech-loading rifles, and steam-powered ships. The relationship of the home front to the battlefront was beginning to change with the use of the telegraph and increased press coverage. Home audiences received news from the Crimean front lines more rapidly and in more detail than ever before. Reports of incompe-

tence, poor sanitation, and the huge death toll outraged the public, inspiring a few to go to the front to help. Florence Nightingale became the best known of these sojourners: she seized the moment to escape the confines of middle-class domesticity by organizing a battlefield nursing service to care for the British sick and wounded. (See The Mission of Mercy, below.) Through her tough-minded organization of nursing units, she not only improved the sanitary conditions of the troops both during and after the war but also pioneered nursing as a profession. (See the excerpt on Mrs. Seacole opposite.)

More immediately, the war accomplished Napoleon III's goal of severing the alliance between the Habsburgs and Russia, the two conservative powers on which the Congress

The Mission of Mercy
Florence Nightingale organized British health-care services during the Crimean War, inspiring a committed cadre of women volunteers to leave domestic life for the battlefront. As disease took its heavy toll, Nightingale introduced sanitary measures into the care of the wounded and sick, dramatically reducing the death rate. Jerry Barrett's romantic portrayal of her greeting the wounded at Scutari hardly captures the strenuous and tough-minded efforts involved in her work. Why would the artist portray the exacting, industrious Nightingale as a romantic, ladylike heroine? *National Portrait Gallery, London.*

Mrs. Seacole: The *Other* Florence Nightingale

Another highly skilled medical worker besides Florence Nightingale made an impact on the battlefields in Crimea. Mary Seacole (1805–1881), daughter of a free black Jamaican woman and a Scottish army officer, had learned about medicine from her mother and from doctors who passed through Kingston, staying at the family's boardinghouse. In addition to a gift for healing, Mrs. Seacole (as she was always called) had a passion for travel—to Europe, the United States, and Panama—which she supported by tending other travelers. When the Crimean War broke out, she chafed—like Nightingale herself—to be at the battlefront. Arriving in Crimea in 1855, Mrs. Seacole saved many desperately ill soldiers who lacked all medical care.

[Sick soldiers] could and did get at my store sick-comforts and nourishing food, which the heads of the medical staff would sometimes find it difficult to procure. These reasons, with the additional one that I was very familiar with the diseases which they suffered most from and successful in their treatment (I say this in no spirit of vanity), were quite sufficient to account for the numbers who came daily to the British Hotel for medical treatment.

That the officers were glad of me as a doctress and nurse may be easily understood. When a poor fellow lay sickening in his cheerless hut and sent down to me, he knew very well that I should not ride up in answer to his message empty-handed. And although I did not hesitate to charge him with the value of the necessaries I took him, still he was thankful enough to be able to *purchase* them. When we lie ill at home surrounded with comfort, we never think of feeling any special gratitude for the sick-room delicacies which we accept as a consequence of our illness; but the poor officer lying ill and weary in his crazy hut, dependent for the merest necessaries of existence upon a clumsy, ignorant soldier-cook, who would almost prefer eating his meat raw to having the troubles of cooking it (our English soldiers are bad campaigners), often finds his greatest troubles in the want of those little delicacies with which a weak stomach must be humoured into retaining nourishment.

Source: Mary Grant Seacole, *Wonderful Adventures of Mrs. Seacole in Many Lands* (New York: Oxford University Press, 1988), 125–26.

of Vienna peace settlement had rested since 1815. It thus ended Austria's and Russia's grip on European affairs and undermined their ability to contain the forces of liberalism and nationalism. Russia's catastrophic defeat thereby forced the authoritarian state to embark on a long-overdue renovation of the empire.

Spirit of Reform in Russia

Defeat in the Crimean War not only thwarted Russia's territorial ambition but also forced the country onto the path of reform. Hundreds of peasant insurrections had erupted during the decade before the Crimean War. Serf defiance ranged from malingering while at forced labor to boycotting vodka to protest its heavy taxation. "Our own and neighboring households were gripped with fear," one aristocrat reported, because everyone expected "a serf uprising at any minute." Although economic development spread in parts of eastern Europe, the Russian economy stagnated compared with that of western Europe. Old-fashioned farming techniques led to depleted soil and food shortages, and the nobility was often contemptuous of ordinary people's suffering. Works of art such as *A Hunter's Sketches* (1852), by novelist Ivan Turgenev,♦ contributed to a spirit of reform with their sympathetic portrayals of serfs

♦**Turgenev:** tur GAYN yuhf

and frank depiction of brutal masters. A Russian translation of Harriet Beecher Stowe's antislavery novel *Uncle Tom's Cabin* (1852) also struck a responsive chord. When Russia lost the Crimean War, the educated public, including some government officials, found the poor performance of serf-conscripted armies a disgrace and the system of serf labor an intolerable liability.

Emancipation of the Serfs. Confronted with the need for change, Alexander proved more flexible than his father, Nicholas I. Well educated and more widely traveled, Alexander ushered in what came to be known as the age of Great Reforms, granting Russians new rights from above as a way of ensuring that violent action from below would not force change. The most dramatic reform was the emancipation of almost fifty million serfs beginning in 1861. By the terms of emancipation, communities of former serfs, headed by male village elders, received grants of land. The community itself, traditionally called a **mir,**◆ had full power to allocate this land among individuals and to direct their economic activity. Thus, although emancipation partially laid the groundwork for a modern labor force in Russia, communal landowning and decision making prevented unlimited mobility and the development of a pool of free labor.

The condition attached to these so-called land grants was that peasants were not *given* land along with their personal freedom: they were forced to "redeem" the land they farmed by paying the government through long-term loans, which in turn compensated the original landowners. The best land remained in the hands of the nobility, and most peasants ended up owning less land than they had tilled as serfs. These conditions, especially the huge burden of debt and communal regulations, blunted Russian agricultural development for decades. But idealistic reformers believed that the emancipation of the serfs, once treated by the nobility virtually as livestock, had produced miraculous results. As one of them put it, "The people are without any exaggeration transfigured from head to foot. . . . The look, the walk, the speech, everything is changed."

The state also reformed local administration, the judiciary, and the military. The government compensated the nobility for loss of peasant services and set up **zemstvos**◆—regional councils through which aristocrats could direct neglected local matters such as education, public health, and welfare. Aristocratic dominance assured that the zemstvos would remain a conservative structure, but they became a countervailing political force to the distant central government, especially as some nobles profited from the relaxation of censorship and of restrictions on travel to see how the rest of Europe was governed. Their vision broadened as they saw new ways of solving social and economic problems. Simultaneously, judicial reform gave all Russians, even former serfs, access to modern civil courts, rather than leaving them at the mercy of a landowner's version of justice or secret, blatantly preferential practices. The principle of equality of all persons before the law, regardless of social rank, was introduced in Russia for the first time. Military reform followed in 1874 when the government ended the twenty-five-year term of conscription, substituting a six-year term and attention to education, efficiency, and humane treatment of recruits. These changes improved the fitness of Russian soldiers, bringing them closer to the level of their counterparts in western Europe.

From Reform to Rebellion. Alexander's reforms assisted modernizing and market-oriented landowners in Russia just as enclosures and emancipation had done much earlier for landowners in western Europe. At the same time, the changes diminished the personal prerogatives of the nobility, leaving their authority weakened and sparking intergenerational rebellion. "An epidemic seemed to seize upon [noble] children . . . an epidemic of fleeing from the parental roof," one observer noted. Rejecting aristocratic leisure, youthful rebels from the upper class valued practical activity and sometimes identified with peasants and workers. Some formed communes where they hoped to do humble manual labor, whereas others turned to higher education, especially the sciences. Rebellious daughters of the nobility

◆**mir:** mihr

◆**zemstvos:** ZEHMPST vohs

flouted parental expectations by cropping their hair short, wearing black, and escaping from home through phony marriages so they could study in European universities. This repudiation of traditional society led Turgenev to label radical youth as nihilists (from the Latin for "nothing"), those who do not believe in any values whatsoever. In fact, it showed a defiant spirit percolating in Russian society.

The atmosphere of nation building also inspired resistance among Russian-dominated ethnic groups, including an uprising by aristocratic and upper-class nationalist Poles, who sought full independence for Poland in 1863. By 1864, however, Alexander II's army had regained control of the Russian section of Poland, having used reforms to buy peasant support in defeating the rebels. In the Caucasus◆ and elsewhere, Alexander responded to nationalist unrest with repression and programs of intensive **Russification**—a tactic meant to reduce the threat of future rebellion by national minorities within the empire by forcing them to adopt Russian language and culture.

In this era of the Great Reforms, the tsarist regime only partially succeeded in developing the administrative, economic, and civic institutions that buttressed the nation-state elsewhere. The tsar and his inner circle tightly held the reins of government, allowing few to share in power. Elsewhere the sense of common citizenship took shape in the nineteenth century, but in imperial Russia the persistence of autocracy and the abuse of large numbers of the population hindered the development of a shared national identity.

> **Review:** What were the main results of the Crimean War?

❖ War and Nation Building

Politicians in the German and Italian states used the opportunity provided by the weakened concert of Europe to unify their countries quickly and violently through warfare. When national disunity threatened, the United States also waged a bloody civil war to ensure its borders and smooth the way for further expansion. Historians sometimes treat the rise of powerful **nation-states** such as Italy, Germany, and the United States and an accompanying sense of national identity among their peoples as part of an inevitable process. However, millions of individuals in the Austrian Empire, Ireland, and elsewhere maintained a regional or local sense of identity rather than a national one.

Cavour, Garibaldi, and the Process of Italian Unification

Despite the failure of the revolutions of 1848 in the Italian states, the issue of Risorgimento◆ (literally meaning "rebirth," especially associated with the movement for Italian unification) continued to simmer, aided by the disintegration of diplomatic stability across Europe. This time the clear leader of the Risorgimento would be the kingdom of Piedmont-Sardinia, in the economically modernizing north of Italy. The kingdom rallied to the operas of Verdi, and its national spirit was fortified by railroads, a modern army, and the support of France against the Austrian Empire, which still dominated the peninsula.

Cavour. The architect of the new Italy was the pragmatic Camillo di Cavour (1810–1861), prime minister of the kingdom of Piedmont-Sardinia from 1852 until his death. A rebel in his youth, Cavour had conducted agricultural experiments on his aristocratic father's land. He organized steamship companies, played the stock market, and inhaled the heady air of modernization during his travels to Paris and London. Cavour promoted economic development rather than democratic uprising as the means to achieve a united Italy. As prime minister to the capricious and scheming king, Victor Emmanuel II (r. Italy 1861–1878), he helped develop a healthy Piedmontese economy, a modern army, and a liberal political climate as the foundation for Piedmont's control of the unification process (Map 23.2).

To unify Italy, however, Piedmont would have to confront Austria, which governed the provinces of Lombardy and Venetia and

◆**Caucasus:** KAW kuh suhs

◆**Risorgimento:** ree zawr jih MEHN toh

MAP 23.2 Unification of Italy, 1859–1870
The many states of the Italian peninsula had different languages, ways of life, and economic interests. The northern kingdom of Sardinia, which included the commercially advanced state of Piedmont, had much to gain from a unified market and a more extensive pool of labor. Although King Victor Emmanuel's and Giuseppe Garibaldi's armies brought these states together as a single country, it would take decades to construct a culturally, socially, and economically unified nation. Given that people in the new Italian nation-state did not speak a common language or share the same economic prosperity, what held them together?

northern Italy in April 1859. The cause of Piedmont now became the cause of nationalist Italians everywhere, even those who had supported romantic republicanism in 1848. Political liberals in Tuscany and other central Italian states rose up on the side of Piedmont. Using the newly built Piedmontese railroad to move troops, the French and Piedmontese armies achieved rapid victories at Solferino and Magenta. Suddenly fearing the growth of Piedmont as a potential competing force, Napoleon independently signed a peace treaty with Habsburg emperor Francis Joseph that seemed in effect to end the war. Its terms gave Lombardy but not Venetia to Piedmont, and the rest of Italy remained disunited.

Garibaldi. Napoleon had plans for controlled liberation of Lombardy and Venetia and for the continuation of a disunited Italy, but they were derailed. Support for Piedmont continued to swell inside Italy, while a financially strapped Austria stood by, unable to keep control of events in the peninsula. Ousting their rulers, citizens of Parma, Modena, Tuscany, and the Papal States (except Rome, which French troops had occupied) elected to join Piedmont. In May 1860, Giuseppe Garibaldi (1807–1882), a committed republican, inspired guerrilla fighter, and veteran of the revolutions of 1848, set sail from Genoa with a thousand red-shirted volunteers (many of them teenage boys) to liberate Sicily, where peasant revolts against landlords and the corrupt government were under way in anticipation of the Risorgimento. In the autumn of 1860, the victorious

exerted strong influence over most of the peninsula. Cavour turned for help to Napoleon III, who at a meeting in the summer of 1858 promised French assistance in exchange for the city of Nice and the region of Savoy. Napoleon III expected that France rather than Austria would influence the peninsula thereafter. Sure of French help, Cavour provoked the Austrians to invade

forces of King Victor Emmanuel descending from the north and Garibaldi moving up from the south finally met in Naples. Although some of his followers still clamored for social reform and a republic, Garibaldi threw his support to the king. In 1861, the kingdom of Italy was proclaimed with Victor Emmanuel at its head.

Exhausted by a decade of overwork, Cavour died within months of leading the unification, leaving lesser men to organize the new Italy. The task ahead was enormous and complex: for instance, 90 percent of the peninsula's inhabitants did not even speak Italian but rather local languages or dialects. The political side held difficulties too: consensus among Italy's elected political leaders was often elusive once the war was over, and admirers of Cavour, such as Verdi (who had been made senator), fled the heated political scene. Economically, the wealthy commercial north and the impoverished agricultural south remained at odds over issues such as taxation and development, as they do even today. Finally, Italian borders did not yet seem complete because Venetia and Rome remained outside them, under Austrian and French control, respectively. But the legend of an Italian struggle for freedom symbolized by the figure of Garibaldi and his Red Shirts romanticized the economic and military Realpolitik that had made unification possible. Pride in the Italian nation infused many a citizen of the new country (see the illustration opposite).

Bismarck and the Realpolitik of German Unification

The most momentous act of nation building for the future of Europe and the world was the creation of a united Germany in 1871. This too was the product of Realpolitik, undertaken once the concert of Europe was smashed and the champions of the status quo defeated. Employing the old military caste to wage war, yet enjoying support from economic modernizers who saw profits in a single national market, the Prussian state brought a vast array of cities and kingdoms under its control within a single decade. From then on, Germany prospered, continuing to consolidate its economic and political

might. By the end of the nineteenth century, it would be the foremost continental power.

Bismarck's Rise to Power. The architect of the unified Germany was Otto von Bismarck (1815–1898), the Prussian minister-president. Bismarck came from a traditional Junker (Prussian landed nobility) family on his father's side; his mother's family included high-ranking bureaucrats and literati of the middle class. At university, the young Bismarck had gambled and womanized, interested only in a course on the economic foundations of politics. After failing in the civil service, he worked to modernize operations on his landholdings while leading an otherwise loutish life. His marriage

Seamstresses of the Red Shirts
Sewing uniforms and making battle flags, European women like these Italian volunteers saw themselves as contributors to the nation. Many nineteenth-century women participated in nation building as "republican mothers" by donating their domestic skills and raising the next generation of citizens to be patriotic. What advantages did the nation-state bring to women like these in the nineteenth century?

to a pious Lutheran woman worked a transformation and gave him new purpose. In the 1850s his diplomatic service to the Prussian state made him increasingly angry at the Habsburg grip on German affairs and the roadblock it created to the full flowering of Prussia. Establishing Prussia as a respected and dominant power became his cause.

In 1862, William I (king of Prussia, r. 1861–1888; German emperor, r. 1871–1888—see the illustration below) appointed Bismarck prime minister in hopes that he would quash the growing power of the liberals in the Prussian parliament. The liberals, representing the prosperous professional and business classes, had gained parliamentary strength at the expense of conservative landowners during the decades of industrial expansion. Indeed, the liberals' wealth was crucial to the Prussian state's ability to augment its power.

Desiring Prussia to be like western Europe, the liberals advocated the extension of political rights and increased civilian control of the military. William I, along with members of the traditional Prussian elite such as Bismarck, rejected the western European model. Against the liberals' will, Bismarck rammed through programs to build the army and thwart civilian control. "Germany looks not to Prussia's liberalism, but to its power," he preached. "The great questions of the day will not be settled by speeches and majority decisions—that was the great mistake of 1848 and 1849—but by iron and blood."

Prussia's Wars of Unification. After his triumph over the parliament, Bismarck led Prussia into a series of wars, against Denmark in 1864, against Austria in 1866, and, finally, against France in 1870. Using war as a political tactic, he kept the disunited German states from choosing Austrian leadership and instead united them around Prussia. Bismarck drew Austria into a joint war with Prussia against a rebellious Denmark in 1864 over its proposed incorporation of the provinces of Schleswig♦ and Holstein, with their partially German population. Their joint victory resulted in an agreement that Prussia would administer Schleswig, and Austria, Holstein. Such an arrangement stretched Austria's geographic interests far from its central European base.

Austria proved weaker than Prussia, as the Habsburg lands both lagged in economic development and suffered from a swelling national debt and the restlessness of its many national minorities. Bismarck, however, encouraged Austria's pretensions to its former grandeur and influence. He simultaneously fomented disputes over the administration of

Emperor William I of Germany, 1871
The defeat of France in the Franco-Prussian War of 1870–1871 ended with the proclamation of the king of Prussia as emperor of a unified Germany. Otto von Bismarck, who had orchestrated the wars of unification, appropriately appears in Anton von Werner's rendering as the central figure attired in heroic white. The event in the French palace of Versailles symbolized the militaristic and antagonistic side of state building, especially the Franco-German rivalry that would disastrously motivate European politics in the future. *AKG London.*

♦**Schleswig:** SHLAYS vihk

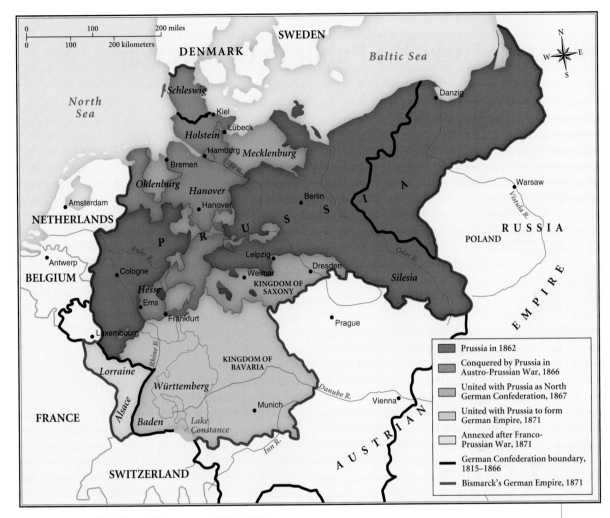

MAP 23.3 Unification of Germany, 1862–1871

In a complex series of diplomatic maneuvers, Prussian leader Otto von Bismarck welded disunited kingdoms and small states into a major continental power independent of the other dominant German dynasty, the Habsburg monarchy. Prussia's use of force against Denmark, the Habsburg Empire, and France unified Germany politically, and almost immediately that unity unleashed the new nation's economic potential. An aristocratic and agrarian elite remained firmly in power, but a rapidly growing working class would soon become a political force to be reckoned with. How did defeating its neighbors allow Prussia to create a unified nation?

Schleswig and Holstein, goading a puffed-up and confident Austria into declaring war on Prussia itself. In the summer of 1866, Austria went to war with the support of most small states in the German Confederation. Within seven weeks the modernized Prussian army, using railroads and breech-loading rifles against the outdated Austrian military, had won decisively. The smart and masterful victory allowed Bismarck to drive Austria from

the German Confederation, create a North German Confederation led by Prussia, and coordinate economic and political programs (Map 23.3).

To bring the remaining German states into the rapidly developing nation, Bismarck next moved to entrap France in a war with Prussia. During the Austro-Prussian War, Bismarck had suggested to Napoleon III that his neutrality would bring France new territory,

Bismarck Tricks the Public to Get His War

By 1870 Otto von Bismarck had gained the allegiance of most of the German states (excluding Austria) by waging two successful wars and thus showing the military muscle of Prussia. Defeating France, he believed, would pull in the remaining independent German states—most notably Bavaria—and unite Germany. To this end he doctored a document sent by the Prussian king to the French ambassador over the contested issue of succession to the Spanish throne and released the edited version to the press. He knew that its newly contrived imperious tone would offend the French parliament. Realpolitik, then as now, involved manipulating the press. Here Bismarck describes his actions.

All considerations, conscious and unconscious, strengthened my opinion that war could only be avoided at the cost of the honor of Prussia and of the national confidence in her. Under this conviction I made use of the royal authorization . . . to publish the contents of the telegram; and in the presence of my two guests [General Moltke and General Roon] I reduced the telegram by striking out words, but without adding or altering anything, to the following form:

"After the news of the renunciation of the hereditary prince of Hohenzollern had been officially communicated to the imperial government of France by the royal government of Spain, the French ambassador at Ems made the further demand of his Majesty the king that he should authorize him to telegraph to Paris that his Majesty the king bound himself for all future time never again to give his consent if the Hohenzollerns should renew their candidature. His Majesty the king thereupon decided not to receive the French ambassador again, and sent to tell him, through the aid-de-camp on duty, that his Majesty had nothing further to communicate to the ambassador."

The difference in the effect of the abbreviated text of the Ems telegram as compared with that produced by the original was not the result of stronger words, but of the form, which made this announcement appear decisive, while [the original] version would only have been regarded as a fragment of a negotiation still pending and to be continued at Berlin.

After I had read out the concentrated edition to my two guests, Moltke remarked: "Now it has a different ring; in its original form it sounded like a parley; now it is like a flourish of trumpets in answer to a challenge." I went on to explain: "If, in execution of his Majesty's order, I at once communicate this text, . . . not only to the newspapers, but also by telegraph to all our embassies, it will be known in Paris before midnight, and not only on account of its contents, but also on account of the manner of its distribution, will have the effect of a red rag upon the Gallic bull."

Source: Otto von Bismarck, *Memoirs* in James Harvey Robinson and Charles Beard, eds., *Readings in Modern European History* (Boston: Ginn, 1909), 2:158–59.

thus heating up nationalist sentiments for and against this expansion in both France and Germany. The atmosphere became even more charged when Spain proposed a minor Prussian prince to fill its vacant royal throne. This candidacy at once threatened the French with Prussian rulers on two of their borders and inflated Prussian pride. Bismarck used the occasion to get nationalist sentiments onto the news pages in both countries by editing a diplomatic communication (the so-called Ems telegram, named after the spa town in which it was issued) to make it look as if the King of Prussia had insulted France over the issue of the vacant throne. Release of the revised version to journalists inflamed the French public into demanding war (see Bismarck's account above). The parliament gladly declared it on July 19, 1870, setting in motion the alliances Prussia had created with the other German states. The Prussians captured Napoleon III with his army on September 2, 1870, and the Second Empire fell two days later.

Birth of the German Empire. With Prussian forces still besieging Paris, in January 1871 in the Hall of Mirrors at Versailles, King William of Prussia was proclaimed the kaiser, or emperor, of a new, imperial Germany. The terms of the peace signed in May of that year required France to cede the rich industrial provinces of Alsace and Lorraine to Germany and to pay a multibillion-franc indemnity. Without French protection for the papacy, Rome became part of Italy. Germany was now poised to dominate continental politics.

Prussian military might served as the foundation for German state building, and a complex constitution ensured the continued political dominance of the aristocracy and monarchy—despite the growing wealth and influence of the liberal business classes. The kaiser, who remained Prussia's king, controlled the military and appointed Bismarck to the powerful position of chancellor for the Reich (empire). The German states balanced monarchical authority somewhat through the Bundesrat, a body composed of representatives from each state. The Reichstag,♦ an assembly elected by universal male suffrage, ratified all budgets but had little room to initiate bills or programs. In framing this constitutional settlement, Bismarck accorded rights such as suffrage in the belief that the masses would uphold autocracy out of their fear of "the domination of finance capital"— shorthand for "liberal power." He balanced this move, however, with an electoral system in populous and powerful Prussia in which the votes from the upper classes counted more than those from the lower. He had little to fear from liberals, who, dizzy with German military success, came to support the blend of economic progress, constitutionalism, and militaristic nationalism that Bismarck represented.

Francis Joseph and the Creation of the Austro-Hungarian Monarchy

There was no blueprint for nation building. Just as the Crimean War left Russia searching for solutions to its social and political problems, so the confrontations with Cavour and Bismarck left the Habsburg Empire de-

feated and at bay. At first, the Habsburg Empire emerged from the revolutions of 1848 and 1849 renewed by the ascension of Francis Joseph (r. 1848–1916), who favored absolutist rule. A tireless worker, Francis Joseph enhanced his authority through stiff, formal court ceremonies, playing to the popular fascination with the trappings of power. Though the emperor stubbornly resisted change, official standards of honesty and efficiency improved, and the government promoted local education. The German language was used by the administration and taught by the schools, but the government respected the rights of national minorities—the Czechs and Poles, for instance—to receive education and communicate with officials in their native tongue. Above all, the government abolished most internal customs barriers, freed trade with Germany, fostered a boom in private railway construction, and attracted foreign capital. The capital city of Vienna underwent extensive rebuilding, and people found jobs as industrialization progressed, if unevenly.

The Austro-Hungarian Monarchy, 1867

In a fast-moving age, the absolutist emperor could not match Bismarck's pace in advancing modernization and the power of the state. Too much of the old regime remained as a roadblock to change, while prosperous liberals prevented measures that would strengthen the state. They resented the swarm of police informers, the virtually free hand of the Catholic church in education and in civil institutions such as marriage, and their own lack of representation in such important policy matters as taxation and finance. Thus, liberals blocked funds for modernizing the military, and there was no one to override them to bring about change.

After Prussia's victory over Francis Joseph's scaled-back armies in 1866, the most disaffected but wealthy part of the empire, Hungary, became the key to stability and even to the empire's existence. The leaders of the Hungarian agrarian elites forced the emperor to accept a **dual monarchy**—that is, one in which the Magyars had home rule

♦**Reichstag:** RYKS tahk

over the Hungarian kingdom. This agreement restored the Hungarian parliament and gave it control of internal policy (including the right to decide how to treat Hungary's national minorities). Although the Habsburg emperor Francis Joseph was crowned king of Hungary and Austro-Hungarian foreign policy was coordinated from Vienna, the Hungarians mostly ruled themselves after 1867 and hammered out common policies such as tariffs in acrimonious negotiations with Vienna. The new political arrangement served as still another roadblock to strengthening the empire as a whole.

The dual monarchy of Austria-Hungary was designed specifically to address the Hungarian demands, but in so doing it strengthened the voices of Czechs, Slovaks, and at least half a dozen additional national groups in the Habsburg Empire wanting the same kind of self-rule. Czechs who had helped the empire advance industrially, for example, desired Hungarian-style liberties. For some of the dissatisfied ethnic groups, **Pan-Slavism**—

that is, the transnational loyalty of all ethnic Slavs—became a rallying cry, as the various Slav peoples saw themselves as linked through a common heritage across national boundaries. Instead of looking toward Vienna, they turned to the largest Slavic country—Russia—as a focal point for potential unity. As the nation-state grew in strength, transnational movements like Pan-Slavism would emerge to provide alternative allegiances for those not recognized as equal citizens in their home countries. With so many competing ethnicities, the Austro-Hungarian monarchy remained a dynastic state in which people could rouse loyalty to the Habsburg dynasty but had increasing difficulty relating to one another as members of a single nation.

Political Stability through Gradual Reform in Great Britain

In contrast to the turmoil on the continent, Britain appeared the epitome of liberal progress. By the 1850s, the monarchy symbolized domestic tranquillity and propriety. Unlike their predecessors, Queen Victoria (r. 1837–1901) and her husband, Prince Albert, were considered models of morality, emblematic of British stability and middle-class virtues (see the illustration shown here). Britain's parliamentary system incorporated new ideas and steadily brought more men into the political process. Economic prosperity further fortified peaceful political reform, except for Ireland's continued suffering and thwarted demands for justice. Smooth governmental decision making was fostered by an ever-flexible party system: the Tory Party evolved into the Conservatives, who favored a more status-oriented politics but still went along with the evolving liberal consensus around economic development and representative government. The Whigs changed

Muslim Quarter and Bazaar
Nineteenth-century Europeans were a diverse people, composed of many religions, ethnicities, and ways of life. In the Balkans, many were Muslims, as this marketplace in Sarajevo, Bosnia, illustrates. The goal of finding a common cultural ground eluded the peoples of the Balkans. The Habsburg monarchy, which annexed Bosnia-Herzegovina in 1908, exerted its influence in the area to keep peoples divided and to play one against the other. *Graphische Sammlung Albertina, Wien.*

names, too, and became the Liberals. In 1867, the Conservatives, led by Benjamin Disraeli, passed the Second Reform Bill, which made a million more men eligible to vote.

Political parties supported reforms because pressure groups now influenced the party system. The Law Amendment Society and the Social Science Association, for example, lobbied for laws to improve social conditions, and women's groups advocated the Matrimonial Causes Act of 1857, which facilitated divorce, and the Married Women's Property Act of 1870, which allowed married women to own property and keep the wages they earned. Dissension over new policies was papered over by plush ceremonies that united not only critics and activists but also, and more important, different social classes.

Whereas previous monarchs' sexual infidelities had incited mobs to riot, the monarchy of Queen Victoria and Prince Albert, with its newly devised celebrations of royal marriages, anniversaries, and births, drew respectful crowds. Promoting the monarchy in this way was so successful that the term *Victorian* came to symbolize almost the entire century and could refer to anything from manners to political institutions. The aristocracy, maintaining power despite the rising wealth of liberal businessmen, built gigantic country houses in such traditional English architectural styles as Queen Anne and Georgian, still further anchoring the monarchical heritage in the modern age. Yet Britain's politicians were as devoted to Realpolitik as those in Germany, Italy, or France, especially using violence to expand their overseas empire and increasingly to control Ireland. The violence was far beyond the view of most British people, however, allowing them to imagine their nation as peaceful, advanced, and united.

Civil War and Nation Building in the United States and Canada

In North America, increasing nationalism and powerful economic growth characterized the nation-building experience. The United States entered a midcentury period of upheaval with a more democratic political culture than existed in Europe. Virtually universal white male suffrage, a rambunctiously independent press, and mass polit-

Queen Victoria and Prince Albert
Mid-nineteenth-century rulers started using the new photographic technology to make themselves respectable and celebrated figures. Queen Victoria and her consort, Prince Albert, were expert publicists, often posing as an ordinary middle-class couple and the epitome of domestic order. Their photos were sold or given away on small cards called *cartes de visites*, a means used by many leaders to spread their fame. How does this presentation of Victoria and Albert differ from those of monarchs in the eighteenth century such as Catherine the Great (page 706), or Napoleon (page 786)? *The Royal Archives © Her Majesty Queen Elizabeth II.*

ical parties endorsed the accepted view that sovereignty derived from the people.

The United States continued to expand its territory to the west (Map 23.4). In 1848, victory in its war with Mexico almost doubled the size of the country: Texas was officially annexed, and large portions of California and the Southwest extended U.S. borders into formerly Mexican land. Politicians and citizens alike favored banning the native Indian peoples from these western lands. Complicating matters, however, was the question

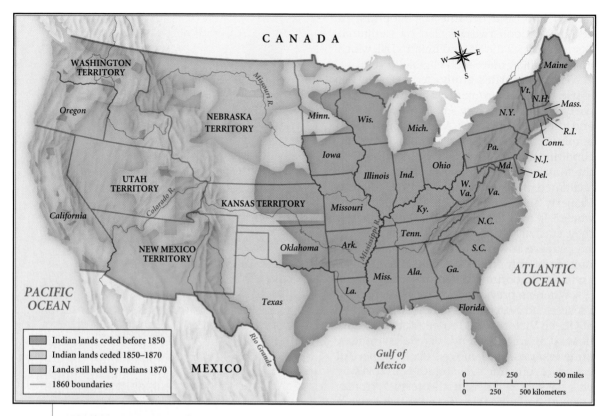

MAP 23.4 U.S. Expansion, 1850–1870

Like Russia, the United States expanded into adjacent regions to create a continental nation-state. Conquering indigenous peoples and taking over their territories, the United States differed from Russia, however, by herding native peoples into small confined spaces called reservations so that settlers could acquire thousands of square miles for farming and other enterprises. Gradually some native Americans acquired the right to vote, and the U.S. government granted full citizenship for all in 1925. What are the differences between U.S. expansion in North America and the expansion of the British in India (see page 896)?

of whether the West would be settled by free white farmers or whether southern slaveholders could bring in their slaves.

The issue polarized the country. In the North, the new Republican Party emerged to demand "free soil, free labor, free men," although few Republicans endorsed the abolitionists' demand to end slavery. With the 1860 election of Republican Abraham Lincoln to the presidency, most of the slaveholding states seceded to form the Confederate States of America. Between 1861 and 1865, the United States was torn apart by a devastating civil war.

Under Lincoln's leadership, the North fought to uphold the Union. Lincoln did not initially aim to abolish slavery, but in January 1863 his Emancipation Proclamation came into force as a wartime measure, offi-

cially freeing all slaves in the Confederate states and turning the war into a fight not only for union but also for blacks' liberation from slavery. After the summer of 1863, the North's superior industrial strength and military might overpowered and physically destroyed much of the South. By April 1865, the North had prevailed, even though a Confederate sympathizer had assassinated Lincoln. Distancing the United States still further from the colonial plantation model, constitutional amendments ended slavery and promised full political rights to free African American men.

Northerners hailed their victory as the triumph of American values, but racism remained entrenched throughout the Union. By 1871, northern interest in promoting African

American political rights was waning, and southern whites began regaining control of state politics, often by organized violence and intimidation. The end of northern occupation of the South in 1877 put on hold for nearly a century the promise of rights for blacks.

The North's triumph had profound effects elsewhere in North America. It allowed the reunited United States to contribute to Napoleon III's defeat in Mexico in 1867. The United States also demanded the annexation of Canada in retribution for Britain's partiality to the Confederacy because of its dependence on cotton. To head off this threat, the British government allowed Canadians to form a united, self-governing dominion. Dominion status answered Canadian appeals for home rule and lessened domestic opposition to Britain's control of Canada.

> **Review:** What role did warfare play in the various nineteenth-century nation-building efforts?

❖ Establishing Social Order

The age of nation building disturbed everyday life, often bringing chaos and sometimes dramatic public protest. Thus, government officials developed mechanisms to forge internal social unity and order that served to clean up or offset the violence and change by which the nation-state was expanding. Confronted with growing populations and crowded cities, governments throughout Europe intervened to guard social peace by attending to public health and safety. Many liberal theorists advocated a laissez-faire government that left social and economic life largely to private enterprise. Nevertheless, having confidence in the benefits of European institutions in general, bureaucrats and reformers paid more attention to citizens' lives and with the help of missionaries and explorers spread European influence to the farthest reaches of the globe.

Bringing Order to the Cities

European cities became the backdrop for displays of state power and national solidarity; thus, efforts to improve sanitation and control disease redounded to the state's

credit. Governments focused their refurbishing efforts on their capital cities, although many noncapital cities acquired handsome parks, widened streets, and erected stately museums and massive city halls. In 1857, Francis Joseph ordered the old Viennese city walls to be replaced with concentric boulevards lined with major public buildings such as the opera house and government offices (see the illustration on the next page). Opera houses and ministries tangibly represented national wealth and power, and the broad boulevards allowed crowds to observe royal pageantry. These wider roads were also easier for troops to navigate than the twisted, narrow medieval streets that in 1848 had concealed insurrectionists in cities like Paris and Vienna—an advantage that convinced some otherwise reluctant officials to approve the expense. Impressive parks and public gardens showed the state's control of nature, while they helped order people's leisure time. Revamped European cities inspired awe among the citizens of the various nation-states and throughout their empires.

Another effect of refurbishing cities was to highlight class differences. Construction first required destruction, and officials chose to eliminate poor neighborhoods, dislocating tens of thousands of city dwellers. The new boulevards often served as boundaries marking rich and poor sections of the city. In Paris, the process of urban change was called **Haussmannization,**❖ named for the prefect Georges-Eugène Haussmann, who implemented a grand design that included eighty-five miles of new city streets, many lined with showy dwellings for the wealthy. In London, improved architectural design, including Victorian ornamentation, many believed, would blot out the ugliness of commerce and industry. Moreover, the size and spaciousness of the many new banks and insurance companies built there "help[ed] the impression of stability," as an architect put it, and this would foster social order. Civic pride would also result from urban renewal, replacing rebellion.

Yet there were problems in merely focusing on ornament and grandeur. Amid signs of economic prosperity, the devastation

---

❖**Haussmannization:** hows muhn ih ZAY shuhn

blamed prostitutes, not their clients, for its spread. The police picked up any suspect woman on the street, passed her to public health doctors who examined her for syphilis, and incarcerated her for mandatory treatment if she was infected. As states began monitoring prostitution and other social matters like public health and housing, they had to add new departments and agencies. In 1867, Hungary's bureaucracy handled fewer than 250,000 public welfare cases; twenty years later, it dealt with more than a million.

The middle classes recognized the potential for influential jobs in the expansion of these bureaucratic agencies and lobbied to eliminate aristocrats' stranglehold on the top positions. They argued that civil service jobs should be awarded according to talent and skill rather than political loyalty or high birth. In Britain, a civil service law passed in 1870 required competitive examinations to assure competency in government posts—an idea in the air since the West had come in contact with the Chinese examination system. Citizens thus demanded that the state itself conform to middle-class ideas of fairness, competence, and opportunity.

Schooling and Professionalizing Society

Increased emphasis on empirical knowledge and objective standards of evaluation enhanced the status of certain professions, even as it changed their nature. Growing numbers of middle-class doctors, lawyers, managers, professors, and journalists gained prestige for employing science, information, and standards in their work. Governments began to allow professional people to influence state policy and to determine rules for who would and would not be admitted to their fields. Such legislation had both positive and negative effects: groups could set high standards, but otherwise qualified people were sometimes prohibited from working because they lacked the established credentials or connections. The German medical profession, for example, was granted authority to control the licensing of physicians, which led to more rigorous university training for future doctors but also pushed midwives out of medicine and caused the arrest of healers not trained in medical school. Science, too, became

the province of the trained specialist rather than the experienced amateur; scientists were likely to be employed by universities and institutes, funded by the government, and provided with equipment and assistants. Like other members of the middle class, professors of science often interpreted their work as part of a national struggle for prestige and excellence.

Nation building required major improvements in the education of all citizens, professional or not. Bureaucrats and professionals called for radical changes in the scope, curriculum, and faculty of schools—from kindergarten to university—to make the general population more fit for citizenship and useful in furthering economic progress. Ongoing expansion of the electorate along with lower-class activism prompted one British aristocrat to say of the common people, whom he feared were gaining influence, "We must now educate our masters!" Governments also introduced compulsory schooling to reduce illiteracy rates, which were more than 65 percent in Italy and Spain in the 1870s and even higher in eastern Europe. As ordinary people were allowed to participate in government, books taught them about the responsibilities of citizenship, along with practical knowledge necessary for an industrial society.

Accomplishing this goal was not always easy. At midcentury, various religious denominations supervised schools and charged tuition, making primary education an option chosen only by prosperous or religious parents. After the 1850s many leaders felt that liberal rationalism should supplant religious fervor as a guiding principle for instruction. In 1861, an English commission on education concluded that instead of knowledge of the Bible, "the knowledge most important to a labouring man is that of the causes which regulate the amount of his wages, the hours of his work, the regularity of his employment, and the prices of what he consumes." To cohere as citizens of a nation, the young had to learn its language, literature, and history. Supplanting religion was one challenge for the secular and increasingly knowledge-based state.

Enforcing school attendance was another challenge. Though the Netherlands, Sweden, and Switzerland had functioning primary school systems before midcentury, rural parents in these and other countries did not automatically make use of the opportunity. They depended on their children to perform farm chores and often believed that young people would gain the knowledge necessary for life in the fields or the household. Urban homemakers from the lower classes needed their children to help with domestic tasks such as fetching water, disposing of waste, tending younger children, and scavenging for household necessities such as stale bread from bakers or soup from local missions. Yet even among the working poor, education, like other aspects of nation building, ultimately became a shared value and led to a craze for learning, which made traveling lecturers, public forums, reading groups, and debating societies popular among the middle and working classes.

The secondary school also expanded, reflecting the demands of both an industrial society and a bureaucratic state. In Prussia, a system of secondary schools (*Gymnasia*) offered a liberal arts curriculum that trained students for a variety of careers. In the 1860s, however, new *Realschulen,*♦ or technical schools, less prestigious at the time, emphasized math, science, and modern languages for those who would not attain a Gymnasium degree or go on to attend the university. Secondary education remained a luxury for the privileged few, however, and in some countries such as Russia it was even suspect. Authoritarian officials saw the study of modern subjects such as science as potentially subversive of the old order.

Reformers pushed to allow young women to attend more advanced and more complex courses than they had been offered in the past. In France and Russia, government leaders themselves saw that "public education has had in view only half the population—the male sex," as the Russian minister of education wrote to Tsar Alexander II in 1856. Both Napoleon III and Alexander II sponsored secondary- and university-level courses for women as part of their programs to control the modernization of society. In Britain, the founders of two women's colleges—Girton (1869) and Newnham (1871)—at Cambridge University believed that exacting standards in women's higher education would provide an example of a modern curriculum, reward merit, and thus improve the low standards of scholarship prevalent in the men's colleges of Cambridge and Oxford. The modern need for highly competent elites thus challenged the gentlemanly ideal that education merely served to indicate social status. Nonetheless, higher education for women remained a hotly contested issue. The vast majority of people felt that knowledge of religion, sewing, deportment, and writing was adequate for women. On the other side, reformers from across the political spectrum argued that women who knew some science, history, and literature would rear their children better and prove more interesting wives.

Education also opened professional doors to women, who came to attend universities—in particular, medical schools—in Zurich and Paris in the 1860s. Despite criticism that their practicing medicine would weaken the system of separate spheres, women doctors thought that they could protect female patients' modesty better than male doctors and could bring feminine values to health care. The growing need for educated citizens also offered the opportunity for large numbers of women to enter teaching, a field once dominated by men. Hundreds of women founded nurseries, kindergartens, and primary schools based on the Enlightenment idea that developmental processes start at an early age. In Italy, these efforts coincided with the founding of a unified nation, and women there founded schools as a way to expand knowledge and teach civics lessons, thus providing a service to the fledgling state. Yet the idea of women teaching also aroused intense opposition. "I shudder at philosophic women," wrote one critic of female kindergarten teachers. Seen as radical because it enticed middle-class women out of the home, early childhood education, or the "kindergarten movement," was as controversial as most other educational reforms.

Spreading Western Order beyond the West

In an age of nation building and industrial development, colonies took on new importance, adding a political dimension, including direct rule from the homeland, to the

---

♦ **Realschulen:** ray AHL shoo lehn

economic role that global trade already played in national prosperity. After midcentury Great Britain, France, and Russia revised their colonial policies by instituting direct rule, expanding colonial bureaucracies, and in many cases providing a wider array of social and cultural services, such as schools. For instance, in the 1850s and 1860s provincial governors and local officials promoted the extension of Russian borders to gain control over nomadic tribes in central and eastern Asia. As in areas like Poland and the Ukraine, the state instituted common educational and religious policies, often enforcing the use of the Russian language and the practice of Russian orthodoxy as a means to social order.

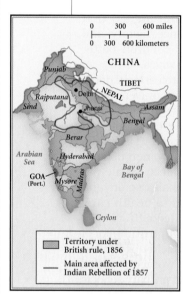

Indian Resistance, 1857

Great Britain, the era's mightiest colonial power, made a dramatic change of course toward direct political rule during these decades. Before the 1850s, British liberals desired commercial gain from colonies, but, believing in laissez-faire, they kept political involvement in colonial affairs minimal. In India, the East India Company ruled on Britain's behalf, and many regional rulers awarded the company commercial advantages. Since the eighteenth century, the East India Company had expanded its dominion over various kingdoms on the Indian subcontinent, becoming the major tax collector for the region and building railroads throughout the countryside to make commerce and revenue collecting more efficient. As the British bureaucratic and economic presence grew, enterprising Indian merchants and financiers enhanced their wealth by dealing with the Europeans through trade and tax collection. Other local men enlisted in the British-run Indian civil service and the colonial army, which became one of the largest standing armies in the world.

In 1857, a contingent of these Indian troops, both Muslim and Hindu, violently rebelled against the expanded British presence and the disregard it entailed for their autonomy and local beliefs. Ignoring the Hindu ban on beef and the Muslim prohibition of pork, the British forced Indian soldiers to use cartridges greased with cow and pig fat. This was not their main grievance, though. The soldiers, angered at tightening British control, stormed and conquered the old Moghul capital at Delhi and declared the independence of the Indian nation—an uprising that became known as the Indian Rebellion. Simultaneously, there erupted civil rebellions, composed both of leaders who were being displaced and the general populace who backed them. The virtually powerless emperor, Bahadur Shah, explained the rebellion as one against "the tyranny and oppression of the infidel and treacherous English." The rani ("queen") Lakshmibai,♦ widow of the ruler of the state of Jhansi♦ in central India, led a separate military revolt when the East India Company tried to take over her lands after her husband died. Brutally put down by British-led Indian forces from other regions, the Indian Rebellion of 1857 and the Jhansi revolt gave birth to Indian nationalism. (See "New Sources, New Perspectives," page 898.) They also persuaded the British government to issue the Government of India Act of 1858, which established direct British control of India.

A system of rule emerged in which close to half a million Indians governed the Asian subcontinent under the supervision of a few thousand British men. Indians also collected taxes and distributed patronage. Colonial rule meant both blatant domination and more subtle intervention in everyday life. Simultaneously, however, ordinary Indians benefited in some places from improved sanitation and medicine. Following the British attack on their cultural practices, some upper-class Indians came to reject Indian customs such as infanticide, child marriage, and *sati*—a widow's self-immolation on her husband's funeral pyre. British notions of a scientifically ordered society also proved attractive to some Indians, who sent their children to British schools for training. The unity

---

♦**Lakshmibai:** LAHK shmee BY
♦**Jhansi:** JAHNT see

that British rule gave to what were once small localities and princedoms with separate allegiances promoted nationalism that, paradoxically, would soon be used against them.

French political expansion was similarly a matter of push, pull, and paradox. The French government pushed to establish its dominion over Cochin♦ China (modern southern Vietnam) in the 1860s. Missionaries in the area, ambitious French naval officers stationed in Asia, and even some local peoples—as in the case of Indian merchants and financiers—urged the French government to make successive attacks in the region to establish even greater control. Like the British, the French brought improvements, such as the Mekong Delta project that increased the amount of cultivated land and spurred rapid growth in the food supply. Sanitation and public health programs proved a mixed blessing, because they led to population growth that strained other local resources. Furthermore, landowners and French imperialists siphoned off most of the profits from economic improvement. The French also undertook a cultural mission to transform cities like Saigon with signs of Western urban life such as tree-lined boulevards that emulated those of Paris. French literature, theater, and art were popular not only with colonial officials but also with upper-class Indochinese.

Strategic commercial and military advantages remained an important motivation for some European overseas ventures in this age of Realpolitik. The Crimean War had shown the great powers that the Mediterranean basin was pivotal. Napoleon III, remembering his uncle's campaign in Egypt, took an interest in building the Suez Canal, which would connect the Mediterranean with the Red Sea and the Indian Ocean and thus dramatically shorten the route from Europe to Asia. Upon completion of the work in 1869, canal mania erupted. Verdi composed the opera *Aïda*, set in ancient Egypt, and Europeans developed a craze for anything Egyptian, adopting new styles in textile design, furniture, architecture, and art.

The rest of the Mediterranean and the Ottoman Empire felt the heightened presence of the European powers. Driving into the North African hinterland, the French army occupied all of Algeria by 1870, the year in which the number of European immigrants to the region reached one-quarter million. There was also a pull: as elsewhere, French rule in Algeria was aided by the attraction of local people to European goods, technology, and institutions. Merchants and local leaders cooperated in building railroads, sought bank loans and trade from the French, and sent their children to European-style schools. Many local peoples, however, resisted the invasions by continuing to attack soldiers and settlers. Others died from European-spread diseases. By 1872, the native population in Algeria had declined by more than 20 percent from five years earlier.

Its vastness allowed China to escape complete takeover, but the Qing♦ empire was rapidly declining from its populous and prosperous peak in the eighteenth century. Traders and Christian missionaries from European countries, carrying their message of Christian salvation, made inroads for the Western powers. Directing the Christian message to a population that had almost doubled during the preceding century and now numbered about 430 million, missionaries spread Christianity in a society already destabilized by demographic growth, defeat in the Opium War, and economic pressures from European trade. These contacts with the West had helped generate the mass movement known as the Taiping♦ ("Heavenly Kingdom"). Its millions of adherents wanted an end to the ruling Qing dynasty, the elimination of foreigners, more equal treatment of women, and land reform. By the mid-1850s, the Taiping controlled half of China. The Qing regime, its dynasty threatened, promised the British and French greater influence in exchange for aid. The result was a bloody civil war that lasted until 1864 and killed some thirty to sixty million Chinese (compared with 600,000 dead in the U.S. Civil War). When peace finally came, Western governments controlled much of the Chinese customs service and had virtually unlimited access to the country.

♦**Cochin:** KOH chihn

♦**Qing:** CHIHNG
♦**Taiping:** TY PIHN

Édouard Manet, *Déjeuner sur l'herbe* (*Luncheon on the Grass*, 1863)
The leading painters of the Parisian art world rejected the highly idealized paintings of nudes and romanticized historical scenes. In Manet's portrayal of a picnic, the clothed men sitting alongside the nude and seminude women, with their garments tossed about, mocked such idealism and romanticization. Critical art like Manet's annoyed many genteel citizens in the art-viewing public. What is the difference between the female nude in this painting and the ones in the Orientalist painting in Chapter 21 (page 794)? *Bridgeman-Giraudon/Art Resource, NY.*

This disregard for the classical tradition of showing women in mythical or idealized settings was too much for the critics. "A sort of female gorilla," one wrote of *Olympia*. "Her greenish, bloodshot eyes appear to be provoking to the public," wrote another. Shocking at first, graphic portrayals that shattered comforting illusions became a feature of modern art.

Opera. Unlike most of the visual arts, opera was commercially profitable, accessible to most classes of society, and thus effective artistically for reaching the nineteenth-century public. Verdi used musical theater to contrast noble ideals with the corrosive effects of power, love of country with the inevitable call for sacrifice and death, and the lure of passion with the need for social order. *La Traviata* (1853) stunned audiences with the tragedy of a tubercular courtesan who falls in love with a respectable middle-class man. In a series of lyrical arias, the characters express the lure of a heartfelt passion at odds with the need for stable families.

The German Richard Wagner,◆ the most flamboyant and musically innovative composer of the era, hoped to revolutionize opera by fusing music and drama to arouse the audience's fear, awe, and engagement with his vision. A gigantic cycle of four operas, *The*

◆**Wagner:** VAHG nur

Ring of the Nibelungen reshaped ancient German myths into a modern, nightmarish allegory of a world doomed by its obsessive pursuit of money and power and redeemable only through unselfish love. Wagner's operas were also influenced by the flood of philosophic and religious ideas coming from Asia—above all, Buddhism. His lovers in *Tristan and Isolde*, like characters in other operas, portray higher states of being through subduing the will and by dying in purifying flames. Wagner was a complex composer and thinker, and his opera *The Mastersingers of Nuremberg* (*Die Meistersinger,*♦ 1862–1867) was a nationalistic tribute to German culture. The piece was said to be implicitly anti-Semitic because of its rejection of influences other than German ones in the arts. Wagner's flair for publicity, self-dramatization, musical innovation, and complex national and international themes ultimately made him a major force in philosophy, politics, and the arts. By becoming a grand symbol himself, he excelled in fulfilling the nationalizing and unifying potential in all cultural works.

All of the arts, no matter how controversial, shaped the cultural attitudes of the decades 1850–1870. Favoring realism and the rising nation-state, the arts provided visions that helped unite isolated individuals into a public with a shared, if debated, cultural experience. Artists implicitly promoted nation building even as they experimented with new forms.

Religion and Secular Order

Organized religion formed one bulwark of traditional social and political order after the revolutions of 1848, but the expansion of state power set the stage for clashes over its influence. Should religion have the same hold on government and public life as in the past, thus competing with loyalty to the nation? The views were mixed and would remain so. In the 1850s, many politicians supported religious institutions and attended public church rituals because they were another source of order. Simultaneously, some nation builders, intellectuals, and economic liberals came to reject the competing jurisdiction and religious worldview of established churches, particularly Roman Catholicism. Bismarck was one of these; he came to judge that the church impeded the growth of nationalist sentiment. He thus mounted a full-blown **Kulturkampf**♦ ("culture war") against religion. The German government expelled the Jesuits from Germany in 1872, increased state power over the clergy in Prussia in 1873, and introduced obligatory civil marriage in 1875. Bismarck had miscalculated his own ability to manipulate politics, however, for both conservatives and Catholics rebelled against policies of religious repression as part of state building. The Roman Catholic church insisted on its political influence and explicitly attacked nineteenth-century visions of progress and reform embodied in such institutions as secular public schools. Competition between church and state for power and influence heated up in the age of Realpolitik.

Catholic Reaction. The Catholic church felt assaulted by a growing rationalism that was supposed to replace religious faith and by the state building of Italy and Germany that competed for people's traditional loyalty. In addition, nation building had resulted in the extension of liberal rights to Jews, whom Christians often considered enemies. Attacking reform, Pope Pius IX issued *The Syllabus of Errors* (1864), which put the church and the pope at odds "with progress, with liberalism, and with modern civilization." In 1870, the First Vatican Council approved the dogma of papal infallibility. This teaching proclaimed that the pope, under certain circumstances, must be regarded by Catholics as speaking divinely revealed truth on issues of morality and faith. In 1878 a new pontiff, Leo XIII, began the process of reconciliation with modern politics by encouraging up-to-date scholarship in Catholic institutes and universities and by accepting aspects of democracy. Leo's ideas marked a dramatic turn, ending the Kulturkampf and fortifying beleaguered Catholics across Europe.

Religious doctrine continued to have powerful popular appeal, but the place of

---

♦*Die Meistersinger:* dee MY stur sihn gur

♦*Kulturkampf:* kul TUR kahmpf

organized religion in society at large was changing. On the one hand, church attendance declined among workers and artisans; on the other, many in the upper and middle classes and most of the peasantry remained faithful. The Orthodox church of Russia and eastern Europe with its Pan-Slavic appeal fostered nationalism among oppressed Serbs and became a rallying point. Women's spiritual beliefs became more intense, with both Roman Catholic and Russian Orthodox women's religious orders increasing in size and number; men, by contrast, were falling away from religious devotion. Many urban Jews assimilated to secular, national cultures, abandoning religious practice. The social composition of those faithful to religion had come to take a distinctly different shape from the days when it included everyone.

In 1854, the pope's announcement of the doctrine of the Immaculate Conception (stating that Mary, alone among all humans, had been born without original sin) was followed by an outburst of popular religious fervor, especially among women. In 1858, a young peasant girl, Bernadette Soubirous,♦ began having visions of the Virgin Mary at Lourdes in southern France. In these visions Mary told Bernadette to drink from the ground, at which point a spring appeared. Crowds comprised mostly of women besieged the area to be cured of ailments by the waters of Lourdes. In 1867, less than ten years later, a railroad track was laid to Lourdes to enable millions of pilgrims to visit the shrine on church-organized trips. The Catholic church thus showed that it was not passé— it could use such modern means as railroads, medical verifications of miraculous cures, and journalism to make Lourdes itself the center of a brisk commercial as well as religious culture. The cultural unity of the nation-state could be achieved by old and venerable institutions like churches, if they too followed these innovative paths to modern power.

The Challenge from Natural Science.

Almost contemporaneously with Soubirous's vision, the English naturalist Charles Darwin (1809–1882) published *On the Origin of*

♦**Soubirous:** soo bee roo

Species (1859), a challenge to the Judeo-Christian worldview that humanity was a unique creation of God. In this book and in later writings, Darwin argued that life had taken shape over countless millions of years before humans existed and that human life was but the result of this slow development, called evolution. Instead of God miraculously bringing the universe and all life into being in six days as described in Genesis, Darwin held that life developed from lower forms through a primal battle for survival and through the sexual selection of mates— processes called natural selection, which others of Darwin's contemporaries had also identified. An eminently respectable Victorian gentleman, Darwin announced that the Bible gave a "manifestly false history of the world." Darwin's theories also undermined certain liberal, secular beliefs. Enlightenment principles, for example, had glorified nature as tranquil and noble and had viewed human nature as essentially rational. The theory of natural selection, in which the fittest survive, suggested a different kind of human society, one composed of combative individuals and groups constantly at war with one another to prevail in hostile surroundings.

Darwin's findings and other innovative biological research influenced contemporary beliefs about society. Working in obscurity with pea plants in his monastery garden in the 1860s, Gregor Mendel (1822–1884) discovered the principles of heredity, from which the science of genetics later developed. Investigation into the female reproductive cycle led German scientists to discover the principle of spontaneous ovulation—the automatic release of the egg by the ovary independent of sexual intercourse. This discovery caused theorists to conclude that men had aggressive and strong sexual drives because reproduction depended on their sexual arousal. In contrast, the spontaneous and cyclical release of the egg independent of arousal indicated that women were passive and lacked sexual feeling.

Darwin also tried to use biological findings to explain social phenomena. The legal, political, and economic privilege of white European men in the nineteenth century, he maintained, naturally derived from their being more highly evolved than white women or people of color. Despite recognizing a common ancestor for all humans, Darwin held that people of color, or "lower races," were far behind whites in intelligence and civilization. As for women, "the chief distinction in the intellectual powers of the two sexes," Darwin declared, "is shewn by man's attaining to a higher eminence in whatever he takes up." A school of Social Darwinism grew out of this Darwinist thought. Social Darwinists used a distorted version of evolutionary theory to lobby for racist, sexist, and nationalist policies. Their arguments were influential in the years to come.

From Natural Science to Social Science

The spread of Darwinist ideas accelerated the search for alternatives to the religious understanding of social order as divinely ordained. Theorists and critics sought to devise hardheaded and secular explanations of how society functioned. Simultaneously, the theories of the French social philosopher Auguste Comte♦ (1798–1857), whose ideas formed the basis of a "positive science" of society and politics, inspired a host of reform organizations. **Positivism** claimed that careful study of facts would generate accurate, or "positive," laws of society. Comte's *System of Positive Politics, or Treatise on Sociology* (1851) proposed that social scientists construct knowledge of the political order as they would an understanding of the natural world, that is, according to informed secular investigation. This idea inspired people to believe they could solve the problems spawned by economic and social change. Comte also encouraged women's participation in reform because he deemed "womanly" compassion and love as equally fundamental to social harmony as was scientific public policy. Positivism led not only to women's increased social and political activism but also to the growth of the social sciences, which developed during this period, largely under the banner of positivism. Sociology, the scientific study of human society, was primary among these influential new disciplines.

Darwin Ridiculed, c. 1860
Charles Darwin's theories claimed that humans evolved from animal species and rejected the long-standing explanation of a divine human origin. His scientific ideas so diverged from people's beliefs that cartoonists lampooned both the respectable Darwin and his theory. Despite the controversy, evolution withstood the test of further scientific study. What message might this cartoon have conveyed to a nineteenth-century viewer? **For more help analyzing this image**, see the visual activity for this chapter in the Online Study Guide at **bedfordstmartins.com/hunt**. *Hulton Archive/Getty Images.*

For a time, the celebrated English philosopher John Stuart Mill (1806–1873) became an enthusiast of Comte, whose theories led Mill to espouse widespread reform and mass education and to support the complete

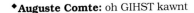

♦**Auguste Comte:** oh GIHST kawnt

enfranchisement of women. His political treatise *On Liberty* (1859) couched his aspiration for a general social improvement in a concern that superior people not be brought down or confined by the will of the masses. Influenced by his wife, Harriet Taylor Mill, he notoriously advocated the extension of rights to women and introduced a woman suffrage bill into the House of Commons after her death. The bill's defeat prompted Mill to publish *The Subjection of Women* (1869), a work recapitulating his studies with his wife. Translated into many languages and influential in eastern Europe, Scandinavia, and the Americas, *The Subjection of Women* presented the family as maintaining an older kind of politics devoid of modern concepts of rights and freedom. Mill also proposed that the aura of women's voluntary obedience and love in marriage was necessary to mask the gross inequalities between men and women in the household. To make a woman appear "not a forced slave, but a willing one," he said, she was trained from childhood not to value her own talent and independence but to embrace "submission and yielding to the control of others." Critiquing accepted rules for men's and women's roles, *The Subjection of Women* became an internationally respected guide for a growing women's movement committed to obtaining basic rights.

The progressive side of Mill's social thought was soon lost in a flood of Social Darwinist theories. Even before *Origin of Species*, Herbert Spencer's *Social Statics* (1851) advocated the study of society but also promoted laissez-faire and unadulterated competition, claiming that the "unfit" should be allowed to perish in the name of progress. Spencer's opposition to public education, social reform, and any other attempt to soften the harshness of the struggle for existence struck a receptive chord among the middle and upper classes. The spread of his views contributed to the surge of Social Darwinism in the next decades.

These various visions of social order—all of them believed to be scientific and thus true—would become dominant in future national debates over policy in the West. The influence of Darwinism and Mill's liberalism, like that of the arts, religion, and science, would be to shape public culture, setting the subjects and terms of social and political thought.

In an age of nation building, culture often enhanced the political call for realistic, hard-headed thinking about social order.

> **Review:** What were the results of the increasing spread of the scientific method to social thought?

❖ Contesting the Growing Power of the Nation-State

By the end of the 1860s, the unchecked growth of the state and the ongoing process of economic change had led to palpable tensions in European society. New theories of work life and politics appeared to counter nationalism and capitalism—most notably those of economist and philosopher Karl Marx, who advocated socialism and international rather than national loyalties. Workers throughout the West protested the terms of work and the upheavals in everyday life caused by the expanding power of the state, as governments ripped apart cities for improvements and sent workers scurrying for new places to live. In France anger at defeat in the Franco-Prussian War and at economic hardship made these tensions erupt into a bitter, if brief, civil war. In the spring of 1871, the people of Paris, blaming the centralized state for the French surrender to the Germans, declared Paris a commune—a community of equals without bureaucrats and pompous politicians. Marx's books analyzing the growth of capitalism and national politics—as well as the Paris Commune—provided workers with a popular and politically galvanizing account of events. From the 1870s on, these two phenomena—the writings of Karl Marx and the fury of working people—renewed fear among the middle classes that both nation-state and social order might be violently destroyed.

The Rise of Marxism

Marxism arose with urbanization and the spread of industry to cities and towns across Europe. Increasingly well educated by an ambitious nation-state, urban workers frequented cafés and pubs to hear news and share with one another impressions of political and economic change. After a period of repression in the 1850s following their failed revolutions, workers' organizations slowly reemerged as a political force in the West. Like other interest groups, workers' organizations were part of a pattern of horizontal allegiances, in which people with similar backgrounds came together to shape the political process. Such allegiances replaced the old vertical allegiances that reflected not similarity and equality but the hierarchy and subordination of the old regime.

In the 1850s, governments often outlawed unions, fearing that they would challenge political order. Unions that existed in those years were thus secret, poorly coordinated, and shaped by a wide range of programs for change, including the ideas of former printer Pierre-Joseph Proudhon♦ (1809–1865). In the 1840s, Proudhon had coined the explosive saying "Property is theft," suggesting that ownership robbed propertyless people of their rightful share of the earth's benefits. He opposed the centralized state and proposed that society be organized instead around natural groupings of men in artisans' workshops. These workshops and a central bank crediting each worker for his labor would replace government and would lead to a mutualist social organization. Proudhon heartily opposed any mingling of men and women in political life; he believed the mutualist organization of men in public should be matched by the seclusion of their wives laboring at home for their husbands' comfort.

Another theory that attracted workers at the time was anarchism. Anarchists maintained that the existence of the state was the root of social injustice. According to Russian nobleman and anarchist leader Mikhail Bakhunin,♦ the slightest infringement on freedom, especially by the central state, was unacceptable. The political theory of **anarchism** thus advocated the destruction of all state power. At a London meeting in 1864, workers from Italy, Germany, Britain, and France accepted both anarchism and Proudhon's mutualism as guiding ideas for the la-

bor movement. However, Karl Marx was a third major presence at this founding meeting of the International Workingmen's Association, and he set out to battle these two very popular, rival theories. These doctrines, Marx insisted, were emotional and wrongheaded, lacking the sound, scientific basis of his own theory, subsequently called **Marxism**. Marx's analysis, expounded most notably in *Das Kapital*, adopted the liberal idea, dating back to John Locke in the seventeenth century, that human existence was defined by the necessity of working as a way of fulfilling basic needs such as food, clothing, and shelter. *Das Kapital*, published between 1867 and 1894, was based on mathematical calculations of production and profit that would justify a Realpolitik for the working classes. Marx held that the fundamental organization of any society, including its politics and culture, derived from the relationships arising from work or production. This idea, known as materialism, meant that the foundation of a society rested on class relationships—such as those between serf and medieval lord, slave and master, or worker and capitalist. Marx called the type of class relationships that developed around work the mode of production: for instance, feudalism, slavery, or capitalism. Rejecting the liberal focus on individual rights, he emphasized the unequal class relations caused by feudal lords, slaveholders, and capitalists or the bourgeoisie—that is, those who took control of the "means of production" in the form of the capital, land, tools, or factories necessary to fulfill basic human needs. When capitalist control disappeared, a classless society of workers—that is, a socialist one—would arise.

Economic liberals expected the free market to produce balance and a harmony of interests, but Marx saw social organization and productive life not as harmonious but in conflict because of economic oppression. He believed that workers' awareness of their oppression would produce class consciousness among those in the same predicament and ultimately lead them to revolt against their exploiters. Such revolt, not reform or legislation, would be the mechanism for historical change. Capitalism would be overthrown by these workers—the **proletariat**—and the reign of socialism would ensue. Like Darwin,

♦**Pierre-Joseph Proudhon:** pyehr zhaw ZEHF proo DAWN
♦**Mikhail Bakhunin:** myih kuh YEEL buh KOON yihn

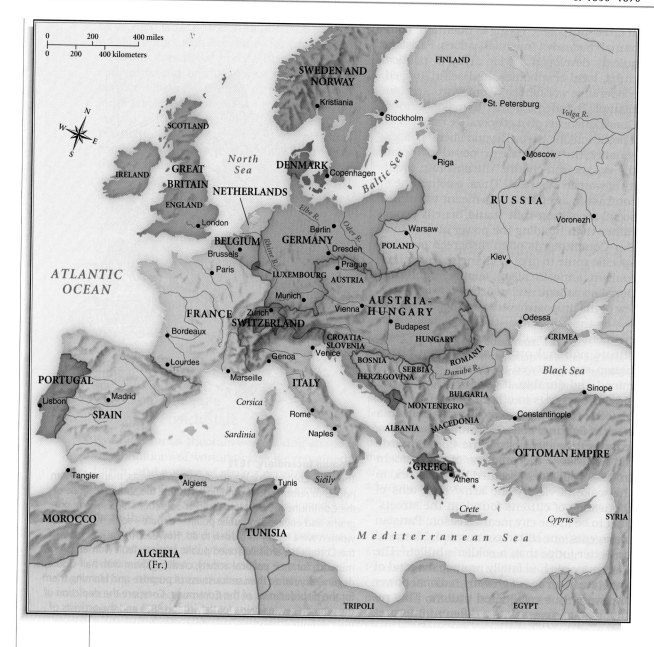

MAPPING THE WEST Europe and the Mediterranean, 1871

European nation-states consolidated their power by building unified state structures and by developing the means for the diverse peoples within their borders to become socially and culturally integrated. They were also rapidly expanding outside their boundaries, extending the economic and political reach of the nation-state. North Africa and the Middle East—parts of the declining Ottoman Empire—particularly appealed to European governments because of their resources and their potential for further European settlement. They offered a gateway to the rest of the world. Compare this map of Europe with that from two decades earlier (page 868) to explain the progress of nation-state building. What aspects of nation building does this map show, and what aspects do not appear on the map?

the collapsed boundaries between the male political sphere and the female domestic sphere. Karl Marx disagreed: he portrayed the Commune as a class struggle of workers attacking upper-class interests, which were embodied in the centralized state. Executions and deportations by the thousands virtually shut down the French labor movement, while memories of the Commune kept fear of workers smoldering in middle- and upper-class hearts across Europe.

> **Review:** Why did Marx and members of the Paris Commune object to modern social order and the expanding powers of the nation-state?

Conclusion

Throughout modern history the development of nation-states has been neither inevitable nor uniform nor peaceful. This was especially true in the nineteenth century, when ambitious politicians, resilient monarchs, and determined bureaucrats transformed very different countries into various kinds of states by a variety of methods and policies. Nation building was most dramatic in Germany and Italy, where states were unified through military force and where people of many political tendencies ultimately agreed that national unity surpassed most other causes. Compelled by military defeat to shake off centuries of tradition, the Austrian and Russian monarchs instituted reforms as a way of keeping their systems viable, but the results were different, even unique. The Habsburg Empire became a dual monarchy, an arrangement that gave the Hungarians virtual home rule and that raised the level of disunity. Russian reforms left the authoritarian monarchy intact and even protected the social and political order. In eastern Europe, the middle class was far less powerful than in western Europe, and reform came from autocratic leaders who imposed it from above to preserve the system rather than from popular agitation to democratize it.

After decades of romantic fervor, hard-headed realism in politics became a much-touted norm, often with unexpected consequences. Proponents of realism, Darwin and Marx developed theories disturbing to those who maintained an Enlightenment faith in social and political harmony. Realist novels and artworks jarred polite society, and, like the operas of Verdi, portrayed dilemmas of the times. The policies of the growing state apparatus that were meant to bring order often brought disorder, such as the destruction of entire neighborhoods and violence toward people in far-off lands. Schooling, however, taught the lower classes to be orderly citizens, and urban renewal ultimately improved cities and public health to complement nation building. Yet when the ordinary people of the Paris Commune rose up to protest the loss of French power and prestige, they also aimed to defy the trend toward state building. Their actions raised difficult questions. How far should the power of the state extend in both domestic and international affairs? Would nationalism be a force for war or for peace? As these issues ripened, the next decades saw extraordinary economic advances, and an unprecedented surge in Europe's global power.

Suggested References

The End of the Concert of Europe

Historians have often neglected the inglorious Crimean War despite its impact on European politics. Much of the best new literature focuses not only on political changes but also on the war's social impact in Russia. Worobec's book gives a searching look at Russian peasant life in this age of transition.

Edgerton, Robert B. *Death or Glory: The Legacy of the Crimean War.* 1999.

Hazareesingh, Sudhir. *From Subject to Citizen: The Second Empire and the Emergence of Modern French Democracy.* 1998.

*Seacole, Mary. *Wonderful Adventures of Mrs. Seacole in Many Lands.* 1857.

Worobec, Christine. *Peasant Russia: Family and Community in the Post-Emancipation Period.* 1991.

Wortman, Richard S. *Scenarios of Power: Myth and Ceremony in Russian Monarchy.* 2 vols. 1995–2000.

---

*Primary source.

War and Nation Building

Nation building has produced a varied literature ranging from biographies to studies of ceremonials and the presentation of royalty as celebrities and unifying figures. Two Web sites show the complexities of this process: Brown University's Victorian Web demonstrates the connections among royalty, politicians, religion, and culture; and Bucknell University's Russian Studies site opens to the strains of the Russian national anthem, composed in the reign of Nicholas I to foster reverence for the dynasty and homeland.

Blackbourn, David. *Fontana History of Germany, 1780–1918: The Long Nineteenth Century.* 1997.

Breuilly, John. *The Formation of the First German Nation-State, 1800–1871.* 1996.

DiScala, Spencer. *Italy: From Revolution to Republic, 1700 to the Present.* 1995.

Homans, Margaret. *Royal Representations: Queen Victoria and British Culture, 1837–1876.* 1998.

Russian Studies: **http://www.departments.bucknell.edu/Russian**.

Smith, Paul. *Disraeli: A Brief Life.* 1996.

The Victorian Web: **http://landow.stg.brown.edu/victorian/victov.html**.

Establishing Social Order

Nation building entailed state-sponsored activities stretching from promoting education to rebuilding cities. New histories show the process of creating a sense of nationality through government management of people's environment, such that citizenship became part of everyday life. Hine and Faragher show the intersection of U.S. expansionism and nation building.

Hamm, Michael F. *Kiev: A Portrait, 1800–1917.* 1993.

Hine, Robert V., and John Mack Faragher. *The American West: A New Interpretative History.* 2001.

Hoffenberg, Peter H. *An Empire on Display: English, Indian, and Australian Exhibitions from the Crystal Palace to the Great War.* 2001.

Johanson, Christine. *Women's Struggle for Higher Education in Russia, 1855–1900.* 1987.

Jordan, David. *Transforming Paris: The Life and Labor of Baron Haussmann.* 1995.

Lebra-Chapman, Joyce. *The Rani of Jhansi: A Study in Female Heroism in India.* 1986.

Rotenberg, Robert. *Landscape and Power in Vienna.* 1995.

The Culture of Social Order

Like the biographies of politicians, the biographies of artists and intellectuals have proved crucial to understanding the period of realism and Realpolitik. They show artists, intellectuals, and scientists addressing the central issues of their day amid dramatic social change. Kaufman's book shows the connection between religious fervor, tourism, and commercial development in the West.

Bordenheimer, Rosemarie. *The Real Life of Mary Ann Evans: George Eliot, Her Letters and Fiction.* 1994.

*Darwin, Charles. *Autobiography.* 1969.

Gieson, Gerald L. *The Private Science of Louis Pasteur.* 1996.

Kaufman, Suzanne. *Lourdes and the Making of Mass Culture in Modern France.* 2004.

Mayr, Ernst. *One Long Argument: Charles Darwin and the Genesis of Modern Evolutionary Thought.* 1991.

*Turgenev, Ivan. *A Hunter's Sketches.* 1852.

Contesting the Growing Power of the Nation-State

The teachings of Karl Marx and the story of the Paris Commune haunted Europeans in the mid-nineteenth century. The following works capture the fear of the working classes that shaped middle-class thought, and they show the energy that working- and middle-class people alike put into politics in this period of nation building. Northwestern University has digitized its collection on the Siege of Paris and the Commune.

Gullickson, Gay. *Unruly Women of Paris: Images of the Commune.* 1996.

McClellan, David. *Karl Marx: His Life and Thought.* 1978.

Nord, Philip. *The Republican Moment: Struggles for Democracy in Nineteenth-Century France.* 1995.

Siege of Paris Collection, Northwestern University: **http://www.library.northwestern.edu/spec/siege**.

CHAPTER REVIEW

KEY TERMS

anarchism (907)

dual monarchy (887)

Haussmannization (891)

Kulturkampf (903)

Marxism (907)

Meiji Restoration (898)

mir (880)

nation-state (881)

Pan-Slavism (888)

positivism (905)

proletariat (907)

realism (899)

Realpolitik (873)

Russification (881)

zemstvos (880)

REVIEW QUESTIONS

1. What were the main results of the Crimean War?
2. What role did warfare play in the various nineteenth-century nation-building efforts?
3. How did colonial expansion change in the period of nation building?
4. What were the results of the increasing spread of the scientific method to social thought?
5. Why did Marx and members of the Paris Commune object to modern social order and the expanding powers of the nation-state?

MAKING CONNECTIONS

1. How did realism in social thought break with Enlightenment values?
2. Why did some nation-states tend toward secularism while the kingdoms that preceded them were based on religion?
3. How was the Paris Commune related to earlier revolutions in France? How did it differ from them?

FOR FURTHER EXPLORATION

To assess your mastery of the material in this chapter, see the Online Study Guide at **bedfordstmartins.com/hunt**.

To read additional primary-source material from this period, see Chapter 23 in *Sources of The Making of the West*, Second Edition.

Industry, Empire, and Everyday Life, 1870–1890

BETWEEN 1870 AND 1890, MARIANNE NORTH, an unmarried Englishwoman, traveled the globe several times. The end of the nineteenth century was a time of vast migration, some of it in search of a better life, some of it for imperial conquest, and some of it, as in the case of Marianne North, in pursuit of knowledge. North was a botanical illustrator and "plant hunter," one of those avid Europeans who on their own or under government sponsorship searched the world over for plants to classify, grow, and put to commercial use. North ventured to India, North and South America, Java, Borneo, South Africa, and many other distant points setting up her easel and making scientific drawings of plants. She discovered at least five new species (officially named after her) and a new type of tree as well as collected thousands of plants to send back to botanical gardens in England. When she became too frail to travel, she organized a permanent museum in London to display her botanical drawings to the public (see the illustration on page 916). Her goal was promoting ordinary people's knowledge of the British Empire: "I want them to know," she announced, "that cocoa doesn't come from the coconut."

Historians have aptly labeled the decades from 1870 to 1890 an era of industry and empire in the West. The Western powers were

---

Thomas Roberts, *Coming South* (1886)
The exodus of Europeans to every part of the world swelled from the middle of the nineteenth century. Most of this migration occurred for political and economic reasons, with the most beleaguered segments of the population likely to cross thousands of miles by ship to find opportunity and political freedom. In the nineteenth century employment agencies enticed male and female workers to travel to areas with labor shortages. Non-profit organizations also encouraged single women to migrate in hopes of righting the gender imbalance in most colonies. Other Western migration was temporary, like that of scientists, writers, soldiers, and missionaries. The Australian painter Thomas Roberts, who had himself migrated from London in 1869 at the age of 13, depicted these voyages on ship as so calm and boring as to test one's sanity, an atmosphere described similarly in migrants' diaries and letters. Other artists portrayed migration as tumultuous, especially at dockside, as people jostled to get on board or wept at separation—sometimes permanent—from families and loved ones. *National Gallery of Victoria, Melbourne, Australia. Gift of Col. Aubrey Gibson in Memory of John and Anne Gibson. Bridgeman Art Library.*

Universal Exposition of 1889
French politicians launched the Universal Exposition, or World's Fair, of 1889 in Paris to celebrate what they called the "progress resulting from one hundred years of freedom." The exposition featured the latest industrial inventions as well as musical and artistic displays from the cultures France had conquered. The greatest attraction, however, was the Eiffel Tower, constructed in two years, to much criticism. "Hideous, horrible," one Catholic leader called it, a "skeleton in stark contrast" to the city's majestic cathedrals. Nevertheless, tens of thousands flocked to ascend this masterpiece of engineering technology—the same technology Gustave Eiffel had used to provide the iron skeleton supporting the Statue of Liberty. Electric illumination and electric elevators enhanced the tower's technological impact. What were the purposes of an exposition like that of 1889? *Private Collection/Archives Charmet/Bridgeman Art Library.*

in Paris for the Universal Exposition of 1889, stood as a monument to the age's engineering wizardry; visitors rode to its summit in electric elevators (see the illustration above).

To fuel the West's explosive industrial growth, the leading industrial nations mined and produced massive quantities of coal,

iron, and steel during the 1870s and 1880s. Production of iron increased from 11 million to 23 million tons. Even in relatively underdeveloped Spain, iron-ore mining unearthed a total of 6 million tons in 1890, up from 130,000 tons in 1861—an almost 5,000 percent increase. Steel output grew just as impressively in the industrial nations, increasing from 500,000 to 11 million tons in the 1870s and 1880s. Manufacturers used the metal to build the more than 100,000 locomotives that pulled trains during these years—trains that transported 2 billion people annually.

Historians used to contrast a "second" Industrial Revolution, with its concentration on heavy industrial products, to the "first" one of the eighteenth and early nineteenth centuries, in which innovations in textile making and the use of steam energy predominated. But many historians now believe that the distinction applies mainly to Britain: in countries where industrialization came later, the two stages occurred simultaneously. Numerous textile mills were installed on the continent later than in Britain, for instance, at the same time as blast furnaces were constructed. Although industrialization led to the decline of cottage production in traditional crafts like weaving, home industry—or **outwork**, defined as the process of having some aspects of industrial work done outside factories in individual homes—persisted in garment making, metalwork, and such "finishing trades" as porcelain painting and button polishing. The coexistence of home and factory enterprise continued through all the changes in manufacturing, to the present day.

Industrial innovations also transformed agriculture. Chemical fertilizers boosted crop yields, and reapers and threshers mechanized harvesting. In the 1870s, Sweden produced a cream separator, a first step toward mechanizing dairy farming. Wire fencing and barbed wire replaced wooden fencing and stone walls, both of which were labor-intensive to create. Refrigeration allowed fruits, vegetables, and meat to be transported without spoiling, thus diversifying and increasing the urban food supply. Tin from colonial trade facilitated large-scale commercial canning, which made many foods available year-round to people in the cities.

Challenge to British Dominance. In the last decades of the century, Britain's rate of industrial growth slowed, as its entrepreneurs remained wedded to older, successful technologies. Although Great Britain maintained its high output of industrial goods and profited from a multitude of worldwide investments, two countries began surpassing it in research, technical education, innovation, and rate of growth: Germany and the United States.

In the aftermath of the Franco-Prussian War, Germany received the territories of Alsace and Lorraine, which had textile industries as well as rich iron deposits. Investing heavily in research, German businesses rapidly devised new industrial processes and began to mass-produce goods that other countries had originally manufactured. Germany also spent as much money on education as on its military in the 1870s and 1880s. This investment resulted in highly skilled engineers and technical workers whose productivity enabled Germany's electrical and chemical engineering capabilities to soar.

The United States began an intensive exploitation of its vast natural resources, including coal, metal ores, gold, and oil. The value of U.S. industrial goods spurted from $5 billion in 1880 to $13 billion two decades later. Whereas German accomplishments rested more on state promotion of industrial efforts, U.S. growth often involved innovative entrepreneurs, such as Andrew Carnegie in iron and steel and John D. Rockefeller in oil. The three-way industrial rivalry among Germany, the United States, and Great Britain would soon have political and diplomatic repercussions.

Areas of Slower Industrialization. With the exception of Belgium, which had been the first continental country to industrialize, other countries trailed the three industrial leaders. French industry grew steadily, but French businesses remained smaller than those in Germany and the United States. Although France had some huge mining, textile, and metallurgical establishments, many businessmen retired early to imitate the still-enviable aristocratic way of life. In Spain, Austria-Hungary, and Italy, industrial development was primarily a local phenomenon. Austria-Hungary had densely industrialized areas around Vienna and in Styria and Bohemia, but the rest of the country remained tied to traditional, unmechanized agriculture. Italy's economy continued to industrialize in the north while remaining rural and agricultural in the south. The Italian government spent more on building Rome into a grand capital than it invested in economic growth. A mere 1.4 percent of Italy's 1872 budget went to education and science, compared with 10.8 percent in Germany. The commercial use of electricity helped Scandinavians, who were poor in coal and ore, to industrialize in the last third of the nineteenth century. Sweden and Norway became leaders in the use of hydroelectric power and the development of electrical products; Denmark developed a major commercial sector in animal and dairy products. Despite these innovations, however, Scandinavia retained its mostly rural character.

Russia's road to industrialization was tortuous, slowed partly by its relatively small urban labor force. Many Russian peasants who may have wished to take advantage of the opportunities of industrialization were tied to the mir, or landed community, by the terms of the serf emancipation. Some villages sent men and women to cities, but on the condition that they return for plowing and harvesting. Nevertheless, by the 1890s, Moscow, St. Petersburg, and a few other cities had substantial working-class populations. The Russian minister of finance Sergei Witte attracted foreign capital, entrepreneurs, and engineers and used them to construct railroads, including the Trans-Siberian Railroad (1891–1916), which upon completion stretched 5,787 miles from Moscow to Vladivostok (see the illustration on the next page). The burgeoning of the railroads combined with growth in metallurgical and mining operations strengthened Russia as an industrial and military power. As in most of eastern Europe, however, the peasants bore the main burden of financing Russia's industrial growth, especially in the form of higher taxes on vodka. Thus, neither they nor the underpaid Russian workers could afford to buy the goods their country

Trans-Siberian Railroad

Begun in 1892, the Trans-Siberian railroad, the major east–west transportation line across the Russian Empire, took several decades to complete. From farms in western Siberia the line brought goods to markets in major cities, while in the more sparsely populated east the railroad mostly served to transport troops to secure imperial conquests and guard frontiers. The railroad also became a feature of around-the-world tourism; voyagers traveled in luxurious, if very slow, Trans-Siberian railway coaches. The infrastructure of the line, however, was cheaply built and caused incredible difficulties both in wartime and in peacetime. How did the Trans-Siberian Railroad strengthen the Russian empire? *Sovfoto.*

produced. Russia offered a prime example of the complexities of industrialization and its uneven benefits.

Facing Economic Crisis

Although innovations and business expansion often conveyed a sense of optimism, economic conditions were far from rosy throughout the 1870s and 1880s. Within two years of the end of the Franco-Prussian War, prosperity abruptly gave way to a severe economic depression in many industrial countries. The crisis of 1873 was followed by almost three decades of economic fluctuations, most alarmingly a series of sharp downturns whose severity varied from country to country. People of all classes lost their jobs or businesses and faced consequences ranging from long stretches of unemployment to bankruptcy. Economists of the day were stunned by the relentlessness and per-

vasiveness of the slump. Because economic ties bound industrialized western Europe to international markets, recession affected the economies of such diverse regions as Australia, South Africa, California, Newfoundland, and the West Indies.

These dramatic fluctuations differed from the economic cycles that were the rule before 1850, in which failure on the land led to higher food prices and then to failure in manufacturing. Although suffering problems of its own, agriculture was no longer so dominant that its fate determined the welfare of other sectors of the economy. By the 1870s, industrial and financial setbacks were sending businesses into long-term tailspins. Innovation created new or modernized industries on an unprecedented scale, but economic disaster constantly loomed.

Economic crises were possible in a time of industrial progress because economists, industrialists, and government officials did not yet clearly understand the workings of industrialized, interconnected economies. As industrialization advanced, entrepreneurs encountered fundamental problems. First, the start-up costs of new enterprises skyrocketed. Textile mills had required relatively modest amounts of capital in comparison to factories producing steel and iron. To use the terms of modern economists, **capital-intensive industry** replaced labor-intensive industry: growth of the former required the purchase of expensive machinery, not merely the hiring of more workers. Second, the distribution and consumption of goods were inadequate to sustain industrial growth. Increased productivity in both agriculture and industry led to rapidly declining prices. Wheat, for example, dropped to one-third its 1870 price by the 1890s. Consumers, however, did not always benefit from this deflation: wages were slashed and unemployment rose during the economic downturns. Nor could they always afford the new goods. Industrialists had made their fortunes by emphasizing production, not consumption. The series of slumps refocused entrepreneurial policy on finding ways to enhance sales and distribution and to control markets and prices.

In response to nervous business owners and to those fearful of potential social unrest, governments took steps to foster economic prosperity. New laws spurred the development of the **limited liability corporation**, which protected investors from personal responsibility for the firm's debt. Before limited liability, businesses drew the capital they needed primarily from their own family assets, and financial backers were individually responsible for the firm's financial difficulties. In one case in England, a former partner who had failed to have his name removed from a legal document after leaving the business remained responsible to creditors when the company went bankrupt. He lost everything he owned except a watch and the equivalent of $100. The end of personal liability greatly increased investor confidence with regard to financing business ventures.

Public financing in stocks and bonds promised investors wide opportunities to gain high profits. Stock markets had existed prior to the changes in liability laws, but they had dealt mainly in government bonds and in government-sponsored enterprises such as railroads. By the end of the century, stock markets were trading heavily in industrial corporate stock owned by many individuals, and investors thus raised money from a larger pool of private capital than before. At the center of an international economy linked by telegraph, telephone, railways, and steamships, the London Stock Exchange in 1882 traded industrial shares worth £54 million, a value that surged to £443 million by 1900. The capacity to raise capital for financing industry soared.

Less personal financial liability and new sources of capital did not eliminate business difficulties, however. In another adaptive move, firms in the same industry banded together in cartels and trusts to control prices and competition. Cartels (the organization of industries into a monopoly for fixing prices) flourished particularly in German chemical, iron, coal, and electric industries. For example, the Rhenish-Westphalian Coal Syndicate, founded in 1893, eventually dominated more than 95 percent of coal production in Germany. Although business owners might continue publicly to advocate free trade, their own cartels broke with free-trade practices by restricting output and setting prices.

Trusts appeared first in the United States. In 1882, John D. Rockefeller created the Standard Oil Trust by acquiring stock from many different oil companies and placing it under the direction of trustees. The trustees then controlled so much of the companies' stock that they could set prices for the entire industry. They could even dictate to the railroads the rates for transporting the oil. Trusts and cartels also oversaw the vertical integration of industries, in which, for example, a steel company acquired mining operations in ore and coal as well as railroads to distribute its output. Such acquisitions ensured access to raw materials, lower production costs, and greater control of product distribution.

Like the establishment of cartels and trusts, government imposition of tariffs expressed declining faith in classical liberal economics. Much of Europe had adopted free trade after midcentury, but during the recessions of the 1870s, huge trade deficits—caused when imports exceed exports—soured many Europeans on the concept. A country with a trade deficit had less capital available to invest internally; thus, fewer jobs were created and the chances of social unrest increased. Farmers in many European countries were hurt when improvements in transportation made it possible to import perishable food, such as grain from the United States and Ukraine. France and Germany were particularly vulnerable to trade deficits in the last three decades of the century. In response, governments in both countries approved tariffs throughout these decades. Farmers, capitalists, and even many workers supported these taxes on imports to prevent competition from foreign goods. Governments in the West responded to calls for economic nationalism, and by the early 1890s all but Belgium, Britain, and the Netherlands had ended free trade.

Revolution in Business Practices

Industrialists tried to minimize the damage of economic downturns by revolutionizing the everyday conduct of their businesses. A generation earlier, a factory owner was directly involved in every aspect of his business and often learned to run the firm through trial and

TAKING MEASURE

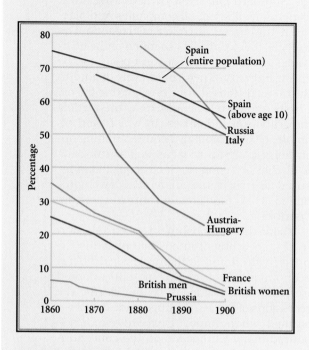

The Decline of Illiteracy
The development of mass politics and the consolidation of the nation-state depended on building a cohesive group of citizens, informed about the progress of the nation. Increasing literacy was thus a national undertaking but one with varying rates of success in different nations, ranging from low levels of illiteracy in Prussia to high levels in Austria-Hungary and Russia. Even in regions of high illiteracy, however, governments successfully encouraged people to read. In what ways does the rate of literacy reflect other developments in the countries represented above? *Theodore Hamerow, The Birth of New Europe: State and Society in the Nineteenth Century (Chapel Hill: University of North Carolina Press, 1983), 85.*

error. In the late 1800s, industrialists began to hire managers to run their increasingly complex day-to-day operations. Managers who specialized in sales and distribution, finance, and purchase of raw materials made decisions and oversaw the implementation of their policies. One German steel magnate told his managers to hire "supervisors and supervisors of supervisors to watch what our men are doing," all to the end of raising productivity.

The White-Collar Sector. The rise of the manager was accompanied by the emer-

gence of a "white-collar" service sector. Businesses employed secretaries, file clerks, and typists to guide the flow of business information. Banks that accepted savings from the general public and that invested those funds heavily in business needed tellers and clerks; railroads, insurance companies, and government-run telegraph and telephone companies all needed armies of office workers.

Workers with mathematical skills and literacy acquired in the new public primary schools staffed this service sector, which provided in particular clean work for educated, middle-class women (see "Taking Measure," on this page). Women eventually predominated among service employees. At the beginning of the century, middle-class women still tended businesses with their husbands. In the next few decades, however, the ideology of domesticity developed to dictate that these women should not work outside the home. By the late nineteenth century, the costs of middle-class family life, especially children's education, were becoming a burden. Many middle-class people could not even afford to marry. Whether to help pay family expenses or to support themselves, both unmarried and married women of the respectable middle class increasingly took jobs. Employers, as one put it, found in the new women workers a "quickness of eye and ear, and the delicacy of touch" essential to office work. By hiring women for newly created clerical jobs, business and government contributed to a dual labor market in which certain categories of jobs were predominantly male and others were overwhelmingly female. Since women had few other employment options, businesses in the service sector saved significantly by paying women chronically low wages—much less than they would have had to pay men for the same work.

The Department Store. Just as industrial capitalism had transformed the scale of production, the rise of consumer capitalism eventually transformed the scale of consumption. The principal institution of this change was the department store. Founded after midcentury in the largest cities, department stores gathered an impressive variety of goods in one place in imitation of the Middle

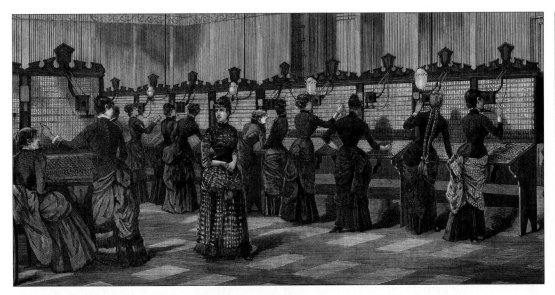

Copenhagen's Central Telephone Exchange (c. 1884)
European governments established telephone and telegraph services for individual customers late in the nineteenth century. These services were part of the rapid advance in transport and communications that characterized the modern West. Middle-class women, like these in Copenhagen's Telephone Exchange, staffed many white-collar positions that made up the new service sector. Schooling prepared more people to perform non-manual labor such as servicing telephone customers by connecting them with one another and monitoring calls or, in the case of department store clerks, selling consumer goods and calculating sales. The rise of the service economy centered in communications, banking, and consumption expanded job opportunities. *Mary Evans Picture Library.*

Eastern bazaar. Created by daring entrepreneurs such as Aristide and Marguerite Boucicaut♦ of the Bon Marché in Paris (shown on the next page) and John Wanamaker of Wanamaker's in Philadelphia, department stores eventually replaced the single-item stores that people entered knowing clearly what they wanted to purchase.

These modern palaces sought to stimulate consumer desires with luxurious fabrics, delicate laces, and richly embellished tapestries. The items spilled over railings and counters, not in the calculated order inherent in rational, middle-class ideals, but in intentional and glorious disarray. Shoppers no longer bargained over prices; instead they reacted to sales, a new marketing technique that could incite a buying frenzy. Because most men lacked the time for shopping expeditions, department stores appealed mostly to women, who came out of their domestic sphere into a new public role. Women ex-

plained their forays outside the home as necessary to enhance their home and family lives. Attractive salesgirls, another variety of service workers, were hired to inspire customers to buy. Shopping was not only an urban phenomenon: enticing mail-order catalogs from the Bon Marché or Sears, Roebuck arrived regularly in rural areas, replete with all the luxuries and household items contained in the exotic, faraway dream world of the city.

Consumerism was shaped by imperialism. Wealthy travelers like Marianne North journeyed on well-appointed oceanliners, carrying quinine, antiseptics, and other medicines as well as cameras, revolvers, and the latest in rubber goods and apparel. Coffee, tea, sugar, tobacco, cocoa, and cola from the colonies were stimulants whose consumption became more widespread. Tons of palm oil from Africa were turned into both margarine, increasing fat in the European diet, and fine soap, allowing Westerners to see themselves as cleaner and

♦**Boucicaut:** boo see KOH

The Great Staircase of the Bon Marché (c. 1880)
The Bon Marché in Paris was one of the West's premier department stores. It centralized consumption in a single large place and in so doing became the object of wonder and excitement as well as criticism. The vast array of goods caused customers to flock to these stores and gape in amazement at the luxurious displays and sheer abundance. Critics, however, charged that these stores turned sober housewives into irrational shoppers, wasteful of family resources. Instead of entering a fabric store, for example, with a clear idea of their needs, they let their fantasies run wild in a store like the Bon Marché. As a result, respectable shopkeepers with only small establishments were driven out of business as their customers defected. Consumption as a whole expanded with the birth of the department store shopper. © Snark/Art Resource, NY.

more civilized. Industry and empire jointly shaped everyday life, as a voracious desire to consume and own—whether industrial goods or colonies—took root in Western culture.

> **Review:** What economic and political factors led to the rise of the department store?

❖ The New Imperialism

In the last third of the nineteenth century, industrial demand and rampant business rivalry added fuel to the contest for territory in Africa and Asia. The new imperialism—unlike the trader-based domination of preceding centuries—brought direct European rule to many regions of these two continents.

Just as the British government took over from the East India Company trading house, other governments became directly involved in expansion. Champions of nation building came to connect industrial prosperity and imperial expansion with national identity. "Nations are not great except for the activities they undertake," declared a French advocate of huge imperial acquisitions in 1885. Conquering foreign territory appeared to heap glory on the nation-state. While the new imperialism aimed to advance Western religions and culture, the expansion of the West simultaneously increased the subjugation of local peoples, inflicting violence and radically altering their lives.

Taming the Mediterranean

European countries eyed the African and Asian shores of the Mediterranean for a primary reason, based on the old imperialism: the chance to profit through trade. Great Britain and France were especially eager to do business with Egypt, a convenient and profitable stop on the way to Asia. There, enterprising rulers had not only made Cairo into a bustling metropole but also helped boost commerce and manufacturing, the combined value of imports and exports jumping from 3.5 million Egyptian pounds in 1838 to 21 million in 1880 and to 60 million in 1913. European capital investment in the region rose, first in ventures such as the Suez Canal in the 1860s and then in the laying of thousands of miles of railroad track, the improvement of harbors, and the creation of telegraph systems. But all of these ventures cost local entrepreneurs dearly: Egyptians paid 12 percent interest rates on loans for improvements while Europeans paid 5 percent. Having invested in the

Suez Canal and in other businesses, the British and French in 1879 took over the Egyptian treasury, said to be a guarantee for their financial investments. After invading Egypt in 1882, which they claimed was necessary to put down those Egyptian nationalists who protested the takeover of the treasury, the British effectively seized control of the government as a whole. Despite heated parliamentary opposition at home, Britain forced the reshaping of the Egyptian economy from a system based on multiple crops that maintained the country's self-sufficiency to one that emphasized the production of a few crops—mainly cotton, raw silk, wheat, and rice, which were especially useful to European manufacturing. Colonial powers, local landowners, and moneylenders profited from these agricultural changes, while the bulk of the rural population barely eked out an existence.

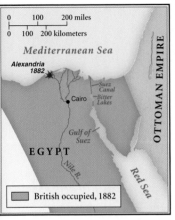

The Suez Canal and British Invasion of Egypt, 1882

As further insurance for their Mediterranean claims, the French occupied neighboring Tunisia in 1881. Businessmen from Britain, France, and Germany flooded Asia Minor, the portion of Asia at the eastern end of the Mediterranean, with cheap goods, driving artisans from their trades and into low-paid work building railroads or processing tobacco. Instead of basing wage rates on gender (as they did at home), Europeans used ethnicity and religion, paying Muslims less than Christians, and Arabs less than other ethnic groups. Such practices, as well as contact with European technology and nationalism, planted the seeds for anticolonial movements.

Scramble for Africa

Sub-Saharan Africans also felt the heavier hand of European ambition after the British takeover of the Egyptian government. Economic relations between Africans and Europeans were not new, but contact between the two continents had principally involved the trade of African slaves for European manufactured goods. The slave trade had drastically diminished by this time, and Europeans' principal objective was expanding trade in Africa's raw materials, such as palm oil, cotton, diamonds, cocoa, and rubber. Additionally, with its industrial and naval supremacy and its empire in India, Britain hoped to keep the southern and eastern coasts of Africa secure for stopover ports on the route to Asia.

Except for the French conquest of Algeria, commerce had rarely involved Europe in direct political control in Africa. Yet in the 1880s, European influence turned into direct control as one African territory after another fell to European military force (Map 24.1 on the next page). The French, Belgians, Portuguese, Italians, and Germans jockeyed to dominate peoples, land, and resources— "the magnificent cake of Africa," as King Leopold II of Belgium (r. 1865–1909) put it. Driven by insatiable greed, Leopold claimed the Congo region of central Africa, thereby initiating competition with France for that territory and inflicting on its peoples unparalleled acts of cruelty. German chancellor Otto von Bismarck, who saw colonies mostly as political bargaining chips, established German control over Cameroon and a section of East Africa. Faced with competition, the British poured millions of pounds into preserving their position by dominating the continent "from Cairo to Cape Town," as the slogan went, and the French cemented their hold on large portions of western Africa.

The scramble for Africa escalated tensions in Europe and prompted Otto von Bismarck, now the German chancellor, to call a conference of European nations at Berlin. The fourteen nations at the conference, held in a series of meetings in 1884 and 1885, decided that control of settlements along the African coast guaranteed rights to internal territory. This agreement led to the strictly linear dissection of the continent; geographers and diplomats cut across indigenous boundaries of African culture and ethnic life. The Berlin conference also banned the sale of alcohol and controlled the sale of arms to native peoples. In theory the meeting was supposed to reduce bloodshed and temper

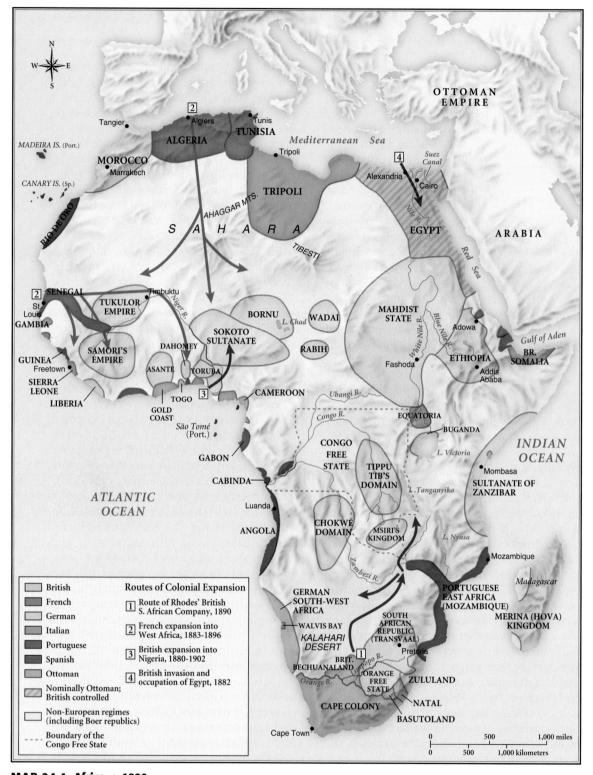

Legend:

British
French
German
Italian
Portuguese
Spanish
Ottoman
Nominally Ottoman; British controlled
Non-European regimes (including Boer republics)
Boundary of the Congo Free State

Routes of Colonial Expansion

1 Route of Rhodes' British S. African Company, 1890
2 French expansion into West Africa, 1883–1896
3 British expansion into Nigeria, 1880–1902
4 British invasion and occupation of Egypt, 1882

MAP 24.1 Africa, c. 1890

The "scramble for Africa" entailed a change in European trading practices, which generally had been limited to the coastline. Trying to conquer, economically penetrate, and rule the interior ultimately resulted in a map of the continent that made sense only to the imperial powers, for it divided ethnic groups and made territorial unities that had nothing to do with Africans' sense of geography or patterns of settlement. This map shows the unfolding of that process and the political and ethnic groupings to be conquered. This map doesn't yet show the partitioning of Africa that will appear in chapter 25. How do these divisions compare to national boundaries in Europe?

ambitions in Africa, but in reality European leaders were intent on maintaining and expanding their power, and savagely greedy individuals like King Leopold continued to plunder the continent and terrorize its people (as shown in the photo on this page). Journalistic reports of vast chunks of land trading hands only whetted the popular appetite for more imperialist ventures.

Technological development of powerful guns, railroads, steamships, and medicines dramatically expanded and facilitated Western domination, accelerating European penetration of all the continents after more than three centuries of exploration and trade. The gunboats that forced the Chinese to open their borders to opium played a part in forcing African ethnic groups to give up their independence. Quinine and guns were also important factors in African conquest. Before the development of medicinal quinine in the 1840s and 1850s, the deadly tropical disease malaria had threatened to decimate any European party embarking on exploration or military conquest, giving Africa the nickname "White Man's Grave." The use of quinine, extracted from cinchona bark from the Andes, to treat malaria sent death rates among missionaries, adventurers, traders, and bureaucrats plummeting.

While quinine saved white lives, technology to take lives was also advancing. Improvements to the breech-loading rifle and the development of the machine gun, or "repeater," between 1862 and the 1880s dramatically increased firepower. Europeans carried on a brisk trade selling inferior guns to Africans on the coast, while peoples of the interior still used bows and arrows. Muslim slave traders and European Christians alike crushed African resistance with blazing gunfire: "The whites did not seize their enemy as we do by the body, but thundered from afar," claimed one local African resister. "Death raged everywhere—like the death vomited forth from the tempest."

Nowhere did this destructive capacity have greater effect than in southern Africa, where farmers of European descent and immigrant prospectors, rather than military personnel, battled the Xhosa,♦ Zulu, and

The Violence of Colonization

King Leopold, ruler of the Belgian Congo, was so greedy and ruthless that his agents squeezed the last drop of rubber and other resources from local peoples. Missionaries reported such atrocities as the killing of workers whose quotas were even slightly short or the amputation of hands for the same offense. Belgian agents collected amputated hands and sent them to government officials to show Leopold that they were enforcing his kind of discipline. What attitudes allowed for such amputations, and what might have prompted the photographer to take this photo? *Anti-Slavery International.*

other African peoples for control of the frontier regions of Transvaal, Natal, the Orange Free State, Rhodesia, and the Cape Colony. Although the Dutch originally settled the area in the seventeenth century, the British had gained control by 1815. Thereafter, descendants of the Dutch, called Boers♦ (Dutch for "farmers"), were joined by British immigrants in their fight to wrest farmland and

♦**Xhosa:** KOH suh

♦**Boers:** bawrs

Malian Young Men's House
Europeans claimed that sub-Saharan Africans had no culture and especially no technical knowledge. Skilled road builders, textile designers, and manufacturers of weapons, Africans had also constructed intricate mosques, private dwellings, and communal buildings (such as this one for young men in Mali) long before the arrival of Europeans in the African interior. European painters, architects, and sculptors soon adapted features from African styles and even wholly modeled their designs on those of artists beyond the West. *Carollee Pelos/Jean-Louis Bourgeois.*

Wherever necessary to ensure profit and domination, Europeans either destroyed African economic and political systems or transformed them into instruments of their rule. A British governor of the Gold Coast put the matter succinctly in 1886: the British would "rule the country as if there were no inhabitants," as if local traditions of political and economic life did not exist. Indeed, most Europeans considered Africans barely civilized, despite the wealth local rulers and merchants accumulated in their international trade in raw materials and slaves, and despite individual Africans' accomplishments in fabric dyeing, road building, and architecture. Unlike the Chinese and Indians, whom Europeans credited with a scientific and artistic heritage, Africans were seen as valuable only for manual labor. By confiscating Africans' land, Europeans forced native peoples to work for them to earn a living and to pay the taxes they imposed. Subsistence agriculture, often performed by women and slaves, thus declined in favor of mining and farming cash crops. Standards of living dropped for Africans who lost their lands without realizing the Europeans were claiming permanent ownership. Systems of family and community unity provided support networks for Africans during this upheaval in everyday life.

Acquiring Territory in Asia

Britain justified the invasion of African countries as strategically necessary to preserve its control of India's quarter of a billion people, but in reality from the 1870s on, the expansion of European power was occurring around the world. Much of Asia, with India as the centerpiece, was integrated into Western empires.

Although half a million Indians held bureaucratic positions in India under British authority, British domination was blatant. In 1876, the British Parliament declared Queen Victoria the empress of India. British policy forced the end to indigenous production of finished goods such as cotton textiles that would compete with Britain's own manufactures. Instead the British wanted cheaper raw materials such as wheat, cotton, and jute to supply their industries. Enclaves of British

mineral resources from natives. British businessman and politician Cecil Rhodes (1853–1902), sent to South Africa for his health just as diamonds were being discovered in 1870, cornered the diamond market and claimed a huge amount of African territory with the help of official charters from the British government, all before he turned forty. Pushing hundreds of miles into the interior of southern Africa (a region soon to be named Rhodesia after him), Rhodes moved into gold mining too. His ambition for Britain and for himself was boundless: "I contend that we are the finest race in the world," he explained, "and that the more of the world we inhabit the better it is." Although notions of European racial superiority had been advanced before, racist attitudes now justified converting trade with Africans into conquest and political control of their lands (see "Imperialism's Popularity among the People" on the next page). Within just a few decades, Darwinism had evolved from a contribution to science to a racist justification for imperialism.

civil servants, who sought prosperity and social advancement for governing the vast subcontinent, enforced segregation and an inferior status on all classes of Indians. Discriminated against but educated, the Indian elite in 1885 founded the Indian National Congress. One group among its many prosperous members accepted British liberalism in economic and social policy, but others challenged Britain's right to rule. In the next century, the Congress would develop into a mass movement.

To the east, British military forces took control of the Malay peninsula in 1874 and of the interior of Burma in 1885. In both areas, political instability often threatened secure trade. The British depended on the region's tin, oil, rice, teak, and rubber as well as its access to the numerous interior trade routes of China. The presence of British troops guaranteed the order necessary to expand railroads for more efficient export of raw materials and the development of Western systems of communication. Once secured, the relative tranquillity also allowed the British to build factories and from there to create an industrial base in China.

The British added to their holdings in Asia partly to counter Russian and French annexations. Since 1865, Russia had been absorbing the small Muslim states of central Asia, including Turkestan and provinces of Afghanistan (Map 24.2 on the next page). Besides extending into the Ottoman Empire, Russian tentacles reached Persia, India, and China, often encountering British competition. The Trans-Siberian Railroad allowed Russia to be-

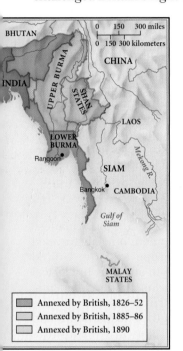

British Colonialism in the Malay Peninsula and Burma, 1826–1890

gin integrating Siberia—considered a distant colony in the eighteenth and early nineteenth centuries. Hundreds of thousands of hungry peasants moved to the region and trade routes to cities in the west expanded. France meanwhile used favorable treaties backed by the threat of military action to create the Union of Indochina from the ancient states of Cambodia, Tonkin, Annam, and Cochin China in 1887 (the latter three now constitute Vietnam). Laos was added to Indochina in 1893.

To those who opposed this expansion as "spending our money on distant adventures," advocates of imperialism pointed out that, in the example of France, Europe had a

Imperialism's Popularity among the People

Henry Stanley (1841–1904) was an unscrupulous English adventurer in Africa, who regularly killed and abused indigenous peoples to gain their land and wealth on behalf of such clients as Leopold of Belgium. Yet the press boosted sales by recounting his adventures as those of a brave and rugged soldier—an ambassador of civilized values. The celebratory tone infiltrated popular culture, as in the song below. Recounting Stanley's search for an important African leader, Emin Pasha, it brought London music hall audiences to their feet in an orgy of thunderous applause for their hero.

Oh, I went to find Emin Pasha, and started
    away for fun,
With a box of weeds and a bag of beads, and
    some tracts and a Maxim gun . . .
I went to find Emin, I did, I looked for him far
    and wide;
I found him right, I found him tight, and a lot
    of folks beside,
Away through Darkest Africa, though it cost
    me lots of tin,
For without a doubt I'd rind him out, when I went
    to find Emin!

Source: Ernest Short, *Fifty Years of Vaudeville* (New York: Eyre and Spotteswoode, 1946), 43.

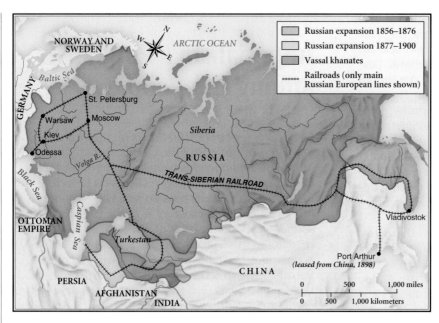

MAP 24.2 Expansion of Russia in Asia, 1865–1895
Russian administrators and military men continued enlarging Russia, bringing in Asians of many different ethnicities, ways of life, and religions. Land-hungry peasants in western Russia followed the path of expansion into Siberia and Muslim territories to the south. In some cases they drove native peoples from their lands, but in others they settled unpopulated frontier areas. As in all cases of imperial expansion, local peoples resisted any expropriation of their livelihood, while the central government tried various policies for integration. What differences do you observe about Russian expansion as opposed to British, French, American, and Dutch expansion? With whom would the Russians most likely clash?

"civilizing mission." The French thus taught some of their colonial subjects to speak French and learn French literature and history. The emphasis was always on European, not local people's culture. In Africa, an exam for students in a school run by German missionaries asked them to write on "Germany's most important mountains" and "the reign of William I and the wars he waged." The deeds of Africa's great rulers and the accomplishments of its kingdoms disappeared from the curriculum. While Europeans believed in instructing colonial subjects, they did not believe that they were equally capable of achieving great things.

Japan's Imperial Agenda

Japan escaped the new European imperialism by its rapid transformation into a modern industrial nation with its own imperial agenda. A Japanese print of the 1880s illustrates both traditional ways and the Western influence behind Japan's burgeoning power (opposite). The picture's costumed women, strolling with their parasols amid flowering cherry trees, might have been rendered centuries earlier; but a steaming locomotive in the background symbolizes change. The Japanese embraced foreign trade and industry. "All classes high and low shall unite in vigorously promoting the economy and welfare of the nation," ran one of the first pronouncements of the new Meiji regime that had come to power in 1868. The Japanese had long acquired knowledge from other countries. Unlike China, Japan endorsed Western-style modernization.

In the 1870s, Japanese government officials traveled to Europe and the United States to study technological and industrial developments. Western dress became the rule at the imperial court, and when fire destroyed Tokyo in 1872 a European planner directed the rebuilding in Western architectural style. Opposition to such changes was not tolerated, as the new central government, led by some of the old samurai, or warrior elite, crushed massive rebellions by those who resisted modernization. The Japanese adapted samurai traditions such as spiritual discipline and the drive to excel for a large, technologically modern military, filled by universal conscription. By 1894, Japan had become powerful enough to force traders to accept its terms for commerce and diplomatic relations.

The Japanese government instigated the turn toward industry. Japanese legal scholars, following German models, helped draft a constitution in 1889 that emphasized state power rather than individual rights. The state also stimulated economic development by building railroads and shipyards and establishing financial institutions. Unlike other

Modernization in Japan
Japan modernized with breathtaking speed, as this view of a railroad station demonstrates. Japan both borrowed from the West and loyally supported its own traditions. Thus, while many Japanese donned Western clothes, others remained wedded to local costumes and to native scenery such as cherry trees. In this woodcut by Ando Hiroshige II—son of an artist imitated by many in the West—the train schedule appears across the top of the depiction. How do industrial and traditional values intermingle in this woodcut? *Laurie Platt Winfrey Inc.*

The Union of Indochina, 1893

modernizing economies it kept its borrowing from Europe to a bare minimum. Then in the 1880s, when the cost of modernization had drained resources, the government auctioned off its businesses to private entrepreneurs, thereby collecting essential revenue to stabilize its finances. State support led daring innovators like Iwasaki Yataro, founder of the Mitsubishi firm, to develop heavy industries such as mining and shipping. In Japan, unlike the rest of Asia, the adaptation of Western-style enterprises became a patriotic goal. Like its Western models, Japan started intervening in Asian affairs in hopes of expanding its influence and resource base.

The Paradoxes of Imperialism

Imperialism ignited constant, sometimes heated debate because of the many paradoxes in its meaning and scope. Although it was meant to stabilize great-power status, imperialism intensified distrust in international politics. New countries vied with old ones for a share of world influence. In securing India's borders, for example, the British faced Russian expansion in Afghanistan and along the borders of China. Imperial competition even made areas of Europe, such as the Balkans, more volatile than ever as governments tried to control disputed territory of the weakening Ottoman Empire.

Politicians were at odds about the economic value of empire. The search for new markets often proved more costly than profitable to societies. Britain, for example, spent

An ABC for Baby Patriots (1899)

Pride in empire began at an early age, when learning the alphabet from this kind of book helped develop an imperial sensibility. The subject of geography became important in schools during the decades between 1870 and 1890 and helped young people know what possessions they could claim as citizens. In British schools, the young celebrated the holiday Empire Day with ceremonies and festivities emphasizing imperial power. If you were a nineteenth-century parent, how would you explain the importance of this book to your child's development? *Mary F. Ames. Reference (shelfmark) 2523 c 24. Bodleian Library, University of Oxford.*

enormous amounts of tax revenue to maintain its empire even as its industrial base began to decline. Yet for certain businesses, colonies provided crucial markets: late in the century, French colonies bought 65 percent of France's exports of soap and 41 percent of its metallurgical exports. Imperialism provided huge numbers of jobs to people in European port cities, but—whether they benefited or not—taxpayers in all parts of a nation paid for colonial armies, increasingly costly weaponry, and administrators.

Imperialism did not always fulfill the intentions of its practitioners. Goals such as fostering national might, boosting national loyalty, and Christianizing colonized peoples often proved unattainable. Many believed that, through imperialist ventures, "a country exhibits before the world its strength or weakness as a nation," as one French politician announced. Governments worried that imperialism—because of its expense and the constant possibility of war—might weaken rather than strengthen them. Another French statesman argued that France "must keep its role as the soldier of civilization." But it was unclear whether imperialists should emphasize soldiering—that is, conflict, con-

quest, and murder of local peoples—or the exporting of culture and religion. The French tried both in Indochina, building a legacy of resistance that continued unabated until the mid-twentieth century.

Hoping to spread their religion, European missionaries ventured to newly secured areas of Africa and Asia. A woman missionary working among the Tibetans reflected a common view when she remarked that the native peoples were "going down, down into hell, and there is no one but me . . . to witness for Jesus amongst them." Europeans were confident in their religious and cultural superiority. In the judgment of many, Asians and Africans were beneath Europeans, variously characterized as lying, lazy, self-indulgent, or irrational. One English official pontificated that "accuracy is abhorrent to the Oriental mind." At the height of imperialism, such beliefs offered still another justification for conquest and dominion: the civilizing process of colonization would eventually make conquered peoples grateful for what Europe had brought them. Paradoxically, this cultural pride prompted "civilizers" such as missionaries to collaborate with the most brutal military measures to accomplish their goals.

Western scholars and travelers had long studied Asian and African languages and cultures or, like Marianne North, had sought botanical and other scientific knowledge. Yet even the best scholars' study of foreign cultures was tinged with bias. Scholars of Islam characterized Muhammad as a mere imitation of Jesus, for example. Alternatively, some Europeans—from novelists to military men—considered conquered peoples better than Europeans because they were unspoiled by civilization. "At last some local color," enthused one colonial officer, fresh from industrial cities of Europe, on seeing Constantinople. This romantic, misinformed, "orientalizing" vision of an ancient center of culture, similar to eighteenth-century condescension toward the "noble savage," had little to do with the reality of conquered peoples' lives. We see these paradoxes clearly in hindsight. At the time belief in the superiority of European ways hid many of them—above all the paradox that people who believed in national independence invaded the territory of people thousands of miles away and claimed the right to rule them.

> **Review:** What were the differences between the new imperialism and European states' earlier relationships with regions beyond the West?

❖ The Transformation of Culture and Society

Advancing industrialization and empire not only made the world an interconnected marketplace but also transformed everyday culture and society. Success in manufacturing and foreign ventures created millionaires, and the expansion of a professional middle class and development of a service sector meant that more people were affluent enough to own property, see some of the world, and provide their children a cosmopolitan education. Consumers in the West could purchase goods that poured in from around the world. Many Europeans grew healthier, partly because of improved diet and partly because of government-sponsored programs aimed at promoting the fitness necessary for citizens of imperial powers.

Industrial and imperial advance affected many working-class people in the West differently than it did the middle classes. In many cases it replaced their labor with new machinery while offering them opportunities for mobility as European societies opened up the globe. From the mid-nineteenth century on, millions migrated to the United States, Canada, Australia, Argentina, Brazil, and Siberia. In the process they imported culture. Artists captured the imperial and industrial spectacle in increasingly iconoclastic works influenced by non-Western styles. Their art, like the everyday lives of those they depicted, was transformed in the industrial, imperial crucible.

The "Best" Circles and the Expanding Middle Class

The profits from industry and empire added new members to the upper class, or "best" circles, so called at the time because of their members' wealth, education, and social status. People in the best circles often came from the aristocracy, which retained much of its power and was still widely emulated. Increasingly, however, aristocrats had to share their social position with new millionaires from the ranks of the bourgeoisie. In fact, the very distinction between aristocrat and bourgeois became blurred, as monarchs gratefully endowed millionaire industrialists and businesspeople with aristocratic titles for their contributions to national wealth. Moreover, down-at-the-heels aristocrats were only too willing to offer their children in marriage to families from the newly rich. Such arrangements brought a much-needed infusion of funds to old, established families and the cachet of an aristocratic title to upstart families. Thus, the American heiress Winaretta Singer (of Singer sewing machine fame) married Prince Edmond de Polignac of France, and Jeanette Jerome, daughter of a wealthy New York financier, married England's Lord Randolph Churchill (their son Winston later became England's prime minister). Millionaires discarded the modest ways of a century earlier to build palatial country homes and villas, engage in conspicuous displays of wealth, and wall themselves off from the poor in segregated neighborhoods. To justify

Tiger Hunting in the Punjab
Big-game hunting became the imperial sport of choice, as this Indian work of art so beautifully shows. European and American hunters took the sport over from local Asians and Africans who had previously depended on the hunt for their livelihood. Now these Asians and Africans served the Western amateurs, many of whom were in wretched physical shape and totally inexperienced in hunting big game. Nonetheless, Western manliness was coming to depend on such feats, as imperialists saw those who continued the old aristocratic fox hunt as effeminate. Though not apparent in this illustration, some Western women enjoyed hunting too. As a chivalrous gesture, men would let women issue the coup de grace, or death shot, should a tiger materialize during the hunt. © *Victoria and Albert Museum, London/Art Resource, NY.*

hunting—as reshaped by imperial contact (see the illustration on this page). Fox and bird hunting had been aristocratic pastimes in parts of Europe for centuries, but big-game hunting in Asia and Africa now became the rage. European hunters forced native Africans, who had depended on hunting for income or food and for group unity, to work as guides, porters, and domestics for European hunters instead. Mastering activities like big-game hunting or foreign games like polo demonstrated that Europeans could conquer both territory and the more intangible things like culture (see "Did You Know?" opposite). Collectors on the hunts brought exotic specimens back to Europe for zoological exhibits, natural history museums, and traveling displays, all of which flourished during this period. Stags' heads, elephant tusks, and animal skins also decorated European homes.

Members of the upper class did their best to exclude others by controlling their children's social lives. Parents of marriageable women watched them closely to preserve their chastity and to keep them from socializing with lower-class men. Upper-class men had liaisons with lower-class women—part of the double standard that saw promiscuity as normal for men and as immoral for women—but few thought of marrying them. Parents still arranged many marriages directly, but other courtships were initiated during visiting days, on which occasions prominent hostesses held an open house under rather formal conditions. Such regular social contact sometimes provided the foundation for matrimonial decisions.

Upper-class women devoted themselves to maintaining standards of etiquette and social conduct, having children, and directing staffs of servants. They took their role seriously, keeping detailed accounts of their expenditures and monitoring their children's religious and intellectual development. Their pursuit of fashion in home furnishing took on imperial motifs in these decades, featuring Persian-inspired designs in textiles, Oriental carpets, wicker furniture, and Chinese porcelains. With the importation of plants such as azaleas and rhododendrons from around the world, gardens replaced parks and lawns—another domestic element for upper-class women to oversee. Being an active consumer

their success, the wealthy often appealed to a Social Darwinist principle that their ability to accumulate money demonstrated the natural superiority of the rich over the poor.

Sport and leisure brought upper-class men together in their favorite activity—

DID YOU KNOW?

Polo and Social Class

Today's historians often see the introduction of sports by the imperial powers in colonized regions as a form of domination. By organizing teams of cricket or rugby players in West Africa, India, or the Caribbean, for instance, the British were said to be imposing Western ideas of what sports and sportsmen were on peoples with other traditions. In this interpretation, imperialists replaced local cultures with their own.

But imperialism has always been a two-way street despite great differences in power between colonizers and colonized. While playing cricket in the colonies, the British upper classes became hooked on polo, an Asian sport that imperial forces learned in India. Played on horseback, *puhluh* was a team sport that allowed a cavalry-based fighting force (both men and horses) to stay in shape during long, idle intervals. Chutneys, curries, verandahs, jodhpurs, and the game of pachisi were some of the cultural elements that the West borrowed

Anglo-Indian Polo Team
Team sports underwent rapid development during the imperial years, as spectators rooted for the success of their football team in the same spirit they rooted for their armies abroad. Some educators believed that team sports molded the male character so that men could be more effective soldiers against peoples of other races. Thus, this mixed team of polo players was uncharacteristic. In cricket, soccer, and other sports, city challenged city, nation challenged nation, and race often challenged race. How have the development and cultural exchange of sports promoted racism, nationalism, and militarism? How have they lessened racism, nationalism, and militarism? *Hulton Archive/ Getty Images.*

from India in the nineteenth century. Westerners have largely forgotten the imperial origins of polo, which seems to many people emblematic of Britain's celebrated, aristocratic way of life.

---

of fashionable clothing was time-consuming. In contrast to men's plain garments, upper-class women's elaborate costumes featured constricting corsets, long voluminous skirts, bustles, and low-cut necklines for evening wear. Upper-class women, symbols of elite leisure, tried to offset the drabness of industrial life with the rigorous practice of art and music. One Hungarian observer wrote, "The

piano mania has become almost an epidemic in Budapest as well as Vienna." Some women were also quite active outside the home, engaging in religious and philanthropic activities and taking a particular interest in the welfare of lower-class women.

Below the best circles, or "upper crust," the "solid" middle class was expanding, most notably in western and central Europe. (In eastern Europe this did not happen naturally, and the Russian government often sought out foreigners to build its professional and entrepreneurial classes.) Although middle-ranked businessmen and professionals could sometimes mingle with those at the apex of society, their lives remained more modest. They employed at least one servant, to give the appearance of leisure to the middle-class woman in the home. Professional men working at home did so from the best-appointed, if not lavish, room. Middle-class domesticity substituted cleanliness and polish for upper-class conspicuous consumption. The soap and tea used in the middle-class home were becoming signs—along with hard work—of a racial superiority and higher status not accessible to the colonized peoples who actually produced those goods.

Professional Sports and Organized Leisure

As nations competed for territory and economic markets, male athletes banded together to organize team sports that eventually replaced village games. Large audiences now backed a particular team, as soccer, rugby, and cricket drew mass followings and integrated migrants as well as the lower and higher classes into a common culture. The heightened emphasis on group competition also found favor with the reading public; newspapers reported the results of all sorts of contests, including cross-country bicycle races sponsored by tire makers who wanted to prove the superiority of their product. These evolved into international events such as the Tour de France, first held in 1903. Tests of speed measured by clocks and involving the use of machines like bicycles and cars replaced older forms of competition such as cockfighting and sack racing. Competitive sports began to be seen as valuable to national strength and spirit. "The Battle of Waterloo was won on the playing fields of Eton," ran the wisdom of the day, suggesting that the games played in school could mold the strength and character of an army.

Team sports—like civilian military service—helped differentiate male and female spheres and thus promoted a social order based on distinction between the sexes. Some team sports for women emerged, such as soccer, field hockey, and rowing, but in general women were encouraged to engage in individual sports (see the illustration shown here of women bicycle racing). "Riding improves the temper, the spirits and the appetite," wrote one sportswoman. "Black shadows and morbid fancies disappear." Rejecting the idea of women's natural frailty, reformers introduced exercise and gymnastics into schools for girls, often with the idea that these would strengthen them for motherhood and thus help build the nation-state. So-called Swedish exercises for young women spread through respec-

Victorian Women's Bicycle Race
The bicycle represented freedom for millions of young people, and many credit it with changes in social customs that gradually appeared in these decades. In clubs or groups of friends, the young went off riding for miles; the bicycle was particularly liberating for young women, giving them exercise and a chance to see a bit more of the world. Their clothing changed subtly too as full skirts and abundant petticoats were soon found cumbersome and even unsafe. The bicycle also provided easier transportation for working people. *Collection of Sally Fox.*

table homes across Europe, and, as knowledge of the world developed, some women began to practice yoga.

The middle classes believed their leisure pursuits should be edifying as well as fun. Thus, mountain climbing became a popular middle-class hobby. As the editor of a Swedish publication of 1889 explained, "The passion for mountain-climbing can only be understood by those who realize that it is the step-by-step achievement of a goal which is the real pleasure of the world." Working-class people adopted middle-class habits by joining clubs for such pursuits as bicycling, touring, and hiking. Clubs that sponsored trips often had names like the Patriots or the Nationals, again associating physical fitness with national strength. The new emphasis on healthy recreation gave individuals a greater sense of individual freedom and power and thereby contributed to a developing sense of citizenship based less on constitutions and rights than on an individual nation's exercise of raw power. A farmer's son in the 1890s boasted that with a bicycle, "I was king of the road, since I was faster than a horse."

Working People's Strategies

Working people had for centuries migrated from countryside to city and from country to country to make a living. After the middle of the nineteenth century, empire and industry were powerful factors in migration. Older cities of Europe like Riga, Marseille, and Hamburg offered secure ports of entry, new industrial jobs, and opportunities for global trade, while new colonies provided land, posts for soldiers and administrators, and the possibility of unheard-of wealth in diamonds, gold, and other natural resources. City workers adapted to new conditions as industry made further inroads into the social and economic fabric.

Migration. Some Europeans followed an imperialist pattern of migration, moving well beyond their national borders to those countries where land was being taken from native peoples for white settlements (see "Contrasting Views," page 940). In parts of Europe, the land simply could not produce enough to support a rapidly expanding population. For example, Greek shipbuilding in ancient times had stripped the vast forests of Sicily, leaving the soil eroded and nearly worthless. By the end of the nineteenth century, hundreds of thousands of Sicilians were leaving, often temporarily, to find work in the industrial cities of northern Europe or the United States. The British Isles, especially Ireland, yielded one-third of all European emigrants between 1840 and 1920, first because of the potato famine and then because of uncertain farm tenancy and periodic economic crises. Between 1886 and 1900, half a million Swedes out of a population of 4.75 million quit their country (Figure 24.1 on the next page). Millions of rural Jews, especially from eastern Europe, left their villages for economic reasons, but Russian Jews also fled in the face of vicious anti-Semitism. Russian mobs brutally attacked Jewish communities, destroying homes and businesses and even murdering some Jews. These ritualized attacks, called pogroms, were scenes of horror. "People who saw such things never smiled anymore, no matter how long they lived," recalled one Russian Jewish woman who migrated to the United States in the early 1890s.

Commercial and imperial prosperity determined destinations. Most migrants went to North and South America, Australia, and New Zealand, as news of opportunity reached Europe. Moreover, the railroad and steamship made journeys across and out of Europe more affordable, more comfortable, and faster, even though most workers traveled in steerage, with baggage and supplies and few amenities. Once established elsewhere, migrants frequently sent money back home; the funds could be used to provide education or set up family members in small businesses, thus contributing to advancement. European farm families often received a good deal of their income from husbands or grown sons and daughters who had left. Nationalist commentators in Slovakia, Poland, Hungary, and other parts of eastern and central Europe bemoaned the loss of ethnic vigor as the young and active departed, but peasants themselves welcomed the arrival of "magic dollars" from their kin. Migrants appreciated the chance to begin anew without the deprivation and social constrictions of the old world. One settler in

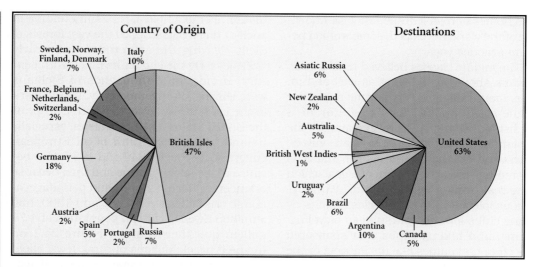

FIGURE 24.1 European Emigration, 1870–1890

The suffering caused by economic change and by political persecution motivated people from almost every European country to leave their homes for greater security elsewhere. North America attracted more than two-thirds of these migrants, many of whom followed reports of vast quantities of available land in both Canada and the United States. Both countries were known for following the rule of law and for economic opportunity in urban as well as rural areas. Which countries accounted for the largest share of emigrants and why? *Theodore Hamerow,* The Birth of New Europe: State and Society in the Nineteenth Century *(Chapel Hill: University of North Carolina Press, 1983), 169.*

the United States was relieved to escape the meager peasant meal of rye bread and herring: "God save us from . . . all that is Swedish," he wrote home sourly.

Migration out of Europe often meant the end to the old way of life. Workers immediately had to learn new languages and civic practices and to compete for jobs in growing cities where they formed the cheapest pool of labor, often in factories or sweatshops. Women who stayed at home, however, tended to associate with others like themselves, preserving traditional ways. More insulated, they might never learn the new language or put their peasant dresses away. Their children and husbands more often devalued their pasts as they were forced to build a life in schools and factories of the new world.

More common than international migration was internal migration from rural areas to European cities, accelerating the urbanization of Europe. The most urbanized countries were Great Britain and Belgium, followed by Germany, France, and the Netherlands. In Russia, only 7 percent of the population lived in cities of 10,000 or more; in Portugal the figure was 12 percent. Cities of more than

100,000 grew the most, but every urban area attracted rural people seeking employment. Migrants returned to the countryside at harvest time. Temporary migrants to the cities worked as masons, cabdrivers, or factory hands to supplement declining income from agriculture; in the winter, those remaining on the land turned to cottage industry, making bricks, pottery, sieves, shawls, lace, locks, and samovars. To maintain their status as independent artisans, handweavers sent their wives and daughters to towns to work in factories.

Adaptation to Industrial Change. Changes in technology and management practices eliminated outmoded jobs and often made the work of those who survived job cuts more difficult. Workers complained that new machinery sped up the pace of work to an unrealistic level. For example, employers at a foundry in suburban Paris required workers using new furnaces to turn out 50 percent more metal per day than they had produced using the old furnaces. Stepped-up productivity demanded much more physical exertion to tend and repair machines, often at a faster pace, but workers did not receive additional pay for their extra efforts. Workers also grumbled about the proliferation of managers; many believed that foremen, engineers, and other supervisors interfered with their work. For women, supervision sometimes brought on-the-job harassment, as in the case of female workers in a German food-canning plant who kept their jobs only in return for granting sexual favors to the male manager.

On the one hand, employers could increasingly use untrained workers, often women, and pay them less than skilled workers. On the other hand, inventions always demanded new skills for those who had to understand work processes or repair machinery. Employers began to use the concept of skill (based in the old craft traditions) to segment the labor force. They created a hierarchy of formal skill levels, although sometimes the designations were arbitrary.

Many in the urban labor force continued to do outwork at home. Every branch of industry, from metallurgy to toy manufacturing to food processing, employed women at home—and their work was essential to the family economy. They painted tin soldiers, wrapped chocolate, made cheese boxes, decorated porcelain, and polished metal. Factory owners liked the system because low piece rates made outworkers desperate for work under any conditions and thus willing to work extremely long days. A German seamstress at her new sewing machine reported that she "pedaled at a stretch from six o'clock in the morning until midnight. . . . At four o'clock I got up and did the housework and prepared meals." Owners could lay off women at home during slack times and rehire them whenever needed with little fear of organized protest.

Economic change and the periodic recurrence of hard times had uneven consequences for people's everyday lives. In the late nineteenth century, joblessness and destitution threatened. Some city workers prospered by comparison to those left behind in rural areas, though a growing number lost the steadiness of traditional artisanal work. By and large, however, the urban working class was better informed and more connected to the progress of industry and empire than their rural counterparts were.

Reform Efforts for Working-Class People

The cycle of boom and bust, the uneven prosperity of industrialism, and the upheaval of migration caused social problems that many in the middle and upper classes sought to address through reform organizations and charities. Settlement houses, clinics, and maternal and child wellness societies seemed to rise overnight in cities, quickly becoming a common sight. Young men and women, often from universities, flocked to staff these new organizations, especially the settlement houses, where the reformers took up residence in poor neighborhoods to study and help the people. Believing in the scientific approach to social problems, they thought that study would uncover the causes of social ills and point the way to solutions. One group devoted to this enterprise was the Fabian Society in London, a small organization established in 1884. Committed to a socialism based on reform and state planning rather than revolution, the Fabians helped found the Labour Party in 1893 as a way of incorporating social improvement into politics. Still other reformers were motivated by a strong religious impulse. "There is Christ's own work to be done," wrote one woman who volunteered to inspect workhouse conditions.

A Social Darwinist fear that Europeans would lack the fitness to survive in a competitive world drove philanthropists and government agencies to intervene more in the lives of working-class families. They sponsored health clinics and milk centers to provide good medical care and food for children and instructed mothers in child-care techniques, including breast-feeding—an important way, reformers maintained, to promote infant health. Some schools distributed free lunches, medicine, and clothing and inspected the health and appearance of their students. These attempts to improve urban life had their downside, however, as when government officials or private reformers deemed themselves the overseers of the working-class family and entered apartments with impunity. Such intrusions pressured poor, overworked mothers to conform to standards for their children—such as

CONTRASTING VIEWS

Experiences of Migration

In the nineteenth century millions of migrants moved thousands of miles from their homelands. The vast distances traveled and the permanent relocation of these migrants were among the issues generating a wide range of responses. Both migrants and those left behind showed acceptance and enthusiasm alternating with opposition and anger. The conflicting reactions appeared in official reports, local newspapers, poems, and very personal letters. While officials pointed with relief to the economic benefits of emigration (Document 1), people left behind were often heartbroken and destitute (Document 2). Migrants themselves had vastly differing experiences, adding to debate over migration (Documents 3 and 4).

1. THE GOVERNMENT VIEW

The preamble to the Hungarian census for 1890 was blunt and unambiguous on the subject. It saw emigration exclusively in financial terms:

Emigration has proved to be a veritable boom. The impoverished populace has been drawn off to where it has found lucrative employment; the position of those left behind, their work opportunities and standard of living, have undoubtedly improved thanks to the rise in wages, and thanks to the substantial financial aid coming into the country: sums of from 300,000 to 1,500,000 florints.

Source: Quoted in Julianna Puskas, "Consequences of Overseas Migration for the Country of Origin: The Case of Hungary," in Dirk Hoerder and Inge Blank, eds., *Roots of the Transplanted: Late 19th Century East Central and Southeastern Europe* (Boulder: East European Monographs, 1994), I:397.

2. THOSE LEFT BEHIND

Teofila Borkowska, from Warsaw, Poland, reacted to her husband's resettlement in the United States in two letters from 1893 and 1894. Stripped of a family group, Teofila had a difficult time surviving, and her husband, Wladyslaw Borkowski, never did return.

1893. Dear Husband: Up to the present I live with the Rybickis. I am not very well satisfied, perhaps because I was accustomed to live for so many years quietly, with you alone. And today you are at one end of the world and I at the other, so when I look at strange corners [surroundings], I don't know what to do from longing and regret. I comfort myself only that you won't forget me, that you will remain noble as you have been. . . . I have only the sort of friends who think that I own thousands and from time to time someone comes to me, asking me to lend her a dozen roubles.

1894. Up to the present I thought and rejoiced that you would still come back to Warsaw, but since you write that you won't come I comply with the will of God and with your will. I shall now count the days and weeks [until you take me to America]. . . . Such a sad life! I go almost to nobody, for as long as you were in Warsaw everything was different. Formerly we had friends, and everybody was glad to see us, while now, if I go to anybody, they are afraid I need something from them and they show me beforehand a different face.

Source: Letter from Teofila Borkowska to Wladyslaw Borkowski, in William Thomas and Florian Znaniecki, *The Polish Peasant in Europe and America* (New York: Dover, 1958), July 21, 1893, April 12, 1894, II: 874–75.

finding them respectable shoes—that they could ill afford.

To counteract the burdens facing the working-class family, some professionals began to make available birth-control infor-mation in the belief that small families were more likely to survive the rigors of urban life. In the 1880s, Aletta Jacobs (1851–1929), a Dutch physician, opened the first birth-control clinic, which specialized in promoting

3. MIGRATION DEFENDED

In some cases emigrants were said to be unpatriotic and cowardly for leaving their homeland just to avoid hard economic times. To charges against Swedish emigrants, one journalist, Isador Kjelberg, responded with the following defense.

Patriotism? Let us not misuse so fine a word! Does patriotism consist of withholding the truth from the workingman by claiming that "things are bad in America"? I want nothing to do with such patriotism! If patriotism consists of seeking, through lies, to persuade the poorest classes to remain under the yoke, like mindless beasts, so that we others should be so much better off, then I am lacking in patriotism. I love my country, as such, but even more I love and sympathize with the human being, the worker. . . . Among those who most sternly condemn emigration are those who least value the human and civic value of the workingman. . . . They demand that he remain here. What are they prepared to give him to compensate the deprivations this requires? . . . It is only cowardly, unmanly, heartless, to let oneself become a slave under deplorable circumstances which one *can* overcome.

Source: Quoted in H. Arnold Barton, *A Folk Divided: Homeland Swedes and Swedish Americans, 1840–1940* (Carbondale: Southern Illinois University Press, 1994), 72–73.

This anonymous Swedish poem combined a political defense of migration with an economic one.

I'm bound for young America,
Farewell old Scandinavia.
I've had my fill of cold and toil,
All for the love of mother soil.
You poets with your rocks and rills
Can stay and starve—on words, no frills.
There, out west, a man breathes free,
While here one slaves, a tired bee,
Gathering honey to fill the hive
Of wise old rulers, on us they thrive.
In toil we hover before their thrones,
While they take to slumber, like lazy drones.

Drunk with our nectar they've set us afright,
But opportunity has knocked, and we'll take our flight.

Source: Quoted in ibid., 137.

4. THE PERILS OF MIGRATION

A contrasting view of emigration to the United States appeared in the following Slovak song.

My fellow countryman, Rendek from Senica, the
 son of poor parents
Went out into the wide world. In Pittsburgh he
 began to toil.
From early morning till late at night he filled
 the furnaces with coal.
Faster, faster, roared the foreman, every day. . . .
Rendek toiled harder
So as to see his wife.
But alas! He was careless
And on Saturday evening late
He received his injuries.
At home his widow waited
For the card which would never come.
I, his friend, write this song
To let you know
What a hard life we have here.

Source: Quoted in Frantisek Bielik, Horst Hogh, and Anna Stvrtecka, "Slovak Images of the New World: 'We Could Pay Off Our Debts'" in Dirk Hoerder and Inge Blank, eds., *Roots of the Transplanted: Late 19th Century East Central and Southeastern Europe* (Boulder: East European Monographs, 1994), I:388.

QUESTIONS TO CONSIDER

1. Did the vast nineteenth-century migration ultimately enrich or diminish European culture and society?
2. How would you characterize the experience of migration for families and individuals?
3. How did migration affect the national identity of both receiving countries and European countries of origin?

the new, German-invented diaphragm. Jacobs was moved to act by the plight of women in Amsterdam slums who were worn out by numerous pregnancies and whose lives, she believed, would be greatly improved by limiting their fertility. Working-class women themselves sought out these clinics, and knowledge of birth-control techniques spread by word of mouth among workers. But the churches adamantly opposed this trend, and

Mary Cassatt, *The Letter* (c. 1890)
Mary Cassatt, an American artist who spent much of her time in Europe, was one of the many Western artists smitten by Japanese prints. Like them, she worked to learn Japanese techniques for printmaking but she also reshaped her painting style to follow Japanese conventions in composition, perspective, and the use of color. Cassatt is known for her many depictions of Western mothers and children and of individual women. In this painting the woman herself even looks Japanese. Compare the ingredients and style of this portrait to that of Germaine de Staël on page 795. **For more help analyzing this image**, see the visual activity for this chapter in the Online Study Guide at **bedfordstmartins.com/hunt**. *The Art Institute of Chicago.*

trial years, "living flowers should inspire a living ornament," as May Morris explained. Theirs was called the "arts and crafts" style, which they hoped would build enthusiasm for handcrafted products. Industrial advance led to frequent enthusiasm for "craft" goods from an earlier age, albeit made from industrial materials and modeled on foreign designs.

By the 1870s painters felt intense competition from a popular industrial inven-

tion—the camera. Photographers could produce cheap copies of paintings and create more realistic portraits than painters could, at affordable prices. In response, painters altered their style, at times trying to make their work look as different from photographs as possible. Using thousands of dots and dabs, French painter Georges Seurat◆ (1859–1891) depicted the Parisian suburbs' newly created parks with their Sunday bicyclists and walking paths along which white-collar workers in their store-bought clothing, carrying books or newspapers, paraded like the well-to-do. Another French artist, Edgar Degas (1834–1917), focused on portraying women—from ballet dancers to laundry women—in various states of exertion and fatigue brought on by work in the fast-paced economy. He did much of his work, however, in fuzzy pastels with blurred lines that captured the mental haze of relentless physical labor while distinguishing his art from the photographic realism of the camera.

Degas and Seurat, although their styles varied, both have been characterized as avant-garde and impressionist. The term **impressionism** was first used to criticize the work of French artist Édouard Manet (1832–1883), but eventually it was used to emphasize the artist's attempt to capture a single moment by focusing on the ever-changing light and color found in ordinary scenes. Using splotches and dots, impressionists moved away from the precise realism of earlier painters; their challenge to the norm made the impressionists simultaneously avant-garde. Claude Monet (1840–1926), for example, was fascinated by the way light transformed an object, and he often portrayed the same place—a bridge or a railroad station—at different times of day. Vincent Van Gogh (1853–1890) used vibrant colors in great swirls to capture sunflowers, haystacks, and the starry evening sky. Such distortions of reality made the impressionists' visual style seem outrageous to those accustomed to realism, but others enthusiastically greeted impressionism's luminous quality. Industry contributed to the new style, as factories produced a range of pigments that allowed artists to use a wider, more intense spectrum of colors than ever before.

◆**Georges Seurat:** zhawrzh su RAH

In both composition and style, impressionists borrowed heavily from Asian art and architecture. The concept of the fleetingness of situations came from a centuries-old and well-developed Japanese concept—*mono no aware* (serenity before and sensitivity to the fleetingness of life). The color, line, and delicacy of Japanese art (which many impressionists collected) is evident, for example, in Monet's later paintings of water lilies, his studies of wisteria, and even his re-creation of a Japanese garden at his home in France as the subject for artistic study. Similarly, the American expatriate Mary Cassatt (1845–1926) used the two-dimensionality of Japanese art in *The Letter* (1890–1891) and other paintings (Cassatt, *The Letter*). Other artists, like Degas, imitated Asian art's use of wandering and conflicting lines to orchestrate space on a canvas, and Van Gogh filled the background of portraits with copies of intensely colored Japanese prints, even imitating classic Japanese woodcuts. The graphic arts and literature advanced the West's ongoing borrowing from other cultures, while responding to the changes brought about by industry and the new consumerism.

Review: How did industry and empire influence art and everyday life?

❖ The Birth of Mass Politics

Struggles for political voice, especially through the vote, accompanied imperial and economic expansion. Industrial growth and urban development strengthened networks of political communication, continuing the work of institutions such as schools, urban agencies, and government bureaucracy in producing national consciousness. As national consciousness grew among workers, western European governments continued to allow more men to vote. Even high-ranking politicians such as William Gladstone, the prime minister of Great Britain, had to campaign by railroad to win votes from a far-flung electorate. Although only men profited from electoral reform, the era's expanding franchise marked the beginning of mass politics—a hallmark of the twentieth-century West.

Without the franchise, women still participated in a range of political activism. Among the authoritarian monarchies, Germany had manhood suffrage, but in more autocratic states to the east—notably Russia and the Ottoman Empire—violence and ethnic conflict resulted from a political system that often resembled the rule imposed on colonized peoples rather than citizens.

Workers, Politics, and Protest

Workers in the 1870s–1890s coalesced politically to exert pressure on governments and businesses. Though strikes and activism were reactions to workplace hardships, they depended on community bonds forged by homemakers and neighborhood groups. With the backing of their neighbors and fellow laborers, workers in these decades built effective unions and powerful political parties—many of them based on a Marxist platform. The unions and parties acted in the public sphere to protect workers from the dizzying, often brutal pace of industrial change and to guarantee that they received a fair wage. Workers banded together at the grass roots in clubs and reading societies, yet they also aimed to unify across national boundaries. The Second International, founded in 1889, served to combat the growing nationalism that separated workers rather than binding them in a common cause.

Unions and Strikes. As the nineteenth century entered its final decades, economic uncertainties led workers to organize formal unions, which attracted the allegiance of millions. Unions demanded a say in working conditions and aimed, as one union's rule book put it, "to ensure that wages never suffer illegitimate reductions and that they always follow the rises in the price of basic commodities." Businessmen and governments viewed striking workers as insubordinate, threatening political unrest and destructive violence. Even so, strong unions appealed to some industrialists because a union could make strikes more predictable (or even prevent them), present demands more coherently, and provide a liaison for labor–management relations.

From the 1880s on, the pace of collective action for better pay, lower prices, and better working conditions accelerated. In 1888, for example, hundreds of young women who made matches, the so-called London matchgirls, struck to end the fining system, under which they could be penalized an entire day's wage for being a minute or two late to work. This system, the matchgirls maintained, helped companies reap profits of more than 20 percent. Newspapers and philanthropists picked up the strikers' story, helping them win their case. Soon thereafter, London dockworkers and gasworkers protested their precarious working conditions. Across Europe, the number of strikes and major demonstrations rose from 188 in 1888 to 289 in 1890. On May 1, 1890, for example, sixty thousand workers took to the streets of Budapest to agitate for suffrage and safer working conditions. Day laborers on Hungarian farms struck in 1891.

Housewives, who often acted in support of strikers, carried out their own protests against high food prices. In keeping with centuries of women's protest, they confiscated merchants' goods and sold them at what they considered a just price. "There should no longer be either rich or poor," argued organized Italian peasant women. "All should have bread for themselves and for their children. We should all be equal." They took other kinds of action, too: school officials or police looking for truant children met a phalanx of housewives ready to hide the children so that they could continue to help with work at home. When landlords evicted tenants, women would gather in the streets and replace household goods as fast as they were removed from the rooms of ousted families. Meeting on doorsteps or at fountains, laundries, pawnshops, and markets, women initiated rural newcomers into urban ways and developed a unity similar to that created by workers in the factory. Like strikes, political activism grew not just from the shop floor but also in neighborhoods.

Fearing threats to industrial and agricultural productivity, governments increasingly responded with force, even though most strikes were about the conditions of everyday life for workers and not about political revolution. In the face of government reaction,

unions did not back down or lose their commitment to solidarity. Craft-based unions of skilled artisans, such as carpenters and printers, were the most active and cohesive, but from the mid-1880s on, a **new unionism** attracted transport workers, miners, matchgirls, and dockworkers. These new unions were nationwide groups with salaried managers who could plan massive general strikes across the trades, focusing on such common goals as the eight-hour workday, and thus paralyze an entire nation. Although small, local workers associations remained, the large unions of the industrialized countries of western Europe, like cartels and trusts, increasingly influenced business practices and society's views of workers.

Political Parties.   New political parties also engaged the masses in political life by addressing working-class issues. Workingmen helped create the Labour Party in England, the Socialist Party in France, and the Social Democratic Parties of Sweden, Hungary, Austria, and Germany—most of them inspired by Marxist theories. Germany was home to the largest socialist party in Europe after 1890. Socialist parties attracted workingmen because they promised the triumph of new male voters who could become a powerful collective force in national elections.

Those who accepted Marx's assertion that "workingmen have no country" went further, founding an international movement that could address workers' common interests across national boundaries. In 1889, some four hundred socialists from across Europe met to form the **Second International**, a federation of working-class organizations and political parties that replaced the First International, founded by Marx before the Paris Commune. This meeting adopted a Marxist revolutionary program from the start, but it also advocated suffrage where it still did not exist and better working conditions in the immediate future.

Members of the Second International determined to rid the organization of anarchists, who flourished in the less industrial parts of Europe—Russia, Italy, and Spain. In these countries anarchism got heavy support from peasants, small property owners, and agricultural day laborers, for whom the industrially based theories of Marx had less appeal. In an age of crop failures and stiff international competition in agriculture, many rural people looked to the possibility of life without the domination of large landowners and government. Many advocated extreme tactics, including physical violence and even murder. "We want to overthrow the government . . . with violence since it is by the use of violence that they force us to obey," wrote one Italian anarchist. In the 1880s, anarchists bombed stock exchanges, parliaments, and businesses. Members of the Second International felt that such random violence was counterproductive.

Workingwomen joined these parties, but in much smaller numbers than men. Not able to vote in national elections and usually responsible for housework in addition to their paying jobs, women had little time for party meetings. Furthermore, their low wages hardly allowed them to survive, much less to pay party or union dues. Many workingmen opposed their presence, fearing women would dilute the union's masculine camaraderie. Contact with women would mean "suffocation," one Russian workingman believed, and end male union members' sense of being "comrades in the revolutionary cause." Unions glorified the heroic struggles of a male proletariat against capitalism, and Marxist leaders continued to maintain that injustice to women was caused by capitalism and would disappear in the socialist society following the coming revolution. As a result, although the new political organizations encouraged women's support, they saw women's concerns about lower wages and sexual coercion in the workplace as basically unimportant.

Outside the informal ties of neighborhoods and the factory, a range of organizations forged worker solidarity through popular community activities that intertwined politics with everyday life. The gymnastics and choral societies that had once united Europeans in nationalistic fervor now served working-class goals. Songs emphasized worker freedom, progress, and eventual victory. "Out of the dark past, the light of the future shines forth brightly," went one Russian workers' song. Socialist gymnastics, bicycling, and marching societies rejected competition and prizes as middle-class preoccupations, but they valued physical fitness for what it could do to the "outer and inner organism" and for helping workers in the "struggle for existence"— a reflection of the spread of Darwinian thinking. Workers also held festivals and gigantic parades, most notably on May 1, proclaimed by the Second International as a labor holiday. Like religious processions of an earlier time, parades were rituals that fostered unity. European governments frequently prohibited such public gatherings, fearing they were tools for agitators.

Expanding Political Participation in Western Europe

Western European countries moved toward mass politics more rapidly than did countries to the east. Ordinary people everywhere in the West were becoming aware of politics through newspapers, which, combined with industrial and imperial progress, were an important nationalizing force. In western Europe in particular, people's access to newspapers and their political participation meant that politicians depended for election more on the will of the people and less on the power of small cliques.

Mass Journalism.   The rise of mass journalism after 1880 gave Europeans ready access to information (and misinformation) about politics and world events. The invention of automatic typesetting and the production of newsprint from wood pulp lowered the costs of printing; the telephone allowed reporters to communicate news to their papers almost instantly. Once philosophical and literary in content, many daily newspapers emphasized the sensational, using banner headlines, dramatic pictures, and gruesome or lurid details—particularly about murders and sexual scandals—to sell papers. In the hustle and bustle of industrial society, one editor wrote, "you must strike your reader right between the eyes." A series of articles in 1885 in London's *Pall Mall Gazette* on the "white slave trade" warned the innocent not to read further. The author then proceeded to describe how young women were "snared, trapped," and otherwise forced into prostitution through sexual violation and drugs. Stories of imperial adventurers and exaggerated accounts of wasted women workers and their unborn babies similarly drew ordinary people to the mass press.

Journalism created a national community of up-to-date citizens, whether or not they could vote. Stories of crime and corruption appealed to the growing body of publicly educated, critical readers. Newspapers were meant not for quiet reflection at home or in the upper-class club but for quick reading on mass transportation and on the streets. Elites grumbled that the sensational press was itself a sign of social decay. But for up-and-coming people from the working and middle classes it provided an avenue to success. As London, Paris, Vienna, Berlin, and St. Petersburg became centers not only of politics but also of news, a number of European politicians got their start working for daily newspapers. In this context of growing political literacy, politicians in western Europe incorporated more people into the political process.

British Political Reforms. In the fall of 1879, William Gladstone (1809–1898), leader of the British Liberals, whose party was then out of power, waged an experimental campaign in northern England and in Scotland for a seat in the House of Commons. During this campaign, Gladstone spoke before thousands of workers, calling for greater self-determination in India and Africa and summoning his audiences to "honest, manful, humble effort" in the middle-class tradition of "hard work." Newspaper reports around the country highlighted his trip and, along with mass meetings, fueled public interest in politics. Queen Victoria bristled at Gladstone's speaking tour and at his attacks on her empire; she vowed that he would never again serve as prime minister. Gladstone's Liberals won, however, and he did become prime minister.

Gladstone's campaign exemplified the trend toward expanded participation in Britain's political life. The process had begun with the Reform Bill of 1832, which extended the franchise to middle-class men. The Ballot Act of 1872 made voting secret, a reform supported by those who wished to limit the influence of landlords and employers on their workers. Most significant, the **Reform Act of 1884** doubled the electorate, to around 4.5 million

men, enfranchising many urban workers and artisans and thus diminishing traditional aristocratic influence in the countryside.

As the number of British men entering political life as first-time voters increased, Liberals and Conservatives alike found it necessary to establish national political clubs as a means to gain party loyalty. These clubs competed with the insular groups of parliamentary elites who ruled through "wire-pulling," as one member of the House of Lords put it. These small cliques had heretofore determined the course of party politics. In contrast, broadly based interest groups such as unions, businessmen's associations, and national political clubs began to open up politics by appealing to many more voters.

British political reforms immediately affected Irish politics by arming disaffected tenant farmers with the secret ballot, making them less like colonized peoples than before. The political climate in Ireland was explosive mainly because of the repressive tactics of absentee landlords, many of them English and Protestant. These landlords evicted unsuccessful and prosperous tenants alike so that they could raise rents for newcomers. In 1879, opponents formed the Irish National Land League and launched fiery protests. Irish tenants elected a solid bloc of nationalist representatives to the British Parliament.

The Irish members of Parliament, voting as a group, had sufficient strength to defeat legislation proposed by either the Conservatives or the Liberals. Irish leader Charles Stewart Parnell (1846–1891) demanded British support for **home rule**—a system giving Ireland its own parliament—in return for Irish votes (see Parnell's portrait on the next page). Gladstone, who served four nonconsecutive terms as prime minister between 1868 and 1894, accommodated Parnell with bills on home rule and tenant security. But Conservatives called home rule "a conspiracy against the honor of Britain." When they were in power (1885–1886 and 1886–1892), they cracked down on Irish activism. Scandals reported in the press ultimately ended Parnell's political career. The first came late in the 1880s, when journalists at the London *Times* fabricated letters implicating Parnell in the assassination of English officials. Parnell

Charles Stewart Parnell, Irish Hero
Charles Stewart Parnell gained the support of both the moderates and the radicals working for Irish home rule. Many saw Ireland as the first of England's colonial conquests—a land that was both ruled and exploited economically like a colony. Son of a landowning Protestant and a skilled parliamentary politician, Parnell threw himself into the Irish cause by paralyzing the British Parliament's conduct of business. He was even able to topple the parliamentary leadership. In retaliation, the government used forgeries and other unsavory means to destroy Parnell; but in the end, scandal in his personal life lost him the vital support of the public. How had the means of perpetrating scandal changed since its use in the French Revolution? *Mary Evans Picture Library.*

was cleared of this charge, but in 1890 the news broke of his affair with a married woman, and he died in disgrace soon after. Following his death, Irish home rule still remained as divisive an issue as ever.

France's Third Republic. In France, the **Third Republic** was a hotly contested political institution from its beginning in 1870 to its collapse seventy years later. It was always a question of whether it would last and whether it was worth keeping. Universal manhood suffrage already existed as a result of classical liberalism's expansion to politics, but intrigue and scandal, magnified by press coverage, threatened the functioning of popular politics. Following the Second Empire's defeat in the Franco-Prussian War, the Third Republic began shakily with monarchist political factions—Bonapartist, Orléanist, and Bourbon—struggling to control the National Assembly and to restore their respective families to power. But the republican form of government, which French supporters had been trying to solidify for almost a century, was saved when the monarchists' compromise candidate for king, the comte de Chambord, stubbornly refused to accept the tricolored flag devised in the French Revolution. Associating the tricolor with regicide, he would accept only the white flag adorned with fleur-de-lis of the Bourbons and thus lost the chance to revive the monarchy. In 1875, a new constitution created a ceremonial presidency and a premiership dependent on support from an elected Chamber of Deputies. An alliance of businessmen, shopkeepers, professionals, and rural property owners hoped the new system would prevent the kind of strong-arm politics that had ended previous republics.

Fragile constitutional compromises, menaced by a highly partisan press, kept the Third Republic on shaky ground in the midst of economic downturns, widespread corruption, and growing anti-Semitism. Support for republican government was rocked by newspaper stories about members of the Chamber of Deputies selling their votes to business interests, and the press contributed to unrest by linking economic swings to the alleged machinations of Jewish businessmen. As a result, public sentiment turned against Jews for the failures of republican government and the economy. Confidence in republican politics plummeted in 1887 when the president's son-in-law was discovered to have sold memberships in the Legion of Honor. An aborted coup by the dashing and highly popular general Georges Boulanger soon thereafter showed the fragility of the republic and thus of political liberalism. Boulanger gathered the support of those disgusted with the messiness of parliamentary politics; his own last-minute failure of will sealed the coup's failure, preserving the republic from the menace of yet another strongman.

Republican leaders attempted to coalesce citizens by fortifying civic institutions, most notably instituting compulsory and free public education in the 1880s. In public schools, secular, republican-minded teachers supplanted Catholic clergy, who often favored a restored monarchy, and a centralized curriculum featured patriotic primers and courses in French geography, literature, and history. To perpetuate a republican ethos, the government established secular public high schools for young women, seen as the educators of future citizens. Mandatory military service for men inculcated the values of national identity and pride in place of regional and rural identities. In short, it turned peasants into Frenchmen.

Political Liberalism Rejected. Although many western European leaders believed in economic liberalism, constitutionalism, and efficient government, these ideals did not always translate into universal manhood suffrage and other forms of political liberalism in the less powerful western European countries. Spain and Belgium abruptly awarded suffrage to all men in 1890 and 1893, respectively, but both governments remained monarchies. Denmark and Sweden continued to limit political participation, and reform in the Netherlands in 1887 and 1896 increased manhood suffrage to only 14 percent. An 1887 law in Italy gave the vote to all men who had a primary school education, but this affected only 14 percent of the men.

In Italy the accession of liberals to power under the constitutional monarchy had many flaws. The process of unification left a towering debt and massive pockets of discontent, including Catholic supporters of the pope

and impoverished citizens in the south. Without receiving the benefits of nation building—education, urban improvements, industrial progress, and the vote—the average Italian feared the devastating effects of national taxes and the draft on the family economy. Italians were beginning to develop an unhappiness with constitutional government that would have dramatic implications.

Power Politics in Central and Eastern Europe

Germany, Austria-Hungary, and Russia diverged from the political paths taken by western European countries. These countries industrialized at varying rates—Germany rapidly and Russia far more slowly. Literacy and the development of a civic, urban culture were more advanced in Germany and Austria-Hungary than in Russia. Even Russia, however, saw the development of a modern press, although with a far smaller readership than elsewhere. Nonetheless in all three countries, agrarian political forces remained powerful, often working to block improvements in transport, sanitation, and tariff policy that would support a growing urban population.

Bismarck's Germany. Bismarck had upset the European balance of power, first by humiliating France in the Franco-Prussian War and then by creating a powerful, unified Germany, exemplified in explosive economic growth and in rapid development of every aspect of the nation-state, from transport to its thriving capital city, Berlin (Map 24.3). His goals achieved, he now desired stability and a respite from war and so turned to diplomacy. Fearing that France would soon seek revenge against the new Reich and needing peace to consolidate the nation, he pronounced Germany "satisfied," meaning that it sought no new territory. To ensure Germany's long-term security in Europe, in 1873 Bismarck forged an alliance with Austria-Hungary and Russia, called the Three Emperors' League. The three conservative powers shared a strong interest in maintaining the political status quo.

At home, Bismarck, who owned land and invested heavily in industry, joined with the liberals to create a variety of financial institutions such as a central bank to further German commerce and industry. Religious leaders mustered their forces to defeat his Kulturkampf against religious institutions, leading Bismarck to find another supposed enemy of the new regime. He stopped persecuting Catholics and turned his attention to socialists and liberals. He used unsuccessful assassination attempts on Emperor William I as a pretext to outlaw the Social Democratic Party in 1878. Simultaneously, hoping to wean the working class from socialism, between 1882 and 1884 Bismarck sponsored an accident and disability insurance program—the first of its kind in Europe and an important step in broadening the mandate of government to encompass social welfare. In 1879, he assembled a conservative Reichstag coalition that put through tariffs protecting German agriculture and industry from foreign competition but also raising the prices of consumer goods. This increased cost of basic necessities like food chipped away at industrial profits because owners had to pay their workers more. Ending his support for laissez-faire economics, Bismarck also severed his working relationship with political liberals. The agrarian conservatives, who disliked the growing power of industry and increasing urbanization, found their status enhanced by Bismarck's apparent attacks on the political force of Germany's burgeoning industrial sector.

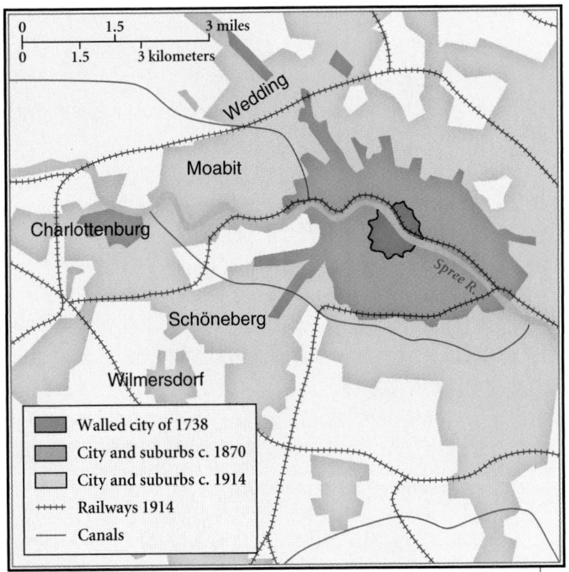

Authoritarian Austria-Hungary.

Like Germany, Austria-Hungary frequently relied on liberal economic policies. From the 1860s, liberal businessmen succeeded in industrializing parts of the empire, and the prosperous middle classes erected conspicuously large homes, giving themselves a prominence in urban life that rivaled the aristocracy's. They persuaded the government to enact free-trade provisions in the 1870s and to search out foreign investment to build up infrastructure, such as railroads.

Yet despite such influences, Austria-Hungary remained resolutely monarchist and authoritarian. Liberals in Austria—most of them ethnic Germans—saw their influence eroded under the leadership of Count Edouard von Taaffe,♦ Austrian prime minister from 1879 to 1893. Taaffe built a coalition of

♦**von Taaffe:** fawn TAHF uh

MAP 24.3 Expansion of Berlin to 1914
"A capital city is essential for the state to act as a pivot for its culture," the German historian Heinrich von Treitschke asserted. No other capital city grew as dramatically as Berlin after German unification in 1871. Industrialists and bankers set themselves up in the new capital, while workers migrated there for jobs, swelling the population. The city was newly dotted with military monuments and with museums to show off its culture. Describe the growth of Berlin as this map conveys it. What is the virtue of a map versus a photograph of bustling Berlin?

clergy, conservatives, and Slavic parties and used its power to weaken the liberals. In Bohemia, for example, he designated Czech as an official language of the bureaucracy and school system, thus breaking the German speakers' monopoly on officeholding. Reforms outraged people at whose expense other ethnic groups received benefits, and those who won concessions, such as the Czechs, continued to clamor for even greater autonomy. In this way the government played nationalities off one another and ensured the monarchy's predominance as the central mechanism for holding competing interest groups together in an era of rapid change. Even with the success of these divide-and-rule tactics, Emperor Francis Joseph and his ministers feared the influence of the most powerful Slavic nation—Russia—on the ethnic minorities living within Austria-Hungary. Francis Joseph considered the

MAP 24.4 The Balkans, c. 1878

After midcentury, the map of the Balkans was almost constantly redrawn. This resulted in part from the weakness of the dominant Ottoman Empire, but also from the ambitions of inhabitants themselves and from great power rivalry. In tune with the growing sense of national identities based on shared culture, history, and ethnicity, various Balkan peoples sought to emphasize small-group identities rather than merging around a single dominant group such as the Serbs. Yet there was also a move by some intellectuals to transcend borders and create a southern Slav culture. How might the geography of the Balkan states and the surrounding region explain these tendencies?

government that Russia declared war on Turkey in 1877, supposedly to protect Orthodox Christians. With help from Romania and Greece, Russia defeated the Ottomans and by the Treaty of San Stefano (1878) created a large, pro-Russian Bulgaria.

The Russo-Turkish War and the ensuing treaty sparked an international uproar that almost resulted in general war. Austria-Hungary and Britain feared that an enlarged Bulgaria would become a Russian satellite that would enable the tsar to dominate the Balkans. To the Austrians this appeared the potential trigger to an uprising of its restless minorities. British prime minister Benjamin Disraeli moved warships into position against Russia in order to halt the advance of Russian influence in the eastern Mediterranean, so close to Britain's routes through the Suez Canal. The public was drawn into foreign policy: the music halls and newspapers of England echoed a new jingoism, or political sloganeering, that throbbed with sentiments of war: "we don't want to fight,/ but by Jingo if we do, /We've got the ships, /we've got the men, /we've got the money too!"

The other great powers, however, did not want a Europe-wide war, and in 1878 they attempted to revive the concert of Europe by meeting at Berlin under the auspices of Bismarck, who saw this potential war as inopportune. The Congress of Berlin rolled back the Russian victory by partitioning the large Bulgarian state that Russia had carved out of Ottoman territory and denying any part of Bulgaria full independence from the Ottomans (Map 24.4). Austria occupied (but did not annex) Bosnia and Herzegovina♦ as a way of gaining clout in

appeal of the Pan-Slavic movement dangerous to the stability of his empire.

The Balkans, where the competing forces of modernization and Ottoman decay aroused political ambition in nationalists wanting independence, became the scene of the next European struggle. Slavs in Bulgaria and Bosnia-Herzegovina revolted against Turkish rule in 1876, killing Ottoman officials. As the Ottomans slaughtered thousands of Bulgarians, two other small Balkan states, Serbia and Montenegro, rebelled against the sultan. Russian Pan-Slavic organizations sent aid to the Balkan rebels and so pressured the tsar's

---

♦**Herzegovina:** hehr tsuh goh VEE nuh

the Balkans; Serbia and Montenegro became fully independent. Nonetheless, the Balkans remained a site of political unrest and great-power rivalries.

Following the Congress of Berlin, the European powers attempted to guarantee stability through a complex series of alliances and treaties. Anxious about Balkan instability and Russian aggression, Austria-Hungary forged a defensive alliance with Germany in 1879. The **Dual Alliance**, as it was called, offered protection against Russia, whose threat to Hungarian control of its Slavic peasantry, a German diplomat wrote, "was on [the Hungarian government's] mind day and night." In 1882, Italy joined this partnership (henceforth called the Triple Alliance), largely because of Italy's imperial rivalries with France. Because tensions between Russia and Austria-Hungary remained high, Bismarck signed the Reinsurance Treaty (1887) with Russia to stifle Habsburg illusions about having a free hand in dealing with Pan-Slavism.

Unrest in Russia. Although Russia enjoyed some international success in the late nineteenth century, its internal affairs were in disarray. By 1871, the era of Great Reforms had run its course, and Russia remained almost the only European country without a constitutional government. Reform-minded youth increasingly turned to revolutionary groups for solutions to political and social problems. One such group, the Populists, wanted to rouse the debt-ridden peasantry to revolt. Other people formed tightly coordinated terrorist bands with the goal of assassinating public officials and thus forcing change. The secret police, relying on informers, rounded up hundreds of members of one of the largest groups, Land and Liberty, and subjected them to torture, show trials, and imprisonment. When in 1877 a young radical, Vera Zasulich, tried unsuccessfully to assassinate the chief of the St. Petersburg police, the people of the capital city applauded her act

Vera Zasulich
A radical activist, Vera Zasulich launched the violent phase in Russian protest when in 1877 she shot the governor-general of St. Petersburg after he ordered the beating of a political prisoner for not raising his cap to the governor. The religiously inspired daughter of a military official, Zasulich, like her two activist sisters, worked to mitigate the brutal conditions in her country. Reformers began to duplicate the violence of the government and assassinated Tsar Alexander II in 1881. *ItarTass/Sovfoto.*

and acquittal, so great was their horror at the brutal treatment of young radicals from respectable families (see the portrait of Vera Zasulich, above).

Writers added to the intense debate over Russia's future. Novelists Leo Tolstoy, author of the epic *War and Peace* (1869), and Fyodor Dostoevsky, a former radical who changed position, both opposed the revolutionaries' desire to overturn the social order; they believed that Russia above all required spiritual regeneration. Tolstoy's novel *Anna Karenina* (1877) tells the story of an impassioned, adulterous love affair, but it also weaves in the spiritual quest of Levin, a former "progressive" landowner who, like Tolstoy, eventually rejects modernization and idealizes the peasantry's tradition of stoic endurance. Dostoevsky satirized Russia's radicals in *The Possessed* (1871), a novel in which a group of revolutionaries carries out one central act: the murder of one of its own members. In Dostoevsky's view, the radicals could only act destructively and were incapable of offering any positive solution to Russia's ills.

The more radical revolutionary groups did seek to change Russia by violent action rather than by spiritual uplift. In 1881, the People's Will, a splinter group of Land and Liberty impatient with its failure to mobilize the peasantry, killed Tsar Alexander II in a bomb attack. His death, however, failed to provoke the general uprising the terrorists expected. Alexander III (r. 1881–1894), rejecting further liberal reforms, unleashed a new wave of oppression against religious and ethnic minorities and gave the police virtually unchecked power. Popular books and drawings depicted Tatars, Poles, Ukrainians, and others as horrifying, uncivilized, or utterly ridiculous—and thus always a menace to the health of Russian culture. Intensified Russification that enforced the use of the Russian language and the observance of Russian Orthodox church rituals aggravated old grievances among oppressed nationalities such as the Poles, but it also turned the once-loyal German middle and upper classes of the Baltic provinces against Russian rule, with serious long-term consequences.

The five million Russian Jews, confined to the eighteenth-century Pale of Settlement (the name for the restricted territory in which they were permitted to live), endured particularly severe oppression. Local officials instigated pogroms against Jews, whose distinctive language, dress, and isolation in ghettos made them easy targets. Government officials encouraged people to blame Jews for escalating living costs—though the true cause was the policy of making the peasantry pay for industrialization by raising taxes.

As the tsar responded to internal turmoil with even greater repression, Bismarck's delicate alliance of the three conservative powers was unraveling. A brash but deeply insecure young kaiser, William II (r. 1888–1918), mounted the German throne in 1888. William chafed under Bismarck's tutelage, and his advisers flattered the young man into thinking that his own personal talent made Bismarck a hindrance, even a rival. William dismissed Bismarck in 1890 and, because he ardently supported German nationalism, let the alliance with Russia lapse in favor of a strong relationship with the supposedly kindred Austria-Hungary. Fatefully, he had opened the door to a realignment of the great powers just as imperial rivalries were intensifying antagonisms among the European nation-states and empires.

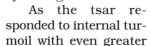

Russia: The Pale of Settlement in the Nineteenth Century

Review: What were the major changes in political life from the 1870s to the 1890s, and which areas of Europe did they most affect?

Conclusion

The period from the 1870s to the 1890s has been called the age of industry and empire because Western society pursued both these ends in a way that rapidly transformed Europe and the world. In these decades the West appeared at the top of its form. Industrial innovation and national growth caused much of Europe to thrive and become more populous and urban. Europeans proudly spread their supposedly superior culture globally and, like Marianne North, searched out whatever other peoples and places could offer by way of knowledge, experience, and wealth. The great powers undertook a new imperialism, carving up territory and establishing direct rule over foreign peoples. As they tightened connections with the rest of the globe, Europeans felt the influence of other civilizations. In politics, reformers drew lower-class men into active citizenship by extending suffrage. Humanitarian commitment prompted the development of philanthropic agencies and promoted the development of a more activist state that worked to make citizens of imperial countries more fit.

Yet as workers struck for improved wages and conditions and the impoverished migrated to find a better life, Western society showed its fissures and divisions. While newspapers, novels, and the arts helped inform people of profound social and international changes, they also raised questions about poverty and hopelessness. By the 1890s, the advance of industry and empire was bringing unprecedented tensions to national politics, the international scene, and everyday life. Racism, anti-Semitism, and ethnic chauvinism were spreading, sanctioned in most strata of society, and the costs of empire to conquered peoples were beyond measure. Politics in the authoritarian countries was taking a more conservative turn, resisting participation and reform, while to the west democratization advanced. These differences would ultimately be of consequence for the West as a whole.

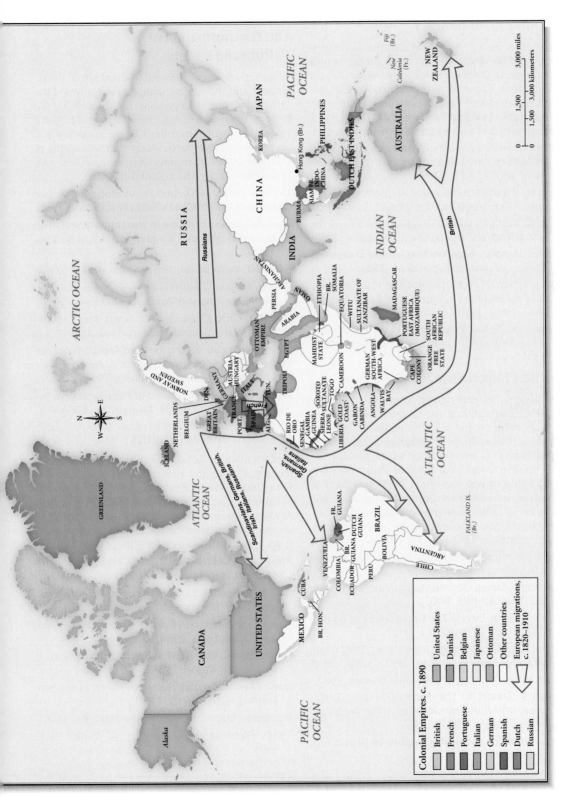

MAPPING THE WEST The West and the World, c. 1890
European influence was reaching its height in the late nineteenth century as European trade and political reach spanned the globe. Needing markets for the vast quantities of goods that poured from European factories and access to raw materials to produce the goods, governments asserted that the Western way of life should be spread to the rest of the world and that resources would be best used by Europeans. Explorations and scientific discoveries continued both to build the knowledge base of European peoples and to enhance their ability for greater conquest. Simultaneously, millions of Europeans left their homes to find a better life elsewhere. What has changed geographically in Europe's relationship with the world since the Spanish and Portuguese took colonies in the late fifteenth and early sixteenth centuries?

Suggested References

The Advance of Industry

Industry in the 1870s–1890s advanced on every front, from the development of new products and procedures to the reorganization of work life and consumption. Crouzet's sweeping new work on the creation of economic structures contrasts with other recent studies (such as Rappaport's) on the impact of consumers and taste in driving economic change.

Crossick, Geoffrey, and Serge Jaumin, eds. *Cathedrals of Consumption: The European Department Store, 1850–1939*. 1999.

Crouzet, Francois. *A History of the European Economy, 1000–2000*. 2001.

Franzoi, Barbara. *At the Very Least She Pays the Rent: Women and German Industrialization*. 1985.

Malone, Carolyn, *Women's Bodies and Dangerous Trades in England, 1880–1914*. 2003.

Marks, Steven G. *Road to Power: The Trans-Siberian Railroad and the Colonization of Asian Russia, 1850–1917*. 1991.

Rappaport, Erika. *Shopping for Pleasure: Women in the Making of London's West End*. 2000.

The New Imperialism

New studies of imperialism show not only increasing conquest and the creation of an international economy but also the cultural impulses behind it. Cannadine's book offers a readable— and debatable— interpretation of the social relations involved. The University of Pennsylvania's African studies Web site offers vivid depictions of African art and architecture, such as that confiscated for Western museums, while the Chrétien study investigates not only European imperialism in Africa but also its long-term effects.

African Studies Center: http://www.sas.upenn.edu/African _Studies/AS.html.

Cannadine, David. *Ornamentalism: How the British Saw Their Empire*. 2001.

Chrétien, Jean-Pierre, *The Great Lakes of Africa: 2,000 Years of History*. 2003.

Crosby, Alfred W. *Ecological Imperialism: The Biological Expansions of Europe, 900–1900*. 1993.

Ferro, Marc. *Colonization: A Global History*. 1997.

Headrick, Daniel R. *The Tools of Empire: Technology and European Imperialism in the Nineteenth Century*. 1981.

Keene, Donald. *Emperor of Japan: Meiji and His World*. 2002.

*Stanley, Sir Henry. *Autobiography*. 1909.

Wildenthal, Lora. *German Women for Empire, 1884–1945*. 2001.

The Transformation of Culture and Society

Historians have come to see that industrial development and the spread of imperialism affected the smallest details of everyday life as well as the larger phenomena of class formation and massive regional and global migration. Beckles and Stodart, and Blakely, give particularly rich portrayals of cultural mixture, exploitation, motivation, and resistance under the colonial regime.

Beckles, Hilary McD., and Brian Stodart, eds. *Liberation Cricket: West Indies Cricket Culture*. 1995.

Blakely, Allison. *Blacks in the Dutch World: The Evolution of Racial Imagery in Modern Society*. 1993.

*Bonnell, Victoria, ed. *The Russian Worker*. 1983.

Callen, Anthea. *The Art of Impressionism: Painting Technique and the Making of Modernity*. 2000.

Hoerder, Dirk. *Cultures in Contact: World Migrations in the Second Millennium*. 2002.

Maynes, Mary Jo. *Taking the Hard Road: Life Course in French and German Workers' Autobiographies in the Era of Industrialization*. 1995.

McReynolds, Louise. *Russia at Play: Leisure Activities at the End of the Tsarist Era*. 2003.

The Birth of Mass Politics

Historical study of politics in this period entails looking at both government policies and the activism based on neighborhood solidarity, the growth of unions, and the rise of the mass media. The Avalon Project at the Yale Law School provides access to major treaties and conventions, making it an excellent resource for this period.

Applegate, Celia. *A Nation of Provincials: The German Idea of Heimat*. 1990.

Avalon Project at Yale Law School: http://www.yale.edu/lawweb/avalon/avalon.htm.

Hoppen, K. Theodore. *Ireland since 1800: Conflict and Conformity*. 1999.

Rogger, Hans. *Jewish Policies and Right-Wing Politics in Imperial Russia*. 1986.

Ross, Ellen. *Love and Toil: Motherhood in Outcast London, 1870–1918*. 1993.

Todorova, Maria. *Imagining the Balkans*. 1997.

*Verga, Giovanni. *The House by the Medlar Tree*. 1981.

*Primary sources.

CHAPTER REVIEW

IMPORTANT EVENTS

1860s–1890s	Impressionism flourishes in the arts; absorption of Asian influences
1870s–1890s	Vast emigration from Europe continues; the new imperialism
1873	Extended economic recession begins with global impact
1876	Invention of the telephone
1879	Dual Alliance formed between Germany and Austria-Hungary
1882	Triple Alliance formed between Germany, Austria-Hungary, and Italy; Britain invades Egypt
1882–1884	Bismarck sponsors social welfare legislation
1884	British Parliament passes the Reform Act, doubling the size of the male electorate
1884–1885	European nations carve up Africa at the Berlin conference
1889	Japan adopts constitution based on European models; Socialists meet in Paris and establish the Second International

KEY TERMS

capital-intensive industry (920)

Dual Alliance (953)

home rule (948)

impressionism (944)

limited liability corporation (921)

new unionism (946)

outwork (918)

Second International (946)

Reform Act of 1884 (948)

Third Republic (949)

REVIEW QUESTIONS

1. What economic and political factors led to the rise of the department store?
2. What were the differences between the new imperialism and European states' earlier relationships with regions beyond the West?
3. How did industry and empire influence art and everyday life?
4. What were the major changes in political life from the 1870s to the 1890s, and which areas of Europe did they most affect?

MAKING CONNECTIONS

1. Compare the political and social goals of the newly enfranchised male electorate with those of people from the "best circles."
2. Describe the effects of imperialism on European politics and society as a whole.

FOR FURTHER EXPLORATION

To assess your mastery of the material in this chapter, see the Online Study Guide at **bedfordstmartins.com/hunt**.

To read additional primary-source material from this period, see Chapter 24 in *Sources of The Making of the West*, Second Edition.

Modernity and the Road to War, c. 1890–1914

IN THE FIRST DECADE OF THE TWENTIETH CENTURY, a wealthy young Russian man traveled from one country to another to find relief from neurasthenia, a common malady in those days. Its symptoms included fatigue, lack of interest in life, depression, and sometimes physical sickness. In 1910, the young man encountered Sigmund Freud, a Viennese physician whose unconventional treatment— eventually called psychoanalysis—took the form of a conversation about the patient's dreams, sexual experiences, and everyday life. Over the course of four years, Freud uncovered his patient's deeply rooted fear of castration disguised as a phobia of wolves—thus the name Wolf-Man by which he comes down to us. Often building his theories from information about colonized peoples and cultures, Freud worked his cure, as the Wolf-Man himself put it, "by bringing repressed ideas into consciousness." Freud's theories laid the groundwork for an understanding of the human psyche that has endured, with modifications and some controversy, to our own time.

The Wolf-Man was emblematic of his age. Born into a family that owned vast estates, he reflected the growing prosperity of Europeans, albeit on a grander scale than most. Simultaneously, countless individuals seemed anguished and mentally disturbed, and suicides abounded—the Wolf-Man's own sister and father died from intentional drug overdoses. European society as a whole subjected itself to agonized

---

Edvard Munch, *The Scream* (1893)
In some of his paintings Norwegian artist Edvard Munch captured the spirit of the turn of the century using delightful pastel colors to convey the leisured life of people strolling in the countryside. Impressionists similarly depicted modern life in paintings of animated conversations in outdoor cafés and gardens. But modern life at this time also had its tortured side, which Munch was equally capable of portraying. *The Scream* is taken as emblematic of the torments of modernity as the individual turns inward, beset by neuroses, self-destructive impulses, and even madness. Today some believe that *The Scream* reflects Munch's violent reaction to the earlier eruption of a volcano. While some—like the two other figures in the painting— could react calmly to whatever modern life had to offer, others like the screamer were agonized at every turn of events. It can also be suggested that the screamer, like Europe, travels the road to World War I. *National Gallery, Oslo, Norway. © Scala/Art Resource. © Copyright 2005 The Munch Museum/The Munch-Ellingsen Group/Artists Rights Society (ARS), NY.*

questioning about the family, gender relationships, empire, religion, and the consequences of technology and progress. Conflict reigned throughout Europe and the world, as an array of powers (including Japan) fought their way into even more territories and took political control. Every sign of imperial wealth brought on an apparently irrational sense of Europe's decline. British writer H. G. Wells saw in this era "humanity upon the wane . . . the sunset of mankind."

Governments expanded the male electorate during this period in the hope of making politics more harmonious and manageable. Ethnic chauvinism, anti-Semitism, and militant nationalism only increased the violence of political rhetoric, however. Women suffragists along with politically disadvantaged groups such as the Slavs and Irish demanded full rights, but the liberal ethos of tolerance receded before a wave of political assassinations and public brutality. While the great powers fought to dominate people around the world, their competition for empire fueled an arms race that threatened to turn Europe—the "most civilized" region of the world, according to its leaders—into a savage battleground.

These were just some of the conflicts associated with modernity—a term often used to describe the accelerated pace of life, the rise of mass politics, and the decline of a rural social order that were so visible in the West from the late nineteenth century on (see "Terms of History," page 962). Modernity also refers to the response of artists and intellectuals to this rapid change. The celebrated "modern" art, music, science, and

philosophy of this period still resonate for their brilliant, innovative qualities. Yet these same innovations were often considered offensive at the time: cries of outrage at the new music echoed in concert halls, while educated people were utterly shocked at Freud's ideas that sexual drives motivate even the smallest children. Every advance in science and the arts simultaneously had consequences that undermined the middle-class faith in artistic and scientific progress.

When the heir to the Austro-Hungarian throne was assassinated in June 1914, few gave any thought to the global significance of the event, least of all the Wolf-Man, whose treatment with Freud was just ending and who viewed that fateful day of June 28 simply as the day he "could now leave Vienna a healthy man." Yet the assassination was the catalyst for an eruption of discord that had simmered for several decades, as the nations of Europe lurched from one diplomatic crisis to another. The consequences of the resulting disastrous war, World War I, like the insights of Freud, would shape modern life.

❖ Private Life in the Modern Age

Western ideals of a comfortable family life flourished because of Europe's improved standard of living. The prosperity brought by industrialization and empire, however, challenged traditional social norms just the way imperial and technological advance had up-

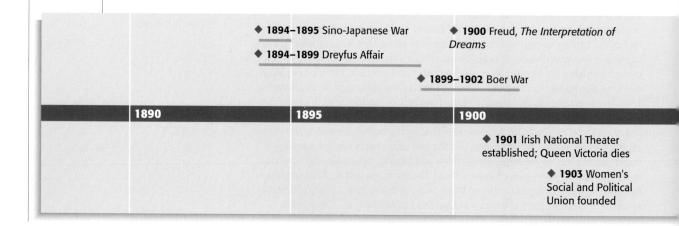

◆ **1894–1895** Sino-Japanese War

◆ **1894–1899** Dreyfus Affair

◆ **1900** Freud, *The Interpretation of Dreams*

◆ **1899–1902** Boer War

1890	**1895**	**1900**

◆ **1901** Irish National Theater established; Queen Victoria dies

◆ **1903** Women's Social and Political Union founded

set international politics and worker confidence in the economic future. A falling birthrate, a rising divorce rate, and growing activism for marriage reform provoked intense debate by the turn of the century. Some among the elites acknowledged homosexuality as a way of life, while others made it the topic of politics. Middle-class women took jobs and became active in public to such an extent that some feared the disappearance of distinct gender roles. Women's visibility in public life prompted one British songster in the late 1890s to write:

> Rock-a-bye baby, for father is near
> Mother is "biking" she never is here!
> Out in the park she's scorching all day
> Or at some meeting is talking away!

Discussions of gender roles and private life contributed to rising social tensions because they upset so many traditional ideals. They also fueled the optimism of reformers that Western society was making constant progress and becoming more rational and egalitarian. Freud and other scientists tried to study such phenomena dispassionately and eventually formulated new theories of the human personality. Public discussions of private life—especially when they became intertwined with politics—demonstrated the close connection of private and public concerns.

Population Pressure

Urgent concerns over trends in population, marriage, and sexuality clogged the agendas of politicians and reformers from the 1890s on, and they still do so in the present day. The staggering population increases of the eighteenth century had continued through the nineteenth. At the turn of the century, cities looked chaotic as population soared and changed the urban landscape by filling it with rural people and migrants—even some from other ethnicities and continents. Faced with the urban masses, often crowded into tenements and shacks, Social Darwinists warned of racial decay and Western leaders faced tense population dilemmas. Reformers, politicians, and critics of public life were seriously concerned over the quantity and quality of population.

Europe's Population Soars. Dramatic increases in the European population continued as the twentieth century opened. Germany increased in size from 41 million people in 1871 to 64 million in 1910; tiny Denmark, from 1.7 million in 1870 to 2.7 million in 1911. Such growth resulted from improvements in sanitation and public health that extended the life span and reduced infant mortality. To cope with their burgeoning populations, Berlin, Budapest, and Moscow were torn apart and rebuilt, following the lead of Vienna and Paris. The German government pulled down eighteenth-century Berlin and reconstructed the city with new roadways and mass-transport systems as the capital's population grew to over 4 million. Rebuilding to absorb population growth was not confined to capitals of the most powerful states: Balkan cities like Sofia, Belgrade, and Bucharest gained tree-lined boulevards, public buildings, and better sanitation.

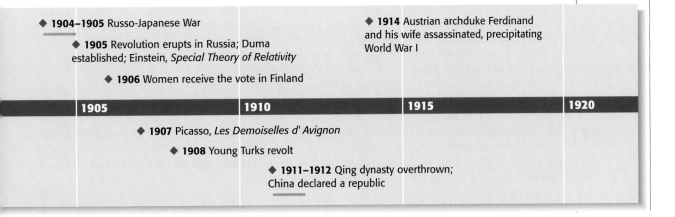

◆ **1904–1905** Russo-Japanese War

◆ **1905** Revolution erupts in Russia; Duma established; Einstein, *Special Theory of Relativity*

◆ **1906** Women receive the vote in Finland

◆ **1914** Austrian archduke Ferdinand and his wife assassinated, precipitating World War I

| 1905 | 1910 | 1915 | 1920 |

◆ **1907** Picasso, *Les Demoiselles d' Avignon*

◆ **1908** Young Turks revolt

◆ **1911–1912** Qing dynasty overthrown; China declared a republic

TERMS OF HISTORY

Modern

The word *modernus* was introduced into Latin in the sixth century; after that, the claim to being modern occurred in many centuries and cultures. Shakespeare, for example, referred to "modern ideas" in his plays. By the second half of the nineteenth century, historians were heatedly debating where "modern" history began: with Abraham? with Charlemagne? or with the Renaissance?

Despite the many claims to being modern, the term has fastened itself most firmly around the period from the end of the nineteenth century through the first half of the twentieth. Its most specific historical use has been to describe the art, music, and dance that flourished at that time. When used in this sense, *modern* indicates a sharp break with lyrical romantic and classical music and dance and also with the conventions for representing objects in the arts. The blurred images of the impressionists and the jarring music of Arnold Schoenberg are part of modern art. The sexual rawness of *Madame Bovary* (see Chapter 23) or of Sigmund Freud's analysis of the Wolf-Man's dreams gave a further ingredient into the multifaceted meanings of the word *modern*. Sometimes this intellectual break with the cultural past is referred to as modernism.

At the end of the nineteenth century the word *modern* referred to social phenomena. Women who went to work or entered universities or began careers in the new field of social work were called modern women. They believed that by showing themselves capable and rational they could attain social progress and end restrictions placed on them. Some of them lived different lives from those women who had large families and confined themselves to the domestic sphere. This departure from tradition also made them appear modern.

In seeking an education and hoping for progress toward rationality in the law, these women were invoking a meaning of the word *modern* dating back to the Enlightenment. Progress, rational thought, and science have also been taken as the bedrock of the modern. *Modernization*—another derivative of the word *modern*—refers to the kind of scientific and technological progress that came with industrialization and the rise of commercial agriculture as they began to shape the nineteenth and twentieth centuries. Indoor plumbing, electricity, telephones, and automobiles were signs of modernity. As a result, modern artists painted teeming cities, industrial workers, world's fairs, and other scenes associated with the modernization of the late nineteenth century. In the second decade of the twentieth century, other artists started converting parts of industrial products like the toilet and the automobile into works of art.

Modern may be a popular word because it contains paradoxical meanings that make it multipurpose. While associated with the triumph of industry and rational thought at the turn of the century, cultural modernism brought a glorification of the so-called primitive and non-Western, whether in representational art, music, literature, or philosophy. The great innovative composer Richard Wagner gained inspiration from Indian philosophy, while the philosopher Friedrich Nietzsche read Asian religious and philosophical writings. Pablo Picasso derived some of his modern style from African art, while the clean lines of modern architecture—the turn away from Victorian curlicues and gaudy colors—were modeled on the pure forms of native American, African, Asian, and Middle Eastern dwellings.

Complex, paradoxical, and dense with meaning, *modern* may not always be precise enough to be useful. But its very breadth explains why *modern* remains a crucial—and debated—term of history.

In many countries the number of urban residents was surpassing that of the rural population, and the multitudes began to live their lives among strangers, getting their news from impersonal media like newspapers instead of trading stories with neighbors. Some ruling elites from the countryside protested the independence and unruliness of urban dwellers.

Alarm over the Falling Birthrate.

While the absolute size of the population was rising in much of the West, the birthrate (measured in births per thousand people) was falling because of urbanization and industrialization. The birthrate had been decreasing in France since the eighteenth century; other European countries began experiencing the decline late in the nineteenth century. The Swedish rate dropped from thirty-five births per thousand people in 1859 to twenty-four per thousand in 1911; even populous Germany went from forty births per thousand in 1875 to twenty-seven per thousand in 1913.

Rural community norms, such as postponing marriage until the late twenties when couples were too old to produce large numbers of children, broke down under rapid economic change. Urbanization released the grip of rural community decision making in reproductive matters. In an age when agriculture was also becoming industrialized, farm families needed fewer hands, and individual couples determined their own birth-control practices to limit their family's size. Abstinence was a common method, but the spread of new birth-control practices that would encompass most of the globe by the end of the twentieth century mainly accounted for modern Europe's ebbing birthrate. In cities, pamphlets and advice books for those with enough money and education spread information about coitus interruptus—the withdrawal method of preventing pregnancy. Technology also played a role in curtailing reproduction: condoms, improved after the

Large German Family
Improved medicine, hygiene, and diet at the turn of the century helped more people survive infancy and childhood. Thus, in many cases family size grew larger, as this photo from a working-class apartment suggests. Even those opposed to birth control were appalled that lower-class families were becoming larger than those of the "best circles," where family limitation was increasingly practiced. What Social Darwinist ideas could be used to describe this family? How would a birth-control activist describe it? Might these two groups have the same ideas about the family? *AKG London.*

vulcanization of rubber in the 1840s, proved fairly reliable in preventing conception, as did the German-invented diaphragm. Abortions were also legion, if still legally sanctioned.

The wider use of birth control stirred controversy. Critics accused middle-class women, whose fertility was falling most rapidly, of holding a "birth strike." Anglican bishops, meeting early in the twentieth century, deplored family limitation, especially by artificial means, as "demoralizing to character and hostile to national welfare." Politicians worried about a crisis in masculinity that would detract from military strength. But U.S. president Theodore Roosevelt blamed middle-class women's selfishness for the population decline, calling it "one of the most unpleasant and unwholesome features of modern life." The "quality" of those being born worried activists and politicians: If the

Oscar Wilde
The Irish-born writer Oscar Wilde symbolized the persecution experienced by homosexuals in the late nineteenth century. Tried for and convicted of having sexual relations with another man, Wilde served time in prison—a humiliation for a husband, father, acclaimed author, and witty playwright. Wilde's writings aimed to suggest that the complexities of human society made narrow moral codes harmful. *Library of Congress.*

Oscar Wilde (1854–1900), who was sentenced to two years in prison for indecency—a charge that referred to his sexual affairs with young men (see the illustration on this page). After Wilde's conviction one newspaper rejoiced, "Open the windows! Let in the fresh air!" Between 1907 and 1909, German newspapers also publicized the scandal around men in Kaiser William II's closest circle who were condemned for homosexuality and transvestitism. Amid growing concern over population and family values, the public received assurances from the government itself that William's own family life "provides the entire country with a fine model." Sexuality thus took on patriotic overtones: the accused homosexual elite in Germany was said by journalists to be out to "emasculate our courageous master race." Although these cases paved the way for growing sexual openness in the next generations, they also showed that sexual issues were becoming regular weapons in politics.

Sciences of the Modern Self

Scientists and Social Darwinists, working during the height of European power, found cause for alarm not only in the condition of the working class but also in modern society's host of mental complaints such as fatigue and irritability. Most of these illnesses originated in the "nerves," they reasoned, which were troubled by the hectic pace and demands of urban living. Sciences of the mind such as psychology and psychoanalysis arose to treat everyone, not just the insane.

New Approaches to Mental Ailments. A rash of books in the 1890s expounded on the subject of modern nervous ailments. The most widely translated of them, *Degeneration* (1892–1893), written by Hungarian-born physician Max Nordau,♦ blamed overstimulation for both individual and national deterioration. According to Nordau, increasingly bizarre modern art, male lethargy, and female hysteria were all symptoms of overstimulation and reflected a general downturn in the human species. The standard Social Darwinist cure for such mental decline was imperial adventure, renewed virility, and increased childbearing. Medical scientists also studied the criminal, classifying typologies of the deviant mind and creating the field of criminology. They invented intelligence tests that they said could measure the capacity of the human mind more accurately than a schoolteacher could. In Russia, physiologist Ivan Pavlov (1849–1936) proposed that conditioning mental reflexes—that is, causing a subject to associate a desired response with a previously unrelated stimulus—could modify behavior. His experiments, especially his success in changing the

♦**Max Nordau:** mahks NAWR dow

behavior of a dog, were among those that formed the basis of modern psychology.

Freud and Psychoanalysis. Sigmund Freud (1856–1939) devised an approach to modern anxieties that, he claimed, avoided traditional moral evaluations of human behavior. He became convinced that the human psyche was far from rational. Dreams, he explained in *The Interpretation of Dreams* (1900), reveal a repressed part of personality—the "unconscious"—where all sorts of desires are more or less hidden. Freud also believed that the human psyche is made up of three competing parts: the ego, the part that is most in touch with external reality; the id (or libido), the part that contains instinctive drives and sexual energies; and the superego, the part that serves as the force of conscience. Freud's theory of human mental processes and his method for treating their malfunctioning came to be called **psychoanalysis**. Like Darwin's ideas, Freud's notions challenged accepted liberal belief both in a unified, rational self that acted in its own interest and, by implication, in the certainty of progress. Nonetheless, Freud placed his work squarely in the scientific tradition and announced his conclusions as resulting from observation, not religion.

Freud shocked many contemporaries by insisting that all children have sexual drives from the moment of birth, but he also believed that many of these sexual impulses have to be repressed for the individual to attain maturity and for society to remain civilized. Attaining one's adult sexual identity is always a painful process because it depends on repressing infantile urges, which include bisexuality and incest. Thus, the Wolf-Man's nightmare of white wolves outside his window symbolized his unresolved sexual feelings for members of his family. Freud claimed that certain aspects of gender roles— such as motherhood—are normal and that throughout their lives women in general achieve far less than men do. At the same time, he believed that adult gender identity results not from anatomy alone (motherhood is not the only way to be female) but from inescapable mental processing of life experiences as well. He thus made gender more complicated than simple biology would suggest. Finally, Freud's psychoanalytic theory maintained that girls and women have powerful sexual feelings, an assertion that broke with existing ideas of women's passionlessness.

The influence of psychoanalysis became pervasive in the twentieth century, offering paradoxes and representing yet another turn toward global thinking. (See "New Sources, New Perspectives," page 968.) For example, free association of ideas and interpretation of

Freud's Office
Sigmund Freud's therapy room, where his patients experienced the "talking cure," was filled with imperial trophies such as Oriental rugs and African art objects. Freud himself was fascinated by cures brought about through shamanism, trances, and other practices of non-Western medicine as well as through drug-induced mental states. In 1938, Freud fled to England to escape the Nazis. This photo shows his office in London. What impression might Freud's office have left on his patients? How might it have helped the talking cure? *Mary Evans Picture Library/Sigmund Freud copyrights.*

NEW SOURCES, NEW PERSPECTIVES

Psychohistory and Its Lessons

In the last fifty years, historians have radically changed the way they write history. In the nineteenth century, history books mostly recounted the deeds of kings and emperors, discussed royal genealogy, and listed wars and peace treaties. Determined to be factual, historians laid out the fine points of laws, charters, and treaties and they checked their sources in archives.

Much has changed since then, partly because of the rise of psychology and psychoanalysis as the twentieth century opened. Confronted with strikes, mass demonstrations, anarchist deeds, anti-Semitism, and other forms of political violence, some observers tried to explain a phenomenon they called crowd psychology. According to this view, psychic states are important factors in shaping some public events.

Not surprisingly, Sigmund Freud studied great historic figures like Leonardo da Vinci from a psychoanalytic perspective, exploring the connection between repressed childhood fantasies and later towering accomplishments. Freud also explained the outbreak of World War I as more of a psychic than a diplomatic event. He saw the war as a form of collective death wish. He subjected both individuals and entire societies to psychoanalytic probing. Few historians followed Freud's lead.

In 1957, William Langer, president of the American Historical Association, charged his fellow scholars with being foolishly backward in their methods. Unlike scientists, he claimed, historians did not try new systems or techniques such as psychoanalysis that might advance their understanding of the past. Others joined the debate, finding that traditional history sometimes attributed actions to gossipy traits such as ambition, greed, hate, and great intelligence. But what was the "scientific" depth in such characterizations? Another criticism of history by those interested in psychology and psychoanalysis was that, if it did take human agency into account, it usually saw historical figures as acting rationally in their self-interest. Trauma, the irrational, uncontrollable drives, and unconscious motivations had no role to play in understanding historical figures.

Psychohistory was born in these discussions. A major study by psychoanalyst Erik Erikson, *Young Man Luther* (1958), announced that the Protestant Reformation originated in the childhood traumas of Martin Luther. Identity crises stemming from his relationship with his father caused Luther to search for and reject father figures, not only his own father but the pope. Erikson's book caused a stir among historians, changing the way people approached Luther and starting an entirely new school of historical thought.

Not surprisingly, some of the most compelling examples of psychohistory have focused on the lives of individuals and the development of political movements. Historians interested in psychoanalysis have tried to find in Kaiser William II's childhood answers to his rejection of Bismarck, his turn to an aggressive foreign policy, and his participation in World War I. On a collective level, analyses of Adolf Hitler's and Benito Mussolini's followers have seen mass psychic needs and traumas as motivating their blind worship of these vicious dictators. But the intense nationalism that most people in the modern world have increasingly felt for their countries has also become a phenomenon that psychohistorians examine.

Psychohistory remains controversial to this day. While its practitioners expand the field of historical explanation, its critics find that it can

dreams are mainstays in psychoanalysis derived from the African and Asian influences on Freud's thought: the "talking cure," as it was quickly labeled, gave rise to a general acceptance of talking out one's problems. As psychoanalysis became a respected means of recovering mental health, terms such as *neurosis*, *unconscious*, and *libido* came into widespread use. By way of paradox, Freud attributed girls' complaints about unwanted

Kaiser William and Edward VII's Family

Psychotherapy aimed to cure the individual in good part by discussing family relationships and the fantasies built around them. Psychohistory often draws its analyses from these same relationships, as in the case of Martin Luther, for example, and his father. The royal families of Europe are ripe for such analysis because, as the photo shows, German and British monarchs (Edward VII, right; and William, second from right) were closely related; so too were the Russians, Germans, and British. These relationships raise potential questions about the outbreak of World War I as the work of complex family dynamics. *Hulton Archive/Getty Images.*

be formulaic by fitting the behavior of historical characters into Freud's schema. Other critics find that psychohistory is too imprecise and speculative because it is not based on the same kinds of hard, documentary evidence that historians have been trained to use. Nonetheless, psychohistorians have made a good case that if we are going to look at personalities, character, and relationships, we should do so in the most informed way possible. Their rationale makes psychohistory appear to be a necessity.

QUESTIONS TO CONSIDER

1. What are the advantages and disadvantages of psychohistory?
2. How would you set out to investigate the psychological reasons for the actions of William II, Emmeline Pankhurst, Marie Curie, or Gavrilo Princip? Would you look at their character, their childhood, their social background, or other parts of their lives?
3. Can we write history without talking about the emotions, mental habits, and human relationships of major figures? Should we avoid psychologizing when thinking about the past?

FURTHER READING

Binion, Rudolph. *Frau Lou: Nietzsche's Wayward Disciple.* 1968.

Erikson, Erik. *Young Man Luther: A Study in Psychoanalysis and History.* 1958.

Journal of Psychohistory.

Kohut, Thomas A. *Wilhelm II and the Germans: A Study in Leadership.* 1991.

sexual advances or abuse to fantasy caused by "penis envy," an idea that led members of the new profession of social work to believe that most instances of such abuse had not actually occurred. On the one hand, Freud was a meticulous scientist, examining symptoms, urging attention to the most minute evidence from everyday life, and demanding that sexual life be regarded with a rational rather than a religious eye. On the other hand, he was a pessimistic visionary who had abandoned the optimism of the Enlightenment and pre-Darwinian science by claiming that humans were motivated by irrational drives toward death and destruction and that these urges shaped society's collective mentality. Freud would later interpret World War I's vast devastation of humanity as bearing out his bleak conclusions.

Review: How did ideas about the self and about personal life change at the turn of the century?

❖ Modernity and the Revolt in Ideas

Although the intellectuals and artists who participated in the turmoil and triumph of turn-of-the-century society did not know it at the time, their rejection of accepted beliefs and artistic forms announced a new era. In science, theories that time is relative and that energy and mass are interchangeable rocked established truths about time, space, matter, and energy. Art and music became unrecognizable. Artists and musicians who deliberately produced shocking, lurid works were, like Freud, heavily influenced by advances in science, critical thinking, and empire. Amid contradictions such as the blending of the scientific and the irrational, and of the "West" and "non-West," intellectuals and artists helped launch the disorienting revolution in ideas and creative expression that we now identify collectively as **modernism**.

The Challenge to Positivism

Late in the nineteenth century, at the height of empire and reform efforts, many philosophers and social thinkers rejected the century-old faith that by using scientific methods one could discover enduring social laws. This belief, called positivism, had emphasized the permanent nature of fundamental laws and had motivated reformers' attempts to perfect legislation based on studies of society. Challenging positivism, the philosophers Wilhelm Dilthey (1833–1911)

in Germany and John Dewey (1859–1952) in the United States declared that because human experience is ever changing, theories and standards cannot be constant or enduring. Just as scientific theory was modified over time, so must social theories and practice react pragmatically to the immediate conditions at hand. In the same vein, German political theorist Max Weber (1864–1920) maintained that the sheer numbers involved in policymaking would often make decisive action by bureaucrats impossible—especially in times of crisis, when a charismatic leader might usurp power because of his ability to make flexible and instinctive decisions. Thus, the development of impartial forms of government such as bureaucracy carried the potential for undermining the rule of law. The turn-of-the-century thinkers, called relativists and pragmatists, influenced thinking about society throughout the twentieth century.

The most radical scholar was the German philosopher Friedrich Nietzsche (1844–1900), who called himself neither a relativist nor a pragmatist but a nihilist. Early in his career he developed the challenging distinction between the "Apollonian," or rational, side of human existence and the "Dionysian" side, with its expression of more primal urges. Nietzsche believed that people generally cling to the rational, Apollonian explanations of life because Dionysian ideas about nature, death, and love such as those found in Greek tragedy are too disturbing. Nietzsche maintained that all assertions of scientific fact and theory were mere illusions. Knowledge of nature had to be expressed in mathematical, linguistic, or artistic representation; truth thus existed only in the representation itself, for humans could never experience unfiltered knowledge of nature or reality. This aspect of Nietzsche's philosophy would lead to the late-twentieth-century school of thought called postmodernism.

Much of Nietzsche's writing consisted of aphorisms—short, disconnected statements of truth or opinion—a form that broke with the logical rigor of traditional Western philosophy. Nietzsche used aphorisms to convey the impression that his ideas were a single individual's unique perspective, not universal truths that thinkers since the Enlightenment had claimed were attainable. Influenced by a range of Asian philosophy that had filtered into Western thought, Nietzsche was convinced that late-nineteenth-century Europe was witnessing the decline of dogmatic truth, most notably in religion. In this belief, he made his announcement that "God is dead, we have killed him." Far from arousing dread, the death of God, according to Nietzsche, would give birth to a joyful quest for new "poetries of life" to replace worn-out religious and middle-class rules. Not the rule-bound bourgeois but the untethered "superman" was Nietzsche's highly influential model.

Nietzsche's thought, especially the idea of the individual as manifesting a vital life energy he called "the will to power," inspired reformers, intellectuals, and students. As a teacher, Nietzsche was so compelling that his first students thought they were hearing another Socrates. But after he contracted syphilis and became insane in the last eleven years of his life, his sister edited his diatribes against middle-class values into attacks on Jews. On her brother's death, she revised his complicated concepts of the will to power and of superman so as to appeal to nationalists and to justify violent anti-Semitism and competition for empire. Nietzsche's legacy was thus a mixed one, influencing not only the ideas of the militarist and racist right-wing political parties but also the works of avant-garde artists and thinkers.

Revolutionizing Science

While philosophers like Nietzsche questioned the ability of traditional science to provide timeless truths, scientific inquiry itself flourished and the scientific method gained authority. Technological breakthroughs and improvements in public hygiene earned science prestige in the population at large even as discoveries by pioneering researchers shook the foundations of traditional scientific certainty. In 1896,

Antoine Becquerel (1852–1908) discovered radioactivity and also suggested the mutability of elements by the rearrangement of their atoms. French chemist Marie Curie (1867–1934) and her husband, Pierre Curie (1859–1906), isolated the elements polonium and radium, which are more radioactive than the uranium Becquerel used. From these and other discoveries, scientists concluded that atoms are composed of subatomic particles moving about a core. Instead of being solid, as scientists had believed since ancient times, atoms are largely empty space and act not as a concrete substance but as an intangible electromagnetic field. German physicist Max Planck (1858–1947) announced his influential quantum theorem in 1900; it demonstrated that a flow of energy is emitted in irregular packets, not in a steady stream.

Scientists had already demonstrated that light has a uniform velocity regardless of the

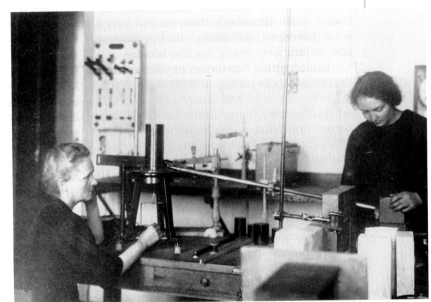

Marie Curie and Her Daughter
Recipient of two Nobel Prizes, Marie Curie came from Poland to western Europe to study science. Curie's extraordinary career made her the epitome of new womanhood; her daughter Irene Joliot-Curie followed her mother into the field and also won a Nobel Prize. Both women died of leukemia caused by their exposure to radioactive materials. Today a reconstruction of the Curie laboratory as a museum contains a display of the intense radioactivity still in the scientific instruments they used a century ago. Given that other women have made important contributions to the sciences and literature, why would the Curies be so celebrated? *ACJC—Archives Curie et Joliot-Curie.*

inner reality—called expressionism—broke with middle-class optimism. Norwegian painter Edvard Munch (1863–1944) aimed "to make the emotional mood ring out again as happens on a gramophone." His painting *The Scream* (1893; see page 958) used twisting lines and a depiction of tortured skeletal human form to convey the horror of modern life that many artists perceived. German avant-garde artist Gabriele Münter (1877–1962) and Russian painter Wassily Kandinsky (1866–1944) opened their "Blue Rider" exhibit of "expressive" work that made use of geometric forms and striking colors. The artists of the Blue Rider group imitated the paintings of children and the mentally ill to achieve their depiction of psychological reality. Kandinsky, who employed these forms and colors to express an inner, spiritual truth, is often credited with producing the first fully abstract paintings around 1909. Shapes in these paintings no longer showed any resemblance to physical objects or reality. The expressionism of Oskar Kokoschka (1886–1980), who worked in Vienna, was even more intense, displaying ecstasy, horror, and hallucinations. As a result, his work—like that of other expressionists and cubists before World War I—was a commercial failure in an increasingly complex marketplace that featured not only museum curators but also professional dealers and art "experts." Trade in art became professionalized, as had medicine and government work before it, even as modern artists sought to shatter traditional norms.

Art Nouveau. Only one innovative style emerged an immediate commercial success: **art nouveau** ("new style") won approval from government, critics, and the masses. Creating everything from dishes and advertising posters to streetlamps and even entire buildings in this new style, designers manufactured beautiful things for the general public. As one French official said about the first version of art nouveau coins issued in 1895, "Soon even the most humble among us will be able to have a masterpiece in his pocket." Adapted from Asian design, the organic and natural elements of art nouveau were meant to offset the fragmentation of factory and office work with images depicting the unified forms of nature. The impersonality of machines was replaced by intertwined vines and flowers and the softly curving bodies of female nudes that would psychologically soothe the individual viewer—an idea that directly contrasted with Picasso's artistic vision. Gustav Klimt (1862–1918), son of a Czech goldsmith, flourished in Viennese high society because his paintings captured the psychological essence of dreamy, sensuous women. Their bodies took the shape of mosaics inspired by Turkish and Egyptian styles and were liberally dotted with gold. Art nouveau was the notable exception to the public outcries over innovations in the visual arts.

Musical Iconoclasm

"Astonish me!" was the motto of modern dance and music, both of which shocked audiences in the concert halls of Europe. American dancer Isadora Duncan (1877–1927) took Europe by storm at the turn of the century when, draped in a flowing garment, she danced barefoot in the first performance of modern dance. Drawing on sophisticated Japanese practices, hers was nonetheless called a primitive style that, as one journalist put it, "lifted from their seats people who had never left theater seats before except to get up and go home." Similarly, experimentation with forms of bodily expression animated the Russian Ballet's 1913 performance of *The Rite of Spring*, by Igor Stravinsky (1882–1971), the tale of an orgiastic dance to the death performed to ensure fertile soil and a bountiful harvest. The choreography of its star, Vaslav Nijinsky (1890–1950) created a scandal. Nijinsky and the troupe struck awkward poses and danced to rhythms intended to sound primitive. At the work's premiere in Paris, one journalist reported that "the audience began shouting its indignation. . . . Fighting actually broke out among some of the spectators." Such controversy made *The Rite of Spring* a box-office hit, although critics called its choreographer a "lunatic" and the music itself "the most discordant composition ever written."

Music had been making this turn for several decades. Having heard Asian musicians at international expositions, French composers like Claude Debussy (1862–1918) transformed their style to reflect non-European musical patterns and themes. The twentieth century opened with *Scheherazade* by Frenchman Maurice Ravel (1875–1937) and *Madame Butterfly* by the Italian composer Giacomo Puccini♦ (1858–1924), both with non-Western subject matter. Using non-Western tonalities, sound became jarring to many listeners. Austrian composer Richard Strauss (1864–1949) upset convention by using several musical keys simultaneously in his compositions. Like the fragmented representation of reality in cubism, atonality or several tonalities at once distorted familiar harmonic patterns for the audience. Strauss's operas *Salome* (1905) and *Elektra* (1909) reflected a modern fascination with violence and obsessive passion. A newspaper critic claimed that Strauss's dissonant works "spit and scratch and claw each other like enraged panthers." The Hungarian pianist Béla Bartók (1881–1945) incorporated folk melodies into his compositions in order to elevate Hungarian ethnicity above the Habsburg Empire's multinationalism. His music disturbed some audiences because of its nationalism and others because of its dissonance.

The early orchestral work of Austrian composer Arnold Schoenberg (1874–1951), who also wrote cabaret music to earn a living, shocked even Strauss. In *Theory of Harmony* (1911), Schoenberg proposed eliminating tonality altogether; a decade later he devised a new twelve-tone scale. "I am aware of having broken through all the barriers of a dated aesthetic ideal," Schoenberg wrote of his music. But new aesthetic models distanced artists like Schoenberg from their audiences, separating high from low culture even more and ending the support of many in the upper classes, who found this music not only incomprehensible but also unpleasant. The artistic elite and the social elite parted ranks. "Anarchist! Nihilist!" shouted Schoenberg's audiences, showing their contempt for modernism and bringing the language of politics into the arts.

Review: How did modernism transform the arts and the world of ideas?

♦**Giacomo Puccini:** JAH koh moh poot CHEE nee

Léon Bakst, *Nijinsky in* L'Après-Midi d'un Faune (Nijinsky in *The Afternoon of a Faun*, 1912)
Theater sets, costume designs, and performance itself resonated with the experimental climate of early-twentieth-century Europe. Léon Bakst, a Russian painter and set designer, used the art nouveau style to capture the faunlike character of ballet star Vaslav Nijinsky. Yet on the eve of World War I, Nijinsky was part of a revolution in ballet that introduced jerky, awkward, pounding movements to indicate the primal nature of dance. How is this depiction of a creative artist new? Compare it to the portrait on page 815. *Wadsworth Atheneum, Hartford. The Ella Gallup Sumner and Mary Catlin Sumner Collection Fund.*

❖ Growing Tensions in Mass Politics

Alongside modernist disturbances in intellectual life, the political atmosphere grew charged despite the advance of liberal opinions that opened the door to growing tolerance and political representation for workingmen.

Networks of communication, especially the development of journalism, enhanced the impact of expanded male suffrage in Europe, leading to the creation of mass politics. Working-class people seemed to come into their own once they had the vote: politicians had to campaign publicly and frequently to win their support. Simultaneously, however, political activists were no longer satisfied with the liberal rights sought by reformers a century earlier, and some strenuously opposed them. Militant nationalists, anti-Semites, socialists, suffragists, and others demanded changes that challenged the liberal status quo. Traditional elites, resentful of the rising middle classes and urban peoples, aimed to stem constitutional processes and the development of modern life. Mass politics soon threatened social unity, especially in central and eastern Europe, where governments often answered reformers' demands with repression.

Labor's Expanding Power

European leaders watched with dismay the rise of working-class political power late in the nineteenth century. Laboring people's growing confidence came in part from expanding educational opportunities. Workers in England, for example, avidly read works by Shakespeare and took literally his calls for political action in the cause of justice. Unions gained members among factory workers, while the Labor and Socialist Parties won seats in parliaments as men in the lower classes received the vote. In Germany, Kaiser William II had allowed antisocialist laws to lapse after dismissing Bismarck as chancellor in 1890. Through continuous grassroots organizing at the local level, the Social Democratic Party, founded by German socialists in 1875, became the largest parliamentary group in the Reichstag by 1912. Similar parties across Europe helped elect workers' representatives into parliaments, where they focused on passing legislation that benefited workers and their families.

Growing strength, especially electoral victories, raised issues for socialists. Some felt uncomfortable sitting with the upper classes in parliaments. Others worried that their participation as heads of governmental ministries would produce reform but compromise their ultimate goal of revolution. Often these deputies refused seats in the government. Between 1900 and 1904, the Second International wrestled with the issue of revisionism—that is, whether socialists should accept such incremental gains in power for laboring people rather than pushing for a violent revolution to overthrow governments. Powerful German Marxists argued that such reformism would only buttress capitalism and rule by the wealthy, who would continue to rule while throwing small crumbs to a few working-class politicians. Stormy discussions divided these German purists, who were shut out of high government positions by conservatives in the military and aristocracy, from the socialist delegates of France, England, and Belgium who had gained influential posts in their governments.

Some working-class parties were forced to operate in exile because they were utterly excluded from mass politics. The Russian government, for instance, outlawed political parties, persecuted activists, and gave the vote to only a limited number of men when it finally introduced a parliament in 1905. Thus, Russian activist V. I. Lenin (1870–1924), who would take power during the Russian Revolution of 1917, migrated to western Europe after his release from confinement to Siberia and earned a reputation among Marxists for hard-hitting journalism and political intrigue. Lenin advanced the theory that a highly disciplined socialist elite—rather than the working class as a whole—would lead a lightly industrialized Russia immediately into socialism. At a 1903 party meeting of Russian Marxists, he briefly gained the upper hand when a group of his opponents walked out of the proceedings. In the ensuing votes, Lenin's supporters eked out slim victories for control of the party. Thereafter, his faction of Bolsheviks, so named after the Russian word for "majority" (which they had temporarily formed in these successful votes), constantly struggled to suppress the Mensheviks, who had been the dominant voice in Russian Marxism until Lenin outmaneuvered them. Neither of these factions, however, had as large a constituency within Russia as the Socialist Revolutionaries, whose objective was to politicize peasants rather than industrial workers as the prelude to a populist revolution. All of these groups prepared for the revolutionary moment through study, propaganda efforts, and organizing—not through the electoral politics successfully employed elsewhere in Europe.

During this same period, anarchists, along with some trade union members known as syndicalists, kept Europe in a panic with their terrorist acts. Anarchism flourished in the less industrial parts of Europe—Russia, Italy, and Spain, where many rural people hoped for a life without the domination of large landowners and government. Members of these groups advocated extreme tactics, including physical violence and even murder. "We want to overthrow the government . . . with violence since it is by the use of violence that they force us to obey," wrote one Italian anarchist. In the 1880s, anarchists bombed stock exchanges, parliaments, and businesses; by the 1890s, they were assassinating heads of state: Spanish premier Antonio Canovas del Castillo in 1897, Empress Elizabeth of Austria-Hungary in 1898, King Umberto of Italy in 1900, and President William McKinley of the United States in 1901, to name a few famous victims. Syndicalists advocated the use of direct action, such as general strikes and sabotage, to bring industry and government under the control of labor unions by paralyzing the economy.

Whether active in representative or authoritarian countries, whether peaceful or violent, working-class organizations caused the upper and middle classes grave anxiety. Despite growing acceptance of representative institutions and despite the spread of education, many in the "best circles" still believed that they alone should hold political power. Politicians from the old landowning and military elites of eastern and central Europe were often the most adamant in their rejection of mass politics, and many of them hoped to reverse the trend toward constitutionalism, worker activism, and reform.

Rights for Women and the Battle for Suffrage

Singly or in groups, women continued to agitate for the benefits of liberalism such as the right to their wages and to parliamentary representation. In most countries women could not vote, exercise free speech, or own property if married. Laws in France, Austria, and Germany curtailed women's political activism and even made their attendance at political meetings a crime. There were many battlefields besides the one for legal rights. German women focused on widening opportunities for female education and for teaching. Their activism aimed to achieve the German cultural ideal of *Bildung*—the belief that education can build character and that individual development has public importance. In several countries, women continued to monitor the regulation of prostitution. Their goal was to prevent prostitutes from being imprisoned on suspicion of having syphilis when men with syphilis faced no such incarceration. Other women took up pacifism as their special cause. Many of them were inspired by Bertha von Süttner's popular book, *Lay Down Your Arms* (1889), which emphasized the terror inflicted on women and families by the ravages of war. (Later, von Süttner would influence Alfred Nobel to institute a peace prize and then win the prize herself in 1903.)

By the 1890s, many activists concluded that only the right to vote would correct the problems caused by male privilege that they were combating in piecemeal fashion. Thereafter, **suffragists** created major organizations involving millions of activists, paid officials, and permanent offices out of the earlier reform groups and women's clubs. Using skills gained from this organizing, British suffrage leader Millicent Garrett Fawcett (1847–1929) pressured members of Parliament for women's right to vote and participated in national and international congresses on behalf of suffrage. Across the Atlantic, American Susan B. Anthony (1820–1906) traveled across the country to speak at mass suffrage rallies, organized suffrage societies, edited a suffragist newspaper, raised money for the movement, and founded the International Woman Suffrage Association in 1904. Its leadership argued that despite men's promises to protect women in exchange for their inequality and disfranchisement, the system of male chivalry had led to exploitation and abuse. Power and privilege—no matter how couched in expressions of goodwill—worked against those without them. "So long as the subjection

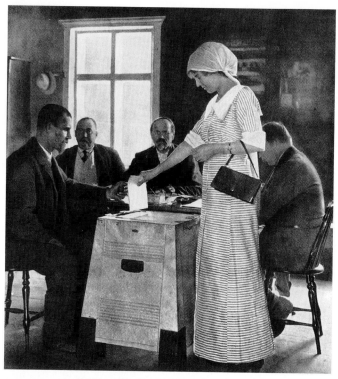

Woman Suffrage in Finland
In 1906, Finnish women became the first in Europe to receive the vote in national elections when the socialist party there—usually opposed to feminism as a middle-class rather than a working-class project—supported woman suffrage. The Finnish vote elated activists in the West, now linked together by many international organizations and ties, because it showed that more than a century of lobbying for reform could lead to gains. What impact might this photograph have had on working-class women and men or middle-class women and men in other European countries? *Mary Evans Picture Library.*

of women endures, and is confirmed by law and custom, . . . women will be victimized," a leading British suffragist claimed. Other activists believed that women had attributes needed to counterbalance masculine qualities in the running of society. The characteristics that came from mothering should shape a country's destiny as much as qualities that stemmed from work in industry and trade, they asserted.

Women's rights activists were predominantly, though not exclusively, from the middle class. Not having to earn a living, they simply had more time to be activists, and a higher level of education allowed them to read the works of feminist theorists such as Harriet

Taylor and John Stuart Mill. They attended theater productions of Norwegian playwright Henrik Ibsen's jarring plays about rebellious heroines or read novels such as Sigrid Undset's *Jenny* (1911), which told the story of a woman artist deliberately choosing motherhood but not marriage. They saw feminism in part through the lens of their middle-class cultural life. But working-class women also participated, though many distrusted the middle class and believed suffrage to be less crucial than women's pressing economic concerns. Textile workers of Manchester, England, for example, put together a vigorous suffrage movement connecting the vote to improved working conditions. Although some union women participated heartily in feminist activism, socialists and suffragists usually differed over issues of class and gender.

In 1906 in Finland, suffragists achieved their first major victory when the Finnish parliament granted women the vote (see the photo on this page). But the failure of parliaments elsewhere in Europe to enact similar legislation provoked some suffragists to violence. Part of the British suffragist movement adopted a militant political style when Emmeline Pankhurst (1858–1928) and her daughters founded the Women's Social and Political Union (WSPU) in the belief that women would accomplish nothing unless they threatened men's property. Starting in 1907, members of the WSPU held parades in English cities, and in 1909 they began a campaign of violence, blowing up railroad stations, slashing works of art, and chaining themselves to the gates of Parliament. Easily disguising themselves as ordinary shoppers in the new consumer economy, they carried little hammers in their handwarming muffs to smash the plate-glass windows of department stores and shops. Parades and demonstrations made suffrage a public spectacle, and outraged men responded by attacking the marchers violently. Arrested for disturbing the peace, the marchers went on hunger strikes in prison. Like striking workers, these women were willing to use confrontational tactics to obtain rights, and like anarchists they were not afraid to damage property. As politicians continued to refuse the vote to women, militant suffragists added to the tensions of urban life.

Liberalism Modified

Governments in western Europe, where liberal institutions were seemingly well entrenched, sought to control the conflicts of the late nineteenth century with pragmatic policies that often struck at liberalism's very foundations. Some politicians and reformers ended laissez-faire trade policies by instituting protective tariffs; others decided that government needed to intervene beyond economic matters and expand social welfare legislation—another break with the liberal idea that governments should not tamper with the free development of either the economy or society. Although many programs addressed urban needs insufficiently, they added to the growing apparatus of the welfare state in which government actively promoted social well-being.

Testing Liberalism in Britain. In 1905, the British Liberal Party won a solid majority in the House of Commons and seemed determined to enact social legislation to gain working-class support. "We are keenly in sympathy with the representatives of Labour," one Liberal politician announced. "We have too few of them in the House of Commons." The government initiated a system of unemployment relief for the unemployed in the National Insurance Act of 1911 funded by new taxes on the wealthy. When the Conservatives in the House of Lords resisted the higher taxation, the Liberal government threatened to add to the number of lords and thus dilute the power and prestige of the nobility. The newcomers, unlike their recalcitrant peers, would guarantee to vote for reform. Under this threat, the lords approved the Parliament Bill of 1911, which eliminated their veto power.

Britain modified liberalism in the social arena, while the Irish question tested its commitment to such liberal values as autonomy, opportunity, and individual rights. In the 1890s, new groups formed to foster Irish culture as a way of heightening the political challenge to Britain's continuing colonization of the country. In 1901, the circle around the modernist poet William Butler Yeats (1865–1939) and the charismatic patriot and actress Maud Gonne (1866–1953) founded the Irish National Theater. Gonne took Irish politics into everyday life by opposing British efforts to woo the loyalty of the young. Every time an English monarch visited Ireland, he or she held special receptions for children. Gonne and other Irish volunteers sponsored competing events, handing out candies and other treats for patriotic youngsters. "Dublin never witnessed anything so marvelous," enthused one home rule supporter, "as the procession . . . of thirty thousand school children who refused to be bribed into parading before the Queen of England."

Speaking Gaelic instead of English, singing Gaelic songs, using Catholicism as a rallying point, and generally reconstructing an "Irish way of life," the promoters of Irish culture threw into question the educated class's preference for everything English. This cultural agenda took political shape with the founding in 1905 of Sinn Fein♦ ("We Ourselves"), a group that strove for complete Irish independence. In 1913, Parliament approved home rule for Ireland, but the outbreak of World War I prevented the legislation from taking effect and cut short dreams of independence.

Unrest in Italy. Liberal Italian nation builders, left with a towering debt from unification and with massive pockets of discontent, drifted more rapidly from liberalism's moorings. Corruption plagued Italy's constitutional monarchy, which had not yet developed either the secure parliamentary system of England or the authoritarian monarchy of Germany to guide its growth. To forge a national consensus in the 1890s, prime ministers used patriotic rhetoric, bribes to gain support from the press, and imperial adventure, culminating in a second thwarted attempt to conquer Ethiopia in 1896. Riots and strikes, followed by armed government repression, erupted, until Giovanni Giolitti (1842–1928), who served as prime minister for three terms between 1903 and 1914, adopted a policy known as *trasformismo* (from the word for "transform"), by which he used bribes, public works programs, and other benefits to localities to influence their deputies in parliament. Political opponents called Giolitti the "Minister of the Underworld" and accused him of preferring to buy the votes of local bosses rather than to spend money to develop the Italian economy. Giolitti's attempt to achieve consensus met

♦**Sinn Fein:** SHIHN FAYN

instead with unrest in the rapidly industrializing cities of Turin and Milan and in the depressed agrarian south. Urban and rural workers alike demanded change, especially of the restricted suffrage that allowed only three million of more than eight million adult men to vote. Giolitti appeased the protesters by instituting social welfare programs and, in 1912, virtually complete manhood suffrage.

Anti-Semitism, Nationalism, and Zionism in Mass Politics

In the two decades leading up to World War I, politicians used anti-Semitism and nationalism to attract support and to win elections. Amid change and complexity, they suggested that anti-Semitism and increased patriotism would easily resolve all problems. At all levels of society, many voters responded enthusiastically. They accepted that Jews were villains responsible for the perils of modern society, and they viewed the nation-state as the hero in the struggle to survive. In both republics and monarchies, anti-Semitism and nationalism played key roles in mass politics by providing a focus for the creation of a radical right increasingly committed to combating the radical left of social democracy. Adopting the imperiled nation as its theme and using the Social Darwinist category of race to identify threats to the nation, the right fundamentally changed the older notion of nationalism based on liberal ideas of constitutional rule and equality of all citizens. Liberals had hoped that voting by the masses would make politics more harmonious as parliamentary debate and compromise smoothed out class differences. The new politics shaped by right-wing leaders—usually representatives of the agrarian nobility, aristocrats who controlled the military, and highly placed clergy—dashed those hopes.

Authoritarianism in Russia. A more traditional form of anti-Semitism existed in Russian politics. The Russian tsar Nicholas II (r. 1894–1917) confronted modern life with unswerving beliefs in orthodoxy in religion, autocracy in politics, and anti-Semitism and Russification in social policy. In this he followed the lead of his father, Alexander III, whose reign had opened in 1881 with an outbreak of vicious pogroms against Jews. Taught as a child to hate Jews, Nicholas believed that any failure in Russian policy was the fault of the Jews. In his reign many high officials eagerly endorsed anti-Semitism to gain his favor. Pogroms became a regular feature of the Easter holiday in Russia, and he explained to his mother that in the face of such violence he would never order soldiers to "fire on Christians to protect Jews." Nicholas increasingly limited where Jews could live and how they could earn a living. Although Nicholas was crueler to Jews than parliamentary politicians of the right in France, Germany, and Austria-Hungary, there was an old-fashioned nature to his cruelty and he did not manipulate parliamentary politics via anti-Semitism. Anti-Semitism was integral to his autocracy and orthodoxy, but it was not yet a tool in modern party politics.

The Dreyfus Affair in France. The most notorious instance of anti-Semitism in mass politics occurred in France, where the political compromise that had created the Third Republic after defeat in the Franco-Prussian War produced institutional fragility. Although an alliance of businessmen, shopkeepers, professionals, and rural property owners backed republican government, destabilizing economic downturns, widespread corruption, attempted coups, and the politics of anti-Semitism threatened political chaos at every turn. The press attributed failures of almost any kind to Jews, and despite an excellent system of primary education promoting literacy and rational thinking, the public was quick to agree. The clergy and monarchists also contributed to the belief that the republic was backed by a conspiracy of Jews.

Amid rising anti-Semitism, a Jewish captain in the French army, Alfred Dreyfus, was charged with spying for Germany in 1894. Dreyfus had attended the elite École Polytechnique in Paris and become an officer in the French military, whose upper echelons were traditionally aristocratic, Catholic, and monarchist. Dreyfus's conviction and harsh exile to Devil's Island failed to stop the espionage, but the republican government adamantly upheld his guilt. Then several newspapers received proof that the army had used perjured testimony and fabricated documents to convict Dreyfus. In 1898, the celebrated French novelist Émile Zola published an article titled *"J'accuse"*♦ (I accuse) on the front page of a Paris daily. Zola cited a list of military lies and cover-ups perpetrated by highly placed government officials to create an illusion of Dreyfus's guilt.

The article was explosive because it named the guilty parties and endorsed liberal government based on truth, tolerance, and the rule of law. "I have but one passion, that of Enlightenment," wrote Zola. His piece led to public riots, quarrels among families and friends, and denunciations of the army, eroding public confidence in the republic and in French institutions. The government finally pardoned Dreyfus in 1899, ousted from office the aristocratic and Catholic officers held responsible, and ended religious teaching orders to ensure a secular public school system that taught liberal values of tolerance. Nonetheless, the Dreyfus Affair made anti-Semitism a standard tool of politics by producing hate-filled slogans that shaped mainstream politics (see the cartoon shown here).

Nationalist and Anti-Semitic Politics in Germany. The ruling elites in Germany also used anti-Semitism as a political weapon to garner support from those who feared the consequences of Germany's sudden and overwhelming industrialization. The agrarian elites, unlike French conservatives, still controlled the highest reaches of government and influenced the kaiser's policy. But the basis of their power was rapidly eroding; agriculture, from which they drew their fortunes and social prestige, declined as a percentage of gross national product from 37 percent in the 1880s to only 25 percent early in the 1900s. As new opportunities lured rural people away from the land and as industrialists grew wealthier, the agrarian elites came to loathe industry and the working class for coming to challenge their entrenched rule. As a Berlin newspaper noted, "The agrarians' hate for cities . . . blinds them to the simplest needs and the most natural demands of the urban population." In contrast to Bismarck's astute wooing of the masses through social programs, William II's aristocracy often encouraged anti-

Public Opinion in the Dreyfus Affair: "Ah! The Dirty Beast!"
The French army used forged documents and perjured testimony to convict Captain Alfred Dreyfus of espionage. In a climate of escalating anti-Semitism, the conviction of a Jew struck many in the public as yet another narrow escape for the country. Only intense detective work by pro-Dreyfus activists and lobbying by Dreyfus's family convinced republican leaders that the system of equal rights was imperiled not by Dreyfus but by the bigotry of the army and those right-wing politicians who had trumped up the case against him. What meaning is conveyed by this illustration? For what audience is it intended? *Photothèque de Musées de la Ville de Paris Toumazet.*

Semitism, both in the corridors of power and in the streets.

Conservatives and a growing radical right claimed that Jews, who made up less than 1 percent of the German population, were responsible for the disruption of traditional society and charged them with being the main beneficiaries of economic change. In the

♦*J'accuse*: zhah KOOZ

1890s, nationalist and anti-Semitic political pressure groups flourished, spewing diatribes against Jews and "new women" but also against Social Democrats, whom they branded as internationalist, socially destructive, and unpatriotic. In the 1890s, the new Agrarian League played to the fears of small farmers by accusing Jews of causing agricultural booms and busts; it thus led other parties to imitate its hate-filled speeches against an array of groups. Expression of extremist hatreds and violent feelings of nationalism rather than rational programs to meet the problems of economic change became regular features of political campaigns. The right invented a modern politics that rejected parliamentary consensus building, relying instead on mouthing slogans and creating enemies.

Ethnic Politics in Austria-Hungary. People in the dual monarchy of Austria-Hungary also expressed their political and economic discontent using militant nationalism and anti-Semitism, but here nationalism was colored by the presence of many competing ethnic groups. Foremost among the nationalists were the Hungarians, who wanted autonomy for themselves while forcibly imposing Hungarian language and culture on all other ethnic groups in Hungary. The demands for greater Hungarian influence (or Magyarization, from Magyars, the principal ethnic group) seemed justified: Budapest was a thriving industrial city, and the export of Hungarian grain from the vast estates of the Hungarian nobility balanced the monarchy's foreign trade deficit. With vociferous nationalism and separatism mounting, the Independence Party disrupted the Hungarian parliament so regularly that it weakened the orderly functioning of the government.

Although capable of causing trouble for the empire, Hungarian nationalists, who mostly represented agrarian wealth, were

Principal Ethnic Groups in Austria-Hungary, c. 1900

vulnerable to the resistance of other nationalities and to the demands of a growing industrial proletariat. On the land, the policy of Magyarization resulted in the formation of strong political groups among the regions ethnic groups—Slovaks, Romanians, and Ruthenians. Strikes erupted to protest horrendous labor conditions, and in the fall of 1905, a hundred thousand activists demonstrated in front of the Hungarian parliament for the vote. In the face of this resistance, Hungarians intensified Magyarization, even decreeing that all tombstones be engraved in Magyar. Emperor Francis Joseph temporarily brought the Hungarian nationalists to bay by threatening to introduce universal manhood suffrage, which would allow both the Magyars' lower-class and non-Magyar opponents to vote. Although numerous nationality groups and the many Jews who settled in Budapest assimilated Magyar ways, the uncompromising and chauvinist nature of Hungarian policies toward both imperial government in Vienna and different ethnic groups within the empire made for instability throughout Austria-Hungary.

Hungarian policies changed the course of Habsburg politics by arousing other nationalists to intensify their demands for rights. Croats, Serbs, and other Slavic groups in the south organized and called for equality with the Hungarians. The central government gave more privileges to the Czechs and allowed them to increase the proportion of Czech officials in the government because growing industrial prosperity in their region gave them more influence. But every step toward recognition of Czech ethnicity provoked outrage from the traditionally dominant ethnic Germans, further straining the political fabric of the empire. When Austria-Hungary decreed in 1897 that government officials in the Czech region of the empire would have to speak Czech as well as German, the Germans rioted.

Tensions mounted as politicians in Vienna linked the growing power of Hungarian and Czech politicians to Jews. A prime instigator of the "politics of the irrational"—as historians often label this ultranationalist and anti-Semitic phenomenon—was Karl Lueger (1844–1910), whose newly formed Christian Social Party attracted members from among the aristocracy, Catholics, artisans, shopkeepers, and white-collar workers. In speeches around the city's neighborhoods, Lueger used hatred to appeal to those groups for whom modern life meant a loss of privilege and security. In 1895, he was elected mayor of Vienna after using rough language and verbal abuse against Jews and ethnic groups in his campaigns. Lueger's ethnic nationalism and anti-Semitism attracted raucous crowds and destabilized the multinational coexistence on which Austria-Hungary was based. By the turn of the century, many politicians were harping on Jewishness as a symbol in their election campaigns, calling Jews the "sucking vampire" of modernity and blaming them for the tumult of migration, social dislocation, and just about anything else people did not like. Politics became a thing not of parliaments but of the streets, bloated with racism and inflaming the atmosphere.

The Jewish Response to Anti-Liberal Politics.

The prevailing view in the West that Jews were inferior to Christians provoked varying responses from Jews themselves. Jews in western Europe had responded to increased legal tolerance by moving out of Jewish neighborhoods, intermarrying with Christians, and in some cases converting to Christianity—practices known as assimilation. Many Jews also favored the German Empire because classical German culture seemed more appealing than the Catholic ritual promoted by Austria-Hungary. By contrast, Jews in Russia and Romania were increasingly singled out for persecution, legally disadvantaged, and forced to live in ghettos. If Jews from these countries wanted refuge, the nearby cities of central and eastern Europe offered opportunity. By 1900, many Jews were prominent in cultural and economic affairs in cities across the continent even as others were discriminated against and victimized elsewhere. Some Jews adopted the cosmo-

politan culture of Vienna or Magyar ways in Budapest; for example, despite escalating anti-Semitism, the celebrated composer Gustav Mahler (1860–1911), the budding writer Franz Kafka, and the pioneer of psychoanalysis Sigmund Freud flourished in Habsburg society.

Most Jews, however, were not so accomplished or prosperous as these cultural giants, and their migration to the United States and other countries in reaction to both pogroms and economic change filled towns and cities with poor day laborers and struggling artisans (Map 25.1). Amid this vast migration

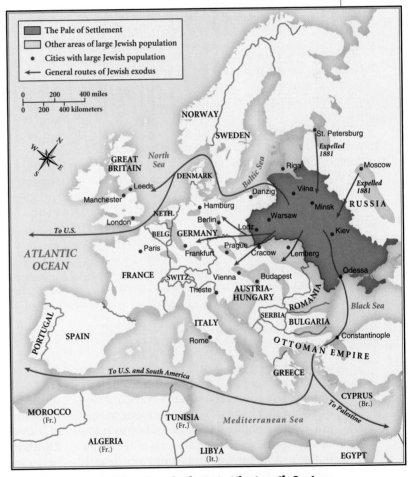

MAP 25.1 Jewish Migrations in the Late Nineteenth Century
Pogroms in eastern Europe, increasingly violent anti-Semitism across the continent, and the search for opportunity led Jews to many parts of the world. Between 1890 and 1914 some five million Jews left Russia alone. They migrated to European cities and, as Zionism progressed, to Palestine. The development of manufacturing in the United States offered a wealth of new opportunities, especially the chance to live where the rule of law was somewhat better established than in Russia. Why did the migration of Jews vary from region to region?

Leon Pinsker Calls for a Jewish State

In 1882 the Ukrainian physician Leon Pinsker published a pamphlet called Auto-Emancipation *in which he analyzed the situation of the Jews in Europe. This pamphlet convinced some in Europe—most notably Theodor Herzl—that Jews could never be assimilated to European culture no matter how many dropped their religion in favor of Christian ways. This pamphlet ultimately led to the migration of Jews to Palestine, despite Pinsker's own conviction that the Middle East was not necessarily the right place for creating a Jewish nation.*

This is the kernel of the problem, as we see it: *the Jews comprise a distinctive element among the nations under which they dwell, and as such can neither assimilate nor be readily digested by any nation.* . . .

A fear of the Jewish ghost has passed down the generations and the centuries. First a breeder of prejudice, later . . . it culminated in Judeophobia.

Judeophobia is a psychic aberration. As a psychic aberration it is hereditary, and as a disease transmitted for two thousand years it is incurable. . . .

The Jews are aliens who can have no representatives, because they have no country. Because they have none, because their home has no boundaries within which they can be entrenched, their misery too is boundless. . . .

. . . If we would have a secure home, give up our endless life of wandering and rise to the dignity of a nation in our own eyes and in the eyes of the world, we must, above all, not dream of restoring ancient Judaea. We must not attach ourselves to the place where our political life was once violently interrupted and destroyed. The goal of our present endeavors must be not the "Holy Land," but a land of our own. We need nothing but a large tract of land for our poor brothers, which shall remain our property and from which no foreign power can expel us. There we shall take with us the most sacred possessions which we have saved from the shipwreck of our former country, the *God-idea* and the *Bible.* It is these alone which have made our old fatherland the Holy Land, and not Jerusalem or the Jordan. Perhaps the Holy Land will again become ours. If so, all the better, but *first of all,* we must determine—and this is the crucial point—what country is accessible to us, and at the same time adapted to offer the Jews of all lands who must leave their homes a secure and indisputed refuge, capable of productivization. . . .

Source: Robert Chazan and Marc Lee Raphael, eds., *Modern Jewish History: A Source Reader* (New York: Schocken Books, 1974), 161, 163, 165–66, 169–71, 171–74.

and continued persecution, a spirit of Jewish nationalism arose. "Why should we be any less worthy than any other . . . people," one Jewish leader asked. "What about our nation, our language, our land?" Jews began organizing resistance to pogroms and anti-Semitic politics, and intellectuals drew on Jewish folklore, language, customs, and history to establish a national identity parallel to that of other Europeans.

In the 1880s, the Ukrainian physician Leon Pinsker (1821–1891), seeing the Jews' lack of national territory as fundamental to the persecution heaped on them, advocated the migration of Jews to Palestine (see his

statement above). In 1896, Theodor Herzl (1860–1904), strongly influenced by Pinsker, published *The Jewish State*, which called not simply for migration but for the creation of a Jewish nation-state, a goal known as **Zionism**. A Hungarian-born Jew, Herzl experienced anti-Semitism firsthand as a Viennese journalist and a writer in Paris during the Dreyfus Affair. He became driven to found a Jewish state, searching Europe for financial backing, technical advice, and a political structure for the venture. His constituency should have been prosperous Jews, but many of them had assimilated and thought his ideas mad. However, with the support of poorer eastern European Jews, he succeeded in calling the first International Zionist Congress (1897), which endorsed settlement in Palestine. By 1914, some eighty-five thousand Jews had moved into Palestine.

> **Review:** What were the points of tension in European political life at the turn of the century?

❖ European Imperialism Contested

Inflamed nationalism across the West made it difficult for nations to calm domestic politics and the traumas of modern industrial life. In 1897, the poet Rudyard Kipling (1865–1936) marked the fiftieth anniversary of Queen Victoria's reign with "Recessional," a somber poem comparing the British Empire to ancient cities whose glory had long since faded:

> Far-called our navies melt away—
> On dune and headland sinks the fire—
> Lo, all our pomp of yesterday
> Is one with Nineveh and Tyre.

Kipling's turn to pessimistic sentimentalism was apt, first because holding imperial territory was aggravating relations among the European powers and second because colonized peoples were challenging European control. Japan had become an Asian power, and nationalist movements for independence were gaining strength, a development that eventually led to new rebellions against European rule.

The Trials of Empire

After centuries of global expansion, imperial adventure soured for Britain and France as the twentieth century opened. Such newcomers as Italy and Germany had difficulty acquiring territory outside Europe, and they fought for a place at the imperial table. Increasing competition among a greater number of nations for colonies and escalating tensions between the French and British in Africa and elsewhere raised serious questions about the future of imperialism. "Where thirty years ago there existed one sensitive spot in our relations with France, or Germany, or Russia," the British economist J. A. Hobson wrote in 1902, "there are a dozen now; diplomatic strains are of almost monthly occurrence between the Powers." For their part, colonized people were fighting back with stubborn vigor.

Boer War. Accustomed to crushing resistance to their imperial ambitions, the British experienced a bloody defeat in 1896, when Cecil Rhodes, prime minister of the Cape Colony in southern Africa, directed a raid into the neighboring territory of the Transvaal. The foray was intended to stir up trouble between the Boers, descendants of early Dutch settlers, and the more recent immigrants from Britain who had come to southern Africa in search of gold and other riches. Rhodes hoped the raid would justify a British takeover of the Transvaal and the Orange Free State, which the Boers independently controlled. The Boers, however, easily routed the raiders, forcing Rhodes to resign in disgrace.

Other Europeans gloated over the British loss. Kaiser William II telegraphed his congratulations to the Transvaal president for "maintaining the independence of the country against attacks from without." Unaccustomed to defeat, the British government did not accept it easily: for the next three years it fought the **Boer War** directly against the Transvaal and the Orange Free State, causing unease and even outrage in Britain. As foreign correspondents unexpectedly flocked to South Africa, they reported on appalling bloodshed, heavy casualties, and the unfit condition of the average British soldier. Most alarmingly to those who liked to think of Britain as the most civilized country in the world, news arrived back in the capital of rampant disease and inhumane treatment of South Africans herded into a shocking and unfamiliar institution—the concentration camp, which became the graveyard of tens of thousands. Back home in England, right-minded thinkers began to see imperialism as barbarism. Britain finally annexed the area after defeating the Boers in 1902, but the cost of war in money, destruction, demoralization, and loss of life was enormous (Map 25.2).

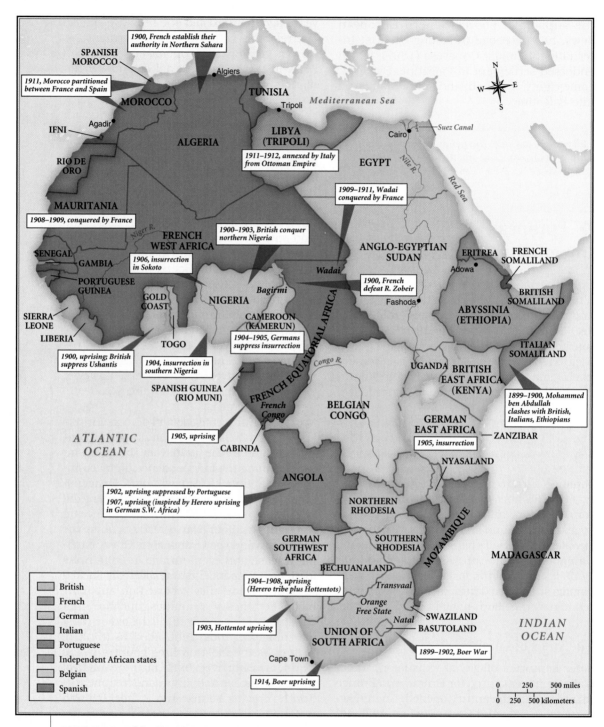

MAP 25.2 Africa in 1914

Uprisings intensified in Africa in the early twentieth century as Europeans tried both to consolidate their rule through bureaucratization and military action and to extract more wealth from the Africans. At the same time as Europeans were putting down the rebellions against their rule, a pan-African movement arose, attempting to unite Africans as one people. As in Asia and the Middle East, the more the colonial powers tried to impose their will, the greater the political forces—including the force of political ideas—that took shape against them. What impression does this map give of the status of European imperialism in Africa? Compare it to the map of Africa in chapter 24.

Newcomers Face Setbacks. Almost simultaneously, Spain lost Cuba, Puerto Rico, and the Philippines to the United States as a result of its defeat in the Spanish-American War of 1898. The United States was not a novice to imperialism. It had successfully crushed native Americans, killing many and confining survivors to reservations, and in 1898 it annexed Hawaii. Both Cuba and the Philippines had begun vigorous efforts to free themselves from Spanish rule. U.S. politicians saw their chance. Urged on by the expansionist-minded Theodore Roosevelt, then assistant secretary of the navy, and the inflammatory daily press, the United States intervened to help the independence movements. Instead of allowing the independence that victory called for, however, the U.S. government annexed Puerto Rico and Guam and bought the Philippines from Spain. Cuba was theoretically independent, but the United States monitored its activities.

War revealed the fragility of established European empires and the unpredictability of imperial fortunes. Even the triumphant United States, encouraged by Kipling to "take up the white man's burden" by bringing the benefits of Western civilization to those liberated from Spain, had to wage a bloody war against the Filipinos, who wanted independence, not another imperial ruler. Reports of American brutality in the Philippines, where some 200,000 local people were slaughtered, further disillusioned the Western public, who liked to imagine native peoples joyously welcoming the bearers of civilization.

Despite these setbacks, the emerging powers had an emotional stake in gaining colonies. In the early twentieth century, Italian public figures bragged about the Italians becoming Nietzschean supermen by conquering Africa and restoring Italy to its ancient position of world domination. After a disastrous war against Ethiopia in 1896, Italy won a costly victory over the Ottoman Empire in Libya. These wars roused Italian hopes for national grandeur only to dash them when such grandeur proved elusive or costly.

Germany likewise demanded a place at the imperial table and an end to the virtual British-French monopoly of colonial power. Foremost among the new competitors for empire, German bankers and businessmen were

ensconced throughout Asia, the Middle East, and Latin America. Several centuries after other European states, Germany sent linguists, ethnographers, and museum curators to study other cultures and obtain their treasures. Despite some successes, there was no unalloyed glory. Germany, too, met humiliation and constant problems, especially in its dealings with Britain and France and with those local peoples abroad who resisted the German takeover in Africa and elsewhere. As Italy and Germany aggressively pursued new territory, the rules set

The Struggle for Ethiopia, 1896

for imperialism at the Congress of Berlin a generation earlier gave way to increasingly heated rivalry and nationalist fury.

Japan Victorious. Japan's rise as an imperial power further eroded Europeans' confident approach to imperialism. The Japanese had started building an empire by invading the Chinese island of Formosa (present-day Taiwan) in 1874 and continued by forcing trading treaties on Korea in 1876 (Map 25.3). In 1894, Japan sparked the Sino-Japanese War against China, which ended China's domination of Korea. The European powers, alarmed at Japan's victory, forced it to relinquish other gains, a move that outraged and affronted the Japanese. Japan's insecurity had risen with Russian expansion to the east and south in Asia. Pushing into eastern Asia, the Russians had built the Trans-Siberian Railroad through Manchuria, sent millions of Russian settlers eastward, and sponsored anti-Japanese groups in Korea, making the Korean peninsula appear, as a Japanese military leader put it, like "a dagger thrust at the heart of Japan." Angered by the continuing presence of Russian troops in Manchuria, the Japanese attacked tsarist forces at Port Arthur in 1904.

The conservative Russian military proved inept in the ensuing Russo-Japanese War,

because of growing resistance to the empire and to European influence. Just as the Habsburgs used the transnational appeal of Catholicism to quash nationalist aspirations, Sultan Abdul Hamid II (r. 1876–1909) tried to revitalize the multiethnic empire by using Islam to counteract the rising nationalism of the Serbs, Bulgarians, and Macedonians. Instead, he unwittingly provoked a burgeoning Turkish nationalism in Constantinople itself. Turkish nationalists rejected the sultan's pan-Islamic solution and built their movement on the uniqueness of their culture, history, and language, as many European ethnic groups were doing. Using the findings of Western scholarship, they first traced the history of the group they called Turks to change the word *Turk* from one of derision to one of pride. Nationalists also tried to purge their language of words from Arabic and Persian, and they popularized the folklore of rural Turkish peoples scattered across territories from eastern Europe through Asia. The events of 1904–1905 electrified these nationalists with the vision of a modern Turkey becoming "the Japan of the Middle East," as they called it. In 1908, a group of nationalists called the Young Turks took control of the government in Constantinople, which had been fatally weakened by nationalist agitation and by the empire's economic dependence on Western financiers and businessmen.

The Young Turks' triumph motivated other groups in the Middle East and the Balkans to demand an end to Ottoman domination in their regions as well. These groups adopted Western values and platforms, and some, such as the Egyptians, had strong contingents of feminist-nationalists who mobilized women to work for independence. But the Young Turks, often aided by European powers with financial and political interests in the region, brutally tried to repress the uprisings in Egypt, Syria, and the Balkans that their own success had encouraged.

The rebellions became part of the tumult shaping international relations in the decade before World War I. Empires, whether old or young, were the scene of growing resistance in the wake of Japanese, Russian, and Turkish events. In German East Africa, colonial forces countered native resistance in 1905 with a scorched-earth policy of destroying homes, livestock, food, and other resources. The Germans eventually killed more than 100,000 Africans there. The French closed the University of Hanoi, executed Indochinese intellectuals, and deported thousands of suspected nationalists merely to maintain a tenuous grip on Indochina. A French general stationed there summed up the fears of many colonial rulers in the new century: "The gravest fact of our actual political situation in Indochina is not the recent trouble in Tonkin [or] the plots undertaken against us but in the muted but growing hatred that our subjects show toward us."

Review: Why did events in overseas empires from the 1890s on prove discouraging to many Europeans back home?

❖ Roads to War

International developments simultaneously aggravated competition among the great powers and caused Western nationalism in its many varieties to swell. In the spring of 1914, U.S. president Woodrow Wilson (1856–1924) sent his trusted adviser Colonel House to Europe to assess the rising tensions among the major powers. "It is militarism run stark mad," House reported, adding that he foresaw an "awful cataclysm" ahead. Government spending on what people called the "arms race" had stimulated European economies; but arms were not stockpiled for economic growth only. As early as the mid-1890s, one socialist had called the situation a "cold war" because the hostile atmosphere made physical combat seem imminent. By 1914, the air was even more charged, with militant nationalism in the Balkan states and conflicts in domestic politics also setting the stage for war. Although historians have long debated whether World War I could have been avoided, they have never reached a consensus. Considering the feverish background of prewar change, they have had to content themselves with tracing the steps Europeans took along the road toward mass destruction.

Competing Alliances and Clashing Ambitions

As the twentieth century opened, the Triple Alliance that Bismarck had negotiated among Germany, Austria-Hungary, and Italy confronted an opposing alliance between France and Russia, created in the 1890s. The wild card in the diplomatic scenario was Great Britain, traditional enemy of France, nowhere more than in the contest for colonial power. Constant rivals in Africa, Britain and France edged to the brink of war in 1898 at Fashoda in the Sudan. The French government, however, backed away and both nations were frightened into getting along for mutual self-interest. To prevent another Fashoda, they entered into secret agreements, the first of which (1904) guaranteed British claims in Egypt and French claims in Morocco. This agreement marked the beginning of the British-French alliance called the **Entente Cordiale**. Despite the alliance, Britain's response to a European war remained in question; even French statesmen feared that their ally might remain neutral.

Germany's Imperial Demands. Germany under Kaiser William II became dissatisfied with its international status and inflamed rather than calmed the diplomatic atmosphere. Bismarck had maintained a policy of proclaiming Germany a "satisfied" nation, working to balance great-power interests, and avoiding the draining fight for colonies. To the contrary, the kaiser, emboldened by Germany's growing industrial might, strode onto the imperial stage with a big appetite for world power. Convinced of British hostility toward France, William II used the opportunity presented by the defeat of France's ally Russia to contest French claims in Morocco. A man who boasted and blustered and was easily prodded to rash actions by his advisers, William landed in Morocco in 1905, thus challenging French predominance in what became known as the First Moroccan Crisis. To resolve the situation, an international conference met in Spain in 1906, where Germany confidently expected to gain concessions and new territories. Instead the powers, now including the United States, decided to support French rule. The French

and British military, faced with German aggression in Morocco, drew closer together.

Germany found itself weak diplomatically and strong economically, a situation that made its leaders more determined to compete for territory abroad. When the French finally took over Morocco in 1911, Germany triggered the Second Moroccan Crisis by sending a gunboat to the port of Agadir and demanding concessions from the French. This time no power—not even Austria-Hungary—backed the German move. No one acknowledged this dominant country's might, nor did the constant demands for recognition encourage anyone to do so. The British and French now made binding military provisions for the deployment of their forces in case of war, thus strengthening the Entente Cordiale. Smarting from its setbacks on the world stage, Germany refocused its sights on its role on the continent and on its own alliances.

Crises in the Balkans. Germany's bold territorial claims, along with public uncertainty about the binding force of alliances, unsettled Europe, particularly the Balkans. German statesmen began envisioning the creation of a **Mitteleuropa**♦—a term that literally meant "central Europe" but that in their minds also included the Balkans and Turkey. The Habsburgs, now firmly backed by Germany, judged that expansion into the Balkans and the resulting addition of even more ethnic groups would weaken the claims of any single ethnic minority in the Dual Monarchy. Russia, however, saw itself as the protector of Slavs in the region and wanted to replace the Ottomans as the dominant Balkan power, especially after Japan had crushed its hopes for expansion to the east. Austria's swift annexation of Bosnia-Herzegovina during the Young Turk revolt in 1908 enraged not only the Russians but the Serbs as well, because these southern Slavs wanted Bosnia as part of an enlarged Serbia. The Balkans thus whetted many appetites (Map 25.4).

Even without the greedy eyes cast on the Balkans by outside powers, the situation would have been extremely complex given the tensions created by political modernity. The

♦**Mitteleuropa:** miht loy ROH pah

An Historian Promotes Militant Nationalism

As the nineteenth century came to an end, competitive nationalism in preparation for war was everywhere, even in classrooms. History had developed into a "science" by this time, and historians were supposed to be neutral, basing their conclusions on solid, documentary evidence and erasing all trace of religious or national bias from their work. In the climate of military buildup, competition for empire, and a prowar spirit, the goal of dispassionate objectivity weakened. Supporting his nation was a driving force in the writing and teaching, of, among others, Heinrich von Trietschke of the University of Berlin, who delivered his lectures glorifying Germany's wars to throngs of cheering students and army officers.

The next essential function of the State is the conduct of war. The long oblivion into which this principle had fallen is a proof of how effeminate the science of government had become in civilian hands. In our century sentimentality was dissipated by Clausewitz, but a one-sided materialism arose in its place, after the fashion of the Manchester school, seeing in man a biped creature, whose destiny lies in buying cheap and selling dear. It is obvious that this idea is not compatible with war, and it is only since the last war [1870–71] that a sounder theory arose of the State and its military power.

Without war no State could be. All those we know of arose through war, and the protection of their members by armed force remains their primary and essential task. War, therefore, will endure to the end of history, as long as there is multiplicity of States. The laws of human thought and of human nature forbid any alternative, neither is one to be wished for. The blind worshipper of an eternal peace falls into the error of isolating the State, or dreams of one which is universal, which we have already seen to be at variance with reason.

Even as it is impossible to conceive of a tribunal above the State, which we have recognized as sovereign in its very essence, so it is likewise impossible to banish the idea of war from the world. It is a favourite fashion of our time to instance England as particularly ready for peace. But England is perpetually at war; there is hardly an instant in her recent history in which she has not been obliged to be fighting somewhere. The great strides which civilization makes against barbarism and unreason are only made actual by the sword.

Source: Heinrich Treitschke, *Politics*, Hans Kohn, ed., Blanche Duddale and Torben de Bille, trans. (New York: Harcourt, 1965), 37–38.

Naval construction also played a sensational role in nationalist politics. To defend against the new powerful, accurate weaponry, ships were made out of metal rather than wood after the mid-nineteenth century. In 1905, the English launched H.M.S. *Dreadnought*, a warship with unprecedented firepower and the centerpiece of the British navy's plan to construct at least seven battleships per year. Germany followed British navy building step by step and made itself a great land and sea power. Grand Admiral Alfred von Tirpitz (1849–1930) encouraged the insecure William II to view the navy as the essential ingredient in making Germany a world power and oversaw an immense buildup of the fleet. Tirpitz admired the American naval theorist Alfred Thayer Mahan (1840–1914) and planned to build naval bases as far away as the Pacific, following Mahan's conclusion that command of the seas determined international power. The German drive to build battleships further motivated Britain to ally with France in the Entente Cordiale. Britain raised its annual naval spending from $50 million in the 1870s to $130 million in 1900; Germany, from $8.75 million to $37.5 million; France, from $37 million to $62.5 million (Figure 25.1 on page 995). The Germans announced the fleet buildup as "a peaceful policy," but, like the British buildup, it led only to a hostile international climate and intense competition in weapons manufacture.

Public relations campaigns and internal politics were important to shaping military policy (see "An Historian Promotes Militant Nationalism" on page 996). When critics of the arms race suggested a temporary "naval holiday" to stop British and German building, British officials opposed the moratorium by warning that it "would throw innumerable men on the pavement." Colonial leagues of those pushing for imperial expansion, nationalist organizations, and other patriotic groups lobbied for military spending, while enthusiasts in government publicized large navies as beneficial to international trade and domestic industry. To enlarge the German fleet, Tirpitz made sure the press connected naval buildup to the cause of national power and pride. The press accused Social Democrats, who wanted an equitable tax system more proportionate to wealth, of being unpatriotic. The Conservative Party in Great Britain, eager for more battleships, made popular the slogan "We want eight and we won't wait." The remarks of a French military leader typified the sentiments of the time, even among the public at large. When asked in 1912 about his predictions for war and peace, he responded enthusiastically, "We shall have war. I will make it. I will win it."

1914: War Erupts

June 28, 1914, began as an ordinary, even happy day not only for Freud's patient the Wolf-Man but also for the Austrian archduke Francis Ferdinand and his wife, Sophie, as they ended a state visit to Sarajevo in Bosnia. The archduke, in full military regalia, was riding in a motorcade to bid farewell to various officials when a group of young Serb nationalists threw bombs in an unsuccessful assassination attempt. The full danger did not register, and after a stop the archduke and his wife set out again. In the crowd was another nationalist, Gavrilo Princip, who for several weeks had traveled clandestinely to reach this destination, dreaming of reuniting his homeland of Bosnia-Herzegovina with Serbia and smuggling weapons with him to accomplish his end. The unprotected and unsuspecting Austrian couple became Princip's victims, as he shot both dead.

Some in the Habsburg government saw an opportunity to put down the Serbians once and for all. Evidence showed that Princip had received arms and information from Serbian officials, who directed a terrorist organization from within the government. Endorsing a quick defeat of Serbia, German statesmen and military leaders urged the Austrians to be unyielding and reiterated promises of support in case of war. The Austrians sent an ultimatum to the Serbian government, demanding public disavowals of terrorism, suppression of terrorist groups, and the participation of Austrian officials in an investigation of the crime. The ultimatum was severe. "You are setting Europe ablaze," the Russian foreign minister remarked of the Austrians' humiliating demands made on a sovereign state. Yet the Serbs were conciliatory, accepting all the terms except the presence of Austrian officials in the investigation. Kaiser William was pleased: "A great

Archduke Francis Ferdinand and His Wife in Sarajevo, June 1914
Archduke Francis Ferdinand, heir to the Austro-Hungarian monarchy, was a thorn in the side of many politicians because he did not want to favor Hungarian interests over other ethnic ones in his kingdom. His own family life was also unusual for royalty in those days in that his wife, Sophie, and he had married for love and did not like to be apart. Thus, the couple were traveling together to Bosnia in 1914 and were jointly assassinated—the immediate prelude to the outbreak of World War I. How was the assassination of the archduke and his wife related to the other factors that led to World War I? *Mary Evans Picture Library.*

Legend:
- Triple Alliance, 1882–1915
- Triple Entente, 1907–1917

MAPPING THE WEST   Europe at the Outbreak of World War I, August 1914

All the powers expected a great, swift victory when war broke out. Sharing borders, many saw a chance to increase their territories; and as rivals for trade and empire, they were almost all convinced that war would bring them many advantages. But if European nations appeared well prepared and invincible at the start of the war, relatively few would survive the conflict intact. Where are the particular "hot spots" in Europe in which resentments and conflicting ambitions were centered?

moral success for Vienna! All reason for war is gone." His relief proved unfounded. Austria-Hungary, confident of German backing, used the Serbs' resistance to only one of the ultimatum's terms as the pretext for declaring war against Serbia on July 28.

Complex and ineffectual maneuvering now consumed statesmen, some of whom tried very hard to avoid war. The tsar and the kaiser sent pleading letters to one another not to start a European war. The British foreign secretary proposed an all-European conference, but to no avail. Germany displayed firm support for Austria in hopes of convincing the French and British to shy away from the war. The failure of either to fight, German officials believed, would subsequently keep Russia from mobilizing. Additionally, German military leaders had become fixed on fighting a short, preemptive war that would provide territorial gains leading toward the goal of a Mitteleuropa; imposing martial law as part of such a war would justify arresting the leadership of the German Social Democratic Party, which threatened conservative rule.

The European press caught the war fever of the expansionist, imperialist, and other pro-war organizations, even as many governments were torn over what to do. Likewise, military leaders, especially in Germany and Austria-Hungary, promoted mobilization rather than diplomacy in the last days of July. The Austrians declared war and then ordered mobilization on July 31 without fear of a Russian attack. They did so in full confidence of German military aid, because as early as 1909 the German chief of staff Helmuth von Moltke had promised that his government would defend Austria-Hungary, believing Russia would not dare intervene. But Nicholas II ordered the Russian army to mobilize in defense of Russia's Slavic allies the Serbs. Encouraging the Austrians to attack Serbia, the German general staff mobilized on August 1. France declared war by virtue of its agreement to aid its ally Russia, and when Germany violated Belgian neutrality on its way to invade France, Britain entered the war on the side of France and Russia.

> **Review:** What were the major factors leading to the outbreak of World War I?

Conclusion

Rulers soon forgot their last-minute hesitations in the general celebration that erupted with the war. "Old heroes have reemerged from the books of legends," wrote a Viennese actor after watching the troops march off. "A mighty wonder has taken place, we have become *young*." Both sides exulted, believing in certain victory. A short conflict, people maintained, would resolve tensions ranging from the rise of the working class to political problems caused by global imperial competition. Disturbances in private life and challenges to established certainties in ideas would disappear, it was believed, in the crucible of war. German military men saw war as an opportune moment to round up social democrats and reestablish the traditional deference of an agrarian society. Liberal government based on rights and constitutions, some believed, had simply gone too far in its production of new groups aspiring to full citizenship and political autonomy.

Even as modernity seemed to be an enemy, it had also given rise to the new technology, mass armies, and techniques of persuasion to support military buildup that moved the elites to embrace war. The arms race had stimulated militant nationalism and brought many Europeans to favor war over peace. Modernity had helped blaze the path to war: *The Rite of Spring*, the ballet that opened in Paris in 1913, had taken as its theme the ritualistic attraction of death. Facing continuing violence in politics, incomprehensibility in the arts, and problems in the industrial order, Europeans had come to believe that war would save them from the perils of modernity. The sense of decline and the worry over imperial tensions that so characterized the years before 1914 would end once and for all. "Like men longing for a thunderstorm to relieve them of the summer's sultriness," wrote one Austrian official, "so the generation of 1914 believed in the relief that war might bring." Such a possibility caused Europeans to rejoice. But tragically, their elation was short-lived. Instead of bringing the refreshment of summer rain, war opened an era of political turmoil, widespread suffering, massive human slaughter, and even greater doses of modernity.

Suggested References

Private Life in the Modern Age

Historians are engaged in serious study of the transformations of everyday life brought about by industrial and imperial advance in the early twentieth century. Women's striving for personal autonomy was expressed in dozens of novels about the "new woman," including the famous *Keys to Happiness*, now available in an English translation.

Duberman, Martin, Martha Vicinus, and George Chauncey Jr. *Hidden from History: Reclaiming the Gay and Lesbian Past.* 1989.

Gillis, John. *A World of Their Own Making: Myth, Ritual, and the Quest for Family Values.* 1996.

Roberts, Mary Louise. *Disruptive Acts: The New Woman in Fin-de-Siècle France.* 2002.

*Verbitskaya, Anastasia. *The Keys to Happiness.* 1908–1913 [trans. by Beth Holmgren and Helen Goscilo, 1999].

Walkowitz, Judith. *City of Dreadful Delight: Narratives of Sexual Danger in Late-Victorian London.* 1993.

Modernity and the Revolt in Ideas

Some of the most controversial historical writing sees the road to World War I as paved with cultural conflict. Many of the studies here suggest that new forms of art, music, dance, and philosophy were as central to the challenges Europe faced as were ethnic, economic, and international turmoil. The Web offers good cultural sites for this important period.

Art nouveau: **http://www.nga.gov/feature/nouveau/nouveau.htm**.

Eksteins, Modris. *Rites of Spring: The Great War and the Birth of the Modern Age.* 1989.

Everdell, William R. *The First Moderns: Profiles in the Origins of Twentieth-Century Thought.* 1997.

Kern, Steven. *The Culture of Space and Time, 1880–1918.* 1983.

*Mann, Thomas. *Buddenbrooks.* 1901.

Nineteenth- and twentieth-century philosophy: **http://www.epistemelinks.com/index.asp**.

Safranski, Rüdiger. *Nietzsche: A Philosophical Biography.* 2002.

Staller, Natasha. *A Sum of Destructions: Picasso's Cultures and the Creation of Cubism.* 2001.

Growing Tensions in Mass Politics

Historians are uncovering the dramatic changes in political life and the rise of mass politics across Europe, including the development of suffragist movements. Rose shows that mass education gave the working class a foundation in the works of Shakespeare and other classical writers. Still another major phenomenon was a spreading political hatred and the rise of aggressive nationalism to replace nationalism based on constitutional values.

Burns, Michael. *Dreyfus: A Family Affair.* 1992.

Chickering, Roger. *We Men Who Feel Most German: A Cultural Study of the Pan-German League, 1886–1914.* 1984.

Dennis, David B. *Beethoven in German Politics, 1870–1989.* 1996.

Kent, Susan. *Gender and Power in Britain, 1640–1990.* 1999.

Kornberg, Jacques. *Theodor Herzl: From Assimilation to Zionism.* 1993.

* Primary source.

Lendavi, Paul. *The Hungarians: A Thousand Years of Victory in Defeat.* 2003.

Rose, Jonathan. *Intellectual Life of the British Working Class.* 2001.

European Imperialism Contested

In the midst of raucous political and social debate, the European powers faced growing resistance to their domination and increasingly serious setbacks. Many historians now judge Europe to have played a less commanding role in the rest of the world than the leading empires claimed. Imperial instability, as some studies show, paved the road to war. The fascination with the major non-Western contender—Japan—can be traced on the Japanese history Web site.

Japanese history: **http://www.csuohio.edu/history/japan/index.html**.

Gooch, John, ed. *The Boer War: Direction, Experiences, Image.* 2000.

Kansu, Aykut. *The Revolution of 1908 in Turkey.* 1997.

*Pruitt, Ida. *A Daughter of Han: The Autobiography of a Chinese Working Woman.* 1945.

Sinha, Mrinalini. *Colonial Masculinity: The "Manly Englishman" and the "Effeminate Bengali" in the Late Nineteenth Century.* 1995.

Weeks, Theodore R. *Nation and State in Late Imperial Russia: Nationalism and Russification on the Western Frontier.* 1996.

Roads to War

Why World War I broke out remains a widely debated topic. There are always newcomers to the discussion devoted to assessing the responsibility for the war's beginning, some fixing on a single country and others investigating the full range of diplomatic, military, social, and economic conditions. Trenches on the Web looks at military conditions before war erupted.

Ascher, Abraham. *The Revolution of 1905: Russia in Disarray.* 1988.

Clark, Christopher. *William II.* 2000.

Hermann, David G. *The Arming of Europe and the Making of the First World War.* 1996.

Hobson, Rolf. *Imperialism at Sea: Naval Strategic Thought, the Ideology of Sea Power, and the Tirpitz Plan, 1875–1914.* 2002.

Manning, Roberta. *The Crisis of the Old Order in Russia.* 1982.

Trenches on the Web: **http://www.trenchesontheweb.com**.

Williamson, Samuel. *Austria-Hungary and the Origins of the First World War.* 1991.

CHAPTER REVIEW

IMPORTANT EVENTS

1894–1895	Japan defeats China in the Sino-Japanese War
1894–1899	Dreyfus Affair lays bare anti-Semitism in France
1899–1902	Boer War fought between Dutch descendants and the British in South African states
1900	Sigmund Freud publishes *The Interpretation of Dreams*
1901	Irish National Theater established by Maud Gonne and William Butler Yeats; death of Queen Victoria
1903	Emmeline Pankhurst founds the Women's Social and Political Union to fight for women's suffrage in Great Britain
1904–1905	Japan defeats Russia in the Russo-Japanese War
1905	Revolution erupts in Russia; violence forces Nicholas II to establish an elected body, the Duma; Albert Einstein publishes his paper titled "Special Theory of Relativity"
1906	Women receive the vote in Finland
1907	Pablo Picasso launches cubist painting with *Les Demoiselles d'Avignon*
1908	Young Turks revolt against rule by the sultan in the Ottoman Empire
1911–1912	Revolutionaries overthrow the Qing dynasty and declare China a republic
1914	Assassination of the Austrian archduke Francis Ferdinand and his wife by a Serbian nationalist precipitates World War I

KEY TERMS

art nouveau (974)

Boer War (985)

Duma (989)

Entente Cordiale (993)

Mitteleuropa (993)

modernism (970)

new woman (965)

psychoanalysis (967)

suffragists (977)

Zionism (984)

REVIEW QUESTIONS

1. How did ideas about the self and about personal life change at the turn of the century?
2. How did modernism transform the arts and the world of ideas?
3. What were the points of tension in European political life at the turn of the century?
4. Why did events in overseas empires from the 1890s on prove discouraging to many Europeans back home?
5. What were the major factors leading to the outbreak of World War I?

MAKING CONNECTIONS

1. How did changes in society at the turn of the century affect the development of mass politics?
2. How was culture connected to the world of politics in the years 1890–1914?

FOR FURTHER EXPLORATION

To assess your mastery of the material in this chapter, see the Online Study Guide at **bedfordstmartins.com/hunt**.

To read additional primary-source material from this period, see Chapter 25 in *Sources of The Making of the West*, Second Edition.

War, Revolution, and Reconstruction, 1914–1929

JULES AMAR FOUND HIS TRUE VOCATION in World War I. A French expert on improving the efficiency of industrial work, Amar switched his focus after 1914 as hundreds of thousands of men returned from the battlefront missing body parts. Plastic surgery developed rapidly, as did the construction of masks and other devices to hide deformities. But Amar, who devised artificial limbs and appendages in these traumatic years, sought to create prostheses that would allow the wounded soldier to return to normal life by "mak[ing] up for a function lost, or greatly reduced." So he designed arms that featured hooks, magnets, and other mechanisms with which the veteran could hold a cigarette, play a violin, and, most important, work with tools such as typewriters. Mangled by the weapons of modern technological warfare, the survivors of World War I would be made whole, it was thought, by technology such as Amar's.

Amar dealt with the human tragedy of the "Great War," so named by contemporaries because of its staggering human toll— forty million wounded or killed in battle. The Great War was also what historians call a **total war**, meaning one built on full mobilization of soldiers, civilians, and the technological capacities of the nations involved. The Great War did not settle problems or restore social order as the European powers hoped it would. Instead, the war produced political cataclysm, overturning the Russian, German, Ottoman, and Austro-Hungarian empires. The crushing burden of war on the European powers accelerated the rise of the United States, while service in the war intensified the demands of colonized peoples for autonomy.

Grieving Parents

Before World War I the German artist Käthe Kollwitz gained her artistic reputation with woodcuts of handloom weavers whose livelihoods were threatened by industrialization. From 1914 on, she depicted the suffering and death that swirled around her and never with more sober force than in these two monuments to her son Peter, who had died on the western front in the first months of battle. Today one can still travel to his burial place in Vladslo, Belgium, to see this father and mother mourning their loss, like millions across Europe in those heartbreaking days. *The John Parker Picture Library. © 2005 Artists Rights Society (ARS), New York/VG Bild-Kunst, Bonn.*

For all the vast changes that the Great War ushered in, it also hastened transformations under way before it started. Nineteenth-century optimism, already tinged with a sense of decline, gave way to a more pervasive postwar cynicism. Many Westerners turned their backs on politics and attacked life with frenzied gaiety in the Roaring Twenties, snapping up new consumer goods, drinking in entertainment provided by films and radio, and enjoying personal freedoms that Victorianism had forbidden. Others found reason for hope in the new political systems the war made possible: Soviet communism and Italian fascism. Modern communication technologies such as radio gave politicians the means to promote a utopian mass politics that paradoxically was antidemocratic, militaristic, and eventually dictatorial. Already weakening during the prewar period, the gentlemanly political tone of William Gladstone's day had been devastated by total war.

Seen as a solution to the conflicts of modernity, a war that was long anticipated and even welcomed in some quarters destabilized Europe and the world far into the next decades. From statesmen to ordinary citizens, many Europeans like Amar would spend their best peacetime efforts to make war-ravaged society function normally, while others saw that task as utterly futile, given the globally transformative force of the Great War. During the 1920s, bitterness continued to haunt everyday life, while many simultaneously believed that peacetime would usher in a better society.

❖ The Great War, 1914–1918

When war erupted in August 1914, the ground had been prepared with long-standing alliances, the development of strategies for war, and the buildup of military technologies such as heavy artillery, machine guns, and the airplane. Seeing precedents in Prussia's rapid victories in the 1860s and 1870 and the swift blows that Japan dealt Russia in 1904–1905, most people felt that this would be a short, decisive conflict. But the unforeseen happened: this war would last for more than four years, and it would be a total war, mobilizing entire societies and producing the unprecedented horror that made World War I "great."

Blueprints for War

World War I pitted two sets of opponents formed roughly out of the alliances developed during the previous fifty years. On one side stood the Central Powers (Austria-Hungary and Germany), which had evolved from Bismarck's Triple Alliance, and on the other the Allies (France, Great Britain, and Russia), which had emerged as a bloc from the Entente Cordiale between France and Great Britain and the 1890s treaties between France and Russia. In 1915, Italy, originally part of the Triple Alliance, joined the Allies in hopes of postwar gain. The two sides expanded globally almost from the start: in late August 1914, Japan, eager to extend its empire into China, went over to the Allies,

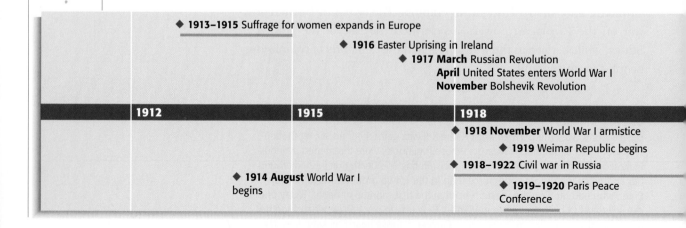

◆ **1913–1915** Suffrage for women expands in Europe

◆ **1916** Easter Uprising in Ireland

◆ **1917 March** Russian Revolution
April United States enters World War I
November Bolshevik Revolution

1912	**1915**	**1918**

◆ **1918 November** World War I armistice

◆ **1919** Weimar Republic begins

◆ **1918–1922** Civil war in Russia

◆ **1914 August** World War I begins

◆ **1919–1920** Paris Peace Conference

while in the fall the Ottoman Empire united with the Central Powers against its traditional enemy, Russia (Map 26.1).

The antagonists fought with the same ferocious hunger for power, prestige, and prosperity that had inspired imperialism. Of the Central Powers, Germany aspired to a far-flung empire to be gained by annexing Russian territory and incorporating parts of Belgium, France, and Luxembourg. Some German leaders wanted to annex Austria-Hungary as well. Austria-Hungary hoped to retain its great-power status in the face of competing nationalisms within its borders. Among the Allies, Russia wanted to reassert its status as a great power and as the protector of the Slavs by adding a reunified Poland to the Russian Empire and by taking formal leadership of other Slavic peoples. The French, too, craved territory, especially the return of Alsace and Lorraine, taken from them after the Franco-Prussian War of 1870–1871, to secure its boundaries with Germany. The British sought to cement their hold on Egypt and the Suez Canal, as well as to secure the rest of their world empire. By the Treaty of London (1915), France and Britain promised Italy territory in Africa, Asia Minor, the Balkans, and elsewhere in return for joining the Allies.

The colonies provided massive assistance and were also a battleground. Some one million Africans, another one million Indians, and more than a million members of the British commonwealth countries served on the battlefronts, while the imperial powers also conscripted still uncounted numbers of colonists as forced laborers both at home and on the battlefront. For instance, a million Kenyans and Tanzanians alone are estimated to have been conscripted for portage and other menial labor in the battle for east Africa. Fighting occurred across north and sub-Saharan Africa, with colonial troops playing a major role. Reliant on Arab, African, and Indian troops, the British waged successful war on Turkey and Germany, menacing Germany's longtime interests by taking Baghdad in 1917 and also taking Palestine, Syria, and Mesopotamia. When the Russian Revolution broke out in 1917, the war moved into the Caucasus in a fight for the rich Baku oilfields, expanding the British theater of war. In sub-Saharan Africa, a vicious campaign for east Africa occurred over the course of the war, resulting not only in loss of life among the African troops used against one another on behalf of the imperialist powers but also among the civilian population whose resources were confiscated and villages burned. The Japanese seized German assets in China to enlarge their influence on the mainland permanently.

Unprecedented use of machinery also determined the course of war. In August 1914, machine guns and rifles, airplanes, battleships, submarines, and motorized transport—cars and railroads—were at the disposal of armies; new technologies like chlorine gas, tanks, and bombs would develop between 1914 and 1918. Countries differed, however, in their experience with and quantities of weapons of war. British generals who had fought fifteen years earlier in the Boer War (1899–1902) knew the destructive capacity of these weapons, while

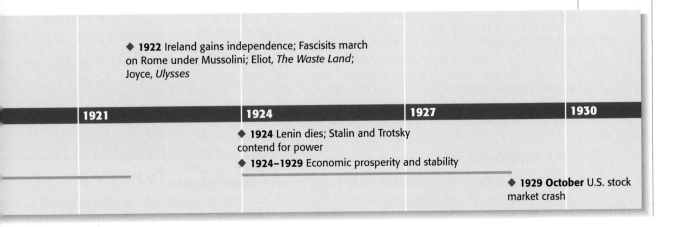

◆ **1922** Ireland gains independence; Fascisits march on Rome under Mussolini; Eliot, *The Waste Land*; Joyce, *Ulysses*

| 1921 | 1924 | 1927 | 1930 |

◆ **1924** Lenin dies; Stalin and Trotsky contend for power

◆ **1924–1929** Economic prosperity and stability

◆ **1929 October** U.S. stock market crash

A French Regiment Leaves for the Front, August 1914
Bands played, crowds cheered, and bicyclists led the way as bayonet-equipped soldiers marched eagerly to war. The mood changed quickly as machine guns and poison chemicals brought the bravest men down. People in cities, working to provide munitions and supplies, soon felt the pinch of inflation and later many lacked food. Men returned permanently disabled, even mentally deranged from their experience. And as four major empires—Ottoman, Russian, Austro-Hungarian, and German—collapsed, the war's bright beginnings disappeared from memory. What accounts for people's high-spirited attitude as this most devastating of wars erupted? © *Collection Roger Viollet/Getty Images.*

the Germans were far more advanced in strategy and weaponry than either the Russians or the Austrians. The war itself became a lethal testing ground as both new and old weapons were used, often ineffectively. Nonetheless, officers on both sides believed in a **cult of the offensive**, in which continuous spirited attacks and high troop morale were thought to be decisive. Despite the availability of newer, more powerful war technology, an old-fashioned vision of war made many officers unwilling to abandon the more familiar sabers, lances, and bayonets. In the face of massive firepower, the cult of the offensive would cost millions of lives.

The Battlefronts

The first months of the war crushed hope of quick victory. All the major armies mobilized rapidly. The Germans were guided by the **Schlieffen Plan**, named after its author, Alfred von Schlieffen, a former chief of the general staff. The plan essentially outlined a way to combat antagonists on two fronts by concentrating on one foe at a time. It called for a rapid and concentrated blow to the west against Russia's ally France, which would lead to that nation's defeat in six weeks, accompanied by a light holding action to the east. The western armies would

The Schlieffen Plan

then be deployed against Russia, which, it was believed, would mobilize far more slowly.

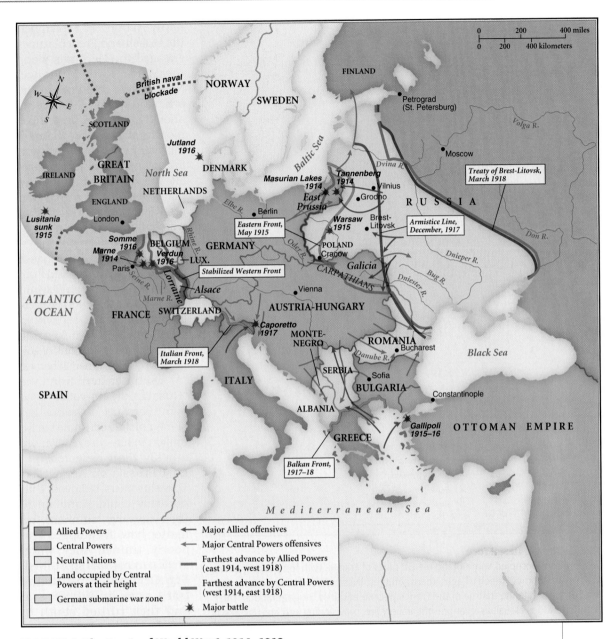

MAP 26.1 The Fronts of World War I, 1914–1918
Because the western front remained relatively stationary, devastation of land and resources was intense. All fronts, however, destroyed segments of Europe's hard-won industrial and agricultural capacity, while the immobile trenches increased military casualties whenever heavy artillery fire pounded them. Men engaged in trench warfare for so long developed an intense camaraderie based on their mutual suffering and deprivation.

The attack on France was to proceed through Belgium, whose neutrality was guaranteed by the European powers. German planners had not counted on the unexpected—resistance from Belgium and bad luck—and the other great powers were similarly unprepared for the unexpected—prolonged and devastating carnage with no hint of a victory in sight.

Indecisive Offensives: 1914–1915. The Belgian government rejected an ultimatum to allow the uncontested passage of the German

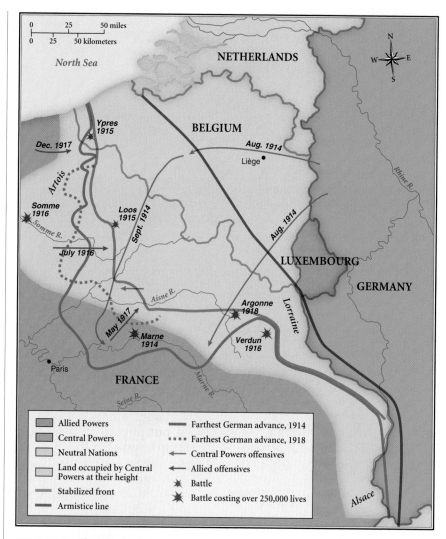

MAP 26.2 The Western Front
The western front occupied some of the richest parts of France, with long-lasting consequences. Destruction of French villages, roads, bridges, livestock, and property was the worst in Europe, while the trauma of the French people endured for generations. The effects of horrendous casualties, ever-present artillery fire, provisioning and hospital needs, and the demands of military and medical personnel changed everyone's way of life and made most people fear another war more than anything else. What different effects would trench warfare have on civilians and military personnel?

northern front. In September, the British and French armies engaged the Germans along the Marne River in France. Neither side could defeat the other, and casualties were shocking: in the first three months of war, more than 1.5 million men fell on the western front alone. Firepower with guns like the 75-millimeter howitzer that were accurate, mobile, and good at long range turned what was supposed to be an offensive war of movement into a stationary, defensive impasse along a line that stretched from the North Sea through Belgium and northern France to Switzerland (Map 26.2). Deep within parallel lines of trenches dug along this front, millions of soldiers lived in nightmarish homes.

On the eastern front, the "Russian steam-roller"—so named because of the number of men mobilized, some twelve million in all—drove far more quickly than expected into East Prussia on August 17. The Russians believed that no army could stand up to their massive numbers, no matter how ill equipped and poorly trained they were. Their success was short-lived. The Germans crushed the tsar's army in East Prussia and then turned south to Galicia.◆ Victory boosted German morale and made heroes of the military leaders Paul von Hindenburg (1847–1934) and Erich Ludendorff (1865–1937), who thereupon demanded more troops for the eastern front. Despite heartening victories, by year's end German triumphs in the east had failed to knock out the Russians and had also misdirected the Schlieffen Plan, which called for only light holding action to the east until the western front had been won.

army through the country. Thus at the beginning of August 1914, the Germans quickly reached Luxembourg and Belgium, but instead of allowing passage the Belgians offered spirited resistance. Meanwhile, the main body of French troops, tricked by German diversionary tactics, attacked the Germans in Alsace and Lorraine instead of meeting the invasion from the north. Belgian resistance slowed the German advance, allowing British and French troops to reach the

◆**Galicia:** guh LIH shee uh

War in the Skies (1914)
As the war started, modern artists saw aviators and the machines they piloted as symbols of a new age that offered humans the thrilling potential to transcend time and space. The Great War, however, featured the airplane as the new weapon in what British writer H.G. Wells called the "headlong sweep to death." Daring pilots or "aces" took the planes on reconnaissance flights, flew them over targets for bombing, and guided them in the experimental phenomenon of aerial combat, as shown in this engraving from an Italian newspaper of a French airplane shooting down a German one. Death now rained from the skies, and pilots themselves had as mixed an experience of war as did frontline soldiers. After destroying a German aircraft early in the war, one French ace announced his great joy. But later he described the experience as "horrible." And added "I remained traumatized for some time."
The Art Archive/Domenica del Corriere/Dagli Orti.

War at sea proved equally indecisive. Confident in Britain's superior naval power, the Allies blockaded ports to prevent supplies from reaching Germany and Austria-Hungary. William II and his advisers planned a massive submarine, or U-boat (*Untersee-boot*, "underwater boat"), campaign against Allied and neutral shipping around Britain and France. In May 1915, German submarines sank the British passenger ship *Lusitania* and killed 1,198 people, including 124 Americans (Map 26.3 on the next page). Despite U.S. outrage, President Woodrow Wilson maintained a policy of neutrality; Germany, unwilling to provoke Wilson further, called off unrestricted submarine warfare. In May 1916, the navies of Germany and Britain finally clashed in the North Sea at the inconclusive battle of Jutland, which demonstrated that the German fleet could not master British seapower.

Ideas of a negotiated peace were discarded: "No peace before England is defeated and destroyed," the kaiser railed against his cousin King George V. "Only amidst the ruins of London will I forgive Georgy." French leadership called for a "war to the death." General staffs on both sides continued to prepare fierce attacks several times a year. Indecisive campaigns opened with heavy artillery pounding enemy trenches and gun emplacements. Troops then responded to the order to go "over the top" by scrambling out of their trenches and into battle, usually to be mowed down by machine-gun fire from defenders secure in their own trenches. On the western front, throughout 1915 the French assaulted the enemy in the north to drive the Germans from industrial regions, but they accomplished little, and casualties of 100,000 and more for a single campaign became commonplace. On the eastern front, Russian armies captured parts of Galicia in the spring of 1915 and lumbered toward Hungary. The Central Powers struck back in Poland later that year, bringing the front closer to Petrograd (formerly St. Petersburg), the Russian capital. The Austro-Hungarian armies routed the Serbs in 1915 and then engaged the newly mobilized Italian army.

Mounting Catastrophe: 1916. The next year was even more disastrous. To cripple French morale, the Germans launched massive assaults on the fortress at Verdun, firing as many as a million shells in a single day. Combined French and German losses totaled close to a million men. Nonetheless, the

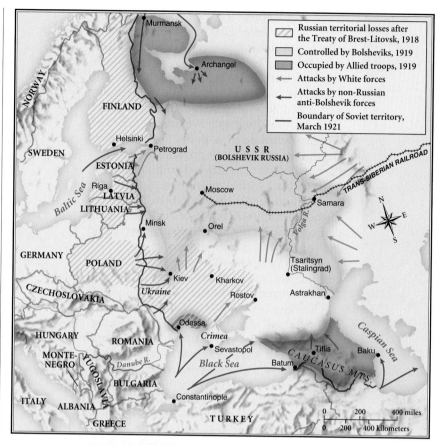

MAP 26.3 The Russian Civil War, 1917–1922

Nationalists, aristocrats, middle-class citizens, and property-owning peasants tried to combine their interests to defeat the Bolsheviks, but they failed to create an effective political consensus. As fighting covered a broad swathe of the countryside, the result was more suffering for ordinary people, whose produce was confiscated to fight the civil war. The Western powers and Japan also sent in troops to put down this revolution that so threatened the economic and political order. How widespread was discontent with Bolshevism as expressed in the military attacks against the regime?

fifties, and the German general staff decided it would take over Austrian military operations. The war was sapping Europe's strength and individual sovereignty.

The Soldiers' War. Had the military leaders thoroughly dominated the scene, historians judge, all armies would have been utterly demolished in nonstop offensives by the end of 1915. Yet ordinary soldiers in this war were not automatons in the face of what seemed to them suicidal orders. Some battalions went for long stretches with hardly a casualty, and these low rates stemmed from agreements among troops to avoid battles. Enemies facing each other across the trenches frequently ate their meals in peace, for example, even though the trenches were within hand-grenade reach. Throughout the war, soldiers fraternized on both fronts. They played an occasional game of soccer, shouted across the trenches, exchanged mementos, and made gestures of agreement not to fight. A British veteran of the trenches explained to a new recruit that the Germans "don't want to fight any more than we do, so there's a kind of understanding between us. Don't fire at us and we'll not fire at you." Burying enemy dead in common graves with their own fallen comrades, many ordinary soldiers came to feel more warmly toward enemies who shared the trench experience than toward civilians back home.

Newly forged bonds of male camaraderie alleviated some of the misery of trench life and aided survival. Sharing the danger of death and the deprivations of front-line experience weakened traditional class distinctions. In some cases, upper-class officers and working-class draftees became friends in that "wholly masculine way of life uncomplicated by women,"

French held. Hoping to relieve their allies, the British unleashed an artillery pounding of German trenches in the Somme region in June 1916. In several months of battle at the Somme, 1.25 million men were killed or wounded, but the final result was stalemate. By the end of 1916, the French had absorbed more than 3.5 million casualties. To help the Allies engaged at Verdun and the Somme, the Russians struck again, driving once more into the Carpathians, recouping territory, and menacing the Habsburg Empire. Only the German army stopped the Russian advance. Amid huge losses, the Habsburg army recruited men in their mid-as another British soldier put it. Soldiers picked lice from one another's bodies and clothes, revered section leaders who tended their blistered feet, and came to love one another, sometimes even passionately. Positive memories of this front-line community survived the war and influenced postwar politics.

Troops of colonized soldiers from Asia and Africa had different experiences, especially as they were often put in the very front ranks, where the risks were greatest. European observers noted that these soldiers suffered particularly from the rigors of a totally unfamiliar climate and strange food as well as from the ruin inflicted by Western war technology. Yet, as with class divisions, racial barriers sometimes fell, for instance, whenever a European understood enough to alleviate the distress that cold inflicted. Colonial troops' perspectives changed, too, as they saw their "masters" completely undone and "uncivilized." For when fighting did break out, trenches became a veritable hell of shelling and sniping, flying body parts, rotting cadavers, and blinding gas. Some soldiers became hysterical or succumbed to shell shock through the sheer stress and violence of battle. Alienation and cynicism rose: "It might be me tomorrow," a young British soldier wrote his mother in 1916. "Who cares?" Many had gone to war to escape ordinary life in industrial society; however, they learned, as one German put it, "that in the modern war . . . the triumph of the machine over the individual is carried to its most extreme form." They took this hard-won knowledge into battle, pulling their comrades back when an offensive seemed lost or too costly.

The Home Front

World War I took place off the battlefield too. Even before the war had reached the stage of catastrophic impasse, it had become total. Total war meant the indispensable involvement of civilians in the war industry: manufacturing the shells and machine guns, poisonous gases, bombs and airplanes, and eventually tanks that were the backbone of technological warfare. Increased production of coffins, canes, wheelchairs, and the artificial limbs devised by the likes of Jules Amar

was also a wartime necessity. Because soldiers would have utterly failed without them, civilians had to work overtime for, believe in, and sacrifice for victory. To keep the war machine operating smoothly, governments oversaw factories, transportation systems, and resources ranging from food to coal to textiles. Such tight government control would have outraged many liberals before the war but was now accepted as a necessary condition for victory.

Politics Suspended. Initially all political parties on both sides put aside their differences. Many socialists and working-class people who had formerly criticized the military buildup announced their support for the war. For decades socialist parties had preached that "the worker has no country" and that nationalism was mere ideology meant to keep workers disunited and subjected to the will of their employers. In August 1914, however, the socialist rank and file, along with most of the party leaders, became as patriotic as the rest of society. Feminists divided over whether to maintain their traditional condemnation of militarism or to support the war. Although many feminists actively opposed the conflict, the British suffrage leader Emmeline Pankhurst and her daughter Christabel were among the many activists who became militant nationalists, even changing the name of their suffrage paper to *Britannia*. Parties representing the middle classes shelved their distrust of the socialists and working classes. In the name of victory, national leaders wanted to end political division of all kinds: "I no longer recognize [political] parties," William II declared on August 4, 1914. "I recognize only Germans." The new political climate of unity was called the *Burgfriede*◆ ("domestic peace") in Germany and the *union sacrée*◆ ("sacred union") in France. Ordinary people, even those who had been at the receiving end of discrimination, came to believe that a new day of unity was dawning. One rabbi proudly echoed the kaiser: "In the German fatherland there are no longer any Christians and Jews, any believers and disbelievers, there are only Germans."

◆ *Burgfriede:* burg FREE duh
◆ *union sacrée:* oon yohn sah KREH

Governments Mobilize the People. Governments mobilized the home front with varying degrees of success. All countries were caught without ready replacements for their heavy losses of weapons and military equipment and soon felt the shortage of food and labor, too. War ministries set up boards to allocate labor on the home front and the battlefront and to give industrialists financial incentives to encourage productivity. In several countries, emergency measures allowed the drafting of both men and women for military or industrial service, further blurring dis-

tinctions between military and civilian life. But the Russian bureaucracy only reluctantly and ineffectively cooperated with industrialists and other groups that could aid the war effort. Desperate for factory workers, the Germans forced Belgian citizens to move to Germany, housing them in prison camps. In the face of rationing, municipal governments set up canteens and day-care centers. Rural Russia, Austria-Hungary, Bulgaria, and Serbia, where youths, women, and old men struggled to sustain farms, had no such relief programs.

Governments throughout Europe passed sedition laws that made it a crime to criticize official policies. To ensure civilian acceptance of longer working hours and shortages of consumer goods, governments created propaganda agencies to tout the war as a patriotic mission to resist villainous enemies (see the French propaganda poster on this page). British propagandists fabricated atrocities the German "Huns" supposedly committed against Belgians, and German propaganda warned that French African troops would rape German women if Germany was defeated. In Russia, Nicholas II changed the German-sounding name of St. Petersburg to the Russian Petrograd in 1914. Efforts were often clumsy: the British film *The Battle of the Somme* (1916) was so obviously sanitized of the war's horrors that soldiers in the audience roared with laughter, though civilians found it riveting. The Russians, hoping to ensure support of the many ethnicities in the empire, plastered Polish towns with posters promising national independence. It printed the Polish flag upside down, however, infuriating rather than attracting the Poles.

Playing on fears and arousing hatred, propaganda rendered a compromise peace unlikely. Nonetheless, some individuals sought to shatter the nationalist consensus supporting the war. In 1915, activists in the international women's movement met in The Hague, site of late-nineteenth-century peace conferences, in their own effort to end the war. "We can no longer endure . . . brute force as the only solution of international disputes," declared Dutch physician Aletta Jacobs. Despite their lack of success, many spent the remainder of the war urging statesmen to work out a peace settlement. In Austria-

War Propaganda, 1915
"Never Forget!" screams the headline of this French propaganda poster depicting an assaulted woman in despair. Intended to incite sentiment against the Germans, the poster suggested what German passage through neutral Belgium came to be called—the rape of Belgium. Propaganda offices for the Allies sent out reports of women attacked and children massacred as the German armies moved through Belgian territories. Why would propaganda experts use an image of a civilian woman instead of a male soldier to represent war's horrors? *Mary Evans Picture Library.*

Hungary, nationalist groups agitating for ethnic self-determination hampered the empire's war effort. The Czechs undertook a vigorous anti-Habsburg campaign at home, while exiled politicians in Paris established the Czechoslovak National Council to lobby Western governments for recognition of Czech rights. In the Balkans, Croats, Slovenes, and Serbs formed a committee to plan a South Slav state carved from Habsburg possessions and other Balkan territory. The Allies encouraged such independence movements as part of their strategy to defeat the Habsburgs.

The Civilians' War.   The war upset the social order as well as the political one. In the war's early days many women had lost their jobs when luxury shops, textile factories, and other nonessential establishments closed. With men at the front, many women headed households with little support and few opportunities to work. But governments and businesses soon recognized the amount of labor it would take to wage technological war. As more and more men left for the trenches, women who had lost their jobs in nonessential businesses as well as many low-paid domestic workers took over higher-paying jobs in formerly restricted munitions and metallurgical industries. In Warsaw they drove trucks, and in London they conducted streetcars. Some young women drove ambulances and nursed the wounded near the front lines.

The press praised women's patriotism in adopted new roles, but women's assumption of men's jobs looked to many like social disorder. From the start, a steady flood of wounded and weak men returned home to women who had adapted resourcefully and taken full charge. Workingmen commonly protested that women, in the words of one metalworker, were "sending men to the slaughter." Men feared that when the war was over women would remain in the workforce, robbing men of the breadwinner role. Many people, even some women, objected to women's loss of femininity. "The feminine in me decreased more and more, and I did not know whether to be sad or glad about this," wrote one Russian nurse about adopting rough male clothing near the battlefield. But others criticized young female munitions workers for squandering their pay on

A Woman Munitions Worker in World War I, England (1917)
The transfer of tens of millions of men from the workforce to military service left a huge deficit of workers. Simultaneously, millions of women lost the support of a male wage, while they themselves were often laid off from jobs in the consumer sector that were deemed superfluous. Women thus had to work out of economic necessity during the war, and the military effort needed them in manufacturing jobs. These jobs paid salaries far beyond traditional women's jobs, which often brought accusations that extra money was making women frivolous and that their cravings were needlessly sending men to their deaths. By contrast, others applauded women's energy, patriotism, and sacrifice. Praise turned to dismay, however, when the armies began forming units of women: " 'She-Men,' who wished to be armed to the teeth," one aristocrat called them; and a letter to a London newspaper in 1915 called them "ridiculous" and insulting to the dignity of the nation. Why did gender issues remain highly debated even amid the crisis of war? ©*Hulton-Deutsch Collection / Corbis.*

ribbons and jewelry and echoed other prewar gender tensions.

Although many soldiers from different social backgrounds felt bonds of solidarity in the trenches, wartime conditions increasingly pitted civilians against one another or against the government. Workers toiled longer hours eating less, while many in the upper classes bought abundant food and fashionable clothing on the black market (outside the official system of rationing). Governments allowed many businesses high rates of profit, a step that resulted in a surge in the cost of living and thus contributed to social strife. Shortages of staples like bread, sugar, and meat grew worse across Europe, while the Germans called the brutal winter of 1916–1917 the turnip winter because turnips were often the only available food. A German roof workers' association pleaded for relief: "We can no longer go on. Our children are starving." Dredging up prewar hatred, some explained deprivation as the work of the Jews. Civilians in occupied areas and in the colonies suffered the most oppressive working conditions. The combatants deported or conscripted able-bodied people in territories they occupied. The French forcibly transported some 100,000 Vietnamese to work in France for the war effort. Africans also faced grueling forced labor along with skyrocketing taxes and prices, as the disruption of agriculture caused shortages. All such actions, like increasing class divisions, further politicized ordinary people whether in the colonies or at home in Europe.

> **Review:** What factors contributed to making World War I a total war?

❖ Protest, Revolution, and War's End, 1917–1918

By 1917, the situation was becoming desperate for politicians, the military, and civilians alike, and discontent on the home front started shaping the course of the war. Neither patriotic slogans before the war nor propaganda during it had prepared people for wartime suffering. Cities across Europe experienced civilian revolt; soldiers mutinied, and nationalist struggles continued to plague Britain and Austria-Hungary. Soon revolution was sweeping Europe, toppling the Russian dynasty for good, and threatening the entire continent not just with war but with civil war.

War Protest

On February 1, 1917, the German government, hard-pressed by the public clamor over mounting casualties and by the military's growing control over decision making, resumed unrestricted submarine warfare.

The military made the irresistible promise to end the war in six months by cutting off imported food and military supplies to Britain and thus forcing the island nation to surrender before the United States could come to its rescue. The British responded by mining harbors and the seas and by developing the convoy system of shipping, in which a hundred or more warships and freighters traveling the seas together could drive off the submarines. The Germans' submarine gamble failed to defeat the British. Moreover, unrestricted submarine warfare brought the United States into the war in April 1917, after German U-boats had sunk several American ships.

Political opposition increased in Europe, and deteriorating living conditions sparked outright revolt by civilians. "We are living on a volcano," warned an Italian politician in the spring of 1917. High prices and food shortages plagued everyday life (Figure 26.1). Food shortages in cities of Italy, Russia, Germany, and Austria provoked riots by women who were unable to feed their families. As inflation mounted, tenants conducted rent strikes, factory hands and white-collar workers alike walked off the job, and female workers protested the skyrocketing cost of living and their fatigue from overwork. Amid protest, the new emperor of Austria-Hungary secretly asked the Allies for a negotiated peace to avoid a total collapse of his empire. In the summer of 1917, the German Reichstag made overtures for a "peace of understanding and permanent reconciliation of peoples." Woodrow Wilson further weakened civilian resolve in Germany and Austria-Hungary in January 1918 by issuing his Fourteen Points, a blueprint for a new international order that held out the promise of a nonvindictive peace settlement to war-weary citizens of the Central Powers. The Allies faced dissent too. In the spring of 1917, French soldiers mutinied against further bloody and fruitless offensives, and wartime protest in Russia turned into outright revolution.

Revolution in Russia

Of all the warring nations, Russia sustained the greatest number of casualties—7.5 million by 1917. Slaughter on the eastern front drove hundreds of thousands of peasants

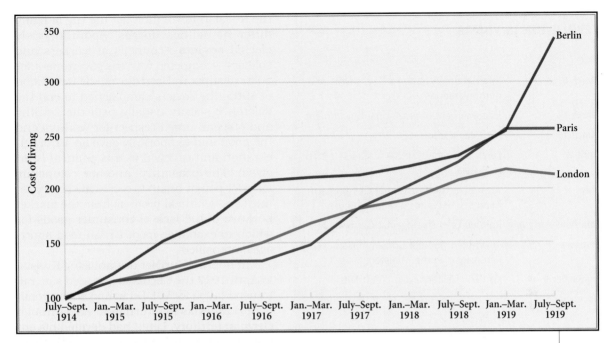

FIGURE 26.1 The Rising Cost of Living During World War I
The diversion of resources to the military resulted in a soaring cost of living for civilians. As men went to the front and as some remaining agricultural workers could find higher pay in factories, a decline in agricultural output led to scarcity and thus rising prices for food. Finally, housing came to be in short supply as resources were directed to the war effort rather than used to construct needed buildings. Even after the war, prices rose in Germany because the Allies maintained their blockade to keep the pressure on the peacemaking process. How was the pace of inflation connected to the course of the war itself? *Jay Winter and Jean-Louis Robert,* Capital Cities at War: Paris, London, Berlin, 1914–1919 *(Cambridge: Cambridge University Press, 1997), 259.*

into the Russian interior, bringing hunger, homelessness, and disease. In March 1917,* crowds of workingwomen swarmed the streets of Petrograd demanding relief from harsh conditions. As these women were turned away from stores, they fell in with other protesters commemorating International Women's Day and began looting shops for food. Factory workers and other civilians joined them. Russia's comparative economic underdevelopment overwhelmed the government's ability to provide basic necessities on the home front.

Many in the army, instead of remaining loyal to the tsar, were embittered by the massive casualties caused by their inferior weapons and their leaders' foolhardy tactics.

Since the Revolution of 1905 the masses had become politicized, leading to rising protest against the government's incompetence and Nicholas II's stubborn resistance to change. Unlike other heads of state, Nicholas failed to unify the bureaucracy and his peoples in a concerted wartime effort. Grigori Rasputin, a combination of holy man and charlatan, held Nicholas and his wife, Alexandra, in his thrall by claiming to control the hemophilia of their son and heir. Rasputin's disastrous influence on state matters led educated and influential leaders to withdraw their support. "Is this stupidity or treason?" one member of the Duma asked of the corrupt, impotent wartime administration. When the riots erupted in

---

*Until February 1918, Russia remained on the Julian calendar, which was thirteen days behind the Gregorian calendar used by the rest of Europe. Hence, the first phase of the revolution occurred in March according to the Gregorian calendar (but February in the Julian calendar), the later phase in November using the Gregorian calendar (October according to the Julian). All dates used in this book follow the Gregorian calendar.

REVOLUTION IN RUSSIA

1917

March 8	International Women's Day, strikes and demonstrations
March 12	Establishment of Provisional Government
March 15	Nicholas II abdicates
April 17	Lenin and other Bolshevik leaders return to Russia
May	Turmoil in the Provisional Government; Kerensky becomes a leading figure
Late June–early July	Russian offensive against Germany fails
Mid-July	Attempted popular uprising fails; Kerensky is Prime Minister
September 9–14	Kornilov military coup d'état fails
November 6–7	Bolshevik seizure of power on behalf of soviets
November 25	Constituent assembly elections held
1918	
January 18	Constituent assembly closed down by Bolsheviks
1918–1922	Civil war
1924	Union of Soviet Socialist Republics formally established; death of Lenin
1928–1929	Stalin takes full power

March 1917, Nicholas for once saw the reality of the situation and knew it was hopeless. He abdicated, bringing the three-hundred-year-old Romanov dynasty to an abrupt end.

The Provisional Government. Politicians from the old Duma formed a new ruling entity called the **Provisional Government**. At first hopes were high that under the Provisional Government, as one revolutionary poet put it, "our false, filthy, boring, hideous life should become a just, pure, merry, and beautiful life." Composed essentially of moderate aristocrats and members of the middle class, the Provisional Government had to pursue the war successfully, manage internal affairs better, and set government on a firm constitutional footing to establish its credibility. However, it did not rule alone, as

the Russian Revolution felt the tug of many different political forces. Spontaneously elected **soviets**—councils of workers and soldiers—competed with the government for political support. Born during the Revolution of 1905, the soviets campaigned to end the deference society usually paid the wealthy and officers, urged respect for workers and the poor, and temporarily gave an air of celebration and carnival to this political cataclysm. The peasantry, another competing force for power, began to confiscate gentry estates and withheld produce from the market because of the lack of consumer goods for which to exchange food. Urban food shortages intensified.

In hopes of further destabilizing Russia, in April 1917 the Germans provided safe rail transportation for V. I. Lenin and other prominent Bolsheviks to return from exile through German territory. Lenin had devoted his entire existence to bringing about socialism through the force of his small band of Bolsheviks, and as a political exile he had no parliamentary experience. Upon his return to Petrograd, Lenin issued the April Theses, a radical document that called for Russia to withdraw from the war, for the soviets to seize power on behalf of workers and poor peasants, and for all private land to be nationalized. The Bolsheviks aimed to supplant the Provisional Government by challenging its legitimacy with the slogans "All power to the soviets" and "Peace, land, and bread."

Time was running out for the Provisional Government, which saw a battlefield victory as the only way to ensure its position. On July 1, the Russian army attacked the Austrians in Galicia but was defeated once again. The new prime minister, the Socialist Revolutionary Aleksandr Kerensky (1881–1970), used his commanding oratory to arouse patriotism, but he lacked the political skills needed to fashion an effective wartime government. In Petrograd, groups of workers, soldiers, and sailors—many of them Bolsheviks—agitated for the soviets to replace the Provisional Government. Instead of clamping down, the Provisional Government found itself once more dependent on the people when a military coup, led by General Lavr Kornilov, broke out. Depending on its sworn enemies, the Provisional Government had shown itself once again

Lenin Addressing the Second All-Russian Congress of Soviets
In the spring of 1917, the German government craftily let Lenin and other Bolsheviks travel from their exile in Switzerland back to the scene of the unfolding revolution in Russia. A committed revolutionary instead of a political reformer, Lenin used his oratory and skilled maneuvering to convince many in the soviets to follow him in overthrowing the Provisional Government, taking Russia out of the war, and implementing his brand of communism. What impression of Lenin and his audience does this artist hope to convey? *Novosti (London).*

impotent, failing to enact reforms, summon a constituent assembly to plan a new permanent government, or win the war. The army had become, as one critic put it, "a huge crowd of tired, poorly clad, poorly fed, embittered men"—eager for radical change.

The Bolshevik Takeover. The **Bolshevik Revolution** took place in November 1917. Urged on by Lenin, the Bolshevik leadership seized power on behalf of the soviets while simultaneously asserting its own right to form a government. When in January 1918, elections for a constituent assembly failed to give the Bolsheviks a plurality, the party used troops to disrupt the assembly and took over the

government by force. They seized town and city administrations, closing down the zemstvos (local councils) and other institutions in the countryside where opposition support was keen (see "Outbreak of the Russian Revolution," page 1018). In the winter of 1918–1919, the Bolshevik government, observing Marxist doctrine, abolished private property, nationalizing factories in order to restore production, which had fallen off precipitously. The Provisional Government had allowed both men and women to vote in 1917; Russia was thus the first great power to legalize universal suffrage—a hollow privilege once the Bolsheviks limited slates to candidates from the Communist Party.

Outbreak of the Russian Revolution

It is only clear in retrospect when a full-fledged and sustainable revolution has broken out. Here an eighteen-year-old student describes what happened when news of the St. Petersburg revolt reached Moscow in the late winter of 1917. Crowds had already formed when the young man decided to see what was happening in the streets.

In the crowd were many students who explained that a revolution had begun in St. Petersburg. The news swept through them like a breeze and created an extraordinary atmosphere. People began to embrace and kiss; strangers became close friends; some wept for joy. In five to ten minutes people seemed reborn. A pretty girl came up to me and took me by the hand, as though we had known each other for ages. Then hand-in-hand, in a warm embrace, and without asking each other's name, we proceeded toward the Krutitskie barracks. . . .

The crowd grew bigger and bigger, and somewhere in the distance one could hear the well-known refrain of a revolutionary song. By this time it was so crowded that it was quite impossible to get to one side or the other. We continued to hold hands, as though we might get lost. Slowly, barely perceptibly, the human stream moved toward the Red Gates, where I knew there was another barracks. It was the same scene there, except that the soldiers were shouting loudly, waving and greeting us. We couldn't make out what they said. Near Pokrovka we ran into a group of police officers, but instead of greeting them with good-natured jokes, thousands of

voices yelled fierce, threatening cries: "Pharaohs! Your time is up! Get away for your own good!" . . . We moved slowly and could see neither the front nor the back of the crowd, for the street was blocked solid. For the first time in my life I sensed that atmosphere of joy, when everyone you meet seems close to you, your flesh and blood, when people look at one another with eyes full of love. To call it mass hypnosis is not quite right, but the mood of the crowd was transmitted from one to another like conduction, like a spontaneous burst of laughter, joy, or anger.

The majority of the crowd consisted of people who that morning had been praying for the good health of the imperial family. Now they were shouting, "Down with the Tsar!" and not disguising their joyful contempt. My companion was a good example. She showered me with questions: Where are we going? Why are we marching? Why is there a revolution? How will we manage without a tsar? It seemed like a mere holiday to her—Sunday's carnival procession, complete with mass participation. Tomorrow— Monday—humdrum working life would begin again, just as usual. Without asking a question, as though talking to herself, she suddenly said: "How good it would be if there was another revolution tomorrow!" What could I say? Tomorrow? Probably tomorrow the police would arrest us. But today there was a festival on the streets.

Source: Eduard Dune, *Notes of a Red Guard*. Translated and edited by Dianne Koenker and S. A. Smith (Champaign, Illinois, 1993), 32,34.

The Bolsheviks asked Germany for peace and agreed to the Treaty of Brest-Litovsk◆ (March 1918), which placed vast regions of the old Russian Empire under German occupation. The treaty partially realized the German ideal of a central European region, or Mitteleuropa, under German control. Because the loss of millions of square miles put Petrograd at risk, the Bolsheviks relo-

◆**Brest-Litovsk:** BREHST lih TAWFSK

cated the capital to Moscow and formally adopted the name Communists (taken from Karl Marx's writings) to distinguish themselves from the socialists/social democrats who had voted for the disastrous war in the first place. Lenin agreed to the catastrophic terms of the treaty not only because he had promised to bring peace to Russia but also because he believed that the rest of Europe would soon rebel against war and overthrow the capitalist order.

Civil War in Russia

Resistance to Bolshevik policies, especially those that nationalized private property, mushroomed into full-fledged civil war with the pro-Bolsheviks (the "Reds") pitted against an array of antirevolutionary forces (the "Whites") (see Map 26.3, page 1010). Among the Whites, the tsarist military leadership, composed of many landlords and supporters of aristocratic rule, took to the field whatever troops it could muster. Dispossessed businessmen and the liberal intelligentsia soon lent their support. Many non-Russian nationality groups—formerly incorporated into the empire through force, Russification (which suppressed non-Russian languages and culture), and other bureaucratic efforts—fought the Bolsheviks because they saw their chance for independence. Before World War I ended, Russia's former allies, notably the United States, Britain, France, and Japan, landed troops in the country both to block the Germans and to stop Bolshevism. To compete effectively with the Bolsheviks, however, the counterrevolutionary groups desperately needed a strong leader and unified goals. Instead, the groups competed with one another: the pro-tsarist forces, for example, alienated those aspiring to nation-state status, such as the Ukrainians, Estonians, and Lithuanians. Ultimately, without a common purpose or unified command, the opponents of revolution could not win.

The civil war shaped communism. Leon Trotsky (1879–1940), Bolshevik commissar of war, built a highly disciplined army by ending democratic procedures, such as the election of officers, that had originally attracted soldiers to Bolshevism. Lenin and Trotsky introduced the policy of war communism, whereby urban workers and troops moved through the countryside, brutally confiscating grain from the peasantry to feed the army and workforce. The Cheka (secret police) set up detention camps for political opponents and black marketers and often shot them without trial. The expansion of the size and strength of the Cheka and the Red Army—the latter eventually numbered five million men—accompanied the expansion of the bureaucracy, making the government more authoritarian and undermining the promise of Marxism that revolution would bring a "withering away" of the state.

As the Bolsheviks clamped down on opposition during the bloody civil war, they organized their supporters to foster revolutionary Marxism across Europe. In March 1919, they founded the Third International, also known as the Comintern (Communist International), for the explicit purpose of replacing the Second International with a centralized organization dedicated to preaching communism. By mid-1921, the Cheka had shored up Bolshevism in Russia and the Red Army had secured the Crimea, the Caucasus, and the Muslim borderlands in central Asia. When the Japanese withdrew from Siberia in 1922, the civil war ended in central and east Asia. The Bolsheviks were now in charge of a state as multinational as the old Russian Empire had been.

The Russian Revolution, as led by the Bolsheviks, promised bold experiments in social and political leadership. But although the revolution had turned out the inept Romanovs and the privileged aristocracy, civil war turned Russia into a battlefield where disease, hunger, and death prevailed. Moreover, the brutal way the Bolsheviks came to power—by crushing opposition of all stripes—ushered in a political style and direction far different from earlier socialist hopes.

Ending the War, 1918

Having pulled Russia out of World War I, the Bolsheviks left the rest of Europe's leaders confronting a new balance of forces. Facing war protest as well, these leaders were also left fearing that communism might lie in their future.

The Central Powers made one final attempt to smash through the Allied lines using a new offensive strategy. It consisted of concentrated forces piercing single points of the enemy's relatively thin defense lines and then wreaking havoc from the rear. The Central Powers had overwhelmed the Italian army at Caporetto in the fall of 1917 with these tactics. In the spring of 1918, a similar offensive on the all-important western front ground to a bloody halt within weeks. By then the British and French had started making limited but effective use of tanks supported by airplanes. Although the first tanks were cumbersome, their ability to withstand machine-gun fire made offensive attacks possible. In the summer of 1918, the Allies, now fortified by the Americans, pushed back the Germans all along the western front and headed toward Germany. The German armies, suffering more than two million casualties between spring and summer, rapidly disintegrated.

By October 1918, the desperate German command helped create a civilian government to take over from its own dictatorial rule of the home front. It thus hoodwinked inexperienced politicians to take responsibility for the defeat and to ask for peace. Deflecting blame from the military, generals proclaimed themselves still fully capable of winning the war. Weak-willed civilians, they claimed, had dealt the military a "stab in the back" that forced a surrender. Amid this blatant political deceit, naval officers called for a final sea battle, sparking mutiny against what the sailors saw as a suicide mission. The sailors' rebellion capped years of indignities at the hands of high-ranking officers whose champagne-filled diet contrasted with the sailors' increasingly meager fare of turnips and thin soup. The sailors' revolt spread to the workers, who demonstrated in Berlin, Munich, and other major cities. The uprisings provoked Social Democratic politicians to declare a German republic in an effort to prevent revolution. On November 9, 1918, Kaiser William II fled as the Central Powers collapsed on all fronts. Since the previous winter, Austria-Hungary had kept many combat divisions at home simply to maintain civil order. At the end of October, Czechs and Slovaks had declared an independent state, and the Croatian parliament simultaneously announced Croatia's independence.

Finally, on the morning of November 11, 1918, delegates from the two sides signed an armistice. The guns fell silent on the western front six hours later. In the course of four years, European civilization had been sorely tested, if not shattered. Conservative figures put the battlefield toll at a minimum of ten million deaths and thirty million wounded, incapacitated, or eventually to die of their wounds. In every European combatant country, industrial and agricultural production had

plummeted, and much of the reduced output had been put to military use. Asia, Africa, and the Americas, which depended on European trade, also felt the painful impact of Europe's declining production. From 1918 to 1919, the weakened global population suffered an influenza epidemic that left as many as one-hundred million more dead.

Besides illness, hunger, and death, the war also provoked tremendous moral questioning. Soldiers returning home in 1918 and 1919 flooded the book market with their memoirs, trying to give meaning to their experiences. Some 2,500 war poets published in Britain alone. Whereas many had begun by emphasizing heroism and glory, others were cynical and bitter by war's end. They insisted the fighting had been absolutely meaningless. Total war had drained society of resources and population and had inadvertently sown the seeds of future catastrophes.

> **Review:** Why did people revolt during World War I, and what turned revolt into outright revolution in Russia?

❖ The Search for Peace in an Era of Revolution

Amid the quest for peace, revolutionary fervor swept the continent, especially in the former empires of Germany and Austria-Hungary. In Moscow, Lenin welcomed the emperors' downfall as a phase of world revolution that would usher in an age of working-class internationalism. Until 1921, the triumph of socialism seemed plausible; many of the newly independent peoples of eastern and central Europe fervently supported socialist principles. The revolutionary mood captured workers and peasants in Germany too. In contrast, many liberal and right-wing opponents hoped for a political order based on military authority of the kind they had relied on during the war. Faced with a volatile mix of revolution and counterrevolution, diplomats from around the world arrived in Paris in January 1919 to negotiate the terms of peace, though without fully recognizing the magnitude of the changes brought about by war.

Europe in Turmoil

Urban people and returning soldiers ignited the protest that swept Europe in 1918 and 1919. In January 1919, the red flag of socialist revolution flew from the city hall in Glasgow, Scotland, while in cities of the collapsing Austro-Hungarian Monarchy workers set up councils to direct factory production and to influence politics. Many soldiers did not disband at the armistice but formed volunteer armies, making Europe ripe not for parliamentary politics but for revolution by force. Germany was politically unstable, partly because of the shock of defeat. Independent socialist groups and workers' councils vied with the dominant Social Democrats for control of the government, and workers and veterans took to the streets to demand food and back pay. Whereas in 1848 revolutionaries had marched to city hall or the king's residence, these protesters took over newspapers and telegraph offices, thus controlling the flow of information. Some were inspired by one of the most radical socialist factions, the Spartacists, led by cofounders Karl Liebknecht♦ (1871–1919) and Rosa Luxemburg (1870–1919). Unlike Lenin, the two Spartacist leaders favored political uprisings that would give workers political experience and thus eliminate the need for an all-knowing party leadership. They argued for direct worker control of institutions, but they shared Lenin's dislike for parliamentary politics.

Social Democratic leader Friedrich Ebert (1871–1925), who headed the new German government, shunned revolution and backed the creation of a parliamentary republic to replace the kaiser's rule. Splitting with his former socialist allies, he called on the German army and the Freikorps♦—a roving paramilitary band of students, demobilized soldiers, and others—to suppress the workers' councils and demonstrators. He thus appeared to endorse the idea that political differences could be settled with violence. "The enthusiasm is marvelous," wrote one young soldier. "No mercy's shown. We shoot even the wounded. . . . We were much more humane against the French in the field." Members of

♦**Liebknecht:** LEEP knehkt
♦**Freikorps:** FRY kawr

the Freikorps hunted down Luxemburg and Liebknecht and murdered them.

Protest continued even as a constituent assembly meeting in the city of Weimar in February 1919 approved a constitution and founded a parliamentary republic called the **Weimar Republic**. This time the right rebelled, for the military leadership dreamed of a restored monarchy: "As I love Germany, so I hate the Republic," wrote one officer. Facing a military coup by Freikorps officers, Ebert called for a general strike that abruptly averted a takeover of the new republic by showing the clear lack of popular support for a military regime. In so doing, the Weimar Republic had set the dangerous precedent of relying on street violence, paramilitary groups, and protests to solve political problems.

Revolutionary activism surged and was smashed. In the late winter of 1919, leftists proclaimed soviet republics—governments led by workers' councils—in Bavaria and Hungary. These soon fell before the assault of the volunteer armies and troops. The Bolsheviks tried to establish a Marxist regime in Poland in the belief that its people wanted a workers' revolution. Instead, the Poles resisted and drove the Red Army back in 1920, while the Allied powers rushed supplies and advisers to Warsaw. Though this and other revolts failed, they provided further proof that total war had loosened political and social order.

The Paris Peace Conference, 1919–1920

As political turmoil engulfed peoples from Berlin to Moscow, a peace conference opened in Paris in January 1919. Visions of communism spreading westward haunted the assembled statesmen, but the desperation of millions of war-ravaged citizens, the status of Germany, and the reconstruction of a secure Europe topped their agenda. Leaders such as French premier Georges Clemenceau had to satisfy their angry citizens who demanded revenge or, at the very least, compensation for their suffering. France had lost 1.3 million people—almost an entire generation of young men—and more than a million buildings, six thousand bridges, and thousands of miles of railroad lines and roads. Great Britain's representative, Prime

Minister David Lloyd George, caught the mood of the British public by campaigning in 1918 with such slogans as "Hang the kaiser." Italians arrived on the scene demanding the territory promised to them in the 1915 Treaty of London. Meanwhile, U.S. president Woodrow Wilson, head of the new world power that had helped achieve the Allied victory, had his own agenda. His **Fourteen Points**, on which the truce had been based, were steeped in the language of freedom and called for open diplomacy, arms reduction, an "open-minded" settlement of colonial issues, and the self-determination of peoples.

The Fourteen Points did not represent the mood of all the victors, however. Allied propaganda had made the Germans seem like inhuman monsters, and many citizens demanded a harsh peace. Moreover, some military experts feared that Germany was using the armistice only to regroup for more warfare. Indeed, Germans widely refused to admit that their army had lost the war. Eager for army support, Ebert had given returning soldiers a rousing welcome: "As you return unconquered from the field of battle, I salute you." Thus, conservative leaders among Wilson's former allies campaigned to make him look naive and deluded. "Wilson bores me with his Fourteen Points," Clemenceau complained. "Why, the good Lord himself has only ten."

Nevertheless, Wilson's Fourteen Points appealed to European moderates and persuaded Germans that the settlement would not be vindictive. His commitment to *settlement* as opposed to *surrender* contained tough-minded stipulations, for Wilson wisely recognized that Germany was still the strongest state on the continent. He merely pushed for a treaty that balanced the strengths and interests of various European powers. Economists and other specialists accompanying Wilson to Paris agreed that, harshly dealt with and humiliated, Germany might soon become vengeful and chaotic—a lethal combination that could lead to the growth of unsavory political movements.

The Peace of Paris Treaties. After six months, the statesmen and their teams of experts produced the **Peace of Paris** (1919–1920), composed of a cluster of individual treaties (Map 26.4). These treaties shocked the countries that had to accept them, and in retrospect historians see how they destabilized eastern and east-central Europe (see "Contrasting Views," page 1024). The treaties separated Austria from Hungary, reduced Hungary by almost two-thirds of its inhabitants and three-quarters of its territory, broke up the Ottoman Empire, and treated Germany severely. They replaced the Habsburg Empire with a group of small, internally divided, and relatively weak states: Czechoslovakia, Poland, and the Kingdom of the Serbs, Croats, and Slovenes, soon renamed Yugoslavia. After a century and a half of partition, Poland was reconstructed from parts of Russia, Germany, and Austria-Hungary, with one-third of its population ethnically non-Polish. The statesmen in Paris also created a Polish Corridor that connected Poland to the Baltic Sea and separated East Prussia from the rest of Germany. Austria and Hungary were both left reeling at their loss of territory and resources, while many of the new states became rivals and were for the most part politically and economically weak.

The Treaty of Versailles with Germany was the centerpiece of the Peace of Paris, however. France recovered Alsace and Lorraine, and the victors would temporarily occupy the left, or western, bank of the Rhine and the coal-bearing Saar basin. Wilson accepted his allies' expectations that Germany would pay substantial reparations for civilian damage during the war. The specific amount was set in 1921 at the crushing sum of 132 billion gold marks. Germany also had to reduce its army, almost eliminate its navy, stop manufacturing offensive weapons, and deliver a large amount of free coal each year to Belgium and France. Furthermore, it was forbidden to have an air force and had to give up its colonies. The average German saw in these terms an unmerited humiliation that was compounded by Article 231 of the treaty, which described Germany's "responsibility" for damage "imposed . . . by the aggression of Germany and her allies." The outraged German people interpreted this as a **war guilt clause**, which blamed Germany for the war and allowed the victors to collect reparations from economically viable Germany rather than from decimated Austria. War guilt made Germany an outcast in the community of nations.

MAP 26.4 Europe and the Middle East after the Peace Settlements of 1919–1920
The political landscape of central, east, and east-central Europe changed dramatically as a result of the Russian Revolution and the Peace of Paris. The Ottoman, German, Russian, and Austro-Hungarian Empires were either broken up altogether into multiple small states or territorially reduced in size. The settlement left resentments among Germans and Hungarians and created a group of weak, struggling nations in the heartland of Europe. The victorious powers took over much of the oil-rich Middle East. Why is it significant that the postwar geopolitical changes were so concentrated in one section of Europe?

The League of Nations. Besides redrawing the map of Europe, the Peace of Paris set up an organization called the **League of Nations**, whose responsibility for maintaining peace— a principle called collective security—was to replace the divisive secrecy of prewar power politics. As part of Wilson's vision, the league would guide the world toward disarmament, arbitrate its members' disputes, and monitor labor conditions around the world. Returning to prewar isolationism, the U.S. Senate, in a humiliating defeat for the president, failed to ratify the peace settlement and refused to join the league. Moreover, both

CONTRASTING VIEWS

Arguing with the Victors

The end of World War I aroused hopes around the world. The conquered expected a fair-minded treaty based on Wilson's Fourteen Points, while a variety of other peoples saw in that same document the promise of "self-determination." In particular, men living under colonial domination, such as many in Africa and the Arab states, had taken part in the conflict because the Allies had promised new rights in return for fighting this bloody and destructive war. The emir Faisal had led troops to bring about freedom and Arab unity (Document 1). Like some representatives at the Pan-African Congress, even those Africans who had not fought saw peacemaking as a process that should forge a better future. Many wanted full political rights and parliamentary representation if not outright independence (Document 2).

In Paris in 1919, representatives of the victorious powers were besieged by outsiders to Western government, each making a claim for special attention to their needs or for concrete action to realize the noble rhetoric of the Fourteen Points. Feminist-pacifists wanted to ensure the pacifist cause (Document 3), while a Polish representative articulated a concern that Jews had taken too many good jobs in the new Poland (Document 4). The proposals to the peacemakers produced few results.

1. CLAIMING INDEPENDENCE FOR THE MIDDLE EAST

Arabs had hotly debated whether to join with the Allied colonizers in World War I, but promises of independence won them over. Some Arabs argued for independence of individual areas in the Middle East and for resolutions to competing claims of the Arabs and of new Jewish settlers in the region. Emir Faisal, who had commanded Arab forces in the war, presented the pan-Arab ideal.

The aim of the Arab nationalist movement is to unite the Arabs eventually into one nation. . . .

I came to Europe on behalf of my father and the Arabs of Asia to say that they are expecting the powers at the Conference not to attach undue importance to superficial differences of condition among us and not to consider them only from the low ground of existing European material interests and supposed spheres of influence. They expect the powers to think of them as one potential people, jealous of their language and liberty, and they ask that no step be taken inconsistent with the prospect of an eventual union of these areas under one sovereign government.

Source: Stephen Bonsal, *Suitors and Suppliants: The Little Nations at Versailles* (Port Washington: Kennikat Press, 1969), 32–33.

2. THE VOICE OF PAN-AFRICANISTS

African and African American leaders believed it would be opportune for them to meet in a Pan-African Congress while the Paris Peace Conference was going on. For some time an idea of a single African people had been forming among leading black intellectuals, and Pan-African meetings had taken place from the late nineteenth century on. The demands were legion, but above all the congress, by mid-February 1919, had resolved to seek better treatment from the colonial powers.

Resolved

That the Allied and Associated Powers establish a code of law for the international protection of the natives of Africa. . . .

The Negroes of the world demand that hereafter the natives of Africa and the peoples of African descent be governed according to the following principles:

1. The land: the land and its natural resources shall be held in trust for the natives and at all times they shall have effective ownership of as much land as they can profitably develop. . . .

3. Labor: slavery and corporal punishment shall be abolished and forced labor except in punishment for crime. . . .

5. The state: the natives of Africa must have the right to participate in the government as fast as their development permits, in conformity with the principle that the government exists for the natives, and not the natives for the government.

Source: Quoted in W. E. B. Du Bois, *The World and Africa* (New York: International Publishers, 1946), 11–12.

3. PACIFISTS' GOALS FOR THE PEACE PROCESS

Pacifist women were angered that the peace conference would be held in Paris instead of in a noncombatant or neutral country. Situating it where wartime hatred was at a fevered pitch, they argued, would not allow the conquered to receive a fair hearing. The continuing blockade of the Central Powers after the armistice was increasing suffering and causing deaths. Themselves meeting in neutral Switzerland, pacifist women speeded the dispatch of their resolutions to Paris when the Treaty of Versailles was announced.

The International Congress of Women regards the famine, pestilence, and unemployment extending throughout great tracts of central and eastern Europe and into Asia as a disgrace to civilization.

It therefore urges the Governments of all the Powers assembled at the Peace Conference immediately to develop the inter-allied organizations formed for purposes of war into an international organization for purposes of peace, so that the resources of the world—food, raw materials, finance, transport—shall be made available for the relief of the peoples of all countries from famine and pestilence.

To this end it urges that immediate action be taken . . . to raise the blockade.

The terms of the peace tacitly sanction secret diplomacy, deny the principles of self-determination, recognize the rights of victors to the spoils of war, and create all over Europe discords and animosities, which can only lead to future war. . . . By the financial and economic proposals a hundred million people of this generation in the heart of Europe are condemned to poverty, disease,

and despair, which must result in the spread of hatred and anarchy within each nation.

Source: James Weber Linn, *Jane Addams: A Biography* (New York: Greenwood, 1968), 342–43.

4. ANTI-SEMITISM AT THE PEACE TABLE

Some of the new nations of eastern Europe were using anti-Semitism to focus their unity and independence. A Polish leader lobbied the Allies to exercise a police power in the newly independent Poland, where major problems would be rural crowding and inability to make ends meet on the land.

We have too many Jews, and those who will be allowed to remain with us must change their habits. I recognize that this will be difficult and will take time. The Jew must produce and not remain devoted exclusively to what we regard as parasitical pursuits. Unless restrictions are imposed upon them soon, all our lawyers, doctors, and small merchants will be Jews. They must turn to agriculture, and they must at least share small business and retail stores with their Polish neighbors. I readily admit that there is some basis in the Jewish contention that in days past it was difficult for them to own land or even to work the fields of others as tenants; that they were often compelled by circumstances beyond their control to gain their livelihood in ways which are hurtful to Polish economy. Under our new constitution all this will be changed, and for their own good I hope the Jews will avail themselves of their new opportunities. I say this in their own interest as well as in the interest of restored Poland.

Source: Bonsal, *Suitors and Suppliants*, 124.

QUESTIONS TO CONSIDER

1. Describe the various contending claims beyond those of the official combatant powers. Did the victorious powers heed these voices when forging the peace?

2. How were the various demands at the peace conference related to the politics and conditions of World War I?

3. Do any of the demands seem more justifiable in addressing the peacetime needs of Europe and the world?

Germany and Russia initially were excluded from the league and were thus blocked from acting in legal concert with other nations.

The covenant, or charter, of the League of Nations organized the administration of the colonies and territories of Germany and the Ottoman Empire—such as Togo, Cameroon, Syria, and Palestine—through a system of mandates. The victorious powers exercised political control over mandated territory, but local leaders retained limited authority. The league covenant justified the **mandate system** as providing governance by "advanced nations" over territories "not yet able to stand by themselves under the strenuous conditions of the modern world." However, colonized people and other people of color, who had served and fallen on the battlefield, began to challenge the claims of their European masters. They had seen how savage and degraded were these people who claimed to be racially superior, politically advanced, and leaders of global culture. "Never again will the darker people of the world occupy just the place they had before," the African American leader W. E. B. Du Bois◆ predicted in 1918. The mandate system continued the practice of apportioning the globe among European powers at a time when those powers were bankrupt and weak. Like the Peace of Paris, it aroused anger and resistance.

Economic and Diplomatic Consequences of the Peace

The financial and political settlement in the Peace of Paris had repercussions in the 1920s and beyond. Western leaders worried deeply about two intertwined issues in the aftermath of the war. The first was economic recovery and its relationship to war debts, the restoration of European trade, and German reparations. The second was ensuring that peace lasted.

Economic Dilemmas. France, the hardest hit by wartime destruction and billions of dollars in debt to the United States, estimated that Germany owed it at least $200 billion. The British, by contrast, worried about maintaining their empire and restoring trade with Germany, not about exacting huge

◆**Du Bois:** doo BOYS

reparations. Nevertheless, both France and Britain depended on some monetary redress to pay their war debts to the United States because Europe's share of world trade had plunged during the war. Germany claimed that the demand for reparations strained its government, already beset by political upheaval. But hardship was not the result of the Peace of Paris alone. The kaiser had refused to raise taxes, especially on the rich, to

Inflation in Germany (1923)
The German government resisted paying reparations by inflating the currency and slowing down the shipments of manufactured goods that were a condition of the reparations program. French troops were sent into the Ruhr manufacturing region to take goods by force, but angry workers refused to work for the occupiers. To pay the workers and service its debt, the government printed money so rapidly that inflation brought the value of the German mark from 4.2 marks to the dollar to 4.2 trillion marks to the dollar, which destroyed savings and increased resentment in Germany. As children played with worthless marks, shown in this picture, a new administration came to power in the summer, promising to resolve the currency situation and to deal with the reparations issue with practical measures, rather than futile resistance. **For more help analyzing this image**, see the visual activity for this chapter in the Online Study Guide at **bedfordstmartins.com/hunt**.
AKG Images.

pay for the war, so the new republic had to pay reparations and to manage the staggering war debt. As an experiment in democracy, the Weimar Republic needed to woo the citizenry, not alienate it by hiking taxes. In 1921, when Germans refused to present a realistic payment scheme, the French occupied several cities in the Ruhr until a settlement was reached.

Embroiled with powers to the west, the German government deftly sought economic and diplomatic relations in eastern Europe. It reached an agreement to foster economic ties with Russia, desperate for western trade, in the Treaty of Rapallo (1922). Its relations with powers to the west, however, continued to deteriorate. In 1923, after Germany defaulted on coal deliveries, the French and Belgians sent troops into the Ruhr basin, planning to use its abundant resources to recoup their wartime expenditures. Urged on by the government, Ruhr citizens fought back, shutting down industry by staying home from work. The German government printed trillions of marks to support the workers and to pay its own war debts with practically worthless currency. Soon Germany was in the midst of a staggering inflation that demoralized its citizens and gravely threatened the international economy: at one point a single U.S. dollar cost 4.42 trillion marks, and wheelbarrows of money were required to buy a turnip. The spirit of the League of Nations demanded a resolution to this economic chaos through negotiations. The Dawes Plan (1924) and eventually the Young Plan (1929) reduced payments to the victors and restored the value of German currency. Nonetheless, the inflation had wreaked enduring psychological havoc, wiped out people's savings, and ruined those living on fixed incomes (see the photo opposite).

Ensuring Peace. A second pressing issue in addition to economic recovery involved ensuring that peace would last. Statesmen recognized that peace demanded disarmament, a return of Germany to the fold, and security for the new countries of eastern Europe. It took hard diplomatic bargaining outside the league to produce two plans in Germany's favor. At the Washington Conference in 1921, the United States, Great Britain, Japan, France, and Italy agreed to reduce their number of battleships

and to stop constructing new ones for ten years. Four years later, in 1925, the league sponsored a meeting of the great powers, including Germany, at Locarno, Switzerland. The Treaty of Locarno provided Germany with a seat in the League of Nations as of 1926. In return, Germany agreed not to violate the borders of France and Belgium and to keep the nearby Rhineland demilitarized— that is, unfortified by troops.

To the east, the door seemed open to a German attempt to regain territory lost to Poland, to form a merger with Austria, or to launch aggression against the states spun off from Austria-Hungary. To meet the threat, Czechoslovakia, Yugoslavia, and Romania formed the Little Entente in 1920–1921. This was a collective security agreement to protect themselves from their two powerful neighbors, Germany and Russia, and to guard against Hungarian expansionism. Then, between 1924 and 1927, France allied itself with the Little Entente and with Poland. The major European powers, Japan, and the United States also

The Little Entente

signed the Kellogg-Briand Pact (1928), which formally rejected international violence. The nations failed, however, to commit themselves to concrete action to prevent its outbreak.

The publicity and planning that yielded the international agreements during the 1920s sharply contrasted with old-style diplomacy, which was conducted in secret and subject to little public scrutiny or democratic influence. The development of a system of collective security and the new openness suggested a diplomatic revolution that would promote peace in international relations. Despite this promise, openness allowed diplomats of the era to feed the press reports calculated to arouse the masses. For example, much of the German populace was lashed into a nationalist frenzy by the press and opposing parties whenever Germany's diplomats, who were successfully working to undo the Treaty of Versailles by reducing reparation payments, for example, seemed to

Western Europe. In France and Britain, parties of the right had less effect than elsewhere because parliamentary institutions were better established and the upper classes were not plotting to restore an authoritarian monarchy. In France, politicians from the conservative right and moderate left successively formed coalitions and rallied general support to rebuild war-torn regions and to force Germany to pay for the reconstruction. Hoping to stimulate population growth after the devastating loss of life, the French parliament made the distribution of birth-control information illegal and abortion a severely punished crime.

Britain encountered postwar boom and bust and continuing strife in Ireland. Ramsay MacDonald (1866–1937), elected the first Labour prime minister in 1924, represented the political ambitions of the working masses. Like other postwar British leaders, he had to swallow the paradoxical fact that although Britain had the largest world empire, many of its industries were obsolete or in poor condition. A showdown came in the ailing coal industry, where prices fell and wages plummeted once the Ruhr mines reopened and offered tough competition to British mines. On May 3, 1926, workers launched a nine-day general strike against wage cuts and dangerous conditions in the mines. The strike provoked unprecedented middle-class resistance. University students, homemakers, and businessmen shut down the strike by driving trains, working on docks, and replacing workers in other jobs. Thus, citizens from many walks of life revived the wartime spirit to defend the declining economy.

In Ireland, the British government met bloody confrontation over the continuing failure to implement home rule. Irish republicans had attacked government buildings in Dublin on Easter Monday 1916 in an effort to wrest Irish independence from Britain. Ill-prepared, their effort was easily defeated and many of them were

The Irish Free State and Ulster, 1921

executed. The severe punishment only intensified demands for home rule, and in January 1919, republican leaders announced Ireland's independence from Britain and created a separate parliament. The British government refused to recognize the parliament and sent in the Black and Tans, a volunteer army of demobilized soldiers named after the color of their uniforms. Terror reigned in Ireland, as both the pro-independence forces and the Black and Tans waged guerrilla warfare, taking hostages, blowing up buildings, and even shooting into crowds at soccer matches. By 1921, public outrage forced the British to negotiate a treaty. It reversed the Irish declaration of independence and made the Irish Free State a self-governing dominion owing allegiance to the British crown. Northern Ireland, a group of six northern counties containing a majority of Protestants, gained a separate status: it was self-governing but still had representation in the British Parliament. Incomplete independence and the rights of religious minorities remained contentious issues.

The Colonies. European powers encountered rebellion in overseas empires as well. Colonized peoples who had fought in the war expected more rights and even independence. Indeed, European politicians and military recruiters had actually promised the vote and many other reforms in exchange for support. But colonists' political activism, now enhanced by increasing education, trade, and experience with the West, mostly met a brutal response. Fearful of losing India, British forces massacred protesters at Amritsar◆ in 1919 and put down revolts against the mandate system in Egypt and Iran in the early 1920s. The Dutch jailed political leaders in Indonesia; the French punished Indochinese nationalists. For many Western governments, maintaining empires abroad was crucial to ensuring democracy at home, as any hint of declining national prestige fed antidemocratic forces.

Despite resistance, the 1920s marked the high tide of imperialism and saw a fresh burst of imperialist activity. Britain and France, enjoying new access to Germany's colonies in Africa and to the spoils of the fallen Ottoman

◆**Amritsar:** uhm RIHT sur

Empire in the Middle East, were at the height of their global power. Although bankrupted and shell-shocked by the war, these countries along with Holland, Belgium, Japan, and Australia took advantage of the growing profitability that enterprises around the world could bring. Middle Eastern and Indonesian oil, for instance, fueled the growing number of automobiles, airplanes, trucks, ships, and buses and heated homes. Products like hot chocolate and tropical fruit became regular items in the diet.

The balance of power among the imperial nations was changing, however. The most important change was the real competition for markets, resources, and influence with Japan. During the war, Japanese industrialization altered dramatically from the production of textiles to heavy industrial output such as shipbuilding and metallurgy. Japan's industrial development advanced because the Western powers outsourced their wartime needs for industrial goods. As Japan took shipping, financial, and other business from Britain and France, its prosperity skyrocketed and Japan began edging Britain out as the dominant power in China. The Japanese government touted its success across the region and pointed to its achievements as a sign of hope for non-Westerners. Japan's prosperity, the country's politicians claimed, would pull its neighbors from Western oppression. Strongly nationalist, the government was nonetheless accommodating toward the Western powers because it could not yet afford to compete militarily. Thus, although outraged that the Western powers at Paris had refused a nondiscrimination clause in the charter of the League of Nations, the Japanese government cooperated in the Anglo-American dominated peace, even agreeing to the settlement at the naval conference in Washington that set the ratio of English, American, and Japanese shipbuilding at 5:5:3. "Rolls Royce, Rolls Royce, Ford," a Japanese official commented bitterly.

Reconstructing the Economy

New worldwide economic competition was as big a challenge to recovery as were global political struggles. During the war the European economy had lost many of its international markets to India, Canada, Australia, Japan, and the United States. Nonetheless, the war had forced many European manufacturers to become more efficient and had expanded the demand for automotive and air transport, electrical products, and synthetic goods. The prewar pattern of mergers and cartels continued after 1918, giving rise to gigantic food-processing firms such as Nestlé in Switzerland and petroleum enterprises such as Royal Dutch Shell. Owners of these large manufacturing conglomerates wielded more financial and political power than entire small countries. By the late 1920s, Europe had overcome the wild economic swings of the immediate postwar years and was enjoying renewed economic prosperity.

Despite this growth, the United States had become the trendsetter in economic modernization. European businessmen made pilgrimages to Henry Ford's Detroit assembly line, which by 1929 produced a Ford automobile every ten seconds. Ford touted this miracle of productivity as resulting in a lower cost of living and increased purchasing power for workers. Indeed, whereas French, German, and British citizens in total had fewer than two million cars, some seventeen million cars were on U.S. streets in 1925.

Scientific management, sometimes called the science of work, also aimed to raise productivity. American efficiency expert Frederick Taylor (1856–1915) developed methods to streamline workers' tasks and motions for maximum productivity. European industrialists adopted Taylor's methods during the war and after, but they were also influenced by European psychologists who emphasized the mental aspects of productivity and the need for a balance of work and leisure activities, such as cinema and sports, for both workers and managers. In theory, increased productivity not only produced prosperity for all but also aimed to bind workers and management together, avoiding Russian-style worker revolution. In practice, streamlining did help reduce working hours in many industries, a result that encouraged union leaders to embrace modernization and the "cult of efficiency." For many workers, however, the emphasis on efficiency seemed inhuman, with restrictions on time and motion so severe that often they were allowed to use the bathroom only on a fixed schedule. "When I left the factory, it followed me," wrote one worker. "In my dreams I was a machine."

The managerial sector in industry had expanded during the war and continued to do so thereafter. Workers' initiative became devalued, with managers alone seen as creative and innovative. Managers reorganized work procedures and classified workers' skills. They categorized "female" jobs as those requiring less skill and therefore deserving of lower wages, thus adapting the old segmentation of the labor market to the new working conditions. With male workers' jobs increasingly threatened by labor-saving machinery, unions usually agreed that women should receive lower wages to keep them from competing with men for scarce high-paying jobs. Like the managerial sector, union bureaucracy had ballooned during World War I to help monitor labor's part in the war. Union bureaucrats became specialized, composed of negotiators, membership organizers, educators and propagandists, and political liaisons. Playing a key role in politics, unions could mobilize masses of people, as they demonstrated when they blocked coups against the Weimar government in the 1920s and organized the 1926 general strike in Great Britain.

Restoring Society

Postwar society met the returning millions of brutalized, incapacitated, and shell-shocked veterans with combined joy and apprehension. Many veterans harbored hostility toward civilians who had rebelled against wartime conditions, these soldiers charged, instead of patriotically enduring them. The world to which the veterans returned differed from the home they had left: the war had blurred class distinctions, giving rise to expectations that life would be fairer afterward. The massive casualties had fostered social mobility by allowing commoners to move up to the ranks of officers, positions often monopolized by the prewar aristocracy. Members of all classes had rubbed shoulders in the trenches. The enormous loss of life and the enduring wounds inspired in many a newfound sense of community. His son killed on the battlefield, author Rudyard Kipling was

among those who influenced the decision that all memorials to individual soldiers would be the same—whether the soldier was rich or poor. Wealth, he maintained, should not allow some to "proclaim their grief above other people's grief" when rich and poor had died the same death in the same cause. The identical, evenly spaced crosses of military cemeteries made all the dead equal, as did the mass "brothers' graves" at the battlefront where all ranks lay side by side in a single burial pit.

In contrast to expectations veterans often had no jobs; and some soldiers found that their wives and sweethearts had abandoned them—a wrenching betrayal for those who had risked their lives to protect the homeland. Middle-class daughters began to work outside the home; their mothers did their own housework because former servants could earn more money in factories. Women of all classes cut their hair, wore sleeker clothes, smoked, and had money of their own. In the United States this postwar version of the "new woman" was called the flapper. Patriotic when the war erupted, civilians, especially women, sometimes felt estranged from these returning warriors who had inflicted so much death and who had lived daily with filth, rats, and decaying human flesh. Civilian anxieties were often valid. Tens of thousands of German, central European, and Italian soldiers refused to disband; a few British veterans even vandalized university classrooms and assaulted women streetcar conductors and factory workers. Women who had served on the front could empathize with the soldiers' woes. But many suffragists in England, for instance, who had fought for an end to separate spheres before the war, now embraced gender segregation, so fearful were they of returning veterans.

Confronting the appeal of Bolshevism, governments tried to make civilian life as comfortable as possible to reintegrate men into society and prevent revolution. Politicians believed in the stabilizing power of traditional family values and supported social programs such as pensions, benefits for out-of-work men, and housing for veterans to alleviate their pent-up anger. The new housing—"homes for heroes," as politicians called the program—was a vast improvement over nineteenth-century working-class tenements. In Vienna,

Frankfurt, Berlin, and Stockholm, modern housing projects provided collective laundries, day-care centers, and rooms for group socializing; they featured gardens, terraces, and balconies to provide a soothing, country ambience that offset the hectic nature of industrial life. Inside, they boasted modern kitchens, indoor plumbing, central heating, and electricity. Borrowing the clean lines of East Asian and African dwellings to create a sense of modernity, domestic architects avoided ornate moldings, plaster-work, and curlicues—now seen as old-fashioned. The bungalow, a style started in India, formed the basis for early suburban developments and for the beach homes that higher productivity would allow the middle classes to enjoy.

Despite government efforts to restore traditional family values, war had dissolved many middle-class conventions, among them attempts to keep unmarried young men and women apart. Freer relationships and more open discussions of sex characterized the 1920s. Middle-class youth of both sexes visited jazz clubs and attended movies together. Revealing bathing suits, short skirts, and body-hugging clothing emphasized women's sexuality, seeming to invite men and women to join together and replenish the postwar population. Still, the context for sexuality remained marriage. In 1918, British scientist Marie Stopes published the best seller *Married Love*, and in 1927, the wildly successful *Ideal Marriage: Its Physiology and Technique* by Dutch author Theodor van de Velde appeared. Both described sex in rhapsodic terms and offered precise information about birth control and sexual physiology. Changing ideas about sex were not limited to the middle and upper classes; one Viennese reformer described working-class marriage as "an erotic-comradely relationship of equals" rather than the economic partnership of past centuries. The flapper, a sexually liberated working-woman, vied with the dedicated housewife to

Einstein Tower (1919-1921)
While the war profoundly disillusioned many in the West, peace aroused utopian hopes for a better future, and this utopianism influenced building design. The post-war years saw the construction of modern apartment buildings with conveniences such as laundries and a spare, clean architectural style—some of these buildings were intended to be "homes for heroes." This radical break with ornate Victorian styles appears in this specially designed observatory that could also serve as a house for the celebrated physicist Albert Einstein. Its flowing lines continued the prewar trend in modern art to let forms express inner states. In this case, architect Erich Mendelsohn, who favored fantasy and utopianism in his designs at the time, shows the expressive possibilities of building materials. Design would become sparer still as the 1920s progressed. *Astrophysikalisches Institut Potsdam. Photo: Dr. J Rendtel, Potsdam, Germany.*

represent the ordinary woman in the public's eyes. Meanwhile, such writers as the Briton D. H. Lawrence and the American Ernest Hemingway glorified men's sexual vigor in, respectively, *Women in Love* (1920) and *The Sun Also Rises* (1926). Mass culture's focus on heterosexuality encouraged the return to normality after the gender disorder that troubled the prewar and war years.

As images of men and women changed, people paid more attention to bodily improvement. The increasing use of toothbrushes and toothpaste, safety and electric razors, and deodorants reflected new standards for personal hygiene and grooming. For Western women, a multibillion-dollar cosmetics industry sprang up almost overnight. Women went to beauty parlors regularly to have their short hair cut, set, dyed, conditioned, straightened, or curled. They also tweezed their eyebrows, applied makeup, and even submitted to cosmetic surgery. Ordinary women painted their faces as formerly only prostitutes had done and competed in beauty contests that judged physical appearance. Instead of wanting to look plump and prosperous, people aimed to become thin and tan. The proliferation of boxers, hikers, gymnasts, and tap dancers spurred people to exercise and to participate in amateur sports. Modern industry encouraged consumers' new focus on personal health, which coincided with its need for a physically fit workforce.

As prosperity returned, people could afford to buy more consumer goods. Thanks to the gradual postwar increase in real wages, middle- and upper-class families snapped up sleek modern furniture, washing machines, and vacuum cleaners. Other modern conveniences such as electric irons and gas stoves appeared in better-off working-class households. Installment buying, popularized from the 1920s on, helped people finance these purchases. Housework became more mechanized, and family intimacy increasingly depended on machines of mass communication like radios, phonographs, and the less expensive automobiles. At the same time, these new domestic products that transformed private life brought unforeseen changes in the public world of culture and mass politics.

> **Review:** What were the major social and economic problems facing postwar Europe, and how did leaders address them?

❖ Mass Culture and the Rise of Modern Dictators

Wartime propaganda had aimed to unite all classes against a common enemy. In the 1920s, the process of incorporating diverse groups into a homogeneous Western culture, increasingly seen as a mass culture, continued. The instruments of mass culture—primarily radio, film, and newspapers—expanded their influence in the 1920s. Whereas some intellectuals urged elites to form an experimental avant-garde that refused to cater to "the drab mass of society," others wanted to use modern media and art to reach and even control the masses. Mass media had the potential for creating an informed citizenry and thus enhancing democracy. Paradoxically, it also provided the tools for dictatorship in the troubled postwar climate. Authoritarian rulers—Benito Mussolini, Joseph Stalin, and ultimately Adolf Hitler—were thus able to control the masses in unprecedented ways.

Culture for the Masses

An array of media had received a big boost from the war. Bulletins from the battlefront had whetted the public's craving for news and real-life stories, and sales of nonfiction books soared. After years of deprivation, people were driven to achieve material success, and they devoured books that advised how to gain it. A biography of Henry Ford, telling his story of upward mobility and technological accomplishment, became a best seller in Germany. With postwar readers avidly pursuing practical knowledge, institutes and night schools became popular, and school systems promoted reading in geography, science, and history. Photographs, the radio, and movies also contributed to the formation of national culture.

In the 1920s, filmmaking changed from an experimental medium to a thriving international business in which large corporations set up theater chains and marketed films worldwide. The war years, when the U.S. film industry began to outstrip the European, gave rise to specialization: directors, producers, marketers, photographers, film editors, and many others subdivided the process. A "star" system turned film personalities into celebrities, promoted by professional publicity and royal lifestyles. Films of literary classics and political events developed people's sense of a common heritage. Thus, the British government sponsored documentaries that articulated national goals, while Bolshevik leaders also supported filmmaking, underwriting the innovative work of director Sergei Eisenstein (1898–1948). His films *Potemkin* (1925) and *Ten Days That Shook the World* (1927–1928) presented a Bolshevik view of history to Russian and international audiences.

Films incorporated familiar elements from other cultural forms to cement viewer loyalty. The piano accompaniment that went along with the action of silent films derived from music halls; comic characters, farcical plots, and slapstick humor were borrowed from street or burlesque shows and from trends in postwar living. The popular comedies of the 1920s satirized men and women who botched the job of achieving emotional intimacy or featured the flapper and made her more visible to the masses. Lavish cinema houses attracted some hundred million weekly viewers, the majority of them women. As popular films and books crossed national borders, a cosmopolitanism and global culture for an international audience flourished.

Cinematic portrayals also played to postwar fantasies and fears, even global ones. In Germany, where filmmakers used expressionist sets and costumes to make films frightening, the influential hit *The Cabinet of Doctor Caligari* (1919) depicted events in an insane asylum as horrifying symbols of state power. Popular detective and cowboy films portrayed heroes who could restore wholeness to the disordered world of murder, crime, and injustice. The plight of gangsters appealed to war veterans, who had been exposed to the cheap value of life in the modern world. English comedian, actor, and producer Charlie Chaplin (1889–1977) created the character of the Little Tramp, who won international popularity as the defeated hero, the anonymous modern man, trying to keep his dignity in a mechanical world. All of these films played in theaters internationally, reflecting the restoration of global culture. Films featured characters from around the world, especially set in the popular new areas of North Africa and the Middle East, whose deserts became a common backdrop for plays and operettas too. Sporting events like cricket and boxing became internationalized in the 1920s and 1930s as the British competed with teams from other parts of the Commonwealth. Clips from these matches were then shown as newsreels before feature films.

Film remained experimental well into the 1920s, but radio was even more so. Developed from the wireless technology of Italian inventor Guglielmo Marconi, which had been introduced at the turn of the century, radio broadcasts in the first half of the 1920s were heard by mass audiences in public halls (much like film theaters) and featured orchestras and song followed by audience discussion. The radio quickly became a relatively inexpensive consumer item, and the public concert or lecture could now penetrate the individual's private living space. Specialized programming for men (such as sports reporting) and for women (such as advice on home management) soon followed. By the 1930s, radio was available for politicians to reach the masses wherever they might be—even alone at home (see "Taking Measure," page 1036).

Cultural Debates over the Future

Cultural leaders in the 1920s either were obsessed by the horrendous experience of war or—like the modernists before the war—held high hopes for creating a fresh, utopian future that would have little relation to the past. Those haunted by the war produced bleak or violent visions, and such visions were a theme in German art especially. The sculpture and woodcuts of German artist Käthe Kollwitz (1867–1945), whose son died in the war, portrayed bereaved parents, starving children, and other heart-wrenching, antiwar images. Others, gaining connections with a wider world because of the extent of the war, thought that Europeans needed to search for answers in other cultures. Seeing Europe as decadent, some turned to the spiritual richness of Asian philosophies and religions. Some fixed on the pacifist leader for Indian independence Mohandas Gandhi,♦ and an "Asiatic fever" seemed to grip intellectuals, including influential writers like Virginia Woolf and important filmmakers like Sergei Eisenstein.

Other artists employed satire, irony, and flippancy to express postwar rage and revulsion at civilization's apparent failure. George Grosz♦ (1893–1959), stunned by the carnage like so many other German veterans, joined Dada, an artistic and literary movement that had emerged during the war. With a meaningless name, Dada produced works marked by nonsense, incongruity, and

---

♦**Mohandas Gandhi:** moh huhn DAHS GAHN dee
♦**Grosz:** gorzh

TAKING MEASURE

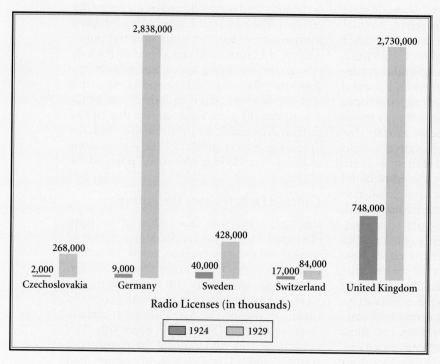

Radio Licenses (in thousands)

1924 — 1929

The Growth of Radio, 1924–1929
The spread of radio technology, like the earlier development of printing, advanced the cultural and political unity of citizens in a nation-state. The most industrially and commercially developed societies witnessed the most rapid diffusion of radios, which were both programmed and taxed by governments. Because of this centralized control, historians can compare the country-by-country use of radio in Europe and in much of the rest of the world. Of the five countries represented here, which experienced the most rapid spread of radio technology? Can you suggest reasons for their lead in accepting radio?

shrieking expressions of alienation. Grosz's paintings and cartoons of maimed soldiers and brutally murdered women reflected his psychic wounds and his self-proclaimed desire "to bellow back." In the postwar years, the modernist tradition of shocking audiences became more savage and often more hateful of ordinary people. Avant-garde portrayals of seediness and perversion in everyday life flourished in cabarets and theaters in the 1920s and reinforced veterans' visions of civilian decadence.

The art world itself became a battlefield, especially in defeated Germany, where it paralleled the Weimar Republic's contentious politics. Popular writers such as Ernst Jünger◆ glorified life in the trenches and called for the militarization of society to restore order. In contrast, Erich Maria Remarque cried out for an end to war in his controversial *All Quiet on the Western Front* (1928). This international best seller depicted the life shared by enemies on the battlefield,

thus aiming to dampen the national hatred stoked by wartime propaganda. Remarque's novel was part of a flood of popular, and often bitter, literature appearing on the tenth anniversary of the war's end.

Poets reflected on postwar conditions in more general terms, using styles that rejected the comforting rhymes or accessible metaphors of earlier verse. T. S. Eliot, an American-born poet who for a time worked as a banker in Britain, portrayed postwar life as petty and futile in "The Waste Land" (1922) and "The Hollow Men" (1925). The Irish nationalist poet William Butler Yeats joined Eliot in mourning the replacement of traditional society with its moral conviction and religious values by a new, superficial generation gaily dancing to jazz and engaging in promiscuous sex and vacuous conversation. Yeats's "Sailing to Byzantium" (1928), reflecting his own turn to cultures outside of Europe, starts:

That is no country for old men. The young
In one another's arms, birds in the trees
—Those dying generations . . .

◆**Jünger:** YOON gur

Both poets had an uneasy relationship with the modern world and at times advocated authoritarianism rather than democracy.

The postwar arts produced many a utopian fantasy turned upside down; dystopias of life in postrevolutionary, traumatized Europe proliferated. The bizarre expressionist stories of Franz Kafka, an employee of a large insurance company in Prague, showed the world as a vast, impersonal machine. His novels *The Trial* (1925) and *The Castle* (1926) evoked the hopeless condition of individuals caught between the cogs of society's relentlessly turning gears. His theme seemed to capture for civilian life the helplessness that soldiers had felt at the front. As an old social order collapsed in the face of political and technological innovation, other writers depicted the complex, sometimes nightmarish inner life of individuals. French author Marcel Proust,♦ in his multivolume novel *Remembrance of Things Past* (1913–1927), explored the workings of memory, the passage of time, and sexual modernity through the life of a narrator. At the beginning of the first volume, the narrator recalls a childhood obsession with his mother's absence as he tries to fall asleep at night. He witnesses progressively disturbing obsessions, such as violent sexuality and personal betrayals of love. The haunted inner life analyzed by Sigmund Freud was infiltrating fiction: for Proust, redemption lay in producing beauty from the raw material of life, not in promoting outmoded conventions of decency and morality.

Irish writer James Joyce and British writer Virginia Woolf shared Proust's vision of an interior self built on memories and sensations. Joyce's *Ulysses* (1922) and Woolf's *Mrs. Dalloway* (1925) illuminated the fast-moving inner lives of their characters in the course of a single day. In one of the most celebrated passages in *Ulysses*, a long interior monologue traces a woman's lifetime of erotic and emotional sensations. The technique of using a character's thoughts to propel a story was called stream of consciousness. For Woolf, the war had dissolved the solid society from which absorbing stories and fascinating characters were once fashioned.

Otto Dix, *The Cardgame* (1920)
The Cardgame shows the human legacy of war in mutilated bodies and destroyed minds. Even though some veterans would see armed struggle as the highest expression of manhood, the artist and ex-soldier Otto Dix depicted the faces of fallen soldiers with worms crawling through them. He portrayed postwar society as being run by corrupt profiteers and filled with decrepit prostitutes and others seeking mindless pleasure. World War I had shown life to be a game of chance to be played even after one had been beaten. It was this antiwar and pessimistic spirit that caused the Nazis to hate artists like Dix and to condemn their work. *Private Collection, Konstanz. ©Erich Lessing / Art Resource, NY. ©2005 Artist Rights Society (ARS), NY / VG Bild-Kunst, Bonn.*

Her characters experience fragmented conversations, momentary sensations, and incomplete relationships. Her novel *Orlando* (1928; see page 1038) also reflected the current interest in Eastern ideas of reincarnation and the self's travels through time. In the novel, the hero Orlando lives hundreds of years and in the course of his long life is eventually transformed into a woman.

There was another side to the postwar story, one based not on the interior life of a traumatized society but on the promise of

♦**Proust:** proost

Virginia Woolf's *Orlando* (1928)

Virginia Woolf's celebrated work featured innovations such as stream of consciousness and observations on the feelings of the modern self. She also observed changing sex roles, especially prominent after World War I, and the unequal status of women. She wrote Orlando *to show the fluidity of these roles in contrast to her contemporaries' belief in women's "eternal nature." In this witty fantasy the hero, born in the sixteenth century, wakes up mysteriously to find himself in the eighteenth century as a heroine.*

Virginia Woolf (1925) Along with Marcel Proust and James Joyce, Virginia Woolf represented the peak of literary modernism with her emphasis on interior states of mind and disjointed, dreamlike slices of reality. Woolf's novels such as Mrs. Dalloway also captured the unappreciated centrality of women, who provided an array of personal and emotional services to their families and more highly valued husbands. Woolf boldly announced that for a woman to be as creative as a man depended on her being partially relieved of the burdens of family—most notably having "a room of one's own" in which to develop that creativity. *Time Life Pictures/Getty Images.*

Orlando had become a woman—there is no denying it. But in every other respect, Orlando remained precisely as he had been. The change of sex, though it altered their future, did nothing whatever to alter their identity. Their faces remained, as their portraits prove, practically the same. His memory—but in future we must for convention's sake, say "her" for "his," and "she" for "he"—her memory then, went back through all the events of her past life without encountering any obstacle. Some slight haziness there may have been, as if a few dark drops had fallen into the clear pool of memory; certain things had become a little dimmed; but that was all. The change seemed to have been accomplished painlessly and completely and in such a way that Orlando herself showed no surprise at it. Many people, taking this into account, and holding that such a change of sex is against nature, have been at great pains to prove (1) that Orlando had always been a woman, (2) that Orlando is at this moment a man. Let biologists and psychologists determine. It is enough for us to state the simple fact; Orlando was a man till the age of thirty; when he became a woman and has remained so ever since.

But let other pens treat of sex and sexuality; we quit such odious subjects as soon as we can. Orlando had now washed, and dressed herself in those Turkish coats and trousers which can be worn indifferently by either sex; and was forced to consider her position. That it was precarious and embarrassing in the extreme must be the first

thought of every reader who has followed her story with sympathy. Young, noble, beautiful, she had woken to find herself in a position than which we can conceive none more delicate for a young lady of rank. We should not have blamed her had she rung the bell, screamed, or fainted. But Orlando showed no such signs of perturbation. All her actions were deliberate in the extreme, and might indeed have been thought to show tokens of premeditation. First, she carefully examined the papers on the table; took such as seemed to be written in poetry, and secreted them in her bosom; next she called her Seleuchi hound, which had never left her bed all these days, though half famished with hunger, fed and combed him; then stuck a pair of pistols in her belt. . . .

Source: Virginia Woolf, *Orlando, A Biography* (New York: Penguin, 1946), 85–86.

technology. Avant-garde artists before the war had celebrated the new, the futuristic, the utopian. Like Jules Amar crafting prostheses for shattered limbs, they were optimistic that technology could make an entire society whole after the slaughter. The aim of art, observed one of them, "is not to decorate our life but to organize it." The group of German artists called the Bauhaus◆ (after the idea of a craft association, or *Bauhütte*) created streamlined office buildings and designed functional furniture, utensils, and decorative objects, many of them inspired by forms from "untainted" East Asia and Africa. Russian artists, temporarily entranced by the Communist experiment, optimistically wrote novels about cement factories and ballets about steel—the latter an element common to artificial limbs and advanced, utopian design.

Artists fascinated by technology and machinery were drawn to the most modern of all countries—the United States. Hollywood films, glossy advertisements, and the bustling metropolis of New York tempted careworn Europeans. They loved films and pulp stories devoted to the Wild West and to the carefree modern American "girl." They were especially attracted to jazz, the improvisational music that emanated from Harlem. African American jazz musicians showed a resiliency of spirit, although Europeans could still feel superior to those of dark skin color in "primitive" costumes. Performers like Josephine Baker (1906–1976) and Louis Armstrong (1900–1971) became international sensations when they toured Europe's capital cities. Like jazz, the New York skyscraper pointed to the future. Skyscrapers rising in New York provided Europeans with a potent example of avant-garde expression that rejected a terrifying past and boldly shaped the future.

The Communist Utopia

Communism also promised a shining future and a modern, technological culture. But the Bolsheviks encountered powerful obstacles to consolidating their rule. In the early 1920s, peasant bands called Green Armies revolted

◆**Bauhaus:** BOW hows

against the policy of war communism that confiscated their agricultural produce. Industrial production stood at only 13 percent of its prewar output; the civil war had produced massive casualties; shortages of housing affected the entire population; and millions of refugees clogged the cities and roamed the countryside. In the early spring of 1921, workers in Petrograd and sailors at the nearby naval base at Kronstadt revolted, protesting their short rations and the privileged standard of living that Bolshevik supervisors enjoyed. They called for "soviets without Communists"—that is, a return to the early promises of the Bolsheviks for a worker state.

The government had many of the rebels shot, but the Kronstadt revolt pushed Lenin to institute reform. His New Economic Policy (NEP) returned parts of the economy to the free market, a temporary compromise with capitalist methods that allowed peasants to sell their grain freely and to profit from free trade in consumer goods. Although the state still controlled large industries and banking, the NEP encouraged people to produce, sell, and even, in the words of one leading Communist, "get rich." Consumer goods and more food to eat soon became available. Some peasants and merchants did indeed get rich, but many more remained impoverished. The rise of these wealthy "NEPmen," who bought and furnished splendid homes and who cared only about conspicuous consumption, belied the Bolshevik credo of a classless utopia.

Protest erupted within Communist ranks and prompted change. At the 1921 party congress, a group called the Worker Opposition objected to the party's usurpation of economic control from worker organizations and pointed out that the NEP was an agrarian program, not a proletarian one for workers. In response to charges of growing bureaucratization, Lenin suppressed the Worker Opposition faction and set up procedures for purging dissidents—an innovation that would become a deadly feature of Communist rule. Bolshevik leaders also tightened their grip on politics by making the Communist revolution a cultural reality that would inform people's daily lives and reshape their thoughts. Party leaders invaded the

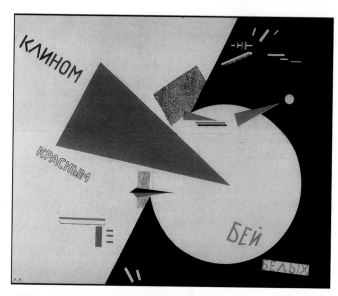

Eli Lissitsky, *Beat the Whites with the Red Wedge* (1919)
Russian artist Eli Lissitsky traveled throughout Europe to bring news of Soviet experimentation. In particular, the Soviets were taken with the new physics and their works of art surrounded the viewer with geometric forms. But abstract art was also political: in this 1919 painting, the "red wedge" uses the force of physical principles to defeat the objectively greater counterrevolutionary power of the "whites." Some revolutionary artists believed that the purity of the forms they used best represented the pure motives and high ideals of the revolutionary cause. Why might artists have moved, within a brief seventy-year period, from the realism of the 1850s and 1860s to the full abstraction of the 1920s? *David King Collection © 2005 Artists Rights Society (ARS), NY/VG Bild-Kinst, Bonn.*

countryside to set up classes in a variety of political and social subjects, and volunteers harangued the public about the importance of literacy—only 40 percent on the eve of World War I. To facilitate social equality between the sexes, as had been part of the Marxist vision of the future, the state made birth control, abortion, and divorce readily available through its agencies. As commissar for public welfare, Aleksandra Kollontai♦ (1872–1952) promoted birth-control education and the establishment of day care for children of working parents. To promote literacy, she wrote simply worded novels about love and work in the new socialist state for ordinary readers.

The bureaucracy swelled to bring modern culture to every corner of life, and *hygiene* and *efficiency* became watchwords, as they were in the rest of Europe. Such agencies as the Zhenotdel♦ (Women's Bureau) sought to teach women about their rights under communism and about modern sanitary practices. Efficiency experts aimed to replace tsarist backwardness with technological modernity based on the American techniques of Henry Ford and Frederick Taylor. The short-lived government agency Proletkult tried to develop proletarian culture through such undertakings as workers' universities, a workers' encyclopedia, a workers' theater, and workers' publishing. Russian artists experimented with blending high art and technology in mass culture, and composers punctuated their music with the sound of train or factory whistles. The poet Vladimir Mayakovsky edited a journal advocating utilitarian art, wrote verse praising his Communist passport and essays promoting toothbrushing, and staged uproarious farces for ordinary citizens. The early days of Bolshevik rule saw interesting and enduring experiments in all of the arts and in mass culture.

As with war communism, many resisted the reshaping of culture to "modern" or "Western" standards. Bolsheviks threatened everyday customs and the distribution of power within the family. As Zhenotdel workers moved into the countryside, for example, they attempted to teach women to behave as men's equals. Peasant families were still strongly patriarchal, however, and Zhenotdel activists threatened gender relations. In Islamic regions of central Asia, incorporated from the old Russian Empire into the new Communist one, Bolsheviks urged Muslim women to remove their veils and change their way of life, but fervent Muslims often attacked both Zhenotdel workers and women who followed their advice.

In the spring of 1922, Lenin suffered a debilitating stroke, and in January 1924, amid ongoing cultural experimentation, factional fighting, and repression, the architect of the Bolshevik Revolution died. The party congress declared the day of his death a permanent holiday, changed the name of Petrograd to Leningrad, and elevated the deceased leader into a secular god. After Lenin's death, no one was allowed to criticize any-

♦**Kollontai:** kuh luhn TY

♦**Zhenotdel:** ZHEHN aht dyul

thing associated with his name, a situation that paved the way for future abuses of power by Communist leaders.

Joseph Stalin (1879–1953), who served in the powerful post of general secretary of the Communist Party, led the deification of Lenin and was chief mourner at his funeral. Stalin organized the Lenin cult, which included the public display of Lenin's embalmed corpse—still on view today. He dealt with thousands of local party officials, which gave him enormous national patronage, and in 1924 welded both Russian and non-Russian regions into the Union of Soviet Socialist Republics (USSR), which gave him a claim to executive accomplishment. Wary of Stalin's growing influence and ruthlessness, Lenin in his last will and testament had asked that "the comrades find a way to remove Stalin." Stalin, however, prevented Lenin's will from being publicized and proceeded to discredit his chief rival, Trotsky, as an unpatriotic internationalist who was unwilling to concentrate on the tough job of modernizing the Soviet Union. With the blessing of Trotsky's other rivals, Stalin had him shipped out of the country. Bringing in several hundred thousand new party members who owed their positions in government and industry to him, Stalin built a loyal base of people whose success testified to the new opportunities that the Bolsheviks had ushered in. By 1928–1929, he had achieved virtually complete control of the USSR.

Fascism on the March in Italy

The political chaos and postwar discontent in Italy brought to power Benito Mussolini (1883–1945), who, like the Bolsheviks, promised an efficient utopia. Italian anger was first aroused when the Allies at Paris refused to honor the territorial promises of the Treaty of London. Domestic unrest swelled when peasants and workers protested their economic plight, made worse by the slump of the early 1920s. Since the late nineteenth century, many Europeans had come to blame parliaments for their ills, so Italians were responsive when Mussolini, a socialist journalist who turned to the radical right, built a personal army (the Black Shirts) of veterans and the unemployed to overturn parliamen-

tary government. In 1922, his supporters, known as Fascists, started a **march on Rome**, forcing King Victor Emmanuel III (r. 1900–1946) to make the dynamic Mussolini prime minister.

The Fascist movement flourished in the soil of poverty, social unrest, and wounded national pride. It attracted to its bands of Black Shirts many young men who felt cheated of glory by the Allies and veterans who missed the vigor of military life. The fasces,♦ an ancient Roman symbol depicting a bundle of sticks wrapped around an ax with the blade exposed, served as the movement's emblem; it represented both unity and force to Mussolini's supporters. Unlike Marxism, Fascism scoffed at coherent ideology: "Fascism is not a church," Mussolini announced upon taking power in 1922. "It is more like a training ground." **Fascism** was thus defined by its political grounding in the promotion of male violence and its opposition to the so-called antinationalist socialist movement and parliamentary rule.

Mussolini consolidated his power by making criticism of the state a criminal offense and by violently steamrolling parliamentary opposition. His Fascist bands demolished socialist newspaper offices, attacked striking workers, used their favorite tactic of forcing castor oil (which caused diarrhea) down the throats of socialists, and even murdered certain powerful opponents. Yet this brutality and the sight of the Black Shirts marching through the streets like disciplined soldiers signaled to many Italians that their country was ordered and modern. Large landowners and businessmen approved Fascist attacks on strikers, and they supported the movement financially. Their generous funding allowed Mussolini to build a large staff by hiring the unemployed and thus fostering the belief that Fascists could spark the economy when no one else could.

In addition to violence, Mussolini used mass propaganda to build support for a kind of military campaign to remake Italy. A society of extremes with severe rural poverty and thriving modern businesses such as the automobile industry, Italy welcomed the

♦**fasces:** FAS eez

Mussolini and the Black Shirts
For movements like fascism, the best society was one controlled by militarized politics that killed its critics and those of opposing political persuasions. Fascism saw parliamentary democracies as effeminate and doomed in the modern world, which would need dictators and obedient warriors to make it strong, efficient, and machinelike. Thus, in the name of promoting state power, Mussolini gained adherents both within and outside of Italy. How does this image reflect the values of Mussolini's fascism? *Farabolafoto.*

unity Mussolini promised to achieve. The mass media, addressing everyone, symbolized that unity. Peasant men huddled around radios to hear him call for a "battle of wheat" to enhance farm productivity. Peasant women, responding to his praise for maternal duty, adulated him for appearing to value womanhood. In the cities the government launched avant-garde architectural projects, designed new statues and public adornments, and used public relations promoters to advertise its achievements. His support of literary and cultural elites turned them into supporters. The modern city became a stage set built by technology for Fascist spectacle, as modernist buildings rose to house the Fascist bureaucracy and the Party's museums. Old residential neighborhoods fell to the wrecking machines, allowing road-builders to put in broad avenues for Fascist parades. Mussolini claimed that he made the trains run on time, and this one triumph of modern technology fanned people's hopes that he could restore order out of wartime and postwar chaos.

Mussolini added a strong dose of traditional values and prejudices to his modern order. Although an atheist, he recognized the importance of Catholicism to most Italians. In 1929, the Lateran Agreement between the Italian government and the church made the Vatican a state under papal sovereignty. The government recognized the church's right to determine marriage and family doctrine and endorsed its role in education. In return, the church ended its criticism of Fascist tactics. Mussolini also introduced a "corporate" state that denied individual political rights in favor of duty to the state. Corporatist decrees in 1926 organized employers, workers, and professionals into groups or corporations that would settle grievances and determine conditions of work. These decrees outlawed independent labor unions and peasant groups, effectively ending societal and workplace activism. Mussolini drew more applause from business leaders when he announced cuts in women's wages; and then late in the 1920s he won the approval of civil servants, lawyers, and professors by banning women from those professions. Mussolini did not want women out of the workforce altogether but aimed to confine them to low-paying jobs as part of his scheme for reinvigorating men.

Mussolini's admirers were numerous across the West and included Adolf Hitler, who throughout the 1920s had been building a paramilitary group of storm troopers and a political organization called the National Socialist German Workers' Party, or Nazis. During his brief stint in jail for the Beer Hall Putsch in 1923, Hitler wrote *Mein Kampf*◆ (*My Struggle*, 1925), which articulated both a vicious anti-Semitism and a political psychology for manipulating the masses. Hitler was fascinated by the dramatic success of the Fascists' march on Rome, by Mussolini's legal accession to power, and by his ability to thwart socialists and trade unionists. But the austere conditions that had allowed Mussolini to rise to power in 1922 no longer existed in Germany.

◆ *Mein Kampf:* myn KAHMPF

Although Hitler was welding the Nazi Party into a strong political instrument, the Weimar parliamentary government was actually working as the decade wore on.

Review: How did the postwar cultural atmosphere encourage both beneficial innovations and the trend toward dictatorship?

Conclusion

The year 1929 was to prove just as fateful as 1914 had been. In 1914, an orgy of death had begun, leading to tens of millions of casualties, the destruction of major dynasties, and the collapse of aristocratic classes. For four years war promoted the free play of military technology, virulent nationalism, and the control of everyday life by bureaucracy. While dynasties collapsed, the centralization of power increased the scope of the nation-state. The Peace of Paris in 1919 left Germans bitterly resentful, and it formally created new states in eastern and central Europe built on principles of nationalist ethnic unity—a settlement that, given the intense intermingling of ethnicities, religions, and languages in the area, failed to guarantee a peaceful future.

War furthered the development of mass society. It leveled social classes on the battlefield and in the graveyard, standardized political thinking through wartime propaganda, and extended many political rights to women for their war effort. Peacetime turned improved techniques of wartime production toward churning out consumer goods and technological innovations like the prostheses built by Jules Amar, air transport, cinema, and radio transmission for greater numbers of people. Modernity in the arts intensified after the war, probing the nightmarish battering endured by all segments of the population.

By the end of the 1920s, the legacy of war had been to so militarize politics that strongmen had come to power in Hungary, Poland, Romania, the Soviet Union, and Italy, with Adolf Hitler waiting in the wings in Germany. Many Westerners were impressed

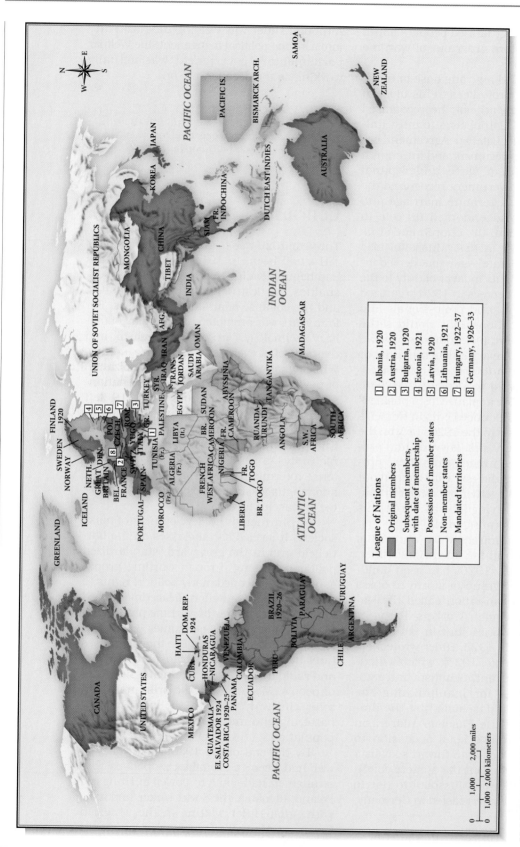

MAPPING THE WEST Europe and the World in 1929

The map reflects the partitions and nations that came into being as a result of war and revolution, while it obscures the increasing movement toward throwing off colonial rule. This was the true high point of empire: the drive for empire would diminish after 1929 except for Italy, which still craved colonies, and Japan, which continued searching for more land and resources to fuel its rapid growth. Describe the membership of the League of Nations as it existed after the war? Were there common bonds among these nations?

League of Nations

- Original members
- Subsequent members, with date of membership
- Possessions of member states
- Non-member states
- Mandated territories

1 Albania, 1920
2 Austria, 1920
3 Bulgaria, 1920
4 Estonia, 1921
5 Latvia, 1920
6 Lithuania, 1921
7 Hungary, 1922–37
8 Germany, 1926–33

by the tough, modern efficiency of the Fascists and Communists, who made parliaments and citizen rule seem out-of-date, even effeminate. Fascist and Communist commitment to violence, compared to that in the war, seemed tame. When the U.S. stock market crashed in 1929 and economic disaster circled the globe, authoritarian solutions and militarism continued to look appealing. What followed was a series of catastrophes even more devastating than World War I.

Suggested References

The Great War, 1914–1918

The most recent histories of the Great War consider its military, technological, psychic, social, and economic aspects. This vision of the war as a phenomenon occurring beyond the battlefield as well as on it characterizes the newest scholarship.

Davis, Belinda. *Home Fires Burning: Food, Politics, and Everyday Life in World War I Berlin.* 2000.

Echenberg, Myron. *Colonial Conscripts: The "Tirailleurs Sénégalais" in French West Africa, 1857–1960.* 1990.

*Hasek, Jaroslav. *The Good Soldier Schweik.* 1920.

Leed, Eric J. *No Man's Land: Combat and Identity in World War I.* 1979.

Panchasi, Roxanne. "Reconstructions: Prosthetics and the Rehabilitation of the Male Body in World War I." *Differences.* 1995.

Roshwald, Aviel, and Richard Stites, eds. *European Culture in the Great War: The Arts, Entertainment, and Propaganda, 1914–1918.* 1999.

Schmitt, Bernadotte E., and Harold C. Vederler. *The World in the Crucible, 1914–1919.* 1984.

World War I Documents Archive: http://www.lib.byu.edu/%7Erdh/wwi.

Protest, Revolution, and War's End, 1917–1918

Histories of the war's end account for the cataclysmic setting: deprivation, ongoing mass slaughter, and the eruption of revolution. Peacemaking also occurred, and that too was complex. In all, the violence of the postwar scene has made historians call into question the idea that wars end with an armistice.

Barry, John. *The Great Influenza: The Epic Story of the Greatest Plague in History.* 2004.

Fitzpatrick, Sheila. *The Russian Revolution, 1917–1932.* 1995.

Horne, John, ed. *State, Society and Mobilization in Europe during the First World War.* 2000.

Lewis, David Levering. *W. E. B. Du Bois: The Fight for Equality and the American Century, 1919–1963.* 2000.

Smith, Leonard V., et al. *France and the Great War 1914–1918.* 2003.

Welch, David. *Germany, Propaganda, and Total War, 1914–1918: The Sins of Omission.* 2000.

The Search for Peace in an Era of Revolution

Peacemaking was a fraught process, occurring amid revolution, the flu pandemic, and starvation. Many aspired to a lasting peace and to social justice. Both dreams were to be dashed, as the story of individuals and the fate of institutions like the League of Nations show. Thompson investigates the new mandates.

Cooper, John Milton. *Breaking the Heart of the World: Woodrow Wilson and the Fight for the League of Nations.* 2001.

Marks, Sally. *The Ebbing of European Ascendency: An International History of the World.* 2002.

Thompson, Elizabeth. *Colonial Citizens: Republican Rights, Paternal Privilege, and Gender in French Syria and Lebanon.* 2000.

A Decade of Recovery: Europe in the 1920s

Two themes shape the history of the 1920s: recovery from the trauma of war and revolution and ongoing modernization of work and social life. The great technological innovations of the prewar period such as films and airplanes receive sophisticated treatment by historians for their impact on people's imagination. The radio is another phenomenon just beginning to find its historians.

Hau, Michael. *The Cult of Health and Beauty in Germany: A Social History, 1890–1930.* 2003.

Kent, Susan. *Making Peace: The Reconstruction of Gender in Postwar Britain.* 1994.

*Primary source.

Lerner, Paul. *Hysterical Men: War, Psychiatry, and the Politics of Trauma in Germany, 1890–1930.* 2003.

Nolan, Mary. *Visions of Modernity: American Business and the Modernization of Germany.* 1994.

Schwartz, Vanessa, and Leo Charney, eds. *Cinema and the Invention of Modern Life.* 1995.

Mass Culture and the Rise of Modern Dictators

Mass communications advances in cinema and radio provided new tools for the rule of modern dictators who arose from the shambles of war and revolution. Many of the most interesting recent studies look at the cultural components of the consolidation of dictatorial power, while not forgetting the violence that was a particular feature of authoritarian rule in the postwar twentieth century.

Berezin, Mabel. *Making the Fascist Self: The Political Culture of Interwar Italy.* 1997.

Harsch, Donna. *German Social Democracy and the Rise of Nazism.* 1994.

*Kollontai, Aleksandra. *Love of Worker Bees.* 1923.

Northrop, Douglas. *Veiled Empire: Gender and Power in Stalinist Central Asia.* 2004.

Sneeringer, Julia. *Winning Women's Votes: Propaganda and Politics in Weimar Germany.* 2002.

Tumarkin, Nina. *Lenin Lives! The Lenin Cult in Soviet Russia.* 1997.

---

*Primary source.

CHAPTER REVIEW

IMPORTANT EVENTS

1914 August	World War I begins
1913–1925	Suffrage for women expands in much of Europe
1916	Irish nationalists stage Easter Uprising against British rule
1917 March	Revolution in Russia overturns tsarist autocracy
1917 April	The United States enters World War I
1917 November	Bolshevik Revolution in Russia
1918 November	Armistice ends fighting of World War I revolutionary turmoil throughout Germany; the kaiser abdicates
1918–1922	Civil war in Russia
1919	The Weimar Republic established
1919–1920	Paris Peace Conference redraws the map of Europe
1922	Ireland is split in two: the independent Irish Free State in the south and British-affiliated Ulster in the north; Fascists march on Rome; Mussolini becomes Italy's prime minister; T. S. Eliot publishes "The Waste Land"; James Joyce publishes *Ulysses*
1924	Lenin dies; Stalin and Trotsky contend for power
1924–1929	Period of general economic prosperity and stability
1929 October	Stock market crash in United States

KEY TERMS

Bolshevik Revolution (1017)

cult of the offensive (1006)

Fascism (1041)

Fourteen Points (1022)

League of Nations (1023)

mandate system (1026)

march on Rome (1041)

Peace of Paris (1022)

Provisional Government (1016)

Schlieffen Plan (1006)

soviets (1016)

total war (1003)

war guilt clause (1022)

Weimar Republic (1021)

REVIEW QUESTIONS

1. What factors contributed to making World War I a total war?
2. Why did people revolt during World War I, and what turned revolt in to outright revolution in Russia?
3. What were the major outcomes of the postwar peacemaking process?
4. What were the major social and economic problems facing postwar Europe, and how did leaders address them?
5. How did the postwar cultural atmosphere encourage both beneficial innovations and the trend toward dictatorship?

MAKING CONNECTIONS

1. How was postwar mass politics shaped by the experience of war?
2. What social changes from the war carried over into the postwar years and why?

FOR FURTHER EXPLORATION

To assess your mastery of the material in this chapter, see the Online Study Guide at bedfordstmartins.com/hunt.

To read additional primary-source material from this period, see Chapter 26 in *Sources of The Making of the West*, Second Edition.

An Age of Catastrophes, 1929–1945

WHEN ETTY HILLESUM MOVED TO AMSTERDAM in the early 1930s to attend law school, an economic depression gripped the world. A resourceful young Dutch woman, Hillesum pieced together a living as a housekeeper and part-time language teacher. The pressures and pleasures of everyday life blinded her, however, to Adolf Hitler's spectacular rise to power in Germany on a platform demonizing her fellow Jews for the economic slump. World War II ruptured her world and woke her up. The German conquest of the Netherlands in 1940 led to direct persecution of Dutch Jews, bringing Hillesum to the shattering realization, noted in her diary: "What they are after is our total destruction." The Nazis started relocating Jews to camps in Germany and Poland. Hillesum went to work for Amsterdam's Jewish Council, which was compelled to organize the transportation of Jews to the east. Changing from self-absorbed student to heroine, she did what she could to help other Jews and meticulously recorded the deportation. "I wish I could live for a long time so that one day I may know how to explain it," she wrote. When she was taken prisoner, she smuggled out letters, bearing witness to the brutal treatment in the transit camps. Etty Hillesum never fulfilled any of her life's ambitions: she died in the Auschwitz death camp in November 1943.

The U.S. stock market crash of 1929 opened a horrific era in world history, when people, old or young like Etty Hillesum, first

Nazis on Parade
By the time Hitler came to power in 1933, Germany was mired in the Great Depression. Hated by Communists, Nazis, and conservatives alike, the republic had few supporters. To a nation still reeling from its defeat in World War I, the Nazis looked as if they would restore national power by defeating enemies—not the Allies but the Jews, Slavs, gypsies, and other groups both within and outside Germany's borders. Hitler took his cue from Mussolini by promising an end to democracy and tolerance. He did so in Germany and then sent his troops into the rest of Europe, including Holland, France, Poland, Czechoslovakia, and the Soviet Union. Compare the excitement of soldiers marching to war in World War I (page 1006) and the visual power of Nazi soldiers marching through the streets during the depression. **For more help analyzing this image,** see the visual activity for this chapter in the Online Study Guide at **bedfordstmartins.com/hunt**. *Hugo Jaeger/Time Life Pictures/Getty Images.*

experienced economic distress and then felt the full horror of war and genocide. During the Great Depression of the 1930s, suffering was global, intensifying social grievances throughout the world. In Europe, many people turned to military-style strongmen for solutions to economic and social ills. Chief among them, Adolf Hitler roused the German masses to pursue national greatness by scorning democratic rights and rooting out what he considered to be inferior, menacing people like Jews, Slavs, and Gypsies. Similarly authoritarian, militaristic, and fascist regimes spread to Portugal, Spain, Poland, Hungary, Japan, China, and elsewhere, trampling on representative institutions. Joseph Stalin oversaw the Soviet Union's rapid industrialization, but in the process he justified the killing of millions of citizens as necessary to Soviet growth.

The international scene was also perilous because elected leaders in the democracies reacted cautiously to the simultaneous phenomena of the depression and fascist aggression. In an age of mass media, civilian leaders appeared weak and fearful of conflict, while dictators in uniform looked bold and decisive. Only the German invasion of Poland in 1939 finally pushed the democracies to strong action, as World War II erupted in Europe. By 1941 the war had spread to the rest of the world with the United States, Great Britain, and the Soviet Union and others allied in combat against Germany, Italy, Japan, and their allies. Tens of millions would perish in this war because both technology and ideology had become more deadly than they

had been just two decades earlier. Half the dead were civilians, among them Etty Hillesum, whose only crime was being a Jew.

❖ The Great Depression

The depression triggered both by the U.S. stock market crash of 1929 and by economic developments around the world threw tens of millions out of work and brought suffering to rural and urban folk alike. The whole world felt the depression's impact as commerce and investment in industry fell off, social life and gender roles were upset, and the birthrate plummeted. From peasants in Asia to industrial workers in Germany and the United States, the lives of large segments of the global population were ravaged.

Economic Disaster Strikes

In the 1920s, U.S. corporations and banks as well as millions of individual Americans had recklessly invested their money or, more often, borrowed money to invest in the stock market, which seemed to churn out endless profits. Using easy credit, they bought shares in popular companies based on electric, automotive, and other new technologies with complete confidence in ever-rising stock prices. By the end of the decade, the Federal Reserve Bank—the nation's central bank, which controlled financial policy—tightened the availability of credit in an attempt to stabilize the market. To meet the new restrictions, brokers had to demand that their

◆ **1929** U.S. stock market crashes; global depression begins; Soviet war against kulaks; Thomas Mann wins Nobel Prize

◆ **1933** Hitler comes to power

◆ **1936** Purges show trials in USSR
◆ **1936–1939** Spanish Civil war

◆ **1938** Virginia Woolf, *Three Guineas*

1925	1930	1935

clients immediately pay back the money they had borrowed to buy stock. As stocks were sold to cover the borrowed funds, the market collapsed. Between early October and mid-November 1929, the value of businesses listed on the U.S. stock market dropped from $87 billion to $30 billion. For individuals and for the economy as a whole, it was the beginning of economic catastrophe.

The crash helped bring on a global depression because the United States, a leading international creditor, had financed the economic growth of the previous five years. Suddenly strapped for credit, U.S. financiers cut back on loans and called in debts, undermining banks and industry at home and abroad. The recent U.S. lead in industrial production and the rise of Japanese manufacturing compounded the collapse in Europe. From the aging industries of Britain to the fledgling factories of eastern Europe, a decline in consumer buying and overproduction further eroded the European economy.

The Great Depression left no sector of the world economy unscathed, but government actions made the depression worse. To spur their economies, governments used standard tools such as budget cuts and high tariffs against foreign goods. Although part of accepted economic theory at the time, these policies further dampened spending and trade in the great industrial powers. By 1933, almost six million German workers, or about one-third of the workforce, were unemployed, and many others were underemployed. France had a more self-sufficient economy. Big businesses like the innovative Citroën car

manufacturer began to fail, however, and by the mid-1930s more than 800,000 French people had lost their jobs. Great Britain, with its textile, steel, and coal industries near ruin because of out-of-date techniques and foreign competition, had close to three million unemployed in 1932.

In the agricultural sector, where prices had been declining for several years because of technological innovation and abundant harvests around the world, creditors confiscated farms and equipment. With their incomes crumbling, millions of small farmers had no money to buy the chemical fertilizers and motorized machinery they needed to remain competitive, and they too went under. Eastern and southern European peasants, who had pressed for the redistribution of land after World War I, especially suffered because they could not afford to operate their newly acquired farms. In Poland, many of the 700,000 new landowners fell into debt trying to make their farms viable—a situation that was widespread across the eastern European region. Eastern European governments often ignored the farmers' plight as they poured available funds into industrialization—a policy that increased tensions in rural society.

Social Effects of the Depression

The picture of society during the Great Depression was more complex than utter ruin, however. First, the situation was not uniformly bleak. Despite the slump, modernization proceeded. Bordering English slums, one traveler in the mid-1930s noticed, were "filling stations

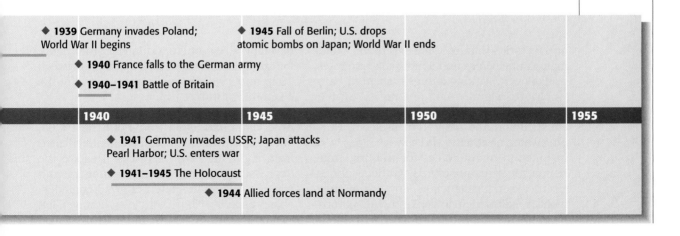

Hunger Marchers in London (1934)
The interwar years were full of civilian protests against government policies. In 1934, these unemployed hunger marchers rallied in London's Trafalgar Square to oppose government cuts in
unemployment benefits during the grim years of the Great Depression. Some marchers were
impressed by the different political system in the USSR, where there was full employment during
the entire 1930s, and became committed Communists; others strove to maintain a middle-class
respectability, even when unemployed—as seen in the proper dress of these hunger strikers. Still
other kinds of politics sprang up in the streets: In Germany there were attempted coups against
the government and by the late 1920s Nazi paramilitary troops regularly marched through city
streets to show their power and their contempt for democratic politics. *©Bettmann/Corbis.*

and factories that look like exhibition buildings, giant cinemas and dance halls and cafés,
bungalows with tiny garages, cocktail bars,
Woolworth's [and] swimming pools." Municipal and national governments continued road
construction and sanitation projects. Running water, electricity, and sewage pipes were
installed in many homes for the first time.
New factories manufactured synthetic fabrics,
electrical products such as stoves, and automobiles—all of them in demand. With government assistance, eastern European industry

developed: Romanian industrial production,
for example, increased by 55 percent between
1929 and 1939 throughout the worst of the
economic slump.

Second, the majority of Europeans and
Americans had jobs throughout the 1930s,
and people with steady employment benefited
from a drastic drop in prices. Despite the
depression, service workers, managers, and
business magnates often enjoyed considerable prosperity. Those with jobs, however, felt
the looming threat of becoming unemployed

and having to scrape, like thousands of others around them, for a bare existence. In towns with heavy industry, sometimes more than half the population was out of work. In England in the mid-1930s, close to 20 percent of the population lacked adequate food, clothing, or housing. In a 1932 school assignment, a German youth wrote: "My father has been out of work for two and a half years. He thinks that I'll never find a job." Despite the prosperity of many people, a storm cloud of fear and resentment settled over Western society.

Economic catastrophe upset social life and strained gender relations. Unemployed men sometimes stayed home all day, increasing the tension in small, overcrowded apartments. Women could often find low-paying jobs doing laundry and cleaning house for others. Men who stayed at home took over housekeeping chores, but some felt that this "women's work" demeaned their masculinity. As many women became breadwinners, albeit for low wages, men could be seen standing on street corners begging—a rearrangement of gender expectations that fueled discontent. Young men in cities faced severe unemployment. Some loitered in parks, intruding in areas usually frequented by mothers and their children and old people. As the percentage of farmworkers in the western European population decreased, rural men also faced the erosion of patriarchal authority, once central in overseeing farm labor and allocating property among heirs. Demagogues everywhere berated parliamentary politicians for their failure to stop the collapse of traditional values. The climate was thus primed for Nazi and fascist politicians who promised to restore prosperity and male dignity.

Politicians of all stripes used the continuing slide in the birthrate to stir already troubled political waters. They forecast national collapse, claiming that the declining birthrate (after a brief postwar upturn) combined with a declining economy signaled a crisis. The reason for the decline was clear: in difficult economic times, people chose to have fewer children. There was another reason too. Mandatory education and more years of required schooling, enforced more strictly after World War I, resulted in reduced income and greater expenses for parents.

Working-class children no longer brought in wages to supplement the family's income and were no longer available to help the family in other ways; instead, they cost money while they went to school. Family-planning centers opened, receiving a warm reception, and knowledge of birth control spread across the working and lower-middle classes, who continued the half-century-long trend of cutting family size.

Many politicians, however, used the population "crisis" to gain votes by igniting racism: "superior" peoples were selfishly failing to breed, they charged, while "inferior" peoples were lurking to take their place. This racism took a violent form in eastern Europe, where the rural population rose because of increased life expectancy despite an overall drop in birthrate. But increased population compounded the burdens of eastern European farm families, who faced an unprecedented struggle for survival. Throughout eastern Europe, peasant political parties blamed Jewish bankers for farm foreclosures and Jewish civil servants (of whom there were actually very few) for new taxes and inadequate relief programs. Thus, population issues along with economic misery fueled ethnic hatred, racial tensions, and anti-Semitism. Social issues inflamed the public sphere as they had before World War I.

The Great Depression beyond the West

The effects of the depression extended beyond the West, further accelerating the pace of change and spread of discontent in European empires. World War I and postwar investment had generated economic growth, a rising population, and explosive urbanization in Asia, Africa, and Latin America. Japan in particular had become a formidable industrial rival, while between 1920 and 1940, Shanghai ballooned from 1.7 million to 3.75 million residents and Calcutta from 1.8 million to 3.4 million. The depression, however, cut the demand for copper, tin, and other raw materials and for the finished products made in urban factories beyond the West. Rising agricultural productivity drove down the price of foodstuffs like rice and coffee, and this proved disastrous for people who had been forced to grow a single cash crop. However,

imperial landlords and traders had cut to make up for their own economic shortfalls. Discontent ran deep. Millions of African and Asian colonial troops had fought for Britain and France in World War I, but these countries had given little back to their colonial populations. In fact, the League of Nations charter had pointedly omitted any reference to the principle of racial equality demanded by people of color at the Paris conference. Their resolve fortified by these slights, by the model of Japan's growth, and by their own industrial development, colonial peoples turned to winning independence.

India was a prime example of visibly rising anger toward colonialism. Upper-class Indians, who had organized to gain rights from Britain in the late nineteenth century, were joined in the 1930s by millions of working people, including hundreds of thousands of veterans of World War I. Mohandas Gandhi (1869–1948, called Mahatma, or "great-souled") emerged as the charismatic leader for Indian independence. Of privileged birth and trained in England as a Western-style lawyer, Gandhi embraced Hindu self-denial and rejected the elaborate trappings of British life, wearing, for example, simple clothing made of thread he had spun. He advocated **civil disobedience**—deliberately but peacefully breaking the law—which he professed to model on British suffragists' tactics and on the teachings of Jesus, Buddha, and other spiritual leaders (see the illustration on this page). Boycotting British-made goods and disobeying British laws, Gandhi aimed to end the deference Indians had traditionally shown the British. The British jailed Gandhi repeatedly and tried to split the independence movement by encouraging the Muslim League and promoting Hindu-Muslim antagonism. As in Europe itself, an inflamed atmosphere set the stage for the future.

In the Middle East, Westernizer Mustafa Kemal, or Atatürk ("first among Turks," 1881–1938), led the Turks to found an independent republic in 1923 and to craft a capitalist economy. In an effort to nationalize and modernize Turkish culture, Kemal moved the capital from Constantinople to Ankara in 1923, officially changed the ancient Greek name Constantinople to the Turkish name Istanbul in 1930, mandated Western dress for men and

Gandhi Leading the Salt March (1930)
Mohandas Gandhi appealed to the masses, not just to the middle- and upper-class constituency of the Indian National Congress, which had emphasized reform and participation in government. Instead, Gandhi addressed the entire colonial system that prevented ordinary Indian people from using the country's national resources such as salt. Violating British laws, which prohibited Indians from gathering this natural product, Gandhi led the people in an act of civil disobedience—his march to the sea to harvest the salt. How might South Asians, other colonized peoples, and Europeans have reacted to this 1930 photo? © Bettmann/Corbis.

the economic picture was uneven in the colonies as well as in Europe. For instance, established industrial sectors of the Indian economy like textiles gained strength, with India achieving virtual independence from British cloth.

Economic distress added to smoldering grievances. During the economic crisis, colonial farmers withheld produce like cocoa from the imperial wholesalers, and strikes erupted across the colonies to restore the wages that

women, introduced the Latin alphabet, and abolished polygamy. In 1936, women received the vote and were made eligible to serve in the parliament. Persia similarly loosened the European grip on its economy, forced the negotiation of oil contracts that kept Western countries from taking the oil virtually free, updated its government, and in 1935 changed its name to Iran. In 1936, Britain agreed to end its military occupation of Egypt (though not the Suez Canal), fulfilling its promise of Egyptian self-rule granted in 1922. Subject peoples were becoming too well organized to accept colonial shackles any longer.

Pressured by rising tariffs in Europe that dampened their trade and obsessed by their own declining population, the French made fewer concessions in their colonies. Like all imperial countries, they came to depend more, not less, on what the empire could provide economically. The French also depended on the colonies for sheer numbers of people. France's trade with its colonies increased as that with Europe lagged, and the demographic surge in Asia and Africa bolstered French optimism. As one official put it, "One hundred and ten million strong, France can stand up to Germany." Like other Western-educated native leaders, Ho Chi Minh,♦ founder of the Indochinese Communist Party, contested his people's subjection, but in 1930 the French government brutally crushed the peasant uprising he led. Thus preoccupied with their empires, Britain and France fortified their troops stationed around the world and let totalitarian forces spread unchecked throughout Europe during the crisis-ridden 1930s.

Review: How did the Great Depression affect society and politics?

❖ Totalitarian Triumph

Representative government collapsed in many countries under the sheer weight of social and economic crisis. After 1929, Italy's Benito Mussolini, the Soviet Union's Joseph Stalin, and Germany's Adolf Hitler were able to mobilize vast support for their violent regimes.

♦**Ho Chi Minh:** HOH CHEE MIHN

Many people admired Mussolini and Hitler for the discipline they brought to social and economic life. Eager to achieve national greatness, many citizens simply overlooked the brutal side of modern dictatorship. In an age of crisis, utopian hopes also led many to support political violence as a sign of restored power. Unity and obedience—not freedom and rights—were seen as keys to rebirth. The common use of violence has led scholars to apply the term totalitarianism to the Fascist, Nazi, and Communist regimes of the 1930s (see "Terms of History," page 1056). The term refers to highly centralized systems of government that attempt to control society and ensure conformity through a single party and police terror. Forged in the crucible of war and its aftermath, totalitarian governments broke with liberal principles of freedom and natural rights and came to wage war on their own citizens.

The Rise of Stalinism

In the 1930s, Joseph Stalin led the astonishing transformation of the USSR from a rural society into a formidable industrial power. Having taken firm control against Lenin's express wishes, Stalin ended the New Economic Policy (NEP), Lenin's temporary compromise between Marxism and capitalism, with the first of several five-year plans presented in 1929.

Transforming the Economy. Stalin's **five-year plans** outlined a program for massive increases in the output of coal, iron ore, steel, and industrial goods over successive five-year periods. Without an end to economic backwardness, Stalin warned, "the advanced countries . . . will crush us." He thus established central economic planning—a policy used on both sides in World War I and increasingly favored by economists and industrialists around the world. Between 1928 and 1940, the number of Soviet workers in industry, construction, and transport grew from 4.6 million to 12.6 million. From 1927 to 1937, production in metallurgy and machinery rose 1,400 percent. Stalin's first five-year plan helped make the USSR a leading industrial nation.

Central planning helped create a new elite of bureaucrats and industrial officials; the number of managers in heavy industry grew

TERMS OF HISTORY

Totalitarianism

Totalitarianism is a word loaded with controversy, but when first introduced in Italy, Mussolini's government adopted it as a mark of pride. In 1923, Mussolini proposed a law by which the political party that garnered the most votes would seat 75 percent of the delegates in Italy's parliament. Until then, Italy's many political parties had formed coalitions that acted together to govern. The proposed law would help Mussolini's small but powerful Fascist Party rule alone, transforming its temporary popularity into real dominance.

One journalist cried foul, claiming that this proposal would eliminate both majority rule and minority coalitions in favor of a "totalitarian" system. He was beaten to death by Mussolini's thugs. Then, in a surprising turn, the Fascists embraced the term, proclaiming the superiority of an all-encompassing state led by a virile and forward-looking party. Their model was the "total state" under conditions of "total war" when efficient military rule stamped out effeminate principles of conscience, rights, and freedom. The Nazis also picked up on the term, hailing the effective totalitarian party that could make workers and soldiers like steel in body and in spirit. Some even pointed approvingly at the USSR's five-year plans and its use of coercion to create uniform political thinking as a "modern" kind of state power.

As refugees fled Europe in the 1930s, they contributed another ingredient to the definition of totalitarianism, a system they abhorred. Refugee intellectuals saw totalitarianism as stemming from the rational thought of the eighteenth century and the aim of the scientific revolution and the Enlightenment to dominate nature. Analogously, to their mind, the system of free trade and capitalist industrialization aimed at domination of the economy and resources. By these arguments, the Soviets were as guilty of totalitarianism as the Fascists and Nazis. As the cold war took shape in 1945, people who defended the USSR and hailed its contribution in the war to defeat Hitler and Mussolini turned against the term as a common definition for all three dictatorships. In the cold war, the United States wanted to view the Soviet system as identical to Nazism, while the USSR's defenders now envisioned the word *totalitarianism* as cold war propaganda and rejected its use. So heated became the debate over

by almost 500 percent between 1929 and 1935. Mostly party officials and technical experts, these managers dominated Soviet workers by limiting their ability to change jobs or move from place to place. Nonetheless, skilled workers as well as bureaucrats benefited substantially from the redistribution of privileges that accompanied industrialism and central planning. Compared with people working the land, both managers and workers in industry had better housing and wages, while Communist officials enjoyed additional perquisites such as country homes, food unavailable to the masses, and luxurious vacations.

Unskilled workers faced a grim plight, often with real dedication. Newcomers from the countryside were herded into barracklike dwellings, even tents, and subjected to dangerous factory conditions. Many took pride in the skills they acquired. "We mastered this profession—completely new to us—with great pleasure," a female lathe operator recalled. More often, however, workers fresh from the countryside lacked the technical education and even the tools necessary to accomplish goals prescribed by the five-year plan. Because fulfilling the plan had top priority as a measure of progress toward Communist utopia, official lying about productivity became ingrained in the economic system. Both the grim conditions and honest commitment to Communist goals turned the Soviet Union from an illiterate peasant society to an advanced industrial economy in a single decade. Intense

the concept and application of *totalitarianism* as a descriptive historical term that many scholars ceased to use it.

Others, however, believe the term merits rethinking now that the cold war is over. A totalitarian state, as its definition evolved late in the twentieth century, was one that intensified government's concern with private life and individual thought, leaving no realm of existence outside the state's will. Censorship of speech, suppression of parliamentary and freely chosen representative rule, and violent elimination of disagreement were crucial ingredients of a totalitarian system. Laws regulating reproduction and family life were also central, especially those that either criminalized or enforced birth control and abortion. Hitler, Mussolini, Stalin, and later Mao Zedong of China all made state control of reproduction pivotal to their regimes. Totalitarian regimes also relied on violence to forge unity: control of military or paramilitary weaponry and modern communications technology allowed for the programming of thought and the elimination of enemies, including those who simply had different ideas. Many believe that totalitarianism can work only in a society where the state uses advanced technology and advanced communications to mold individual thought.

Nonetheless, it is important to note the vast differences among totalitarian states: the socialist economy of the Soviet Union differed from the economies of both Nazi Germany and Fascist Italy. Moreover, systems lumped under the word *totalitarian* had different intellectual roots. Nationalism was key in the rise of fascism and Nazism, whereas communism began as an international workers' movement and forced people of many ethnicities to live together. Anti-Semitism also infected totalitarian societies in varying degrees: in Italy, Jews were rarely persecuted (and frequently protected from Nazis), Stalin purged individual Jews without singling out the entire race for extermination, and Nazism had the elimination of the Jews as central to its mission.

QUESTIONS TO CONSIDER

1. What is the relationship of totalitarian states to the tradition of rights and individual freedom?
2. What are shared characteristics of totalitarian rule?
3. What was the relationship between the rise of totalitarianism and World War I?

FURTHER READING

Arendt, Hannah. *The Origins of Totalitarianism.* 1951.

Gleason, Abbott. *Totalitarianism: The Inner History of the Cold War.* 1995.

Tormey, Simon. *Making Sense of Tyranny: Interpretations of Totalitarianism.* 1995.

---

suffering was tolerated because Soviet workers believed in the ethos of "constant struggle, struggle, and struggle" to achieve a Communist society, in the words of a worker. As another put it, "Man himself is being rebuilt."

In country and city alike work was politicized. Stalin demanded more grain from peasants (who had prospered under the NEP), both to feed the urban workforce and to export as a way to finance industrialization. Peasants resisted government demands by cutting production or withholding produce from the market. Faced with such recalcitrance, Stalin announced a new revolutionary challenge: the "liquidation of the kulaks"♦

(see "The War on Kulaks," page 1058.) The word *kulak*, which literally means "fist," was a derogatory term for prosperous peasants, but in practice it applied to anyone who opposed Stalin's plans to end independent farming. By the late 1920s, party workers were scouring villages for produce and forced villagers to identify the kulaks among them. Propaganda units instilled hatred for anyone connected with kulaks. One Russian remembered believing they were "bloodsuckers, cattle, swine, loathsome, repulsive: they had no souls; they stank." As "enemies of the state," whole families and even entire villages were robbed of their possessions, left to starve, or even murdered outright. Confiscated kulak land formed the basis of the

---

♦**kulaks:** koo LAHKS

The War on Kulaks

Elena Trofimovna Dolgikh was born in Russia in 1910, before World War I and the Bolshevik Revolution. For her family, the war against prosperous farmers called kulaks began even before Stalin launched his first five-year plan. In response to shortages, Communists began confiscating grain and evicting peasant families as early as 1927 and 1928. In an interview given after the collapse of communism in 1989 she described the early attack on kulaks.

In our area collectivization began in '27. That's when people were labeled kulaks and dispossessed. . . . And here's what happened: First of all, they drove the kulaks from their homes. Well, they gave away our horse and the rest—cups, spoons, ladles—all of it they started to sell to people who had not been labeled kulaks. And there were people who were willing to buy those cups, spoons, and ladles. And all of our family was deported to the mountains, to some valley there. So they began to dig shelters. They weren't allowed to take anything with them—only the clothes on their backs. Everything was sold, all that "kulak" wealth. Of course, they confiscated the apiary. This happened toward winter, and that very first winter they let the bees freeze to death. When Granddaddy learned of this, he was struck dead, his heart ruptured, as they said later, because he loved the apiary, he loved the bees. There were melon fields, and everything was ruined. He and Kostia [a brother] went to some village—I don't remember the name of it—where Grandma's sister lived in the mountains. They went on foot and asked for alms. Some gave, some didn't. . . .

[My brother Serezha] was fifteen, and at some point they rounded up all the young fellows from those shelters . . . and drove them on foot 150 kilometers. . . . And it was there . . . that he worked on the construction of the coal and metallurgical complex for several years. In the winter they had to dig ditches, foundation pits, and they were only released when the project was completed, when the first blast furnace was ready to be started up. He and the others had to wear sacks used to store salt. . . . They had no bedding, nothing. They kept dying off, and their bodies were hauled away somewhere.

Source: Barbara Engel and Anastasia Posadskaya-Vanderbeck, eds., *A Revolution of Their Own: Voices of Women in Soviet History* (Boulder: Westview, 1998), 166.

---

kolkhoz, or collective farm, where peasants were all to live, creating a Communist agricultural system using cooperative farming, shared facilities, and modern machinery. Traditional peasant life was brought to a violent end.

Transforming Society. Once the state had politicized work life as central to the achievement of communism, economic failure took on political meaning. Such failure was legion because the inexperience of factory workers, farmers, and party officials with advanced industrialization often meant an inability to meet quotas. In the face of the murder of farmers and the experiment with collectivization, the grain harvest declined from 83 million tons in 1930 to 67 million in

1934 and Soviet citizens starved. Stalin blamed failure on "wreckers," saboteurs of communism, and he instituted **purges**—that is, state violence in the form of widespread arrests, imprisonments in labor camps, and executions—to rid society of these villains. These purges encompassed nearly all segments of society, but "bourgeois" engineers were the first group condemned for causing low productivity. Trials of prominent figures followed, beginning in 1936. When Sergei Kirov, the popular first secretary of the Leningrad Communist Party, was murdered, Stalin used his death (which he may have instigated) as the pretext to try former Bolshevik leaders in a series of "show trials"—trials based on trumped-up charges, fabricated evidence, and coerced confessions.

The government charged these Bolsheviks with conspiring to overthrow Soviet rule. Tortured and coerced to confess in court, most of those found guilty were shot. Yet there was a bizarre atmosphere of acceptance among the top leadership, who saw the purges as good for the future of socialism. Just before his execution, one Bolshevik loyalist and former editor of the party newspaper *Pravda* wrote to Stalin praising the "great and bold political idea behind the general purge" that was clearly part of the process toward democracy. "I could not hope to be left out. . . . It would be petty of me to put the fortunes of my own person on the same level as those tasks of world-historical importance, which rest above all on your shoulders."

The spirit of purge swept all levels of society, and no rung of the Soviet power structure escaped. One woman poet described the scene in towns and cities: "Great concert and lecture halls were turned into public confessionals. . . . People did penance for [everything]. . . . Beating their breasts, the 'guilty' would lament that they had 'shown political short-sightedness' and 'lack of vigilance' . . . and were full of 'rotten liberalism.'" In 1937 and 1938, military leaders were arrested and executed without public trials; some ranks were entirely wiped out. Although it appeared a suicidal massacre at a time when Hitler threatened war, thousands of high military posts became open to new talent. Stalin would not have to worry about an officer corps wedded to old ideas, as had happened in World War I. Simultaneously, the government expanded the system of prison camps, founded under Lenin, into an extensive network stretching several thousand miles from Moscow to Siberia. Called the Gulag—an acronym for the administrative arm of the government that ran the camps—the system held millions of prisoners under lethal conditions. Prisoners did every kind of work from digging canals to building apartment buildings in Moscow. Some one million died annually as a result of the harsh conditions, which included insufficient food and housing and twelve- to sixteen-hour workdays at crushing physical labor. Regular beatings and murders of prisoners rounded out Gulag life, as it became another aspect of Soviet violence.

Before the outbreak of World War II in 1939, casualties of the Soviet system far exceeded those in Nazi Germany up to that point. This bloody period of Soviet history has thus provoked intense debate among historians trying to understand the phenomenon of mass murder. Were the purges carefully planned and directed solely by Stalin, who actually watched the trials from a secret booth in the courtroom? Or were they initiated by the Communist Party's rank and file? Some historians see the purges as a clear-headed attempt on Stalin's part to eliminate barriers to total control, while others view them as the machinations of a psychopath. More recently, historians have judged the purges to result from power struggles among party officials looking for a quick route to the top. People in the lower ranks denounced their superiors to cover the way they themselves had falsified statistics, been lenient on kulaks, or lacked the proper vigilance. Still other interpretations see many denunciations and confessions as sincere expressions of workers' commitment to rooting out enemies of their proletarian utopia. Evidence shows that, in a way, the wide range of purges was a sign of social equality; no one—not even members of Stalin's family and close circle—was exempt. These debates help us attribute responsibility for the horrendous suffering and loss of life; they also add to our understanding of Communist policy in the 1930s and the nature of the Soviet regime. Even amid historical controversy regarding causes, we may be certain about the outcome: the ongoing arrests, incarcerations, and executions removed rivals to Stalin's power.

The 1930s also marked a sharp reversal of toleration in Soviet social life, as sexual freedom also retreated. Much like the rest of Europe, the USSR experienced a rapid decline in its birthrate in the 1930s. This drop, combined with the need to replace the millions of people lost since 1914, motivated Stalin to end the reproductive freedom of the early revolutionary years in order to increase the birthrate. The state restricted access to birth-control information and abortion. More lavish wedding ceremonies came back into fashion, divorces became difficult to obtain, and the state criminalized homosexuality.

N. J. Altman, *Anna Akhmatova*
This modernist painting portrays the poet Anna Akhmatova in 1914, when she was a centerpiece of literary salon life in Russia and the subject of several avant-garde portraits. In the 1930s and 1940s, Akhmatova gave poetic voice to Soviet suffering, recording in her verse ordinary people's endurance of purges, deprivation, and warfare. As she encouraged people to resist the Nazis during World War II, Stalin allowed her to revive Russian patriotism instead of socialist internationalism. What role do poets and artists play in times of suffering? Why are they considered role models when their activity is so different from other people's? *State Russian Museum, St. Petersburg/The Bridgeman Art Library. © Estate of N. J. Altman / RAO, Moscow/VAGA, NY.*

Whereas Bolsheviks had once derided the family as a "bourgeois" institution, propaganda now referred to the family unit as a "school for socialism." Yet women in rural areas made gains in literacy and received improvements in health care. Positions in the lower ranks of the party opened to women as the purges continued, and women increasingly were accepted into the professions. However, the physical and mental stress on women, particularly those in the industrial workforce, increased. After long hours in factories, workingwomen also stood in lines for scarce consumer goods and performed all household and child-care tasks under harsh conditions.

Cultural life was equally paradoxical under Stalin, for it brought an end to avant-garde experimentation. Simultaneously, modernist intellectuals continued to promote their ability to mobilize the masses by appealing to the unconscious and the emotions in their work. Stalin endorsed this role by calling artists and writers "engineers of the soul," but he controlled their output through the Union of Soviet Writers. The union assigned housing, office space, supplies, equipment, and secretarial help and even determined the types of books authors could write. In return, the "comrade artist" adhered to the official style of "socialist realism," derived from the 1920s focus on the common worker as a type of social hero. Some artists, such as the poet Anna Akhmatova (1889–1966; see the illustration on this page), refused to accept this system.

> *Stars of death stood above us, and Russia,*
> *In her innocence, twisted in pain*
> *Under blood-spattered boots . . .*

wrote Akhmatova in those years. Writers and artists went underground, secretly creating works that are still coming to light. Many others, including the composer Sergei Prokofiev (1891–1953), found ways to accommodate their talents to the state's demands. Prokofiev composed scores both for the delightful *Peter and the Wolf* and for Sergei Eisenstein's 1938 film *Alexander Nevsky*, a production that transparently compared Stalin to the towering medieval rulers of the Russian people. Aided by adaptable artists, workers, and bureaucrats, Stalin stood triumphant as the 1930s drew to a close. He was, as two different workers put it, "our beloved Leader" and "a god on earth."

Hitler's Rise to Power

Hitler ended German democracy. Since the early 1920s, he had tried to rouse the German masses to crush the fragile Weimar Republic. In his coup attempt of 1923, in his influential book *Mein Kampf* (My Struggle, 1925), and in his leadership of the Nazi Party, he drummed at a message of anti-Semitism and the rebirth of the German "race." When the Great Depression struck Germany, his party began to outstrip its rivals in elections, thanks in part to massive support from some big businessmen. Among these supporters, for example, was film and press mogul Alfred Hugenberg. Hugenberg's press relentlessly slammed the Weimar government, blaming it for the disastrous economy and inflaming wounded German pride over the defeat in World War I. Nazi supporters took to the streets, jousting with young Communist groups who agitated on behalf of the new Soviet experiment. Hugenberg's press always reported that Communist thugs had attacked upright Nazis, drawing sympathy and further support from the middle classes.

Parliamentary government virtually ground to a halt in the face of economic crisis and real differences over solutions, adding to the social disarray. The Reichstag, or German assembly, failed to approve emergency plans to improve the economy, as Nazi and Communist deputies disrupted its sessions and thus discredited democracy among the people. Hitler's followers made parliamentary government look even more inept by rampaging through the streets and attacking Jews, Communists, and Social Democrats. By targeting all these as a single, monolithic group of "Bolshevik" enemies, the Nazis won wide approval for confronting those who were said to have brought on the depression. Many thought it was time to replace democratic government with a bold, new leader who would take on these so-called enemies military style, without qualms or fussy legal procedures.

As a result of the depression, media publicity, and its own street tactics, Hitler's National Socialist German Workers' Party (NSDAP)—the Nazi Party—which had received little more than 2 percent of the vote in 1928, won almost 20 percent in the Reichstag elections of 1930 and more than doubled its representation in 1932. Many of Hitler's supporters, like Stalin's, were young and idealistic. In 1930, 70 percent of party members were under forty, a stark contrast to the image of Weimar politicians as aged and ineffectual. To youth, the future looked bleak, and they were full of idealism that a better world was possible if Hitler took control. Although businessmen provided substantial sums of money, every class supported the Nazis. The largest number of supporters came from the industrial working class because they had the most voters, but white-collar workers and the lower-middle class joined the party in percentages out of proportion with their numbers in the population. The years of inflation that wiped out savings left them with especially bitter memories, and they too were ready for Hitler even if he did seem a little rough around the edges.

Hitler's modern propaganda techniques helped build his appeal. Thousands of recordings of Hitler's speeches and other Nazi mementos circulated among the citizenry. Teenagers painted their fingernails with swastikas, a Buddhist symbol adopted by the Nazis,

Toys Depicting Nazis
As a totalitarian ideology, Nazism was part of everyday life. Nazi insignia decorated clothing, dishes, cigarette lighters, and even fingernails. People chose their loved ones according to Nazi rules, sent young people to Nazi clubs and organizations, and bought Nazi toys like these for their children's playtime. Nazi songs, Nazi parades and festivals, and Nazi art filled leisure hours. How important are ordinary objects in the development of political attitudes? *Imperial War Museum, London.*

and soldiers flashed metal match covers with Nazi insignia. Nazi rallies were masterpieces of political display in which Hitler mesmerized the crowds as their strong, vastly superior *Führer*, or "leader." Frenzied and inspirational, he represented neither the calculating politician nor the rational bureaucrat but "the creative element," as one poet put it. In actuality, however, Hitler viewed the masses only as tools, and he had contempt for them. In *Mein Kampf* he discussed his philosophy of how to deal with them:

> The receptivity of the great masses is very limited, their intelligence is small. In consequence of these facts, all effective propaganda must be limited to a very few points and must harp on those in slogans until the last member of the public understands what you want him to understand.

With Hitler, as with Stalin, mass politics reached terrifying and cynical proportions; Hitler's media techniques, however, were to endure, some believe to influence today's political styles.

Nazi success in the 1932 Reichstag elections was made more alarming because the Communists also did very well. The leader of one of these two parties was the logical choice as chancellor, and this fact upset conservative politicians in the government. Germany's conservative elites—from the military, industry, and the state bureaucracy—loathed and feared the Communists for their opposition to private property. They favored Hitler as a common type they believed to be easily manipulated. They invited him in January 1933 to become chancellor, and he accepted.

The Nazification of German Politics

Hitler took office amid jubilation in Berlin, as tens of thousands of Hitler's paramilitary supporters, called storm troopers, paraded through the streets with blazing torches. Millions celebrated Hitler's ascent to power. "My father went down to the cellar and brought up our best bottles of wine. . . . And my mother wept for joy," one German recalled. "Now everything will be all right," she said. Instead of being easy to manipulate, Hitler took command brutally, quickly installing himself and his party as dominant and closing down representative government with an ugly show of force.

Terror in the Nazi State.   Within a month of Hitler's taking power, the elements of Nazi political domination were in place. When the Reichstag building was gutted by fire in February 1933, Nazis blamed the Communists and used the fire as the excuse for suspending civil rights, imposing censorship of the press, and prohibiting meetings of the opposition. Hitler had always claimed that all political parties except the NSDAP were his enemies. "Our opponents complain that we National Socialists, and I in particular, are intolerant and intractable," he declared. "They are right, we are intolerant! I have set myself one task, namely to sweep those parties out of Germany."

Storm troopers' political violence became a way of life. They harassed many democratic politicians into silent passivity. At the end of March, intimidated Reichstag delegates let pass the **Enabling Act**, which suspended the constitution for four years and allowed Nazi laws to take effect without parliamentary approval. Solid middle-class Germans approved the Enabling Act as a way to advance the creation of a *Volksgemeinschaft*♦ ("people's community") of like-minded, racially pure Germans—Aryans in Nazi terminology. Heinrich Himmler headed the elite Schutzstaffel (SS), an organization that protected Hitler, and he commanded the Reich's political police system. The Gestapo, or Prussian political police run by Hermann Goering, also enforced complete obedience to Nazism. These organizations had vast powers to arrest people and either execute them or imprison them in concentration camps, the first of which opened at Dachau♦ near Munich in March 1933. The Nazis filled it and later camps with political enemies like socialists, and then with Jews, homosexuals, and others said to interfere with the Volksgemeinschaft. As one Nazi leader proclaimed:

> [National socialism] does not believe that one soul is equal to another, one man equal to another. It does not believe in rights as such. It aims to create the German man of strength, its task is to protect the German people, and all . . . must be subordinate to this goal.

♦*Volksgemeinschaft:* FOHLKS geh myn shaft
♦**Dachau:** DAH kow

Hitler deliberately blurred authority in the government and party so that confusion and bitter competition reigned. He thus prevented the emergence of coalitions against him and allowed himself to arbitrate the confusion, often with violence. When Ernst Roehm, leader of the SA (storm troopers) and Hitler's longtime collaborator, called for a "second revolution" to end the corrupt influence of the old business and military elites on the Nazi leadership, Hitler ordered Roehm's assassination. The bloody Night of the Long Knives (June 30, 1934), during which hundreds of SA leaders and innocent civilians were killed, enhanced Hitler's support among conservatives. They saw that he would deal ruthlessly with those favoring a leveling out of social privilege. Nazism's terroristic politics remained as the foundation of Hitler's Third Reich, which succeeded the First Reich of Charlemagne and the Second of Bismarck and William II.

Nazi Economic and Social Programs. New economic and social programs, especially putting people back to work, were also crucial to the survival of Hitler's regime. Economic revival built popular support, strengthened military industries, and provided the basis for German expansion. The Nazi government pursued **pump priming**, that is, stimulating the economy through public works programs and other infusions of funds to the public— by building tanks and airplanes and the Autobahn, or highway system. From farms to factories, the government demanded high productivity, and unemployment declined from a peak of almost 6 million in 1932 to 1.6 million by 1936. As labor shortages began to appear in certain areas, the government conscripted single women into service as farmworkers and domestics. The Nazi Party closed down labor unions, and government managers classified jobs, determined work procedures, and set pay levels, rating women's jobs lower than men's regardless of the level of expertise required. Imitating Stalin, Hitler instituted central planning, announcing a four-year plan in 1936 with the secret aim of preparing Germany for war by 1940. His programs produced large deficits, which the spoils of future conquests were supposed to eliminate.

Hitler had unprecedented power over the workings of everyday life, including gender roles. In June 1933, a bill took effect that encouraged Aryans (those people defined as racially German) to marry and have children. The bill provided for loans to Aryan newlyweds, but only to those couples in which the wife left the workforce. The loans were forgiven on the birth of the pair's fourth child. Nazi marriage programs enforced racial ideology as well as gender ideology; women were supposed to be subordinate so men would feel tough and industrious despite military defeat and economic depression. The ideal woman gave up her job, gave birth to many children, and completely surrendered her will to that of men. She "joyfully sacrifices and fulfills her fate," as one Nazi leader explained.

Nazism impoverished culture and everyday life. Although 70 percent of households had radios by 1938, the programming broadcast was severely censored. Books like Erich Maria Remarque's *All Quiet on the Western Front* were banned, and in May 1933 a huge book-burning ceremony rid libraries of works by Jews, socialists, homosexuals, and modernist writers out of favor with the Nazis. Modern art in museums and private collections was either destroyed or confiscated, and laws took jobs from Jews and women and bestowed them on Nazi party members. In the Hitler Youth, a mandatory organization for boys and girls over age ten, children learned to report those adults they suspected of disloyalty to the regime, even their own parents. People boasted that they could leave their bicycles out at night without fear of robbery, but their world was also filled with informers—some 100,000 of them on the Nazi payroll. In general, the improved economy led many to believe that Hitler was working an economic miracle while restoring pride in Germany and the harmonious community of an imaginary past. For hundreds of thousands, if not millions, of Germans, however, Nazi rule in the 1930s brought anything but community.

Nazi Racism

The Nazis defined Jews as an inferior "race" dangerous to the superior Aryan or Germanic "race" and responsible for most of Germany's problems, including defeat in World War I

public statements to sustain—not to denounce—faith in democratic rights and popular government. Eager to separate FDR's administration from Hoover's position, First Lady Eleanor Roosevelt rushed to greet the next group of veterans marching on Washington, and FDR himself received the delegation at the White House. The Roosevelts insisted that justice and human rights must not be surrendered in difficult times. "We Americans of today . . . are characters in the living book of democracy," FDR told a group of teenagers in 1939. "But we are also its author." Lynchings, racial violence, and harsh discrimination continued to cause enormous suffering in the United States during the Roosevelt administration, and the economy did not fully recover. But the president's media success and bold programs kept the masses committed to a democratic future.

Sweden. Sweden also developed a coherent program for solving economic and population problems. It too reconceived the government's role as central to promoting social welfare and economic democracy. Although Sweden had industrialized later than western Europe and the United States, it had a tradition of community cooperation in overcoming social and economic difficulties. Sweden succeeded in turning its economy around in the 1930s and instituted central planning and social welfare programs. It also devalued the currency to make Swedish exports more attractive on the international market. Thanks to pump-priming programs, Swedish productivity rose by 20 percent between 1929 and 1935, a time when other democracies were still experiencing decline.

Sweden addressed the population problem with government programs, but without the racist and antidemocratic coercion of totalitarianism. Alva Myrdal (1902–1986), a leading member of parliament, believed that fertility rates depended on both the economy and individual well-being. It was undemocratic, she maintained, that "the bearing of a child should mean economic distress" to those wanting children. Acting on Myrdal's advice to promote "voluntary parenthood," the government started a loan program for married couples in 1937 and introduced prenatal care, free childbirth in a hospital, a food

relief program, and subsidized housing for large families. By the end of the decade, almost 50 percent of all mothers in Sweden received government aid, most importantly in the form of a **family allowance** to help cover the costs of raising children. Long a concern of feminists and other social reformers, care of families became integral to the tasks of the modern state, which now saw itself as responsible for citizen welfare in hard times. Because all families—rural and urban, poor or prosperous—received these social benefits, there was widespread and consistent support for this experiment with developing a welfare state.

Britain and France. The most powerful democracy, the United States, had withdrawn from world leadership by refusing to participate in the League of Nations, leaving Britain and France with greater responsibility for international peace and well-being than their postwar resources could sustain. Britain was already mired in economic difficulties when the Great Depression hit. Faced with falling government revenues, Prime Minister Ramsay MacDonald, though leader of the Labour Party, reduced payments to the unemployed, and Parliament effectively denied unemployment insurance to women even though they had contributed to the unemployment fund. To protect jobs, the government imposed huge protective tariffs that actually discouraged a revival of international trade and did not relieve British misery. Only in 1933, with the economy continuing to worsen, did the government begin to take effective steps with massive programs of slum clearance, new housing construction, and health insurance for the needy. British leaders saw pump-priming methods of recovery as risky and untried, and thus they resorted to them only when all else had failed.

Depression struck later in France, but the country endured a decade of public strife in the 1930s due to severe postwar demoralization, stagnant population growth, and wage cuts. Deputies with opposing views on the economic crisis frequently came to blows in the Chamber of Deputies, and governments were voted in and out with dizzying rapidity. Parisians took to the streets to protest the government's belt-tightening policies, and right-wing paramilitary groups mushroomed, attracting the unemployed, students, and veterans to the cause of ending representative government. In February 1934, the paramilitary groups joined Communists and other outraged citizens in riots around the parliament building. "Let's string up the deputies," chanted the crowd. "And if we can't string them up, let's beat in their faces, let's reduce them to a pulp." Hundreds of demonstrators were wounded and killed, but the antirepublican right lacked both substantial support outside Paris and a leader like Hitler or Mussolini capable of unifying its various groups. As in other parts of Europe, hard times and the attractions of military dictatorship menaced democratic institutions.

Shocked into action by the force of fascism, French liberals, socialists, and Communists established an antifascist coalition known as the **Popular Front**. Until that time, such a merging of groups had been impossible in democratic countries because of Stalin's strict opposition to Communist collaboration with liberals and socialists, who disavowed Communist-style revolutions. Thus, leaders of Communist parties followed instructions not to cooperate, no matter how much they might agree that fascism had to be opposed. As fascism spread throughout Europe, however, Stalin reversed course and allowed Communists to join such efforts to protect democracy. For just over a year in 1936–1937 and again very briefly in 1938, the French Popular Front led the government, with the socialist leader Léon Blum (1872–1950) as premier. Like the American New Dealers and the Swedish Social Democrats, the Popular Front instituted long-overdue reforms. Blum extended family subsidies and welfare benefits, and he appointed women to his government (though women still were not allowed to vote). In June 1936, the government guaranteed workers two-week paid vacations, a forty-hour workweek, and the right to collective bargaining. Working people would long remember Blum as the man who improved their living standards and provided them with benefits and the right to vacations (see the illustration on this page).

During its brief life, the Popular Front offered the masses a youthful but democratic political culture. "In 1936 everyone was twenty years old," one man recalled,

Family at Normandy Beach
In the midst of the depression of the 1930s, the working classes nonetheless gained a taste of leisure when the French government under Léon Blum mandated paid vacations for all workers. As other governments followed this lead, tourism became a booming business in the West. Citizens from all walks of life traveled to see their own country, witness its geographic differences, and visit its historic monuments. How did instituting vacations promote and reflect changing political and social values? *Private Collection.*

evoking the atmosphere of idealism. Local cultural centers sprang up, and to express their opposition to fascism, citizens celebrated democratic holidays like Bastille Day with new enthusiasm. But despite this support from workers, the Popular Front governments were politically weak. Fearing for their investments, bankers and industrialists greeted Blum's appointment by sending their capital out of the country, leaving France financially strapped. "Better Hitler than Blum" was the slogan of the upper classes. Blum's government fell when it lost the left by refusing material support in the fight against fascism in Spain. As in Britain, memories of World War I caused leaders to block crucial assistance to foreign democratic forces such as the republicans in Spain and to keep the domestic military budgets small. The collapse of the antifascist Popular Front showed the difficulties that pluralistic and democratic societies faced in crisis-ridden times.

Central and Eastern Europe. Fledgling democracies in central Europe, hit hard by the depression, also fought the twin struggle for economic survival and representative government, but less successfully. In 1932, Engelbert Dollfuss came to power in Austria, dismissing the parliament and ruling briefly as a dictator. Despite his authoritarian stance, Dollfuss would not submit to the Nazis, who stormed his office and assassinated him in 1934 in an unsuccessful attempted coup. In Hungary, where outrage over the Peace of Paris remained intense, a crippled economy allowed right-wing general Gyula Gömbös◆ to take over in 1932. Gömbös reoriented his country's foreign policy toward Mussolini and Hitler. He stirred up anti-Semitism and ethnic hatreds and left considerable pro-Nazi feeling after his death in 1936. In democratic Czechoslovakia, the Slovaks, who were both poorer and less educated than the urbanized Czechs, built a strong Slovak Fascist Party. In Poland, Romania, Yugoslavia, and Bulgaria, ethnic tensions simmered and the appeal of fascism grew as the Great Depression lingered.

Cultural Visions in Hard Times

Postwar cultural leaders mobilized to meet the crisis of hard times and political menace, making films, writing novels, and producing art that captured the spirit of everyday struggle. Some empathized with the situations of factory workers, homemakers, and shopgirls straining to support themselves and their families; others looked to interpret the lives of an ever-growing number of unemployed and destitute. Artists portrayed the inhuman, regimented side of modern life. In 1931, French director René Clair's film *Give Us Liberty* related the routine of prison to work on a factory assembly line. Charlie Chaplin's film *Modern Times* (1936) showed his famous character, the Little Tramp, as a worker in a modern factory who was so molded by his monotonous job that he assumed anything he could see, even a coworker's body, needed mechanical adjustment. These sympathetic representations of the modern factory worker in hard times made Chaplin a hit even in the Soviet Union, where productions from capitalist countries were not supposed to receive such a warm welcome.

◆ **Gyula Gömbös:** DYUL ah GUHM buhsh

Media sympathy poured out to victims of the economic crisis, with women portrayed alternately as the cause and as the cure for society's problems. *The Blue Angel* (1930), a German film starring Marlene Dietrich, contrasted a woman's power to the ineffectuality of an impractical professor and thus symbolized how a vital, modern woman could destroy men—and civilization. In comedies and musicals, by contrast, heroines behaved bravely, pulling their men out of the depths of despair and setting things right again. In such films as *Keep Smiling* (1938), the British comedienne Gracie Fields portrayed spunky working-class women who remained cheerful despite the challenges of living in hard times.

Ridiculed in the past, techniques of modern art became standard tools for popular culture and advertising. Graphic artists used montage, which overlaid two or more photos or parts of photos, to grab visual attention in the cultural battles of the 1930s. Some intellectuals turned away from experimentation with nonrepresentational forms as they drove home their antifascist, pacifist, or pro-worker beliefs. Popular Front writers created realistic studies of human misery and the threat of war that haunted life in the 1930s. The British writer George Orwell described his experiences among the poor of Paris and London, wrote investigative pieces about the unemployed in the north of England, and published an account of atrocities committed by both sides during the Spanish Civil War (1936–1939).

After several decades during which abstract art had often avoided giving direct political messages, art during the Great Depression and the struggle against fascism returned to affirming values—especially those of rational thought, individual rights, and the dignity of the poor. German writer Thomas Mann (1875–1955) was outraged at Hitler's ascent to power and went into exile even though he was of Christian birth. He based a series of novels on the Old Testament hero Joseph to convey the struggle between humanist values and barbarism. The fourth volume, *Joseph the Provider* (1944), eulogized Joseph's welfare state, in which the granaries were full and the rich paid taxes so the poor might live decent lives. One of the last works of English writer Virginia Woolf, *Three Guineas* (1938), rejected experimental forms such as interior monologues for a direct attack on militarism, poverty, and the oppression of women, claiming they were interconnected parts of a single, devastating ethos undermining Europe in the 1930s.

While writers rekindled moral concerns, scientists in research institutes and universities continued to point out limits to human understanding—limits that seemed at odds with the megalomaniacal pronouncements of dictators. Astronomer Edwin Hubble (1889–1953) in California determined in the early 1930s that the universe was an expanding entity. Czech mathematician Kurt Gödel (1906–1978) maintained that all mathematical systems contain some propositions that are undecidable. The German physicist Werner Heisenberg developed the uncertainty, or indeterminacy, principle in physics. Scientific observation of atomic behavior, according to this theory, actually disturbs the atom and thereby makes precise formulations impossible. Even scientists, Heisenberg asserted, had to settle for statistical probability. Limits to understanding, approximation, and probability were not concepts that military dictators welcomed, and even people in democracies had a difficult time reconciling these new ideas with the certainty of which science and technology had once boasted.

Religious leaders helped foster a spirit of resistance to dictatorship among religious people. Notable clergymen hoped for a re-Christianization of ordinary people so that they might have spiritual alternatives to fascist preachings. The Swiss theologian Karl Barth (1886–1968) encouraged opposition to the Nazis, teaching that the faithful had to take seriously scriptural justifications of resistance to oppression. In his 1931 social encyclical, a letter addressed to the world on social issues, Pope Pius XI (r. 1922–1939) condemned the failure of modern societies to provide their citizens with a decent life and supported government intervention to create better moral and material conditions. The encyclical, *Quadragesimo Anno,* seemed to some an endorsement of the heavy-handed intervention of the fascists, however. In Germany, nonetheless, German Catholics opposed Hitler, and religious commitment inspired many other individuals to oppose the rising tide of fascism through the churches.

> **Review:** How did the democracies work to maintain their values while facing the twin challenges of economic depression and the rise of fascism?

❖ The Road to Global War

The economic crash intensified competition for wealth and influence among the major powers in the 1930s, as politicians sought to solidify their control of people and resources. External colonies were more important than ever during the depression, continuing to enrich individual investors while softening the effects in Europe. Of the British in Malaya, one businessman said, "It was impossible not to make money." Europeans who migrated to the colonies also enjoyed living sociably together away from the humdrum struggles in Europe: imperial officials and businesspeople had, according to one woman colonialist, "a very good time" full of "sunshine, servants, wonderful memories." Governments did not let up on the collection of taxes and other charges, despite hardships of the ordinary colonized person. However, no matter the wealth and self-satisfaction colonies brought, Britain and France could simply not afford to govern and protect their vast holdings should concerted challenges arise. This paradox, which continued to define imperialism, increased the tendency toward war and violence during the Great Depression.

In the context of depression and the weakened condition of the imperial leaders, contenders for empire arose. Seeking relief from economic catastrophe and a boost to their prestige, Hitler, Mussolini, and Japan's military leaders marched the world toward another catastrophic war. These leaders believed that their nations deserved to rule a far larger territory as part of their special destiny. At first, statesmen in Britain and France hoped that sanctions imposed by the League of Nations would be able to contain this new aggression. Others, believing that the powers had rushed into World War I, counseled the appeasement of Mussolini and Hitler. The

THE ROAD TO WORLD WAR II

1929	Global depression begins with U.S. stock market crash
1931	Japan invades Manchuria
1933	Hitler comes to power in Germany
1935	Italy invades Ethiopia
1936	Civil war breaks out in Spain; Hitler remilitarizes the Rhineland
1937	Japan invades China
1938	Germany annexes Austria; European leaders meet in Munich to negotiate with Hitler
1939	Germany seizes Czechoslovakia; Hitler and Stalin sign nonaggression pact; Germany invades Poland; Britain and France declare war on Germany

widespread desire for peace in the 1930s sprang from fresh and painful memories: the destruction of World War I and the economic turmoil of the Great Depression. But it left many people blind to Japanese actions in China, Hitler's outright expansionism, and the Fascist attack on the Spanish republic. So brutal were the interwar years that some historians claim that, along with World Wars I and II, they make up a single "Thirty Years' War" of the twentieth century.

A Surge in Global Imperialism

The 1930s brought the last surge of global imperialism and one that ultimately led to a thoroughly global war. As a whole, it was the most important grab for land of the century, shaping international politics down to the present because of its immense consequences. In Palestine, European Jews continued to arrive and claim the area as theirs. The numbers escalated sharply as Hitler enacted his harsh anti-Jewish policies in 1933 and as people across Europe and Asia felt the impact of the economic slump. To prevent the migration of Jews and the unemployed to their own countries, the major European states encouraged emigration to Palestine. As immigration soared, the Arabs, who even with the rapidly growing numbers of Europeans made up more than two-thirds of the population, under-

took a prolonged general strike in 1936. Nationalist politicians from the region saw in the revolt evidence of a common threat to Arabs everywhere, and pan-Arabism suddenly intensified. Japan, Germany, and Italy joined in the competition for land and resources—both close at hand and far away—to continue their economic development.

Japan's Expansionism. Japan's military leaders chafed to control more of Asia and saw China, Russia, and the other Western powers as obstacles to the empire's prosperity and the fulfillment of its destiny. In the 1920s Japan experienced some of the turmoil that afflicted industrializing countries. Along with the development of literacy and mass politics, the country suffered from a weak monarchy in the person of Emperor Hirohito, who was barely of age. This caused a crisis of legitimacy that stimulated groups with competing ambitions to seek control of the government. Japan's military leaders developed the ideology that the military was an institution unto itself, an "emperor's army" independent of civilian control and indeed one whose well-being was separate from that of the nation. Nationalist groups encouraged these leaders to prize the military success of Japan as the basis of a new world order. By the 1930s, the young emperor and his advisers had helped reactivate emotional support for the imperial system and convince the people that Japan deserved an extensive empire (Map 27.1). Renewed military vigor was seen as key to pulling agriculture and small business from the depths of economic depression. Japan's claims to racial superiority and territorial entitlement to the lands of inferior people linked it with Germany and Italy in the 1930s, setting the stage for a powerful global alliance.

The army took the lead in making these claims a reality: in September 1931, a railroad train in the Chinese province of Manchuria blew up, and Japanese officers used the explosion, which they had actually set, as an excuse to invade the territory, set up a puppet government, and push farther into China. The public agreed with journalistic calls for aggressive expansion to restore the economy and lagging prestige, while businessmen wanted new markets and resources for their burgeoning but wounded industries. From 1931 on, Japan continued its aggression in China, not only rousing the Chinese but also angering the United States, on which it depended for natural resources and markets. Ideologically, the Japanese military leadership saw itself as fully justified in breaking the stranglehold of the status quo. "Unequal distribution of land and resources causes war," an adviser to Hirohito announced before an enthusiastic public. Advocating Asian conquest as part of Japan's "divine mission," the military extended its influence in the government. By 1936–1937, Japan was spending 47 percent of its budget on arms.

The situation in East Asia had international repercussions. Japanese military success added to the threat Japan posed to the West, as Japanese goods found even bigger markets in Asia thanks to the conquest of new regions. The League of Nations condemned the invasion of Manchuria, but it imposed no sanctions that would have put economic teeth into its condemnation. Meanwhile, the rebuff outraged the Japanese public and goaded the government to ally with Hitler and Mussolini. In 1937, Japan undertook another major attack on China, justifying its offensive as a first step toward liberating the region from Western imperialism. Hundreds of thousands of Chinese were massacred in the "Rape of Nanjing"—an atrocity so named because of the brutality toward girls and women and the grim acts of torture perpetrated by the Japanese. President Roosevelt immediately announced an embargo on U.S. export of airplane parts to Japan and later enforced stringent economic sanctions on the crucial raw materials that

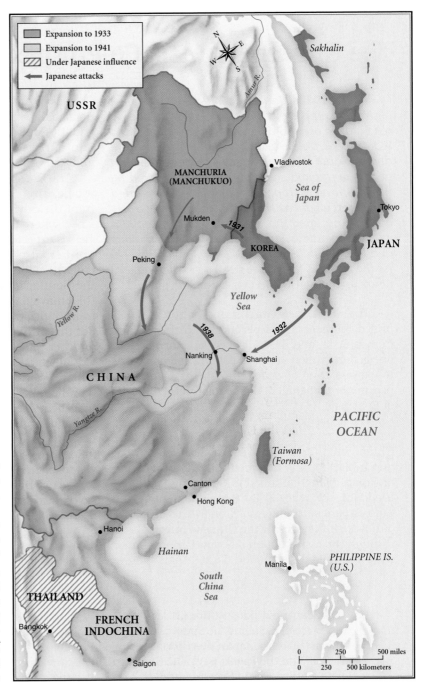

MAP 27.1 The Expansion of Japan, 1931–1941

Japanese expansion in the twentieth century approximated that of Russia and the United States in the nineteenth century: that is, it incorporated neighboring regions of Korea, Taiwan, and Manchuria with the vast area of China an inviting target. Governments of modernizing states believed that actual possession of territories was necessary for the resources, workforce, and markets they provided. But Japan's ambition fell afoul of the United States' own Pacific goals and made these two powers suddenly become deadly rivals. Why would Japan believe itself more entitled than the United States and Europe to a privileged position in the economic and political direction of East Asia?

The Greater East Asia Co-Prosperity Sphere

During the 1930s, Japan entered a new phase of imperial expansion in the Pacific, after having already taken over Korea and Formosa before World War I. To keep pace with its rapidly developing industrial and military capacities, Japan needed access to raw materials and markets blocked by the U.S. and European powers. As it invaded China and other Pacific nations, the Japanese government declared that expansion was actually a move to liberate Asians from Western imperialism and form an independent "Co-Prosperity Sphere" for the region. This secret 1942 government planning paper outlines Japan's expansion goals.

The states, their citizens, and resources, comprised in those areas pertaining to the Pacific, Central Asia, and the Indian Oceans formed into one general union are to be established as an autonomous zone of peaceful living and common prosperity on behalf of the peoples of the nations of East Asia. . . .

The above purpose presupposes the inevitable emancipation or independence of Eastern Siberia, China, Indo-China, the South Seas, Australia, and India. . . . It is intended that the unification of Japan, Manchoukuo, and China in neighborly friendship be realized by the settlement of the Sino-Japanese problems through the crushing of hostile influences in the Chinese interior, and through the construction of a new China in tune with the rapid construction of the Inner Sphere.

Aggressive American and British influences in East Asia shall be driven out of the area of Indo-China and the South Seas, and this area shall be brought into our defense sphere. The war with Britain and America shall be prosecuted for that purpose.

The Russian aggressive influence in East Asia will be driven out. Eastern Siberia shall be cut off from the Soviet regime and included in our defense sphere. For this purpose, a war with the Soviets is expected. It is considered possible that this Northern problem may break out before the general settlement of the present Sino-Japanese and the Southern problems if the situation renders this unavoidable. Next the independence of Australia, India, etc. shall gradually be brought about. For this purpose, a recurrence of war with Britain and her allies is expected. . . . Occidental individualism and materialism shall be rejected and a moral world view, the basic principle of whose morality shall be the Imperial Way, shall be established. The ultimate object to be achieved is not exploitation but co-prosperity and mutual help, not competitive conflict but mutual assistance and mild peace, not a formal view of equality but a view of order based on righteous classification, not an idea of rights but an idea of service, and not several world views but one unified world view.

Source: Ryusaku Tsunoda, Wm. Theodore de Bary, Donald Keene, *Sources of Japanese Tradition.* (New York: Columbia University Press, 1958) 802–3, 805.

---

drove Japanese industry. Nonetheless, the Western powers, including the Soviet Union, did not effectively resist Japan's territorial expansion in Asia and the Pacific (see "The Greater East Asia Co-Prosperity Sphere," above).

Germany and Italy Contest the Status Quo. Like Japanese leaders, Mussolini and Hitler called their countries have-nots and demanded a change in the status quo. Mussolini threatened "permanent conflict" to expand Italy's borders, while Hitler's agenda included breaking free from the Versailles treaty's military restrictions and gain-

ing more **Lebensraum,**♦ or living space, in which "superior" Aryans could thrive. This space would be taken from the "inferior" Slavic peoples and Bolsheviks, who would be moved to Siberia or would serve as slaves. Both dictators portrayed themselves as peace-loving men who resorted to extreme measures only to benefit their country and humanity. Their anticommunism appealed to statesmen across the West, and Hitler's anti-Semitism even found widespread support. Some thus favored accommodating these

---

♦**Lebensraum:** LAY buhnz rown

two dictators' demands to control more land at the expense of others.

Both leaders' moves against the international status quo were open and audacious. In the autumn of 1933, Hitler announced Germany's withdrawal from the League of Nations. In 1935, Hitler loudly rejected the clauses of the Treaty of Versailles that limited German military strength; he reintroduced military conscription and publicly started rearming, although Germany had been rearming in secret for years. Mussolini also chose 1935 to invade Ethiopia, one of the very few African states not overwhelmed by European imperialism. The attack was intended to demonstrate his regime's youth and vigor and to raise Italy's standing among the colonial powers. "The Roman legionnaires are again on the march," one soldier exulted. The poorly equipped Ethiopians resisted, but their capital,

The Ethiopian War, 1935–1936

Addis Ababa, fell in the spring of 1936. The League of Nations voted to impose sanctions against Italy, but Britain and France opposed an embargo with teeth in it—one on oil—and thus kept the sanctions from being effective while also suggesting a lack of resolve to fight aggression. The fall of Ethiopia was a searing moment for many Africans, and memories of Italy's boastful assertions of African racial inferiority fortified many African national liberation movements in later years.

Profiting from the diversion of Italy's attack on Ethiopia, in March 1936 Hitler defiantly sent his troops into what was supposed to be a permanently demilitarized zone in the Rhineland. The inhabitants greeted the Germans with wild enthusiasm, and the French, whose security was most endangered by this action, also protested to the League of Nations instead of countering with an invasion, as they had done in the Ruhr in 1923. The British

accepted the fait accompli, and the two dictators thus appeared as powerful military heroes forging, in Mussolini's muscular phrase, a "Rome–Berlin Axis." Next to them, the politicians of France and Great Britain looked timid, unfit, and defeatable.

The Spanish Civil War, 1936–1939

Spain joined the wave of authoritarianism inundating Europe, despite the country's attempts early in the 1930s to turn toward democracy. In 1931 Spanish republicans overthrew their monarchy, which for centuries had fortified the rule of large landowners and the domination of the Catholic clergy. As Spain fitfully developed an industrial capacity in cities like Barcelona and Bilbao, these ruling elites kept an impoverished peasantry in their grip, making Spain a country of economic extremes. Urban groups reacted enthusiastically to the end of the dictatorship and began debating the course of change, with Communists, socialists, anarchists, constitutionalists, and other splinter groups all holding differing views on a democratic future. For republicans, the air was electric with promise. As public debate developed, one woman recalled, people sat for hours dreaming dreams: "We saw a backward country suddenly blossoming out into a modern state. We saw peasants living like decent human beings. We saw men allowed freedom of conscience. We saw life, instead of death in Spain."

Groups on the left were so embroiled in battling one another to get their way, however, that the republic had a hard time putting in place a political program that would gain it widespread support in the countryside. Instead, they preferred symbolic acts such as releasing political prisoners and doling out coveted municipal jobs to the urban unemployed. Thus, although they wanted political and economic modernization, the Spanish republicans failed to mount a unified effort against their reactionary opponents, an especially grave failure in hard economic times. Specifically, instead of building popular loyalty and diminishing the strength of the right wing by enacting land reform, the various antimonarchist factions struggled among themselves to dominate the

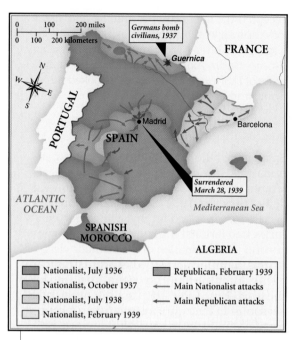

MAP 27.2 The Spanish Civil War, 1936–1939
Republican and antirepublican forces bitterly fought
one another to determine whether Spain would be
a democracy or an authoritarian state. Germany and
Italy sent military assistance to the rebels, notably airplanes to experiment with bombing civilians, while
volunteers from around the world arrived to fight for
the losing cause of the republic. Defeating these ill-
organized groups, General Francisco Franco instituted
a pro-fascist government that sent many to jail and
into exile.

new government. In 1936, pro-republican
forces temporarily banded together in a Popular Front coalition to win elections and prevent the republic from collapsing under the
weight of internal squabbling and growing
monarchist opposition. With the Popular
Front victory, euphoria swept the country
and unemployment abated.

In response, the forces of the right drew
closer together, making use of their considerable wealth to undermine the government.
In 1936, a group of army officers staged an
uprising against the republican government
in Madrid. The rebellious officers soon found
a determined leader, General Francisco Franco
(1892–1975), who was able to both unify the
right and make use of its greater resources.
The rebels, who now comprised monarchists,
landowners, the clergy, and the fascist Falange

Party, soon had the help of fascists in other
parts of Europe. Committed citizens—male
and female—took up arms and formed volunteer units of republican fighters to meet
the grave military challenge. In their minds,
citizen armies symbolized republicanism, while
professional troops followed the aristocratic
rebels. As civil war gripped the country, the
republicans generally held Madrid, Barcelona, and other commercial and industrial areas. The rebels found most support in the
agricultural west and south (Map 27.2).

The struggle became a rehearsal for
World War II when Hitler and Mussolini sent
military personnel in support of Franco, gaining the opportunity to test new weapons and
to practice the terror bombing of civilians. In
1937, German planes attacked the town of
Guernica,◆ mowing down civilians in the
streets. This gratuitous slaughter inspired
Pablo Picasso's memorial mural to the dead,
Guernica (1937), in which the intense suffering is starkly displayed in monochromatic
grays and whites to capture a sense of moral
decay as well as physical death. The Spanish
republican government appealed everywhere
for assistance, but only the Soviet Union
answered (see the illustration on the facing
page). Stalin withdrew his troops and tanks
in 1938 as government ranks floundered, however. Britain and France refused to provide
aid despite the outpouring of popular support
for the cause of democracy. Instead, a few
thousand volunteers from a variety of countries—including many students, journalists,
and artists—fought for the republic. With
Hitler and Mussolini on a rampage in Europe, "Spain was the place to stop fascism,"
these volunteers believed. The conflict was
bitter and bloody, with widespread atrocities
committed on both sides. But the splinter
groups and random armies with which the
Republic defended itself could not hold, while
the aid Franco received ultimately proved
decisive. His troops defeated the republicans
in 1939, bringing another victory to the cause
of authoritarianism in Europe. Franco dealt
his defeated enemies a harsh peace: tens
of thousands fled his government's brutal
revenge while critics found themselves jailed
and worse.

◆**Guernica:** gehr NEE kah

The "MILITARY" PRACTICE OF THE REBELS

IF YOU TOLERATE THIS YOUR CHILDREN WILL BE NEXT

The Spanish Republic Appeals for Aid
The government of the Spanish Republic sent out modern advertising and propaganda to attract support from the remaining democracies—especially Great Britain and France. Antiwar sentiment remained high among the British and French, however. Thus, despite the horrifying and deliberate bombing of civilians by Franco's German allies, aid for the republic failed to arrive. What are the modernist techniques used in this propaganda photo? *Imperial War Museum, London.*

Hitler's Conquest of Central Europe, 1938–1939

The fall of central Europe that ultimately led to World War II began with Hitler's annexation of Austria in 1938. Many Austrians had actually wished for such a merger, or *Anschluss,* after the Paris peace settlement stripped them of their empire. So Hitler's troops simply entered Austria, and the enthusiasm of Nazi sympathizers among the Austrians made the Anschluss appear to support the Wilsonian idea of self-determination. The annexation began the so-called unification of Aryan peoples into one greater German nation and marked the first step in taking over

the resources of central and eastern Europe. Austria was declared a German province, the Ostmark, and Hitler's thugs ruled once-cosmopolitan Vienna. An observer later commented on the scene:

> University professors were obliged to scrub the streets with their naked hands, pious white-bearded Jews were dragged into the synagogue by hooting youths and forced to do knee-exercises and to shout "Heil Hitler" in chorus.

Nazis also generated support in Austria by solving the intractable problem of unemployment—especially among the young and out-of-work rural migrants to the cities. Factories sprang up overnight, mostly to foster rearmament, and new "Hitler housing" was of a quality that suggested the dignity of workers as propounded by the Nazis. "We were given work!" Austrians continued to say long afterward, defending their embrace of the Third Reich. It eliminated some of the pain Austrians had suffered when their empire had been reduced to a small country after World War I.

The Anschluss enhanced the image of German omnipotence, allowing Hitler to turn rapidly to Czechoslovakia and its rich resources. Overpowering this democracy did not appear as simple a task as seizing Austria, however. Czechoslovakia had a large army and formidable border defenses and armament factories, and most Czech citizens were prepared to fight for their country. However, Hitler gambled correctly that the other Western powers would not interfere, especially as the Nazi propaganda machine poured tremendous abuse on Czechoslovakia for allegedly persecuting its German minority. By October 1, 1938, Hitler warned, Czechoslovakia would have to grant autonomy (amounting to Nazi rule) to the German-populated border region, the Sudetenland, or face German invasion.

As the October deadline approached, the British prime minister Neville Chamberlain, the French premier Edouard Daladier, and Mussolini met with Hitler and agreed not to oppose Germany's claim to the Sudetenland. The strategy of preventing a war by making concessions for legitimate grievances (in this case, the alleged affront to Germans in the Peace of Paris) was called **appeasement**. At the time it was widely seen as a positive act,

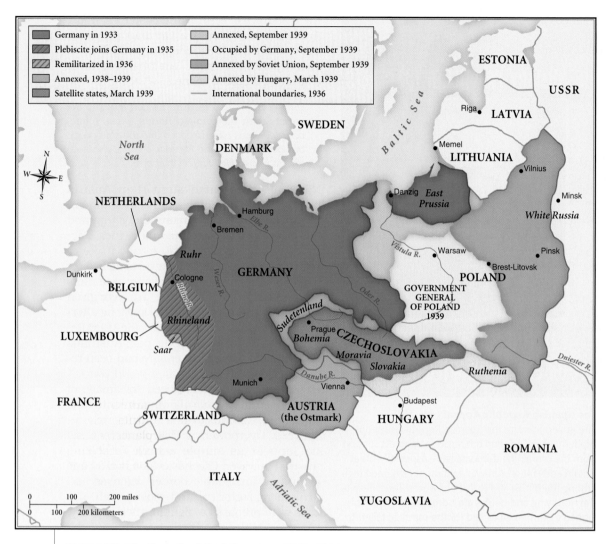

MAP 27.3 The Growth of Nazi Germany, 1933–1939

German expansion was rapid and surprising, as Hitler's forces and Nazi diplomacy achieved the annexation of the new states of central and eastern Europe. Although committed to defending the sovereignty of these states through the League of Nations, French and British diplomats were more concerned with satisfying Hitler in the mistaken belief that doing so would prevent his claiming more of Europe. In the process, Hitler acquired the human and material resources of adjacent countries to support his Third Reich. What is the relationship between the expansion of Germany in the 1930s and the Peace of Paris after World War I?

and the agreement between Germany and Great Britain prompted Chamberlain to announce that he had secured "peace in our time." Stalin, excluded from the Munich deliberations, learned from the conference that the democracies were not going to fight to protect eastern Europe. Having portrayed himself as a man of peace, Hitler waited until March 1939 to invade the rest of Czechoslovakia (Map 27.3). Britain and France responded to that act by promising military support to Poland, Romania, Greece, and Turkey in case of Nazi invasion. In May 1939, Hitler and Mussolini countered this agreement by signing a pledge of offensive and defensive support called the Pact of Steel.

Some historians have sharply criticized the Munich Pact because it bought Hitler time to build his army and seemed to give him the green light for further aggression. They believe that a confrontation might have stopped Hitler and that even if war had resulted, the democracies would have triumphed at less cost than they later did. According to this view, each military move by Germany, Italy, and Japan should have been met with stiff opposition, and the Soviet Union should have been made a partner to this resistance. Others counter that appeasement provided France and Britain precious time to beef up their own armies, which the Munich crisis caused them to begin doing. The Munich Pact and the surrounding public debate about Nazi aggression also helped prepare citizens in the democracies for the possibility of another war. Finally, there were those at the time who believed that Germany deserved to have Czechoslovakia— so unfairly had the Peace of Paris treated the defeated great power.

Hitler's audacity knew no bounds. To the astonishment of public opinion in the West, on August 23, 1939, Germany and the USSR signed a nonaggression agreement. The **Nazi-Soviet Pact** provided that if one country became embroiled in war, the other country would remain neutral. Moreover, the two dictators secretly agreed to divide Poland and the Baltic States—Latvia, Estonia, and Lithuania—at some future date. The Nazi-Soviet Pact ensured that, should war come, the democracies would be fighting a Germany that feared no attack on its eastern borders. The pact also benefited the USSR. Despite Hitler's many threats to wipe the Bolsheviks off the face of the earth, Stalin needed extra time to reconstitute his officer corps destroyed in the purges. In the belief that Great Britain and perhaps even France would not fight because his aggression had met no resistance so far, Hitler now moved to enlarge his empire further and aimed his forces at Poland. The contest for territory and resources was set to become another world war.

Review: How did the aggression of Japan, Germany, and Italy create the conditions for global war?

❖ World War II, 1939–1945

The global catastrophe that quickly came to be called the Second World War opened when Hitler launched an all-out attack on Poland on September 1, 1939. In contrast to 1914, no jubilation in Berlin accompanied the invasion; when Britain and France declared war two days later, the mood in those capitals was similarly grim. Although Japan, Italy, and the United States did not join the battle immediately, their eventual participation spread the fighting throughout the world. By the time World War II ended in 1945, many Europeans were starving; much of the continent lay in ruins; and unparalleled atrocities, including technological genocide, had killed six million Jews and six million Slavs, gypsies, homosexuals, and other civilian enemies of fascism.

The German Onslaught

German ground forces quickly defeated the ill-equipped Polish troops by launching an overpowering **Blitzkrieg**❖ ("lightning war"), in which they concentrated airplanes, tanks, and motorized infantry to encircle Polish defenders and capture the capital, Warsaw, with overwhelming speed. Allowing the army to conserve supplies, Blitzkrieg assured Germans at home that the human costs of gaining Lebensraum would be low. On September 17, 1939, the Soviets invaded Poland from the east to make their own conquest. By the end of the month, the Polish army was in shambles and the victors had divided the country according to the Nazi-Soviet Pact. Hitler sold the war within the Reich as one of self-defense, especially from what propagandists called the "warlike menace" of world Jewry.

Hitler ordered an attack on France for November 1939, but his generals, who feared that Germany was ill prepared for total war, convinced him to postpone the offensive until the spring of 1940. In April 1940, the Blitzkrieg crushed Denmark and Norway; the battles of Belgium, the Netherlands, and France followed in May and June. On June 5, Mussolini, eyeing future spoils for Italy, invaded France from

❖**Blitzkrieg:** BLIHTS kreeg

the southeast. The French defense and its British allies could not withstand the German onslaught. Trapped on the beaches of Dunkirk in northern France, 370,000 British and French soldiers were rescued in a heroic effort by an improvised fleet of naval ships, fishing boats, and pleasure craft. A dejected French government surrendered on June 22, 1940, leaving Germany to rule the northern half of the country, including Paris. In the south, named Vichy◆ France after the spa town where the government sat, the reactionary and aged World War I hero Henri Philippe Pétain was allowed to govern. Stalin used the diversion in western Europe to annex the Baltic States of Estonia, Latvia, and Lithuania.

Britain now stood alone. Blaming Germany's rapid victories on his policy of appeasement, the British swept Chamberlain out of office and installed as prime minister Winston Churchill, an early advocate of resistance to Hitler. After Hitler ordered the bombardment of Britain in the summer of 1940, Churchill rallied the nation by radio—now in millions of British homes—to protect the ideals of liberty with their "blood, toil, tears, and sweat." In the battle of Britain—or Blitz, as the British called it—the German Luftwaffe (air force) bombed public buildings and monuments, harbors and weapons depots, and industry. Using the wealth of their colonies, the British poured resources into antiaircraft weapons, its highly successful code-detecting group called Ultra, and development of its advantage in radar. At year's end, the British air industry was outproducing that of the Germans by 50 percent.

By the fall of 1940, German air losses forced Hitler to abandon his plan for a naval invasion of Britain. Forcing Hungary, Romania, and Bulgaria to join with him, Hitler gained access to more food and oil. He then made his fatal decision to attack what he called the

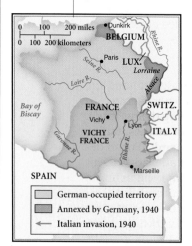

The Division of France, 1940

"center of judeobolshevism"—the Soviet Union. In June 1941, the German army crossed the Soviet border, as Hitler broke the Nazi-Soviet Pact and promised to "raze Moscow and Leningrad to the ground." Deployed along a two-thousand-mile front, three million German and other Axis troops quickly penetrated Soviet lines. Stalin initially disappeared for several days but then rallied to direct the defense. By July, however, the German army had rolled to within two hundred miles of Moscow. Using a strategy of rapid encirclement, German troops had killed, captured, or wounded more than half the 4.5 million Soviet soldiers defending the borders.

Amid success, Hitler blundered. Considering himself a military genius and the Slavic people inferior, he proposed attacking Leningrad, the Baltic States, and the Ukraine simultaneously, whereas his generals wanted to concentrate on Moscow. Following this cumbersome strategy lost precious time, and driven by Stalin, local party members, and rising patriotic resolve, the Soviet people fought back. The onset of winter turned Nazi soldiers to frostbitten wretches because Hitler had feared that equipping his army for Russian conditions would suggest that a prolonged campaign lay in store—the scenario that did in fact materialize. Keeping civilians focused on victory and enjoying abundance so that they would not rebel against war thus brought additional suffering on the battlefront. Yet Hitler remained so convinced of imminent victory in the USSR that he switched German production from making tanks and artillery to making battleships and airplanes. Consequently, Germany's ill-supplied armies succumbed to the weather, disease, and ultimately a shortage of equipment. As the war became worldwide, Germany faced another obstacle: fighting a global war from a strictly European base and with far less familiarity of a global terrain than its enemies had. What it did have was an inflated and poorly calculated view of its own might.

War Expands: The Pacific and Beyond

As the German army stalled in the Soviet Union, an all-out dramatic attack ignited war in the Pacific. The outbreak of war in Europe had intensified U.S.-Japanese com-

◆**Vichy:** VIH shee

petition, as Japan had taken control of parts of the British Empire, bullied the Dutch in Indonesia, and invaded French Indochina to procure raw materials for its industrial and military expansion. The militarist Japanese government decided that it should settle matters with the West once and for all. In December 1941, Japanese planes bombed American naval and air bases at Pearl Harbor in Hawaii and then decimated a fleet of airplanes in the Philippines. Roosevelt summoned the U.S. Congress to declare war on Japan. By the spring of 1942, the Japanese had conquered Guam, the Philippines, Malaya, Burma, Indonesia, Singapore, and much of the southwestern Pacific. Like Hitler's expansionist drive, the Japanese victories strengthened the military's ideology that the empire was fulfilling its destiny. "The era of democracy is finished," the foreign minister announced confidently, despite Japan's dependence on the United States for trade, raw materials, technology, and loans. Officials marketed Emperor Hirohito to the region as the pan-Asian monarch who would lead the liberation and promote the well-being of Asians everywhere.

Germany quickly joined its Japanese ally and declared war on the United States—an appropriate enemy, Hitler proclaimed, as it was "half Judaized and the other half Negrified." Mussolini followed suit. The United States was not initially prepared for a prolonged struggle, partly because isolationist sentiment remained strong: its armed forces numbered only 1.6 million, and no plan existed for producing the necessary guns, tanks, and airplanes. Also working against war preparedness was ambivalence toward the Soviet Union even in the face of Hitler's attack, and Stalin himself reciprocated the mistrust. Yet despite the odds against such cooperation, Hitler's four enemies came together in the Grand Alliance of Great Britain, the Free French (an exile government led by General Charles de Gaulle and based in London), the Soviet Union, and the United States.

Given the urgency of war and the partners' competing interests, the Grand Alliance and the larger coalition with twenty other countries—known collectively as the Allies—had much internal strife to overcome in their struggle against the Axis powers—Germany, Italy, and Japan. Yet in the long run, the Allies had a distinct advantage. Their potential for war in terms of manpower and resources was vast. The extensive terrain they controlled gave them access to more goods from around the world, and these allowed them to survive the war. The globalization of the war brought into play Britain's traditional naval strength and its leaders' and troops' experience in combat on many continents. In the face of these advantages, the irrational ideology of the Axis powers only added to the problems of waging effective war.

The War against Civilians

Everyone was a target in World War II, and the war killed far more civilians than soldiers. The Axis and the Allies alike bombed cities simply to destroy civilian will to resist—a debatable tactic that seemed to inspire defiance rather than surrender. Allied firebombing of Dresden and Tokyo were but two instances that killed tens of thousands of civilians, but Axis attacks far outweighed these. The British people, not British soldiers, were the target of the battle of Britain, and as the German army swept through eastern Europe, it slaughtered Jews, Communists, Slavs, and others Nazi ideology deemed "racial inferiors" and enemies. In Poland, the SS murdered hundreds of thousands of Polish citizens or relocated them in forced labor camps. As land and homes were confiscated, they were given to "racially pure" Germans from other central European countries and from Germany. Literate people were the most vulnerable, because Hitler, like Stalin, saw them as the foundation of a civil society that he was determined to destroy. A ploy of the Nazis was to test captured people's reading skills, suggesting that those who could read would be given clerical jobs while those who could not would be relegated to hard labor. Those who could read, however, were lined up and shot. Because many in the German army initially rebelled at this inhuman mission, special Gestapo forces took up the charge of herding their victims into woods, to ravines, or even against town walls where they would be shot en masse. The Japanese did the same in China, southeast Asia, and on the islands in the Pacific. The number of civilians murdered in China alone is said to be at least 2.5 million, with untold millions murdered elsewhere.

The Holocaust. The extermination of Jews during the war became a special focus of Nazi murderers. Herded into urban ghettos, stripped of their possessions, and living on minimal rations, eastern European Jews died of starvation and disease—the Nazis' initial plan for reducing the Jewish population. There was also direct murder. Around Soviet towns, Jews were usually shot in pits, some of which they had been forced to dig themselves. After shedding their clothes and putting them in ordered piles for later Nazi use, ten thousand or more at a time were killed, often with the help of anti-Semitic villagers. However, the "Final Solution"—the Nazis' diabolical plan to exterminate all of Europe's Jews systematically—was not yet fully under way.

A bureaucratically organized and efficient technological system for rounding up Jews and transporting them to extermination sites had, however, taken shape by the fall of 1941. On the eve of war in 1939, Hitler had predicted "the destruction of the Jewish race in Europe." Although no clear order written by Hitler exists, his responsibility for it is clear: he discussed the Final Solution's progress, issued oral directives for it, and from the beginning made lethal anti-Semitism a basis for Nazism. Modern social and legal science and technology, managed by efficient scientists, doctors, lawyers, and government workers also made the Holocaust work. Six camps in Poland were developed specifically for the purposes of mass murder, though some, like Auschwitz-Birkenau,♦ served as both extermination and labor camp (Map 27.4). Using techniques developed in the T4 project that killed disabled and elderly people from 1939 on, the camp at Chelmno first gassed Christian Poles and Soviet prisoners of war. Specially designed crematoria for the mass burning of corpses started functioning in 1943. By then, Auschwitz had the capacity to burn 1.7 million bodies per year. About 60 percent of new arrivals—particularly children, women,

♦**Auschwitz-Birkenau:** OWSH vihts BIHR kuh now

MAP 27.4 Concentration Camps and Extermination Sites in Europe
This map shows the major extermination sites and concentration camps in Europe, but the entire continent was dotted with thousands of lesser camps to which the victims of Nazism were transported. Some of these lesser camps were merely way stations on the path to ultimate extermination. In focusing on the major camps historians often lose sight of the ways in which evidence of deportation and extermination blanketed Europe.

and old people—were selected directly for murder in the gas chambers; the other 40 percent labored until, utterly used up, they too were sent to their deaths.

Death and Life in the Camps. Extermination camps received their victims from across the continent. In the ghettos in various European cities, councils of Jewish leaders, such as the one in Amsterdam where Etty Hillesum worked, were ordered to determine those to be "resettled in the east." For weakened, poorly armed ghetto inhabitants, open resistance meant certain death. When Jews rose up against their Nazi captors in Warsaw in 1943, they were mercilessly butchered (see Persecution of Warsaw Jews, page 1081). For all their bluster, the Nazis took pains to cloak their true purposes in the extermination camps in order to prevent up-

Persecution of Warsaw Jews
Hitler was determined to exterminate Jews, Slavs, Gypsies, homosexuals, and others he deemed "undesirable"; he often enlisted community leaders to cooperate in deportation and even executions. In the 1930s, people fled Germany; later, more fled the countries the Nazis conquered. In the city of Warsaw, where Jews were crowded into the ghetto and deprived of food and fuel, the Jewish uprising brought massive retaliation. How is this picture an example of World War II as a total war? © Bettmann/Corbis.

risings and disorder. Bands played when trainloads of victims arrived; some were given postcards with reassuring messages to mail home. Survivors later noted that the purpose of the camps was so unthinkable that potential victims could not begin to imagine that they were to be killed en masse. Those not chosen for immediate murder had their heads shaved, were showered and disinfected, and were then given prison garments—many of them used and so thin that they offered no protection against winter cold and rain. So began life in "a living hell," as one survivor wrote.

The camps were scenes of struggle for life in the face of torture and death. Instead of the minimum of two thousand calories needed to sustain adult life, overworked inmates usually received less than five hundred calories per day, leaving them vulnerable to typhus and other diseases that swept through the camps. Surviving prisoners sometimes went mad, as did many of the guards. In the name of advancing "racial science," doctors performed unbelievably cruel medical experiments and operations with no anesthesia on pregnant women, twins, and other innocent people. The brutality of the camp guards and the harshness of the living conditions failed to crush everyone's spirit, though: prisoners forged new friendships that helped in the struggle for survival, and women especially observed religious holidays, celebrated birthdays, and re-created other sustaining aspects of domestic life. Thanks to those sharing a bread ration and doing him favors, wrote the Auschwitz survivor Primo Levi, "I managed not to forget that I myself was a man." In the end, six million Jews, the vast majority from eastern Europe, along with an estimated five to six million gypsies, homosexuals, and Slavs, and countless others were murdered in the Nazi genocidal fury. What has stayed vivid in human memory is the planned, bureaucratic organization of this vast and unspeakable crime

NEW SOURCES, NEW PERSPECTIVES

Museums and Memory

Historical monuments and museums that house historical artifacts have in recent years received unprecedented attention. Both of these institutions are testimonials to historical events because they provide records of those events and show that people were deeply moved by them. Monuments to World War I keep the memory of the Great War alive in villages and cities, while Holocaust museums are found in dozens of countries, many far from the region where the Holocaust took place.

But is the impression conveyed by a tragic photo or the memory of an event the same as its history? Historians wrestle with this question and for the most part regard photographs and oral testimony as legitimate kinds of evidence. However, many judge such institutions as Holocaust museums as only partially about the history of the Holocaust. Instead, a Holocaust museum tells a great deal about the nation or group that builds it. It tells about the "memory" that the nation or group wants average people to have of the Holocaust.

Holocaust memorials have had a complicated development that is instructive to historians. Some Holocaust memory sites sprang up spontaneously in concentration camps as memorials constructed by survivors themselves. Stones, writings, plaques, flowers and plants, and other objects were used to testify to what had happened in the camp. In many cases, these initial memorials were replaced when local and national governments stepped in to take over the site, sometimes waiting years between destroying the spon-

Holocaust Memorial Museum
Designed to evoke a sense of awe at the unprecedented suffe[r] caused by the mass murder of the Jews, the Holocaust Memo[rial] Museum in Washington, D.C., displays pictures of thousands [of] Germany's victims. Other museums around the world focus [on] different aspects of Hitler's policy of extermination, emphasiz[ing] the many nationalities of his victims or the variety of reasons [for] their slaughter. *Johnson/Getty Images.*

perpetrated by apparently civilized humans. (See "New Sources, New Perspectives," above.)

Societies at War

Even more than World War I, World War II depended on industrial productivity geared totally toward war and mass killings. The Axis countries remained at a disadvantage throughout the war despite their initial conquests. Although the war accelerated eco-

nomic production by some 300 percent between 1940 and 1944 in all belligerent countries, the Allies produced more than three times Axis output in 1943 (Figure 27.1). Even while some of its lands were occupied and many of its cities besieged, the Soviet Union increased its production of weapons. Both Japan and Germany made the most of their lower capacity, notably in the strategy of Blitzkrieg. Hitler had to avoid imposing wartime austerity because he had come to

taneous memorials and replacing them with an official one. The concentration camp at Dachau, near Munich, fell into disrepair until a group of survivors, including many Catholic clergy, demanded that the camp be made into a permanent museum and memorial, with the crematorium and other grisly features preserved. Although townspeople and local government resisted, Dachau and its crematorium became one of the most visited camps and indeed came to symbolize the Holocaust in all its horror. Yet Dachau was not primarily an extermination site for Jews, Slavs, and Gypsies but rather a grim concentration camp where Hitler put political prisoners, many of them Catholic clergy. It is so often visited because it is on the tourist route, close to a beautiful city. Indeed, among the plaques in this on-site museum, one invites visitors to tour the other cultural institutions and scenery of the area while another asks them to remember that vast numbers of those interned were Polish and Catholic. All of these factors in the politics of memories—official and unofficial, competing and contested—need to be taken into account by historians.

In the case of Holocaust museums, official memories can clash with memories of actual survivors who, for instance, do not like what is often the most aesthetic or avant-grade in terms of art and architecture. They generally reject abstract art, feeling that a more realistic depiction of their suffering seems most important. As for architectural design, the American Holocaust Museum was redone so that it would not look grimly out of place but would instead fit in with the tranquil style of the central museum mall in Washington, D.C., and thus be another nice tourist attraction. His-

torians question the way certain objects like shoes or eyeglasses are displayed to create a certain memory effect. They note that costume designers puff up prison uniforms to make them look more lifelike and to stir people emotionally.

Holocaust museums have offered a powerful, vivid, and emotionally charged experience of history. In contrast, historians pride themselves on eliminating emotions and biases in ascertaining facts, calculating cause and effect, and reaching historical judgments. Though each provides an important representation of the past, the relationship between memory and history remains fraught with questions—and never more so than in the case of the Holocaust.

QUESTIONS TO CONSIDER

1. What is the difference between a historical textbook and a historical monument?
2. Do you trust a history book more than you trust a museum? How do people compare and evaluate the presentation of the past in either one?
3. Why do museums and public exhibitions of art and artifacts arouse more debate than do history books?

FURTHER READING

Gillis, John R. *Commemorations: The Politics of National Identity.* 1994.

Sherman, Daniel J., and Irit Rogoff, eds. *Museum Culture: Histories, Discourses, Spectacles.* 1994.

Young, James Edward. *The Texture of Memory: Holocaust Memorials and Meaning.* 1993.

power promising to end economic suffering, not increase it. The use of millions of slave laborers and resources from occupied areas helped, but neither Japan nor Germany took the resources and morale of its enemies into full account.

Allied governments were overwhelmingly successful in generating civilian participation, especially among women. In the Axis countries, where government policy particularly exalted motherhood and kept women from

the best-paying jobs, officials began to realize that women were desperately needed in offices and factories. Even changing the propaganda to emphasize the need for everyone to take a job did not convince women that they should take the low-paid work offered them. In contrast, Soviet women constituted more than half the workforce by war's end. They dug massive antitank trenches around Moscow and other threatened cities, and 800,000 volunteered for the military, even

the fascist countries. Couples in Germany and Italy limited family size in defiance of pro-birth policies. German teenagers danced the forbidden American jitterbug, thus defying the Nazis and forcing the police to monitor their groups. Historians question still another incident of resistance in Germany. In July 1944, a group of German military officers, fearing their country's military humiliation, made another of several attempts to assassinate Hitler. Only wounded but shaken, Hitler mercilessly tortured and killed hundreds of conspirators, opponents, and innocent friends and family members, imprisoning still others as well. Some ask whether this attempt came too late in the war to count as resistance. However, as a noted scholar points out, some five million Germans alone, and millions more of other nationalities, lost their lives in the last nine months of the war. Had Hitler died even as late as the summer of 1944, the relief to humanity would have been considerable.

The Axis Crushed in Europe.   Amid civilian resistance, Allied forces started tightening a noose around the Axis in mid-1942 (Map 27.5), and Allied victory began to look certain by 1943. Nonetheless, Hitler and his minions continued to promote an unrealistic expectation of German victory, announcing, for example, that the United States was "a big bluff." A major turning point came in August 1942, when the German army began a siege on Stalingrad, a city whose capture would give Germany access to Soviet oil and cut Soviet access to its own interior. Months of ferocious house-to-house fighting ended when the Soviet army captured the ninety thousand German survivors in February 1943. Meanwhile, the British army in North Africa held against German troops under German field marshall Erwin Rommel, an adept practitioner of the new kind of mobile warfare. Although Rommel let his tanks improvise creatively, moving hundreds of miles from supply lines, he could not overcome the Allies' access to secret German communication codes. This access ultimately helped the Allies successfully capture Morocco and Algeria in the fall of 1942. After driving Rommel out of Africa, the Allies landed in Sicily in July 1943, provoking a German in-

vasion during which they took over the war effort from the Italians. A slow, bitter fight for the Italian peninsula followed, lasting until April 1945, when Allied forces finally triumphed. After Italy's liberation, partisans shot Mussolini and his mistress and hanged their dead bodies for public display.

The victory at Stalingrad marked the beginning of the costly Soviet drive westward, during which the Soviets bore the brunt of the Nazi war machine. From the air, Britain and the United States pounded German cities with strategic bombing aimed at demoralizing ordinary Germans and destroying war industries. But it was an invasion from the west that Stalin needed, and on June 6, 1944, known as D-Day, the combined Allied forces under the command of U.S. general Dwight Eisenhower attacked the heavily fortified French beaches of Normandy and then fought their way through the German-held territory of western France. In late July, Allied forces broke through German defenses and a month later helped liberate Paris, where rebellion had erupted against the Nazis. The Soviets meanwhile took the Baltic States and entered Poland, pausing only to resupply while craftily allowing the Germans to put down a spontaneous uprising of the Polish resistance in August 1944. German elimination of the Polish resistance allowed the Soviets a freer hand in eastern Europe after the war. Facing more than twice as many troops as on the western front, the Soviet army took Bulgaria and entered Romania at the end of August, and then faced fierce German fighting in Hungary during the winter of 1944–1945. British, Canadian, U.S., and other Allied forces were simultaneously fighting their way

MAP 27.5 World War II in Europe and Africa ▶
World War II inflicted massive loss of life and destruction of property on civilians, armies, and all the infrastructure—including factories, equipment, and agriculture—needed to wage total war. Thus, the war swept the European continent as well as areas in Africa colonized by or allied with the major powers. Ultimately the Allies crushed the Axis by moving from east, west, and south to inflict a total defeat. What indications are there on the map that this war would be hard on civilians?

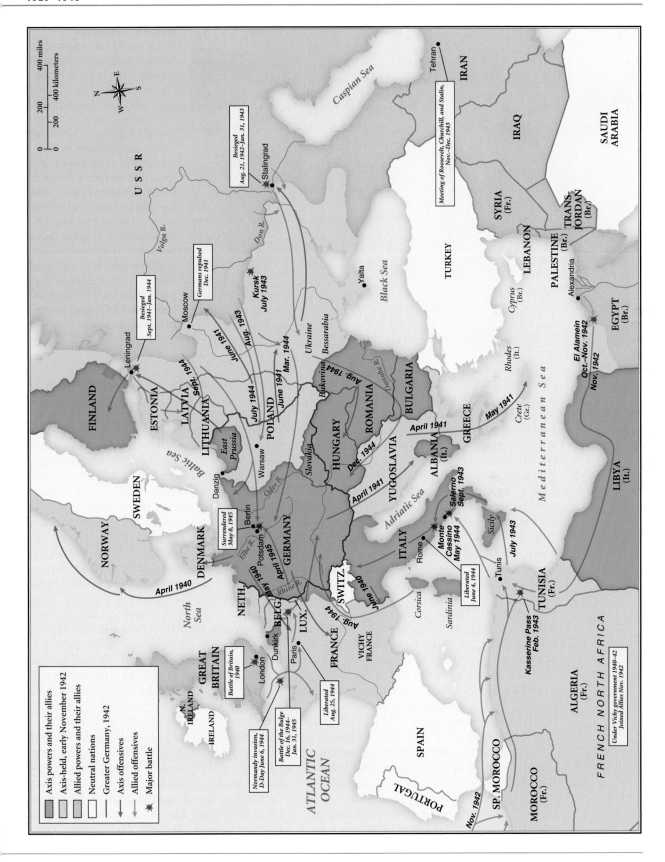

Legend
- Axis powers and their allies
- Axis-held, early November 1942
- Allied powers and their allies
- Neutral nations
- Greater Germany, 1942
- Axis offensives
- Allied offensives
- Major battle

400 miles
400 kilometers

N

USSR

Caspian Sea

Besieged Aug. 21, 1942–Jan. 31, 1943
Stalingrad

Tehran
IRAN

IRAQ

SAUDI ARABIA

Meeting of Roosevelt, Churchill, and Stalin, Nov.–Dec. 1943

SYRIA (Fr.)

TRANS JORDAN (Br.)

LEBANON (Br.)

PALESTINE (Br.)

Alexandria

EGYPT (Br.)

Volga R.

Don R.

Germans repulsed Dec. 1941

Moscow

Kursk July 1943

Ukraine

Bessarabia

Black Sea

Yalta

TURKEY

Cyprus (Br.)

Rhodes (It.)

El Alamein Oct.–Nov. 1942
Nov. 1942

Besieged Sept. 1941–Jan. 1944
Leningrad

FINLAND

ESTONIA

LATVIA

LITHUANIA

East Prussia

Danzig

Warsaw

June 1941
Aug. 1943
Sept. 1944
July 1944
June 1941
Mar. 1944
Aug. 1944

Baltic Sea

SWEDEN

NORWAY

DENMARK

Oder R.

POLAND

Slovakia

Bukovina

HUNGARY

ROMANIA

Danube R.

BULGARIA

April 1941

GREECE

May 1941

Crete (Gr.)

Mediterranean Sea

LIBYA (It.)

April 1940

Surrendered May 8, 1945
Berlin
Potsdam

GERMANY

Elbe R.

April 1945

May 1940

Rhine R.

SWITZ.

YUGOSLAVIA

Adriatic Sea

ALBANIA (It.)

April 1941

Salerno Sept. 1943

Monte Cassino May 1944

ITALY

Rome

Liberated June 4, 1944

Sicily

July 1943

Tunis

Corsica

Sardinia

TUNISIA (Fr.)

Kasserine Pass Feb. 1943

North Sea

NETH.

BELG.

LUX.

FRANCE

VICHY FRANCE

Aug. 1944

June 1940

Paris

Dunkirk

Battle of Britain, 1940

London

GREAT BRITAIN

N. IRELAND

IRELAND

Liberated Aug. 25, 1944

Normandy invasion, D-Day June 6, 1944

Battle of the Bulge Dec. 16, 1944– Jan. 31, 1945

ATLANTIC OCEAN

SPAIN

PORTUGAL

SP. MOROCCO (Fr.)

MOROCCO (Fr.)

ALGERIA (Fr.)

FRENCH NORTH AFRICA

Under Vichy government 1940–42 Joined Allies Nov. 1942

Nov. 1942

Battle of Leningrad
In the face of Nazi invasion, Soviet citizens reacted heroically, moving entire factories to the interior of the country and building fortifications. Nowhere was their resolve so tested as in Leningrad (St. Petersburg), where two million are estimated to have died during a Nazi siege lasting more than two years. Before the invasion of Normandy in 1944, the people of the USSR bore the brunt of Nazi military might in Hitler's attempt to defeat "judeo-bolshevism." How does this picture of citizen defense of Leningrad differ from illustrations of Nazi power? How could the Nazis have been defeated in such events as this siege? *Sovfoto.*

eastward to join the Soviets in squeezing the Third Reich to its final defeat.

As the Allies advanced, Hitler decided that Germans were proving themselves unworthy of his greatness and deserved to perish in a cataclysmic conflagration. He thus refused to surrender and thereby spare Germans further death and destruction from the continued massive bombing. As the Soviet army took Berlin, Hitler committed suicide with his wife, Eva Braun. Although many soldiers remained committed to the Third Reich, Germany finally surrendered on May 8, 1945.

The Atomic Bomb and the Defeat of Japan. The United States and its allies had followed a "Europe first" strategy for conducting the war. They had nonetheless pursued the Japanese in the Pacific relentlessly. In 1940 and 1941, Japan had ousted the Europeans from many colonial holdings in Asia, but the Allies turned the tide in 1942 despite their diminished forces, by destroying some of Japan's formidable naval power in battles at Midway Island and Guadalcanal (Map 27.6). Unlike the United States, Japan lacked the capacity to recoup losses of ships or of manpower, while the Allies had not only their own productive power but also

access to matériel manufactured in Australia, India, and elsewhere around the world. The Allies stormed one Pacific island after another, gaining more bases from which to cut off the import of supplies and to launch bombers toward Japan itself. Short of men and weapons, the Japanese military resorted to kamikaze tactics, in which pilots deliberately crashed their planes into American ships, killing themselves in the process. In response, the Allies stepped up their bombing of major cities, killing more than 100,000 civilians in their spring 1945 firebombing of Tokyo. The Japanese leadership still ruled out surrender.

Meanwhile a U.S.-based international team of more than 100,000 workers, including scientists, technicians, and other staff, had developed the atomic bomb. The Japanese practice of dying almost to the man rather than surrendering caused Allied military leaders to calculate that defeating Japan might cost the lives of hundreds of thousands of Allied soldiers (and even more Japanese). On August 6 and 9, 1945, the U.S. government thus unleashed its new atomic weapons on Hiroshima and Nagasaki, respectively, killing 140,000 people instantly; tens of thousands later died from burns, wounds, and other afflictions (see Hiroshima Victim, page 1090).

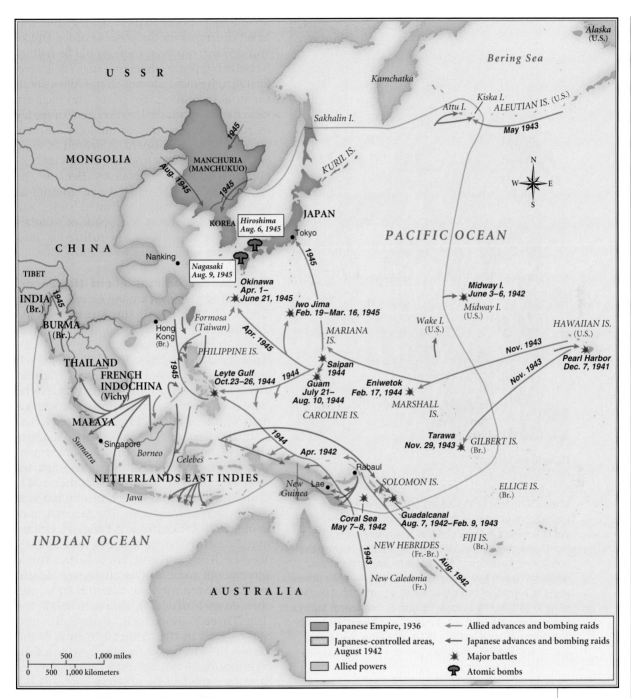

The following labels appear on the map:

Alaska (U.S.)

Bering Sea

U S S R

Kamchatka

Kiska I.

Attu I.   ALEUTIAN IS. (U.S.)

Sakhalin I.   May 1943

MONGOLIA   1945

MANCHURIA (MANCHUKOO)

Aug. 1945   1945

KURIL IS.

KOREA   Hiroshima Aug. 6, 1945

JAPAN   Tokyo

PACIFIC OCEAN

N   W   E   S

CHINA   Nanking

Nagasaki Aug. 9, 1945

TIBET

Okinawa Apr. 1– June 21, 1945

Midway I. June 3–6, 1942

Midway I. (U.S.)

INDIA (Br.)   1945

Iwo Jima Feb. 19–Mar. 16, 1945

Wake I. (U.S.)

HAWAIIAN IS. (U.S.)

BURMA (Br.)   Hong Kong (Br.)

Formosa (Taiwan)

Apr. 1945

MARIANA IS.

Nov. 1943

Pearl Harbor Dec. 7, 1941

THAILAND

PHILIPPINE IS.

Saipan 1944

Nov. 1943

FRENCH INDOCHINA (Vichy)   1945

Leyte Gulf Oct.23–26, 1944   1944

Guam July 21– Aug. 10, 1944

Eniwetok Feb. 17, 1944

MARSHALL IS.

MALAYA

CAROLINE IS.

Singapore   Borneo

Sumatra

Celebes

1944

Tarawa Nov. 29, 1943   GILBERT IS. (Br.)

NETHERLANDS EAST INDIES

Java

Apr. 1942

New Guinea   Lae   Rabaul

SOLOMON IS.

ELLICE IS. (Br.)

Coral Sea May 7–8, 1942

Guadalcanal Aug. 7, 1942– Feb. 9, 1943

FIJI IS. (Br.)

INDIAN OCEAN

NEW HEBRIDES (Fr.-Br.)

1943   Aug. 1942

New Caledonia (Fr.)

AUSTRALIA

0   500   1,000 miles
0   500   1,000 kilometers

Legend:
- Japanese Empire, 1936
- Japanese-controlled areas, August 1942
- Allied powers
- Allied advances and bombing raids
- Japanese advances and bombing raids
- Major battles
- Atomic bombs

MAP 27.6 World War II in the Pacific

As in Europe, the early days of World War II gave the advantage to the Axis power Japan as it took the offensive in conquering islands in the Pacific and territories in Asia—many of them colonies of European states. Britain countered by mobilizing a vast Indian army, while the United States, after the disastrous losses at Pearl Harbor and in the Philippines, gradually gained the upper hand by costly assaults, island by island. The Japanese strategy of fighting to the last person instead of surrendering when a loss was in sight was one factor in President Truman's decision to drop the atomic bomb in August 1945. How does the war in the Pacific look different from the war in Europe and North Africa?

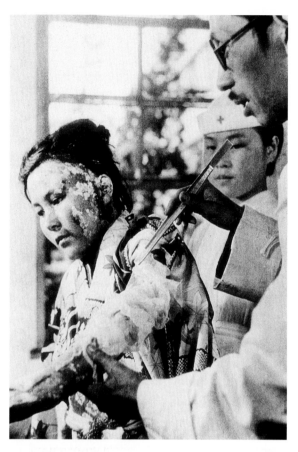

Hiroshima Victim
On August 6 and 9, 1945, the United States dropped the first atomic weapons on Hiroshima and Nagasaki, respectively, killing tens of thousands of Japanese instantly and leaving tens of thousands more to die of their injuries and the aftereffects. A few days later Japan surrendered, but controversy has swirled around the decision to drop the bomb ever since. Some see it as a racist act, no atomic weapons having been dropped on Germany, while others see it as a justified act of warfare in a conflict that threatened to cost countless more casualties because of Japan's policy of no surrender. What might have been the reaction at the time to such a photo in Japan, China, the United States, and Europe? *Tokyo/Fuji/Sumiko Kurita/Gamma.*

Although hardliners in the Japanese military wanted to continue the war, on August 14, 1945, Japan surrendered.

An Uneasy Postwar Settlement

Envisioning a postwar settlement had been a major priority throughout the war, and the Allies had held critical meetings during the

hostilities not only to plan strategy but also to set the terms for the postwar order. Unlike World War I, however, there would be neither a celebrated peace conference nor a definitive, formal agreement among all the Allies about the final resolution. Yet peace and recovery were more important than ever, as Europe lay in ruins and as tens of millions starved, wandering the continent in search of food, shelter, and security from the armies that occupied virtually every country. Because the victorious Allies distrusted one another in varying degrees, with the United States and the Soviet Union on the brink of another struggle for supremacy, the future for most Europeans looked grim.

Wartime Agreements about the Peace. Wartime agreements among members of the Grand Alliance about the future reflected their ongoing differences, and these hard-won agreements would come to rouse intense postwar debate. In 1941, Roosevelt and Churchill forged the Atlantic Charter, which condemned aggression, reaffirmed the ideal of collective security, and endorsed the right of all people to choose their governments. Not only did the Allies come to focus on these points, but so did colonized peoples to whom, Churchill said, the charter was not meant to apply. In October 1944, Churchill and Stalin agreed on the postwar distribution of territories. The Soviet Union would control Romania and Bulgaria, Britain would control Greece, and they would jointly oversee Hungary and Yugoslavia. These agreements went against Roosevelt's faith in collective security, self-determination, and open doors in trade. In February 1945, the "Big Three"—Roosevelt, Churchill, and Stalin—met in the Crimean town of Yalta. Roosevelt advocated the institution of an organization to be called the United Nations to replace the League of Nations as a global peace mechanism and supported future Soviet influence in Korea, Manchuria, and the Sakhalin◆ and Kurile Islands. The last meeting of the Allied leaders took place at Potsdam, Germany, in the summer of 1945, where they agreed to give the Soviets control of eastern Poland, to cede a large stretch of

◆**Sakhalin:** SAH kuh leen

eastern Germany to Poland, and to adopt a temporary four-way occupation of Germany that included France as one of the supervising powers. Yet as victory unfolded, the Allies scrambled to outmaneuver one another.

The War's Grim Legacy. The Great Depression had inflicted global suffering, while the Second World War left an estimated 100 million dead, more than fifty million refugees without homes, and one of the most tragic moral legacies in human history. Thus, making peace proved a prolonged and bitter process—and one that was hardly over in 1945. Forced into armies or into labor camps for war production, colonial peoples were in full rebellion or close to it. For a second time in three decades, they had seen their imperial masters killing one another, slaughtered by the very technology that was supposed to make European civilization superior. Deference to Europe was virtually finished, with independence a matter of time.

Western values at home were imperiled as well. Rational, democratic Europe had succumbed to continuous wartime values, and it was this Europe that George Orwell captured in his novel *1984* (1949). Poor food and worn clothing, grimy streets and dwellings, people prematurely aged and careworn—all characterized both London of the 1940s and Orwell's fictional state, Oceania. Orwell had worked for the wartime Ministry of Information (called the Ministry of Truth in the novel) and churned out doctored news for wartime audiences. Information and truth hardly mattered: words had taken on sanitized meaning during the war as *disengagement* replaced *retreat, battle fatigue* substituted for *insanity,* and *liberating* a country could mean invading it and slaughtering its civilians. Millions rejoiced at the demise of Nazi evil in 1945, but Orwell saw as part of war's legacy the end of prosperity, the deadening of creativity, and the intrusion of big government into everyday life. For Orwell, bureaucratic domination depended on the perpetuation of conflict, and fresh conflict was indeed brewing in the race for Berlin and Japan even before the war ended. As Allied powers competed for territory, a new struggle called the cold war was taking root.

Review: What were the major consequences of World War II?

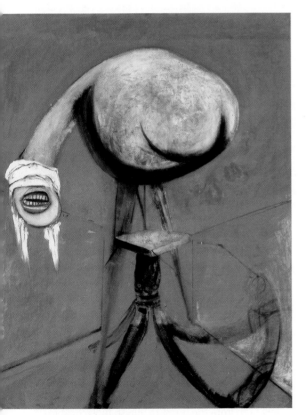

Francis Bacon, *Three Studies for Figures at Base of Crucifixion* (c. 1944)
At the end of the war, English artist Francis Bacon depicted the traditional Western subject of the crucifixion, but in a way that converted the human figure into a grotesque monster. His figures often reflect horror, disgust, and real debasement and thus seem to describe the human condition at the end of World War II and the Holocaust. *Tate Gallery, London/Art Resource, NY.*

Conclusion

The Great Depression brought massive social dislocation and fear. It provided a setting in which dictators thrived because they promised to restore national greatness and bring economic prosperity. Enticed by the mass media, people turned away from representative institutions and toward dynamic, if brutal, leaders. Memories of World War I permitted Hitler and Mussolini to menace

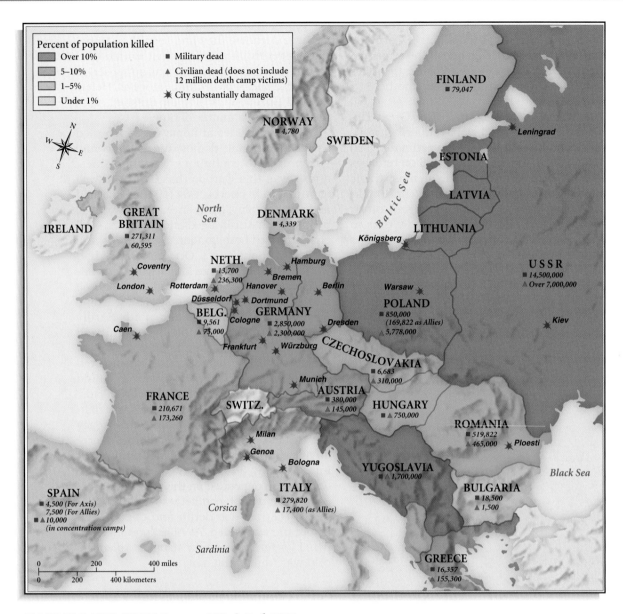

Percent of population killed
- Over 10%
- 5–10%
- 1–5%
- Under 1%

■ Military dead
▲ Civilian dead (does not include 12 million death camp victims)
✳ City substantially damaged

FINLAND ■ 79,047

NORWAY ■ 4,780

SWEDEN

Leningrad

ESTONIA

LATVIA

North Sea

DENMARK ■ 4,339

LITHUANIA

Königsberg

GREAT BRITAIN ■ 271,311 ▲ 60,595

IRELAND

USSR ■ 14,500,000 ▲ Over 7,000,000

Coventry

NETH. ■ 13,700 ▲ 236,300

Hamburg

London Rotterdam Hanover Bremen Berlin Warsaw

Düsseldorf Dortmund

BELG. ■ 9,561 ▲ 75,000

Caen

Cologne

GERMANY ■ 2,850,000 ▲ 2,300,000

Dresden

POLAND ■ 850,000 (169,822 as Allies) ▲ 5,778,000

Kiev

Frankfurt Würzburg

CZECHOSLOVAKIA ■ 6,683 ▲ 310,000

FRANCE ■ 210,671 ▲ 173,260

SWITZ.

Munich

AUSTRIA ■ 380,000 ▲ 145,000

HUNGARY ■ ▲ 750,000

ROMANIA ■ 519,822 ▲ 465,000 Ploesti

Milan

Genoa

Bologna

YUGOSLAVIA ■ ▲ 1,700,000

Black Sea

SPAIN ■ 4,500 (For Axis) 7,500 (For Allies) ■ ▲ 10,000 (in concentration camps)

Corsica

ITALY ■ 279,820 ▲ 17,400 (as Allies)

BULGARIA ■ 18,500 ▲ 1,500

Sardinia

GREECE ■ 16,357 ▲ 155,300

0   200   400 miles
0   200   400 kilometers

MAPPING THE WEST Europe at War's End, 1945
While all of Europe was severely shocked during the age of catastrophe, wartime damage left scars that would last for decades. Major German cities were bombed to bits, while the Soviet Union suffered an unimaginable toll of well over twenty million deaths due to the war alone. In addition to the vast civilian and military losses shown on this map, historians estimate that no less than twelve million people were murdered in the Nazi death camps. Everything from politics to family life needed rebuilding. The chaos fueled postwar tensions stemming both from the quest to punish those held responsible for such suffering and from the superpowers' determination to gain the political allegiance of recovering countries in the cold war. Explain the relative difference in loss of life in Eastern Europe and Western Europe. *From* The Hammond Atlas of the Twentieth Century *(London: Times Books, 1996), 102.*

Europe unimpeded throughout the 1930s. When a coalition formed to stop them, it was an uneasy one among the imperial powers France and Britain, the Stalinist Soviet Union, and the industrial giant the United States. World War II ended European dominance. Its economies were shattered, its population was reduced, its colonies were on the verge of independence, and its peoples were starving and homeless.

The costs of a bloody war—one waged against civilians as much as armies—taught the victorious powers different lessons. The United States, Britain, and France were convinced that a minimum of citizen well-being was necessary to prevent a recurrence of fascism. Soviet citizens hoped that their lives would become easier and more open. The devastation of the USSR's population and resources, however, made Stalin increasingly obsessed with national security and reparations. Britain and France confronted the final eclipse of their imperial might, underscoring Orwell's insight that the war had transformed society irrevocably. The militarization of society and the deliberate murder of millions of innocent citizens like Etty Hillesum were a permanent blight on the European legacy. Nonetheless, backed by vast arsenals of sophisticated weaponry, the competing visions of former Allies regarding how to deal with Germany and eastern Europe led the United States and the Soviet Union to threaten one another—and the world—with yet another war.

Suggested References

The Great Depression

Historians look to the depression as a complex event with economic, social, and cultural consequences, but in addition they see its impact as yet another indication of the tightening of global economic connections. To follow some of the political implications for European empires, see in particular Columbia University's South Asia Web site, which explores Gandhi's economic resistance to British colonialism.

Balderston, Theo, ed. *The World Economy and National Economics in the Interwar Slump.* 2003.

Evans, Richard J., and Dick Geary. *The German Unemployed: Experiences and Consequences of Mass Unemployment from the Weimar Republic to the Third Reich.* 1987.

Roszkowski, Wojciech. *Landowners in Poland, 1918–1939.* 1991.

Rothermund, Dietmar. *The Global Impact of the Great Depression, 1929–1939.* 1996.

South Asia and Gandhi: **http://www.columbia .edu/cu/libraries/indiv/area/sarai.**

Totalitarian Triumph

The vicious dictators Stalin, Hitler, and Mussolini are among the most popular subjects for historians and readers alike. Recent histories study their mobilization of art and the media and consider people's complex participation in totalitarian regimes. Studies like those of Gellately and Stolzfus, Kaplan, and Engel and Posadskaya-Vanderbeck have provided us with fascinating if grim insights into studies of everyday life.

Ben-Ghiat, Ruth. *Fascist Modernities: Italy, 1922–1945.* 2001.

Burleigh, Michael. *The Third Reich: A New History.* 2000.

*Engel, Barbara Alpern, and Anastasia Posadskaya-Vanderbeck, eds. *A Revolution of Their Own: Voices of Women in Soviet History.* 1998.

Fritzsche, Peter. *Germans into Nazis.* 1998.

Gellately, Robert, and Nathan Stolzfus, eds. *Social Outsiders in Nazi Germany.* 2001.

Kaplan, Marion. *Between Dignity and Despair: Jewish Life in Nazi Germany.* 1998.

Viola, Lynn, ed. *Contending with Stalinism: Soviet Power and Popular Resistance in the 1930s.* 2003.

Democracies on the Defensive

The democracies attacked the depression from a variety of perspectives ranging from state policy to film and the arts, yet another indication of how complex politics can be. Further departure from liberal policies, whether in trade or in the development of the activist welfare state, also have attracted historical study.

Kalvemark, Ann-Sofie. *More Children or Better Quality? Aspects of Swedish Population Policy.* 1980.

Kennedy, David M. *Freedom from Fear: The American People in Depression and War, 1929–1945.* 1999.

Lavin, Maud, et al. *Montage and Modern Life, 1919–1942.* 1992.

Rearick, Charles. *The French in Love and War: Popular Culture in the Era of the World Wars.* 1997.

Richards, Jeffrey, ed. *The Unknown 1930s: An Alternative History of the British Cinema, 1929–39.* 1998.

*Primary source.

The Road to Global War

The road to war encircled the globe, involving countries seemingly peripheral to the struggles among the antagonists. The perennial question for many historians is whether Hitler could have been stopped, but with globalization there is new attention to the beginnings of war beyond the West as a prelude to decolonization.

Bix, Herbert P. *Hirohito and the Making of Modern Japan.* 2000.

Crozier, Andrew. *The Causes of the Second World War.* 1997.

Knight, Patricia. *The Spanish Civil War.* 1991.

*Mangini González, Shirley. *Memories of Resistance: Women's Voices from the Spanish Civil War.* 1995.

Watt, D. Cameron. *How War Came: The Immediate Causes of the Second World War.* 1989.

World War II, 1939–1945

In a vast literature historians have charted the war's innumerable and global horrors, with issues of the Holocaust, industrial killing, and the nature of racial thinking drawing particular attention. The U.S. Holocaust Memorial Museum provides online exhibits giving the history of the Holocaust in different locations. While looking at the social aspects of war, historians have intensely debated the development of the cold war within the "hot" war.

Beevor, Anthony. *The Fall of Berlin 1945.* 2002.

Browning, Christopher. *The Origins of the Final Solution: The Evolution of Nazi Jewish Policy, September 1939–March 1942.* 2004.

*Dawidowicz, Lucy S. *A Holocaust Reader.* 1976.

Dower, John W. *War without Mercy: Race and Power in the Pacific War.* 1986.

Holocaust Museum: http://usholocaustmuseum.org.

James, Harold. *The Deutsche Bank and the Nazi Economic War Against the Jews: The Expropriation of Jewish-Owned Property.* 2001.

Miner, Steven Merritt. *Stalin's Holy War: Religion, Nationalism, and Alliance Politics, 1941–1945.* 2003.

Rhodes, Richard. *The Making of the Atomic Bomb.* 1986.

Slaughter, Jane. *Women in the Italian Resistance, 1943–1945.* 1997.

Weinberg, Gerhard. *A World at Arms: A Global History of World War II.* 1994.

---

*Primary source.

CHAPTER REVIEW

IMPORTANT EVENTS

1929 The U.S. stock market crashes; global depression begins; Soviet leadership initiates war against prosperous farmers, the kulaks; German Thomas Mann wins the Nobel Prize for literature

1933 Hitler comes to power in Germany

1936 Show trials begin in the USSR; Stalin purges top Communist Party officials and military leaders; the Spanish Civil War begins

1938 Virginia Woolf publishes *Three Guineas*

1939 Germany invades Poland; World War II begins; the Spanish Civil War ends

1940 France falls to the German army

1940–1941 The British air force fends off German attacks in the battle of Britain

1941 Germany invades the Soviet Union; Japan attacks Pearl Harbor; the United States enters the war

1941–1945 The Holocaust

1944 Allied forces land at Normandy, France

1945 The fall of Berlin; United States drops atomic bombs on Hiroshima and Nagasaki; World War II ends

KEY TERMS

appeasement (1075)

Blitzkrieg (1077)

civil disobedience (1054)

Enabling Act (1062)

family allowance (1066)

five-year plans (1056)

Lebensraum (1072)

Nazi-Soviet Pact (1077)

Nuremberg Laws (1064)

Popular Front (1067)

pump priming (1063)

purges (1058)

REVIEW QUESTIONS

1. How did the Great Depression affect society and politics?

2. What role did violence play in the Soviet and Nazi regimes?

3. How did the democracies work to maintain their values while facing the twin challenges of economic depression and the rise of fascism?

4. How did the aggression of Japan, Germany, and Italy create the conditions for global war?

5. What were the major consequences of World War II?

MAKING CONNECTIONS

1. Compare fascist ideas of the individual with the idea of individual rights that drove the American and French revolutions.

2. What are the major differences between World War I and World War II?

FOR FURTHER EXPLORATION

To assess your mastery of the material in this chapter, see the Online Study Guide at **bedfordstmartins.com/hunt**.

To read additional primary-source material from this period, see Chapter 27 in *Sources of The Making of the West*, Second Edition.

Remaking Europe in the Shadow of Cold War,

C. 1945–1965

AFTER THE UNITED STATES DROPPED two atomic bombs on Japan in 1945, the Union of Soviet Socialist Republics raced to catch up with its rival in atomic weaponry. In late August 1949, the Soviet Union detonated its own atomic bomb. Two days after President Harry S Truman announced the news of this test, Billy Graham, a young Baptist preacher, based his sermon at a revival meeting on the fearsome event. Graham warned that U.S. officials believed "we have only five to ten years and our civilization will be ended." He announced that Russia had aimed bombs to strike New York, Chicago, and Los Angeles, where the revival was taking place. "Time is desperately short....Prepare to meet thy God," he warned. People flocked to hear Graham talk about the end of the world, launching the evangelist's astonishing career of spiritual and political influence in the United States and around the globe.

Graham's message—"We don't know how soon, but we do know this, that right now the grace of God can still save a poor lost sinner"—captured the extremes of postwar sentiment in an atomic age. On the one hand, the global postwar situation was tragic. One hundred million people had died; Europe and Japan were prostrate, and their people starving; evidence of genocide and other inhumanity was everywhere; the menace of nuclear annihilation loomed. It was to this menace that Graham referred. The old international order was gone, replaced by the rivalry of the United States and the Soviet Union for control of a devastated Europe, whose political and

---

The Atomic Age
The atomic bombs dropped on Hiroshima and Nagasaki in 1945 were followed by several decades of increasingly powerful detonations for testing purposes. The Soviet Union practiced underground testing, while the United States carried out above-ground tests in the Pacific region. Protests against testing developed in the 1950s, many of them citing the hazards of radioactivity and the growing threat of nuclear annihilation. Simultaneously, nuclear power was converted to peacetime use, notably serving both as a source of energy and as a therapy for cancer. What feelings might pictures of nuclear mushroom clouds have aroused in citizens in Europe, the Soviet Union, and the United States? © *Corbis*.

economic systems had collapsed. The nuclear arsenals of these two superpowers—a term coined in 1947—grew massively in the 1950s, but they were enemies who did not fight outright. Thus, their terrifying rivalry was called the **cold war**. The cold war divided the West and caused acute anxiety, even for someone like Graham from the victorious and wealthy United States.

On the other hand, the defeat of Nazism inspired an upsurge of hope, a revival of religious feeling like Graham's, and a new commitment to humanitarian goals. Heroic effort had defeated fascism, and that defeat raised hopes that a new age would begin. Atomic science promised advances in medicine, and nuclear energy was trumpeted as a replacement for coal and oil. The creation of the United Nations heralded an era of international cooperation. Around the globe, colonial peoples won independence from European masters, while in the United States the civil rights movement gained new momentum. The welfare state expanded, and by the end of the 1950s economic rebirth, stimulated in part by the cold war, had made much of Europe more prosperous than ever before. An "economic miracle" had occurred, and, unbelievably, just a decade after the war Europeans were beginning to enjoy the highest standard of living they had ever known.

Extremes of hope and fear infused the atomic age, as society, culture, and the international order were all transformed. Gone was the definition of a West comprising Europe and its cultural offshoots such as the United States and an East comprising Asian countries like India, China, and Japan. During the cold war, the word *West* came to stand for the United States and its client countries in western Europe, while *East* meant the Soviet Union and its tightly controlled bloc in eastern Europe. Still another terminology arose in the 1950s, one that divided the globe into the first world, or capitalist bloc of countries; the second world, or socialist bloc; and the **third world**, or countries emerging from imperial domination. As the world's people redefined themselves politically and culturally, the superpowers took the world to the brink of nuclear disaster when the United States discovered Soviet missile sites on the island of Cuba. From the dropping of the atomic bomb on Japan in 1945 to the Cuban missile crisis of 1962, Graham's dread that "we are moving madly toward destruction" gripped much of the world, albeit in the midst of prosperity and Europe's rebirth.

❖ World Politics Transformed

World War II ended the global leadership of Europe. Many countries lay in ruins by the summer of 1945, and conditions would deteriorate before they got better. Though victorious, bombed and bankrupt Britain could not feed its people. In contrast, the United States, whose territory was virtually untouched in the war, emerged as the world's sole economic giant, and the Soviet Union, despite suffering immense destruction, retained formidable military might. Having occupied Europe as part of the victorious alliance against Nazism

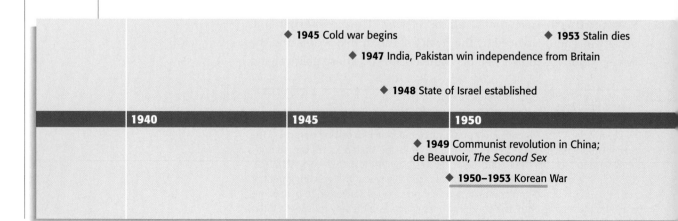

♦ **1945** Cold war begins   ♦ **1953** Stalin dies

♦ **1947** India, Pakistan win independence from Britain

♦ **1948** State of Israel established

1940	1945	1950

♦ **1949** Communist revolution in China; de Beauvoir, *The Second Sex*

♦ **1950–1953** Korean War

and fascism, the two superpowers used Germany—at the heart of the continent and its politics—to divide Europe in two. By the late 1940s, the USSR imposed Communist rule throughout most of Eastern Europe and in the 1950s quashed rebellions against its dominance there. Western Europeans found themselves at least partially constricted by the very U.S. economic power that helped them rebuild, as the United States maintained air bases and nuclear weapons sites on their soil. The age of bipolar world politics had begun, with Europe as its testing ground.

Europe Prostrate

In contrast to World War I, when devastation was limited to the front lines around the trenches, armies in World War II had fought a war of movement and massive air strikes that leveled thousands of square miles of territory. Across the continent, whole cities were clogged with rubble; homeless survivors wandered the streets. In Sicily and on the Rhine River, almost no bridge remained standing; in the Soviet Union, seventy thousand villages and more than a thousand cities lay in shambles. Everywhere people were suffering. In the Netherlands, the severity of Nazi occupation left the Dutch population close to death, relieved only by a U.S. airlift of food. In Britain, basic commodities were difficult to obtain, and many died in the bitterly cold winter of 1946–1947 because of a shortage of fuel. Italian bakers sold bread by the slice. When Allied troops passed through German towns, the famished inhabitants lined the roads in hopes that someone would toss them something to eat. "To see the children fighting for food," one British soldier noted, "was like watching animals being fed in a zoo." There was social disarray, even chaos, at the war's end but no mass uprisings as after World War I. Until the late 1940s, people were too exhausted by the struggle for bare survival.

The tens of millions of refugees suffered the most. Many had been inmates of prisons and death camps, and, weakened and ill, they were now released into a world where resources were slim and old ways of living destroyed. Others, especially some twelve million ethnic Germans, fled westward to escape the victorious but destructive Red Army as it inflicted a grim occupation on eastern Europe. Native Germans in the western occupied zones viewed refugees as competitors for food and work and often provided a cold welcome. Many refugees ultimately found homes in countries that experienced little or no war damage, such as Denmark, Sweden, Canada, and Australia. Following the exodus of refugees from the east, western Europe became one of the world's most densely populated regions (Map 28.1). The USSR lobbied hard for the repatriation of several million Soviet prisoners of war and forced laborers, and the Allies transported the majority of the Russian refugees back to the Soviet Union. "Contaminated" by Western ideas, according to Soviet leaders, they faced execution until the Allies slowed the process, leaving hundreds of thousands of Soviets to join the ocean of refugees in western Europe.

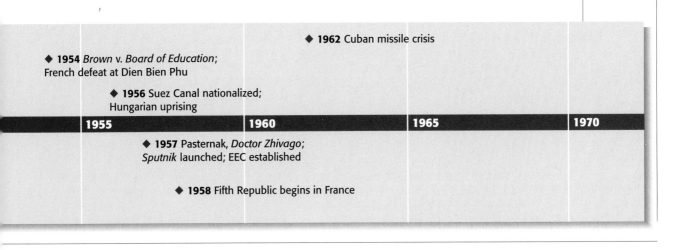

◆ **1962** Cuban missile crisis

◆ **1954** *Brown* v. *Board of Education*;
French defeat at Dien Bien Phu

◆ **1956** Suez Canal nationalized;
Hungarian uprising

| 1955 | 1960 | 1965 | 1970 |

◆ **1957** Pasternak, *Doctor Zhivago*;
Sputnik launched; EEC established

◆ **1958** Fifth Republic begins in France

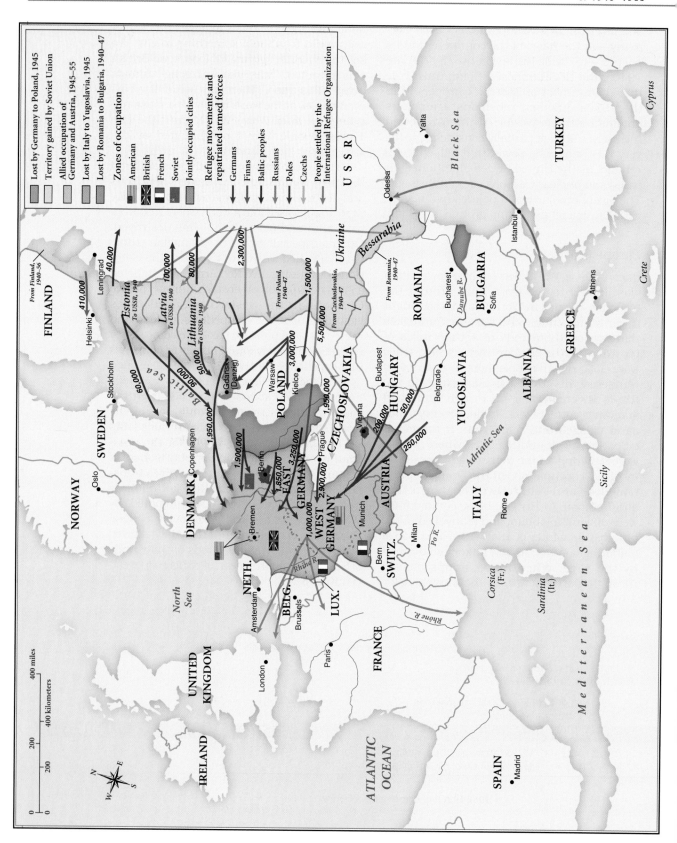

Legend:

Lost by Germany to Poland, 1945

Territory gained by Soviet Union

Allied occupation of Germany and Austria, 1945–55

Lost by Italy to Yugoslavia, 1945

Lost by Romania to Bulgaria, 1940–47

Zones of occupation
American
British
French
Soviet
Jointly occupied cities

Refugee movements and repatriated armed forces
Germans
Finns
Baltic peoples
Russians
Poles
Czechs

People settled by the International Refugee Organization

◀ **MAP 28.1 The Impact of World War II on Europe**
European governments, many of them struggling to provide food and other necessities for their populations, found themselves responsible for hundreds of thousands, if not millions, of new refugees. Simultaneously, millions of prisoners of war, servicemen, and slave laborers were returned to the Soviet Union, many of them by force. This situation unfolded amid political instability and even violence. How would you describe the movement of refugees and soldiers in Europe conveyed by this map? What impact did this movement have on political and social life?

Survivors of the concentration camps also discovered that their suffering had not ended with Germany's defeat. Many returned diseased and disoriented, while others often had no home to return to, as property had been confiscated and entire communities destroyed. Moreover, anti-Semitism—official policy under the Nazis—lingered in popular attitudes. In the summer of 1946, a vicious crowd in Kielce,◆ Poland, rioted against 250 returning Jewish survivors, killing at least 40. Elsewhere in eastern Europe, such violence was common. Meanwhile, some officials across Europe even denied that unprecedented atrocities had been committed and wanted to refuse Jews any help. Survivors crammed into the port cities of Italy and other Mediterranean countries, eventually to escape Europe for Palestine, where Zionists had been settling for half a century. Unwilling or unable to help Hitler's most abused victims, many European countries had simply lost the capacity for moral and economic leadership.

New Superpowers: The United States and the Soviet Union

Only two powerful countries were left in 1945: the United States and the Soviet Union. The United States was now the richest country in the world. Its industrial output had increased by a remarkable 15 percent annually between 1940 and 1944, a rate of growth that was reflected in workers' wages. By 1947, the United States controlled almost two-thirds of the world's gold bullion. It also

◆ **Kielce:** kee EHLT say

controlled more than half of the commercial shipping, up from almost one-fifth of the total in the 1930s. With continued spending on industrial and military research adding prosperity to victory, a confident mood swept the United States at the end of the war. Casting aside the post–World War I policy of nonintervention, Americans embraced their position as global leaders. Many had learned about the world while tracking the war's progress; hundreds of thousands of soldiers, government officials, and relief workers had direct experience of Europe, Africa, and Asia. Although some feared a postwar depression and many shared Billy Graham's worries about nuclear annihilation, a wave of suburban housing development and consumer spending kept the economy buoyant. Temporarily reversing the trend toward a lower birthrate that had existed for most of the century, a baby boom exploded from the late 1940s through the early 1960s in response to the economic abundance.

The Soviets also emerged from the war with a well-justified sense of accomplishment. Withstanding horrendous losses, they had resisted the most massive onslaught ever launched against a nation. Instead of the international isolation dealt Russia after World War I, Soviet leadership expected equality in decision making with the United States, and indeed many Europeans and Americans had great respect for the Soviet contribution to Hitler's defeat. Ordinary Soviet citizens believed that a victory that had cost the USSR some 25 million lives would bring improvement in their everyday conditions and a continuation of the war's relatively relaxed politics. Rumors spread among the peasants that the collective farms would be disbanded and returned to them as individual property now that the war was won and agriculture modernized. "Life will become pleasant," one writer prophesied. "There will be much coming and going, and a lot of contacts with the West." The Stalinist goals of industrialization and defense against Nazism had been won, and thus many Soviets expected an end to decades of hardship, even an end to censorship and repressive government.

Stalin took a different view and moved ruthlessly to reassert control. In 1946, his new five-year plan set increased production goals and mandated more stringent collectivization of agriculture. For him, rapid recovery meant more work, not less, and more order, not greater freedom. Stalin cut back the army by two-thirds to beef up the labor force and also turned his attention to the low birthrate, a result of wartime male casualties and women's long, arduous working days, which discouraged them from adding child care to their already heavy responsibilities. He introduced an intense propaganda campaign emphasizing that women should hold down jobs and also fulfill their "true nature" by producing many children. A crackdown on freedom took place, and a new round of purges began in which people were told that enemies among them were threatening the state. Jews were especially targeted, and in 1953 the government announced that doctors—most of them Jews— had long been assassinating Soviet leaders, murdering newborns and patients in hospitals, and plotting to poison water supplies. Hysteria gripped the nation, as people feared for their lives. "I am a simple worker and not an anti-Semite," one Moscow resident wrote, "but I say…it's time to clean these people out." In these ways, Stalinism was reborn and an atmosphere developed that was ripe for cold war.

Origins of the Cold War

In the immediate postwar years, the United States and the Soviet Union launched a cold war that would afflict the world for more than four decades. No peace treaty officially ended the conflict with Germany as a written record of contest and compromise or of things gone wrong, as in the Peace of Paris of 1919–1920. As a result, the origins of the cold war remain a matter of debate, with historians faulting both sides for starting this fearsome rivalry (see "New Sources, New Perspectives," page 1104). Some point to consistent U.S., British, and French hostility to the Soviets that began as far back as the Bolshevik Revolution of 1917 and continued through the Depression and World War II. These powers opposed the Communists' abolition of private property and Russia's withdrawal from World War I. Others stress

Stalin's aggressive policies, notably the Nazi-Soviet alliance in 1939 and his quick claims on the Baltic States and Polish territory when World War II broke out. In this view, other countries naturally feared a Soviet expansionism that knew no limits.

During the war, suspicion ran deep and the Grand Alliance was always a troubled one. Stalin felt that Churchill and Roosevelt were deliberately letting the USSR bear the brunt of Hitler's onslaught on the continent as part of their anti-Communist policy. He rightly viewed Churchill in particular as interested primarily in preserving Britain's imperial power, no matter what the cost in lives of Soviet citizens. At the time, some Americans believed that dropping the atomic bomb on Japan would also frighten the Soviets from land grabs, and the new U.S. president, Harry Truman, was far tougher than Roosevelt with regard to Soviet needs. He cut off aid to the USSR almost the instant the last gun was fired, fueling Stalin's belief that the United States was aiming for his country's utter collapse. Given what Stalin interpreted as a menace from the West, especially in a revived Germany, and his own country's exhausted condition, he saw the USSR as needing not just a temporary military occupation but also a permanent "buffer zone" of European states loyal to the USSR as a safeguard. Across the Atlantic, Truman saw the Soviet occupation of eastern Europe as heralding an era of Communist takeovers around the world. By 1946, members of the U.S. State Department were describing Stalin as yet another neurotic Asian tyrant, driven to continue the centuries-old Russian thirst for world domination.

The cold war thus became a series of moves and countermoves in the shared occupation of the rich European heartland by two very different countries. In line with its geopolitical needs, the USSR repressed democratic coalition governments of liberals, socialists, Communists, and peasant parties in central and eastern Europe between 1945 and 1949. It imposed Communist rule almost immediately in Bulgaria and Romania. In Romania, Stalin cited citizen violence in 1945 as the excuse to demand an ouster of all non-Communists from the civil service and cabinet. In Poland, the Communists fixed the election results of 1945 and 1946 to create the illusion of approval for communism. Nevertheless, the Communists had to share power between 1945 and 1947 with the popular Peasant Party, which had a large constituency of rural workers and peasant landowners. The Allies protested many of these moves by the Communists as the cold war advanced.

The United States put its new interventionist spirit to work, promoting American influence. It acknowledged Soviet authority in areas it occupied but worried that Communist power would spread to western Europe. The difficult conditions of postwar life made Communist programs that promised better conditions increasingly attractive to workers, while Communist leadership in the Resistance gave the party a powerful allure. Both U.S. and British concern mounted when Communist insurgents had enough of a following to threaten the right-wing monarchy the British had installed in Greece in 1944. In March 1947, Truman reacted to the Communist threat by announcing what quickly became known as the **Truman Doctrine**, the countering of political crises with economic and military aid. The president requested $400 million in military aid for Greece and Turkey, where the Communists were also exerting pressure. Fearing that Americans would balk at backing Greece, U.S. congressmen would agree to the program only if Truman would "scare the hell out of the country," as one put it. Truman thus publicized an expensive aid program as necessary to fortify the world against a tide of global Soviet conquest. The show of American support convinced the Communists to back off, and in 1949 the Greek rebels declared a cease-fire.

In 1947, the United States also devised the **Marshall Plan**—a program of massive economic aid to Europe—to alleviate some of the hardships that were making ordinary people in western Europe find communism attractive. "The seeds of totalitarian regimes are nurtured by misery and want," the president warned in the same speech that introduced the Truman Doctrine. Named after Secretary of State George C. Marshall, the program's direct aid would immediately improve everyday life, while the loans and other financial credit aimed to restart the flow of international trade. The government claimed that the Marshall Plan was not directed "against any country or doctrine but against hunger, poverty, desperation, and chaos." By the early 1950s, the United States had sent Europe more than $12 billion in food, equipment, and services and the Marshall Plan did its intended political work by reducing the appeal of communism in the countries of western Europe that received the aid.

Stalin saw the aid as a U.S. political ploy that caught him without similar largess to offer to his client countries in eastern and central europe. He thus clamped down still harder on eastern European governments, eliminating the last remnants of democracy in Hungary and Poland and preventing governments in his sphere of influence from responding to the U.S. offer of assistance. For

THE COLD WAR

1945–1949	USSR establishes satellite states in eastern Europe
1947	Truman Doctrine announces American commitment to contain communism; U.S. Marshall Plan provides massive aid to rebuild Europe
1948–1949	Soviet troops blockade Berlin; United States airlifts provisions to Berliners
1949	West Germany formed; Western nations form North Atlantic Treaty Organization (NATO); Soviet bloc establishes Council for Mutual Economic Assistance (COMECON); USSR tests its first nuclear weapon
1950–1953	Korean War
1950–1954	U.S. senator Joseph McCarthy leads hunt for American Communists
1953	Stalin dies
1955	USSR and Eastern bloc countries form military alliance, the Warsaw Pact
1956	Khrushchev denounces Stalin in "secret speech" to Communist Party Congress; Hungarians revolt unsuccessfully against Soviet domination
1959	Fidel Castro comes to power in Cuba
1961	Berlin Wall erected
1962	Cuban missile crisis

NEW SOURCES, NEW PERSPECTIVES

Government Archives and the Truth about the Cold War

As the modern nation-state grew in the nineteenth century, historians came increasingly to rely on official government archives to answer questions arising from ideological disputes. The cold war was one such battle of charges and countercharges. Government archives have thrown light on the accusations of both sides. Participants and eyewitnesses, it is believed, are not reliable because of their bias. Instead, trained scholars, ridding themselves of bias, carefully examine government records, preserved in official repositories where tampering cannot take place.

The opening of USSR archives in the late 1980s and 1990s after the fall of Soviet communism gave answers to many cold war questions. In 1956, in the midst of superpower rivalry, Nikita Khrushchev first threw official light on the slaughter connected with Stalin's regime. In Khrushchev's partial revelation of truths, V. I. Lenin and Joseph Stalin were presented as distinctly different political beings, with Lenin an ideologue and benefactor and Stalin a creature of excess. The Soviet archives, however, revealed a more vicious Lenin, one who demanded from the start of the Bolshevik regime the kind of brutality that Khrushchev had pinned on Stalin alone. Lenin and his contemporaries started the reliance on wholesale massacre of the upper classes, peasants, dissenters, and even ordinary citizens. At the same time, the archives discredited the U.S. claim that the Soviet Union in the 1950s was out to conquer the world. Instead, scholars found both Stalin and Khrushchev fearful of a U.S. nuclear attack and eager to come to terms. Their bluster and brinkmanship, the archives showed, often arose from a need to appear dominant to Soviet satellite states and to the new challenger for Communist leadership—the People's Republic of China.

Much official U.S. archival material still remains closed to scholars, but the Freedom of Information Act (1966, amended 1974) allows historians to press for access and at times to obtain it. Official U.S. documents have opened up debate about the dropping of the atomic bomb, with some scholars concluding that it was not merely a matter of ending the war with Japan in the most expeditious way. Instead, brandishing atomic weapons served U.S. cold war ends of scaring the Soviets. Tapes released from John F. Kennedy's administration have shown the president differing from his generals, most of whom wanted a nuclear war during the Cuban missile crisis. Kennedy, far from being the consistent cold warrior he sought to portray, pulled back from the brink.

For all that new archival evidence can reveal, reliance on this material has many pitfalls. First, one train of thought leads to the mistaken belief that if an archive contains no written evidence of an event, the event is open to question. For instance, if there is no written order from Adolf Hitler to start the Holocaust, some have argued, it means that he did not know about the event or even that it did not occur. Second, faith in archives also makes them susceptible to forg-

instance, Czechoslovakia, which by Eastern European standards had prospered under a Communist-led coalition, welcomed the Marshall Plan as the beginning of East-West reconciliation. This illusion ended, however, during a purge of non-Communist officials that began in the autumn of 1947. By June 1948, Czechoslovakia's socialist president, Edouard Beneš,◆ had resigned and been replaced by a Communist figurehead. The pop-

◆ **Edouard Beneš:** EH doo ahrt BEH nehsh

Russian Secret Archives

The opening of archives across the former Soviet bloc had many consequences. In the former East Germany, for instance, names of secret police informers were made public and many people had their reputations utterly tarnished for their collaboration with the Communist government. The opening of the archives also exposed the cases of those convicted with trumped-up evidence (some pictured here), most of them sent to camps and to their deaths long since. The probable existence of such secret archives and concealed official information around the world has made historians and the families of victims fight for access. Simultaneously, politicians in the democracies are currently struggling to keep their archives closed, especially to scholars with training in assessing them. *ITAR-TASS/Sovfoto.*

eries and the planting of evidence, as has happened with some Russian documents of the 1990s. Finally, excessive faith in archival documents, some critics say, skews history by suggesting that the most important kind of history comes from official government sources. These critics point out that important historical evidence lies as well in sources ranging from newspapers, family account books, diaries, and personal letters to novels, paintings, and architecture, especially when many kinds of sources are used to verify one another.

QUESTIONS TO CONSIDER

1. Are archives overseen by government officials more or less likely to be biased than other sources? How can we know the extent to which they are telling the truth?
2. Make a list of the most reliable sources for discovering historical truth and provide reasons for your ranking these sources as reliable.

FURTHER READING

Andrew, Christopher, and Vasili Mitrokhin. *The Mitrokhin Archive: The KGB in Europe and the West.* 1999.

Courtois, Stephane, et al. *The Black Book of Communism: Crimes, Terror, Repression,* trans. Johnathan Murphy and Mark Kramer. 1999.

Zubok, Vladislav, and Constantine Pleshakov. *Inside the Kremlin's Cold War: From Stalin to Khrushchev.* 1996.

ulace accepted the change so passively that Communist leaders said the takeover was "like cutting butter with a knife." The Soviet Union had successfully created a buffer of satellite states in eastern Europe directed by what it called people's governments.

The only exception to the Soviet sweep in eastern Europe came in Yugoslavia, under the Communist ruler known as Tito (Josip Broz, 1892–1980). During the war, Tito led the powerful anti-Nazi Yugoslav "partisans." After the war, he drew on support from Serbs,

Croats, and Muslims to mount a Communist revolution. His revolution, however, was explicitly meant to avoid Soviet influence. Eager for Yugoslavia to develop industrially rather than simply serve Soviet needs, Tito

Yugoslavia after the Revolution

remarked, "We study and take as an example the Soviet system, but we are developing socialism in our country in somewhat different forms." Stalin was furious; in his eyes, commitment to communism meant obedience to him. Nonetheless, Yugoslavia emerged from its Communist revolution as a culturally diverse federation of six republics and two independent provinces within Serbia. Tito's break with Stalin further fueled the purges in the USSR because the Soviet government could point to Tito as a vivid example of the treachery supposedly at work even in the depths of communist belief. Holding diverse groups of south Slavs together until his death in 1980, Tito's forceful personality and strong organization also held the Soviets at bay.

The Division of Germany

The cold war became most menacing when the superpowers struggled for control of Germany. The agreements reached at Yalta provided for Germany's occupation by troops divided among four zones, each of which was controlled by one of the four principal victors in World War II— the United States, the Soviet Union, Britain, and France. However, the superpowers disagreed on fundamental matters in German history. Many in the United States had come to believe that there was something inherently wrong with the character of Germans—a fatal, evil flaw responsible for two world wars and the Holocaust. After the war, the U.S. occupation forces undertook a reprogramming of German cultural attitudes by controlling the press and censoring all media in the U.S. zone to ensure that they did not express fascist or authoritarian values. In contrast, Stalin believed that Nazism was merely an extreme form of capitalism. His solution was to con-

fiscate and redistribute the estates of wealthy Germans to ordinary people and supporters.

A second disagreement, this one over Germany's economic potential, led to that nation's partition. According to the American plan for coordinating the various segments of the German economy, surplus produce from the Soviet-occupied areas would feed urban populations in the western zones; in turn, industrial goods would be sent to the USSR. The Soviets upset this plan. Following the Grand Alliance agreement that the USSR would receive reparations from German resources, the Soviets dismantled industries and seized German equipment, shipping it all to the Soviet Union. They transported skilled workers, engineers, and scientists to the USSR to work virtually as slave laborers. The Soviets also manipulated the currency in their zone, enabling the USSR to buy German goods at unfairly low prices.

The struggle between the superpowers was escalating. The western Allies struck back by agreeing to merge their zones into a West German state. Instead of continuing to curtail German power, as wartime agreements called for, the United States began an economic buildup under the Marshall Plan to make the western zone of Germany a buffer against the Soviets. By 1948, notions of a permanently weakened Germany came to an end, as the United States enlisted many former Nazi officials as spies and bureaucrats. On July 24, 1948, Stalin retaliated by using Soviet troops to blockade Germany's capital, Berlin. Like Germany as a whole, the city had been divided into four occupation zones, even though it was located more than one hundred miles deep into the Soviet zone and was thus cut off from western territory. Expecting the United States and its allies to capitulate, the Soviets declared that Berlin was now part of their zone of occupation and refused to allow western vehicles to travel through the Soviet zone, including Berlin. The United States responded decisively, flying in millions of tons of provisions to the stricken city. During the winter of 1948–1949, the Berlin airlift—Operation Vittles, as U.S. pilots called it—even funneled in coal to warm some two million isolated Berliners (Map 28.2). Given the immense quantities of fuel and food needed to pro-

MAP 28.2 Divided Germany and the Berlin Airlift, 1946–1949
Berlin, controlled by the United States, Great Britain, France, and the Soviet Union, was deep in the Soviet zone of occupation and became a major point of contention among the former allies. When the USSR blockaded the western half of the city, the United States responded with a massive airlift. To stop movement between the two zones, the USSR built a wall in 1961 and used troops to patrol it. What reasons does the map suggest for the attention to Berlin during the cold war?

MAP 28.3 European NATO Members and the Warsaw Pact in the 1950s
The two superpowers intensified their rivalry by creating large military alliances: NATO, formed in 1949, and the Warsaw Pact, formed in 1955 after NATO invited West German membership. International politics revolved around these two alliances, which faced off in the heart of Europe. War games for the two sides often assumed a massive war concentrated in central Europe over control of Germany.

vision the city and the limited number of transport planes, pilots kept the plane engines on to achieve a rapid turnaround that would ensure the necessary number of flights each day. Cold war culture increasingly centered on heroic deeds enacted in Berlin long after the end of the blockade in May 1949, as many Westerners came to see Berlin as the centerpiece of a moral crusade. The divided city became the symbol of the cold war.

Accelerating cold war tensions led to the formation of competing military alliances (Map 28.3). The United States, Canada, and their allies in western Europe and Scandinavia formed the **North Atlantic Treaty Organization (NATO)** in 1949. NATO provided a unified military force for its member countries. In 1955, after the United States forced France and Britain to invite

West Germany to join NATO, the Soviet Union retaliated by establishing with its satellite countries the military organization commonly called the Warsaw Pact. By that time, both the United States and the USSR had accelerated their arms buildups. Each had tested highly destructive hydrogen bombs and increased its potential for annihilating the enemy with nuclear weapons. These two massive regional alliances, armed to the teeth, formed the military muscle for cold war politics and definitively replaced the individual might of the European powers.

Review: What major events led to the development of the cold war between the superpowers?

❖ Political and Economic Recovery in Europe

The ideological clash between the United States and the Soviet Union served as a background to the remarkable economic and political recovery that took place in Europe even as the cold war unfolded. The first order of business on the political front was a highly charged eradication of the Nazi past and the inauguration of peacetime governments. Simultaneously, western Europe revived its democratic political structures, its individualistic culture, and its productive capabilities. Eastern Europe restlessly endured a far less prosperous and far more repressive existence under Stalinism, although even there the conditions of everyday life improved as peasant societies were forced to modernize. Some consumer goods industries and basic health services were restored. By 1960, people across the continent had escaped the poverty of the depression and war to enjoy a higher standard of living than ever before in their history. This rapid revival was even called the **economic miracle**, especially in the case of West Germany's striking prosperity. As governments took increasing responsibility for the health and well-being of citizens, the cold war era also became the age of the welfare state.

Dealing with the Nazi Past

In May 1945, Europeans lived under a complex system in which local resistance leaders, Allied armies of occupation, international relief workers, and the remnants of bureaucracies—among them Nazi sympathizers—shared jurisdiction. Amid confusion, starvation, and a thriving black market, the goals of feeding civilians, dealing with the tens of millions of refugees, purging Nazis, and setting up new governments all competed for attention. Members of governments-in-exile returned to claim their rightful share of power, but they often met up with occupying armies that covered much of the continent and were often a law unto themselves. The Soviets were especially feared for inflicting rape and robbery—abuses they justified by pointing to the twenty million and more

deaths at the hands of the Nazis. Distributing food and clothing, other armed forces tried to instill order even though there was a lively trade in food for sex among various soldiers in all armies and starving civilians. The desire for revenge against Nazis hardened with the discovery of the death camps' skeletal survivors and the remains of the millions murdered there. Swift vigilante justice by civilians released pent-up rage and aimed to punish collaborators for their complicity in genocide and occupation crimes. In France, villagers often shaved the heads of women suspected of associating with Germans and made some of them parade naked through the local streets (see the photo opposite). Members of the resistance executed tens of thousands of Nazi officers and collaborators on the spot and without trial. These became the founding acts of a reborn European political community.

Allied representatives undertook a more systematic "denazification" that ranged from forcing German civilians to view the death camps to investigating and bringing to trial suspected local collaborators. The trials conducted at Nuremberg, Germany, by the victorious Allies in the fall of 1945 used the Nazis' own documents to provide a horrifying panorama of crimes by Nazi leaders. Although international law lacked a precedent for defining genocide as a crime, the judges at Nuremberg found sufficient cause to impose death sentences on half of the twenty-four defendants, among them Hitler's closest associates, and give prison terms to the remainder. The Nuremberg trials introduced current notions of prosecution for crimes against humanity and an international politics based on demands for human rights.

Allied prosecution of Nazi and fascist leadership never succeeded completely because some of the leaders most responsible for war crimes disappeared. Furthermore, many Germans were skeptical about denazification. As women in Germany endured starvation, the menace of occupying forces, and the forced labor of clearing rubble in bombed-out cities, the belief spread among the German population that they were the main victims of the war. German civilians also interpreted the trials of Nazis as a characteristic retribution of victors rather than a

The Punishment of Collaborators
Women who had romantic involvements with Germans were called "horizontal collaborators" to suggest that they were traitorous prostitutes. With heads shaved and often stripped of their clothing, they were forced to parade through cities and towns enduring verbal and other abuse. The public shaming of these women, a vivid part of the memory of the war, served as the background for the film *Hiroshima Mon Amour,* which gripped audiences late in the 1950s. Many local collaborators of both sexes dealt with occupying troops on a daily basis, but some 80 percent of all those whose heads were shaved were women. To what should we attribute this discrepancy? *Robert Capa/Magnum Photos Inc.*

well-deserved punishment of the guilty. Soon the new West German government proclaimed that the war's real casualties were the German prisoners of war held in Soviet camps. Allied officials themselves, eager to restore government services and pursue the cold war, often came to rely on the expertise of high-ranking fascists and Nazis. The Nazi past haunted European cultural life and politics even to this day. While many were rightly horrified at the unprecedented murder and genocide, others attempted to paper over these grim truths. Political expediency led Westerners pursuing the cold war to forgive some Nazis quite easily.

Rebirth of the West

Against all political and economic odds, Europe revived at an accelerating pace in the 1950s. In western Europe, reform-minded civilian governments reflected the broad coalitions that had opposed the Axis. They conspicuously emphasized democracy to show their rejection of the totalitarian regimes that had earlier attracted so many Europeans—and with such dire consequences. Rebuilding devastated towns and cities spurred industrial recovery, while bold projects for economic cooperation like the European Common Market and the conversion of wartime technological know-how to peacetime use produced a brisk trade in consumer goods and services in western Europe by the late 1950s. Memories of the war remained vivid, but prosperity restored confidence and hope for a better future.

Democratic Politics Restored.   Resistance leaders had the first claim on political office in postfascist western Europe and began asserting their rights to authority in postwar government. In France, the leader of the Free French, General Charles de Gaulle, governed briefly as chief of state, and the French approved a constitution in 1946 that established the Fourth Republic and finally granted the vote to French women. Wanting a conservative political system that would grant him more authority, de Gaulle soon resigned in favor of left-wing and centrist forces. Meanwhile, Italy replaced its constitutional monarchy with a full parliamentary system that also allowed women the vote for the first time. As in France, a resistance-based government initially took control. Then, late in 1945, the socialist and labor politicians were replaced by a coalition headed by the conservative **Christian Democrats**, descended from the traditional Catholic centrist parties of the prewar period. As in Italy, other parts of Europe saw the growing influence of Christian parties because of their participation in the resistance.

The Communist Party also attracted the vocal loyalty of a consistently large segment of the western European population. Symbol of the common citizen, the ordinary Soviet soldier was a hero to many western Europeans outside occupied Germany, as were the resistance leaders—many of them Communist until late in the war when the impending Nazi collapse lured mainline politicians to join the anti-Nazi bandwagon. People still remembered the common man's plight in the depression of the 1930s. Thus, in Britain, despite the wartime successes of Winston Churchill's Conservative Party leadership, the Labour government of Clement Attlee appeared more likely to fulfill promises to share prosperity equitably among the classes through expanded social welfare programs and the nationalization of key industries. The exceedingly hard times of the immediate postwar years only added to the voices raised for governments that would represent the millions of ordinary people who had suffered, fought, and worked incredibly hard during the war.

In West Germany, however, communism and the left in general had little appeal, so sure was the hold of the Western allies and so distasteful were the Communist takeovers going on to the east. In 1949, centrist politicians helped create a new state, the German Federal Republic, whose constitution aimed to prevent the emergence of a dictator, to guarantee individual rights, and to build a sound economy. West Germany's first chancellor was the seventy-three-year-old Catholic anti-Communist Konrad Adenauer, who allied himself with the economist Ludwig Erhard. Committed to the free market, Erhard had stabilized the postwar German currency so that commerce could resume. The economist and the politician successfully guided Germany away from both fascism and communism and restored the representative government that Hitler had overthrown.

Paradoxically, given its leadership in the fight against fascism, the United States was the country in which individual freedom and democracy were imperiled after the war. Two events—a successful test of an atomic bomb by the Soviet Union in 1949 and the Communist revolution in China—brought to the fore Joseph McCarthy, a U.S. senator foreseeing a reelection struggle. To strengthen his following in advance of the election, McCarthy warned of a great conspiracy to overthrow the United States. As during the Soviet purges, people of all occupations including government workers, filmstars, and union leaders were called before congressional panels to confess, testify against friends, and to ask themselves whether they had ever had Communist thoughts or sympathies. The atmosphere was electric with confusion and a sense of betrayal, for only five years before the mass media had run glowing stories about Stalin and the Soviet system. During the war, Americans were told to think of Stalin as a friendly "Uncle Joe." By 1952, however, more than six million Americans had been investigated, imprisoned, or fired from their jobs. McCarthy had books like Thomas Paine's *Common Sense*, written in the eighteenth century to support the American Revolution, removed from government shelves, and he personally oversaw book burnings. Although the Senate finally voted to censure McCarthy in the winter of 1954, the assault on freedom had been devastating and anticommunism dominated political life.

Economic Rebirth.   Given the wartime destruction, the economic rebirth of western Europe was even more surprising than the revival of democracy. In the first weeks and months after the war, the job of rebuilding often involved menial physical labor that mobilized entire populations. With so many men dead, wounded, or detained as prisoners of war, German housewives, called women of the ruins, earned their living clearing rubble by hand (see the photo of women clearing rubble in Berlin). Initially governments diverted labor and capital into rebuilding infrastructure — transportation, communications, industrial capacity—and away from producing consumer goods. However, the scarcity of those goods sparked unrest and made communism politically attractive because it proclaimed less interest in the revival of big business than in the ordinary person's standard of living. In the midst of growing discontent over suffering and even starvation, the Marshall Plan boosted recovery with American dollars; food and consumer goods became more plentiful; and demand for automobiles, washing machines, and vacuum cleaners accelerated economic growth. Increased production in all sectors wiped out most unemployment. Labor-short northern Europe even arranged for "guest workers" to migrate from impoverished regions like Sicily to help rebuild cities.

The postwar recovery also featured the adaptation of wartime technology to consumer industry and the continuation of military spending. Civilian travel expanded as nations organized their own air systems based on improved airplane technology. Developed to relieve wartime shortages, synthetic goods such as nylon now became part of peacetime civilian life. Factories churned out a vast assortment of plastic products, ranging from pipes to household goods to rainwear. In the

Women Clearing Berlin
The amount of destruction caused by World War II was staggering, requiring the mobilization of the civilian population in Berlin, where women were conscripted to sort the rubble and clear it away. Scenes like this were ultimately used as propaganda in the cold war to make it seem as if the Germans were the victims rather than the perpetrators of the war. That German soldiers in the Nazi army were held in Soviet camps and were only slowly repatriated added to the image of Soviet rather than German aggression in World War II. Such depictions also made the Germans appear weak and helpless before a threatened menace, as in the photos of weak and ravaged Belgian women in World War I propaganda on page 1012. Would you describe this as a propaganda photo? Why or why not? **For more help analyzing this image**, see the visual activity for this chapter in the Online Study Guide at **bedfordstmartins.com/hunt**. *AKG Photo, London.*

climate of cold war, however, military needs remained high: governments ordered bombs, fighter planes, tanks, and missiles (Figure 28.1). They also continued to sponsor military research. The outbreak of the Korean War in 1950, and the U.S. need for manufactured goods to wage that war, further sustained economic growth in Europe. Ultimately, the cold war prevented a repeat of the 1920s, when reduced military spending threw people out of jobs and thus fed the growth of fascism.

Large and small states alike developed (or in some cases redeveloped) prosperous, modern economies. In the twelve principal countries of western Europe, the annual rate of economic growth had been 1.3 percent per inhabitant between 1870 and 1913. Between 1950 and 1973 those countries almost tripled that rate, attaining an annual rate of growth per capita of 3.8 percent. Among the larger powers, West Germany surprisingly became the economic leader by the 1960s. The smaller Scandinavian countries also achieved a notable recovery: Sweden succeeded in the development of automobile, truck, and shipbuilding industries. Finland modernized its industry in order to pay the reparations demanded by the Soviet Union for resisting its invasion; it also modernized the agricultural sector, which freed up farmers to move into factory work. Scandinavian women joined the workforce in record numbers, which also boosted economic growth and expanded prosperity.

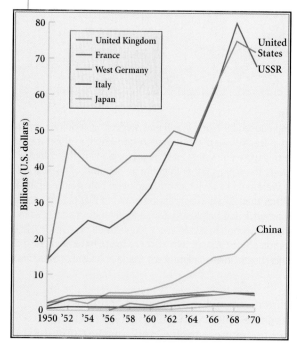

FIGURE 28.1 Military Spending and the Cold War Arms Race, 1950–1970
As soon as the war ended, the United States and the Soviet Union started a massive arms buildup that would continue into the 1980s. Because it had not suffered destruction during the war, the United States could afford spending hundreds of billions of dollars on weapons. The Soviet Union could not, and its citizens were comparatively deprived of consumer goods as a result of these expenditures. By the end of the twentieth century, the United States and Russia held vast arsenals of nuclear and other weapons and, along with France, led the way in selling arms to the rest of the world. The arms race in the early twentieth century helped produce World War I. Why has the arms buildup since World War II not produced a world war to date?

The thirty years after World War II were a golden age of European economic growth.

Birth of the Common Market. As a final ingredient in the postwar recovery, international cooperation and planning led to the creation of the Common Market and ultimately the European Union of the 1990s. The Marshall Plan demanded as a condition for assistance that recipients undertake far-reaching economic cooperation. In 1951, Italy, France, Germany, Belgium, Luxembourg, and the Netherlands formed the European Coal and Steel Community (ECSC). This organization managed joint production and prices among its members. Most important, it arranged for the abundant West German output of coal and steel to benefit all of western Europe. According to the ECSC's principal architect, Robert Schuman, the economic cooperation created by the organization would make another war "materially impossible." Simply put, the bonds of common productivity and trade would keep France and Germany from another cataclysmic war. (See "The Schuman Plan on European Unity, 1950," page 1114.)

In 1957, the six ECSC members took another major step toward regional prosperity when they signed the Treaty of Rome. The treaty provided for a more general trading partnership called the **European Economic Community (EEC)**, known popularly as the **Common Market**. The EEC reduced tariffs among the six partners and worked to develop common trade policies. It brought under one cooperative economic umbrella more than 200 million consumers and would eventually add several hundred million more. According to one of its founders, the EEC aimed to "prevent the race of nationalism, which is the true curse of the modern world." Increased cooperation produced great economic rewards for the six members, whose rates of economic growth soared. Britain pointedly refused to join the partnership at first; membership would have required that it surrender certain imperial trading rights among its Commonwealth partners such as Australia, New Zealand, and Canada. Since 1945, British statesmen had shunned the developing continental trading bloc because, as one of them put it, participation would make Britain "just another European country." Even without Britain, it

TAKING MEASURE

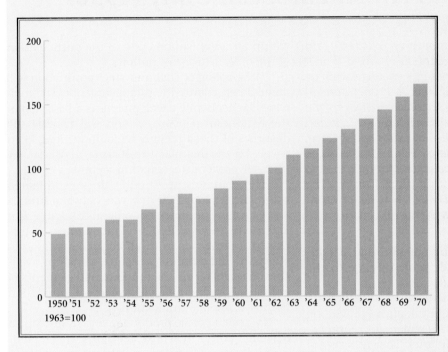

1963=100

World Manufacturing Output, 1950–1970
During the long boom from the 1950s to the early 1970s, the world experienced increased industrial output, better agricultural production, and rising consumer spending. This era of prosperity resulted not only from the demand generated by the need to rebuild Europe and other areas affected by the war but also from the adaptation of war technology to peacetime uses. The General Agreement on Trade and Tariffs (GATT) was also implemented after the war, lowering tariffs and thus advancing trade. What factors were behind the conditions shown in the chart? From Hammond Atlas of the Twentieth Century *(London: Times Books, 1987), 127.*

was clear to some that the future lay with the rising prosperity of a new western Europe joined in the Common Market.

Behind the move to the Common Market stood the adoption of the economic planning and coordination by specialists employed during wartime. Called technocrats after 1945, specialists were to base decisions on expertise rather than on personal interest; those working for the Common Market were to disregard the self-interest of any one nation and thus reduce the potential for irrationality and violence in politics, both domestic and international. Administered by a commission in Brussels, the Common Market was the daily task of experts, whose functions transcended the borders of the nation-state and thus exceeded the power of elected politicians. Some critics insisted (and some still insist even today) that expert planning would diminish democracy by putting massive control in the hands of bureaucracy, not legislatures. Defenders were just as insistent that planning and cooperation would be the surest tools of prosperity and peace.

The Welfare State: Common Ground East and West

On both sides of the cold war, governments intervened forcefully to ameliorate social conditions with state-financed programs such as pensions and insurance. This system of intervention became known as the **welfare state**, indicating that states were no longer interested solely in maintaining order and augmenting their power. Veterans' pensions and programs were primary, but the welfare state had concerns beyond simply sustaining those who had sacrificed in wartime. Because the European population had declined during the war, almost all countries now desperately supported reproduction and family life with direct financial aid. Imitating the sweeping Swedish programs of the 1930s, nations expanded or created family allowances, health-care and medical benefits, and programs for pregnant women and new mothers. The French gave larger family allowances for each birth after the first; for many French families, this allowance provided as much as a third of the household income.

The Schuman Plan on European Unity (1950)

One method of reviving European productivity and well-being after the devastation of World War II was for countries to pool natural resources such as coal and steel. Robert Schuman, French foreign minister from 1948 to 1953, was an architect of the European Coal and Steel Community, instituted after the war to share resources among France, Germany, and other nations. Schuman, however, foresaw more long-term benefits, including lasting peace and the unification of all of Europe. The Schuman Plan, excerpted below, is widely viewed as a blueprint for today's European Union.

World peace can only be safeguarded if constructive efforts are made proportionate to the dangers which threaten it. . . .

Europe will not be made all at once, nor according to a single, general plan. It will be formed by taking measures which work primarily to bring about real solidarity. The gathering of the European nations requires the elimination of the age-old opposition of France and Germany. The action to be taken must first of all concern these two countries.

With this aim in view, the French Government proposes to take immediate action on one limited but decisive point. The French Government proposes that Franco-German production of coal and steel be placed under a common high authority within an organisation open to the participation of the other European nations.

The pooling of coal and steel production will immediately ensure the establishment of common bases for economic development as a first step in the federation of Europe, and will change the destinies of those regions which have long been devoted to the manufacture of arms, to which they themselves were the constant victims.

The common production thus established will make it plain that any war between France and Germany becomes not only unthinkable, but materially impossible. The establishment of this powerful entity, open to all countries willing to take part, and eventually capable of making available on equal terms the fundamental elements of industrial production, will give a real foundation to their economic unification. . . .

By pooling basic production and by creating a new high authority whose decisions will be binding on France, Germany and the other countries that may subsequently join, these proposals will lay the first concrete foundation for a European Federation which is so indispensable to the preservation of peace.

Source: U.S. Department of State Bulletin, June 12, 1959, 936–37. Reprinted in Documents on European Union, eds., A.G. Harryvan and J. van der Harst (New York: St. Martin's, 1997), 61–62.

Aspects of the welfare state reflecting gender bias worked to the detriment of women. Britain's maternity benefits and child allowances, announced in a wartime report, favored women who did not work outside the home by providing little coverage of workingwomen. The West German government passed strict legislation that forced employers to give women maternity leaves, thus discouraging them from hiring women. It also cut back or eliminated pensions and benefits to married women. In fact, West Germans bragged about removing women from the workforce, claiming that this distinguished democratic practices from Communist ones. The refusal to build day-care centers or to allow stores to remain open in the evening so that workingwomen could buy food for their families led West Germany to have among the lowest rate of female employment of any industrial country. Another result of West Germany's policies regarding women was a high rate of female poverty in old age.

By contrast, in eastern Europe and the Soviet Union, where wartime loss of life had been enormous, women worked nearly full-time and usually outnumbered men in the workforce. Like many countries of western Europe, however, child-care programs, family allowances, and maternity benefits were designed to encourage pregnancies by working women. A national health program provided medical and health services, as in most countries to the west. There were marked differences in everyday life that undermined the drive to increase population, however. The scarcity of consumer goods, the housing shortages, and the lack of household conveniences in the eastern bloc discouraged workingwomen from having large families. Because women had sole responsibility for onerous domestic duties on top of their paying jobs, their already heavy workload increased with the birth of each additional child. As a result, the birthrate in Communist states stagnated.

Across Europe welfare-state programs aimed to improve people's health. State-funded medical insurance, subsidized medical care, or nationalized health-care systems covered health-care needs in most industrial nations except the United States. The combination of better material conditions and state provision of health care dramatically extended life expectancy and lowered rates of infant mortality. Contributing to the overall progress, the number of doctors and dentists more than doubled between the end of World War I and 1950, and vaccines greatly reduced the death toll from such diseases as tuberculosis, diphtheria, measles, and polio. In England, schoolchildren stood on the average an inch taller than children the same age had a decade earlier. As people lived longer, governments began to establish programs for the elderly.

State initiatives in other areas played a role in the higher standard of living. A growing network of government-built atomic power plants brought more thorough electrification of eastern Europe and the Soviet Union. Governments legislated better conditions and more leisure time for workers. Beginning in 1955, Italian workers received twenty-eight paid holidays annually; in Sweden they received twenty-nine vacation days, a number that grew in the 1960s. Planning also helped provide a more varied diet and more abundant food, with meat, fish, eggs, cheese, milk, and fresh fruit supplementing the older grain-based foods. Housing shortages posed a daunting challenge after three decades of economic depression and destructive war. Postwar Europeans often lived with three generations sharing one or two rooms. Eastern Europeans faced the worst conditions, whereas Germans and Greeks fared better because only 20 to 25 percent of prewar housing had been lost. To rebuild, governments sponsored a postwar housing boom. New cities formed around the edges of major urban areas in both East and West. Many buildings went up slapdash, and restored towns took on an undistinguished look and a constantly deteriorating condition. Westerners labeled many Eastern-bloc apartments environmentally horrible, meaning that they were a blight on cities and towns across the Soviet landscape (see the illustration below).

Postwar Housing

The housing situation was dire in much of Europe because of the massive bombings and the destruction caused by armies on both sides crisscrossing the continent. Although financially strapped, governments poured resources into rebuilding during the immediate postwar years, but often they lacked the money for anything but minimal dwellings. This was especially the case in the Soviet Union, which faced the dual cost of repairing massive devastation and simultaneously financing the rocketry and weapons systems needed to pursue the cold war. Because of Stalin's cold war preparations, housing construction was postponed. Residential buildings, such as those in the Moscow suburbs, shown above, did not begin construction in earnest until after Stalin's death, when the living standard of ordinary people began to receive government attention. *Stan Wayman/Time Life Pictures/Getty Images.*

Recovery in the East

To create a Soviet bloc according to Stalin's prewar vision of industrialization, Communists revived the crushing methods that had served before to transform peasant economies. In eastern Europe, Stalin enforced collectivized agriculture and badly needed industrialization through the nationalization of private property. In Hungary, for example, Communists seized and reapportioned all estates over twelve hundred acres. Having gained support of the poorer peasants through this redistribution, Communists later dispossessed everyone of their prized lands and pushed them into cooperative farming. Only in Poland did a substantial number of private farms remain. The process of collectivization was brutal and slow everywhere, and rural people looked back on the 1950s as dreadful. But some among those in the countryside felt that ultimately their lives and their children's lives had improved. "Before we peasants were dirty and poor, we worked like dogs....Was that a good life? No sir, it wasn't....I was a miserable sharecropper and my son is an engineer," said one Romanian peasant. Despite modernization, government investment in agriculture was never high enough to produce the bumper crops of western Europe, and lack of motivation among farmers—even their outright hostility toward the new system—worked against the success of collective farming.

Transforming the Soviet Bloc. An admirer of American industrial know-how, Stalin prodded all the socialist economies in his bloc to match U.S. productivity. The Soviet Union formed regional organizations like those to the west, instituting the Council for Mutual Economic Assistance (COMECON) in 1949 to coordinate economic relations among the satellite countries and Moscow. Modernization of production in the Soviet bloc opened new technical and bureaucratic careers, and modernizers in the satellite states touted the virtues of steel plants and modern transport. The terms of the COMECON relationship thwarted development of the satellite states, for the USSR was allowed to buy goods from its clients at bargain prices and sell to them at exorbitant ones. Nonetheless, these formerly peasant states became oriented toward technology and bureaucratically directed industrial economies. Tired of the struggles on the land, rural people moved to cities, where they received better education, health care, and ultimately jobs, albeit at the price of repression. The Roman Catholic church, which often protested the imposition of communism, was crushed as much as possible or infiltrated by government agents. Old agrarian elites, professionals, intellectuals, and other members of the middle class were discriminated against, imprisoned, or executed. Political prisoners in East German camps did hard labor in uranium and other dangerous mines.

Science and culture were the building blocks of Stalinism in the satellite countries as well as in the USSR. State-instituted programs aimed to build loyalty to the modernizing regime; thus, citizens found themselves obliged to attend adult education classes, women's groups, and public ceremonies. An intense program of Russification and de-Christianization forced students in eastern Europe to read histories of the war that ignored their own country's resistance and gave the Red Army sole credit for fighting the Nazis. They replaced national symbols with Soviet ones. For example, Hungarians had to accept a new flag with a Soviet red star beaming rays onto a hammer and sickle; the Hungarian colors were reduced to a small band on the flag. Utter historical distortion, revivified anti-Semitism, and rigid censorship resulted in what one staunchly socialist writer in the USSR characterized as "a dreary torrent of colorless, mediocre literature." Stalin also purged prominent wartime leaders to ensure obedience and conformity. Marshal Zhukov, a popular leader of the Soviet armed forces, was shipped to a distant command, while Anna Akhmatova, the great poet whose widely admired writing had emphasized perseverance and individual heroism during the war, was confined to a crowded hospital room because she refused to glorify Stalin in her postwar poetry.

The Death of Stalin. In March 1953, amid looming troubles, Stalin died, and it soon became clear that the old ways would not hold. Political prisoners in the labor camps who had

ELŐRE A BÉKE ÉS A SZOCIALIZMUS
IFJU HARCOSAINAK KONGRESSZUSÁÉRT
1950. JUNIUS 17-18

Re-creating Hungarian Youth
People across Europe focused on the well-being of young people after World War II, and in the Soviet sphere this took the form of education in Communist ways. Youth groups, such as those in the early Stalinist USSR, served this end, and vivid posters in the Soviet realist style carried inspirational messages: "Forward for the Congress of the Young Fighters of Peace and Socialism," reads this typical message to Hungarian youth in 1950. Why was the condition of youth so important a concern after World War II? Why was youth so prominent in popular culture during this period? *Magyar Nemzeti Múzeum, Budapest (Hungarian National Museum).*

started rioting late in the 1940s now pressed their demands for reform. In the spring of 1953, more than a million were released from the Gulag, or prison camp system, and returned home with horrific stories to tell. At the other end of the social order, Soviet officials enjoyed country homes, luxury goods, and plentiful food, but many of them had come to distrust Stalinism and were ready for some changes. A power struggle ensued

within the Soviet government, and protests took place across the satellites and at home. In response, the government beefed up the production of consumer goods—a policy called goulash communism because it resulted in more food for ordinary people. There was still lingering uncertainty, however, about the post-Stalin future.

In 1955, Nikita Khrushchev♦ (1894–1971), an illiterate coal miner before the revolution, outmaneuvered other rivals to emerge the undisputed leader of the Soviet Union, but he did so without the usual executions. Khrushchev listened to popular complaints in both city and countryside about conditions and continued to divert resources to consumer goods. The next year he attacked Stalinism. At a party congress, Khrushchev denounced the "cult of personality" Stalin had built about himself and announced that Stalinism did not equal socialism, thus shifting all the problems with communism onto a single individual. The "secret speech"—it was not published in the USSR but became widely known—sent tremors through Communist parties around the world and was a sensation at home. People experienced, in the words of one writer, "a holiday of the soul." Debates broke out in public, and books appeared championing the ordinary worker against the party bureaucracy. The climate of relative toleration for free expression was called the **thaw**. It was to prove an erratic and uneven Soviet policy.

In this climate of uncertainty and change, protest erupted once more in early summer 1956, when discontented Polish railroad workers struck for better wages. Popular support for their cause ushered in a more liberal Communist program. Inspired by the Polish example, Hungarians rebelled against forced collectivization in October 1956—"the golden October," they would call their uprising. As in Poland, economic issues, especially announcements of reduced wages, also sparked outbreaks of violence, but the protest soon targeted the entire Communist system. Tens of thousands of protesters filled the streets of Budapest and succeeded in returning a popular hero, Imre Nagy,♦ to power. When Nagy announced that Hungary might leave

♦ **Nikita Khrushchev:** nyih KEE tuh kroosh CHAWF
♦ **Imre Nagy:** IHM reh NAHD yuh

the Warsaw Pact, Soviet troops moved in, killing tens of thousands and causing hundreds of thousands more to flee to the West. Nagy was hanged. Crushing the Hungarian Revolution vividly displayed the limits to the thaw, but the simultaneous U.S. refusal to intervene in Hungary showed that, despite a rhetoric of liberation, the United States would not risk World War III by militarily challenging the Soviet sphere of influence.

The failure of eastern European uprisings overshadowed significant changes since Stalin's death. In the process of defeating his rivals, Khrushchev ended the Stalinist purges and reformed the courts, which came to function according to procedures instead of staging the show trials of the past. The gates of the Gulag opened further, and the secret police lost many of its arbitrary powers. A new sense of security acquired from increased productivity, military buildup, and stunning successes in aerospace development helped promote the thaw. In 1957, the Soviets successfully launched the first artificial earth satellite, *Sputnik*, and in 1961 they put the first cosmonaut, Yuri Gagarin, in orbit around the earth. The Soviets' edge in space technology shocked the Western bloc and motivated the creation of the U.S. National Aeronautics and Space Administration (NASA). Soviet successes indicated that the USSR was on the way to achieving Stalin's goal of modernization.

Nevertheless, Khrushchev alternately bullied dissidents and showed himself open to changing Soviet culture. For example, he forced Boris Pasternak to refuse the 1958 Nobel Prize in literature because his novel *Doctor Zhivago* (1957) cast doubt on the glory of the Communist revolution and affirmed the value of the individual. Yet in 1961 he allowed the publication of Aleksandr Solzhenitsyn's *One Day in the Life of Ivan Denisovitch*, a chilling account of life in the Gulag. Under the thaw, Khrushchev himself made several trips to the West and was more widely seen by the public than Stalin. More confident and more affluent, the Soviets took steps to reduce their diplomacy's paranoid style and concentrated their efforts on spreading socialism in the emerging nations of Asia, Africa, and Latin America. Despite the USSR's more relaxed posture, the cold war advanced, as both superpowers sought influence in these new nations and continued to move the world to the nuclear brink.

> **Review:** What factors drove economic recovery in western Europe? In eastern Europe?

❖ Decolonization in a Cold War Climate

World War II dealt the final blow to the ability of European powers to maintain their vast empires, and the cold war added to opportunities for new nations to emerge with the help of the superpowers. Despite their postwar weakness, Britain, France, the Netherlands, and others futilely attempted to stamp out nationalist groups that had strengthened during the war and to reimpose their control. As before, colonized peoples had been on the front lines defending the West; and as before, they had witnessed the full barbarism of Western warfare. Excluded from victory parades and other ceremonies so that the great powers could maintain the illusion of Western supremacy, adult men in the colonies still did not receive the political rights promised them. Moreover, the successive wars had allowed local industries to develop, as the imperial powers lost their ability both to maintain their own consumer manufacturing and to stamp out local initiatives. As a result of the war, people in Asia, Africa, and the Middle East, often led by individuals steeped in Western values and experienced in military and manufacturing technology, embraced the cause of independence and often clashed with the West in bloody warfare.

The path to achieving independence—a process called **decolonization**—was paved with difficulties. In Africa, a continent whose peoples spoke more than five thousand languages, the European conquerors' creation of convenient administrative units such as Nigeria and Rhodesia had obliterated living arrangements that had relied on ethnic ties and local cultures. In addition, religion played a divisive role in independence movements. In India, Hindus and Muslims battled one another even though they shared the goal of eliminating the British. In the Middle East and North Africa, pan-Arab and pan-Islamic movements might seem to have been unifying forces. Yet many Muslims were not Arab, not all Arabs were Muslim, and Islam itself encompassed many competing beliefs and sects. Differences among religious beliefs, ethnic groups, and cultural practices—many of them invented or promoted by the colonizers to divide and rule—worked against political unity. Despite these complications, various peoples in what was coming to be called the third world succeeded in gaining

Jawaharlal Nehru, Prime Minister of India (1952)
Jawaharlal Nehru (1889-1964) led his newly independent country of India from 1947 to 1964, during its first years of freedom from British rule. Trained as a lawyer in English universities, Nehru became an adamant opponent of the British after they massacred hundreds of his countrymen at Amritsar in 1919, and the British imprisoned him during World War II. In the cold war, both sides needed to compete in order to make India an ally. However, U.S. presidents and diplomats hesitated wooing this crucial leader in part because of their suspicions about the toughness of a man who wore what appeared to them a dress along with a rose pinned to it. Nehru and his compatriots were said to be too "feminine" to be reliable in an age of robust cold-war heroes like James Bond. Nehru chose to maintain India, though a populous Asian democracy, as a neutral country. ©*Bettmann/Corbis.*

independence while they offered a new field for competition between the United States and the Soviet Union in the cold war.

The End of Empire in Asia

At the end of World War II, leaders in Asia began to mobilize the mass discontent that had intensified during the war and, often facing stiff resistance from white settlers, were able to drive out foreign rulers. Declining from an imperial power to a small island nation, Britain was the biggest loser. In 1947 it parted with India, whose independence it had promised in the 1930s. When the war broke out, independence was postponed and some two million Indian men were mobilized to fight in the Middle East and Asia. Local industry became an important supplier of war goods, and Indian business leaders bought out British entrepreneurs short of cash. But during this period of economic prosperity for some, food shortages created by British wartime policies drove people to overcrowded cities, and political fissures between Hindus and Muslims, long encouraged by the British, widened.

The British faced the inevitable after the war and decreed that two countries should emerge from the old colony, so great was the mistrust between the Indian National Congress and Muslim League parties. Thus, in 1947 India was created for Hindus and Pakistan—itself later divided into two parts—for Muslims. Yet during the independence year, political tensions exploded among opposing members of the two religions. Hundreds of thousands were massacred in the great shift of populations between the two nations. In 1948, a radical Hindu assassinated Gandhi, who though a Hindu himself had continued to champion religious reconciliation. Britain retained control of Hong Kong; but before two decades of the postwar era had passed, almost half a billion Asians had gained their freedom from the rule of fifty million British (see Mapping the West, page 1134).

In 1949, a Communist takeover in China brought in a government led by Mao Zedong◆ (1893–1976) that was no longer the plaything of the traditional colonial powers. Chinese

◆ **Mao Zedong:** MOW zuh DOONG

communism in the new People's Republic of China emphasized above all the welfare of the peasantry rather than the industrial proletariat and was thus distinct from Marxism and Stalinism. Mao instituted social reforms such as civil equality for women but at the same time copied Soviet collectivization, rapid industrialization, and brutal repression of the privileged classes.

The United States and the Soviet Union were deeply interested in East Asia, the United States because of the region's economic importance and the USSR because of its shared borders. Thus, the Chinese victory spurred both superpowers to increase their involvement in Asian politics. They faced off indirectly in Korea, which had been split at the thirty-eighth parallel after World War II. In 1950, the North Koreans, with the support of the Soviet Union, invaded U.S.-backed South Korea. The United States maneuvered the United Nations' Security Council into approving a "police action" against the North, and its forces quickly drove well into North Korean territory, where they were met by the Chinese army. After two and a half years of stalemate, the opposing sides finally agreed to a settlement in 1953: Korea would remain split at its prewar border, the thirty-eighth parallel. The United States lost more than fifty thousand men in the Korean War and increased its military spending from $10.9 billion in 1948 to almost $60 billion in 1953. The expansion of the cold war to Asia prompted the creation of an Asian counterpart to NATO: the Southeast Asia Treaty Organization (SEATO), established in 1954. Another side effect of the Korean War was the rapid reindustrialization of Japan to provide the United States with supplies.

The cold war spread to Indochina, where nationalists had been struggling against the

The Korean War, 1950–1953

postwar revival of French imperialism. Their leader, the European-educated Ho Chi Minh (1890–1969), preached both nationalism and socialism and built a powerful organization, the Viet Minh, to fight colonial rule. He advocated the redistribution of land held by big landowners, especially in the rich agricultural area in southern Indochina where some six thousand owners possessed more than 60 percent of the land. Viet Minh peasant guerrillas ultimately forced the technologically advanced French army, which was receiving aid from the United States, to withdraw from the country after the bloody battle of Dien Bien Phu in 1954. Later that year, the Geneva Convention carved out an independent Laos and divided Vietnam into North and South, each free from French control. The Viet Minh was ordered to retreat to an area north of the seventeenth parallel. But superpower intervention undermined the peace treaty while risking nuclear war and subjecting native peoples to the force of their military might. The United States, continuing to assist the corrupt government in the south, was acquiring a reputation as an imperialist power of the old school, and nowhere more so than in Vietnam.

Indochina, 1954

The Struggle for Identity in the Middle East

Independence struggles in the Middle East gained in force because of the world's growing need for oil and the ability of small countries to maneuver between the superpowers. As in the rest of the world after the war, Middle Eastern peoples renewed their commitment to independence and resisted attempts by the major powers to reimpose imperial control. Weakened by the war, British oil companies wanted to tighten their grip on profits, as the value of this energy source soared. But the British leaders arrogantly behaved as if they were still dominant. For example, Winston Churchill, paying a visit to Saudi Arabia during negotiations over the renewal of Britain's oil rights in the country, insisted that he be served alcohol and cigars, sneering at the Islamic prohibitions against alcohol and tobacco. The outcome was that Saudi Arabia turned to the United States, saying that the superpower could take over the oil consortium so long as Britain was kept out. The cold war also gave Middle Eastern leaders an opening to bargain with the superpowers, playing them against each other. Middle Eastern countries, mandated to Britain and France after World War I, not only gained their full independence after the war but began building their economic clout as well.

The legacy of the Holocaust, however, complicated the Middle Eastern political scene as the Western powers' commitment to secure a Jewish settlement in the Middle East further stirred up Arabs' determination not to be pushed out of their homeland. When World War II broke out, 600,000 Jewish settlers and twice as many Arabs lived, in intermittent conflict, in British-controlled Palestine. In 1947, an exhausted Britain ceded the area to the United Nations (UN) to work out a settlement between the Jews and the Arabs. In the aftermath of the Holocaust, the UN voted to partition Palestine into an Arab region and a Jewish one (Map 28.4). Conflicting claims, however, led to war, and Jewish military forces prevailed. On May 14, 1948, the state of Israel came into being. "The dream had come true," Golda Meir, the future prime minister of Israel, remembered, but "too late to save those who had perished in the Holocaust." Israel opened its gates to immigrants, driving its expansionist ambitions against those of its Arab neighbors.

One of those neighbors, Egypt, had gained its independence from Britain at the end of the war. Britain, however, retained its dominance in shipping to Asia through control of the Suez Canal, which was owned by a British-run company. In 1952, Colonel Gamal Abdel Nasser (1918–1970) became

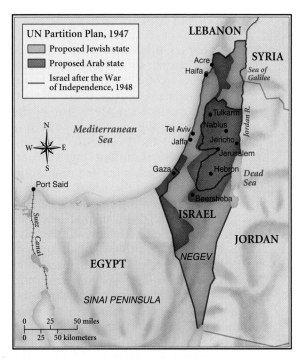

MAP 28.4 The Partition of Palestine and the Creation of Israel, 1947–1948
The creation of the Jewish state of Israel in 1948 against a backdrop of ongoing wars among Jews and indigenous Arab peoples made the Middle East a powder keg until the present day. The struggle for resources and for securing the borders of viable nation-states was at the heart of these bitter contests, threatening to pull the superpowers into a third world war. What does the position of countries on the map indicate about the likelihood that a dispute would arise in this region?

Egypt's president on a platform of economic modernization and true national independence. A prime goal was reclaiming the Suez Canal, "where 120,000 of our sons had lost their lives in digging it [by force]," he stated. In July 1956, Nasser nationalized the canal and thereby became a heroic figure to Arabs in the region. Britain, supported by Israel and France, attacked Egypt, bringing the Suez crisis to a head while the Hungarian revolt was in full swing. The British branded Nasser another Hitler and hoped that the Hungarian revolt would distract the superpowers. But American opposition, born from concerns that Egypt would turn to the USSR, made the British back down. Nasser's triumph inspired confidence that the Middle East could confront the West and win.

New Nations in Africa

In sub-Saharan Africa, nationalist leaders roused their people to challenge Europe's increasing demand for resources and labor, which resulted only in poverty for African peoples. "The European Merchant is my shepherd, and I am in want," went one African version of the Twenty-third Psalm. Disrupted in their traditional agricultural patterns, many Africans flocked to shantytowns in cities during the war, where they kept themselves alive through scavenging, making crafts, and doing menial labor for whites. At war's end, Kwame Nkrumah♦ (1909–1972) led the diverse inhabitants of the British-controlled West African Gold Coast in Gandhian-style passive resistance. After years of arresting and jailing the protesters, the British withdrew, allowing the state of Ghana to come into being in 1957. Nigeria, the most populous African region, became independent in 1960 after the leaders of its many regional groups and political organizations reached agreement on a federal-style government. In these and other African states where the population was mostly black, independence came less violently than in mixed-race territory (Map 28.5).

The eastern coast and southern and central areas of Africa had numerous European settlers, who violently resisted independence movements. In British East Africa, where white settlers ruled in splendor and where blacks lacked both land and economic opportunity, violence erupted in the 1950s. African men formed rebel groups named the Land Freedom Army but nicknamed Mau Mau. With women serving as provisioners, messengers, and weapon stealers, Mau Mau bands, composed mostly of war veterans from the Kikuyu ethnic group, tried to recover land from whites. In 1964, Kenya gained formal independence, but only after the British had slaughtered some ten to fifteen thousand Kikuyus.

France—although eager to regain its great-power status after its humiliating defeat and occupation in World War II—easily granted certain demands for independence, such as those of Tunisia, Morocco, and West Africa, where there were fewer white settlers, more limited economic stakes, and less military involvement. Elsewhere, French struggles against independence movements were prolonged and bloody. The ultimate test of the French empire came in Algeria. When Algerian nationalists rebelled against the restoration of French rule in the final days of World War II, the French army massacred tens of thousands of protesters. The liberation movement resurfaced with ferocious intensity as the Front for National Liberation in 1954. In response, the French dug in, sending more than 400,000 troops. Neither side fought according to the rules of warfare: Algerian women, shielded by gender stereotypes, planted bombs in European cafés and carried weapons to assassination sites; the French savagely tortured Algerian Arabs. "The loss of Algeria," warned one statesman, "would be an unprecedented national disaster." Yet protests in Paris greeted reports of the army's barbarous practices against the Muslim population, while the French military and settlers in Algeria met the antiwar movement with terrorism against citizens in France. They threatened coups, set off bombs, and assassinated politicians in the name of keeping Algeria French.

France's Fourth Republic collapsed over Algeria, and Charles de Gaulle came back to power in 1958. In return for leading France out of its Algerian quagmire, de Gaulle demanded the creation of a new republican government, one with a strong president who chose the prime minister and could exercise emergency power. As his plans to decolonize Algeria unfolded, terrorism against the French government escalated. By 1962, de Gaulle had negotiated independence with the Algerian nationalists who had successfully turned world opinion against France. Hundreds of thousands of *pieds noirs*♦ ("black feet"), as the French condescendingly called Europeans in Algeria, as well as their Arab supporters fled to France. The Dutch and Belgian empires also disintegrated. Similarly, violent resistance to the reimposition of colonial rule led to the establishment of the large independent states of Indonesia and the

---

♦ **Kwame Nkrumah:** KWAH may ehn KROO mah

♦ *pieds noir:* pyay NWAR

Congo (now known as the Democratic Republic of the Congo).

As independent nations emerged from colonialism and as the continent received immigrants from former colonies, structures arose to promote international security and worldwide deliberations that included voices from the new states. Foremost among these, the **United Nations (UN)** convened for the first time in 1945. One notable change ensured it a greater chance of success than the League of Nations: both the United States and the Soviet Union were active members from the outset. The charter of the UN outlined a collective global authority that would adjudicate conflicts and provide military protection if any members were threatened by aggression. In 1955, Achmed Sukarno, who succeeded in wrenching Indonesian independence from the Dutch, sponsored the Bandung Convention of nonaligned nations to set a common policy for achieving modernization and facing the major powers. Both the UN and the meetings of emerging nations began shifting global issues away from those of the Western powers. North–south inequities and human rights nudged their way into public consciousness.

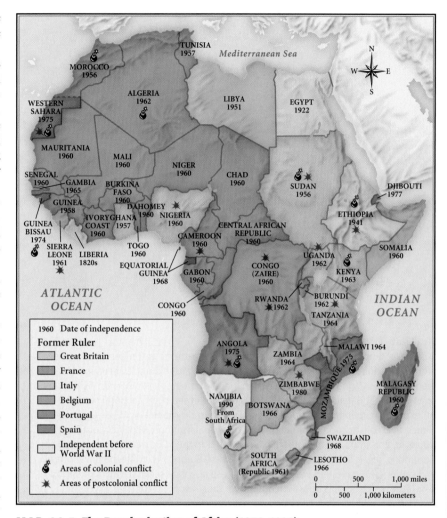

MAP 28.5 The Decolonization of Africa (1951–1990)
The liberation of Africa from European rule was an uneven process, sometimes occurring peacefully and at other times demanding armed struggle to drive out European settlers, governments, and armies. The difficult—and costly—process of nation building following liberation involved setting up state institutions, including educational and other services. Creating national unity out of many ethnicities also took work, except where the struggle against colonialism had already brought people together. To what extent did new African nations keep the borders imposed by the European imperial powers as shown in Map 25.2?

The Arrival of New Europeans

Amid the uncertainties of wars of liberation and the struggles to achieve solid economic independence, people from the former colonies began migrating to Europe—a reversal of the nineteenth-century trend of migration out of Europe. The first influx of non-European newcomers came from Britain's Caribbean possessions right after the war.

Next, labor shortages in Germany, France, Switzerland, and elsewhere compelled governments to negotiate with southern European countries for temporary workers. The German situation was particularly dire because in 1950 the working-age population (people between the ages of fifteen and sixty-four) was composed of 15.5 million men and 18 million women. In an ideological climate that kept women out of the workforce, the

The First "New" Europeans (1949)

World War II not only disrupted every-day life and patterns of trade in Europe, but around the globe. Some of the first people to immigrate to Europe after World War II were from the Caribbean (like these men in the photograph) and South Asia. Many arrived in Great Britain from the late 1940s onward in search of economic well-being. An expanding welfare state hired some of them to do menial work in hospitals, clinics, and construction, no matter what their qualifications. Race riots erupted, however, and immigration was so extensive that in the 1950s the British House of Commons began debating the rights of these new Europeans. While the government and businesses in western Europe needed these new laborers to rebuild after World War II, some Europeans questioned whether these workers—or their wives and children—should be allowed to become citizens. *Hulton Deutsch Collection/Corbis.*

The agreements stipulated that immigrant workers would have only temporary resident status, with a regular process of emigration back to their homeland. Turks and Algerians would arrive in Germany and France, respectively, to work for a set period of time, return home temporarily to see their families, then arrive in Europe for another period as guest workers. Initially, these workers were housed in barracks-like dormitories and few Europeans paid any attention to the quality of their lives. Instead of settling into community affairs, they created their own enclaves. They were welcomed because they took few social services, not even needing education because they came as adults. For businesspeople and policymakers alike, temporary workers made good economic sense. Virtually none of the welfare-state benefits would apply to them; often their menial work was off the books. "As they are young," one French business publication explained, "the immigrants often pay more in taxes than they receive in allowances." Most immigrants did jobs that people in the West were not likely to want: they collected garbage, built roads, held factory jobs, and cleaned homes. Although men predominated among migrant workers, women performed similar chores for less pay.

Immigrants saw Europe as a land of relatively good government, wealth, and opportunity. Others simply appreciated the conditions of everyday existence. As one Chinese immigrant to Spain put it: "If you want to be a millionaire, you must go to Singapore; if you want to be rich, you must go to Germany; but if you want good weather and an easy life, go to Spain." The advantages of living in Europe, especially the higher wages and jobs, became so overwhelming that clandestine workers began arriving. As early as the late 1960s, regularly admitted laborers formed only 12 percent of the non-European workforce and illegal workers some 88 per-

government needed immigrants. After southern European reserves proved insufficient, Germany and France turned to North African and then to sub-Saharan countries in the 1960s. During the cold war, countries in the Soviet bloc took refugees from war-torn Southeast Asia. Then, in the late 1970s, clandestine workers from Africa and Asia began entering countries like Italy that had formerly exported labor. Scandinavia received immigrants from around the world who flocked there because of reportedly greater opportunity and social programs to integrate newcomers. Immigrants from Surinam and Indonesia headed toward the Netherlands. By the 1980s, some 8 percent of the European population was foreign-born, compared to 6 percent in the United States.

cent. As empires collapsed, the composition of the European population in terms of race, religion, ethnicity, and social life began to change, becoming more multicultural and diverse than ever before in modern times. Many white Europeans looked back nostalgically on their imperial history and produced exotic films and novels about conquest and its pageantry. New nations emerged, their hopes high but their futures uncertain because of the costs of nation building and the legacy of colonial institutions and economic exploitation.

> **Review:** How did former imperial powers come to be dependent on temporary workers from the former colonies?

❖ Cultural Life on the Brink of Nuclear War

Both World War II and the cold war shaped postwar leisure and political culture. People engaged in heated debate over the responsibility for Nazism, the cause of ethnic and racial justice, and the merits of the two superpowers. During this period of intense self-scrutiny, they discussed and even fought over the course of decolonization and the Americanization that seemed to accompany the influx of U.S. dollars, consumer goods, and cultural media. Were they becoming too materialistic, like the Americans, or too intolerant like the Soviets? As Europeans examined their warlike past and the prosperity of the present, the cold war menaced hopes for peace and stability. In 1961, the USSR demanded the construction of a massive wall that physically divided the city of Berlin in half. In October 1962, the world held its breath while the leaders of the Soviet Union and the United States nearly provoked nuclear conflagration over the issue of missiles on the island of Cuba. In hindsight, the existence of extreme nuclear threat in an age of unprecedented prosperity seems utterly bewildering, but for those who lived on the precipice of global annihilation, the dangers were all too real.

Restoring "Western" Values

After the depravity and inhumanity of Nazism, cultural currents in Europe and the United States reemphasized universal values and spiritual renewal. Some, like Billy Graham, saw the churches as central to the restoration of values through an active commitment to "re-Christianizing" Europe and the United States. Their success was only partial, however, as the trend toward a more secular culture continued. In the early postwar years, people in the U.S. bloc emphasized the triumph of a Western heritage, a Western civilization, and Western values over fascism, and they characterized the war as one "to defend civilization [from] a conspiracy against man." This definition of *West* often emphasized the heritage of Greece and Rome and the rise of national governments in England, France, and western Europe as they encountered "barbaric" forces, be these nomadic tribes, Nazi armies, Communist agents, or national liberation movements in Asia and Africa. University courses in Western civilization flourished after the war to reaffirm those values. At the same time, the postwar renewal of humanitarianism pushed issues of cultural pluralism and human rights to the fore.

Holocaust and Resistance Literature. Memoirs of the death camps and tales of the resistance were compelling reading material. Rescued from the Third Reich in 1940, Nelly Sachs won the Nobel Prize in literature in 1966 for her poetry about the Holocaust. Anne Frank's *Diary of a Young Girl* (1947), the poignant record of a teenager hidden with her family in the back of an Amsterdam house, was emblematic of the survival of Western values in the face of Nazi persecution. Confronted with the small miseries of daily life and the grand evils of Nazism, Anne never stopped believing that "people are really good at heart." Governments erected permanent plaques at spots where resisters had been killed, organizations of resisters commemorated their role in winning the war, and their biographies filled magazines and bookstalls. Although resistance efforts were publicized, discussion of collaboration threatened to open old wounds. Thus, French filmmakers, for instance, avoided the subject for decades

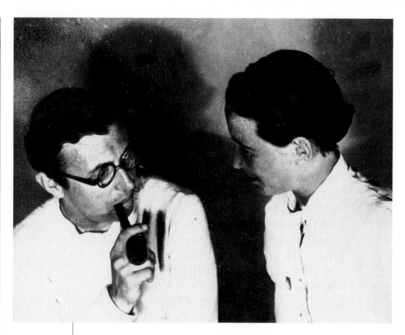

Jean-Paul Sartre and Simone de Beauvoir

The postwar period saw the rise of glossy, richly illustrated weekly magazines featuring news and pop culture. The faces of even the most complex philosophers became well known to the public, while their private lives intrigued readers. The public personae of these two existentialists, who were seen to promote the revival of human values after the nightmare of fascism, hid the twisted relationship Sartre and de Beauvoir actually had. Why did the intellectual life of Sartre, de Beauvoir, and their circle receive such media attention after World War II? Does the photo give any hints, or is it merely part of the attention itself? *Editions Gallimard.*

after the war. Many a politician with a Nazi past returned easily to the new cultural mainstream even as the stories of resistance took on mythical qualities.

Existential Philosophy. By the end of the 1940s, **existentialism** became the rage among the cultural elites and students in universities. It explored the meaning (or lack of meaning) of human existence in a world where evil flourished. Two of its leaders, Albert Camus (1913–1960) and Jean-Paul Sartre (1905–1980), had written for the resistance during the war, although Nazi censors had allowed the production of Sartre's plays. Existentialists confronted the question of "being," given what they perceived as the absence of God and the breakdown of morality. Their answer was that being, or existing, was not the automatic process either of God's creation or of birth into the natural world. One was not born with spiritual goodness in the image of a creator, but instead one created an "authentic" existence through action and choice. Camus's novels, such as *The Stranger* (1942) and *The Plague* (1947), dissected the evils of a corrupt political order and pondered human responsibility in such situations. Sartre's writings emphasized political activism and resistance under totalitarianism. Despite the fact that they had

never confronted the enormous problems of making choices while living under fascism, young people in the 1950s found existentialism compelling and made it the most fashionable philosophy of the day.

In 1949, Simone de Beauvoir♦ (1908–1986), Sartre's lifetime companion, published the twentieth century's most important work on the condition of women, *The Second Sex*. Beauvoir believed that most women had failed to take the kind of action necessary to lead authentic lives. Instead they lived in the world of biological necessity, devoting themselves exclusively to reproduction and motherhood. Failing to create an authentic self through considered action and accomplishment, they had become its opposite—an object, or "Other." Moreover, instead of struggling to define themselves and assert their freedom, women passively accepted their own "Otherness" and lived as defined by men. Beauvoir's classic book was a smash hit, in large part because people thought Sartre had written it. Both were celebrities, for the media spread the new commitment to humane values just as it had previously spread support for Nazism and for its wartime enemies.

♦ **Simone de Beauvoir:** see MAWN duh bohv WAHR

Race and Human Rights. While Europeans debated decolonization among people of color in Africa and Asia, intellectuals spawned new theories of what their liberation would mean. The first half of the century had witnessed the rise of pan-Africanism, but it was in the 1950s and 1960s that the immensely influential Frantz Fanon (1925–1961), a black psychiatrist from the French colony of Martinique, began analyzing liberation movements. He wrote that the mental functioning of the colonized person was "traumatized" by the violence and the brutal imposition of an outside culture as the only standard of value. Ruled by guns, the colonized person knew only violence and would thus naturally decolonize by means of violence. Translated into many languages, Fanon's *Black Skin, White Masks* (1952) and *The Wretched of the Earth* (1961) posed the question of how to decolonize one's mind.

Simultaneous with decolonization, in the 1950s the commitment to the civil rights cause of such long-standing organizations as the National Association for the Advancement of Colored People (NAACP, founded 1909) intensified. African Americans had fought in the war to defeat the Nazi idea of white racial superiority; as civilians, they now hoped to advance that ideal in the United States. In 1954, the U.S. Supreme Court declared segregated education unconstitutional in *Brown v. Board of Education*, a case initiated by the NAACP. On December 1, 1955, in Montgomery, Alabama, Rosa Parks, a part-time secretary for the local branch of the NAACP, boarded a bus and took the first available seat in the so-called white section at the front. When a white man found himself without a seat, the driver screamed at Parks, "Nigger, move back." Sitting in the front violated Southern laws, which encompassed a host of inequitable, even brutal policies toward African Americans. Parks confronted that system through the studied practice of civil disobedience. She refused to move back, and her action led to a boycott of public transportation that pushed the civil rights movement into the African American community as a whole.

The culture of rights and humane values generated further organizing. A variety of civil rights groups boycotted discriminatory businesses, "sat in" at segregated facilities, and registered black voters disfranchised by local regulations. Many talented leaders emerged, foremost among them Martin Luther King Jr. (1929–1968), a Baptist pastor from Georgia whose oratorical power galvanized activists to nonviolent resistance despite brutal white retaliation. He advocated "soulforce"—Gandhi's *satyagraha,* or "holding to truth"—to counter aggression. The postwar culture of nonviolence would shape the civil rights movement for a few years. Soon, however, the voices of thinkers like Fanon would merge with those of the civil rights movement to revolutionize attitudes toward race and rights.

Rising Consumerism and Shifting Gender Norms

Government spending on reconstruction, productivity, and welfare helped prevent the kind of upheaval that had followed World War I. Nor did the same tensions prevail among men and women: men returned from World War II much less frustrated than they had been in the 1920s because of the decisive result of World War II. A rising birthrate and bustling youth culture made for an upsurge in consumer spending that edged out wartime thriftiness. So veterans had fewer worries about jobs. Nonetheless, the war affected men's roles and sense of themselves. Young men who had missed World War II adopted the rough, violent style of soldiers, and roaming gangs posed as tough military types. While Soviet youth admired aviator aces, elsewhere groups such as the "teddy boys" in England (named after their Edwardian style of dressing) and the *gamberros* ("hooligans") in Spain took their cues from pop culture in music and film.

The leader of rock-and-roll style and substance was the American singer Elvis Presley. Sporting slicked-back hair and an aviator-style jacket, Presley bucked his hips and sang sexual lyrics to screaming and devoted fans. Rock-and-roll concerts and movies galvanized youth across Europe, including the Soviet bloc, where teens demanded the production of blue jeans and leather jackets. In a German nightclub late in the 1950s, members of a rock group of Elvis fans called the

Zbigniew Cybulski, the Polish James Dean
Zbigniew Cybulski depicted a tortured young resistance fighter in the film *Ashes and Diamonds* (1958) by Andrzej Wajda. Cybulski's character is to assassinate a Communist resistance leader on what turns out to be the last day of World War II, and his human dilemma around the act is set amid the chaos in Poland at war's end. Like existentialist philosophers and other cinema directors at the time, Wajda captured the debate over human values and the interest in young heroes of the postwar era. Why would this character be attractive to audiences in eastern Europe? *Photofest.*

and Francis Crick had discovered the structure of the gene. Portraying himself as an enthusiastic bad boy, Watson described how he had rifled people's desk drawers (among other dishonest acts) to become a scientific hero. In the revival of West German literature, Heinrich Böll published *The Clown* (1963), a novel whose young middle-class hero takes to performing as a clown and begging in a railroad station. Böll protested that West Germany's postwar goal of respectability had allowed the resurgence of precisely those groups of people who had produced Nazism. Across the Atlantic, the American "Beat" poets, who affected a dirty, bearded, and sometimes crazy appearance, like prisoners or camp survivors, critiqued traditional ideals of the upright and rational male achiever.

Both high and low culture revealed that two horrendous world wars had weakened the Enlightenment view of men as rational, responsible breadwinners. The 1953 inaugural issue of the American magazine *Playboy*, and the hundreds of magazines that came to imitate it, ushered in a startling depiction of a changed male identity. *Playboy* differed from typical pornographic magazines: along with pictures of nude women, it featured serious articles, especially on the topic of masculinity. This segment of the media presented modern man as sexually aggressive and independent of dull domestic life—just as he had been in the war. Breadwinning for a family only destroyed a man's freedom and sense of self, this new male culture claimed. The notion of men's liberty had come to include not just political and economic rights but also freedom of sexual expression outside the restrictions of the family.

In contrast, Western society promoted a postwar model for women that differed from their wartime experience. Instead of being essential workers and heads of families in the absence of their men, postwar women were made to symbolize the return to normalcy—a domestic, nonworking norm. Late in the 1940s, the fashion house of Christian Dior launched a clothing style called the "new look". It featured a pinched waist, tightly fitting bodices, and voluminous skirts. This restoration of the nineteenth-century female silhouette invited a renewal of clear gender roles. Women's magazines publicized the new look

Quarrymen performed, yelling at and fighting with one another as part of their show. They would soon become known as the Beatles. Rebellious young American film stars like James Dean in *Rebel Without a Cause* (1955) and Marlon Brando in *The Wild One* (1953) created the beginnings of a conspicuous postwar youth culture. The rebellious and rough masculine style appeared also in literature such as James Watson's autobiography, *The Double Helix* (1968), explaining how he

Consumerism, Youth, and the Birth of the Generation Gap

Young people were at the cutting edge of consumerism and other aspects of Americanization and economic revival. The generation gap, so much talked about in the 1960s, was taking shape earlier because of youthful openness on matters of the body and sexuality. Not so mired in the war as their parents, the young were ready for adventure—and adults worried about the consequences. Here an Austrian working-class woman (born in 1933) who sewed for a living describes her youth around 1955.

I bought myself records, American blues and jazz, Benny Goodman and Louis Armstrong. I was happy dancing the boogie-woogie. . . .

In fashion I was always very much in opposition to my mother. First, there was craze around nylon stockings, which were very expensive, and which almost everyone bought. We wore long checked skirts, not made of sheep's wool but of a "mixed" wool that was produced out of rags. Then came a short skirt, just above the knee. When I went dancing, however, everyone wore tight, fashionable skirts. One really had to get oneself into them with a shoehorn, and one's backside stood out. I then sewed a kind of cascade on one side, and thus attired, I proudly went dancing.

At first one wore hair long. But my boss was at me so much about it that I had it cut. Then with the new permanents from America one got a totally new look which was flat in the back with a garland of curls around the rest. But fashion changed fast, at one minute such a hairdo was modern, but then one had to put a comb in to push it up higher.

My home was very nice, with a great deal of love, and because of that my parents gave me a lot of freedom although my mother was always concerned. Above everything she always worried: "What will the neighbors think?"

We only spoke about sex with our schoolmates. Certainly nothing about it came from my parents, nothing either from the school. No, one could not ask about such things . . . . Everything was taboo. And boys and girls were strictly segregated from one another in the school. I remember at carnival time a boy came to school dressed as a girl and was sent right home.

Source: Birgit Bolognese-Leuchtenmüller et al., eds., *Frauen der ersten Stunde 1945–1955.* (Vienna: Medieninhaber Europaverlag, 1985), 20–21. Translation by Bonnie G. Smith.

and urged a return to domesticity and thus normalcy. Even in the hard-pressed Soviet Union, recipes for homemade face creams passed from woman to woman and beauty parlors did a brisk business. New household products such as refrigerators and washing machines raised standards for women's accomplishment in the home by giving them the means to be "perfect" housewives.

However, new-look propaganda did not mesh with reality or even with all social norms. Dressmaking fabric was still being rationed in the late 1940s; even in the next decade, women could not get enough of it to make voluminous skirts. In Europe, where people had barely enough to eat, the underwear needed for new-look contours simply did not exist. In Spain, women were said to perform their role best by being religious and concerned with the spiritual well-being of their families. The frequent, even excessive activity known as consumerism, however, emphasized the physical beauty available through cosmetics and clothing; it urged women to buy things that would make their families look better too (see "Consumerism, Youth, and the Birth of the Generation Gap," above). European women continued to work

The New Look
Immediately after the war, the French fashion industry swung into action to devise styles for the return to normal life. Cinched, even corseted waists and voluminous skirts suggested the nineteenth century rather than the depression and war years, when some women had started regularly wearing trousers. The highly restrictive femininity was also part of the cold war, as the leisured ideal demanded by the new look for middle-class Western women contrasted with the more practical styles in the Soviet Union. Although western Europe was hard hit by the war, governments imported foreign workers to rebuild; in the USSR, in contrast, more than 90 percent of women worked to rebuild their devastated country. Why did the image of women after World War I become so modern, while the image of women after World War II became more traditional, especially in western Europe and the United States? *Liaison Agency.*

outside the home after the war; indeed, mature women and mothers were working more than ever before—especially in the Soviet bloc (Figure 28.2, opposite). The female workforce was going through a profound revolution as it gradually became less youthful and more populated by wives and mothers who would hold jobs all their lives despite being bombarded with images of nineteenth-century middle-class femininity.

The advertising business presided over the creation of cultural messages as well as over the rise of the new consumerism that accompanied recovery. Guided by marketing experts, western Europeans were imitating Americans by driving some forty million motorized vehicles, including motorbikes, cars, buses, and trucks. They drank Coca-Cola and used American detergents, toothpaste, and soap. The number of radios in homes grew steadily—for example, by 10 percent a year in Italy between 1945 and 1950—and the 1950s marked a high tide of radio influence. The development of television spread in the United States, where two-thirds of the population had sets in the early 1950s, while in Britain only one-fifth did. Only in the 1960s did television become an important consumer item for most Europeans. In the 1950s, radio was still king and consumerism a growing mass phenomenon.

The Culture of Cold War

Radio was at the center of the cold war. As superpower rivalry heated up, radio's propaganda function remained at the fore, as it had in wartime. During the late 1940s and early 1950s, the Voice of America, with its main studio in Washington, D.C., broadcast in thirty-eight languages from one hundred transmitters and provided an alternative source of news for people in eastern Europe. The Soviet counterpart broadcast in Russian around the clock but initially spent much of its wattage jamming U.S. programming. Russian programs stressed a uniform Communist culture and values; the United States, by contrast, emphasized diverse programming and promoted debate about current affairs. The contrast was meant to show commitment to socialist values versus commitment to choice and free speech.

	Member Countries of Council of Mutual Economic Assistance[1]		Member Countries of European Economic Community[2]	
	1950	1960	1950	1960
Female as % of total population	54.9	53.9	51.8	51.6
Female labor force as % of total labor force	48.5	48.7	31.1	31.4
Distribution of female labor force (%):				
Agriculture	63.3	50.0	26.1	16.8
Industry	16.9	22.6	29.3	31.3
Services	19.8	27.4	44.6	51.9

[1]Albania, Bulgaria, Czechoslovakia, East Germany, Hungary, Poland, Romania, and USSR

[2]Belgium, Denmark, France, West Germany, Ireland, Italy, Luxembourg, Netherlands, and United Kingdom

FIGURE 28.2 Women in the Workforce, 1950–1960
In contrast to the situation after World War I, women did not leave the workforce in great numbers after World War II. In fact, Europe faced labor shortages. In countries of the Soviet bloc, women vastly outnumbered men because so many men had died in the war, and the task of rebuilding demanded every available worker. In western Europe, women's workforce participation was lower, and countries like West Germany tried to keep women out of the labor pool to distinguish themselves from the Communist bloc. Note the increase in women's service-sector employment in just one decade. From World Employment 1996–1997: National Policies in a Global Context *(Geneva: International Labour Office, 1996), 7.*

Its issues and events conveyed by radio and other media, the cold war had a far-reaching emotional impact. The public heard reports of nuclear buildups; tests of emergency power facilities sent them scurrying for cover. In school, children rehearsed for nuclear war, while at home families built bomb shelters in their backyards. Books like George Orwell's *1984* (1949) were claimed by ideologues on both sides as vindicating their beliefs. Ray Bradbury's popular *Fahrenheit 451* (1953), whose title indicated the temperature at which books would burn, condemned cold war curtailment of intellectual freedom. In the USSR, official writers churned out spy stories, and espionage novels topped best-seller lists in the West. *Casino Royale* (1953), by the British author Ian Fleming, introduced James Bond, who tested his wit and physical prowess against Communist and other political villains. Soviet pilots would not take off for flights when the work of Yulian Simyonov,♦ the Russian counterpart of Ian Fleming, was playing on radio or television. Reports of Soviet -and U.S.-bloc characters—fictional or real—facing one another down became part of everyday life.

Culture as a whole came under the cold war banner. Even as Europe's major cities rebuilt their war-ravaged opera houses and museums, they could not hold back the "Americanization" they saw taking place in Europe. While many Europeans were proponents of American business practices, the Communist Party in France led a successful campaign to ban Coca-Cola for a time in the 1950s. Soviet magazines carried fashion photos touted as decently attractive in contrast to the highly sexualized garments for women to the

♦ **Yulian Simyonov:** ool ee AHN sihm YAWN uhv

Bomb Shelter
Americans expressed their fear of nuclear annihilation by building tens of thousands of individual bomb shelters. Stocked with several months' supply of canned food and other goods, the shelters were to protect a family from the nuclear blast itself and from the disorder that might follow nuclear war. The government also prepared shelters to shield top officials and to ensure the continuation of civil society despite vast casualties and massive destruction. *Bettman/Corbis.*

West. Both sides also tried to win the war by pouring vast sums of money into high culture, though the United States did it by secretly channeling government money into foundations to award fellowships to artists and writers or promote favorable journalism around the world. As leadership of the art world passed to the United States, art became part of the cold war. Abstract expressionism, practiced by American artists such as Jackson Pollock, produced nonrepresentational works by dripping, spattering, and pouring paint. Abstract expressionists spoke of the importance of the artist's self-discovery, spiritual growth, and sensations in the process of painting. "If I stretch my arms next to the rest of myself and wonder where my fingers

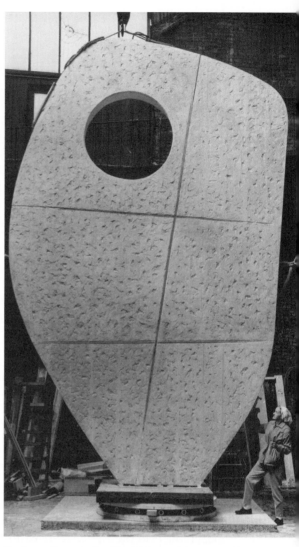

Barbara Hepworth, *Single Form* **(1961–1964)**
Like others in the West, British sculptor Barbara Hepworth was strangely buoyed by the war, hoping that it meant the dawn of a new age. Full of renewed energy, Hepworth believed that art should follow pure forms, which some called "primitive," as a way of expressing enduring values. Her twenty-one-foot abstract sculpture *Single Form*, shown here as a plaster cast, was installed at the United Nations building in New York to commemorate the life of her friend Dag Hammarskjöld, who served as secretary-general of the United Nations from 1953 until his death in 1961. *Single Form* followed the clean lines of an earlier version of the sculpture—one much loved by Hammarskjöld. "[We] depend on the pure courage of the UN," Hepworth wrote of the sculpture created to honor Hammarskjöld's life and work. *Plaster for bronze, BH325, height: 21 feet, 1961-64, Photo: Morgan-Wells, London. © Bowness, Hepworth Estate*

are, that is all the space I need as a painter," commented Dutch-born Willem de Kooning on his relationship with his canvas. Said to exemplify Western freedom, such painters were given shows in Europe and awarded commissions at the secret direction of the U.S. Central Intelligence Agency.

The USSR openly promoted an official Communist culture. When a show of abstract art opened in the Soviet Union, Khrushchev yelled at the exhibition itself that it was "dog shit." Pro-Soviet critics in western Europe saw U.S.-style abstract art as "an infantile sickness" and supported socialist realist art with "human content," showing the condition of the workers and the oppressed races in the United States. In Italy, the neorealist technique was developed by filmmakers such as Roberto Rossellini in *Open City* (1945) and Vittorio De Sica in *The Bicycle Thief* (1948). Such works challenged Hollywood-style sets and costumes by using ordinary characters living in devastated, impoverished cities. By depicting stark conditions, neorealist directors conveyed their distance both from middle-class prosperity and from fascist bombast. "We are in rags? Let's show everyone our rags," said one Italian director. Many of these directors associated support for the suffering masses with the Communist cause. Seen or unseen, the cold war entered the most unsuspected aspects of cultural life.

Kennedy, Khrushchev, and the Atomic Brink

It was in this pervasive climate of cold war that John Fitzgerald Kennedy (1917–1963) became U.S. president in 1960. Kennedy represented American affluence and youth but also the nation's commitment to cold war. Kennedy's media advisers and ghostwriters recognized how perfect a match their articulate, good-looking president was to the power of television. A war hero and early fan of the fictional cold war spy James Bond, Kennedy intensified the arms race and escalated the cold war. Some of this escalation occurred over the nearby island of Cuba, where in 1959 Fidel Castro had come to power and allied his government with the Soviet Union after being rebuffed by the United States. In the spring of 1961, Kennedy, assured by the

Central Intelligence Agency (CIA) of success, launched an invasion of Cuba at the Bay of Pigs to overthrow Castro. The invasion failed miserably and humiliated the United States.

Tensions kept growing. In the summer of 1961, East German workers, supervised by police and the army, stacked bales of barbed wire across miles of the city's east–west border to begin construction of the Berlin Wall. The divided city had served as an escape route by which some three million people had fled to the West. Kennedy responded at home with a call for more weapons and an enhanced civil defense program. In October 1962, matters came to a head in the **Cuban missile crisis**, when the CIA reported the installation of Soviet medium-range missiles in Cuba (Map 28.6). Kennedy now responded forcefully, calling for

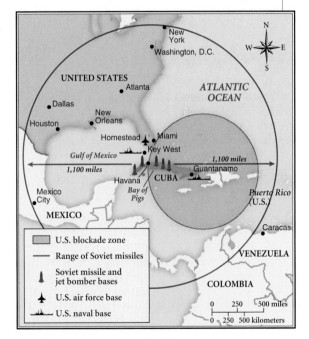

MAP 28.6 The Cuban Missile Crisis, 1962
Just off the coast of the southeastern United States, Cuba posed a threat to North American security once the Soviet Union began stocking the island with missiles. The United States reacted vigorously, insisting on the dismantling of missile sites and an end to the Soviets' supplying Cuba with further weaponry. Although his generals were prepared for nuclear war with the Soviet Union, President Kennedy refused to take this step despite his cold war stance on many other issues. Soviet premier Khrushchev similarly backed down from a military confrontation. Explain the placement of missiles in Cuba and the U.S. reaction to it.

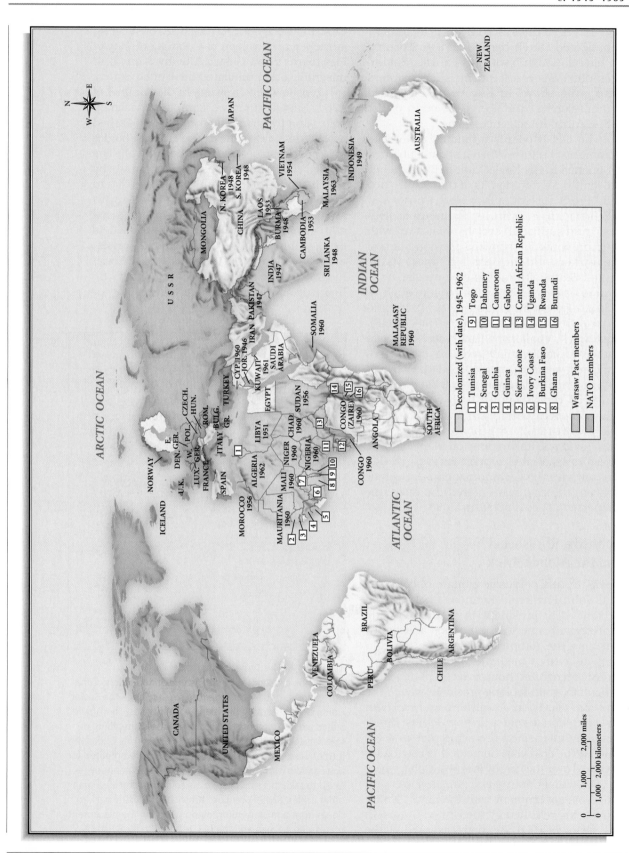

◄ **MAPPING THE WEST**
The Cold War World, c. 1960
Superpower rivalry between the United States and the Soviet Union resulted in the division of much of the industrial world into cold war alliances. Simultaneously, the superpowers vied for the allegiance of the newly decolonized countries of Asia and Africa by providing military, economic, and technological assistance. Wars such as those in Vietnam and Korea were also products of the cold war. How might this map be said to convey the idea that a first, second, and third world existed? How does this map differ from the map on page 955?

a blockade of ships headed for Cuba and threatening nuclear war if the missiles were not removed. For several days the world stood on the brink of nuclear disaster. Then, between October 25 and 27, Khrushchev and Kennedy negotiated an end to the crisis. Kennedy spent the remainder of his short life working to improve nuclear diplomacy; Khrushchev did the same. The two leaders, who had looked deeply into the nuclear future, clearly feared what they saw. In the summer of 1963, less than a year after the shock of the Cuban missile crisis, the United States and the Soviet Union signed a test-ban treaty outlawing the explosion of nuclear weapons in the atmosphere and in the seas. Backing away from the brink, the treaty held out hope that the cold war and its culture would give way to something better.

Review: How did the cold war affect everyday culture and social life?

Conclusion

World War II began the atomic age and transformed international power politics. Two superpowers, the Soviet Union and the United States, each controlling atomic arsenals, replaced the former European leadership and engaged in a menacing cold war. The cold war saturated everyday life, giving birth to cold war religion in the preachings of the Reverend Billy Graham and to a postwar revival of religious faith. In secular life, bomb shelters, spies, purges, and witch hunts kept

people thinking that war was at hand. Postwar diplomacy created a cold war division of Europe into an eastern bloc dominated by the Soviets and a freer western bloc mostly allied with the United States. It was in this grim international atmosphere that starving, homeless, and refugee people faced the task of rebuilding a devastated Europe.

Yet both halves of Europe recovered almost miraculously in little more than a decade. The east, where wartime devastation was greatest, experienced less prosperity, while in western Europe wartime technology and planning served as the basis for new consumer goods and improved health. Spurred on by aid from the United States, western Europe formed a successful Common Market that became the foundation for greater European unity. As a result of the war, Germany recovered as two countries, not one, and the weakened European powers shed their colonies. Newly independent nations emerged in Asia and Africa, opening the possibility for a more equitable distribution of global power. Often serving as pawns in the cold war, these new countries faced the problem of guaranteeing their economic future. As the West as a whole grew in prosperity, its cultural life focused paradoxically on eradicating the evils of Nazism while enjoying the new phenomenon of mass consumerism. But, like newly independent nations, the West had above all to survive the atomic rivalry of the superpowers.

Suggested References

World Politics Transformed

In the past decade, the opening of Soviet archives and closer research in American records have allowed for more informed views of the diplomacy and politics of the cold war in Europe and around the world. Although few defend Stalin, we now benefit from balanced assessments of superpower rivalry. Two Web sites on the cold war contain biographies of the main players, time lines, and miscellaneous details, while a third describes how nuclear weapons actually work and how they cause destruction.

Cold war: **http://library.thinkquest.org/ 10826.mainpage.htm**; **http://history .acusd.edu/gen/20th/coldwar0.html**; **http:// nuclearwar.org**.

Cronin, James. *The World the Cold War Made: Order, Chaos, and the Return of History.* 1996.

Eisenberg, Carolyn Woods. *Drawing the Line: The American Decision to Divide Germany, 1944–1949.* 1996.

Gaddis, John. *We Now Know: Rethinking Cold War History.* 1997.

Hogan, Michael J. *A Cross of Iron: Harry S. Truman and the Origins of the National Security State, 1945–1954.* 1998.

*Pasternak, Boris. *Doctor Zhivago.* 1958.

Zubkova, Elena. *Russia after the War: Hopes, Illusions, and Disappointments, 1945–1957.* 1998.

Political and Economic Recovery in Europe

Though painstaking and complex, recovery in its material and political forms yielded a distinctly new Europe whose characteristics historians are still uncovering. Because of the opening of the archives, historical attention has focused on charting Soviet occupation, recovery, and Communist takeover.

Herf, Jeffrey. *Divided Memory: The Nazi Past in the Two Germanies.* 1997.

Kenney, Padraic. *Rebuilding Poland: Workers and Communists, 1945–1950.* 1997.

Milward, Alan S. *The United Kingdom and the Economic Community.* 2002.

Moeller, Robert, ed. *West Germany under Construction: Politics, Society, and Culture in the Adenauer Era.* 1997.

Naimark, Norman M. *The Russians in Germany: A History of the Russian Zone of Occupation, 1945–1949.* 1995.

Taubman, William. *Khrushchev: The Man and His Era.* 2003.

Decolonization in a Cold War Climate

Novelists, philosophers, and historians debate the impact and issues of decolonization. Powerful evocations of the brutality of the process appear

---

*Primary source.

most often in novels such as *Cracking India*, which was made into the film *Earth*.

Connelly, Matthew. *A Diplomatic Revolution: Algeria's Quest for Independence and the Origins of the Post–Cold War Era.* 2002.

*Fanon, Frantz. *The Wretched of the Earth.* 1961.

Hargreaves, J. D. *Decolonization in Africa.* 1996.

Macey, David. *Frantz Fanon: A Biography.* 2000.

McIntyre, W. David. *British Decolonization, 1946–1997: When, Why, and How Did the British Empire Fall?* 1999.

*Sidhwa, Bapsi. *Cracking India: A Novel.* 1992.

Yergin, Daniel. *The Prize: The Epic Quest for Oil, Money, and Power.* 1991.

Cultural Life on the Brink of Nuclear War

Cold war culture, including the growth of consumerism, make the 1950s a fertile field for research, especially as new sources become available. Historians like Saunders have focused on governments' direction of high culture to the point that some artists and writers were made "stars" because of government intervention, while Engel's new work points to the lows of consumerism in the plight of the Soviet Union's women.

Bayin, Andre. *French Cinema from the Liberation to the New Wave.* 2000.

*Beauvoir, Simone de. *The Mandarins.* 1956.

Engel, Barbara Alpern. *Women in Russia, 1700–2000.* 2004.

Heineman, Elizabeth D. *What Difference Does a Husband Make? Women and Marital Status in Nazi and Postwar Germany.* 1999.

Kuisel, Richard. *Seducing the French: The Dilemma of Americanization.* 1993.

Poiger, Ute G. *Jazz, Rock, and Rebels: Cold War Politics and American Culture in a Divided Germany.* 2000.

Saunders, Frances Stonor. *Who Paid the Piper?* 1999.

Swann, Abram de. *In Care of the State: Health Care, Education, and Welfare in Europe and the United States in the Modern Era.* 1988.

CHAPTER REVIEW

IMPORTANT EVENTS

1945 Cold war begins

1947 India and Pakistan win independence from Britain

1948 State of Israel established

1949 Mao Zedong leads Communist revolution in China; Simone de Beauvoir publishes *The Second Sex*

1950 Korean War begins

1953 Stalin dies; Korean War ends

1954 *Brown v. Board of Education* prohibits segregated schools in the United States; Vietnamese forces defeat the French at Dien Bien Phu

1956 Egyptian leader General Abdel Nasser nationalizes the Suez Canal; uprising in Hungary against USSR

1957 Boris Pasternak publishes *Doctor Zhivago*; USSR launches *Sputnik*; Treaty of Rome establishes the European Economic Community (Common Market)

1958 Fifth Republic begins in France

1962 The United States and USSR face off in the Cuban missile crisis

KEY TERMS

Christian Democrats (1110)

cold war (1198)

Cuban missile crisis (1133)

decolonization (1118)

economic miracle (1108)

European Economic Community (EEC or Common Market) (1112)

existentialism (1126)

Marshall Plan (1103)

North Atlantic Treaty Organization (NATO) (1107)

thaw (1117)

third world (1098)

Truman Doctrine (1103)

United Nations (UN) (1123)

welfare state (1113)

REVIEW QUESTIONS

1. What major events led to the development of the cold war between the superpowers?

2. What factors drove economic recovery in western Europe? In eastern Europe?

3. How did former imperial powers come to be dependent on temporary workers from the former colonies?

4. How did the cold war affect everyday culture and social life?

MAKING CONNECTIONS

1. What was the political climate after World War II and how did it differ from the political climate after World War I?

2. What were the relative strengths of the two European sides in the cold war?

3. How did World War II shape cultural life after the war?

4. Why did decolonization follow the war so immediately?

FOR FURTHER EXPLORATION

To assess your mastery of the material in this chapter, see the Online Study Guide at **bedfordstmartins.com/hunt**.

To read additional primary-source material from this period, see Chapter 28 in *Sources of The Making of the West*, Second Edition.

Postindustrial Society and the End of the Cold War Order, 1965–1989

IN JANUARY 1969, JAN PALACH, a twenty-one-year-old philosophy student, drove to a main square in Prague, doused his body with gasoline, and set himself ablaze. Before killing himself he left a statement in his coat—deliberately put to one side—demanding an end to Soviet-style repression in Czechoslovakia. It promised more such suicides unless the government lifted state censorship. The manifesto was signed: "Torch No. 1." Across a stunned nation, black flags were flown, close to a million people flocked to Palach's funeral, and shrines to his memory seemed to spring up overnight. In the next months, more Czech youth followed Palach's grim example and became torches for freedom.

Before his self-immolation, Jan Palach was an ordinary, well-educated citizen of the technological and postindustrial age. Having recovered from the war, the West was in the midst of still another astonishing transformation, shifting from a manufacturing economy based in heavy industry to a service economy that depended on technical knowledge in such fields as engineering, health care, and finance. This new service economy was seen as a postindustrial one. To staff it, institutions of higher education sprang up at a dizzying rate and drew in more students than ever before—among them Jan Palach. But those young people—along with women, minorities, and

---

Shrine to Jan Palach

Jan Palach was a martyr to the cause of an independent Czechoslovakia, free to pursue a non-Soviet destiny. His self-immolation on behalf of that cause roused the nation. As makeshift shrines sprang up and multiplied throughout the 1970s and 1980s, they served as common rallying points that ultimately contributed to the overthrow of Communist rule. Václav Havel, the future president of a liberated Czechoslovakia, was arrested early in the momentous year of 1989 for commemorating Palach's sacrifice at the shrine. In light of so many other deaths in the Soviet bloc, why did Jan Palach's death become so powerful a force? © *Mark Garanger/Corbis.*

many other activists in the 1960s and 1970s—struck out against war and cold war, inequality and repression, and even against knowledge and technology themselves. From Czechoslovakia to the United States and around the world, protests arose against the way in which postindustrial nations in general and the superpowers in particular were directing society. Before long, countries in both the Soviet and U.S. blocs were on the verge of political revolution.

While reformers questioned the values of technological and cold war society, whole nations challenged the superpowers' monopoly of international power. An agonizing war in Vietnam sapped the resources of the United States, and China confronted the Soviet Union with increasing confidence. The oil-producing states of the Middle East formed a cartel and reduced the flow of oil to the leading industrial nations in the 1970s. The resulting price increases helped bring on a recession, throwing the future of the postindustrial order into question. Others resorted to terrorism to achieve their ends, and all the wealth and military might of the superpowers could not guarantee that they would emerge victorious in this age of increasingly global competition. An invisible erosion of Soviet legitimacy took place, and soon a reform-minded leader—Mikhail Gorbachev—directed the USSR to change course. It was too late: in 1989, the Soviet bloc collapsed, inspired by countless acts of protest, not least of them the individual heroism of Jan Palach and the other human torches.

❖ The Revolution in Technology

The protests of the 1960s and after took place in the midst of incredible technological advance. These advances steadily boosted prosperity and changed daily life in the West, where people awoke to instantaneous radio and television news, worked with computers, and used revolutionary contraceptives to control reproduction. Satellites orbiting the earth reported weather conditions, relayed telephone signals, and collected military intelligence. Smaller gadgets—electric popcorn poppers, portable radios and tape players, automatic garage door openers—made life more pleasant. The reliance of humans on machines led one philosopher to insist that people were no longer self-sufficient individuals, but rather cyborgs—that is, humans who needed machines to sustain ordinary life processes.

The Information Age: Television and Computers

Information technology catalyzed social and political change in these postindustrial decades just as innovations in textile making and the spread of railroads had in the nineteenth century. This technology's ability to transmit knowledge, culture, and political information globally appeared even more revolutionary. Mass journalism, film, and radio had begun to forge a more homogeneous society based on shared information and

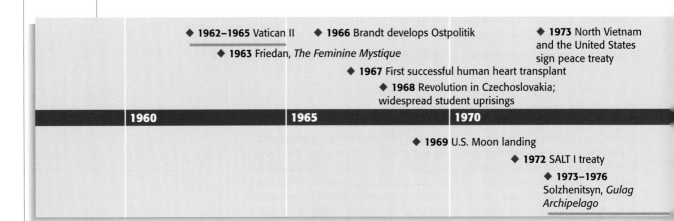

◆ **1962–1965** Vatican II ◆ **1966** Brandt develops Ostpolitik ◆ **1973** North Vietnam and the United States sign peace treaty
◆ **1963** Friedan, *The Feminine Mystique*
◆ **1967** First successful human heart transplant
◆ **1968** Revolution in Czechoslovakia; widespread student uprisings

1960   **1965**   **1970**

◆ **1969** U.S. Moon landing
◆ **1972** SALT I treaty
◆ **1973–1976** Solzhenitsyn, *Gulag Archipelago*

images in the first half of the twentieth century; in the last third of the century, television, computers, and telecommunications made information even more accessible and, some critics said, made culture more standardized. Once-remote villages were linked to urban capitals on the other side of the world thanks to videocassettes, satellite television, and telecommunications. Because of technology, the age of protest was also the age of communications events.

Television. Americans embraced television in the 1950s; following the postwar recovery, it was Europe's turn. Between the mid-1950s and the mid-1970s, Europeans rapidly adopted television as a major entertainment and communications medium. In 1954, just 1 percent of French households had television; by 1974, almost 80 percent did. With the average viewer tuning in about four and a half hours a day, the audience for newspapers and theater declined. "We devote more . . . hours per year to television than [to] any other single artifact," one sociologist commented in 1969. As with radio, European governments funded television broadcasting with tax dollars and controlled TV programming to avoid what they perceived as the substandard fare offered by American commercial TV; instead they featured drama, ballet, concerts, variety shows, and news. Thus, the welfare state, in Europe at least, assumed a new obligation to fill its citizens' leisure time. It thereby gained more power to shape daily life.

With the emergence of communications satellites and video recorders in the 1960s, state-sponsored television encountered competition. Satellite technology allowed for the transmission of sports broadcasts and other programming to a worldwide audience. Feature films on videotape became readily available to television stations (although not yet to individuals) and competed with made-for-television movies and other programs. The competition increased in 1969 when the Sony Corporation introduced the first affordable color videocassette recorder to the consumer market. What statesmen and intellectuals considered the junk programming of the United States—soap operas, game shows, sitcoms—arrived dubbed in the native language, amusing a vast audience with the joys, sorrows, tensions, and aspirations of daily life. Critics charged that both state-sponsored and commercial television avoided extremes to keep sponsors happy, spoon-feeding audiences only "official" or "moderate" opinions. They complained that, although TV provided more information than had ever been available before, the resulting shared culture represented the lowest common denominator.

East and west, television exercised a powerful political and cultural influence. Even in a rural area of the Soviet Union more than 70 percent of the inhabitants watched television regularly in the late 1970s; the rest continued to prefer radio. Educational programming united the far-flung population of the USSR by broadcasting shows designed to advance Soviet culture. At the same time, with travel impossible or forbidden to many, shows about foreign lands were among the most popular—as were postcards from these

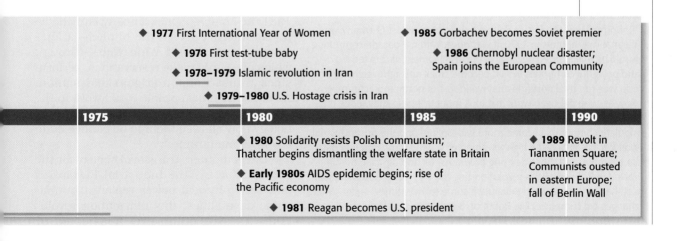

◆ **1977** First International Year of Women

◆ **1978** First test-tube baby

◆ **1978–1979** Islamic revolution in Iran

◆ **1979–1980** U.S. Hostage crisis in Iran

◆ **1985** Gorbachev becomes Soviet premier

◆ **1986** Chernobyl nuclear disaster; Spain joins the European Community

| 1975 | 1980 | 1985 | 1990 |

◆ **1980** Solidarity resists Polish communism; Thatcher begins dismantling the welfare state in Britain

◆ **Early 1980s** AIDS epidemic begins; rise of the Pacific economy

◆ **1981** Reagan becomes U.S. president

◆ **1989** Revolt in Tiananmen Square; Communists ousted in eastern Europe; fall of Berlin Wall

lands, which became household decorations. Heads of state could usually preempt regular programming. In the 1960s, French president Charles de Gaulle addressed his fellow citizens frequently, employing the grandiose gestures of an imperial ruler to stir patriotism. As electoral success in western Europe increasingly depended on cultivating a successful media image, political staffs came to rely on media experts as much as they did policy experts.

Computers.   Just as revolutionary, the computer reshaped work in science, defense, and ultimately industry. Computers had evolved dramatically since the first electronic

Advances in Computing
"Robotron" was the first mainframe computer in East Germany, and, like many computers in 1970, it was huge. Within a decade computing would be miniaturized because of the development of chip technology, and powerful computers would become small and lightweight. Robotron was run by a postindustrial workforce of nonmanufacturing employees, who did clean work that took more technical knowledge than muscle power. As computing became miniaturized, the ability to manipulate computers became more widespread and the postindustrial workforce itself became highly segmented among those entering data, for example, and those devising programs. Technology, like that involved in Robotron, was revolutionizing the way people worked, just as it had in the Industrial Revolution some two centuries earlier. What changes did computers like Robotron bring to modern life in the West? *AKG Images.*

ones, among them the Colossus, which the British used in 1943 to decode Nazi military and diplomatic messages. Several countries had devised these machines for processing information, all of them primitive by later standards in being gigantic, slow, noisy, and able only to decode. With growing use in civilian industry and business after the war, computing machines shrank from the size of a gymnasium in the 1940s to that of an attaché case in the mid-1980s. They also became both far less expensive and fantastically more powerful than the Colossus, thanks to the development of increasingly sophisticated digital electronic circuitry implanted on tiny silicon chips, which replaced the clumsy radio tubes used in 1940s and 1950s computers. Within a few decades, the computer could perform hundreds of millions of operations per second and the price of the integrated circuit at the heart of computer technology would fall to less than a dollar, allowing businesses and individuals access to computing ability at a reasonable cost.

Computers changed the pace and patterns of work not only by speeding up and easing tasks but also by performing many operations that workers had once done themselves. In garment making, for example, experienced workers no longer painstakingly figured out how to arrange patterns on cloth for maximum efficiency and economy. Instead, a computer specified instructions for the optimal positioning of pattern pieces, and trained workers, usually women, followed the machine's directions. By the end of the 1970s, the miniaturization of the computer had made possible a renewal of the eighteenth-century cottage industry, and in 1981 the French phone company launched a public Internet server, the Minitel—a forerunner of the World Wide Web—through which one could make reservations, perform stock transactions, and gain information. As in earlier times, people could work in the physical isolation of their homes, but technology now allowed them to be connected to a central mainframe.

Did computers transform society for the better? Whereas the Industrial Revolution had seen physical power replaced by machine capabilities, the information revolution witnessed brainpower augmented by computer technology. Many believed that computers would profoundly expand mental life, providing, in the words of one scientist, "boundless opportunities . . . to resolve the puzzles of cosmology, of life, and of the society of man." Others maintained that computers programmed people, reducing human capacity for inventiveness, problem solving, and initiative. As the 1970s closed, such predictions were still untested as the information revolution moved toward a more dramatic unfolding in the 1980s and 1990s.

The Space Age

When the Soviets launched the satellite *Sputnik* in 1957, they ignited competition with the United States that was quickly labeled the space race. John F. Kennedy became determined to beat the Soviets in space by putting a man on the moon by the end of the 1960s. The result was increasingly complex space flights that tested humans' ability to survive the process of space exploration, including weightlessness. Astronauts walked in space, endured weeks (and, later, months) in orbit, docked with other craft, fixed satellites, and carried out experiments for the military and private industry. Meanwhile, a series of unmanned rockets filled the earth's gravitational sphere with weather, television, intelligence, and other communications satellites.

In July 1969, a worldwide television audience watched as U.S. astronauts Neil Armstrong and Edwin "Buzz" Aldrin walked on the moon's surface—the climactic moment in the space race. The space race also drove Western cultural developments. Astronauts and cosmonauts were perhaps the era's most admired heroes: Yuri Gagarin, John Glenn, and Valentina Tereshkova—the first woman in space (see illustration on the next page)—topped the list. A whole new fantasy world developed. Children's toys and games revolved increasingly around space. Films such as *2001: A Space Odyssey* (1968) portrayed space explorers answering questions about life that were formerly the domain of church leaders. Likewise, in the internationally popular television series *Star Trek*, members of the starship *Enterprise*'s diverse crew wrestled with the problems of maintaining humane values against less-developed, often menacing

THE SPACE AGE	
1957	Soviet Union launches the first artificial satellite, *Sputnik*
1961	Soviet cosmonaut Yuri Gagarin orbits the earth; capsule carrying Alan Shepard Jr. makes first U.S. suborbital flight
1965	United States launches first commercial communications satellite, *Intelsat I*
1969	U.S. astronauts Neil Armstrong and Edwin Aldrin walk on moon's surface
1970s–present	Soviet Union and United States individually and in collaboration with various countries perform space station maneuvers, lunar probes, and other scientific experiments
1971	Soviet Union attempts unsuccessfully to put *Salyut 1*, a space station, into orbit
1973	United States puts *Skylab*, an experimental space station, into orbit
1976	*Viking* spacecraft explores Mars
1979–1986	Spacecraft *Voyager* makes successful flybys of Jupiter, Saturn, and Uranus

civilizations. In the Eastern bloc, Polish author Stanislaw Lem's novel *Solaris* (1971) similarly portrayed space age individuals engaged in personal quests and likewise drew readers and ultimately viewers into a futuristic fantasy.

The space age grew out of cold war concerns, but it also offered the possibility of more global political cooperation. Although advances in rocket technology allowed for powerful and destructive missiles, it also promoted international efforts. From the 1960s on, U.S. spaceflights often involved the participation of other countries such as Great Britain and the Netherlands. In 1965, an international consortium headed by the United States launched the first commercial communications satellite, *Intelsat I*, and by the 1970s some 150 countries worked together at more than four hundred stations worldwide to maintain global satellite communications. Although some 50 percent of satellites were for spying purposes, the rest promoted international communication and were sustained by transnational collaboration.

Valentina Tereshkova, Russian Cosmonaut
People sent into space were heroes, representing modern values of courage, strength, and well-honed skills. Insofar as the space age was part of the cold war race for superpower superiority, the USSR held the lead during the first decade. The Soviets trained both women and men, and the 1963 flight of Valentina Tereshkova—the first woman in space—supported Soviet claims of gender equality in contrast to the all-male superstar image of the early U.S. space program. The achievements of both countries led to the launching of communications satellites that produced the globalizing communications revolution of the next decades. Does it make a difference that men and women go into space even though most analysts agree that humans are not necessary to space exploration and experimentation? *Hulton Archive/Getty Images.*

Lunar landings and experiments in space advanced pure science in the midst of space race hype. Astronomers, for example, previously dependent on remote sensing for their work, used mineral samples from the moon to calculate the age of the solar system with unprecedented precision. Unmanned spacecraft provided data on cosmic radiation, magnetic fields, and infrared sources. Although the media touted the human conquerors of space, breakthroughs in space exploration and astronomy were utterly dependent on a

range of technology, including the radiotelescope, which depicted space by receiving, measuring, and calculating nonvisible rays. These findings reinforced the so-called big bang theory of the origins of the universe, first posited in the 1930s by American astronomer Edwin Hubble and given crucial support in the 1950s by the discovery of a low level of radiation permeating the universe in all directions. Based on the earlier work of Albert Einstein and Max Planck, the big bang theory explains the development of the universe from a condition of extremely high density and temperature some ten billion years ago. Nuclei emerged when these conditions dissipated in a rapid expansion of space—the big bang.

Revolutions in Biology, Reproductive Technology, and Sexual Behavior

Sophisticated technologies extended to the life sciences, bringing dramatic new health benefits and ultimately changing reproduction itself. In 1952, scientists Francis Crick, an Englishman, and James Watson, an American, discovered the configuration of **DNA**, the material in a cell's chromosomes that carries hereditary information. Simultaneously, other scientists were working on "the pill"—an oral contraceptive for women that tapped more than a century of scientific work in the field of birth control. Still other breakthroughs lay ahead—ones that would revolutionize conception and make scientific duplication of species possible.

Understanding DNA. Crick and Watson, working from laboratories in Cambridge, England, solved the mystery of the gene and thus of biological inheritance when they demonstrated the structure of DNA. They showed how the double helix of the DNA molecule splits in cellular reproduction to form the basis of each new cell. This genetic material, biologists concluded, provides a chemical pattern for an individual organism's life. Beginning in the 1960s, genetics and the new field of molecular biology progressed rapidly. Growing understanding of nucleic acids and proteins advanced knowledge of viruses and bacteria that effectively ended the ravages of polio, tetanus, syphilis, tuberculosis, and such dangerous childhood diseases as mumps and measles in the West.

Understanding how DNA works allowed scientists both to alter the makeup of plants and to bypass natural animal reproduction in a process called cloning—obtaining the cells of an organism and dividing or reproducing them (in an exact copy) in a laboratory. In 1997 one group of researchers produced a cloned sheep named "Dolly," though the breakthrough was marred by the fact that she suffered an array of disabilities and died six years later. Cloning raised the question of whether scientists should interfere with so basic and essential a process as reproduction, and the question became more urgent when in 2002 an Italian doctor claimed to have cloned several humans—a claim disbelieved by many scientists. Similarly, the possibility of genetically altering species and even creating new ones (for instance, to control agricultural pests) led to concern about how such actions would affect the balance of nature. In 1967, Dr. Christiaan Barnard of South Africa performed the first successful heart transplant, and U.S. doctors later developed an artificial heart. Commentators debated the selection process for these scarce, reusable organs and asked whether the enormous cost of new medical technology to save a few people would be better spent on helping the many who lacked even basic medical and health care.

Transforming Reproduction. Technology also influenced the most intimate areas of human relations—sexuality and procreation. In traditional societies, community and family norms dictated marital arrangements and sexual practices, in large part because too many or too few children threatened the crucial balance between population size and agricultural productivity. As Western societies industrialized and urbanized, however, not only did these considerations become less urgent but the growing availability of reliable birth-control devices permitted young people to begin sexual relations earlier, with less risk of pregnancy. These trends accelerated in the 1960s as the birth-control pill, first produced in the United States and tested on women in developing areas, came on the Western market. By 1970, its use was spreading around the world. Millions also sought out voluntary surgical sterilization through tubal ligations and vasectomies. New techniques brought abortion, traditionally performed by amateurs, into the hands of medical professionals, making it a safe procedure for the first time.

Childbirth and conception itself were similarly transformed. Whereas only a small minority of Western births took place in hospitals in 1920, more than 90 percent did by 1970. Obstetricians now performed much of the work midwives had once done. As pregnancy and birth became a medical process, innovative new procedures and equipment

Thalidomide Children
In the last third of the twentieth century, increasingly destructive side effects of powerful medicines became apparent. Women who had taken the drug thalidomide gave birth to children with severe disabilities, and the public condemned companies selling untested products. The race to profit from scientific and technological developments sometimes ignored human well-being. Children affected by thalidomide, once they became adults, were among those who launched the disability rights movement. What questions about medicine and health care does the use of thalidomide raise? **For more help analyzing this image,** see the visual activity for this chapter in the Online Study Guide at **bedfordstmartins.com/hunt**. *Deutsche Press Agentur.*

made it possible to monitor women and fetuses throughout pregnancy, labor, and delivery. The number of medical interventions rose: cesarean births increased by 400 percent in the United States in the 1960s and 1970s, and the number of prenatal visits per patient in Czechoslovakia, for example, rose by 300 percent between 1957 and 1976. In 1978, the first "test-tube baby," Louise Brown, was born to an English couple. She had been conceived when her mother's eggs were fertilized with her father's sperm in a laboratory dish and then implanted in her mother's uterus—a complex process called **in vitro fertilization**. If a woman could not carry a child to term, the laboratory-fertilized embryo could be implanted in the uterus of a surrogate, or substitute, mother. Researchers even began working on an artificial womb to allow for reproduction entirely outside the body—from storage bank to artificial embryonic environment.

A Sexual Revolution?   The globally expanding media helped spread knowledge of birth-control procedures after World War II and made public discussions of sexual matters explicit, technical, and widespread. Popular use of birth control allowed Western society to be saturated with highly sexualized music, literature, and journalism without a corresponding rise in the birthrate—evidence of the increasing separation of sexuality from reproduction. Statistical surveys showed that regular sexual activity began at an ever-younger age, and people talked more openly about sex—another component of cultural change. Finally, in a climate of increased publicity to sexuality, more open homosexual behavior became apparent, along with continued efforts to decriminalize it across the West. The Western media announced the arrival of a "sexual revolution." However, sexual revolutions had been trumpeted with each advance in birth-control technology beginning in the nineteenth century, showing once again the social and political impact of technological transformation.

> **Review:** How did the scientific advances from the 1950s and 1960s challenge established patterns of thought and social behavior?

❖ Postindustrial Society and Culture

Reshaped by soaring investments in science and the spread of technology, Western countries in the 1960s started on what has been labeled a postindustrial course (see "Terms of History," opposite). Instead of being centered on manufacturing and heavy industry, postindustrial society emphasized the distribution of services such as health care and education. The service sector was the leading force in the economy, and this meant that intellectual work, not industrial or manufacturing work, had become primary in creating jobs and profits. Moreover, all parts of society and industry interlocked, forming a system constantly in need of complex analysis. These characteristics of postindustrial society would carry over from the 1960s and 1970s into the next century; they also laid the groundwork for further globalization.

Multinational Corporations

One of the major innovations of the postindustrial era was the growing number of **multinational corporations**. These companies produced goods and services for a global market and conducted business worldwide, but unlike older kinds of international firms, they established major factories in countries other than their home base. For example, of the five hundred largest businesses in the United States in 1970, more than one hundred did over a quarter of their business abroad, with IBM operating in more than one hundred countries. Although U.S.-based corporations led the way, European and Japanese multinationals like Volkswagen, Shell, Nestlé, and Sony also had a broad global scope.

Some multinational corporations had bigger revenues than entire nations. They appeared to burst the bounds of the nation-state as they set up shop in whatever part of the world offered cheap labor. Their interests differed starkly from those of ordinary people with local or national identities. In the first years after the war, multinationals preferred European employees, who constituted a highly educated labor pool, had developed consumer habits, and eagerly sought secure

TERMS OF HISTORY

Postindustrial

In 1973, U.S. sociologist Daniel Bell's book *The Coming of Postindustrial Society* announced a momentous change in Western society. The economies of the major powers had stopped being predominantly manufacturing and had become instead postindustrial. By this, Bell meant not that there was no more industrial production of cars, household goods, and materials such as steel but rather that service industries like health care, education, and financial services had become the largest sector of the economy. Statistics from Europe and the United States bore him out.

Bell also spotted the knowledge- or information-based characteristics of postindustrial society. Decisions in individual enterprises as well as in technological society as a whole could no longer spring from hunches and small bits of information. Instead, the management of any entity depended on systems analysis, which aimed to take into account every factor pertinent to the system, be it a factory, a financial institution, or a government. Under these circumstances, those who knew how to obtain, produce, and manipulate vast quantities of knowledge could be far more important than those who could not.

The term *postindustrial* was part of a trend prevalent in these years to use the prefix *post* with an array of words, employed first in the term *post-war*. *Postwar* came to mean the period between the end of World War II and economic recovery from it, from 1945 to about 1960, even though Europe and the world still reverberated with the legacy of the Holocaust and wartime devastation for many decades. *Post*s proliferated in these years: *postmodern*, *post-Western*, *post-human*, and *post-Marxist*, to name a few of the most important uses.

The term *postmodern* arose after the various rebellions of the 1960s had challenged the rational, progressive, and technology-proud attitudes connected with the Enlightenment, the first wave of modernity. Enlightenment thinkers associated modernity with the triumph of science and Enlightenment faith that precise knowledge would yield an ever better future. In the 1960s, students and environmentalists maintained that bombs, pollution, and the rising tide of cancer—not progress—had been the major results of modernity. Over the next decades postmodernity would criticize even more aspects of the Enlightenment.

The word *post-human* also began to emerge during these decades, associated at first with the development of robots to do factory work and artificial organs and body parts to treat health conditions. Not only had machines replaced people in factories, critics observed, but ordinary people could not live without machines in their lives. The so-called virtual reality of the Internet age contributed yet another sense to the word *post-human* as people developed relationships that were purely electronic.

The word *post-Marxism* can be dated to the years before the collapse of communism when socialist countries introduced elements of the market economy. Hungary was notable in opening the road to post-Marxism economically, helping to set the stage for the collapse of communism in the 1980s and 1990s. Others maintain that post-Marxism began with the inability of the Communist system to meet the technological demands of the postindustrial age. As technology and information determined the well-being of industries, consumers, and social programs, ideology got in the way of efficiency and alienation prevented coordination and cooperation.

The emergence of a postindustrial social and economic order may well leave us wondering what will succeed it as an organizing principle for human productivity. The emergence of such concepts as *postindustrial* and *post-Marxist* suggests that theorists are seeing further change already at hand. Historians, however, counterbalance these analyses by suggesting that most proclamations of change and most visions of the future have deep roots in the past.

FURTHER READING

Bell, Daniel. *The Coming of Postindustrial Society: A Venture in Social Forecasting.* 1973.

Hayles, N. Katherine. *How We Became Posthuman: Virtual Bodies in Cybernetics, Literature, and Informatics.* 1999.

Seidman, Steven, ed. *The Postmodern Turn: New Perspectives on Social Theory.* 1994.

work. Then, beginning in the 1960s, multinationals moved more of their operations to the emerging economies of formerly colonized states to reduce labor costs, taxes, and regulations in the West. Although multinational corporations provided jobs in developing areas, profits usually enriched foreign stockholders and thus looked to some like imperialism in a new form.

Many European firms believed that they could stay competitive only by expanding, merging with other companies, or becoming partners with government in doing business. In France, for example, a massive glass conglomerate merged with a metallurgical company to form a new group specializing in all phases of construction—a wise move given the postwar building boom. European firms increased their investment in research and used international cooperation to produce major new products. This new emphasis on research was a crucial ingredient in postindustrial society. The British-French Concorde supersonic aircraft, which, beginning with its first flight in 1976, flew from London to New York in under four hours, was one result. Another venture was the Airbus, a more practical series of passenger jets inaugurated in 1972 by a consortium of European firms. Both projects attested to the strong relationship among government, business, and science as well as to the international cooperation in manufacturing among members of the Common Market (Map 29.1). The relationship allowed for successful competition with U.S.-based multinational giants. Whereas U.S. production surpassed the combined output of West Germany, Great Britain, France, Italy, and Japan in the immediate postwar years, by the mid-1970s the situation was reversed.

The New Worker

In its formative stage, industrial production had depended on workers who often labored to exhaustion, endured malnourishment, and lived in a state of poverty that sometimes led to violence. This scenario changed fundamentally in postwar Europe with the reduction of the blue-collar workforce, resource depletion in coal mines, the substitution of foreign oil for coal and of plastics for steel, the

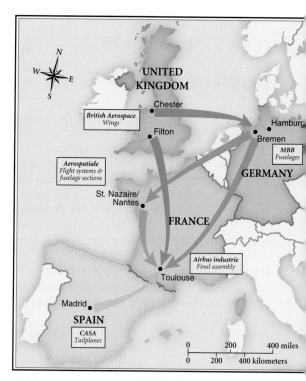

MAP 29.1 The Airbus Production System

The international consortium Airbus marked an important step in the economic and industrial integration of Europe. It also advanced the revitalization of the individual national economies by establishing new manufacturing centers away from capital cities and by modernizing older ones. Its formation presaged the international mergers and cooperative production that would characterize the late twentieth and early twenty-first centuries; today Airbus is a global enterprise with locations offering parts and service around the world, including the United States, China, and India. How does the production of the Airbus differ geographically from the early production of textiles in a nineteenth-century factory?

growth of off-shore manufacturing, and automation in industrial processes. Work in manufacturing was simply cleaner and more mechanized than ever before. Within firms, the relationship of workers to bosses shifted as management started grouping workers into teams that set their own production quotas, organized and assigned tasks, and competed with other teams to see who could produce more. As workers adopted attitudes and gained responsibilities that had once been managerial prerogatives, union membership declined.

In both the U.S. and Soviet blocs, a new kind of working class emerged, consisting of white-collar service personnel. Its rise undermined economic distinctions based on the way one worked, for those who performed service work or had managerial titles were not necessarily better paid than blue-collar workers. The ranks of service workers swelled with researchers, health-care and medical workers, technicians, planners, and government functionaries. Employment in traditional parts of the service sector—banks, insurance companies, and other financial institutions—also surged because of the vast sums of money needed to finance technology and research. Entire categories of employees such as flight attendants devoted much of their skill to the psychological well-being of customers. The consumer economy provided more jobs in restaurants and personal health, fitness and grooming, and in hotels and tourism. By 1969, the percentage of service-sector employees had passed that of manufacturing workers in several industrial countries: 61.1 percent versus 33.7 percent in the United States; and 48.8 percent versus 41.1 percent in Sweden (see "Taking Measure," shown below).

Postindustrial work life had some different ingredients in the Soviet bloc. Late in the 1960s, Communist leaders announced a program of "advanced socialism" that included more social leveling, greater equality of salaries, and nearly complete absence of private production. The percentage of farmers remained higher in the Soviet bloc than in western Europe. A huge difference between professional occupations and those involving physical work also remained in socialist countries because of declining investment

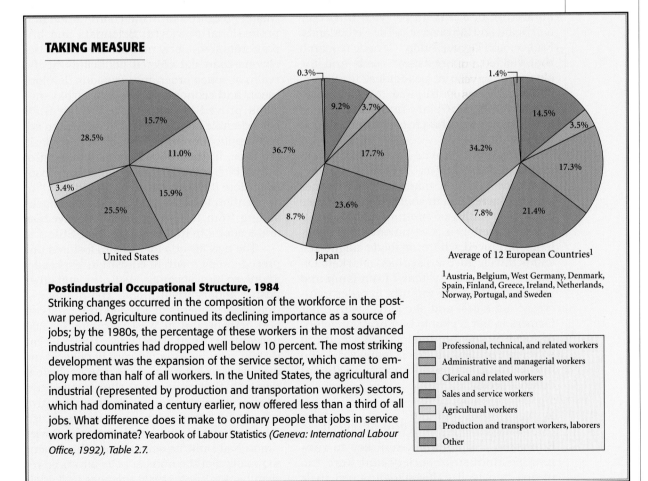

TAKING MEASURE

United States

Japan

Average of 12 European Countries[1]

[1]Austria, Belgium, West Germany, Denmark, Spain, Finland, Greece, Ireland, Netherlands, Norway, Portugal, and Sweden

Postindustrial Occupational Structure, 1984
Striking changes occurred in the composition of the workforce in the postwar period. Agriculture continued its declining importance as a source of jobs; by the 1980s, the percentage of these workers in the most advanced industrial countries had dropped well below 10 percent. The most striking development was the expansion of the service sector, which came to employ more than half of all workers. In the United States, the agricultural and industrial (represented by production and transportation workers) sectors, which had dominated a century earlier, now offered less than a third of all jobs. What difference does it make to ordinary people that jobs in service work predominate? Yearbook of Labour Statistics *(Geneva: International Labour Office, 1992), Table 2.7.*

- Professional, technical, and related workers
- Administrative and managerial workers
- Clerical and related workers
- Sales and service workers
- Agricultural workers
- Production and transport workers, laborers
- Other

in advanced machinery and cleaner work processes. Less mobility existed between the two classifications, but much as in the U.S.-led bloc, gender also shaped the workforce into two groups, with men generally earning higher pay for better jobs and women relegated to lower pay and lesser jobs. Somewhere between 80 and 95 percent of women worked in socialist countries, mostly under these conditions.

Farm life was updated, even bureaucratized across the West. By the 1970s, one could travel for miles in Europe without seeing a farmhouse. Small landowners sold family plots to farmers engaged in agribusiness—that is, vast acreage devoted to commercial rather than peasant farming. Governments, farmers' cooperatives, and planning agencies took over decision making from the individual farmer; they set production quotas and handled an array of marketing transactions. In the 1960s, agricultural output rose an average of 3 percent per year in Greece and Spain and 2.5 percent in the Netherlands, France, and Great Britain. Genetic research that yielded pest-resistant seeds and the skyrocketing use of pesticides, fertilizers, and machinery contributed to growth. Between 1965 and 1979, the number of tractors in Germany more than tripled from 384,000 to 1,340,000.

Bureaucracy played its part too: for example, in the 1970s a French farmer, Fernande Pelletier, made a living on her hundred-acre farm in southwestern France in the new setting of international agribusiness. Advised by a government expert, Pelletier produced whatever foods might sell competitively in the Common Market. On expert advice, she switched from lamb and veal to foie gras and walnuts in order to increase her sales, and she joined with other farmers in her region to buy heavy machinery and to sell her products. Agricultural solvency required as much managerial and intellectual effort as did success in the industrial sector.

The Boom in Education and Research

Education and research were key to running postindustrial society and were the means by which nations maintained their economic and military might. In the West, common sense, hard work, and creative intuition had launched the earliest successes of the Industrial Revolution. By the late twentieth century, success in business or government demanded humanistic or technological expertise and ever-growing staffs of researchers. As one French official put it, "the accumulation of knowledge, not of wealth, . . . makes the difference" in the quest for power.

Investment in research fueled military and industrial leadership. The United States funneled more than 20 percent of its gross national product into research in the 1960s, in the process siphoning off many of Europe's leading intellectuals and technicians in a so-called brain drain. Complex systems—for example, nuclear power generation with its many components, from scientific conceptualization to plant construction to the publicly supervised disposal of radioactive waste—required intricate coordination and professional oversight. Scientists and bureaucrats frequently made more crucial decisions than did elected politicians in the realm of space programs, weapons development, and economic policy. Soviet-bloc nations proved less adept at linking their considerable achievements in science to actual applications because of bureaucratic red tape. In the 1960s, some 40 percent of Soviet-bloc scientific findings became obsolete before the government approved them for application to technology. An unseen backsliding from the superpower effectiveness and leadership had begun in the USSR.

The new criteria for success fostered unprecedented growth in education, especially in universities, scientific institutes, and other postsecondary institutions. The number of university students in Sweden rose by about 580 percent and in West Germany by 250 percent between 1950 and 1969. Great Britain established a network of polytechnic universities to encourage the technical research that traditional elite universities often scorned. France set up administrative schools for future high-level experts in administration. By the late 1970s, the Soviet Union had built its scientific establishment so rapidly that the number of its advanced researchers in the natural sciences and engineering surpassed that of the United States. Meanwhile, institutions of higher learning added courses in business and management, information technology, and systems analysis—most notably in western Europe and the United States.

In principle, education made the avenues to success more democratic by basing them on talent instead of wealth. In fact, however, societal leveling did not occur in most western European universities, and instruction often remained rigid and old-fashioned. Although eighteenth-century Europeans had pioneered educational reform, students in the 1960s reported that teachers lectured even young children, who spoke in class only to echo the teacher or to recite homework memorized the night before. At the university level, as one angry student put it, the professor was "a petty, threatened god" who puffed himself up "on the passivity and dependence of students." Such judgments would soon provoke young people to rebel against the traditional authority of teachers, officials, and parents.

A Redefined Family and a Generation Gap

Just as education changed dramatically to meet the needs of postindustrial society, the contours of the family and the nature of parent–child relationships shifted from what they had been a century earlier. Family roles were transformed, and the relationship between parents and children—long thought to be natural and unchangeable—looked different, alarmingly so to some conservatives. Even though television and media commentators delivered messages about what the family should be, technology, consumer goods, and a constant flow of guest laborers and migrants from the former colonies produced social and cultural change, including enormous variety in what households actually were. Households were now headed by a single parent, by remarried parents merging two sets of unrelated children, by unmarried couples cohabitating, or by traditionally married parents who had few—or no—children. Households of same-sex partners also became more common. At the end of the 1970s, the marriage rate in the West

had fallen by 30 percent from its 1960s level. Despite a rising divorce rate, the average marriage lasted one-third longer than it had a century earlier because of increased longevity. After almost two decades of baby boom, the birthrate dropped significantly. On average, a Belgian woman, for example, bore 2.6 children in 1960 but only 1.8 by the end of the 1970s. Although the birthrate fell, the percentage of children born outside of marriage soared.

Daily life within the family changed. Technological consumer items saturated domestic space, as radio and television often formed the basis of the household's common social life. Appliances such as dishwashers, washing machines, and clothes dryers became more affordable and more widespread, reducing (in theory) the time women had to devote to household work and raising standards of cleanliness. More women worked outside the home during these years to pay for the prolonged economic dependence of children, but working mothers still did the housework and child care almost entirely themselves.

To advance in a knowledge-based society, children did not enter the labor force until their twenties but instead attended school, thus requiring their parents' financial and emotional support. Whereas the early modern family organized labor, taught craft skills, and monitored reproductive behavior, the modern family seemed to have a primarily psychological mission. Parents were to provide emotional nurture while their children learned intellectual skills in school. They could also count on psychologists, social workers, and other social service experts to provide counseling in dealing with the stress that resulted from the emphasis on academic accomplishment. Television programs portrayed a variety of family experiences on soap operas, sitcoms, and family-oriented game shows, giving viewers an opportunity to see how other families dealt with the tensions of modern life.

Most notably, postindustrial society transformed teenagers' lives. A century earlier, teens had been full-time wage earners; now, most were students, financially dependent on their parents into their twenties. Amid the anxieties caused by this prolonged childhood, youth simultaneously gained new roles

The Beatles (1969)
"Let It Be" went the lyrics to one of the last songs of this world famous group before they disbanded to go their separate ways as performers. The Beatles represented both the aspirations of a rising generation of youth and the booming consumer culture that created the Beatles' look, sound, and message. Their records were simultaneously directed by astute marketing experts for big record companies and filled with what seemed liberating allusions to the drug culture and Asian spirituality. What was the appeal of the Beatles and the other celebrated rock stars who followed in their wake? © Bruce McBroom/Camera Press/Retna Ltd.

as consumers. Advertisers and industrialists saw the baby boomers as a multibillion-dollar market and wooed them with consumer items associated with rock music—records, portable radios, stereos. Replacing romantic ballads, rock music celebrated youthful rebellion against adult culture in biting, critical, and often explicitly sexual lyrics. Sex roles for the young did not change, however. Despite the popularity of a few individual women rockers, promoters focused on men, whom they depicted as heroic, surrounded by worshiping female "groupies." The new models for youth such as the Beatles were themselves the products of advanced technology and savvy marketing for mass consumption. "What's your message for American teenagers?" the Beatles were asked. "Buy some more Beatles records," they responded. But the Beatles also offered a special zest and even spirituality, derived from going to India and introducing its instruments and ideals in their songs. The mixture of high-tech music, pop-star marketing, and the youthful hysteria of fans contributed to a sense that there was a unique youth culture and a growing generation gap.

Art, Ideas, and Religion in a Technocratic Society

Cultural trends evolved with the march of consumer society and with technology itself. Like modernists in the past, a new generation of artists addressed growing consumerism and the world of space, electronics, and computers in their art. Even as colonies ripped away from the old colonial powers, their influence on the Western mind remained strong, continuing to turn musicians, scholars, and religious leaders in their direction for new ways of thinking. Conversely, many of these intellectuals enjoyed increasing international recognition and global markets—like the multinationals themselves. With the development of computers, they buttressed their prestige by employing complex statistical and other scientific methods.

The Visual Arts. A new trend in the visual arts was called **pop art**. It featured images from everyday life and employed the glossy techniques and products of what these artists called admass, or mass advertising. "There's no reason," the group maintained of modern society's commercialism, "not to consider the world as one gigantic painting." Robert Rauschenberg, a leading U.S. practitioner, made collages from comic strips, magazine clippings, and fabric to fulfill his vision that "a picture is more like the real world when it's made out of the real world." The movement had become a financial success by the early 1960s, attracting such maverick American artists as Jasper Johns and Andy Warhol, who advanced the parody of modern commercialism. Warhol showed, for example, how the female body, the classic form that attracted nineteenth-century male art buyers, was used to sell everything mass culture had to offer in the 1960s and 1970s. He depicted Campbell's soup cans as they appeared in advertisements and sold these works as elite artistic creations.

Swedish-born artist Claes Oldenburg (b. 1929) portrayed the grotesque aspects of ordinary consumer products in *Giant Hamburger with Pickle Attached* (1962) and *Lipstick Ascending on Caterpillar Tractor* (1967). "High art" picked up not merely commercial goods but actually "low" objects such as scraps of metal, cigarette butts, dirt, and even excrement. The Swiss sculptor Jean Tinguely used rusted parts of old machines to make fountains that could move. His partner Niki de Saint-Phalle then constructed huge, gaudy figures—many of them inspired by the folk traditions of the Caribbean and Africa—to decorate them. Their colorful, mobile fountains adorned main squares in Stockholm, Montreal, Paris, and other cities (see *Fontaine Stravinsky*, below).

Niki de Saint-Phalle, *Fontaine Stravinsky* (1983)
Niki de Saint-Phalle's exuberant and playful art, seen in the fountains of Paris and cities around the world, captured the accessibility of pop art. Her other work drew inspiration from Caribbean and African styles and celebrated women of decolonizing countries. Living during the rebirth of activism, de Saint-Phalle lined up suspended bags of paint and machine-gunned them to create a spattered canvas—her answer to the alleged "macho" or bad-boy style of abstract expressionists like Jackson Pollock. How does the presence of such works of art change the nature of public space?
© 2005 Artists Rights Society (ARS), NY/ADAGP, Paris. Photo: Barbara Alper/Stock Boston.

To mock this mocking world of art, German artist Sigmar Polke did cartoonlike drawings of products and of those who craved them.

Music. The American composer John Cage (1912–1992) worked in a similar vein when he added sounds produced by such everyday items as combs, pieces of wood, and radio noise into his musical scores. Buddhist influence led Cage to incorporate silence in music and to compose by randomly tossing coins and then choosing notes by the corresponding numbers in the ancient Chinese *I Ching* (Book of Changes). These techniques continued the trend away from classical melody that had begun with modernism. The development widened the gulf between the composer and the larger public: many listeners simply hated such music. Other composers, called minimalists, simplified music by featuring repetition and sustained notes as well as by rejecting the "masterpiece" tradition of lush nineteenth-century symphonies and piano music. Arno Part, the famed Estonian composer, wrote minimalist pieces in the 1970s using only three or four notes in total; he called this style "starvation" music to underscore the lack of both freedom and goods in the Soviet bloc.

Some musicians stressed modern technology; they introduced tape recordings into vocal pieces and used computers and synthesizers both to compose and to perform their works. German composer Karlheinz Stockhausen introduced electronic music into classical composition in 1953; Cage also used it soon after. Influenced by his own travels, Stockhausen continued the modern style of fully exploring non-Western tonalities in such 1970s pieces as *Ceylon*. But even though this music echoed the electronic and increasingly interconnected state of human society, its concert audiences diminished because new music continued to seem dissonant and even shrill. At the same time, improved recording technology and mass marketing brought music of all varieties to a wider home audience than ever before.

Social Science. The social sciences reached the peak of their prestige during these decades, often because of their increasing use of statistical models and predictions made possible by advanced electronic computations. Sociologists and psychologists produced empirical studies that were more detailed than ever before and that purported to demonstrate rules for understanding individual, group, and societal behavior. Anthropology was among the most exciting of the social sciences, for it brought to the young university student information about societies that seemed immune to modern technology and industry. The sense of escape and adventure was more vivid than ever before, as colorful ethnographic films captured alternative lifestyles and exotic practices. While studying people who came to be called "the other," the young had their sense of freedom reinforced by the vision of going back to nature.

Simultaneously, the social sciences also undermined some of the foundations for the belief that individuals had true freedom. French anthropologist Claude Lévi-Strauss (b. 1908) developed a theory called structuralism, which insisted that all societies function within controlling structures—kinship and exchange, for example—that operate according to coercive rules similar to those of the unbreakable conventions in language. Structuralism challenged existentialism's tenet that humans could create a free existence and shook the social sciences' faith in the triumph of rationality. Lévi-Strauss's book *The Savage Mind* (1966) also demonstrated that people outside of the West had not a scientific but an improvisational style that could be extremely effective. In the 1960s and 1970s, the findings of the social sciences generally paralleled concerns that technology was creating a society of automatons and that complex managerial systems would eradicate individualism and human freedom.

Religion. Church officials and parishioners made an effort to bring religion up to date with the changing times, which tended to see merit in a variety of cultures and thus promoted toleration. Responding to what he saw as a crisis in faith caused by affluence and secularism, Pope John XXIII (r. 1958–1963) in 1962 convened the Second Vatican Council, known as **Vatican II**. The Council modernized the liturgy, democratized many church procedures, and at the last session in 1965 renounced church doctrine that condemned the Jewish people as guilty of killing Jesus. Vatican II promoted ecumenism—that is, mutual cooperation among the world's faiths. In the face of scientific advance, Pope John's successor, Paul VI (1963–1978), kept Catholic opposition to artificial birth control alive, but he also became the first pontiff to demonstrate global concerns by visiting Africa, Asia, and South America. A succession of popes, most notably Polish-born John Paul II, encouraged Catholicism in the Soviet bloc, strengthening religion as a primary focal point for anticommunism there.

In some parts of the West, there was a notable upsurge in postwar religious fervor. In the face of scientific advance, growing numbers of U.S. Protestants joined sects that stressed the literal truth of the Scripture and denied the validity of past scientific discoveries such as the age of the universe and the evolution of the species. In western Europe, however, Christian churchgoing remained at a low ebb. In the 1970s, for example, only 10 percent of the British population went to religious services—about the same number that attended live soccer matches. Most striking was the changing composition of the Western religious public. Immigration of people from former colonies and other parts of the world increased the strength of the non-Christian religions such as Islam and varieties of Hindu faiths. Cities and towns came to house mosques, Buddhist temples, and shrines to other creeds. New religious values mixed sometimes easily and sometimes tensely with both Western European Judeo-Christianity and the antireligious culture of the Soviet bloc.

Review: What major changes took place in the formation of postindustrial society?

❖ Protesting Cold War Conditions

Affluence, scientific sophistication, and military might elevated the United States and the Soviet Union to the peak of their power in the 1960s. By 1965, however, the six nations of the Common Market had replaced the United States as the leader in worldwide trade and the marketing of new technologies and other products, and they often acted in their own self-interest across the U.S.–Soviet divide. In 1973, Britain joined the Common Market, followed by Ireland and Denmark. The market's exports now amounted to almost three times those of the United States. Communist China, along with countries in eastern Europe, contested Soviet leadership, and many decolonizing regions refused to become pliable allies to the superpowers. The struggle for Indochinese independence had never ended, and by the mid-1960s a devastating war in Vietnam was under way. At the end of the 1970s, the USSR became embroiled in an equally devastating war in Afghanistan. Another serious challenge to the cold war order also came from rising citizen discontent and from dramatic protest like that of Jan Palach. From the 1960s until 1989, people rose up against the consequences of technological development, the lack of fundamental rights, and the potential for nuclear holocaust latent in the cold war. Leaders of emerging nations in the Middle East and elsewhere struck back too, eroding industrial economies in the West and further shaking up the international political order of the cold war.

Cracks in the Cold War Order

Across the social and political spectrum there were calls for at least softening the effects of the cold war in this age of unprecedented progress and technological prowess. The new Soviet middle class of bureaucrats and managers demanded a better standard of living and a reduction in the cold war animosity that made everyday life so menacing. In western European countries, voters elected politicians in the late 1960s who promoted an increasing array of social programs designed to ensure the economic democracy of the welfare state. A significant minority shifted their votes away from the centrist Christian Democratic coalitions that supported U.S. political goals. Instead they voted for Socialist, Labor, and Social Democratic parties in hopes of shifting priorities from the cold war to ordinary people's needs during this period of rapid change. Leaders also developed new diplomatic strategies to deal with the cold war.

Germany and France. The German and French governments both made solid and highly visible changes in policy, which, though different, refused to uphold cold war. In Germany, Social Democratic politicians had enough influence to shift money from defense spending to domestic programs. Willy Brandt (1913–1992), the Socialist mayor of West Berlin, became foreign minister in 1966 and pursued an end to frigid relations with Communist East Germany. This policy, known as **Ostpolitik**, thus unsettled cold war thinking. It gave West German business leaders what they wanted: "the depoliticization of Germany's foreign trade," as one industrialist put it, and an unlocking of Soviet-bloc consumerism. West German trade with eastern Europe grew rapidly; however, it left the relatively poorer countries of the Soviet bloc strapped with mounting debt—some $45 billion annually by 1970.

To break the cold war stranglehold on international politics, French president Charles de Gaulle poured more money into French nuclear development, withdrew French forces from NATO, and signed trade treaties with the Soviet bloc. Communist China and France also drew closer. However, de Gaulle protected France's good relations with Germany to prevent further encroachments from the Soviet bloc. At home, de Gaulle's government sponsored construction of modern housing and mandated the exterior cleaning of all Parisian buildings—a massive project taking years—to wipe away more than a century of industrial grime. With his haughty and stubborn pursuit of French grandeur, de Gaulle offered the European public an alternative to submissively obeying the superpowers.

The Soviet Union. Brandt's Ostpolitik and de Gaulle's assertiveness had their echoes in Soviet-bloc reforms. Pushing de-Stalinization, the Soviet premier Nikita Khrushchev took the dangerous course of trying to reduce Communist officialdom's privileges. Khrushchev's blunders—notably his humiliation in the Cuban missile crisis, his

ineffectual schemes to improve Soviet agriculture, and his inability to patch the rift with China—were highly visible and led to his ouster in 1964. Nevertheless, the new leadership of Leonid Brezhnev♦ (1909–1982) and Alexei Kosygin♦ (1904–1980) initially continued attempts at reform, encouraging plant managers to turn a profit and allowing the production of televisions, household appliances, and cheap housing to alleviate the discontent of an increasingly better-educated and better-informed citizenry. The government also loosened restrictions to allow cultural and scientific meetings with Westerners, another move that relaxed the cold war atmosphere in the mid-1960s. The Soviet satellites in eastern Europe grasped the economic opportunity presented by Moscow's relaxed posture. Poland allowed private farmers greater freedom to make money, and Hungarian leader János Kádár introduced elements of a market system into the national economy.

In the arts, Soviet-bloc writers continued for a time to thaw the frozen monolith of socialist realism and slavish praise for the Soviet past. Ukrainian poet Yevgeny Yevtushenko exposed Soviet complicity in the Holocaust in *Babi Yar* (1961), a passionate protest against the slaughter of tens of thousands of Jews near Kiev during World War II. Challenging the celebratory nature of socialist art, East Berlin writer Christa Wolf showed a couple tragically divided by the Berlin Wall in her novel *Divided Heaven* (1965). But repression returned later in the 1960s and 1970s, however, as the Soviet government took to bulldozing outdoor art shows, thereby forcing visual artists to hold secret exhibitions in their apartments and even to turn their living spaces into a new kind of art: the installation. Installations include the arrangement of multiple components often including everyday objects in large spaces. Dissident artists' paintings depicted Soviet citizens as worn and tired in grays and other monochromatic color schemes instead of the brightly attired and heroic figures of socialist realism. For their part, writers relied on samizdat culture, a key form of dissident ac-

---

♦**Leonid Brezhnev:** lay oh NEED BREHZH nehf
♦**Alexei Kosygin:** uhl yihk SYAY kuh SEEG ihn

Krusikov Street (1977)
"Always forward, never backward," was what the father of Soviet Communism V. I. Lenin and sub-sequent leaders of the USSR demanded of Soviet citizens. All artists, writers, composers, and per-formers in the USSR, were supposed to follow Communist Party directives in their work, spreading such ideals as found in Lenin's slogan. Dissident artists, however, slyly undermined the Commu-nist message, as in this depiction of Lenin and contemporary Soviets by Eric Bulatov. Despite the accepted socialist realist style of painting, the portrayal shows the leader going forward but the citizens moving in the opposite direction, which can only be called backward. This was just one dissident style among many adopted by dissident artists, who prepared the ground for a full-scale revolt against the Soviet system. It was thus with good reason that the government of the USSR mostly destroyed such works whenever they were displayed in public. *Jane Voorhees Zimmerli Art Museum, Rutgers University. The Norton and Nancy Dodge Collection of Nonconformist Art from the Soviet Union. ©Artists Rights Society (ARS), NY/ADAGP, Paris. Photo: Jack Abraham.*

tivity in which uncensored publications were reproduced by hand and passed from reader to reader, thus building a foundation for the successful resistance of the 1980s.

The United States. In the United States, other issues challenged the cold war for front-page attention. The assassination of President John F. Kennedy in November 1963 shocked the nation and the world. But only momentarily did it still escalating demands for civil rights for African Americans and other minorities. White segregationists mur-dered, maimed, and arrested those attempt-ing to integrate lunch counters, register black voters, or simply march on behalf of freedom. This violent racism was a weak link in the American claim to moral superiority in the cold war, and in response to the murders and destruction, Kennedy had introduced civil

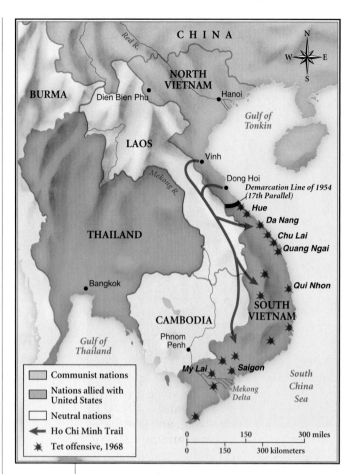

MAP 29.2 The Vietnam War, 1954–1975
The local peoples of Southeast Asia had long resisted incursions by their neighbors. They also resisted French rule from the end of the nineteenth century, never more fiercely than in the war that liberated them after World War II. Ill-prepared by comparison with the French, the Vietnamese nonetheless triumphed in the battle of Dien Bien Phu in 1954. But the Americans soon became involved, trying to stem what they saw as the tide of Communist influence behind the Vietnamese liberation movement. The ensuing war in Vietnam in the 1960s and 1970s spread into neighboring countries, making the region the scene of vast destruction. How were the Vietnamese wars after 1945 related to the struggle between Japan and the United States for resources in the region in the 1930s and in World War II? Or were these two distinct contests?

rights legislation and forced the desegregation of schools and universities. Lyndon B. Johnson (1908–1973), Kennedy's successor, steered the Civil Rights Act through Congress in 1964. This legislation forbade

segregation in public facilities and created the Equal Employment Opportunity Commission (EEOC) to fight job discrimination based on "race, color, national origin, religion, and sex." Southern conservatives had tacked on the provision against sex discrimination in the vain hope that it would doom the bill. Modeling himself on his hero Franklin Roosevelt, Johnson envisioned what he called a Great Society, in which new government programs would improve the chances of the forty million Americans living in poverty. He sponsored myriad reform programs, among them Project Head Start for disadvantaged preschool children and the Job Corps for training youth. Black novelist Ralph Ellison called Johnson "the greatest American president for the poor and the Negroes."

However, the cold war did not go away; in fact, the United States became increasingly embroiled beyond its borders in Vietnam (Map 29.2). After the Geneva settlement in 1954, the United States escalated its commitment to the corrupt and incompetent leaders in non-Communist South Vietnam. North Vietnam, China, and the Soviet Union backed the rebel Vietcong, or South Vietnamese Communists. The strength of the Vietcong seemed to grow daily, and by 1966, the United States had more than half a million soldiers in South Vietnam. Before the war ended in 1975, the United States would drop more bombs on North Vietnam than the Allies had launched on Germany and Japan combined during World War II. Early in the war, Johnson's advisers appeared on television, predicting imminent victory despite mounting U.S. casualties and the need to draft young men, many of them unwilling to go. But after decades of anticolonial struggle, the insurgents rejected a negotiated peace. Confronting growing antiwar sentiment, increasing military costs, and declining popularity, President Johnson announced in March 1968 that he would not run for president again.

The Explosion of Civic Activism

In the midst of cold war, technological transformation, and bloody conflict, a new social activism emerged. Prosperity and the rising benefits of a postindustrial, service-oriented economy made people ever more eager for peace. Students, after two decades of study, did not want to end their lives on faraway battlefields, as their fathers and grandfathers had done. Still other activists—among them minorities and women—simply wanted a fair chance at education, jobs, and political influence. Students, blacks and other minorities, Soviet-bloc citizens, women, environmentalists, and homosexuals sometimes brought their societies to the brink of revolution during what became increasingly fiery protests. Most were against the cold war order, and most wanted to share equally in postindustrial well-being.

Civil Rights. The U.S. civil rights movement expanded its bold activism, and others joined in to make demands for fair treatment. In 1965, César Chávez (1927–1993) led vulnerable Mexican American migrant workers in the California grape agribusiness to strike for better wages and working conditions. Deeply religious and ascetic, Chávez helped Hispanic Americans define their identity and struggle against deportation, inferior schooling, and discrimination.

Meanwhile, the African American civil rights movement took a dramatic turn as urban riots erupted across the United States in 1965 and subsequent summers. Frustrated and angry, many activists changed their struggle into a militant celebration of their race under the banner "Black is beautiful." The issue they faced was one they felt they had in common with decolonizing people: how to shape an identity different from that of white oppressors. Some urged a push for "black power" to reclaim rights instead of begging for them nonviolently. Separatism, not integration, became the goal of still others; small cadres of militants even took up arms, believing that, like decolonizing people elsewhere, they needed to protect themselves against the violent whites around them.

Youth Activism. The 1960s pulsated with young people's activism. As a result of the new turn in black efforts for change, white American university students who had participated in the early stages of the civil rights movement found themselves excluded from leadership positions. Many of them soon joined the swelling protest against techno-

logical change, consumerism, and the Vietnam War. European youth were also feverish for reform. In the mid-1960s, university students in Rome occupied an administration building after right-wing opponents assassinated one of their number during a protest against the 200-to-1 student–teacher ratio. In 1966, Prague students held carnival-like processions, commemorated the tenth anniversary of the 1956 Hungarian uprisings, and took to chanting, "The only good Communist is a dead one." The "situationists" in France called on students to wake up from the slumbering pace of mass society and student life by jolting individuals to action with shocking graffiti and street theater.

Throughout the 1960s, students criticized the traditional university curriculum and flaunted their own countercultural values. They questioned how studying Plato or Dante would help them after graduation. "How to Train Stuffed Geese" was French students' satirical version of the teaching methods inflicted on them. "No professors over forty" and "Don't trust anyone over thirty" were powerful slogans of the day. Long hair, communal living, and a repudiation of personal hygiene announced students' rejection of middle-class values, as did their denunciation of sexual chastity. With the widespread use of the pill, abstinence became unnecessary as a method of birth control, and students made the sexual revolution explicit and public with open promiscuity. Marijuana use became common among students, and amphetamines and barbiturates added to the drug culture, which had its own rituals, songs, and gathering places. Scorned by students, businesses nonetheless made billions of dollars not only by selling blue jeans, dolls dressed as "hippies," natural foods, and drugs but also by packaging and managing the stars of the counterculture.

The Women's Movement. Women's activism erupted across the political spectrum (see "Contrasting Views," page 1160). Working for reproductive rights, women in France helped end the ban on birth control in 1965. More politically conventional middle-class women eagerly responded to the international best seller *The Feminine Mystique*

CONTRASTING VIEWS

Feminist Debates

The feminist movement of the late twentieth century provoked the most pronounced and widespread debate over gender in recorded history. Discussion often reached a heated pitch, as it did in other reform movements of the day. Hardly the single movement described by journalists, feminism had a variety of concerns, often depending on nationality, ethnicity, sexual orientation, and class. These could produce conflict among activists and serious divisions on goals and policies, as the authors of the Combahee River Statement demonstrated (Document 1). At times, concerns over issues like equal opportunity in the workplace were directed at government policies, as in the case of the Soviet worker (Document 2). Italian feminists saw all the disabilities imposed by government as characteristic of larger problems (Document 3), while Germans explicitly connected the cause of feminism to that of environmentalism (Document 4).

1. CRITICIZING FEMINISM

In the United States, black women, like several other minority groups, found themselves marginalized in both the feminist and civil rights movements. In 1977, some of them issued the Combahee River Statement.

Black, other third world, and working women have been involved in the feminist movement from its start, but both outside reactionary forces and racism and elitism within the movement itself have served to obscure our participation. . . .

Black feminist politics also have an obvious connection to movements for Black liberation,

particularly those of the 1960s and 1970s. . . . It was our experience and disillusionment within these liberation movements, as well as experience on the periphery of the white male left, that led to the need to develop a politics that was antiracist, unlike those of white women, and antisexist, unlike those of Black and white men. . . .

Above all else, our politics initially sprang from the shared belief that Black women are inherently valuable, that our liberation is a necessity not as an adjunct to somebody else's but because of our need as human persons for autonomy.

Source: "The Combahee River Collective Statement" in *Feminism in Our Time: The Essential Writings, World War II to the Present,* ed. Miriam Schneir (New York: Vintage, 1994), 177–79.

2. CRITICIZING SOCIALISM

Official policy in the Soviet Union stated that socialism had brought women full equality, eliminating the need for feminism. In the 1970s, however, Russian women in clusters announced their dissatisfaction with so-called equality under socialism. Tatyana Mamonova, the editor of a collection of Russian women's writings such as this from a railroad worker, was ultimately expelled from the USSR.

It is becoming increasingly clear that the current equality means only giving women the right to perform heavy labor . . . [I]n our day the woman, still not freed from the incredible burden of the family, strains herself even harder in the service of society. The situation . . . is true not only in large cities but also in villages. On collective and state farms, women do the hardest and most exhausting work while the men are employed as administrators, agronomists, accountants, warehouse managers, or high-paid tractor and combine drivers. In other words, men do the work that is more interesting and more profitable and does not damage their health.

Source: Tatyana Mamonova, ed., *Women and Russia: Feminist Writings from the Soviet Union* (Boston: Beacon Press, 1984), 8.

3. POLICY AND PATRIARCHY

In Italy, as in the Soviet Union, feminism had an underground quality to it involving mimeographed tracts and graffiti on buildings; women formed their own bookshops and published small newspapers. But others lobbied hard to get legislation on divorce and abortion changed, while in 1976 the Feminist Movement of Rome issued this article in its paper.

Patriarchal society is based on authoritarian-exploitative relationships, and its sexuality is sadomasochistic. The values of power, of the domination of man over the other [woman], are reflected in sexuality, where historically woman is given to man for his use. . . .

The idea of woman as man's property is fundamental to her oppression and she is often the only possession that dominant men allow exploited men to keep. . . .

In other words woman is given to the (exploited) man as compensation for his lack of possessions. . . .

We denounce as the latest form of woman's oppression the idea of a "sexual revolution" where woman is forced to go from being one man's object to being everybody's object, and where sadomasochistic pornography in films, in magazines, in all the forms of mass media that brutalize and violate woman, is bandied about as a triumph of sexual liberty.

Source: "Male Sexuality—Perversion," *Movimento Femminista Romano* (1976), quoted in *Italian Feminist Thought: A Reader*, eds. Paola Bono and Sandra Kemp (Oxford: Blackwell, 1991), 68–69.

4. FEMINISM AND ENVIRONMENTALISM

"Green" feminists took a different approach, such as announced in this "Manifesto of the 'Green' Women." It was originally a 1975 speech made in West Germany in the context of men's landing on the moon and other accomplishments in space.

Man has actually landed on the moon—an admirable feat. . . . We "Green" women . . . believe that men belong to our environment. In order to rescue that environment for our children, we want to confront this man, this adventurer and moon explorer. A female cosmonaut from a so-called socialist republic doesn't justify this energy-wasting enterprise for us at a time when three-fourths of the earth's population is suffering from malnutrition.

Our inability to solve immediate problems may tempt us into escape—to the moon, into careerism, escape into ideologies, into alcohol or other drugs. But one group cannot escape completely: women, society's potential mothers, who must give birth to children, willingly or unwillingly, in this polluted world of ours.

Source: Delphine Brox-Brochot, "Manifesto of the 'Green' Women," in *German Feminism: Readings in Politics and Literature*, eds. Edith Hoshino Altbach et al. (Albany: State University of New York Press, 1984), 314.

QUESTIONS TO CONSIDER

1. Was the feminist movement of the 1960s and 1970s primarily an offshoot of other reform movements of the day, or did it have a character of its own?

2. In what ways was feminism in these decades a unified movement, and in what ways was it a set of multiple movements?

3. What issues are raised by these activists?

Gay Activists in London
The reformist spirit of the 1960s and 1970s changed the focus of homosexuals' activism. Instead of concentrating mostly on legal protection from criminal prosecution, gays and lesbians began affirming a special and positive identity. As other groups who had endured discrimination began making similar affirmations, "identity politics" was born. Critics charged that traditional universal values were sufficient and that homosexuals and others constituted special-interest groups. Gays, women, and ethnic or racial minorities countercharged that the universal values first put forth in the Enlightenment seemed to apply only to a privileged few. In what ways were gays' demonstrations similar to those of women, colonized people, union activists, and civil rights organizers over the past centuries? In what ways did they differ? © Hulton Archive/Getty Images.

(1963) by American journalist Betty Friedan. Pointing to the stagnating talents of many housewives, Friedan helped organize the National Organization for Women (NOW) in 1966 "to bring women into full participation in the mainstream of American society now." NOW advocated equal pay and a variety of other legal and economic reforms. In Sweden, women lobbied to make tasks both at home and in the workplace less gender-segregated, and in these same years a few Soviet women began speaking out against their low and unpaid work that kept the USSR running.

Those engaged in the civil rights and student movements soon realized that many of those protest organizations devalued women just as society at large did. Male activists adopted the leather-jacketed machismo style of their film and rock heroes, but women in the movements were often judged by the status of their male-protester lovers. "A woman was to 'inspire' her man," African American activist Angela Davis complained, adding that women aiming for equality supposedly "wanted to rob [male protesters] of their manhood." A speaker in Frankfurt, West Germany, interrupted a student meeting, demanding "that our problems be discussed substantively. It is no longer enough that women are occasionally allowed to say a few words."

Women also took to the streets on behalf of such issues as abortion rights or the decriminalization of gay and lesbian sexuality (see Gay Activists in London, shown here). Many flouted social conventions in their attire, language, and attitudes. Renouncing brassieres, high-heeled shoes, cosmetics, and other adornments, they spoke openly about taboo subjects such as their sexual feelings and even announced that they had resorted to illegal abortions. This brand of feminist activity was meant to shock polite society—and it did. At a Miss America contest in 1968, women protesters crowned a sheep the new beauty queen. West German women students tossed tomatoes at male protest leaders in defiance of standards for ladylike behavior. Many women of color, however, broke with feminist solidarity and spoke out against the "double jeopardy" of being "black and female." Soon there were concrete changes. In Catholic Italy, feminists won the rights to divorce, to gain access to birth-control information, and to obtain legal abortions. The demand for rights as well as for equal pay, job opportunities, and protection from rape, incest, and battering framed the major legal struggles of thousands of women's groups in the 1970s.

1968: Year of Crisis

The West seethed with protest and calls for reform finally boiled over in 1968. In January, on the first day of Tet, the Vietnamese New Year, the Vietcong and the North Vietnamese attacked more than one hundred South Vietnamese towns and American bases, inflicting heavy casualties. The Tet offensive, as it came to be called, caused many to conclude that the war might be unwinnable and gave the antiwar movement around the world crucial momentum. Meanwhile, in Czechoslovakia, a quieter movement against Soviet cold war domination had taken shape. The atmosphere in that country, as elsewhere, soon became explosive.

Violence Erupts. On April 4, 1968, Martin Luther King Jr. was assassinated by a white racist, and more than a hundred cities in the United States erupted in violence as African Americans vented their anguish and rage. Rejecting the nonviolence of King, formerly pacifist black leaders turned their rhetoric to violence: "Burn, baby, burn," chanted rioters who destroyed the grim inner cities around them. On campuses, strident confrontation over the intertwined issues of war, technology, racism, and sexism closed down classes.

Student dissent was escalating everywhere, but the most dramatic protests occurred in France. In January, students at Nanterre, outside of Paris, had gone on strike, invading administration offices to protest their inferior education and status. They called themselves a proletariat—an exploited working class—and, rejecting the Soviets, considered themselves part of a New Left. When students at the prestigious Sorbonne in Paris took to the streets in protest, police assaulted them. The Parisian middle classes reacted with unexpected sympathy to the student uprising because of their own resentment of bureaucracy. They were also horrified

at seeing the elite and brutal police force—the CRS—beating middle-class students and passersby who expressed their support.

French workers joined in: some nine million went on strike, occupying factories and calling not only for higher wages but also for participation in everyday decision making. To some, the revolt of youth and workers looked as if it might spiral into another French revolution, so unified were the expressions of political alienation. The normally decisive president Charles de Gaulle seemed paralyzed at first, but he soon sent tanks into Paris. In June, he announced a raise for workers, and businesses offered them a strengthened voice in decision making. Many citizens, having grown tired of the street violence, the destruction of so much private property, and the breakdown of services (for example, the garbage was not collected for weeks), began to sympathize with the government instead of the students. Although demonstrations continued throughout June, the student movement in France at least had been closed down. The revolutionary moment had passed.

The Prague Spring. The 1968 revolt in Prague began within the Czechoslovak Communist Party itself. In the autumn of 1967 at a party congress, Alexander Dubček,♦ head of the Slovak branch of the party, had called for more social and political openness. Attacked as an inferior Slovak by the leadership, Dubček nonetheless struck a chord among frustrated party officials, technocrats, and intellectuals; Czechoslovaks began to dream of creating a new society—one based on "socialism with a human face." Party delegates elevated Dubček to the top position, where he quickly changed the Communist style of government, ending censorship, instituting the secret ballot for party elections, and allowing

Prague Spring, 1968

♦**Dubček:** DOOB chehk

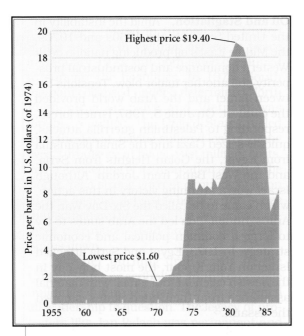

FIGURE 29.1 Fluctuating Oil Prices, 1955–1985
Colonization allowed the Western imperial powers to obtain raw materials at advantageous prices or even without paying at all. Even with decolonization, European and American firms often had such entrenched roots in newly independent economies that they were able to set the terms for trade. OPEC's oil embargo and price hikes of the 1970s were signs of change, which included the exercise of decolonized countries' control over their own resources. Not only did OPEC's action lead to a decade of painful economic downturn, but it also encouraged some European governments to improve public transportation, encourage the production of fuel-efficient cars, and impose policies that would make individual consumers cut back their dependence on oil.

50 percent in Europe and the United States and inflation to soar. By the end of 1973, the inflation rate jumped to over 8 percent in West Germany, 12 percent in France, and 20 percent in Portugal. Eastern-bloc countries, dependent on Soviet oil, fared little better because the West could no longer afford their products and the Soviets boosted the price of their own oil. Skyrocketing interest rates discouraged both industrial investment and consumer buying. With prices, unemployment, and interest rates soaring—an unusual combination of economic conditions dubbed **stagflation**—some in the West came to realize that both energy resources and economic growth had limits. Western Europe drastically cut back on its oil dependence by undertaking conservation, enhancing public transportation, and raising the price of gasoline to encourage the development of fuel-efficient cars.

Dominance of the world by the U.S. bloc deteriorated further. In 1976, Jimmy Carter, a wealthy farmer and governor of Georgia, narrowly won the U.S. presidential election but could do little to return the economy to its pre-Vietnam and pre–oil embargo prosperity. His administration eventually faced an insurmountable crisis in the Middle East. Late in the 1970s, students, clerics, shopkeepers, and unemployed men in Iran began a religious agitation that brought to power the Islamic religious leader Ayatollah Ruhollah Khomeini.◆ Employing audiocassettes to spread his message, he called for a transformation of the country into a truly Islamic society, which meant the renunciation of the Western ways advocated by the shah, who as a result was deposed. In the autumn of 1979, revolutionary supporters of Khomeini took hostages at the American embassy in Teheran and would not release them. The paralysis of the United States in the face of Islamic militancy, along with the soaring inflation following another round of OPEC price hikes, suggested the possibility of a permanent decline of the West.

The Western Bloc Meets Challenges with Reform

As the 1980s opened, stagflation and the realignment of global economic power forced non-Communist governments in the West to put their economic houses in order. On top of the economic challenge was the growing phenomenon of **terrorism**—that is, coordinated and targeted political violence by opposition groups. The unprecedented mix of terrorism, the energy crisis, soaring unemployment, and double-digit inflation sparked the election of conservative politicians, who maintained that decades of supporting a wel-

◆**Khomeini:** koh MAY nee

The Middle East and the Politics of Oil

When Middle Eastern countries took control of the price and volume of oil they sold, Western leaders were taken aback, so thoroughly accustomed were the United States and its allies to setting the conditions of trade. OPEC leaders were lampooned in cartoons as the global economic crisis unfolded. Stagflation hit Western economies hard, while everyone came to terms with the new force of oil in international politics. What attitudes are expressed in this illustration? *Rosen-Albany Times-Union, NY/Rothco.*

"AND ANYWHERE KHALID WENT, THE LAMB WAS SURE TO GO!"

fare state were at the heart of economic problems. Across the West, tough times intensified feelings that the unemployed and new immigrants from around the world were responsible for the downturn in postindustrial progress. Nineteenth-century emphases on competitiveness, individualism, and revival of privilege for the "best circles" replaced the twentieth-century trend toward advancing economic democracy to combat totalitarianism. Postindustrial society changed political course.

Terrorism. The terrorism at the U.S. embassy in Iran was part of a trend that had actually begun in the West. In the 1970s, terrorist bands in Europe responded to the restoration of political order and the worsening economic conditions with kidnappings, bank robberies, bombings, and assassinations. Disaffected and well-to-do youth, steeped in extreme theories that said Western society was decaying, often joined these groups. Eager to bring down the Social Democratic coalition that led West Germany throughout the 1970s, the Red Army Faction assassinated prominent businessmen, judges, and other public officials. Practiced in assassinations of public figures and random shootings of pedestrians, Italy's Red Brigades kidnapped and then murdered the head of the dominant Christian Democrats in 1978.

Advocates of independence for the Basque nation in northern Spain assassinated Spanish politicians and police officers.

In Britain, nationalist and religious violence in the 1970s pitted the Catholics in Northern Ireland against the dominant Protestants. Catholics experienced job discrimination and a lack of civil rights. Demonstrators urged union with the Irish Republic, and with protest escalating, the British government sent in troops. On January 30, 1972, which became known as Bloody Sunday, British troops fired at demonstrators and killed thirteen, setting off a cycle of violence that left five hundred dead in that single year. Protestants fearful of losing their dominant position combated a reinvigorated Irish Republican Army (IRA), which carried out bombings and assassinations to achieve the union of the two Irelands in order to end

Nationalist Movements of the 1970s

Soldiers and Civilians in Northern Ireland
Separatist, civil rights, and terrorist movements made everyday life unpredictably dangerous in the last third of the twentieth century, as activists increasingly directed their violence against ordinary people. The world wars had often targeted civilians, and those leading internal struggles did so even when the declared wars were over. In Belfast, Northern Ireland, British troops fought to put down the Irish Republican Army and restore unity. Civilians were often drawn into the conflict. It was only late in the 1990s that both sides called a halt to the killing and agreed to negotiate. How did the politics of violence in the late-twentieth-century West differ from or resemble the politics of violence in the thirty years before World War I? *Brian Aris/Camera Press London.*

the oppression of Catholics (see Soldiers and Civilians in Northern Ireland, above).

Terrorists failed in their goal of overturning the existing democracies, and, sorely tried as it was, parliamentary government scored a few important successes in the 1970s. The Iberian Peninsula, suffering under dictatorship since the 1930s, regained its freedom and set out on a course of greater prosperity. The death of Spain's Francisco Franco in 1975 ended more than three decades of dictatorial rule. Franco's handpicked successor, King Juan Carlos, surprisingly steered his nation to Western-style constitutional monarchy, facing down threatened military coups. Portugal and Greece also ousted right-wing dictators, thus paving the way for their integration into western

Europe and for substantial economic growth. Despite these democratic advances, a consensus emerged from the economic crisis, political terrorism, and failures in leadership that the West was in trouble.

Thatcher Reshapes Political Culture.
More than anyone else, Margaret Thatcher (b. 1925), the outspoken leader of Britain's Conservative Party from 1979 to 1990, reshaped the West's political and economic ideas to meet the crisis. Coming to power amid continuing economic decline, revolt in Northern Ireland, and labor unrest, the combative prime minister eschewed the politics of consensus building. Believing that only a resurgence of private enterprise could revive the sluggish British economy, Thatcher lashed

out at union leaders, Labour Party politicians, and people who received welfare-state benefits as enemies of British prosperity. Her anti-welfare-state policies struck a revolutionary chord, and she called herself "a nineteenth-century liberal" in reference to the economic individualism of that age. In her view, business leaders and entrepreneurs were the key members of society. Although immigrants often worked for the lowest wages and contributed to profits, she characterized as inferior the unemployed and those who came from Britain's former colonies, saying that neither group contributed to national wealth. Under Thatcher, even workers blamed labor leaders or newcomers for Britain's trauma.

The policies of "Thatcherism" were based on monetarist, or supply-side, theories associated most prominently with U.S. economist Milton Friedman. Monetarists contend that inflation results when government pumps money into the economy at a rate higher than a nation's economic growth rate. Thus, they advocate a tight rein on the money supply to keep prices from rising rapidly. Supply-side economists maintain that the economy as a whole flourishes when businesses grow and their prosperity "trickles down" throughout the society. To implement such theories, the British government cut income taxes on the wealthy to spur new investment, increasing sales taxes to compensate for the lost revenue. The result was an increased burden on working people, who bore the brunt of the sales tax. Thatcher also vigorously pruned government intervention in the economy: she sold publicly owned businesses and utilities such as British Airways, refused to prop up "outmoded" industries such as coal mining, and slashed education and health programs. As their influence spread through the West and the world, the package of economic policies came to be known as **neoliberalism** (see Margaret Thatcher's Economic Vision, on page 1172).

In the first three years of Thatcher's government, the British economy did not respond well to her shock treatment. The quality of universities, public transportation, highways, and hospitals deteriorated, and leading scholars and scientists left the country in a renewal of the brain drain. In addition, social unity fragmented. In 1981, blacks and Asians rioted in major cities. Thatcher's popularity sagged. She revived it by going to war with Argentina in 1982 over ownership of the Falkland Islands off the Argentinian coast. When inflation ultimately dissipated, historians and economists debated whether the change resulted from Thatcher's policies or from the lack of spending power that burdened the poor and unemployed. In any case, Thatcher's program became the standard. Britain had been one of the pioneers of the welfare state, and now it pioneered in changing course.

In Thatcher's Footsteps. In the United States, Ronald Reagan (b. 1911) followed a similar road to combat the economic crisis. Dividing citizens into the good and the bad, Reagan vowed to promote the values of the "moral majority," which included commitment

Margaret Thatcher at Conservative Party Conference (1983)
As British prime minister for more than a decade, Margaret Thatcher profoundly influenced the course of modern government by rolling back the welfare state. Thatcher was convinced and convinced others that the welfare state did not advance society and its citizens but made them lazy when it rewarded useless people with handouts. Her tenure in office encouraged other politicians, from Ronald Reagan to Helmut Kohl, to execute similar cuts in social programs. More than any other head of state during this period she set the course for domestic policy into the twenty-first century. Why was cutting social programs attractive to voters late in the twentieth century? © Bettmann/Corbis.

Margaret Thatcher's Economic Vision

Margaret Thatcher, Britain's longest serving prime minister, changed Western thinking about the importance of the welfare state. Many Europeans saw the welfare state as a mainstay of democracy, which would alleviate the hardships that had turned workers toward either socialism, from Bismarck's time onward, or toward Mussolini's and Hitler's fascism, during the difficult years between the difficult interwar years. Thatcher, however, thought programs to provide healthcare, education, and housing coddled the lazy. She thought the money for such programs should be invested in private industry, to produce a profit and to encourage more investment and greater productivity. Here she outlines her thoughts on public spending to members of the Conservative Party.

. . . I and my colleagues say that to add to public spending takes away the very money and resources that industry needs to stay in business, let alone to expand. Higher public spending, far from curing unemployment, can be the very vehicle that loses jobs and causes bankruptcies in trade and commerce. That is why we warned local authorities that since rates [taxes] are frequently the biggest tax that industry now faces, increases in them can cripple local businesses. . . .

That is why I stress that if those who work in public authorities take for themselves large pay increases, they leave less to be spent on equipment and new buildings. That in turn deprives the private sector of the orders it needs, especially some of those industries in the hard pressed regions. Those in the public sector have a duty to those in the private sector not to take out so much in pay that they cause others' unemployment. That is why we point out that every time high wage settlements in nationalised monopolies lead to higher charges for telephones, electricity, coal, and water, they can drive companies out of business and cost other people their jobs.

If spending money like water was the answer to our country's problems, we would have no problems right now. If ever a nation has spent, spent, spent, and spent again, ours has. Today that dream is over. All of that money has got us nowhere, but it still has to come from somewhere. Those who urge us to relax the squeeze, to spend yet more money indiscriminately in the belief that it will help the unemployed and the small businessman, are not being kind or compassionate or caring. They are not the friends of the unemployed or the small business. They are asking us to do again the very things that caused the problems in the first place. . . .

I am accused of lecturing or preaching about this. I suppose it is a critic's way of saying, "Well, we know it is true, but we have to carp at something." I do not care about that. But I do care about the future of free enterprise, the jobs and exports it provides, and the independence it brings to our people.

Source: Juliet S. Thompson and Wayne C. Thompson, ed., Margaret Thatcher: Prime Minster Indomitable (Boulder: Westview, 1994), 230-31.

to Bible-based religion, dedication to work, sexual restraint, and unquestioned patriotism. Chastizing so-called spendthrift and immoral "liberals," he introduced "Reaganomics"—a program of whopping income tax cuts for the wealthy combined with massive reductions in federal spending for student loans, school lunch programs, and mass transit. Like Thatcher, Reagan believed that tax cuts would lead to investment and a reinvigo-rated economy; federal outlays for welfare programs, which he felt only encouraged bad Americans to be lazy, would generally be unnecessary thereafter.

In foreign policy, Reagan spent most of his time in office warning of the Communist threat. The longtime cold warrior labeled the Soviet Union an "evil empire" and demanded huge military budgets to counter the Soviet arms buildup of the 1970s. Reagan announced the Strategic Defense Initiative (SDI), known popularly as Star Wars, a costly plan to put lasers in space to defend the United States against a nuclear attack. The combination of tax cuts and military expansion had pushed the federal budget deficit to $200 billion by 1986.

Other western European leaders also limited welfare-state benefits in the face of stagflation, though without Thatcher's and Reagan's socially divisive rhetoric. West German leader Helmut Kohl, who took power in 1982, reduced welfare spending, froze government wages, and cut corporate taxes. By 1984, the inflation rate was only 2 percent and West Germany had acquired a 10 percent share of world trade. Unlike Thatcher, Kohl did not fan class and racial hatreds. The politics of divisiveness was particularly unwise in Germany, where terrorism on the left and on the right continued to flourish. Moreover, the legacy of Nazism loomed menacingly. When an unemployed German youth said of immigrant Turkish workers, "Let's gas 'em," the revival of Nazi language appalled many in Germany's middle class rather than gaining their support.

France took a different political path, though by 1981 stagflation had put more than 1.5 million people out of work and reduced the economic growth rate to an anemic 1.2 percent. The French elected a socialist president, François Mitterrand (1916–1996), who nationalized banks and certain industries and stimulated the economy by wage increases and social spending—the opposite of Thatcherism. New public buildings like museums and libraries arose along with new subway lines and improved public transport. Financial leaders reacted by sending capital abroad rather than investing it at home, and in Mitterrand's second term, conservatives captured the majority of seats in the assembly, which entitled them to choose the prime minister. When the conservative prime minister Jacques Chirac succeeded Mitterrand as president, he adopted neoliberal policies. Repercussions similar to those elsewhere in Europe emerged as the politically racist National Front Party won 10 percent and sometimes more of the vote with promises to deport African and Middle Eastern immigrants and cut French ties with nonwhite nations.

Revival in Smaller States. Meanwhile, a cluster of smaller states without heavy defense commitments enjoyed increasing prosperity, though many slashed away at welfare programs. In Spain, tourist dollars helped rebuild the southern cities of Grenada and Córdoba, and the country joined the Common Market in 1986. In Ireland, a surge of investment in education for high-tech jobs combined with low wage rates to attract much new business to the country in the 1990s. Prosperity and the increasingly unacceptable death toll led to a political rapprochement between Ireland and Northern Ireland in 1999. Austria prospered, too, in part by reducing government pensions and aid to business. Austrian chancellor Franz Vranitsky summed up the changed focus of government in the 1980s and 1990s: "In Austria, the shelter that the state has given to almost everyone—employee as well as entrepreneur—has led . . . a lot of people [to] think not only what they can do to solve a problem but what the state can do. . . . This needs to change." The century-long growth of the welfare state seemed to be over by the 1990s.

Almost alone, Sweden maintained a full array of social programs for everyone. The government also offered each immigrant a choice of subsidized housing in neighborhoods inhabited primarily by Swedes or primarily by people from the immigrant's native land. Such programs were expensive: the tax rate on income over $46,000 was 80 percent. Despite a highly productive workforce, Sweden dropped from fourth to fourteenth place among nations in per capita income by 1998. Although the Swedes reduced their costly dependence on foreign oil by cutting consumption in half between 1976 and 1986, their welfare state came to seem extreme to many citizens. As elsewhere, immigrants were cast as a major threat to the country: "How long will it be before our Swedish children will have to turn their faces toward Mecca?" ran one politician's campaign speech in 1993.

Collapse of Communism in the Soviet Bloc

Beginning in 1985 reform came to the Soviet Union as well, but instead of fortifying the economy, it provoked more rebellion. Within four years, communism collapsed throughout the Soviet bloc. Reform came at a time of ongoing protest by workers, artists, and intellectuals. Communications, international trade, and democratic movements were pulling apart a vast region that communism had structured for almost half a century. A deteriorating economy and a corrupt system of political and economic management prevented any kind of cure. Years of stagnant and then negative growth led to a deteriorating standard of living. After working a full day, Soviet homemakers stood in long lines to obtain basic commodities; housing and food shortages necessitated the three-generation household, in which grandparents took over tedious homemaking tasks from their working children and grandchildren. "There is no special skill to this," a seventy-three-year-old grandmother and former garbage collector remarked. "You just stand in line and wait." Even so, people often went away empty-handed as basic household supplies like soap disappeared instantly from stores. One cheap and readily available product—vodka—often formed the center of people's social lives. Alcoholism reached crisis levels, diminishing productivity and tremendously straining the nation's morale.

Mikhail Gorbachev Attempts Reform. In 1985 a new leader, Mikhail Gorbachev, unexpectedly opened an era of change. The son of peasants, Gorbachev had risen through the party ranks as an agricultural specialist and had traveled abroad to gain a firsthand glimpse of life in the West. He saw that economic stagnation had many ramifications. Ordinary people decided not to have children, and fertility fell below replacement levels throughout the Soviet bloc, except for the Muslim areas of Soviet Central Asia. The country was forced to import massive amounts of grain because 20 to 30 percent of the grain that was produced in the USSR rotted before it could be harvested or shipped to market, so great was the inefficiency of the state-directed economy. Industrial pollution, spewed out by enterprises responsible only for meeting production quotas, reached scandalous dimensions. A massive and privileged party bureaucracy hobbled innovation and failed to achieve socialism's professed goal of a decent standard of living for working people. To

match American military growth, the Soviet Union diverted 15 to 20 percent of its gross national product (more than double the U.S. proportion) to armaments, further crippling the economy's chances of raising living standards. As this combustible mix of problems heated up, a new generation was coming of age that had no memory of World War II or Stalin's purges. One Russian observer found members of the younger generation "cynical but less afraid." "They believe in nothing," a mother said of Soviet youth in 1984.

Gorbachev knew from experience and travels to western Europe that the Soviet system was woefully inadequate, and he quickly proposed several unusual programs that went hand in hand. A crucial economic reform, **perestroika** ("restructuring"), aimed to reinvigorate the Soviet economy by improving productivity, increasing the rate of capital investment, encouraging the use of up-to-date technology, and gradually introducing such market features as prices and profits. The complement to economic change was the policy of **glasnost** (usually translated as "openness" or "publicity"), which called for disseminating "wide, prompt, and frank information" and for allowing Soviet citizens new measures of free speech (see Gorbachev's statements on reform, opposite). When officials complained that glasnost threatened their status, Gorbachev replaced more than a third of the Communist Party's leadership in the first months of his administration. The pressing need for glasnost became most evident after the Chernobyl♦ catastrophe in 1986, when a nuclear reactor exploded and spewed radioactive dust into the atmosphere. Bureaucratic cover-ups delayed the spread of information about the accident, with lethal consequences for people living near the plant.

After Chernobyl, even the Communist Party and Marxism-Leninism were opened to public criticism. Party meetings suddenly included complaints about the highest leaders and their policies. Television shows adopted the outspoken methods of American investigative reporting; one program showed an interview with an executioner of political prisoners and exposed the plight of

---

♦**Chernobyl:** chur NOH buhl

Mikhail Gorbachev on Reform in the USSR

Some people—especially Westerners—have interpreted Gorbachev's reforms as noble and enlightened, opening the way to free markets and free speech. Others, especially in the Soviet Union, saw him as simply another member of the Communist establishment, hoping to prop up a rotten system. "A flatterer," one critic called him, "who can live for free in luxurious villas at our expense." For such critics Gorbachev's reforms were merely machinations by a Soviet leader hoping to boost productivity so that there would be more to siphon off. The following passage from Gorbachev's 1987 book on perestroika reveals the complex relationship between Gorbachev's program and the Communist status quo.

Perestroika is closely connected with socialism as a system. That side of the matter is being widely discussed, especially abroad, and our talk about perestroika won't be entirely clear if we don't touch upon that aspect.

Does perestroika mean that we are giving up socialism or at least some of its foundations? Some ask this question with hope, others with misgiving.

There are people in the West who would like to tell us that socialism is in a deep crisis and has brought our society to a dead end. That's how they interpret our critical analysis of the situation at the end of the seventies and beginning of the eighties. We have only one way out, they say: to adopt capitalist methods of economic management and social patterns, to drift toward capitalism.

They tell us that nothing will come of perestroika within the framework of our system. They say we should change this system and borrow from the experience of another socio-political system. To this they add that, if the Soviet Union takes this path and gives up its socialist choice, close links with the West will supposedly become possible. They go so far as to claim that the October 1917 Revolution was a mistake which almost completely cut off our country from world social progress.

To put an end to all the rumors and speculations that abound in the West about this, I would like to point out once again that we are conducting all our reforms in accordance with the socialist choice. We are looking within socialism, rather than outside it, for the answers to all the questions that arise. We assess our successes and errors alike by socialist standards. Those who hope that we shall move away from the socialist path will be greatly disappointed. Every part of our program of perestroika—and the program as a whole, for that matter—is fully based on the principle of more socialism and more democracy.

More socialism means a more dynamic pace and creative endeavor, more organization, law and order, more scientific methods and initiative in economic management, efficiency in administration, and a better and materially richer life for the people.

More socialism means more democracy, openness and collectivism in everyday life, more culture and humanism in production, social and personal relations among people, more dignity and self-respect for the individual.

More socialism means more patriotism and aspiration to noble ideals, more active civic concern about the country's internal affairs and about their positive influence on international affairs.

In other words, more of all those things which are inherent in socialism and in the theoretical precepts which characterize it as distinct socioeconomic formation.

We will proceed toward better socialism rather than away from it. We are saying this honestly, without trying to fool our own people of the world. Any hopes that we will begin to build a different, non-socialist society and go over to the other camp are unrealistic and futile. Those in the West who expect us to give up socialism will be disappointed. It is high time they understood this, and, even more importantly, proceeded from that understanding in practical relation with the Soviet Union.

Source: Mikhail Gorbachev, *New Thinking for Our Country and the World* (New York: Harper & Row: 1987), 36-37.

Gorbachevs and Reagans at the Ranch
Ronald Reagan raised the temperature of the cold war with a massive arms buildup in the 1980s that caused the U.S. budget deficit to soar. When Mikhail Gorbachev came to power in the USSR, he changed course, encouraging freer speech, seeking innovation in the economy, and reducing cold war tensions. The two leaders' regular meetings helped slow down the arms race, but Gorbachev's policies also inadvertently helped bring down the Soviet system of eastern European satellites. How is this photograph related to the end of the cold war? *Ruelas, L.A. Daily News/Sygma.*

Glasnost and perestroika dramatically affected superpower relations as well. Recognizing how severely the cold war arms race was draining Soviet resources, Gorbachev almost immediately began scaling back missile production. His unilateral actions gradually won over Ronald Reagan. In 1985, the two leaders initiated a personal relationship and began defusing the cold war. "I bet the hard-liners in both our countries are bleeding when we shake hands," said the jovial Reagan at the conclusion of one meeting. In early 1989, Gorbachev at last withdrew his country's forces from the debilitating war in Afghanistan, and by the end of the year the United States started to cut back its own vast military buildup.

Rebellion in Poland. As Gorbachev's reforms in the USSR started spiraling out of his control, they did so in an atmosphere of rising dissent across the Soviet bloc, but most notably in Poland. Already in the summer of 1980, Poles had reacted furiously to government-increased food prices by going on strike. As the protest spread, workers at the Gdańsk shipyards, led by electrician Lech Walesa and crane operator Anna Walentynowicz, created an independent labor movement called **Solidarity**. The organization soon embraced much of the adult population, including a million members of the Communist Party. Both intellectuals and the Catholic church, long in the forefront of opposition to socialist secularization, supported Solidarity workers as they occupied factories in protest against inflation, the scarcity of food, and other deteriorating conditions of everyday life. The members of Solidarity waved Polish flags and paraded giant portraits of the Virgin Mary and Pope John Paul II (b. 1920)—a Polish native.

Having achieved mass support at home and worldwide sympathy through media coverage, Solidarity leaders insisted that the

Leningrad's homeless children. Instead of publishing made-up letters praising the great Soviet state, newspapers were flooded with real ones complaining of shortages and abuse. One outraged "mother of two" protested that the cost-cutting policy of reusing syringes in hospitals was a source of AIDS. "Why should little kids have to pay for the criminal actions of our Ministry of Health?" she asked. Debate and factions arose across the political spectrum. In the fall of 1987, one of Gorbachev's erstwhile allies, Boris Yeltsin, quit the governing Politburo after denouncing perestroika as insufficient to produce real reform. Yeltsin's political daring, which in the past would have consigned him to oblivion (or Siberia), inspired others to organize in opposition to the crumbling ruling orthodoxy. By the spring of 1989, in a remarkably free balloting in Moscow's local elections, not a single Communist was chosen.

government recognize it as an independent union—a radical demand under communism. As food became scarce and prices rose, tens of thousands of women marched in the streets crying, "We're hungry!" They, too, protested working conditions, but as both workers and the only caretakers of home life, it was the scarcity of food that sent them into the streets. The Communist Party teetered on collapse, until the police and the army, with Soviet support, imposed a military government and in the winter of 1981 outlawed Solidarity. Continued efforts by reporters and dissidents, using global communications, kept Solidarity alive as a force both inside and outside of Poland. Stern and puritanical, General Wojciech Jaruzelski took over as the head of Poland's new regime in 1981, but the general could not push repression too far: he needed new loans from the U.S.-led bloc to keep the sinking Polish economy afloat. Workers, additionally, kept meeting, creating a new culture outside the official Soviet arts and newscasts. Poets read dissident verse to overflow crowds, and university professors lectured to Solidarity members on such forbidden topics as Polish resistance in World War II. Ongoing activism in Poland set the stage for communism's downfall.

The Revolutions of 1989. The year 1989 has been designated the twentieth century's *annus mirabilis*, or year of miracles, because of the sudden and unexpected disintegration of Communist power. Inspired by Gorbachev's visit to China's capital, Beijing, in the spring of 1989 thousands of students massed in the city's Tiananmen Square, the world's largest public square, to demand democracy. They used telex machines and e-mail to rush their messages to the international community, and they effectively conveyed their goals through the cameras that Western television trained on them. China's aged Communist leaders, while pushing economic modernization and even allowing market operations, refused to consider the introduction of democracy. As workers began joining the pro-democracy forces, the government crushed the movement and executed as many as a thousand rebels.

The protests in Tiananmen Square were galvanizing nonetheless. In June 1989, the Polish government, weakened by its own bungling of the economy and lacking Soviet support for further repression, held free parliamentary elections. Solidarity candidates overwhelmingly defeated the Communists, and in early 1990, Walesa became president, hastening Poland's rocky transition to a market economy. Gorbachev pointedly reversed the Brezhnev Doctrine, refusing to interfere in the political course of another nation. As it became evident that the Soviet Union would not intervene in Poland, the fall of communism repeated itself in country after country.

Communism collapsed first in Poland and then in Hungary because of those countries' early introduction of free-market ingredients. In Hungary, which had experimented with "market socialism" since the 1960s, even officials began to realize that political democracy had to accompany economic freedom. Citizens lobbied against ecologically unsound projects like the construction of a new dam. They encouraged boycotts of Communist holidays and on March 15, 1989, they commemorated instead the anniversary of the Hungarian uprising—the "battle of the holidays" it was called. Finally, when these popular demands for liberalization led the Parliament in the fall of 1989 to dismiss the Communist Party as the official ruling institution, people tore down Soviet and Communist symbols across the country.

The most potent symbol of a divided Europe—the Berlin Wall—stood in the midst of a divided Germany. East Germans had attempted to escape over the wall for decades, and since the early 1980s dissidents had held peace vigils in cities across East Germany. In the summer of 1989, crowds of East Germans flooded the borders of the crumbling Soviet bloc, and hundreds of thousands of protesters rallied throughout the fall against the regime. Satellite television brought them visions of postindustrial prosperity and of free and open public debate in West Germany. The crowds intensified in November, when Gorbachev, taken as a hero by many, visited the country. On November 9, an ambiguous statement from the government encouraged guards to allow free passage across the wall. Protest turned to festive holiday: West Berliners handed out bananas, a consumer good that had been in short supply in the Eastern zone, and that fruit became the unofficial symbol of a newfound liberation. As they strolled freely

Reunited Berliners Welcome the New Year.
On New Year's Eve, 1989, Berliners—and indeed supporters from around the world—celebrated the fall of the Berlin wall and the prospect of a new Germany. The exuberant crowd tore the Communist seal from the flag and then hoisted it above the Brandenburg Gate as fireworks added to the intense emotion of the moment. Disposing of the remnants of Communism lay in the future, and for many the transition would prove difficult. Rebuilding Berlin after Communism, like the rebuilding of most of eastern Europe, lasted into the twenty-first century.
Ullstein-Boening, Berlin.

in the streets, East Berliners saw firsthand the goods available in a successful postindustrial society. Soon thereafter, citizens—east and west—released years of frustration by assaulting the Berlin Wall with sledgehammers and bringing home chunks as souvenirs. The government finished the wall's complete destruction in the fall of 1990.

In Czechoslovakia, which after 1968 had been firmly restored to Soviet-style rule, people also watched the progress of glasnost expectantly. Persecuted, dissidents had nonetheless maintained their critique of Communist rule. In an open letter to the Czechoslovak Communist Party leadership, playwright Václav Havel accused Marxist-Leninist rule of making people materialist and indifferent to civic life. In 1977, Havel, along with a group of

fellow intellectuals and workers, signed Charter 77, a public protest against the regime that resulted in the arrest of the signers. In the mid-1980s these dissidents watched Gorbachev on television calling for free speech, though never mentioning reform in Czechoslovakia. Demonstrators protested in the streets for democracy, but the government cracked down by turning the police on them, arresting Havel again in January 1989 for commemorating the death of Jan Palach. The turning point came in November 1989 when Alexander Dubček, leader of the Prague Spring of 1968, addressed the crowds in Prague's Wenceslas Square with a call for the ouster of Stalinists from the government after the police had beaten students. Almost immediately, Communist leadership resigned. Capping the country's "velvet revolution," as it became known for its lack of bloodshed, the formerly Communist-dominated parliament elevated the dissident Havel to the presidency.

The world's attention now fastened on an unfolding political drama in Romania. From the mid-1960s on, Nicolae Ceaușescu♦ had ruled as the harshest dictator in Communist Europe since Stalin. In the name of modernization, he destroyed whole villages; to build up the population, he outlawed contraceptives and abortions, a restriction that led to the abandonment of tens of thousands of children. He preached the virtues of a very slim body so that he could cut rations and use the savings on his pet projects such as buying up private castles and other property. Most Romanians lived in utter poverty as Ceaușescu determined to channel almost all the country's resources into building himself an enormous palace in Bucharest. To this end, he tore down entire neighborhoods and dozens of historical buildings, and so much did he torture any opponents that the gaudy project seemed to have unanimous support. Yet in early December 1989, an opposition movement rose up and workers kept up a string of demonstrations against the dictatorial government. Most of the army rose up, too, and crushed the forces loyal to Ceaușescu. On Christmas Day, viewers watched on television as the dictator and his wife were tried by a military court and then executed. For many, the death of Ceaușescu meant that the very worst of communism was over.

Homeless Romanian Children (1995)
These children were among the many who lived without families around the railroad station in Romania's capital city, Bucharest. Nicolae Ceaușescu's regime prohibited birth control and abortion in order to increase the supply of workers while simultaneously cutting back on food rations. The redirected funds were then used on lavish homes for Ceaușescu and his family. Children were the victims of this policy, even after Ceaușescu was overthrown, as families simply abandoned children they could not support. In order to survive, the children scavenged, stole, begged, and did small tasks. They often slept on baggage carts at the railroad station (like the children in this photograph) — never losing their haunted expressions. Young children in orphanages sometimes fared better, especially if they were adopted by couples from other countries. ©*Barry Lewis/Corbis.*

> **Review:** What factors led to the collapse of communism in the Soviet bloc?

♦**Nicolae Ceaușescu:** nee koh LY chow SHEHS koo

Conclusion

The fall of the Berlin Wall in 1989 symbolized the end of the cold war, even though the USSR still stood as a bulwark of communism. Collapse of communism in the Soviet satellites was an utter surprise, for U.S.-bloc analysts had erroneously reported throughout the 1980s that the Soviet empire was in dangerously robust health. But no one should have been unaware of dissent or economic discontent. Since the 1960s, a surge of rebellion among youth, ethnic and racial minorities, and women condemned conditions across the West, along with criticizing the threat posed by the cold war. By the early 1980s, wars in Vietnam and Afghanistan,

MAPPING THE WEST The Collapse of Communism in Europe, 1989–1990
The 1989 overthrow of the Communist party in the USSR satellite countries of Eastern Europe occurred with surprising rapidity. The transformation began in Poland when Polish voters tossed out Communist party leaders in June 1989, and then accelerated in September when thousands of East Germans fled to Hungary, Poland, and Czechoslovakia. Between October and December, communist regimes were replaced in East Germany, Czechoslovakia, Bulgaria, and Romania. Within three years the Baltic States would declare their independence, the USSR itself would dissolve, and the breakup of Yugoslavia would lead to war in the Balkans.

protests against privations in the Soviet bloc, the power of oil-producing states, and the growing political force of Islam had weakened superpower preeminence. Reformers like Margaret Thatcher, Ronald Reagan, and Mikhail Gorbachev tried with varying degrees of success to put their postindustrial and cold war houses in order. The first two were successful, while Gorbachev brought on collapse by introducing glasnost and pere-

stroika—each a policy aimed at political and economic change.

Glasnost and perestroika were supposed to bring about the high levels of postindustrial prosperity enjoyed outside the Soviet bloc. Across the West, including the USSR, an unprecedented technological development had transformed businesses, the exploration of space, and the functioning of government. It also had an enormous impact on everyday life. Work changed, as society reached a stage called postindustrial, in which the service sector predominated. New patterns of family life, new relationships among the generations, and revised standards for sexual behavior also characterized these years. But it was only in the United States and western Europe that the consumer benefits of postindustrialization had reached ordinary people, for the attainment of a thoroughgoing consumer, service, and high-tech society demanded levels of efficiency, coordination, and cooperation that had not been reached in the Soviet bloc. For the most part, the old coercion that drove rapidly industrializing economies still prevailed.

There were complaints everywhere, nonetheless, about the dramatic changes that postindustrial society entailed and, ironically, about its failure to materialize sufficiently. The protesters of the late 1960s addressed postindustrial society's stubborn problems: concentrations of bureaucratic and industrial power, social inequality, environmental degradation, even uncertainty about humankind's future. In the Soviet sphere, these protests never stopped but were never heeded until the collapse of Soviet domination of eastern Europe in 1989. Soon communism would be overturned in the USSR itself. However, the triumph of democracy in the former Soviet empire opened an era of painful adjustment, impoverishment, and violence for hundreds of millions of people. Ending the cold war, it also accelerated the process of globalization.

Suggested References

The Revolution in Technology

Wartime technological development came to have profound consequences for the peacetime lives of individuals and for society. The works listed here describe the new technologies and analyze their importance, with authors divided on whether the new developments should be feared or embraced. Fordham University's history Web site has a section on recent developments in science and technology.

Bauer, Martin W., and George Gaskell, eds. *Biotechnology: The Making of a Global Controversy.* 2002.

Fordam University, Internet Modern History Sourcebook: **http://www.fordham.edu/ halsall/mod/modsbook59.html**.

Hecht, Gabrielle. *The Radiance of France: Nuclear Power and National Identity after World War II.* 1998.

Natalicchi, Giorgio. *Wiring Europe: Re-Shaping the European Telecommunications Regime.* 2001.

Singer, Edward Nathan. *The Twentieth Century Revolution in Technology.* 1998.

*Stanworth, Michelle, ed. *Reproductive Technologies: Gender, Motherhood, and Medicine.* 1987.

Postindustrial Society and Culture

Changes in the way people worked became striking in the 1960s, causing social observers to analyze the social and cultural meaning of the transformation. Many critics agree that technology's creation of a postindustrial workplace changed not only the way people worked but also how they lived in families and interacted with peers.

Evans, Christopher. *The Micro Millennium.* 1979.

Hochschild, Arlie. *The Time Bind: When Work Becomes Home and Home Becomes Work.* 1997.

Proctor, Robert. *Cancer Wars: The Politics behind What We Know and Don't Know about Causes and Trends.* 1994.

Ramet, Sabrina P., and Gordana P. Crnković, eds. *Kazaaam! Splat! Ploof! The American Impact on European Culture since 1945.* 2003.

Roulleau-Berger, Laurence. *Youth and Work in the Post-Industrial City of North America and Europe.* 2003.

Sinfield, Alan. *Literature, Politics, and Culture in Post-war Britain.* 1989.

Protesting Cold War Conditions

Historians look to domestic politics, international events, and social change to capture the texture of the tumultuous 1960s. The momentous changes on so many fronts are beginning to receive synthetic treatment in books such as Suri's, which connects the move for détente with domestic protest around the world. The Martin Luther King Web site introduces visitors to the biography, speeches, sermons, and major life events of the slain civil rights leader.

*Dubček, Alexander. *Hope Dies Last: The Autobiography of Alexander Dubček.* 1993.

*Primary source.

Fink, Carole et al., eds. *1968: The World Transformed.* 1998.

*Guy-Sheftall, Beverly, ed. *Words of Fire: An Anthology of African-American Feminist Thought.* 1995.

*Lévi-Strauss, Claude. *Tristes Tropiques.* 1961.

The Martin Luther King Jr. Papers Project at Stanford University: `http://www.stanford.edu/group/King`.

Ross, Kristin. *May '68 and Its Afterlives.* 2003.

Suri, Jeremi. *Power and Protest: Global Revolution and the Rise of Détente.* 2003.

Varon, Jeremy. *Bringing the War Home: The Weather Underground, the Red Army Faction, and Revolutionary Violence in the Sixties and Seventies.* 2004.

The Erosion of Superpower Mastery Ends the Cold War

As the superpowers continued their standoff, historians found that myriad global changes affected their status and that protest continued at home. Many interesting Web sites explore the development of green parties over the past three decades, the most inclusive being that of the global organization with links to green parties of all continents and countries. Protest also continued in the Soviet bloc: the dissident art of the Soviet Union is striking for its deft and moving critique of life under communism. Attempts at reform succeeded in the United States and western Europe, but eastern Europe saw the surprising collapse of communism and the end of the cold war in 1989.

*Gorbachev, Mikhail. *Memoirs.* 1996.

Green Parties worldwide: `http://www.greens.org`.

Kligman, Gail. *The Politics of Duplicity: Controlling Reproduction in Ceauşescu's Romania.* 1998.

Laqueur, Walter. *The Age of Terrorism.* 1987.

Olson, James S., and Randy Roberts. *Where the Domino Fell: America and Vietnam, 1945–1990.* 1996.

Reiton, Earl A. *The Thatcher Revolution: Margaret Thatcher, John Major, Tony Blair, and the Transformation of Modern Britain.* 2002.

Rosenfeld, Alla, and Norton T. Dodge. *From Gulag to Glasnost: Nonconformist Art from the Soviet Union.* 1995.

Rothschild, Joseph, and Nancy M. Wingfield. *Return to Diversity: A Political History of East Central Europe.* 2000.

*Solzhenitsyn, Aleksandr Isaevich. *The Gulag Archipelago.* 1973–1976.

Sternhal, Suzanne. *Gorbachev's Reforms: De-Stalinization through Demilitarization.* 1997.

Weigel, George. *Witness to Hope: The Biography of Pope John Paul II.* 1999.

CHAPTER REVIEW

IMPORTANT EVENTS

1962–1965	Vatican II reforms Catholic ritual and dogma
1963	Betty Friedan publishes *The Feminine Mystique*
1966	Willy Brandt becomes West German foreign minister and develops Ostpolitik, a policy designed to bridge tensions between the two Germanies
1967	South Africa's Dr. Christiaan Barnard performs first successful human heart transplant
1968	Revolution in Czechoslovakia against communism; student uprisings throughout Europe and the United States
1969	U.S. astronauts walk on the moon's surface
1972	SALT I treaty between the United States and Soviet Union
1973	North Vietnam and the United States sign treaty ending war in Vietnam; OPEC raises price of oil and imposes oil embargo on the West
1973–1976	Aleksandr Solzhenitsyn publishes *Gulag Archipelago*
1977	Feminists gather in Houston to mark the first International Year of Women
1978	The first test-tube baby is born in England
1978–1979	Islamic revolution in Iran; hostages taken at U.S. embassy in Teheran
1980	An independent trade union, Solidarity, organizes resistance to Polish communism; Prime Minister Margaret Thatcher begins dismantling the welfare state in Britain
Early 1980s	AIDS epidemic strikes the West
1981	Ronald Reagan becomes U.S. president
1985	Mikhail Gorbachev comes to power in the USSR
1986	Explosion at Soviet nuclear plant at Chernobyl; Spain joins the Common Market
1989	Chinese students revolt in Tiananmen Square and government suppresses them; Communist governments ousted in eastern Europe; fall of the Berlin Wall

KEY TERMS

DNA (1144)
glasnost (1174)
in vitro fertilization (1146)
multinational corporation (1146)
neoliberalism (1171)
perestroika (1174)
pop art (1152)
OPEC (1167)
Ostpolitik (1156)
samizdat (1156)
Solidarity (1176)
stagflation (1168)
terrorism (1168)
Vatican II (1154)

REVIEW QUESTIONS

1. How did the scientific advances from the 1950s and 1960s challenge established patterns of thought and social behavior?
2. What major changes took place in the formation of postindustrial society?
3. What were the main issues for protesters in the 1960s, and how did governments address them?
4. What factors led to the collapse of communism in the Soviet bloc?

MAKING CONNECTIONS

1. What were the differences between industrial society of the late nineteenth century and postindustrial society of the late twentieth century?
2. Why were there so many protests, acts of terrorism, and uprisings across the West in the decades between 1960–1990?
3. What have been the long-term consequences of Communist rule between 1917 and 1989?

FOR FURTHER EXPLORATION

To assess your mastery of the material in this chapter, see the Online Study Guide at bedfordstmartins.com/hunt.

To read additional primary-source material from this period, see Chapter 29 in *Sources of The Making of the West*, Second Edition.

The New Globalism: Opportunities and Dilemmas,
1989 to the Present

ON JANUARY 1, 2002, PEOPLE in twelve countries of the European Union (EU) woke up to find their centuries-old national currencies gone, replaced by a single unit of money—the **euro**. The bills were all standard, designed to represent the EU's shared ideals, represented by the image of bridges. The design of the coins was different, however. One side of the coin was common, while on the other each country was, for an allotted number of coins, allowed to put a unique national symbol. Supporters of the currency pointed to the savings on currency exchanges for businesses, consumers, and international travelers, while its detractors felt that a traditional bulwark of the nation-state—a controlled, independent monetary system—would be undermined, and perhaps national integrity with it. Thus, Britain, Sweden, and Denmark refused to join the currency system despite being members of the EU. For those adopting the euro, funds for industry and commerce moved unhampered. Having the new currency in their pockets also gave psychological advantages to EU citizens. "People with the same money don't go to war with one another," a French nuclear scientist remarked. An Italian student enthused that the euro provided "a sense of belonging to a European Union and I think it's beautiful that there's this big European country."

The Euro
These new bills went into circulation on January 1, 2002, even though banks and other financial institutions began using the euro monetary unit two years earlier. The design of the euro bills and coins, like everything else in the European Union, represented compromise and unity. The bills' designer used architectural imagery of windows and bridges, suggesting openness, light, connectedness, and boundary crossing. Reflecting the compromise between Europe and individual states, the head side of the coins bears a common image, while the tail sides contain symbols chosen by individual nations within the euro zone. Europeans were generally enthusiastic about the common currency for many reasons both idealistic and practical: it allowed for more effective bargain hunting, while it also represented yet another step in ending the divisive nationalism that had plagued the history of the West. Why might some Europeans object to the euro? *Royalty Free/Corbis.*

For these people, the euro represented post–cold war opportunity—an opportunity to start the new millennium with the risks of disastrous wars perhaps permanently diminished.

The end of the cold war rivalry between the superpowers and their allies paved the way for a more intimately connected world, and the euro was just one concrete example of weakening national boundaries. The collapse of communism in Europe spread after 1989 to include Yugoslavia and then the Soviet Union itself—another major piece of the globalization puzzle. After that, the former Common Market transformed itself into the European Union and in 2004 admitted many states from the former Soviet empire in Eastern Europe. Instead of being forced to adhere to the demands of one superpower or the other, nations around the world had more opportunity to trade and interact with each other freely, and technology moved openly from region to region. Further advances in communication added to the potential for Europe-wide and global relationships; spurred by the fall of the Soviet realm, these advances paved the way for the West as a whole to enter the global age. The world was no longer divided in two with all the guarded borders and burdensome restrictions the cold war division implied. Rather, a denser web of economic and social ties bound peoples and cultures together.

The globalizing world brought challenges, opportunities, disasters, and astonishing accomplishments. Migration from eastern to western Europe accelerated in the 1990s as an unexpected consequence of the Soviet collapse. As the costs of the welfare state were cut across the West, governments increased subsidies and incentives for businesses facing global competition from the rising economic power of Japan, China, and other Asian countries. International business mergers accelerated from the 1990s on. The global age brought the vast international and national migration of tens of millions of people; an expanding global marketplace; and an accelerated cultural exchange of popular music, books, films, and television entertainment. Less hopefully, it also encompassed the international impact of lethal disasters such as AIDS, environmental degradation, genocide, and terrorism. The global age was indeed one of golden opportunities and unprecedented dilemmas.

While the end of superpower rivalry made global exchange easier, it also resulted in the dominance of a single power, the United States, in world affairs. As the United States sought to exercise global power through warfare, however, the West itself seemed to fragment. European states, more interested in peace than war, started to resist the United States just as the Soviet satellites had pulled away from the USSR. As global events progressed, new forces arose to rival those of the West, not only the economic power of the Asian and Middle Eastern countries but also the cultural might of Islam. Some observers predicted a huge "clash of civilizations" based on the total incompatibility of Western civilization and cultures beyond the West. Others, however, saw a different clash—one between a Europe reborn after decades of

◆ **1990s** Internet revolution
◆ **1990–1991** Persian Gulf War

◆ **1991** Civil war in Yugoslavia; failed coup in the Soviet Union

◆ **1995** International congress of women at Beijing

◆ **1997** Economic problems for the Pacific tigers

1985　　　　**1990**　　　　**1995**

◆ **1992** Soviet Union dissolves

◆ **1993** Toni Morrison wins Nobel Prize

◆ **1989** Tiananmen Square uprising; Berlin Wall falls

◆ **1994** Mandela elected in South Africa; Russia invades Chechnya; EU formed

disastrous wars as a nonmilitaristic group of nations allied with other peace-seeking states confronting an imperial United States that, like Europe in the nineteenth century, was increasingly at war around the world. Instead of bringing connections and understanding, globalization in either of these scenarios could entail global holocaust.

For historians, understanding the recent past is a challenge in itself. Every day since 1989 has been filled with news, and never more so than after September 11, 2001. This news receives virtually instantaneous reporting because of global communication technology. Unlike journalists, historians do not choose from this mass the most sensational story of the moment or the one that will attract the greater readership. Rather, they are interested in judging which items from the unfiltered mass of technologically transmitted news are actually true and, of these, which will be important in the long run. Moving beyond a single U.S.-based newspaper or television station, historians want to identify social, cultural, and political events that are uniquely important or generally significant for people's everyday lives, and they need time to collect facts from more than one national tradition. They make the most reliable evaluations when phenomena are no longer "news"—that is, after a good period of time has shown their staying power and influence.

When we first started writing this book, we held our breath in the face of rapidly changing events and judged that the fall of communism and the increasing interconnectedness of the world's peoples and cultures

were the challenges not only of the moment but also of history. In this second edition we persisted in that judgment although the fall of communism and coming of globalism had brought greater perils than we had seen only five or six years earlier. Other forces, such as the Internet, had missed our notice altogether despite the fact that the system had been around for several decades. Today, almost a decade after we made our first selections of important trends, we judge the gradual unification of the entire European continent as potentially momentous. We also see the forces of terrorism and possibly a new fragmentation of the West itself into U.S. and European blocs as events with historical staying power. As an experiment in history, you might note the important events of the months in which you take this course, put your list away for several years or more, and then see if they—along with the events discussed in this chapter—stand the test of time.

❖ Soviet Collapse Releases Global Forces

Rejection of communism spread in the 1990s, turning events in unpredictable and ever more violent directions. Yugoslavia and then the Soviet Union itself fell apart. Like Hungarians and Czechs in the early-twentieth-century Habsburg Empire, nationality groups in the USSR began to demand political and cultural autonomy. The Soviet empire had held together more than one hundred ethnic

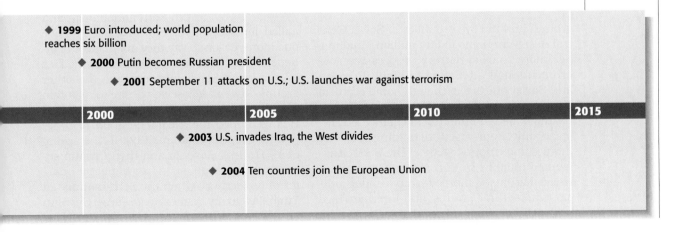

◆ **1999** Euro introduced; world population reaches six billion

◆ **2000** Putin becomes Russian president

◆ **2001** September 11 attacks on U.S.; U.S. launches war against terrorism

| 2000 | 2005 | 2010 | 2015 |

◆ **2003** U.S. invades Iraq, the West divides

◆ **2004** Ten countries join the European Union

MAP 30.1 Eastern Europe in the 1990s

In the 1990s, the countries of Eastern Europe tried to forge their own destiny free from the direction of either the Russia or the United States. The transition, as the new situation came to be called, was far from easy. Old states like Czechoslovakia fragmented and many state borders were contested. Turning definitively from Russia, the leadership of these countries began to look to Western Europe, most of them eventually opting for membership in the European Union. Compare this map to the sharp divisions between Eastern and Western Europe shown in Map 28.3. What are the most significant changes to the region in the post-cold world era?

unstable years of the early 1990s, ambitious politicians used ethnicity as their most effective political slogan, and ethnic violence became the major political tool, continuing to shape post-Communist politics into the new millennium. (Map 30.1) Alongside such human issues in post-Soviet society lay the question of who would control the massive Soviet arsenal of nuclear weapons and the further one of how global politics would shape up without cold war guidelines.

The Breakup of Yugoslavia

Ethnic nationalism came to replace communism in Yugoslavia, shaping political debate for the first time in decades. Tensions erupted in Yugoslavia in 1990 when a Serb Communist, Slobodan Milosevic, won the presidency of Serbia and began to assert Serb ascendancy instead of communism in the Yugoslav federation as a whole. Other ethnic groups in Yugoslavia resisted Milosevic's militant pro-Serb nationalism and called for secession. "Slovenians . . . have one more reason to say they are in favor of independence," warned one of them in the face of mounting Serb claims to rule the other groups. Against Milosevic's desire to maintain a centralized state, Slovenia, Croatia, and Bosnia hoped for a confederation of independent republics (Map 30.2). In the spring of 1991, first Slovenia and then Croatia seceded, but Croatia soon lost almost a quarter of its territory when the Serb-dominated Yugoslav army, eager to enforce Serbian supremacy, invaded. An even more devastat-

groups, and the five republics of Soviet Central Asia were home to fifty million Muslims. For more than a century, successive governments had attempted to instill Russian and Soviet culture, although some cultural autonomy was allowed. The policy of Russification failed to build full allegiance but instead only improvised at holding the vast multiethnic empire together. The USSR fragmented quickly. In Yugoslavia, Communist rulers had also enforced unity among religious and ethnic groups, and intermarriage among them occurred regularly. During the

ing civil war engulfed Bosnia-Herzegovina, where the republic's Muslim majority tried to create a multicultural and multiethnic state. Many Bosnian Serb men formed a guerrilla army, backed by the covert military support of Milosevic's government, and gained the upper hand. A United Nations (UN) arms embargo prevented the Bosnian Muslims from equipping their forces adequately to defend themselves even as the Serbs took to massacring them.

Violence in the Balkans was relentless and unspeakable—all in the name of creating "ethnically pure" states in a region where ethnic mixture, not ethnic purity, was the norm. During the 1990s, civilians died by the tens of thousands, as Serbs under Milosevic's leadership pursued a policy they called **ethnic cleansing**—that is, genocide—against the other nationalities. They raped women to leave them pregnant with Serb babies as another form of conquest. Men and boys were taken away and murdered. Croatian forces also murdered people of other ethnicities, and each competing force took aim at the cultural heritage of its opponent. Military units on all sides destroyed libraries and museums, architectural treasures like the Mostar Bridge, and cities rich with history such as Dubrovnik. Ethnic cleansing thus entailed eliminating both actual people and all traces of their complex past. Many in the West explained violence in the Balkans as part of "age-old" blood feuds typical of a backward, almost "Asian" society. Others saw ethnic rivalry using genocide to achieve national power as a modern phenomenon practiced by a variety of politicians, including Adolf Hitler. Still others

MAP 30.2 The Former Yugoslavia, c. 2000
After a decade of destructive civil war, UN forces and UN-brokered agreements attempted to protect the civilians of the former Yugoslavia from the brutal consequences of post-Communist rule. Ambitious politicians, most notably Slobodan Milosevic, used the twentieth-century Western strategy of fostering ethnic and religious hatred as a powerful tool to build support for themselves while making those favoring peace look softhearted and unfit to rule. What issues of national identity does the breakup of Yugoslavia indicate? Have these changed since the nineteenth century?

blamed the former great powers for stirring up many of these tensions in the first place.

The civil wars in Yugoslavia shook Europeans' confidence that they had finally put an end to their heritage of slaughter. Western values were tested still further when, late in the 1990s, Serb forces, having withdrawn from Croatia, moved to attack Muslims of Albanian ethnicity living in the Yugoslav province of Kosovo. From 1997 to 1999, hundreds of thousands of Albanian Kosovars fled their homes as Serb militias and the Yugoslav army slaughtered the civilian population.

Yugoslavia in 1990, before Destruction of the Mostar Bridge (top) and after (bottom) In modern history the construction of a nation-state has depended on the growth of institutions such as armies and bureaucracies and the promotion of a common national culture. In an effort to dominate Bosnia and Croatia, Serbs destroyed non-Serb architecture, books, and such ancient symbols as the Mostar Bridge. Why was it important for the various factions to attack and destroy cultural objects in the breakup of Yugoslavia and successive wars? *Top: Sygma; bottom: Stephane Cardinale/Sygma.*

was turned over to the International Court of Justice, or World Court, in the Netherlands to be tried for crimes against humanity. In 2003, Milosevic loyalists, many of them in line to be rounded up for trial in the World Court, assassinated the new Serbian president. Across both western and eastern Europe, the language of racial, ethnic, and religious hatred was influencing political agendas, nowhere more violently than in the former Communist states.

The Soviet Union Comes Apart

Amid the ongoing genocide in the former Yugoslavia came the total collapse of the Soviet Union in 1992. A string of secessions in the 1990s and into the next century held the potential for widespread destabilization of regional and perhaps global politics. By 1990, perestroika had failed to revitalize the Soviet economy; people confronted soaring prices, the specter of unemployment, and even greater scarcity of goods than

NATO pilots bombed the region in an attempt to drive back the army and Serb militias. Amid incredible violence and suffering, UN peacekeeping forces stepped in to enforce an interethnic truce, but people throughout the world felt that this intervention came far too late, reflecting great-power self-interest rather than a true commitment to maintaining peace and protecting human rights. Alongside the decimated independent republics of Slovenia, Bosnia, and Croatia, a new regime emerged in Serbia, and Milosevic

they had endured in the past. Although Mikhail Gorbachev announced late that year that there was "no alternative to the transition to the market [economy]," his plan was too little, too late and satisfied no one. After the Russian parliament's election of Boris Yeltsin as president of the Russian Republic over a Communist candidate in 1991, a group of eight antireform hard-liners, from the Soviet vice president to the powerful head of the Soviet secret police, or KGB, tried to overthrow the government. Holding Gorbachev under house arrest, coup leaders claimed to be rescuing the Soviet Union from the "mortal danger" posed by "extremist forces." Yeltsin, defiantly standing atop a tank outside the Russian Republic's parliament building, called for mass resistance. Hundreds of thousands of residents of Moscow and Leningrad filled the streets, and units of the army defected to protect Yeltsin's headquarters. People used fax machines and computers to coordinate internal resistance and send messages to the rest of the world. The coup was in complete disarray in the face of citizen determination not to allow a return of Stalinism, or indeed of any form of Soviet orthodoxy.

Yeltsin Defeats the Communists.   After the failed coup, the Soviet Union disintegrated. People tore down statues of Soviet heroes; Yeltsin outlawed the Communist Party newspaper, *Pravda*, and sealed the KGB's files. At the end of August 1991, the Soviet parliament suspended operations of the Communist Party itself. The Baltic States of Estonia, Latvia, and Lithuania declared their independence in September, and one republic after another followed their lead. Bloody ethnic conflicts erupted in the disintegrating Soviet world. In the Soviet republic of Tajikistan,♦ native Tajiks rioted against Armenians living there; in Azerbaijan,♦ Azeris and Armenians clashed over contested territory; and in the Baltic States, anti-Semitism revived as a political tool. The USSR finally dissolved on January 1, 1992. Twelve of the fifteen former Soviet republics banded together in a Commonwealth of Independent States (CIS), but that hardly ended the disintegration of Russian power (Map 30.3 on the next page).

The coup and the drive for dissolution of the USSR so tainted Gorbachev that he abandoned politics, leaving Yeltsin as head of the Russian state. The change to a market economy under Yeltsin introduced new problems. Plagued by corruption, the Russian economy entered an ever-deepening crisis. Yeltsin's political allies bought up national resources, stripped them of their value, and sent billions of dollars out of the country. By

♦**Tajikistan:** tah jih kih STAN
♦**Azerbaijan:** a zur by JAHN

1999, Yeltsin's own family appeared to be deeply implicated in stealing the wealth once seen as belonging to all the people. Managers, military officers, and bureaucrats took whatever goods they could lay their hands on, including weaponry, and sold it. Ethnic and religious battles continued for the entire decade of the 1990s, and the government undertook disastrous policies. In an attempt to consolidate support, Yeltsin launched military action against Muslim dissenters in the province of Chechnya, inflicting destruction and massive casualties on both sides. The political right appealed to nationalist sentiments in Russia, and ethnic hatred became a standard tool in the new multiparty politics. Political disorder was matched by social disarray as organized criminals interfered in the distribution of goods and services and assassinated legitimate entrepreneurs, legislators, and anyone who criticized them. As a result, Western powers drastically reduced the aid they were willing to supply Russia to rebuild its infrastructure. In 1998, the Russian government devalued its currency and defaulted on its loans, bringing temporary chaos to world financial markets. As the Russian parliament pursued an investigation in the business dealings of Yeltsin, his family, and his allies, Yeltsin resigned on December 31, 1999. He appointed a new protégé, Vladimir Putin, as interim president.

Vladimir Putin Takes Charge.   Putin was a little-known functionary in Russia's new security apparatus, which had evolved from the old KGB. Observers thought that in the upcoming presidential elections of spring 2000 he would garner about 1 percent of the vote. Putin surprised everyone, however; though associated with the Yeltsin family corruption, he proved himself a leader committed to legality. "Democracy," he announced, "is the dictatorship of law." The electorate voted him in, abandoning old Communist bosses, rabid nationalists, and new robber barons alike. With a solid mandate, Putin proceeded to drive from power the biggest figures in regional government, usually the henchmen of the robber barons, and he fired their associates who held high positions in the central government. Ultimately, he also sent into exile Boris Berezovsky, who

MAP 30.3 Countries of the Former Soviet Union, c. 2000

Following an agreement of December 1991, twelve of the countries of the former Soviet Union formed the Commonwealth of Independent States (CIS). Dominated by Russia and with Ukraine often disputing this domination, the CIS worked to bring about common economic and military policies. As nation-states dissolved rapidly in the late twentieth century, regional alliances and coordination were necessary to meet the political and economic challenges of the global age. What is the relationship between the breakup of the Soviet Union over the course of the 1990s and international events in the 1990s and early twenty-first century?

had gained his billions of dollars from wheedling control of the Russian media and oil. Faced with a desperate situation, Putin aimed to restore "strong government" and end the influence of a "handful of billionaires with only egotistical concerns." Putin's popularity rose even more when in 2003 the government arrested yet another billionaire, the head of the Yukos Oil Company. The pillaging of the country—the source of ordinary citizens' recent suffering—was finally being punished. Yet while cleaning up the government and the economy, Putin continued the destructive war in Chechnya to quell the independence movement. Casualties, atrocities, disease, and physical devastation of the cities continued as a virtual plague on all concerned.

An Elusive Market Economy

Developing a free market and a republican government brought misery to Russia and the rest of eastern Europe. The conditions of everyday life grew increasingly dire as salaries went unpaid, food remained in short supply, and essential services disintegrated. In 1994, inflation soared at a rate of 14 percent a month in Russia, while industrial production dropped by 15 percent. People took drastic steps to stay alive. Hotel lobbies became clogged with prostitutes because women were the first people fired as governments privatized industry and cut service jobs. Unpaid soldiers sold their services to the Mafia. Ordinary citizens stood on the sidewalks of major cities selling their household possessions. Simultaneously, a pent-up demand was unleashed for items never before available. An enormous underground economy existed in goods such as automobiles stolen from people in other countries and then driven or shipped to Russia.

There were, of course, many pluses: people were able to travel freely for the first time, and the media were more open than ever before in Russian history. Some workers, many of them young and highly educated, profited from contacts with technology and business. However, their frequent emigration to more prosperous parts of the world further depleted Russia's human resources. "I knew in my heart that communism would collapse," said one ex-dissident, commenting

sadly on the exodus of youth from his country, "but it never crossed my mind that the future would look like this." At the same time, as the different republics that had once comprised the Soviet Union became independent, the hundreds of thousands of Russians who had earlier been sent there by the state as colonizers returned as refugees to put further demands on the chaotic Russian economy. Some 900,000 returned in 1993 alone. The dismantling of communism was thus more complicated and painful than anyone had imagined it would be.

The Economic Agenda.   For many in the former Soviet bloc, the first priority was getting economies running again—but on new terms. Replacing a government-controlled economy with a market one could not happen naturally or automatically but rather required government planning. Given the spiraling misery, however, many opposed the introduction of new market-oriented measures. In Russia, members of collective farms fought to preserve them as a means of security in a rapidly changing world. With the farms up for sale, most collective farmers faced landlessness and starvation. The countries that experienced the most success were those in which administrators had introduced ingredients of free trade, such as allowing farmers to sell their produce on the open market or encouraging independent entrepreneurs or even government factories to deal in international trade. Countries also had to recognize that the emergence of a free market needed time— and governmental support. Hungary and Poland thus emerged from the transition with less strain, because both had favored market elements early on and had hired advisers to speed the transformation of the economy. They set up business schools and other institutions to foster modern trade and industry with comparative ease. Foreign capital arrived as well, anchoring these two countries securely to the world economy.

Elsewhere, however, the transition happened differently. The former Soviet Union itself, in the words of one critic, became simply one vast "kleptocracy" in the 1990s as the country's resources—theoretically the property of all the people—were stolen for individual gain. In this regard, one Polish adviser noted,

Czech Prostitute on the Border with Germany
The collapse of communism and the Soviet Union created financial disaster, particularly for women who represented more than two-thirds of all the unemployed. Communists advocated the belief that all people, regardless of gender, should work and that they should be paid equally. While this equality never worked in practice, it did provide jobs so that women could support themselves and their children. Under the free market system, women were eliminated from good jobs and given lower pay. Many resorted to prostitution, especially seeking clients from the West. The global sex industry expanded, using ads for attractive women with good skills and then forcing them into prostitution by confiscating their passports and identity papers. More casual prostitution took place on borders with more prosperous countries such as Germany, shown here. *Sean Gallup/Getty Images.*

democracy and a successful transition went hand in hand, for unless the people were represented and institutionally powerful enough to prevent it, former dictatorial leaders and administrators would operate as criminals. In the long run, the worst-case scenario involved post-Communist countries dealing with a cancerous inheritance of corruption, tax evasion, and off-the-books dealing. Moreover, because the socialist leadership had removed their economies from global developments, they had not benefited from technological change, leaving plants and personnel hopelessly out of date, even worthless. In these countries, competition and free trade meant closing plants and firing all the workers.

Talent Flees the Region.   A final element in post-Soviet economic difficulties stemmed from a brain drain that plagued the region. The fall of the Soviet empire and the economic chaos that followed brought a rush of migration from eastern Europe to western Europe, often involving those with marketable skills. The countries that received the most migrants were Austria and Germany, which bordered the former Soviet satellites. Migrants left for several reasons, including the lack of jobs, the upsurge of ethnic hatreds, and the availability of higher remuneration for well-educated workers in other countries. Escaping anti-Semitism also played a role: post-Communist politicians used the cruel rallying cry of hatred of Jews to build a following, just as Hitler and many others had done so effectively in the past. Banditry and violence inflicted by organized crime added to the disadvantages of remaining in eastern Europe and helping transform the economy. Some migrants from the east, fearful of reprisals, sought political asylum.

The everyday amenities of western Europe included safe water, better housing, better roads, and at least a minimal level of social services. Although western Europe was now on a firm neoliberal course of cutting the social programs of the welfare state, in formerly Communist countries benefits had disappeared entirely. Pensions for veterans and retired workers were rarely paid, and even when paid were often worthless given the soaring inflation; day-care centers, kindergartens, and homes for the elderly closed their doors; and hospitals and health care deteriorated. Salaries of government employees plummeted. In these circumstances, the benefits of citizenship in western European countries appeared even more desirable.

Chechnya and Central Asian States: The Quest for Independence and Influence

Although Gorbachev had pulled the Soviet Union out of its disastrous war with Afghanistan, his successors opened another war to prevent the secession of oil-rich Chechnya and to provide a nationalist rallying cry to shore up domestic support for the administration. For decades, Chechens had been integrated into the bureaucracy and military. The Soviets had effectively squashed ethnic hostility of and toward Chechens, deporting those who used ethnic politics and importing peoples to regions where ethnic concentrations needed diluting. In the fall of 1991, the National Congress of the Chechen People took over the government of the region from the USSR, moving toward the same kind of independence sought by the Baltic nations and other former Soviet states. In June 1992, after the collapse of the Soviet Union, Chechen rebels got control of massive numbers of Russian weapons, including airplanes, tanks, and some forty thousand automatic weapons and machine guns.

In December 1994, the Russian government sealed the Chechen borders and invaded. A high Russian official defended the war as crucial to bolstering Yeltsin's position: "We now need a small victorious war. . . . We must raise the President's rating." Yeltsin, prompted by his advisers, announced the impossibility of negotiating with the Chechens to counteract the Russian population's opposition to the war. In 1996, the KGB assassinated the Chechen leader Dzhokhar Dudayev with a rocket as he spoke on his cell phone, but the war persisted. There was intense suffering among the Chechen themselves and retaliatory terrorist attacks in Russian cities, particularly Moscow. As the war dragged on, Chechnya's capital city of Goszny was pounded to bits, but Russian casualties mounted too—as did protest against continuing the conflict. In 2002, Chechen loyalists took hundreds of hostages in a Moscow theater; they were killed by nerve gas in a successful liberation attempt that also killed almost two hundred of the hostages. The Chechen war, which continued to unfold tragically and endlessly even as Russia was trying to create a new future, only compounded Russia's problems of establishing a sound economy and credible post-Communist government.

As the war in Chechnya continued, the newly independent states of Central Asia became enmeshed in the politics of oil and Islam, as did much of the rest of the world. Led by strong men, if not dictators, the states of Kazakhstan♦ and Uzbekistan♦ became es-

Terrorist Attack on a Moscow Bus, 1996
Terrorism became more widespread from the 1970s onward, taking many forms and espousing many causes. Although terrorists often targeted prominent individuals for kidnapping and assassination, they also engineered wider attacks on random citizens to increase the loss of life. Post-Soviet Russia experienced such attacks at the hands of breakaway Chechens, whose independence Russia violently resisted. But large-scale bombings occurred in the Paris subway, on London streets, and on Spanish railways, causing these countries to cover public wastebaskets and to train people to be vigilant about parcels in streets, public buildings, and train and subway stations. Terrorism instilled a generalized feeling of fear that the wartime targeting of civilians had become a regular threat in peacetime.
© *Ivo Lorenc/Corbis Sygma.*

pecially involved in the intertwined issues of terrorism, local political factionalism, and the global economy, particularly centered on issues of oil. Uzbekistan lent its territory to various groups of anti-Western radicals for the purposes of recruiting and training militant activists. Kazakhstan had huge resources to exploit, which allowed it to play Western oil companies off against Muslim interests in the region. As in some of the other newly independent nations of the former USSR, such as Ukraine, critics of the strongmen were murdered. Democracy and human rights were not an issue: they simply did not exist.

Review: What were the major issues facing the former Soviet world in the 1990s and early 2000s?

♦**Kazakhstan:** kah zahk STAHN
♦**Uzbekistan:** ooz BEHK uh stan

❖ Global Opportunities Transcend the Nation-State

Although the end of the Soviet system fractured one large regional economy, it gave further impetus to European unification. The European Community was robust compared to former Soviet-bloc countries, many of which applied for membership. Europe as a whole was poised to enter a new phase—one based on further steps toward unity. This move toward unity stood in marked contrast to the wars and civil strife that plagued many other regions of the world, and the union's economic success provoked the formation of the North American Free Trade Agreement (NAFTA), which established a free-trade zone of the United States, Canada, and Mexico. As new forms of world governance and large regional blocs took shape, people debated whether the nation-state would disappear in Europe as an outmoded vestige of a bloody past.

Europe Looks Beyond the Nation-State

The peoples of Europe took immense strides in the 1990s to move their institutions beyond those of the traditional nation-state. The Common Market had opened the pathway to unified supranational policy in economic matters, and its evolution into the European Union expanded that cooperation to political and cultural matters. The nationalist function of cities diminished as major urban areas like London and Paris became packed with people from other countries, who in turn brought new ideas and attractive new customs. These trends, however, aroused resistance from those who wanted to preserve their own traditions and who felt the loss of a face-to-face, local way of life. For many, globalization posed the problem of preserving the best of global, national, and local relationships, although these might be in conflict.

From Common Market to European Union. In 1992, the twelve countries of the Common Market ended national distinctions in the spheres of business activity, border controls, and transportation, effectively closing down passport controls at most of their common borders. Citizens of the member countries carried a common burgundy-colored passport, and governments, whether municipal or national, had to treat all member nations' firms the same. In 1994, by the terms of the **Maastricht⁺ Treaty**, the European Community became the **European Union (EU)**, and in 1999 a common currency—the euro—came into being, first for transactions among financial institutions and then in 2002 for general use by the public. Common policies governed everything from the number of American soap operas aired on television to pollution controls on automobiles to the health warnings on cigarette packages. The EU parliament convened regularly in Strasbourg, France, while subgroups met to negotiate further cultural, economic, and social policies. With the adoption of a common currency, an EU central bank came into being to guide interest rates and economic policy.

The EU continued to play a pacifying role in Europe. It was Greece that pushed for the admission of its traditional enemy Turkey in 2002 and 2003 despite the warnings of a former president of France that a predominantly Muslim country could never fit in with the Christian traditions of EU members. Many EU members disputed this appraisal, but Greece took the lead, having developed diplomatic ties with Turkey. "Turkey has been a great European power since the sixteenth century," Greek prime minister Costas Simitis maintained in 2003. Rejecting religious criteria to resolve political issues, Costas pointed to the common desire of Turks and other Europeans for "democratization and economic stability"—both of them fundamental tenets of the EU. Both Greece and Turkey stood to benefit by having their disputes adjudicated by the larger body of European members, principally by being able to cut that part of their defense budget used for weaponry against the other country. Like the rivalry between Germany and France, that between Turkey and Greece, it was hoped, would dissolve if bound by the strong economic and political ties of the EU.

Drawbacks to EU membership remained, however. The EU enforced no common regu-

---

⁺**Maastricht:** MAHS trihkt

latory practices, and the common economic policies demanding cooperation among its members were not always observed. Individual governments set up hurdles and barriers for businesses, for instance obstructing transnational mergers they did not like. One government might secretly block the acquisition of a company based on its own soil no matter what the advantages to shareholders, economy, the workforce, or unified Europe's consumers. Nonetheless, countries of eastern Europe clamored to join, working hard to meet not only the EU's fiscal requirements but also those pertaining to human rights and social policy (Map 30.4 shown here). As the EU grew more powerful, nations once committed to remaining outside the euro or the EU itself scheduled referenda to rethink membership. In 2003, a draft constitution for the EU was formulated to forge an even tighter bond among member states.

East Joins West. The EU's attractions became clear to eastern Europe, as demonstrated in the case of Greece, long considered the poor relative of the other member countries. Greece joined the European Community in 1981; its per capita gross domestic product was 64 percent of the European average in 1985 and 58.5 percent in 1990. However, Greek leaders and the EU made a real effort during the 1990s to bring the country closer to EU norms. By the early twenty-first century, thanks to advice from the EU and an infusion of funds—8.3 percent of the total EU budget—Greece had reached 80 percent of the EU per capita gross domestic product. It also aimed to develop economic

MAP 30.4 The European Union in 2004
The European Union (EU) appeared to increase the economic health of its members despite the rocky start of its common currency: the euro. The EU helped end the traditional competition between its members and facilitated trade and worker migration by providing common passports and business laws, and open borders. But many critics feared a loss of cultural distinctiveness among peoples, in an age of mass communications, if the economic union turned into a political one. What advantages does the expansion of the EU provide to Europe and to the world? What are the disadvantages?

relations in the Balkan and Eastern Mediterranean.

Hoping for similar gains, the countries to the east moved toward EU membership throughout the 1990s. The collapse of the Soviet system advanced privatization of industry, as governments offered basic services for sale to the highest bidder. Often, only companies in the wealthy western countries of the EU could afford to purchase eastern European assets. For example, the Czech Republic in 2001 sold its major energy

Moscow "Hyperstore"
Daily life in the post-Soviet world was one of extremes. At first, many experienced a sudden collapse in their standard of living, which was already low because of the planned economy that diverted many resources to building cold war weapons. Within several years, entrepreneurs set up vast "hyperstores" filled with more goods than most Muscovites had ever seen before—testimony to the potential for a better life that globalization offered. Along with the unprecedented array of goods, the collapse of communism brought new dangers as well, such as bombings on public transportation and in apartment buildings, hostage-takings, and an increased mafia presence. What is the relationship, if any, between the post-communist terrorism that menaced Russians (as shown on page 1197) and the appearance of mass consumerism in their society? *Peter Blakely/CORBIS SABA.*

and eastern Europe (Estonia, Latvia, Lithuania, Poland, the Czech Republic, Slovakia, Hungary, Slovenia, Malta, and Cyprus), and in May of that same year the Declaration of Rome announced an affiliation between NATO and Russia—once the enemy that spawned NATO's creation. On the eve of Poland's admission to the EU, its standard of living was 39 percent of EU standards, up from 33 percent in 1995. The Czech Republic and Hungary enjoyed 55 and 50 percent, respectively, but in all three cases these figures masked the discrepancy between the ailing countryside and thriving cities. Further, in these countries a far larger proportion of income went to purchasing food rather than leisure and other nonessentials, and on the eve of entering the EU, citizens in eastern Europe were not always happy at the prospect. "It's bad," a farmer in the Czech Republic maintained. "The European Union is already imposing various quotas and regulations on us." A retiree foresaw the cost of beer going up and added, "If I wanted to join anything in the West, I would have defected." Still others felt that having just established an independent national identity, it was premature to join yet another body that would swallow them up.

The economic life of eastern Europe had nonetheless picked up considerably by 2000. In contrast to the first bleak years of massive layoffs, soaring inflation, and unpaid salaries, in 2002 residents of Poland, Slovenia, and Estonia had purchasing power some 40 percent higher than in 1989. Latvia, Romania, and Bulgaria were at the bottom of the former Communist states. Even there, however, a greater number of residents enjoyed freezers, computers, and portable telephones. Automobile purchases were increasing by 10 to 12 percent a year, but 30 to 40 percent of the people were automatically excluded from the consuming public because they simply lacked the wherewithal to make what would be considered in western Europe basic purchases. The shopping malls that rose mostly around capital cities testified to the urban nature of the benefits of the free economy. They also showed that eastern Europe was seen as a great new market consisting of 100 million customers for superstores like the furniture giant IKEA or the electronics firm Electroworld. "When Electroworld

distributor Transgaz and eight other regional distributors for 4.1 billion euros to a German firm. Lower wages and costs of doing business in eastern Europe attracted foreign investment, which reached its peak of $20 billion in 2000. The most attractive countries for investment were Poland, the Czech Republic, Hungary, and Slovenia—the most developed state spun off from Yugoslavia. Although the economies of these four countries grew at a faster rate than elsewhere in Europe, unemployment remained high, and they still had no safety net should their economies slow. (See the excerpt from Václav Havel's speech, opposite.)

In 2002, members of the EU voted to admit ten new members, mostly from central

Václav Havel, "Czechoslovakia Is Returning to Europe"

Czech playwright and longtime anti-Communist activist Václav Havel became the first president of his country after the Communist Party was ousted in 1989. Havel was an idealist who believed that the people of eastern Europe had gained important insights from their experience of Soviet domination. This speech provides a backdrop to the admission of eastern European countries to the European Union in 2004. Despite fears among more prosperous EU countries that the lower standard of living in eastern Europe will drag the EU down, there is also a strong sense that the EU is incomplete without them. Havel details what eastern Europeans have to offer, even to those who have long enjoyed greater freedom and prosperity.

Czechoslovakia is returning to Europe. . . . We are doing what we can so that Europe will be capable of really accepting us, its wayward children. Which means that it may open itself to us, and may begin to transform its structures—which are formally European but de facto Western European . . .

The Communist type of totalitarian system has left . . . all the nations of the Soviet Union and the other countries the Soviet Union subjugated in its time, a legacy of countless dead, an infinite spectrum of human suffering, profound economic decline, and above all enormous human humiliation. It has brought us horrors that fortunately you have not known.

At the same time, however—unintentionally, of course—it has given us something positive: a special capacity to look, from time to time, some-what further than someone who has not undergone this bitter experience. A person who cannot move and live a somewhat normal life because he is pinned under a boulder has more time to think about his hopes than someone who is not trapped that way. . . .

For this reason, the salvation of the human world lies nowhere else than in the human heart, in the human power to reflect, in human meekness and in human responsibility. . . . If we are no longer threatened by world war, or by the danger that the absurd mountains of accumulated nuclear weapons might blow up the world, this does not mean that we have definitively won. We are in fact far from the final victory. . . .

In other words, we still don't know how to put morality ahead of politics, science and economics. We are still incapable of understanding that the only genuine backbone of all our actions—if they are to be moral—is responsibility. Responsibility to something higher than my family, my country, my company, my success. Responsibility to the order of Being, where all our actions are indelibly recorded. . . .

I end where I began: history has accelerated. I believe that once again it will be the human mind that will notice this acceleration, give it a name, and transform those words into deeds.

Source: From speech delivered to the Joint Session of Congress, Washington, D.C., on February 21, 1990. Reprinted in *Vital Speeches of the Day*, March 15, 1990, 329–30.

opened in Budapest [April 2002], it provoked a riot. Two hundred thousand people crowded to get in the doors," reported one observer. A French entrepreneur, commenting on the rapid development of the superstore in the Czech Republic, called it a marvel: "In France it took thirty years to build a network of stores . . . but in the East we only needed three years to provision the entire country with them." Critics worried that eastern Europeans had fallen prey to uncontrolled materialism and frenzied shopping, a Western disease they called "Consomania."

Consumption patterns evolved over the first decades of the free market. At first, people spent money on any available product; it was, according to one eastern European businessperson, "a social act, indicating that one had joined consumer society." However, people learned to read labels and to use the superstores, where prices were lower. Because of relentless housing shortages, young adults with incomes lived with their parents, giving them significant purchasing power and making them the target of advertisers. Italian fashions, fast cars, and exotic products especially sold among the young. Joining the consumer world was a sign of belonging to a global community of those free and prosperous enough to consume.

Globalizing Cities and Fragmenting Nations

The West in the transitional period of the 1990s and early 2000s both fragmented into more nation-states and consolidated new forms—most notably the global city. These were cities whose institutions, functions, and visions were overwhelmingly global rather than regional or national. They contained stock markets, legal firms, insurance companies, financial service organizations, and other enterprises that operated across local and national borders, linking to similar enterprises in other global cities. Within these cities there came together high-level decision makers who interacted with one another primarily to set global economic policy and to enact global business. The high-powered and high-priced nature of such global business operatives made life in global cities extremely costly, driving middle managers and engineers to lower-priced living quarters in the suburbs that nonetheless provided good schools and other amenities for well-educated white-collar earners. However, living in very squalid conditions in the global cities were the very lowest paid of service providers—the maintenance, domestic, and other workers whose menial labor was essential around the clock to the needs and comfort of those at the top.

Global cities were those with the best transport or telecommunication facilities. They thus became centers for migration, whether of highly skilled or more modest workers. Paris, London, and New York were not just cosmopolitan but global, with direct and constant contact around the world. As a result citizens of other cities who took pride in

maintaining a distinctive national culture or way of life denounced them. Global cities also drew criticism for their very concentrated wealth, seen to be taken at the expense of poorer people in southern countries. The need to populate global cities with the working poor gave rise to new enterprises, such as recruiters to fill jobs for which local peoples had no taste. In other cases, however, globalization produced intentional diasporas of willing migrants, such as the estimated ninety thousand Japanese in England in the mid-1990s who staffed Japan's global businesses. Because these migrants did not aim to become citizens, they made no economic or political claims on the adopted country and were thus sometimes said to be invisible migrants. For global citizens, there were no more "traumas of exile" because they could commune with massive numbers of like-minded wanderers in their communities and partake of the multiculturalism of the cities themselves. Global cities were said to produce a "deterritorialization of identities"— meaning that many urbanites lacked both a national and a local sense of themselves, so much did they travel the world.

Ironically, as globalization took hold economically and culturally, political borders grew smaller. There were more nations in Europe in 2000 than there had been in 1945, as individual nation-states fragmented under the rising tide of ethnic distinctiveness. Despite two centuries aimed at Slavic unification and the trend toward larger nation-states, ethnic groups separated in the 1990s and early twenty-first century. In 1993, Czechoslovakia split into the Czech Republic and Slovakia (see Map 30.1 on page 1188). As noted earlier in this chapter, Yugoslavia came apart into several states and Russia fought to keep Chechnya from becoming independent as many other states of the former Soviet Union had become.

Activists launched movements for regional autonomy in places such as France, Italy, and Spain. Some Bretons and Corsicans demanded their independence from France, the latter violently attacking national officials. Basque nationalists in northern Spain continued to assassinate tourists, police, and other public servants in an effort to gain autonomy. The push for an independent northern Italy began somewhat halfheartedly, but when politicians saw its attractiveness to voters, they became adamant in their demands and the movement grew. Given the presence of global cities and fragmenting nations, new combinations of local and global identities took shape. These developments, plus the overall consolidation shown in the growth of the European Union, made the status of the nation-state uncertain.

Global Organizations

Globalization spawned the proliferation of supranational organizations, many of them regulating international finance and trade but others addressing social issues. The **World Bank** and the International Monetary Fund had been in existence for several decades, but as national economies interacted more closely, these supranational organizations gained in power and new ones such as the World Trade Organization came into being (1995). Raising money from individual governments, the International Monetary Fund made loans to developing countries but on the condition that they restructure their economies according to neoliberal principles. Other supranational organizations were charitable foundations, many of them based in Europe and the United States. Because some—the Rockefeller, Ford, and Open Society Foundations, for example—controlled so much money, **nongovernmental organizations (NGOs)** often had considerable international power. After the fall of the Soviet bloc, NGOs used their resources to shape economic and social policy and the course of political reform. Some charitable and activist NGOs, like the French-based Doctors Without Borders, gained money through global contributions and used it to provide medical attention in such places as the former Yugoslavia, where people facing war otherwise had no medical help. Small, locally based NGOs excelled at inspiring grassroots activism. All of these various organizations, both small and large, were in tune with the globalization process, and the larger ones were often criticized for exercising their power with no regard for democratic processes.

While the World Bank, World Trade Organization, and International Monetary Fund forced poorer nations to adopt free trade in exchange for loans and financial aid, the European Union and the United States enacted huge tariffs to prevent cheap goods from competing with their own products. In 2002, the U.S. government under George W. Bush, a staunch advocate of free trade, levied large tariffs on steel in order to win the votes of workers in this declining industry. The European Union threatened retaliation with its own list of U.S. goods to be taxed. The biggest threat, however, came from the financial help given to European and U.S. agribusiness by propping up prices, enacting tariffs, and providing outright subsidies—all of which artificially made them profitable in the world market even though poor countries with lower wages produced less expensive food. Tariffs and subsidized profits, it was estimated, diverted $100 billion worth of business away from poorer nations even though their goods were better bargains for consumers.

Activists began movements to attack globalization itself. In 1998, Bernard Cassen of France founded one of them, the Association for the Benefit of Citizens (or ATTAC, after its French name). The organization, which soon had adherents in forty different countries, stood against the control of globalization by the forces of high finance: "Commercial totalitarianism is not free trade." ATTAC took its major policy goal from U.S. economist and Nobel Prize winner James Tobin: to tax financial transactions (just as the purchase of household necessities were taxed) and to create with the tax a fund for people living in underdeveloped countries. Cassen sided with European integration and opposed the "balkanization" of regions and countries. Instead of obstructing globalization, ATTAC believed, countries needed to show policy alternatives. The organization held well-attended conferences to find new directions, especially to help countries hurt in the crush of global development. ATTAC was but one of several antiglobalization movements, some of which organized mass demonstrations during a variety of international economic meetings.

Review: What trends suggest that the nation-state was a declining institution at the beginning of the twenty-first century?

❖ Global Challenges and Discontents

It is now a common belief that we live in a global age, but once our historical vision widens to encompass the globe we see a picture of uneven development and much room for debate about the state of our planet and its peoples. Despite prosperity for many, the end of the cold war ushered in many challenges. First, the health of the world's peoples and their environment came under a multipronged attack from nuclear disaster, acid rain, and surging population. Second, economic prosperity and physical safety continued to elude great masses of people, especially in the southern half of the globe. Third, as suprastate organizations developed, transnational allegiances and religious and ethnic movements also vied for power and influence. Growing prosperity in regions outside the West gave these movements not only financing but also confidence in the idea that it was time for the West to surrender some of its power.

Pollution and Population

Whereas industrialization and a growing population had once appeared wholly positive, people in the late twentieth century became more than ever aware of their dangers and limits. Despite spreading ecological awareness, technological development continued to threaten the environment. The aftermath of the 1986 nuclear explosion at Chernobyl left thousands perishing slowly from the effects of radiation. Levels of radioactivity rose for hundreds of miles in all directions, and by the 1990s cancer rates in the region were soaring, particularly among children.

Other environmental problems were more insidious but also had devastating global effects. Fossil-fuel pollutants such as those from natural gas, coal, and oil mixed with atmospheric moisture to produce acid rain, a poisonous brew that destroyed forests in industrial areas. In eastern Europe, the unchecked use of fossil fuels ravaged forests and inflicted ailments such as chronic bronchial disease on children. In less indus-

trial areas, the world's rain forests were hacked down at an alarming rate to develop the land for cattle grazing or for cultivation of cash crops. Clearing the forests depleted the global oxygen supply and threatened the biological diversity of the entire planet. By the late 1980s, scientists determined that the use of chlorofluorocarbons (CFCs), chemicals found in aerosol and refrigeration products, had blown a hole in the earth's ozone layer, the part of the blanket of atmospheric gases that prevents harmful ultraviolet rays from reaching the planet. Simultaneously, automobile and industrial emissions of chemicals were adding to that thermal blanket. The result was **global warming**, an increase in the temperature of the earth's lower atmosphere. Changes in temperature and dramatic weather cycles of drought or drenching rain indicated that a greenhouse effect might be permanently warming the earth. Already in the 1990s the Arctic pack ice was breaking up, allowing Finland to ship oil along the once-iced-over route in 2002. Scientists predicted dire consequences: the rate of global ice melting, which had more than doubled since 1988, would raise sea levels 27 centimeters by 2100, flooding coastal areas, disturbing fragile ecosystems, and harming the fresh water supply.

Rising activism protesting unbridled industrial growth took decades to develop as an effective political force. An escapee from Nazi Germany, E. F. "Fritz" Schumacher, produced one of the bibles of the environmental movement, *Small Is Beautiful* (1973), which spelled out how technology and industrialization actually threatened the earth and its inhabitants. Behind him stood the legacy of American Rachel Carson, author of a powerful critique—*Silent Spring* (1962), which advocated the immediate rescue of rivers, forests, and the soil from the ravages of factories and chemical farming. In West Germany, environmentalism united members of older and younger generations around a political tactic called citizen initiatives, in which groups of people blocked everything from public transportation fare increases to plans for urban growth. In 1979, the Green Party was founded in West Germany and across Europe Green Party candidates came to force other politicians to voice their con-

Petra Kelly, Activist for the Green Party

Petra Kelly was a typical transnational, who had been born in Germany but who received some of her childhood education in the United States. When her younger sister died of cancer, Kelly became an environmentalist and active member of the German Green Party. Kelly, like many Greens, came to believe that environmentalism involved more than simply eliminating carcinogens in the air. The movement needed to advocate a new lifestyle in general and new forms of political participation. In the excerpt below, Kelly outlines the goals of the Green Party.

The Green Party must remain a movement for non-violent change, and, at the same time, it must use parliament to make the case for non-violence to the electorate. One of the most important tasks for a parliamentary, extra-parliamentary party is to campaign for the recognition and protection of human rights. Food, health care, work, housing, freedom of religion and belief, freedom of assembly, freedom of expression, humane treatment of prisoners—all these human rights have been formally recognized by the member states of the United Nations, and all of them continue to be abused. These rights derive from a human being's right to life. Abuse of human rights can lead to the outbreak of war. Respect for human rights can help to build peace.

The Greens demand the unconditional abolition of all weapons of mass destruction. This demand is addressed to everybody, immediately and without exception, regardless of whether or when others make the same move. The destruction of mankind is the most heinous crime against

humanity imaginable. There can be no justification for it or for any action which might cause such destruction.

The Greens seek a new life-style for the Western world, as well as in their own personal lives. They would like to see an alternative way of life without exploitation, and they aim for non-violent relationships with others and with themselves. . . . We should muster some solidarity, some friendship, in the face of our throw-away life-style. More important than material goods, is enhancing the quality of life and living in harmony with the need for the preservation of nature and cyclical renewal. This is one of the most important objectives that the Greens are working for in the new political culture.

However, there can be no future for the Greens if they go in for gaining power in the same way as the established parties. The Greens are ready to work with others if the demand that parliament should speak the language of the people is finally met. So far, parliaments have acted simply as the executive body of the bureaucracy in the ministries, especially where important proposals such as airports or nuclear power stations are concerned. . . .

We are, and I hope we will remain, half party and half local action group—we shall go on being an anti-party party. The learning process that takes place on the streets, on construction sites, at nuclear bases, must be carried into parliament.

Source: Petra Kelly, *Fighting for Hope* (Boston: South End Press, 1984), 19–21.

cern for the environment. (See "Petra Kelly, Activist for the Green Party" above.) As the horrific effects of utterly unchecked pollution in eastern Europe became known, protest mounted and solutions began to unfold.

Europeans attacked environmental problems on both the local and global levels.

Some European cities—Frankfurt, for example—developed car-free zones, and the city of Venice operated completely without the use of automobiles. In Paris, when levels of emissions reached a certain level, the use of automobiles was restricted, and when the pollution reached dangerous levels, cars were banned altogether. The Smart, a very small car using reduced amounts of fuel, became a fashionable way in Europe to reduce dependence on fossil fuels. Cities also developed bicycle lanes on major city streets. To reduce dependence on fossil fuels, some areas of Europe developed wind power to such an extent that 20 percent of the country's electricity was generated by wind. To eliminate pollution, Denmark banned the use of aluminum cans in favor of glass containers, and many cities in the West began to recycle waste materials. These were success stories, involving changing habits and dependencies, by some of the most industrialized countries in the world. Many of these countries added their signatures to the Kyoto Protocol, an international treaty fashioned in 1997 to reduce the level of emissions and other pollutants around the world. But here, as in other policies, the West was fragmenting: the United States and Russia—among the world's top polluters—rejected the treaty, making cooperation on the environment a dead issue.

Population and Disease

Nations with less-developed economies struggled with the pressing problem of surging population, while the global public health establishment confronted the spread of deadly disease. The cause of the population surge was complex. Whereas by 1995 Europe was actually experiencing negative growth (that is, more deaths than births), the less industrially developed countries accounted for 98 percent of worldwide population growth in part because the spread of Western medicine enabled people there to live much longer than before. By late 1999, the earth's population had reached six billion, with a doubling forecast for 2045 (see "Taking Measure," opposite). In nonindustrial countries, birthrates were much higher than in the West, while life expectancy rose by an average of sixteen years between 1950 and 1980. The world's sole remaining superpower did not fare particularly well by this measure of social health: by 1995, the United States had fallen from the

Windmills in the Netherlands
The oil crisis of the 1970s caused so much havoc in the world economy that many European states encouraged the development of alternate sources of energy. Surprisingly, entrepreneurs turned to an older source of power—that provided by the wind—and constructed these modern windmills that dot many coastal regions of northern Europe. Whereas windmills several centuries earlier had powered tools that ground grain, these mills generated energy that was stored and then sold to regional power companies. What made the windmill an attractive means of generating power? © *Benoit Roland/ The Image Works.*

top twenty in longevity for both women and men. However, life expectancy in the Soviet Union and then in its successor states was catastrophic, falling steadily from a peak of seventy years for Russian men in the mid-1970s to fifty-three in 1995 and to fifty-one at the beginning of the twenty-first century. Meanwhile, fertility rates were declining. They had been dropping in the West for decades. In the less economically developed world they also began to fall noticeably by 1995. Though birthrates in these countries were higher than in the West, some 58 percent of couples in the emerging economies were estimated to use birth control. Many took the slowdown in population increase as a heartening sign of the potential for taming calamitous growth. Migration and urbanization only added to the problems faced by nations lacking the industrial resources to care for their swelling numbers.

TAKING MEASURE

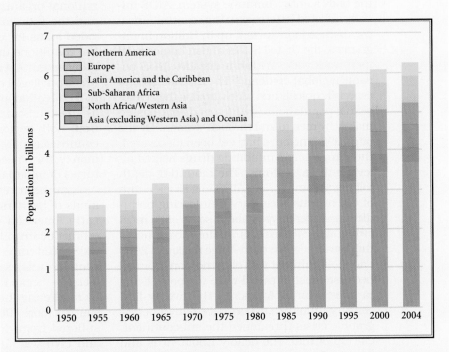

World Population Growth, 1950–2004

In the twenty-first century, a major question is whether the global environment can sustain billions of people indefinitely. In the early modern period, local communities had lived according to unwritten rules that balanced population size with the productive capacities of individual farming regions. Centuries later, the same need for balance had reached global proportions. As fertility dropped around the planet because of contraception, population continued to grow because of improved health. The political, social, and environmental results remain unclear. What are the major population issues demonstrated by this chart?

Western medicine and better health found their way into the less-developed world in the form of vaccines and drugs for diseases such as malaria and smallpox. However, half of all Africans did not benefit from basic public health facilities such as safe drinking water. Drought and poverty, along with the maneuvers of politicians in some cases, spread famine in regions like the Sudan, Somalia, and Ethiopia. Critics pointed to medical practices in the industrialized nations that focused on high-tech solutions to health problems and provided a disproportionate amount of expensive and high-tech hospital services to the upper classes. Specialists performed heart bypass surgery, transplanted organs, and treated cancer with radiation and chemotherapy, while preventive care for the masses received less attention. The poor and unemployed suffered more chronic illnesses than those who were better off, but they received less care. The distribution of health services became a hotly debated issue in the general argument about whether technological solutions could remedy global problems.

Disease, like population and technology, operated on a global terrain. In the early 1980s, both Western values and Western technological expertise were challenged by the spread of a global epidemic disease: acquired immuno-deficiency syndrome (AIDS). An incurable, highly virulent killer that effectively shuts down the body's entire immune system, AIDS initially afflicted heterosexuals in central Africa; the disease later turned up in Haitian immigrants to the United States and in homosexual men worldwide. Within a decade, AIDS became a global epidemic. The disease spread especially quickly and widely among the heterosexual populations of Africa and Asia, passed mainly by men to and through women. By the late 1990s, no cure had yet been discovered, though protease-inhibiting drugs helped alleviate the symptoms. The mounting death toll made some equate AIDS to a Black Death of the twentieth century, reinforcing prejudices and stereotypes about some of its most vulnerable victims. As millions contracted the disease—some thirty-three million in 2000 had it—treatment was often not forthcoming because most of the ill were too poor, living in sub-Saharan Africa. As the twenty-first century unfolded, an unprecedented demographic crisis threatened the subcontinent. On top of that, the deadly Ebola virus and dozens of other viruses smoldered like a global conflagration in the making. Interconnectedness via disease became all too real once again in 2003, when an unknown respiratory illness traveled the world: in the space of a month, severe acute respiratory syndrome (SARS) caused hundreds of deaths. Despite quarantines and surveillance of travelers, economic activity in Asia plunged, threatening the world economy, if only temporarily. Although it was rapidly brought under control through global medical cooperation, SARS showed the potential for medical and economic crisis in the global age.

North versus South?

During the 1980s and 1990s, world leaders tried to address the growing economic schism between the earth's northern and southern regions. Other than Australians and New Zealanders, southern peoples generally suffered lower living standards and measures of health than northerners. Recently emerging from colonial rule and economic exploitation by northerners, citizens in the southern regions could not yet count on their new

governments to provide welfare services or education. Their funds generally coming from the wealth of the northern countries, international organizations like the World Bank and the International Monetary Fund provided loans for economic development, but the conditions tied to them, such as cutting government spending, led to criticism that underprivileged citizens gained no real benefit if education and health care had to be cut as a result. Some twenty-first-century leaders from both regions advocated that wealthy countries simply give southern countries the money they needed in recognition of centuries of imperial pillage.

Southern regions experienced different kinds of barriers to economic development. Latin American nations grappled with government corruption, multibillion-dollar debt, widespread crime, and grinding poverty, though some countries—prominent among them Mexico—began to strengthen theireconomies by marketing their oil and other natural resources more effectively. Sub-Saharan Africa suffered from drought, continuing famine, and civil war. In lands such as Rwanda, military rule, ideological factionalism, and ethnic antagonism encouraged under imperialism produced a lethal mixture of conflict and genocide in the 1990s. Millions perished; others were left starving and homeless due to a kleptocracy that drained resources. Although African countries began turning away from military dictatorship and toward parliamentary government, global economic advance was uneven on that continent, and in the twenty-first century the scourge of AIDS added to the weight of Africa's problems.

Emerging economies in the Southern Hemisphere as a whole continued to increase their share of the world's gross domestic product during the 1980s and 1990s, and some achieved political gains as well. In South Africa, native peoples began winning the struggle for political rights when, in 1990, the moderate government of F. W. de Klerk released political leader Nelson Mandela, imprisoned for almost three decades because of his antiapartheid activism. De Klerk followed Mandela's release with a gradual dismantling of apartheid, including the desegregation of parks and beaches. In 1993, the government agreed to a democratic constitution that granted the vote to the nonwhite majority while guaranteeing whites and other minorities civil liberties. The next year, Mandela became the country's president in a landslide victory, formalizing the institution of a multiracial democracy in which international business made strides. In India, Rajiv Gandhi, the grandson of India's first prime minister, Jawaharlal Nehru, worked for education, women's rights, and an end to bitter local rivalries, but his assassination in 1991 raised the question of whether India would continue to have the strong leadership necessary to attract investment and thus to continue modernization. That question was especially difficult to answer. India developed strong leadership in communications and other technology alongside the rise of Hindu nationalism and movements that actually obstructed, even through violence, India's global reach.

Islam Confronts the West

The Iranian hostage crisis that began in 1979 showed religion, nationalism, and the power of oil uniting to make the Middle East an arbiter of international order. The charismatic leaders of the 1980s and 1990s—Iran's Ayatollah Ruhollah Khomeini; Libya's Muammar Qaddafi;◆ Iraq's Saddam Hussein; and Osama bin Laden, leader of the al-Qaeda transnational terrorist organization—variously promoted a pan-Arabic or pan-Islamic world order that gathered increasing support. Khomeini's program—"Neither East, nor West, only the Islamic Republic"—had wide appeal. Turning from the Westernization that had flourished under the shah, his regime in Iran required women once again to cover their bodies almost totally in special clothing, restricted their access to divorce, and eliminated a range of other rights. Buoyed by the prosperity that oil had brought, Islamic revolutionaries believed these restrictions would restore the pride and Islamic identity that imperialism had stripped from Middle Eastern men. Khomeini built widespread support among the Shi'ite Muslims by proclaiming the ascendancy of the Shi'ite clergy. Even though they were numerous and

◆**Qaddafi:** kuh DAH fee

even constituted the majority in parts of the Middle East, the Shi'ites had long been ruled by the Sunnis.

Power in the Middle East remained dispersed, however, and Islamic leaders did not achieve their unifying goals. Instead, war plagued the region, as Saddam Hussein of Iraq sought to make his country the dominant power and launched an attack on Iran in 1980. Hussein feared that Iraq's Shi'ite minority might be convinced by Iran's example to rebel against his regime, and he sought to channel their aggression through a patriotic crusade against the non-Arab Iranians. The United States provided Iraq with massive aid in the struggle against the power of Muslims in Iran. But eight years of combat led to stalemate and extensive loss of life on both sides. Simultaneously, the Soviet Union had become embroiled against Islam when it supported a coup by a Communist faction against the government in Afghanistan in 1979. Tens of thousands of Soviets fought in Afghanistan, using the USSR's most advanced missiles and artillery to combat a powerful group of Muslim resisters. The United States, China, Saudi Arabia, and Pakistan provided aid to this resistance movement, some of which later coalesced into the Taliban. The losing war in Afghanistan so riled the Soviet population and drained resources that the Soviet leaders withdrew the troops in 1989. Power in Afghanistan remained contested until the late 1990s when the fundamentalist Taliban movement succeeded in imposing a strict regime, creating millions of political and religious refugees.

As the USSR's empire fell apart, Saddam Hussein was the first to test the post–cold war waters. At the end of the Iran-Iraq war in 1988, Iraq staggered under a heavy debt and a lowered standard of living. Hussein viewed the annexation of neighboring Kuwait, whose 600,000 citizens enjoyed the world's highest per capita income, as a way to rebuild his economy. In 1990, he invaded the oil-rich country. Contrary to Hussein's expectations that he would be left alone, the deployment of Iraqi troops on the Saudi Arabian border galvanized a UN coalition (joined by the USSR) to stop the Iraqi invasion. A multinational force led by the United States pummeled the Iraqi army (Map 30.5, page 1208).

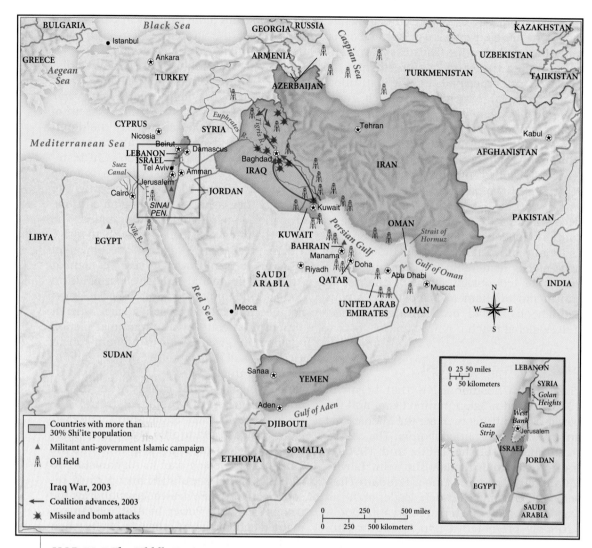

MAP 30.5 The Middle East, c. 2003

Tensions among states in the Middle East, especially the ongoing conflict between the Palestinians and Israelis, became more complicated in the 1990s. As Islam took center stage in politics, Middle Eastern populations divided over such issues as the extent of religious determination of state policies, the rule of religion in everyday life, and access to human rights including freedom of speech and of movement. Conflicts erupted around some of these questions because, as elsewhere, they were also vehicles for political ambition. The increasing demands of globalization in the 1990s pulled other citizens in the direction of secularization, high-tech international partnerships, and a reduction in the costly politics of violence. In 2001, however, violence escalated among Arabs and Israelis, bringing tensions in the region close to the breaking point. In 2003, the situation in the Middle East grew more uncertain and violent when the United States and Britain led an invasion in Iraq to seize its weapons of mass destruction and to overthrow the government of the dictator Saddam Hussein.

The Middle East remained in turmoil, and discontent mounted, even while efforts to resolve conflicts between the Israelis and the Palestinians continued. Peace talks broke down in 2001. As Israeli settlers began taking more Palestinian land, in the late 1990s, Palestinian suicide bombers began murdering Israeli civilians. The Israeli government retaliated with missiles, machine guns, and tanks, often killing Palestinian civilians in turn. Throughout the 1980s and 1990s, terrorists from the Middle East and North Africa planted bombs in many European cities, blew up airplanes, and bombed the Paris subway system. These attacks, causing widespread destruction and loss of life, were said to be punishment for the West's support for both Israelis and the repressive regimes in the Middle East.

On September 11, terrorism finally caught the full attention of the United States. In an unprecedented act, Muslim militants hijacked four planes in the United States and flew two of them into the World Trade Center in New York and one into the Pentagon in Virginia. The fourth plane crashed in Pennsylvania. The hijackers, all but one of whom were from Saudi Arabia, were inspired by the wealthy radical leader, Osama bin Laden, who sought to end the presence of U.S. forces in Saudi Arabia. These hijackers trained in bin Laden's terrorist camps in Afghanistan and learned to pilot planes in the United States. The loss of more than three thousand lives led the United States to declare a "war against terrorism." The administration of U.S. president George W. Bush forged a multinational coalition, which included the vital cooperation of Islamic countries such as Pakistan. The coalition enjoyed quick successes in driving out the ruling Taliban party in Afghanistan, though it failed in its major goal of capturing bin Laden.

Terrorism became one of the most frightening global challenges of the twenty-first century, and there was real cooperation in the wake of the September 11 attacks, as European countries rounded up terrorists and conducted the first successful trials of them in the spring of 2003. However, ultimately the West fragmented its efforts when the United States claimed that Iraq's Saddam Hussein had menacing weapons of mass destruction and suggested ties between Saddam Hussein and bin Laden's terrorist group. The most powerful European states, including Germany, Russia, and France, refused to back the invasion of Iraq the United States undertook in March 2003. Many people in the United States were furious. Bumper stickers appeared saying "First Iraq, Next France," and bars and pubs held regular happy hours to encourage "French bashing." Although British prime minister Tony Blair supported the U.S. effort, the separation grew wider as the United States suggested that Syria and Iran would need to

Europeans React to 9/11 Terror
On September 11, 2001, terrorists killed thousands of people from dozens of countries in airplane attacks on the World Trade Center in New York. Throughout the world, people expressed their shock and sorrow in vigils, and like this British tourist in Rome, they remained glued to the latest news. Terrorism, which had plagued Europeans for several decades, easily traveled the world in these days of more open borders, economic globalization, and cultural exchange, finally reaching the sole superpower left after the collapse of the Soviet Union. © *Pizzoli Alberto/Corbis Sygma.*

be invaded as well. Casualties and resistance to the U.S. occupation mounted, even as Saddam Hussein himself was captured in late 2003. Europeans in general, including the British public, accused the United States of becoming a world military dictatorship in order to preserve its only remaining value—wasteful consumerism. The United States countercharged that the Europeans were too selfish in their enjoyment of democracy and creature comforts to fund military defense of freedom under attack. There was a sense that the West was coming apart.

The Rise of the Pacific Economy

Additional evidence of weakening Western leadership came from the global diffusion of industry and technology in the last third of the twentieth century. Just as economic change in the early modern period had redirected European affairs from the Mediterranean to the Atlantic, so explosive productivity from Japan to Singapore in the 1980s and 1990s spread economic power from the Atlantic region to the Pacific. In 1982, the Asian Pacific nations accounted for 16.4 percent of global gross domestic product, a figure that had doubled since the 1960s. By 1989, the share of East Asia's world production was more than 25 percent as that of the West declined. By the mid-1990s China alone was achieving economic growth rates of 8 percent per year and more, while Japan had developed the second largest national economy after the United States, with Germany in third place.

South Korea, Taiwan, Singapore, and Hong Kong were popularly called **Pacific tigers** for the ferocity of their growth in the 1980s and 1990s. China, pursuing a policy of economic modernization and market orientation, saw phenomenal economic growth in the 1990s as well. Japan, however, had led the charge of Asian economies. Investment in high-tech consumer industries drove the Japanese economy. Thus, in 1982, Japan had 32,000 industrial robots in operation; western Europe employed only 9,000, and the United States had 7,000. In 1989, the Japanese government and private businesses invested $549 billion to modernize industrial capacity, a full $36 billion more than American public and private investment combined. Such spending paid off substantially, as buyers around the world snapped up automobiles, televisions, videocassette recorders, and computers from Japanese or other Asian Pacific companies. As the United States poured vast sums into its cold war military budget, Asian Pacific funds purchased U.S. government bonds, thus financing America's ballooning national debt. Forty years after its total defeat in World

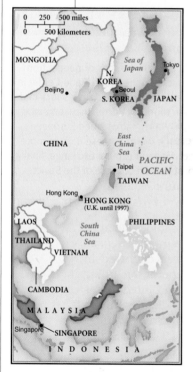

Tigers of the Pacific Rim, c. 1995

War II, Japan was bankrolling its former conqueror and its citizens had come to be the world's leading savers.

Despite rising national prosperity, individual Asian workers, particularly outside of Japan, often paid dearly for this newly created wealth. For example, women in South Korea and Taiwan labored in sweatshops to produce clothing for such U.S.-based companies as J. C. Penney and Calvin Klein. Using the lure of a low-paid and docile female workforce, governments were able to attract electronics and other industries. However, educational standards rose, along with access to birth control and other medical care for these women. Despite the persistent grip of authoritarian government, some of the Pacific tigers ranked high by UN standards for human development.

Mounting economic difficulties plagued Japan and the other Pacific tigers in the 1990s and early twenty-first century. Financial scandals and widespread corruption, which the government refused to address, destabilized the Japanese economy. The stock market plunged, as did the value of the yen. Domestic consumers cut back, and some of those interested in saving sent their money abroad for higher returns. From 1997 on, Japan's depressed economy menaced the region and the world, and little reform was in sight. A severe business crisis struck the Pacific rim as currency speculation and irresponsible and corrupt financial practices—labeled crony capitalism—first brought down the Thai currency in 1997 and then toppled politicians and industrial leaders in Indonesia, South Korea, and elsewhere in the region; by 2001, the economic downturn had spread to Europe and the United States. Europeans were slow to reduce the heavy welfare costs paid by businesses that might have restimulated investment and thus economic growth. Only China continued its expansion. Other economic leaders, notably the Japanese, vacillated amid a growing recognition that in the twenty-first century, global industrial and financial health depended on the highly developed and emerging economies outside the West as well as on the West itself.

Review: What were the most important challenges facing the West in the new millennium?

❖ Global Culture and Society in the New Millennium

As the final years of the millennium unfolded, thinkers began to debate the future, with scenarios changing as rapidly as global politics and economics did. Some saw the world's peoples rapidly absorbing Western cultural values with the adoption of the West's systems of technology, representative government, and the free market. An opposing view predicted a clash of civilizations in which increasingly incompatible religions and cultures would lead to future global strife. These thinkers believed that Islam, with more than one billion followers, would confront Western values rather than absorb them. Finally, there was the prediction of the collapse of the West itself because the United States continued to venture forth as the determining force in the world, opposed by much of Europe, which—as in the case of the Iraq invasion—suddenly refused to obey U.S. requests for cooperation in successive invasions of sovereign states.

Yet the migration that had accelerated since the 1990s, the movement of disease and climate, the information revolution, and the global sharing of culture argued against the cultural purity of any group—including the West. "Civilizations," as Nobel Prize winner Amartya Sen wrote after the terrorist attacks of September 11, "are hard to partition . . . , given the diversities within each society as well as the linkages among different countries and cultures." In the 1980s and 1990s, Western society changed even more rapidly than when it came into intense contact with the rest of the globe hundreds of years earlier. Moreover, national boundaries in the traditional European center of the West were weakening politically and economically, given the growing strength of the European Union and the simultaneous influx of migrants. Culture ignored national boundaries, as East, West, North, and South became saturated with one another's cultural products. Observers even labeled the new millennium an era of denationalization— meaning that national cultures as well as national boundaries were becoming less distinct. But there is no denying that even while the West absorbed peoples and cultures, it continued to exercise not only economic but also cultural influence over the rest of the globe. This influence, like global military power, was also debated and contested. (See "Contrasting Views," page 1212.)

Redefining the West: The Impact of Global Migration

The global movement of people was massive in the last third of the twentieth century and into the twenty-first. Uneven economic development, political persecution, and warfare (which claimed more than 100 million victims worldwide after 1945) sent tens of millions in search of opportunity and safety. In the 1970s alone, more than 4.7 million people moved to the United States. By 2001, France had some six million Muslims within its borders and Europe as a whole had between thirty-five and fifty million. But other parts of the world were as full as the West of people from other cultures on the move. The oil-producing nations of the Middle East employed millions of foreign workers, who generally constituted one-third of the labor force. Singapore and Nigeria were also home to still further millions of foreign-born inhabitants. The ongoing violence in Africa sent Rwandans, Congolese, and others to South Africa, as its government became dominated by blacks. War in Afghanistan increased the number of refugees to Iran to close to two million in 1995, while the Iraq-Iran war and successive attacks on Iraq by the West had sent still further millions fleeing. By 2000, there were some 120 million migrants worldwide.

Migrants often earned desperately needed income for family members who remained in the native country, and in some cases they propped up the economies of entire nations. In the southern African country of Lesotho, where the soil had been ruined by overuse during colonial rule, between 40 and 50 percent of national income came from migrant workers, particularly from those who toiled in the mines of South Africa. In countries as different as Yugoslavia, Egypt, Spain, and Pakistan, money sent home from abroad constituted up to 60 percent of national income. In places where immigration was restricted, millions of people nevertheless

CONTRASTING VIEWS

The Debate over Globalization

Globalization has transformed the workings of government and industry, provoked the rise of thousands of organizations devoted to supporting and combating it, and expanded educational offerings to meet its needs. As part of the controversy over its value were hardheaded economic arguments on both sides: whereas a Harvard professor advocated the global scale of business (Document 1), two environmental scientists saw globalization as a disaster for the future of agriculture in India (Document 2). Another component of globalization—migration—aroused real opposition. According to a British newspaper editor, it led to political instability (Document 3). Rightist French politician Jean-Marie Le Pen preached "cultural diversity" for the world, by which he meant that the many peoples and cultures should be kept separate, with strict control of migration and of immigrants (Document 4).

1. GLOBALIZATION BUILDS THE ECONOMIC FUTURE

Rosabeth Moss Kanter, a renowned management consultant and professor, cited the advantages of globalization in 1994.

[G]lobalization encourages the formation of alliances and partnerships—cooperative relationships that extend each partner's global reach while each contributes its local competence. . . . Some countries require local partners in order for companies to do business there. But even where this is not required, many companies recognize the benefits of establishing alliances to combine technologies or develop market access quickly. Connection to a global network allows smaller companies to gain the purchasing power or market clout of larger ones.

Source: Rosabeth Moss Kanter, Afterword to *Global Strategies: Insights from the World's Leading Thinkers*, ed. Percy Barnevik and Rosabeth Moss Kanter (Cambridge: Harvard Business Review Books, 1994), 230.

2. DESTRUCTION OF AN AGRICULTURAL WAY OF LIFE

Scientists Vandana Shiva and Radha Holla-Bhar have protested the ways in which economic globalization has affected the environment and local farmers in their native India.

Until very recently in India, biodiversity was something held entirely in common by local communities of people. Resources and knowledge about forest or agricultural properties were freely shared. Whether it was seeds of the farm or plants of the forest, all were clearly understood to be part of the cultural, spiritual, and biological commons.

The idea that the commons could be divided up, purchased, and owned by individuals or companies for their own commercial purposes was unknown to Indian farmers until the early 1960s, when certain international conventions established "plant breeder's rights." These new "rights" allowed commercial plant breeders to take traditional indigenous varieties of seed, for example, "improve" them (often by very minor alterations of genetic structure), and then patent and commercialize them, eventually selling back the patented seeds to the communities that first provided them freely.

This globalization of the South's biodiversity commons was a windfall for northern corporations, which began a race to patent and privatize as much of this natural commons as possible, without ever paying royalties to the original breeders and farmers . . . who gathered all the knowledge about them.

The issue came to a crisis during the GATT [General Agreement on Tariffs and Trade] negotiations [1986], when the United States and other northern countries imposed their new rules of Trade-Related Intellectual Property Rights. . . . The northern countries argued that when southern farmers attempted to retain free use of their own seeds, developed by them over thousands of years, it was a form of piracy. . . .

Before GATT, Indian law excluded the private ownership of patent rights in biological materials. This helped ensure that entitlements to food and nutrition remained as broad-based as possible.

Source: Vandana Shiva and Radha Holla-Bhar, "Piracy by Patent: The Case of the Neem Tree," in *The Case against the Global Economy and for a Turn toward the Local*, ed. Jerry Mander and Edward Goldsmith (San Francisco: Sierra Club Books, 1996), 146–48.

3. THE PERILS OF GLOBAL MIGRATION

In 1995, Martin Woollacott, deputy editor of the influential British newspaper the Guardian, *found the global migration of peoples and their settlement in diasporas or communities of migrants from a different native land far from positive.*

Diasporas have many beneficial effects on both host and migrant communities, but they may also breed pathological attitudes among a small minority. Some may fight their own wars on foreign soil. Or diaspora communities can provide inadvertent cover, in their separateness from the main society, for terrorists and extremists from inside or outside who want to attack their hosts. . . . The global village can be a violent place. Its curse is that new combination of intimacy and aggression, with societies so penetrated by each other physically and culturally that awful damage can be wreaked at close quarters in a way that was not possible in the past.

Source: Martin Woollacott, "Living in the Age of Terror," *Guardian*, August 22, 1995.

4. GUARDING THE NATION FROM GLOBAL MIXTURE

In France, Jean-Marie Le Pen led a popular political party, the National Front, committed to renewed nationalism in the face of globalization. Here is an excerpt from his platform.

The French will have priority when it comes to being hired. In the event of group redundancies, they will be the first to keep their jobs. The immigrants who will be induced to going back to their country of origin will liberate numerous jobs for the French. Through the application of new protectionism, jobs will be protected against unauthorized competition from countries where wages and social protection are low. . . .

Foreigners whose resident's permit has expired and immigrant unemployed people with no more unemployment allowance rights will be repatriated to their country of origin in humane and dignified conditions. Expulsions of illegal immigrants and delinquents will be effectively upheld. French people will be given priority for social allowances, housing and jobs. Family allowances and the Minimum Revenue for Insertion (RMI) will be reserved for our compatriots, and will therefore be revalued. In order to avoid all disguised immigration the right of asylum will be strictly limited, family regrouping will be abolished and French naturalization will become more difficult.

Source: mosaique@mosaique.worldnet.net. Copyright Mosaïque, March 1995.

QUESTIONS TO CONSIDER

1. Describe and analyze the areas in which globalization seems to raise the most questions.

2. In what ways are issues around globalization centuries-old points of contention?

3. Is it possible or desirable to change the course of globalization?

4. List the benefits of globalization and assess whether the benefits outweigh the costs, some of which are presented in these documents.

The Headscarf Controversy in Germany
For centuries people in Western countries have debated the relationship between religion and the nation-state. In particular, that debate targeted the need for religiously neutral education in order to develop citizens with impartial judgment and undivided national loyalties. In an age of global migration, the issue of religion in the schools has resurfaced, this time focusing on the headscarfs worn by many Muslim women. Critics see this religious garb in the schools as weakening the commitment to secular education. In 2004, France banned all conspicuous religious attire in schools, including headscarves, yarmulkes, and crosses. Although in 2003 Germany upheld the right of the teacher Fereshta Ludin, pictured above, to wear her headscarf while teaching on the grounds of religious freedom, it simultaneously asserted the right of children to a religiously neutral education. Such complex debates show how individual rights, born in the eighteenth and nineteenth centuries, have become open to intense questioning in the twenty-first century world. *Photo: Michael Latz/ddp, Berlin.*

successfully crossed borders: from Mexico or China into the United States; over unguarded African frontiers; and between European states. Such migrants, unprotected by law, risked exploitation and abuse of their human rights. Those at greatest risk were the eastern European and Asian prostitutes, many of whom were coerced into international sex rings that controlled their passports, wages, and lives. Foreign workers were convenient scapegoats for native peoples suffering from economic woes such as unemployment caused by downsizing. Political parties with racist programs came to life in Europe, where unemployment was a problem from the mid-1970s on. Yet the West remained a place of opportunity and hope despite all obstacles.

Among migrants to the West, women had little to say in decisions about leaving home; a patriarchal head of the household generally made such choices. Once abroad, migrant women suffered the most from unstable working conditions and usually obtained more menial, lower-paying jobs than migrant men or native Europeans. They were also more likely than men to be refused political asylum. Rape and other violence against them, even during civil war, were classified as part of everyday life, not politics. The offspring of immigrants often had a difficult time being accepted even when they were citizens of their parents' adopted land. Unemployment hit them especially hard because "whites" and native-born people received preference. They also struggled with questions of identity, sometimes feeling torn between two cultures. Young black immigrants in particular forged transnational identities, for example, when they created music combining elements of African, Caribbean, Afro-American, and European cultures. As tens of millions of people migrated in the 1980s and 1990s, belief in a national identity based on a single, unique culture was losing credibility.

Global Networks and the Economy

Rapid technological change in electronic communications also made traditional national borders appear permeable, if not obsolete, and it made the world's economy far more global than ever before. In 1969, the U.S. Department of Defense developed a computer network to carry communications in case of nuclear war. This system and others like it in universities, government, and business grew into an unregulated system of more than ten thousand networks globally. These came to be known as the Internet—shorthand for *internetworking.* By 1995, users in more than 137 countries were connected to the Internet, creating new "communities" based on business needs, shared cultural interests, or other factors that transcended common citizenship in a particular nation-state. Communicating via the Internet allowed users often to escape state regulation such as censorship. An online global marketplace emerged, offering goods and services ranging from advanced weaponry to organ transplants. While enthusiasts claimed that the Internet could promote world democracy, critics

Call Center in Chandigarh, India
Modern communications now permits the outsourcing not just of manufacturing jobs, which began after World War II, but of service jobs to places like eastern Europe, Africa, and South Asia. In many countries, citizens are bi- and poly-lingual, enabling them to service customers in Europe and the United States, such as these telemarketers in India, who are calling consumers in the United States to persuade them to switch long-distance telephone plans. New Web sites like callcentersindia.com offer "one-stop shopping for Indian call centers," which includes consulting, training, and site visits for businesses that want to set up their own call centers to take advantage of the comparatively low wages and reduced benefits. What are the advantages and disadvantages of a division of labor that operates internationally? *Pablo Bartholomew/NetPhotograph.com*

charged that communications technology favored elites and disadvantaged those without computer skills. Yet these skills advanced so quickly that in 2001 countries like Estonia, Hungary, and the Czech Republic as well as Morocco, India, and the Philippines were successfully luring businesses to employ their help desk and other call-center service workers. By the early twenty-first century, three percent of India's domestic product came from the outsourcing work it did for English-speaking governments and private industries based in Europe, the United States, and the South Pacific. The Internet allowed some service industries to globalize as the manufacturing sector had done.

Globalization of the economy affected the West in complex ways. Those who worked in outsourcing enterprises were more likely

than those in domestic firms to participate in the global consumer economy, much of it for Western goods. A twenty-one-year-old Indian woman, working for a service provider in Bangalore under the English name Sharon, was able to buy a cell phone from the Finnish company Nokia and other consumer items with her salary. "As a teenager I wished for so many things," she said of her job. "Now I'm my own Santa Claus." The Irish and the eastern Europeans benefited from the booming global economy of the 1990s. Their new disposable income gave them access to luxury automobiles, CD players, and personal computers that would have been far beyond their means a decade before. The downside for ordinary Western workers was that this global revolution threatened their jobs. In Germany, where taxes for social security and other welfare-state financing comprised 42 percent of payroll costs in 2003, the incentive for business to move to countries with lower costs was strong. Here again, the West parted ways. For instance, book publishers in such places as France and Canada were enticed to outsource more of their work to pools of comparatively low-paid, highly educated editors in the United States who received fewer benefits. Thus, an editor in western Europe might now compete for work with an editor in the United States. Globalization redistributed jobs and reworked economic networks.

The Global Diffusion of Culture

Culture has long transcended political boundaries, and in fact archaeologists point to its diffusion as a constant of tens of thousands of years of human history. In the ancient world, the Romans studied the work of Greek philosophers; in the eighteenth and nineteenth centuries, Western scholars immersed themselves in Asian languages. In the postwar period, cultural exchange accelerated vastly through new forms of transportation and communication: tourism, for instance, became the largest single industry in Britain and in many other Western countries by the early 1990s. Throngs of visitors from Japan and elsewhere testified to the powerful place the West held in the world's imagination. Chinese students in Tiananmen Square in 1989 had rallied around their own representation of the Statue of Liberty (which itself was a gift from France to the United States). In Japan, businesspeople wore Western-style clothing and watched soccer, baseball, and other Western sports using English terms, but the connections flew in many directions.

Remarkable innovations in communications integrated cultures and made the earth seem a much smaller place, though possibly one with a Western flavor. Videotapes and satellite-beamed telecasts transported American television shows to Hong Kong and Japanese movies to Europe and North America. American rock music sold briskly in Russia and elsewhere in the former Soviet bloc. When more than 100,000 Czechoslo-

vakian rock fans, including President Václav Havel, attended a Rolling Stones concert in Prague in 1990, it was clear that despite half a century of supposedly insular Communist culture, Czechs and Slovaks had tuned in to the larger world. Sports stars like the Brazilian soccer player Pelé, the American basketball hero Michael Jordan, and Japanese baseball ace Ichiro Suzuki became better known to countless people than their own national leaders were. In today's world, millions of people might even, at the same moment, be spectators at a live event anywhere on the planet, whether a World Cup competition or an Academy Awards broadcast from Hollywood. With their messages conveyed around the world, even today's moral leaders—the Nobel Peace Prize winners Nelson Mandela, former president of South Africa; the Dalai Lama, the spiritual leader of Tibet; and Aung San Suu Kyi,♦ opposition leader in Burma—are global figures.

Culture from Beyond the West. As it had done for centuries, the West continued to devour material from other cultures—whether Hong Kong films, African textiles, Indian music, or Latin American pop culture. Publishers successfully marketed the outpouring of written work by major non-Western artists and intellectuals, and Hollywood made many of their novels into internationally marketed films. Such literature won both popular and critical acclaim and exerted a strong influence on European and North American writers. The lush, exotic fantasies of Colombian-born Nobel Prize winner Gabriel García Márquez, for example, attracted a vast Western readership. His novels, including *One Hundred Years of Solitude* (1967) and *Love in the Time of Cholera* (1988), portray people of titanic ambitions and passions who endure war and all manner of personal trials. Another Nobel Prize recipient who won high regard in the West was Egyptian writer Naguib Mahfouz.♦ Having immersed himself in his youth in great Western literature, Mahfouz authored more than forty books. His celebrated *Cairo Trilogy*, written in the 1950s, describes a middle-class family—

♦**Aung San Suu Kyi:** AWN SAHN SOO CHEE
♦**Naguib Mahfouz:** nuh GEEB mahk FOOS

from its practice of Islam and seclusion of women to the business and cultural life of men in the family. British colonialism forms the trilogy's backdrop; it impassions the protagonists and shapes their lives and destinies. In the eyes of many Arab observers, Mahfouz was a safe choice for the Nobel Prize in 1988, not only because he produced a literature about the history of colonialism but also because he had adopted a European style. "He borrowed the novel from Europe; he imitated it," charged one fellow Egyptian writer. "It's not an Egyptian art form. Europeans . . . like it very much because it is their own form." The globally read Egyptian Nawal el-Saadawi was also accused of producing exotic accounts of women's oppression to appeal to Western feminists. Thus, although non-Western literature reshaped Western taste, it sometimes provoked charges of inauthenticity in its authors' homelands.

Immigrants to Europe described how the experience of Western culture felt to the transnational person. The popular writer Buchi Emecheta, in her novel *In the Ditch* (1972) and her autobiography *Head above Water* (1986), explored her experiences as a newcomer to Britain. Her *Joys of Motherhood* (1979) was an imaginary foray back in time to probe the nature of mothering under colonial rule in her native Lagos, Nigeria. While critiquing colonialism and the welfare state from a non-Western perspective, Emecheta, like many writers and politicians from less-developed countries, felt the lure of Western education and Western values. International conflict around artistic expression became dangerous. Salman Rushdie, also an immigrant to Great Britain (from India), produced the novel *The Satanic Verses* (1988), which ignited outrage among Muslims around the world because it appeared to blaspheme the prophet Muhammad. From Iran, the Ayatollah Khomeini promised both a monetary reward and salvation in the afterlife to anyone who would assassinate the writer. In a display of Western cultural unity, international leaders took bold steps to protect Rushdie until the threat was lifted a decade later.

The mainstream became fraught with conflict as groups outside the accepted circles engaged in artistic production. From within the West, novelist Toni Morrison, who in 1993

Toni Morrison Receiving the Nobel Prize
The first African American woman to receive the Nobel Prize, Toni Morrison had used her literary talent to depict the condition of blacks under slavery and after emancipation. Morrison also published cogent essays on social, racial, and gender issues in the United States. *Pressens Bild/Gamma Liaison.*

became the first African American woman to win the Nobel Prize in literature, described the nightmares, daily experiences, and dreams of the descendants of men and women who had been brought as slaves to the United States. But some parents objected to the inclusion of Morrison's work in school curricula. Critics charged that, unlike Shakespeare's universal Western truth, the writing of African Americans, Native Americans, and women represented only a partial vision, not great literature. In both the United States and western Europe, politicians on the right saw the presence of multiculturalism as a sign of deterioration similar to that brought about by racial mixing. It was an era of culture wars—much like that ushered in by the Nazis and by the cold warriors of both the USSR and United States—when strong political attacks on new kinds of thinking and writing took place.

Building Post-Soviet Culture. In the former Soviet bloc, artists and writers faced unique challenges. The collapse of the Soviet Union put literary dissidents out of business. Those who had helped bring down the Soviet regime had lost their subject matter—the critique of a tyrannical system. Tied as their work was to the drama of the Soviet empire, there was no drama left. Moreover the lack of state support meant that authors had to sell their products on the free market in countries where economic conditions were so harsh as to make books an unaffordable luxury. Additionally, there was no consensus on what the post-Communist arts should be. Was everything that had appeared under the Soviets utterly worthless because it was produced by a corrupt system? Some seemed to think so, for shortlisted novels for major prizes in the 1990s were those influenced by Buddhist and other worldwide texts and such writers as Hermann Hesse and Thomas Mann. The post-Soviet legacy was to look beyond the region itself for models to replace Communist ones.

However, in music and the other arts much energy was spent on simply absorbing all the underground arts that had been hidden since 1917. The situation was utterly astonishing as the work of literally dozens of first-rate composers, for example, emerged. They had written their classical works in private for fear that they might contain phrasings, sounds, and rhythms that would be called subversive. Meanwhile, they had often earned a living writing for films, as did Giya Kancheli, who wrote immensely popular music for more than forty films. Other work could now become even better known. Alfred Schnittke (1934–1998) produced rich compositions—dozens of operas, symphonies, chamber music pieces, concertos, and other works—that were extremely sad, punctuated with anger in loud bursts of dissonance, and set in a somber bass register. The public also discovered virtually unknown composers, such as Galina

Ustvolskaya, a protégé and lover of Soviet composer Dmitry Shostakovich. Ustvolskaya lived in poverty because she refused to join the Communist cultural system; her music surfaced for the public only after the USSR collapsed, as did unknown works of classical writers like Mikhail Bulgakov (1891–1940), famous for his novel *The Master and Margarita* (published 1966–1967).

Cultural reappraisals were often the order of the day in eastern Europe, and the entire intellectual world adjusted to the novel atmosphere of artistic freedom. Old works were unearthed, and dissident writing was harshly criticized. Eastern-bloc writers who formerly found success in the West seemed less heroic—and less talented—in the wide-open post-Soviet world. Milan Kundera's work, for example, lost its luster. It was, according to one critic, merely a phenomenon of the West's prosperous book contracts, not literature but merely a "line of business." eastern European artists both reappraised their cultural past and tried to redefine the future of creativity.

U.S. Cultural Dominance. The political and economic power of the United States gave its culture an edge. U.S. success in "marketing" culture, along with the legacy of British imperialism, helped make English the dominant international language by the end of the twentieth century. Such English words as *stop*, *shopping*, *parking*, *okay*, *weekend*, and *rock* infiltrated dozens of non-English vocabularies. English became an official language of the European Union, but it functioned across Europe as the main language of such educational institutions as the Central European University in Budapest and the European University Institute in Florence. It has united the scientific community as well as guiding travelers. In the 1960s, French president de Gaulle, fearing the corruption of the French language, had banned such new words as *computer* in government documents, and his path was followed by succeeding administrations; but such a directive did not stop the influx of English into scientific, technical, diplomatic, and daily life. Nonetheless, in another sign of cultural divide, the European Union's parliament, as well as national cultural ministries, has regulated the amount of American programming on television and in cinemas.

American influence in film was dominant, making such films as *Titanic* (1997) and *The Matrix Reloaded* (2003) works that earned hundreds of millions of dollars from global audiences. American pop music and television stars filled the pages of foreign magazines because of their international appeal. Simultaneously, however, the United States itself welcomed films from around the world—whether the Chinese *Crouching Tiger, Hidden Dragon* (2000), the Mexican *Y Tu Mamá También* (2001), or the Italian *Life Is Beautiful* (1997)—the number one favorite foreign film in the United States. "Bollywood" films—happy, lavish films from the Indian movie industry—had a huge following in all Western countries, even influencing the plots of some American productions. The fastest-growing media in the United States in the twenty-first century was Spanish-language television, just one more indication that culture even in the United States was based on mixture and global exchange.

Postmodernism. Some have called the global culture of the late twentieth and early twenty-first centuries **postmodernism**, defined in part as intense stylistic mixing in the arts without a central unifying theme or privileged canon. Striking examples of postmodern art abounded in Western society, including the AT&T building in New York City, the work of architect Philip Johnson. Although the structure itself, designed in the late 1970s, looked sleek and modern, its entryway was a Roman arch, and its cloud-piercing top suggested eighteenth-century Chippendale furniture. The buildings of Johnson and other postmodernists appealed to the human past and drew from cultural styles that spanned millennia and continents without valuing one style above others. The Guggenheim Museum in Bilbao, Spain, designed by American Frank Gehry, was similarly bizarre by classical or even "modern" standards as it represented forms, materials, and perspectives that by rules of earlier decades did not belong together. Finally the postunification rebuilding of Berlin was accomplished by architects from around the world in a variety of hybrid styles.

Other intellectuals defined the postmodern in political terms as an outgrowth of the

The "Dancing Building," Prague
This building—also nicknamed "Fred and Ginger" after the famed American dancers—rose in the 1990s on the site of an accidental bombing by U.S. forces in World War II. American architect Frank Gehry and Czech architect Vladimir Milunic hoped to achieve something light and pleasure-giving—a mark of postmodern style. Critics, however, felt that the building looked more like a crushed can of Coca Cola and that it served as an ugly reminder of American militarism and consumerism. Others lamented that in the place of a good Czech building something American would arise on exactly the spot where Americans had left their destructive mark. Defenders, however, pointed to the international cooperation of the design team and the fact that its eccentric look called attention to the destruction instead of simply papering over the wartime devastation with a mere restoration of the original building. Why are cultural works such as paintings, novels, and architecture the subject of such debate in today's world? *Ben R. Hays/brhphoto.com*

demise of the eighteenth-century Enlightenment ideals of human rights, individualism, personal freedom, and their guarantor—the Western nation-state. A structure like the Bilbao Guggenheim was just an international tourist attraction that had no Spanish roots or purpose; consumption, global technology, mass communications, and international migration made citizenship, nationalism, and rights irrelevant to its meaning. It was a rootless structure, unlike the Louvre in Paris. Moreover, the end of imperialism meant an end to the white privilege behind modern civil rights as defined in the eighteenth century. The 1982 American film *Blade Runner*, for example, depicted a dangerous, densely packed, multiethnic Los Angeles patrolled by police with high-tech gear—a metropolis with no place for national or personal identity or human rights. For postmodernists of a political bent, computers had replaced the autonomous, free self and bureaucracy had rendered representative government obsolete.

A third definition of the postmodern involved investigating the "unfreedom" or irrationality that shaped human life. Thus, French psychoanalyst Jacques Lacan, whose writing deeply influenced Western literary criticism in the 1990s, maintained that people operate in an unfree, predetermined world of language. In becoming social, communicating beings, we must bow to these laws, implanted in us at birth. Another prominent French thinker, Michel Foucault, deplored the easy acceptance of such liberal ideas as the autonomous self, the progressive march of history, and the advance of freedom. For him, the sexual revolution had not been liberating at all; rather, sexuality was merely a way in which humans expressed power over one another and through which society, by allowing greater sexual expression, actually controlled individuals. Some postmodern thinkers thus questioned the West's conviction that it had achieved freedom: even in the most intimate part of human experience, people were inescapably locked in a grid of social and individual constraint.

The issues raised by postmodernism—whether in architecture, ideas, or the popular media—focused on the basic ingredients of Western identity as it had been defined over the past two hundred years. Postmodernism was part of a great enterprise of rethinking and questioning that accompanied globalization. We can point to such critical thinking—whatever its momentary conclusions—as itself a key ingredient in the making of the West.

Review: What social and cultural questions has globalization raised?

Conclusion: The Making of the West Continues

Although some postmodernists have proclaimed an end to centuries of faith in progress, they themselves have worked within the modern Western tradition of constant criticism and reevaluation. Moreover, said their critics, the daunting problems of contemporary life—population explosion, resource depletion, North–South inequities, global pollution, ethnic hatred, and global terrorism—demanded, more than ever, the exercise of humanistic values and the renewal of a rational commitment to progress. Postmodernists and other philosophers countered with the question of "unintended consequences," that is, the question of whether one could begin to know the consequences of an act. Who would have predicted, for example, the human misery resulting from the fall of the Soviet empire?

The years since 1990 have proved both sides correct. The collapse of communism signaled the eclipse of an ideology that was perhaps noble in intent but deadly in practice. Events from South Africa and Northern Ireland, for example, indicated that certain long-feuding groups were wearying of conflict and groping for peace, even as other peoples took up arms against their neighbors. Yet the unintended consequences of communism's fall were bloodshed, sickness, and hardship, while the global age ushered in by the Soviet collapse has brought denationalization to many regions of the world. Instead of being advocates for peace, prosperous militants from Saudi Arabia, Egypt, Indonesia, and the Philippines have unleashed unprecedented terrorism on the world, while many in Africa and Asia also face disease and the dramatic social and economic change associated with the global age.

Western traditions of democracy, human rights, and economic equality have much to offer. Given that these were initially intended only for certain people, global debates about

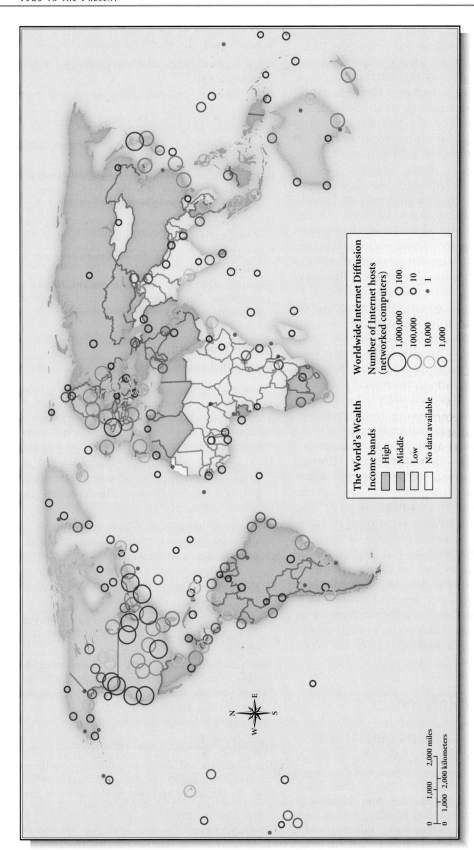

MAPPING THE WEST The World in the New Millennium

By the twenty-first century, the Internet had transformed communications and economic organization into an inter-connected global network. People in the so-called North had greater access to this network in 2004 and for the most part enjoyed greater wealth. Despite globalization, historians still find local and national conditions of political, social, and economic life important in telling the full story of peoples and cultures. In what ways does this map indicate a closely connected world? From www.mids.org (Austin: Matrix Information and Directory Services, Inc.)

their value abound. The nation-state, which protected those values for privileged Westerners, is another legacy that must be rethought in an age of transnationalism, when more people than ever are demanding the dignity of citizenship. At the same time, the West faces questions of its own unity and cultural identity—an identity made from the far-flung cultural, natural, and human resources of Asia, Africa, and the Western Hemisphere. Non-Westerners have challenged, criticized, refashioned, and made enormous contributions to Western culture; they have also served the West's citizens as slaves, servants, and menial workers. Whether the West survives as a unit or not, one of the greatest challenges to the West and the world in this global millennium is to determine how peoples and cultures can live together on terms that are fair for everyone.

A final challenge to the West is living with the inventive human spirit. In the past five hundred years, the West has benefited from its scientific and technological advances. Longevity and improved material well-being have spread to many places. In the past century, communication and information technology brought people closer to one another than ever before. Simultaneously, through the use of technology the period from the last century and to the present one has become the bloodiest era in human history. War, genocide, and terrorism are among technology's hallmarks, posing perhaps the greatest challenge to the West and to the world. The making of the West has been a constantly inventive undertaking, but also a deadly one. What mixture of peoples and cultures will face the paradoxical challenge of technology to protect the creativity of the human race in the century that now stretches before us?

Suggested References

Soviet Collapse Releases Global Forces

Historians will be telling and retelling this story, for the full consequences of communism's collapse are still unfolding. As new archives open, scholars like Wachtel explain the post-Communist situation in terms of long-standing trends such as the obstacles to creating cultural unity

among peoples of the former Yugoslavia. Engel is excellent on the effects on Russian women.

Engel, Barbara. *Women in Russian History, 1700–2000.* 2004.

Glenny, Misha. *The Fall of Yugoslavia: The Third Balkan War.* 1996.

*Gorbachev, Mikhail. *Memoirs.* 1996.

Jarausch, Konrad. *The Rush to German Unity.* 1994.

Kazanov, Anatoly M. *After the USSR: Ethnicity, Nationalism, and Politics in the Commonwealth of Independent States.* 1995.

Kotkin, Stephen. *Armageddon Averted: The Soviet Collapse, 1970–2000.* 2001.

Naimark, Norman. *Fires of Hatred: Ethnic Cleansing in Twentieth-Century Europe.* 2001.

Wachtel, Andrew B. *Making a Nation, Breaking a Nation: Literature and Cultural Politics in Yugoslavia.* 1998.

Global Opportunities Transcend the Nation-State

The many new institutional forms, such as global cities and rising regionalism, are outlined in Applegate and Sassen, among others. The advance of the European Union is one of the transnational stories of the 1990s and the twenty-first century.

Applegate, Celia. "A Europe of Regions: Reflections on the Historiography of Sub-National Places in Modern Times." *The American Historical Review.* 1999.

European Union: http://europa.eu.int.

Piening, Christopher. *Global Europe: The European Union in World Affairs.* 1997.

Redmond, John, and Glenda S. Rosenthal. *The Expanding European Union: Past, Present, Future.* 1998.

Sassen, Saskia. *Globalization and Its Discontents: Essays on the New Mobility of People and Money.* 1998.

Shalin, Jamal, and Michael J. Wintel, eds. *The Idea of a United Europe: Political, Economic, and Cultural Integration Since the Fall of the Berlin Wall.* 2000.

Global Challenges and Discontents

The international scene is politically challenging and, one should add, dangerous. But in this time, the forces of overpopulation, disease, and

*Primary source.

pollution remain potentially destructive. Huntington and Kagan give two different pictures of world events.

Bess, Michael. *The Light-Green Society: Economic and Technological Modernity in France.* 2003.

Huntington, Samuel P. *The Clash of Civilizations and the Remaking of the World Order.* 1996.

Kagan, Robert. *Of Paradise and Power: America and Europe in the New World Order.* 2003.

Morris, Benny. *Righteous Victims: A History of the Zionist-Arab Conflict, 1881–1999.* 2000.

Rashid, Ahmed. *Jihad: The Rise of Militant Islam in Central Asia.* 2002.

United Nations. *State of the World Population: People, Poverty, and Possibilities.* 2003.

Global Culture and Society in the New Millennium

The fate of cultural identity in an age of globalization engages a wide range of investigation and theorizing. In an age of migration and the Internet, people need to rethink long-standing identities and individual relationships, as Turkle, among others, suggests. Western prosperity is both enhanced and challenged by this technology. The Public Broadcasting Service's Web site offers a wide array of information on current issues.

Agre, Philip. *Computation and Human Experience.* 1997.

Bales, Kevin. *Disposable People: New Slavery in the Global Economy.* 1999.

*Emecheta, Buchi. *The Joys of Motherhood.* 1979.

Hoerder, Dirk. *Cultures in Contact: World Migrations in the 2nd Millennium.* 2002.

Iriye, Akira. *Cultural Internationalism and World Order.* 1997.

*Morrison, Toni. *Paradise.* 1998.

Public Broadcasting Service: http://www.pbs.org.

Smith, Andrea, ed. *Europe's Invisible Migrants.* 2002.

Turkle, Sherry. *Life on the Screen: Identity in the Age of the Internet.* 1995.

CHAPTER REVIEW

IMPORTANT EVENTS

1989	Chinese students revolt in Tiananmen Square and government suppresses them; fall of the Berlin Wall
1990s	Internet revolution
1990–1991	War in the Persian Gulf
1991	Civil war erupts in the former Yugoslavia; failed coup by Communist hard-liners in the Soviet Union
1992	Soviet Union is dissolved
1993	Toni Morrison becomes the first African American woman to win the Nobel Prize
1994	Nelson Mandela elected president of South Africa; Russian troops invade Chechnya; European Union officially formed
1995	International congress of women at Beijing
1997	Collapse of Thai currency launches economic problems for Pacific tigers
1999	Euro introduced in the European Union; world population reaches six billion
2000	Vladimir Putin becomes president of Russia
2001	Terrorist attack on the United States and declaration of a "war against terrorism"
2003	United State invades Iraq; the West divides on this policy; draft European Union constitution
2004	Ten countries join the European Union

KEY TERMS

ethnic cleansing (1189)

euro (1185)

European Union (EU) (1196)

global warming (1202)

Maastricht Treaty (1196)

nongovernmental organizations (NGOs) (1201)

Pacific tigers (1210)

postmodernism (1219)

World Bank (1201)

REVIEW QUESTIONS

1. What were the major issues facing the former Soviet world in the 1990s and early 2000s?
2. What trends suggest that the nation-state was a declining institution at the beginning of the twenty-first century?
3. What were the most important challenges facing the West in the new millennium?
4. What social and cultural questions has globalization raised?

MAKING CONNECTIONS

1. In what ways were global connections at the beginning of the twenty-first century different from the global connections at the beginning of the twentieth century?
2. How did the Western nation-state of early twenty-first century differ from the Western nation-state at the opening of the twentieth century?

FOR FURTHER EXPLORATION

To assess your mastery of the material in this chapter, see the Online Study Guide at **bedfordstmartins.com/hunt**.

To read additional primary-source material from this period, see Chapter 30 in *Sources of The Making of the West*, Second Edition.

Appendix

Useful Facts and Figures

PROMINENT ROMAN EMPERORS

Julio-Claudians

27 B.C.E.–14 C.E.	Augustus
14–37	Tiberius
37–41	Gaius (Caligula)
41–54	Claudius
54–68	Nero

Flavian Dynasty

69–79	Vespasian
79–81	Titus
81–96	Domitian

Golden Age Emperors

96–98	Nerva
98–117	Trajan
117–138	Hadrian
138–161	Antonius Pius
161–180	Marcus Aurelius

Severan Emperors

193–211	Septimius Severus
211–217	Antoninus (Caracalla)
217–218	Macrinus
222–235	Severus Alexander

Period of Instability

235–238	Maximinus Thrax
238–244	Gordian III
244–249	Philip the Arab
249–251	Decius
251–253	Trebonianus Gallus
253–260	Valerian
270–275	Aurelian
275–276	Tacitus
276–282	Probus
283–285	Carinus

Dominate

284–305	Diocletian
306	Constantius
306–337	Constantine I
337–340	Constantine II
337–350	Constans I

(Continued)

337–361	Constantius II
361–363	Julian
363–364	Jovian
364–375	Valentinian I
364–378	Valens
367–383	Gratian
375–392	Valentinian II
378–395	Theodosius I (the Great)

The Western Empire

395–423	Honorius
406–407	Marcus
407–411	Constantine III

409–411	Maximus
411–413	Jovinus
412–413	Sebastianus
423–425	Johannes
425–455	Valentinian III
455–456	Avitus
457–461	Majorian
461–465	Libius Severus
467–472	Anthemius
473–474	Glycerius
474–475	Julius Nepos
475–476	Romulus Augustulus

PROMINENT BYZANTINE EMPERORS

Dynasty of Theodosius

395–408	Arcadius
408–450	Theodosius II
450–457	Marcian

Dynasty of Leo

457–474	Leo I
474	Leo II
474–491	Zeno
475–476	Basiliscus
484–488	Leontius
491–518	Anastasius

Dynasty of Justinian

518–527	Justin
527–565	Justinian I
565–578	Justin II
578–582	Tiberius II
578–582	Tiberius II (I) Constantine
582–602	Maurice
602–610	Phocas

Dynasty of Heraclius

610–641	Heraclius
641	Heraclonas
641	Constantine III
641–668	Constans II
646–647	Gregory
649–653	Olympius
669	Mezezius
668–685	Constantine IV
685–695	Justinian II (banished)
695–698	Leontius

698–705	Tiberius III (II)
705–711	Justinian II (restored)
711–713	Bardanes
713–716	Anastasius II
716–717	Theodosius III

Isaurian Dynasty

717–741	Leo III
741–775	Constantine V Copronymus
775–780	Leo IV
780–797	Constantine VI
797–802	Irene
802–811	Nicephorus I
811	Strauracius
811–813	Michael I
813–820	Leo V

Phrygian Dynasty

820–829	Michael II
821–823	Thomas
829–842	Theophilus
842–867	Michael III

Macedonian Dynasty

867–886	Basil I
869–879	Constantine
887–912	Leo VI
912–913	Alexander
913–959	Constantine VII Porphrogenitos
920–944	Romanus I Lecapenus
921–931	Christopher
924–945	Stephen
959–963	Romanus II

Useful Facts and Figures

963–969	Nicephorus II Phocas
976–1025	Basil II
1025–1028	Constantine VIII (IX) alone
1028–1034	Romanus III Argyrus
1034–1041	Michael IV the Paphlagonian
1041–1042	Michael V Calaphates
1042	Zoe and Theodora
1042–1055	Constantine IX Monomchus
1055–1066	Theodora alone
1056–1057	Michael VI Stratioticus

Prelude to the Comnenian Dynasty

1057–1059	Isaac I Comnenos
1059–1067	Constantine X (IX) Ducas
1068–1071	Romanus IV Diogenes
1071–1078	Michael VII Ducas
1078–1081	Nicephorus III Botaniates
1080–1081	Nicephorus Melissenus

Comnenian Dynasty

1081–1118	Alexius I
1118–1143	John II
1143–1180	Manuel I
1180–1183	Alexius II
1183–1185	Andronieus I
1183–1191	Isaac, Emperor of Cyprus

Dynasty of the Angeli

1185–1195	Isaac II
1195–1203	Alexius III
1203–1204	Isaac II (restored) with Alexius IV
1204	Alexius V Ducas Murtzuphlus

Lascarid Dynasty in Nicaea

1204–1222	Theodore I Lascaris
1222–1254	John III Ducas Vatatzes
1254–1258	Theodore II Lascaris
1258–1261	John IV Lascaris

Dynasty of the Paleologi

1259–1289	Michael VIII Paleologus
1282–1328	Andronicus II
1328–1341	Andronicus III
1341–1391	John V
1347–1354	John VI Cantancuzenus
1376–1379	Andronicus IV
1379–1391	John V (restored)
1390	John VII
1391–1425	Manuel II
1425–1448	John VIII
1449–1453	Constantine XI (XIII) Dragases

PROMINENT POPES

314–335	Sylvester
440–461	Leo I
590–604	Gregory I (the Great)
687–701	Sergius I
741–752	Zachary
858–867	Nicholas I
1049–1054	Leo IX
1059–1061	Nicholas II
1073–1085	Gregory VII
1088–1099	Urban II
1099–1118	Paschal II
1159–1181	Alexander III
1198–1216	Innocent III
1227–1241	Gregory IX
1243–1254	Innocent IV
1294–1303	Boniface VIII
1316–1334	John XXII
1447–1455	Nicholas V
1458–1464	Pius II

1492–1503	Alexander VI
1503–1513	Julius II
1513–1521	Leo X
1534–1549	Paul III
1555–1559	Paul IV
1585–1590	Sixtus V
1623–1644	Urban VIII
1831–1846	Gregory XVI
1846–1878	Pius IX
1878–1903	Leo XIII
1903–1914	Pius X
1914–1922	Benedict XV
1922–1939	Pius XI
1939–1958	Pius XII
1958–1963	John XXIII
1963–1978	Paul VI
1978	John Paul I
1978–	John Paul II

THE CAROLINGIAN DYNASTY

687–714	Pepin of Heristal, Mayor of the Palace
715–741	Charles Martel, Mayor of the Palace
741–751	Pepin III, Mayor of the Palace
751–768	Pepin III, King
768–814	Charlemagne, King
800–814	Charlemagne, Emperor
814–840	Louis the Pious

West Francia

840–877	Charles the Bald, King
875–877	Charles the Bald, Emperor
877–879	Louis II, King
879–882	Louis III, King
879–884	Carloman, King

Middle Kingdoms

840–855	Lothair, Emperor
855–875	Louis (Italy), Emperor
855–863	Charles (Provence), King
855–869	Lothair II (Lorraine), King

East Francia

840–876	Ludwig, King
876–880	Carloman, King
876–882	Ludwig, King
876–887	Charles the Fat, Emperor

GERMAN KINGS CROWNED EMPEROR

Saxon Dynasty

962–973	Otto I
973–983	Otto II
983–1002	Otto III
1002–1024	Henry II

Franconian Dynasty

1024–1039	Conrad II
1039–1056	Henry III
1056–1106	Henry IV
1106–1125	Henry V
1125–1137	Lothair II (Saxony)

Hohenstaufen Dynasty

1138–1152	Conrad III
1152–1190	Frederick I (Barbarossa)
1190–1197	Henry VI
1198–1208	Philip of Swabia
1198–1215	Otto IV (Welf)
1220–1250	Frederick II
1250–1254	Conrad IV

Interregnum, 1254–1273:
Emperors from Various Dynasties

1273–1291	Rudolf I (Habsburg)
1292–1298	Adolf (Nassau)
1298–1308	Albert I (Habsburg)
1308–1313	Henry VII (Luxemburg)
1314–1347	Ludwig IV (Wittelsbach)
1347–1378	Charles IV (Luxemburg)
1378–1400	Wenceslas (Luxemburg)
1400–1410	Rupert (Wittelsbach)
1410–1437	Sigismund (Luxemburg)

Habsburg Dynasty

1438–1439	Albert II
1440–1493	Frederick III
1493–1519	Maximilian I
1519–1556	Charles V
1556–1564	Ferdinand I
1564–1576	Maximilian II
1576–1612	Rudolf II
1612–1619	Matthias
1619–1637	Ferdinand II
1637–1657	Ferdinand III
1658–1705	Leopold I
1705–1711	Joseph I
1711–1740	Charles VI
1742–1745	Charles VII (not a Habsburg)
1745–1765	Francis I
1765–1790	Joseph II
1790–1792	Leopold II
1792–1806	Francis II

RULERS OF FRANCE

Capetian Dynasty

987–996	Hugh Capet
996–1031	Robert II
1031–1060	Henry I
1060–1108	Philip I
1108–1137	Louis VI
1137–1180	Louis VII
1180–1223	Philip II (Augustus)
1223–1226	Louis VIII
1226–1270	Louis IX (St. Louis)
1270–1285	Philip III
1285–1314	Philip IV
1314–1316	Louis X
1316–1322	Philip V
1322–1328	Charles IV

Valois Dynasty

1328–1350	Philip VI
1350–1364	John
1364–1380	Charles V
1380–1422	Charles VI
1422–1461	Charles VII
1461–1483	Louis XI
1483–1498	Charles VIII
1498–1515	Louis XII
1515–1547	Francis I
1547–1559	Henry II
1559–1560	Francis II
1560–1574	Charles IX
1574–1589	Henry III

Bourbon Dynasty

1589–1610	Henry IV
1610–1643	Louis XIII
1643–1715	Louis XIV
1715–1774	Louis XV
1774–1792	Louis XVI

After 1792

1792–1799	First Republic
1799–1804	Napoleon Bonaparte, First Consul
1804–1814	Napoleon I, Emperor
1814–1824	Louis XVIII (Bourbon Dynasty)
1824–1830	Charles X (Bourbon Dynasty)
1830–1848	Louis Philippe
1848–1852	Second Republic
1852–1870	Napoleon III, Emperor
1870–1940	Third Republic
1940–1944	Vichy government, Pétain regime
1944–1946	Provisional government
1946–1958	Fourth Republic
1958–	Fifth Republic

MONARCHS OF ENGLAND AND GREAT BRITAIN

Anglo-Saxon Monarchs

829–839	Egbert
839–858	Ethelwulf
858–860	Ethelbald
860–866	Ethelbert
866–871	Ethelred I
871–899	Alfred the Great
899–924	Edward the Elder
924–939	Ethelstan
939–946	Edmund I
946–955	Edred
955–959	Edwy
959–975	Edgar
975–978	Edward the Martyr
978–1016	Ethelred the Unready
1016–1035	Canute (Danish nationality)
1035–1040	Harold I
1040–1042	Hardicanute
1042–1066	Edward the Confessor
1066	Harold II

Norman Monarchs

1066–1087	William I (the Conqueror)
1087–1100	William II
1100–1135	Henry I

House of Blois

1135–1154	Stephen

House of Plantagenet

1154–1189	Henry II
1189–1199	Richard I

(Continued)

1199–1216	John	
1216–1272	Henry III	
1272–1307	Edward I	
1307–1327	Edward II	
1327–1377	Edward III	
1377–1399	Richard II	

House of Lancaster

1399–1413	Henry IV
1413–1422	Henry V
1422–1461	Henry VI

House of York

1461–1483	Edward IV
1483	Edward V
1483–1485	Richard III

House of Tudor

1485–1509	Henry VII
1509–1547	Henry VIII
1547–1553	Edward VI
1553–1558	Mary
1558–1603	Elizabeth I

House of Stuart

1603–1625	James I
1625–1649	Charles I

Commonwealth and Protectorate (1649–1660)

1653–1658	Oliver Cromwell
1658–1659	Richard Cromwell

House of Stuart (Restored)

1660–1685	Charles II
1685–1688	James II
1689–1694	William III and Mary II
1694–1702	William III (alone)
1702–1714	Anne

House of Hanover

1714–1727	George I
1727–1760	George II
1760–1820	George III
1820–1830	George IV
1830–1837	William IV
1837–1901	Victoria

House of Saxe-Coburg-Gotha

1901–1910	Edward VII

House of Windsor

1910–1936	George V
1936	Edward VIII
1936–1952	George VI
1952–	Elizabeth II

PRIME MINISTERS OF GREAT BRITAIN

Term	Prime Minister	Government
1721–1742	Sir Robert Walpole	Whig
1742–1743	Spencer Compton, Earl of Wilmington	Whig
1743–1754	Henry Pelham	Whig
1754–1756	Thomas Pelham-Holles, Duke of Newcastle	Whig
1756–1757	William Cavendish, Duke of Devonshire	Whig
1757–1761	William Pitt (the Elder), Earl of Chatham	Whig
1761–1762	Thomas Pelham-Holles, Duke of Newcastle	Whig
1762–1763	John Stuart, Earl of Bute	Tory
1763–1765	George Grenville	Whig
1765–1766	Charles Watson-Wentworth, Marquess of Rockingham	Whig
1766–1768	William Pitt, Earl of Chatham (the Elder)	Whig
1768–1770	Augustus Henry Fitzroy, Duke of Grafton	Whig
1770–1782	Frederick North (Lord North)	Tory
1782	Charles Watson-Wentworth, Marquess of Rockingham	Whig

Useful Facts and Figures

1782–1783	William Petty FitzMaurice, Earl of Shelburn	Whig
1783	William Henry Cavendish Bentinck, Duke of Portland	Whig
1783–1801	William Pitt (the Younger)	Tory
1801–1804	Henry Addington	Tory
1804–1806	William Pitt (the Younger)	Tory
1806–1807	William Wyndham Grenville (Baron Grenville)	Whig
1807–1809	William Henry Cavendish Bentinck, Duke of Portland	Tory
1809–1812	Spencer Perceval	Tory
1812–1827	Robert Banks Jenkinson, Earl of Liverpool	Tory
1827	George Canning	Tory
1827–1828	Frederick John Robinson (Viscount Goderich)	Tory
1828–1830	Arthur Wellesley, Duke of Wellington	Tory
1830–1834	Charles Grey (Earl Grey)	Whig
1834	William Lamb, Viscount Melbourne	Whig
1834–1835	Sir Robert Peel	Tory
1835–1841	William Lamb, Viscount Melbourne	Whig
1841–1846	Sir Robert Peel	Tory
1846–1852	John Russell (Lord)	Whig
1852	Edward Geoffrey–Smith Stanley Derby, Earl of Derby	Whig
1852–1855	George Hamilton Gordon Aberdeen, Earl of Aberdeen	Peelite
1855–1858	Henry John Temple Palmerston, Viscount Palmerston	Tory
1858–1859	Edward Geoffrey–Smith Stanley Derby, Earl of Derby	Whig
1859–1865	Henry John Temple Palmerston, Viscount Palmerston	Tory
1865–1866	John Russell (Earl)	Liberal
1866–1868	Edward Geoffrey–Smith Stanley Derby, Earl of Derby	Tory
1868	Benjamin Disraeli, Earl of Beaconfield	Conservative
1868–1874	William Ewart Gladstone	Liberal
1874–1880	Benjamin Disraeli, Earl of Beaconfield	Conservative
1880–1885	William Ewart Gladstone	Liberal
1885–1886	Robert Arthur Talbot, Marquess of Salisbury	Conservative
1886	William Ewart Gladstone	Liberal
1886–1892	Robert Arthur Talbot, Marquess of Salisbury	Conservative
1892–1894	William Ewart Gladstone	Liberal
1894–1895	Archibald Philip–Primrose Rosebery, Earl of Rosebery	Liberal
1895–1902	Robert Arthur Talbot, Marquess of Salisbury	Conservative
1902–1905	Arthur James Balfour, Earl of Balfour	Conservative
1905–1908	Sir Henry Campbell-Bannerman	Liberal
1908–1915	Herbert Henry Asquith	Liberal
1915–1916	Herbert Henry Asquith	Coalition
1916–1922	David Lloyd George, Earl Lloyd-George of Dwyfor	Coalition
1922–1923	Andrew Bonar Law	Conservative
1923–1924	Stanley Baldwin, Earl Baldwin of Bewdley	Conservative
1924	James Ramsay MacDonald	Labour
1924–1929	Stanley Baldwin, Earl Baldwin of Bewdley	Conservative
1929–1931	James Ramsay MacDonald	Labour
1931–1935	James Ramsay MacDonald	Coalition
1935–1937	Stanley Baldwin, Earl Baldwin of Bewdley	Coalition
1937–1940	Neville Chamberlain	Coalition
1940–1945	Winston Churchill	Coalition
1945	Winston Churchill	Conservative
1945–1951	Clement Attlee, Earl Attlee	Labour
1951–1955	Sir Winston Churchill	Conservative

(Continued)

PRIME MINISTERS OF GREAT BRITAIN (continued)

Term	Prime Minister	Government
1955–1957	Sir Anthony Eden, Earl of Avon	Conservative
1957–1963	Harold Macmillan, Earl of Stockton	Conservative
1963–1964	Sir Alec Frederick Douglas-Home, Lord Home of the Hirsel	Conservative
1964–1970	Harold Wilson, Lord Wilson of Rievaulx	Labour
1970–1974	Edward Heath	Conservative
1974–1976	Harold Wilson, Lord Wilson of Rievaulx	Labour
1976–1979	James Callaghan, Lord Callaghan of Cardiff	Labour
1979–1990	Margaret Thatcher (Baroness)	Conservative
1990–1997	John Major	Conservative
1997–	Tony Blair	Labour

RULERS OF PRUSSIA AND GERMANY

1701–1713	*Frederick I
1713–1740	*Frederick William I
1740–1786	*Frederick II (the Great)
1786–1797	*Frederick William II
1797–1840	*Frederick William III
1840–1861	*Frederick William IV
1861–1888	*William I (German emperor after 1871)
1888	Frederick III
1888–1918	*William II
1918–1933	Weimar Republic
1933–1945	Third Reich (Nazi dictatorship under Adolf Hitler)
1945–1952	Allied occupation
1949–1990	Division of Federal Republic of Germany in west and German Democratic Republic in east
1990–	Federal Republic of Germany (reunited)

*King of Prussia

RULERS OF AUSTRIA AND AUSTRIA-HUNGARY

1493–1519	*Maximilian I (Archduke)
1519–1556	*Charles V
1556–1564	*Ferdinand I
1564–1576	*Maximilian II
1576–1612	*Rudolf II
1612–1619	*Matthias
1619–1637	*Ferdinand II
1637–1657	*Ferdinand III
1658–1705	*Leopold I
1705–1711	*Joseph I
1711–1740	*Charles VI
1740–1780	Maria Theresa
1780–1790	*Joseph II
1790–1792	*Leopold II

1792–1835	*Francis II (emperor of Austria as Francis I after 1804)
1835–1848	Ferdinand I
1848–1916	Francis Joseph (after 1867 emperor of Austria and king of Hungary)
1916–1918	Charles I (emperor of Austria and king of Hungary)
1918–1938	Republic of Austria (dictatorship after 1934)
1945–1956	Republic restored, under Allied occupation
1956–	Free Republic

*Also bore title of Holy Roman Emperor

LEADERS OF POST-WORLD WAR II GERMANY

West Germany (Federal Republic of Germany), 1949–1990

Years	Chancellor	Party
1949–1963	Konrad Adenauer	Christian Democratic Union (CDU)
1963–1966	Ludwig Erhard	Christian Democratic Union (CDU)
1966–1969	Kurt Georg Kiesinger	Christian Democratic Union (CDU)
1969–1974	Willy Brandt	Social Democratic Party (SPD)
1974–1982	Helmut Schmidt	Social Democratic Party (SPD)
1982–1990	Helmut Kohl	Christian Democratic Union (CDU)

East Germany (German Democratic Republic), 1949–1990

Years	Communist Party Leader
1946–1971	Walter Ulbricht
1971–1989	Erich Honecker
1989–1990	Egon Krenz

Federal Republic of Germany (reunited), 1990–

1990–1998	Helmut Kohl	Christian Democratic Union (CDU)
1998–	Gerhard Schroeder	Social Democratic Party (SPD)

RULERS OF RUSSIA, THE USSR, AND THE RUSSIAN FEDERATION

c. 980–1015	Vladimir
1019–1054	Yaroslav the Wise
1176–1212	Vsevolod III
1462–1505	Ivan III
1505–1553	Vasily III
1553–1584	Ivan IV
1584–1598	Theodore I
1598–1605	Boris Godunov
1605	Theodore II
1606–1610	Vasily IV
1613–1645	Michael
1645–1676	Alexius
1676–1682	Theodore III
1682–1689	Ivan V and Peter I
1689–1725	Peter I (the Great)
1725–1727	Catherine I
1727–1730	Peter II
1730–1740	Anna
1740–1741	Ivan VI
1741–1762	Elizabeth
1762	Peter III
1762–1796	Catherine II (the Great)
1796–1801	Paul
1801–1825	Alexander I
1825–1855	Nicholas I
1855–1881	Alexander II
1881–1894	Alexander III
1894–1917	Nicholas II

Union of Soviet Socialist Republics (USSR)*

1917–1924	Vladimir Ilyich Lenin
1924–1953	Joseph Stalin
1953–1964	Nikita Khrushchev
1964–1982	Leonid Brezhnev
1982–1984	Yuri Andropov
1984–1985	Konstantin Chernenko
1985–1991	Mikhail Gorbachev

Russian Federation

1991–1999	Boris Yeltsin
1999–	Vladimir Putin

*USSR established in 1922

RULERS OF SPAIN

1479–1504	Ferdinand and Isabella
1504–1506	Ferdinand and Philip I
1506–1516	Ferdinand and Charles I
1516–1556	Charles I (Holy Roman Emperor Charles V)
1556–1598	Philip II
1598–1621	Philip III
1621–1665	Philip IV
1665–1700	Charles II
1700–1746	Philip V
1746–1759	Ferdinand VI
1759–1788	Charles III
1788–1808	Charles IV
1808	Ferdinand VII
1808–1813	Joseph Bonaparte
1814–1833	Ferdinand VII (restored)
1833–1868	Isabella II
1868–1870	Republic
1870–1873	Amadeo
1873–1874	Republic
1874–1885	Alfonso XII
1886–1931	Alfonso XIII
1931–1939	Republic
1939–1975	Fascist dictatorship under Francisco Franco
1975–	Juan Carlos I

RULERS OF ITALY

1861–1878	Victor Emmanuel II
1878–1900	Humbert I
1900–1946	Victor Emmanuel III
1922–1943	Fascist dictatorship under Benito Mussolini (maintained in northern Italy until 1945)
1946 (May 9–June 13)	Humbert II
1946–	Republic

SECRETARIES-GENERAL OF THE UNITED NATIONS

		Nationality
1946–1952	Trygve Lie	Norway
1953–1961	Dag Hammarskjöld	Sweden
1961–1971	U Thant	Myanmar
1972–1981	Kurt Waldheim	Austria
1982–1991	Javier Pérez de Cuéllar	Peru
1992–1996	Boutros Boutros-Ghali	Egypt
1997–	Kofi A. Annan	Ghana

UNITED STATES PRESIDENTIAL ADMINISTRATIONS

Term(s)	President	Political Party
1789–1797	George Washington	No party designation
1797–1801	John Adams	Federalist
1801–1809	Thomas Jefferson	Democratic-Republican
1809–1817	James Madison	Democratic-Republican
1817–1825	James Monroe	Democratic-Republican
1825–1829	John Quincy Adams	Democratic-Republican
1829–1837	Andrew Jackson	Democratic
1837–1841	Martin Van Buren	Democratic
1841	William H. Harrison	Whig
1841–1845	John Tyler	Whig
1845–1849	James K. Polk	Democratic
1849–1850	Zachary Taylor	Whig
1850–1853	Millard Filmore	Whig
1853–1857	Franklin Pierce	Democratic
1857–1861	James Buchanan	Democratic
1861–1865	Abraham Lincoln	Republican
1865–1869	Andrew Johnson	Republican
1869–1877	Ulysses S. Grant	Republican
1877–1881	Rutherford B. Hayes	Republican
1881	James A. Garfield	Republican
1881–1885	Chester A. Arthur	Republican
1885–1889	Grover Cleveland	Democratic
1889–1893	Benjamin Harrison	Republican
1893–1897	Grover Cleveland	Democratic
1897–1901	William McKinley	Republican
1901–1909	Theodore Roosevelt	Republican
1909–1913	William H. Taft	Republican
1913–1921	Woodrow Wilson	Democratic
1921–1923	Warren G. Harding	Republican
1923–1929	Calvin Coolidge	Republican
1929–1933	Herbert C. Hoover	Republican
1933–1945	Franklin D. Roosevelt	Democratic
1945–1953	Harry S. Truman	Democratic
1953–1961	Dwight D. Eisenhower	Republican
1961–1963	John F. Kennedy	Democratic
1963–1969	Lyndon B. Johnson	Democratic
1969–1974	Richard M. Nixon	Republican
1974–1977	Gerald R. Ford	Republican
1977–1981	Jimmy Carter	Democratic
1981–1989	Ronald W. Reagan	Republican
1989–1993	George H. W. Bush	Republican
1993–2001	William J. Clinton	Democratic
2001–	George W. Bush	Republican

MAJOR WARS OF THE MODERN ERA

1546–1555	German Wars of Religion
1526–1571	Ottoman wars
1562–1598	French Wars of Religion
1566–1609, 1621–1648	Revolt of the Netherlands
1618–1648	Thirty Years' War
1642–1648	English Civil War
1652–1678	Anglo-Dutch Wars
1667–1697	Wars of Louis XIV
1683–1697	Ottoman wars
1689–1697	War of the League of Augsburg
1702–1714	War of Spanish Succession
1702–1721	Great Northern War
1714–1718	Ottoman wars
1740–1748	War of Austrian Succession
1756–1763	Seven Years' War
1775–1781	American Revolution
1796–1815	Napoleonic wars
1846–1848	Mexican-American War
1853–1856	Crimean War
1861–1865	United States Civil War
1870–1871	Franco-Prussian War
1894–1895	Sino-Japanese War
1898	Spanish-American War
1904–1905	Russo-Japanese War
1914–1918	World War I
1939–1945	World War II
1946–1975	Vietnam wars
1950–1953	Korean War
1990–1991	Persian Gulf War
1991–1997	Civil War in the former Yugoslavia
2003	Iraq War

Glossary of Key Terms

This glossary of key terms contains definitions of words and ideas that are central to your understanding of the material covered in this textbook. Each term in the glossary is in boldface in the text when it is first defined, then listed again in the corresponding Chapter Review section to signal its importance. We have also included the page number on which the full discussion of the term appears so that you can easily locate the complete explanation to strengthen your historical vocabulary.

For words not defined here, two additional resources may be useful: the index, which will direct you to many more topics discussed in the text, and a good dictionary.

Abbasids (326): The caliphal dynasty that came to power in 750. The Abbasids built their capital at Baghdad, where they exercised considerable power over the entire Islamic world until the late ninth century.

abolitionists (713): Advocates of the abolition of the slave trade and of slavery.

Absolutism (621): A system of government in which the ruler claimed sole and uncontestable power.

agora (93): The central market square of a Greek city-state, a popular place to gather for conversation.

agricultural revolution (676): Increasingly aggressive attitudes toward investment in and management of land that increased production of food in the 1700s; this revolution developed first in England and then spread to the continent.

aids (382): Payments paid by a vassal to his lord on important occasions, such as the knighting of the lord's eldest son or the marriage of his eldest daughter.

Albigensians (420): The name given by its opponents to a religious movement of dualists centered in Albi, in southern France. The Albigensians were considered heretics, and a crusade was launched against them.

Anabaptists (561): Sixteenth-century religious dissenters who believed that humans have free will and that people must knowingly select the Christian faith through rebaptism as adults. They advocated radical separation from society; though originally pacifist, some chose violent paths to religious renewal.

anarchism (907): The belief that people should not have government; it was popular among peasants and workers in the last half of the nineteenth century and the first decades of the twentieth.

Angevins (406): The dynasty from Anjou that came to the English throne with Henry II. Also called Plantagenets.

Anglo-Saxon England (308): England *after* the invasions of the Angles and Saxons (which began in the 440s) and *before* the Norman conquest in 1066.

apocalypticism (51): A religious belief about the end of the world; literally, "uncovering the future."

apostate (254): Literally, "renegade from the faith"; the emperor Julian (r. 361–363), who rejected Christianity and tried to restore traditional religion as the state religion, was given the nickname "the Apostate."

apostolic succession (228): The principle by which Christian bishops traced their authority back to Jesus's apostles.

appeasement (1075): The strategy of preventing a war by making concessions for legitimate grievances.

areté (53): Greek for "excellence"; a competitive value that defined the Greek social elite.

Arianism (257): The Christian doctrine named after Arius, who argued that Jesus was "begotten" by God and did not have an identical nature with his Father.

art nouveau (974): A successful style in the arts, household and fashion design, and graphics that featured flowing, sinuous lines that contrasted with the mechanical influence of the early twentieth century. It borrowed many of its motifs from Asian and African art and was internationally popular.

asceticism (260): The practice of self-denial (from the Greek *askesis*, "training"), as in the lives of monks; a doctrine for Christians emphasized by Augustine.

atheist (712): A person who does not believe in the existence of God.

Atlantic revolutions (749): A term historians use to refer to protest movements that appeared on both sides of the Atlantic in the late 1780s: the new United States prepared a new constitution after winning its independence from Great Britain, while organized revolts occurred in the Dutch Republic, the Austrian Netherlands, and France.

Atlantic system (666): The triangular pattern of trade established in the 1700s that bound together western Europe, Africa, and the Americas. Europeans sold slaves from western Africa and bought commodities such as coffee and sugar that were produced by the new colonial plantations in North and South America and the Caribbean.

auctoritas (207): Literally, "moral authority"; the authority derived from respect on which the Roman princeps' power rested.

Augustus (206): The title meaning "divinely favored" that Rome's Senate granted Octavian and that became shorthand for "Roman imperial ruler."

auto da fé (528): Literally, "demonstration of faith"; the ritual of public confession that was one of the punishments given to heretics by the Inquisition in the fifteenth century.

ban (347): The rights to collect taxes, hear court cases, levy fines, and muster men for defense. It was largely understood as a complex of royal rights, but around 1000, local rulers as well as kings began exercising them.

baroque (607): An artistic style of the seventeenth century that featured curves, exaggerated lighting, intense emotions, release from restraint, and even a kind of artistic sensationalism; like mannerism, it departed from the Renaissance emphasis on harmonious design, unity, and clarity.

Beguines (420): Women in northern Europe who chose a life of celibacy outside of a cloister. Taking no permanent vows, the women lived in community houses and earned their living as laundresses and the like.

benefices (486): In the Catholic church, ecclesiastical offices funded by an endowment.

Blitzkrieg (1077): Literally, "lightning war"; a strategy for the conduct of war in which motorized firepower quickly and overwhelmingly attacks the enemy, leaving it in a state of shock and awe and unable to resist psychologically or militarily.

Boer War (985): The war between Britain and Boer (originally Dutch) inhabitants of South Africa for control of the region. Lasting between 1899 and 1902, the war convinced many British people that empire was wrong or at least too costly to maintain.

Bolshevik Revolution (1017): The overthrow of Russia's Provisional Government in the fall of 1917 by V. I. Lenin and his Bolshevik forces because of the government's continuing defeat in the war, its failure to bring political reform, and a further decline in the conditions of everyday life.

buccaneers (674): Pirates of the Caribbean who governed themselves and preyed on international shipping.

bureaucracy (627): A network of state officials carrying out orders according to a regular and routine line of authority.

Byzantine Empire (272): Historians' name for the eastern Roman Empire from about 500 to 1453, derived from Byzantium, the original name of Constantinople.

capital-intensive industry (920): A mid- to late-nineteenth-century development in industry that required great investments of money for machinery and infrastructure to make a profit; it contrasts with labor-intensive industry.

castellan (347): A person who controlled a castle. After around 1000, these castles were the seats of local power in France.

chansons de geste (415): Long vernacular poems about knightly and heroic deeds.

Chartism (855): The movement of supporters of the People's Charter (drawn up in Britain in 1838), which demanded universal manhood suffrage, vote by secret ballot, equal electoral districts, annual elections, and the elimination of property qualifications for and the payment of stipends to members of Parliament. Chartism attracted many working-class adherents.

chivalry (415): The proper, ideal comportment of a knight, who was constrained by a code of refinement, fair play, and piety.

cholera (829): An epidemic, usually fatal disease that appeared in the 1830s in Europe; it is caused by a waterborne bacterium that induces violent vomiting and diarrhea and leaves the skin blue, eyes sunken and dull, and hands and feet ice cold.

Christ (226): Greek for "anointed one" (the corresponding Hebrew word is *Messiah*); in apocalyptic religious thinking, the agent of God sent to conquer the forces of evil.

Christian Democrats (1110): Powerful center to center-right political parties that evolved in the late 1940s from former Catholic parties of the pre–World War II period.

Christian humanists (550): Humanists who in the sixteenth century dreamed of ideal societies based on peace and morality, and who sought to realize the ethical ideals of the classical world. Desiderius Erasmus (c. 1466–1536) and Thomas More (1478–1535) are representative of these thinkers.

city-state (9): A state consisting of an urban center exercising political and economic control over the countryside around it.

Civil Code (792): The French legal code formulated by Napoleon in 1804 (hence also called the Napoleonic Code); it assured equal treatment under the law to all classes of men and guaranteed religious liberty but curtailed many of the rights of women.

civil disobedience (1054): Deliberately but peacefully breaking the law, a tactic used by Mohandas Gandhi in India and earlier by British suffragists to protest oppression and obtain political change.

civilization (4): A way of life that includes political states based on cities with dense populations, large buildings constructed for communal activities, diverse economies, a sense of local identity, and some knowledge of writing.

classicism (654): A style of painting and architecture that reflected the ideals of the art of antiquity; in classicism, geometric shapes, order, and harmony of lines took precedence over the sensuous, exuberant, and emotional forms of the baroque.

cold war (1098): The rivalry between the United States and the Soviet Union following World War II that lead to massive growth in nuclear weapons on both sides.

coloni (251): Tenant farmers in the Roman Empire who became bound by law to the land they worked and whose children were legally required to continue to farm the same land.

Colosseum (218): Rome's giant amphitheater for gladiatorial shows and other spectacles.

commercial revolution (360): Historians' term to describe the collective effect of the development of a profit economy, growth of cities, increased trade, and the rise of powerful new groups of merchants and artisans at the end of the eleventh/beginning of the twelfth century.

common law (407): The law of all of England. Its first chief architect was King Henry II, who sent his justices to every locality in his realm, declared certain crimes to be under his jurisdiction, and opened up new possibilities for property litigation under royal aegis.

commune (364): Sworn associations of citizens who formed a legal corporate body. Communes were the normal institution of self-government in medieval towns.

communists (855): Those socialists who after 1840 (when the word was first used) advocated the abolition of private property in favor of communal, collective ownership.

conservatism (808): A political doctrine that emerged after 1815 and rejected much of the Enlightenment and the French Revolution, preferring monarchies over republics, tradition over revolution, and established religion over Enlightenment skepticism.

constitutionalism (622): A system of government in which rulers had to share power with parliaments made up of elected representatives.

consuls (789): The title given to the three leaders of the new French government installed in 1799; in fact, Napoleon as First Consul held the reins of power.

consumer revolution (676): The rapid increase in consumption of new staples produced in the Atlantic system as well as of other items of daily life, such as mirrors, that were previously unavailable or beyond the reach of ordinary people.

Continental System (801): The system inaugurated by Napoleon's order in 1806 that France and its satellites boycott British goods; after some early successes in blocking British trade, the system was undermined by smuggling.

conversos (528): Jews in the Iberian peninsula who converted to Christianity in the fifteenth century.

Corn Laws (853): Tariffs on grain in Great Britain that benefited landowners by preventing the import of cheap foreign grain; after agitation by the Anti–Corn Law League, the tariffs were repealed by the British government in 1846.

Cuban missile crisis (1133): The confrontation in 1962 between the United States and the USSR over Soviet installation of missiles off the American coast; both John F. Kennedy and Nikita Khrushchev backed down from using nuclear weapons to resolve the situation.

cult of the offensive (1006): A military strategy of constantly attacking the enemy, believed to be the key to winning World War I. Given the firepower of both sides, however, this strategy boosted casualties and failed to bring victory to either side.

cuneiform (12): The earliest form of writing, invented in Mesopotamia and done with wedge-shaped characters.

curials (251): The social elite in the Roman Empire's towns who were responsible for collecting taxes for the imperial government and paying for any shortfalls themselves.

daguerreotype (834): A form of photography named after its inventor, Jacques Daguerre.

Dark Age (45): An extended period of economic depression and depopulation.

this treaty, the European Community became the European Union (EU) in 1994.

Maat (21): The Egyptian goddess ("What Is Right") embodying truth, justice, and cosmic order.

madrasa (330): A school located within or attached to a mosque.

mandate system (1026): The League of Nations covenant that granted the victors of World War I political control over Germany's former colonies.

mannerism (607): A late-sixteenth-century style of painting in which a distorted perspective created bizarre and theatrical effects that contrasted with the precise, harmonious lines of Renaissance painting.

manor (357): A great estate consisting (normally) of arable fields, vineyards, meadows, and woodland, ordinarily owned by a lord (which could as easily be a monastery or a church as a layperson) and cultivated by serfs.

march on Rome (1041): The threat by Benito Mussolini and his followers in 1922 to take over the Italian government in a military convergence on Rome; the march forced King Victor Emmanuel II to make Mussolini prime minister.

Marshall Plan (1103): A post–World War II program funded by the United States to get Europe back on its feet economically and thereby reduce the appeal of communism. It played an important role in the rebirth of European prosperity in the 1950s.

martyr (228): Greek for "witness," designating someone who dies for his or her religious belief.

Marxism (907): A body of thought about the organization of production, social inequality, and the processes of revolutionary change as devised by the philosopher and economist Karl Marx.

materialism (150): The philosophical doctrine that only things made of matter truly exist.

mean (130): Aristotle's term for the balance in desires that people needed to achieve to live just and worthwhile lives.

Mediterranean polyculture (33): The cultivation of olives, grapes, and grains in a single, interrelated agricultural system.

Meiji Restoration (898): A change in the Japanese government in 1867 that reinstalled the emperor as legitimate ruler in place of the military leader, or shogun.

mercantilism (628): The doctrine that governments must intervene to increase national wealth by whatever means possible.

mercenary (469): A soldier who fights for money. Mercenaries first appeared in the fourteenth century after the Black Death caused nobles to seek new sources of revenue; they stood in contrast to citizens who fought for their cities or peasants conscripted to serve their lords.

Merovingian dynasty (307): The dynasty that ruled as kings of the Franks from about 486 to 751.

mestizo (674): A person born to a Spanish father and Native American mother.

metaphysics (128): Ideas about the ultimate nature of reality beyond the reach of human senses.

Methodism (721): A religious movement founded by John Wesley that broke away from the Anglican church in Great Britain and insisted on strict self-discipline and a "methodical" approach to religious study and observance. Wesley emphasized an intense personal experience of salvation and a life of thrift, abstinence, and hard work.

metic (97): A foreigner granted a permanent residency permit in a Greek city-state in return for obligations to pay taxes and do military service.

mir (880): A Russian farm community fortified by the emancipation of the serfs in 1861 that provided for holding the land in common and regulating the movements of any individual by the group. The mir hindered the free movement of labor and individual agricultural enterprise, including modernization.

Mitteleuropa (993): Literally, "central Europe," but used by influential military leaders in Germany before World War I to refer to land in both central and eastern Europe that they hoped to acquire as a substitute for vast colonial empires in Africa and Asia. This territory ultimately formed a war aim in World War I and for Hitler thereafter.

modernism (970): Changes in the arts at the end of the nineteenth century that featured a break with realism in art and literature and with lyricism in music.

monotheism (25): The belief in only one god, as in Judaism, Christianity, and Islam.

Moors (480): Muslims in Spain and Portugal under Christian rule in the mid-fourteenth century.

moral dualism (50): The concept that the world is the arena of an ongoing battle between the opposing divine forces of good and evil.

Moriscos (587): Muslim converts to Christianity in Spain who remained secretly faithful to Islam; they were expelled from Spain in 1614.

mos maiorum (165): Literally, "the way of the elders"; the set of Roman traditional values.

motet (445): A two- or three-part polyphonic song that interweaves vernacular and sacred texts.

multinational corporation (1146): A business that operates in many foreign countries by sending large segments of its manufacturing, finance, sales, and other business components abroad.

mystery cult (97): A set of prayers, hymns, ritual purification, sacrifice, and other forms of worship undertaken to gain divine protection; each cult was connected to a particular divinity and centered on initiation into secret knowledge about the divine and human worlds.

mysticism (491): A belief that the emotional and individual experience with God is more important than external religious behavior. The Free Spirits of the late Middle Ages practiced an extreme form of mysticism.

nationalism (814): A political doctrine that holds that all peoples derive their identities from their nations and should have states to express their common language and shared cultural traditions.

nation-state (881): A sovereign political entity of modern times based on representing a united people.

NATO (North American Treaty Organization) (1107): The security alliance formed in 1949 to provide a unified military force for the United States, Canada, and their allies in Western Europe and Scandinavia. The corresponding alliance of the Soviet Union and its allies was known as the Warsaw Pact.

Nazi-Soviet Pact (1077): The agreement reached in 1939 by Germany and the Soviet Union in which both agreed not to attack the other in case of war. The agreement secretly divided up territory that would later be conquered.

neoliberalism (1171): A theory promoted by Margaret Thatcher, Britain's prime minister from 1979 to 1990, and those who followed her calling for a return to liberal principles of the nineteenth century, including the reduction of welfare-state programs and the cutting of taxes for wealthy people in order to promote economic growth.

Neolithic [period] (P-4): "New Stone" period; the period of the Stone Age during which people developed agriculture and domesticated animals.

Neolithic Revolution (P-8): The changes in human life in the New Stone Age produced by the invention of agriculture and the domestication of animals.

Neoplatonism (233): The spiritual philosophy developed by Plotinus (c. 205–270) that was based on Plato's ideas and very influential for Christian intellectuals.

new unionism (946): A mid- to late-nineteenth-century development in working-class organizing that entailed nationwide unions with bureaucracies and a membership of all kinds of workers, including unskilled ones; they replaced local craft-based unions.

new woman (965): A woman of the turn of the twentieth century, often from the middle class, who dressed practically, moved about freely, lived apart from her family, and supported herself.

nominalism (488): A late medieval philosophy that holds that concepts have no reality in nature but exist only as representations, or merely as words.

Nongovernmental organizations (NGOs) (1201): Charitable foundations and activist groups such as Doctors Without Borders that often work internationally on political, economic, and relief issues; also, philanthropic organizations such as the Rockefeller, Ford, and Open Society Foundations that shape economic and social policy and the course of political reform.

Nuremberg laws (1064): Legislation in 1935 that deprived Jewish Germans of their citizenship and imposed many other hardships on them.

Old Believers (635): A Russian Orthodox religious group that rejected church efforts to bring Russian worship in line with Byzantine tradition.

OPEC (Organization of Petroleum Exporting Countries) (1167): A consortium that regulated the supply and export of oil and that acted with more unanimity after the United States supported Israel against the Arabs in the wars of the late 1960s and early 1970s.

opium (830): An addictive drug derived from the heads of poppy plants; it was imported to Europe from the Ottoman Empire and India, available in various forms, and often used by ordinary people until restricted in 1868.

optimates (189): The Roman political faction supporting the "best," or highest, social class; established during the late republic.

orders (176): The two groups of people in the Roman republic—the patricians (aristocratic families) and the plebeians (everyone else).

Ostpolitik (1156): A policy initiated by Willy Brandt in the late 1960s in which West Germany sought better economic relations with the Communist countries of eastern Europe.

ostracism (91): Athenian democracy's annual procedure to block tyranny by sending a citizen into exile for ten years by a vote of six thousand citizens in the assembly.

outwork (918): The process of having some aspects of industrial work done outside factories in individual homes.

Pacific tigers (1210): Countries of East Asia so named because of their massive economic growth, much of it from the 1980s on; foremost among these were Japan and China.

palace society (33): The political and social organization of Minoan and Mycenaean civilization, with palace complexes as their administrative centers.

Paleolithic [period] (P-4): "Old Stone" period; the period of the Stone Age before people farmed for a living.

Pan-Slavism (888): A movement in the nineteenth century for the unity of all Slavs across national and regional boundaries.

parish (563): The basic territorial organization of the Catholic and main Protestant churches.

parlements (623): High courts in France (the term comes from the French *parler*, "to speak"). Each region had its parlement; the parlements could not propose laws, but they could review laws presented by the king and refuse to register them (the king could also insist on their registration).

patria potestas (167): Literally, "father's power"; the legal right of a father in ancient Rome to own the property of his children and slaves and to control their lives.

patron-client system (166): The interlocking network of mutual obligations between Roman patrons (social superiors) and clients (social inferiors).

Pax Romana (204): The period of "Roman peace" under the principate in the first and second centuries C.E.

Peace of God (349): A movement begun by bishops in the south of France first to limit the violence done to property and later (with the Truce of God) to limit fighting between warriors.

Peace of Paris (1022): The series of peace treaties that provided the settlement of World War I. These treaties were resented, especially by Germany, Hungary, and states of the Middle East in which England and France took over the government.

perestroika (1174): Literally, "restructuring"; an economic policy instituted in the 1980s by Soviet premier Mikhail Gorbachev calling for the introduction of market mechanisms and the achievement of greater efficiency in manufacturing, agriculture, and services.

philosophes (708): Public intellectuals of the Enlightenment who wrote on subjects ranging from current affairs to art criticism with the goal of furthering reform in society. (The word in French means "philosophers.")

Pietism (683): A Protestant revivalist movement that emphasized deeply emotional individual religious experience.

plantation (667): A large tract of land producing staple crops such as sugar, coffee, and tobacco; farmed by slave labor; and owned by a colonial settler who emigrated from western Europe.

plebiscites (179): Laws passed by the Plebeian Assembly in the Roman republic.

polis (57): The Greek term for an independent city-state based on citizenship.

political states (P-15): People living in a definite territory and organized under a system of government with powerful leaders, officials, and judges.

politiques (585): Political advisers during the French Wars of Religion who argued that compromise in matters of religion—limited toleration for the Calvinists—would strengthen the monarchy.

polyphony (446): Music that consists of two or more melodies performed simultaneously.

polytheism (12): The worship of multiple gods.

pop art (1152): A style in the visual arts that mimicked advertising and consumerism and that used ordinary objects as a part of paintings and other compositions.

Popular Front (1067): An alliance of political parties that joined together in the 1930s to resist fascism despite deep philosophical differences.

populares (189): The Roman political faction supporting the common people established during the late republic.

positivism (905): A theory, developed in the mid-nineteenth century, at the foundation of the social sciences that the study of facts would generate accurate, or "positive," laws of society; these laws could, in turn, help in the formulation of policy and legislation.

postmodernism (1219): A term applied in the late twentieth century to both an intense stylistic mixture in the arts without a central unifying theme or privileged canon and a critique of Enlightenment and scientific beliefs in rationality and the possibility for precise knowledge.

praetorian guard (207): The group of soldiers stationed in Rome under the emperor's control; first formed by Augustus.

predestination (558): John Calvin's doctrine that God preordained salvation or damnation for each person before creation; those chosen for salvation were considered the "elect."

primogeniture (348): The right to inheritance of the firstborn.

principate (204): The political system invented by Augustus as a disguised monarchy with the *princeps* ("first man") as emperor.

proletarians (179): In the Roman republic, the mass of people so poor they owned no property.

proletariat (907): The working class or, in Marxist terms, those who do not control the means of production such as factories, tools, workshops, and machines.

proscription (192): The procedure devised under Roman general Lucius Cornelius Sulla of posting a list of those supposedly guilty of treasonable crimes so that they could be executed and their property confiscated.

Protestants (548): Members of the Christian branch that formed when Martin Luther and his followers broke from the Catholic church in 1517; the name was first used in 1529 in an imperial diet by German princes who protested Emperor Charles V's edict to repress religious dissent.

Provisional Government (1016): The initial government to take control in Russia after the overthrow of the Romanov empire in 1917. The government was composed of aristocrats and members of the middle class, often deputies in the Duma, the assembly created after the Revolution of 1905.

psychoanalysis (967): Freud's theory of human mental processes and his method for treating their malfunctioning.

pump priming (1063): An economic policy used by governments to stimulate the economy through public works programs and other infusions to public funds.

purges (1058): The series of attacks instituted by Joseph Stalin on citizens of the USSR in the 1930s and later. The victims were accused of being "wreckers," or saboteurs of communism, while the public grew hysterical and pliable because of its fear.

Puritans (589): Strict Calvinists who opposed all vestiges of Catholic ritual in the Church of England.

radical democracy (90): The ancient Athenian system of democracy, established in the 460s and 450s B.C.E., that extended direct political power and participation in the court system to the mass of adult male citizens.

raison d'état (597): French for "reason of state." The political doctrine, first proposed by Cardinal Richelieu of France, which held that the state's interests should prevail over those of religion; Richelieu, for example, allied with the Lutheran king of Sweden even though he himself was a leading official of the Catholic Church.

rationalism (77): The philosophic idea that people must justify their claims by logic and reason.

realism (899): A style in the arts that arose in the mid-nineteenth century and was dedicated to depicting society realistically without romantic or idealistic overtones.

Realpolitik (873): Policies associated initially with nation building that are said to be based on hard-headed realities rather than the romantic notions of earlier nationalists. The term has come to mean any policy based on considerations of power alone.

reconquista (367, 480): The Christian reconquest of Spain.

redistributive economy (15): A system in which state officials control the production and distribution of goods.

Reform Act of 1884 (948): The British act that granted the right to vote to a mass male citizenry.

reliefs (382): Money payments made by a vassal to his lord upon inheriting a fief.

Renaissance (505): The rebirth of classical poetry, prose, and art in Europe that began in the fourteenth century; the word *renaissance* can also refer to other earlier cultural rebirths.

res publica (172): Literally, "the people's matter" or "the public business"; the Romans' name for their republic.

restoration (808): The Congress of Vienna's policy, after the fall of Napoleon, to "restore" as many regimes as possible to their former rulers.

rococo (681): A style of painting that emphasized irregularity and asymmetry, movement and curvature, but on a smaller, more intimate scale than the baroque.

Romanesque (390): The term for the art and architecture in western Europe of the period before around 1150, characterized by monumentality and solidity enlivened by sculpture and painting.

Romanization (221): The spread of Roman law and culture in the provinces of the Roman Empire.

romanticism (720, 815): An artistic movement of the early nineteenth century that glorified nature, emotion, genius, and imagination.

ruler cults (155): Cults that involved worship of a Hellenistic ruler as a savior god.

Russification (881): A program for the integration of Russia's many nationality groups involving the forced acquisition of Russian language and the practice of Russian orthodoxy as well as the settlement of ethnic Russians among other nationality groups.

salons (711): Informal gatherings, usually sponsored by middle-class or aristocratic women, that provided a forum for new ideas and an opportunity to establish new intellectual contacts among supporters of the Enlightenment; works that could not be published officially were read aloud. (The word in French means "living rooms.")

samizdat (1156): A key form of dissident activity in the Soviet Union and its satellite countries of eastern Europe in the 1960s and 1970s; individuals reproduced uncensored publications by hand and passed them from reader to reader, thus building a foundation for the successful resistance of the 1980s.

sans-culottes (761): The name given to politically active men from the lower classes (French for "without breeches"); they worked with their hands and wore the long trousers of workingmen rather than the knee breeches of the upper classes.

Sassanid Empire (284): The empire of the Sassanid dynasty of Persia, which lasted from 224 until its conquest by Islamic armies in 637–651.

satrap (49): A regional governor in the Persian empire.

Schlieffen Plan (1006): The strategy in World War I named for former chief of the German general staff Alfred von Schlieffen that called for attacks on two fronts—concentrating first on France to the west and then turning east to attack Russia.

scholasticism (443): The body of theological and philosophical thought of the scholastics, the scholars of the medieval universities, which combined the authority of the church fathers with that of Aristotle.

scientific method (611): A combination of experimental observation and mathematical deduction to determine the laws of nature; it became the secular standard of truth and as such challenged the hold of both the churches and popular beliefs.

scutage (409): A money payment paid by a vassal in lieu of military service. King John of England demanded scutage rather than service because vassals owed service for only forty days whereas hired soldiers would work as long as they were paid.

Sea Peoples (37): The diverse groups of raiders who devastated the eastern Mediterranean in the period of calamities around 1200–1000 B.C.E.

Second International (946): A transnational organization of workers established in 1889, mostly committed to Marxian socialism.

secularization (606): The trend toward making religious faith a private domain rather than one directly connected to state power and science; it prompted a search for nonreligious explanations for political authority and natural phenomena.

Seljuk Turks (372): A Sunni Muslim Turkic group whose migration westward, into areas that had been controlled by Byzantium and various local Muslim rulers, set off the First Crusade.

serfs (345): Semifree peasants. Serfs could not legally leave the land they tilled; they owed labor services and either produce or money to their lord whose land it was. Yet they were not slaves: they had the right to marry, to keep part of their produce, and to remain on the land.

simony (366): Derived from the name of Simon Magus, a magician in the New Testament who offers St. Peter money to have the power to confer the Holy Spirit (Acts 8:9–24), the term came to mean the giving of gifts or money for church offices.

social contract (650): The doctrine found in the writings of Hobbes and Locke that all political authority derives not from divine right but from an implicit contract between citizens and their rulers.

social question (840): An expression common in the 1830s–1850s that reflected a widely shared concern about the effects of industrialization and urbanization on the fabric of social life.

socialism (813): A social and political doctrine that advocated the reorganization of society to overcome the new tensions created by industrialization; early socialists emphasized the need to restore social harmony through communities based on cooperation rather than competition.

Socratic method (109): Socrates' method of conversation, in which he asked probing questions to make his listeners examine their most cherished assumptions before drawing conclusions.

Solidarity (1176): An outlawed Polish labor union of the 1980s that contested Communist Party programs and eventually succeeded in ousting the party from the Polish government.

Sophists (106): Competitive intellectuals and teachers who offered a new form of education and new philosophical and religious ideas beginning about 450 B.C.E.

soviets (1016): Councils of workers and soldiers first formed in Russia in the Revolution of 1905; they took shape to represent the people in the early days of the 1917 Russian Revolution. These groups saw themselves as a more legitimate political force than the Provisional Government.

stagflation (1168): The combination of a stagnant economy and soaring inflation; a period of stagflation occurred in the West in the 1970s as a result of an OPEC embargo on oil.

Stoicism (151): The most influential Hellenistic philosophy, which taught the goal of living a virtuous life in harmony with nature.

subjectivism (106): The belief, especially associated with the Sophist Protagoras, that there is no absolute reality behind and independent of appearances.

successor kings (139): Alexander's commanders (Antigonus, Seleucus, and Ptolemy) who took over portions of his empire to create personal monarchies after his death.

suffragists (977): Women around the turn of the twentieth century who worked actively for the right to vote.

summa (443): A scholastic treatise. These characteristically took up a topic and explored it exhaustively, resulting in a "summary" of all opinions and their resolution.

symposium (plural: symposia) (99): A drinking party for Greek men with entertainment ranging from philosophical conversation to hired female companions (see *hetaira*).

temperance movement (845): A movement in the United States and Europe begun in the early nineteenth century to discourage consumption of alcohol.

Terror (763): The emergency government established under the direction of the Committee of Public Safety during the French Revolution; the government aimed to establish a republic of virtue, but to do so it arrested hundreds of thousands of political suspects and executed thousands of ordinary people.

terrorism (1168): Coordinated and targeted political violence by opposition groups.

tertiaries (441): Laypeople who affiliated themselves with the friars and adopted many of their pious practices while living in the world.

tetrarchy (247): Literally, "rule by four"; devised by Diocletian to put into practice his principle of subdivision of power in ruling the Roman Empire.

thaw (1117): The climate of relative toleration for free expression in the Soviet bloc after the death of Joseph Stalin, in 1953. The thaw alternated with periods when the government returned to repression.

Thermidorian Reaction (770): The violent backlash against the rule of Robespierre that began with his arrest and execution; most of the instruments of the Terror were dismantled, and supporters of the Jacobins were harassed or even murdered.

Third Republic (949): The government that succeeded Napoleon III's Second Empire after its defeat in the Franco-Prussian War of 1870–1871 and lasted until France's defeat in World War II (1940).

third world (1098): A term devised after World War II to designate those countries outside either the capitalist world of the U.S. bloc or the socialist world of the Soviet bloc—most of them emerging from imperial domination.

tithe (347, 601): A tax equivalent to one-tenth of the parishioner's annual income taken by the church.

Torah (51): The first five books of the Hebrew Bible; also referred to as the Pentateuch. It contains early Jewish law.

total war (1003): A war built on full mobilization of soldiers, civilians, and the technological capacities of the nations involved. The term also refers to a highly destructive war and one that is both a physical war and a war for ideas and ideologies.

trireme (89): An ancient Greek warship rowed by 170 oarsmen sitting on three levels and equipped with a ram.

trivium (386): The first three—the foundational subjects—of the seven liberal arts: grammar, rhetoric, and logic (or dialectic).

troubadours (413): Vernacular poets in southern France who sang of love, longing, and courtesy.

Truman Doctrine (1103): The United States' policy to limit communism after World War II by countering political crises with economic and military aid.

tsar (530): The Russian imperial title first taken by Muscovite prince Ivan III (r. 1462–1505); also spelled *czar*, from Caesar.

Twelve Tables (177): The first written Roman law code, enacted between 451 and 449 B.C.E.

Umayyad caliphate (298): The successors of Muhammad who traced their ancestry to Umayyah, a member of Muhammad's tribe. The first of these caliphs was related to Muhammad because he married two of the Prophet's daughters. The dynasty lasted from 661 to 750.

ummah (294): The community of believers following Muhammad.

United Nations (UN) (1123): An organization for collective security and deliberation set up as World War II closed; it replaced the ineffective League of Nations and has proved active in resolving international conflicts both through negotiation and by the use of force.

vassalage (344): The rights and duties of a vassal, a free warrior who was nevertheless the dependent of another, his lord.

Vatican II (1154): A Catholic Council held between 1962 and 1965 to modernize some aspects of church teachings (such as condemnation of Jews), to update the liturgy, and to promote cooperation among the faiths (i.e., ecumenism).

vernacular literature (497): Works written in the languages spoken by the people as opposed to being written in Latin; such literature blossomed in the fourteenth century.

Visigothic Spain (310): Spain under the Visigoths. Beginning in the mid-fifth century,

Visigothic rule ended with the conquest of most of Spain by Islamic armies in 711.

Vulgate (562): The authoritative Latin version of the Catholic Bible, the only one authorized prior to the Protestant Reformation.

war guilt clause (1022): The part of the Treaty of Versailles that assigned blame for World War I to Germany.

Weimar Republic (1021): The parliamentary republic established in 1919 in Germany to replace the imperial form of government.

welfare state (1113): A system comprising state-sponsored programs for citizens, including veterans' pensions, social security, health care, family allowances, and disability insurance. Most highly developed after World War II, the welfare state intervened in society to bring economic democracy (to supplement political democracy) by setting a minimum standard of well-being.

wergild (270): Under Frankish law, money or goods a murderer had to pay as compensation for his crime; most went to the victim's kin, but the king received about one-third.

Westernization (688): The effort, especially in Peter the Great's Russia, to make society and social customs resemble counterparts in western Europe, especially France, Britain and the Dutch Republic.

wisdom literature (23): Fables, proverbs, essays, and prophecies teaching morality and proper behavior.

working class (811): The term introduced in the early nineteenth century for those who worked in the new factories of industrial production.

World Bank (1201): An international institution of credit created in the 1940s. With the globalization of finances and of national economies from the 1980s on, it became increasingly powerful.

zemstvos (880): Regional councils of the Russian nobility established after the emancipation of the Serfs in 1861 to deal with education and local welfare issues.

ziggurat (10): A large Mesopotamian temple with a stair-step design.

Zionism (984): A movement that began in the late nineteenth century among European Jews to found a Jewish state.

Additional Credits

Chapter 1, page 17: "Hammurabi's Laws for Physicians." From translation adapted in *Ancient Near Eastern Texts Relating to the Old Testament*, 3rd. ed. with supplement, by James B. Pritchard. Copyright © 1950, 1955, 1969, renewed 1978 by Princeton University Press. Reprinted by permission of Princeton University Press. **Page 26:** "Declaring Innocence on Judgement Day in Ancient Egypt." From *The Book of the Dead*. Reprinted in *Ancient Egyptian Literature: A Book of Readings*, translated by Miriam Lichtheim, Vol II: *The New Kingdom*. Published by the University of California Press (1976). © 1973–1980 by the Regents of the University of California. Reprinted courtesy of the University of California Press.

Chapter 3, page 107: "Sophists Arguing both Sides of a Case." Excerpt from *Dissoi Logio* 1. 1-6. Translation adapted from *The Older Sophists* by Rosamund Kent Sprague, ed. Copyright © 1972 by Rosamund Kent Sprague. Reprinted by permission of the University of South Carolina Press. **Page 117:** Taking Measure: "Military Forces of Athens and Sparta at the Beginning of the Peloponnesian War." Adapted from Fig. 4.10 in *Risk and Survival in Ancient Greece: Reconstructing the Rural Domestic Economy* by Thomas W. Gallant. Copyright © 1991 by Thomas W. Gallant. Courtesy of Stanford University Press.

Chapter 4, page 141: "Ethnic Tension in Ptolemaic Egypt." From *Greeks in Ptolemaic Egypt: Case Studies in the Social History of the Hellenistic World*, with translation adapted by Naphtali Lewis. Copyright © 1986 by Naphtali Lewis. Reprinted by permission of Oxford University Press.

Chapter 8, page 288: Taking Measure: "Church Repair." Adaptation of three figures (8a, 8b, and 8c) from *The Sixth Century: Production, Distribution and Demand* by Richard Hodges and William Bowden. Copyright © 1998, Brill Publishers, via Copyright Clearance Center. Reprinted by permission.

Chapter 9, page 337: "Dhuoda's Handbook for Her Son." From *Handbook for William: A Carolingian Woman's Counsel for Her Son*. Translated with Introductions and Notes by Carol Neel. Copyright © 1991. University of Nebraska Press. Reprinted by permission. **Page 345:** "The Chronicle of Fulcher of Chartres." Edited text from pp. 35–37 in *The First Crusade: The Chronicle of Fulcher of Chartres and Other Source Materials*, edited Edward Peters. Copyright © 1971 Edward Peters. Reprinted by permission of the University of Pennsylvania Press.

Chapter 10, page 370: "A Byzantine View of Papal Primacy." From *Byzantium: Church, Society, and Civilization Seen through Contemporary Eyes* by Deno John Geanakoplos. Quoting from *Byzantium and the Roman Primacy*, translated by Edwin A. Quain, S.J. Copyright © 1966/79 Fordham University Press. Reprinted by permission of the publisher. **Page 378:** "Genoese Traders in Palestine." Excerpt from pp. 88–89 in *Medieval Trade* in the Mediterranean World: Illustrative Documents. Translated with Introductions and Notes by Robert S. Lopez & Irving W. Raymond. Copyright © 1955 by Columbia University Press. Reprinted with the permission of the publisher. **Page 374:** "The Jewish Experience, as told by Solomon Bar Simson." Edited text from pp. 21–23 in *The Jews and the Crusaders: The Hebrew Chronicles of the First and Second Crusaders*, translated and edited by Shlomo Eidelberg. Copyright © Shlomo Eidelberg. Reprinted by permission of the author. **Page 383:** Taking Measure: "Slaves in England in 1086 as Reported in Domesday." Excerpted data from appendices 1, 3, 13, and 14 (for map w/table) in *Domesday England* by H.C. Darby. Copyright © 1977 by H.C. Darby. Reprinted with the permission of Cambridge University Press.

Chapter 11, page 425: Adaptation of 2 maps from p. 146 in *Atlas of Medieval Europe*, edited by Angus Mackay and David Ditchburn. Copyright © Routledge. Reprinted with the permission of Taylor & Francis, Ltd.

Chapter 13, page 474: Edited text from pp. 30, 48–49, 64–65, 223–24, 233 in *Joan of Arc: By Herself and Her Witnesses* by Regine Pernoud. © 1994 by Regine Pernoud. Reprinted by permission of Madison Books. **Page 494:** Excerpt from *Piers the Ploughman* by William Langland, translated by J.F. Goodridge (Penguin Classics, 1959, Revised Edition, 1966). Copyright © J.F. Goodrich, 1959, 1966. Reprinted by permission of Penguin Books, Ltd. **Page 485:** Taking Measure: "Population Losses and the Plague." Excerpted text from table 1, p. 36 in *The Fontana Economic History of Europe: The Middle Ages* by Carlo M. Cipolla, ed. © 1974 by Carlo M. Cipolla/Fontana Books. Reprinted by permission of HarperCollins Publishers, Ltd. **Page 498:** Excerpt from *The Book of the City of Ladies* by Christine de Pizan, translated by Rosalind Brown-Grant (Penguin Classics, 1999). Translation © Rosalind Brown-Grant, 1999. Reprinted by permission of Penguin Group Ltd.

Chapter 15, page 551: Excerpt from *Utopia* by Thomas More, translated by Paul Turner (Penguin Classics, 1961). Copyright © Paul Turner, 1961. Reprinted by permission of Penguin Books, Ltd. **Page 556:** "Erasmus Writes to Martin Luther" Excerpt from p. 317 in *Essential Works of Erasmus*, edited by W.T.H. Jackson. © 1965 Bantam, Doubleday Dell a division of Random House, Inc.

Chapter 16, page 594: "The Horrors of the Thirty Years' War." Excerpt from pp. 6–7 in *The Adventures of Simplicius Simplicissimus*, translated by George Schulz-Behrend, 2nd ed. Copyright © 1993 by George Schulz-Behrend. Reprinted by permission of Camden House. **Page 613:** "Galileo Writes to Kepler."

Index

A note about the index:

Names of individuals appear in bold face; biographical dates are included for major historical figures.

Letters in parentheses following pages refer to:
- (i)   illustrations, including photographs and artifacts
- (f)   figures, including charts, graphs, and tables
- (m)   maps
- (b)   boxed features (such as "Contrasting Views")

continued

continued

continued

continued

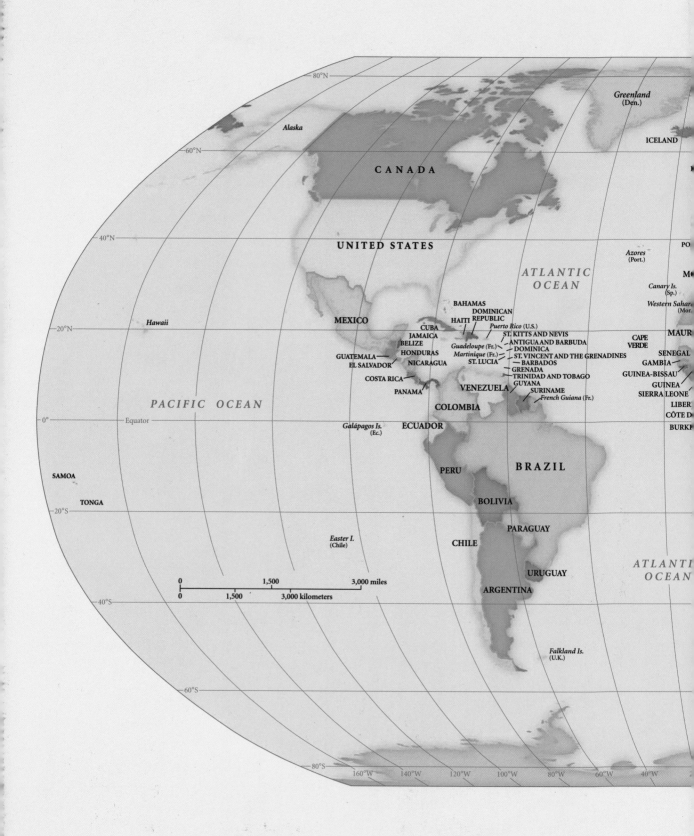

80°N

Greenland
(Den.)

Alaska

ICELAND

60°N

C A N A D A

40°N

UNITED STATES

*ATLANTIC
OCEAN*

PO

Azores
(Port.)

M

Canary Is.
(Sp.)

20°N

Hawaii

MEXICO

BAHAMAS

DOMINICAN
REPUBLIC

HAITI

Western Sahara
(Mor.)

CUBA

Puerto Rico (U.S.)

MAUR

JAMAICA

ST. KITTS AND NEVIS

BELIZE

ANTIGUA AND BARBUDA

CAPE
VERDE

Guadeloupe (Fr.)

DOMINICA

SENEGAL

GUATEMALA

HONDURAS

Martinique (Fr.)

ST. VINCENT AND THE GRENADINES

GAMBIA

EL SALVADOR

ST. LUCIA

BARBADOS

NICARAGUA

GRENADA

GUINEA-BISSAU

TRINIDAD AND TOBAGO

GUINEA

COSTA RICA

GUYANA

SIERRA LEONE

PANAMA

VENEZUELA

SURINAME

LIBER

French Guiana (Fr.)

CÔTE D

COLOMBIA

BURKI

0°

Equator

Galápagos Is.
(Ec.)

ECUADOR

B R A Z I L

PACIFIC OCEAN

PERU

SAMOA

BOLIVIA

TONGA

20°S

PARAGUAY

Easter I.
(Chile)

CHILE

*ATLANTI
OCEAN*

URUGUAY

0   1,500   3,000 miles

ARGENTINA

0   1,500   3,000 kilometers

40°S

Falkland Is.
(U.K.)

60°S

80°S

160°W   140°W   120°W   100°W   80°W   60°W   40°W